Routledge
International O

This is a comprehensive history of international organizations from their very beginning at the Congress of Vienna in 1815 up to the present day, and provides the reader with nearly two centuries of world history seen from the perspective of international organizations. It covers the three main fields of international relations, security, economics and the humanitarian domain, which often overlap in international organizations. As well as global and intercontinental organizations, the book also covers regional international organizations and international NGOs on all continents.

The book progresses chronologically, but also provides a thematic and geographical coherence so that related developments can be discussed together. A series of detailed tables, charts and information boxes explain the chronologies, structures and relationships of international organizations. There are biographies, histories and analysis of hundreds of international organizations.

This is an essential reference work with direct relevance to scholars in international relations, international political economy, international economics and business and security studies.

Bob Reinalda is Senior Lecturer in International Relations at the Department of Political Science, Nijmegen School of Management at Radboud University Nijmegen, the Netherlands. He has written extensively about the history of social movements; NGOs; autonomous policy making by, decision making within and implementation by intergovernmental organizations; and the Bologna Process.

Routledge History of International Organizations

From 1815 to the present day

Bob Reinalda

LONDON AND NEW YORK

First published 2009
by Routledge
2 Park Square, Milton Park, Abingdon, Oxon OX14 4RN

Simultaneously published in the USA and Canada
by Routledge
711 Third Avenue, New York, NY 10017

Routledge is an imprint of the Taylor & Francis Group, an informa business

First issued in paperback 2013

© 2009 Bob Reinalda

Typeset in Bembo by
Taylor & Francis Books

British Library Cataloguing in Publication Data
A catalogue record for this book is available from the British Library

Library of Congress Cataloging in Publication Data
  Reinalda, Bob.
The Routledge history of international organizations : from 1815 to the present
day / Bob Reinalda.
    p. cm.
  1. International agencies–History. 2. International organization–History. I.
Title.
JZ4839.R45 2009
341.209–dc22

                                                 2008050977

ISBN 978-0-415-47624-9 (hbk)
ISBN 978-0-203-87657-2 (ebk)
ISBN 978-0-415-85044-5 (pbk)

Contents

Part XII: Development aid, environmental protection and human rights as normative powers: NGO pressure on governments through intergovernmental organizations 1960–80

Part XIII: International organizations in the 1980s: The Cold War intensifies and neoliberalism replaces Keynesianism

Figures

Abbreviations

ABAC	APEC Business Advisory Council
ABC	atomic, biological and chemical weapons
ABM	anti-ballistic missile systems
ACABQ	Advisory Committee on Administrative and Budgetary Questions
ACM	Arab Common Market
ACP	African, Caribbean and Pacific region
ACS	Association of Caribbean States
ADB	Asian Development Bank
AEC	ASEAN Economic Community
AfDB	African Development Bank
AFL	American Federation of Labor
AFL-CIO	American Federation of Labor-Congress of Industrial Organizations
AFTA	ASEAN Free Trade Area
AIP	ASEAN Industrial Project
ALADI	Asociación latinoamericana de integración (Latin American Integration Association)
ALALC	Asociación latinoamericana de libre cambio (Latin American Free Trade Association)
AMU	Arab Maghreb Union
ANZCERTA	Australia New Zealand Closer Economic Relations Trade Agreement
ANZUK	Australia, New Zealand, the UK
ANZUS	Australia, New Zealand, the US
APEC	Asia Pacific Economic Cooperation
APT	ASEAN Plus Three
ARF	ASEAN Regional Forum
ASC	ASEAN Security Community
ASCC	ASEAN Socio-Cultural Community
ASEAN	Association of Southeast Asian Nations
ASEM	Asia Europe Meeting

ATTAC	Association for the Taxation of Financial Transactions in the Interest of the Citizen
AU	African Union
BCBS	Basel Committee on Bank Supervision
BIAC	Business and Industry Advisory Committee
BINUB	UN Integrated Office in Burundi
BIRPI	Bureaux internationaux réunis pour la protection de la propriété intellectuelle
BIS	Bank for International Settlements
BONUCA	UN Peacebuilding Office in the Central African Republic
BSEC	Black Sea Economic Cooperation
BWC	Biological Weapons Convention
CABEI	Central American Bank for Economic Integration
CAC	Office of the Special Representative of the Secretary-General for Children and Armed Conflict
CACM	Central American Common Market
CAEU	Council of Arab Economic Unity
CAFTA	Central American Free Trade Agreement
CAN	Comunidad andina de naciones (Andean Community of Nations)
CARE	Cooperative for American Remittances to Europe/Cooperative for Assistance and Relief Everywhere
CARICOM	Caribbean Community and Common Market
CARIFTA	Caribbean Free Trade Association
CAT	Committee Against Torture
CAT	Convention against Torture and Other Cruel, Inhuman or Degrading Treatment or Punishment
CBD	Convention on Biological Diversity
CBSS	Council of Baltic Sea States
CCD	Conference of the Committee on Disarmament
CCEET	Centre for Cooperation with the European Economies in Transition
CCW	Convention on Conventional Weapons
CD	Conference on Disarmament
CDB	Caribbean Development Bank
CEAO	Communauté économique de l'Afrique de l'ouest
CEDAW	Committee on the Elimination of Discrimination Against Women
CEDAW	Convention on the Elimination of All Forms of Discrimination against Women
CEEAC	Communauté économique des états de l'Afrique centrale (Economic Community of Central African States)
CEE	Central and Eastern Europe
CEEC	Committee of European Economic Cooperation
CEET	Central and Eastern European Team
CEFTA	Central European Free Trade Agreement
CEMAC	Communauté économique et monétaire de l'Afrique centrale (Economic and Monetary Community of Central Africa)
CENTO	Central Treaty Organization
CEPT	common effective preferential tariff

CERD	Committee on the Elimination of Racial Discrimination
CESCR	Committee on Economic, Social and Cultural Rights
CEWARN	Conflict Early Warning and Response Mechanism
CFC	Common Fund for Commodities
CFCs	chlorofluorocarbons
CFE	Conventional Armed Forces in Europe
CFSP	Common Foreign and Security Policy
CHR	Commission on Human Rights
CIEC	Conference on International Economic Cooperation
CIME	Committee on International Investments and Multinational Corporations
CIOS	Comité international de l'organisation scientifique
CIS	Commonwealth of Independent States
CITES	Convention on International Trade in Endangered Species of Wild Fauna and Flora
CMC	Cluster Munition Coalition
CMEA	Council for Mutual Economic Assistance
CMI	Chiang Mai Initiative
CMW	Committee on Migrant Workers
COCOM	Coordinating Committee for Multilateral Export Controls
COMECON	*see* CMEA
COMESA	Common Market for Eastern and Southern Africa
Cominform	Communist Information Bureau
Comintern	Communist International
CONDECA	Consejo de defensa centroamericano (Central American Defence Council)
CONGO	Conference of Non-Governmental Organizations in Consultative Status with the United Nations Economic and Social Council
COP	Conference of Parties
COPUOS	UN Committee on the Peaceful Use of Outer Space
Coreper	Comité des représentents permanents (Committee of Permanent Representatives)
CRC	Committee/Convention on the Rights of the Child
CRIC	Committee for the Review of the Implementation of the Convention
CRPD	Committee/Convention on the Rights of Persons with Disabilities
CSCE	Conference on Security and Cooperation in Europe
CSD	Commission on Sustainable Development
CSME	CARICOM Single Market and Economy
CSW	Commission on the Status of Women
CTBT	Comprehensive Nuclear-Test-Ban Treaty
CTBTO	Comprehensive Nuclear-Test-Ban Treaty Organization
CUSTA	Canada US Free Trade Agreement
CWC	Chemical Weapons Convention
DAC	Development Assistance Committee
DDA	Department for Disarmament Affairs
DESA	Department of Economic and Social Affairs
DGACM	Department of General Assembly and Conference Management

DM	Department of Management
DOMREP	Mission of the Representative of the Secretary-General in the Dominican Republic
DP	displaced person
DPA	Department of Political Affairs
DPI	Department of Public Information
DPKO	Department of Peacekeeping Operations
DSB	Dispute Settlement Body
EAC	East African Community
EAFTA	East Asia Free Trade Area
EBRD	European Bank for Reconstruction and Development
EC	European Community/Communities
ECA	Economic Commission for Africa
ECB	European Central Bank
ECCM	East Caribbean Common Market
ECE	Economic Commission for Europe
ECLA	Economic Commission for Latin America
ECLAC	Economic Commission for Latin America and the Caribbean
ECO	Economic Cooperation Organization
ECOMOG	ECOWAS Cease-Fire Monitoring Group
ECOSOC	Economic and Social Council
ECOWAS	Economic Community of West African States
ECSC	European Coal and Steel Community
ECT	Energy Charter Treaty
EDC	European Defence Community
EEA	European Economic Area
EEC	European Economic Community
EFTA	European Free Trade Association
EMI	European Monetary Institute
EMS	European Monetary System
EMU	Economic and Monetary Union
ENDC	Eighteen-Nation Disarmament Committee
ENMOD	Environmental Modification Techniques
EOSG	Executive Office of the Secretary-General
EPC	European Political Cooperation
EPO	European Patent Office
EPTA	Expanded Programme of Technical Assistance
EPU	European Payments Union
EPU	European Political Union
ESCAP	Economic and Social Commission for Asia and the Pacific
ESCB	European System of Central Banks
ESCWA	Economic and Social Commission for Western Asia
EU	European Union
EURASEC	Eurasian Economic Community
Euratom	European Atomic Energy Community
FAO	Food and Agriculture Organization
FCCC	UN Framework Convention on Climate Change
FDI	foreign direct investment

FRETILIN	Frente Revolucionária de Timor-Leste Independente (Revolutionary Front for an Independent East Timor)
FSAP	Financial Sector Assessment Programme
FSF	Financial Stability Forum
FSU	Former Soviet Union
FTAA	Free Trade Area of the Americas
GAB	General Agreement to Borrow
GAC	Governmental Advisory Committee
GATS	General Agreement on Trade in Services
GATT	General Agreement on Tariffs and Trade
GCC	Gulf Cooperation Council
GDP	gross domestic product
GEF	Global Environment Facility
GNP	gross national product
GPS	General Preferential System
GSTP	Global System of Trade Preferences among Developing Countries
GUAM Group	Georgia, Ukraine, Azerbaijan and Moldova
GUUAM Group	GUAM Group plus Uzbekistan
Habitat	UN Conference on Human Settlements/UN Centre for Human Settlements
HDI	Human Development Index
HIPC	heavily indebted poor country
HPI	Human Poverty Index
HRC	Human Rights Committee
HRC	Human Rights Council
IAEA	International Atomic Energy Agency
IALL	International Association for Labour Legislation
IANSA	International Action Network on Small Arms
IAW	International Association of Women
IBFAN	International Baby Food Action Network
IBRD	International Bank for Reconstruction and Development
ICANN	Internet Corporation for Assigned Names and Numbers
ICAO	International Civil Aviation Organization
ICBL	International Campaign to Ban Landmines
ICC	International Chamber of Commerce
ICC	International Criminal Court
ICCPR	International Covenant on Civil and Political Rights
ICCPR-OP1	Optional Protocol to the ICCPR
ICCPR-OP2	Second Optional Protocol to the ICCPR, Aiming at the Abolition of the Death Penalty
ICEM	Intergovernmental Committee for European Migration
ICERD	International Convention on the Elimination of All Forms of Racial Discrimination
ICES	International Council for the Exploration of the Sea
ICESCR	International Covenant on Economic, Social and Cultural Rights
ICFTU	International Confederation of Free Trade Unions
ICISS	International Commission on Intervention and State Sovereignty
ICJ	International Court of Justice

ICM	Intergovernmental Committee for Migration
ICPD	International Conference on Population and Development
ICRC	International Committee of the Red Cross
ICRMW	International Convention on the Protection of the Rights of All Migrant Workers and Members of Their Families
ICSID	International Centre for Settlement of Investment Disputes
ICTR	International Criminal Tribunal for Rwanda
ICTY	International Criminal Tribunal for the Former Yugoslavia
ICW	International Council of Women
IDA	International Development Association
IDB	Inter-American Development Bank
IDP	internally displaced person
IEA	International Energy Agency
IEC	International Electrotechnical Commission
IFAD	International Fund for Agricultural Development
IFC	International Finance Corporation
IFCTU	International Federation of Christian Trade Unions
IFF	Intergovernmental Forum on Forests
IFI	International Financial Institution
IFOR	Implementation Force
IFTU	International Federation of Trade Unions
IGAD	Inter-Governmental Authority on Development
IGADD	Inter-Governmental Authority on Drought and Development
IGCR	Intergovernmental Committee for Refugees
IGO	intergovernmental organization
IIL	Institute of International Law
ILA	International Law Association
ILC	International Law Commission
ILO	International Labour Organization
ILPF	International League for Peace and Freedom
IMC	International Maritime Committee
IMCO	Intergovernmental Maritime Consultative Organization
IMF	International Monetary Fund
IMFC	International Monetary and Financial Committee
IMO	International Maritime Organization
IMO	International Meteorological Organization
INF	Intermediate-Range Nuclear Forces
INGO	international non-governmental organization
INSTRAW	International Research and Training Institute for the Advancement of Women
INVO	Iraq Nuclear Verification Office
IOC	International Olympic Committee
IOM	International Organization for Migration
IPA	Inter-Parliamentary Assembly
IPC	Intellectual Property Committee
IPCC	Intergovernmental Panel on Climate Change
IPEC	International Programme on the Elimination of Child Labour
IPF	Intergovernmental Panel on Forests

IRO	International Refugee Organization
IRU	International Radio Telegraph Union
ISA	International Federation of National Standardizing Associations
ISAF	International Security Assistance Force
ISG	Intersessional Support Group
ISM	Intersessional Meeting
ISO	International Organization for Standardization
ITC	International Trade Centre
ITF	International Transportworkers Federation
ITO	International Trade Organization
ITTA	International Tropical Timber Agreement
ITTO	International Tropical Timber Organization
ITU	International Telegraph Union/International Telecommunication Union
IUCN	International Union for the Protection of Nature/International Union for the Conservation of Nature and Natural Resources – The World Conservation Union
IWC	International Whaling Commission
IWSA	International Woman Suffrage Alliance
JIAS	Joint Interim Administrative Structure
KFOR	Kosovo Force
LAFTA	Latin American Free Trade Association
LAIA	Latin American Integration Association
LDC	least-developed country
LLDC	landlocked developing country
LSI	Labour and Socialist International
MAD	mutual assured destruction
MAI	Multilateral Agreement on Investments
MAP	Mediterranean Action Programme
MARPOL	International Convention on the Prevention of Pollution from Ships
MBFR	Mutual and Balanced Force Reductions
MCCA	Mercado común centroamericano (Central American Common Market)
MDB	multilateral development bank
MDGs	UN Millennium Development Goals
MERCOSUL	MERCOSUR in Portuguese
MERCOSUR	Mercadó común del cono sur (Southern Common Market)
METO	Middle East Treaty Organization
MICIVIH	International Civilian Mission to Haiti
MIGA	Multilateral Investment Guarantee Agency
MINOPUH	UN Civilian Police Mission in Haiti
MINUGUA	UN Verification Mission in Guatemala
MINURCA	UN Mission in the Central African Republic
MINURCAT	UN Mission in the Central African Republic and Chad
MINURSO	UN Mission for the Referendum in Western Sahara
MINUSTAH	UN Stabilization Mission in Haiti
MONUA	UN Observer Mission in Angola
MONUC	UN Organization Mission in the Democratic Republic of Congo

MPLA	Popular Movement for the Liberation of Angola
MSF	Médecins Sans Frontières
NAACP	National Association for the Advancement of Colored People
NACC	North Atlantic Cooperation Council
NAFTA	North American Free Trade Agreement
NAM	Movement of Non-Aligned Countries/Non-Aligned Movement
NAT	North Atlantic Treaty
NATO	North Atlantic Treaty Organization
NEPAD	New Partnership for Africa's Development
NGO	non-governmental organization
NIC	newly-industrializing country
NIE	newly-industrializing economy
NIEO	New International Economic Order
NLF	National Liberation Front
NNWS	non-nuclear weapons states
NPFL	National Patriotic Front of Liberia
NPT	Non-Proliferation Treaty
NWS	nuclear weapons states
OAPEC	Organization of Arab Petroleum Exporting Countries
OAS	Organization of American States
OAU	Organization of African Unity
OCAM	Organisation commune africaine et mauricienne
OCCM	Oslo Conference on Cluster Munitions
OCHA	Office for the Coordination of Humanitarian Affairs
ODA	official development assistance
ODCCP	Office for Drug Control and Crime Prevention
ODIHR	Office for Democratic Institutions and Human Rights
OECD	Organization for Economic Cooperation and Development
OECS	Organization of Eastern Caribbean States
OEEC	Organization for European Economic Cooperation
OHCHR	Office of the UN High Commissioner for Human Rights
OHRLLS	Office of the High Representative for the Least Developed Countries, Landlocked Developing Countries and Small Islands Developing Countries
OILPOL	International Convention for the Prevention of Pollution of the Sea by Oil
OIOS	Office of Internal Oversight Services
OIP	UN Office for the Iraq Programme
OLA	Office of Legal Affairs
OMV	ongoing monitoring and verification
ONUB	UN Operation in Burundi
ONUC	UN Operation in the Congo
ONUCA	UN Observer Group in Central America
ONUSAL	UN Observer Mission in El Salvador
OPANAL	Organismo para la proscripción de las armas nuclearas en la América Latina y el Caribe (Agency for the Prohibition of Nuclear Weapons in Latin America and the Caribbean)
OPBW	Organization for the Prohibition of Biological Weapons

OP-CAT	Optional Protocol to the Convention against Torture and Other Cruel, Inhuman or Degrading Treatment or Punishment
OP-CEDAW	Optional Protocol to the Convention on the Elimination of Discrimination against Women
OP-CRC-AC	Optional Protocol to the Convention on the Rights of the Child on the Involvement of Children in Armed Conflict
OP-CRC-SC	Optional Protocol to the Convention on the Rights of the Child on the Sale of Children, Child Prostitution and Child Pornography
OP-CRPD	Optional Protocol to the Convention on the Rights of Persons with Disabilities
OPCW	Organization for the Prohibition of Chemical Weapons
OPEC	Organization of Petroleum Exporting Countries
OSCE	Organization for Security and Cooperation in Europe
PAHO	Pan-American Health Organization
Parlandino	Parlamento andino (Andean Parliament)
PCIJ	Permanent Court of International Justice
PFII	UN Permanent Forum on Indigenous Issues
PfP	Partnership for Peace
PFP	Policy Framework Paper
PICE	Programme for Integration and Economic Cooperation
PID	Political Intelligence Department
PIT	Partners in Transition Countries
PIU	public international union
PLO	Palestine Liberation Organization
PMC	Post-Ministerial Conference
PNET	Peaceful Nuclear Explosion Treaty
POP	persistent organic pollutant
PrepCom	Preparatory Committee
PRGF	Poverty Reduction and Growth Facility
PSO	Peacebuilding Support Office
PTA	Preferential Trade Area for Eastern and Southern African States
PTBT	Partial Test Ban Treaty
Quad	Canada, the Commission of the EEC/EU, Japan, the US
R2P	Responsibility to Protect
RCD	Regional Cooperation for Development
RILU	Red International of Labour Unions
RTAA	Reciprocal Trade Agreements Act
RUF	Revolutionary United Front of Sierra Leone
SAARC	South Asian Association for Regional Cooperation
SACEUR	Supreme Allied Commander Europe
SADC	Southern African Development Community
SADCC	Southern African Development Coordination Conference
SAEU	South Asian Economic Union
SAFTA	Agreement on the South Asian Free Trade Area
SALT	Strategic Arms Limitation Talks
SALW	small arms and light weapons
SAP	Structural Adjustment Programme
SAPTA	SAARC Preferential Trading Arrangement

SCO	Shanghai Cooperation Organization
SDA	Social Dimensions of Adjustment
SDI	Strategic Defence Initiative
SDR	Special Drawing Right
SEATO	Southeast Asia Treaty Organization
SECAL	Sectoral Adjustment Loans
SEECP	South-East European Cooperation Process
SELA	Sistema económico latinoamericano (Latin American Economic System)
SFOR	Stabilization Force
SHAPE	Supreme Headquarters Allied Powers Europe
SI	Socialist International
SICA	Sistema de la integración centroamericana (Central American Integration System)
SOLAS	International Convention for the Safety of Life at Sea
SORT	Strategic Offensive Reductions Treaty
SPA	SADC Programme of Action
SPF	South Pacific Forum
START	Strategic Arms Reduction Talks/Treaty
SUNFED	Special UN Fund for Economic Development
SWAPO	South West Africa People's Organisation
TRAFFIC	Trade Records Analysis of Fauna and Flora in Commerce
TREVI	Terrorism, Radicalism, Extremism, Violence International
TRIPS	Trade-Related Intellectual Property Rights
TTBT	Threshold Test Ban Treaty
TUAC	Trade Union Advisory Committee
UDAO	Union douanière des états de l'Afrique occidentale
UDC	Union of Democratic Control
UDEAC	Union douanière et économique de l'Afrique centrale
UEMOA	Union économique et monétaire ouest-africaine (West African Economic and Monetary Union)
UK	United Kingdom of Great Britain and Northern Ireland
UMOA	Union monétaire ouest africaine
UN	United Nations
UNAEC	UN Atomic Energy Commission
UNAIDS	Joint UN Programme on HIV/AIDS
UNAMA	UN Assistance Mission in Afghanistan
UNAMET	UN Mission in East Timor
UNAMI	UN Assistance Mission for Iraq
UNAMIC	UN Advance Mission in Cambodia
UNAMID	African Union/UN Hybrid Operation in Darfur
UNAMIR	UN Assistance Mission for Rwanda
UNAMIS	UN Advance Mission in the Sudan
UNAMSIL	UN Assistance Mission in Sierra Leone
UNASOG	UN Aouzou Strip Observer Group
UNASUR	Unión de naciones sudamericanas (Union of South American Nations)
UNAVEM	UN Angola Verification Mission

UNC	UN Command in Korea
UNCC	UN Compensation Commission
UNCCD	UN Convention to Combat Desertification
UNCDF	UN Capital Development Fund
UNCED	UN Conference on Environment and Development
UNCHE	UN Conference on the Human Environment
UNCHS	UN Centre for Human Settlements (Habitat)
UNCIO	United Nations Conference on International Organization
UNCITRAL	UN Commission on International Trade Law
UNCLOS	UN Conference on the Law of the Sea
UNCOD	UN Conference on Desertification
UNCRO	UN Confidence Restoration Organization in Croatia
UNCTAD	UN Conference on Trade and Development
UNDC	UN Disarmament Commission
UNDCP	UN Drug Control Programme
UNDOF	UN Disengagement Observer Force (Golan Heights)
UNDP	UN Development Programme
UNEF I	First UN Emergency Force (Suez Crisis)
UNEF II	Second UN Emergency Force (Yom Kippur War)
UNEP	UN Environment Programme
UNESCO	UN Educational, Scientific and Cultural Organization
UNFF	UN Forum on Forests
UNFICYP	UN Peace-keeping Force in Cyprus
UNFPA	UN Fund for Population Activities/UN Population Fund
UNGOMAP	UN Good Offices Mission in Afghanistan and Pakistan
UNHCR	(Office of the) UN High Commissioner for Refugees
UNHSP	UN Human Settlements Programme
UNICEF	UN International Children's Emergency Fund/UN Children's Fund
UNICRI	UN Interregional Crime and Justice Institute
UNIDIR	UN Institute for Disarmament Research
UNIDO	UN Industrial Development Organization
UNIFEM	UN Development Fund for Women
UNIFIL	UN Interim Force in Lebanon
UNIIMOG	UN Iran–Iraq Military Observer Group
UNIKOM	UN Iraq–Kuwait Observation Mission
UNIOSIL	UN Integrated Office in Sierra Leone
UNIPOM	UN India-Pakistan Observation Mission
UNITA	National Union for the Total Independence of Angola
UNITAF	Unified Task Force
UNITAR	UN Institute for Training and Research
UNMEE	UN Mission in Eritrea and Ethiopia
UNMIBH	UN Mission in Bosnia and Herzegovina
UNMIH	UN Mission in Haiti
UNMIK	UN Interim Administration Mission for Kosovo
UNMIL	UN Mission in Liberia
UNMIN	UN Mission in Nepal
UNMIS	UN Mission in the Sudan
UNMISET	UN Mission of Support in East Timor

UNMIT	UN Integrated Mission in Timor-Leste
UNMOGIP	UN Military Observer Group in India and Pakistan
UNMOP	UN Mission of Observers in Prevlaka (Croatia)
UNMOT	UN Mission of Observers in Tajikistan
UNMOVIC	UN Monitoring, Verification and Inspection Commission
UNOCI	UN Operation in Côte d'Ivoire (Ivory Coast)
UNODC	UN Office on Drugs and Crime
UNOG	UN Office in Geneva
UNOGBIS	UN Peacebuilding Support Office in Guinea-Bissau
UNOGIL	UN Observation Group in Lebanon
UNOMIG	UN Observer Mission in Georgia
UNOMIL	UN Observer Mission in Liberia
UNOMOZ	UN Operation in Mozambique
UNOMSIL	UN Observer Mission in Sierra Leone
UNOMUR	UN Observer Mission in Uganda-Rwanda
UNON	UN Office in Nairobi
UNOPS	UN Office for Project Services
UNOSOM	UN Operation in Somalia
UNOV	UN Office in Vienna
UNOWA	Office of the Special Representative of the Secretary-General for West Africa
UNPOS	UN Political Office for Somalia
UNPREDEP	UN Preventive Deployment Force (Macedonia)
UNPROFOR	UN Protection Force (former Yugoslavia)
UNPSG	UN Civilian Police Support Group
UNRISD	UN Research Institute for Social Development
UNRRA	United Nations Relief and Rehabilitation Administration
UNRWA	UN Relief and Works Agency for Palestine Refugees in the Near East
UNSCO	Office of the UN Special Coordinator for the Middle East
UNSCOL	Office of the UN Special Coordinator of the Secretary-General for Lebanon
UNSCOM	UN Special Commission (on Iraq)
UNSECOORD	Office of the UN Security Coordinator
UNSF	UN Security Force (in Dutch New Guinea)
UNSMA	UN Special Mission to Afghanistan
UNSMIH	UN Support Mission in Haiti
UNSSC	UN System Staff College
UNTAC	UN Transitional Authority in Cambodia
UNTAES	UN Transitional Administration for Eastern Slavonia, Baranja and Western Sirmium
UNTAET	UN Transitional Administration in East Timor
UNTAG	UN Transition Assistance Group (Namibia)
UNTCOK	UN Temporary Commission on Korea
UNTEA	UN Temporary Executive Authority
UNTMIH	UN Transition Mission in Haiti
UNTOP	UN Tajiskistan Office of Peacebuilding
UNTSO	UN Truce Supervision Organization

UNU	UN University
UNV	UN Volunteers
UNWTO	World Tourism Organization
UNYOM	UN Yemen Observation Mission
UPEACE	University for Peace
UPOV	International Union for the Protection of New Varieties of Plants
UPU	Universal Postal Union
US	United States of America
WAMA	West African Monetary Agency
WAMZ	West African Monetary Zone
WEF	World Economic Forum
WEU	Western European Union
WFC	World Food Council
WFP	World Food Programme
WFTU	World Federation of Trade Unions
WHO	World Health Organization
WILPF	Women's International League for Peace and Freedom
WIPO	World Intellectual Property Organization
WMO	World Meteorological Organization
WP3	Working Party 3
WSF	World Social Forum
WSSD	World Summit for Social Development
WSSD	World Summit on Sustainable Development
WTO	World Trade Organization
WWF	World Wildlife Fund/World Wide Fund for Nature
ZOPFAN	Zone of Peace, Freedom and Neutrality

Introduction

A comprehensive history

This book tells the history of international organizations since 1815. Thus far a comprehensive account of this actor in international relations has been lacking. Accounts available are restricted in time, often have an inventory character (Lyons 1963; Charnovitz 1997) or discuss specific topics (Reinsch 1911; Van der Linden 1987; Murphy 1994). The realist vision of international relations regards nation-states as the main actors and international organizations as insufficiently interesting, because the great powers dictate the game. This vision's dominance caused international organizations to be neglected, both theoretically and empirically. However, in theoretical debates during the past 25 years, more attention has been paid to cooperation between states and contributions of international organizations to international relations. This applies to the debate on international regimes, which confirmed that even distrustful states may cooperate on a long-term basis through decision-making approaches and social-constructivism, which stressed the relevance of new ideas, expertise and authority. These debates gradually entailed greater empirical attention. Recently some international organizations have started 'intellectual history projects', but these often restrict themselves to one organization or are limited by the organization's vision of its past and its position. The historical overview presented in this book is inspired by political science and attempts to cover the full genesis and evolution of international organizations, taking into account the entire period (from 1815 to the summer of 2008, when the war between Georgia and Russia troubled the balance of power), all policy fields (security, economics and humanity), and both intergovernmental and non-governmental organizations (IGOs and NGOs).

Organization of the text

This text is based on previous research on intergovernmental and private organizations and on research resulting from the objective to map the emergence and evolution of international organizations. Although most references in the text are to literature, many original documents have been used. Nowadays, search engines help to find documents,

1

such as international treaties and programmes, on the Internet, in addition to those which are available in archives and literature. Boxes in the text of this book contain background information, elaborations, overviews and tables. For reasons of simplicity, all boxes and tables are called 'Figures'. They are numbered per chapter and are meant to provide more specific information and to follow the line of an issue or organization. For convenience, all paragraphs have subheadings. Anyone wanting to trace a certain topic can do this via the table of contents, the index and the (sub)headings of sections and paragraphs. Each chapter starts with a boxed table of contents giving the sections and figures of that chapter. For references the author–date system is used, which refers to a bibliography at the end of the book (alphabetically ordered and chronologically by author). For reasons of readability the acronym NGO is used, rather than INGO (international NGO).

Acknowledgments

In the 1990s, Bertjan Verbeek and I started a research programme on, respectively, the autonomous policy making of international organizations, decision making within them and (with Jutta Joachim) implementation by them, which resulted in three edited volumes (Reinalda and Verbeek 1998; Reinalda and Verbeek 2004; Joachim et al. 2008). At the Nijmegen Department of Political Science, Robert H. Lieshout asked me to lecture on international organizations and allowed me to do this according to my understanding of the topic. The discussion forum he established for the international relations staff, called WOIB, can be considered a green zone within a by now rather bureaucratic academic world. WOIB has only one goal, which is debate in order to get better insights and improved texts. John Groom offered Bertjan Verbeek and myself an introduction to the European Consortium for Political Research, which gave us the opportunity to establish an international network of researchers and helped us to publish our volumes on international organizations in the ECPR series published by Routledge. I am particularly grateful to them, to my students, to my co-participants in international panels and workshops and to my English corrector, Annemarie Weitzel. I am looking forward to comments on both details and the entire process since 1815.

Part I

1815: British hegemony and the invention of the multilateral conference plus follow-up conference

The Concert of Europe and the Central Commission for the Navigation of the Rhine

The first part of this historical overview starts with an elaboration of political science views on the emergence and evolution of international organizations (Chapter 1). It then describes how British postwar institutional strategy during the Congress of Vienna created the practice of multilateral conferences with follow-up conferences. In the security field this resulted in the Concert of Europe (Chapter 2). In the economic field the promotion of free trade was helped by the wording of the principle of 'free navigation of rivers' by the Congress of Vienna, which also created the first intergovernmental organization, the Central Commission for the Navigation of the Rhine, tasked with monitoring this principle's implementation (Chapter 3).

Emergence and evolution of international organizations

1.1 Do international organizations matter?

Two kinds of international organization: IGOs and INGOs

Two kinds of international organization exist: *inter*-governmental and *non*-governmental ones. This book discusses both, because their histories, as was found, are intertwined more closely and from an earlier date than is often assumed. *Intergovernmental organizations* (IGOs in international relations theory jargon) have nation-states as their members, *international non-governmental organizations* (INGOs) have national NGOs. Whereas IGOs are established and governed by governments, INGOs with public goals are set up by citizens, who through these private organizations are politically active at both the national and the international level. IGOs and INGOs have three characteristics in common: they are based on a covenant (a text drafted by the founders which defines the objectives and the organization's design), a permanent secretariat performing ongoing tasks and (in the case of IGOs) three or more member states, or (in the case of INGOs) member NGOs from three or more states.

Varying interest in international organizations

The question of whether international organizations matter in international politics, in particular compared with nation-states, has been a topic of dispute. The dominant realist school in international relations theory regards nation-states as the main players and international organizations as barely relevant, INGOs even less so than IGOs (see Figure 1.1 for the various schools in this field). Historians using a similar realist premise have been mainly interested in states and only just, or not at all, in cooperation within IGOs or the resulting roles of IGOs. They regard IGOs as forums where governments representing states meet. As a result, very few overviews of international organizations are available, whether or not inspired by political science, or they are organizational dictionaries and inventories. Within political science, interest in international organizations has fluctuated, as Miles Kahler showed in an overview of the international relations field. During the 1950s international organizations were 'hardly regarded as the most exciting frontiers of research in the field' and for two decades they, as well as international law, remained 'a backwater' (Kahler 1997, 29 and 33). International relations specialists followed what was happening at the United Nations (UN) and its specialized organizations. Their observations were published in the journal *International Organization*, founded in 1947. In 1956 Inis Claude published his book *Swords into Plowshares, The Problems and Progress of International Organization* (Claude 1966³). In this comprehensive and well-balanced treatise an acceptable realist scepticism predominates, unlike in books by orthodox realists such as Edward Carr and Hans Morgenthau, who emphasize the 'idealist' character international organizations supposedly have (Carr 1940) (Morgenthau 1948; revised 1978). During the 1960s a new research programme was developed, focusing on decision making within international organizations and the ensuing roles they play. The programme's two main publications are *Beyond the Nation-State* by Ernst Haas, published in 1964, and *The Anatomy of Influence* edited by Robert Cox and Harold Jacobson and published in 1973 (Haas 1968²; Cox and Jacobson 1973). In the early 1970s international relations theory widened its scope, when so-called transnationalism included actors other than states as well, among them transnational corporations and interest groups (Keohane and Nye 1972). The transborder activities and political leverage of these societal actors enhanced the interdependence between national societies and nation-states. Their roles questioned the assumption of states being the only or primary actors in world politics. Notwithstanding this widening trend, international organizations barely had a chance of being studied because of the thesis put forward in – ironically – *International Organization*: that the formal and bureaucratic character of international organizations blocked a proper view of world politics. Research should not focus on organizations, but on broader, more informal forms of cooperation, such as *international regimes*. Regimes are frameworks of rules, expectations and prescriptions that states and other actors may agree on in specific policy fields, based on commonly perceived needs. Although regime theory and its ensuing *neoliberal institutionalism*, elaborated by Robert Keohane (who defined the term *institution* more broadly than organization by including IGOs, INGOs, regimes and conventions), paid attention to more actors than just states and to cooperation between states, IGOs and international law have remained underexposed in this approach, which was soon guiding the journal *International Organization*. The research programme set up by Haas, Cox and Jacobson, focusing on what takes place within international organizations, did not get a chance to develop further. Neoliberal curiosity about NGOs remained limited, because the power resources of NGOs were restricted in comparison with those of nation-states. The elaboration of *neorealism* by Kenneth Waltz in his book *Theory of International Politics* (1979) narrowed the perspective of the regime theory, because of its return to realist assumptions that great powers dominate world politics and that international bureaucracies are uninteresting and irrelevant. According to Waltz bureaucracies are mainly concerned with securing the continuity and health of the organization, while their leaders are not masters of the matters their organizations deal with (Waltz 1979, 111). Once again, this lack of interest by both neoliberals and neorealists kept research on international organizations restricted. It was not until the 1990s that an awareness of their importance began to grow. This was related to their steering role in the process of globalization that was taking place, their contributions to solving military conflicts and civil wars around the end of the Cold War and the increased role of critical but widely supported NGOs. The generally limited scientific interest in IGOs and NGOs was increasingly confronted with the fact that states have successfully used IGOs and international agreements, and within that multilateral context have appreciated the expert input from NGOs. This left scientific schools paying more attention to the contributions from actors other than states and to the character of bureaucracies' greater room for manoeuvre. The sociologically-oriented social-constructivist approach developed a new research programme on IGOs and NGOs, which took into account the ideas of citizens focused on change as well as the bureaucratic workings and authority of IGOs.

Figure 1.1 Schools within international relations theory

The main schools in international relations theory are *realism* and *liberal institutionalism*, with more systematically elaborated variants in *neorealism* and *neoliberal institutionalism*. Power politics are central to **realism**. The nation-state is the major international actor, trying to survive in a hostile environment by forming and using power. Ideas about sovereignty and self-help assume a separation between domestic and foreign politics, of which the latter is crucial to survival. **Liberal institutionalism** starts from the idea that democratic institutions can tame the power drive of human beings and states. Democratic states, international organizations and common rules may contribute to peace and security. Domestic and foreign politics are intertwined when states recognize common interests. David Baldwin (1993) summarized the debate between the two neo-variants.

Social-constructivism is a critical school. It rejects the positivist premise of neorealism and neoliberal institutionalism, which assumes an external and objective reality in this way: the anarchic situation which exists between states as a result of the absence of a highest authority is considered as 'given'. Constructivists, however, regard the social world, including international relations, as a human construction. That construction is a dynamic process, in which ideas are being developed and knowledge and understandings are being shared (an intersubjective activity). Anarchy then is not a given, but, according to Alexander Wendt, 'what states make of it' (Wendt 1992, 72). The way social structures are defined depends on their shared understandings. The intersubjective understanding in a *security dilemma* is a social structure in which states are so distrustful that they make worst-case assumptions about each other's intentions. As a result they define their interests in self-help terms. But in a *security community* the social structure is based on shared knowledge, with trust between states to resolve their disputes by means other than force, notwithstanding their ongoing promotion of national interests. Constructivists therefore are looking for ways in which international actors change their behaviour as a result of changes in ideas and shared understandings. With regard to IGOs, they are interested in critical ideas put forward by NGOs during the agenda-setting phase and the emergence and acceptance of new norms by IGOs, followed by their acceptance and internalization by a broader public of states and citizens (Finnemore and Sikkink 1998). Constructivists are also interested in rational–legal authority as characteristic of bureaucracies and the ways in which this kind of authority contributes to the more autonomous roles IGOs play in international relations (Barnett and Finnemore 2004). Boas and McNeill (2004) used a constructivist approach in the field of international organizations and development.

Within international relations theory, **four phases with regard to international organizations** may be discerned. During the *first phase* of classical realism, international organizations are agents controlled by the great powers, without contributions of their own to international relations. During the *second phase* of the research programme started by Haas, Cox and Jacobson, international organizations are interesting institutions because the outcome of the political games that are being played within the organizations may add to their autonomous contributions and policies. During the *third phase* of the international regimes discussion, international organizations can help states to solve collective action problems by considering a long-term perspective rather than taking into account short-term interests. However, although it was proved that long-lasting cooperation between states is possible and that international organizations act as intervening variables, attention was barely drawn to the organizational or bureaucratic aspects of this cooperation. During the *fourth phase* of constructivism, attention is paid to what is happening within organizations (for instance, in socialization processes) and to the roles international organizations play on the basis of their rational–legal authority. They affect state behaviour through ideas and expertise based on bureaucratic authority. Although NGO contributions to transnational and international relations were observed during the 1970s, neither neoliberal institutionalism nor neorealism took private actors seriously. This was different with constructivism, because it supported the preceding researchers of NGO contributions to international relations, in particular by focusing on transnational advocacy networks.

Nation-states and international organizations: principals and agents?

The realist subordination of IGOs to nation-states is well expressed in the rational model of principals and agents. This model's premise is that an actor (the *principal*) delegates some authority to a body (the *agent*) without renouncing this authority. The purpose of this relationship is that the actor will perform certain tasks for the principal. The relationship between the member states of an IGO and the organization's bureaucracy (the secretary-general and his or her international staff) may well be discussed as a principal–agent model. The member states are the principals and decide what the IGO's staff shall and may do. In case the secretariat does not fulfil its functions, either by doing too little or too much, or by handling it differently, the member states, in particular the great powers among them, may call the secretariat to order. They may even revoke the delegated authority and the IGO's existence will then come to an end. But reality is not as simple as this model, because the agent (the IGO) may create some room for manoeuvre for itself as there are several principals rather than one. Member states seldom agree among themselves, or in all respects (states represented by various departments are not unitary actors). A secretary-general able to lead an IGO may use this disagreement in favour of the objectives of the organization as defined in its constitution (Reinalda and Verbeek 2004, 22). Furthermore, by the time the IGO starts monitoring the implementation of the decisions taken, the principal–agent relationship is turned around, with the IGO as principal demanding that the member states (agents) implement the international decisions. If member states do this insufficiently, the IGO may act by 'naming and shaming' the non-implementing states in front of the 'international community'.

Autonomous roles of IGOs due to leadership and internal capacities

IGOs playing a role of their own thanks to the room for manoeuvre that states allow to arise, or due to the non-implementation of common decisions, will keep struggling with the demands of the major member states. Member states provide the organizations' resources (the power of the purse), may withhold the political will to implement and as principals control the IGOs. However, the fact that states, in their interactions with IGOs, are able to restrict them, for instance through rules and procedures imposed on IGOs, does not mean that IGOs are defenceless against this state control. An organization's *institutional design* is focused on being effective. This implies an IGO's leadership (the challenge to move unwilling states towards decisions and implementation), as well as its mobilization of internal resources such as using available expertise, creating specific organs, providing technical and other support, or sending independent observers or brokers. In this context the rational–legal authority of modern bureaucracies comes into play, with its characteristics of hierarchy, continuity, impersonality (the work is done according to fixed rules) and expertise (functionaries are selected according to capability, education and training and have access to information in files). IGOs may gain rational–legal authority by acting according to agreed rules and using their experience and expertise from their files. They may enhance this authority by also building up moral authority based on good performance, long-lasting and highly-qualified expertise in various fields and an expansion of assigned tasks. Unlike the *logic of consequentialism* which dominates among rivalling and calculating states, the *logic of appropriateness* may find an opportunity with IGOs, given their functioning according to independent and impartial rules and their inclination to follow ways once entered (*path dependency*) in order to find appropriate solutions in line with norms previously set, or to be developed, for the problems they are confronted with (March and Olsen 1989). If IGOs are able to show leadership and use their internal capacities, they may play a role of their own, even during longer periods, commonly sticking to roads once taken. Often these roles are barely recognizable to outsiders, because IGOs may act rather cautiously and out of sight in order not to antagonize certain member states. The roles of an IGO's staff usually remain fairly invisible, because the staff will not make them explicit. The result counts, not the mentioning of their roles. But if the IGO's roles are effective, it becomes harder for states to deny their results. The ways in which IGOs use their internal capacities and institutional memory have hardly been researched, due to the absence of interest in the functioning of international bureaucracies, but it may be assumed that states control IGOs to a lesser extent than most international relations theories suppose. However, it can also happen that the autonomy and the authority that IGOs have built up diminish, or even are lost. This implies that the extent of autonomy and authority can fluctuate over time (Reinalda 1998).

IGOs as dynamic actors

States are primarily interested in the promotion of their national interests. According to realists, they avoid becoming dependent on other states or self-willed IGOs. But the more profitable cooperation between states in IGOs is, the more difficult it will be to revoke delegated authority. States may do so, since they have only delegated and not renounced it. However, revoking authority may entail such high costs and loss of trust that states prefer to continue their cooperation. It should be added that IGOs that are threatened in their existence will be inclined to fight back in order to survive. They will attempt to become indispensable, for instance by providing comparative overviews and long-term trends based on essential data they have available as the result of regularly collected information about a large number of nation-states. These data are the result of monitoring the states' implementation behaviour of international agreements and services and may be used as a means in a struggle for survival. Most of the time IGOs manifest themselves as dynamic actors. If necessary, they provide broad interpretations of their objectives as formulated in their covenants or articles of agreement and refer to 'implied powers' (Bowett 1982, 338). They adapt to changing situations and demands, argue convincingly that new problems are covered by their mandates, or they themselves add new ambitions. Once established, IGOs take on a life of their own and develop their own inner dynamics (Cox and Jacobson 1973, 7). The nature of bureaucracies may also cause *dysfunctional* behaviour and make IGOs overreach themselves. This can happen if an IGO's leadership receives insufficient response to its activities and produces 'groupthink' or 'tunnel vision'. IGOs may also cause states that are being helped to not look actively for better solutions. Or they may cause international disagreements by behaving partially rather than acting independently (Barnett and Finnemore 1999). IGO roles are not by definition the correct ones.

This book starts from those international relations approaches that offer insights into the roles of IGOs and NGOs, be it liberal institutionalism, transnationalism, regime theory, critical theory, decision-making approaches or constructivism. However, some realist scepticism should be kept in mind. One should not be blind to the fact that major powers' actions and weight do restrict the functioning of IGOs and NGOs. But this does not take place to the extent predicted by the principal–agent model.

1.2 Political science views on the emergence and evolution of international organizations

Multilateral conferences as the foundation of organizations

How did IGOs emerge? This book regards the invention of the multilateral conference plus follow-up conference in 1815, the closing year of the Congress of Vienna, as the foundation of IGOs. The practice that followed this invention provided the groundwork for today's IGOs. The invention involves governments of states convening a *multilateral conference* (of three or more states), setting an agenda and discussing the problems raised. At the conference they will consider causes and possible solutions and finally take decisions that are guidelines for solving the problems on the agenda. What matters after this common decision-making process is the implementation by the participating states. In order to gain insights into their national implementation activities, the participating states will convene a *follow-up conference*, which will use national reports to assess whether states have acted according to the common guiding principles. If all states have implemented the decisions correctly, nothing remains to be done. If this is not, or insufficiently, the case, and that is a more common occurrence, it makes sense to discuss the new situation.

This discussion usually leads to new, or adapted, decisions in favour of further implementation. The carrying out of those new decisions may be discussed at another follow-up conference. The process thus reproduces itself and evolves into an *ongoing cycle*. During a large part of the nineteenth century, convening multilateral conferences was an *ad hoc* matter. But the continuation and further development of common problems and solutions caused a *process of institutionalization* of multilateral conferences and their follow-up conferences, with regularity and continuity as its main characteristics. This resulted in the creation of IGOs with a regularly meeting *general conference* and a *permanent secretariat*, that is, an international staff holding permanent appointments and headed by a secretary-general. The creation of a permanent secretariat changed the previous series of conferences into an organization (Claude 1966, 175). Conferences were no longer called by heads of state, but by organizations. They did this more regularly and soon more systematically as a result of experience and expertise. This took place from 1865. The necessary preparation for the conferences gave the IGO functionaries power over the agenda: 'sending out invitations, deciding on a venue, negotiating a preliminary agenda, arranging for transportation and housing of some delegates, preparing meeting rooms, performing conference services (including translation, editing, and copying) and following up on the conference by publishing and circulating documents, circulating conventions for signature, and keeping track of ratifications'. By 1910 the regular, mostly annual, general conferences of IGOs outnumbered the previous *ad hoc* conferences called at the invitation of heads of state and their governments (Murphy 1994, 111–12). This did not exclude the calling of later *ad hoc* multilateral conferences with follow-up conferences. The Bologna Process set up in 1999 to harmonize higher education in Europe consists of regular multilateral conferences and is institutionalizing, but it still lacks a permanent secretariat (see Figure 43.2).

The hegemon's role: the postwar institutional strategy

The invention of the multilateral conference plus follow-up conference in 1815 was a process set in motion by nation-states, which within less than a century would lead to institutionalization and acceptance of IGOs in international relations. The strongest and leading state, the *hegemon*, initiated this new practice. Although this vision corresponds with the realist school, the hegemon does not seek *maximum* promotion of its interests, as realists suppose, but from a longer-term perspective is satisfied with *optimal* promotion. This creates the leeway in which multilateral conferences and IGOs may emerge. John Ikenberry, who combines realist and liberal-institutionalist views, argues that the creation of international institutions takes place after the end of major wars, when a new distribution of power emerges and creates new asymmetries between powerful and weak states. The hegemon may then resort to institutional strategies as mechanisms to establish restraints on indiscriminate and arbitrary state power and 'lock' in a favourable and durable postwar order. IGOs offer leading states the opportunity 'to restrain themselves and thereby dampen the fears of domination and abandonment by secondary states' (Ikenberry 2001, 15). Ikenberry's main argument is that the United Kingdom (UK) and the United States (US) played sophisticated power games with an institutional strategy after the major wars that ended in 1815, 1919 and 1945. 'They sought to establish mutually agreed-upon rules and principles of order, and they appeared to realize that to do so required not just wielding material capabilities but also restraining the use of that power' (Ikenberry 2001, 12). Their strategies resulted, respectively, in the Concert of Europe,

11

the League of Nations and the UN. That the hegemon's attitude may also have a negative effect was seen during the Cold War, when Ronald Reagan's US Presidency, starting in 1981, marked a turning point in the post-1945 period. He highlighted his policies toward the Soviet Union, replaced Keynesianism, which was the corner stone of the UN's economic and social activities, by neoliberalism and further pressurized the UN system, in particular by restricting its budgets. This strategy severely weakened the institutional set-up created in 1945.

The continued existence of IGOs

Apart from the emergence of IGOs, their *continued existence* should be dealt with. Their very existence may be endangered by exogenous shocks. The First World War was such a shock. However, most of the IGOs created at the end of the nineteenth century survived it. Continuity of IGOs may also be discussed if the power relations between states shift or the hegemon's preferences change, as in the early 1980s. However, neither the weakening of American hegemony during the 1970s nor the Reagan policies of the 1980s resulted in a dismantling of IGOs or an enfeeblement of international regimes. Obviously, the institutional set-up is stable and able to adapt to changing circumstances. The so-called path-dependency approach assumes that organizations evolve in ways that 'even if not predictable ex ante – nonetheless follow a particular logic that makes sense only against the backdrop of the institutional context in which the "next steps" are inevitably negotiated' (Thelen 2003, 220). These ways imply limitations, but do not exclude institutional adaptation or innovation. IGOs, for instance, may develop new arrangements which are added to existing organizations. Instead of dismantling the old organizations, a process of 'layering' takes place, involving the partial renegotiating of some elements of a given set of organs while leaving others in place. Another kind of change takes place through 'conversion' of roles and functions. Set in motion by shifts in their environment or the incorporation of groups that were previously on their margins, IGOs may turn to new aims by using their capacities in new ways or in the service of new goals (Thelen 2003, 226–28). According to Haas, IGOs may adapt and even learn. Adaptation, in the sense of adding new activities and dropping old ones (similar to layering), refers to incremental change with an emphasis on altering means of actions without worrying about their coherence with existing goals. However, the behaviour of IGOs will change if actors question implicit theories underlying programmes and examine their original values. This learning, which does not occur very often, is associated with a form of managed organizational change. The stimuli that lead to learning mostly come from the external environment in which the organization is placed and in which something went wrong, in the sense that IGOs persist in making decisions that produce outcomes not desired by the member states or themselves. Clusters of bureaucratic entities within governments and IGOs together discuss these developments, with the aim not of dismantling the organizations, but of finding solutions for the problems (Haas 1990).

The interplay between international and domestic politics

The ongoing international political process that follows agenda setting at multilateral conferences or within IGOs can be presented as an *input–output model*. This starts with governments of states revealing their political wishes about one or more common problems. These are *inputs* for a multilateral conference or an IGO. Via a *throughput* process in the 'black box' of the conference or organization, the various wishes and related solutions are geared to one another, usually through the wording of international standards that should be guiding what is to be undertaken at the (sub)national level in order to solve the problems. The throughput phase ends with a decision, in the form of a multilateral agreement containing the agreed-upon standards and decision-making procedures for what is to be done. Services, such as financial or technical support, may be part of these decisions. In their turn, these international *outputs* serve as inputs for the states concerned. What follows parallels the ratification process of international treaties, by taking the international decisions to the national parliaments which may agree and ratify. If they do so, they are supposed to adapt national legislation and regulations and to change existing practices in accordance with the international standards. The national reports about implementation activities and results, which states regularly have to send to IGOs, can be regarded as inputs in the *feedback loop* for the follow-up conference or IGO body that will assess these reports and, if required, take further decisions. This input–output cycle shows how international (global or regional) politics are intertwined with domestic politics. Because IGO functionaries contribute to the political process during the entire cycle of agenda setting, the throughput process, the implementation process, the monitoring and the renewed decision-making phase (Joachim *et al.* 2008), it also shows that IGOs are more than just a forum where governments meet.

Governments negotiating at two levels

In this interplay between international and domestic politics, governments are more or less simultaneously negotiating the same issues at two levels: *nationally* within their own political systems and *internationally* within the multilateral conference to which they are a party or the IGO of which they are a member. In political science this combination is described as *two-level games*. Governments therefore are exposed to tensions following both from the debates and power relations within their national political system, and from those within the international arrangement. This combination offers governments opportunities to use arguments from one system in the other. They may use arguments from domestic politics internationally in order to influence the outcome of international agreements, or, the other way round, use international policies or intentions as arguments in domestic politics. Between the two levels, a time difference exists. The time perspective in national systems is definitely shorter than in international arrangements. In the case of democracies with regular elections the general time perspective is four years, with governments and/or their parties then trying to be re-elected. Dependent on the kind of change that is on the agenda, the international time perspective is far longer, a decade rather, or even more.

Private actors also play two-level games

States and IGOs are not the only players in this international political process. Private actors also participate. Large economic actors such as transnational corporations or sectoral interest groups may lobby. Promotional pressure groups, NGOs or social movements may advocate their views. During the throughput phase, independent experts or epistemic communities may bring forward new ideas and solutions for specific problems. Private actors can engage in the international political cycle from an *external* position, by influencing public opinion or lobbying governments and IGO functionaries, but they may also acquire an *internal* position, such as consultative status at a multilateral conference or with an IGO. In that case they have gained *access* to the institution. Access substantially enhances their opportunities to influence debates, because they are able to deliver contributions as regards content and they may coalesce politically with other actors. Furthermore, they often are able to report about national attitudes towards implementation. Private actors being active within national political systems (by putting leverage on their governments), as well as at multilateral conferences or within IGOs (by lobbying and using their consultative status), are also playing two-level games. They will be most influential with regard to their governments if they manage to exert a pincer movement by pressurizing their government simultaneously both nationally and internationally, for instance by referring to violations of international norms. Governments and IGOs engage private actors because of the expertise they themselves do not have available, or have only to a lesser extent. By engaging non-governmental or private actors, who will 'explain' the international decisions to their domestic constituencies, governments and IGOs also hope to find social support for these decisions. Private actors may further be strategic partners in domestic political games. In the same way as power differences play a role between states and IGOs, they also do so between on the one hand governments and IGOs, and on the other NGOs, whose main power resources are expertise and the ability to coalesce politically. Compared with governments, NGOs are weaker players within IGOs, as is also indicated by the term 'consultative' to describe their status. But NGOs promoting new ideas and bringing along resources of their own, as well as manifesting themselves as able political players, are not less interesting or less influential. This is certainly true for NGOs with strong roots in civil society, where citizens have engaged in social and other issues and in finding organizational solutions for those issues.

Two subsystems within IGOs

The outcome of the decision-making process within IGOs can be regarded as the result of two subsystems, according to Cox and Jacobson (1973). The *representative subsystem* is based on voting by governments interested in the promotion of their national interests. The *participant subsystem* takes into account all actors and also includes the influence of the representatives of NGOs (on the basis of their consultative status) and other IGOs (on the basis of their observer status), as well as IGO functionaries, independent experts and even representatives of the media (because they cover issues on the agenda and influence public opinion). The final outcome may be the result of the representative subsystem of governments being the deciding factor. However, in practice this seldom happens. For reasons of needing to find social support and having to take into account the inputs of other actors, the outcome more often depends on a combination of the two subsystems according to a scale, with combinations varying from weak towards strong influence from one or other of the two subsystems. While the salience of issues may favour the representative subsystem of governments, the participant subsystem of all actors should be taken into account. Large organizations are ruled by coalitions of interests depending on mutual accommodation. Although international bureaucracies often are considered a unitary actor, they may instead be a pluralistic whole of actors, with intra- and inter-organizational turf wars and loyalty conflicts experienced by international civil servants (bureaucratic politics). International consensus can come about as the result of continuous bargaining between governmental delegates, the organization's bureaucracy, independent experts and representatives of NGOs and other IGOs, in which the organization's leadership (the secretary-general) may take the lead and may persuade member states and other actors to move in a certain direction.

Promotion of trade, peace and human dignity

From their position in the international political process, with its two-level games and bureaucratic politics, IGOs contribute to solving common problems and attaining specific goals in international relations. They help nation-states to adapt to changing environments and to overcome problems related to these changes. Those who created IGOs had three motives, according to Harold Jacobson: the promotion of trade, peace and human dignity. In accordance with these motives IGOs have helped states: 1) to adapt to the dynamics of technological developments and the international economy (*trade motives*); 2) to create, maintain or improve political structures at global and regional levels that promote security (*peace motives*); and 3) to strengthen the states' national socio-economic basis by promoting social welfare and human rights (*humanitarian motives*) (Jacobson 1979, 64). Often a combination of these motives is found. It is assumed that a lively trade combined with respect for human rights will enhance the chances of peaceful relations between states even more strongly than each motive on its own will do. This book studies all three motives, including their combinations.

States can attain their goals more efficiently

The neoliberal instutionalist Keohane (1984) proved that international regimes and institutions enable states to attain their goals more efficiently. In an interdependent world, in which states and economies are dependent on each other, regimes and institutions facilitate cooperation through the functions they perform for states, such as diminishing their transaction costs, providing information about each other and thus reducing uncertainty. They render it possible for governments to enter into mutually beneficial agreements with one another. Although states remain the most important actors, they understand that they will profit from lasting cooperation, because this will bring them more efficiency than if each state acts on its own. Keohane's premise in this context that the bureaucratic character of IGOs and their specific contributions to international relations are of little relevance has been challenged and refuted by decision-making approaches and constructivism.

IGOs socialize states

Constructivists question the dominant premise that state preferences in an anarchic world are a given and that the source of these preferences is located within the state. They disagree with this view because it is static and not really interested in changes in state behaviour. Instead, constructivists start from the idea that states which are confronted with new international problems may *not* always know what they want and are receptive to teaching on what are appropriate and useful actions to take. This means, according to Martha Finnemore, that state preferences are malleable and that the source of the changes in preferences may be located outside the state (Finnemore 1996, 11). She argues that one cannot understand what states want without understanding the international social structure of which they are a part. 'States are embedded in dense networks of transnational and international social relations that shape their perceptions of the world and their role in that world. States are *socialized* to want certain things by the international society in which they and the people in them live' (Finnemore 1996, 2). IGOs, as parts of these networks, are actors who socialize states to accept new political goals and new values that will have an impact on their behaviour and on the workings of international relations. International standards developed by IGOs hence influence state behaviour. In other words, this view also regards IGOs as actors helping states to adapt to changed circumstances and to efficiently solve problems related to these changes. IGOs based on rational–legal authority will perform better the greater their authority. Sources for new ideas for IGOs may be transnational advocacy networks, NGOs or experts who are able to make states and IGOs aware of problems and possible solutions according to international standards. Unlike neoliberal institutionalists, constructivists are interested in the workings and effects of international bureaucracies as well as in the inputs by private actors into intergovernmental decision making.

Global governance

The working of the described combination of states, IGOs and private actors aimed at solving problems is called governance. This somewhat vague term refers to such elements as control, steering and command. It received its own meaning in the international system of states, in which – unlike in hierarchical national political systems – a highest authority is lacking. There is no world government, but there is governance. Global governance, however, is not a perfect system, according to Craig Murphy, who classifies it as 'poorly done and poorly understood'. Contemporary global governance 'avoids attacking state sovereignty, favours piecemeal responses to crises, and has emerged at a time when creative intellectual leadership was not matched by courageous leadership' (Murphy 2000, 789). Keohane is also critical: 'Globalization depends on effective governance, now as in the past. Effective governance is not inevitable. If it occurs, it is more likely to take place through interstate cooperation and transnational networks than through a world state. But even if national states retain many of their present functions, effective governance of a partially – and increasingly – globalized world will require more extensive institutions. Governance arrangements to promote cooperation and help resolve conflict must be developed if globalization is not to stall or to go into reverse' (Keohane 2001, 1). The design of global (and regional) governance therefore needs attention. The study of IGOs, both in their relations with nation-states and as agents in their own right, as well as INGOs or other transnational networks, can be a helpful tool. This book aims to deepen the study of international governance by providing a comprehensive history of international organizations from 1815 until the early twenty-first century.

1815: the British postwar institutional strategy and the Concert of Europe

> Diplomacy by conference became an established fact of life in the nineteenth century
>
> (Claude 1966, 21)

2.1 The Congress of Vienna in 1814–15 and the transformation of European politics

The balance of power restored in Vienna

The two conferences in 1648 that agreed the peace treaties of Westphalia have been called the first European Congresses, as they laid the foundation for the modern European nation-state characterized by principles such as sovereignty and the balance of power (see Figure 2.1 for the development of the Westphalian state). The peace treaties of Utrecht (1713) and Vienna (1815) confirmed these principles. In Vienna such confirmation was required because Napoleon Bonaparte had upset the European balance of power with his campaigns of conquest. He had violated various international principles that France itself had declared during the French Revolution of 1789, such as national self-determination, non-intervention in other states and the rejection of wars of conquest. After the battle of Paris in early 1814 Napoleon abdicated and the Bourbons returned to the throne. On 30 May 1814, eight states signed the *Peace of Paris* to settle the end of the wars with France. Broadly speaking they restored the French territorial borders of 1792. Other matters were to be completed at the Congress of Vienna, which assembled between 8 September 1814 and 9 June 1815. At the Congress the Austrian Prince Klemens von Metternich presided, chairing the committee of the eight states that had signed the Paris Peace Treaty. The major decisions, however, were taken by the four triumphant great powers: Austria, Prussia, Russia and the UK. The event, with over 200 delegations, was impressive. 'Never had such a brilliant gathering been seen. All the states of Europe sent representatives; and many defunct states, such as the formerly sovereign princes and ecclesiastics of the late Holy Roman Empire, sent lobbyists to urge their restoration.' The four major powers took the decisions and restored the European balance of power, but this distinction between 'great' and 'small' powers was new. 'Indeed it was at the Congress of Vienna that the terms great and small entered clearly into the diplomatic vocabulary.' France remained a great power. 'Europe was at peace, a treaty having been signed with the late enemy; France also was represented at the Congress, by none other than Talleyrand, now minister to Louis XVIII' (Palmer and Colton 1971, 454). The main effort of the Congress was based on the European states' desire to prevent the domination of a single great power in the way Napoleon had tried to achieve. Such a situation had to be offset by 'an ingenious calculation of forces, a transfer of territory and "souls" from one government to another, in such a way as to distribute and balance political power among a number of free and sovereign states' (Palmer and Colton 1971, 455). It was hoped that a proper balance would also produce a lasting peace.

The transformation of European politics

For a long time the Congress of Vienna was regarded as an event that took dynastic rather than national interests into consideration. By repairing the rights of former rulers, rather than considering the future interests of nation-states, it was supposed to be oriented toward the past instead of the future. However, P.W. Schroeder argues that in Vienna a transformation of European politics was taking place (Schroeder 1996). The UK convinced the great powers that they together were the guardians who had the duty to maintain and improve the balance of power. In Vienna they recognized that the state system as it had developed up to the nineteenth century was no longer adequate, given its focus on the pretensions and claims of sovereign rulers. The conviction grew that for the nineteenth century it had become necessary and possible 'to modify the free-wheeling irresponsibility of sovereign states to a greater extent than had been done under traditional international law, and to remedy the international institutional vacuum by creating and putting to work some agencies which would serve the community of states as a whole'. This putting to work of international 'agencies' was done by 'statesmen who sought new arrangements and devices whereby the sovereign units of the old system could pursue their interests and manage their affairs in the altered circumstances of the age of communication and industrialism' (Claude 1966, 19–20). Although the term 'great power' remained the cornerstone of the Concert of Europe's legitimacy, the great powers became aware that in the longer run they also needed the support of the smaller states. They could not avoid these states' involvement if they wanted them to consent to their decisions. They could arrange this by consulting them and, if required, by reinforcing the rights of the smaller states.

Citizens lobbying at the Congress of Vienna

Apart from in its final session, the Congress of Vienna did not meet in plenary but in committees. Lobbying took place during receptions, concerts, suppers, hunting parties or balls: *Le Congrès ne marche pas, il danse*, according to the Prince de Ligne. Apart from princes and government representatives, citizens also came to Vienna in order to lobby for their interests. Representatives of the Jewish communities of Frankfurt and the German

Hanseatic cities submitted petitions and asked for a meeting with Metternich. The Congress of Vienna approved a provision providing for the civil rights of Jews in Article XVI of the constitution which the Congress drafted for the new confederation of German and Austrian states: the Austrian-led German Confederation. Equally, German publishers had sent a representative to Vienna in order to seek protections. This resulted in a constitutional provision calling for liberty of the press and measures against literary piracy (Charnovitz 1997, 195–96). Finally, representatives of the movement for the abolition of slavery and the slave trade exerted influence by their presence in Vienna (see §4.1).

Figure 2.1 The Westphalian state and the balance of power

From ancient times until the Middle Ages (from around 3500 BC to 1500) various international systems existed around civilizations such as those in China, Egypt or Mesopotamia. Thereafter one comprehensive international system of nation-states gradually emerged. **Modern state building** started with the Italian Wars of 1494–1518. The decline of the Holy Roman Empire (the German Empire) prevented the functioning of feudal states and free cities originating in the Middle Ages. The end of the Thirty and Eighty Years' Wars in 1648 resulted in an international treaty which put into words the foundations for modern states. The two *Peaces of Westphalia* were concluded in the cities of Osnabrück and Münster between, respectively, France, the German emperor and Sweden, and Spain and the Republic of the United Netherlands.

During these peace negotiations, **general principles** were phrased with regard to territorial states and the relations between them. These can be found in Articles 64, 65 and 67 of the agreed *Treaty of Westphalia* that was signed on 24 October 1648. Article 64 discusses territoriality, the right of a state to choose its own religion and the right of non-intervention by other states. Article 65 elaborates sovereign authority with regard to foreign policy, whereas Article 67 states the right of a sovereign state to determine its domestic politics without foreign interference. This internal and external sovereignty has remained the main characteristic of the territorial or *Westphalian state* (Van Kersbergen *et al.* 1999, 77–78). When these principles were transformed into actual forms of states and government (a declared principle is not yet a reality), authorities began to define exact territorial borders and within those borders started to centralize authority in a national government. This process of state building after the Middle Ages, which was accompanied by a large number of wars between, and within, states, has taken centuries. Initially it remained restricted to Europe and Northern America but later, in particular in the twentieth century, it also developed elsewhere.

As a result of the Treaty power relations in Europe changed dramatically. The Holy Roman Empire fell apart, Spain lost its position as a great power and France started to become one. The management of the **balance of power** in the Westphalian state system is based on a combination of extensive competition between states and flexible **alliances** (temporary military cooperation arrangements aimed at withstanding a common enemy). It is expected that if all states seek to maximize their power, stability will result from maintaining a balance of power, lubricated by fluid alliance systems (Kegley 1995, 5). Balance of power systems are regarded as **stable** to the extent that they satisfy three conditions: an *alliance structure* in which the distribution of benefits reflects the distribution of power among its members; a substantial *ideological agreement* among the principal powers on what the system is intended to protect; and commonly *accepted procedures* for managing changes within the system. Options for restoring a balance of power are expansion of the alliance, negotiations on economic or territorial concessions or limited war (Pelz in Hogan and Paterson 1991, 113).

2.2 The British postwar institutional strategy and multilateral diplomacy

Multilateral conferences as instruments

The second Peace of Paris of 20 November 1815 marked the beginning of a new era with multilateral conferences and follow-up conferences. After his return from his exile island Elba, Napoleon grabbed power again but was finally defeated at Waterloo and once again sent into exile. This second Peace of Paris also marked the early stages of the *Quadruple Alliance* between Austria, Prussia, Russia and the UK. This alliance, led by monarchs who turned against Bonapartism in France, was charged to guarantee the implementation of what had been decided in Vienna and Paris. For this purpose it used an intergovernmental structure based on regularly convened multilateral conferences with broad purposes and an open agenda. The mechanism of conferences and follow-up conferences began to function in accordance with Article 6 of the Treaty concluded in Paris in 1815. 'To facilitate and to secure the execution of the present Treaty, and to consolidate the connections which at the present moment so closely unite the Four Sovereigns for the happiness of the world, the High Contracting Parties have agreed to renew their Meetings at fixed periods, either under the immediate auspices of the Sovereigns themselves, or by their respective Ministers, for the purposes of consulting upon their common interests, and for the considerations of the measures which at each of these periods shall be considered the most salutary for the response and prosperity of Nations, and for the maintenance of peace in Europe' (cited in Willetts 1996, 18; Richardson 1999, 50).

The Quadruple Alliance and British long-term strategy

That common values also played a role was revealed by the coinciding creation of the *Sacred Alliance* of Austria, Prussia and Russia by the Christian monarchs of these three states. The British monarch stayed out of this. The idea of a postwar continuation of cooperation was attributed to the Russian Tsar Alexander, but John Ikenberry argues that this alliance building resulted from the British desire to create a durable, and for the UK profitable, world order. In January 1814 the UK (the hegemon of the nineteenth century) had already suggested to its military allies that France should be included in the alliance. Although all kinds of territorial disputes arising from the Napoleonic Wars still needed to be settled, Foreign Secretary Viscount Castlereagh arranged that these matters were to be achieved in negotiations during the postwar congress by using the principles of compensation and balance. The Quadruple Alliance took shape with the signing of the *Treaty of Chaumont* in March 1814, which included agreed-upon war aims such as a confederated Germany, an Italy of independent states, an independent Switzerland, a free Spain under the Bourbon dynasty and an enlarged Netherlands. But most consequentially, the Treaty obligated 'the powers to continue the alliance for 20 years after the war ceased, and to agree to protect each other against a resurgent France' (Ikenberry 2001, 96). The UK recognized that in order to achieve such a far-reaching settlement it had to be generous during the negotiations in Vienna and to be lenient with regard to matters that in the long term were less important. It managed to do so by using its financial resources and making concessions. The Congress of Vienna appointed a Statistical Commission and charged it with evaluating the territories under discussion and delimitating territories by 'objective' standards of number, quality and types of population (Morgenthau 1993, 44). This contributed to a refinement of the compensation system and allowed more precise management as well as concessions. The British strategy was more than a settlement among the great powers, as the UK insisted that the created order should also offer protection to the smaller powers. They no longer needed to find a compromise with France because the great powers had already done so. 'Britain responded to incentives to use the war and its aftermath to lock in a Europe-wide settlement' (Ikenberry 2001, 90).

Consultation as a process of learning

The establishment of the new principle of joint consultation by states required the development of techniques and the creation of psychological prerequisites in order to make these kinds of multilateral negotiation successful. International cooperation needed more than good intentions. Governments and their representatives had to develop the devices which are essential for the efficient conduct of multilateral conferences and to adopt the attitudes which are necessary for harmonious consultation. They needed to gain experience before they would understand all procedural and diplomatic innovations. 'Statesmen learned something about the arrangements and procedures, and became imbued with some of the temperamental attributes, which make possible the give and take of genuine multilateral negotiation' (Claude 1966, 23). This learning process took time. It was not an isolated phenomenon, as it took place in an institutional context that was evolving with regard to issues such as diplomatic relations, the relationship with the press, the balance of power, the course of events during a multilateral conference, as well as the multilateral treaty containing the agreed-upon conclusions. Eventually these various nineteenth-century developments cumulated in the so-called multilateral diplomatic process (see Figure 2.2).

Diplomatic relations regulated

The Congress of Vienna produced new regulations for diplomatic relations which simplified the functioning of both bilateral and multilateral diplomacy. The typical disputes about the precedence of state representatives at official ceremonies were resolved by referring to the neutral moment of accreditation. The diplomat holding the oldest accreditation became the doyen. Four successive classes of diplomatic representative were acknowledged: ambassadors and papal nuncios; extraordinary envoys and plenipotentiary ministers; envoys; and *chargés d'affaires*. The precedence of states at multilateral conferences was agreed upon as alphabetically in order of their French names. Generally speaking, the rules that developed in order to protect diplomats (privileges and immunities) would also apply to multilateral conferences and IGOs. Codification of these customary diplomatic practices took place in 1961 in a convention on diplomatic relations and in regulations by intergovernmental organizations.

Changes in diplomacy

The major change taking place in the diplomatic community from the second half of the nineteenth century onwards was in its composition. The diplomatic corps had, in origin, an aristocratic base. This was to change gradually into a more citizen-based community, even if aristocratic titles have remained present within foreign ministries to this day. The old aristocratic diplomatic community had developed its skills through breeding and upbringing rather than by formal training. The new diplomatic community, however, resulted from career paths with formal training and individual exams organized by the ministry. A side effect of this modern type of organization was that the ministry gained a stronger grip on the diplomats and hence on diplomacy itself. Furthermore, due to the greater relevance of economic affairs, consular relations became more important. For consular positions the ministry often appointed people with economic and trade experience. A final change in the diplomatic corps was the rise of non-European diplomats from the early twentieth century onwards, first from Asia (Japan) and later from Latin America.

The role of the press and the first press communiqué (1818)

The conference in Aix-la-Chapelle in 1818 (see Figure 2.3) was the first multilateral conference in times of peace. It attracted many journalists who were eager to report the event. This meant that the conference chair had to consider what exactly he would disclose to them. Aix-la-Chapelle is considered the beginning of public international diplomacy, as a press communiqué was released followed by a verbal explanation by the chair.

Institutional innovation of the balance of power

The institutional innovations of the balance of power introduced by the UK as part of its postwar strategy consisted of three core mechanisms: an alliance extended into peace time based on some measure of restraint of power; a multilateral conference system as a process of consultation among the great powers, with joint management of conflict and the adjudication of territorial disputes; and finally 'a diffuse promulgation of norms and rules of European public law, which together were intended to give the institutional, territorial, and great-power arrangements in Europe a certain sense of legal-based legitimacy and authority' (Ikenberry 2001, 98). The drafting of precise and detailed regulations in its *Final Act*, including the constitution of the German Confederation, gave the Congress of Vienna to some extent the character of a legislative assembly, with the Final Act as a moment in the development of international public law (Ikenberry 2001, 105).

The course of events at multilateral conferences

The initiative in convening a multilateral conference may be taken by various actors. Often it was taken by a government that had an interest in the topic to be discussed. At other times the initiative was a private one, originating from the aristocracy, industrialists or organized citizens. Sometimes various governments asked a particular government to take the initiative. Usually the government that set the convening process in motion acted as the host of the conference, providing meeting places and secretarial assistance as well as persons who were significant enough to preside at the meetings. Their origin was not necessarily governmental. The general model used was one of a *preparatory conference* of technical experts and permanent civil servants, which, if successful, was followed by a *diplomatic conference* where governmental representatives would take decisions. Representatives of NGOs could be present in both cases and influence debates with expertise or suggestions. Whereas the first kind of conference could only pass resolutions meant to influence governments, the second kind could agree to, and sign, treaties or conventions which were binding and would add to the development of international law or result in the creation of an IGO. Diplomats at multilateral conferences were bound by strict instructions from their governments. If these instructions were to remain silent, the diplomat might abstain from voting on particular issues in order not to reveal his government's position. This practice did not survive, since generally speaking openness helped to discuss problems and solutions jointly and was crucial for winning social support from the citizens or other states. Initially, agreement at the conference did not imply that a government or its legislature accepted the negotiated results of the multilateral conference, for this was seen as an institution in itself set apart from the national political system. However, national systems progressively began to accept the outcomes of multilateral conferences, given their benefits and advantages for themselves and also for their citizens or firms. At their discretion, governments sometimes decided to employ diplomats of high standing and at other times experts. 'The professional diplomatist was naturally much better equipped than the "expert" to hammer a broad proposal into an acceptable form' and as a rule was more acutely aware of the limits of the possible or able to keep the expert within reasonable bounds. However, these diplomats themselves had to learn to take into consideration that experts had ideas, which from their points of view made sense as well (Lyons 1963, 22). The success of the telegraph undermined the traditional diplomat's autonomy, as more information from different sources became available more quickly than before. The argument that he had not been able to contact his government could no longer be used by the diplomat who wanted to gain time.

The multilateral treaty

The main institutional elaboration of the traditional interstate treaty in the nineteenth century was the *multilateral convention*, 'hammered out in committee and conference of many states, voted upon as if it were a legislative bill, and adopted to serve as a joint legislative enactment'. Claude regards this instrument 'a clumsy and inadequate device for international legislation'. But its creation 'out of the old materials of the treaty device was nevertheless a major triumph' of the nineteenth-century conferences and intergovernmental organizations (Claude 1966, 32–33). In practice, states encapsulated everything that had been settled and agreed upon in one complete document as *Acte finale*, *Acte général* or *Protocol final*. 'This contained a summary of the work done and had annexed to it the various documents which had been signed' by the governments, initially by the foreign minister and from the twentieth century onwards also by the ministers of specific departments (Lyons 1963, 24). Practice soon revealed that conventions and treaties on the same topics concluded at a later date would fall back on the older ones. They built on what the older agreements contained. States that were not parties to a convention often showed their willingness to recognize, and follow, the norms and

Figure 2.2 The multilateral diplomatic process

After some time, the **multilateral diplomatic process** that followed from the invention of the multilateral conference plus follow-up conference in 1815 developed along more or less established lines, without excluding variations. Solutions found to solve problems in one place might later be used elsewhere. If, for instance, a multilateral conference fails to reach agreement but the states nonetheless show sufficient political will to continue, they may establish a committee with fewer participants. If this committee manages to reach a compromise, the plenary meeting will take this as the basis for its further negotiations. In this way, the conference of American republics of 1901 in Mexico City prevented itself from failing (see §7.4). Other conferences accepted or developed the same procedure. The respective elements of the multilateral diplomatic process are:

- *joint meetings* of states represented by their governments;
- *agenda setting* as a tool to gain insight into the issues to be discussed (common problems) and to prepare decision making;
- *joint analysis* of the issues on the agenda with the purpose of determining the direction of possible solutions;
- *being open* to inputs of expertise by others (experts, NGOs and IGOs);
- *decision making* resulting in a written international agreement;
- *signing* of the agreement by *governments*;
- putting the international agreement to the *national parliament* in order to have it ratified – *ratification* can be done with reservations, but once ratified the state has the obligation to adapt its national legislation and regulations to the international agreement and subsequently to adapt its practice to the new legislation;
- *reporting* about the success or failure of implementation by the government to the international body that monitors the international agreement's national implementation;
- *joint assessment* of the implementation as reported, entailing consequences in case of insufficient implementation such as further action or revision of decisions;
- recognition by *third states* that were not engaged in the drafting of the international agreement, followed by their accession and ratification.

procedures embodied in that convention. Usually they also became parties to it. The conventions resulting from these multilateral conferences enabled the further development of international law and multilateral diplomacy. A summary of the ensuing multilateral diplomatic process is given in Figure 2.2.

2.3 The Concert of Europe as a collective security regime

The Concert of Europe: norms, rules and procedures

During the nineteenth century, multilateral conferences proved an appropriate way to reach international agreements and to monitor their implementation. In the field of security this conferencing took place until the end of the century, often after a political or military conflict (see Figure 2.3 for an overview). The conferences lend themselves to discussing and establishing relations among states, to correcting violations of agreements and to the further specification of those agreements. In order to maintain the agreed order and the functioning of the balance of power, the great powers committed themselves to joint action. They had a whole range of agreed means available, such as norms, rules for behaviour and procedures. The essential *international norms* of the Concert of Europe as it developed after Vienna and Paris were self-restraint, consultation in times of crisis, willingness to act together, refusal to act unilaterally and constant assurances to one another of their pacific intent and commitment to the maintenance of stability. The essential *rules of behaviour* alongside these norms were the use of conference diplomacy to deal with crises, the approval of territorial changes by the great powers, the protection of the essential members of the system and the absence of challenges to the interests and honour of the great powers. Among the *common procedures* were the mutual consultation and collective decision making, the creation of buffer states, the establishment of neutral states and demilitarized zones, the localization of regional conflicts, the limitation of resources in third areas, the delineation of interests and areas of involvement, the intervention by multilateral action, the peaceful settlement of disputes and the communication and provision of advance notification (Richardson 1999, 52).

Four phases during the years 1815–56

Four distinct phases in the years between 1815 and 1856 characterize the Concert of Europe's existence as a security regime:

- 1815–18 as a phase of technical cooperation with activities directed at the defeated France;
- 1818–22 as the proper congress system with conferences in Aix-la-Chapelle (1818, about France), Troppau (1820, about insurrections and Naples), Laibach (1821, about the Naples revolution) and Verona (1822, about Italy, Spain and the Eastern Question);
- 1822–48 as a period of subtle but significant management of the security relations of the great powers;
- 1848–56 as a period of regime decay between the revolutions of 1848 and the outbreak of the Crimean War (1854–56).

During its second phase, the Concert of Europe adapted institutionally to the circumstances, 'when it no longer needed ambassadors taking care of the administration of France'. The joint occupation of France ended after the conference in 1818 when France was admitted to the Concert. The Concert 'changed its form to regular meetings at a higher level of representation in the form of congresses'. It also adapted when the UK 'decided to undermine this form by refusing to participate in the congress system out of opposition to the plans of other members'. The Concert at that point became 'a more *ad hoc* but still effective meeting of major players'. However, the tensions undermined the unity of the great powers and the Concert failed 'once some of the major players were transformed by domestic events'. It was badly weakened and finally it could not adapt 'when two of its members went to war against each other' in 1854 (Richardson 1999, 68).

Figure 2.3 Multilateral security conferences during the nineteenth century

Year	City	Subject
1814–15	Vienna	Peace treaty, Quadruple Alliance
1818	Aix-la-Chapelle	France
1820	Troppau	Revolutions, Naples
1821	Laibach	Naples revolution
1822	Verona	Italy, Spain, Eastern Question
1830–32	London	Belgium
1831–32	Rome	Reform of the Papal States
1838–39	London	Belgium
1839	Vienna	Eastern Question
1840–41	London	Eastern Question
1850–52	London	Schleswig-Holstein
1853	Vienna	Eastern Question
1855	Vienna	Eastern Question
1856	Paris	Peace treaty Crimean War
1858	Paris	Principalities
1860–61	Paris	Syria
1864	London	Schleswig-Holstein
1867	London	Luxembourg
1869	Paris	Crete
1871	London	Black Sea
1876–77	Constantinople	Eastern Question
1878	Berlin	Eastern Question
1880	Madrid	Morocco
1884–85	Berlin	Africa
1889	Washington DC	Trade and arbitration
1889–90	Brussels	Slave trade
1899	The Hague	Law of war and arbitration

Source: (Richardson 1999, 78); the conferences of 1889 and 1899 have been added.

The importance of the nineteenth-century conference system

Despite the demise of the Concert of Europe with the Crimean War of 1854, the great powers maintained their joint consultation at multilateral conferences on issues of security and high politics during the rest of the century. This barely played a role in the wars of Italian and German unification, but it did in the Eastern Question and Africa. The Concert did not initiate a process of institutionalization, but it adapted by broadening the range of topics on the agenda. The conferences did not take place regularly, but on an ad hoc basis. As a security regime it depended on the willingness of the great powers, which did not need to discuss the sovereignty of nation-states. They adhered to unanimous decision making and to maintaining the status quo, since these would not damage their national interests. For them the Concert of Europe was not a mechanism of change or transformation. Both the Concert of Europe during its existence in the first half of the century and the conferences convened during the second half of the century contributed to the stability of European interstate relations. The system was restricted in its impact, as it contributed more to 'the awareness of the problems of international collaboration than to their solution, and more to opening up the possibilities of multilateral diplomacy than to realizing them' (Claude 1966, 24). Nonetheless, the Concert of Europe produced the prototype for an executive council of the great powers that was later found in the League of Nations (1919) and the UN (1945).

Increasingly a matter of all states

Simultaneously, a change occurred within the sequence of conferences which was to give the smaller powers a more important position in the conference system. Participation was not restricted to the great powers, but to an increasing extent became a matter for all states. Despite the great powers' inclination to handle things behind the scenes, the other states' engagement grew stronger during the later years of the nineteenth century. This broader base enhanced the legitimacy of the decisions jointly taken at the various multilateral conferences. The number of nation-states in 1815 was 23. This number rose to 38 in 1850, 42 in 1900 and 44 in 1914. Although the number of states increased (almost doubled in 100 years), numbers also decreased as a result of Italian and German unification (see Appendix 1 for an overview of all states by continent since 1815). The convention that multilateral conferences were, in essence, great-power affairs was left behind with the Hague Peace Conferences of 1899 and 1907, since almost all then existing states participated on a more equal footing than they had done during the Concert of Europe.

3

The Central Commission for the Navigation of the Rhine and burgeoning free trade

3.1 The Central Commission for the Navigation of the Rhine (1815): freedom of navigation

Cooperation aimed at free navigation of international rivers

The main economic issue on the agenda of the Congress of Vienna was securing *freedom of navigation* on international rivers. Whereas the use of rivers was suited to modern water transport, the existing systems of legal and other tolls, dating from the Middle Ages, were increasingly regarded as impediments to the promotion of trade. The Congress of Vienna therefore made provisions to secure the freedom of navigation on the Rhine and other international rivers by creating a form of international authority in order to remove tolls and other obstacles. The principle of free navigation had been discussed before. During the seventeenth and eighteenth centuries, the doctrine of *innocent passage* was developed for situations where the use of rivers caused no harm or damage to riparian states. After the French Revolution, France had used its might to open the Scheldt and Meuse rivers and had argued that the Rhine should also be opened. This resulted in the removal of some existing regulations, and in 1804 France and the Hapsburg Empire agreed to consider the Rhine as common to them both as far as navigation was concerned. They made arrangements for a joint toll system and police administration and established a 'common authority' in Mainz. This first effective experiment in setting up a regime for an international river lasted for ten years. Its experiences played a role during the peace settlements of 1814–15. In May 1814 Article 5 of the Treaty of Paris declared the principle of free navigation. 'The navigation of the Rhine, from the point where it becomes navigable to the sea, and *vice versa*, shall be free, so that it can be interdicted to no one.' The ways in which the dues were to be levied and other aspects were to be discussed by the Congress of Vienna, but these should be regulated 'in the mode the most impartial and the most favourable to the commerce of all nations' (cited in Lyons 1963, 54).

The Committee of Navigation at the Congress of Vienna

The *Committee of Navigation* in Vienna consisted of the representatives of Austria, France, five German states (Baden, Bavaria, Hesse-Darmstadt, Nassau and Prussia), the Netherlands and the UK. Whereas France and the UK promoted a Rhine 'entirely free to the commerce and navigation of all nations', Prussia and other riparian states managed to include the qualifying clause 'in respect of commerce'. The latter interpretation found its expression in Article 109 of the Final Act of the Congress of Vienna. 'The navigation of the rivers ... along their whole course from the point where each of them becomes navigable to its mouth shall be entirely free and shall not, as far as commerce is concerned, be prohibited to anyone.' Regulations for policing and navigation 'shall be alike for all and as favourable as possible to the commerce of all nations' (cited in Lyons 1963, 55). The regime for international rivers as it was established in Vienna can be found in Articles 108–16 of the Final Act. They include the basic principle as well as uniform arrangements for the whole length of the river on issues such as collecting dues, policing the river, repairing the riverbed and the towpaths and the prevention of fraud and smuggling. Appendix 16B contains 32 more specific Articles about the Rhine; Appendix 16C contains seven Articles about the Neckar, the Main, the Moselle, the Meuse and the Scheldt. The freedom of navigation as it had been applied to the Rhine was to be applied correspondingly to these rivers.

The Central Commission for the Navigation of the Rhine (1815) as a learning process

On 8 June 1815 the *Central Commission for the Navigation of the Rhine* began to function in order to promote and maintain the freedom of navigation and the equality of treatment of all states. Its first members were France, the five German states and the Netherlands. The city of Mayence, which had been French but at the Congress of Vienna was allocated to Hesse-Darmstadt, became the Commission's seat. It took the member states a long time to reach agreement about the functioning of the Commission. This was caused by the fact that the states' representatives, among themselves and in contacting their governments, had to clarify the exact interpretation of all legal clauses and also, particularly, because of the strong articulation of their interests by Prussia and the Netherlands (Van Eysinga and Walther 1969, 25). Nonetheless, this thorny learning process among negotiating and cooperating diplomats did not remain without results – in 1832, after 17 years of struggling for power, Prussia and the Netherlands agreed upon the regime for governing the traffic on the river Rhine. In 1868 the ensuing *Act of Mayence* was replaced by the *Act of Mannheim*, which name referred to the Commission's new seat from 1860 onwards. The new Act detailed regulations that discriminated markedly against non-riparian states.

The achievements of cooperation

The two agreements concluded by the Central Commission for the Navigation of the Rhine proved that economic cooperation between nation-states, in this case for the promotion of water transport, was achievable. The agreed-upon results were documented and subsequently implemented. The Commission was given the powers to regularize, to establish commissions in order to prepare decisions and to amend its own rules. It also had available a court of appeal, so as to establish unambiguous jurisdiction in cases of disputes over river problems. All members had one vote. In practice, decisions were taken not according to the formal rule of unanimity but more flexibly, in order to show progress in the Commission's achievements. For instance, decisions were made dependent on the length of the riverbanks in each member state, as that better represented the interests of the riparian states, or majority voting was introduced. The conditions of the Commission's functioning were redefined after the First and after the Second World War (see Figure 3.1).

Figure 3.1 The development of the Central Commission for the Navigation of the Rhine since 1919

During the creation of the League of Nations in 1919, the new foundations for the **Central Commission for the Navigation of the Rhine** were dealt with in Articles 354–62 of the Treaty of Versailles. The Commission's seat was moved from Mannheim in Germany to Strasbourg in France, where the Commission took possession of the former *German Imperial Palace* and renamed it *Le Palais du Rhin*. After the Second World War, the Commission's constitution was amended first in 1945 and then in 1950. This was followed in 1963 by a further amendment and in 1970 by a by-law with regard to policing the river. A tripartite commission on the working conditions of Rhine boatmen began its work in 1959, after an agreement signed at conferences called by the International Labour Organization (ILO) in 1950 and 1954. It reports annually on the application of the agreement.

In 1996, on the occasion of its **150th anniversary**, the Central Commission for the Navigation of the Rhine left behind its usual reserve with regard to public ceremony by organizing festivities and presenting a new flag (Van Eysinga and Walther 1969, 193). As the Rhine became more and more a river inside the European Union, the Commission, much to its dissatisfaction, felt pressure from 'Brussels' to take over its activities. However, it is resisting such a move.

3.2 The transition from mercantilism to free trade

Changing international trade policies

Trade has continuously been important in ideas about international cooperation. In his book *Mare liberum* (1609), Hugo Grotius argued that nations have the right to trade with each other, and that its denial will cause wars. His plea for the free use of the sea for seafaring trade came up against existing protectionist regulations from states promoting their own interests through restrictions on fisheries or passage. The main economic policy of the European states after the Middle Ages consisted of encouraging exports and discouraging imports, especially through the use of tariffs. The aims of this *mercantilism* were support for national prosperity and enhancement of national power. The stronger their economies, the more military capacity states would have available, both in terms of strike power and of their capability to modernize their weaponry. In domestic politics, government interventions were aimed at control of markets through support of producers. In the context of trade promotion, European states supported ship building and colonial strategies. They also tried to get hold of as much gold as possible in order to strengthen the financial basis for their international trade. Other states' interests were of minor importance, as shown in the expression 'beggar thy neighbour'. National interests were pivotal in their foreign economic policies. However, during the late eighteenth and early nineteenth centuries these mercantilist policies were called into question as a result of passionate pleas in favour of free trade (see Figure 3.2). Free trade would not end national interests, but required government intervention in order to promote a different kind of economic foreign policy.

Figure 3.2 Adam Smith's defence of free trade (1776)

Adam Smith articulated the basics of the new economic liberalism in his book *An Inquiry into the Nature and Causes of the Wealth of Nations* (1776). He disagreed with the mercantilist idea that state power depended on wealth and that states should keep their wealth within their borders. Instead, he argued that states would profit from trade and exchange under conditions of competition. He favoured international development through a division of labour based on the exchange of goods and strong competition. He attacked antiquated government restrictions because they hindered industrial expansion and created inefficiency and high prices. Although a strong sentiment for free trade existed in the UK and the US, many still clung to mercantilism.

In 1817 **David Ricardo**, with his theory of comparative advantage, proved that all states profit from international trade if they concentrate on the production and export of goods in which they have comparative advantages over other states. Economic forces should not be restricted by governments, they should be left to compete freely. Free trade occurs if no restrictions are imposed on the import of goods, such as tariffs or technical demands. From an economic perspective, free trade is appreciated as an incentive to competition and efficiency. Social consequences are irrelevant in this economic liberalism.

Burgeoning free trade in the nineteenth century

Pursuing free trade as an international economic principle implied acceptance of new ideas and different political decision making by nation-states. The declaration of the principle of free navigation of international rivers and the establishment of a monitoring intergovernmental organization by the Congress of Vienna marked the beginnings of this international change. In 1820 the UK began promoting free trade by reducing some of its import duties and other trade restrictions. In 1846 it repealed its corn laws of 1815, which had introduced import tariffs to support domestic corn prices. This marked another step towards free trade. On the Continent, Prussia encouraged free trade among the various German states and through trade agreements between the Zollverein and other states. This Prussia-led German customs union would not evolve into an intergovernmental organization, but would end in German unification.

3.3 The Zollverein (1834–71): concerted (free) trade policies and German unification

The weak German Confederation (1815–66)

The *German Confederation* established by the Congress of Vienna consisted of 38 states in the territory of the former Holy Roman Empire: 34 monarchies and four free cities. Its aim was common foreign action while maintaining its members' autonomy. As a result of its moderate objectives, its composition, the functioning of its organs, the existing power configuration, its conservative nature with regard to liberalization and its constitutional limitations, the Confederation did not evolve into the decisive factor in German unification. The eventual unification was not the result of political unity, but rather of economic concerted action set in motion by the customs union of German states created by Prussia: the *Zollverein*.

The strong Prussia-led Zollverein (1834–71)

The main problem for the German states proved to be their isolation among themselves, as a result of a variety of complicated customs systems, trade barriers and border procedures which made travelling and the transportation of goods extremely difficult. In 1819 German commercial and industrial businessmen drafted petitions in favour of the removal of all customs barriers between German states (Mattli 1999, 112–13). Prussia took the lead by abolishing all its internal duties and tolls between 1816 and 1818, by establishing a common external tariff for the whole of Prussia and by standardizing its tariffs. In fact it moved from protectionism to moderate free trade. Other states followed the Prussian example. Some of them established customs unions among themselves: in 1825 the South German Zollverein was created by Bavaria and Württemberg; in 1828 the North German Zollverein by Prussia, Mecklenburg and Hesse-Darmstadt; and in 1829 the Middle German Zollverein under the leadership of Saxony. Leaving aside the various withdrawals and accessions of states, the general Zollverein of 1833 resulted from these predecessors. This came into operation in 1834, originally with 17 member states but soon showing a gradual growth in membership (Mattli 1999, 4). In its first phase, from 1834 to 1867, the customs union was administered by a Congress in which every state had a single vote. The Prussian tariff protected the states from foreign competition, whereas among themselves free trade was the rule. From 1839 onwards, the Zollverein concluded trade agreements with third-party states, among them the Netherlands (1839), Belgium (1844), France (1862) and the UK (1865). These agreements and lower tariffs had positive effects on the volume of trade and the quality of products. For instance, the amount of unrefined sugar exported by the Netherlands to Germany increased robustly, whereas the export of low-quality rag-and-bone material almost disappeared. This phase ended in 1866 with Prussia's military victory over Austria, which within the German Confederation had tried to stir up trouble against Prussia in other states. This conflict soon ended in the overthrow of Austria by Prussia, with its modern armaments and its use of the new railroads for transporting its troops. Chancellor Bismarck 'hastened to make peace before the other European powers, which he had first hoodwinked and now stunned, could realize what had happened' (Palmer and Colton 1971, 571–72). This implied the end of the German Confederation. During the second phase of its existence, from 1867 to 1871, the Zollverein was administered by a *Federal Council* of government representatives, who decided by an absolute majority. Prussia presided at the Council, holding 17 of the 58 votes. A new *Customs Parliament* was composed of deputies elected by popular vote. It had legislative powers and it, too, made decisions by majority vote. With the use of these institutions and the economic power of the Zollverein, the German states moved in the direction of a federal state, which was eventually established thanks to Bismarck's dexterity after the victory in the Franco–German War of 1871.

Explanations

Walter Mattli explains the Zollverein as a process of integration, in which Prussian leadership and German industrial and commercial pressure groups played key parts in bringing about cooperation and eventually national unification. Two areas of innovation supported these political processes: improvements in river transport, with a steamboat on the Rhine as early as 1816, and the introduction of the railway from 1835. 'The railway served not only to reduce transaction costs and widen markets, but also provided the single most powerful stimulus to Germany's industrial development and growth. It created an unprecedented demand for iron as well as other materials used in the manufacture of cars and construction of fixed facilities; moreover, the railway needed these goods in a wide variety of finished forms, ranging from relatively simple items like rails and wheels to complicated engines and machines, all of which gave a special push to the metal working and engineering trades' (Mattli 1999, 114–15). This demand side of industrial groups met with the supply side of Prussian leadership. As the largest and richest German state, Prussia, through the Zollverein, offered an institutional framework, which allowed technological innovation to take place and the old problem of smuggling to be controlled. Prussia served as the recipient of requests for union membership but cannot be said to have abused its position. 'Its fellow-members joined the union voluntarily and were free to leave as they pleased. No state ever left; all remained members and had strong material incentives to do so. ... The gains in revenue soothed the pain of losing independence' (Mattli 1999, 122). Unlike the Central Commission for the Navigation of the Rhine, the Zollverein did not grow into an enduring intergovernmental organization. Instead, the Zollverein in its second phase proved to be the institutional framework for the completion of German unification. With the creation of the German empire in 1871, the Zollverein came to an end. Industrial, commercial and trade policies became matters for the federal government. The fact that economic cooperation under the leadership of a regional great power could lead to a federal state turned into an argument against this kind of cooperation in the Western Hemisphere (see §11.5 about the 1889 conference in Washington).

Part II

Transnational networks of citizens

From the anti-slavery movement in 1815 to the International Committee of the Red Cross of 1863

The second part of this overview traces the emergence of transnational citizens' networks out of the background of ideas on popular sovereignty and human rights declared during the War of American Independence and the French Revolution. Unlike the anti-slavery and peace movements, citizens' striving for democratic rights remained nationally rather than transnationally oriented (Chapter 4). After citizens had started to take care of the wounded on the battlefields, an extraordinary NGO came into existence, the International Red Cross, which was made responsible for monitoring the intergovernmental Geneva Convention on Wounded Soldiers and, later, the other Geneva Conventions (Chapter 5).

Citizens organizing transnationally in support of slavery abolition and peace

4.1 The international movement advocating the abolition of slavery

Private societies dealing with social problems

The creation of issue-oriented NGOs, against slavery or poverty, began with small groups of citizens becoming aware of ethical and social problems. They combined their critical attitude with the assumption that part of the solution was to form societies and associations aiming to deal with these problems. This engagement resulted in group activities, organized by the associations and sometimes by the churches. The actions often included appeals to local or national authorities. The creation of societies, associations or committees in the UK from the mid-eighteenth century onwards was related to the emergence of 'the polite society of gentry and nobility' and the increased mobility made possible by advances in the design of carriages and improvements in the road system (Seary 1996, 17). The nineteenth century saw the rise of the middle classes and an increase in the number of people with the time, education and resources to take part in such societies and activities. Because several states had faced similar problems and their citizens had begun corresponding with each other about them, or had established other kinds of transborder contact such as visits, meetings or conferences, private transnational networks emerged. This development formed part of the transformation of nation-states into democracies, which was taking place against the background of the new ideas about popular sovereignty and human rights that were declared during the War of American Independence in 1776 and the French Revolution of 1789 (see Figure 4.1). The nineteenth-century European world grew smaller politically as the topics citizens engaged in were being discussed at multilateral conferences and in the press. This happened in an era that saw a substantial degree of peace, from 1815 until 1848 and from 1878 until the First World War. 'For much of the nineteenth century it was possible to think of Europe as a continent where issues were pan-European and could be addressed in pan-European ways' (Seary 1996, 18).

The rise of the anti-slavery movement

Early opposition to slavery dated back to the seventeenth century, but at the end of the eighteenth century citizens began to set up societies with the aim of pressurizing governments into supporting the abolition of slavery. In the early nineteenth century, contacts between groups in several countries resulted in the formation of anti-slavery transnational advocacy networks. In 1787 the British Methodists Thomas Clarkson and William Wilberforce established the *Society for Effecting the Abolition of the Slave Trade*, which launched a public campaign. In France the *Société des amis des noirs*, founded in 1788, had some immediate success during the revolution one year later, when slavery was formally ended. But this statement remained largely without practical consequences. In the UK, it was not until 1807 that the slave trade was abolished by an Act of Parliament. In 1811 another Act was needed to close loopholes, as in practice the trade continued to exist. The movement nonetheless met with great sympathy. In 1791–92 400,000 people signed petitions against the slave trade, and in 1814 750,000 abolitionists did so (Keck and Sikkink 1998, 44). Some of the arguments against slavery expressed by concerned Quakers, Mennonites and Methodists, as well as by people appealing to the ideals of the Enlightenment, were *ethical*. Other arguments were *economic* in nature. In line with Adam Smith's new liberal ideas, the modern economy and society would not profit from an 'old' type of labour such as slavery, but rather from workers in a free labour market. The corollary to these arguments was the ideal of *emancipation*, in the sense of freeing the slaves and assigning them equal rights. The British movement regarded slavery as evil and abolition of the slave trade as a means eventually to end this evil. This implied international engagement, as abolishment would involve states other than the UK, among them France, Portugal, Spain, the US and various Latin American states. Despite progress – during the Napoleonic Wars Denmark, Sweden and the Netherlands withdrew from the slave trade – the trade remained profitable, given the weight of slave labour in the economies of the southern US and many Latin American states.

Figure 4.1 Enlightenment, popular sovereignty and human rights

The foundation of the ideal type of democratic state was laid during the **Enlightenment**. In this culturally historic time period of roughly the eighteenth century, philosophy and science flourished. Popularization and education enabled others, particularly young people, to share in the benefits of new knowledge and insights. Ideas about mutual equality and individual freedoms gained weight. Unreasonable traditions, such as the persecution of witches or the torture of prisoners, were attacked and tolerance in matters of religion emerged. Ideas about the emancipation of Jews, slaves and women were part of this line of reasoning. With regard to the state and politics, a more positive portrayal of mankind came into being than the one held by realists. People were considered as being capable of cooperating and improving socially, notwithstanding their ability to cause conflict. Their malicious behaviour was the result not of their character as human beings, but of the social institutions that promoted conflict behaviour rather than harmony. Liberals rejected the fairly undemocratic plea by Thomas Hobbes in his *Leviathan* (1651) to bring an end to the anarchic situation in the 'state of nature' between men and between states by setting up a sovereign power (Leviathan) to command and protect both. They concurred rather with political theorist Jean Bodin, who had argued in his *Six Books on the State* (1576) that even a sovereign is subject to certain rules *vis-à-vis* citizens and other sovereigns. The seventeenth-century political philosopher John Locke, in his *Two Treatises of Civil Government* (1690), had defended a 'limited government' based on consent by, and an active role for, its citizens. The creation of **democratic institutions** would allow citizens to accept the curtailment of their various rights and provide them with procedures in order to, if necessary, correct their government. The model for legitimate government was found in the idea of a **social contract**, which regards sovereignty as the result of a contract between the members of a society. This implies that citizens accept the sovereign power, but are also guaranteed certain inalienable rights and liberties. Jean Jacques Rousseau had developed this idea more fully in his book *Du Contrat Social* (1762).

The idea of **popular sovereignty** followed from these lines of argument on democracy and social contract. In essence, it regards the will and consent of the people as the source of all political power and of a state's legitimacy. The foundation of the US in 1776 made this idea explicit, given the first words of its Constitution of 1787: 'We the People of the United States ... do ordain and establish the Constitution of the United States of America.' The *Declaration of Independence* of 4 July 1776 had already stressed that 'all men are created equal; that they are endowed by their Creator with certain unalienable rights; that among these are life, liberty, and the pursuit of happiness; that, to secure these rights, governments are instituted among men, deriving their just powers from the consent of the governed; that whenever any form of government becomes destructive of these ends, it is the right of the people to alter or to abolish it, and to institute new government, laying its foundation on such principles, and organizing its power in such form, as to them shall seem most likely to effect their safety and happiness.' In 1791 the idea of freedom was developed further in the first ten amendments to the American Constitution, known as the **Bill of Rights**. These limit the powers of the federal government and protect the rights of the citizens. This also happened in France. The **Declaration of the Rights of Man and the Citizen**, issued during the French Revolution, became part of the French Constitution of 1791. It recognizes the individual's freedoms, such as those of speech, of the press and of religion. It regards the people as sovereign and citizens as equal according to their ability rather than through being born into a specific class. It also introduced a new, more equal approach to taxes.

The mere proclamation of these declarations about human rights did not yet make them effective. The way to transform the new ideas into political reality was through **political struggle by citizens**. The emergence of parliamentary institutions within the Westphalian states as a result of this struggle reflects the change in the relationship between sovereign and subjects towards more influence for the citizens. From the nineteenth century onwards, and thanks to the ongoing struggle by citizens, the rights formulated in the American and French human rights declarations became embedded in the constitutions of other states, with national variations depending on national preferences and power relations. The aim of this political process and struggle was the guarantee that in modern democracies citizens are protected against misuses by their governments. This enduring political struggle included the restriction of the monarch's power through a stronger accountability of the executive to the parliamentary representation of the people, the separation of powers between the legislative, executive and judiciary in a *trias politica*, and more power to the people through gradual extension of the popular vote.

The declaration against the slave trade by the Congress of Vienna (1815)

Since the British anti-slavery movement's target was to stop the transatlantic slave trade by the principal European trading states France, Portugal and Spain, it decided to address the Congress of Vienna, expecting that it could win general agreement among the major powers to bring the trade to an end. The movement presented 800 petitions to the British House of Commons, spurring the British government to press for action in Vienna by including the issue on the agenda. Representatives also left for Vienna to explain their views (Charnovitz 1997, 192). 'British opinion was mobilised, the great abolitionist Wilberforce himself circularized several of the leading figures at the Vienna Congress.' In Vienna, British Foreign Secretary Castlereagh, 'while not unnaturally regarding his instructions on this point as something of a diplomatic handicap', addressed the issue as well as possible. 'His orders were to obtain immediate abolition of the slave-trade by the European powers; to win recognition of the right of mutual search within limited areas; and to get the powers to agree to sanctions, i.e. the exclusion of colonial produce from those countries which would not consent to abolition' (Lyons 1963, 288). His proposals met with severe opposition, but Portugal and Spain made the grudging concession that, with compensation from the UK, they would abolish the trade within eight years. The only agreement that the Congress of Vienna could achieve was a declaration condemning the slave trade. This declaration, however, was the first to contain an internationally agreed-upon socio-economic principle – the universal abolition of the slave trade – formulated with the intent of changing an existing situation. The signatory powers declared 'in the face of Europe that, considering the universal abolition of the slave trade as a measure particularly worthy of their attention, conformable to the spirits of the times and to the generous principles of their august sovereigns, they are animated with the sincere desire of concurring in the most prompt and effectual execution of this measure by all the means at their disposal, and of acting in the employment of these means with all the zeal and perseverance which is due to so great and noble a cause' (cited in Lyons 1963, 288).

Transnational contacts

During the 1830s, British and American societies promoting the abolition of slavery grew into widely-supported movements. The strong transatlantic ties of critical Methodists, Presbyterians, Quakers and Unitarians enabled an information exchange between groups on both sides of the ocean, telling each other about organizational experiences, positions and activities. In addition to letters and publications, they also exchanged speakers. The British encouraged their American counterparts to spur American churches into taking positions against slavery. 'Many of these tactics originated in Britain and the transnational network served as a vehicle for diffusing tactical recipes and collective action repertoires from one domestic social movement to another' (Keck and Sikkink 1998, 45).

The International Anti-Slavery Conference in London (1840)

In 1839 the *British and Foreign Anti-Slavery Society* was established with the aim of changing public opinion. In June 1840 it convened the International Anti-Slavery Conference in London, which was attended by large delegations from France, the UK and the US. Its intention was to work for the abolition of slavery and the slave trade throughout the world 'by moral, religious and other influences, no sanction being given to the use of force' (Lyons 1963, 291). The transnational contacts resulted in a second conference in 1843, which was followed by sending British delegations to states such as France, Portugal, Spain and the US in order to encourage citizens further to establish societies and to pressurize their governments. One of their main tactics was the use of *information politics* or the promotion of change by publicly reporting facts. This public pressure was intended to hold a government accountable for situations and to create debates about causes and solutions. In the case of the anti-slavery movement, information politics included the publication of testimonials from individuals and the novel *Uncle Tom's Cabin* by Harriet Beecher Stowe (1852), which had first appeared in serial form in an anti-slavery newspaper. After accusations of falsification and exaggeration, Stowe published the factual *A Key to Uncle Tom's Cabin* (1853) in defence of its authenticity. She also came to Europe for speaking tours. The anti-slavery campaign met the definition of a transnational advocacy network as 'a set of relevant organizations working internationally with shared values, a common discourse, and dense exchanges of information' (Keck and Sikkink 1998, 46). European pressures thus contributed to changes in American views.

The American Civil War 1861–65

The transnational dimension was most influential and decisive in the US when government links with civil society were impaired. Since the Southern states dominated American political institutions and the Northern states were eager to prevent a break-up of the Union, the abolitionist issue was excluded from the political agenda. However, thanks to their British connections, the American abolitionist groups continued their political activities by introducing petitions and resolutions: 'by joining with British activists and at times leveraging the power of the British government on behalf of the antislavery cause, they could amplify their own voices' (Keck and Sikkink 1998, 48). In other words, the transnational advocacy network helped the American anti-slavery movement to continue its agitation in a period of rigid domestic political relations. This rigidity did not disappear until the outbreak of the American Civil War in 1861.

Problematic implementation and monitoring

Despite its principal importance, the declaration on the abolition of the slave trade by the Congress of Vienna remained studiously vague as to means, dates and negotiation procedures for actually implementing the agreed-upon principle. In the same year France formally abolished the trade, but did not enforce the new law until after 1830. The UK concluded a series of treaties with Spain and Portugal and paid large amounts of compensation in return for the ending of the trade, but the legal changes in these states in 1820 and 1825, respectively, remained largely ineffective. The main reason for this was that although legal abolition took place, this was not enforced. The best way to improve this situation was to initiate a joint naval supervision along the African coast. Given its supremacy at sea and its activities off the West African coast to intercept slave ships where possible, the UK was the obvious power to act. However, most states found it difficult to agree with the UK on a reciprocal right of search, whereby the warships of any one of the contracting parties would be entitled to stop ships flying the other parties' flags and take them to ports where joint Courts of Mixed Commission would be empowered to apply the anti-slave-trade laws of the countries concerned. In practice it would be mainly the UK that implemented such an agreement. The US in particular refused to agree to this situation. The inevitable result was that 'slavers, when hard-pressed by British cruisers, had only to hoist American colours (though they might actually be of any nationality) to avoid being stopped and searched' (Lyons 1963, 290). The further restriction of the slave trade and the abolition of slavery was a matter of gradual progress. As a result of political changes in 1853, Brazil stopped the importing of slaves. Partly due to ongoing public pressure, slavery was abolished in Uruguay (1842), France (1848), Argentina (1853), Peru (1854) and, after a clever move by Abraham Lincoln (the 13th amendment), the US (1855). It was easier to control the slave trade off the West African coast than off East Africa, where Arab traders did not bother with the principle agreed in Vienna. This general situation did not change until the 1880s, when the great powers agreed upon a division of Africa and began to restrict the slave trade within their colonial spheres of influence (see Figure 4.2).

Figure 4.2 International instruments against slavery 1885–1930

The multilateral conference on Africa in Berlin (1885) paid lip service to the desirability of suppressing the slave trade after having discussed the idea of preventive action. However, this time joint action followed. The multilateral diplomatic conference of 16 states in Brussels in 1889–90 concerned itself directly with the slavery problem and drafted a code of anti-slave-trade regulations which was both detailed and practical. The final act came to be known as the **Brussels General Act**. It made the colonial powers responsible for developing machinery of repression and for proceeding with the task of raising the economic and moral standards of the natives within their several jurisdictions in order to counterbalance the economic causes of the trade.

Two common institutions were established to monitor the General Act's implementation. In 1890 the **International Maritime Bureau against the Slave Trade** was created on the island of Zanzibar for the purpose of checking naval transportation and providing up-to-date information to the naval officers. The five powers that primarily assumed the preventive operations at sea (France, Germany, Italy, Portugal and the UK) were represented in the Bureau. It began to function in 1892. A second **Bureau** was established in Brussels, and attached to the Belgian Foreign Office, for the purpose of collecting information and publishing documents and statistics with respect to the slave trade. It was responsible for circulating the texts of all laws and regulations that applied the General Act, as well as for providing statistical information about the trade and the number of slaves arrested and liberated, and about the related traffic in firearms, ammunition and liquor. The Bureau also set up measures to prevent the false use of its colours by slavers, and elaborated regulations concerning the use of the flag and the procedures to be followed in stopping and searching suspected vessels. The international machinery that existed from 1890 onwards helped to further suppress the slave trade, but it was unable to prevent the persistence of this trade, in particular in Muslim countries in Africa and Asia. Nonetheless, the conclusion of the Brussels General Act of 1890 and the establishment of the Bureaux in Zanzibar and Brussels provided joint practical regulations and monitoring capacities, which promoted the implementation of the internationally-agreed principles on ending slavery (Reinsch 1911, 64; Lyons 1963, 293–95).

Article 22 of the League of Nations' Covenant expressly forbade the slave trade in mandates that had no self-ruling rights. It upheld the international convention of 1890 and other international conventions. In 1922 the League established a Temporary Commission on Slavery, from 1924 the Advisory Committee of Experts on Slavery, which prepared an anti-slavery convention. In 1926 the League adopted the *International Convention on the Abolition of Slavery and Slave Trade*, which forbade all types of slavery and prohibited all compulsory, non-remunerated labour for all work and services that were not public. Within four years, 44 states had signed it. The ILO was asked to deal with the related issue of forced labour, in order to reduce slavery and forced labour in domestic and colonial labour relations. In 1930 this resulted in the ILO's *Forced Labour Convention*.

4.2 The peace movement, its international congresses and the idea of arbitration

The idea of arbitration and the Jay Treaty of 1794

Like the advocates of the abolition of slavery, those advocating peace found their inspiration both in a critical religious conviction and in free trade as economic policy. Quakers, for instance, are convinced that waging war is incompatible with Christianity. Following the end of the Napoleonic Wars in 1815, Quakers were among the first to establish peace societies in the UK and the US. They published pamphlets, organized speaker tours and founded periodicals. In 1819 the British Peace Society, which placed particular emphasis on the power of the press, began to publish the *Herald of Peace*. The first American periodical was the *Friend of Peace* of 1821. In 1828, 36 Quaker and other societies merged into the *American Peace Society*, which aimed at 'amicable discussion and arbitration' between states and at 'settling all controversies by an appeal to reason' (Carter 1992, 3). This appeal to arbitration and reason reaches back to the treaty concluded between the UK and the US in 1794 to settle disagreements between the two states. Named after its American negotiator James Jay, it is known as the *Jay Treaty*. Jay regarded arbitration as a means to prevent conflicts, rather than to end hostilities. His followers expected that treaties which made provisions for arbitration would contribute to a more durable form of peaceful coexistence and to a firmer foundation for society. As well as in the Jay Treaty, provisions for arbitration were included in numerous treaties concluded between the US and Latin American states during the nineteenth century, such as those with Panama (1826), Colombia and Chile (1880) (Eyffinger 1996, 28–29). The Harvard-educated sea captain William Ladd, the man who had brought about the merger of the various peace societies, argued that the American Peace Society's aim had to be 'to increase and promote the practice already begun of submitting national differences to amicable discussion and arbitration' (Lyons 1963, 310).

Goya's etchings of war cruelties

The emergence of peace societies in 1815 was also related to the nature of the wars which revolutionary and later Napoleonic France had fought from 1791 until 1815. These modern wars marked a change in the nature of war, popularizing the idea of the nation in arms. 'Certainly the wars prompted a romantic nationalism and a glorification of war and the figure of the soldier.' But there was also awareness of the destructiveness and waste of war, of burned and sacked towns and villages, ravages of famine and thousands of fighting men killed. The Spanish painter Francisco de Goya documented all these cruelties and disasters in his paintings and etchings made during the wars in Spain. His images were disseminated widely thanks to new etching techniques. 'Goya's etchings of "The Disasters of War" depicted the mutual atrocities resulting from the Spanish people's guerrilla resistance to the Napoleonic army of occupation' (Carter 1992, 2). The old ethical critiques of warfare found new arguments in the present, whereas arbitration emerged as a means to avoid such cruelties.

Expectations with respect to free trade and peace

The emerging discourse in favour of free trade fostered the reflection on peace and peaceful means. During the 1830s and 1840s, as industrialism was spreading, free trade advocates such as John Bright and Richard Cobden campaigned in the UK for the repeal of the Corn Laws, arguing that free trade was a policy of peace. They regarded trade as a more effective means of exerting influence in the world than the bullying of other states, and they expected that strong economic interests as a result of intensive trade would bring governments to leave behind their old-fashioned ideas about war. 'It is commerce which is rapidly rendering war obsolete, by strengthening and multiplying the personal interests which are in natural opposition to it', according to John Stuart Mill in his *Principles of Political Economy* of 1848 (cited in Lyons 1963, 312). During the 1840s these free trade advocates became allied to the original Quaker-influenced peace groups. They gained support from businessmen who would profit from free trade. They also found support in Continental Europe, for instance in Berlin, where the Englishman John Prince Smith was influencing the free trade policies of the Zollverein, and in France, where the economist Frédéric Bastiat was developing his theory of free trade. Factors such as Protestantism, liberal politics and a free-enterprise economy provided a favourable setting for the promotion of peace societies in the UK and the US, followed by their spread to the Continent, in particular to Western Europe. In Central and Eastern Europe, conservative powers such as Austria and Russia were far less in favour of liberal and democratic aspirations. They regarded the balance of power stemming from the Concert of Europe and wars as more appropriate means to create peace than free trade. The peace movement in the Anglo-Saxon world was split between free trade advocates who gave primacy to free trade, and more committed religiously-inspired pacifists who wished to oppose all wars and promoted Christian non-violence. To gain support in Continental Europe, both emphases were omitted from compromise policies (Carter 1992, 4–5).

The international peace congress of 1843 about arbitration

Peace societies were established in Switzerland in 1830 and in France in 1832. On the initiative of British and American peace societies, the first international peace congress took place in London from 22 to 24 June 1843, with 292 participants from the UK, 36 from the US and six from Continental Europe. Quite a few of these had also been present at the anti-slavery conference in London three years earlier. The major topics at the congress were arbitration, as developed by Jay, and the vision of a Congress and a Court of Nations as expounded by Ladd, who had died in 1841. Henry Macnamarra, who elaborated Ladd's ideas, anticipated that the building of international legislative and judicial institutions would be a long-term process, whereas in the short term all efforts should be concentrated on the realization of the arbitration clause in line with Jay's vision. The London congress eventually adopted two resolutions. It recommended to all governments the adoption of the principle of arbitration 'for the adjustment of all international differences'. It also recommended the creation of a 'Congress of Nations to settle and perfect the code of international law, and a High Court of Nations to interpret and apply that law for the settlement of all national disputes' (Van der Linden 1987, 150). The British political establishment and press were not impressed. Despite the very moderate programme and the generally respected middle-class character of the peace societies, *The Times* denounced the congress as 'a particularly extreme and pernicious example of the "disease" of the "fanaticism of association"'. It commented scathingly on 'the vagaries and delusions of those unhappy individuals who … profess no less than the total abolition throughout the terrestrial globe of war' (cited in Carter 1992, 5).

The revolutions of 1848

The congress participants regarded their resolutions as the beginning of more and similar activities. A second international peace congress, which was also to discuss disarmament, was scheduled for 1848. However, the revolutionary events taking place in Europe during that year prevented this from taking place. In France the revolution emanated from the economic crisis of 1847. After an insurrection in Paris, which gave rise to the petite bourgeoisie and to the 'fourth estate' (the working classes), the French king was ousted in 1848. The revolution spread through Western and Central Europe, resulting in several liberal constitutions, with the movements in Italy and Germany taking on a strongly nationalistic character. The French revolution of 1848 was followed by the reactionary *coup d'état* led by Louis-Napoleon in 1851. The period 1852–70 is known as one dominated by nationalism and by the focusing of British foreign policy on British power and prestige. British Foreign Secretary Henry Palmerston tried to maintain British hegemony on the pretext of 'right or wrong, my country'. The peace activists who had to postpone their 1848 peace congress decided to delay it for a year, but still to hold it in Paris. In June 1949 they were bolstered up by Cobden's arbitration motion in the House of Commons, in which he encouraged the UK to enter into agreements with other states and to resolve conflicts between them through arbitration. Linked with this plea for peace was his attack on the rising cost of weaponry in the UK. His motion was defeated, but the widely publicized debate resulted in petitions in favour of arbitration.

The international peace congress of 1849

The second international peace congress took place in August 1849 in Paris, with nearly 700 British delegates, 100 French, 21 Belgian, 20 American and about 30 from other states. This time the Continent was better represented than in 1843. The already famous author Victor Hugo acted as chairman of the congress, and in his welcoming speech referred to the possibility of the 'United States of Europe', something which would reverberate down the years. The congress marked the peak of the international peace movement and deserved this reputation, as it took place on the Continent and attracted enormous public attention. 'Paris fell under the spell of the congress. The whole press felt compelled to write about it, be it either positively, negatively, or derisively. The cartoonists and the theatres paid attention to it; Daumier even devoted seven caricatures in Le Charivari to the subject. As Paris was the nerve-centre of European news, the cause of the peace movement attracted for the first time much international attention.' Cobden wrote to his wife: 'All our good Quaker friends are in capital spirits. There can be no doubt that our meetings will have done good. Everybody has been talking about them during the week, and the subject of peace has for the first time had its hearing, even in France' (Van der Linden 1987, 338–39). The peace movement remained an overwhelmingly Anglo-Saxon affair though, with smaller follow-up conferences in the UK in October and November, from which Hugo was absent, unlike free trade advocate Bastiat.

The international peace movement divided

The international peace congress that took place in Frankfurt in 1850 saw a clash on the question of whether the condemnation of war should be total. On one side were the religiously-inspired pacifists; on the other those who approached the issue of international relations on a more realistic basis. The latter argued with Cobden that 'governments should be pressed to disarm on the ground that their existing commitments placed a heavy burden of taxation upon their peoples' (Lyons 1963, 316). The final resolution bore this view's imprint and meant a defeat for those who preferred a total condemnation of war. 1851 saw another international peace congress in London, heavily attended again but mainly by British participants, who also visited the Great Exhibition at the Crystal Palace, a forerunner of the world expositions (see §9.2). These congresses could not hide that the peace movement was waning in the 1850s. The decade opened with 'ominous anticipations of the shape of things to come. In England, the belligerent attitude of Lord Palmerston was in the ascendant and a second attempt by Cobden to carry a disarmament motion in the House of Commons was a failure' (Lyons 1963, 317). The two peace congresses of 1853 were held under the advancing shadow of the Crimean War, which resulted from the balance-of-power principle of curbing Russian territorial ambitions. The wave of revolutions, furthermore, had provided democratic and nationalist justifications for violent rebellion and wars of liberation. In contrast to the pacifist character of the early Anglo–American peace societies, European radicals now argued that democratic and nationalist freedoms should be secured as the basis for just and lasting peace, and they abandoned their pacifism. The American peace societies were also divided over the issue of slavery, which during the early 1860s was the cause of the American Civil War. Some committed abolitionists abandoned their pacifism as well. No international peace congresses were held between 1853 and 1871 (Carter 1992, 5).

4.3 Democracy, women's equality and workers' rights as national themes

No transnational advocacy networks for democracy

The struggle for electoral suffrage, often in combination with related issues, was fought by citizens who were excluded from the national political system, such as women and workers. At the end of the eighteenth and the beginning of the nineteenth centuries both groups became conscious of this political exclusion. The basis for their politico-social movements was laid during the first half of the nineteenth century, but unlike the anti-slavery and peace movements, the women's and workers' movements did not succeed in establishing transnational ties until the 1860s. However, ideas were developed, printed and also distributed to other states, where they were read and discussed.

No political rights for American women (1776)

During the War of American Independence and the French Revolution, some women devoted themselves to achieving equal political rights. In 1776 Mercy Otis Warren and Abigail Smith Adams demanded the right of political representation for American women. Adams attempted to use her influence on her husband, who was engaged in drafting the American Constitution. In letters she argued that women should be allowed the vote. 'Do not put such unlimited power in the hands of the Husbands. Remember all Men would be tyrants if they could. If particular care and attention is not paid to the Laidies we are determined to foment a Rebelion, and will not hold ourselves bound by any Laws in which we have no voice, or Representation' (cited in Tuttle 1986, 11). Future President John Adams, however, did not take her request or threat seriously. The Constitution of 1787 simply ignored the subject of political representation for women.

Women's influence during the French Revolution

Women's suffrage was not discussed during the regulation of electoral suffrage by the French National Assembly in October 1789. The influential abbot Emanuel Sieyès favoured individual freedom, but was an opponent of general suffrage. He feared that the poor would sell their votes and argued that women, just like children and foreigners, were not entitled to participate in public bodies. Charles Talleyrand, as a representative of the clergy, also denied women their national citizenship. In those turbulent days, however, Paris women were political actors. In early October, working class women rebelled over the widespread famine, demanding bread and labour. They succeeded in gaining possession of rifles from the city hall and marched to Versailles, where they demanded access to the National Assembly. In the afternoon a delegation left for the palace of Louis XVI. While the king received this delegation, the others waited in the rain outside. On behalf of all the women, Louise Chably informed him about the famine. The president of the National Assembly used the opportunity to insist once again that the king sign the *Declaration of the*

Rights of Man and the Citizen, which the Assembly had approved in August. The king now finally did so, which according to Jean Jaurès meant that his signing was the result of the pressure from Paris working class women. During this period, author of plays and social treatises Olympe de Gouges founded several women's organizations. As most of these women knitted during the meetings, they became known as *les tricoteuses*. In September 1791 De Gouges published her pamphlet *Declaration of the Rights of Women*, in which she protested against the omission of women in the official declaration of human rights. She incited women to demand equal social and political rights, which to her included suffrage as well as access to official positions and activities. In April 1792 Etta Palm petitioned the National Assembly on behalf of women's organizations, arguing in favour of equal rights for women in education, employment, politics and law. But feminism did not last long during the French Revolution. In 1793 De Gouges was sent to the guillotine for her resistance against the reign of terror by Maximilien de Robespierre. The National Assembly forbade and dissolved all women's organizations.

Arguments in favour of women's rights

These events did not stop the political struggle by women, who continued to elaborate ideas about equal rights and opportunities. In 1792 the British author Mary Wollstonecraft, who was sympathetic to the French Revolution, published her book *A Vindication of the Rights of Women*. She argued that the upbringing and education of girls and women should be such that their talents could be used in society in the same way as those of boys and men. Although many judged her for her adventurous and unconventional life, her book was widely read in the UK and elsewhere. The Frenchwoman Flora Tristan, who escaped an unhappy marriage and travelled to the UK and to her father's country Peru, resisted slavery and supported both women's emancipation and social reform. Like Wollstonecraft, she believed that women and men possessed the same potential for development and that women should be given equal opportunities. In 1843 she published her book *L'Union Ouvrière*, which is the first publication with detailed, but not yet very practical, ideas about establishing an international cooperative movement of workers for peaceful revolution and social reform. Tristan went on a speaking tour around the country to win workers and women over to her ideas. She emphasized the importance of education for working class women, also because women could redeem and elevate men through their superior moral power. She was convinced that misery to a large extent resulted from the fact that women were forgotten and looked down upon. Her views and unconventional behaviour caused such a stir that she wrote just before she died: 'I have nearly the whole world against me. Men because I demand the emancipation of women, the owners because I demand the emancipation of wage-earners' (cited in Rowbotham 1972, 55).

Denied access at the International Anti-Slavery Conference in London in 1840

The denial of access to the American representatives Lucretia Mott and Elizabeth Cady Stanton, as well as other women, to the International Anti-Slavery Conference in London in 1840 caused a process of consciousness-raising. 'Their shared experience of being denied seats at the World Anti-Slavery Convention because of their sex convinced them that women were as much in need of emancipation as were slaves' (Tuttle 1986,

288). It was not until 1848 that the American women's movement came into existence. In July 1848 around 260 women met in Seneca Falls near New York, where they drafted a manifesto with demands, prepared by Stanton and modelled on the American Declaration of Independence. This *Declaration of Sentiments* described the grievances of women in an inventory of rights and privileges that they did not have despite their formal citizenship. The resolutions attached to the document formulated the equal opportunities women should have in order to develop their talents fully in all fields. The resolution on women's suffrage was the most controversial, but eventually it was adopted. The meeting in Seneca Falls is regarded as the beginning of what was later termed the 'first wave' of the women's movement, which during the second half of the century would become an international movement.

The rise of the British workers' movement: Thomas Paine's 'Rights of Man'

The rise of the workers' movement in Europe was different in every state, but also showed similarities in the demands by workers and in the negative and repressive reactions from their governments. As far as the term 'movement' can be used, it referred to national movements. Thomas Paine, who had lived in the US for a number of years, criticized the conservative reactions to the French Revolution in the UK. In 1791–92 he published his *The Rights of Man*, in which he defended radical reform. He considered politics as something that also concerned workers. Paine advocated democracy from an American perspective, by arguing that the government had to promote 'life, liberty and the pursuit of happiness'. If a government failed to do so, it should be overturned. His book was sold widely, but was also banned and Paine had to flee to France to escape arrest. Whereas his book spurred some workers on to demand parliamentary reform and general suffrage, some textile workers who felt threatened in their livelihood reacted to the introduction of a free labour market and of modern technology by destroying the mechanized looms. The first *Luddite* protests (1811–13) were suppressed by the army, through trials resulting in executions and penal transportations, and by new laws, but flared up again in 1815 when the end of the Napoleonic Wars and therefore of the war economy caused an economic crisis in the UK. The return of the soldiers resulted in high unemployment, while the newly-introduced protectionist Corn Laws increased food prices. Once again the government responded with repressive force, trials and legislation.

Social reform and electoral reform

In 1824 the British government decided to end the ban on trade unions, in an effort to better control workers through legal organizations. The elections in 1830 have relevance here because advocates of electoral reform gained stronger positions. The Reform Act of 1832 marked the beginning of some minor electoral reforms. In 1833 a new law restricted child labour somewhat, but the poor law reforms of those years promoted the functioning of a free labour market by forcing workers to look for work wherever it was available. British trade unions were established in various business sectors earlier than anywhere else, fighting against wage reductions and for better payment, shorter working hours and the establishment of medical and pension funds. The socially-engaged industrialist Robert Owen propagated a 'new moral world'. This pioneer of the cooperative movement attempted to show that good labour conditions and wages were consistent with business success.

Owen believed that the combination of work and social life could transform the nature of capitalism. Dissatisfied workers to a certain extent accepted these utopian beliefs, as they proved that a better world was feasible. The Chartist Movement, which arose as a result of the 1832 Reform Act, was supported by skilled artisans, who campaigned for parliamentary reform including votes for all men. It obtained over a million signatures and in 1839 presented its *People's Charter* to the House of Commons, where it was rejected by a majority of 235 to 46. Chartism was a mass movement, but it was unable to succeed, even during the unrest of 1848, and the movement died out. Some German workers in London had connections to more or less revolutionary workers on the Continent in that year, but their contacts remained mostly secret and insignificant (Lyons 1963, 164).

The workers' movement in France

In spite of the ban on workers' organizations in France, which was introduced as part of the Revolution, workers in modern industries began to establish organizations for mutual help. They were supported by utopian socialists. The social philosopher Henri de Saint-Simon, who in 1776 was in the US helping the Americans fight against the UK, wanted not to abolish capitalism, but to reform it. In the early nineteenth century he took up a position against landowners and advocated that industrialists should take control of society. His critical analyses of social conditions and pleas for common ownership of the means of production and for redistribution in the cause of social justice influenced political thinking. Charles Fourier, another French social critic and utopian socialist, proposed the organization of people into *phalanstères* of about 1,800 members, which would allow male and female workers to develop their talents. Worker riots during the July Revolution of 1830 had an impact on the changing political situation, but the main result was a deteriorating economic climate in which the government remained deaf to the workers' demands. That eventually caused new riots, such as in Lyon in 1834, and also contributed to the creation of revolutionary circles. Auguste Blanqui expected the people to support a secret elite of conspirators to carry out a socialist *coup d'état*, but his attempt in 1839 failed due to the fact that the people had not been told and hence did not move. During the February Revolution in 1848, workers, together with the petite bourgeoisie, took part in the uprising, but once again a revolution did not happen for them. The creation of a Constituent Assembly was indeed based on men's suffrage, but the 'left' was not included in the newly-created state organs. New worker uprisings in May and June were severely suppressed. 'Working men of all countries, unite!', the call to action by two German socialists in the concluding section of a manifesto written at the request of a German labour organization in London and published there in 1848, was premature. In contrast to the anti-slavery and peace movements, half way through the nineteenth century no relevant women's or workers' organizations, working internationally with shared values, a common discourse and dense exchanges of information, existed.

The International Red Cross made responsible for the Geneva Convention on Wounded Soldiers (1864)

5.1 The private International Red Cross initiative (1863)

The Crimean War 1854–56

The Crimean War of 1854–56 between Russia and Turkey brought the first half of the nineteenth century to an end. Austria, France, Sardinia (a part of the future Italy) and the UK turned against Russia, whereas Prussia mostly kept aloof from the conflict. As a result of this war, Austria and Russia drifted apart more or less permanently, which caused a profound change in European power relations and offered Prussia the opportunity to press for German unity. In 1856 the *Peace of Paris* concluded the Crimean War, which had weakened the Concert of Europe as an international security regime, but did not end the custom of convening multilateral conferences and concluding treaties (see Figure 2.3). The European nation-states continued their use of conference diplomacy and the balance of power. Even the choice of location for a peace agreement was based on considerations related to a cautious use of the balance of power. 'By carefully choosing the location for a congress the European leadership sought to acknowledge, ratify, and legitimate changes in the balance of power. The choice of Paris in 1856, for example, served to rehabilitate Napoleon and demonstrate that France was restored to great-power status. The choice of Berlin over twenty years later was a reflection of the new role of Germany in the centre of Europe. Berlin also marked the emergence of Italy on (almost) equal terms with the great powers' (Richardson 1999, 69). As a result of the outcome of the Crimean War in 1856, Russia lost its Continental leadership position to France. In addition to this Turkey, a Muslim state (the Ottoman Empire), was represented at the conference in Paris and admitted to the then existing international community of states. It was the first enlargement of the conference system beyond Europe in a strict sense (Jackson 2000, 12).

Codification: the Paris Declaration Respecting Maritime Law (1856)

The conference in Paris settled the relations between the great European powers, but on 16 April the signatory states also issued the *Declaration Respecting Maritime Law*. This Declaration of Paris altered certain rules about the conduct of war at sea (part of the Crimean War took place at sea) and is the first codification of maritime law. At the outbreak of the war the belligerents had agreed certain rules relating to neutral ships and the capture of property at sea. At the peace conference in Paris the seven parties (Austria, France, Prussia, Russia, Sardinia, Turkey and the UK) signed the Declaration, with its three prohibitions and one requirement. It prohibited privateering, the capture of enemy goods except contraband on neutral ships and of neutral goods except contraband on enemy ships. It required blockades to be effective and supported by a force sufficiently strong to actually prevent access to the enemy's coast. Although the Declaration applied only to the parties to it, the rules have since been accepted by a far larger number of states as rules of customary law (Hillier 1994, 292; Malanczuk 1997, 40–41).

Florence Nightingale and the wounded soldiers in the Crimean War

Eight years later, this initiative with regard to rules about the conduct of war was followed by an international convention stemming from citizens taking care of the wounded on the battlefield. Florence Nightingale, born in 1820, succeeded in gaining experience of hospital administration in both the UK and Germany, although her parents would not allow her to become a nurse. When the Crimean War was being fought and she read an account in *The Times* of the unhealthy conditions at the front in Scutari, she offered her help to Secretary of War Sidney Herbert, whom she knew. She was sent to Scutari with 38 nurses, where she attacked the unhygienic conditions by proper organization, making sure of sufficient supplies and looking after the welfare of the wounded, thus reducing the death rate. Because of her searching for wounded in the dark she became known as the 'Lady with the Lamp', and she returned to the UK as a popular heroine. Nightingale used the money the public raised in gratitude for her achievements to modernize and further professionalize nursing in the UK. Notwithstanding Nightingale's famous leadership in Scutari, her efforts in fact had not resulted in fewer deaths but rather in an increased death rate, as was discovered during an investigation led by her. This, however, was not made public by the British government. Following her work in the Crimea the British military medical services were completely overhauled and much expanded in such a way that they could adequately care for the military wounded without civilian assistance. Nightingale's actions resulted in the British attitude that taking care of the wounded on the battlefield was a state obligation (Finnemore 1996, 79).

Henri Dunant and the battle of Solferino (1859)

In 1859 the Swiss banker Henri Dunant travelled in northern Italy, where he could not escape seeing the casualties of the battle of Solferino between French and Austrian troops. He came to the conclusion that barely any doctors or supplies were available to the many thousands of wounded. He joined in the relief work, wrote to friends asking for aid and, after reflection, composed an appeal against the cruelties he had witnessed in *A Memory of Solferino* (1862). The book attracted a great deal of attention, due partly to his proposals on how to avoid such situations, and partly to the general impression that the period of peace that Europe had known was drawing to a close and that modern technology would increase the harm caused by more effective weapons such as faster guns or more destructive bullets. Simultaneously the idea that some problems might be dealt with by cooperation between civilized peoples was gaining currency (Lyons 1963, 296). Dunant's proposal promoted the foundation of national societies to work for better medical provision for the wounded and to take responsibility in times of war with the help of qualified volunteers. Whereas Dunant wanted to convince governments with an appeal to reason, the Swiss philanthropist Gustave Moynier, who from personal experience knew about the working of international conferences, organized preparations to raise sufficient support for an international convention that was to establish the basic rules for the care of the wounded. In 1863 Dunant visited the international statistical congress in Berlin (see §9.1), where he gained insights into the available comparative health and death statistics and succeeded in collecting political support for his plans. Governments also at this Berlin congress showed willingness to attend such a conference if it were called (Lyons 1963, 297).

Preparations for the establishment of an NGO

The cooperation between Dunant, Moynier and a few others (a committee of five) resulted in the calling of a conference in Geneva in October 1863, where representatives from 16 states approved the foundation of private national societies staffed by volunteers and funded by private donations. They were to seek recognition from national governments and could act as neutrals in armed conflict. These results were not easily achieved. The French distrusted the competence and integrity of the volunteers, whereas the British argued that their armies were already taking care of the wounded themselves. The Prussians, who had the tradition of the Knights Hospitallers, regarded the British solution as too expensive but in the end agreed to the proposals (Finnemore 1996, 78–79). The man who had designed the Swiss flag, General G.H. Dufour, restrained those who were too idealistic and advised the delegates to strive to 'mitigate the frightfulness of their consequences as much as possible by supporting those whose task it is to help suffering' (Lyons 1963, 297). As a symbol of neutrality, he recommended that medical units should share a common emblem and suggested that this should be the Swiss flag reversed: a red cross on a white ground. Most representatives at the conference were military physicians, often heads of national military units. Some were representatives of private national associations, who were to promote the establishment of organizations of volunteers and to act as pressure groups to bring the governments of the various states together in a full conference for the purpose of concluding a convention (see §5.2). More than anything else the Geneva conference stimulated the growth of the proposed national societies. In 1875, 22 national Red Cross Societies existed; in 1900, 40. The Red Cross Societies are autonomous institutions at the base of the Red Cross that receive their resources mainly from private donations. They coordinate their activities at regular international conferences. In 1919 the *League of Red Cross Societies* was founded as a link between the societies in response to the, by then, immense scope of activities and the need to cooperate.

The International Committee of the Red Cross (1863)

International policy making by the Red Cross is the work of the *International Committee of the Red Cross* (ICRC). In 1863 the original committee of five was replaced by the *Comité international et permanent de secours aux militaires blessés*, which in 1880 took the name of ICRC. Its remarkable feature is that this international body is entirely Swiss. As an independent governing body of 25 Swiss citizens, the ICRC is based in Geneva. It dealt with 'the national societies (the only proviso it made was that they should be recognised by their own governments), summoned the periodic conferences, negotiated with governments to obtain leave to send neutral observers to theatres of war to see that the Convention was being observed, set up (in 1870) an "International Agency" at Geneva for the relief of war victims and also to provide news of wounded or missing men for their relatives, and from time to time published a bulletin which eventually became the *Revue internationale de la Croix-Rouge*' (Lyons 1963, 301–2). On the insistence of Turkey, the ICRC in 1906 adopted Red Crescent as the name and the emblem to be used in Muslim states.

A complicated NGO

The International Red Cross as an organization consists of three components: the national societies, the League of Red Cross Societies (since 1983 League of Red Cross and Red Crescent Societies; since 1991 International Federation instead of League) and the International Committee of the Red Cross. It is a complex hybrid NGO, as there is an NGO within an NGO (the League) and a transnational organization (the ICRC) which, as a private national organization in Switzerland, sets a global foreign policy. The three components (ICRC, League and national societies) meet together every four years at the *Red Cross Conferences*. These are deliberative rather than operational meetings. They have a small staff concerned with procedural matters. Although the influence of these conferences is widely regarded as 'slight', they are also qualified by the presence, participation and voting of the governments which are signatory to the Geneva Conventions (see below) but definitely not members of the International Red Cross. The background to their presence is that after the Second World War governments became the providers of most of the monetary and material resources for conflict-oriented transnational activities of the Red Cross, but without being able to dictate policy to the ICRC (Forsythe 1976, 610–11). The International Red Cross has taken action in conflict situations while conserving the authority of states, but also circumscribing state behaviour in the name of fundamental human rights. 'On the one hand, the Red Cross, principally through the International Committee of the Red Cross (ICRC), is cooperative toward states and acts discreetly in matters regarded by states as sensitive. On the other hand, the Red Cross has promoted the law of armed conflict to limit states and has accepted quasi-supranational authority in international armed conflicts in the form of the right of automatic ICRC access to certain detainees' (Forsythe 1976, 607). Whatever the International Red Cross is doing, its neutrality remains pivotal. At first, neutrality was essential so that the fighting parties would not attack medical personnel helping wounded soldiers and would not view them as combatants. Later, neutrality evolved into a position that the ICRC should never take sides in hostilities or engage at any time in controversies of a political, racial, religious or doctrinal nature.

5.2 Responsibility for monitoring the Geneva Convention on Wounded Soldiers (1864)

The Geneva Convention (1864)

In 1863 the Swiss Red Cross committee of five, which had convened the first conference in Geneva, succeeded in persuading the Swiss government to take the initiative in approaching other governments with proposals for a diplomatic multilateral conference. In August 1864 15 European states, at the invitation of the Swiss government, convened in Geneva with the aim of concluding a convention. Brazil, Mexico and Turkey were absent but had sent messages that they supported the endeavour. The US sent an observer, representing not the American government but the US Sanitary Commission, which was interested in the subject because of the ongoing Civil War and President Abraham Lincoln's aspiration to keep battlefield behaviour as civilized as possible. In order to promote this objective the US armies were guided by the *Instructions for United States Armies in the Field*, a code drafted by Francis Lieber in 1863 and known as the *Lieber Code*. Moynier and Dufour had prepared a draft convention for the Geneva conference which focused on the recognition by belligerents of the neutral position of ambulances and health personnel. On 22 August the conference adopted the final text as *Convention for the Amelioration of the Condition of the Wounded in Armies in the Field*. They also recognized the Red Cross emblem. Since not all states had sent delegates with the full powers to sign the agreement, only 12 states signed what became known as the *Geneva Convention*. By the end of 1866 20 states had ratified, among them Turkey. The US only ratified in 1882. The Geneva Convention, rather than the Paris Declaration Respecting Maritime Law of 1856, was the prototype of the modern international treaty signed by governments and ratified by their national parliaments. Essential in its origin was the role of 'a few morally committed private individuals – individuals without government positions or political power – and the elite networks they were able to use to build an international organization' (Finnemore 1996, 86).

Continuing extension of the original convention

Due to the ongoing efforts by the International Red Cross to improve and extend its text, the Geneva Convention of 1864 was later called the First Geneva Convention. Rounds of decision making resulted in several revisions and additions, in 1899, 1906, 1907, 1929, 1949, 1977 and 2005. The eventual result comprises four conventions and three protocols (see Figure 5.1). Most remarkable with regard to this intergovernmental set of treaties is that the initiative for monitoring its implementation and for adapting the texts has remained an NGO matter. To adapt the texts, the International Red Cross uses the model of first calling a preparatory conference of experts and then asking the Swiss government to convene a diplomatic multilateral conference.

Figure 5.1 The Red Cross Geneva Conventions (1864, 1899, 1929, 1949)

The Geneva Convention of 1864 became the **First Geneva Convention**. Soon after its conclusion the International Red Cross argued that the Convention, due to its brief and business-like character, had left some vital matters out of consideration, such as maritime warfare, prisoners of war and civilian populations. Another multilateral conference was already held in Geneva in 1868, with the object of extending the Convention to maritime warfare. 14 representatives signed the agreed-upon text, but this could not come into effect as it was not ratified by enough states (Lyons 1963, 302).

Not until the Hague Peace Conference of 1899 was the 1864 Geneva Convention extended in the sense of also applying its principles to maritime warfare. This was done in the **Second Geneva Convention**. In 1906 another conference discussed the adaptation and extension of the Convention of 1864 and this resulted in a more detailed and more precise text, replacing the original. This 1906 text was revised again in 1929. The second Hague Peace Conference of 1907 decided that the new version of 1906 also applied to maritime warfare.

In 1929 the **Third Geneva Convention** was adopted, dealing with the treatment of prisoners of war. This subject had already been raised in 1907. The third Convention lays down the general principle, under which belligerent states must treat captives humanely at all times and entrusts the ICRC with the specific task of forwarding information on prisoners of war.

At the International Red Cross Conference in Stockholm, Sweden, in August 1948 experts drafted **four Geneva Conventions**. These represented modernized and newly adapted versions and codification of the three previous Conventions and the experience gained since they came into effect. The protection of civilians in war times was introduced as a new topic. Following in fact two conferences of experts and other consultations, a diplomatic conference convened by the Swiss Federal Council in Geneva from April until August 1949 and attended by 59 states adopted the four new Conventions. These deal with 1) the amelioration of the conditions of the wounded and sick in armed forces in the field; 2) the amelioration of the condition of wounded, sick and shipwrecked members of armed forces at sea; 3) the treatment of prisoners of war; and 4) the protection of civilians in times of war. The first two Conventions are elaborations of neutrality. The Third Convention updated the treatment of prisoners of war owing to the changes that had occurred in the conduct of war, required humane treatment and adequate feeding, and forbade pressure on prisoners to supply more information than a minimum. The Fourth Convention comprises various prohibitions with regard to citizens in occupied territories, such as deportation, the taking of hostages, torture and collective punishments.

In 1977 **two Additional Protocols** were added relating to the protection of victims in armed international conflicts. These Protocols extended protection to guerrilla combatants fighting wars of self-determination or civil wars in which they exercise control over significant stretches of territory (Bugnion 2000). In 2005 a **Third Additional Protocol** added another neutral emblem, the red crystal, alongside the red cross and the red crescent.

The creation of the Hague system

The arbitration movement and the 1899 and 1907 Peace Conferences in The Hague

Part III charts the spread and advance of ideas about arbitration by citizens, lawyers and parliamentarians and by the NGOs they established. During the last 30 years of the nineteenth century, arbitration and international law developed into normative powers in international relations (Chapter 6). They were part of political debates and contributed to the creation of a Permanent Court of Arbitration at the Hague Peace Conference. Arbitration and international law promoted trust among states and contributed to the beginning of the institutionalization of the Hague system (Chapter 7).

Arbitration and international law as normative powers in international relations

6.1 The *Alabama* case and the Treaty of Washington on arbitration (1871)

The Alabama *issue between the UK and the US*

The idea of arbitration as promoted by the international peace movement during the 1840s (see §4.2) attracted new attention as a result of the *Alabama* issue, so-called after a privateer of that name. During the American Civil War, the Northern states blocked the coasts of the Southern states and the latter retaliated by hiring privateers from other states with the aim of hurting the Northern states' trade. They succeeded in this with the help of the *Alabama* from Liverpool, which from 1862 preyed on Northern shipping until it was sunk by a cruiser in 1864. In the meantime, more privateers had been equipped in the UK. After the end of the Civil War in 1865 the US government accused the UK of violation of neutrality and opening its ports to belligerent ships. The US bitterly demanded compensation.

The Treaty of Washington on arbitration (1871)

Negotiations in May 1871 in Washington DC resulted in an arbitration treaty between the two states known as the *Treaty of Washington*, later also as the *Alabama Treaty*. They agreed to submit the *Alabama* issue to an arbitration tribunal, which was to apply the basic rules specified in the Treaty. These became known as 'the three rules of Washington'. They bound a neutral government to: 1) use 'due diligence' to prevent the fitting out, arming or equipping within its jurisdiction of any vessel which it had reasonable grounds to believe was intended to cruise or to wage war against a power with which it was at peace; 2) not to permit or suffer either belligerent to make use of its ports or waters as the base of naval operations against the other; and 3) to exercise due diligence in its own ports and waters and as to all persons within its jurisdiction to prevent any violation of the foregoing obligations and duties. The UK was of the opinion that the rules had not applied during the *Alabama* issue but agreed to have its behaviour tested against the rules.

Five arbitrators were selected, one from each state and three from neutral ones (Brazil, Italy and Switzerland), who held their proceedings in the *Hôtel de Ville* at Geneva. In September 1872 they handed down their judgement, reached by a majority of four to one, which said that the UK had violated the rules and should pay 15.5 million dollars in compensation. Both parties accepted the award and the UK paid within the time stipulated.

Parliamentary majorities in favour of arbitration

Therefore the rules about the conduct of war at sea laid down by European states in the Paris Declaration Respecting Maritime Law of 1856 (see §5.1) were supplemented in 1871 by new rules about neutrality and a process of arbitration between the UK and the US. These two states decided to regard the three rules of Washington as binding, notwithstanding their disagreement about the precise meaning of due diligence. In practice the interpretation of violating neutrality was to become more precise, eventually holding that neutral governments were prohibited from equipping and arming ships within their territory for the benefit of belligerents. Both the Treaty of Washington and the acceptance of the judgement enhanced the idea of arbitration and its practicability. The demonstration that states were capable of settling disputes in a peaceful way had a normative effect. 'The spectacle of two important countries submitting a dispute of this character to impartial third-party settlement on the basis of law, and the loser complying with the terms of the award, naturally gave a great fillip to the development of the concept of international arbitration as an alternative to allowing political tension to smoulder indefinitely' (Rosenne 1989, 5). The *Alabama* issue gave rise to a great deal of parliamentary consideration of international arbitration. The US and various European states had parliamentary majorities in favour of including arbitration clauses in bilateral and multilateral treaties. During the rest of the century interstate arbitration was prevalent, particularly in tribunals in which either the US or the UK participated (Malanczuk 1997, 293–94). The Universal Postal Union of 1874 (see §8.2) was the first intergovernmental organization with a provision for (compulsory) arbitration in its constitution. Examples of arbitration clauses in multilateral treaties are the Congo river treaty of 1885 (see §10.1) and the Brussels General Act against slavery of 1890 (see Figure 4.2) (Eyffinger 1996, 30).

6.2 The creation of two private institutes for international law in 1873

The Institute of International Law (1873)

In addition to arbitration, international law too gained normative power. Shortly after the *Alabama* issue, citizens founded two private institutes of international law, which can be regarded as NGOs: the Institute of International Law and the International Law Association. In September 1873 the *Institute of International Law* (IIL) was established by Francis Lieber and Gustave Moynier, both engaged in humanitarian projects, the International Red Cross and the formulation of rules about warfare, and G. Rolin-Jacqemyns, editor of the Belgian *Revue de droit international et de législation comparée*, founded in 1869. They succeeded in attracting sufficient support for a permanent organization, on condition that this should be non-governmental and restricted to a group of notable lawyers. Founded at a congress in Ghent, Belgium, the IIL aimed to encourage the general progress of international law. 'It was to work towards the formulation of the general principles of science; to give its support to every serious attempt at gradual and progressive codification of international law; to obtain official recognition of principles of law recognized as being in harmony with the needs of modern societies; to contribute – "within the limits of its competence" – to the maintenance of peace and the observance of the laws of war; to examine difficulties which might arise in the interpretation of law and give, where needed, juridical opinions on doubtful or controversial cases; to forward by publications, by education of public opinion and all other means, "the triumph of those principles of justice and humanity which ought to regulate the relations between peoples"' (Lyons 1963, 219). The IIL was composed of members (limited to 60) to be chosen from a group of 'associates' (also 60), as well as distinguished honorary members. No state was allowed to have more than a 20 per cent share of these categories. An extended governance structure was created for the independent and authoritative functioning of the IIL, which was financed by member subscriptions and grants from foundations. The Nobel Peace Prize awarded to the IIL in 1904 was appreciated from a financial perspective also.

International law documented

From 1877 onwards the IIL published the *Annuaires de l'Institute de droit international*. The institute's activities were summarized as 'constant investigation, discussion and recommendation in some twenty main fields of international law' (Lyons 1963, 220). Knowledge of and insights into international law were documented, for instance by the publication of international treaties and their annotations. G.F. de Martens had already started publishing treaty series between states in 1791. The IIL activities added to the development of international law as a discipline and a legal specialization. The issuing of periodicals of international law, such as in Belgium the *Revue de droit international et de législation comparée* and in France the *Revue générale de droit international* (since 1894), was a new venture during the late nineteenth century.

Expertise on arbitration

The first field the IIL itself investigated was international arbitration, given the 'three rules of Washington'. Its analysis of the *Alabama* case focused on the questions of procedure in international arbitral tribunals. 'These debates resulted in the famous *Projet de règlement pour la procédure arbitrale internationale*, which later constituted one of the major sources of the 1899 Hague Peace Conference' (Eyffinger 1996, 30). As the number and volume of its reports grew, and as it became known that the institute represented the most eminent international lawyers in the world, governments began to pay increasing attention to the IIL: 'many conventions and even bi-partite treaties – especially on the subject of arbitration – were modelled upon its recommendation' (Lyons 1963, 221). This fame turned the IIL lawyers into an 'epistemic community' of experts, who under certain conditions within an intergovernmental arrangement were capable of suggesting international policies. In the case of the IIL this was to reach a high point in the Hague system (see Chapter 7).

The International Law Association (1873)

The second private organization established in 1873 was the *Association for the Reform and Codification of the Law of Nations*, which from 1895 onwards became the *International Law*

Association (ILA). The association was founded in Brussels in October 1873 on the initiative of American lawyers deeply committed to the peace movement. It had a strong Anglo-Saxon orientation and set up its headquarters in London. The association was less exclusive in its membership than the IIL, and in practice spent more time on commercial or private international law than did the IIL. 'It gave more detailed examination than the Institute to such matters as bills of exchange, divorce, international recognition of companies, execution of foreign judgements, and many different aspects of maritime law' (Lyons 1963, 221). The ILA saw the drafting of a code of international law as its first priority, preliminary to the creation of a new system of arbitration.

Dissimilarities and complementarity

From the beginning the two organizations maintained friendly relations and proved to be complementary to each other. There were clear differences between them. The Institute of International Law was a more purely scientific body, while the International Law Association's task was 'to act upon public opinion, upon legislatures and upon governments "by the methods the Americans and the English know so well how to employ"', according to the IIL (Lyons 1963, 221). During the last quarter of the nineteenth century, arbitration based on international law became an issue advocated from different angles and for different purposes by activists from government, business circles and the professional world alike: 'through endless streams of meetings, public lectures, magazines, pamphlets and journals'. It became a general feeling in public opinion 'that the useless and extravagant investments on armaments should, with the passage of time, be replaced by a code of international law, in the same way as law had superseded feudal violence at the dawn of modern times' (Eyffinger 1996, 30). Parliamentarians also strove for arbitration and international rules of law.

6.3 The Inter-Parliamentary Union (1889) favouring arbitration

The peace movement in favour of arbitration

The international peace movement of the 1860s and 1870s had a stronger political orientation than the religiously-inspired movement of the first half of the century. The French peace movement, led by parliamentarian Frédéric Passy, played a role at international congresses alongside the International League for Peace and Freedom (to be discussed later; see §13.2). Arbitration became Passy's main aim. His *Ligue de la paix* first changed its name to *Société des amis de la paix* and then to *Société française de l'arbitration entre nations*. His British counterpart Randal Cremer, who in 1871 had founded the *Workmen's Peace Association*, also believed that arbitration should be made the keystone of the peace movement, as it was practical, had already won wide acceptance and had a unifying effect on the various tendencies within the movement. During the 1870s the peace movement developed various schemes for the functioning of arbitration. Cremer proposed one which included a High Court of Nations and sanctions in case a government ignored the court's decisions: 'the other governments shall thereupon suspend diplomatic intercourse with such government and prohibit commercial intercourse with the nation it represents until it shall conform to the decision of the court' (cited in Lyons 1963, 323).

Establishment of the Inter-Parliamentary Union (1889)

Passy and Cremer collected support in their parliaments for the opening of negotiations on arbitration treaties with other states. In 1887–88 Passy promoted one between France and the US. The idea of concerted action by parliamentarians of different states was raised a few times, but it was Cremer who in 1888 took the initiative by bringing a group of British members of parliament to Paris, where Passy headed a group of French deputies. This bilateral meeting was followed by the first *Inter-Parliamentary Conference* in 1889 with 96 delegates, from France (55), the UK (30), Italy (5), Belgium, Denmark, Hungary, Liberia, Spain and the US (one each). The main issue was the question of how to make their respective governments conclude permanent arbitration treaties and include arbitration clauses in commercial treaties. The meetings made sense and were repeated at intervals of about 18 months. In 1892 a permanent Bureau was set up in Bern, which moved to Brussels in 1899 when an executive Committee was appointed and the name of the conferences was changed to *Inter-Parliamentary Union*. This Union did not think much of utopian visions of general peace, but promoted arbitration. Its aim was 'to unite in common action the members of all parliaments constituted in national groups, to secure recognition in their respective states, either through legislation or by international treaties, of the principle of solving disputes between nations by arbitration or other friendly and judicial means. It has also the further objective of studying other questions of international law, and, in general, problems relating to the development of peaceful relations among peoples' (cited in Lyons 1963, 329).

Division of labour between parliamentarians and peace groups

From 1889 onwards peace groups from different states began organizing annual international conferences under the name of *Universal Peace Congress*. In 1891 they set up a Bureau in Bern. The Inter-Parliamentary Union and the Universal Peace Congress, both presided over by Passy, developed the custom of holding their meetings simultaneously in the same place. Apart from having close relations, the two organizations established a division of labour between them: 'the parliamentarians working on the governments as it were from within, the other exerting a continuous pressure from without. One was essentially political, the other essentially propagandist; one practical, the other idealistic; one limited in scope, the other wide-ranging' (Lyons 1963, 329). The Inter-Parliamentary Union still functions, with the aim of promoting peace, cooperation and representative democracy. At its centennial anniversary in 1989 112 national parliaments were members, while in 2008 there were 150 members plus eight regional parliaments as associate members.

6.4 The Washington conference on trade and arbitration in 1889

Pan-Americanism: trade and arbitration

Recognition of arbitration was also an issue on the agenda of the Pan-American multilateral conference of 1889 in Washington DC. In 1881 Colombia had taken the initiative of calling a conference of states on the American continent to discuss the issue of arbitration in international controversies, but due to the war between Chile and Peru this conference did not take place. US Secretary of State James Blaine fostered the idea and began working towards a Pan-American peace conference on arbitration, for which he found support in Congress. Trade was another strong motive for Pan-Americanism in US foreign policy, after a proposal in the Senate to conclude a series of reciprocity treaties with American states in 1884. The Democratic Party, however, opposed the idea of using diplomatic means for the development of trade. But in 1888 the Democrats did not have a majority in either the Senate or the House of Representatives, which meant that Congress could pass an act on this topic (*Act of Congress of May 24, 1888*), which Democratic President Stephen Cleveland did not sign, but did not veto either. On the basis of this Act the President was allowed to invite the states of the American continent to a Pan-American conference, in order to discuss cooperation on various topics such as the preservation of peace and the promotion of prosperity, the formation of an American customs union, regular and frequent communication between the ports, a uniform system of customs regulations and a uniform system of weights and measures, as well as the protection of intellectual property rights, the adoption of a common silver coin and a definite plan of arbitration for all questions, disputes and differences 'to the end that all difficulties and disputes between such nations may be peaceably settled and wars prevented' (cited in Reinsch 1911, 78).

The Washington conference (1889)

The first conference of American states, chaired by Blaine, who remained Secretary of State under Republican President Benjamin Harrison, opened on 2 October 1889 in Washington with all independent states in the Western Hemisphere represented. Based on the topics mentioned in the US Act of Congress, with private international law added as another, 16 standing commissions were set up to discuss these matters. The only treaty project at the conference was obligatory arbitration for international controversies. The other matters were concluded by resolution or recommendation. As a result of the discussions, obligatory arbitration was to be decreed in all controversies with the exception of those in which the independence of a state was endangered. This conclusion gave the conference an advanced character and the treaty text was signed by the delegates of 11 states. Ratification had to take place before May 1891, but despite a call by Harrison that the US, true to its initiative, should ratify, none of the states that had signed ever ratified the arbitration treaty. This was related to the treaty's broad character and to the fact that the delegates were not entirely clear in their minds about the relationship of such a treaty to the sovereignty of their individual states (Reinsch 1911, 81) (see §11.5 for the far more successful economic aspects of the conference). What distinguished this multilateral conference in Washington from previous conferences, such as in Vienna in 1815 and in Paris in 1856, was that it did not take place as an end to a war, nor was it convened for the settlement of a specific diplomatic problem. Instead, it had the character of a 'general advisory meeting of neighboring countries, summoned for the purpose of bringing these countries into closer touch with one another and of arriving at a better mutual knowledge of their various relations and interests, in order to provide a secure basis for the eventual conclusion of treaties and for coöperation of these governments' (Reinsch 1911, 83). That it was not called to end a war was also true for the conference that was to take place in The Hague ten years later and which also dealt with arbitration, albeit more successfully.

The 1899 and 1907 Peace Conferences in The Hague and the Hague system

Si vis pacem, cole justitiam (if you want peace, cultivate justice)

Maxim at the Peace Palace in The Hague, which differs from the older

Si vis pacem, para bellum (if you want peace, prepare war)

7.1 The Hague Peace Conference on the law of war and arbitration (1899)

The calling of the first Hague Peace Conference

Three weeks after Bismarck's death in 1898, at a time when Germany was flourishing economically but isolated internationally, the Russian Tsar Nicholas II sent a circular letter to the states accredited to his Court, in which he invited governments to a multilateral conference on problems of world peace and disarmament. He regarded the steady increase in weaponry as a threat to peace. His mention of humanitarian objectives could not conceal Russia's self-interest, as the burdens of the arms race were exhausting the Russian treasury. Germany reacted negatively, but the US accepted the invitation. In early 1899 the Tsar sent a second circular letter, in which he outlined the two objectives of the proposed conference as being to set a limit on the progressive increase in arms, and to discuss the prevention of armed conflict through the peaceful means of settlement at the disposal of modern diplomacy such as arbitration and mediation. He mentioned eight issues, including 'the freezing of military effectiveness and budgets; the prohibition of new types of arms; the restriction or prohibition of explosives, bombs dropped from balloons and submarine torpedo-boats, the extension of the attainments of the 1864 Geneva convention to the area of naval warfare; the revision of the unratified 1874 Brussels Declaration on the laws and customs of war; and, lastly, the acceptance of the principles of mediation and optional arbitration as a means of preventing or settling international disputes, and the establishment of a model and uniform practice in these respects' (Eyffinger 1996, 42). This agenda setting linked up with the debates about arbitration and with previous agreements, among them the *Declaration of Brussels*. In 1874, at a meeting in Brussels, 12 states including the great powers had attempted to conclude a treaty concerning the laws and customs of war on land. Given the reluctance of the powers to hamper their own freedom of action so soon after the Franco-Prussian war, they were unable to frame a convention but did produce the Declaration. This influenced the instruction manuals for the use of armies in the field that some governments issued and it served as a draft for the Tsar's initiative (Lyons 1963, 305). In 1899 this initiative resulted in 26 states sending their representatives to The Hague. This city was chosen for various reasons, among them the wish to avoid a great power's capital, the family ties between the Romanovs and the House of Orange, Dutch neutrality, and the Dutch tradition of international law from Hugo Grotius to the successful conferences on private international law in The Hague in 1893 and 1894 presided over by Tobias Asser.

The course of events at the conference

The Hague Peace Conference, with about 100 delegates, took place in the palace *Huis ten Bosch* from 18 May to 29 July. Much to the dislike of the German emperor, the states were placed on an equal footing (one state, one vote). In addition to the states accredited to the St Petersburg Court, three more were invited: Luxembourg, Montenegro and Siam (Thailand). South Africa and most Central and Latin American states were not invited. The US and Mexican delegates were to represent the entire American continent. China, Japan and Korea, together with Siam, represented Asia. Despite its diplomatic relations with the Netherlands, the Holy See was absent because of Italian protests. Three commissions were established to discuss the agenda issues. The *First Commission*, chaired by August Beernaert, considered the limitation of weapons and the humanizing of war. The *Second Commission*, chaired by Frederick de Martens, discussed the extension of the 1864 Geneva Convention to maritime warfare as well as the laws and customs of war. The *Third Commission*, chaired by Léon Bourgeois, reviewed the maintenance of general peace, good offices and mediation, international commissions of inquiry and international arbitration. This last Commission touched on the issue of state sovereignty most directly. It was agreed that the delegates were not to inform the press, as the character of the negotiations did not call for open discussion. Only the president and the Conference Bureau were authorized to give brief summaries of the Commissions' proceedings to the press. This decision was greeted with wide dissatisfaction among the members of the press and the NGO representatives present in The Hague (see below). It was not long before the Conference Bureau relaxed its strict rules somewhat. Afterwards it was concluded that this scenario of observing confidentiality was inexpedient, as it had hampered the general acceptance of what was being discussed during the sessions (Eyffinger 1996, 45) and so did not help to find public support for the agreed-upon international policies.

Influence by NGOs

When it was known that the Peace Conference was to take place, numerous NGOs decided to send representatives to The Hague in order to be visible at the event. They sought to make their influence felt and, it seemed to many observers, conducted themselves as though they were official members. Among the NGOs in The Hague were peace groups, women's organizations and deputations from oppressed peoples such as Armenians, Finns and Macedonians (Charnovitz 1997, 196). In October 1898 the German feminist Margaretha Selenka had convinced the international women's movement to support the Tsar's plan and to put forward the opinion of women. As a result of her dedication, which reached as far as Japan, and with the help of Gabrielle Wiszniewska, Victor Hugo's daughter and president of the International Women's League for General Disarmament founded in 1896, Selenka presented a petition signed by one million women in 18 states to the conference, where she had a short meeting with the president. The International Council of Women, which had set up a Standing Commission on Peace and Arbitration in 1899, also supported the conference's aims. In addition, women organized street demonstrations in The Hague and in other cities, among them Copenhagen, Milan, Paris, Stockholm and Turin. During the conference women such as Selenka and Bertha von Suttner – author of the widely-read anti-war novel *Lay Down Your Arms* (1889) and editor of the pacifist journal with the same name – and other female pacifists made sure that at night, when the official sessions were closed, they would meet the diplomats and ministers during dinner. They could afford this, as many of them were of noble birth and good family and had access to the luxury hotels and restaurants used by the delegates. These conversations gave them insights into the course of events during the official gatherings and also provided them with the opportunity to put forward their views with regard to the position of women and peace (S.E. Cooper in Pierson 1987, 63–64). It was the first time that women's organizations lobbied so specifically and widely at a diplomatic multilateral conference.

NGOs lobbying and passing information

Generally speaking, the NGOs were able to make contact with the official delegates at The Hague. To review the many private petitions the conference even set up a Commission of Correspondence. The activism of the NGOs foreshadowed their later habits of using intergovernmental conferences for coordinated lobbying and mass publicity. In defiance of the conference's official rule of secrecy, the peace activist William Stead published a regular chronicle of the conference in two languages (Charnovitz 1997, 197). His information was also based on what the NGOs discovered during their contacts with delegates, including the conversations of women with the official delegates during meals.

Conference results

The results from the three Commissions and the conference were brought together in a *Final Act* with various conventions and declarations attached to it. The results varied for each Commission. The First Commission on disarmament came with a platitudinous resolution. 'The Conference is of the opinion that the restriction of military charges, which are at present a heavy burden on the world, is extremely desirable for the increase of the material and moral welfare of the world' (cited in Lyons 1963, 346). However, it also produced three declarations prohibiting bombardments from balloons and the use of poisonous gas and dumdum bullets. These efforts to lessen the horrors of modern technology were to be binding on the contracting parties only in the case of war between two or more of them. Almost all states signed and ratified these declarations (as was said, no one regarded them as having much relevance to real life), with the exception of the UK and the US, both states with strong pacifist movements. The UK's refusal to sign was influenced by resentment at the criticism for its previous use of dumdum bullets. The US argued that one should not prevent the modernization of weapons, just the inflicting of senseless cruelty with them. The Second Commission produced two conventions about the law of war at sea and on land. The 'commission put together sixty articles of impressive impact and accomplished more with respect to naval warfare and the wounded than all the previous Red Cross Conferences combined' (Eyffinger 1996, 44). The Third Commission presented a convention comprising 61 articles on peaceful settlement, which promoted arbitration and the establishment of a Permanent Court of Arbitration.

7.2 The establishment of the Permanent Court of Arbitration (1899)

The British proposal

When the British delegate first announced the idea of a permanent international tribunal, which had not been mentioned in the Tsar's circular letter, one could 'have heard a pin drop in the Conference'. 'Members looked at one another for a moment in blank amazement, and not a few felt for the first time that they were face to face with serious business put forward by practical statesmen in grim earnest' (Eyffinger 1996, 47). Soon it turned out that delegates of a number of states, among them Russia, the UK and the US, carried elaborated schemes of such an institution in their pockets and were willing to discuss them. The American government had already suggested the establishment of an international court years before, but both Germany and the UK had reacted with reserve. In 1894 and 1895 the Inter-Parliamentary Union, which regarded an arbitration clause in each international treaty as a *sine qua non*, had drawn up a scheme on which the British proposal at The Hague was actually based (Lyons 1963, 340–41). Various other governments relied on the work on arbitration done by the IIL.

Consulting the German emperor

The Third Commission of the Hague Conference, about arbitration, met only nine times, given the strong German resistance to the idea. The actual work was done by a smaller *Special Committee of Examination* and an extraordinary subcommittee that was established to deal with the variety of schemes put forward, while the British scheme was accepted as the basis for further discussion. The Special Committee met three times a week at a different location and suspended its meetings to consult with the German emperor, who opposed any intervention in domestic politics. Whether the Commission would be successful depended on being obliging and on a visit to the emperor by the German and the American members of the Special Committee. The major concession given to Germany was the replacement of obligatory by optional arbitration. 'It was at this juncture, later critics have argued, that by far the best opportunity to achieve something really spectacular was missed' (Eyffinger 1996, 47). France tried to compensate for this concession by authorizing the secretary-general of the court to draw the attention of conflicting parties to the court. The eventual convention was a compromise in which the various contributions could be recognized: 'Great Britain's scheme for arbitration, Russia's Commissions of Inquiry, France's duty-clause, and the mediation plan to the credit of the US' (Eyffinger 1996, 48).

The Hague Convention on the Pacific Settlement of International Disputes

The essence of the Hague *Convention on the Pacific Settlement of International Disputes* was that contracting parties agreed in cases of serious dispute to have recourse to the good offices or mediation of friendly powers, as far as circumstances allowed. The conference had sometimes used general or broad terms to alleviate the fears of small states of pressure by the great powers, with the result of vagueness, 'a classic example of that most familiar malady of international conferences – anaemia induced by unanimity' (Lyons 1963, 349). An innovation in the Convention was that where disputes arose from a difference of opinion over the facts of a particular situation, the parties should agree to the setting up of an international commission of inquiry to elicit the facts by impartial investigation. Another innovation was the establishment of a Permanent Court of Arbitration in The Hague. This body is somewhat misnamed, as it is neither permanent nor a court. It is rather an institutional framework, open to the parties to avail themselves of at their choice. It consists of a group of potential arbitrators who are nominated for six years by the signatory states. Each state may nominate no more than four persons 'of known competency in questions of international law, of the highest moral reputation and disposed to accept the duties of arbitrators' (Rosenne 1989, 8). To arbitrate on their dispute, states may choose a panel of three or five people, including an independent chair, from this group. A single arbitrator is another possibility.

The coming into force of the Permanent Court of Arbitration (1900)

The *Permanent Court of Arbitration* became active in September 1900, after the Dutch minister of foreign affairs deemed the number of ratifications satisfactory. The Hague Convention was amended in 1907, with the new version coming into force in 1910. The Court's only truly permanent organ is the *International Bureau*, at first located at the Prinsegracht in The Hague and from 1913 onwards in the Peace Palace. The Bureau, headed by a secretary-general, performs all routine administrative tasks, acts as a registry for the Court and its Commissions of Inquiry, keeps the archives and is the channel of communication between parties and arbitrators. Its expenses are borne by the signatory parties in the same proportion as fixed for the International Bureau of the Universal Postal Union in 1874 (see §8.2). The Court's second permanent, but in reality less regularly functioning, organ is the *Administrative Council*. It was meant to consist of professional lawyers, but as a result of German opposition the work remained in the hands of the diplomatic representatives of the signatory powers in The Hague, with the Dutch minister of foreign affairs as president (Lyons 1963, 350). The Council decides by majority vote and has 'the power to control the administrative side of the work of the tribunal and of the international bureau; it appoints and dismisses officials and employees of the latter, fixes their salaries, and controls the expenditure. The council also takes charge of the preparation of an annual report upon the work of the international court and of the administrative bureau, as well as on the budget of disbursements' (Reinsch 1911, 124). In some instances the Council has taken far-reaching decisions. In 1935 it extended the Court's jurisdiction to state versus non-state disputes, in 1937 it authorized its International Bureau to put its offices and organization at the disposal of Conciliation Commissions, and in 1992, 1993 and 1996 it established a number of sets of new optional procedural rules for various types of dispute settlement (Eyffinger 1996, 54) (see Figure 7.1).

Results of the Permanent Court

Given the agreed-upon base of the Permanent Court, it was welcomed as an institution but not too much was expected. Its beginnings were not strong because, for instance, important signatories such as France and the UK did not have their dispute over African matters settled by a Court panel, but rather by a single arbitrator chosen by them. The UK furthermore refused to have the Boer War submitted to the Court. The Court's position was strengthened however when, as a result of the Pan-American Conference of 1901 in Mexico City, the Latin American states decided to become signatories to the Hague Convention *en bloc* (see §7.4). Other positive developments were the inclusion in general treaties of a stipulation that disputes arising out of the particular treaty had to be referred to arbitration, and the signing of general treaties of arbitration also referring to the Permanent Court. Between 1900 and 1914 more than 120 general arbitration treaties were concluded between pairs of states (Rosenne 1989, 9). In the years up to 1907 the Court received four cases, in the period from 1907 to 1914 11, in the interwar period eight, between 1938 and 1954 none, and since 1954 four, which makes a total of 27 arbitral tribunals that were set up within the Court's framework. The tribunals included technical matters such as 'claims, indemnities, damaged interests and financial questions; also, land concessions, border disputes and fishery differences. A few had a distinct political impact, such as the *Casablanca* case and the *North Atlantic Coast Fisheries* case, or concerned intricate juridical problems, as in the *Orinoco*, *Savarkar* and *Islands of Palmas* cases' (Eyffinger 1996, 55). As a result of naval incidents, Commissions of Inquiry were set up four times, in 1904, 1912, 1921 and 1961, and on three occasions the International Bureau put its offices and organization at the disposal of Conciliation Commissions, in 1937, 1954 and 1955 (see Figure 7.1 for the Court's expansion of activities at the end of the twentieth century).

Characteristics of international arbitration

The period 1907–14 was the Permanent Court's heyday. 'At that juncture, most governments were fully satisfied with the machinery as it was: optional, but morally authoritative. Arbitration had become firmly rooted' (Eyffinger 1996, 55). During this period the main rules of international arbitration were firmly drawn. These rules are: disputes arising in the course of the proceedings concerning the tribunal's jurisdiction are to be settled by the tribunal itself; arbitrators should be persons of recognized competence and of integrity; parties are equal with regard to judicial techniques; patterns of procedures have settled themselves as regular; and the agreement to have recourse to arbitration implies the obligation to abide by the tribunal's judgement (Rosenne 1989, 10–11). The outbreak of war in 1914 caused a collapse of the system and damaged the credibility of the peaceful settlement of disputes, but nonetheless it did not bring an end to the existence or functioning of the Permanent Court of Arbitration.

Figure 7.1 The Permanent Court of Arbitration at the end of the twentieth century

In 1959, after a period without much activity, the Administrative Council of the **Permanent Court of Arbitration** made an appeal to its contracting parties to resort to the Court more extensively. It also instructed its Bureau to examine how best to increase the role of the Court. In 1968 these efforts resulted in a cooperation agreement with the *International Centre for Settlement of Investment Disputes* (ICSID) of the International Bank for Reconstruction and Development (see Figure 25.1). At the end of the 1980s and in the 1990s, ICSID arbitral tribunals held hearings at the seat of the Permanent Court. The same happened with hearings by the *Arbitral Court* of the private International Chamber of Commerce (see Figure 12.2). Cooperation between the Permanent Court and the *UN Commission on International Trade Law* (UNCITRAL) further expanded the Court's activities in the field of international commercial arbitration. In 1976 this agreement empowered the Court's secretary-general to designate an 'appointing authority' to break some deadlocks in the appointment of arbitrators in this field. In 1981 the Permanent Court placed its offices and staff at the disposal of the *Iran–US Claims Tribunal*, which was set up to solve the problems that had arisen from the occupation of the US embassy in Tehran in 1979. Although this Tribunal moved into its own buildings, it continued its use of the Court's rooms as a venue for hearings of the full Tribunal. From the 1980s onwards various commercial arbitration institutions have used the Court's facilities, and in 1995 the Permanent Court became a registry for such arbitral tribunals. Since 1994 the Court also acts as a registry for cases arbitrated under the UN Convention on the Law of the Sea.

Between 1960 and 1995 the number of contracting parties increased from 60 to 81. In the early 1990s the Permanent Court developed new initiatives to revitalize its role, within the framework of the UN Decade of International Law. In 1991 it set up a working group to improve its functioning, followed in 1992 by the establishment of an expert group to revise certain specific aspects. These initiatives produced two **new sets of optional procedural rules** for disputes between two states and for cases where only one state is involved. In 1996 new sets of procedural rules followed for inquiry, conciliation and arbitration in disputes in which intergovernmental organizations are involved. In 1987 a dispute between a state (Somalia) and an IGO (the UN Development Programme) had been submitted to the Court. The first conference of contracting parties to the Permanent Court of Arbitration took place in September 1993. It adopted a resolution on the establishment of a *Financial Assistance Fund for Qualified States* and another inviting the secretary-general to appoint a steering committee for a possible revision of the 1907 Convention. The Court strengthened its links with the UN, and in October 1993 it was granted permanent observer status at the UN General Assembly (Eyffinger 1996, 55–56). In 2002 a Court tribunal gave its judgement in a dispute between Ethiopia and Eritrea. The Ethiopian government did not regard it as 'fair' and it was not until the end of 2004 that the government recognized it and sent it to parliament in order to end the controversies with Eritrea. In 2008 the number of contracting parties was 108.

7.3 The awarding of the Nobel Peace Prize since 1901

Nobel's vision of the peace movement

The understanding of the peace effort's importance around the end of the nine-teenth century was both a public and a private one. The industrialist Alfred Nobel was not part of the peace movement, but he was to contribute to it in his own way. He created an international prize for the promotion of peace. Having earned a fortune from his invention of dynamite, which had both a civil and a military use, he began reflecting on the meaning of war and peace. Being a mixture of pessimist and idealist by nature, he 'had a deep distrust of the masses and viewed the influence of "pernicious newspapers" with particular suspicion. At the same time he had a belief, at times a naïve belief, in progress, though he felt it could only be achieved if influence were brought to bear upon governments, not peoples' (Lyons 1963, 335). In 1890 he read Bertha von Suttner's anti-war novel and wrote her a letter. She asked him to support the promotion of peace financially. He did send some money, but questioned the practicality of her kind of agitation and at the time preferred a less ambitious, step-by-step approach, paying attention to arbitration and disarmament. In 1892 he attended the conferences of the International Peace Bureau and the Inter-Parliamentary Conference in Bern, where he met Von Suttner. One year later he developed his plan to use part of his fortune for a prize to be awarded regularly to a man or woman who had done most to advance the idea of general peace in Europe. 'I do not refer to disarmament which can be achieved only by very slow degrees. I do not even refer to compulsory arbitration between the nations; but what I have in view is that we should soon achieve the result – undoubtedly a practical one – that all states should bind themselves to take action against the first aggressor. Wars will then become impossible, and we should succeed in compelling even the most quarrelsome state either to have recourse to a tribunal, or to remain quiet' (cited in Lyons 1963, 337). In his last will and testament of 1895, Nobel decreed that the Nobel Peace Prize should be allotted to 'the person who shall have most or best promoted the fraternity of nations and the abolition or diminution of standing armies and the formation and increase of peace congresses' (Lyons 1963, 338).

Awarding the Nobel Peace Prize

The Nobel Foundation was established to organize the Nobel Peace Prize, which in principle every year awards prizes for physics, chemistry, medical science, literature, peace and, since 1969, also for economics. A committee of five members of the Nor-wegian parliament awards the prize, followed by presentation by the Swedish king. The first presentation took place in 1901, when the Peace Prize was awarded to Henri Dunant and Frédéric Passy. No fewer than 14 of the 19 Peace Prizes awarded between 1901 and 1913 went 'to what one might call the Passy–von Suttner school of thought. They each got one, so did ten other members connected either with the Peace Congresses or the Interparliamentary Union, and in one year (1910) the prize was awarded to the Peace Bureau itself' (Lyons 1963, 338). Between 1901 and 2007 the Peace Prize was awarded 87 times (see Figure 7.2), sometimes to one, at other times to two or even three recipients.

International organizations awarded the Nobel Peace Prize

International organizations are also eligible for the prize, both NGOs and IGOs or a combination of persons and organizations. Eight IGOs have received the award: the Nansen International Office for Refugees (1938), the UN refugee organization UNHCR (twice, in 1954 and 1981), the UN children's fund UNICEF (1965), the International Labour Organization (1969), the UN Peacekeeping Forces (1988), the UN itself (2001), the International Atomic Energy Agency (2005) and the Intergovernmental Panel on Climate Change (2007). Ten NGOs have received the prize: the Institute of International Law (1904), the International Peace Bureau (1910), the International Committee of the Red Cross (three times, in 1917, 1944 and 1963, the latter together with the League of Red Cross Societies), the American Friends Service Committee and the (British) Friends Civil Council (1947), Amnesty International (1977), International Physicians for the Prevention of Nuclear War (1985), the Pugwash Conferences on Science and World Affairs (1995), the International Campaign to Ban Landmines (1997), Médecins Sans Frontières (1999) and the Grameen Bank (2006). The first head of state to be honoured was Theodore Roosevelt, certainly not a pacifist but the man who persuaded two states, Russia and Japan, to lay down their arms. Up to 2007 the states that received most Nobel Peace Prizes were the US (19), the UK and France (8), Sweden (5) and Germany and Northern Ireland (4). The results for each continent are: Europe 36, the Americas 23, Asia 8, the Middle East 4 and Africa 4. Eleven awards were to women. The prize was refused once, by Le Duc Tho from North Vietnam, who was awarded it together with Henry Kissinger.

A prestigious prize

The Nobel Peace Prize is considered a prestigious prize, providing its laureates with both money and publicity. It also causes controversy due to the fact that some politicians are honoured and some are not (Mahatma Gandhi). In some cases the prize implies protection, as with Andre Sacharov and Aung San Suu Kyi. Awarding the Nobel Prize for Physics in 1919 to German physicists, among them the inventor of mustard gas which was used during the First World War, was a painful occasion.

Figure 7.2 Nobel Peace Prize winners since 1901

1901 Jean Henri Dunant (Switzerland) and Frédéric Passy (France)
1902 Elie Ducommun and Charles-Albert Gobat (Switzerland)
1903 Randal Cremer (UK)
1904 **Institute of International Law** (founded in 1873)
1905 Bertha von Suttner (Austria)
1906 Theodore Roosevelt (US)
1907 Ernesto Teodoro Moneta (Italy) and Louis Renault (France)
1908 Klas Pontus Arnoldson (Sweden) and Frederic Bajer (Denmark)
1909 Baron d'Estournelles de Constant (France) and August Beernaert (Belgium)
1910 **International Peace Bureau** (founded in 1891)
1911 Tobias Asser (Netherlands) and Alfred Fried (Austria)

1912 Elihu Root (US)
1913 Henri-Marie Lafontaine (Belgium)
1917 **International Committee of the Red Cross** (founded in 1863)
1919 Woodrow Wilson (US)
1920 Léon Bourgeois (France)
1921 Karl Branting (Sweden) and Christian Louis Lange (Norway)
1922 Fridtjof Nansen (Norway)
1925 Sir Austen Chamberlain (UK) and Charles G. Dawes (US)
1926 Aristide Briand (France) and Gustav Streseman (Germany)
1927 Ferdinand Buisson (France) and Ludwig Quidde (Germany)
1929 Frank B. Kellogg (US)
1930 Nathan Söderblom (Sweden)
1931 Jane Addams and Nicholas Murray Butler (US)
1933 Sir Norman Angell (UK)
1934 Arthur Henderson (UK)
1935 Carl von Ossietzky (Germany)
1936 Carlos Saavedra Lamas (Argentina)
1937 Viscount Cecil of Chelwood (UK)
1938 **Nansen International Office for Refugees** (founded in 1931)
1944 **International Committee of the Red Cross** (founded in 1863)
1945 Cordell Hull (US)
1946 Emily Greene Balch and John R. Mott (US)
1947 **American Friends Service Committee** (US) (founded in 1917) and **Friends Civil Council** (UK) (founded in 1927)
1949 Lord Boyd Orr (UK)
1950 Ralph Bunche (US)
1951 Léon Jouhaux (France)
1952 Albert Schweizer (Alsace)
1953 George C. Marshall (US)
1954 **Office of the UN High Commissioner for Refugees** (founded in 1951)
1957 Lester B. Pearson (Canada)
1958 Dominique George Pire (Belgium)
1960 Philip Noël-Baker (UK)
1961 Dag Hammarskjöld (Sweden)
1962 Linus Pauling (US)
1963 **International Committee of the Red Cross** (founded in 1863) and **League of Red Cross Societies** (founded in 1919)
1964 Martin Luther King Jr (US)
1965 **UN Children's Fund UNICEF** (founded 1946)
1968 René Cassin (France)
1969 **International Labour Organization** (founded in 1919)
1970 Norman E. Borlaug (US)
1971 Willy Brandt (Germany)
1973 Henry Kissinger (US) and Le Duc Tho (North Vietnam; refused)
1974 Sato Eisaku (Japan) and Sean MacBride (Ireland)
1975 Andre Sacharov (Soviet Union)

1976   Mairead Corrigan and Betty Williams (Northern Ireland)
1977   **Amnesty International** (founded in 1961)
1978   Menachem Begin (Israel) and Anwar El Sadat (Egypt)
1979   Mother Teresa of Calcutta (India; naturalized)
1980   Adolfo Pérez Esquival (Argentina)
1981   **UN High Commissioner of Refugees** (founded in 1951)
1982   Alva Myrdal (Sweden) and Alfonso Garcia Robles (Mexico)
1983   Lech Walesa (Poland)
1984   Desmond Tutu (South Africa)
1985   **International Physicians for the Prevention of Nuclear War** (founded in 1980)
1986   Elie Wiesel (US)
1987   Oscar Arias Sánchez (Costa Rica)
1988   **UN Peacekeeping Forces** (since 1948)
1989   Dalai Lama (Tibet)
1990   Mikhail Gorbachev (Soviet Union)
1991   Aung San Suu Kyi (Myanmar)
1992   Rigoberta Menchu (Guatemala)
1993   F.W. de Klerk and Nelson Mandela (South Africa)
1994   Yasser Arafat (Palestine) and Shimon Peres and Yitzhak Rabin (Israel)
1995   Joseph Rothblatt (UK) and **Pugwash Conferences on Science and World Affairs** (founded in 1957)
1996   Carlos Ximenes Belo and José Ramos Horta (Timor)
1997   Jody Williams (US) and **International Campaign to Ban Landmines** (founded in 1991)
1998   John Hume and David Trimble (Northern Ireland)
1999   **Médecins Sans Frontières** (founded in 1971)
2000   Kim Dae Jung (South Korea)
2001   Kofi Annan (Ghana) and **United Nations** (founded in 1945)
2002   Jimmy Carter (US)
2003   Shirin Ebadi (Iran)
2004   Wangari Muta Maathai (Kenia)
2005   **International Atomic Energy Agency** (founded in 1957) and Mohamed El Baradei (Egypt)
2006   **Grameen Bank** (founded in 1983) and Muhammad Yunus (Bangladesh)
2007   **Intergovernmental Panel on Climate Change** (founded in 1988) and Al Gore (US)

7.4 The Latin American states decide to join the Hague system (1901)

Latin America and the Hague system

In October 1901 the second Pan-American conference took place in Mexico City at the invitation of US President William McKinley, with all states from the American continent

75

represented and with arbitration once again on the agenda. The non-ratification of the arbitration treaty signed at the first conference in 1889 (see §6.4) created uncomfortable strains among the participants. To remove these, it was decided to trust the further negotiations to a subcommittee of seven people. This new tactic helped to prevent the conference from being deadlocked. 'This small group exhausted all the expedients of suasion and diplomacy. After long negotiations and careful discussion they finally brought forward a plan of compromise. Through the diplomatic tact of some leading members the elements of opposition had been quieted and a common mode of action made possible. Thus one of the greatest difficulties by which an international conference has ever been confronted was solved by the means of diplomacy and by a mutual forbearance among forces in decided opposition to each other on questions of principle' (Reinsch 1911, 86). The solution the US put forward was to make all American republics signatories to the Hague Convention of 1899 and thus for them to recognize the general principle of arbitration. Mexico and the US, which had been present in The Hague whereas the other states had not been invited, were to urge this case of joining *en bloc* in The Hague. Whether such a communication was truly required can be open to discussion, but it was part of the solution for the existing impasse. Those states willing to sign an obligatory treaty among themselves, including a reference to the Hague Permanent Court of Arbitration, could do so. In the end all states joined the Hague Convention and ten states signed a treaty project for obligatory arbitration (Argentina, Bolivia, El Salvador, Guatemala, Mexico, Paraguay, Peru, Santo Domingo, Uruguay and Venezuela). The conference in Mexico City also adopted a treaty establishing international arbitration in all cases of pecuniary claims, which allowed parties to take advantage of two articles of the Hague Convention. Becoming a signatory to the Hague Convention implied that the Latin American states would adhere to the by then functioning international system or community of states. In 1907 almost all states from the American continent were represented in The Hague for the second Peace Conference.

Central American integration and the 1902 arbitration tribunal

Arbitration played a specific role in the relations between five Central American states at the time. Integration efforts in Central America far pre-dated the US-led Pan-American endeavour from 1889 onwards. They went back to territorial zones created by the Spanish. Inspired by the liberation of Colombia, Ecuador and Peru between 1819 and 1824 and the founding of Bolivia by Simon Bolivar and his plan to unite various Latin American states into one republic, Costa Rica, El Salvador, Guatemala, Honduras and Nicaragua in 1823 founded the Republic of the United Provinces of Central America. This federation, however, dissolved into civil war in 1838. New integration efforts continued to come. In 1902 Costa Rica, El Salvador, Honduras and Nicaragua signed a treaty at Corinto, Nicaragua, providing for obligatory arbitration and the establishment of a permanent International Arbitration Tribunal. This was set up in October 1902 in San José, Costa Rica, but in early 1907 the Tribunal failed to solve a dispute between Honduras and Nicaragua and the latter's president declared the Treaty of Corinto null and void, which implied the tribunal's abolition (Eyffinger 1996, 62).

The creation of the Central American Union (1907)

Mediated by the US, in 1906 on board a US vessel the Central American states signed a treaty which planned a diplomatic conference. This was held later that year in San José.

It drew up a general treaty on peace, friendship and commerce and signed treaties on arbitration and closer economic relations. Nicaragua was absent, but mediation by the US and Mexico brought this state on board too. A peace conference in Washington DC in September 1907 resulted in a general treaty on peace and amity, and in December the intergovernmental *Central American Union* was established. It aimed at 'the peaceful reorganization of the mother country – Central America; public education of an essentially Central American character; commerce between the republics; improvement in the methods of agriculture and the industries; uniformity in civil, commercial, and criminal legislation; uniformity in customs law, in the monetary system, and in weights and measures; and cooperative effort for better sanitation' (Reinsch 1911, 119). In 1908 the Union set up its secretariat under the name the *Central American Bureau* in Guatemala City. It published the journal *Centro América*, prepared the establishment of an educational institute and convened annual conferences. Central American integration, however, remained a matter of weakening (soon, during the 1910s) and occasionally of resurgence (as in 1951 and 1962). The decision was also made in 1907 to establish a *Central American Court of Justice*. This functioned from 1907 to 1917. It was the first international court and also the first one to be authorized to apply its judgements to lawsuits from individuals (Reinsch 1911, 120) (see Figure 7.3).

Figure 7.3 The Central American Court of Justice 1907–17

At the peace conference in Washington DC in 1907, five Central American states signed a convention providing for the establishment of a **Central American Court of Justice**. This Court was to represent the national consciousness of Central America. It had its seat in Carthago, Costa Rica and consisted of five 'justices' who were appointed, one by each republic, for five years. The American millionaire Andrew Carnegie donated money for a building, but this was destroyed by an earthquake before it had opened. The seat of the Court was transferred to San José, where a new building was erected, also paid for by Carnegie. During the ten years of its existence – the convention lasted for ten years and was not renewed – the Court handled ten cases. Five involved individuals, but all were declared inadmissible. Three of the five cases between states were the result of the Court's initiative, but were of minor importance. The other two remained without effect because an outside state was involved. The Court met various problems such as the method of selecting the justices, who in fact remained national subjects as they were paid by their government, and its broad jurisdiction, which allowed individuals to bring lawsuits against governments over the violation of treaties and conventions. The Court was regarded not only as a judicial institution but also as a political one. In 1917 Nicaragua accused it of taking part in intrigues. Nonetheless, the Central American Court of Justice was the first international court in modern history 'with continuing functions; in this respect, it represented a tradition of solidarity in Central America which at the time was unique in the world' (Eyffinger 1996, 63). Its body of jurisprudence and practical experiences played a role in 1922, when as part of the League of Nations the statute of the Permanent Court of International Justice was drafted.

7.5 The second Hague Peace Conference of 1907

NGO pressure in favour of a second peace conference

The outcome of the Hague Peace Conference of 1899 was not the hopeful departure for a new future as many members of the peace movement believed, but rather the culmination of previous developments. Despite continuing pacifism, each year from 1899 to 1914 was a year of crisis, carrying the threat of war. 'It was, indeed, a savage irony that this period, which saw a wide acceptance of the idea of international arbitration at the government level, saw also an intensification of the international anarchy' (Lyons 1963, 355). Calling the second Hague Peace Conference started with private initiatives in the US. In 1903 the American Peace Society urged politicians to present a resolution to Congress to authorize the president 'to invite the governments of the world to join in establishing … a regular international congress to meet at stated periods to deliberate upon the various questions of common interest to the nations and to make recommendations thereon to the governments' (cited in Eyffinger 1996, 57). The Inter-Parliamentary Union, which in 1904 met in St Louis in the US, supported the proposal. In line with his policies for the American continent (see §11.5), President Theodore Roosevelt was willing to further the cause and he asked the secretary of state to approach the governments that were signatory to the Hague Convention by circular letter. He proposed to meet again in The Hague to continue the discussions of 1899, and he suggested a procedure by which states absent in 1899 could be made co-signatories. With the exception of Russia the response was favourable and a second circular letter invited the governments to put forward agenda issues. The Permanent Court of Arbitration's International Bureau was instructed to prepare the agenda. Roosevelt's mediating role in the Russo–Japanese war in 1905 put an end to that conflict and resulted in Russia actually offering to convene the second Hague Peace Conference. Roosevelt agreed, on condition that all American republics were invited. As most Latin American states had no embassies in Moscow and hence could not be approached, this invitation nearly failed, but the problem was solved with the help of other embassies.

The second Hague Peace Conference

The second Hague Peace Conference took place from 15 June to 18 October 1907, with 256 delegates from 44 states, 18 more than in 1899. Europe was represented by the same 20 states as in 1899 plus newly independent Norway. Seventeen of the 19 American republics were represented and four states again from Asia, although the delegation from Korea, which in fact was occupied by Japan at the time, was not admitted. Africa remained as unrepresented as before. The conference worked in a similar manner, this time with four Commissions. Compared with its predecessor, advance with regard to subject matter remained restricted, even though the conference adopted one declaration and 13 conventions: ten new and three revised ones, among them the convention on the Permanent Court. The new conventions dealt with the use of weapons and the rules of war. The issue of disarmament could not be discussed at all, because Germany refused to do so.

The first consultative status and the NGO shadow conference

Once again the Peace Conference in The Hague attracted numerous NGOs. This time the president officially received two of them, the International Council of Women and the Salvation Army, and listened to their opinions about issues on the agenda. This may be regarded as the beginning of granting NGOs consultative status at a multilateral event. During the conference William Stead published a four-page daily newsletter, now with more cooperation from the official conference organization which had learned its lesson from 1899. The NGO activities became more coherent, as every afternoon Stead, Von Suttner and other representatives met for tea and discussions. *Le cercle international*, where participants exchanged information and opinions in lectures and debates, already looked like the later NGO shadow conferences running parallel to multilateral ones. Other NGOs, representing various groups of socialists, anarchists or Zionists, gathered near The Hague, where they made their presence known and commented positively, or negatively, on the official proceedings (Charnovitz 1997, 197).

Amending the 1899 Hague Convention

The 1899 Convention on the Pacific Settlement of International Disputes was amended by the 1907 conference, without fully solving the problems relating to practical arbitration, such as the composition of a tribunal and how to define in advance its precise jurisdiction. Since no standing arbitral machinery existed and many procedural aspects still had to be settled at some point during a case, parties were in fact co-deciding the tribunal's composition and procedures. The wish to leave this *ad hoc* character behind grew stronger and was also based on the knowledge that some issues were better suited than others to arbitration. The experience gained through an enquiry into the Dogger Bank incident of 1904, when Russian ships had fired at British fishing boats believing them to be Japanese torpedo boats, was used to clarify procedures with greater lucidity and in more detail. This applied to the way the commissions were composed, the representation of parties in investigations before them, the power to obtain testimony, the duty of litigants to provide information, the manner of examining witnesses and the way the case was presented (Reinsch 1911, 123). The formulation of the main lines of arbitral procedure was a step 'towards simplifying the drawing up of arbitration agreements and thus reducing the opportunities of frustrating a political decision to resort to arbitration' (Rosenne 1989, 8). The main problems however were not solved, due to German opposition (referred to as *Elephas Germanicus*), and the idea of compulsory arbitration, still favoured at the time, had to be dropped.

Other 1907 conventions

The other conventions agreed in 1907 dealt with the use of force for the recovery of debts, the laws of war on land and at sea and neutrality. The *Convention Respecting the Limitations of the Employment of Force for the Recovery of Contract Debts* (also *Drago–Porter Convention*) prohibited the use of force to recover contract debts unless the debtor state refused to go to arbitration or refused to abide by the arbitral judgement. The Latin American states in particular welcomed this Convention, as it would change the practice of powerful European states using armed force to obtain payment from other states for damage caused to them or their nationals (Malanczuk 1997, 15, 308). The *Convention Relative to the Opening of Hostilities* required war to be preceded by a formal declaration of war or by an ultimatum containing a conditional declaration of war. The practice of confiscating enemy ships in port immediately on the outbreak of war had changed after the Crimean War, as enemy ships were since then given *days of grace* in which to depart. Now this 'grace' principle was embodied in Article 1 of the sixth Convention concluded in The Hague in 1907. The 12th Convention provided for the establishment of an International Prize Court (see Figure 7.4) and the 13th Convention dealt with the rights and duties of neutral states and persons in maritime war. Belligerents were bound 'to respect the sovereign rights of neutral powers and to abstain, in neutral territory or neutral waters, from any act which would, if knowingly committed by any power, constitute a violation of neutrality' (Lyons 1963, 85). This last Convention encapsulated the three 'rules of Washington' of the 1871 arbitration Treaty of Washington, with a more precise description of 'due diligence' (see §6.1).

Further codification of maritime warfare rules (1909)

Subsequent to the Hague Peace Conference governments met in London, where in 1909 they issued the *Declaration of London concerning the Laws of Naval Warfare*, in which they continued the rule making regarding navigation in time of war and the relations between belligerents and neutrals. In this Declaration they defined contraband and blockades more precisely than they had done in 1856 in Paris and later in The Hague. Contraband lists of what was 'absolute' and what was 'conditional' contraband were agreed, as well as a list of what was never to be considered contraband. For a blockade to be binding on neutrals it had to be 'declared and notified, the declaration giving the date of commencement, the geographical extent, and the period of grace granted to neutral vessels to come out of port' (Lyons 1963, 87). Taken together, the conferences in Paris, The Hague and London saw a steady advance towards the definition and codification of rules concerning maritime warfare, even if implementation remained disputed. Although the Declaration of London failed to achieve ratification, parts of it were incorporated into the naval instructions of the various belligerent powers in the First World War (Lyons 1963, 85).

Figure 7.4 Two courts proposed in 1907 that remained ineffective

The 12th Convention adopted by the Hague Peace Conference in 1907 proposed the establishment of an **International Prize Court**, meant to serve as a court of appeal against decisions of national prize courts that had been set up to adjudicate the legality of the capture of ships and goods by navies and commissioned privateers. It also opened the way for claims by individuals such as merchants. Ideas about prize courts had resulted from the 1856 Declaration of Paris and from comprehensive studies and proposals by the Institute of International Law published in 1875 and 1887. The 12th Convention of 1907 formed the basis for the creation of a permanent tribunal with an obligatory competence. It was to remain in force for 12 years, then to be tacitly renewed for six years at a time, unless revoked. It would enter into force if it had a sufficient number of ratifications in 1909 and if parties had agreed on a specific number of judges and deputy-judges. As this last condition was not met the convention did not become operative. The conference in London, which issued the Declaration in 1909, was an effort to agree upon the generally recognized principles of international law within the field of maritime economic warfare. Although the states adopted a Declaration in 1909, followed by an additional Protocol to it in 1910, the ideas about the functioning of the International Prize Court met with such lively opposition from the governments of the UK and the US that, in addition to not reaching agreement over the appointment of the judges, there were no ratifications. Yet the process helped 'to crystallize the concept of an International Bench' (Eyffinger 1996, 64).

One criticism of the Permanent Court of Arbitration was that it did not provide a basis for the cumulation of a body of jurisprudence. Debates on this issue at the Peace Conference of 1907 resulted in a *voeu* and a Draft Convention attached to the Final Act, calling for the creation of a court of 'free and easy access, composed of judges representing the various judicial systems of the world' (Eyffinger 1996, 64). This **Court of Arbitral Justice** was to sit in The Hague as an extension of the Permanent Court and administered by its International Bureau. Like the Prize Court, it was to be a permanent institution. The major obstacle for this project at the Peace Conference was disagreement about the selection of the judges. Although at the time numerous proposals were elaborated, none was included in the Draft Convention. The 1909 London naval conference tried to resolve the deadlock, but failed. During informal negotiations between France, Germany, the UK and the US in Paris in March 1910, a Draft Convention was formulated, and in July this was revised in The Hague. 'It envisaged the selection of a judge by each party to the Convention and included a system of rotation. However, being linked to the plan for the Prize Court, the project foundered upon the failure to create the latter Court' (Eyffinger 1996, 65). It was agreed to discuss the topic further at the third Hague Peace Conference, scheduled for 1915.

The decision to carry on

The 'Hague system' that evolved from the two conferences of 1899 and 1907 was becoming an institution, 'which is to a certain extent self-existent'. The privilege of calling the conference and undertaking the preparatory negotiations could no longer to be claimed by Russia, since the parties in 1907 agreed upon a third conference to be held 'within a period corresponding to that which has elapsed since the preceding conference'. The recommendations by the second conference also called attention to the necessity of preparing the programme a sufficiently long time in advance, to ensure that 'the deliberations may be conducted with the necessary authority and expedition' (Reinsch 1911, 122). In order to meet this objective, it was suggested that governments should charge a preparatory committee with the task of collecting agenda issues and proposals to be submitted to the conference about two years before the possible conference date. The committee should ascertain which subjects were ripe for embodiment in an international regulation and prepare a programme which the governments should decide upon early enough to enable them to examine the subject matter carefully. Furthermore, the committee should develop and propose 'a system of organization and procedure for the conference itself' (Reinsch 1911, 123). In other words, after the convening of two conferences in the field of security, a cautious process of institutionalization began to appear. This series of peace conferences was to take place regularly (every seven years), to be of a preventive nature (as they were not taking place as a termination of war) and to put forward international rules and principles. The whole process was to be supported by the Permanent Court of Arbitration's International Bureau, which in fact was not designed for this task but was simply used for it.

Opening of the Peace Palace in The Hague (1913)

The American millionaire Andrew Carnegie, who had earned his fortune in the steel industry, decided to allot his money to the causes of education, welfare and peace. Between 1904 and 1919 he donated 25 million dollars to the promotion of peace, as he was an opponent of war, but without taking part in the international peace movement. In 1910 he founded the *Carnegie Endowment for International Peace* in Washington DC to carry out research that would help hasten the abolition of war. He also donated money for the erection of three international buildings: the Pan-American Union Building for the International Union of American Republics near the White House in Washington (see §11.5), the above-mentioned building for the Central American Court of Justice, at first in Cartago, Costa Rica, and later in San José (see Figure 7.3), and the Peace Palace in The Hague. This third building was to house a highly-qualified library on international law and diplomacy as well as the Permanent Court of Arbitration. The Dutch government showed reservations towards Carnegie's proposal, as it felt that the signatories to the 1899 Hague Convention rather than a private donor could provide adequate accommodation, but eventually it agreed on condition that an administrative foundation was set up. After a competition among architects the Peace Palace was built between 1907 and 1913, having a fairly eclectic architectural style and mixed furnishing because of the many donations from all over the world. The opening ceremony was in August 1913. The Peace Palace houses a library specialized in international relations literature, the Permanent Court of Arbitration and, since 1922, the Permanent Court of International Justice and its successor, the International Court of Justice. The maxim at the Palace represents the ideas of arbitration and international law as they evolved in the nineteenth century: if you want peace, cultivate justice.

Part IV

Public International Unions 1865–1914

Institutionalization of conferences and the creation of continental markets in Europe and the Americas

Arbitration, international law and trust among states mattered also in the economic field. This fourth part deals with the public international unions states founded from 1865 onwards. These nineteenth-century international organizations responded to the expansion of modern capitalism and technology, which did not take much notice of national borders, as illustrated by the telegraph and postal unions (Chapter 8). A great many of these unions arose out of a series of multilateral conferences and went through a process of institutionalization. They filled the new needs of comparative knowledge and standardization with regard to measuring the Earth, establishing a standard time, equal weights and measures, and protecting intellectual property rights (Chapter 9). In the field of transportation, common regulations were drawn up for international shipping, railways and roads (Chapter 10). The public international unions contributed jointly to the creation of continental markets in Europe and the Americas (Chapter 11).

Creation of the International Telegraph Union (1865) and the Universal Postal Union (1874)

8.1 The invention of the telegraph and the creation of the International Telegraph Union (1865)

The invention of the telegraph

The creation of the first public international union arose from the invention of the telegraph and the need to develop uniform rules for its worldwide use. Carrier pigeons had long been used for long-distance communications. Other possibilities for sending messages from post to post across longer distances were using drum beats, light flashes or a semaphore with flag signals. These worked as long as the weather was good. In the late 1830s and early 1840s progress was made with the electromagnetic telegraph, both in Europe and in the US, where Samuel Morse developed an electronic alphabet (his Morse code) that could carry messages along lines. Governments and businesses alike were interested in these technical inventions, as they allowed military, diplomatic and commercial messages to be sent over long distances in a short time. 'Constructed along railway lines, for example, telegraphy rapidly improved the operation of continental transport. Combined with the printing press, telegraphy enabled the creation of a daily news service. Applied in the financial sector, capital became more mobile and easily exchanged' (Lee 1996, 58). The number of telegraphs increased rapidly. In 1868 almost 20 million domestic telegraphs existed in the US, and 5.7 million international ones. In 1885 the numbers were, respectively, 132 and 13.3 million, and in 1905 310 and 82.2 million (Reinsch 1911, 18). The first submarine telegraph cable was laid between Calais and Dover in 1851, and the first durable transatlantic cable between the UK and the US in 1866. While public ownership characterized European telecommunications, the facilities in the US were mainly privately owned and divided between cartels which together developed into an oligopoly. Governments soon came to the realization that regularity and uniformity were needed to connect the national systems. In Europe agreements and unions were set up, such as in 1850 the *Austro-German Telegraph Union* and in 1855 the *Telegraphic Union of Western Europe* (Belgium, France, Sardinia, Spain and Switzerland). In 1858 Belgium, France, the Netherlands, Prussia, Sardinia and Switzerland adopted the *Bern Telegraph Convention*. This made governments aware that more uniformity and also worldwide regulation were necessary.

The International Telegraph Union (1865)

In 1865, 20 states gathered at a conference in Paris to consolidate and widen the existing agreements into the *International Telegraph Union* (ITU). States were represented by both diplomats and expert delegates of the various national administrations, which gave the conference a dual character and, because of this, resulted in an international *convention* signed by the diplomatic representatives and an international *règlement*, controlling the administrative details, signed by the expert delegates. In 1868 the first regular ITU conference took place in Vienna, once more with both diplomatic and expert representatives. Five more members were admitted, including British India. A Bureau was set up in Bern, which in 1869 began to function as the union's central organ. It was supervised by the Swiss government and its expenses were paid by the administrations of the contracting states in proportion to the size of their telegraph services. With the US government arguing that private companies should be allowed to take a full part in the ITU proceedings, the ITU in 1871 at its conference in Rome decided that representatives of important private telegraph companies were to be admitted as advisory members. This gave the organization a mixed character.

The distinction between convention and règlement

The ITU conference of 1875 in St Petersburg overhauled the convention thoroughly, by defining its functions as 'to collect, arrange and publish information of all kinds relating to international telegraphy, to circulate requests for modifications of tariffs and service regulations, to give notice of the charges adopted, and generally to study all subjects and execute all work entrusted to it in the interest of international telegraphy' (cited in Lyons 1963, 40). The constitutional form of the ITU was reshaped by distinguishing more carefully between the matters to be dealt with in the diplomatic *convention* (which was to remain substantially unaltered) and the *règlement* (which was modified quite frequently). 'The convention was made, in a way, the constitution of the union, laying down the fundamental principles which were accepted as expressing the essential relations and duties of the members and the permanent basis of the administration. The *règlement*, on the other hand, was composed of those administrative regulations by which the details of the administration were fixed, and which were susceptible of gradual modification, corresponding to changes in the character of the administrative relations' (Reinsch 1911, 17). Among the matters laid down in the convention were the general classification of telegrams (state, service and private), the admission of cipher dispatches, conditions for suspending the service, the right to decline responsibility for loss, the secrecy of correspondence and the kind of cables to be used for the international service. The application of the rules and the details of the tariffs were fixed in the *règlement*.

86

The functioning of the organization

It was essential for the functioning of the ITU that governments and telegraphic administrations, with the Bureau as intermediary, kept each other informed about changes, interruptions in communication and improvements in their service. This was encouraged by the Bureau's publication of an annual report about general and national developments, which also included statistics. The government of the state in which the periodic conference was to be held took the initiative of setting the agenda in consultation with other governments. This programme formed the basis of discussion at the conference, which soon appointed commissions to consider specific propositions in detail. The adoption of proposals was by majority of the delegates present, but resolutions were not binding until accepted by all administrations of the contracting states. Notwithstanding this unanimity principle, members were free to conclude special agreements among themselves as long as these did not conflict with the ITU convention. This actually resulted in various unions restricted to special purposes and made the ITU a flexible organization. Changing the constitution required diplomatic action by all signatories (Reinsch 1911, 19).

Accession of states

The US did not join the ITU until 1932, because at the time the US government had a different philosophy regarding the roles of the public and the private sectors, and was unable to apply ITU rules since only a small proportion of telegraph lines were under federal control. Nonetheless the US government was represented at ITU conferences in an observer capacity. Hence it could speak, but not vote. In fact American telegraphy practice paralleled that of the ITU to a large extent. Other large states to join later were Mexico (1908), China (1920) and Canada (1960). In 1875 the ITU, which had established the principle of 'one state, one vote', introduced 'colonial voting'. This allowed member states to vote on behalf of territories under their control and meant that states such as France, Italy, Portugal and the UK had seven votes each. This voting system was finally abolished in 1973, following the gradual granting of independence to colonies (Lee 1996, 60).

Assessing the ITU

The completion and publication of an international telegraphic vocabulary was one of the ITU's most substantial achievements. By 1901 it contained nearly two million terms in many languages (Lyons 1963, 40). In addition to the Central Commission for the Navigation of the Rhine (see §3.1), the ITU was another effort by sovereign states to cooperate administratively in a specific economic field. Government representatives returning home after an ITU conference often had to withstand considerable domestic opposition and needed to explain much before it was possible to implement ITU decisions. The ITU, however, succeeded in contributing to a considerable growth in communications between governments and private sectors in Europe and the world at large. This also promoted the growth of trade. 'Through its mandate of enabling the spread of telecommunications and, in turn, the international flow of goods and services, the ITU would uphold the principles of a free market, open trade and comparative advantage' (Lee 1996, 59). Its proceedings resulted in 'a great simplification of the international service as well as in a considerable reduction in the tariff rates' (Reinsch 1911, 16).

Facing the competition of the telephone and radio

One of the limitations of the ITU was that it saw the advance of new technologies, such as the invention and application of the telephone and radio, as a threat to the established markets of the by then powerful telegraph companies, rather than as a related challenge within its mandate. At the end of the nineteenth century, the postal and telegraphic companies therefore called the new inventions less useful, expensive or unreliable. As a result the ITU made little effort to regulate the new technologies. The UK, which at the time had a near-monopoly in transmissions based on Guglielmo Marconi's invention, tried to prevent other states from using it by means of exclusive contracts. However, this was impossible from a technological point of view and also because the UK was 'a power which had already taken a prominent part in international co-operation' (Lyons 1963, 42). In 1906 a separate organization was set up for wireless telegraphy, the *International Radio Telegraph Union* (IRU). Although it shared the ITU's secretariat and was similar in structure with both a convention and a *règlement*, the IRU allowed much stronger private sector representation in its proceedings than the ITU. The IRU's regulation of the radio frequency spectrum was rather minimalist as it started from the 'first come, first served' principle, closely akin to the *res nullius* idea in international law that territory which is not under the sovereignty of a recognized state may be annexed by means of effective occupation. It was not until the mid-1920s that serious international regulation of radiotelegraphy was agreed upon (Lee 1996, 61–62). In 1934 the ITU and the IRU merged into the *International Telecommunication Union* (also ITU, see Figure 8.1), which was to become a specialized UN agency in 1947.

Figure 8.1 The International Telecommunication Union as the successor of ITU and IRU (1934)

After the end of the First World War, the US gained a stronger international position, with the role of American institutions financing European reconstruction increasing and New York becoming the rival of London as the world financial centre. These developments made the US, aware of the importance of the burgeoning **radio and telephone activities**, encourage the regulation of these communications. At a preliminary radio conference in 1920 it proposed the integration of the ITU and IRU, without as yet receiving support for this proposal within the ITU. However, both organizations began to make organizational changes by creating international consultative committees (CCIs) for telegraphy (CCIT) and telephony (CCIF) in 1925 and for radio (CCIR) in 1927. These committees resolved technical and also political questions in relation to further regulation in the three fields (Lee 1996, 64).

The adoption of the *International Telecommunication Convention* at Madrid in 1932 was followed in 1934 by the merger of the ITU and the IRU to form the **International Telecommunication Union**. However, due to the growing focus among governments on national interests, the regulatory activities of the new ITU remained fairly restricted. 'The fact that only one major conference was held by the ITU between 1933 and 1939, the Administrative Telegraph, Telephone and Radio

Conference of 1938, reflected this lower priority given to international tele-communications. With governments' attention occupied elsewhere, ITU officials spent these years refining existing responsibilities. Application of the principle of "first come, first served", for example, was refined by setting more detailed regulations regarding bandwidths and acceptable levels of emission. The Berne Bureau began to publish lists of "occupied" frequencies to facilitate planning' of the radio frequency spectrum (Lee 1996, 66).

8.2 The Universal Postal Union (1874) as an example for other international organizations

Establishment of the General Postal Union (1874)

International postal traffic was hampered by different tariffs, national and local postal systems which were not geared to each other, and the lack of frequency of delivery. In 1863, at the invitation of the US government, an international postal conference in Paris between 15 states began to clarify the general principles that should determine international postal administration. This conference did not yet produce any treaty regulation, as many practical difficulties in establishing a unified system were exposed. The situation did not change until Prussia in 1867 brought private German companies into public ownership, and in 1869 began to urge the setting up of international agreements. After the Franco–German War of 1870–71, the French government attempted to delay this plan, as it expected it would cause severe financial losses, but eventually France could not resist business interests and public opinion, which were in favour of an international union. In 1874, 22 states gathering in Bern adopted the *Convention establishing the General Postal Union*. This Union's leading principles were the complete freedom of transit from one jurisdiction to another and the creation of a practically unified postal territory comprising all treaty states. The Convention was ratified by the action of the diplomatic representatives of the states in Bern, which resulted in the Convention coming into force in 1875. As in the case of the ITU, the postal union also had a more flexible *règlement* for more detailed specifics. From 1878 onwards the Union's name was *Universal Postal Union* (UPU).

The differentiated membership dues as an example

The UPU set up a membership dues system that was copied by a number of other international organizations. In order to determine the proportion of budget charges each member state had to bear, the UPU *règlement* divided the states into seven classes, with varying levels of dues related to characteristics of the state. This was further detailed in such ways that it was very practical. A difference with the ITU was that colonies could be members, with one vote each for large or one vote per group for smaller colonies. In practice, colonies would not always vote with their colonial powers (Reinsch 1911, 23–24). The Union's original combination of a diplomatic conference with a conference of postal administrations was not successful and meant that the latter stopped meeting. The permanent International Bureau of the UPU eliminated the need for a formal conference for any and every amendment, by developing a practice whereby the International

Bureau circulated proposals for amendment by post and, depending on the amendment, then sent a notification of acceptance by either two-thirds or a simple majority, which made the amendment binding on all members. This was a marked departure from the requirement of specific consent in traditional multilateral conferences (Bowett 1982, 7). The services the UPU provided were so valuable that 'no state with any pretensions to civilisation could afford to stay outside. Once inside, it was for all important purposes governed by the will of the majority' (Lyons 1963, 47). In case of disagreement, there was a provision for arbitration.

The UPU's success

The UPU was both successful and efficient. The main conflicts during conferences arose over representation on important committees, which tended to be dominated by the great powers. One issue was the right of an administration to charge a transit rate for postal material passing through its territory. 'Those countries, and this included most of the larger ones, which were in the main stream of international commerce naturally stood to benefit from a charge of this kind; smaller, peripheral powers, such as the South American republics, stood to lose, and from time to time tried to secure the abolition of such charges. They did not succeed in this, though their protests were by no means ineffective, for in fact transit charges remained moderate' (Lyons 1963, 47). The UPU developed into 'a clearing house for information on national postal systems as well as the agency managing the international postal regime and setting international rates' (Murphy 1994, 87–88). Like the ITU, the UPU helped to lower international rates and in that way aided internationally-active businesses that were the largest users. Simultaneously, the international regime helped governments 'to keep their subsidies to national mail services low, in part because the flow of international mail increased to the point that new economies of scale could be achieved, but also by limiting a government's responsibility for lost or damaged mail' (Murphy 1994, 89). The UPU furthermore invented new services such as an international reply coupon, which enabled correspondents to overcome national currency restrictions because the UPU balanced the international accounts of national postal administrations. The international identity card service the UPU established proved superfluous, because at the end of the nineteenth century passports were not that important in crossing borders. Just like the ITU, the UPU failed to recognize the importance of the telephone and to develop an international telephone regime until the 1920s (Murphy 1994, 88–89). In 1948 the UPU became a specialized UN agency. It has its seat in Bern, Switzerland, where the UPU monument erected in 1909 can be found.

8.3 The relevance of the nineteenth-century public international unions

Public international unions

In connection with the spread of modern capitalism and the need to facilitate transborder traffic and transport, a new form of international organization came into being from 1865 onwards (see Figure 8.2 for an overview of IGOs and public international unions established between 1815 and 1914). For most of the *public international unions* (PIUs) the organization was based on a multilateral convention, which defined their often 'functional' aims such as regulating telecommunications or postal traffic. Although these activities are often referred to as 'technical' or apolitical, they were related to direct government involvement and national interests if one takes into consideration the necessary infrastructure (transport and communication facilities) and their security aspects (the use of these facilities by the army in times of crisis or war) or their impact on the national economy's performance. The unions were permanent intergovernmental organizations. This does not mean that governments were the only representatives. Since in many states postal services or railways were in public ownership but in others were privately-owned, this was reflected in the governance structures of the unions. Eventually, however, the various types of mixed institution, both public and private as regards formation or composition, changed into an intergovernmental form, without excluding arrangements for influence by actors other than governments (Reinsch 1911, 144). In 1919 the Covenant of the League of Nations refused admission to public international unions if they were not strictly intergovernmental and established by general treaties (Bowett 1982, 10).

Three causes for formation of PIUs

Three causes for the formation of public international unions can be discerned. The first is the inconveniences and delays which occur if one cannot transit from one national territory to another because of the existence of different administrative systems and regulations. Stimulated by the demand for regulation and by the need to find technical solutions to gear the various systems to each other, international organizations were set up, for example, to promote technical unification of the railways (1882) and the regulation of international railway transport of freight (1890) (see Figure 8.2). The second cause for international action was found in the need to raise the level of competition and in the fear of unfair competition. 'It was soon discovered that after a nation had, within its territory, introduced some improvement in the condition of its industries and its labor, such as required an additional expenditure of money, its industries might, at least for a while, be seriously threatened by the competition of those countries in which such regulations had not as yet been adopted' (Reinsch 1911, 13). Disadvantages in international competition prompted, for instance, the international protection of patents and copyrights and international labour standards. The third cause arose from non-regulated dangers, such as the bringing in of epidemics through faster ships arriving from the colonies, or the stealing of submarine telegraph cables on the high seas.

Three purposes of PIUs

Paul Reinsch discerns three general purposes of public international unions. The first is a mutuality of advantages to be secured for the citizens of all states engaged in the unions. This purpose is not to change national laws, but rather to secure for the subjects of one state the advantages of legislative and administrative arrangements in others. It requires no new laws, only international arrangements to gear national laws and regulations to one another. The second purpose is the regulation of the administrative activities connected with these worldwide interests. This may require a new law or the modification of national procedural methods, which the various national administrations bind themselves to respect. The third purpose is the creation of private international law which serves to free business intercourse and action from all kinds of difficulties and obstructions. Whereas the keyword for the first two purposes is *uniformity* (unification of the

Figure 8.2 IGOs and public international unions established between 1815 and 1914

Year of formation	Name of organization	Year of dissolution
1815	Central Commission for the Navigation of the Rhine	
1838	Superior Council of Health	
1856	European Commission for the Control of the Danube	1939; re-established 1953
1864	Geodetic Association; since 1867: International Geodetic Association	Privatized during the First World War
1865	International Telegraph Union; since 1934: International Telecommunication Union	
1865	International Commission for the Cape Spartel Light in Tangier	1959
1866	International Union of Prut (River)	1914
1874	General Postal Union; since 1878: Universal Postal Union	
1875	International Bureau of Weights and Measures	
1875	International Penitentiary Commission	1944
1882	International Conference for Promoting Technical Unification on the Railways	
1883	International Union for the Protection of Industrial Property (Paris Union)	
1884	International Association of Railway Congresses	
1885	International Commission for the Navigation of the Congo	1914
1886	International Exchange Service	1939
1886	International Union for the Protection of Literary and Artistic Works (Bern Union)	
1888	Suez Canal Administration	1914
1890	International Union of Railway Freight Transportation; also Central Office for International Railway Transport	1939; re-established 1945
1890	International Maritime Bureau against the Slave Trade	1914; some functions transferred to League of Nations and UN
1890	International Union for the Publication of Customs Tariffs	
1890	International Union of American Republics	
1898	International Finance Commission at Athens	1914
1899	Permanent Court of Arbitration	
1900	International Commission for the Decennial Revision of the Nomenclature of the Causes of Death	1948; most functions transferred to League of Nations and UN
1901	International Council for the Exploration of the Sea	
1902	International Arbitration Tribunal (at San José)	1907
1902	International Secretariat for the Unification of Pharmacological Terms	1914
1902	International Sugar Union	1914
1902	Pan-American Sanitary Bureau; later Pan-American Sanitary Organization and Pan-American Health Organization	

Figure 8.2 (continued)

Year of formation	Name of organization	Year of dissolution
1903	International Association of Seismology	Privatized during the First World War; dissolved in 1922
1905	Commission for International Financial Control in Macedonia	1914
1905	International Institute of Agriculture	
1906	Universal Radiotelegraph Union	1926
1907	Central American Court of Justice	1917
1907	International Bureau for Information and Enquiries Regarding Relief to Foreigners	1921
1907	International Central American Bureau	1926
1907	International Prize Court	1914
1907	International Office of Public Health	1947
1907	International Physiological Laboratories on Monte-Rosa	1939
1908	International Commission on the Teaching of Mathematics	1939
1908	International Pedological Institute	1941
1909	Central Bureau for the International Map of the World	Most functions transferred to League of Nations and UN; dissolved in 1953
1909	International Opium Commission	
1909	Permanent International Association of Road Congresses	
1910	International Commission for the Scientific Exploration of the Mediterranean	
1910	International Institute of Administrative Sciences	
1910	Permanent South American Railway Congress Association	
1911	Postal Union of the Americas and Spain	
1912	International Association of Public Baths and Cleanliness	1923
1912	Whangpu Conservancy Consultative Board	
1913	International Bureau of Commercial Statistics	1939

Sources: Murphy (1994) 47–8; Reinsch (1911); Wallace and Singer (1970) 250–1, with small changes.

substantive law governing any international interest and the simplification of the various national administrations based upon a common standard), the keyword for the third is *mutuality of advantages*, as it should mean that the subjects of each of the member states of public international unions shall be able to share in the legal advantages granted to the subjects of every other member state (Reinsch 1911, 130–31, 156–58).

Permanent cooperation and sovereignty under pressure

As sovereign as states have remained, the number and extent of their international activities were impressive. 'It is not so much the case that nations have given up certain parts of their sovereign powers to international administrative organs, as that they have, while fully reserving their independence, actually found it desirable, and in fact necessary, regularly and permanently to coöperate with other nations in the matter of administering economic and cultural interests. Without legal derogation to the sovereignty of individual states, an international *de facto* and conventional jurisdiction and administrative procedure is thus growing up, which bids fair to become one of the controlling elements in the future political relations of the world' (Reinsch 1911, 14). However, the relationship between international cooperation and national sovereignty remained under pressure. 'Men and nations want the benefits of international organization, but they also want to retain the privileges of sovereignty which are inseparable from international disorganization' (Claude 1966, 35).

Parallel domestic and international developments

The establishment of public international unions through multilateral conferences as a way to adapt to new forms of social complexity was paralleled by developments within domestic systems, such as further centralization of authority at national level and expansion of governmental institutions. 'In the nations most affected by the technological and industrial revolution, central governments were gaining in importance, compared with local and provincial governments, as agencies of administrative regulation, and they were expanding their administrative jurisdiction to cover aspects of economic and social life which had for some time been regarded as outside the province of government' (Claude 1966, 30). The creation of international organizations supplemented the administrative work of national governments, and included many problems which had been outside the scope of traditional diplomacy. Whereas the domestic institutions were instruments of authoritative governments, the public international unions were instruments of voluntary cooperation between states. They were not set up to create supranational organizations, rather 'they undertook to establish international mechanisms for doing a kind of job that had never been done before' (Claude 1966, 32). The unions in fact helped governments, according to Inis Claude: 'they served as collective points and clearing houses for information, centers for discussion of common problems by governments, instruments for achieving the coordination by agreement of national policies and practices, and agencies for promoting the formulation and acceptance of uniform or minimum standards in the fields of their concern' (Claude 1966, 31).

The role of the aristocracy

Craigh Murphy regards the public international unions as forums where actors other than governments, such as citizens and aristocrats, also played roles. In various nineteenth-century nation-states in Europe the *ancien régimes* had not yet completely disappeared. Some initiatives for multilateral conferences or public unions originated from monarchs and were related to their national interests. Other initiatives, however, came from, or were supported by, lower ranks of the aristocracy with an eye for the new transborder problems in relation to other trends. They were willing to sponsor conferences or support international experiments, thereby also hoping to maintain their influence. The success of various nineteenth-century multilateral conferences and international unions depended on 'many potential sponsors with different interests and aspirations, rather than on a single dominant power with only one set of interests' (Murphy 1994, 78). Powers that dominated an issue were rarely the ones that succeeded as sponsors of international agreements on that issue, whereas the aristocracy's support gave multilateral conferences and public unions time to prove the value of their activities in practice.

Public system builders

The multilateral conferences of the nineteenth century could be convened with relative ease, discussed a great variety of topics and, in addition to diplomats, empowered a wide range of experts and professionals as the voice of their states. All these characteristics gave the conference system 'a striking ability to uncover previously unrecognized common interests and to generate useful suggestions for new international regimes' (Murphy 1994, 62). They actually helped states to lower their transaction costs. Those engaged deepest in multilateral conferences by designing and administering rail, health, relief and other systems were public system builders in the true sense of the word. They were not in it for private gain, but to create transparent and comprehensive public systems that were to promote communications within and between states (Murphy 1994, 64). Figure 8.2 provides an overview of 51 IGOs and public international unions established between 1815 and 1914. As the following chapters will show, many of these unions resulted from multilateral conferences plus follow-up conferences that after some time institutionalized.

Standardization and intellectual property regulated internationally

9.1 Measurement of the Earth, the standard time and the international map of the world

The need for knowledge: statistical congresses

The advancement of modern industry and the expansion of commerce and transport made governments conscious of the need for general and comparable scientific knowledge about the Earth, the seas, the time, the condition of the soil and the weather. To provide a reliable basis for government action, it was necessary to conduct investigations in nearly every branch of their administrative activities. Private and public multilateral conferences and organizations proved outstanding ways to provide such knowledge, although national interests sometimes surfaced as obstacles to progress. From 1853 onwards international statistical congresses, with representatives from both science and governments participating, were being organized to improve the science of statistics. In 1885 the private *International Statistical Institute* was established in The Hague. When Henri Dunant was setting up the International Red Cross in 1863, he first visited the international statistical congress in Berlin, where he attended the fourth section. Numerous civilian and military doctors in this section were concerned with comparative health and mortality statistics. Dunant learned about the latest scientific developments and, equally importantly, he made contacts with delegates, promoting his ideas and inviting influential people to attend the upcoming Red Cross conference in Geneva. By the end of the conference he had provisional acceptances from a number of states (Finnemore 1996, 76–77).

Measuring the Earth

Gradually it became clear to governments that financing scientific research not only produced scientific insights, but also had practical benefits. In Europe the Prussian government was taking the lead. Urged on by a general, who himself was a mathematician, the Prussian government in 1862 convened a conference in Berlin with the aim of founding an association to compare and harmonize the geodetic work that various states were carrying out at the time. In 1864, 14 states established the *Geodetic Association*, which in 1867 changed its name to *International Geodetic Association*. This permanent organization held a General Conference every three years and had a governing Commission and a central Bureau, located at Potsdam under the direction of the Prussian institute of geodesy. Because this Prussian control proved a hindrance to the Association's further international development, the organization was modified in 1886 by giving the Bureau an independent budget, made up of contributions from the member states according to population. In 1895 another revision of the convention was needed to make the Association even more independent. Its original purpose was to standardize geodetic research in Central Europe, but the Association's scope was subsequently widened to embrace all of Europe and eventually the entire globe. This meant that its work would not be completed by the end of the century, as had been expected, but would have to be continued. The International Association did not specify the methods of observation or computation for any country, but through the exchange of ideas and experiences succeeded in 'making the methods used in various countries more nearly uniform and progressive than they would otherwise be' (Reinsch 1911, 69). The Association, which in 1914 had 20 members, was privatized during the First World War (Lyons 1963, 229–30).

Earthquake research

The study of the causes and consequences of earthquakes was also an issue for harmonization between states. From 1871 onwards scientists had convened international congresses, and after the first general conference in 1901 it was agreed to create a public international union. In 1903 this resulted in a meeting of 19 official governmental representatives, who established the *International Association of Seismology* (Reinsch 1911, 70). It had three organs, an Assembly, a Permanent Commission and a Central Bureau. The Commission was composed of government representatives, and exercised general supervision over the Association's work. The Bureau collected data, set up investigations and published reports. In order to gain more insights into the workings of earthquakes, it established observatories in states where they were unknown or could not be financed. One of the results was a unified code for making observations. Although the organization's functioning to a large extent remained informal, it drew upon the resources of governments for its activities and publications. Governments considered the results of value to them in cases where they had to deal with disturbances by earthquakes. During the First World War the Association was privatized, but it was unable to survive in this way and it was dissolved in 1922 (Lyons 1963, 230–32).

Knowledge about the weather: from NGO to IGO (1878–1950)

In contrast to the two public international unions just discussed, the organization set up by meteorologists was not intergovernmental but was an NGO, which was not transformed into an IGO until half-way through the twentieth century. In 1872 a conference of meteorologists in Leipzig put in place an *International Meteorological Committee*, which was to arrange further periodic conferences. It evolved in 1878 into the *International Meteor-ological Association* and in 1891 into the *International Meteorological Organization* (IMO). It consisted of the directors of national meteorological services, who were members in their functional capacities and not as governmental representatives. In some states their insti-tutions were government agencies, in others private ones. The Organization worked through highly-specialized commissions, which were concerned with subjects such as the magnetism of the Earth, scientific observation of the atmosphere (mostly by balloon), radiation, solar observation, weather-and-storm-warnings at sea, and cloud formations (Lyons 1963, 236–37). During the first half of the twentieth century the Organization gradually took on a more intergovernmental character, but it was not until 1947 that a (still mixed) international conference reached agreement on its new character (Charnovitz 1997, 200). In March 1950 the *World Meteorological Organization* (WMO) replaced the IMO as a specialized UN agency (see Figure 9.1).

Figure 9.1 The World Meteorological Organization of 1950

Unlike its predecessor, the IMO of 1878, the **World Meteorological Organization** (WMO) of 1950 is an IGO. Because its predecessor consisted of the directors of national meteorological services rather than government representatives, the IMO could not adopt international conventions. This handicap eventually resulted in the decision to transform the IMO into an intergovernmental and specialized UN agency. What did not change was the fact that experts were the main actors in the WMO's activities. Decision making within the IMO is a matter of consensus build-ing rather than of voting. However, the fairly informal processes of coalition and majority building formalized to some extent over time (Schemeil 2004).

Most WMO activities take place within its eight **programmes**, among them the *World Weather Programme*, the *World Climate Programme*, the *World Climate Research Programme*, the *Atmospheric Research and Environment Programme* and the *Hydrology and Water Resources Programme*. Even though the work to a large extent is highly technical, these programmes touch upon huge political and social responsibilities, as they are related to sensitive issues such as climate change, the availability of drinking water, or the disparity between the more and the less developed countries. The WMO co-sponsored the *Intergovernmental Panel on Climate Change* (IPCC) of 1988 (see §40.2) and plays a role in the implementation process of the *Framework Convention on Climate Change* of 1992 (see §40.2). Data about weather also have a commercial aspect, as they are sold to news agencies and the media.

The prime meridian and standard time (1884)

At the end of the eighteenth century, cartography in France made strong progress, with the completion of the national topographical map during the French Revolution and its distinctive innovations. It covered the entire state and was based on established facts. In

1792 two astronomers had left Paris in opposite directions to determine the circumference of the Earth and thus to establish a new standard unit of measure: the metre. This was to replace the numerous measures that were being used locally, estimated at some 250,000 in France alone. To determine the length of the meridian arc between Dunkirk and Barcelona, one astronomer went from the north (Dunkirk), the other from the south. They used the most up-to-date techniques and instruments, such as Snellius's triangulation and Borda's repeating circle. It was expected that they would finish the work within a year, but due to the effects of the revolution and the war between France and Spain it was seven years before the two men returned to Paris (Alder 2002). The invention of lithography in 1796 allowed the printing of practical maps with coloured sections and lines. Other states followed France's example and during the nineteenth century cartography flourished, both for military and for commercial use. By around 1900 the number of printed national atlases had greatly increased. In the 1880s geographers had urged their governments to fix a prime meridian. Astronomers supported this. While originally 'apparent solar time' was used, states had begun to introduce 'mean time': Switzerland in 1780, the UK in 1792 and France in 1816. However, this did not meet the requirements of modern technology any better, since railways and the telegraph, for logistical reasons, needed a 'standard time', which was to be achieved by the synchronization of clocks in different geographical locations within a time zone. In 1847 British railways urged the government to use the mean time of Greenwich, where observations of lunar distances had been taking place for a long time, as the new standard time. This resulted in a switch from mean to standard time, in those days also known as 'railway time'. In 1883 the heads of the major American railways decided to adopt the standard time system based on 'Greenwich', which was soon accepted by most states in the US and resulted in recognizable time zones. In the same year, astronomers at a conference in Rome agreed on the meridian that passes through Greenwich as the prime meridian, establishing it as being at zero degrees longitude. This Greenwich meridian had been mentioned on sea maps and was used by mariners to calculate longitude. The multilateral conference held at Washington DC in 1884 was entirely intergovernmental. It passed a resolution, with Brazil and France voting against, recommending the universal acceptance of the meridian of Greenwich as the prime meridian. It also adopted the plan for a universal day, in order to have time in all parts of the world corresponding (Reinsch 1911, 69).

The International Commission of Time (1912)

The universal acceptance of standard time was not immediate. In 1904 astronomers began preparations for an *International Commission of Time*. This Commission met for the first time in 1912 and needed several decades to actually divide the world into time zones starting from Greenwich Mean Time and to administer summer time. In 1912 the *International Time Bureau* was established at the Paris Observatory, with the task of combining different measurements of universal time and to participate in the research of time keeping. The attempt to regulate its status through an international convention failed because of non-ratification during the First World War. In 1919 it was decided that the International Time Bureau should become the executive body of the International Commission of Time, which was made one of the commissions of the then newly-founded International Astronomical Union. In 1925 it succeeded in reaching agreement to abolish the difference between the old astronomical convention of calling noon zero hour and the civil convention of referring to midnight as zero hour, in favour of the latter. Modern techniques have allowed more precise measurements of Universal Time, the term globally adopted in 1928 as more exact than Greenwich Mean Time. In 1987 the responsibilities of the International Time Bureau for combining different measurements of time were taken over by the International Bureau of Weights and Measures (see §9.2) (Guyot 1968).

The Bureau for the International Map of the World (1909)

An international congress of geographers in 1891 put forward the plan that 'civilized' states should cooperate in the production of a 1:1,000,000-scale map of the world. Their 1901 congress took the suggestion up, and the work of a commission resulted in 1909 in the establishment by 24 states of the *Central Bureau for the International Map of the World* in London (Reinsch 1911, 71). With the help of first the League of Nations and then the UN, the Bureau was able to continue its work on this enormous project, although it was difficult to produce results during times of war. At the same time the two world wars brought progress in mapping uncharted parts of the world. During the First World War aerial photography was introduced and the equipment improved constantly. The entire project was to consist of 2,500 maps, each representing four degrees of latitude and six degrees of longitude. In 1939 400 of 975 prioritized maps were published, but the US Air Force assessed that in 1940 less than 10 per cent of the world was mapped in a way helpful to pilots. During the Second World War the great powers mapped vast areas of the uncharted parts of the Earth (the World Aeronautical Charts). During the Cold War, military mapping resulted in the two sides plotting the spheres of influence, as both alliances needed maps that were easily exchangeable between the armies of their members. The UN tried to use aerial surveying to support economic development projects such as infrastructure works. Apart from Europe and the Americas, the other parts of the world remained under-mapped or hardly-mapped, for instance Antarctica. In the 1980s the total number of maps produced had not yet reached a thousand and not all of them met the standards set by the Central Bureau. The UN stopped issuing its regular reports about the project, which slowly died, also because states produced their own national maps. The increased road traffic as well as tourism had resulted in the production of a variety of national and regional road maps, such as the *Michelin* series in France. Further advances in techniques and the use of computers and satellites eventually helped cartography. The *International Hydrographic Bureau* had been set up in 1919 to improve hydrography and to produce maps of seas and other waterways. This private bureau was transformed into an IGO in 1970 as the *International Hydrographic Organization*.

Esperanto as a universal language

Another attempt to improve international contacts was the search for a truly universal language. Some states tried to obtain general recognition for French as the international language, or *lingua franca*, given its use by diplomats and in international law, but efforts in 1905 and 1908 to establish a federation for the promotion of this idea did not meet with support outside the French-speaking world. The creation of a new and artificial language was given a better chance. Between 1815 and 1914, 40 undertakings were started, among them Volapük (1880) and Esperanto (1887) (Lyons 1963, 209). The international congresses discussing Volapük were dominated by conflicts, partly because of the authoritarian character of its creator. The Esperanto congresses, on the contrary, developed well and helped improve the structure of the language. Esperanto found supporters and practitioners in many states, followed by the creation of a *Universala Esperanto-Asocio* in

1908. In 1954 Esperanto was recognized by UNESCO. It still has practitioners, but has never met the high expectations of its creators. In the meantime English has turned into the main *lingua franca*, although French kept its traditional position in international law.

9.2 Identical weights and measures all over the world

World exhibitions since 1851

One of the consequences of the advance of industrial capitalism, with its use of modern technology, was competition between states in the economic and technological fields. To stimulate the sale of new methods and products and to demonstrate the achievements of particular national industries, a new phenomenon was introduced from 1851 onwards: the international industrial exhibition or 'world exposition'. These exhibitions, at which both states and national industries were represented as well as the Zollverein, attracted worldwide attention and can be considered as expressions of internationalist feelings and transborder engagement in the use and spread of modern techniques. It started with the Great Exhibition in London, which was followed by world exhibitions in, among other cities, Paris (1855), London (1862), Paris (1867) and Vienna (1873). Between 1851 and 1914, 42 such international displays were held in 30 cities all over the world, including Philadelphia (1876), Sydney (1879), Chicago (1893) and St Louis (1904). In an effort to attract more people, the exhibitions began to display objects in addition to just showing economic and technical performances, such as Japanese art in 1867, which excited those European artists who later became known as impressionists.

Internationally-oriented cities

Major cities such as Paris, London and Brussels were obvious appropriate venues for international congresses. The French government made special arrangements to ensure sufficient conference locations and hotel accommodation, and subsidized translations and publications for the *Exposition Universelle* in Paris in 1878. In that year 32 out of 47 international congresses took place in Paris. This city could be easily reached, while French was the *lingua franca*. For the centenary of the French Revolution in 1889 the French government created more facilities, with the result that 87 out of the 97 international congresses that year took place in the French capital. Berlin qualified as a venue because it was the centre of a rising industrial power, whereas London was the financial centre of the world, the heart of an empire and the headquarters of many humanitarian organizations. States such as Switzerland and Belgium pointed out their politically neutral status and were taken seriously for that reason. The cities hosting a number of public and private international organizations between 1815 and 1914 were: 96 organizations in Paris, 71 in Brussels (plus another 40 in other Belgian cities), 47 in London, 20 in Berlin, 15 in Geneva, ten in Rome and eight in Bern (plus another 19 in other Swiss cities) (Lyons 1963, 16–17).

The International Bureau of Weights and Measures (1875)

The international exhibitions brought to light how many different weights and measures existed among states and helped to promote a call for more unity. The international geodetic conference in Berlin in 1867 pronounced itself in favour of the universal use of

101

the metric system and suggested the creation of an official international commission to supervise the keeping and duplication of standard units of measure. In 1869 the French government created an internationally-constituted *Metric Commission*, which after an interruption due to the Franco–German War led to a diplomatic conference in 1875 and the adoption of the *Metre Convention*. Under this agreement the *International Bureau of Weights and Measures* was set up in Sèvres near Paris. Its duties were 'to make all necessary comparisons and verifications of new prototypes of the metre and the kilogramme; to preserve the international prototypes; to undertake periodic comparisons between the prototypes and the national standards; to compare the new prototypes with the non-metrical standards employed in various countries; to assist in determining geodesic standards and to undertake whatever comparative studies might be required by governments, learned societies, or even by individual artists and savants' (Lyons 1963, 123). The French government arranged for the International Bureau's buildings and personnel to be free from taxation (Reinsch 1911, 36). The Convention was modified in 1921 and Consultative Committees were established for electricity (1927), photometry (1933), thermometry (1937), the definition of the metre (1952), the definition of the second (1956), ionizing radiation (1956), units (1964), radiometry (1971) and amount of substance (1980).

Standardization and normalization

The drive towards unification and standardization in electricity came from electrical engineers, who at an international conference in Paris in 1881 adopted technical terms for units of electricity, such as the ohm, the ampere and the volt. A multilateral conference of 25 governments in 1882 adopted resolutions establishing rules for electricity, and this was followed by other such conferences (Reinsch 1911, 69). During the world exhibition in St Louis in 1904, the proposal to create a permanent body to ensure continuity between congresses met with wide support. In 1906 the *International Electrotechnical Commission* (IEC) was set up as an NGO, but with national committees formed either by national electrical societies or by governments. Its function was 'to classify machines, materials and standards so as to achieve the widest possible harmony between national usages' (Lyons 1963, 235). Standardization spread to areas other than electricity, often through copying the methods of the electrical societies. In 1926 national organizations and associations in a number of fields established the *International Federation of National Standardizing Associations* (ISA), which existed until 1942. Is successor, the *International Organization for Standardization* (ISO), came into being in 1947 in Geneva and was concerned with standardization in all technical and non-technical fields except electrical and electronic engineering. This NGO has as its members those national organizations which are most representative of standardization in their state, irrespective of whether they are public (as in the UK and the US) or governmental (as in many other states). Standards are regularly reviewed in line with ongoing technological advances and improvements.

9.3 Protection of industrial intellectual property and copyright

The Paris Convention on Industrial Property (1883)

The origin of the international industrial property regime was mainly a private one. The topic of patent reform was discussed at the world exhibition of 1873 in Vienna, where inventors were reluctant to exhibit their inventions if foreigners were free to copy them in detail, and then at a congress which prepared the way for further meetings. During the world exhibition in Paris in 1878, the French government convened a multilateral conference, with representatives from governments and private businesses and organizations. Their aim was a unification of national laws in the manner of the Universal Postal Union, but this was unsuccessful, as they were not empowered to take such firm decisions. However, a commission was set up to provide a draft for a project to establish an international union. This was more successful and the commission called upon the French government to convene a diplomatic conference, which met in Paris in 1880. The conference showed a majority in favour of an international union and even produced a draft convention, adopted by 11 states at the diplomatic conference of 1883 in Paris as the *Paris Convention for the Protection of Industrial Property*. This established the *Paris Union*. Its purpose was not the unification of the respective laws of the member states, but rather 'the creation of administrative rules by which the citizens of one state would be permitted, without expensive formalities, to come under the protection of the patent and trade-mark laws of the other contracting states' (Reinsch 1911, 36). The Paris Union's secretariat was sited in Bern. This *International Bureau for Industrial Property* had its functions confined to correspondence, investigation, statistics, the publication of the journal *La propriété industrielle* and the preparation of the conferences. Various member states were hesitant about making the International Bureau an office for the registration of trademarks and patents. Some other members agreed among themselves that if a trademark was registered in one of the states, it had the effect of being protected in all other states without any further special registration in any of them. This form of a restricted union under the more general Paris Convention proved a great simplification. When Germany and the US became members in the early twentieth century both the Paris Union and its International Bureau were strengthened. The Bureau became more independent and also became an office for the registration of trademarks (Reinsch 1911, 37).

Copyright protection

The first international congress on authors' copyright was convened as early as 1858 and was attended by six official and a few informal government delegates, 54 delegates from learned societies and over 250 individuals. The congress approved some resolutions, but these remained without effect. However, the necessity for some form of international copyright began to be understood. If copyright was solely nation-based, authors and publishers were aware of the risk of successful books being published in other states without either of them being paid (Woolf 1916, 306–7). The French author Victor Hugo presided at a literary congress during the world exhibition of 1878 in Paris. This resulted in an association, later the *International Literary and Artistic Association*, and in a conference in 1883, with authors, artists and jurists drafting proposals for a convention. The Swiss government agreed with this endeavour and convened a diplomatic conference in 1884, with the president and vice-president of the Association as members of their government delegations. The outcome of this conference was the formation of the *International Union for the Protection of Literary and Artistic Property*, later known as the *Bern Union*. The text of the agreement was redrafted at another diplomatic conference in 1885 and was eventually approved by a third one in Bern in 1886 (Reinsch 1911, 37–38; Charnovitz 1997, 201–2).

The Bern Convention on Rights of Authors (1886)

The *Bern Convention for the Protection of the Rights of Authors over their Literary and Artistic Works* stipulated that authors who are citizens of one of the contracting states shall have their works protected in all the other states. During the process of reaching agreement two different schools of thought existed, paralleling the discussion on industrial rights, 'one in favor of complete unification of the laws of copyright, and the other in favor of assuring to the foreign author uniformity of rights' (Woolf 1916, 307), with the latter triumphant. In 1888 the Bern Union set up a Bureau as its central organ, which published the journal *Le droit d'auteur*. The Bern Convention was revised in 1896, when an interpretative declaration and an additional act were issued, and in 1908, when a complete code intended to displace the former conventions was adopted. The new code meant that foreign authors were no longer protected according to the laws of their own state, but by the laws of the state in which protection was sought. The reason for this was the great difficulty national judges had in ascertaining the exact copyright law of other states. Although this Convention constituted a universal code, it was rather 'a model to which future development will conform, than an act whose integral acceptance on the part of all the members of the union is assured' (Reinsch 1911, 40). But even states that were not signatories began to regulate or alter their laws. The US was prevented from becoming a member of the Bern Union because of a law that made printing by American printers obligatory. This subordinated 'the primordial right of authors to the narrow interest of American printers and their employers' (cited in Woolf 1916, 308). It was not until 1989 that the US signed the Bern Convention. After a century, roughly 100 states were signatories to the Bern Convention, but not all of them to the same version. The Convention was modified several times, in Berlin (1908), Rome (1928), Brussels (1948), Stockholm (1967) and Paris (1971), the major differences being translation rights. The *Convention of Rome*, signed in 1961, gives similar protection to performing artists, producers of phonograms and broadcasting organizations.

The BIRPI Bureau (1892)

The two Bureaus in Bern, for industrial property and for copyright, were merged in 1892 as the *Bureaux internationaux réunis pour la protection de la propriété intellectuelle* (BIRPI), which introduced the overarching term 'intellectual property'. Just like its predecessors, BIRPI was under the control of the Swiss foreign ministry. Compared with the public international unions for telecommunications, postal services and railways, the relations between the two intellectual property unions and governments were less direct. Leonard Woolf gave a more positive assessment of the Paris Union than Paul Reinsch. 'This Union has affected a partial unification of patent and trade-mark laws, for it assures to the citizens of any State within the Union the advantages and protection in any other State which the latter accords by its laws to its own nationals. Professor Reinsch calls this an administrative arrangement, and in a sense, of course, it is, but it is also a partial unification of national laws, for the first effect of the convention is that every State has to treat the foreigner in the same way in its patent laws' (Woolf 1916, 309). He was also positive about the International Bureau. 'A certain number of the States in the Union, by a subsidiary agreement, have made the Bureau a true international registry of trade-marks, and a trade-mark registered there and in one of those States is protected in each of the others. It may be mentioned that, between 1893 and 1911, 11,684 trade-marks were registered at the International Bureau, of which over 6,000 were French' (Woolf 1916, 310). In 1967 the *World Intellectual Property Organization* (WIPO) was created as a specialized UN agency, covering the two regimes and expanding them (see Figure 9.2).

Figure 9.2 Establishment of the World Intellectual Property Organization (WIPO) (1967)

The two international regimes for intellectual property functioned in practice, but due to their nineteenth-century character as unions they came to be regarded as somewhat old-fashioned during the second half of the twentieth century. The ongoing internationalization of production, combined with technological progress and refinement during the 1960s when new electrical appliances such as TVs and tape recorders were developed and traded in the world market, made it necessary to revise both regimes. There was also discussion on whether a new organization which was part of the UN would be more effective and have a wider impact. These considerations resulted in a new convention, signed in Stockholm, Sweden, in 1967, establishing the **World Intellectual Property Organization** (WIPO). The new Organization became effective in 1970, and was composed of its own member states as well as those states that were also members of the Paris and Bern Unions. In December 1974 WIPO became a specialized UN agency.

The Geneva-based WIPO promotes the **protection of intellectual property** and supervises administrative cooperation between the Paris, Bern and other intellectual Unions regarding agreements on trademarks, patents and protection of artistic and literary work. Membership rose from 61 in 1970 to 175 in 2000 and to 184 by 2008. WIPO's main area of activity has remained the progressive development of international law in its field, including global protection systems and services. It now seeks to harmonize national legislation and procedures, to provide services for international applications, to exchange information, to provide training and legal and technical assistance to developing states, and to facilitate the resolution of disputes. The advancement of digital techniques and the Internet have posed new challenges regarding the protection and enforcement of intellectual property rights. In 1999 WIPO organized the first international conference on electronic commerce and intellectual property.

Reproduction in the Americas

The conference of the International Union of American Republics (see §11.5) in Mexico City in 1902 adopted conventions on patents, trademarks and copyright, which were confirmed by the following conference of 1906 in Rio de Janeiro, Brazil. The Union established two international bureaus for the registration of patents, trademarks and copyrights, one in Havana, Cuba, for the northern part of the continent and another in Rio for the southern part (Reinsch 1911, 97). The conference in Buenos Aires, Argentina, in 1910 adopted three new conventions for patents, trademarks and copyright, which had benefited from the advances achieved by the Bern and Paris Unions. The

Bern Convention had in fact formed the basis of the convention on literary and artistic property, while the treaty on patents had gained from recent thoughts on, and experience with, the Paris Convention. The original idea that the two American bureaus not only should undertake the registry of trademarks, but should also be the depositories of international patents and copyrights, was abandoned after the European experience was studied. It was decided to confine the function of the bureaus entirely to the registration of trademarks. With regard to industrial and intellectual property they should act only as general information offices, like BIRPI in Bern (Reinsch 1911, 110–12). The registration of inventions was handled mainly by national patent offices (see Figure 9.3).

Figure 9.3 Patent offices for the registration of inventions

Anyone who wants to register an invention needs to do this at a **national patent office**. One of the characteristics of the procedure is that registration means making the invention public, as the government offers the inventor limited property rights in exchange for sharing the details of the invention. In 1947 France and the three Benelux countries established the *International Patent Institute* (originally Bureau) in The Hague to do preliminary research into the originality of inventions that were to be registered nationally. Membership was open to all members of the Paris Union, but in 1970 no more than nine states had joined. In the early 1950s the Council of Europe had also promoted stronger European coordination through two European conventions, one on the formalities of patent applications (1953) and the other on international classification of patents (1954). This eventually resulted in the signing of the *European Patent Convention* in Munich, Germany, in 1973 by the 16 members of the European Economic Community and the European Free Trade Association, and the setting up of the **European Patent Office** (EPO) in October 1977. This European Patent Office was considered a counterweight to the mighty American and Japanese patent offices. In the same year, agreement was reached on a European system for the grant of patents. The Hague International Patent Institute became part of the European Patent Office in 1978. As a result of these joint European activities patents are no longer granted nationally, but for all its member states. In 2000 EPO received its millionth patent application and in 2008 it has 34 member states.

Regulation of international shipping, railway and road traffic

10.1 The relevance of international river commissions: the Danube Commission of 1856

Free navigation on the Danube

Like the Congress of Vienna, the Congress of Paris, which ended the Crimean War in 1856, dealt with the free navigation of rivers, this time the Danube. As Turkey controlled its middle and lower courses but had not been party to the Congress of Vienna, no agreement about this river had been made. Austria had been granted the right to navigate the middle and lower Danube in an Austro-Turkish treaty of 1616, while by a treaty of 1774 Russia was allowed to navigate the lower Danube. In the nineteenth century, Austrian and Russian control increased as Turkish influence waned. An Anglo-Austrian and a Russo-Austrian convention of, respectively, 1838 and 1840 promoted free navigation along the entire river. The Russian defeat in the Crimea presented another opportunity to further free navigation of the Danube. Articles 15–19 of the *Treaty of Paris* regulated the traffic. Article 15 linked directly to the principles and rules laid down at Vienna, by stipulating that 'those principles shall in future be applied to the Danube and its mouths'. The signatories declared that 'this arrangement henceforth forms a part of the public law of Europe and take it under their guarantee'. The remaining articles dealt with the removal of tolls and tariffs and it was stated that, except for police and quarantine regulations, 'no obstacle whatever shall be opposed to free navigation' (cited in Lyons 1963, 59).

The European Commission for the Control of the Danube (1856)

The Treaty of Paris set up two controlling bodies, the European Commission for the Control of the Danube and the Riparian Commission. The *European Commission for the Control of the Danube* consisted of delegates from the seven parties to the peace settlement. Its function was to execute the work necessary to remove obstacles to navigation and to clear the river's mouth of sand. The European Commission was empowered to decide on dues by majority vote in order to meet its expenses, but on condition that 'the flags of all nations shall be treated on a footing of perfect equality' (cited in Lyons 1963, 60). The European Commission was indeed established, but it was planned to be temporary, to be replaced by a permanent commission of riparian states: Austria, Bavaria, Turkey and Württemberg, as well as the Danubean principalities (later Bulgaria, Romania and Serbia). Power politics and disagreement, however, prevented the proper implementation of the Treaty. By referring to older agreements and making deals with Bavaria and Württemberg, Austria succeeded in excluding the upper part of the river, between Ulm in Southern Germany and the Iron Gates near the Yugoslav–Romanian border, from the scope of the new rules. The *Act of Navigation*, agreed upon by the riparian states in 1857, in Article 8 clearly favoured riparian states over outsiders by reserving use of the upper Danube to the vessels of the riparian states. At the follow-up conference in Paris in 1858, Austria disagreed with the UK and France, which stood up for the principle of free navigation without reservations, whereas Austria insisted that it was implementing the original ideas established in Vienna. As a result of this disagreement, the Riparian Commission in the end did not come into being (it finally lapsed in 1866), whereas the European Commission, which was efficiently taking care of clearing the mouth of the river, was granted periodic renewals of its mandate.

An empowered IGO

The European Commission's rights and duties concerning the lower part of the Danube were embodied in the *Public Act* of 1865, which was ratified in 1866. It gave the European Commission considerable authority, affirmed by Article 53 at the 1878 conference in Berlin (see Figure 2.3). This laid down that the European Commission was to continue discharging its duties, exercising them 'in complete independence of the territorial authority' (cited in Lyons 1963, 61). This implied free navigation from the mouth of the Danube up to the Iron Gates. In 1878 Romania also became a member of the Commission. The Commission's activities contributed to the use of the river as a channel for trade and as such enhanced the economic activities and welfare of this part of Europe. An *Additional Act* to the 1865 Act, ratified in 1881, gave the European Commission quasi-sovereign powers as far as navigation was concerned. 'It appointed, paid and dismissed its own officials, who were chosen without distinction of nationality and who in fact took an oath to the Commission. Disputes were settled in its name; it exercised financial control; it provided for the maintenance of lighthouses; it undertook works in the river without reference to the territorial authority (Roumania), and as a sanction for its authority it could call at need upon warships stationed by the powers at the mouths of the Danube to take action against those who infringed its regulations' (Lyons 1963, 62). Admitting the possibility of the use of force made the European Commission for the Control of the Danube a special IGO. Its members enjoyed diplomatic immunity and they frequently resorted to majority voting (Bowett 1982, 6) (see Figure 10.1 for the further development of the international shipping regime on the Danube).

Figure 10.1 The Danube international shipping regime in the twentieth century

In 1919 the Treaty of Versailles granted four rivers international status, including the Danube. The peace treaty of St Germain, which established the new republic of Austria, affirmed the international status of the upper Danube. In 1921 a *Danube Statute* was agreed in Paris in order to promote free navigation of the river, its tributaries and canals, for all states. The **European Commission for the Control of the Danube** was allowed to resume its operations, but saw its authority restricted to the stretch between the Black Sea and Braila. A new **International Commission of the Danube** was set up for the Danube from Braila to Ulm. It consisted of two representatives from German riparian states, one each from the other riparian states and one each from the non-riparian states represented in the European Commission. Navigation was to be unrestricted and open to all flags, on a footing of perfect equality, on the entire navigable portion of the river.

In 1934 the powers of the two German riparian states were transferred to the Third Reich, which required a new diplomatic agreement on German representation on the Commission. From 1936 the German part of the Danube was controlled by Nazi Germany, and during the Second World War hostilities severely obstructed navigation. After the war, when the Soviet Union had become a riparian state, negotiations began about re-establishing the pre-war situation with respect to the Commissions and the free navigation. This, however, was watered down during negotiations from 1946 onwards. At a conference in Belgrade in 1948 the original regime was effectively abolished, as the Soviet Union, which controlled the seven votes of the riparian states, disregarded the proposals from France, the UK and the US. A new *Danube Convention* was agreed without the participation of the three latter states. The newly-established **Danube Commission** replaced its two predecessors. It was controlled by the Danubian states Bulgaria, Czechoslovakia, Hungary, Romania, the Soviet Union, the Ukraine and Yugoslavia. Austria became a member in 1960, while Germany had to wait until 1998 before it was granted membership. The powers of this Commission were far more restricted than those of its predecessors. After the disintegration of Yugoslavia, the Soviet Union and Czechoslovakia in the 1990s, the Commission's 11 members were Austria, Bulgaria, Croatia, Germany, Hungary, Moldova, Romania, Russia, Serbia, Slovakia and the Ukraine. As a result of NATO bombings during its military actions against the Federal Republic of Yugoslavia in 1999, bridges were destroyed and blocked the river. Because the Federal Republic of Yugoslavia was unwilling to cooperate in removing the obstacles, it was not until November 2001 that free navigation was restored. The re-opening followed political changes in the Federal Republic of Yugoslavia and financial aid from the European Union, which contributed 22 of the 26 million euros needed. The Commission is still considering how best to adapt its convention to the changed political situation. In 1998, 13 states established the **International Commission for the Protection of the Danube River** to promote and coordinate sustainable and equitable water management. It deals not only with the actual river, but also with the whole river basin.

International River Commissions for the Congo and the Yellow River

Further international river commissions were established, among them for the Elbe (1821), Douro (1835), Scheldt (1839), Po (1849), Prut (1866), Congo (1885) and two Chinese rivers (1901, 1912). None was comparable in importance and power with the Rhine and Danube Commissions (Bowett 1982, 6–7). The proposal to apply the idea of free navigation to the Congo came from the Institute of International Law, which wanted to prevent certain powers gaining a stranglehold on commerce in this part of Africa. Governments concerned took up the proposal elaborated by the Institute and discussed them at the conference of Berlin in 1884–85 (see Figure 2.3). The ensuing *Act of Navigation for the Congo River* established a wide interpretation of free navigation for the Congo, which 'without excepting any of its branches or outlets, is, and shall remain, entirely free for the merchant-ships of all nations ... for the transport of goods or passengers' (cited in Lyons 1963, 63). The Act made no distinction between the subjects of riparian and non-riparian states. The Congo Commission, which was to regulate the traffic, was modelled on the Danube Commission, but it never came into being, as in practice the Act was administered by the five colonial powers in the region. The provision in this Act that free navigation should remain in force even in time of war was an innovation. The *Whangpu Conservancy Consultative Board*, established for the Yellow River in China in 1912, included five members appointed by foreign governments and one appointed by the Chinese Chamber of Commerce (Charnovitz 1997, 211–12). During the twentieth century, more international river or lake commissions were set up, such as in Africa for the Nile (1929), the Niger and Lake Chad (1964), the Senegal (1972), the Mano (1973), the Great Lakes (1976), the Kagera (1977) and the Gambia (1978). In Latin America a commission was established for the Rio de la Plata (1969) and in Asia for the Mekong (1995). Due to the increasing pressure on freshwater resources and the related socio-economic problems, it is expected that the governance of transboundary rivers will become the subject of a renewed use of international river commissions (Finger *et al.* 2006).

The pollution of the Rhine as a long-lasting problem

Ships' engines, increased traffic, dumping of oil and waste, city outflows into rivers and other civil engineering projects built around and in the River Rhine had a serious impact on the quality of the river's water and health. The water became dirtier and fish were slowly disappearing. In 1885 five riparian states signed the *Salmon Treaty* and established the *International Salmon Commission* to protect salmon against further decline. The Salmon Commission began to remove obstacles and to encourage the release of young salmon into the river. The first stipulation to prevent water pollution was found in Article 10 of the 1887 *Convention Laying Down Uniform Provisions on Fishing in the Rhine and its Tributaries*, agreed between Baden, Alsace-Lorraine and Switzerland (see Figure 10.2 for the later regime protecting the Rhine against pollution).

Passage through the Suez Canal (1888) and the Panama Canal (1901)

The passage of ships through straits such as the Dardanelles and the Bosphorus was a matter for the great powers. The *Treaty of Adrianople* in 1829 conceded the right of passage through these straits to the merchant ships of all powers at peace with Turkey.

Figure 10.2 The international regime protecting the Rhine against pollution

During the 1920s the riparian states noticed a process of salification occurring in the River Rhine, as a result of phosphates from fertilizers and waste from potash mines in the Alsace. Halfway through the 1930s, the salmon had vanished almost entirely. The Netherlands, however, did not get any response to its complaints to Germany and France. In 1946 the Netherlands asked Switzerland to take part in the debate and urged the Central Commission for the Navigation of the Rhine to discuss the problem. Although this issue was not within its precise mandate, the Commission asked the member states to inform their governments about the river's poor water quality. At the initiative of the Swiss government another conference on the salmon was convened in Basel in 1948, which resulted in the establishment of the **International Commission for the Protection of the Rhine against Pollution** in 1950. It began to function on a semi-official basis, but the agreement to clean up the Rhine, signed in Bern in 1963, gave it an official and permanent basis. However, its powers remained restricted.

As water pollution steadily worsened, mainly due to the waste from potash mines in the Alsace and the increased use of chemicals, ministers from various states met for the first time in 1972 to discuss this problem. They decided that pollution had to be dealt with and they agreed about the division of expenses between them. That pollution was also on the public agenda can be explained by a rising environmental awareness and publicity from action groups, among them the **International Rhine Action Group**, established in 1973 to 'save' the River Rhine from dying and to stir up public opinion. In 1976 the members of the International Commission signed the *Convention for the Protection of the Rhine against Chloride Pollution*, which had the aim of reducing the Rhine's salt content from 500 to 200 milligrams per litre along the German–Dutch border. Implementation was not as fast as agreed and the agreement needed to be updated several times. In 1986 pollution received renewed attention when a fire broke out at the Sandoz chemical plant near Basel, with chemicals flushing into the river and causing an ecological catastrophe. This disaster enabled the International Commission for the Protection of the Rhine against Pollution to set higher goals in its *Rhine Action Programme for Ecological Rehabilitation*, with **the return of the salmon** by 2000 as its symbolic aim. As was done a century before, young salmon were released into the river. Not all pollution problems have currently been solved, as various toxins still seep into the river and the return of salmon and other fish has remained limited.

The Treaty of Paris in 1856 confirmed the rule forbidding such use by warships, but the *Treaty of London* in 1871 granted Turkey the right to open the Dardanelles to friendly and allied warships if the implementation of the Treaty of Paris required this. Paralleling what had been arranged for the River Congo in 1885, the *Convention of Constantinople Respecting the Free Navigation of the Suez Maritime Canal*, better known as the *Suez Canal Convention* (1888), laid down the right of passage for all ships, of commerce or of war and without distinction of flag, through the Suez Canal during war and peace. This canal and its ports had been constructed on the initiative of Ferdinand de Lesseps between

111

1859 and 1869. The Convention stipulated that blockading or obstructing the canal was not allowed. The signatories comprised all great European powers at the time: Austria-Hungary, Germany, France, Italy, the Netherlands, Russia, Turkey and the UK. For the purpose of supervising the Convention and enforcing the neutrality of the canal a Commission was set up, similar to the one for the Congo, which consisted of the consuls of the signatory states in Egypt (Reinsch 1911, 74). The British government was the most influential in the Suez Canal Administration, as in 1875 it had bought half of the canal's shares, and from 1882 it occupied Egypt. Disagreement with France over the implementation of the Convention lasted until 1904, when the 1888 Convention was finally implemented. Freedom of passage prevailed, 'even if British sea-power was more effective than the Convention in achieving it' (Lyons 1963, 74). The World Wars and the conflicts in the Middle East after 1948 resulted in the disregarding of the rights laid down in the Convention, but the nationalization of the Suez Canal Administration by Egypt in 1956 did not alter the international canal regime. The Panama Canal, opened in 1914, had similar status. This canal was administered on the basis of the *Panama Canal Convention* of 1903 by the US, under supervision of the army. The UK and the US had agreed in 1901, in the *Hay–Paucefote Treaty*, that the canal was free and open to vessels of commerce and war of all nations. By the treaty concluded with Panama, the canal was also declared neutral, or inviolable, with free access at all times to the vessels of all nations (Lyons 1963, 73).

Navigable waterways of international concern (1921)

The underlying principles of international river and canal commissions were reflected in the *Convention on the Regime of Navigable Waterways of International Concern*, adopted by 40 states in 1921 in Barcelona. The Statute attached to it defines what navigable waterways of international concern are, and formulates the principle of the free exercise of navigation by vessels flying the flag of the contracting states. These states shall be treated on a footing of perfect equality. No distinction shall be made between the nationals, the property and the flags of the different riparian and non-riparian states, with only one exception for riparian states, which have the right to reserve for their own flag the domestic transport of passengers and goods. The Statute furthermore regulates issues such as policing, dues, customs formalities, the use of port facilities, the removal of obstacles and the establishment of international commissions. The Convention of Barcelona summarized and generalized the previous experience of the governance of rivers and other waterways by bringing them under the heading of navigable waterways of international concern.

10.2 Sea-shipping regulations by governments

The freedom of the seas

Only a few of the sea-shipping regulations established during the nineteenth century had a public character and, as far as they were international, they rarely resulted from international cooperation. As the UK was the supreme naval state, it set the rules and expected other states to follow them. Some of the international machinery created towards the end of the nineteenth century did result from joint deliberations, but it was based on private and informal rather than public regulation, and was formulated by professional rather than diplomatic experts. The most important principle in the use of the sea for economic and other purposes was the *freedom of the seas*, which provides unrestricted access to the high seas and to waters outside national territory, and prevents states from subjecting these to their sovereignty. The use of the sea and the exploration of its natural resources are open to all states. During the nineteenth century the states to guarantee this principle were the great sea powers, the UK (*Britannia rules the waves*) and the US (in the Western Hemisphere). The exception was a three-mile zone of territorial waters, based on the range of an eighteenth-century gun. Although some states claimed wider limits, the UK and the US did not recognize these, and the UK had refused to have the issue put on the agenda of the Congress of Vienna. In practice the passage of merchant ships through the territorial waters of other states was allowed, following the principle of 'innocent passage' (see §3.1). The application of this principle to warships remained a more controversial issue.

British rules on navigation and codes of signals

In 1840 the UK published a first general set of rules on navigation, governing collisions at sea and salvage. These were subsequently expanded and in 1862 were attached to the *Merchant Shipping Amendment Act*. Two years later the US also adopted these rules, and within a decade more than 30 states accepted the British rules as obligatory (Lyons 1963, 79). The first code of signals between ships and between ships and land-based stations (semaphores) was also a British initiative. It was published in 1857 and adopted by France in 1864. The two states invited others to adopt it, and 30 states had done so by the end of the century. Revisions of the code of signals were discussed at multilateral conferences in 1879 and 1889, but instead of setting up international conventions the work was entrusted to the British government, which in 1910 published a new edition of the *International Code of Signals*. There was 'international acquiescence in the standards set by a single country rather than joint action by a number of countries' (Lyons 1963, 81).

The lighthouse near Tangier (1865)

The intergovernmental exception to this dominance by the UK, and the first IGO to have the US as a member (Jacobson 1979, 37), was the *International Commission for the Cape Spartel Light in Tangier*. The International Commission was set up by 14 states in 1865 because of the frequency of shipwrecks at this dangerous cape near the Strait of Gibraltar. To facilitate trade a lighthouse was built, which was placed under the sovereignty and ownership of the Sultan of Morocco but had neutral status. The International Commission, composed of the diplomatic representatives in Tangier, had restricted powers. It was created because Morocco was a weak state. In 1892 a semaphore station was also sited there, under the direction of Lloyd's of London and under the general supervision of the diplomatic representatives. The multilateral conference of Algeciras in 1906 was another reaction to the weakness of the Moroccan state and resulted in an extension of international supervision, in particular through international control of the police in the coastal area (Reinsch 1911, 75; Lyons 1963, 81–82). In 1923 these practical arrangements for international supervision resulted in a Statute which made the city an international zone under international administration (see Figure 10.3).

Protection of submarine cables

In the 1880s some limited public regulation for the use of the sea was created, dealing with the protection of submarine cables, the behaviour of fishermen and the sale of liquor.

113

Figure 10.3 The international administration of Tangier 1923–56

In 1912 Morocco was, effectively, partitioned between France and Spain although it remained a topic of debate. The city of **Tangier** was made an international zone in 1923, under the joint administration of France, Spain and the UK, and from 1928 also Italy. This was settled in the *Tangier Statute*, which stipulated an International Legislative Assembly for the zone composed of 27 representatives, an international administration and an international tribunal, the Mixed Court of Tangier. The city and its surroundings were declared neutral and were demilitarized. From 1940 until 1945 its control by Spain meant the Statute was not functioning, but in 1945 the Allied powers forced Spain to leave. In 1956, when full sovereignty was restored to Morocco, Tangier was reunited with the rest of the country and the Statute was terminated.

The completion of submarine telegraph cables meant a huge amount of business from the 1860s onwards, but there were also the issues of damage and theft. Protection was complicated because the cables rested on the seabed, which was part of the freedom of the seas. The problem was studied by lawyers, telegraphic experts, electrical engineers and diplomats at several conferences. In 1879 the Institute of International Law proposed an international convention for the arrest of delinquents on the high seas. The US supported the idea, but it was the French government that in 1881 issued invitations for a diplomatic conference, following a resolution adopted by an international congress of electrical engineers. The conference took place in Paris in 1882, with 33 states and the International Telegraph Union represented, and with both diplomats and experts. The US delegation had to decline an active role due to a lack of instructions from its government. The conference drafted the *Convention for the Protection of Submarine Telegraph Cables*, which in March 1884 was adopted by diplomatic representatives at another conference in Paris. Taking precautions to protect cables was made obligatory for fishermen and navigators. Ships suspected of having wilfully or negligently damaged cables were to be arrested by commissioned ships of the signatory states. 'The arrest is made for the purpose of ascertaining from the ship's papers all necessary data with respect to it. An authentic written minute (*procès-verbal*) is made out on the basis of the facts thus ascertained and of the injuries observed. This document has legal force before the national tribunals of the delinquent, to which jurisdiction for the trial of such cases is reserved' (Reinsch 1911, 63).

Within the bounds of possibility

The clause in this and other conventions, that jurisdiction over an offender was restricted to the national authority of the state to which the offender belonged, showed the limitations of internationalism at the time. 'The powers could agree to co-operate in the supervision of the conventions, in the detection or prevention of offences, and in bringing offenders to justice. But the actual meting out of justice remained an attribute of sovereignty and as such was sacrosanct' (Lyons 1963, 78). No international agreement was reached on insurance for sea shipping. In 1885 the Institute of International Law had developed a code for uniform law on maritime insurance, but governments did not adopt it. The same was true for the *York–Antwerp Rules*, developed in 1890 by the International Law Association at two conferences, in York, England and Antwerp, Belgium. These rules governed marine risks and the contributions to be made by the various interests concerned in a general average. A new effort to create a convention in 1901 remained without success, given the divergence in the different national practices. But although the York–Antwerp Rules were not embodied in a formal instrument, they were widely adopted as standard practice (Lyons 1963, 83).

Rules for fishermen on the North Sea

The *North Sea Convention*, adopted by six North Sea states in 1882, arose out of a concern for the protection of fishermen from each other once they reached the fisheries. It prohibited boats arriving on the fishing grounds from interfering with nets already cast or fouling another boat's fishing gear. It laid down that fishing boats had to be registered under a national scheme and that this scheme was to be communicated to the other signatories. To supervise the Convention, ships commissioned by the signatory states were allowed to stop a suspect vessel and demand to inspect its papers. If necessary the captain might conduct a suspect fishing boat to a port in its own territory and deliver the crew to their own national authority. However, inspection of documents of registration, of the marking and numbering of fishing implements, and of the presence on board of forbidden instruments was confined to commissioned ships from the same state as the fishing boat. At the time the Convention entrusted considerable powers to the commissioned ships of all contracting parties: 'even though the document reveals evident anxiety not to expose the nationals of one party to the tender mercies of the naval patrols of other parties more than was absolutely necessary, it marks nonetheless a real limitation by consent of fishing rights on the high seas' (Lyons 1963, 76). In 1887 this Convention was supplemented by another, concluded at The Hague, on the surveillance and control of floating liquor shops, intended to prevent misbehaviour and fights by crew members through restriction of the sale of liquor. It copied the way of policing from the previous Convention (Reinsch 1911, 62–63).

Exploration of the sea (1902) and a ban on seal hunting (1911)

Marine scientists convinced governments of the necessity to undertake internationally-organized hydrographic and biological research in the northern seas of Europe (Reinsch 1911, 70; Lyons 1963, 232–33; Charnovitz 1997, 199). The Swedish government invited the interested states to a conference in Stockholm in 1899, and a second conference in 1901 decided to create the *International Council for the Exploration of the Sea* (ICES), which began its work in 1902. ICES was provided with a Council, a Central Bureau and an international Laboratory. The Laboratory was for some time headed by the Norwegian explorer Fridtjof Nansen, who also was to play a role in international politics, such as during the split between Sweden and Norway in 1905 and his later work for the League of Nations. The ICES constitution was revised in 1964. Due to its continuous hydrographical observations, ICES has been able to provide extensive knowledge of, for instance, the migration of fish, the uses of plankton and the presence of flora and fauna in the polar region. That animals can be threatened by ruthless exploitation and that a further reduction in numbers can be prevented was shown by the international convention of 1911, agreed between Japan, Russia, the UK and the US, which prohibited the killing, taking and hunting of seals within an area that included the Behring Sea, Kamchatka and the Seas of Okhotsk and Japan (Lyons 1963, 77). The *International Commission for the Scientific Exploration of the Mediterranean* was set up in 1910 in a similar way to ICES.

The consequences of the Titanic's sinking (1912)

After the sinking of the *Titanic*, which had been believed to be unsinkable, an international conference was convened in 1913 and a convention signed in 1914, along the lines of the saying about locking the stable door after the horse has bolted. This *International Convention for the Safety of Life at Sea* (SOLAS) contained regulations and recommendations about ship construction, lifeboats, ship wireless systems, fire protection and safety certificates. It was the foundation for later and more encompassing conventions on the safety of life at sea (see §32.5). Additionally, it initiated the formation and international funding of an *International Ice Patrol*, which was to monitor and report on the location of icebergs in the northern Atlantic Ocean. The actual patrol was carried out by the US Coast Guard. In 1929 at a second conference on safety of life at sea in London, the SOLAS Convention, was replaced by another, more detailed and updated version. Many seafaring states signed these safety conventions.

10.3 Sea-shipping regulations on a private basis

Shipping cartel building from 1875

Steamships and telegraphic communications had changed the business of delivering cargoes and conveying passengers, but had also confronted shipping firms with questions about the functioning of their economic sector, particularly 'questions of rates, of dividing the market equitably and avoiding cut-throat competition'. These issues were discussed at what the companies called 'conferences' or 'rings', which can best be described as *cartels*. A British governmental investigative commission defined this form of economic cooperation, which had first developed in the UK, as 'a combination, more or less close, of shipping companies formed for the purpose of regulating or restricting competition in the carrying trade on a given route or routes' (Lyons 1963, 67). The first cartel dates back to 1875 and concerned freight transport between Manchester and Calcutta. Others followed. Modern technology had resulted in larger ships, and made good connections and working to fixed time schedules possible. But an increase in available tonnage also meant falling freight rates. The shipping companies were faced with a problem. 'On the one hand they had to try to obtain remunerative rates; on the other hand they had to conform to the standards set by the technological revolution by giving regular and advertised sailings whether full or not full' (Lyons 1963, 67). This problem was solved by pulling together. To limit competition so as to maintain stable freight rates, the shipping companies made agreements among themselves to charge the same rates and they devised measures such as an attractive rebate system to counter competition from outsiders. The cartel system spread to other trades and to other parts of the world. By 1913 there were some 80 different international shipping agreements, mostly dating back to the 1890s. 'Whatever form the co-operation took, it was usually based on three main principles – division of area between lines, extension of the rebate system to continental lines, and general agreement upon the actual rates to be charged' (Lyons 1963, 69). Emigration from Europe to America (see §11.1) was the only shipping trade with tariffs fixed on the basis of intergovernmental agreements, dating from 1885, 1892 and 1908.

The private International Maritime Committee (1897) and maritime law

A proposal from the Scandinavian states in 1888 to create an international bureau to deal with technical shipping matters was debated in Washington DC in 1889 at the conference on the code of signals (see §10.2), but it was not supported by Germany and the UK, which considered it unnecessary. The *International Maritime Committee* (IMC), established in 1897 by international lawyers concerned with the law of the sea, ship owners, merchants and underwriters, who were all in favour of more regulation, was an NGO (Charnovitz 1997, 202). The IMC aimed at unification of maritime law, the establishment of national associations and united action. It held regular conferences, each with a temporary bureau, but it also established a permanent Bureau in Antwerp. By 1910 the IMC had 17 national associations. It drafted conventions on maritime law and had achieved sufficient authority to approach the Belgian government over convening diplomatic conferences. The diplomatic conference of 1910 produced two conventions, on the avoidance of collisions at sea and on assistance and salvage. With regard to the Declaration of London of 1909 (see §7.5), the IMC cooperated with the Inter-Parliamentary Union. Conferences prepared by the IMC resulted in numerous conventions. The IMC illustrated how 'a highly qualified professional group, by acting together at the international level, were able to influence the policies of governments, and indeed to transform that division of international law with which they were concerned' (Lyons 1963, 222).

The private Permanent International Association of Navigation Congresses (1902)

Another NGO in the shipping field was the *Permanent International Association of Navigation Congresses*. It was created in 1902 through a merger of two earlier series of conferences, one on marine works and the other on inland navigation. Its aim was to encourage the progress of inland and marine navigation, as well as the improvement of ports, canals and rivers. When governments began to attend the conferences, which to start with were mostly attended by individuals and delegates of national associations, the International Association's character became somewhat semi-public or even corporatist. Its major asset was its expertise, expressed in statistical and other reports. By 1910 1,390 private associations and 25 governments were engaged in the Association's activities and conferences (Reinsch 1911, 35). It was considered a very important pressure group for navigation interests (Lyons 1963, 66).

10.4 Cooperation in the fields of international railway and road connections

International railway connections

International railway collaboration was mentioned in §8.3 in the context of public international unions. In 1846 Prussia had begun to bring more uniformity in the carriage and to regulate the character and amount of the traffic between the many German states by establishing an association of German railway administrations. For practical reasons, railway administrations in the states surrounding Germany joined this German association. From 1860 onwards the railway companies coordinated their transborder connections at *European Time-Table Conferences* twice a year, one for the winter and another for the summer timetable. Given the related public responsibilities, governments soon engaged in securing technical uniformity and standardization. At the initiative of the Swiss government, an exploratory international conference took place in 1882 in Bern. Further conferences were convened in 1886 and 1907. The *Convention for Promoting Technical Uniformity in Railways* adopted in 1886 was adhered to by most European countries. Due to technical advances it was thoroughly revised in 1907, and dealt 'in the most minute detail with the gauge of the track, the condition and maintenance of rolling-stock, loading of goods-wagons and the sealing of carriages passing through customs' (Lyons 1963, 52).

The International Union of Railway Freight Transportation (1890)

As early as 1875 two Swiss railway experts had argued in favour of an international union for railway transportation. But it took three conferences, in 1878, 1881 and 1886, to draft a detailed constitution and a *règlement* for the Central Bureau of an international union. Ultimately, at the conference of 1890, nine states adopted the final text. In 1892 the *International Union of Railway Freight Transportation*, which was established on the basis of this *Convention concerning the Carriage of Goods by Rail*, had been ratified by a sufficient number of states and it began its work in 1893. Its Central Bureau was supervised by the Swiss government, which is relevant because of the Bureau's function of arbitration in disputes between parties to the Convention. The Convention established the fundamental principle that transportation is obligatory. Therefore no article of ordinary merchandise could be refused acceptance. Other important clauses referred to the continuity of transportation under a single bill of lading, uniform regulations with regard to packing, the transport of dangerous substances and responsibility for delays, losses and damages to goods. In 1896 the first conference to consider the Convention's revision took place (Reinsch 1911, 28–32). The achievements of the International Union were soon recognized, as it secured a broad uniformity of practice in the conveyance of freight by rail throughout most of Western and Central Europe. It facilitated the transit of goods from one state to another, and a constant flow of published material about the actual tariffs in the various states prevented excessive charges, as these were criticized and challenged by other members of the International Union. There was no compulsion for members to observe the Union's rules, but an ingenious system of blacklisting was adopted 'whereby a company which defaulted on its debts could be reported by its own government to the central office as no longer fulfilling its obligations, whereupon it would be deleted from the list of recognised companies and this deletion notified to all the contracting states' (Lyons 1963, 50–51). It was not until 1924 that a similar convention for passenger traffic came into force. The Swiss government had already proposed this in 1905, but at the time other states had felt no need for it.

The International Association of Railway Congresses (1885)

In 1885 the *International Association of Railway Congresses* had been established by various railways and governments. It included a larger number of member states than the European-based International Union of 1890. In 1910, 48 states and 413 railways were members of this semi-public International Association. Its purpose was an exchange of experiences in railway management (Reinsch 1911, 32–33; Charnovitz 1997, 202). The *International Union of Railways*, set up in 1922, combined railway administrations in Europe, northern Africa and the Middle East, with the aims of standardization and technical modernization. In the field of transborder connections the railways were more restricted than sea shipping, and close cooperation between railway administrations and governments existed on issues such as technical standardization, freight transport and later also passenger transport.

International regulations for motor cars (1909)

International regulation of road traffic was also on the agenda of multilateral conferences. In 1909 17 European states and the US concluded the *Convention with Respect to the International Circulation of Motor Vehicles* in Paris. Apart from government delegates, most national delegations included representatives of automobile and touring clubs (Charnovitz 1997, 209). Before drivers were allowed to cross borders they had to have their cars inspected and approved by the appropriate national authorities. Motor cars needed a number plate, a horn, two front lights, one rear light and a plate showing the state of origin through abbreviations such as CH, F or GB (Lyons 1963, 52–53). The most remarkable thing about this 1909 conference was that the delegates of some states did not represent their ministry of foreign affairs, but acted on behalf of another ministry of their government. Those ministers representing a specific ministry brought with them their expertise in the relevant field, but at the time did not have the formal right to make binding decisions on behalf of their state. If they signed a convention, this would only ensure the enforcement of it by the ministry which they represented. It gave the convention the lesser status of an administrative arrangement (Reinsch 1911, 33). This fairly new situation did not prevent the Convention from being signed by the delegates of 16 governments, followed by a sufficient number of ratifications in 1910 for it to enter into force. There were more multilateral conferences and conventions to come in this field of international road transport, and in the longer term the signing of conventions by ministers other than the minister of foreign affairs would also be binding on their state.

11

Public international unions and the creation of continental markets in Europe and the Americas 1860–1910

11.1 Free trade, customs tariffs, migration and capital export

Domestic social and political changes

The movement which followed Adam Smith's plea for the cause of free trade had its first success in the UK as a result of interacting social reforms, which were to take place also in other modernizing nation-states. British reforms included the emancipation of Catholics (1829), the redistribution of parliamentary seats which would end the preferential treatment of landowners over the rising industrial cities, the Reform Movement (1832) that strengthened the middle classes, the abolition of slavery (1833), the creation of a labour inspectorate and social legislation in compensation for the dissatisfaction among the emerging working class (see §4.3), and more scope for trade unions and cooperatives during the economically hard 1840s, when crop failure and unemployment caused hunger and poverty. Whereas industrialists in favour of free trade and the repeal of the Corn Laws sought the workers' support with the slogan 'cheap bread', landowners and the Tory party defended the Corn Laws because they kept corn prices high. The potato blight of 1845 and the huge famine it caused in Ireland settled the dispute in favour of the free trade advocates. In 1846 the Corn Laws were repealed, as were some protective shipping laws in 1849. Now that the entrepreneurs had defeated the landowners, the UK could develop industrially and trade its industrial products internationally. Owing to its technical and economic lead it had little to fear from other states. Since wars on the Continent prevented a regular supply of corn, food prices had remained high, but large imports from the US would change this situation. These were made possible because railways in the mid-west of the US opened up the large-scale cultivation of corn, while steamships made transport to Europe profitable and less expensive. The economic success of this change and its ensuing welfare, partly as a result of freer trade, made the UK an example to be copied. The Great Exhibition of 1851 at the Crystal Palace in London displayed this.

Economic internationalism despite political nationalism

The pros and cons of free trade were being discussed by citizens and industrialists in several states. So-called *Cobden Clubs*, named after the English cotton entrepreneur and parliamentarian Richard Cobden, who promoted the repeal of the Corn Laws and the introduction of free trade, referred to the British success and promoted the cause of free trade on the Continent (Charnovitz 1997, 194). Other states started to follow British free trade policy, with France accepting free trade in 1860. During the 1860s the Netherlands began to abolish the system of forced farming in the Dutch East Indies, and through a new agricultural law of 1870 opened up this colony to private capital. Although several states returned to protectionist tariffs in the 1880s, the UK, Belgium and the Netherlands continued with their free trade orientation. The tariffs were 'impediments rather than barriers'. The extreme mobility of goods across political frontiers remained a characteristic of the international economy until 1914. 'Politically, Europe was more than ever nationalistic; but economic activity, under general liberal conditions in which business was supposed to be free from the political state, remained predominantly international and globe-encircling' (Palmer and Colton 1971, 618–19) (see Figure 11.1 for the relaxed relationship between national identity and international orientation).

Figure 11.1 State and national identity in the nineteenth century

The term **nation** refers to citizens' common cultural elements such as language and social traditions. On closer consideration, it becomes clear that one seldom finds a group of citizens who are a perfect match in all cultural aspects. During the nineteenth century the idea of 'nation' was further developed in connection with modern state building, particularly the process of political centralization taking place in the rising 'nation-state'. Political power was being concentrated in the states' capitals, unless such power was given explicitly to lower tiers of government such as those of provinces or cities. While establishing its national political institutions, the national government created and favoured a common identity through symbols and meanings that citizens were shown and taught at school. This process of **national identification** with the state was taking place more strongly, more quickly and more intensively in some states than in others. The identification of citizens with their state and their acceptance of the political power of government were strongest in states with a representative democracy, in which representatives elected by citizens take the decisions and control the government.

Symbols such as flags, hymns, royal robes, orbs or ceremonies opening the parliamentary year represented the new **national identity**. In addition to these governmental symbols, so-called *lieux de mémoires* began to be cherished as more or less tangible recollections which kept the memory alive of events that were considered important for the national identity, such as battles, disasters or occupations. These were reflected in buildings, statues and museums, and in national myths, stories and history books. During the process of decolonization in the twentieth century, similar processes of national consciousness-raising took place among peoples that had been colonized and oppressed. As soon as their national liberation struggles had ended successfully state building began, including the creation of national identity symbols based on their new independence and their original culture.

Because of the identification of citizens with their nation-state, the creation of a national identity implied a **strengthening of the Westphalian state** (see Figure 2.1), with stronger ties between state and citizens. But this might also mean that the stronger national identity would hinder and impede those citizens who were undertaking transnational or international activities. This, however, was not so much the case if citizens were also able to identify with the international system, as this took national differences into consideration and recognized cooperation between states as meaningful. In practice the rise of national identity during the nineteenth century did not conflict with the international system, as long as governments themselves were interested in international developments and approved and promoted the transnational economic and social activities of their citizens. The activities of public international unions favouring the international economy or social developments had a stimulating effect on this **international orientation**, without harming the ties between citizens and their nation-state.

The Cobden–Chevalier Treaty (1860)

In 1860 the UK and France signed the *Cobden–Chevalier Treaty*, named after the parliamentarians who had initiated it. This treaty removed many of the existing trade barriers and greatly reduced the duties on various export products. The result was that the exports between the two states more than doubled, and it was followed by similar treaties with and between other European states. An innovation in these treaties was that even bilateral agreements were starting to have a significant multilateral element, with the adoption of the *most-favoured-nation principle* (Murphy 1994, 131). This principle was part of the Cobden–Chevalier Treaty. In international trade it means that the status awarded to one state must also be awarded to another, and that all trade advantages, such as low tariffs, that are granted to one state must also be granted to any other state.

The Union for the Publication of Custom Tariffs (1890)

The rise in the number of export and import duties levied during the 1880s created an obstacle to international trade, as many states did not publish them. Only a few states (Belgium, France, Germany, Italy, Spain, Switzerland and the UK) published them in detail, and even these details were often inadequate. In 1888 25 states and colonies met in Brussels on the initiative of Belgium to achieve a more constructive attitude and to improve the international knowledge of tariffs. Although support was shown, it took two more years of detailed discussion before the states signed a convention with the object of setting up a bureau to collect, translate and publish the tariffs from around the world. In

1890 the *International Union for the Publication of Customs Tariffs* was established. Its Bureau was sited in Brussels and was under the supervision of the Belgian foreign ministry. Its duty was to supply copies of laws and administrative regulations referring to customs tariffs with the least possible delay and to publish them in *The International Customs Bulletin*. Over more than 20 years the Bureau published roughly 100 volumes with details of 464 tariff systems and 1,813 supplements and revisions (Reinsch 1911, 42; Lyons 1963, 125).

The European import surplus and the export of services

The great macro-economic achievement of particularly Western Europe during the 'long' nineteenth century was that it succeeded in paying for the huge imports that its industrial development needed. Except for Austria-Hungary, the Balkan states and Russia, all European states imported more than they exported. 'Great Britain and the industrial countries of Europe together (roughly Europe's "inner zone"), at the beginning of the twentieth century, were drawing in an import surplus, measured in dollars, of almost $2,000,000,000 every year.' These imports were to some extent paid for by the export of European manufactures, while the difference was made up by 'invisible' exports of services such as shipping, insurance services rendered to foreigners and interest on money lent or invested, which were 'all bringing in foreign exchange'. Shipping and insurance were particularly important. 'An Argentine merchant in Buenos Aires, to ship hides to Germany, might employ a British vessel; he would pay the freight charges in Argentine pesos, which might be credited to the account of the British shipowner in an Argentine bank; the British shipowner would sell the pesos to someone, in England or elsewhere in Europe, who needed to buy Argentine meat. The far-flung British merchant marine thus earned a considerable amount of the food and raw materials needed by Britain. To insure themselves against risks of every conceivable kind people all over the world turned to Lloyds of London. With the profits from selling insurance the British could buy what they wished. Governments or business enterprises borrowed money in Europe, and mainly in England; the interest payments, putting foreign currencies into European and British hands, constituted another invisible export by which an excess of imports could be financed' (Palmer and Colton 1971, 619).

The importance of nineteenth-century migration

The voluntary mass migration flows of the nineteenth century supported and enhanced these economic developments. 'Around 60 million persons left Europe for the Americas, Oceania, and South and East Africa. An estimated 10 million voluntarily migrated from Russia to Central Asia and Siberia. A million went from Southern Europe to North Africa. About 12 million Chinese and 6 million Japanese left their homelands and emigrated to Eastern and Southern Asia. One and a half million left India for South Eastern Asia and South and West Africa' (Hirst and Thompson 1996, 23). Although most emigrants were poor, the millions of Europeans in their new states created new societies which basically had a European character. Furthermore, they would to a large extent buy European manufactures and export to Europe those products that it needed, such as food, cotton and minerals.

The importance of capital export

The emerging worldwide division of labour was effective, because Europe exported the capital necessary to 'get the new settlers and the new worlds into production'. In other words, the European states not only used their capital to raise their own standard of living, but also diverted some of it to developments elsewhere. 'It meant that British, French, Dutch, Belgian, Swiss, and eventually German investors in the desire to increase their income bought the stocks of foreign business enterprises and the bonds of foreign businesses and governments; or they organized companies of their own to operate in foreign climes; or their banks granted loans to banks in New York or Tokyo, which then lent their funds to local users' (Palmer and Colton 1971, 620). An example are the investments in railways in the US, Latin America and Russia. None of these enterprises could have been realized without the help of foreign loans and shares. Although the term 'transnational corporation' dates back only to the 1960s, the process of international industrial production was a nineteenth-century affair, following on from the colonial trading systems of the seventeenth and eighteenth centuries. 'Here the early pre-eminence of British firms as multinational producers becomes apparent. Initially North and South America presented the most favourable investment opportunities, but these were soon followed by Africa and Australasia. There is some dispute as to whether "colonial investments" should be considered a true precursor of FDI [foreign direct investment], but production for the local market began in this way. Technical and organizational developments after the 1870s allowed a wider variety of similar products to be produced domestically and abroad within the boundaries of the same firm, while the exploration and development of minerals and other raw material products also attracted large amounts of FDI' (Hirst and Thompson 1996, 19).

Centralized versus decentralized states

Internationalization in the period from 1870 to 1914 depended on the political choices of rivalling national interest groups and the identity of the politically-dominant coalition they produced. In states with a centralized structure, such as the UK and France, policies favouring internationalization had a better chance of being adopted than in decentralized states such as Germany and the US. 'Decentralized structures allowed potential losers to curb public policies favorable to capital market internationalization, whereas centralized structures allowed expected winners to promote such policies. As a result, economies with centralized states ended up being the most dependent on the international capital market, whereas economies with decentralized states took a less active part in the globalization of finance' (Verdier 1998, 2).

11.2 The gold standard and monetary unions

The gold standard and the Bank of England

The international monetary system of the nineteenth and the first three and a half decades of the twentieth century was based on the gold standard as adopted by the UK in 1816. During the 1870s other European states and the US adopted the same standard, which defined the British currency as the equivalent of a certain amount of gold. Fluctuations in the rate of exchange could be controlled if national monetary authorities, in particular states' treasuries and the central banks that came into existence, respected certain rules. In the case of export of gold as a result of a balance of payments deficit, a *deflationary* policy was required (decreasing the amount of money available and the national price level); in the case of import of gold as a result of a balance of payments surplus, an *inflationary* policy (increasing the available amount of money and the national price level) was needed. During the nineteenth century the currencies of 'civilized' states, such as pounds, dollars, francs and marks, could be exchanged for gold, or the other way around, thanks to the UK's national bank, the *Bank of England*. The main currencies were freely exchangeable, which promoted international trade. Whoever was trading in a specific state was not obliged to buy from that country or to spend the money there, but was free to use the proceeds of the sale elsewhere.

Monetary arrangements

Between 1870 and 1914 the main European and American currencies had substantially the same value, with relatively stable exchange rates. These states assumed that no 'civilized' state's currency ever 'fell': 'such things might happen in Turkey or China, or in the French Revolution, but not in the world of practical men, modern progress, and civilized affairs' (Palmer and Colton 1971, 622). If the financial system of a state did get into trouble, joint international action could help, for instance through the establishment of a 'commission' for financial affairs by the main creditor states. This happened in 1878 for Turkey, in 1880 for Egypt, in 1897 for Greece and in 1906 for Macedonia. In 1901 a commission of bankers was set up in Shanghai, as laid down in a protocol, to facilitate the payment of indemnity instalments (Reinsch 1911, 75). In 1906 the international conference of Algeciras, which set up the international police control in Tangier (see §10.2), also established a committee on customs valuation, which included members of the Moroccan government, the national bank of Morocco, the diplomatic corps at Tangier and one agent of the consortium of banks that had made a loan to Morocco in 1904 (Charnovitz 1997, 211). At the end of the nineteenth century, the gold standard got into trouble because the production of gold lagged behind the expanding production of industrial and agricultural products, but this was resolved when new sources of gold were discovered. The standard was difficult for states that did not have sufficient gold.

Monetary unions in the nineteenth century

During the nineteenth century some regional monetary unions were established to improve the exchange of their currencies (J. Foreman-Peck in Tilly and Welfens 2000, 89–93), the first one being the monetary union which quickly followed the establishment of the *Zollverein* of 1834 (see §3.3). In 1857 the *Austro-German Monetary Union* was set up which accepted the Prussian silver standard, but as a result of war in 1859 this did not last despite later efforts. In contrast to Germany, Italian monetary unification occurred almost simultaneously with its political unification in 1861. At the end of the 1850s there were four different currencies in the various Italian states, but monetary unification through the *Italian Monetary Union* was already complete in 1863. It soon made Italy a low-tariff customs union. During the 1860s problems arose as a result of France linking its currency to both the gold and the silver standard. French coins were also used in Belgium, Italy and Switzerland, which formed a kind of satellite currency zone. When gold prices fell, silver began to disappear from circulation. The *Latin Monetary Union* set up in 1865 by Belgium, France, Greece, Italy and Switzerland tried to solve the problem (Mattli 1999, 4). An international monetary conference in 1867 in Paris, where delegates from 20 states met, proposed a world gold currency that conformed with the pound, but this was unsuccessful as the UK remained aloof. In 1878 the Latin Monetary Union changed over to the gold standard. At a number of conferences (in 1885, 1893, 1898, 1902 and 1908) this Union settled issues such as the means of preventing the exportation of coin, the amount of fractional currency to be allowed for each state and the per capita amount of silver coin to be issued. Denmark and Sweden, later joined by Norway, preferred to have a union of their own rather than joining the Latin Monetary Union, and set up the *Scandinavian Monetary Union* in 1873. During the 1870s this also switched to the gold standard. In practice, however, the gold and silver standards coexisted in many places. In 1892 an international conference was convened in Brussels on the initiative of the US government to discuss ways of maintaining a currency based on the double standard, but no agreement was reached (Reinsch 1911, 76). The gold standard's operation and success depended on historically specific conditions. Governments, for instance, could largely ignore the domestic social and economic consequences of monetary adjustments, particularly deflationary adjustments, given the absence or limited nature of democratic institutions. In other situations the pursuit of protectionist trade policies offered a mechanism for easing the domestic costs of adjustment (Held *et al.* 1999, 197). Both the Latin and the Scandinavian Monetary Union remained in force until obstacles resulting from the First World War prevented their coordination continuing. Their formal dissolutions followed in the early 1920s.

London as the world's international financial centre

As a result of international investments and financial affairs related to British industrial expansion, London became the centre of the global economic and financial system. Older financial centres such as Amsterdam had lost their position during the Napoleonic Wars. In 1818 a syndicate of British banks took over the indemnity of 700 million francs that the victors of 1815 had imposed upon France. It allowed the London-based banks to develop their connections with many government treasuries. In the Crimean War of 1854–56, the London banks floated loans for the Russian government, even while the UK was at war with Russia. London 'became the apex of a pyramid which had the world for its base. It was the main center of exchange of currencies, the clearinghouse of the world's debts, the depository from which all the world borrowed, the banker's bank, the insurance man's resort for reinsurance, as well as the world's shipping center and the headquarters of many international corporations' (Palmer and Colton 1971, 623).

11.3 Agricultural regulations

The International Sugar Union (1902) and its powerful Permanent Commission

In nineteenth-century agriculture, one particular crop was the subject of international coordination. As Europe tried to free itself from its dependency on cane sugar from the colonies, the European beet sugar industry was being stimulated by government subsidies and bounties (bonuses). Because subsidies were financed by taxation, the large-scale national industries on the Continent formed cartels, which meant high domestic prices and low consumption. The free trade-oriented UK did not follow this path and therefore had low domestic prices and high consumption, but it had a problem with the bounties for its West Indian sugar islands. In 1864 Belgium, France, the Netherlands and the UK signed an international convention to solve these problems, but it only lasted for ten years and proved to be inadequate. In 1877 another convention was signed by more states, but this also was ineffective because of the lack of compulsory provisions and the failure of some states to fully live up to the agreement. In 1887 new negotiations began, but it was not until 1902 that the *International Sugar Union* was set up for the purpose of abolishing sugar bounties and placing a fixed limit on import duties. Its members were Austria-Hungary, Belgium, France, Germany, Italy, the Netherlands, Romania, Spain, Sweden and the UK, and they were joined by Luxembourg and Peru (1903), Switzerland (1906) and Russia (1907). The Union's convention created a *Permanent Commission*, charged with supervising the agreement's implementation and composed of delegates of the member states. This Commission was assisted by a Bureau in Brussels whose function was the collection and publication of relevant information. To ensure that states would provide the proper details they had to communicate through the diplomatic channel with the Belgian government, which thus became the 'diplomatic agent' of the International Sugar Union (Reinsch 1911, 51). The Permanent Commission decided by majority vote, each state having one vote. As soon as the Commission determined that some states 'have begun to export sugar, these states, under the agreement, must conform their legislation to the dispositions of the convention. Whenever the commission ascertains the existence of bounties in nonsignatory states, the treaty powers are bound to levy a countervailing duty upon sugar imported from such sources' (Reinsch 1911, 50). These majority decisions had to come into effect within two months of being taken. An appeal could be lodged within eight days and would then be decided on by the Commission within a month. The Permanent Commission also had a strong say in dealing with applications for admission. New applicants could only join with the Commission's approval, which would not be given until 'the sugar laws of the intending entrant had passed a very severe scrutiny'. That the Commission had exceptional powers 'in a field which is not properly technical in character, but economic, and even political' and exercised them for about ten years attracted much attention at the time (Lyons 1963, 106). Its 'power to compel alterations in the jealously guarded tariffs of member-states' was 'a daring step indeed', obviously the result of a learning process from earlier endeavours. Almost from the outset member states began to fidget under the yoke, but most of the time without much effect (Lyons 1963, 110) (see Figure 11.2 for its further existence).

Figure 11.2 The end of the International Sugar Union and
its continuation

If strong disagreement about the application of the tariff rules or the admission of new members of the **International Sugar Union** occurred, intergovernmental negotiation took place, if necessary by calling a conference of member states. In such negotiations the powerful Permanent Commission played an important role. The fact that the discordant elements in the organization 'were reconciled for so long was largely due to its influence' (Lyons 1963, 107). Major problems, however, arose with the UK, as in 1907 it declared its intention to withdraw from the Union after September 1908 unless released from its obligation concerning countervailing duties. The UK had to deal with domestic discontent and with Russian retaliation after imposing countervailing duties on Russian 'bounty-fed' sugar (supported by a bonus system). A major concession was given to the UK through an additional act in order to keep it in the Union, while the Commission dealt with Russia's entry by making a substantial exception for this new member with regard to its westward exports until 1912. After that time Russia wanted to increase its westward exports, as there was a shortage in Western Europe whereas Russia had a surplus. While in 1911 the UK supported Russia in its policy, the other members were against it, demanding that Russia first abolish its bounty system. Because the British delegate was instructed by the Foreign Secretary not to agree to any compromise, the Union's crisis got worse. The Commission was not able to make Russia move from its position, and persisted in its stance. As a result the UK left the Union in September 1913, followed by Italy. The Union's existence came to an end on 1 September 1920. Both the disagreement with the UK and Russia and the First World War had seriously weakened its functioning.

Despite this dissolution of the International Sugar Union, another international agreement and another international institution were accepted. When during the second half of the 1920s the production of sugar continued to exceed its consumption, Belgium, Czechoslovakia, Cuba, Germany, Hungary, the Netherlands and Poland agreed an international convention in 1931. It fixed export quotas for a period of five years, under the authority of the **International Sugar Council** in The Hague. In 1937 a further international sugar conference took place in London, where 22 states agreed upon another convention for five years. In 1953 23 states concluded and ratified a new international sugar convention, which in the context of the UN was renewed by 40 states in 1958.

The International Institute of Agriculture (1905)

Establishing an international institute of agriculture had already been discussed at international conferences in 1848, 1889 and 1891. A private initiative during the last of these conferences resulted in an *International Agricultural Commission*, which every two or three years convened international conferences. These, however, did not lead to government initiatives. They were 'soundingboards for internationally-minded agriculturalists, but had little capacity for positive action' (Lyons 1963, 89). This was also true for the *International Confederation of Agricultural Co-operative Societies*, set up in 1907. Winegrowers were the only group of farmers that received governmental support. In 1878 they established the *Union contre le phylloxéra*, with Austria, France, Germany, Portugal and Switzerland as its first members, a year later followed by ten more member states. This Union enabled them to coordinate activities to fight this infectious disease of vines. Their convention was renewed and extended in 1881 and 1889. The visionary American businessman and fruit farmer David Lubin succeeded in convening an international agricultural conference in Rome in May 1905, opened by the Italian king. Lubin had visualized a bicameral international organization, with an upper tier that included government delegates and a lower tier for representatives from private associations. The organization would have the authority to propose draft agreements for state action on issues such as agricultural credit, pure food and the regulation of forests and watersheds. The Rome conference was attended by representatives of 38 governments and delegates from various private organizations from Europe, the Americas, Asia and Africa. But as a result of a French intervention, the *International Institute of Agriculture* that they established in Rome was a government-only organization, even though it was pointed out that nothing prevented governments choosing delegates from private organizations or taking account of recommendations by them. Despite his initiative and elaborated plan, Lubin himself had not been invited by the king of Italy (Charnovitz 1997, 205). The International Institute's functions were the collection and distribution of information about developments in agriculture, among them payment of rural labour, new plant diseases and agricultural cooperation, insurance and credit, and the presentation for the approbation of governments of measures for the protection of the common interests of agriculturalists. The Institute consisted of a General Assembly and a Permanent Committee. Members were divided into five groups with regard to their contribution to the Institute's expenses, with the number of votes depending on which group they were in. The group that had most votes also had to contribute most.

Its weak political and organizational base

In Lubin's view, the organization determined by the Rome conference far from met his original plan, but despite this and despite not being invited he laboured hard for the ratification of the agreed convention. When by 1908 42 states had ratified it, the International Institute of Agriculture began to function. Contrary to the convention's intentions it soon emerged that the Permanent Committee was the key organ, rather than the General Assembly. The Committee was on the spot and it developed a high degree of continuity. However, it did not grow into an effective body producing international policies, mainly because its members were too directly responsible to their governments. When in 1909 the Committee's president initiated various circulars to governments 'in an effort to get things moving', the other members criticized his behaviour and he had to resign. Another obstacle to international action was its mainly Italian staff: 42 out of a total of 53. The International Institute achieved very little because of this lack of initiative, apart from its research and its publications of information on agricultural matters, among them a statistical yearbook published between 1910 and 1922 and a monthly bulletin of agricultural intelligence and plant diseases. Otherwise the Institute's objectives aimed too high. 'David Lubin had hoped at one time that the Institute might develop a world consensus of the principal crops. But he had not sufficiently realized the incompleteness of existing agricultural statistics, the reluctance of governments either to improve upon them or to communicate them, and their lack of uniformity. Even where a government was willing to provide statistics they might well be defective, and where it was unwilling those which it would produce might be of little use' (Lyons 1963, 101). In other words, the political and organizational basis of the International Institute of Agriculture was too weak.

11.4 Public international unions and the creation of the European continental market

Fostering industry and trade

The creation of a European continental market around the end of the nineteenth century was the result of the public international unions and their activities, according to

Murphy. With their regular multilateral conferences and international agreements, they worked to create the non-coercive part of the international political order that was needed for Europe to take part in the Industrial Revolution (Murphy 1994, 46). The unions completed the necessary public works of the European continental market, in particular by fostering industry and managing potential social conflicts, but also by strengthening states and societies (Murphy 1994, 82–106). Looking at the traffic routes and flow of goods on the map of Europe before 1914 shows that even France, at the time one of the most protectionist industrial powers, was part of this continental economic market (Murphy 1994, 281). The public works fostering industry included infra-structural work for the benefit of telecommunications, railways, shipping and road traffic, the setting of international industrial standards which allowed for comparison and international cooperation, the creation of a working patent system, and the promotion of a trade regime with international statistics as well as a monetary regime which encour-aged investment in industry and trade in industrial goods. For most of these issues, multilateral conferences and public international unions had been the vehicles to set things moving.

Managing potential social conflicts

The patent system developed by the Paris Union for industrial property (see §9.3) was set up in such a way that it allowed its members to demand that 'foreign patents be worked in order to be valid'. 'Edison could not stop a Danish firm from making something like his light bulb in Denmark unless he was willing to start production there himself.' The system created preferences for its less industrialized members, and the more industrialized a state became, 'the more it had an incentive to join the system and enforce the inter-national regime in order to protect its own industries' inventions' (Murphy 1994, 93). This ingenious system promoted international investments, and by protecting intellectual property the Paris Union helped establish a coherent civil order among conflicting interests that would operate in that market (Murphy 1994, 85). Other potential conflicts managed by public international unions were in the field of agriculture, where the information provided by the International Institute of Agriculture helped farmers adapt to the demands of the emerging continental markets and, in fact, the world market. Photographs of the clerical workers of this Institute show that in 1910 they had at their disposal the most modern means of communication and data processing (Murphy 1994, 98, 280). The international conferences and labour conventions of 1906, aimed at the protection of workers (see §14.3), helped to discourage political and social opposition to the new industrial system, with its negative consequences for working men and wage labourers, that was gaining ground in Europe.

Strengthening states and societies

The public international unions' activities tended to strengthen both states and societies (Murphy 1994, 100–106). The rule-creating work of the unions contributed to the expansion of national governmental institutions and helped protect the domestic social orders from disruptive interstate conflicts and the opening up of national markets to international influences. As a result of the often detailed information governments needed to present to international organizations monitoring the implementation of their conventions, governments continued the expansion of statistical departments within ministries or established new statistical institutes. The same applied to supervisory organs and inspections. International jurists and other experts in many fields, often through multilateral conferences, began to exert influence over the ideas of national and sub-national authorities. Internationally-developed ideas about the abolition of slavery, public health regulation and the protection of workers and women thus contributed to the expansion of citizens' rights and to an increase in governmental responsibilities. These processes of strengthening the state and its apparatus as the result of international incentives occurred in many states at the same time as agenda setting in domestic politics by citizens and their organizations or movements, for instance with regard to the promotion of universal suffrage or the abolishment of social wrongs. In states in which this kind of agitation was taking place, this eventually meant a strengthening of civil society (not-withstanding the social unrest it also caused) and thus in the longer term a strengthening of the nation-state, albeit one that was capable of resisting international competition (see also Chapter 14).

11.5 The Union of American Republics and the creation of the American continental market

Differences with the European continental market

The international political structures necessary to create the European continental market in principle were accessible to all nation-states, whereas the market on the American continent was formed by a regional organization that was open only to American republics. The *International Union of American Republics* furthermore covered a wide range of issues, rather than focusing on one specific function in the way done by the public international unions established in Europe. The American union stemmed from the conference on trade and arbitration of 1889 in Washington DC (see §6.4) and still had to develop into an organization. In addition to international law and arbitration, the Washington conference discussed trade-related matters and adopted various resolutions on these issues, which were ratified and implemented nationally as if they were conventions. They concerned postal communication, the Pan-American railway, administrative customs regulations, harbour dues, international monetary affairs including a Pan-American bank, patents and trademarks, weights and measures, sanitary regula-tions, extradition treaties and international private law. Preparatory work in some fields had already been done in Latin America. In 1888 a Latin American congress of interna-tional law had taken place in Montevideo, Uruguay, and sanitary conferences had been held in Rio de Janeiro, Brazil (1887) and Lima, Peru (1889). At the 1889 conference in Washington, Argentina and Chile opposed the plan for an American customs union proposed by the US, as they feared that it would end in a 'complete Zollverein' and in state building similar to what had taken place in Germany under the leadership of Prussia (see §3.3). The US tried to remove this impression, arguing that the plan merely indi-cated that considerations of a commercial nature were to be taken up by the conference. As a result the ensuing resolution was fairly vague (Reinsch 1911, 80), although it sug-gested the creation of an international commercial bureau. The US delegation to the conference included manufacturers, merchants and lawyers, and this multilateral con-ference probably was one of the earliest occasions on which private citizens were included in an official US delegation (Charnovitz 1997, 211).

The International Bureau of the American Republics (1890)

The Washington conference of 1889 established two bodies: an intercontinental railway commission and, as a result of the debate about the customs union, the *International Bureau of the American Republics*. The Bureau's aim was the prompt collection and distribution of commercial information. It was established in Washington DC for a period of ten years, to be renewed unless a majority of its members wished to withdraw, and was placed under the supervision of the US Secretary of State, who appointed the first director in August 1890. The power to control the administrative work was given to a Governing Board, which ten years later served as a model for the Administrative Council of the Permanent Court of Arbitration (see §7.2) in The Hague (Reinsch 1911, 124). Although the International Union of American Republics and its Bureau had an institutional beginning, no agreements about future conferences had been made in 1889. And for the time being these were not going to happen. The Democrats in the US won the elections of 1893, and an initiative by Mexico in 1896 did not find sufficient commitment to convene a second Pan-American conference. Even though Republican President William McKinley was in favour of Pan-Americanism, he was also carried away by the imperialist mood at the time. The war with Spain that resulted from this in 1898 amounted to the entry of the US in world politics. As a result Cuba was given partial independence under a kind of US protectorate, whereas Guam, Puerto Rico and the Philippines became US territories. But in contrast to predictions, the war did not reinforce the differences of opinion between North and South America. There were few declarations by Latin American states in favour of Spain and US interest in Latin America was greater than ever before.

The second conference of American republics (1901)

In October 1901 the second conference of the American republics took place in Mexico City, with all republics represented. During the first weeks relations were uncomfortably strained, particularly on the issue of obligatory arbitration. After the establishment of a subcommittee and long negotiations, a compromise was reached both on arbitration and on joining the Hague system (see §7.4). The consensus on commercial policies reached in Washington in 1889 continued with several conventions. New treaty projects concerned the extradition of criminals, the codification of public and private international law, the mutual recognition of diplomas for professional study, patents and trademarks, copyright and literary property and the rights of aliens. The conference went much further in agreeing international conventions than the previous one. To ensure the periodicity of the Union and the monitoring of the agreements, it was decided to convoke a third conference within five years through the Governing Board of the Bureau in Washington. The intercontinental railway commission of 1890 was reinforced and it was decided to establish an International Sanitary Bureau in Washington. There was decided progress in Pan-American relations. 'For the second time it had been possible, in the presence of radical differences of opinions, to find a basis for mutual understanding and for coöperation in a number of important matters' (Reinsch 1911, 91).

Reinforcement of the International Bureau (1906)

The Governing Board of the International Bureau of the American Republics prepared in detail the third conference of American republics in July and August 1906 in Rio de

Janeiro. 'A complete program had been worked out, containing all the subjects upon which joint action was considered desirable. A set of rules and regulations, also, had been adopted, and the length of the session had been fixed so as not to exceed six weeks' (Reinsch 1911, 93). This saved the delegates a lot of work and time and enabled them to prepare more fully for the issues on the agenda. The conference decided to reorganize the International Bureau, which would have a separate building as was agreed in Mexico City. The Bureau should do more than its purely commercial and informational duties. It could be more effective in carrying out the resolutions of the conferences, by bringing to the attention of the governments the advisability of adopting the recommendations and of handling matters relating to the implementation of the conventions. In fact the International Bureau was now set up as the executive organ of the Union. It was instructed to compile and digest all information regarding treaties and conventions between the American republics and to assist in securing their ratification and implementation. In every American republic that agreed, a *Permanent Commission on Pan-American Affairs* was to be established, which on the one hand was to function as the nucleus of Pan-American interests in that state, and on the other was to assist the International Bureau in carrying out its duties (Reinsch 1911, 95–96). Although the formal rules laid down that the meetings of the conference were secret, representatives of the press and other visitors, such as those representing NGOs, were freely admitted by common consent, 'but as the real business was done in committee, the spirit of the rules was observed' (Reinsch 1911, 100). However, practical experience here was similar to that in The Hague: that openness would promote the understanding of, and social support for, the international decisions.

The Bureau's transformation to Pan-American Union (1910)

The Governing Board of the International Bureau also made the preparations for the fourth conference, in Buenos Aires in 1910. The programme adopted by the Board was accepted by the member states. To secure periodicity the Governing Board was given the power to designate the place and time of the next conferences, which were to be convened every five years. An information centre for what was taking place in the various states was established in Washington, which was to also host the Columbus Memorial Library, and a permanent Pan-American exhibition of products was established in Buenos Aires. The function of director was upgraded to director-general and that of secretary to assistant director. The name of the International Bureau was changed to *Pan-American Union* and the name of the International Union to the shorter *Union of American Republics*. All powers and essential regulations were embodied in a convention or constitution, whereas the details of the daily work were left to the Governing Board and the director-general. They had the power to make decisions through regulations. This transformation of the International Union of American Republics as a series of conferences into the Union of American Republics as an organization with a permanent secretariat was the result of an institutionalization process. 'The draft adopted rests entirely upon experience, and incorporates in a more formal manner the organization already developed by means of the successive resolutions of the conferences and the activities of the union' (Reinsch 1911, 108).

Monroe doctrine, Roosevelt corollary and dollar diplomacy

That the US Secretary of State remained the president of the Governing Board of the Pan-American Union was not acceptable to all members and it was proposed, 'in accordance with the equal dignity of all the members', to make this chairmanship elective. But the US pointed out that 'by common international practice a position of similar importance is usually accorded the minister of foreign affairs of the country in which the union has its seat; and also that the presidency of the Secretary of State would powerfully assist the union and help to increase its dignity and efficiency' (Reinsch 1911, 106). Because the other members could not change this attitude they accepted the US position, while aware that the conferences provided them with the opportunity to air their opinions and feelings. 'Certainly at the conferences the American government has had no policy to force upon the sister republics. Its delegates always accord an impartial hearing to whatever may be proposed by other delegations; they claim no hegemony for the United States, but strive to assist in arriving at a basis for common understanding', according to Reinsch (1911, 116). However, it is difficult not to relate the US multilateral approach on the American continent to the Monroe doctrine and its Roosevelt corollary. The Monroe doctrine of 1823, proclaimed by President James Monroe, in its original vision held that the European powers could no longer interfere in the affairs of the 'New World' of independent nation-states of the Americas. In 1904 the doctrine was amended by Theodore Roosevelt, president from 1901 until 1909, who asserted the right of the US to intervene in Latin American states if they gave cause for US action. This Roosevelt corollary made the US into a 'hemispheric police officer'. Of the 43 armed interventions between 1901 and 1921 by the American presidents Roosevelt, William Taft (1909–13) and Woodrow Wilson (1913–21), 27 took place in Latin America, ten out of 14 initiated by Roosevelt, six out of ten by Taft and 11 out of 19 by Wilson (Kegley and Wittkopf 1996, 41–42). One of the US interventions was in Panama, showing that US interests in the construction of the Panama Canal prevailed over the independence of this state. Roosevelt is regarded as the first US president to embrace unambiguously the principles of power politics. The period from 1900 to 1913 is also described as the time of 'dollar diplomacy'. Taft, who continued Roosevelt's interventionism, used American forces to support American business interests which were mushrooming in the Caribbean and Central America, and described his policies as 'substituting dollars for bullets' (Kegley and Wittkopf 1996, 40). However, it should be noted that these US presidents combined their realist foreign policies with a multilateral strategy on the American continent through the Union of American Republics.

Results of the American multilateral strategy

The progress made in implementing the conventions adopted at the second conference of the International Union of American Republics in 1902 – about the settlement of pecuniary claims (coming into force in 1905), obligatory arbitration, extradition and diploma exchange – remained slow. 'The principal states of South America – Chile, Argentina, and Brazil – had therefore, by 1906, not adopted any of the treaties framed at Mexico. Mexico had ratified two, while the United States had accepted only the convention concerning pecuniary claims' (Reinsch 1911, 92). Results improved after the third conference in Rio (1906). In 1910, 12 of the 20 member states of the Union had ratified the convention on naturalization, 12 the one on pecuniary claims, eight the conventions on patents, trademarks and copyrights, 14 the convention on codification of international law and 11 the one on Pan-American Commissions (table in Reinsch 1911, 121). In relations between the states it was made the practice to exchange messages, such as congratulatory addresses or expressions of condolence on the occasion of disasters or the death of certain personalities. The American republics engaged in greater uniformity of travel documents and customs regulations. There was also progress on issues related to the membership of international organizations, such as accepting a national delegation, although its state had no diplomatic relations with the state hosting the international conference, or accepting a delegation from a state of which the government was not recognized by all member states. In addition to the regular conferences of the Union of American Republics, other more specialized Pan-American conferences were convened, dealing with issues such as health, customs regulations, closer financial relations and science. In 1898 the first Pan-American scientific congress in Latin America took place in Buenos Aires. The first to also invite Native Americans was the scientific congress of 1909 in Santiago, Chile. The follow-up congress of 1915 had a parallel Women's Auxiliary Conference. The delegations included government officials as well as representatives of scientific societies, universities and private associations (Charnovitz 1997, 211). Reinsch was not strongly impressed by the total number of ratifications of the conventions of the Union of American Republics, but he approved the very existence of the union as it gave the representatives of states with different interests the opportunity of 'exchanging views, of measuring each other, and of testing the extent of the sphere of common consent' (Reinsch 1911, 116). Just as the public international unions in Europe had completed the necessary public works for the creation of a continental market, somewhat later the Union of American Republics fulfilled a similar function for the creation of a continental market on the American continent. The main differences are that Europe made use of a large number of specialized unions (in contrast to the all-embracing single one on the American continent), and that in the case of the Western Hemisphere the American Union was under the strong leadership of a single great power. Here the US obviously acted as the regional hegemon, using both force and a multilateral strategy.

Part V

The international foundation for the welfare state 1880–1914

How governments became involved in international labour legislation

The fifth part discusses the creation of private international organizations around the end of the nineteenth century. It starts with the business community, in particular internationally-active large firms that began to form cartels and later established international interest groups, among them the International Chamber of Commerce (Chapter 12). Citizens, who at first had been fighting for democratic rights and emancipation only in domestic politics, now also established transnational advocacy networks and NGOs. Women turned against the 'white slave trade' and devoted themselves to social reform, suffrage and international treaties. Workers established Internationals, but unlike women they did not set up transnational advocacy networks, nor were they involved in international treaties (Chapter 13). That governments eventually did conclude international labour conventions was not set in motion by the labour internationals, but rather by socially-engaged entrepreneurs, economists and lawyers. They argued in favour of an international labour code, established an NGO for that purpose, and caused governments to adopt the first international labour conventions in 1906. These created the necessary international coordination of national labour agreements that were to protect citizens against the consequences of strong free trade conditions, and as such laid the international foundation for the welfare state (Chapter 14).

International business around the end of the nineteenth century

12.1 International trusts, cartels and federations

The rise of the industrial economy and the role of entrepreneurs

Among the explanatory factors in the successes of the nineteenth-century multilateral conferences and public international unions are the industrial economy and the active role of internationally-oriented entrepreneurs. Because the modern Westphalian state allowed for the functioning of an independent commercial class, entrepreneurs had the freedom to develop and implement their own economic strategies. In his book *The Protestant Ethic and the Spirit of Capitalism* (1904–05), Max Weber proposed that after the Middle Ages, warfare and state building ran parallel with the development of the capitalist world economy. The rise of Protestantism and what Weber termed the 'spirit of capitalism' ended the medieval traditionalism, which maintained methods of work according to fixed rules and prescribed quantities. Instead, a stimulus to expand economically developed, albeit in combination with personal thriftiness. The state profited from the creation of the legal, political and social space for this commercial and entrepreneurial class, as it had an increased resource base and developed a more complex class structure and a more pluralist distribution of power and interest within the state, separate from the traditional dynastic ruling establishment. This strengthening of state and society in turn gave impetus to free enterprise (Buzan and Little 2000, 252). Among the negative consequences of this new economic trend was a weakening of social cohesion. Modern urban society replaced traditional communities: *Gesellschaft* instead of *Gemeinschaft*, according to the German sociologist Ferdinand Tönnies. Firms began to develop their own legal identity as public limited companies, which gave them permanent existence as regards ownership. This meant that owners had limited liability for their debts and that the shares could be traded on a stock exchange (as public trade). Modern industrial capitalism did not take much notice of national borders and evolved into a worldwide phenomenon, with capitalism and the modern state reinforcing one another and with economic competition between nation-states playing an increasingly important role. Because of this competition, governments of states in which industrial capitalism was developing involved themselves in the industrialization process. Generally speaking, they did not meddle with the practice of national commercial classes developing their own international strategies. However, governments stayed aloof when they could have promoted these strategies, without necessarily returning to mercantilist policies. 'They strengthened the structures of the state and imposed reforms designed to remove any remaining obstacles that might impede the release of enterprise, market incentives or scientific and technological learning' (Cohen and Kennedy 2000, 79).

Internationally-active large firms

International cooperation between entrepreneurs around the end of the nineteenth century took place against the background of a worldwide economy, with colonial systems and emerging continental markets as well as the creation of internationally-active large firms. Among the characteristics of this worldwide economy were *expanding transport and communication facilities*, such as railways, steel steamships and telegraph and postal communications; the development of *modern industrial sectors* as 'pullers' of national industries and international trade, with the steel industry, machine construction, oil production, car and electrotechnical industries soon replacing the older textile and coal mining industries; and *international movements of capital* focusing on investments in international production, control of markets for raw materials and the securing of markets for industrial products. National economic growth related to international trade and investment movements, and the emerging international division of labour made the engaged states dependent on each other, as they needed each other's (semi)products or parts of their production processes. Simultaneously, competition among them was promoted because their industries had an interest in acquiring a relevantly large share of foreign investments and markets for raw materials and products. While in 1870 the UK was the world's foremost capital exporter, the industrially rapidly developing states of Germany and the US followed between 1885 and 1900, at a time when new technology and international activities demanded greater investments than ever before. Large firms rather than individual entrepreneurs managed to provide the amounts required. The firms' need for capital gave an incentive to banking, and sometimes banks even became the policy makers for national industries. The utilization of new techniques and the rationalization of industrial processes meant that larger enterprises could produce more cheaply and so outcompete smaller ones. Firms grew by reinvesting their profits, by taking over other businesses or by merging with each other. All this reinforced the importance of large firms, which also employed a larger part of the working class.

Formation of monopolies and trusts and cartels

Some firms became so powerful that they succeeded in achieving monopoly positions. They then controlled the supply side of the market and thus eliminated competition. The major reason for entrepreneurs striving to become monopolies was their hope of survival and of gaining greater profits by controlling both prices and markets (Thorp 1924). Industrial combinations varying from price agreements to holdings arose in the 'new' economies of Germany, the US and Japan, which became competitors with the UK, which had industrialized at an earlier stage (see Figure 12.1 for the shifts between great economic powers in the world market). This occurred in industrial sectors such as steel, oil, electrotechnology, cars and chemicals, and in public services such as telephone, gas and electricity. In the 1870s so-called *pools* were formed in the US, of a fairly loose construction, which made agreements on prices and market shares. In the late 1880s previously competing firms began to form *trusts*, by agreeing among themselves their share in common projects. These often secret agreements between entrepreneurs to restrain competition were called *cartels*. As well as through mergers, firms also grew by forming *holdings*, in which the firms kept their formal independence but concentrated the financial control of their firms, as well as of banks, in a joint holding. The so-called Morgan Empire succeeded in taking over a large number of banks and played a role in trust formation in American railways, steel and shipping industries (Ripley 1915). In contrast to Europe, where the economic crisis at the time had a less severe impact, the US reacted to a 'rich man's panic' with strong antitrust legislation, such as the *Sherman Act* of 1890 and the *Clayton Act* of 1914. This legislation focused on preventing the misuse of economic power by trusts, cartels or interlocking directorates between competing banks, competing industrials, and between railroads and their potential suppliers (Fennema 1982, 2).

Figure 12.1 Shifts in the world market

Europe's central position in the international system of states and the world market resulted from the fact that Europe had controlled the sea routes around Africa and across the Atlantic and the Pacific since the fifteenth century. 'By the last decades of the sixteenth century a basic global system of navigation was firmly in place. In line with the ancient and classical pattern of economic systems being larger than military–political ones, this breakthrough in interaction capacity quickly generated a global-scale trading system that not only linked Europe, Africa, and Asia directly, but brought the resources of the Americas into the Eurasian system for the first time' (Buzan and Little 2000, 241–42). It took time for this trading system to become part of a single, full and global network of states, but around the middle of the nineteenth century this was in place, once Western powers had used their force to open up Japan and China, to rearrange control over the interior of Africa and to suppress the still existing pre-international systems in the Western Hemisphere.

After the Middle Ages politics nationalized, but the world market did not fragment. The alternation of rivalry between states and the presence of ascending and declining hegemonic powers resulted in a dynamic system which prevented the world market from being subjected to one great power. Gaining economic and political power, however, meant that some great powers held a Core position in the world economy. They were able to bend the market to their will by devising a system of trade and investment that placed economically and politically weaker states in a Peripheral position, which allowed the Core states to exploit the Peripheral ones. The Dependencia and World-System approaches of Andre Gunder Frank and Immanuel Wallerstein hence reject the claim of modernization theory that the problems of the Periphery were the result of traditionalism or historical backwardness. Instead, industrial capitalism as it developed from the Middle Ages on created an exchange relationship between **Core and Periphery**, with a surplus transfer from the Periphery to the Core, which has allowed the Core to develop further but has kept the Periphery 'underdeveloped'.

A Semi-Periphery came into existence between the Core and the Periphery, which itself was exploited by the Core but *vis-à-vis* the Periphery took a Core position. According to Wallerstein the Semi-Periphery held an intermediary position, with efforts to increase its status and power (Wallerstein 1974). Ascent and decline in the World System has resulted in **shifts in the world market**. Some Core states declined into the Semi-Periphery, whereas others rose out of the Periphery or Semi-Periphery to a higher status. Between 1800 and 1860 the US moved from Periphery to Semi-Periphery status and between 1860 and 1900 from Semi-Periphery to Core status. Between 1870 and 1900 Germany rose from Semi-Periphery to Core; between 1868 and 1900 Japan went from Periphery to Semi-Periphery status and between 1945 and 1970 to a Core position; Taiwan and South Korea moved from Periphery to Semi-Periphery status between 1950 and 1980. Spain, however, moved from Core to Semi-Periphery status between 1620 and 1700 (Shannon 1996, 147) and did not return to a Core position until after it had become a member of the European Union at the end of the twentieth century. During the 1990s states such as Brazil, China and Mexico began to move from their Semi-Periphery status to Core position, while Thailand and South Africa were moving from Periphery to Semi-Periphery.

Hegemonic power occurs if one Core power achieves a position of economic and military superiority over the other Core powers. Economic superiority takes place if that state enjoys a major economic advantage over all other Core states in production (as a result of technological advance), in trade (in volume and as a result of services) and in finance (by providing the largest source of capital for international investments and most financial services, among them the setting of the currency exchange rates). Economic predominance enables the hegemonic state to maintain the largest strategic military forces and 'thus, to intervene militarily all over the world more effectively than any other core state' (Shannon 1996, 137). This military superiority, however, has never been so great as to threaten the actual independence of other Core states. Examples of hegemonic powers are the United Provinces of the Netherlands (1620–50), the UK (1815–1900) and the US (from 1945).

International trusts and cartels

Around the end of the nineteenth century, trust and cartel formation also occurred internationally. 'The great capitalists and captains of industry show by their actions that they are by no means convinced that the national interests of commerce and industry are best served by international competition. ... The trend of modern industry is, as everyone knows, towards combination' (Woolf 1916, 334). This trend showed in international trusts and cartels as well as in international federations of commercial and industrial firms. Due to international competition and problems relating to the emerging international division of labour, international cartels were established. These were 'loose organizations, forming and reforming at frequent intervals and with no very highly developed internal cohesion or discipline'. Their purpose was 'to prevent dumping or to put an end to cut-throat price wars, and their main objective was to dominate the market in their particular commodity' (Lyons 1963, 113). In addition to those in international shipping established from 1875 onwards (see §10.3), cartels were formed for the basic materials needed by modern industry, such as borax, caffeine, cyanide, dynamite, zinc, copper, cement, steel rails, tubes and needles. By the end of the century about 40 of these cartels were known to exist, and by 1914 there were 114. The cartel for explosives consisted of the companies founded by the Swedish inventor of dynamite Alfred Nobel (discussed in §7.3 because of the Nobel Peace Prize). In 1886 his Swedish firm formed the Nobel Trust Company with three British firms, six German companies and one each from Brazil, Mexico and Switzerland, plus cooperation based on agreements about the division of exports with a Paris-led group of firms in France, Italy, Spain and Switzerland. An agreement with Du Pont in the US had to be cancelled as it was in violation of the Sherman Act. The international cartel for the steel rails made by manufacturers in several states was based on an agreement dating back to 1883. It collapsed within a few years, but in 1904 the *International Rail Makers Association* was established, which in fact was a London-based cartel with participants from Belgium, France, Germany and the UK, and later Austria, Russia and Spain, as well as close relations with US Steel. Its aim was 'to delimit markets by allotting to groups of firms from the different countries certain percentages of the export trade, while leaving them in full control of their own home markets'. The importance of oil for sea shipping and the existence of only a few large companies, such as American Standard Oil and British–Dutch Shell–Royal Dutch, made the British government 'aware of the dangers of being at the mercy of private, international companies for a vital part of their war potential'. In May 1914 it therefore decided to become the principal shareholder of the Anglo-Persian Oil Company (Lyons 1963, 117).

International industrial federations

The *Baltic and White Sea Conference*, created in 1905, consisted of ship owners in 11 states in the north of Europe. They had established a Central Bureau, a Governing Council and an annual Conference, based on majority voting. 'It originated from the realization of owners that competition had cut freights for wood from the Baltic to next to nothing. The object of the Association was to regulate competition and to fix a minimum freight tariff' (Woolf 1916, 328–29). Although this organization still resembled a cartel, it was less informal and secret. Its development also revealed that other motives for international cooperation between entrepreneurs in specific sectors were growing in importance, such as the collection and dissemination of reliable statistics and up-to-date information, the development of new methods of production, the protection of industries against periods of depression and the operations of speculators. These objectives were achieved by forming international business federations of entrepreneurs or federations of national associations. Between 1904 and 1910 four such federations were established, for flax-spinning, tailoring, building and cotton-spinning (Lyons 1963, 117–18).

The International Federation of Cotton Spinners (1904)

The oldest federation was the *International Federation of Cotton Spinners*, established by Charles Wright MacAra. He had become an exponent of conciliation between capital and labour, and in 1903 had succeeded in defeating American speculators by persuading the entire Lancashire cotton industry to restrict production for as long as necessary, until the speculators were forced to sell their cotton stocks. After this the industry reverted to normal prices, but MacAra realized that it would be impossible to do this again and therefore began to think in terms of a permanent international organization. He approached Prime Minister Arthur Balfour with a request to call a conference to establish such an organization, but the British government refused. MacAra instead persuaded the British federation of cotton spinners to arrange an unofficial conference itself. This occurred at the same time that David Lubin travelled around Europe to find support for his ideas about an International Institute of Agriculture (see §11.3). Lubin visited MacAra, who introduced him to important institutions and people. Although the men differed in many respects, they shared their devotion to the ideal of international economic cooperation. The international conference of cotton spinners took place in Zurich, Switzerland, in May 1904 and resulted in the planned international federation, which was chaired by MacAra. 'The Federation was joined by, or received co-operation from, every cotton-growing country in the world and its annual congresses became virtually the parliament of the industry. The international committee of the Federation met twice a year, usually in some central city of Europe, and its main function was to collect and circulate to the members accurate information about the state of crops wherever cotton was grown and marketed. In addition, it concerned itself with methods of improving and increasing cotton production; with matters of packing, shipping, storage, and sale; with problems of insurance; even with questions of international arbitration' (Lyons 1963, 119). This international federation can be regarded as the model for many other international industrial federations established during the twentieth century at regional or global level.

12.2 Advocating an international chamber of commerce 1905–19

International conferences of businesspeople

The first time businesspeople discussed trade-related matters at an international conference was in 1869. From 1878 this happened more frequently, and in 1900 they called a conference on customs regulations. These conferences were attended by representatives of companies and commercial organizations such as chambers of industry and commerce, and later also of governments. Delegates from chambers of commerce proposed the establishment of an international chamber and in 1905 they established a *Permanent Committee* for this purpose in Liège, Belgium. This Committee worked out a *règlement* and organized international congresses at regular intervals, which were also attended by government representatives. These congresses aimed at unification of national laws on a variety of topics. The 1910 congress in London adopted resolutions 'demanding a fixed date for Easter; that commerce and industry should be consulted whenever politico-economic international conferences were held; that there should be uniformity of laws regarding cheques; that the laws relating to the enforcement of judgments in foreign countries should be revised; that uniformity in the compilation of custom statistics was "of the highest economic importance" and that this matter should be recommended both to governments and to the International Institute of Statistics; and that an investigation might be made in the different countries on the basis of the question: "What are, in your country, the products, alimentary or otherwise, natural or manufactured, deriving from the soil, the climate or special manufacturing processes, which should be internationally protected?"' (Lyons 1963, 120–21). For the fifth congress in Boston in 1912, US President Taft was authorized to invite other governments to attend. One of the resolutions in Boston supported the establishment of the International Court of Arbitral Justice, as proposed in The Hague in 1907 (see Figure 7.4), for suits between individuals and foreign states (Charnovitz 1997, 209).

Establishment of the International Chamber of Commerce (1919)

It was not until the sixth congress in 1914 that an elaborated constitution for an international chamber was adopted, envisaging biennial congresses, a permanent executive committee and a Bureau in Brussels. The outbreak of the war prevented further action, but at an international trade conference in 1919 in Atlantic City, New Jersey, business-people from Belgium, France, Italy, the UK and the US decided to establish the *International Chamber of Commerce* (ICC). The constituent congress took place in 1920 in Paris, where the constitution and organizational structure were agreed. The aims were promotion of peace, cordial international relations, greater freedom of trade and private enterprise, provision of practical services and representation of business interests at governmental and intergovernmental levels. The ICC became a strong private organization, based in Paris, with its own regulations for the settlement of disputes and practical services that soon were recognized worldwide (see Figure 12.2). In the 1920s the ICC focused on reparations and war debts, with three prominent ICC members serving on the Dawes Commission which forged an international agreement on war reparations in 1924 (see §18.2). When industrial cartels were being discussed during the 1920s, the ICC emphasized in 1927 that these cartels should not lose sight of the interests of workers, merchants and consumers, but it also confirmed the economic importance of establishing international cartels in Europe. National legislatures 'should favour such international cartels in order to facilitate their creation and to promote the development of such combines, without infringing the economic interests of the nations concerned in industry' (De Király 1929, 19). In 1928 the International Law Association discussed the legal aspects of these cartels. During the 1930s the ICC tried to hold back the tide of protectionism and economic nationalism.

Figure 12.2 The relevance of the International Chamber of Commerce (1919)

The private **International Chamber of Commerce** (ICC) of 1919 was designed as a policy-making forum for private business, but its first president Etienne Clémentel also saw the ICC as an international and neutral institution for the settlement of business disputes. In 1923 the **ICC Court of Arbitration** was created in Paris as a neutral body to settle business disputes of an international character by means of arbitration. Actual arbitration could take place elsewhere if parties preferred. The ICC aimed at high-quality verdicts, as it wanted national judiciaries and legal professions to accept and recognize the judgements. Therefore the ICC Court brought its verdicts to the attention of national courts. In the beginning the ICC Court of

Arbitration was engaged in developing schemes of arbitration and justice in fields where public regulation was either weak or lacking.

After the Second World War, the ICC engaged in the drafting and acceptance of an international legal backing for arbitral decisions. This resulted in 1958 in the adoption by the UN of the *Convention on the Recognition and Enforcement of Foreign Arbitral Awards*. In the 1970s the ICC complemented its Court with new facilities for the provision of technical expertise, for marine arbitration and for concluding contracts, through the establishment of the *International Centre for Technical Expertise*, the *International Maritime Arbitration Organization* and the *International Panel on Extortion and Bribery in Business Transactions*. From the 1980s onwards the ICC set up various services to combat commercial crime, such as the *International Maritime Bureau* for dealing with the various types of maritime crime, the *Counterfeiting Intelligence Bureau* and the *Financial Investigation Bureau*. It is assumed that codes of behaviour developed by the world business community itself have a greater impact than public regulation, while in practice the private codes contribute to the further development of international private law. It has remained the ICC's conviction that business operates most effectively with a minimum of government intervention. Although the ICC was one of the pioneers in international self-regulation, its position did not stay unchallenged, as by the end of the twentieth century a number of international law firms became involved in setting international business law precedents (Ronit and Schneider 2000, 18).

Practical facilitation of international trade has proved to be another strong asset of the ICC since the interwar period, including the standardization of banking techniques, trade terms, marketing codes and combined transport rules. During the 1920s the ICC began to formulate uniform trade conditions, model contracts and standard international trade definitions, or *Incoterms*, which have facilitated imports and exports. The first Uniform Customs and Practice for Documentary Credit was published in 1933 and has been followed by updated versions since.

In 1981 the ICC explained in a brochure that many of its activities should be undertaken by the ICC rather than intergovernmental organizations, as the business community is far closer to the market concerned. Members of the business community are supposed to know better what the problems are and what the solutions should be, and are more aware of what the inadequacies of the existing situation cost them every day. 'They cannot afford the unhurried deliberations of an intergovernmental body working on the basis of Conventions that take years to prepare and more years to come into effect.' The ICC is convinced that its organs are well-equipped to keep a continual watching brief on such developments (ICC 1981, 4). Despite this critical **attitude towards IGOs**, the ICC has developed into an international pressure group that is using its consultative status at the UN Economic and Social Council extensively. As an NGO, the ICC has been actively involved in the activities within the UN, its specialized agencies, the Organization for Economic Cooperation and Development, the European Union and other regional IGOs. Its commitment has been the promotion of free enterprise and the greater freedom of trade.

Rising international emancipation movements of workers and women

13.1 The socialist First International of 1864 as a spectre

The international workers' movement in the 1860s

Workers from France and Germany were among the visitors at the world exhibition of 1862 in London. Looking for workers' support, the French government had enabled 750 working men from large cities to travel to the London exhibition. Some were selected by their employers, others by their co-workers. Once in London they met representatives of the British trade unions. When they returned to France they told the home front about the freedom of organization in the UK and argued in favour of abolishing the ban on workers' organizations that dated back to the French Revolution. The German workers who came to London were introduced to politically-engaged German emigrants. After a demonstration in London to support the Polish uprising of 1863, British trade union leaders, a delegation of French workers and representatives of Polish and German workers agreed to establish an international association. The British unions were entrusted with the necessary preparations, and in September 1864 the *International Working Men's Association* was founded, which later became known as the *First International*. A delegation from France, together with workers from Germany, Ireland, Italy, Poland and Switzerland who lived in the UK, decided to establish a Central Council, consisting of representatives from their countries, to set up national committees in their capitals and to investigate the conditions and needs of workers by means of international congresses.

Differences of opinion between socialists and anarchists

A German emigrant, who had just finished an extensive study of the rise of modern capitalism, set himself up as a strategist on the commission that had to draw up the articles of association and a programme for the International. This man, Karl Marx, explained the International's objectives in an *Inaugural Address*, ending with the same call to action as the *Communist Manifesto* of 1848: 'Working men of all countries, unite!' (see §4.3). The address urged workers to organize, with the aim of winning political power so as to achieve the working class's emancipation and a socialist reorganization of society. The International convened a number of international congresses, which in some states supported the already emerging foundation of trade unions and political organizations by workers. The International's congresses and the meetings of its Central Council to a large extent were characterized by differences of opinion about the Association's purpose and the methods to be used. These frictions became worse, as the International in essence was an association of people, rather than a federation of organizations. Formally local or national organizations were sections of the International and were entitled to send delegates to the annual congress, which elected the members of the Central Council. In reality, however, a few people imposed their views during the debates at the Council's meetings and the congresses. Marx had shown already in the *Communist Manifesto* that he was not averse to sharply criticizing those political currents he disapproved of and showing them in a bad light by using negative qualifications such as 'utopian' and 'impractical'. Within the Central Council he pushed what he believed was a sound doctrine, if necessary by intrigue. The substantial influence of the anarchists, headed by his opponent Michael Bakunin, was countered at the congress of the International in The Hague in 1872 by Marx's proposal to transfer the General Council's seat to New York. The congress agreed and the First International practically ceased to exist, even if its formal dissolution did not take place until 1876. Marx, however, had succeeded in weakening Bakunin's influence.

No transnational advocacy network

This premature end made organizing workers once again a national affair, although the seed of internationalism had been sown. The First International succeeded in bringing the word 'International' into the dictionary, in the sense both of joining together internationally and of a political threat. The latter meaning was related to the International's publicly-declared revolutionary purpose and its support for the Paris Commune, the uprising of workers in the French capital in 1871. The International itself was 'a mere beginning in international labour organization', its Central Council 'a brilliant staff without an army'. The International distinguished itself from transnational advocacy networks, such as the anti-slavery and peace movements, which urged people at grassroots level to establish transnational relations, to exchange ideas and to learn from each other's experience. All activities that these networks normally undertook were absent in the International, which was dominated by a few leaders. 'It never succeeded in carrying out many of its objects such as publishing a bulletin, collecting statistics of labor, making reports on working conditions in different countries, or promoting international aid in wage movements' (Lorwin 1929, 58).

13.2 The liberal International League for Peace and Freedom (1867)

The ideals of peace and liberty

The frictions within the First International also played a role at the foundation congress of the *International League for Peace and Freedom* (ILPF) in 1867. Marx had recommended that the International's members should not apply for membership of the League, given its bourgeois-liberal character. However the Central Council proved unable to prevent more than one third of the delegates to the congress of the International, which took place in Lausanne, Switzerland, from 2–8 September, from attending in a personal capacity the congress of the International League, which was held from 9–12 September in Geneva. As a member of the International, Bakunin was also present at the League's congress, where he defended a programme that demanded radical change of the economic system and would lead to the liberation of the working classes and the elimination of the proletariat. When he discovered that he was being rebuffed by both sides and could not succeed in forging a union between the two associations, he dropped the League to set up his own organization (Lyons 1963, 175–76). The League attracted many politically-conscious workers and craftsmen, but its main appeal was the ideals of peace and freedom rather than its economic programme. Prepared thoroughly by French and Swiss peace activists and democrats, the League arose after a long period, during the 1850s and 1860s, without international peace congresses. Its founders appealed to the fact that great military monarchies deprived the people of their most vital liberties, maintained formidable armies and tended to suppress small states. They described the essential condition of a permanent peace between states as: 'liberty for each people and, with respect to their international relations, the establishment of a confederation of free democracies forming the United States of Europe'. The means of preparing and hastening the advent of a confederation of free people were the 'Return to the great principles of the Revolution which will finally become verities; revendication of all individual and political liberties; appeal to all moral energies, revival of conscience; diffusion of popular education; destruction of prejudices of race, nationality, sect, military spirit, etc.; abolition of standing armies; harmony of economic interests by liberty; harmony of politics and morals' (Van der Linden 1987, 682).

Establishment of the ILPF (1867)

The call to support this programme and to establish such a league was well received. Nearly 11,000 signatures, mainly from the Continent, were collected and the number of congress participants was over 6,000, which at the time was huge. The well-known Italian freedom fighter Giuseppe Garibaldi acted as honorary president of the Geneva congress in 1867, which decided to establish the International League for Peace and Freedom. Bakunin's departure meant the end of the debate on the social question and turned the ILPF into a 'real and normal peace society' (Van der Linden 1987, 776). The League was to convene a number of international congresses, the last one in 1879, and raise miscellaneous issues, such as the abolishment of standing armies, the relationship between peace and economic problems, federalism, suffrage, democracy and the question of nationalities. It was also converted to arbitration and, during the 1870s, was an active participant in the legal and political debates on this issue (Van der Linden 1987, 925). The ILPF, which was strongly influenced by Charles Lemonnier, was more than a peace society, given its strong democratic

149

interests and activities. 'It was republican, it was strongly for separation of church and state, it was political in the sense that it looked far beyond international arbitration or even disarmament to a new configuration of the continent' (Lyons 1963, 321). Whereas socialists such as Marx viewed the topics discussed in relation to the working class and the overthrow of capitalism as of primary importance, the League's liberals relied primarily on an enlightened middle class and favoured reforms of the economy. There were also differences in the ways of organizing, not least because the ILPF promoted debate and transnational ties among its members. Both political currents, however, had in common their assumption that peace would ensue once 'arbitrary and corrupt forms of government and sinister interests' had been overthrown by popular democratic pressure (Carter 1992, 6).

13.3 Women joining forces internationally and actions against trafficking in women

Acceptance of women by the ILPF and the foundation of the International Association of Women (1868)

The Swiss pacifist and feminist Marie Goegg-Pouchoulin felt encouraged by the foundation congress of the International League to establish an international women's association. Before the congress had taken place, a debate had been held among the founders on the question of whether women were to be admitted. A majority was in favour both of admitting women and of allowing them, if they wanted, to act as spokesperson, but this was not mentioned in the congress's code of order. No women spoke during the congress and the only (written) contribution by a woman ('ten articles against war') was read by a man. In February 1868 Goegg explained her plan to establish, together with the League, an international women's association in the ILPF's journal *Les Etats Unis d'Europe*. This association should coordinate its actions with the League, but also operate in a separate sphere. The *International Association of Women* (IAW) was founded in May and had the aim of promising the people liberty, education, welfare and fraternal union between them while also working for the intellectual and social improvement of women. Goegg became the IAW's president. Her objective was to organize women from all social classes and to allow them to exercise within a state the same rights as men, to do the same work and to engage in the same professions as men. Her involvement resulted in a statement by the League about the importance of women being socially and politically active. The code of order for the ILPF's second congress explicitly mentioned that women were admitted on the same conditions and with the same rights as men. Goegg's speech at this congress as president of the IAW and her nomination as the League's treasurer were regarded as unprecedented feats (Cooper 1985, 338). Almost all members of the diplomatic corps were present, accompanied by their wives (Van der Linden 1987, 815). Goegg's effort during the same year to also contribute to debates within the First International failed, since the International was not convinced of the necessity of paying particular attention to the position of women.

Equal pay as an international demand

In 1870 the International Association of Women convened its first congress in Bern. Many visitors were intrigued to hear women delivering speeches at a public meeting.

Goegg explained that the IAW wanted to end discrepancies between the sexes and called 'general' suffrage a misleading term as long as women remained excluded. The IAW was in favour of the emancipation of women in the field of education, as that would allow them to develop on an equal footing with men. In addition the IAW promoted the freedom for women to be employed in the labour market, according to the principle of equal pay for equal work. This demand made the IAW the first NGO to raise the issue of equal pay at international level.

The downfall of the IAW (1871)

The IAW organized small conferences, lectures and meetings as well as social gatherings. After setting up 'corresponding societies' of women, it succeeded in establishing 15 sections in France, Germany, Italy, Portugal, Switzerland, the UK and the US, and approached the parliaments in those states regarding its demands. The Franco–German War and the strongly negative reaction of the Swiss government to the Paris Commune of 1871, in particular because of the support of the First International for this uprising, resulted in the suppression of several organizations that had the word 'international' in their names, among them the IAW, because it had had relations with the International. Accused of misuse of power, Goegg had to resign her presidency in August 1871. This did not end the organization's international contacts, but the subtitle of the journal *Espérance*, published by women between the end of 1871 and 1875, no longer had the word 'international' in it. Despite the IAW's downfall, Goegg managed to continue part of her activities within the ILPF, which as a result of its liberal character was less affected by the anti-socialist mood.

Prostitution as repression of women

After some years the limited international contacts between women in the mid-1870s began to grow again and resulted in transnational advocacy networks, resembling the earlier ones in favour of the abolition of slavery and peace. In 1878 an international congress on women's rights was convened in Paris, which was attended by 220 people from 11 states. Two of Goegg's old speeches were reprinted for this meeting with her permission. Whereas the Continental delegations consisted of nearly equal numbers of women and men, there were scarcely any men in those from the UK and the US. Prostitution, also more neutrally referred to as 'vice', became a new issue on the agenda of equality for women. In the UK Josephine Butler had involved herself in the establishment of refuges for ill prostitutes. She regarded prostitution, at the time a taboo for ladies, as a form of persecution of women by men, rather than as a moral issue. She became the leader of a campaign against the state regulation of prostitution under the Contagious Diseases Acts of the late 1860s, which allowed the police to arrest any woman suspected of prostitution and to have her examined medically. If the woman refused she could be sentenced to imprisonment. Butler regarded these Acts as the repression of, and discrimination against, all women. After long, and often militant, campaigning she succeeded in having the Acts repealed in 1886.

Prostitution, temperance and women's suffrage

To gain international support for her work and to establish an international network, Butler undertook speaking tours to Paris, Lyon, Naples, Rome and Geneva in the winter

151

of 1874–75, which resulted in the *British, Continental and General Federation for the Abolition of the State Regulation of Prostitution* (later: International Federation). This NGO convened its first congress in 1875 in Liverpool, and in 1877 held a first international congress on prostitution (Charnovitz 1997, 203). Butler regarded her work in the field of public morals as part of the movement for equal rights. In 1873 she declared that when she was not working for repeal of the Contagious Diseases Acts she would throw her energy into getting suffrage. She saw having the vote as a means of self-preservation for women. After her success in 1886, she decided to move to other fronts of the same battle and began to investigate and expose child prostitution, expanding her campaigns to the Continent. Frances Willard, founder of the *World Women's Christian Temperance Union*, established in the US in 1883, also matched her zeal in the field of public morals with campaigning for suffrage. Her temperance work drew many women into politics for the first time, and the temperance union poured more money and organizers into the women's suffrage campaigns than any of the official suffrage organizations. The Union also engaged in issues of peace and security, and in 1887 set up a Peace Department. To protect girls and young women who had to travel to other cities and abroad, the *Union internationale des amies de la jeune fille* was established in 1877. During the 1880s this private Union managed to set up a network of national committees, which in very practical ways organized help for girls at railway stations and in large cities. The object of this decentralized and stable organization was 'to form a network of protection around every girl obliged to leave her home to earn a living, and so far as possible around every girl alone or in bad surroundings, whatever her nationality, religion or occupation' (Lyons 1963, 277).

The white slave trade exposed

As a result of the activities of the women's organizations in the field of prostitution, the international trafficking in women and girls, also referred to as the 'white slave trade', began to receive more attention. The women's organizations realized that prevention of trafficking across borders and measures against the organizers of the trade were beyond their competence and therefore decided to alert their national governments by raising public awareness. In 1880 Butler published her information on the recruitment of British girls for Belgian brothels and her women's network arranged that newspapers would publish details. Although the accusations were challenged by the Belgian police authorities, public opinion was disconcerted and investigations began. Butler published a detailed statement and was asked by Belgian authorities to repeat her accusations on oath before an English magistrate. This eventually resulted in arrests, trials and the imprisonment of some traffickers in Belgium. In the UK an official commission of inquiry was set up. In 1885 the journalist and peace activist William Stead decided to put some pressure on this still ongoing inquiry by publishing a series of articles and, with the help of the Salvation Army, by demonstrating how easy it was to arrange for the purchase of a young child for a few pounds and to send her to a Continental brothel. He was put on trial after he had entered the girl's room (to secure her) and was sent to prison. Bramwell Booth of the Salvation Army, who had helped to secure the girl, was also put on trial but was acquitted. Their action resulted in immense publicity and, together with disclosures by the official commission of inquiry, in a change in British law (Lyons 1963, 280). New bilateral agreements were adopted, which also decreased the trade in women and girls.

The convention against traffic in women (1904)

During the late 1890s a private organization in the UK called for an international solution to the problem of trade in women. As a result an international congress was held in London in 1899 and the *International Bureau for the Suppression of Traffic in Women and Children* was established (Charnovitz 1997, 203). This private Bureau collected information on girls who were abducted in a number of states and exerted pressure on governments to take measures. At the initiative of France, but as a result of public pressure, a first 'technical' conference was convened in Paris in 1902, with the aim of harmonizing national penal codes against traffickers by establishing a relevant national authority and procedures to inform each other. Fifteen European states and Brazil agreed on a draft convention, but this received insufficient support in domestic politics. A diplomatic congress in 1904, however, agreed the *International Convention for the Suppression of the White Slave Traffic*. This received enough ratifications and came into force in 1905.

Strengthening and expanding the Convention (1910)

As a result of the Convention, national legislation began to be tightened. The trafficking in women within Europe was reduced, but trade with Asia and Latin America increased. These shifts in the market were an incentive for a new round of decision making. In 1906 another conference, of both governments and NGOs, was held in Paris, and adopted resolutions urging governments to be more active. In 1908 private organizations called a conference about obscene publications and pornography, which also discussed the progress with regard to trafficking in women and children. This conference decided to approach the parties to the 1904 Convention, and proposed a strengthening and expansion of the Convention by including the issue of obscene publications. In 1910 a diplomatic conference of governments, with various NGO representatives in their delegations, agreed on a revised and stronger Convention (Charnovitz 1997, 210) and on an international agreement for the suppression of the circulation of obscene publications. Governments undertook to recommend to their legislatures 'the necessary steps to punish these offences according to their gravity', to inform each other through the French government about their legislation and to specify the offences for which extradition might be granted (Lyons 1963, 284). The amended 1910 Convention made the London-based International Bureau a central organ for purposes of communication, while in some states specific police authorities were designated to act as national bureaus (Reinsch 1911, 66).

13.4 International campaigning for women's suffrage

Political rights and social reforms

Elizabeth Cady Stanton, the draughtswoman of the *Declaration of Sentiments* of 1848 (see §4.3), and Susan B. Anthony, who had met her at an anti-slavery meeting in the early 1850s, visited the UK and France in 1883. Stanton believed that the time for international action on women's suffrage had come. The electoral reform of 1869 in the US had given the vote to black men, but had still excluded all women. The women's movement in Europe was supported by the publication of the book *The Subjection of Women* in 1869, written by the English liberal philosopher and economist John Stuart Mill, together with his wife Harriet Taylor and her daughter Helen Taylor (the publisher mentioned only his name). The book was a general plea for the granting of equal rights to women and men in the social and political fields. It was translated into many languages and widely read. At a meeting of British and other European women in Liverpool in 1883, Stanton, Anthony and other champions of women's suffrage set up a *Committee of Correspondence*. This proved fairly unsuccessful, and in 1887 Anthony revived Stanton's initiative. Anthony had once been prevented from speaking at a temperance rally because of her sex and had learned to fight prejudices against women. In 1868 she had founded a radical journal which demanded women's suffrage. Its motto was: 'men, their rights and nothing more; women, their rights and nothing less'. Anthony now proposed to widen the social basis of the international suffrage movement. As well as women fighting for political rights, she wanted to include those favouring reforms in other fields without necessarily being advocates for suffrage. She received support from Frances Willard of the World Women's Christian Temperance Union and from May Wright Sewall, who was engaged in issues such as education, social hygiene and reform clothes (to replace the restrictive corset). Younger women felt more attracted to these non-political reforms than to political rights. Reform movements also occurred elsewhere, such as the campaign in China against foot binding (see Figure 13.1).

Figure 13.1 The campaign against foot binding in China

The non-acceptance of certain social practices with regard to women, followed by actions to change the situation, also took place with regard to **the Chinese habit of foot binding**. Tightly wrapping a young girl's feet to prevent growth was not only painful, but in the end also created an obstacle to a woman's freedom of movement. In the 1870s missionaries working in the Chinese harbour cities that had been opened were among the first to criticize this practice. In the 1890s a wider national reform movement arose in China, but it was suppressed after a while. The campaign against foot binding, initiated by Western women, managed to stay active and it received more and more support and initiatives from Chinese women, who from 1908 onwards were leading the actions. A successful articulation between anti-foot binding and Chinese traditionalism at the turn of the century allowed the campaign to succeed rapidly. After a first anti-foot-binding Edict in 1902, when it came to power in 1911 the new republican and nationalist government banned the practice altogether. This change was the result of a moral and political campaign, using networks 'where both foreign and domestic actors were crucial to the success of the campaign, with foreign actors instrumental in "first rolling the stone" and domestic actors framing the issue to resonate with domestic audiences and generating the broad-based support necessary for success' (Keck and Sikkink 1998, 65).

The establishment of the International Council of Women (1888)

With the encouragement of Willard and Sewall, a conference was called in Washington DC in March 1888 to celebrate the 40th anniversary of the meeting in Seneca Falls and its *Declaration of Sentiments* (see §4.3). Following Anthony's policy, the call went out to 'all women of light and learning, to all associations of women in trades, professions and reforms, as well as to those advocating political rights' (Rupp 1997, 15). Fifty-three women's organizations participated, with 49 delegates from Canada, Denmark, Finland, France, India, Norway, the UK and the US. The meeting was also used to found the *International Council of Women* (ICW), which proclaimed itself in favour of the free opening of all institutions of learning to women, industrial training for both sexes, equal wages to be paid for equal work and an identical standard of personal purity and morality for women and men (ICW 1966, 14). The ICW's objectives were the provision of both a means of communication between women's organizations in all states, and opportunities for women from all parts of the world to meet and discuss questions relating to 'the welfare of the commonwealth and the family'. The constitution laid down that affiliation was open only to national councils of women, thus encouraging the formation of such councils. During the first five years the only national council was the American one, also founded in 1888. This meant that for some time the ICW in effect was a purely American organization, even if some foreign women were members of the Executive Committee. Creating national councils was not yet successful, despite speaking tours by Sewall and others in Europe. The women also visited world exhibitions. During the exhibition of 1889 in Paris, in celebration of the first centenary of the French Revolution, a women's congress under the auspices of the French government took place that helped to spread the idea of national councils. At the world exhibition in Chicago in 1893, the ICW convened a World Congress of Representative Women. During the remainder of the 1890s a number of national councils were established (among them in Canada in 1893, Germany in 1897, and the UK and Sweden in 1898). From 1900 onwards the dominant position of American women on the ICW Executive Committee diminished.

The International Woman Suffrage Alliance splitting off (1904)

The ICW programme was wide-ranging and characterized by a strong idealism, which helped to attract large numbers of women. However, the organization was rather conservative in its policies and even had the reputation of an aristocratic body, in part because of its long-time president Lady Aberdeen (Rupp 1997, 20). The strategy of also attracting non-politicized women did not satisfy those who were fighting for women's suffrage, and resulted in friction and plans to set up a separate suffrage organization. After a preparatory meeting in Washington in 1902, a split took place at the ICW congress in Berlin in 1904. This resulted in the foundation of the *International Woman Suffrage Alliance* (IWSA). Under the leadership of Carrie Chapman Catt, this new organization provided the more radical proponents of women's suffrage with a high-profile forum to exchange views and experience at international level. Six years later the IWSA had affiliates in 25 states.

The women's suffrage campaign

Compared with the ICW, the IWSA represented a minority movement among women and their organizations. Internally there were more fractions and differences of opinion, partly due to the fact that several organizations from one state could be members, partly due to friction on issues such as limited or universal suffrage. Whereas the ICW 'increasingly dominated by aristocrats and patronised by governments, represented its official, "establishment" aspect' (Evans 1977, 252), the IWSA embodied a greater sense of urgency and a dynamic side of feminism. It played a role for national organizations favouring women's suffrage 'both by providing the means for the different national societies to meet and to benefit from each other's experience, and by giving them a sense of solidarity and of belonging to a crusade which was being carried on simultaneously all over the world. In a struggle such as the campaign for women's suffrage, where prejudice died hard and where opposition was often extremely bitter, this sense of solidarity and fellowship was an invaluable support – and the kind of support which only an international association could give' (Lyons 1963, 272). In comparison with the anti-slavery movement, the suffrage campaign relied more on symbolic and pressure politics than on information politics (see §4.1). 'The problem women faced was more about entrenched social attitudes and practices than lack of information or understanding.' In this field it was impossible to use international standards and norms against governments. 'Nowhere did women find powerful foreign organizations or governments willing to use leverage or devote resources to promote woman suffrage beyond their borders, nor were suffrage organizations able to use accountability politics, for no governments accepted international obligations to which they could later be held accountable.' Instead, symbolic politics with striking events such as arrests, meant to draw public attention, and ongoing pressure, both politically and morally, were used: 'when peaceful tactics produced meager results they sometimes turned to civil disobedience and provocation'. The IWSA had a lot in common with the militant British 'suffragettes' led by the Pankhurst family: 'suffrage activists were prepared to break the law to gain attention to their cause, and to go to jail defending their beliefs' (Keck and Sikkink 1998, 54).

13.5 The national orientation of the Second International and international trade unions

The Second International (1889)

At the end of the 1880s, the idea began to emerge among socialist groupings in Europe that the creation of an international organization might support their pursuit of social reform. In the summer of 1886, when an international labour exhibition was held in Paris, French socialists, known as 'Possibilists', and British trade unionists met at an international workers' conference to discuss, among other issues, the relevance of international labour legislation, the regulation of the working day and the usefulness of cooperatives (see Figure 13.2 for the cooperative movement). They decided that the French would call an international workers' congress in Paris in 1889, when the centenary of the French Revolution was to be celebrated. An international trade union congress in London in November 1888 confirmed this decision. In February 1889, however, a group of rival, more Marxist socialists, known as 'Guesdists', also decided to call an international workers' congress in Paris that year. As it proved impossible to join forces, Paris thus hosted two international workers' congresses in July 1889. That organized by the Guesdists, with representatives from European states, Argentina and the US, established the *Second International*, at least that was the name given by the press to this combination of socialist parties from various states.

The First of May (1890)

Until 1900 the Second, or Socialist, International showed itself by organizing international congresses every few years. There was no secretariat or executive body with the authority to issue statements on behalf of the International, and no constitution or code of order. The organization of the congresses was taken care of by the parties in the hosting state. Resolutions adopted at congresses were not binding and had mainly moral importance. It was not until 1900 that this situation changed somewhat, through the establishment of an *International Socialist Bureau* in Brussels. But in the new configuration the socialist parties still remained autonomous entities. The Bureau provided a means of communication between the parties and had to prepare the congresses. Its apparatus, however, was rudimentary and without effective power. An Interparliamentary Commission, set up to coordinate action between the parliamentary groups in each state, was stillborn and in 1906 had its functions taken over by the Bureau, which served chiefly 'as a clearinghouse for information and correspondence' (Lyons 1963, 184). The strongest signal given by this International was the arranging of an international demonstration on 1 May 1890 in favour of the eight-hour day, a demand addressed to both employers and governments, thus laying the foundation for the international socialist tradition of May Day, with its strong connotation of 'international solidarity'.

Inclusion in national politics

Despite its pretence of universality, the core of the Second International consisted of European parties. The American delegates did not play a role of any importance, given the different position of labour in American society, and the delegates from Asia represented little more than a colonial society (India) and an insignificant minority (Japan). At first the congresses of this International were dominated by differences of opinion between the various socialist strands, and between them and the anarchists. But from 1896 onwards the two main issues were the transformation from capitalist to socialist production and property relations, and participation in parliamentary and legislative work. The national political systems provided the main context for these debates, because most workers were 'excluded' from their national systems, given the existing suffrage arrangements. In numerous states, socialist parties were not recognized or even forbidden. Socialist organizations therefore focused on recognition of their demands and participation in national politics through being given the vote and having the opportunity to send their representatives to parliament. This process of recognition of political rights is described as a process of 'inclusion' in national politics.

Politico-strategic debates and differences of opinion

The theoretical debates of the Second International were dominated by the Germans August Bebel and Karl Kautsky. Their main opponent, the Frenchman Jean Jaurès, aroused his co-socialists' wrath by standing up for Alfred Dreyfus, a French officer falsely accused of selling military secrets to Germany in 1894 and sentenced to imprisonment. The outcome of this controversial affair, based on anti-Semitic prejudice, changed power relations in French politics in favour of the left. Alexandre Millerand's acceptance of a ministerial position in 1899 strongly influenced the debate on how to overthrow capitalism. The question was raised of whether capitalism could be transformed gradually, if it was not abolished at once. If so, improvements for the working and middle classes had to be gained step-by-step within national politics, as the German 'revisionist' Eduard Bernstein argued. During the early twentieth century, the more radical socialists defended the 'weapon' of a general strike, meant to overthrow capitalism at once. However, this could only be effective if it was used universally and simultaneously, and with regard to practical international solidarity the Second International was powerless: 'simultaneity depended upon universality, and there was no universality. There was no overwhelming urge to use the weapon in any one country – not even in France' (Lyons 1963, 189).

Special protection of women

In addition to strategy, the struggle against militarism and the issue of international legislation were also found on the agendas of the congresses of the Second International. Peace was seen as a necessary condition for the emancipation of the workers. With regard to women's rights there was a theoretical defence of equal rights for women, but in practice it was hard for women to gain their own place and programme within the movement. In the male-dominated International, women's suffrage was secondary to men's suffrage and the socialists defended the special protection of women with regard to work. Unlike feminists, who regarded special protection (such as the prohibition of night work for women; see §14.2) as discrimination against women, socialists emphasized the role of women in the family and as mothers.

The choice of national defence (1914)

The main characteristic of the Second International as an international institution was that it internationalized the internal controversies of its member parties, rather than affecting its member parties through common policies or bringing about joint action against governments or at intergovernmental level. This made the International a reflection of the development of its individual member parties, as was painfully demonstrated in August 1914, when a majority of national parties opted for national defence and the Second International proved incapable of being a guarantor against war, as it had always promised. While the socialists had denounced the war as a 'universal imperialist aggression' in which socialists should not be engaged, they made a complete about-turn in August, when they converted the war in their minds to 'general national defence'. 'The Second International had failed' (Lorwin 1929, 139). This dramatic choice of a national orientation, without any form of international solidarity, ended the Second International's existence in the summer of 1914. As strong as it had been in fostering a feeling of international solidarity between workers from different states, in the field of international relations the Second International was not a factor of any importance. Its focus on 'inclusion' in national politics had kept the organization, just like its predecessor, restricted to being an international platform for political strategists. Unlike the women's movement, the workers' movement of the Second International had not set up transnational advocacy networks or ventured into international action at intergovernmental level.

The creation of international trade secretariats in the 1890s

The international trade union movement did not arise until the end of the nineteenth century, when trade unions were strong enough to organize internationally. The international trade union congress in 1888 in London, mentioned above, was the first practical effort to bring trade unionists together, although tailors and other occupational groups had had international contacts for a long time, through still-practised guild traditions of sending apprentices on a tour of a number of states to thoroughly learn their

Figure 13.2 The International Co-operative Alliance (1895)

In addition to political parties, action groups and trade unions, the workers' movement had also established producer and consumer cooperatives. For a long time the cooperative movement was a British working-class phenomenon, strongly promoted by Robert Owen, who in 1835 had launched an 'Association of all classes of all nations', for the purpose of promoting his notion of moral regeneration through social and economic cooperation. Although the idea of international cooperation was being expressed more often, it was not until 1895 that the **International Co-operative Alliance** was established at an international conference. Because of insufficient resources this Alliance could do little more than produce international statistics. In 1907 the agricultural cooperative societies decided to found their own international confederation. This, however, was a 'blessing in disguise', as it forced the Alliance to restrain itself and, instead of becoming an international parliament for cooperation, to develop into an organization for advancing the interests of consumers' societies (Lyons 1963, 197). In 1910 the Alliance was strengthened as an organization when various ideological provisos were removed. The most important function this international NGO fulfilled, which it shared with other organizations, was the exchange of views and information through publications and congresses. At the 1913 congress strong feelings of international brotherhood were aroused, which resulted in a long and fervent resolution in favour of international peace. The First World War brought the Alliance to a standstill, but, unlike the Second International, did not cause its downfall, as the cooperatives' activities were too practical. International congresses were resumed in 1921.

trade. Tobacco workers had already formed an international trade secretariat in 1876, but the real beginning of this type of NGO came in the years after 1888: hatters and shoemakers (1889), miners (1890), glassworkers and typographical workers (1892), clothing workers and railwaymen (1893), fur workers and textile workers (1894), lithographers, seafarers and dockers (1896), metal workers (1898), clerical workers (1900) and diamond workers (1905). The number of international trade secretariats was 17 in 1900 and 28 in 1910. The practical work of these *international trade secretariats*, which combined national trade unions of workers in the same occupational group, was to spread information about trade conditions in different states, keep members informed about strikes in their trade, prevent workers from one state acting as strike-breakers in another, make appeals for financial help if there were extensive strikes, and promote trade unionism. As a whole, the work of the secretariats was 'narrow in scope and modest in results' (Lorwin 1929, 99). The work, however, was useful, 'especially in those industries, like merchant shipping, whose international character required some form of international exchange of information' (Windmuller 1980, 24). The secretariats were based on the 'presumed existence of an international community of interests, a set of shared problems and experiences, and an expectation of increased strength through mutual help' (Windmuller 1980, 23). In 1910, 24 out of 28 secretariats were based in Berlin. The most important secretariat outside Germany was that of the transport workers in London. Since most of the national affiliates were part of the socialist movement in their own state, they identified with the Second International. Because the Berlin-based international secretariats used the bureaus of the German national unions, the German socialist workers' movement, which also dominated the Second International, had a strong hold over these international trade secretariats. The job of international secretary was 'a spare-time one and not too exacting, though it is clear from the rules drawn up by these various bodies that their intentions at least were imposing' (Lyons 1963, 158).

International Secretariat of National Centres of Trade Unions (1901)

A second type of international trade unionism came into being in 1901, when national trade union federations (overarching national federations of trade unions from several occupational groups) decided to establish the *International Secretariat of National Centres of Trade Unions*. In this case, too, most of the costs and the work were German concerns. This was acceptable, given the long and successful struggle the German unions had waged against Bismarck's anti-socialist campaign (see §14.1). Another argument in favour of Germany was its central geographical situation and the movement of labour across its many borders, which meant labour problems were thought of in international terms. German trade unions furthermore followed a model of highly-centralized, well-disciplined, financially strong unions, extensive benefit features and peaceful methods of collective bargaining (Lorwin 1929, 102–3). When the International Secretariat was established, organizational views had not been finalized, as debates about setting up permanent international institutions were still going on. There was slow progress in organizational terms in 1903 and 1905, but more and more matters were settled, such as: only national federations could be affiliated and not individual unions; a subscription rate per 1,000 national members; in order to represent a state a delegate must reside in that state; and conferences would take place every other year. Nonetheless, the International Secretariat remained 'a very loose-knit organization' (Lyons 1963, 160). Congressional frequency did not add much to a further strengthening of the organization. The International Secretariat's name was changed to the *International Federation of Trade Unions* (IFTU) in 1913, when it started to issue its own journal in three languages. The International Secretariat's and IFTU's functions remained restricted to the exchange of information, the prevention of strike breaking by the importation of foreign labour and help for strikers.

Subordination to the Second International

With regard to the question of how far the international trade union movement ought to involve itself in politics, the International Secretariat was set up as non-political and concerned only with trade union matters in the strictest sense, while the Second International was responsible for all political and policy questions. Among the International Secretariat's own responsibilities were 'the promoting of closer association between the trade unions of all countries, the collection of uniform trade statistics, the provision of mutual support in industrial conflicts, and all other questions directly relating to the trade union organization of the working-class', but not: 'All theoretical questions and questions affecting the tendencies and tactics of the trade union movement in the various countries' (Lyons 1963, 163). After its reorganization as IFTU in 1913, the international trade secretariats convened their first joint international conference, to discuss the strengthening of their position *vis-à-vis* the IFTU. In 1914 the international trade secretariats represented 5.2 million members of trade unions, the IFTU 6.8 million. The general idea of international trade union organization was based on a 1907 gentleman's agreement, stating that individual unions should be affiliated both to their national trade union federation – and through that to the IFTU – and to their international trade secretariat. In 1913, shortly before the international trade union movement was to be paralysed by the outbreak of the First World War, it was said jokingly that the international organizations, with a total of 12 employees, had grown from a 'mailbox' into a 'well-organised post office' (Reinalda 1997, 12).

International labour conventions (1906) and the foundation for the welfare state

14.1 How governments became involved in international labour regulation

Labour and competition between states

That governments began to conclude international conventions with regard to labour was not a consequence of the international labour movement, although the mere fact of workers organizing nationally and internationally contributed to the process. Rather than by workers' organizations, international regulation of labour was brought about by socially-engaged employers, economists and lawyers, as well as by an NGO that was based on their ideas and actions. The first to argue for this was the entrepreneur Robert Owen, who became known as the 'father of English Socialism'. He believed that modern industrial conditions caused hardship to many workers, which could be avoided by international coordination. In 1818 he even travelled to the diplomatic follow-up conference of Vienna in Aix-la-Chapelle (see Figure 2.3) in order to explain his views to the governmental representatives. He declared that setting the legal limits of the normal working day for the industrial classes of Europe internationally was a priority for the governments of Europe and invited the conference to appoint a commission to report on this subject (Johnston 1970, 5). But his understanding that modern industrial capitalism was creating an international problem, which could be solved by the emerging system of multilateral conferences, was ahead of its time. The governmental representatives did not understand him, taking him for an eccentric (Lyons 1963, 136). The British humanitarian entrepreneur Charles Hindley also had an international perspective, as he explained to the commission investigating factory conditions in the UK in 1833. He feared that a shortening of the working day might be stopped by increased international competition.

He admitted that shorter working hours would raise British prices, but also believed that technical superiority, the skill of the workers and the concentration of British industry would allow successful competition for many years. In case of increased and excessive competition, however, it would be necessary to deal with the problem through bilateral conventions. 'I think it would be as proper a subject of treaty with foreign nations as the annihilation of the slave trade.' In 1840 the French economist Jérome Adolphe Blanqui went one step further, by arguing in the French parliament that the regulation of the working day should be the subject of a multilateral treaty. He suggested that 'all nations should unite in accepting the principle that there should be some agreed limitation of the working-day' (Lyons 1963, 137).

Fears about revolution and pleas for an international labour code

During the 1840s, the Alsatian entrepreneur Daniel Legrand understood the fears concerning rebellious workers and argued that reforming labour legislation might help avert revolution. He approached the French, British, Russian and Swiss governments, as well as the Zollverein, in the hope of inducing them to enact 'an international law to protect the working class against work excessive in amount and at too early an age, the primary and principal cause of its physical deterioration, its moral degradation and its deprivation of the blessings of family life' (Johnston 1970, 6). He wanted to extend the benefits of the Prussian factory law of 1839 as widely as possible, but received no response. In 1844 he drew up a more ambitious proposal, for an international labour code, which he was to elaborate and improve several times. He persisted in approaching princes, ministers and diplomats in Europe and the US. His schemes advocated a 12-hour day and the prohibition of almost all night work. Legrand went further than any of his predecessors, arguing that international regulation would be part of the new trend in world politics. 'International conventions become a necessity and a sacred duty in an epoch in which the happy influence of the gospel on the inhabitants of both hemispheres, the press, industry, commerce and in general all material and spiritual forces point to the solidarity of nations' (Lyons 1963, 139). In 1843 the Belgian expert in criminal law and researcher of industrial relations Edouard Ducpétiaux argued that the already existing benevolent societies should be linked internationally. He did this in an appendix to his study of the physical and moral conditions of young workers in industry. He proposed an *International Association for the Progress of Moral and Social Sciences* in order to spread ideas about charity in an organized way, as it had been done before for the abolition of the slave trade and for temperance. 'The power of the principle of association in forwarding social and humanitarian projects cannot be doubted' (Lyons 1963, 140). It was not until 1856 that the first of a series of private *congrès internationaux de bienfaisance* was held in Brussels. The topic of international factory legislation was postponed until the congress of 1857, when a cautious resolution was passed laying down that 'the principal states act in concert to decide upon international measures for the regulation of industry', albeit without invading the 'legitimate interests of the manufacturers' (Lyons 1963, 141). Ducpétiaux also was ahead of his time.

Domestic politics and governmental international concern: Switzerland

Due to the increasing pace of modern industrialism and the mounting pressure of international competition governments became more aware of the social dimensions of their national economies. The doctrine of *laissez-faire* began to weaken and in 1877 Switzerland passed a federal law to harmonize the situation in all cantons, prohibiting child labour under 14, forbidding night labour for persons between the ages of 14 and 18, and limiting the working day to 11 hours for all workers. The President of the Swiss National Council, Emil Frey, warned the Swiss that a federal solution might not be enough and that Switzerland should consider the possibility of concluding a series of treaties with other states 'in order to secure as close harmony as possible in the factory legislation of the various industrial states'. Swiss manufacturers immediately complained that they could no longer beat foreign competition, and demanded a revision of the law of 1877. Workers' organizations, however, were in favour of retaining it. They petitioned the government, asking it to negotiate with other governments to pave the way for international legislation, 'whether it be in the form of a convention, such as the Geneva Convention on the care of the wounded in war-time, or in the form of such agreements as the Universal Postal Union' (Lyons 1963, 142). In May 1881 the Swiss government took up this demand and explored the attitude of a few governments, but was met with unwillingness to intervene between employers and workers (Johnston 1970, 7).

International workers' congresses on international labour legislation

At a meeting in Zurich in 1883, the disappointed trade unions urged the federal government to reopen negotiations. Simultaneously they approached trade unions in other states, requesting them to support their views on international labour legislation. This action explains why the issue also was on the agendas of the international workers' congresses in 1886, 1888 and 1889 that would lead to the establishment of the Second International (see §13.5). However, the participants in these congresses were concerned with setting up an organization in favour of class war, rather than with discussing international treaties. This meant that international labour legislation played only a minor role at these congresses. But the issue had been raised in the French parliament in 1884, where Count Albert de Mun had asked 'why, if international conventions have been concluded to regulate the laws of war and to facilitate postal services, they should not also be concluded to regulate labour conditions' (Lyons 1963, 141). In 1885 a group of socialist deputies produced a draft law, which also suggested that an international labour office should be established, but it was not adopted (Johnston 1970, 7). In 1887 Swiss trade unions, which had succeeded in obtaining support from some Catholic unions established in France, Germany and Switzerland itself, summoned a congress at Aarau. 'The gathering was notable in that it combined both Catholics and socialists and that both agreed, for the time being at any rate, to sink their doctrinal differences and urge on the Swiss government the necessity of approaching the powers of Europe once more' (Lyons 1963, 143).

The Swiss government calling an international conference (1889)

In March 1889, the Swiss government approached the 13 governments most likely to beinterested by circular letter, proposing a conference to consider certain issues and to recommend to governments whatever might be felt desirable to regulate by international agreement. Issues mentioned were Sunday labour, a minimum age for the admission of children into industry, limitation of the working day for minors, prohibition of the employment of women and minors in unhealthy and dangerous trades and limitation of night work for women and minors, as well as the ways and means of implementing international conventions in these fields. Since by now governments had gained more insight into the international dimensions of labour conditions, most of the states circularized, with the exception of Russia, agreed to participate in the proposed conference. In January 1890 the Swiss government sent a detailed agenda and fixed the date of the conference for 5 May 1890.

Domestic politics and governmental international concern: Germany

The young and energetic German emperor William II, who had come to the throne in 1888, upset the Swiss plans by instructing his Chancellor, Otto von Bismarck, to prepare a similar conference, to be convened by the emperor shortly. Thus the emperor, who did not want to remain in the shadow of Bismarck, put pressure on the powerful Chancellor and also created an opportunity to equalize labour conditions between Germany and France. In his attitude to the labour question the emperor differed sharply from Bismarck, who had been engaged in a long and fervent struggle against the rising socialist movement. From 1878 onwards Bismarck had persecuted numerous socialists under his anti-socialist law, and in order to counter the ensuing dissatisfaction among workers he had begun introducing social insurance schemes. Despite Bismarck's repression of socialists, debates had been held about the relationship between labour legislation and international competition as well as the introduction of international conventions. So-called socialists of the chair (intellectuals known as *Katheder-Sozialisten*) had declared themselves in favour of international treaties, and in 1885 even Bismarck himself had considered the possibility of international solutions, since effective labour legislation would also strengthen the ties between workers and their nation-state. But when a motion favouring international labour legislation was introduced in the German parliament, Bismarck pointed out that a maximum length of the working day in Germany would be possible only if that was agreed internationally 'by means of a union analogous to that of the Universal Postal Union', something he considered 'impossible in the world in which we live' (Lyons 1963, 145). The motion was defeated, but the heated discussions gave publicity to the idea of international labour legislation (Johnston 1970, 7). As a result of the debates and the stronger position of the socialists, Bismarck lost the elections in February 1890 and left politics.

The intergovernmental conference in Berlin (1890)

Meanwhile the Swiss had accepted the new situation, despite their obvious annoyance. The alternative conference called by the emperor was speedily organized to take place in Berlin in March 1890. It was made clear in advance that no conventions would emanate from this multilateral conference. Instead resolutions were to be passed, with 'it is desirable' phrases on issues such as underground employment of women or children, Sunday rest with exceptions and child labour in factories and in unhealthy or dangerous occupations. There was a large measure of agreement about most of these issues, but also a sharp difference of opinion on monitoring the implementation of the resolutions. Germany preferred to restrict this to each government appointing a number of officials to investigate and report annually about the extent of implementation. Their reports would contain relevant statistics, copies of factory laws and other related documents, and would be exchanged at follow-up conferences. The Swiss, however, had further-reaching ideas. 'They wanted "obligatory arrangements" – in effect a convention – to be concluded among the participating states, and they also wanted a permanent bureau to co-ordinate and publish information and to arrange for further conferences. In short, they wished to apply to factory legislation machinery which had already become thoroughly familiar in other fields' (Lyons 1963, 147). Most governments supported the German proposal. This was adopted, however, without providing for follow-up conferences. Despite the meagre result of the negotiations, the conference received wide publicity, and the very fact that an official diplomatic conference had gathered on the issue implied that governments were taking international labour regulation seriously. Various states began to introduce labour regulation and even the German law of 1891, which was the foundation for the labour code for years to come, was influenced by the Berlin conference of 1890.

14.2 An NGO for international labour legislation (1900) and the 1906 labour conventions

Laissez-faire *or intervention?*

The thread of international labour legislation was picked up again in 1897, when the Swiss trade unions, once again as a combination of socialist and Catholic unions, convened an international congress on labour protection in Zurich, with 400 delegates and 200 observers from 13 European states and the US. There were many issues on the agenda and at the end of the congress a series of resolutions was passed, which together constituted an almost ideal programme. The Swiss government was asked to invite other states to consider setting up an international labour office. Almost simultaneously a group of intellectuals composed of lawyers and economists from France, Germany and Switzerland met at a conference, with both *laissez-faire* supporters and *interventionists*, which provided the advocates of international labour legislation (the interventionists) with the arguments for going a stage further. They appointed a commission to draft the statutes of a private, but government-oriented, international association. In July 1900 a meeting in Paris discussed the draft, which was accepted despite strong differences of opinion. A committee of six people was appointed to prepare the first congress, to be held in Switzerland. The *International Association for Labour Legislation* (IALL) was founded in the same year. The Association consisted of national sections and had the *International Labour Office* in Basel as its executive organ.

The International Labour Office in Basel (1901)

The International Labour Office's tasks were to publish all labour laws, reports and other relevant documents, to promote the study of national labour laws and their harmonization, and to maintain relations among reformers in the various states. The Office in Basel began to function in May 1901 and ceased to operate in 1919, when its activities were taken over by the International Labour Organization (ILO) in Geneva (see Chapter 17). While being established the IALL decided to limit its immediate objectives regarding international conventions to two issues that were recognized widely, enabling the IALL to investigate them and to make recommendations to governments. These issues were night work for women and the use of industrial poisons, in particular white lead and phosphorus (Lyons 1963, 151). The reasons for this restriction were that the IALL was not representing employers, trade unions or governments, nor could it demand the necessary information in its investigations into industrial questions. Therefore it suffered from fundamental weaknesses for an organization that promoted international agreements (Johnston 1970, 9). The IALL, however, did collect and analyse information on the two issues and forwarded its reports to governments. With regard to the proposals about women's work, it was known that the social–democrats approved them, as during the 1890s they had discussed special protection of women extensively. In addition to the IALL other international NGOs were also active in the field of labour relations, such as in social insurance, occupational diseases and unemployment (see Figure 14.1).

Figure 14.1 INGOs in the field of labour relations

The *International Association for Labour Legislation* was not the only international NGO concerned with labour issues from a socio-liberal perspective. Other NGOs in this field were the *International Federation for the Observation of Sunday* (founded in 1876), the *Permanent International Committee on Social Insurance* (1889), the *International Congress on Occupational Diseases* (1906) and the *International Association on Unemployment* (1910). The first international congress on unemployment was held in 1906, with representatives from governmental labour bureaus, international trade unions and charitable organizations. The congress recommended the creation of an international employment exchange, but no action was taken (Charnovitz 1997, 204). In 1925 the International Association for Labour Legislation merged with the NGOs for social insurance and unemployment to form the **International Association for Social Progress** (Ghebali 1989, 5; Charnovitz 1997, 194).

Governmental presence and the Franco-Italian Treaty (1904)

Governmental representatives, from both Europe and the US, had already attended the IALL founding conference of 1900 (Charnovitz 1997, 204). Governments were impressed by the usefulness of the work done by the IALL and began to send more official observers to its conferences, with their number rising from four in 1901 to 22 in 1912. The expenses of the International Labour Office were partly paid for out of contributions from national sections, but to a greater extent through subscriptions from governments (Reinsch 1911, 48). Governments also began to agree on labour issues in bilateral treaties. In 1904 France and Italy negotiated a treaty on access to social benefits for each other's workers, an initiative which would be widely copied by other states in Europe, resulting in 27 such agreements by 1914. The *Franco-Italian Treaty* of 1904 changed the existing situation where foreign workers were not entitled to the same privileges with regard to welfare legislation as the natives of the state. In the new Treaty France agreed to give Italian immigrant workers access to the social benefits enjoyed by French workers, while Italy undertook to enact more progressive labour laws so as to bring its legislation in line with France. Both states profited from this Treaty. Remarkably, this and other bilateral treaties were not regarded as substitutes for international conventions, but rather as bridges over which states might proceed towards such conventions. Article 3 of the Treaty read: 'In cases where the initiative is taken by one state to convoke various other states to an international conference with a view to unifying, by common agreement, certain laws for the protection of work-people, the adherence of one of the two contracting states to the proposed conference shall entail in principle a favourable reply from the other contracting state' (cited in Lyons 1963, 156).

The Swiss government's move (1905)

In 1905 the Swiss government once more initiated a call to convene an international conference on labour regulation, regarding the two issues the International Association for Labour Legislation had been investigating. This time it received a greater response. It was agreed to first hold a conference of experts, and then a diplomatic one if agreement among experts seemed feasible. The expert conference of 1905 was attended by governmental delegates from Austria-Hungary, Belgium, Denmark, France, Germany, Greece, Italy, Luxembourg, the Netherlands, Norway, Portugal, Romania, Serbia, Spain, Sweden and the UK. Despite this large attendance, various states that used the poisonous phosphorus extensively in making matches, such as Japan, British India, Egypt and Turkey, had not been invited. This caused a debate on whether it made sense to conclude a convention without them. A draft of only four clauses was agreed, with several states abstaining. Consensus on night work for women was wider, although the UK refused to sign as it claimed that night work for women had already been abolished 30 years earlier. It was agreed to convene a diplomatic conference on both issues in Bern in 1906.

Changes in British domestic politics and the conference in Bern (1906)

The draft *International Convention Respecting the Prohibition of Night Work for Women in Industrial Employment* was accepted with little change. This time the UK agreed. A Liberal victory in the general election of 1906 had changed domestic politics, in the sense that the new government was more committed to social welfare policies. It was also more cooperative in Bern than the previous government had been the year before. It even proposed that a permanent commission be set up to monitor the implementation of the Convention and that it should be made obligatory for disputes to be submitted to arbitration if one party demanded this. The German government strongly opposed these British proposals, as they were an infringement of sovereignty and socialist parties might use arbitration as an instrument in domestic politics. Rejection of the British proposals did not prevent the insertion of a clause making it obligatory for every signatory state to take whatever administrative steps where necessary to ensure the strict implementation of the convention within its national territory. Furthermore a *voeu* was agreed, laying down that it would be desirable for points left unresolved by the convention to be submitted to a commission on which each signatory state would be represented, albeit that this commission would have a 'purely consultative character'. 'In no circumstances would it be able to undertake any inquiry into or interfere in any way in the administrative or other acts of the states' (Lyons 1963, 153). Despite these reservations, there was progress compared with the situation in 1890 and even in 1905. The *International Convention Prohibiting the Use of White (Yellow) Phosphorus in the Manufacture of Matches* was improved somewhat, but did not receive widespread acceptance because of Japan's continued absence. This meant that the governments' readiness to sign it was weak.

Another round of decision making

In 1911 nine states ratified the Convention on Night Work for Women, and in January 1912 it came into force. The Phosphorus Convention also became effective in January 1912, after ratification by six states, soon followed by a few more, among them the UK in 1913. A new conference of experts was called by the Swiss government in 1913. It was attended by governmental representatives from 15 states, who continued the work of the previous conferences by drafting conventions prohibiting night work for all children under 14 and proposing a maximum working day of 10.5 hours and a working week of 60 hours. The diplomatic conference scheduled for September 1914, however, did not take place because of the outbreak of the First World War the month before. Nonetheless, another round of decision making in the field of labour relations had taken place.

14.3 Social protection against the consequences of free trade: the welfare state

The connection between social policy and free trade

As limited as the two 1906 conventions may have been, and as cautiously as governments had proceeded, certainly more cautiously than in the case of telegraph and railway services (Reinsch 1911, 48), the coming into existence of the two conventions was 'an undeniable victory for the principle of intervention and a remarkable illustration of the way in which governments could be moved by private or unofficial pressure when that pressure was skilfully applied' (Lyons 1963, 154). In addition, the process of intervention would move forward. There is a connection between the emergence of social welfare, as a package of labour market regulations and social insurance programmes, within industrializing states at the end of the nineteenth century and the perseverance with free trade and the creation of a continental market at the time. Because historians have regarded the rise of social policy and the trend towards international market integration as separate developments, the impression was given that no connection existed. But it did (Huberman and Lewchuk 2003, 14), and this also explains the national orientation of the workers' movement discussed earlier (see §13.5). The core of this relationship is that workers were able to accept free trade in exchange for the social protection they would receive through 'labour compacts' established by national authorities. *Labour compacts* include regulations with regard to the functioning of the labour market, such as those on the minimum age for child labour, the length of the working day, the prohibition of night labour for children and women and the inspection of factories, as well as social insurance programmes with compensation for accidents, sickness, unemployment and old age. These labour pacts were found in many European states, offering protection for workers against the economic and social consequences of an open economy with fierce international competition, such as existed by the end of the nineteenth century. Within this international context, the national labour compacts formed the foundation for what is termed the 'welfare state'. However, these pacts required international coordination, as Robert Owen and others had argued since 1818.

The trilemma of employers in an open economy

The connection between an open and free trade-oriented economic foreign policy, the standard of living and the demand for social policy presented a trilemma for employers in the late nineteenth century. Rising wages and access to international markets went together, as did social reform and a closed economy, but a combination of increases in wages, social reforms and an open economy was irreconcilable unless employers were helped to avoid the harmful effects of economic policies. 'If employers could not offload

169

their contributions to social entitlements and other programmes, the labour compact would lead to a loss of competitive advantage, a balance of payments crisis and inevitably to downward pressures on wages' (Huberman and Lewchuk 2003, 14).

Governments as parties between employers and workers

At this point governments became significant, as the workers' movement demanded social policies in order to counter the negative consequences of the internationally-developing national economies. Because of the limited impact of international agreements in this respect, governments had to find solutions that satisfied the various parties and interests. 'Faced by the failure of international accords, national authorities had to devise policies that reconciled the interests of workers and employers' (Huberman and Lewchuk 2003, 14). Governments engaged themselves in solving the trilemma, as this would support both a business world capable of international competition and a working class tied to its nation-state through protection against the consequences of this international competition. National cohesion would be the eventual result of this. Governments in Europe had in fact several options. One was to let international competition run its course, but that would lead to a 'race to the bottom', with the lowest standards of social insurance and factory regulation and no national cohesion. The Swiss option was an alternative, as that tried to create a wider European social union with fixed standards for working conditions across the continent laid down in various international conventions. As the Swiss option was not strongly supported, either by governments or by the workers' movement, Europe ended up with a compromise. 'After 1890, it was left to unofficial and independent organisations of reformers and workers, often at an industry level, to exert pressure on national authorities in order to avoid the inevitable "race to the bottom"' (Huberman and Lewchuk 2003, 14).

Free trade and democracy

In terms of *laissez-faire* or tariff protection, this third option meant that the European states in the period up to 1913, when faced by falling world grain prices and strong international competition, did not need to opt for tariff protection. The labour pacts provided workers with sufficient protection against external risks for governments to be able to continue free trade without the need to raise tariffs. Industrial workers in states with extensive labour pacts, such as Belgium and Denmark, even became 'enthusiastic supporters of free trade'. The labour compact varied across Europe. 'Larger states with sizeable domestic markets tended to use labour market and factory regulations; countries with more exposure to international markets, many of which were small, opted for social insurance type programmes' (Huberman and Lewchuk 2003, 34). In the period before the First World War, internationalization could expand as it was associated with increased worker protection, according to Huberman and Lewchuck, while free trade was less well received where workers were forced to be self-reliant. But labour pacts were most extensive where the exposure to free trade was greatest. The number of adult male voters in the population was a significant determinant of the extent of the labour compact, with proportional representation a vehicle for workers to exchange their support of trade for concessions from the state. Hence it made sense that the workers' movement engaged in domestic politics: 'democracy was good for growth because it was good for trade *and* workers' (Huberman and Lewchuk 2003, 34).

14.4 International efforts to improve health and uplift morality

Prevention of transboundary epidemics

During the nineteenth century health care also became part of the social reach of the nation-state, while cooperation between governments in this field was due to efforts to combat transboundary epidemics. From 1830 onwards Europe was confronted with outbreaks of cholera, but it was not until the 1880s that medicine helped to control the outbreaks. There was disagreement on how such diseases spread and which remedies should be used. Some argued that the disease was transmitted from person to person and that quarantine in harbours and at borders was the best remedy. Ports in southern Europe had used this quarantine solution since the fourteenth century. Others argued that illnesses spread because of an infected atmosphere and needed medication. In this alternative solution ports and roads were kept open, ships and vehicles were inspected and infected people removed to specially provided hospitals. This 'British solution' had the advantage of obstructing communication and transport less. The main locations through which epidemics were thought to spread from Asia and the Middle East to Europe were the Bosphorus, the Red Sea (because of the Mecca and Medina pilgrimages) and later the Suez Canal. Faster transport through the introduction of steamships and railways created another problem, as infection with the disease was discovered not during the trip, but only at the destination (Lyons 1963, 238–39). The first international action against such epidemics was the establishment of so-called sanitary councils, as happened in Constantinople (Istanbul) in 1838 and Tangier in 1840. The *Superior Council of Health* in Constantinople consisted of delegates from the Ottoman Empire and the principal maritime powers. Its function was to supervise the sanitary regulation of the port, aiming to prevent the exportation of cholera from Asia to Europe. That a sovereign state allowed an international administration to be active in its territory can be explained by the weakness of the Ottoman Empire and its dependency on the major maritime states (Jacobson 1979, 36).

The international health conference in Paris (1851)

In 1851 the French emperor called a conference in Paris to find a way to combat the cholera epidemics. It was attended by 12 governments and probably is one of the first occasions when technical experts were used. Each government was represented by two delegates, a diplomat and a physician, who voted individually and not as a unit (Charnovitz 1997, 198). A long and detailed convention was drafted, which however remained ineffective as only France, Portugal and Sardinia ratified it and the latter two denounced it again a few years later. A second international conference was convened in Paris in 1859 and, after another cholera epidemic, a third in Constantinople in 1865. Although they had a diplomatic character, these conferences were primarily scientific in their aims, confining themselves to discussions and resolutions rather than drafting treaties (Reinsch 1911, 57). This lack of progress in fighting epidemics was the result of national rivalries and suspicion, disagreement about the right solution and the power struggle between the great powers in the Middle East. Governments preferred to have a free hand, but they also acknowledged that some joint action was necessary to control the outbreaks of epidemics. However, even if they eventually agreed upon a solution, there would still remain the task of imposing it on states such as Persia and the Ottoman Empire, 'where

171

administrative incompetence was no bar to extreme sensitivity about sovereignty' (Lyons 1963, 240). In 1881 the UK reorganized the *Sanitary Council of Egypt* of 1831 in Alexandria. The ensuing *Sanitary, Maritime and Quarantine Council* consisted of nine Egyptian and 14 European members.

Conferences and conventions on cholera 1892–1903

The view that the spread of cholera had to be controlled near waterways such as the Suez Canal gained ground after Robert Koch's identification in Egypt in 1883 of the bacterium that caused the disease. In 1892, 14 states gathered in Venice where they agreed an *International Sanitary Convention* for protection against cholera on the lines of the 'British solution'. It included detailed regulations with regard to a sanitary station, the disinfection of ships and a special hospital. As the Sanitary, Maritime and Quarantine Council in Egypt did not function well, the conference reduced the number of Egyptians from nine to four (Lyons 1963, 240). A new outbreak of cholera in 1892 kept the pressure on, and every conference since then 'has added to the diplomatic work' (Reinsch 1911, 58). The International Sanitary Convention adopted in 1893 by ten European states in Dresden had a broader character, as it dealt with commercial traffic in general, laying down detailed provisions about merchandise. This Convention was also in line with the British solution and made the international notification of the existence of cholera in their territories obligatory upon all states. In order to better control the pilgrim traffic to Mecca and Medina, 12 European states and Persia met in Paris in 1894. The resulting International Sanitary Convention laid down that ships' captains found guilty of infringing the regulations should be fined. The conference in Venice in 1897 adopted another International Sanitary Convention, dealing with preventive measures against the plague, which was signed by 18 states. The conference in Paris in 1903, attended by the non-European states Brazil, Egypt, Persia and the US, in addition to 16 European states, was another step forward, as its purpose was to codify the rules already agreed and to extend regulation to yellow fever as well. The new International Sanitary Convention consisted of three parts: shipping and merchandise, ordinary shipping in the Red Sea and the Persian Gulf, and pilgrimages. It laid down detailed provisions about notification, merchandise, disinfection, quarantine and rats. The Sanitary Council in Constantinople was reorganized, as it was decided to set up an international court of appeal, the *Consular Commission*, to try cases in Turkish ports when the statements of health officials and captains were contradictory (Lyons 1963, 241–42). The conference also agreed, with Austria-Hungary, Germany and the UK voting against, to the suggestion of the 1897 congress in Brussels on hygiene to set up an 'international office of public health'.

The creation of the International Office of Public Health (1907)

The main reasons for such an institution were the shortcomings of the Sanitary Councils in Alexandria, Constantinople, Tangier and also now Tehran, because of frictions between the local representatives on these councils and the European experts, as well as disagreement among the Europeans. In 1907 the states met in Paris to discuss the creation of a central institution to carry out a more strategic war against epidemic diseases. The *International Office of Public Health* was established in Paris, with a permanent Secretariat and a permanent Committee of national health authorities. It was to keep in close contact with the national health authorities and the Sanitary Councils. Its function was 'to collect and bring to the knowledge of the participating states facts and documents of a general character concerning public health and especially regarding infectious diseases, notably cholera, the plague, and yellow fever, as well as the measures taken to check these diseases' (cited in Reinsch 1911, 58). States were obliged to inform the International Office of the steps governments were taking to implement the various sanitary conventions. The International Office, however, had the right to suggest such modifications as it saw fit (which it did, both in 1912 and in 1926). The convention establishing the International Office came into effect for a period of seven years after nine ratifications in 1908, thereafter to be renewed for further periods of seven years. It received wide support, as shown by the fact that in 1910, 14 states had ratified it (Belgium, Brazil, Egypt, France, Italy, the Netherlands, Peru, Portugal, Russia, Serbia, Spain, Tunis, the UK and the US), and by 1915, 32 had. Major abstainers were Germany and Austria-Hungary, which had preferred Berlin as the location for the International Office (Lyons 1963, 244–45). The International Office of Public Health was the second international organization in the field of health. The first was the *International Sanitary Bureau* of the International Union of American Republics (see §11.5), established in 1902. This had been in reaction to the infectious diseases, in particular yellow fever, brought to the US by immigrants from Europe and by ships from Central and Latin America. The International Sanitary Bureau aimed to secure and maintain efficient and modern sanitary conditions in ports and territories, and to reduce quarantine restrictions to a minimum and finally abolish them. In 1905 it drafted a treaty concerning the prevention of epidemics such as cholera, the plague and yellow fever (Reinsch 1911, 60). Both international organizations are precursors of the World Health Organization, created in 1945–46 (see Figure 14.2).

Figure 14.2 The establishment of the World Health Organization (1946)

Establishing the **World Health Organization** (WHO) in 1946 was far from easy. From 1902 the *International Sanitary Bureau* (from 1910: Pan-American Sanitary Bureau) operated in the Western Hemisphere, as did the *International Office of Public Health* from 1907 in Europe and the Middle East. When in 1919 the League of Nations was also charged with the prevention and control of infectious diseases, it proved impossible to join activities or forge a merger because of disagreements between the European states and the US, and resistance by the two organizations. As a result, the League of Nations created its own *Health Organization* (see §18.1), making a total of three institutions.

During the United Nations Conference on International Organization in San Francisco in 1945, all three were represented. Here Brazil and China jointly proposed that a conference be convened to create one international health organization. Their declaration was approved and referred to the UN General Assembly. In March 1946 a preparatory Technical Committee began its work and the International Health Conference was opened in June, at which the draft constitution of the WHO was signed on 22 July 1946. The word 'international' had been replaced by 'world'. For the time being the WHO functioned as an interim organization, as its constitution did not come into force until 7 April 1948 after the 26th ratification. At the end of that year the WHO had 53 members. The International Office of Public Health and the League's Health Organization merged with the WHO, while the Pan-American Sanitary Bureau staunchly defended its existence. This resulted in a US resolution advocating the double allegiance of being a regional organization in harmony with the general policies of the WHO. During a reorganization process in the Americas, the word 'Bureau' in the Sanitary Bureau's name was replaced by 'Organization', and in 1948 the new **Pan-American Health Organization** (PAHO) managed to reach an agreement with the WHO, which recognized the PAHO as both an independent entity and a regional WHO office for the Americas (Pan-American Health Organization 1992, 45). A remarkable shift in the nature of international collaboration in the field of health had taken place. Whereas the initiatives for international cooperation in the field of health prior to 1945 had largely come from the developed states in the North and aimed to protect them from the diseases of the poorer states in the South, the initiative in 1945 was taken by developing states from the South and had a much broader purpose: 'the attainment by all peoples of the highest possible levels of health' (Jacobson 1973, 175).

The International Opium Commission (1906)

In 1906 the International Opium Commission was created. Other health issues discussed internationally at the time were tuberculosis (1905), school hygiene (1907) (Charnovitz 1997, 209–10) and infant mortality (Lyons 1963, 265). In 1874 the Anglo-Oriental Society for the Suppression of the Opium Trade had been established as an NGO that was part of an influential anti-drug movement, which included temperance groups and missionaries. At a public hearing in 1904, convened by US Secretary of State John Hay, NGOs and missionaries urged the US government to persuade the UK to release China from a treaty obligation to tolerate traffic in opium (Charnovitz 1997, 203). As the US government understood that the issue had to be settled internationally, it convened a conference in 1906 in Shanghai, where 13 states created the *International Opium Commission*. Resolutions were adopted, calling for legislation within the states represented forbidding the manufacture and distribution of opium for other than medical purposes (Reinsch 1911, 61). The Commission did the preparatory work for a diplomatic conference in The Hague in 1912, which adopted the *International Opium Convention* to restrict the use of opium to medical purposes. After the First World War it came into force widely, and within the context of the League of Nations the convention was updated and revised in 1925, 1931 and 1936 (see §18.1). These various versions laid the foundation for the UN *Single Convention on Narcotic Drugs* of 1961.

The International Olympic Committee (1896)

Health became part of the public debate in yet another way, apart from as an issue of diseases and addiction. This was because of workers' and women's NGOs' public criticism of the bad housing and insufficient hygiene found in large industrial cities, which caused unhealthy living conditions. They tried to improve this situation through agitation, reform proposals and practical initiatives. The emergence of popular sports also played a role. Whereas originally sports were enjoyed only by the well-to-do, by the end of the nineteenth century many forms of sport also became activities of the middle and lower classes. Baron Pierre de Coubertin of France favoured the revival of the classical Olympic Games in a modern form, partly as a means to improve the physical and moral conditions of young people, partly to promote friendly relations between the peoples of states. He assumed that sport would create feelings of chivalry and respect for the achievements of opponents in both athletes and spectators and that international matches would help to bridge national differences. De Coubertin linked international sports activities with free trade and peace. At a preparatory meeting for his Olympic movement in 1892 he declared: 'The real free trade of the future will be to send our athletes of all kinds to all countries where games are played in order that they may study the methods practised by the greatest exponents of the various arts. On the day that this free trade is accepted in Europe, a great step forward will have been made in the sacred cause of peace' (cited in Lyons 1963, 384). In 1896 his Olympic movement established the private *International Olympic Committee* (IOC) and the first modern games were held in Athens. To strengthen the international foundation of the sports movement, the games were held in a different state every four years. The ambition of keeping sports and politics separate was part of the Olympic ideal. However, it did not prevent De Coubertin, at the age of 51, from placing himself at the French army's disposal in 1914, as he wanted to serve his country. He withdrew from the IOC temporarily. Immediately after the First World War he arranged for the 1920 games to be held in Belgium, in order to invigorate that state. Austria, Germany, Hungary and Turkey were excluded from these games, being regarded as the sources of the evil.

The temperance movement: the Blue Cross (1886)

The temperance movement has been discussed above in the context of women's rights (see §13.3). The American temperance movement began in 1842 as a campaign for total abstinence among young people. The various groups merged into the *Order of Good Templars*, which in 1852 became international, promoting 'the physical and moral development of mankind among all nations by total abstinence as a means of defence'. In Switzerland a temperance organization was founded in 1877, which in 1881 adopted the emblem of the Blue Cross. It copied the Red Cross's structure and in 1886 transformed itself into the *International Blue Cross Federation*, which consisted of fairly autonomous local and national groups. It was one of the most successful agencies in combating drunkenness (Lyons 1963, 268). From 1885 on the Blue Cross also convened international conferences, but these did not result in international conventions, except one involving liquor trade with African natives. The Blue Cross's importance lay in its propaganda for the cause of health (Charnovitz 1997, 208).

Penitentiary reform and combating international crime

The sports and temperance movements had in common their desire to reform social practices, which increasingly were being questioned. Another debate, in the context of prison reform, referred to the connection between crime and punishment. An American initiative resulted in a private international penitentiary congress being held in London in 1872. The congress had a mixed character, as its participants included representatives from governments, prison societies, prisons and societies of jurists (Charnovitz 1997, 199). Steps were taken to form a permanent organization, the *International Penal and*

Penitentiary Commission for the Prevention of Crime and the Treatment of Delinquents. It organized congresses every five years, and its secretariat in Bern collected information on national prison conditions and penal systems. The International Penitentiary Commission of 1875 devoted attention to issues such as the cellular system of punishment, support on discharge, more severe sentences for recidivists, greater lenience for first offenders, and how juvenile delinquency was treated. Governments took this non-governmental Commission seriously and became regular visitors at its congresses. During the congress in London in 1872 24 governments were represented; in Washington DC in 1910 there were 33. Thanks to this Commission, which also used questionnaires (Reinsch 1911, 57), 'knowledge of modern methods of prison administration became virtually worldwide, even if practice often still lagged behind precept' (Lyons 1963, 266). In 1899 jurists established the *International Union of Penal Law*, which in 1911 had national sections in 25 states. Its aim was the scientific study of criminal law. With regard to international crime, the police itself also developed a need for international information, which at the start was solved mostly through bilateral contacts. However, in 1914 a first international conference of police officials, jurists and lawyers was called in Monaco to discuss joint efforts to combat international crime. These contacts were resumed in 1923 at a second conference in Vienna. The *International Criminal Police Commission* established there was an NGO, notwithstanding its members being official police bodies. The Commission was renamed Interpol in 1956 and became an intergovernmental organization in 1971 (Charnovitz 1997, 210).

Well-being of people and protection of nature

The well-being of people and the condition of nature also became issues which were discussed at their own international congresses, supported by governments because of the expert knowledge and policy solutions available there. From 1889 onwards charity, for the first time internationally considered in Brussels in 1856 on the initiative of Ducpétiaux (see §14.1), was debated during a new series of international *Congresses of Public and Private Charity*, which in 1900 formed an International Committee and in 1907 set up a Bureau of Information and Studies. Philanthropic societies and governments alike were interested in discussing issues such as supplying medical assistance to the poor, the rehabilitation of prisoners, the care for abandoned children, the extension of charitable assistance to foreigners on the same terms as nationals, the role of women in charity and the protection of young girls and women (Lyons 1963, 264). International action to protect nature dates back to 1860, when a society for the protection of animals convened an international meeting. In 1884 ornithologists at their first international congress began analytical work for a future convention on bird protection, and in 1895 17 governments held a conference to draft a treaty on birds, with ornithologists as part of their delegations. The failure of ratification meant the treaty did not enter into force, but another diplomatic conference in 1902 redrafted the treaty as the *International Convention for the Protection of Birds*, which did become law. At their fifth international congress in 1910 the ornithologists discussed an international instrument to prohibit trade in birds and feathers and proposed that the next Hague Peace Conference, scheduled for 1915, should draft a convention (Charnovitz 1997, 206). However, the First World War intervened.

Part VI

Laying down the path of collective security

The First World War, the League of Nations founded (1919) and the interwar period

The sixth part deals with the First World War and the interwar period. The war caused a break in the development of international organizations after the 'long' nineteenth century (until 1914), but it also involved a new initiative. The founding of a 'League of Nations' was widely discussed during the war by both citizens and politicians and became part of the institutional strategy devised by the US. The outcome of that strategy was, however, determined not by the US, but by the balance of power between the principal victors at Versailles, where the Covenant of the League of Nations was drawn up (Chapter 15). The League proved to be a suitable medium to restore relations in places where measures had been taken during the peace negotiations, but where acute tensions still existed. This resulted in arrangements such as temporary administration, conflict settlement and the accommodation of large numbers of refugees. Efforts to disarm, however, remained the domain of the great powers, despite attempts by the League of Nations to play a part. The League had barely any grip on the political and military developments of the 1930s because the great powers took little notice of it (Chapter 16).

The First World War and the creation of the League of Nations (1919)

The League ... was not simply the culmination of a long evolutionary process but was also in some respects a radical departure from past practice, owing as much to the immediate circumstances of its creation as to the previous history of international organisation

(Armstrong *et al.* 1996, 7)

15.1 Liberal debates on a postwar League of Nations in the UK

External shock and interrupted evolution

The outbreak of the First World War in August 1914 was an external shock to the evolutionary development of international organizations. The general progress in security in the form of regular Hague Peace Conferences was interrupted and the third Conference, planned for 1915, did not take place (see §7.5). Most public international unions continued, albeit that ten of the 51 that existed in 1914 (see Figure 8.2) came to an end. In the field of security the great powers now prevailed with their power politics. However, during the war the concept of international organization was not absent. It was even central to the thinking on international politics in the UK and the US. The term 'League of Nations' that featured in this thinking stemmed from the book *La société des nations*, published in 1908 by the French politician and jurist Léon

Bourgeois. The British government saw such a League as a means of involving the US in the war, while the US saw it as an opportunity to modernize international and European politics.

A new beginning

As the peace negotiations approached the UK and the US increasingly denied the good experiences of the Hague Peace Conferences. They wanted the League they envisaged to be free of all associations with previous common efforts (Armstrong *et al.* 1996, 12). This 'new' approach was helped by the fact that the official plans for such a League took shape outside the normal channels of the ministries of foreign affairs. Despite this there was continuity, as in the follow-up to the nineteenth-century developments with regard to arbitration and international law, more emphasis was placed on judicial solutions and economic sanctions (see Chapter 7). The liberal political elites in both the UK and the US contributed to the debates, being 'the creators of the background thinking for policy, and often policy makers themselves' (Williams 1998, 21). Andrew Williams calls the US the 'older partner' in relation to ideas on international relations after a peace agreement. He sees the mutual influence of the UK and the US as an intellectual 'input' for the philosophical basis of the peace settlement and the specific proposals for a League of Nations. John Ikenberry, however, is of the opinion that the ideas that inspired Woodrow Wilson in his proposal for a League of Nations 'were first articulated and embraced by British liberals' (Ikenberry 2001, 131). Within the liberal camp two factions existed: an essentially conservative and realist trend and a radical (British) or progressive (American) trend.

British plans for a League of Nations

Regarding ideas on a possible League of Nations, Williams perceives three groups in the liberal British camp. The first was the *Bryce Group*, named after James Bryce, the British ambassador to the US from 1907 to 1913. It argued for the establishment of an alliance between the UK, the US and France with a realist, that is a strictly intergovernmental, organizational structure. This group was considered to be conservative. The second group, the *Union of Democratic Control* (UDC), comprised left-wing Liberals and Labour people. These 'Lib-Labs' emphasized the importance of democratic parties and states for a postwar League. The third group was the *League of Nations Society* (later, after merging with another organization, the *League of Nations Union*), to which among others Jan Smuts and Leonard Woolf belonged. The South African politician Smuts became a member of the British war cabinet led by David Lloyd George in 1917. As South African delegate at Versailles, he would put forward practical ideas about the eventual League during the peace conference (Smuts 1952). Woolf developed a vision of 'world government', by which he meant an international organization jointly established by states (see Figure 15.1).

British government policy

After the outbreak of the war, the British government considered it necessary to tackle German domination on the Continent. The notion of using a 'League of Nations' for this purpose was accepted midway through 1915, and from spring 1916 it became part of

Figure 15.1 Two plans for an international peace organization (1915–16)

During the First World War, various detailed **plans for an international peace organization** were produced. These were based on the idea that peace as a condition had to be actively and jointly promoted. The British social-liberal economist John Hobson did this in 1915, the publisher and publicist Leonard Woolf in 1916. The experiences of the nineteenth-century organizations were manifested in their work, as is evident in the table of contents of both books.

Table of contents: J.A. Hobson, Towards International Government (London, 1915)

  I A league of peace
  II A basis of confederation
  III International arbitration: its scope and method
  IV Settlement by conciliation
  V Court and Council: their appointment and personnel
  VI International force
  VII The economic boycott
  VIII International government in relation to (i) problems of nationality (ii) problems of economic opportunity
  IX The social contract of nations
  X The international mind
  XI Democracy and internationalism

Table of contents: L.S. Woolf, International Government (New York, 1916)

  I International government, international agreement, and international disagreement
  II International organs and organisms
  III The internationalization of administration (a) communications (b) public health and epidemic diseases (c) industry and commerce (d) morals and crime
  IV Cosmopolitan law-making (a) international maritime legislation and the unification of maritime law (b) international labor legislation (c) other examples
  V International society and international standards
  VI The internationalization of commerce, industry and labor
  VII Some conclusions

government policy. The May 1916 memorandum on this by the cabinet secretary Maurice Hankey supported the formation of an international organization. Hankey warned that some states, such as the UK, did believe in the power of international treaties and institutions, but others, such as Germany, did not: 'there could be no reliance on international organs, for example to enforce international arbitration, as a reliance on this would "create a sense of security which is wholly fictitious"'. For the time being another strategic interest was of more importance to the British government, as it saw the League of Nations as 'a vital lever to ensure American involvement in the war' (Williams 1998, 29).

Use of intelligence and historical models

As the end of the war approached at the beginning of 1918, the British government entrusted two bodies with the preparations for negotiations. It formed the *Historical Section* within the Admiralty, which was responsible for the administration and planning of the navy, and set up the *Political Intelligence Department* (PID) in the Foreign Office. Both bodies compiled so-called *Peace Books* for the negotiators. The Historical Section, which was later transferred to the Foreign Office, collected every possible piece of historical, economic and geographical information that could be relevant to the discussions and negotiations, while the Political Intelligence Department coordinated the flow of information from the various ministries. It was the first time in international relations that *intelligence* was collected on such a large scale, and in such a structured way, in preparation for a peace conference. However, this method of working also resulted in politicians and civil servants becoming suspicious. Prime Minister Lloyd George wanted nothing to do with it. Smuts, on the other hand, used this information during the conference, where the *Peace Books* proved their worth (Williams 1998, 27–28). At the beginning of 1918 the government appointed another commission, led by Lord Phillimore, to assess the consequences of a League. This commission issued a report later that year comparing various 'historical models'. Its main conclusion was that an international peace organization could function only if it consisted of democratic states. The expansion of democratic nationalism appeared to be successful but, according to the report, military and absolutist states would remain an obstacle to the functioning of a postwar League of Nations (Ikenberry 2001, 143).

Reverberating British realism

Although the report was criticized, many elements were later evident in the Covenant of the League of Nations. This particularly applies to 'the injunction not to resort to war' and 'the settlement of international disputes'. The report stated that, when necessary in situations of crisis, cooperation between the great powers was more important than regular meetings in an organizational context. 'It thus drew much more on the nineteenth century tradition of the diplomacy of the Congress system than on the conference diplomacy envisaged by the supporters of the League.' Moreover, it was an 'essentially "statist/realist" construct that puts its faith in states and alliances' (Williams 1998, 31). A certain realism also reverberated within the League of Nations Union. Lord Grey thought that a League of Nations had a chance of succeeding only if heads of state and leaders of government took it seriously. States had to understand that participation in a League brought with it responsibilities, in the form of providing help to other states and enforcing sanctions. There was a realization within the Foreign Office that the founding of a League would change an old British liberal tenet. The international system of states would no longer be self-regulating purely on the basis of a harmony of interests. Instead, it had to be acknowledged that 'the nature of modern war, and the existence of "less civilized" states, even among those that were economically developed, made "idealism" something that had to be backed up by the use of force, if necessary' (Williams 1998, 32).

15.2 The United States involved in the war (1917) and Wilson's Fourteen Points (1918)

American plans for a League of Nations

As in the UK, private organizations in the US promoted the forming of a League of Nations. Jane Addams of the *Women's Peace Party*, for example, in 1915 demanded disarmament, democratic control of foreign policy, compulsory arbitration, the freedom of the seas and a Concert of Nations. On the opposite side to this progressive variation of internationalism in the US was the conservative *League to Enforce Peace*. Comparable to the Bryce Group in the UK, this League wanted to make the judicial possibilities against aggression so much stronger that they could be supported by force and legal sanctions.

Wilson's Peace without Victory

US President Woodrow Wilson did not want to become involved in the war (Cooper 2001; Levin 2001). He had presupposed American neutrality and emphasized free trade and shipping. The torpedoing of the British *Lusitania* by Germany in 1915, which cost many of its American passengers their lives, signified a curtailment of the freedom of the seas, as was sharply reflected in public opinion. Through diplomatic memoranda Wilson managed to force Germany to be more restrained, but the continuing German presence in international waters made it clear that the US should take action. Wilson first thought of mediation, but redefining the objectives of the belligerent states quickly took precedence. These had to be formulated in such a way that a world war could not break out again. In a speech in the New Willard Hotel on 27 May 1916, Wilson emphasized the principle that 'every people has a right to choose the sovereignty under which they shall live', while at the same time the world had the right to be protected from 'every disturbance of its peace that has its origins in aggression and disregard of the rights of peoples and nations' (cited in Williams 1998, 34–35). On 22 January 1917 Wilson elaborated on his vision in what was to become known as his *Peace without Victory* speech. He now looked for consultation between the opposing groups of states. With a view to a 'peace without victory', he sketched an institutional framework for his earlier ideas. There should not only be a balance of power, but also 'a community of power; not organized rivalries, but an organized common peace'. He argued for a new diplomacy based on equal rights between states, on governments that had the approval of their citizens, on the freedom of the seas and on equal weaponry as part of a jointly enforced peace (Williams 1998, 35). With this vision of the international system Wilson belonged to the 'interventionist' liberals in the US. The non-interventionists, or isolationists, assumed that a liberal world order must spread as a matter of course. Interventionists, however, were of the opinion that over time progress was unavoidable, but that it could be helped now and again. They followed the older idea of a 'just war'. According to interventionists it could be necessary to take action to help rid the world of oppressive opponents not oriented on freedom, by which during the First World War they meant the autocratic European states that strove to maintain their power.

The US involved in the war (1917)

On 1 February 1917, Germany reacted to Wilson's speech by declaring unlimited submarine warfare including the sinking of American ships. Moreover, Germany secretly sought the support of Mexico by holding out the prospect of returning Texas and California to this state. The torpedoes and the publication of the secret Mexican telegrams gave Wilson sufficient public support to be able to declare war on Germany at the beginning of April. For Wilson it was not the German people who were the opponent, but the antidemocratic militarism in Germany (Ikenberry 2001, 125). To develop his ideas on a peace settlement, which he did not want to make known yet, Wilson instigated the *Inquiry*. This was a body working independently of the State Department. Some members of the Inquiry were later part of the official US delegation at Versailles. The exclusion of the State Department embittered the Secretary of State and meant that the Inquiry barely had access to (or profited from) the normal US diplomatic channels and the information they could provide. The Inquiry produced reports and the *Black Book*, which was important at Versailles. The quality of the American reports was not equal to that of the British *Peace Books*, which were made available to the US but not to France and Italy, causing tension between the Allies (Williams 1998, 37–38).

Wilson's Fourteen Points (1918)

The best-known document resulting from the Inquiry was Wilson's *Fourteen Points* (see Figure 15.2). Wilson announced these on 8 January 1918 in a speech to the American Congress. The first point set out the new 'open diplomacy' he favoured. The second point concerned the absolute freedom of the seas, the third the removal of all economic barriers to international trade and the fourth the reduction in national weaponry. Points 6 to 13 dealt with territorial questions, and points 5 and 14 with the settlement of colonial claims and the establishment of a league, or association, of nations. Wilson assumed that states' imperfection and the structure of the international system were the

Figure 15.2 Woodrow Wilson's Fourteen Points (1918)

I   Open covenants of peace, openly arrived at, after which there shall be no private international understandings of any kind but diplomacy shall proceed always frankly and in the public view.

II   Absolute freedom of navigation upon the seas, outside territorial waters, alike in peace and in war, except as the seas may be closed in whole or in part by international action for the enforcement of international covenants.

III   The removal, so far as possible, of all economic barriers and the establishment of an equality of trade conditions among all the nations consenting to the peace and associating themselves for its maintenance.

IV   Adequate guarantees given and taken that national armaments will be reduced to the lowest point consistent with domestic safety.

V   A free, open-minded, and absolutely impartial adjustment of all colonial claims, based upon a strict observance of the principle that in determining all such questions of sovereignty the interests of the populations concerned must have equal weight with the equitable claims of the government whose title is to be determined.

VI The evacuation of all Russian territory and such a settlement of all questions affecting Russia as will secure the best and freest cooperation of the other nations of the world in obtaining for her an unhampered and unembarrassed opportunity for the independent determination of her own political development and national policy and assure her of a sincere welcome into the society of free nations under institutions of her own choosing; and, more than a welcome, assistance also of every kind that she may need and may herself desire. The treatment accorded Russia by her sister nations in the months to come will be the acid test of their good will, of their comprehension of her needs as distinguished from their own interests, and of their intelligent and unselfish sympathy.

VII Belgium, the whole world will agree, must be evacuated and restored, without any attempt to limit the sovereignty which she enjoys in common with all other free nations. No other single act will serve as this will serve to restore confidence among the nations in the laws which they have themselves set and determined for the government of their relations with one another. Without this healing act the whole structure and validity of international law is forever impaired.

VIII All French territory should be freed and the invaded portions restored, and the wrong done to France by Prussia in 1871 in the matter of Alsace-Lorraine, which has unsettled the peace of the world for nearly fifty years, should be righted, in order that peace may once more be made secure in the interest of all.

IX A readjustment of the frontiers of Italy should be effected along clearly recognizable lines of nationality.

X The peoples of Austria-Hungary, whose place among the nations we wish to see safeguarded and assured, should be accorded the freest opportunity to autonomous development.

XI Rumania, Serbia, and Montenegro should be evacuated; occupied territories restored; Serbia accorded free and secure access to the sea; and the relations of the several Balkan states to one another determined by friendly counsel along historically established lines of allegiance and nationality; and international guarantees of the political and economic independence and territorial integrity of the several Balkan states should be entered into.

XII The Turkish portion of the present Ottoman Empire should be assured a secure sovereignty, but the other nationalities which are now under Turkish rule should be assured an undoubted security of life and an absolutely unmolested opportunity of autonomous development, and the Dardanelles should be permanently opened as a free passage to the ships and commerce of all nations under international guarantees.

XIII An independent Polish state should be erected which should include the territories inhabited by indisputably Polish populations, which should be assured a free and secure access to the sea, and whose political and economic independence and territorial integrity should be guaranteed by international covenant.

XIV   A general association of nations must be formed under specific covenants for the purpose of affording mutual guarantees of political independence and territorial integrity to great and small states alike.

causes of war. He wanted to counter aggression and despotism by applying the principle of national self-determination and by stimulating democratic systems. While authoritarian leaders were interested only in personal gain, glory or power, democracies could prevent these leaders going to war unless there was a good reason to do so. Wilson proposed forming an association of nation-states in which large and small states would give mutual guarantees on their political independence and territorial integrity (see point XIV). Following the motto of the Three Musketeers, 'one for all and all for one', a system of collective security would mean that *all* states would provide help to *every* state that was threatened by aggression. Apart from military deterrence this was about moral strength, which for Wilson was more powerful than physical strength. Peace could be assured only if states had accepted the idea that aggression was wrong (Mansbach 1994, 295). With his Fourteen Points Wilson also turned against the Bolsheviks, who had taken power in Russia. They had reacted positively to his call for a new diplomacy, but 'Wilson's goal was to persuade the people of Europe that American principles, not Bolshevik ones, provided the most enlightened basis for a new postwar order' (Ikenberry 2001, 127).

15.3 The postwar institutional strategy as a result of power negotiations (1919)

Negotiating with European power politicians in Versailles

When Wilson came to Europe in late 1918 after the end of the war, he was hailed as a peacemaker. During the negotiations in Versailles, however, he had to deal with experienced politicians such as the French government leader and minister of war Georges Clemenceau and the British Prime Minister Lloyd George. Wilson based his actions on the 'deal' that the US would join an international peacekeeping league and that the Europeans would agree to a peace settlement on US terms (Ikenberry 2001, 124). In reality, though, there was no unity between the Allies. They had come to little agreement about their objectives in advance. In this sense 1919 differed from both 1815 and 1945, 'when Britain and the United States, respectively, used their dominant wartime position to gain early agreement on common war aims and settlement goals' (Ikenberry 2001, 134). Trying to reach consensus in 1919 consisted of a few Allied conferences prior to the agreement on the suspension of hostilities. 'Clemenceau, Lloyd George, House [Wilson's representative], and Italy's Orlando settled essential points before they were submitted to the Supreme War Council.' Wilson concentrated on the general settlement, trying to strengthen it with liberal ideas, but the representatives of the other great powers intended 'to make good on their own territorial and security goals and commitments to each other'. The result was a series of compromises, 'that left the principles severely in doubt' (Ikenberry 2001, 137). Clemenceau, who derisively called Wilson Jupiter (Williams 1998, 40), in particular wanted to get even with Germany. Wilson's promise of a democratic Germany was not enough for him. He wanted the return of Alsace-Lorraine to France, a permanent occupation of the west bank of the Rhine, and the western parts of Germany split into smaller, autonomous republics. When Clemenceau eventually made some concessions (no permanent occupation and no splitting up), Wilson agreed in order to save the conference. John Maynard Keynes, who was a member of the British delegation, saw Clemenceau as the man who knew what he wanted and who dominated the negotiations. Keynes had little regard for Wilson, who barely had a view on the implementation of his points ('when it came to practice his ideas were nebulous and incomplete. He had no plan, no scheme, no constructive ideas whatever for clothing with the flesh of life the commandments which he had thundered from the White House'), was badly informed about the situation in Europe, was not familiar with details and had a slow-working mind (Keynes 1920, 42–43). Wilson was also forced to make concessions on the reparations, owing to their importance in European public opinion. 'In each of these instances, Wilson resisted where he could and conceded where he had to in order to achieve agreement on his prize element of the treaty, the League of Nations' (Ikenberry 2001, 139). Wilson's relationship with his Secretary of State deteriorated, as he found Robert Lansing too cautious and legalistic. Lansing gave priority to democratization and wanted to strengthen the existing diplomatic elements, such as arbitration and research commissions, in the League of Nations. The result of this disagreement was that Wilson no longer listened to Lansing's analyses (Armstrong *et al.* 1996, 19).

The drafting of the Covenant of the League

The draft text of the Covenant of the League of Nations emerged from a process of negotiation 'involving many disparate elements and contending interests. It was, first and foremost, a compromise between the British and American viewpoints: one which managed to patch over the only partially concealed suspicions each nurtured about the other's true intentions' (Armstrong *et al.* 1996, 24). The British fear of American wealth and trading power featured prominently, while within US domestic politics there was anxiety that the UK would dominate the League. The underlying principles and assumptions with regard to the new international order and the League, as well as the underlying discord, can be summed up in seven points (Armstrong *et al.* 1996, 19–24). The term *collective security* was not used until later, but the idea that Germany could have been constrained by this, and hence the world war would not have broken out, was clear. There was a difference of opinion on what military means would be necessary for this collective security. While France was in favour of an international army with a permanent general staff, Wilson and House argued for economic sanctions. Smuts pointed out that such sanctions would work only if they were ultimately backed up by military force. At Versailles there was agreement on which conflicts could and could not be solved through a legal process. On the whole this meant an extension of *judicial solutions*, including arbitration, compared with the nineteenth century. This understanding was eventually written into a British proposal for a permanent international court of justice. The mention of arbitration in the Covenant was due to the member of the French delegation Léon Bourgeois, who had tried to link the drafting of the peace treaty with the work of the Hague Peace Conferences, but only Portugal had supported him in this (Armstrong *et al.* 1996, 12). Despite this, Bourgeois managed to have arbitration included in Articles 12 and 13. It seemed sensible to control the escalation of conflicts through *crisis management*. By having compulsory moratoria, attempts could be made to settle differences peacefully. Public discussions were considered important, given the intention to end secret diplomacy. The idea of *disarmament* and *weapons control* originated from concern about the arms race that had preceded the war, but here too perspectives differed. France was interested in the disarmament of Germany, the UK in the end of national service and the US in a general agreement on arms limitation, including the production of weapons. The great powers gave little importance to the contribution of the small states, as they regarded the *concert of powers* to be a discussion between themselves. A British proposal to establish Allied control over the postwar reconstruction of Europe, in line with Allied military cooperation during the war, however, met with an American veto. The US did not want any foreign control over goods that were mainly going to be provided by the US. Smuts had suggested the possibility of cooperation in the non–security field. Shortly before the meeting in Versailles this *specialized economic and social cooperation* began to acquire some significance and it also kept it afterwards. It did not, however, become an essential issue. It was only in the sphere of labour that it took the form of a specialized agency of the League of Nations, the International Labour Organization. The League itself was given a few commissions in the economic and social domain, but these were not independent in structure and the public international unions remained outside the workings of the League. Regarding the *organizational principles* of the League, the negotiators agreed on the creation of an executive Council, an Assembly for consultation and an administrative Secretariat. The UK wanted only the great powers to have a say, with the smaller states playing a subordinate role. House was also in favour of excluding the small states, but he found Wilson opposed to him on this point. A suggestion by Smuts and Italy to make the great powers 'permanent members' of the Council and a number of small states 'non-permanent members' received Wilson's approval. This compromise, however, disappeared from the draft texts of the great powers, but due to pressure from the smaller states during the negotiations it was reinstated. The real significance of the Assembly would only become clear in practice. During the negotiations at Versailles Italy succeeded in arranging that the Assembly would not remain an informal entity, but would become a forum in which international law could develop. Italy also managed to change part of the decision-making process by replacing unanimity with two-thirds majority. The function of the secretary-general of the League was to be mainly administrative and concentrated on coordination with other international organizations. The Secretariat, however, eventually would become an international organ (see §15.4).

Wilson fails in American domestic politics

When Wilson returned to the US he failed to gain the Senate's support for the compromise reached at Versailles. Under the leadership of Henri Cabot Lodge, the Senate opposed the proposed League of Nations. The cause of this opposition lay in Wilson's attachment during the negotiations to his brain child, the League. His personal position and House's recommendations had not taken domestic political relationships in the US sufficiently into account. Because he had made his vision an issue in the 1918 elections to Congress, Wilson presented his view of the peace settlement far too much as a Democratic Party rather than an all-American matter. 'This created a party division over Wilson's peace plans, when in reality the division of opinion was much more fragmented, even within the Republican opposition' (Ikenberry 2001, 149). With a Republican majority in the Senate and the House, Wilson's chances of having the League accepted in the US were poor. The opponents' objections were that 'domestic affairs were not explicitly excluded from the League's auspices, that the special relationship between the United States and Latin America, as embodied in the Monroe Doctrine, was not officially acknowledged in the Covenant, that the United States might be saddled with mandated territories against its wishes, and that procedures by which states could withdraw from the League needed to be clarified'. When the negotiators accepted these objections during new discussions in Paris, however, the Senate continued its opposition. This particularly applied to Article 10, 'which contained a diluted version of Wilson's long-cherished principle of guarantees of territorial integrity and political independence' (Armstrong *et al.* 1996, 25). Eventually the Senate formulated 14 reservations about the League, and Article 10 would be agreed to only if Congress explicitly decided to approve such an obligation. Wilson travelled the country to gain the support of the American people, trying to explain that Article 10 was necessary because of the 'conscience of the world'. After suffering a stroke Wilson had to drastically reduce his workload and he eventually lost the 1920 elections. Evidently he had failed to convince Americans of the need for the League of Nations. Under Wilson's successor, the Republican Warren Harding, the US returned to a position of isolationism, at least in relation to Europe. With regard to regional relations in the Western Hemisphere, the Covenant of the League emphatically stated that regional understandings such as the Monroe doctrine, 'for securing maintenance of peace', were not incompatible with the League's own character (Article 21). This formulation of words says more about the power relations during the peace negotiations, in particular the continental power of the US (see §11.5), than about considered reflection on the nature of the universal peace organization.

The ultimate result

In March 1919 the text of the League's Covenant was discussed again at Versailles. Wilson took amendments with him that resulted in new compromises to meet the wishes of the US. The resultant Covenant of the League formed the first part of the *Treaty of Versailles*. This was finished at the end of April, with Germany signing at the end of June. Ultimately the three most important articles of the Covenant were firstly that which stated that the League had the right *to involve itself with any threat to peace* (Article 11.1: 'Any war or threat of war, whether immediately affecting any of the Members of the League or not, is hereby declared a matter of concern to the whole League, and the League shall take any action that may be deemed wise and effectual to safeguard the peace of nations'). Secondly the League was able *to make arrangements to settle differences peacefully* (to be found in Articles 12–14, thereby making judicial decisions possible). Thirdly it was *to be able to impose sanctions against those who contravened the agreements* (Article 16.1: Should any member of the League resort to war, it 'shall *ipso facto* be deemed to have committed an act of war against all other Members of the League, which hereby undertake immediately to subject it to the severance of all trade or financial relations, the prohibition of all intercourse between their nationals and the nationals of the covenant-breaking State, and the prevention of all financial, commercial or personal intercourse between the nationals of the covenant-breaking State and the nationals of any other State, whether a Member of the League or not'). To meet the wishes of France to create a general international staff in some form or other, a *Permanent Commission* was formed, which could advise the Council on military, maritime and air questions (Article 9).

Colonial paternalism, the mandate system and discrimination

With regard to the colonies, Article 22 laid down that the welfare and development of peoples who were not yet able to be independent in the difficult circumstances of the modern world were 'a sacred trust of civilisation'. This echoed the colonial paternalism of earlier times. The areas that the Allied states placed under international control after the war were known as *mandated territories*. The colonial territories of Germany and areas that previously belonged to the Ottoman Empire (Turkey) were assigned to the Allies. Wilson wanted to prevent France and the UK annexing these regions and following a practical suggestion from Smuts the concept of a mandate was devised, whereby a particular state would administer a territory under supervision of the League. In this way Ruanda-Urundi for example went to Belgium. The League controlled the administration of these areas, laid down conditions for it and appointed a *Permanent Mandates Commission* to supervise implementation. This Commission, which met for the first time in October 1921, consisted of 11 members, the majority of whom had to be from states that had not been assigned a mandate. Article 22 paved the way for independence for various groups of states, depending on the level of development of their people. This was higher for instance in Iraq, which could therefore become independent more quickly, than in areas of Africa. New, in comparison with the nineteenth century, was that the states administering the mandates had to report regularly to the League. An amendment by Japan to prohibit racial discrimination had not been accepted during the negotiations in Versailles, since Australia and other members of the British Empire opposed this because of their immigration policy. Racial discrimination was the only point on which Japan had expressed an opinion at the conference, and it had linked the approval of its proposal to a ban on religious discrimination put forward by Wilson, with the result that both types of discrimination remained outside the Covenant.

Social-economic activities and public international unions

At the last moment, the UK succeeded in having an article included in the Covenant which enabled the League to have a coordinating role for specialized agencies (Article 24). The subjects and principles named in Article 23 were: fair and humane conditions of labour for men, women and children, just treatment of the native inhabitants, the trafficking in women and children, the traffic in opium and other dangerous drugs, the freedom of communications and of transit, and the prevention and control of disease. With the exception of the treatment of native inhabitants, these were all matters that had been on the agenda of public and private international unions in the nineteenth century. The unions, however, were not invited to Versailles. They would remain outside the League of Nations with only a few exceptions, such as the 1919 International Hydrographic Bureau, which was placed under the authority of the League in 1921.

15.4 The League of Nations' Secretariat: an international organ rather than a principal's agent

A concept that failed

Before Sir Eric Drummond was asked to become secretary-general, Maurice Hankey had been the candidate for this post. Hankey outlined the organization as he envisaged it at

190

the end of March 1919 and based this on his experience with the war councils, on which representatives of the Allies had cooperated in technical fields such as transport and arms (see §18.1). The core of Hankey's concept was that every member state represented on the Council would nominate a *principal secretary* and an assistant. Both would be members of the Secretariat. These national 'principal secretaries' would function as liaison agents between their respective governments and the secretary-general, and had to have the complete confidence of both sides. It would be their responsibility to arrange meetings of the Council under the supervision of the secretary-general. States that were not members of the Council could also nominate liaison agents. The secretary-general would be able to turn to these national diplomats on matters concerning the governments in question. According to Hankey these should be people 'with mutual knowledge and understanding who are accustomed to work together'. His idea was that the diplomats would be appointed for a period of five years and on returning to the national bureaucracy their work for the League would count as good services rendered (Dubin 1983, 473).

A truly international secretariat

Drummond on the other hand was not in favour of an international secretariat based on national officials who would be loyal to and paid by the member states. At the end of May he put forward an alternative, which sounded daring in the security field but was familiar to the public international unions: 'a truly international secretariat, whose members … must divest themselves of national preconceptions and devote themselves wholeheartedly to the service of the League'. The members of the Secretariat were not to be nominated by governments and should not be representatives of their states. He thought that the most important criterion for nomination was that they were 'really capable men and women of broad vision and flexible mind' (cited in Dubin 1983, 472). Drummond's proposal was the result of ideas he had worked on with James Salter, the British secretary of the Allied Maritime Transport Council (see §18.1), Lord Robert Cecil, the British representative in charge of the negotiations on the League at Versailles, and his French colleague Jean Monnet. They were concerned that national ties would mean that the international Secretariat did not have enough room for manoeuvre and that the organs of the League would not meet frequently enough to be able to make progress.

Salter's vision on a genuinely international administration

A range of proposals was put forward during the preparations for the League's Secretariat. Salter thought that economic affairs would become increasingly important in international relations. He therefore wanted to break the monopoly of the ministries of foreign affairs and have the economics ministers also meet regularly. Moreover, he wanted to establish national secretariats linked to the international Secretariat, in which the national representatives, who were well informed on domestic and international relations, could prepare mutually acceptable proposals. He also wanted to establish a secretariat in each national state that would keep the various ministries and the government continually informed about international developments. With the help of private organizations and the press, this secretariat should also rally popular support for international activities. Special units needed to exist within the international

Secretariat in which ministers and representatives of private organizations could talk to each other regularly. The international Secretariat would have the task of coordinating this multifaceted work and would also have to have sufficient research capacity. Salter did not expect that such an organization could be realized immediately. It would have to be developed gradually by people experienced in international administration (Dubin 1983, 475).

The Secretariat and the dissemination of international values

The US also had a view on the international Secretariat. The members of the Secretariat should be of different nationalities and distance themselves as far as possible from national ties. The organization had to be flexible and form a link between the Council and the Assembly, prepare the meetings and maintain contacts with governments. Governments needed to establish an office within their ministry of foreign affairs to maintain contacts with the League. The Frenchman Jean Monnet found this vision too restricted, arguing that the dissemination of the ideals of the League and the rallying of global public opinion were part of the role of the Secretariat. These activities had to inspire governments to solve differences peacefully through common understanding. Monnet expected that this would be made easier by 'greater interpenetration of peoples', which required permanent contact 'rather than discussion only in the context of conflict' (Dubin 1983, 476). He therefore emphasized the role of the Secretariat in areas such as information campaigns and education.

Canalization or multichannel communication?

During the negotiations on the structure and organization of the Secretariat, compromises were made between the different proposals. Monnet argued fiercely against the 'canalization' of information to and from the Secretariat via the ministries of foreign affairs. He spoke out in favour of other ministries being able to communicate directly with the League's Secretariat and through it with the ministries of other states. The Organization Committee, consisting of the states that were to form the first Council, gave Drummond permission to work on a plan for the Secretariat. The question of canalization or 'multichannel communication', which also included private organizations, was discussed at length, albeit with great reluctance on the side of the governments. Monnet and Drummond tried to convince their own governments of the benefit of multichannel communication, which would change the traditional methods of international relations and influence the departments in the various ministries. Lord Cecil demurred, arguing that some degree of canalization would be necessary if governments were to retain their capacity for unity of action. As a compromise, Monnet and Drummond managed to persuade their governments to create an agency at government level that would coordinate national policy and supply the ministry of foreign affairs with copies of all correspondence with the League (Dubin 1983, 480–81). In practice, IGOs were later to follow the path favoured by Monnet and Drummond, but in 1919 no one dared to do this. The most important victory achieved by Drummond and his supporters was the establishment of a Secretariat with an international staff. This meant that a secretariat based on the principal's agent model of the international war councils, as propounded by Hankey, was rejected.

15.5 Women gain access to the League of Nations: Article 7.3

Women and the struggle for peace

During the course of the nineteenth century women increasingly had begun to play their own role in the international peace movement, often in conjunction with their struggle for equal rights with men. The assumption that they, by reason of motherhood, had a role to play in promoting peace prompted women to undertake diverse activities, varying from involvement in education, which is formative in children's lives, to nursing the wounded in the war and direct political action. The *International Union of Women* founded in 1895 in Paris combined the struggle for women's rights with that against military aspirations and the killing of people. Gabrielle Wiszniewska, daughter of Victor Hugo, was the first chairperson of the *International Women's League for General Disarmament* founded in 1896, also in Paris, which in 1899 changed its name to *Universal Women's Alliance for Peace*. As at the Hague Peace Conferences of 1899 and 1907, the well-to-do women in the movement used their connections to influence men. After their role as lobbyists and advisers during the Conferences, the women's organizations continued to work for peace. Under the leadership of the German-American pacifist Anna Eckstein, hundreds of thousands of signatures were collected in 1910, with the aim of applying pressure to call a third peace conference.

Women's reactions to the outbreak of the First World War

However, in 1914 the women's movement was divided. Just like the socialist workers' movement, many women supported the war policy of their governments. Nevertheless, in various states a part of the women's movement continued to oppose the war and tried to overcome the impediments to travel and communication caused by it. The International Woman Suffrage Alliance did everything it could to distribute its monthly magazine *Ius Suffragii* as widely as possible. It also set up an *International Women's Relief Committee* in London, which gained the support of the Home Office and the American ambassador. In Switzerland women founded the *World Union of Women for International Concord* at the beginning of 1915, which expressed moral support for women and launched several aid and arbitration operations. In the US, women campaigned vehemently against the war. Immediately after war broke out they had formed the *Women's Peace Party*, which they wanted to expand internationally. In January 1915 the Party adopted a programme of seven points, which argued for agreement between states instead of a balance of power, for the removal of the causes of war and for the promotion of peace. Jane Addams, who influenced President Wilson, belonged to this Party. In socialist circles in Europe, Clara Zetkin tried to repair the contacts between women that had been broken by the war. She was the secretary of the *Socialist International Women's Committee* of the Second International, which had been formed in the meantime, and wanted to convene an international women's conference. She did not succeed in organizing such a conference in the Netherlands at the beginning of 1915 as the Dutch government refused to issue visas. At the end of March, however, she managed to do so in Bern, where the first real international protest against the war took place. Despite differences of opinion between socialist and communist women, they adopted a joint resolution against the war.

The peace congress of women in The Hague (1915)

What Zetkin was not able to do, the Dutch doctor and women's activist Aletta Jacobs did. As the congress of the International Woman Suffrage Alliance planned for 1915 in Berlin could not take place and 'something had to be done', Jacobs took the initiative for an international peace congress for women from both belligerent and neutral states. This was held from 28 April to 1 May 1915 in The Hague. The women from Germany, Italy, the Netherlands, Austria-Hungary, the UK and the US who were present condemned the war. They contrasted sisterly support, sympathy and peace proposals with their governments' hunger for war. They specifically condemned the offences against women that the war brought with it and appealed to all governments for immediate peace negotiations and disarmament. The women in The Hague argued that peace could only be assured if women enjoyed equal civil and political rights and responsibilities, because women's influence on national politics would be one of the strongest powers possible to prevent wars. For this reason they should be involved in the forthcoming peace discussions and in a permanent international conference, which had to prepare practical proposals for international cooperation. The congress in The Hague therefore decided to convene an international women's meeting at the same time as the official peace conference after the end of the war in order to influence the peace negotiations.

The International Committee of Women for Permanent Peace (1915)

After much discussion the women's congress decided to send a small delegation of women to the governments of belligerent and neutral states. Over a period of five weeks these delegates visited the governments of eight belligerent and six neutral states. They arranged for the international women's organizations in these states to convene meetings in their capital cities to publicize their intentions. They also arranged meetings with influential people. Almost everywhere these women encountered a willingness to end the war, on condition that an honourable means would be found of achieving peace. An initiative from the neutral states to accomplish this would not be seen as an unfriendly action. However, the women also heard the argument that a nation at war cannot ask for negotiations or express readiness to negotiate without the enemy claiming that this is a sign of weakness, something which would then be exploited when determining the conditions for peace. Therefore the willingness to end the war could not be pursued. The congress in The Hague and the contacts with governments resulted in the *International Committee of Women for Permanent Peace*. The US women involved were soon accused of being traitors to their nation, and especially when the US became involved in the war, feelings against the women fervently advocating peace were so strong that they had to stay in the background.

Public discussion on the Covenant and transforming the Committee into the WILPF (1919)

In May 1919 the International Committee organized a conference in Zurich, thus implementing the 1915 decision to discuss the peace conditions after the end of the war. The conference was attended by 150 delegates from both neutral and belligerent states. The meeting could not take place in Versailles, as France refused to issue visas to the non-Allied women, and problems with border papers had to be overcome for the journey to neutral Switzerland. A group of US women visited the battlefields in France first. Thanks to Jane Addams' good contacts in government circles she succeeded in bringing a copy of the draft peace conditions, including the proposed League of Nations, with her from Paris. This text was put on the agenda at Zurich, the first public meeting to discuss it. The draft was found disappointing, because of the contrast between the peace conditions which were to be enforced and the principles for a just and permanent peace laid down earlier by Wilson. This applied less to the Covenant of the League, although the women did find a real materialization of the idea of a common endeavour lacking. Despite differences in appreciation of the proposed League, the women in Zurich agreed that a global organization, which expressed the will of the nations and was open to all states, should be established. They were also in favour of an immediate reduction in arms on equal terms for all states, open access to raw materials and a ban on the use of military force or food blockades if sanctions were enforced. To make their objections known the congress decided to transform the International Committee into an organization, the *Women's International League for Peace and Freedom* (WILPF), and to send a deputation to Versailles. Because of Addams' connections they were sympathetically received by various national delegations, but they made little impression.

Women's lobby at Versailles

The WILPF was not the only international women's organization represented at the peace conference in Versailles. The *International Council of Women*, under the leadership of Lady Aberdeen, and the *League of Women Suffragists of the Allied Powers and the United States*, a collaboration set up by the International Woman Suffrage Alliance, together asked for a meeting with the commission that had drafted the League's Covenant. They wanted to be heard on a number of issues regarding the legal position of women in the future, with the International Council of Women referring to the fact that they had been consulted by the Hague Peace Conference in 1907 (see §7.1). During this meeting a delegation of 17 women explained their wishes and handed over a memorandum with their demands: the appointment of women to positions in the League of Nations, both in commissions and on the staff; the abolishment of the exploitation of women and children and of prostitution; women's suffrage and equal consultation of women and men in a referendum about changes in the nationality of people; the establishment of an international agency for education; and the formation of an international health organization. The memorandum also included a declaration in favour of the control and reduction of weapons. Wilson reacted sympathetically, but also said that the League of Nations could not solve all problems at once.

An additional article of principal significance

During this mission, Lady Aberdeen was adamant about having a clause included in the Covenant that forbade sexual discrimination in the activities of the League. This was difficult, as general statements about citizens' rights had been rejected during the debate on the rights of minorities, racial equality and freedom of religion as being violations of the sovereignty of states, and the negotiations on racial and religious discrimination had reached an impasse (see §15.3). However, the women's lobbying had some success, because the League's Covenant did ultimately include a third paragraph in Article 7, later known as the 'equality article'. This pertained to the holding of office and read: 'All positions under or in connection with the League, including the Secretariat, shall be open equally to men and women'. In paragraph c of Article 23, moreover, the League was given the task of combating prostitution. Article 7.3 meant that women could be appointed to positions in the League, which in turn implied that they could become actively involved in issues of importance to women. It was not actually stipulated anywhere, but this was something that would develop in practice. Several international women's organizations now concentrated their activities on the League and moved their offices to Geneva. The first resolutions on the work of the League were passed at the congress of the International Council of Women in Oslo in 1920, and as soon as the conference was over the ICW sent them to the secretary-general. A few weeks later the ICW arranged for all its publications to be included in the library of the League. On 15 December ICW vice-chairperson Henni Forchammer, who was in Geneva as technical adviser to the Danish delegation, addressed the Assembly of the League, the first woman to do so (ICW 1966, 47). Through a special confederation they established in Geneva, international women's organizations arranged to have regular contact with delegates and other international figures. Moreover, from 1925 onwards they participated in cross-organization consultations on appointing more women to commissions of the League. Whenever possible they suggested women candidates.

15.6 The League of Nations as a universal organization 1919–46

Preamble to the covenant

The League was founded on 10 January 1920 with the objective 'to promote international co-operation and to achieve international peace and security' (see Figure 15.3 for the text of the preamble to the Covenant). It was located in Geneva in neutral Switzerland and was meant to be a universal organization that all states could join. They retained their sovereignty and were legally equal to each other.

Member states of the League of Nations

In total 62 states became members (see Figure 15.4 for the original members and Appendix 1 for all members). There was an admissions procedure through which a total of 20 states joined. It was also possible to withdraw from the League, and 16 states did so. In addition to most of the Allied victors, 13 neutral states signed up after the founding of the League, but the US did not. On 10 March 1920 there were 42 member states. Germany joined in 1926 and the Soviet Union in 1934. Argentina left in 1921 because the Assembly did not adopt its proposals to amend the Covenant, while Brazil withdrew in 1928 because it had not been given a permanent seat on the Council. In the 1930s Germany, Italy and Japan departed, and the Soviet Union was expelled in 1939 over the war it had started against Finland.

Organs of the League of Nations and associated institutions

The principal organs of the League of Nations were the *Assembly*, the *Council* and the *Permanent Secretariat*. The three 'technical organizations' of the League (in fact commissions and not organizations) in the fields of economics, traffic and health are dealt with in

Figure 15.3 Preamble to the Covenant of the League of Nations

The High Contracting Parties,
In order to promote international co-operation and to achieve international peace and security

by the acceptance of obligations not to resort to war,
by the prescription of open, just and honourable relations between nations,
by the firm establishment of the understandings of international law as the actual rule of conduct among Governments, and
by the maintenance of justice and a scrupulous respect for all treaty obligations in the dealings of organised peoples with one another,

Agree to this Covenant of the League of Nations.

Figure 15.4 The states named in the Covenant of the League of Nations

Original members (signatories of the peace treaty): Belgium, Bolivia, Brazil, the British Empire (including the dominions of Australia, Canada, India, New Zealand and South Africa), China, Cuba, Czechoslovakia, Ecuador (did not ratify and hence did not become a member), France, Greece, Guatemala, Haiti, Hejaz (including Mecca and Medina, united with Nejd in 1932 to form Saudi Arabia; did not become a member), Honduras, Italy, Japan, Liberia, Nicaragua, Panama, Peru, Poland, Portugal, Romania, Serbian-Croatian-Slovenian State, Siam, the United States of America (did not become a member) and Uruguay.

Invited to accede to the treaty: Argentina, Chile, Colombia, Denmark, El Salvador, Mexico (owing to Wilson's opposition not invited but added by the Assembly in 1931), the Netherlands, Norway, Paraguay, Persia, Spain, Sweden, Switzerland and Venezuela.

Chapter 18 (see §18.1). In addition the League established several kinds of commission and committee: permanent and temporary advisory commissions, administrative commissions for particular regions and refugees, and three international institutes. These commissions and institutes were as follows.

Permanent advisory commissions:

- International Committee on Intellectual Cooperation
- Permanent Mandates Commission
- Permanent Advisory Commission on Military, Naval and Air Questions
- Advisory Committee on Opium and Other Dangerous Drugs
- Advisory Committee on the Traffic in Women and Children; 1936: Advisory Committee on Social Questions

Temporary advisory and preparatory commissions:

- Committee for the Progressive Codification of International Law
- Preparatory Commission for the Disarmament Conference

Administrative commissions and officials:

- Governing Commission for the Saar Basin
- High Commissioner for the Free City of Danzig
- High Commissioner for Refugees; 1931: Nansen International Office for Refugees
- Commission for Greek Refugees (Athens)
- Commission for Bulgarian Refugees (Sofia)

International institutes:

- International Institute of Intellectual Cooperation (Paris)
- International Educational Cinematographic Institute (Rome)
- International Institute for the Unification of Private Law (Rome).

The two institutions connected to the League but operating virtually independently were the *Permanent Court of International Justice*, established on the basis of Article 14 of the Covenant, and the *International Labour Organization*, established on the basis of Part XIII of the Treaty of Versailles. Because of the peace treaty the ILO was not based on the Covenant, but it was part of the League system. Article 23 stipulated that the League's member states 'will endeavour to secure and maintain fair and humane conditions of labour for men, women, and children, both in their own countries and in all countries to which their commercial and industrial relations extend, and for that purpose will establish and maintain the necessary international organisations'.

The Assembly

The *Assembly* of the League of Nations was made up of representatives of the member states. Each state could send a maximum of three representatives, who together had one vote. The Assembly met once a year in September, and the meetings were open to the public. The official languages were French and English, and as the interpreters always translated after a speech, work was slowed down. The Assembly chose a new chairperson and six vice-chairpersons every year, who together formed the *Bureau* that organized activities. The Assembly generally made decisions unanimously. Decisions on procedures and the admission of new members, however, required only a two-thirds majority. The Assembly had *six committees*, which also sum up its activities:

- *First Committee*: Constitutional questions (regarding the organization)
- *Second Committee*: Technical organizations (economic, social and technical questions)
- *Third Committee*: Reduction of Armaments (also the Permanent Court)
- *Fourth Committee*: Budget and financial questions (also staff questions)
- *Fifth Committee*: Social and general questions (also admission of new members)
- *Sixth Committee*: Political questions (including mandates and minorities)

Every member state had a representative on each committee.

The Council

The *Council*, the second political organ of the League, had four (later five) permanent members: France, Italy, Japan and the UK with from 1926 to 1933 Germany and from 1934 to 1939 the Soviet Union. There were also four non-permanent members (increased to six from 1922 and nine from 1926) who each held their seat for three years. They were chosen by the Assembly. The Council could be temporarily enlarged when a subject was being dealt with that involved a member state not represented on the Council. It met about five or six times a year with a different chairperson each time. Official discussions were open to the public, but the number of admission tickets available was limited. Other meetings were generally closed, although the minutes were published later. The subjects dealt with were categorized, with each representative on the Council allocated a particular category over which he or she reported to the Council. Each participating state had one vote and decisions were usually made unanimously. One of the reasons for the creation of the Council was to be able to discuss matters in a small committee rather than in the Assembly. The balance of power between states was taken into account when choosing Council members. The Council was not *below* the Assembly but *alongside* it, which meant that agreement between the Council and the Assembly was necessary on many issues: something could be implemented only if both organs had agreed. Claude called the Council a new, institutionalized edition of the Concert of Europe 'incorporating the principles of legal definition of authority and terms of reference, institutional continuity, regularity of session, and balanced composition of great and small power representatives' (Claude 1966, 38).

The Permanent Secretariat

The *Permanent Secretariat* of the League of Nations consisted of a secretary-general, one and later two deputy secretaries-general and three (later four) undersecretaries-general. The secretary-general was appointed by the Council after approval from the Assembly, and all others connected with the Secretariat were also appointed by the Council. The secretary-general held the post for both the Assembly and the Council. Sir Eric Drummond was the first secretary-general of the League. He took office in April 1919 and was succeeded in July 1933 by the Frenchman Joseph Avenol, while the Irishman Séan Lester held the position from August 1940 to April 1946. Jean Monnet was one of the undersecretaries-general (until 1922). Ultimately the League had a staff of about 600 of various nationalities, although their posts were international, as they reported to the secretary-general and not to their own state. They enjoyed diplomatic privileges and immunities in the performance of their job. The Secretariat was located in London from the end of April 1919 until October 1920, when the Geneva office opened for business on 1 November 1920. The Secretariat had *11 sections*: Political Affairs; Legal Affairs; Financial and Economic Affairs; Reduction of Armaments; Transit and Traffic; Mandates; Administration and Minorities; Social Affairs; Health; Intellectual Cooperation and International Bureaus; and Information (for publications and contact with the press). In 1933 a Central Section was added.

NGO influence at the League of Nations

In line with the nineteenth-century tradition of NGO influence on multilateral conferences and within IGOs, internationally-active NGOs could exercise influence at the

League of Nations. As the relationship between the League and NGOs was not formally regulated, there was room for authentic private influence within the League. NGOs could formulate their viewpoints in memoranda which they, like the International Council of Women, submitted to the League. Sometimes their viewpoints or ideas were presented by national delegations with similar points of view. In addition their representatives spoke in commissions, produced reports, started discussions and even proposed resolutions and amendments. In 1932 they were allowed to address the delegates to the League's Disarmament Conference during a plenary session. In the course of the 1930s, however, the relationship between the League and the NGOs deteriorated. The increasingly powerless League gradually curtailed the NGO privileges that had developed over the years.

15.7 The Permanent Court of International Justice 1920–46

The independent selection of judges

Founded in 1920, the *Permanent Court of International Justice* became operational in 1922. As a result of its neutral position during the war, the Netherlands did not succeed in bringing the League of Nations to The Hague, but it was successful with the Court due to it being the Permanent Court of Arbitration's seat. The new Court had permanent judges. The nine (from 1931, 11) judges and four deputy judges were chosen for the first time on 30 January 1922. Each state, regardless of whether it was a member of the League, could designate a so-called 'national group' of four candidates. These groups in turn chose four candidate judges, of whom only two could have the state's nationality, which meant judges chosen were independent of their governments. If the Assembly and the Council of the League, in separate ballots, agreed on a candidate by a majority of votes, then the candidate was appointed. In addition to this appointment procedure there was another connection with the League, as the budget of the Court came out of its own budget, but apart from that the Court functioned independently. Ultimately there were 59 member states of the Court.

Administration of justice and jurisprudence

The purpose of the Court was to administer justice and develop jurisprudence. Between 1922 and 1939, the period during which the Court functioned effectively, 66 cases were presented: 38 contentious cases and 28 advisory cases (Rosenne 1989, 15). In addition the Court made several recommendations to the League. According to Article 14 of the Covenant of the League the Court was competent to 'hear and determine any dispute of an international character which the parties thereto submit to it'. The Assembly drew up the Statute of the Court on 13 December 1920. It added an 'optional clause', which stated that in all cases of a legal character the Court should have compulsory jurisdiction, with an 'additional clause' stipulating that any state could accept the compulsory jurisdiction of the Court on the basis of reciprocity. Adherence to these clauses was optional. In 1929, 41 states had signed the clauses. On 14 September 1929 the Statute of the Court was amended on a number of points and a protocol about the entry of the US was accepted. The US signed the Statute of the Court, after it had been rejected twice by the Senate, with five reservations which the Senate had formulated in January 1926. The other states accepted these special conditions, which restricted the authority of the

Court in relation to the US. From the start an American judge was always a member of the Court. The Soviet Union did not sign the Statute, did not have a judge as a member of the Court and rejected the Court's competence in a dispute in which it was involved itself (Rosenne 1989, 16).

Sources of law and codification

The main sources of law for the Permanent Court were the general principles of international law, rather than the written rules. As there were still few written rules, the existence of the Court prompted the need for codification of international law. In 1929 a first conference of experts was held in The Hague. The judicial department of the Secretariat of the League of Nations, which was responsible for the registration of international treaties, was also given responsibility for the codification and the League set up a temporary commission of experts for this purpose.

Administration of justice and arbitration

When states submitted a dispute to the Court, they could request administration of justice (judgement was made and one of the parties lost the dispute) or arbitration (the interests of both parties were reconciled in an equitable fashion). The Permanent Court of International Justice was authorized to arbitrate, thereby overlapping with the Permanent Court of Arbitration of 1899. This overlap led to a practical division of tasks between the two Courts. The Permanent Court of Arbitration mainly dealt with disputes based on differences about the explanation and application of international treaties and customs, while the Permanent Court of International Justice concentrated on general principles. Under the auspices of the League, the *General Act for the Pacific Settlement of Disputes* was agreed in 1928. Although this made reference to the Convention on the Pacific Settlement of International Disputes as amended in 1907, the new regulation was not a real improvement, apart from on a few points. No more than 23 states accepted the General Act and Spain withdrew in 1939. Only eight states signed the slightly revised version of this General Act which the UN adopted in 1949 (*Revised General Act*) (Malanczuk 1997, 274).

Important cases before the Court

The ILO submitted the first cases to the Court. It requested advisory opinions on the conditions of agricultural workers, the methods of production and the appointment of delegates to its International Labour Conference. The *Wimbledon* case from 1923 established the Court's reputation. The Germans refused the British ship *Wimbledon*, which was on its way to Poland with French weapons, access to the Kiel Canal. Germany appealed to the neutrality rules that applied to it. The Court determined, however, that the free access laid down in the Treaty of Versailles applied to ships from all states that had concluded peace with Germany. It ruled that Germany was wrong and had to pay compensation. The most sensitive subject to come before the Court was the judgement in 1931 on a proposed customs union between Germany and Austria, which conflicted with the provisions of Versailles. Due to the politicized atmosphere that had developed in the meantime, the ruling of the Court had little effect. 'Although the Court took a firm stand against Germany's arguments, this decision highlighted the weakness of the judicial process in the current legal order. Despite all the precautions taken, politicization had brought the Court down' (Eyffinger 1996, 91). The Court continued to play a role in the late 1930s in the approach of the Second World War, however, when a number of important conflicts were submitted, such as those between Germany and Poland and between Latvia, Poland and Germany.

From The Hague to Geneva (1940)

At the beginning of May 1940, just before the German occupation of the Netherlands, the Permanent Court of International Justice moved from The Hague to Geneva in neutral Switzerland. The Court became paralysed by the Second World War, and was abolished at the same time as the League of Nations on 18 April 1946. On the same day it was succeeded by the International Court of Justice in The Hague (see §21.1).

The major powers and collective security in the interwar period

16.1 Temporary administration, conflict settlement and refugee support by the League of Nations

The High Commissioner for Danzig

During the Versailles Conference of 1919, separate measures were taken for different territories, including Danzig, Vilnius, Memel and the Saar Basin. The League of Nations initially played a successful role in tackling the problems relating to these territories. In 1919 the port of Danzig and the area around it, which was part of Prussia, was declared a free city under the supervision of the League of Nations. The League appointed a High Commissioner, who was paid jointly by the city and by Poland. Danzig was also to remain dependent on Poland for its foreign policy. This arrangement produced a difficult relationship with Poland, which the city was reluctant to accept. It meant that Poland lost an important port (the reason why it built a new one in Gdynia) and it continued to consider Danzig as Polish territory. The High Commissioner, a position filled at various times by Britons, Italians, a Dutchman and a Dane, had the task of drafting a constitution for the city and mediating between it and Poland. In the 1920s, despite tensions, the High Commissioner succeeded in both these objectives. In the 1930s the situation became more complex because of Germany's ambitions to reclaim the city as part of its territory.

Involvement in the cities of Vilnius and Memel

At Versailles, after being occupied by the Germans and fighting for its independence during the First World War, Vilnius was assigned to Lithuania. However, it continued to be at the mercy of international politics, with Germany, Poland and Russia each claiming it, and it changed hands several times in 1920. After a peace treaty between Russia and Lithuania in that year, Polish volunteer troops occupied the city. Intervention by the League of Nations in the conflict resulted in a referendum. Early in 1922 the majority of the city's inhabitants voted for Vilnius to be part of Poland, but Lithuania refused to recognize the result as the referendum had been conducted under the super-vision of the Polish volunteers. There were fears that the vote had been an attempt to keep the city under Polish rule. Partly due to the efforts of the League of Nations, a war between Poland and Lithuania was avoided. A Conference of Ambassadors decided to allocate Vilnius to Poland. As compensation, Lithuania took control of the city of Memel (Klaipeda) and the surrounding area early in 1923. This port had been placed under the control of the Allies in 1919 at Versailles, because of its primarily German population, but was to be assigned to Lithuania. The major powers recognized the Lithuanian occupa-tion, on condition that Memel would remain autonomous and the League of Nations could protect its German citizens. A committee was set up under the leadership of the American Norman Davis, which drew up a constitution in which Lithuania guaranteed Poland the same trade and transport rights as other users of the port of Memel. To ensure compliance, a member of the League's Transit Organization (see §18.1) joined the Port Council in Memel as an independent member. Lithuania and the Allies approved the agreement in March 1924 and it entered into force in August 1925. The situation in the city remained tense, however, as the German population still wanted it to be returned to Germany.

The referendum in Upper Silesia (1921)

It was decided at Versailles that the northwest of Silesia, the former southeast of Prussia, would remain part of Germany. This industrialized area had many coal and iron mines. The inhabitants of Upper Silesia, two-thirds of whom were Polish and one-third German, were given the opportunity to vote in a referendum on whether they wished to have German or Polish nationality. In the meantime Allied troops under the control of France occupied the area. A Conference of Ambassadors divided the territory between Poland and Germany, which led to new tensions. In the referendum, which was held in March 1921, the majority voted to be part of Germany but, because of the unrest and violence surrounding the vote, a committee of the League of Nations ruled that the larger part of Upper Silesia should remain Polish. The committee was very thorough in its work and in May 1922 it drafted the *Geneva Convention on Upper Silesia*, which both Germany and Poland accepted. This enabled the region to develop economically, but the League of Nations received regular complaints from minorities in both states.

The Governing Commission for the Saar Basin

At Versailles the Territory of the Saar Basin, a coalmining region on the border of Ger-many and France, was separated from Germany and placed under League of Nations administration for 15 years (1920–35). France was given charge of the coalmines and chaired the international Governing Commission that consisted of representatives from France, three other states and the Saar territory. The five members of the *Governing Commission for the Saar Basin* were appointed by the Council of the League of Nations, initially for a year each but with the power to extend their term. In early 1923 France decided to occupy the Ruhr region. This led to a protest strike by miners and transport workers, which was supported by the international trade union movement (see §17.4). In response, the French chair of the Governing Commission curtailed the civil liberties of the inhabitants of the Saar territory and called in French troops. His actions led to an inquiry the following summer by the Council of the League of Nations, which made it clear that the Saar territory was the responsibility of the League and not of France. As a result, the Governing Commission reversed the measures it had taken.

Settling the disputes on the Åland Islands (1920) and Albania (1921)

One of the League of Nations' earliest successes was the settlement of a conflict between Finland and Sweden. The Åland Islands had long been part of Sweden, but were transferred to Russia in 1809, together with Finland. In 1917 the island's inhabitants demanded autonomy and to be reunited with Sweden. After a protest from Finland, a committee of the League of Nations ruled that the islands would remain part of Finland from 1920. They would be demilitarized and Finland would have to take account of the Swedish character of the population. The ruling was laid down in the 1921 *Convention Relating to the Non-Fortification and Neutralisation of the Åland Islands*. Another success for the League of Nations was preventing the division of Albania in 1921. During the First World War, Albania had been occupied by several states. France and Italy were prepared to withdraw in 1920, and Yugoslavia followed in 1921. Through the intervention of the League, Albania's independence within its 1913 borders was again recognized. Greece accepted this settlement because the League pledged to monitor the situation of the Greek minority in Albania.

Developments around Corfu (1923) and the protest by the small states

In 1923 the murder of an Italian diplomat and four members of his staff, who were in the process of defining the Greek–Albanian border in Corfu, led to Italy bombarding and occupying the island. The Conference of Ambassadors of the three states involved condemned Greece and decided that it should pay compensation, to be set by the Permanent Court of International Justice. This ruling was approved by the Council of the League of Nations, but under pressure from Benito Mussolini, Italy persuaded the ambassadors not to accept a role for the Permanent Court. This led to a protest by the smaller European and the Latin American states in the Assembly of the League of Nations, because the Council of the League had left it to the Conference of Ambassadors to settle the dispute. They appealed to Article 15 of the League's Covenant, which called for disputes to be submitted to the Council, and they stated that the Council should have acted, even if one of its members found it inappropriate. They also felt that an impression had been given that states could use occupation to achieve their aims. Italy's violent action could not be tolerated, even if it were not committed with the intention of provoking a war. The Council accepted this interpretation in a legal statement, but nevertheless left it to the Conference of Ambassadors to settle the matter. 'Though the disappointment of some League supporters did not disappear when the Conference of Ambassadors announced the Italian evacuation of Corfu at the end of September, most small member states in the Assembly felt that their demands had had some effect. To France, which had supported Italy, and Mussolini, it became clear that acts of violence could count on opposition' (Van Ginneken 2006, 63).

Problems over Greece, Turkey and Armenia

After the First World War the Allied powers and Turkey had agreed a peace treaty in Sèvres. As a result, Turkey lost substantial territories in the Ottoman Empire, including Mesopotamia, Palestine, Syria, Armenia and a number of islands in the Mediterranean. Greece had occupied parts of western Turkey after the war, but was driven out again by Turkish troops in 1922. At the suggestion of Fridtjof Nansen, who concerned himself with the fate of refugees fleeing the Graeco–Turkish war (see below), the conflict, which was threatening to escalate, was put before the League of Nations. However, the major powers that occupied Istanbul were not willing to agree to this, and without involving the League of Nations they concluded a peace treaty in Lausanne in 1923, under which most of the territory occupied by Greece was returned to Turkey. As a consequence of the agreed border changes there was mass migration in both directions. A million Greeks were forced to leave Turkey and around 800,000 Turks left Greece. The League of Nations supported Greece in dealing with these mass movements of people. In 1925 the League mediated in a similar border conflict between Greece and Bulgaria. Armenia, which had declared its independence after the First World War, had the sympathy of the Allies, but the region was increasingly the subject of tension between communist Russia and nationalist Turks. In 1915 the Turkish government had decided to deport all Turkish Armenians to Syria and other parts of the Ottoman Empire. During this mass exodus, hundreds of thousands of Armenians were murdered or driven to their deaths as victims of circumstance. At the end of the war the border between Russia and Turkey ran right through the original territory of Armenia, but none of the major powers were prepared to intervene in the resulting skirmishes and migration flows. In April 1920 the Council of the League of Nations decided to initiate a mandate for Armenia. The invitation to the US to take part in the process was accepted by President Woodrow Wilson, but Congress rejected the idea in June. The situation deteriorated as a consequence of increased tensions and the heavy-handed actions of the Turkish army, which had been sent into Armenia. The first meeting of the Assembly of the League of Nations in 1920, however, went no further than expressing its sympathy for the Armenian republic and calling on the two parties to cease hostilities. At the end of 1920, after a communist coup, Armenia became part of communist Russia and later the Soviet Union.

First international intervention in refugee issues

As well as being a polar explorer, Fridtjof Nansen also became known as an international politician. During the First World War he led a Norwegian committee that conducted negotiations in the US on the supply of goods that were important to Norway. He was an observer at Versailles and headed the Norwegian delegation at the first session of the Assembly of the League of Nations, a position he retained until his death in 1930. Neither the Covenant of the League nor the negotiations in Versailles had made any provisions for the repatriation of prisoners of war or refugees. At the insistence of the International Committee of the Red Cross, the League decided to take action, to help the more than a million refugees fleeing Russia after the civil war and the 1917 Revolution and because of the subsequent famine which was to claim five million lives. In April 1920 Nansen was appointed High Commissioner to address the problems of Russian refugees in Europe. This mandate was later extended to cover Greek, Armenian, Bulgarian and other refugees fleeing, among other conflicts, the Graeco–Turkish war.

The legal status of refugees

Nansen succeeded in drawing up a definition of the legal status of refugees, which was expressed in an international identification document. The 'Nansen passport', introduced on the basis of a treaty concluded in Geneva in 1922, allowed refugees who had lost their papers or had no valid papers for other reasons to travel across national borders. This passport, issued by the state in which the refugees were staying, was recognized by more than 50 states. Nansen received very little financial support from the League of Nations for refugee work (4,000 British pounds) and therefore had to seek funds elsewhere, something he did by setting up private committees of sympathetic individuals and organizations in various states. These *Nansen Committees* collected money and were 'responsible' for certain areas in Russia. In addition to the minimal financial support, the limited willingness among states – with the exception of France – to accept large groups of refugees was a disappointment. Within the League of Nations, Nansen set up an informal structure of representatives from the states where Nansen Committees existed. He had a few rooms at the League's Secretariat for his activities and later acquired a small office at the International Labour Organization, where he worked with the ILO to arrange employment for refugees in receiving states and after their repatriation. In 1922 Nansen was awarded the Nobel Peace Prize for this work.

The Nansen International Office for Refugees (1931)

In 1929 the Assembly of the League of Nations decided to bring the office of the High Commissioner under the authority of the secretary-general and incorporate it into the Secretariat. Nansen's death in 1930 meant the end of the High Commissioner and its secretariat, but in the following year the League set up the *Nansen International Office for Refugees*. This Office was under its authority but, again, had hardly any funds. Within a short period it had to deal with large numbers of refugees from Germany, Austria, the Saar territory and Czechoslovakia. In 1933, with the rise of national socialism, the American James McDonald was appointed *High Commissioner for Refugees from Germany*. This position was formally independent of the League of Nations and, because it was also unwilling to provide any funds, McDonald could do little more than coordinate non-governmental organizations and initiatives. He concentrated his efforts on combating immigration restrictions around the world, to ensure that Jewish refugees from Germany could flee to other states. After the introduction of the Nuremberg decrees of 1935, which stripped German Jews of their civil rights, McDonald became disillusioned with the League of Nations. The League adhered to the view that this was an internal German affair in which it was not prepared to take more resolute action, and in December 1935 McDonald resigned (Cutts 2000, 15). After Germany left the League of Nations, the two small offices – the Nansen International Office for Refugees and that of the High Commissioner for Refugees from Germany – were merged. Receiving the Nobel Peace Prize in 1938 gave the Nansen Office a little leverage, and in 1939 Sir Herbert Emerson was appointed High Commissioner. His office in London continued to operate until 1946. This office was also used by the *Intergovernmental Committee for Refugees* (IGCR), set up in 1938 at a conference in Evian to negotiate with Germany on the emigration of Jews. The US was also present in Evian, but did nothing to offer a lifeline to Jewish refugees (Loescher 2001, 32–33).

The conventions on the status of refugees from Germany (1933, 1938)

An international conference on the protection of refugees led to the 1933 *Convention Relating to the International Status of Refugees*. This Convention embraced the general principle that refugees cannot be forced to return to their country of origin. It was, however, ratified by no more than eight states, while the 1938 *Convention Concerning the Status of Refugees from Germany* was ratified by only three states (Cutts 2000, 25–26). Despite the lack of support for these Conventions in the 1930s, they would later form the basis of the 1951 UN Convention Relating to the Status of Refugees (see §22.1). In this way, through its experience and Conventions, the League of Nations laid the basis for refugee work during and after the Second World War.

16.2 Disarmament efforts by the major powers and the League of Nations

The Washington Naval Conference of 1921–22

Although arms control and disarmament were one reason for the establishment of the League of Nations, in Asia these issues were addressed not by the League but by the major powers between themselves. In 1921 the US called the major powers together to discuss the size of their fleets. It recognized Japan as a major power, thereby changing the relationship between Japan and the UK which had been laid down in a British–Japanese alliance in 1902. At the Naval Conference in Washington DC from November 1921 to February 1922, France, Italy, Japan, the UK and the US agreed on the *Washington Naval Treaty*, known as the *Five Power Treaty*, which limited the size and standard of their fleets. The Treaty specified the relative tonnages of the large ships of the five fleets, in the following proportions: US five, UK five, Japan three, France and Italy 1.75 each. In the *Four Power Treaty*, France, Japan, the UK and the US secured their rights in the Pacific and pledged to consult each other in case of aggression in the Far East. In the *Nine Power Treaty*, all the states present (Belgium, China, France, Italy, Japan, the Netherlands, Portugal, the UK and the US) recognized an *open door policy* regarding China. This entailed equal treatment for all states in matters relating to trade with and industrial activity in China, which for China represented recognition of its territorial integrity. This *Washington System* of international relations as created by the major powers functioned effectively in the 1920s, when despite a certain degree of unrest in the region there were no serious international conflicts in the Far East. These treaties show that the well-known isolationism of the US shortly after the First World War was less evident in Asia than in Europe.

The London Naval Treaty (1930)

In 1930 the Washington Naval Treaty was reviewed at a conference in London, where France, Italy, Japan, the UK and the US reached a number of further agreements on warship types and the use of submarines in trade disputes between states. Other states could become party to these agreements, known together as the *London Naval Treaty*. The Treaty, however, ultimately proved ineffective in dealing with new military tensions. Japan withdrew in 1936 and like Italy it did not participate in the *Second Naval Treaty of London* in 1936 (see Figure 16.1 for an overview of the disarmament conferences in the interwar period).

Figure 16.1 Disarmament conferences in the interwar period

Washington Conference 1921–22
Resulted in the *Washington Naval Treaty*, the *Four Power Treaty* and the *Nine Power Treaty*.

Geneva Conference 1925
Resulted in the Geneva Poison Gas Protocol.

London Conference 1930
Resulted in the *London Naval Treaty*.

League of Nations Disarmament Conference in Geneva 1932–34
The prepared Draft Disarmament Convention and other proposals were rejected.

1935
German–British Naval Treaty, which set the ratio of German to British warships at 35:100. This Treaty was cancelled shortly before the start of the Second World War.

London Conference 1936
Second London Naval Treaty. This also included the Soviet Union, but not Italy and Japan. It aimed to impose qualitative limits on naval weaponry.

Disarmament efforts by the League of Nations: Resolution XIV (1922)

The League of Nations had been excluded from the discussions to limit the size of the major powers' fleets, and in the 1920s and 1930s it did not succeed in taking the lead in the disarmament process or in breaking through the lack of political will on the part of the major powers. Article 8 of the League's Covenant stated that 'the maintenance of peace requires the reduction of national armaments to the lowest point consistent with national safety and the enforcement by common action of international obligations'. In 1922 the Assembly unanimously adopted *Resolution XIV*, which expressed the idea that states would be willing to disarm only if there was a treaty safeguarding them against aggression to which all states could be party. At the insistence of France, a proviso was added that states could also conclude regional mutual assistance treaties. A *Temporary Mixed Commission for the Reduction of Armaments*, set up in 1920 and consisting of eminent politicians and experts from the League and the ILO, began to prepare a treaty of mutual assistance. A draft was ready in the summer of 1923 and was sent to the Third Committee of the Assembly, which was concerned with disarmament. The treaty suffered an early demise during 1924, however, when it was publicly rejected by the US, the Soviet Union and the UK, which now argued that the security issue was best addressed through arbitration.

The Geneva Protocol (1924) also scrapped

To make at least some progress, the UK and France submitted a resolution on the combination of arbitration, security and disarmament in September 1924. This resolution aimed to give the League of Nations greater authority over its member states. The background to the resolution was shaped by the developments surrounding Corfu, where the Council had acted with little authority (see §16.1), and France's wish for protection against a possible German invasion. The Assembly approved the resolution and set the First Committee (legal affairs) and the Third Committee (reduction of armaments) to work. This resulted in October 1924 in the *Geneva Protocol* on the peaceful settlement of international disputes and a proposal for a conference on disarmament, after which the Protocol could come into force. The Protocol stipulated general acceptance of the obligatory jurisdiction of the Permanent Court of International Justice in the case of legal disputes. Although the Assembly advised that they should sign the Protocol, few member states actually did. Most of them saw little point in becoming involved in war against a state they were obliged to see as an aggressor out of solidarity, without themselves having any direct interest in doing so. When the new Conservative government in the UK rejected the Protocol it signified its political end. Many later international security treaties were however inspired by the Geneva Protocol and built on its principles. Legal formulations drafted by international organizations clearly do not lose their value and validity as quickly as political agreements.

The Locarno Conference (1925)

The next event of major significance, partly prepared by the League's Temporary Mixed Commission, was the Locarno Conference from 5 to 16 October 1925, where Belgium, France, Germany, Italy and the UK as well as Poland and Czechoslovakia signed eight treaties. These related to the mutual assurance of the Franco–German and Belgian–German borders, arbitration between Germany and Belgium, Germany and France, Germany and Poland, and Germany and Czechoslovakia, and mutual assistance between France and Poland and France and Czechoslovakia in case of aggression by Germany. As a result of these agreements, Germany was able to join the League of Nations in 1926, a condition for all these treaties to come into force. Because Germany was not prepared to accept the provisions of Article 16 of the Covenant on sanctions against states without reservations, these provisos were appended to the Treaties of Locarno.

The Kellogg–Briand Pact (1928)

For a short time during the second half of the 1920s, the League of Nations ideal seemed to be succeeding. In 1928 Germany and other states agreed the *Kellogg–Briand Pact*, named after its initiators the foreign minister of France Aristide Briand and the US Secretary of State Frank Kellogg. The Pact, ultimately signed by 55 states including the major powers, was seen as complementing the Covenant of the League of Nations. The signatories to the Pact rejected war as a means of settling international disputes and as an instrument of national policy. Peaceful means were to be sought to solve conflicts. It brought the US closer to the League. This 'European moment', which was felt between 1924 and 1933, found expression in a movement for Pan-European unity and a proposal by Briand in September 1929 for a European Federal Union (see Figure 16.2).

The 1925 Geneva Poison Gas Protocol

Another factor contributing to this optimism in the 1920s was the adoption of the Geneva Poison Gas Protocol in 1925, which banned the use of poison gas and bacteriological weapons. It was intended to complement the conventions concluded at the Peace Conferences held in The Hague in 1899 and 1907. After the horrific experiences

Figure 16.2 Coudenhove-Kalergi's Pan-European Union (1926) and Briand's proposal for a European Federal Union (1929)

Aristide Briand's statement that 'At Locarno we spoke European, a new language which we shall all have to learn', led John Horne to conduct a study in the use of language during the interwar period. He suggested that between 1924 and 1933 there was a '**European moment**', which was reflected in the language. It had its roots in the efforts of former enemies to dismantle the political and cultural structures that they had mobilized during the First World War. One expression of this was the statement of the British ambassador after returning from Locarno, emphasizing that Germany had taken the initiative for peace in Europe. Efforts were also made to rid the term 'Allies' of its military connotations. The focus was primarily on removing the potentially damaging significance of the divisions created by the war. This 'European' use of language had its origins more in the war and the political and economic dividing lines in the period that followed it, than in any idealized view of a common civilization. The 'European moment' came to an end when the national socialists came to power in Germany in 1933. From then on, it was clear that the time for reconciliation was past and the language once more became that of war (Horne 2004).

Yet there was one movement that emphasized what European states had in common. The European moment and Europe's common destiny became particularly widely known through the book **Pan-Europa**, published in 1923 by the Austrian Richard Coudenhove-Kalergi, and through the author's efforts to achieve a federation of European states. The First World War had made him a staunch advocate of a federation of all European states and their overseas territories, although without the Soviet Union. In 1924 he launched a magazine called *Pan-Europa* and in 1926 he organized the first Pan-European Congress in Vienna, at which he was elected the first chairman of the **Pan-European Union**. Wherever possible he tried to persuade politicians of the value of his federal vision of Europe. The Union has been seen as the forerunner of the European Movement and the European integration ideal of the post-Second World War period (see §23.1).

Briand contributed to this trend in September 1929 with a proposal for a **European Federal Union**, submitted to the European members of the League of Nations. According to Briand, the Locarno Conference and the League of Nations showed that a model for collective security based on negotiation and arbitration could work. A European Federal Union would provide a framework for peaceful relations between France, Germany and the other states. He believed that it could be consolidated by a system of common institutions in Europe. He also saw it as a European counterbalance to US protectionism, and an opportunity to put an end to the economic fragmentation caused by the changes in Eastern Europe since the end of the war. He envisaged achieving the latter aim by setting up common tariff-free zones. Briand's proposals were cautious, as he wished to avoid intervening in the sovereign affairs of the member states or undermining the authority of the League (Horne 2004, 231). Turkey, which had joined the League and part of whose territory was in Europe, was indignant that Briand did not wish to include Turkey in his Union. The proposals were short-lived in any case. With the internal changes in Germany, the opportunity for a European moment had passed.

with poison gas in the First World War, there was a general desire to make sure it was never used again. Restrictions were therefore imposed on Germany, Austria, Hungary and Bulgaria at Versailles. Such a ban was included in the Washington Naval Treaty in 1922 and finally in Geneva in the *Protocol for the Prohibition of the Use in War of Asphyxiating, Poisonous or Other Gasses, and of Bacteriological Methods of Warfare*, which was signed by 29 states on 15 June 1925. The Protocol came into force on 8 February 1928 and was largely respected, although Japan did experiment with the use of gas in occupied Manchuria, and Germany developed a number of poison gases. During the Second World War poison gas was used comparatively rarely, though, and it was then not used again until by Iraq in 1980. The Protocol was superseded by the 1972 UN Biological Weapons Convention (see §24.2).

The Third Red Cross Geneva Convention (1929)

On 27 July 1929 the *Third Red Cross Geneva Convention*, which regulated the treatment of prisoners of war, was concluded. In general terms it required that warring states must treat prisoners of war humanely, provide information on their situation and allow representatives of neutral states access to prisoner-of-war camps. This new Convention and some amendments to the Second Convention of 1906 (see Figure 5.1) represented a further elaboration of the rules to which states had to adhere during war. Again, responsibility for monitoring compliance was entrusted to the private International Red Cross organization.

Preparing the Disarmament Conference

Because disarmament was not progressing very rapidly, at the suggestion of the Netherlands the League of Nations set up the *Preparatory Commission for the Disarmament Conference* in 1925. The US also took part in this Commission, following an invitation from the League. The consultations were difficult, with France, which wished to strengthen its security, on one side, and the UK, the US, Scandinavia, the Netherlands and Germany, on the other. Because France was only prepared to restrict its weaponry if there were compensatory security guarantees, no progress could be made until it had reached a compromise with the UK. This entailed France supporting the British standpoint on naval ordnance and the UK agreeing with France's views on army weapons. This compromise led to the 1930 London Naval Treaty and the *Draft Disarmament Convention*, completed in December of that year, which contained agreements on various points. 'Personnel was to be limited, and where possible reduced, in the number of serving effectives in all formations organized on a military basis, without considerations of trained reserves. The period of service with conscript forces was to be limited. Land-war material was subjected to budgetary limitation, and naval material was to be limited in accordance with the conclusions of the London conference. The budgetary limitation was not applied specifically to air material, which was restricted by numbers and horse-power. But an overhead budgetary limitation was applied to the total expenditure on land, sea, and air forces. Chemical and bacteriological weapons were prohibited. Other articles provided for the exchange of information, and the setting up of a Permanent Disarmament Commission' (Gathorne-Hardy 1952, 195–96). Germany was irritated by the clause that rights and obligations from previous treaties were to be upheld. 'While this was primarily intended by Great Britain and America to apply to the London and Washington

Treaties, it was construed by France and other Powers as maintaining the strict application of the military clauses of the Treaty of Versailles' (Gathorne-Hardy 1952, 196). In January 1931 the Council decided that, given the progress made, the Disarmament Conference would start in Geneva in February 1932. In addition to the member states, future member states and the US were invited to attend.

The League of Nations Disarmament Conference (1932–34)

The League of Nations Disarmament Conference opened on 2 February 1932, with 64 states represented. International women's organizations had set up the *Committee of International Women's Organisations for Peace and Disarmament*, which was usually called the Dingman Committee after its chair Mary Dingman. The constituent organizations had collected signatures in 56 states, with the intention of presenting them jointly to the Disarmament Conference. On 6 February they handed over eight million signatures, after a procession and ceremony led by Mary Dingman and Rosa Manus in which the League's secretary-general Sir Eric Drummond had agreed to take part. The women's organizations were also active during the conference, not allowing their NGO status to stop them from taking part in the debates. Despite the strong desire for world peace, the international situation, including the Japanese invasion of Manchuria (see below), made progress on disarmament impossible. Attempts were made to continue the talks right into 1934, but eventually only technical committees met, making some headway in areas such as the publication of arms budgets, access to information on arms production and the internationalization of civil aviation. The Disarmament Conference held its last meeting on 11 June 1934.

Why the League of Nations made such little progress on disarmament

The main difficulty with the *Draft Disarmament Convention* debated at the Conference was that the underlying problems dividing the major powers had not been solved. The disagreement between the UK and France and the positions of Germany and the Soviet Union made it impossible to draw up a meaningful convention. The most important factors standing in the way of the disarmament envisaged by the League of Nations were the lack of an inherent belief in disarmament among the great powers, the lack of effective leadership within the League at state level on the issue of disarmament, the lack of political will to reach a successful conclusion through negotiation, the lack of political will to give greater significance to the technical agreement already reached by military experts and politicians, and the unwillingness to see the issue of disarmament through the eyes of other states, who were mainly viewed as potential rivals. Despite the failures there were two positive developments. Due to the efforts of the League of Nations, disarmament had become a permanent fixture in the public debate and the experience of the negotiations had shown that they were a learning process that required time. 'They showed the intricacies involved in coming to technical agreements on matters which impinge directly on national power and security, and the attendant need to draft a disarmament agreement with extreme care. In this respect, the work of the technical committees and the Disarmament Secretariat at Geneva were of considerable value. International disarmament is not something that can be negotiated overnight, even with the best of intentions, as American and Soviet negotiators would discover in the 1970s and 1980s' (Richardson 1995, 15). The League of Nations can thus be seen as an valuable learning experience on negotiating bodies and procedures.

16.3 Japan and Germany leave the League of Nations (1933)

Failure and its causes

On the basis of the events of the 1930s, the League of Nations is widely seen as having failed as an institution aimed at achieving and maintaining collective security. Its most serious failures are considered to be the invasions of Manchuria by Japan in 1931, Ethiopia by Italy in 1934, and Poland by Germany and Finland by the Soviet Union in 1939. This is seen as having several causes, including the non-universality of membership, the primacy accorded to national interest and the unwillingness to take an active part in ensuring collective security. The assumed joint sense of community and mutual trust on which a workable collective security system should have been based was absent. As far as the lack of involvement was concerned, significant states were either not members of the League (the US), only became members at a later date (Germany, the Soviet Union), or left the organization (Japan, Germany, Italy). States with authoritarian regimes took little notice of the League's ambitions because they did not serve their expansion-based interests, but democratic states also proved reluctant to work to achieve collective security in the 1930s.

In defence of the League of Nations

In the cases of Manchuria and Ethiopia it is too simple to say that the League of Nations failed. In fact the League did try to pursue a joint policy, but was unable to achieve this because individual states withdrew their support. 'The League institutions were actually taking a stronger stand against Mussolini and the Japanese aggressors than the power brokers in control of foreign policy, who were acting outside the League framework to muddle through and to appease Mussolini and the Japanese. Partly these diplomats realized their position was weak against these aggressors, partly they hoped to get Mussolini to help stop Hitler, and partly they wanted to protect their economic and military assets from attack by the aggressors' (Yoder 1997, 21). The fact that national interests took precedence does not mean that the League of Nations did not try to reach and implement a joint strategy.

Japan's invasion of Manchuria (1931)

The first of a series of dramatic events facing the League of Nations in the 1930s was Japan's invasion of Manchuria in September 1931. The invasion came as a complete surprise to the Assembly, which was meeting at the time. China, which lost part of its territory through the invasion, appealed to the League for help. The background to the events was a radical change in Japanese domestic politics. A group of people who had been excluded from the elite tried to achieve a reversal of the internationalist and pro-Western foreign policy that Japan had been pursuing since it joined the League. They also attempted to reject the 'Washington System' by whipping up strong chauvinist and militarist sentiments (see §16.2). This group of malcontents succeeded in creating an atmosphere of crisis after a Japanese railway line in Manchuria had been blown up. Manchuria had an autonomous position within China and had in fact come within Japan's sphere of influence. The invasion shifted the balance of political power in Japan in favour of the chauvinists and brought Manchuria under direct Japanese control. The Council of the

League of Nations took at face value the statement of the Japanese delegation that Japan had acted in self-defence, and warned both states that they should ensure the dispute did not escalate. When Japan bombed a Chinese town a few weeks later, the Council – at which a representative of the US was also present – adopted a resolution that it should withdraw its troops from Manchuria within three weeks. When this did not happen, the Council agreed to Japan's proposal to set up a commission to study the issue, so prolonging the situation. Efforts by China to get the Council to come to a more balanced decision were fruitless. Even when China, which had first made its appeal under Article 11 of the Covenant, invoked the stronger Articles 10 and 15, the Council still took no action. The attitudes of the major powers – France, the UK and the US – made a resolute response to Japan by the League of Nations as good as impossible. None of these states was prepared to risk a war in the Far East to rectify the situation in Manchuria.

Japan's withdrawal from the League of Nations (1933)

The study commission, led by Lord Lytton, produced a thorough report, but because it tried to do justice to both parties, each could conclude from it what best suited their own interests. 'Its findings of fact were generally condemnatory of Japan, but it proposed a settlement which should fully recognize the rights and interests of that country in Manchuria' (Gathorne-Hardy 1952, 320). A Committee of Nineteen, set up to bring Japan and China closer together, also failed to make any progress. In March 1933 the Assembly adopted the Committee's report, but Japan voted against it and Siam abstained. Japan then left the meeting and shortly afterwards withdrew its membership of the League of Nations. The League had proved incapable of preventing a violation of the territorial integrity of one of its member states.

Germany leaves the League of Nations (1933)

Although Germany made progress in meeting the reparation commitments imposed on it at Versailles (see §18.2), there was less success in the fields of weapons and disarmament. At the Assembly of September 1932, Germany announced that it would not return to the Disarmament Conference unless its demands for equality before the law were met. The major powers were sympathetic to these demands, and in December France, Germany, Italy, the UK and the US issued a statement affirming that the aim of the Disarmament Conference was to grant Germany equality before the law in the context of a system that guaranteed security for all states. At the second session of the Disarmament Conference in February 1933, France tried to make progress with a 'constructive' proposal for a 'Continental Treaty of Mutual Assistance'. However, the UK, Germany and Italy were not in favour of this. For their part the French felt that a British proposal, known as the MacDonald plan, offered them too little security and submitted an amendment to it. This was unacceptable to Germany, now led by Adolf Hitler, because it did not guarantee Germany straightforward equality before the law. Germany seized the opportunity to go its own way, cancelling its membership of the League of Nations in October 1933.

The Disarmament Conference adjourned (1934)

Further attempts to save the Disarmament Conference were unsuccessful. Sweden proposed a limited draft convention, but encountered opposition from France. France did not wish to accept the rearmament of Germany and continued to seek guarantees for its own security. It succeeded in persuading the Soviet Union to join the League of Nations in 1934, but this did not change the tense relations. The Disarmament Conference was adjourned and not reconvened. Although the League solved the Letitia dispute between Colombia and Peru and organized a referendum in the Saar territory (see below), these successes were overshadowed by the failure of the disarmament debate.

The Letitia dispute between Peru and Colombia settled (1933)

In 1932, armed Peruvian citizens had attacked the port of Letitia in Colombia and occupied an area that had belonged to Colombia since 1922. Colombia mobilized troops to win back the territory and, although Brazil tried to mediate, Colombia submitted the dispute to the Council of the League of Nations. After long negotiations the specially set up *Consultative Commission* suggested a procedure to settle the dispute, which included placing Letitia under the control of an international administration led by the League and giving a contingent of Colombian troops the status of an international force. In March 1933, after the assassination of the Peruvian dictator, the new government signed an agreement in Geneva and shortly afterwards the League handed Letitia back to Colombia.

The referendum in the Saar territory (1935)

The referendum organized by the League of Nations in the Saar territory in January 1935 was a success for the League from a logistical point of view. For France, however, it was a great disappointment, as more than 91 per cent of the people of the region expressed a preference to be reunited with Germany. As a consequence the region was returned to Germany at the end of February.

The mandate system in operation

The League of Nations' mandated territories were subject to the mandate system laid down in Article 22 of the Covenant. A distinction was made between A, B and C mandates, which in the 1920s was gradually developed in separate treaties. The A category covered the territories that had previously belonged to the Ottoman Empire and that were relatively highly developed. They included Palestine, Transjordan, Mesopotamia and Syria. What is now Lebanon and Syria came under French mandate, while Palestine, Transjordan and Iraq were British administered. Iraq became an independent state in 1932, after a proposal from the UK, which was struggling with the high costs of the unpopular mandate. The Permanent Mandates Commission had doubts on whether Iraq was capable of operating as an independent state and had demanded – and received – guarantees for the security of minorities. Despite this, Syrian Christians wishing to leave Iraq encountered serious hostility. After a bloodbath had occurred, the Council of the League of Nations, which had declared itself responsible for the minorities in Iraq, sought a safe haven for them. However, France was prepared to accept only 9,000 of the 20,000 Syrian Christian refugees in Syria and the remainder had to stay in Iraq (Van Ginneken 2006, 41). The B category included six regions in Africa that had formerly belonged to Germany. Part of former German East Africa (Tanganyika) was mandated to the UK, while the other part, Ruanda-Urundi, went to Belgium. Togoland and Cameroon were both divided between France and the UK. Of the five C mandated territories, South

West Africa (now Namibia) came under South African administration, the former German islands in the Pacific north of the equator went to Japan, while those south of the equator (the Bismarck and Solomon Islands, North-East New Guinea and Nauru) went to Australia and Western Samoa to New Zealand. The mandate holders reported annually to the League of Nations, and the Permanent Mandates Commission studied the reports and policies pursued and advised the Council.

16.4 The League of Nations imposes sanctions on Italy (1935)

Italian intervention in Ethiopia (1934)

The Italian *duce* Benito Mussolini declared publicly that Italy had been sparsely rewarded for its contribution to the Allied victory in the First World War and saw an opportunity to extend its territories in East Africa, where Italy already had colonies (Eritrea and Somaliland). In 1934 he sent troops to the region and, after an armed encounter with Ethiopian soldiers, Italy demanded an apology and compensation. Ethiopia, then also known as Abyssinia, called on the League of Nations, of which it had been a member since 1923, for assistance. The League set up an arbitration commission, but its authority was to be undermined because the British government was playing a double game. The British League of Nations Society had drawn up a petition on the imposition by the League of sanctions on Italy, which had been signed by no fewer than 11 million people – almost half the electorate. To show its respect for the result of this Peace Ballot, the British government had expressed willingness to support the sanctions, but in secret the government was working on an agreement with Italy. Prior to the Assembly in September 1935 it also agreed with the French government not to impose sanctions on Italy if the latter undertook aggressive action against Ethiopia, and to delay any economic sanctions that might be imposed. Both states wanted to preserve friendly relations with Italy and prevent the spread of the war to Europe. Because of this secret accord the League of Nations was condemned to taking half measures.

Sanctions imposed on an aggressor for the first time (1935)

When the Italians invaded Ethiopia in October 1935, an emergency session of the Assembly decided by 50 to four votes that Article 16 of the Covenant had been violated because war had broken out. As there was no unanimity it was determined that each state should decide for itself on whether to participate in imposing sanctions. Fifty states joined the *Coordinating Committee* set up to monitor the sanctions. Because this Committee was nearly as large as the Assembly itself, it set up a *Committee of Eighteen* to expedite the process. More than 40 states proved willing to cooperate on the measures proposed by the Committee and it was agreed that they would come into force in November. This was the first time that an international organization had imposed sanctions on an aggressor. Much to the alarm of the UK, Canada took this very seriously, calling for a ban on oil exports as well, but the UK was able to delay this proposal. At the same time the Conservatives came to power in the UK, partly on the promise that they would implement the economic sanctions in full. The new government had no intention of actually doing this, however, and found itself in serious trouble when the British–French plan to allow Italy to keep part of Ethiopia was leaked to the French press, causing great consternation. The government immediately retracted this peace plan, but the Foreign Secretary had to resign. The plan was seen by the wider public as a reward for Italy's aggression and treachery to the League of Nations.

Declining support for sanctions and Italy's withdrawal from the League of Nations (1937)

While the Ethiopian affair and the oil embargo were pushed temporarily into the background by the German invasion of the Rhineland (see below), the League of Nations was unable to bring the peace negotiations to a successful conclusion and halt the Italian aggression. In May 1936 Italy occupied Addis Ababa, Ethiopia became a part of Italy and the Italian king also became the Emperor of Ethiopia. Yet support for the League's sanctions declined. 'In the following month there was a very general movement for the abandonment of sanctions, in which policy the British government met with no perceptible opposition from the public opinion of the country. On 6 July the Coordinating Committee of the League recommended that sanctions should be dropped as from 15 July' (Gathorne-Hardy 1952, 417–18). The new situation was increasingly accepted. After the sanctions were lifted more and more states began to recognize Ethiopia as a *de jure* part of Italy, until eventually 28 members of the League did so. When Germany declared its recognition of the situation in October 1936, Mussolini responded with a speech in which he announced the Rome–Berlin axis. In 1937, as a consequence of these developments, Italy renounced its membership of the League of Nations.

16.5 Collective security paralysed

Germany occupies the Rhineland (1936)

The German occupation of the demilitarized Rhineland in March 1936 constituted a violation of the Treaties of Versailles and Locarno. Hitler defended himself with the argument that the Treaty of Mutual Assistance between France and the Soviet Union, ratified by the French government on 26 February, was also a violation of Locarno, a claim that was legally contestable. Hitler's action led to a further deterioration in international relations. He indicated that he was prepared to accept a new system of treaties, which could lead to Germany's return to the League of Nations. Neither the UK nor France was prepared to take military action against Germany. France did, however, call the Council together. This meeting took place not in Geneva but in London, with Italy and Germany present. Consultations between Belgium, France, Italy and the UK produced a resolution that called Germany's action a threat to international security and called for negotiations on the basis of Hitler's proposals. During the session it emerged that most of the members of the Council did not believe that Germany had violated the provisions of the League of Nations Covenant. The Council limited itself to condemning Germany's action, without imposing sanctions, and the intended negotiations on a new treaty system never materialized. Germany's violation of the Treaty of Versailles thus went unpunished. The fact that sanctions, which had already been in place for six months in the case of Ethiopia, had not also been applied to Germany had radical consequences for the significance of collective security, weakening the sanctions against Italy and affecting relations in Europe. 'When it became clear, in the course of the Ethiopian affair, that the status quo in Europe would not be effectively defended, future possibilities for a collective security system or even for an arrangement other than appeasement to accommodate peaceful change, disappeared' (Baer 1973, 178).

Attempts to reform the League of Nations

After the Ethiopian fiasco the League of Nations decided at Chile's suggestion to see if, given the changed nature of political relations in the world, it could reform itself. A *Committee of Twenty-Eight* was set up, which addressed the question of whether the League should actually be able to take action against aggressors (by imposing sanctions), or whether it was better for it to remain a consultative organization, because then more states would join and be part of the process. This was known as the 'universality argument'. In August 1937 a report was completed on Article 16, which concluded that the principle of collective security must not be surrendered, even though it remained difficult to gauge the impact of sanctions in advance. In the summer of 1938 a group of smaller states met in Copenhagen. They concluded that the League's sanctions system could not function in the way it was intended and therefore they thought it better that sanctions be made optional (see §18.3). The Assembly of September 1938 discussed this interpretation of Article 16. There proved to be a majority (29 of the 49 states present) in favour of making Article 16 no longer compulsory. This had far-reaching consequences, as Article 16 now gained an optional character which meant that the system of collective security had effectively ceased to exist.

The end of Czechoslovakia and of the League of Nations' involvement in Memel, Danzig and Vilnius (1939)

The Assembly of the League of Nations in September 1938 was overshadowed by German agitation about the treatment of Germans in Czechoslovakia. At a conference attended by France, Germany, Italy and the UK in Munich on 29 September 1938, France and the UK hoped to avoid war. They agreed with Hitler's demands that Czechoslovakia should drop its claims to the Sudetenland, which Czechoslovakia under pressure agreed to. These developments outside the framework of the League meant that security had once again become a matter for the great powers only. In March 1939 Hitler's Germany occupied the rest of Czechoslovakia and later the same month it annexed Memel. This meant that the League of Nations could no longer protect the various groups of citizens there. The national socialists had gained in strength in Danzig. In May 1933 they had a majority in the city's parliament, but they did not have the two-thirds majority needed to abolish the constitution. By 1937 the constitution and the parliament barely functioned any longer, despite the efforts of the High Commissioner, in the face of much violence, to support them. On 23 August 1939 the constitution was annulled and the League was informed that Danzig was now part of Hitler's Third Reich. On 1 September Germany invaded Poland, which led directly to the outbreak of the Second World War. None of the states brought this invasion before the Council of the League of Nations. On the basis of the non-aggression pact signed by Germany and the Soviet Union on 27 August, in which the two states had specified their spheres of influence in Central Europe, Vilnius was seized by Soviet troops and restored to Lithuania. In 1940 the Soviet Union occupied Lithuania.

The last meeting of the League of Nations (1939)

After the Soviet Union attacked Finland at the end of November 1939 the Council and the Assembly of the League of Nations met one last time in December. At this meeting the Soviet Union was expelled from the League, which was now completely paralysed in terms of ensuring security. At the League of Nations buildings in Geneva only a few staff members remained in the Secretariat, most of whom were involved in the League's economic activities.

Laying down the path of common economic endeavours

The International Labour Organization (1919) and the economic and social activities of the League of Nations

Part VII discusses both the workings of the ILO, the specialized agency of the League of Nations, and the economic and social activities of the League itself. The ILO created a coherent body of standard-setting international conventions and recommendations and a relatively strong mechanism for monitoring the implementation of its conventions. By using the Organization's bureaucratic character in combination with an independent strategy towards its member states, the ILO director-general succeeded in relatively autonomous policy making by his Organization (Chapter 17). The League's activities and policies in fields such as the economy, finance, traffic and health contradict the often negative overall assessments of the League. Looking back, these economic and social activities seem more impressive than the League's political endeavours, which from the beginning were regarded as its most important objective. The 'other' activities, nonetheless, paved the way for the economic and social activities of the UN (Chapter 18).

The normative workings of the International Labour Organization (1919)

17.1 The creation of the first specialized international agency

Continuity and change

The private International Association for Labour Legislation (IALL) of 1900 had insti-gated the first two international labour conventions, which governments signed in 1906 (see §14.2). However, the outbreak of the First World War prevented a discussion of the draft conventions on the IALL's 1914 agenda. Given their weak international orienta-tion, trade unions had virtually not been involved in the IALL's activities. In 1919, however, the IALL's work was continued by the *International Labour Organization* (ILO) in Geneva, consisting of governments, trade unions and employers. The ILO was the first and only specialized agency of the League of Nations. That trade unions in 1919 embraced the idea of international labour law, contrary to their previous attitude, was the result of three developments during the war: the recognition and inclusion of the labour movement in national political systems, the turnaround within the international trade union movement which made it a proponent of international labour law, and the governments' fear of revolution.

Governmental responsibilities for the labour movement

The first factor explaining the change in attitude of the labour movement, which in 1914 by a large majority had opted for national defence in the war cause, was its new governmental responsibilities in a number of states. In France the socialist Albert Thomas had become the minister of defence, and in 1916 a ministry of labour had been set up in the UK, which was headed by a trade union leader and Member of Parliament for the

Labour Party. The new ministers encouraged cooperation between workers and employers. In France new representative organs had been created for workers in the defence industry, and because of a wave of strikes in the UK a commission, presided over by John Whitley, proposed to establish regular consultations between workers and employers for each business sector. At national level these so-called *Whitley Councils*, consisting of one employer, one worker and a neutral chair, resulted in a change in relations between capital, labour and government in the UK. This also happened elsewhere. 'Class collaboration took precedence over the class struggle. Governments played their full part and reacted positively, often by adopting social policy measures during the war itself' (Ghebali 1989, 6). In most states socialist parties were practically the only political groups which, despite *union sacrée* and other forms of collaboration in favour of national defence, continued to control and criticize governments. Their ongoing agitation for social policy measures meant that in domestic politics the labour movement was gaining positions which governments could no longer deny. The combinations of socialist parties and trade unions succeeded in leverage politics by obtaining concessions from governments and, simultaneously, in becoming integral parts of the existing national political orders.

Understanding international competition

Support for the establishment of the ILO by the labour movement was in line with this form of 'inclusion': not for idealistic reasons but rather as a consequence of practical economic realism. The labour movement gradually began to understand that international cooperation in the fields of labour relations and social security was essential to prevent international competitiveness being disturbed by differing national regulations. Like liberal economists and lawyers earlier, socialist parties and trade unions began to comprehend the social disturbances resulting from open economies and the remedy of internationally-coordinated national compacts with regulations for the labour market and systems of social insurance (see §14.3). The labour movements fought for such 'labour compacts' within their national systems: trade unions at industry level, political parties at parliamentary level. National compacts demanded international coordination to prevent unfair competition and a 'race to the bottom'. Trade unions realized that an international regime with common standards in the fields of labour relations and social insurance was needed in order to prevent the welfare state from failing before it had started.

The trade union movement in favour of international labour law

The second explanatory factor was that in 1919 the international trade union movement, unlike previously, wanted to be engaged in international arrangements. It regarded the peace settlement as an opportunity to influence developments in such a way that it would also affect domestic politics. Soon after the outbreak of war, the American Federation of Labor (AFL) had urged the calling of a world labour congress at the same time as the peace conference. Later it was clarified that the AFL, which was not in favour of state intervention, had not considered participating directly in the peace conference: 'labour would be working out its problems while the politicians were working out theirs' (Alcock 1971, 15). But in Europe state intervention was regarded differently, as the trade union movement favoured national regulations because these would cover the entire population. Hence European trade unions wanted to participate in the peace conference and had prepared their demands.

The Allied international trade union conference in Leeds (1916)

Just before the war the international trade union movement had upgraded its weak International Secretariat to the *International Federation of Trade Unions* (IFTU) (see §13.5). The IFTU Secretariat in Berlin, led by Carl Legien, had maintained relations, as far as the war circumstances allowed, with trade union confederations in Central states as well as in some neutral ones, such as the Netherlands. The trade union movement in the Allied states, however, went its own way when in 1916 the French confederation, led by Léon Jouhaux, set up its own international correspondence bureau. In July 1916 Jouhaux and William Appleton, the secretary of the British trade union federation, called an inter-Allied trade union conference in Leeds. Representatives from Belgium, France, Italy and the UK drew up a detailed programme of rights to be recognized in the peace treaty. They also called for an international commission to ensure the adopted rights were implemented by states. Additionally the commission was to prepare future conferences, which governments might convoke to develop further international labour legislation. In essence the conference in Leeds thus took over the workings of the IALL. It called for the creation of an international labour office to study the development of international labour law and coordinate inquiries, and suggested that the IALL's International Labour Office in Basel be used for this purpose, albeit in cooperation with the IFTU (Alcock 1971, 16).

The conferences of trade unions from Central states (1917)

Jouhaux's idea to move the IFTU Secretariat from Berlin to a neutral state was taken by Legien to be a call to break up the IFTU. He therefore convened a counter-conference and prepared a set of counter-proposals which went further than those of Leeds. Legien also believed that the IALL should have the power to convene international congresses for the promotion of labour legislation, 'at which the Contracting Powers were not only to be officially represented but to pledge themselves to carry out the resolutions of these congresses' (Alcock 1971, 17). The conference in June 1917 in Stockholm was attended only by trade unions from the Central powers and a few neutral states. Since it was not representative, Legien asked the Swiss trade unions to call another conference (Windmuller 1980, 28). This met in Bern in October 1917, but once again it was not attended by representatives from the Allied states. Legien's demand that the signatory states had to implement the resolutions of the IALL congresses was not accepted by the Bern conference, which only called for the states 'to aid in the realisation of the resolutions of these congresses' (Alcock 1971, 17).

The international trade union conference in Bern (1919)

After the 1918 armistice, another international trade union conference was held in Bern in February 1919. It was hastily arranged, but was attended by 90 representatives from neutral, Allied and Central states. They became reconciled and decided to proceed with the reconstruction of the IFTU. They endorsed a detailed programme of labour demands, which envisaged the adoption of a comprehensive set of international labour conventions, among them 'an eight-hour day, a weekly rest period of thirty-six consecutive hours, the prohibition of female night labour, a six-hour day for children between sixteen and eighteen years of age, a system of social insurance, freedom of association, a system of employment bureaux, and "the creation of a permanent Commission for the application of international labour legislation'" (Johnston 1924, 35). Trade union representatives used this Bern programme to influence the negotiations in Versailles in the field of labour, both through their national delegations and directly.

Fear of revolution and a social concession

The third factor to explain the turnaround in the attitude of the labour movement was governments' fear of radical social changes. This fear resulted from the revolutionary events in Russia in 1917, where in the end the communist party had seized power. The paradox in the international situation of 1919, the year the League and the ILO were founded, was that governmental negotiators in Versailles feared the *political* aspirations of the working masses and their representatives so strongly that they gave the *social* concession of institutionalized international labour legislation. They did this in the hope that the social democratic and reform-oriented labour movements and Christian organizations would not choose the revolutionary model. Similar to the situation in France in 1848, when the revolutionaries were 'bought off' by the setting up of a ministry of labour, the Allied forces in 1919 added a Part XIII to the Treaty of Versailles about the set-up and principles of the ILO, according to B.W. Schaper (in ILO 1969, 42). Entrepreneurs also feared social unrest and revolution because of the threat of expropriation. The internationally-active French entrepreneur Robert Pinot was, furthermore, afraid of the by then influential British feminist movement. Pinot was not completely wrong in this, since the feminists he referred to opposed special protection of women workers. Unlike most of those engaged in international labour law, they regarded special protection as a form of inequality and hence as discriminatory. These feminists favoured regulations on the basis of equality of the sexes. At the time the newly-founded *International Federation of Working Women* strongly defended this position within the IFTU, despite its minority position (Van Goethem 2006).

No more room for the IALL

The new relations forged in 1919 did not leave any room for the private IALL. Its activities had almost come to a standstill following the outbreak of war, and the establishment of the ILO in fact ended its active existence. The governmental representatives and trade unionists engaged in the Versailles peace negotiations who decided to establish the ILO simply took over the workings and expertise of the IALL, without thanking this predecessor very explicitly. The significance of the IALL as an 'epistemic community' around the turn of the century was continued by another, differently composed group of experts. There was an overlap between the old and the new group, as various officials had been participants in the IALL conferences and were acquainted with its proceedings. The ILO was enabled to take over the libraries of both the IALL and the International Association on Unemployment, so from the beginning the ILO had a significant database at its disposal which immediately could be used for the development of social policies. When, in September 1918, the end of the war was in sight, the intelligence department of the British ministry of labour began to make plans for the peace conference. Its expert on international issues, Edward Phelan, often had represented the UK at IALL conferences. His memorandum shows that the UK was fully aware of its position as a state that was among the most advanced in regulating conditions of employment and was in need of international coordination. 'Once free competition had been restored it would be very difficult to raise the general standard of wages and conditions or even to maintain the present minimum in industries which depended on foreign markets, unless similar standards were applied in all competing markets. But if it were possible to ensure that standards in Europe approximated those in England, there would be little to fear since British workmanship was held to be generally superior' (Alcock 1971, 19).

The Labour Commission in Versailles

After the war's end on 11 November 1918, Phelan and his colleagues, in their preparatory meetings for the peace conference, favoured a permanent organization for dealing with international labour problems, which should contain representatives of governments as well as of workers and employers. This received consent from France and the US. As none of the delegations had prepared their plans in similar detail, the British proposals formed the basis for discussion in the official *Labour Commission*, which with 15 members from nine states began its work in Versailles in February 1919. As a tribute to the US the American trade union leader Samuel Gompers was elected chair. The further design of the ILO, however, was a matter of British and French efforts. Jouhaux, a member of the French delegation at Versailles, made sure the resolutions of the Bern international trade union conference were included in the discussions about the future ILO. After ten weeks of meetings in the French Ministry of Labour, the Labour Commission presented its plan for a 'tripartite' ILO which was empowered to adopt international conventions. After amendments and decision making by the heads of government in April 1919, the text became *Part XIII* of the *Treaty of Versailles*. The preamble to this Part declared that the League of Nations' object of establishing universal peace could be reached only if it was based upon 'social justice'. Conditions of labour had to be improved, as injustice, hardship and privation for large numbers of people could produce 'unrest so great that the peace and harmony of the world are imperilled'. Establishment of the ILO was moved by 'sentiments of justice and humanity as well as by the desire to secure the permanent peace of the world'. While Section I of Part XIII contained the constitution of the ILO (adopted on 11 April), Section II detailed the principles underlying this new organization (adopted on 28 April). The contracting parties recognized that the 'well-being, physical, moral and intellectual, of industrial wage-earners is of supreme international importance'. Holding that 'labour should not be regarded merely as an article of commerce', they believed that there were methods and principles for regulating labour conditions. Section II contained nine principles, among them the right of association for all lawful purposes by the employed as well as the employers, a wage adequate to maintain a reasonable standard of living, an eight-hour day, a 48-hour week, and equal pay for work of equal value for men and women (Johnston 1924, 38–40).

The first ILO conference in Washington (1919)

Even before the establishment of the League of Nations, it was agreed to hold the first ILO conference in Washington DC. Arrangements were made for it to take place in 1919, as there was a general desire to see it happen as soon as possible in view of 'the existing labour ferment' (Alcock 1971, 37). The conference was held between the end of October and the end of November, bringing together governments, workers and employers for the first time on an equal footing. There were delegations from 39 states. All European states were represented, with the exception of the Central Powers, communist

Russia and the hitherto unrecognized Baltic states. Asia had delegations from China, Japan, India and Thailand, the Middle East from Persia. In addition to India two British dominions, Canada and South Africa, were represented for the first time as independent entities. US President Wilson had had great trouble in obtaining the authority of Congress to issue invitations for this conference and to make resources available. When Wilson fell ill, no-one could be found to set the ILO conference in motion. All the delegates found ready when they arrived was a hall in the Pan-American Union building. Meetings could not start until the British Treasury had cabled the necessary money and the Assistant-Secretary of the US Navy, Franklin D. Roosevelt, had put offices in the Navy Building at the disposal of the ILO conference. As Congress had not authorized American participation in the conference and neither the Secretary of Labour nor the Secretary of State wanted to make a decision, the conference could begin only after the president's wife, on behalf of the White House, had ordered the Secretary of Labour to preside (Alcock 1971, 38). This ILO conference in Washington elected the governors of the organization, arranged many practical issues and adopted the first labour conventions: nine conventions and six recommendations, among them the principles of the eight-hour working day and the 48-hour week. The conference admitted Germany and Austria to membership, even before they were allowed into the League of Nations. Jouhaux pointed out that to admit the enemy states was in the spirit of the League but also practically necessary, since without their cooperation no system of international labour legislation could be really effective in Europe (Johnston 1924, 65). The US, however, did not become an ILO member, as the Senate did not ratify the Treaty of Versailles. ILO membership started with 42 states and rose to 62 by 1934, when both the US and the Soviet Union became members. The number then decreased to 50 by 1942. States that left the ILO during the interwar period and during the Second World War included several Latin American states, Germany (1935), Austria (1938), the Soviet Union (expelled in 1939), Japan (1940), Spain (1940) and Romania (1942). In spite of these losses the ILO had a fairly universal membership at the time.

17.2 Albert Thomas's leadership of the ILO

Tripartite decision making

The ILO has three main organs, the *International Labour Conference*, the *Governing Body* and the *International Labour Office*, headed by a director. The annual International Labour Conference is the general assembly of the member states, the Governing Body a kind of executive committee with a coordinating function and the International Labour Office the permanent secretariat. When it became obvious that someone from the UK was going to lead the League of Nations, Jean Monnet arranged that a Frenchman would be the ILO leader. Once appointed, provisionally in 1919 and a year later permanently, Albert Thomas succeeded in securing independent status for the ILO and in transforming the International Labour Office into a strong secretariat. In 1921 the ILO had 262 staff members from 19 states; ten years later more than 400 from 35 states. The ILO's main characteristic is its tripartite decision-making structure composed of governments, trade unions and employers. The origin of 'tripartism' was a British idea set out in 1916 by Leonard Woolf for the London Fabian Society, which was then elaborated more practically by Edward Phelan when preparing his ideas about the ILO as part of the peace conference (Ghebali 1989, 8). Every national delegation to the ILO's annual Labour Conference is composed of two governmental representatives, one trade union representative and one employer representative. The Governing Body is also constituted according to this 2:1:1 formula, originally with 12 governmental, six trade union and six employer representatives. These numbers were increased several times, and in 1975 were 28, 14 and 14. The ILO period under Thomas's leadership can be characterized as one of functional representation. Because the employers and the trade unionists joined together in blocs at the Labour Conference and in the Labour Office, without any compulsion to do so, they discussed the issues on the agenda from a functional rather than a national perspective. By their fairly independent behaviour *vis-à-vis* the national organizations, the '*social partners*' (employers and trade unions) enhanced the ILO's independent character.

The balance of governments and social partners

In this tripartite decision-making structure trade unions and employers were equally strong and, combined, they were as strong as governments. The intention behind giving governments a voice equal to that of the combined social partners was to avoid situations in which national legislatures would reject conventions adopted by a two-thirds majority of the Labour Conference without governments agreeing. Such an outcome would have destroyed the influence and prestige of the Conference (Johnston 1970, 25–26). Governments regarded the representation of social partners in the ILO necessary to ensure that national legislation was drawn up 'in the light of full knowledge of industrial conditions and in order to secure the best possible conditions for their subsequent application' (Alcock 1971, 21). It was doubtful that social partners would be content with merely acting as advisers, given the weight and consequences of the decisions. Initially the employers were the weakest link in this triangle. They did not question the usefulness of the ILO's work, but simply wanted to keep it within certain limits, moderate its pace and reduce its costs. It was not until 1938 that they abandoned their detached attitude when they joined the two other groups in recognizing the need to keep the ILO alive in an emergency. After 16 years of rejection the employers on the Governing Body approved the 1940 budget and defended it jointly with trade unions (Ghebali 1989, 12). Given the wording in the 1919 peace treaty about improvement of labour conditions, the position of workers within the ILO was fundamentally different from that of employers. Workers could not expect ILO impartiality, but rather resolute behaviour for their benefit.

Relations with women's organizations

From the very beginning the ILO attached weight to its relations with the international women's movement, although this relationship was less strongly institutionalized than the one with the trade unions. The international women's organizations lobbied the ILO from the start. The ILO stipulated that if women-related issues were being discussed, at least one of the experts in the delegation to the Labour Conference should be female. Furthermore, one of the female staff members of the International Labour Office in Geneva was made responsible for relations with important international women's organizations and women's sections of national organizations. The International Labour Office was often represented at the congresses of these organizations, which seldom were disinterested in the ILO's work in the field of women's labour, whether they agreed with it or not. An ILO Correspondence Committee on Women's Work was allowed to advise on an *ad hoc* basis.

Thomas's leadership

The director-general (originally director), as the secretary-general of the ILO was called, played the leading part in the course of events within the organization. In 1919 Thomas's candidacy had taken most governments by surprise. They had not agreed among themselves on any candidates and had not given much thought to the requirements of the office. Thomas himself, however, had strong feelings about his position as director. Because he was supported by the trade union movement he could use his position as 'a base for initiative in international policy' (Cox 1973, 103). There were complaints about him being 'the boss' and the organization a 'one man show', but Thomas managed to secure for the director within the ILO's constitutional organs a position 'not unlike that of a minister introducing and defending his proposals in Parliament' (Ghebali 1989, 12). Thomas's successors until 1948 – Harold Butler (1932–38), John Winant (1939–41) and Edward Phelan (1941–48) – followed the path he had opened up.

Independence from the League of Nations

Thomas's initiatives and his political power base resulted in important modifications of the intentions of the ILO founders at Versailles. From when he took office, Thomas had made it clear that the ILO should function sufficiently independently from the League of Nations to have freedom of action *vis-à-vis* the member states. He succeeded in arranging that constitutional links with the League did not block ILO action, by finding a *modus vivendi* on budgetary matters, providing the ILO with sufficient resources and ending shared membership of both organizations. The last promoted the entry of states in favour of ILO membership which were not members of the League. Thomas's leadership turned the ILO into a specialized agency of the League, with its own room for manoeuvre, as was shown during the Second World War when the ILO, unlike the League, fled to Canada where it continued to function as well as possible.

Dependency on member states

Thomas had less freedom with regard to the ILO's member states than *vis-à-vis* the League. The ILO's international labour standards mostly paralleled the democratic and industrially-developed states in Western Europe and northern America, with their specific interest groups such as trade unions, employer federations and women's organizations. Most of these were mainly interested in national situations and did not demand strong international supervision. This made the ILO dependent on the good will and interests of these states and kept its room for manoeuvre 'sharply limited' (Haas 1968, 435). But despite these limitations the first two directors-general succeeded in enlarging the ILO's scope for policies of its own.

The gradual growth of autonomy

The development of more ILO autonomy was a gradual process. The industrial states' willingness to continue the examination of industrial issues at international level had two unintended consequences. The first was an increase in its programmatic range, resulting from the fact that judicial decisions in the context of monitoring the implementation of ILO standards led to additional categories of issues being discussed. 'New tasks have resulted from new inputs, which in turn resulted from interaction with earlier organizational outputs.

The environmental forces, which earlier had evinced little interest in such tasks, acquiesced in them as a consequence of lessons learned and incorporated into their demands and expectations' (Haas 1968, 431). The second unintended consequence was the emergence of an annual review and discussion procedure because of the dissatisfaction of key client groups with the implementation of ratified ILO conventions (see §17.3). Although several member states objected to this development they were unwilling to block it (Haas 1968, 435), and the director-general in turn consciously stimulated this growth by taking up new issues and by supporting proposals for the expansion and enhancement of monitoring procedures.

How the ILO increased its competence

A decision in 1925 resulted in a monitoring procedure for ILO conventions that eventually was stronger than the one agreed in Versailles. A standing committee existed to consider the many annual reports on ratified conventions that member states were obliged to submit. Because this committee found itself unable to cope with the volume of material, a *Committee of Experts* began to function in 1927, as proposed by Thomas. This Committee of Experts had a strict mandate: comparing the texts of national legislation and ratified conventions. It had no power to evaluate performance or to interpret conventions. However, the experts were often faced with situations in which they needed more information than was available from the two texts to assess real implementation. The Committee 'soon enlarged its cocoon', because the experts came up with substantiated proposals for more powers. Because of the constant support of the workers, their proposals had a chance of success (Haas 1968: 253). In 1929 the Committee demanded the power to raise questions regarding the ratified conventions' effectiveness of application. This was consented to as long as no actual investigations were undertaken. Soon after, however, the experts' demands that states be asked to make observations on difficulties encountered in applying conventions, and that

Figure 17.1 The International Management Institute 1927–34

The **International Management Institute** existed from 1927 to 1934. Thomas initiated it jointly with Edward A. Filene, an American businessman who believed that European business did not modernize sufficiently and should have a better knowledge of American management methods. Thomas and Filene shared expectations of what was called 'scientific management'. That labour relations profited from this was shown by collective labour agreements. These collective agreements fitted well with the rational production process, because they contributed to stable expectations that were needed during the production process to supply the required half-finished and final products on time and according to certain standards. In American corporate management, the investigations by F.W. Taylor had added to the rationalization of the production process. In 1924 a congress took place in Prague, Czechoslovakia, that was attended by 50 American 'Taylorists' and management experts. More congresses followed: in 1925 in Brussels, 1927 in Rome, 1929 in Paris, 1932 in Amsterdam, 1935 in London and 1938 in Washington DC. A permanent executive was established, the *Comité international de l'organisation scientifique* (CIOS), which today is called the **World Council of Management** and is still convening congresses.

The message of the 1924 congress was that entrepreneurs and workers should end their mutual antagonism and leave more room for engineers and management experts. The initiative by Thomas and Filene focused on such cooperation within companies. Thomas tried to gain support for the social dimensions of rationalization from the labour movement, Filene from the entrepreneurs. Filene supplied resources, Thomas released some ILO staff members to the project. However, during the early 1930s many companies hit by the economic crisis failed. Within the ILO's Governing Board, Thomas met with more reservations and objections. Although there was a budgetary guarantee until 1937, the International Management Institute had to cut back its activities drastically as a result of the dollar devaluation of 1933. In 1934 it closed down. Given the economic nationalism in most countries, Filene had lost confidence in the project. The importance of **management conferences** as well as the economic activities of the ILO and the League of Nations was not restricted to Europe. 'Japanese delegates returning from the 1925 International Management Congress in Brussels and the 1927 International Economic Conference in Geneva [organized by the League, see §18.2] viewed themselves as part of an international network of Taylorists, destined to engineer in Japan the same leaps in productivity that had already been engineered in the United States and in some European countries' (Sil 2002, 153).

the associations of workers and employers be invited to add their observations to the official reports, were accepted because they were considered reasonable. It was even agreed that governments would be invited to appear before the Committee to explain special difficulties. Other demands, however, were refused, such as a blacklist for persistent violators, the explanation of non-compliance by non-ratifying states or colonial powers, and the creation of specialized bodies. In its reports the Committee was not allowed to use the word 'criticism', but this handicap was solved by changing to the word 'observation'. This evolution resulted from Thomas's strategy of not demanding such powers at the level of the International Labour Conference, but rather at the sublevel of experts. The increase in powers along this 'endogeonous dynamic' would never have been possible at Conference level, where member states would have referred formally to their sovereignty, but was allowed at the level of a sub-organ dealing with practical and rational arguments that could almost not be denied. The Committee of Experts 'slowly stripped itself of its original, purely consultative capacity and took the form of a semi-autonomous organ with its own authority' (Reinalda 1998, 52). Another initiative taken by Thomas was the promotion of modern management methods (see Figure 17.1).

17.3 The international labour code: ILO conventions and recommendations

The ILO's international labour code

The ILO continued the practice of international labour conventions, set in motion in 1906, through adopting by qualified majority at its Labour Conferences international agreements in the form of conventions and recommendations. The difference between the two kinds of agreement stemmed from a problem raised by the US at Versailles. The US federal government 'could not accept the obligation to ratify Conventions dealing with matters within the competence of the forty-eight States of the Union, with which the power of Labour Legislation for the most part rested' (Johnston 1924, 54). The resulting dilemma, of keeping the US out of the ILO or of seriously limiting international labour legislation from the very beginning, was discussed at Versailles by a subcommission of American, Belgian and British delegates. They proposed the solution that the decisions of the Labour Conference could take the form either of (binding) conventions or of recommendations, giving federal states a lesser degree of obligation. Later, the ILO's common practice was to regulate principled matters in a convention and more practical ones affirming the principles in a recommendation, so that the convention and the recommendation paralleled each other with regard to their subject. In drafting the *international labour standards* that are expressed in these conventions and recommendations, the ILO succeeded in taking into consideration the diversity of national conditions and in establishing an effective monitoring machinery for the national implementation of its standards (Valticos 1985, 93–99). Taken together, the ILO conventions and recommendations are known as the *International Labour Code*. This code contains a many-sided international standardization in the fields of labour, social insurance and other topics related to the welfare state. From 1919 to 1939 the ILO adopted 67 conventions and 66 recommendations. Fifty years later, in 1989, there were 169 conventions and 176 recommendations, in 2008 188 and 199, respectively. Figure 17.2 shows the subjects covered

Figure 17.2 Classification of ILO conventions and recommendations by subject

I Basic human rights

- Freedom of association
- Forced labour
- Equality of opportunity and treatment

II Employment

- Employment policy
- Employment services and agencies
- Vocational guidance and training
- Rehabilitation and employment of disabled persons
- Employment security

III Social policy

IV Labour administration

- General
- Labour inspection
- Labour statistics
- Tripartite consultation

V Labour relations

VI Conditions at work

- Wages
- General conditions of employment: hours of work, night work, weekly rest, paid leave
- Occupational safety and health: general provisions; protection against specific risks; protection in given branches of activity: building industry, commerce and offices, construction, dock labour
- Social services, houses and leisure

VII Social security

- Comprehensive standards
- Protection in the various social security branches: medical care and sickness benefit; old age, invalidity and survivors' benefits; employment injury benefit; unemployment benefit; maternity benefit

VIII Employment of women

- Maternity protection
- Night work
- Underground work
- See also under basic human rights: equality of opportunity and treatment

IX Employment of children and young persons

- Minimum age
- Night work
- Medical examination
- Conditions of employment in underground work

X Older workers

XI Migrant workers

XII Indigenous and tribal peoples

XIII Workers in non-metropolitan territories

XIV Particular occupational sectors

- Seafarers; fishermen; inland boatmen; dock workers; plantation workers; tenants and sharecroppers; nursing personnel; hotel and restaurant workers.

Source: (ILO 1992, xxxv–xlv).

by ILO conventions and recommendations. The main ones are basic human rights, employment, social policy, labour administration, labour relations, conditions of work, social security, employment of women, employment of children and young persons, specific groups such as older workers, migrant workers, indigenous and tribal peoples, and workers in non-metropolitan territories, as well as particular occupational sectors.

The establishment of ILO conventions and recommendations

In order to put an issue onto the ILO agenda it must be brought to the attention of the Governing Body, which decides on the agenda of the Labour Conference and is responsible for the budget of the organization. Once the Governing Body agrees, all interested parties in the member states are informed and are enabled to react with an overview of existing legislation as well as a wish list. The International Labour Office follows this by preparing a report that analyses the laws and practices of the member states with regard to the issue at stake. It sends questionnaires to governments, expecting them to consult with trade unions and employer organizations. After having collected these data, it asks the available ILO experts, such as labour law experts or economists, to comment and advise. The Labour Office then writes its report and circulates it to the governments, trade unions and employers' organizations. This report is discussed at the International Labour Conference, which appoints a special commission to see which practical measures the Conference should take in order to debate the issue dealt with in the report. Later, the Conference's standpoint is determined in a public discussion. In drafting conventions the ILO developed the practice of 'double discussion', which means that after this first discussion the Labour Office prepares a second report with a draft instrument for comments and submits this for discussion at the following Labour Conference, where the draft is amended as necessary and proposed for adoption. The ILO labour convention can be compared with a classic treaty, whereby countries commit themselves to implement the standards and decision-making procedures mentioned in it. In order to adopt a convention, a two-thirds majority is needed. Once adopted at the 'second' Labour Conference, governments are required to submit the convention to their national parliament (the competent authority for the enactment of relevant legislation) for it to be ratified. In addition to the formal ratification procedure, the intention here is to bring the convention to the attention of a state's population. If the parliament ratifies and accepts the convention as a legally-binding instrument, the member state has the obligation to apply the convention and to adapt its existing legislation and practices to the standards and norms mentioned in the convention. To prevent states with 'stronger' legislation and regulations than mentioned in the convention weakening their national legislation and regulations, it was agreed that this is not allowed. ILO recommendations are not binding, but they should also be submitted to parliament and, where appropriate, may result in the application of international provisions.

Monitoring national implementation

The time limit for ratification by parliament is one year, and in some exceptional cases 18 months. If a state does not accept a convention it has to inform the International Labour Office about the reasons for delay or non-acceptance. If it does accept the convention, this generally comes into force for that state one year after the date of ratification. The member state then is subject to the ILO's regular supervisory system responsible for ensuring that the convention is applied, which means that it has to report on its enforcement at regular intervals. The Labour Office uses questionnaires to receive information on the extent of implementation. The government's answers must also be presented to the trade unions and employers' organizations, which may lodge complaints. Furthermore, governments are expected to ensure that national institutions responsible for supervision, such as a labour inspectorate, play their roles with regard to monitoring the implementation of international labour standards. The legal experts of the International Labour Office assess the national reports in their capacity of independent experts. They can make remarks and ask governments questions for reasons of clarification in accordance with the powers discussed above. The report by the experts is submitted to a commission at the following International Labour Conference. This commission, which has the function of discussing the progress in implementation, may ask governments for further clarification. If this remains unsatisfactory the Labour Conference can do the same itself, which has a greater impact as it is done in front of all member states. The further enforcement of ILO standards at national level and the criticisms raised will be brought up again at later Labour Conferences in order to ensure that the standards are applied.

17.4 The divided international trade union movement

The division of labour between IFTU and international trade secretariats

For various reasons, the international trade union movement in its role as an ILO participant was not a strong partner. First, the division of labour between international confederations and international trade secretariats was dominated by the former, which did not leave much room for developing international policies. Second, strong antagonism existed both between social democratic and communist trade unions, and between non-religious and religious trade unions. The reconstruction of the International Federation of Trade Unions in 1919 was attended by national federations from 14 states in Europe and northern America. Combined, they represented 17.7 million members, almost three times as many as on the eve of the First World War. This increase in unionization had occurred during and immediately after the war in almost every industrialized state, which gave the trade union movement political momentum (Windmuller 1980, 29). The congress in Amsterdam, which had been called to reconstruct the IFTU adopted a new constitution, moved the Secretariat from Berlin to Amsterdam and appointed two Dutchmen as secretaries: Jan Oudegeest and Edo Fimmen. The practical outcome of the Amsterdam congress was that 'the British bore most of the costs, the Germans won most of the important policy decisions, and the reward of staffing the central organizations was monopolised by the Dutch' (Logue 1980, 43). Fimmen would also play a role as secretary of the largest international trade secretariat, that of transport workers. Following the IFTU, many international trade secretariats also moved their seats to Amsterdam. As previously (see §13.5) a general division of labour between the IFTU and the trade secretariats developed, with the IFTU taking care of major international trade union policies in general, while the trade secretariats concentrated on more practical objectives for their trades. To raise the standards of wages and general conditions of employment in their own industries, the trade secretariats in the various sectors found that they had to cooperate among themselves and with the IFTU, 'if there was to be an advance all along the line'. However, one could not call it an amalgamation into one common force. 'Although consultation and joint action increased as the years went by, the international organizations for the different trades continued to exist side by side with the I.F.T.U., which was responsible for decisions on matters of general concern' (Price 1945, 147). The choice made in 1901 to make nationality rather than profession the basis of international trade unionism was not discussed in 1919. The trade secretariats remained outside the decisions on general policies, which remained firmly in the hands of the IFTU. As a result the IFTU barely had any means of wielding power in the sense of using industrial action, and remained focused on the coordination of national views, with national federations mainly interested in their political and representative functions.

The importance of the international trade secretariats

During the interwar period the international trade secretariats were large representational organizations, representing 12.1 million members in 1919 and 13.3 in 1927. In comparison, IFTU numbers decreased from 22.7 million in 1920 to 13.1 in 1927. In other words, in 1927 the IFTU and the combined trade secretariats represented about the same numbers. The trade secretariats embodied the consciousness of workers in modern industries in an internationalizing context. Although some of the 27 secretariats after the First World War still had a narrow trade or craft base, the general tendency had been to form large industrial secretariats. For instance, bakery workers, brewers, millers and butchers had joined together in a combined food secretariat. Where necessary the larger secretariats arranged for special craft and trade sections, as the *International Transportworkers Federation* (ITF) did by having separate sections for seafarers, dockers, inland navigation, railwaymen and motor vehicle drivers. The three largest international trade secretariats in the interwar period were those of the transport workers (2.2 million in 1927), miners (1.9 million) and metal workers (1.6 million).

The boycott of Hungary (1920)

Immediately after the war the IFTU became socially and politically engaged. After its reconstruction in 1919, Edo Fimmen, secretary of both the IFTU and the ITF, initiated various humanitarian relief actions. By the end of 1919 he had made the two unions send food shipments to the hungry people of Austria and, between 1921 and 1923, to those of Russia. In addition to this humanitarian relief work, he undertook political international action. As a protest against the 'white terror' of the Horthy regime in Hungary, after the repression of the soviet republic of Bela Kun and the suppression of the Hungarian labour and trade union organizations, Fimmen organized a transnational action in which Austrian and Czech transport unions boycotted transportations to and from Hungary for six weeks. Although the boycott during the summer of 1920 was not fully implemented and the Hungarian government launched a counter-boycott with measures against states participating in the boycott, the international trade union action drew international attention to the repressive regime. The Hungarian government felt obliged to receive a fact-finding ILO mission and to negotiate in Vienna with the international trade union movement on ending the boycott measures. The ILO sent a delegation of three people, who stayed in Hungary between 8 August and 10 September, studying relevant Hungarian legislation and comparing it with the Treaty of Versailles, which stipulated the free exercise of trade union rights for the signatories. It also heard from representatives of employers and workers. In 1921 the delegation's report was published in Geneva, once more drawing attention to Hungarian domestic politics (Molnár in Reinalda 1997, 157).

The transnational boycott of munition transports to Poland (1920)

Shortly after the Hungarian boycott Fimmen fairly successfully organized another, even better prepared boycott action to prevent the transport of weapons from Germany through Poland to counter-revolutionary forces in Russia. These preparations for military intervention to overthrow the Soviet Russian government were incompatible with the Treaty of Versailles, but above all they created fear about another war. The IFTU and the ITF once more appealed to the transport workers, this time to refuse to transport arms and munitions destined for Poland. The embargo was effective, as the refusals to load vessels and the halting of munitions trains continued for several months, until negotiations eventually took place between Poland and Russia (Reinalda 1997, 164–66). These 1920 boycotts mark the first time that NGOs, in these cases international trade unions, undertook transnational action against the governments of states.

War on war (1922)

Such politically-inspired trade union activism to keep peace characterized international trade unionism between 1919 and 1922. This was partly due to Fimmen, who for his entire life had been an antimilitarist and a fierce opponent of war, but it was also due to the widely-supported expectation that the trade union movement would contribute to a better world. Fimmen articulated these feelings and turned what many people thought into deeds. In 1914 he was one of those people who were in favour of combating the coming war by any means, among them an international boycott and a general strike. His relief actions for Austria and Russia and his political actions against Hungary and Poland were similarly inspired. At the Hague international congress for peace, organized by the IFTU in December 1922 to strengthen the ties between the trade union organizations, he declared 'war on war'. The struggle for world peace and against war was the highest and most exalted duty for the international trade union movement. However, when in January 1923 Belgian and French forces occupied the German Ruhr area to enforce German war payments (see §18.2), the period of IFTU political activism ended, as the international trade union movement remained inactive. Despite previous commitments, Fimmen was left no room to organize an international action of protest against this occupation. Within the IFTU, and in particular for his co-secretary Oudegeest, nationalism and pragmatism had become more important. Fimmen expressed his disappointment in an article entitled 'Black January' and accepted his defeat.

The ITF setting its own international direction

In 1924 Fimmen lost his IFTU position, as word got around that he, as a social democrat, was prepared to cooperate with the communist trade unions which were led by Russia. He regarded such cooperation as less dangerous than the identification of trade unions with the national bourgeoisie that he saw occurring in many states. He referred to the right-wing military developments taking place in Italy and Germany at the time, which to his mind were a greater danger to world peace. He believed that a vigorous fight through unity of action should be put up against this. Fimmen was one of the few people who recognized the dangers of fascism and national socialism as early as that. His stance of unity with the communists, however, ended in 1929 with Stalin's new 'ultra left' policy, which interpreted social democracy as 'social fascism', and Fimmen withdrew from the cooperation. Having lost his IFTU position in 1924, Fimmen had remained secretary of the transport workers' trade secretariat, despite the fact that his unity policy was criticized there as well, although to a far lesser extent than in the IFTU. The ITF provided Fimmen with an organizational basis from which he managed to continue his activist, unity-oriented attitude and to make it a success for its trade (Reinalda 1997). In his book *Labour's Alternative* (1924) Fimmen tried to understand the internationalization of capitalist interests and to answer the question of how the labour movement could react adequately. Having developed from a local to a national movement, the trade union movement now should understand that a struggle conducted within national limits was becoming more and more inadequate. Given the internationalization of capital and its division of labour on an international scale, the trade unions should unite under international trade secretariats rather than an international confederation of national federations. It was not the national perspective that should come first, but the international one. This meant that the international trade union movement, which in Fimmen's eyes was as yet purely European in scope, had to become a truly global organization with continental secretariats, organizing all the workers of the world, in spite of their origin or colour of skin. Because power relations in the international trade union movement were dominated by the IFTU, and the ITF could do nothing to change this, it began to expand its activities to other continents and to integrate Latin American and Asian trade unions into the ITF. This global model of organization put the ITF ahead of other trade unions. It was important because of both its geographical scope and its conscious effort to unite workers with different skin colours. While Fimmen was arguing that the ITF should organize all workers, be they white, brown, black or yellow, western shipping companies began replacing European crew by cheaper labour from Asia, which caused many sailors to speak about the 'yellow peril' of Asian sailors. The ITF tried to combat this racism, and in 1928 Fimmen noted that white workers often felt more solidarity with other white people than with fellow class members whose skin had a different colour. He argued against such contempt and stressed that the European labour movement had to pay attention to the life and labour of the workers in the colonial countries (Reinalda 1997, 120–21).

ITF action within the ILO

From 1924 onwards the ITF was active within the ILO, backing international conventions and recommendations for transport workers. Since 1919 the IFTU and other international trade secretariats had already established relations with the ILO, but it had taken the ITF some time before it was convinced of the ILO's usefulness and had overcome internal troubles in its seafarers' section. During the interwar period the ILO adopted, also through the influence of the ITF, 17 conventions and 15 recommendations for transport workers, out of an ILO total of 67 conventions and 66 recommendations: 13 conventions and six recommendations for seafarers, one recommendation for fishermen, three conventions and three recommendations for dockworkers, one recommendation for inland waterway workers, one convention and four recommendations for road transport workers, and none for railway workers (Reinalda 1997, 150).

The closed character of the IFTU

The IFTU as an organization had a closed character, as only one national trade union federation per state was admitted as a member. The presumption was that this rule would force national trade unions to unity, but its actual effect was that the IFTU regarded the affiliated national federation as the only correct one with regard to political ideology or trade union principles and strategy. Another consequence was that the IFTU refused to cooperate with trade unions which had a different orientation, whether communist or Christian. On the contrary, the IFTU regarded itself as the most competent international representation of trade unions and tried to gain monopoly positions, which meant a continuous range of conflicts within the entire international trade union movement (Van Goethem 2005). Oudegeest, who had participated in the 1919 ILO conference in Washington DC as a Dutch delegate, claimed that the largest Dutch trade union federation, to which he himself belonged, should have a permanent trade union position in the official Dutch ILO delegation. However, the Permanent Court of International Justice, asked by the ILO for an advisory opinion on this claim, laid down that the Dutch federation and the Christian federations were to alternate in filling the trade union position in the Dutch delegation. Although the IFTU could not take on the leadership of the workers' group in the ILO officially, as it tried to do, it succeeded in doing so informally. From a geographical perspective, however, the IFTU remained a limited organization, as it had great difficulty in reaching beyond the industrialized states of Western Europe. As Fimmen claimed, it was fairly European in scope. The American Federation of Labor had decided to not affiliate and did not reconsider its affiliation with the IFTU until 1935, and then mainly because its rival, the Congress of Industrial Organizations, formed in that year, had good European contacts. 'By affiliating to the IFTU the AFL sought to cut off the international track for its rival' (Van der Linden 2000, 144). It was not until 1937 that the AFL, strongly supported by the British, actually joined the IFTU. The IFTU had little to offer for the colonies, as most trade unions apart from the British were barely interested in the promotion of unions there. British trade unions had a different attitude, as they regarded themselves as part of a worldwide English-speaking community. In the British colonies and dominions they promoted the establishment and working of trade unions and, because by then the US had become an industrial world power, they supported the affiliation of the AFL to the IFTU.

The international Christian trade union federation (1920)

Religious trade unions were established later than socialist ones. This was particularly true of Catholic trade unions and in some states, such as Germany, the Netherlands and Switzerland, also of Protestant ones. In its ideologies these religiously-inspired trade unions turned against capitalism and its related liberal ideas as well as against socialism in its many varieties. Unlike the class-struggle-oriented socialists, the religiously-based trade unions were in favour of class cooperation, stressing spiritual values and Christian solidarity. In 1920 the *International Federation of Christian Trade Unions* (IFCTU) was established in The Hague, representing 3.3 million members. Here too antagonisms between Allied, neutral and Central states played a role and the Dutch had to bridge the divisions by taking the posts of secretary and treasurer under a Swiss president. From an organizational perspective the IFCTU looked like the IFTU. It was however a weak organization, with decreasing membership during the entire interwar period. Relations with the far stronger IFTU were simply hostile. 'The ideological gap was too wide. Besides, the tolerance of the dominant trade unions for dual organization, i.e. for pluralism, has always been extremely limited – nationally and internationally. … What one group regarded as its right to an independent existence was seen by the other as an almost treasonable act against working class unity' (Windmuller 1980, 41).

The international communist trade unions

Hostility between the IFTU and the international communist trade unions was even more intense. The Moscow-led Communist International (see Figure 17.3 for the ideological differences of opinion within the left-wing labour movement) took an antagonist attitude towards all non-communist labour organizations. The *Red International of Labour Unions* (RILU), established in Moscow in 1921, having among its members the large Russian trade unions and minority groups from trade unions in other European states, vehemently opposed the IFTU, which it called the 'Yellow International' or 'International of Amsterdam'. The RILU instructed its affiliates to become active within the large 'Amsterdam'-affiliated unions, in order to oppose official policies and in that way either take over or split these unions. This hostility became a dominant factor in international trade unionism during the interwar period, which also affected the power of trade unions within the ILO. 'Although the IFTU was at all times the more representative and clearly the more experienced organization, its Communist rival was often able to exercise the initiative as the more aggressive and monolithic organization. Its decisions on strategy and tactics usually set the tone for the relationship with the IFTU, the International Trade Secretariats, and individual IFTU affiliates, and there can be little doubt that throughout much of the 1920s the RILU considered itself to be in the ascendancy, while regarding the IFTU as facing inexorable decline and eventual collapse' (Windmuller 1980, 31–32). However, this was not the actual situation. Partly due to its great size and its dominant position within the ILO, the IFTU managed to set the final tone.

Figure 17.3 Tendencies in the twentieth-century international left-wing labour movement

The **First International** existed between 1864 and 1876 (see §13.1), the **Second** or **Socialist International** between 1889 and 1914 (see §13.5). The outbreak of the First World War halted the international contacts of the socialist labour movement, although in March 1915 a group of women succeeded in convening an international socialist women's conference in Bern. At the invitation of Italian and Swiss socialists an international conference was called in Zimmerwald, near Bern, in September 1915, which unanimously turned against the war, despite differences of opinion about the necessity of revolutionary violence. After the war's end social democrats and communists, as the revolutionary socialists called themselves after the October Revolution of 1917 in Russia, began the reconstruction of an international organization.

Russian Bolsheviks, who had turned against the nationalistic policies of the social democratic parties before and during the First World War, emphasized their revolutionary perspective as an alternative to *union sacrée* and reformism. In March

1919 they established the **Communist International** (Comintern, also Third International) in Moscow, which during the 1920s developed into a 'world party' with national sections in several states that had to execute unconditionally the instructions of the Executive in Moscow. The Comintern existed until 1943, when the Soviet Union abolished it.

On the initiative of the British, the former Second International convened two congresses in 1919 to bridge the divisions that had occurred since 1914. As a result the **Labour and Socialist International** (LSI) was established in July 1920 as a continuation of the Second International. It became the main opponent of the Comintern.

Various social democratic parties did not affiliate to the Comintern or the LSI, as Austrian and groups of French and German social democrats still hoped for reconciliation between the two internationals. In February 1920 they established the *International Working Union of Socialist Parties* in Vienna, known as the Vienna Union and as the **Two-and-a-Half International**. When reconciliation proved impossible, these socialists joined the LSI.

When in 1935 the Comintern decided in favour of a United Front against Fascism, based on unity between communists and social democrats, the Comintern obliged its affiliated parties to set aside the old differences of opinion with the social democrats. The LSI, however, remained divided in this respect. Although Popular Front governments were set up in France and Spain, the rift between the two tendencies remained great.

The LSI continued to exist until the beginning of the Second World War. Following several congresses it was decided in July 1950 in Frankfurt am Main to continue the LSI as the **Socialist International** (SI).

In September 1947 the Soviet Union established the **Communist Information Bureau**, or Cominform, in Szklaraska Poreba, Czechoslovakia, as a reaction to the announcement of the Truman doctrine. It was meant to close communist ranks and to force obedience to Soviet policies. In addition to communist parties from Eastern Europe a few West European communist parties joined. However, in the context of some détente between East and West the Cominform was dissolved in 1956.

In September 1938 the **Fourth International** was established by the exiled Russian revolutionary Leon Trotsky and his followers. It accused the Soviet Union of bureaucratic deformation and degeneration. Instead of 'socialism in one country' the Fourth International was in favour of 'permanent revolution' to be exported elsewhere. Joseph Stalin had Trotsky murdered in 1940 in Mexico. This did not dissolve the Fourth International.

The League of Nations' ongoing economic and social activities

18.1 The League of Nations' structures for economic and social activities

Allied war councils

During the First World War the Allied powers had already set up various means of cooperation. As early as August 1914 the *Commission internationale de ravitaillement* was created to coordinate the purchases of the Allied powers in the UK. Two years later, purchases for their civil requirements were also placed under a common structure. The *Wheat Executive*, established in November 1916, acted as an inter-Allied commission for the joint purchase of wheat supplies. The aim was 'to arrange for the wheat supplies (and later for all cereals) of all countries to be bought together and allotted by agreement' (Hill 1946, 14). These 'war councils' are perfect examples of cooperation among the Allied states in specific areas. In December 1917 the *Allied Maritime Transport Council* was founded to ensure the most efficient use possible of the available means of transport. For planning in other areas Programme Committees were set up. In time these merged to form larger bodies such as the *Inter-Allied Munitions Council* and the *Inter-Allied Food Council*. None of these bodies had direct powers of implementation, however. The Transport Council was made up of two ministers from each of the European states involved and two delegates from the US. A group of experts from the UK, the US,

France and Italy carried out its administrative tasks. It was this 'personal integration of the national administrations rather than any formal delegation of executive power (which indeed has been expressly withheld) which accounted for the strength, efficiency, and success of the inter-Allied economic organizations in the later stages of the first World War' (Hill 1946, 15–16).

The Supreme Economic Council (1919)

After the war cooperation was again necessary, due to the urgent need for food and other supplies in those parts of Europe which had been devastated and impoverished by the war. The US government tackled the food shortage. No means was found to finance and distribute basic materials for reconstruction, however, and this hampered the economic recovery. In February 1919 the *Supreme Economic Council* was formed to tackle these economic problems. This had similar characteristics to the war councils, but its activities were restricted to too small an area for it to be a success. The effectiveness of the Council was 'enormously reduced by the concomitant disintegration of the controls, both national and international, which proceeded rapidly during the first half of 1919' (Hill 1946, 15). The US delegates withdrew in August and the final meeting of the Supreme Economic Council took place in March 1920. Some of its tasks were continued by the League of Nations. For example, the Raw Materials Section of the Council conducted research that was later utilized by the Economic and Financial Organization of the League (see below), which took over the statistical work of the Raw Materials Section.

Should the League of Nations have an economic role or not?

The war councils, which had played a role at Versailles during discussions on the establishment of the Secretariat of the League of Nations (see §15.4), proved to be unsustainable in a situation where there was no common enemy. During the Versailles talks there had been a debate on whether a universal organization to promote peace and security ought also to have an economic dimension. The question of whether the League should take on the specialized activities of the public international unions was answered in the negative. Most states had no desire to commit themselves to such activities within the framework of the League. Once the American President Wilson had agreed to the establishment of the ILO, he had little reason to pay much more attention to those sections of the Treaty of Versailles which did not deal with security. Because of changing political relationships at home, the US beat a hasty retreat from all forms of economic cooperation such as the Supreme Economic Council, and also stayed out of the League of Nations and, for the time being, the ILO. In practice, however, the US continued to follow the development of the League of Nations closely and often became involved.

No coordination of the public international unions

The fact that Article 23 of the Covenant of the League of Nations offered the possibility of international action on free economic activity was due to British pressure during negotiations. Article 23 refers to measures 'to secure and maintain freedom of communications and of transit and equitable treatment for the commerce of all members of the League'. Other policy fields mentioned specifically were conditions of labour, traffic in women and children, traffic in opium, and prevention and control of disease. However, public international unions active in these areas were not in favour of cooperation with the League, as this would affect their independence. Article 24 enabled the League to coordinate the economic and social activities of public international unions. 'Coordination' generally refers to preventing the duplication of activities and ensuring cooperation and mutual support, but the Covenant mentioned placing these unions 'under the direction of the League', and it was to this hierarchical arrangement that the unions objected. They preferred to remain independent of any 'political' organization. Additionally, not all the unions' member states were members of the League of Nations and they did not all operate on a strictly intergovernmental basis, as the League required. The same applied to public international unions formed later. The League was thus not able to establish itself as the coordinator of those unions that had remained active during and after the war. The ILO, on the other hand, was created as a specialized agency of the League. In Versailles the career politicians had shown little interest in the creation of the ILO and foreign ministers had attempted to move it down the agenda. However, political leaders such as Clemenceau, Lloyd George and Wilson had persevered and ensured it was founded.

Bodies known as 'organizations'

In line with Article 23, the League of Nations created three specialized sections or 'organizations' dedicated to economic and social policy fields. These were the Economic and Financial Organization, the Transit Organization and the Health Organization. Although these were known as 'organizations', they were in fact bodies within the League. Unlike the ILO and the Permanent Court of International Justice, they had no independent status.

The Economic and Financial Organization

The foundations of the *Economic and Financial Organization* were laid in the summer of 1919, when the secretary-general of the League of Nations appointed a small commission to investigate which economic problems needed urgent international attention. As a result of this it was decided in February 1920 to hold a conference to discuss the worldwide crisis in finance and trade. The conference was held in Brussels (see §18.2) and came out in favour of sustained action by the League. However, it was not until 1923 that the Economic and Financial Organization could begin its work. As a result of this delay, it started work at a time when the immediate and common dangers that it had been set up to tackle had already disappeared (Hill 1946, 23). The new body was charged with the task of advising the Council. For it to be able to do this the Council appointed senior officials from national ministries of finance, directors of central banks and specialists in areas such as trade and monetary affairs. Specialist experts were dominant and functioned more on the basis of their expertise than as national delegates, although they were entrusted with national interests. The Economic and Financial Section of the Permanent Secretariat of the League was responsible for the Economic and Financial Organization's secretariat. The Organization was subdivided into the *Economic Commission* and the *Financial Commission*, with the latter focusing on matters such as an international currency, the use of gold as a means of payment, and relations between the League of Nations and the Bank for International Settlements, established in 1930 (see §18.2). Additionally, specialized subcommittees for areas such as statistics and fiscal affairs were set up. In 1930 the Economic and Financial Organization, with its 53 staff members, was the largest body within the League. After its director Arthur Salter left it in 1931, it was subdivided into the Economic Relations Section and the Financial Section and Economic Intelligence Service.

The meaning of economic 'intelligence'

Through the work done by its two Commissions, the Economic and Financial Organization gradually built up its apparatus, as can be seen in the role of the Economic Intelligence Service. This rather loose grouping of economists and statisticians was able to take over the publication of the *Statistical Bulletin* from the Supreme Economic Council and to continue this work under the League's auspices. The quality of the statistics was enhanced by convening international conferences of experts, giving the League a detailed statistical overview of the monetary and financial situation in many member states. General and comparative statistics of this nature had up to this point been unavailable or hard to come by, even though various public international unions such as the International Union for the Publication of Customs Tariffs (see §11.1) had undertaken work in this area. The Assembly of the League considered these financial and economic publications so important that it decided that they were to be compiled and published on a regular basis. The League's Secretariat was charged with this task. 'The scope of this work of research and exposition was widened from time to time by decisions of later Assemblies, in response, sometimes to a demand from one or more governments, sometimes to the recommendations of conferences, notably the Genoa and Geneva conferences of 1922 and 1927 respectively' (Hill 1946, 95). The *World Economic Survey* was published for the first time in 1932, after which it appeared annually (see Figure 18.2 for an overview of all the League of Nations' regular economic publications). Through its activities in this area the Economic and Financial Organization became a valued forum, within which senior officials, national experts and policy makers could come together, consult one another and exchange information. Regular meetings within the economic institutions of the League enabled the participants to know what was happening in various other states and who was politically and administratively responsible. During the interwar period those sections of the League's Secretariat which handled economic and social matters formed an 'elaborate system of expert committees, and the League of Nations Assembly did provide clearinghouses for transgovernmental linkages' (Dubin 1983, 471).

A growing number of competencies

As in the case of the ILO (see §17.2), the League's Economic and Financial Organization gradually developed a more flexible method of working, and became less dependent on member state governments than had been agreed at its foundation. In practice the Council's formal control over the activities of the Economic Commission and the Financial Commission, which had been emphasized in a resolution of 1920, became much less rigid. The convention that the Council had to approve the Commissions' agenda was swiftly dropped, and from 1929 onwards the Commissions were allowed to publish and send their reports directly to governments without first having to have them discussed by the Council. In 1927 the Economic Commission obtained permission to consult experts, set up special committees and undertake any research that it saw fit

Figure 18.1 The League of Nations' regular economic publications

- *Balances of Payments*
- *International Trade in Certain Raw Materials and Foodstuffs*
- *International Trade Statistics*
- *Money and Banking: Volume I: Monetary Review; Volume II: Commercial and Central Banks*
- *Monthly Bulletin of Statistics*
- *Review of World Trade*
- *Statistical Year-Book*
- *Survey of National Nutrition Policies*
- *World Economic Survey*
- *World Production and Prices*

Source: (Hill 1946, 98).

without having to ask for approval. In 1930 the Council went so far as to invite the Financial Commission to take initiatives and send proposals to the Council in areas which the Commission viewed as particularly important (Hill 1946, 107–8).

The Communications and Transit Organization

The Transit Organization of the League, which soon became the *Communications and Transit Organization*, focused on encouraging free movement between states and the integration of the transport and communication facilities that linked them. The Organization's General Conference was able to make proposals to member states, and the Organization also had its own Consultative Committee and a secretariat provided by the Transit Section of the Permanent Secretariat. There were 18 members on the Consultative Committee, four of whom represented the permanent members of the Council. For the remaining 14 elective places, non-members of the League of Nations could also be considered. The Transit Organization set up subcommittees for areas such as rail transport, inland waterways, harbours, maritime navigation and the distribution of electricity. The Organization paved the way for a number of international treaties on transport (see Figure 18.2, where 14 of the 43 agreements are related to communication and transport). The preparatory work for these agreements was done at international conferences, such as those held in Barcelona (1921), Geneva (1923) and Lisbon (1930). The Transit Organization's other activities included the simplification of travel documents and visa procedures, simplifying cross-border procedures for freight trucks and tourist buses, the distribution of electricity and other forms of energy from one state to another, and the standardization of calendars across different parts of the world. It proved difficult for the trade union movement to access the Transit Organization, as the International Transportworkers Federation (ITF) experienced time and again. The Transit Organization instead favoured contacts with automobile clubs, chambers of commerce and tourist organizations. Working conditions were secondary to this and viewed as the concern of the ILO (Reinalda 1997, 146). As a result the two areas remained separate.

Figure 18.2 Agreements in the economic and social fields
1921–37

Agreements in the economic field:

- International Convention Relating to the Simplification of Customs Formalities, Geneva, 3 November **1923**.
- Convention for the Abolition of Import and Export Restrictions, Geneva, 8 November **1927**.
- International Convention for the Suppression of Counterfeiting Currency, Geneva, 20 April **1929**.
- Protocol to the International Convention for the Suppression of Counterfeiting Currency, Geneva, 20 April **1929**.
- Optional Protocol Regarding the Suppression of Counterfeiting Currency, Geneva, 20 April **1929**.
- Convention Providing a Uniform Law for Bills of Exchange and Promissory Notes, Geneva, 7 June **1930**.
- Convention for the Settlement of Certain Conflicts of Laws in Connection with Bills of Exchange and Promissory Notes, Geneva, 7 June **1930**.
- Convention on the Stamp Laws in Connection with Bills of Exchange and Promissory Notes, Geneva, 7 June **1930**.
- Convention Providing a Uniform Law for Cheques, Geneva, 19 March **1931**.
- Convention on the Stamp Laws in Connection with Cheques, Geneva, 19 March **1931**.
- Convention for the Settlement of Certain Conflicts of Laws in Connection with Cheques, Geneva, 19 March **1931**.
- Final Act of the Conference of Wheat Exporting and Importing Countries, London, 25 August **1933**.
- International Agreement Regarding the Regulation of Production and Marketing of Sugar (and Protocol), London, 6 May **1937**.

Agreements in the communication and transport fields:

- Convention and Statute on Freedom of Transit, Barcelona, 20 April **1921**.
- Convention and Statute on the Regime of Navigable Waterways of International Concern, Barcelona, 20 April **1921**.
- Additional Protocol to the Convention on the Regime of Navigable Waterways of International Concern, Barcelona, 20 April **1921**.
- Declaration Recognising the Right to a Flag of States having no Sea-coast, Barcelona, 20 April **1921**.
- Convention and Statute on the International Régime of Maritime Ports, Geneva, 9 December **1923**.
- Convention on the International Régime of Railways, Geneva, 9 December **1923**.
- Convention Regarding the Measurement of Vessels Employed in Inland Navigation, Paris, 27 November **1925**.

- Agreement Concerning Manned Lightships not on their Stations, Lisbon, 23 October **1930**.
- Agreement Concerning Maritime Signals, Lisbon, 23 October **1930**.
- Convention Concerning the Unification of Road Signals, Geneva, 30 March **1931**.
- Convention on the Taxation of Foreign Motor Vehicles, Geneva, 30 March **1931**.
- Convention for the Regulation of Whaling, Geneva, 24 September **1931**.
- International Convention Concerning the Transit of Animals, Meat and Other Products of Animal Origin, Geneva, 20 February **1935**.
- International Convention Concerning the Export and Import of Animal Products (other than Meat, Meat Preparations, Fresh Animal Products, Milk and Milk Products), Geneva, 20 February **1935**.
- International Convention Concerning the Use of Broadcasting in the Cause of Peace, Geneva, 23 September **1936**.

Agreements in the health field:

- Agreement concerning the Suppression of the Manufacture of, Internal Trade in, and Use of, Prepared Opium (with Protocol), Geneva, 11 February **1925**.
- International Opium Convention (with Protocol), Geneva, 19 February **1925**.
- Convention for Limiting the Manufacture and Regulating the Distribution of Narcotic Drugs (with Protocol of Signature), Geneva, 13 July **1931**.
- Agreement Concerning the Suppression of Opium Smoking, Bangkok, 27 November **1931**.
- International Convention for the Campaign against Contagious Diseases of Animals, Geneva, 20 February **1935**.
- Convention for the Suppression of the Illicit Traffic in Dangerous Drugs, Geneva, 26 June **1936**.

Agreements in the social field:

- International Convention for the Suppression of the Traffic in Women and Children, Geneva, 30 September **1921**.
- International Convention for the Suppression of the Circulation of and Traffic in Obscene Publications, Geneva, 12 September **1923**.
- Convention to Suppress the Slave Trade and Slavery, Geneva, 25 September **1926**.
- Convention Establishing an International Relief Union, Geneva, 12 July **1927**.
- Convention on Certain Questions Relating to the Conflict of Nationality Laws, The Hague, 12 April **1930**.
- Protocol Relating to a Certain Case of Statelessness, The Hague, 12 April **1930**.
- Protocol Relating to Military Obligations in Certain Cases of Double Nationality, The Hague, 12 April **1930**.
- Special Protocol Concerning Statelessness, The Hague, 12 April **1930**.
- International Convention for the Suppression of the Traffic in Women of Full Age, Geneva, 11 October **1933**.

The Health Organization

The *Health Organization* of the League was established in 1922. In 1902 the pan-American International Sanitary Bureau had been set up in Washington DC, followed in 1907 by the International Office of Public Health in Paris (see §14.4). Because of disagreements with the US and the existing institutions' opposition to losing their autonomy, the League of Nations' Health Organization was formed alongside the two bodies, each pursuing its own agenda. In 1926 the International Office of Public Health in Paris extended the remit of the *International Sanitary Convention*, which dated from 1892 and had restricted its activities to cholera (see §14.4), to include smallpox and typhoid, and a regulation was passed in 1935 concerning infection via the air. In 1938 the Paris Office decided to close the International Sanitary, Maritime and Quarantine Council in Alexandria and hand over its powers and material resources to Egypt. Non-members of the League, such as Germany, the US and the Soviet Union, also took part in the work of the Health Organization. The Organization had a Consultative Committee and a secretariat provided by the Health Section of the Permanent Secretariat. At the health conference organized by the League in Warsaw in 1922, plans were developed to combat the spread of infectious illnesses in Africa, the Middle East, the Far East and the Soviet Union. The standardization of vaccinations for diseases such as diphtheria, tetanus and tuberculosis was promoted through establishing and supporting institutions in Singapore (Eastern Bureau of Epidemiological Information), Copenhagen (State Serum Institute) and London (National Institute for Medical Research). When health problems arose, the Health Organization formed a link between governments. It also provided the technical expertise and support they required. International health issues remained on the League's agenda until 1939, with the Health Organization's last conference held in Paris in 1938. The League of Nations' Health Organization was one of the precursors of the World Health Organization, founded in 1946 (see Figure 14.2).

The League's Opium Committee

The *Advisory Committee on Opium and Other Dangerous Drugs*, established in 1920, was charged with strengthening the 1912 Hague International Opium Convention (see §14.4). The League's opium conferences of 1924 and 1925 led to a toughening of this convention and the introduction of practical measures to control the production and refinement of narcotics. In 1931 the regulation of the use of narcotic drugs for medical and scientific purposes was begun (see Figure 18.2 for the conventions). A restriction or ban on the cultivation of plants from which opium can be produced was also discussed. These debates were interrupted by the outbreak of the Second World War and were resumed by the UN, as was the case with many of the League of Nations' policy dossiers. The Opium Committee had a Secretariat, from 1929 a Permanent Central Opium Board, and from 1931 a Supervisory Body.

Social activities of the League: women and children

The most important social topics for the League of Nations were trafficking in women, and the protection of children. Although this was regarded as of secondary importance within the organization and many politicians were sceptical, viewing it as meddling in their domestic affairs, there were some successes in these fields (Walters 1960, 186–87).

In 1921 the League set up a permanent *Advisory Committee on the Traffic in Women and Children*, which from 1924 was subdivided into the *Committee on the Traffic in Women* and the *Committee for the Protection of Children and Young People*. These Committees had a relatively high number of women as members, and NGOs working in these fields attended in an advisory role without voting rights. At Versailles the League of Nations had also assumed responsibility for the international conventions of 1904 and 1910, which governed the traffic in women and in pornography (see §13.3), and in 1921, 1923 and 1933 it initiated new versions of these conventions (see Figure 18.2). The League undertook thorough investigations prior to updating the conventions, in both Europe and the Far East, and further research was carried out subsequently to monitor compliance, with violations reported to the Advisory Committee (Myers 1935, 231–32). On the subject of children, the League published the *Geneva Declaration on the Rights of the Child* in 1924, in which a link was also made between depression and unemployment. In 1934 an Information Centre was established for questions regarding children's welfare. In February 1937 the League held a conference for Far Eastern states in Bandung, in the Dutch East Indies, of which the practical results were the raising of the legal age at which girls were allowed to marry and the abolition of licensed brothels.

Nationality and the legal status of women

Other issues discussed by the League in the 1930s were nationality and the legal status of women. Despite arguments from women's organizations, the Convention on Nationality Laws, which the League passed in 1930 (see Figure 18.2), made no assumption of equality between women and men. However, equality was a topic that women continued to advance within the League of Nations, which led to the publication of two reports by international women's organizations in 1932 that made the case for equality. The Latin American states, which supported this point of view, were unable to enlist the support necessary to change the relevant articles of the 1930 convention. Although an information procedure was accelerated by the League, this offered no prospect of further action. To avoid an impasse, the Latin American states widened the discussion to include the general legal status of women, with the intention of eventually achieving recognition for the principle of the equality of women and men. In 1938 the League established a special commission to investigate the legal status of women, which continued its activities well into the Second World War. In fact the most favourable developments in this area took place within the ILO. Although the ILO had mainly instigated conventions and recommendations for the special protection of women, international women's organizations – such as the International Federation of Business and Professional Women and Open Door International – applied sufficient pressure for the idea of equality to gradually gain acceptance. Pressure for equal pay grew steadily. In 1937 the ILO recognized for the first time that discrimination against women existed and decided that the status of women must change. The ILO became a supporter of women's equal right to paid work, full opportunity in education and recognition of the civil and political rights of women (Riegelman Lubin and Winslow 1990, 48). In 1939 the ILO qualified its special protection of women workers by pointing out that the welfare of all workers should be safeguarded. To reflect the broadening of its interests and activities, the League of Nations in 1936 changed the name of the Advisory Committee on the Traffic in Women and Children to the *Advisory Committee on Social Questions*.

Citizens' expectations and intellectual cooperation

The League of Nations' promotion of cooperation in the intellectual sphere dated from just after the First World War and had its roots in citizens' dismay at the unprecedented savagery of the war. This had also played a role during the Napoleonic Wars of the early nineteenth century (see §4.2). President Wilson and the League had sparked high expectations on the part of citizens with Wilson's new ideas such as 'making the world safe for democracy' and 'open diplomacy'. Newspapers and the radio reinforced these expectations through their thorough reporting of the League's discussions and activities in Geneva. The peace movement, with its demands for 'no more war' and its symbol of a broken firearm, agitated against military activities and also helped spread anti-war attitudes. During the negotiations in Versailles the idea of cooperation between scientists and intellectuals so as to promote better understanding between states had already been floated. However, a Belgian proposal on this subject met with so much resistance among negotiators that it was withdrawn. A Belgian delegate put forward the proposal again during the first meeting of the League's Assembly in 1920. This time it was decided to publish a report on this idea, which in 1922 led to the establishment of an advisory body to the Assembly and the Council: the *International Committee on Intellectual Cooperation*, which was to meet annually. From 1923 on it encouraged the formation of national committees, by which means it was able to collect information from states and involve important people in its work. The Committee had 12 members, later increased to 15, including such notables as Henri Bergson, Albert Einstein and Marie Curie. Women members were explicitly encouraged. The objectives of the Committee were the improvement of the working conditions of qualified personnel and the promotion of the development of international relationships between teachers, artists, scientists and members of other intellectual groups. In 1926 this led to the formation of the *International Institute of Intellectual Cooperation* (see Figure 18.3).

Figure 18.3 The International Institute of Intellectual Cooperation (1926)

The establishment of the *International Committee of Intellectual Cooperation* did not mean that the League of Nations actually had the funds at its disposal to carry out the work. The UK and the Netherlands in particular were against providing the money, as they did not view this work as an appropriate task for governments and the League. France, on the other hand, which under the new government of Édouard Herriot – installed in 1924 – was seeking greater cooperation in Europe, was prepared to establish and finance an institute. The League's Council accepted this French offer, and in 1926 the **International Institute of Intellectual Cooperation** began its work in Paris. It forged contacts with scientific and cultural institutions in 40 states and organized conferences in diverse fields. Subcommissions were formed for sciences, arts and literature. Outsiders were then brought in as experts and paired with members of the League's Committee. One of the activities which the Institute encouraged was joint research by scientists from different states into, among other things, international relations. Thus during the 1930s subjects such as collective security, peaceful change and the use of economic policy as a means to peace were all placed on the agenda. In 1939, just before the outbreak of the Second World War, the subject of international organizations was agreed upon. There were also close ties with the **International Educational Cinematographic Institute**, set up by the Italian government in Rome, since half its governing body members belonged to the International Institute in Paris. In 1946 UNESCO became the successor organization to the International Institute of Intellectual Cooperation.

18.2 A faltering international economy and German reparation payments 1920–32

The international financial conference in Brussels (1920)

The League of Nations held its first economic conference in 1920. The way in which this was organized and the procedures used there set the tone for the future work of the League in the field of economics. Delegates from 39 states, including the non-member states Germany and the US, attended the international financial conference in Brussels. The delegates were appointed by governments, but acted as experts in their field rather than as national representatives. The conference assessed the financial situation in the world and made recommendations to governments. The governments were to strive 'to reduce expenditure, to balance their budgets, to check inflation, to return to the gold standard, to abolish "artificial restrictions" on international trade, and to afford increased facilities for transport'. Additionally the conference emphasized that financial reforms could be successful in the long term only if existing restrictions on trade and industrial development were gradually removed and the prewar free trade situation was restored (Hill 1946, 25). A clear policy was put forward on this, but the scheme to create a system of international credits, named after the Dutch businessman who designed it, C.E. Ter Meulen, was not accepted. Under the Ter Meulen scheme the League was to establish a commission of bankers and business representatives to which governments could apply for foreign credit, with both the businesses and the governments involved offered guarantees. While states with a positive credit status, such as the US, welcomed the plan, they were not prepared to implement it. Some form of collective supervision would be necessary to ensure that problems could be tackled on a state-by-state basis and in a coordinated fashion and the international community was not yet ready to provide such supervision.

Economic assistance to Austria and Hungary 1922–24

An opportunity arose to put some of the League's ideas into practice when it provided economic assistance to Austria, Hungary and Bulgaria. Between 1922 and 1924, and under international supervision, these states received loans and technical support (expertise) for the economic reforms which they needed following the break-up of the Austro-Hungarian Empire. 'Building up the financial system was given high priority throughout the area: a series of economic reforms was carried out everywhere at the threshold of the new era: their patterns – strictly "classicist" patterns – were set by those carried out in two countries, Hungary and Bulgaria, under the aegis of the League of Nations' (Cipolla 1976, 594). This had a stabilizing effect on the region, where the League also helped alleviate the refugee problem of 1922–23 (see §16.1). The efforts were coordinated by the High Commissioner for Refugees and the League of Nations' Health Organization. The Financial Commission developed a programme to house refugees, stabilize the Greek currency and introduce general measures to improve the financial situation in Greece. Similar financial and technical support was given to Albania (in 1923), Estonia (in 1924, 1926 and 1927), Danzig, which needed to establish its own currency and central bank (in 1925 and 1927), and the territory of the Saar Basin (in 1929 and 1931).

The economic and financial conference in Genoa (1922)

In May 1922 the Economic Commission held an economic and financial conference in Genoa, where ways of strengthening trade links were discussed. The problem of awarding most-favoured-nation treatment came to the fore, because both France and Spain at the time decided not to grant it in their trade agreements. The Economic Commission was charged with devising procedures to make improvements. As a result of the conference's recommendation that customs arrangements should be simplified, the Economic Commission began work to improve and strengthen the administrative, legal and fiscal regulations governing trade.

German reparation payments and national short-term interests

The reparations imposed on Germany by the Treaty of Versailles represented a continual concern during the interwar period. The economist John Maynard Keynes, who had been working at the British Treasury and was part of the British delegation at the peace negotiations in Versailles, had resigned his post because of disagreements with Prime Minister Lloyd George over the Treaty's economic provisions. Keynes elaborated his criticisms of this aspect of the Treaty of Versailles in *The Economic Consequences of the Peace*, which was published in 1919 and attracted a great deal of attention. Keynes believed that the reparations imposed on Germany would disadvantage Germany because it would never be able to meet these obligations, and that this would lead to great poverty and have disastrous consequences for European economic prosperity as a whole. The UK and France, however, were much more interested in rebuilding their own economies. They had incurred large debts in the US to finance the war in France and on the Eastern Front, while communist Russia was not prepared to pay back the debts run up by tsarist Russia. The UK and France saw Germany as having caused the war, and considered it in their interest to keep Germany on a tight rein. The US representatives at Versailles were more prepared to take German interests into account and they even favoured the 'grand scheme for the rehabilitation of Europe' put forward by Keynes. However, US politicians in Washington DC did not agree with Keynes's 'mutual Allied debt cancellation', which they thought was too expensive (Williams 1998, 220). As no compromise was made on the reparation scheme, Germany was forced to take out foreign loans to meet its reparation commitments.

Economic nationalism rather than liberal internationalism

Many European states were in a state of economic collapse in 1919, and the situation deteriorated still further at the beginning of the 1920s. The League of Nations, however, did not have enough power to act in any meaningful way. The collapse of the German currency in 1923 had a devastating effect on the German middle classes and this in turn affected French and British trade. The Franco–Belgian occupation of the Ruhr region in 1923 aggravated the situation and these events strengthened isolationist sentiment among Americans, 'who believed the French and British were incapable of any higher feeling than that which directly affected their wallets and Imperial designs'. Little remained of all the good intentions which had been evident at Versailles and liberal internationalism was the main victim, because no state was prepared to return to an open economic system such as had existed pre-1914. Instead there was a return to economic nationalism and protectionism (Williams 1998, 221).

The Dawes Plan for German war debts (1924)

The German currency crisis of 1923 forced a re-evaluation of German reparation payments. An international commission was set up, chaired by the American politician and banker Charles Dawes, which proposed moving to a more flexible arrangement for repayment of the amounts due. This became known as the Dawes Plan and implied the return of US involvement in European politics. Because no international organization existed that could lend money to states, private bankers and businesspeople – rather than ministers of finance – continued to make the decisions on international economic cooperation. It was clear to US bankers that Germany could never repay its loans unless the burden of repayment was reduced and diplomatic relations in Europe, particularly Franco–German relations, were stabilized. It was this private pressure on European and American politicians that led to the acceptance of the Dawes Plan at a conference in London in 1924. 'To put the minds of the bankers at rest, the London conference revised the volume and manner of collection of Germany's reparation payments and … markedly weakened France's ability to enforce the collection of reparations in future. It also redistributed the European balance of power favouring Germany over France, and, once the loan was in place, determined that the Allies would service Germany's loans even if it defaulted on reparations' (Clavin 2000, 37).

The League of Nations' World Economic Conference in Geneva (1927)

Because many states continued to obstruct the restoration of free world trade by placing restrictions on trade, the League of Nations convened the World Economic Conference in Geneva in May 1927. This was not an intergovernmental conference. Many of the delegates were appointed by their governments, but actually attended the conference in their capacity of experts in the field. There were 194 delegates and 157 experts from 50 states, including the US and the Soviet Union. Although the impact of the conference on trade relations was limited in its extent and duration, the basis was laid for a European system of bilateral trade agreements and a remarkable consensus was achieved on the best direction for future policy. This consisted of: 1) a stable system of trade relationships without tariffs or non-tariff barriers on the basis of long-term commercial treaties; 2) the generalization of most-favoured-nation treatment and the progressive removal of non-tariff discrimination; and 3) a reduction in the level of tariffs (Hill 1946, 49). In short, there was still a desire for general free trade. The League was charged with the task of establishing a *Standard Customs Nomenclature*, so that the same customs standards could be applied everywhere. It was also required to codify the arrangements for most-favoured-nation status which were already in existence and to carry out research into the implications of international industrial agreements and cartels. The latter topic was also on the agendas of the International Chamber of Commerce and the International Law Association (see §12.2), and this motivated research into the need for surveillance of trusts and cartels (Wibaut 1935). The conference certainly made it clear that international economic problems needed to be solved collectively, but it provided few means of tackling these problems. The lack of an international economic organization exacerbated the weakness of international economic policy, and the League of Nations, whose functionality was already limited due to the refusal of the US to join, was ineffective (Pinder 1976, 329–30).

Encouragement of international trade

When, in the mid-1920s, Europe found itself in a more economically and financially stable climate, the Economic Commission of the League was able to do more to find ways of promoting the international exchange of goods. Its means of achieving this was through a reduction in import and export prohibitions and restrictions. Twenty-nine states, including the US, discussed this issue at a diplomatic conference in 1927, which agreed the *Convention for the Abolition of Import and Export Restrictions* within a period of six months. Ratification of this Convention proved extremely difficult, however, and two further conferences were necessary in the same year. After this 21 states had ratified, but this was linked to the condition that other explicitly named states should also ratify. The Convention finally came into effect in 1930, based on annual renewal by the US, the UK, Japan and four other states that had few trade restrictions. By 1934 all states had withdrawn from the Convention. Despite this disappointing outcome the League had made progress in eliminating trade restrictions. 'Under the constant stimulus from Geneva, quantitative restrictions on trade were very substantially whittled down, and by 1930 such restrictions no longer constituted a considerable obstacle to international trade' (Hill 1946, 46). There was, however, still no question of free trade.

The Economic Consultative Committee of 1928

The economic activities of the League of Nations in the late 1920s gave rise to a new body, the *Economic Consultative Committee*. This was set up to exist for three years and met in May 1928 and May 1929. Even the US became a member, but the high expectations that surrounded it were not realized. Whatever suggestions the Committee made for collective action, all its proposals ('maximum duties, percentage reductions in duties, concerted reductions of duties on selected groups of commodities') came up against resistance from states concerned only with their own national interests (Hill 1946, 51). Towards the end of 1929 it was obvious that the number of governments imposing tariffs was increasing and, what was more, many industrially-developed states were also turning to agricultural protectionism. International economic relations became even more difficult as a result of the problems with German reparation payments, which were exacerbated by protectionism and the 1929 US stock market crash.

The 1929 stock market crash and subsequent Depression

The improved economic situation in the second half of the 1920s came to an end with the Wall Street stock market crash in New York in October 1929. Shares lost around 40 per cent of their value in one day and an economic collapse followed: production fell by half; investment was slashed; millions of people were left jobless – unprecedented numbers. The crisis spread to Europe because the US withdrew its overseas capital. The Depression reached its lowest point in 1932–33, and it was only in 1937 that the situation began to approach normality again. The causes of the crisis were changes in trading patterns after the First World War, which meant that Japan and the US had acquired significant new markets for their goods in Europe. As a result of agricultural surpluses prices fell drastically, causing a fall in investment and industrial production in Europe. At the same time, belief in the capacity of the US to deliver unlimited economic growth led over time to lively but speculative share trading, causing a structural imbalance in the economic flows between the US and the rest of the world. This issue was not addressed, because at this point the US was neither willing nor able to take on the role, previously performed by the UK, of being the world's economic steward.

The Young Plan (1930) and the cancellation of German reparations (Lausanne 1932)

Following the economic crisis of 1929, US intervention was again needed to solve the problem of German reparation payments, which was being prolonged by other negative economic developments. The international reparation commission was by then under the chairmanship of the US businessman Owen Young. In May 1930 the Young Plan replaced the Dawes Plan, but the economic Depression meant that payments had to be suspended as early as June 1931. This was known as the Hoover moratorium, after the US president of the time, and led eventually to the cancellation of payments under the *Treaty of Lausanne*, signed in July 1932. While the League's Disarmaments Conference was running into difficulties (see §16.2), it was decided in Lausanne that Germany would not have to pay any reparations for three years. After that it would have to pay one more instalment, provided it was able to.

The establishment of the Bank for International Settlements (1930)

It was not the League of Nations which was responsible for the establishment of the *Bank for International Settlements* (BIS) in Basel, Switzerland, in 1930. This Bank was part of the framework of the Young Plan, as agreed at an international conference in The Hague. It involved three treaties. First a Convention was created between the host nation Switzerland on the one side and the governments of Belgium, France, Germany, Italy, Japan and the UK on the other. Then a constituent Charter was drawn up as the actual founding document of the BIS. This was followed by Statutes which laid down the bank's objectives and methods of working. As well as settling German reparation payments, the BIS was given an international coordinating role. The statutory role of this partnership between national central banks was framed more broadly: the promotion of cooperation between central banks and the facilitation of international financial operations. The international economic crisis meant that the Bank was unable to address these broader objectives. In reality the BIS had little practical impact, because states continued to solve their problems on a national basis (Carr 1940, 150; Kenwood and Lougheed 1971, 187–88).

International inactivity

Ideas such as customs unions, free trade areas and other forms of economic cooperation, which were being suggested by the League of Nations on the basis of the available expertise, found few supporters in the international economic and political climate of the 1930s. The contrast between national and international levels could not have been more marked. On the one hand, in accordance with Keynesian theory, states were seeking to address the crisis by gradually implementing more interventionist economic and social policies. At international level, meanwhile, inactivity prevailed (Pinder 1976, 337–38). Keynes himself had been reticent in the discussion about the establishment of the BIS. He had followed closely developments in the international economy, publishing *A Tract on Monetary Reform* in 1923, followed in 1930 by *A Treatise on Money*. Given the reluctance of states to try to find any kind of collective solution, he ruled out the possibility that the BIS would be a first move towards the formation of 'the Super-National Currency Authority which will be necessary if the world is ever to enjoy a rational monetary system' (cited by Bakker 1996, 89). Keynes would be proven correct in this assessment (see Figure 18.4 for the later development of the BIS).

Figure 18.4 The later development of the Bank for International Settlements (1930)

The **Bank for International Settlements** (BIS) took over the functions of the Berlin-based *Agent General for Reparations* and legally represented those institutions which had lent money within the framework of the Dawes Plan and the Young Plan. After the Lausanne conference of 1932 its work regarding German reparations quickly came to an end. The BIS also provided credit support to the German and Austrian central banks during the financial crises of 1931 to 1933. Although central banks had difficulty launching a collective policy on monetary relations, meetings between the central banks' directors and experts did take place in Basel every year from 1930 onwards. Another important point was that the BIS began to undertake its own research into financial and monetary developments and in this way built up its own level of expertise.

It was not until long **after the Second World War** that the BIS developed into a kind of international central bank. A US resolution passed after the establishment of the Bretton Woods arrangements of 1944 proposed the abolition of the BIS, but European central banks rejected this. When the US dollar came under pressure in the 1960s, the BIS acquired a new function and the Americans were invited to take part in its monthly discussion of the stability of international monetary arrangements. In the 1970s, as a result of the oil crisis and the international debt crisis, the BIS was charged with managing flows of capital. The monitoring of internationally-active banks was officially recognized in the 1988 *Basel Capital Accord*, which was revised in 2003 as 'Basel II' (see §41.1). The BIS also carried out monetary functions in the framework of European integration. In 2008, 55 central banks were associated with the BIS.

The Tariff Truce Conference of 1930

In September 1929, as the new economic isolationism began to emerge, the Assembly of the League of Nations adopted up a UK proposal to convene a diplomatic conference to explore how this trend could be reversed. At the beginning of 1930 the states met at what became known as the *Tariff Truce Conference*. The idea of a 'truce' was developed as a direct consequence of the contrasting positions of agricultural states and industrially-developed states. The smaller agricultural states wanted to diminish their trade deficits by imposing tariffs on industrial products, while industrialized states wanted to protect their agricultural interests. However, the trade treaty of limited scope that was agreed at the conference, which stipulated that existing trading agreements could be extended by one year, was ratified by too few states to come into force (Hill 1946, 52).

The Commission of Enquiry for European Union and the conference in Stresa (1932)

Acting on a French initiative, in 1930 the Assembly of the League established the *Commission of Enquiry for European Union*. The activities of the Commission focused particularly on Central and Eastern Europe, where the withdrawal of foreign credit and the fall in agricultural prices had led to the greatest restrictions on trade. The League investigated the possibility of setting up a bank to grant international credit on the basis of mortgages and to put in place favourable short-term tariffs for grain-producing states. The various studies and negotiations undertaken by the Commission were discussed at a conference in Stresa in September 1932, a follow-up to the July conference on German reparations in Lausanne. A detailed plan was put forward to encourage Central and Eastern European states to return to a policy of free trade, but in the end these efforts were in vain: 'the Stresa scheme came to nothing, owing partly to political difficulties, partly to the impossibility of securing the foreign credits on which the scheme was dependent; and the trade policy in that part of Europe became increasingly restrictive and discriminatory' (Hill 1946, 64).

18.3 Regional cooperation as a protectionist solution to the crisis of the 1930s

Trade diversion, as opposed to trade creation

Regionalism in the Western Hemisphere in the late nineteenth and early twentieth century had been aimed at the formation of continental markets and the promotion of free trade. The 'new' regionalism which sprang up in Europe at the end of the 1920s, by contrast, took the form of discriminatory trading blocks and protectionist bilateral agreements. It was, thus, more accurate to talk of *trade diversion*, for the benefit of the particular trading block to which a state belonged, than of *trade creation*, the ultimate goal of free trade. This new regionalism was 'highly preferential' for the participating states and 'more discriminatory' for the rest of the world (Mansfield and Milner 1997, 596–97).

The French customs union (1928) and the British Commonwealth (1931)

This regional solution to European economic problems began in 1928 with the formation of a customs union between France and its colonies. The union placed the French colonies under the economic sovereignty of the French motherland and excluded them economically from the rest of the world. This arrangement ultimately proved so stable that it also formed the basis of the *Union française* of 1946. In 1931 the UK followed suit and formed the *Commonwealth*, which involved reciprocal preferential economic treatment between the component parts of the British Empire, to the disadvantage of the rest of the world (see Figure 18.5).

Figure 18.5 The British Commonwealth of 1931

The **Commonwealth** arose out of the British Empire and included the UK and most of its colonies and dominions. When the UK declared war on Germany in 1914, the dominions (self-governing states, which had considerable autonomy) were not consulted. This applied to Australia, Canada, Newfoundland, New Zealand and South Africa. These dominions did, however, become involved in the war and therefore participated in the British government through the Imperial War Cabinet. They were also involved with the peace conference in Versailles, signatories to the Treaty of Versailles and members of the League of Nations. Their status thus approached that of sovereign states. In 1926 an Imperial Conference took place which transformed the dominions into autonomous areas within the British Empire. From that point on they had equal status and were in no way subordinate to the UK.

At the end of 1931 the **Statute of Westminster**, which laid the basis for the Commonwealth, granted the dominions the status of sovereign powers, although they remained united in their common allegiance to the British Crown as members of the Commonwealth. Participation in this so-called cultural international organization was voluntary. All members, to this day, recognize the reigning British monarch as Head of the Commonwealth, although constitutionally many are republics. In 2008 the Commonwealth had 53 members, whose aim is cooperation and mutual support.

The Conference of Ottawa (1932)

In the summer of 1932 a meeting of Commonwealth members took place in Ottawa, Canada. The aim of this meeting was a trading agreement under which they would grant each other a preferential position. The conference also led to a detailed general agreement on tariffs, which set out how British import duties on goods from the dominions would be lowered for some goods and abolished for others. In return, the dominions would guarantee to import British industrial products. The *Ottawa Agreements* put economic nationalism, in this case in the form of 'Imperial Preference', above free trade. Nevertheless, supporters of free trade within the Commonwealth did succeed in preventing an extreme form of protectionism in Ottawa. 'Although greatly diminished in strength, free traders were able to moderate protectionist policies through the Ottawa Agreements and the Sterling Area' (Lobell 1999, 671). Just like France, the UK was seeking to protect its colonial interests, but some colonies acquired greater self-government and a well-defined status, which meant that there was more autonomy within the British Empire than in the French Union.

Protectionist policies in Europe

Other states in Europe also formed trading blocks. Bulgaria, Hungary, Romania and Yugoslavia put in place a preferential system of tariffs for trade in agricultural products with other European states. In 1934 an agreement was signed in Rome between Hungary, Italy and Austria to establish a preferential trading area. The Baltic states of Estonia, Latvia and Lithuania formed the *Baltic Entente* in the same year. They met in Geneva to emphasize their neutrality, in the face of tensions with Germany and the Soviet Union and over the disputed border areas of Vilnius and Memel. Economically, cooperation was difficult because the states were competitors in terms of agricultural products, but the Baltic Entente survived until 1940, when the Soviet Union annexed the Baltic states. Meanwhile Germany went its own way, formalizing its trading preferences in bilateral agreements.

Trade relations between the US and Latin American states

A policy of reciprocal trade agreements was also being pursued by the US. Most of the two dozen or so trade agreements which were struck during this period were with South and Central American states. The US sought to improve relations with states within its sphere of influence. This was done in the context of the Union of American Republics (see §11.5), which by the end of the 1920s had established specialized institutions for children, women and geography (see Figure 18.6).

Resistance to US domination among American states

In the first half of the twentieth century, the Union of American Republics remained exactly what the name suggested: 'a typical nineteenth-century international union with strictly limited functions' (Armstrong *et al.* 1996, 220). However, every four or five years the conferences of the Union provided the other American states with a forum in which to express their reservations about the right claimed by the US that it could intervene in the affairs of Latin American states. This assumption became a point of increasing contention within the Union, in view of, on the one hand, the increase in the power of the US, and on the other, the economic development of the other American states. The discontent of the Latin American states over US behaviour found expression in terms such as 'Yankee imperialism' and 'Colossus of the North'. In fact the pressure became so great that at the Pan-American conferences of 1933 and 1936 the US formally accepted the principle of non-intervention. In his presidential acceptance speech in 1933 the newly-elected Democratic President Franklin D. Roosevelt announced a *Good Neighbour Policy*. He spoke of 'a good neighbor who resolutely respects himself, and because he does so, respects the rights of others' (cited in Plano and Olton 1982, 387). The man behind this new policy was US Secretary of State Cordell Hull, who expected healthier economic ties to have a positive effect on security relations. In 1933 the conference of the Union of American Republics agreed a treaty of non-intervention. The *Treaty of Montevideo* defined a sovereign state as one with a permanent population, a (more or less) sharply defined territory, a government and the authoritative power to enter into relations with other states (Van Kersbergen *et al.* 1999, 76). In 1934 the US ended restrictions on the recognition of Cuban sovereignty and withdrew its troops from Haiti. Following this political rapprochement there was a period of greater cooperation

Figure 18.6 Specialized Pan-American and Inter-American institutions

1902: The *International Sanitary Bureau* was founded, known from 1910 on as the **Pan-American Sanitary Bureau**, based in Washington DC (see §14.4).

1927: The **Inter-American Children's Institute** was set up. Based in Montevideo, Uruguay, its primary task was to study and find solutions to problems associated with children and the family.

1928: The **Inter-American Commission of Women** was established. Based in Washington DC, this advisory body came into existence as a result of the appearance of women's rights on the agenda at the conference of the Union of American Republics in Santiago, Chile, in 1923. This subject had not originally been on the agenda, and was proposed by a man against the backdrop of a strong women's movement in many Latin American states and in the US. The Commission was given the necessary scope, working on the basis that women should have equal civil and political rights to men. In this area the Union was more progressive than the League of Nations.

1928: The **Pan-American Institute of Geography and History** was founded. Based in Mexico City, the institute was charged with creating maps and with the study of geography and history.

1940: The **Inter-American Indian Institute** was established. Based in Mexico City, the institute coordinated the policy of the member states towards the original inhabitants of the continent and the opportunities available to them, commissioning research in this field.

1942: The **Inter-American Institute on Cooperation for Agriculture** was set up. Based in San José, Costa Rica, the role of this institute was the advancement of agriculture and prosperity in rural areas.

between North, Central and South America, which reached a high point during the Second World War when there was a strong desire to continue this cooperation after the war and to adapt the organization to the new circumstances.

The American Reciprocal Trade Agreements Act (1934)

The protectionist tone of the US was set in the summer of 1930 with the passing of the Republican-initiated *Smoot–Hawley Tariff Act*. This Act protected US interests and had global repercussions, being an invitation for tit-for-tat measures. In 1934, however, President Roosevelt attempted to amend the domestic process required to sanction trade agreements in the US. He wanted to be able to make trade agreements without the need for ratification by the Senate. Reciprocal trade agreements were valued by the rest of the Western Hemisphere, as demonstrated by the Pan-American Economic Conference at the beginning of 1934. The *Reciprocal Trade Agreements Act* (RTAA) of 1934, which was based on reciprocity and the most-favoured-nation principle (both to be included in the later GATT; see §25.3) gave the president what he was demanding. It gave him the authority to raise or lower tariffs himself, stripping Congress of the power to ratify such agreements. This presidential authority had to be extended every three years, however.

In this way Roosevelt was able to conduct an active foreign economic policy and lower the tariffs which had been imposed on the basis of the Smoot–Hawley Tariff Act. Although US interests continued to take top priority in new trade agreements, the RTAA resulted in a significant and lasting fall in US tariffs, which had been rising sharply ever since 1919 (Schnietz 2003, 215, Figure 1). In this regard the US differed from Europe, where regional protectionism remained dominant.

Regional support for the League of Nations: Oslo and Ouchy

At the beginning of the 1930s, two regional agreements were made in Europe aimed at supporting the League of Nation's efforts to promote free trade: the 1930 Convention of Oslo on economic rapprochement and the Convention of Ouchy of 1932. The 1930 *Convention of Oslo*, signed by Denmark, the Netherlands, Norway and Sweden, guaranteed reciprocal consultation before any of these states could impose further restrictions on mutual trade. The 1932 *Convention of Ouchy*, between Belgium, the Netherlands and Luxembourg, set out a plan for the phased reduction of tariffs. The UK was not party to the Convention of Ouchy because it did not wish to commit itself to changing its terms of trade with the three signatories (Hill 1946, 63). The Scandinavian states and the three smaller states involved in the two conventions became collectively known as the *Oslo states*, named after the 1930 Convention. Because the UK, in the Ottawa Agreements of 1932, had decided to orientate itself towards cooperation with the Commonwealth rather than towards Continental cooperation (the Convention of Ouchy), the Netherlands and Belgium sought stronger links with Germany. In May 1933 the Netherlands concluded a trade agreement with Nazi Germany. This strengthened Dutch trading interests, but it also meant that the Oslo states could no longer pursue a collective policy and it gave Germany the chance to provoke disagreements among the smaller states. However, joint Belgian and Dutch plans for a customs union and the failure of the World Economic Conference organized by the League of Nations in London in 1933 (see §18.4) actually drove the Oslo states closer together. In effect the bilateral treaties following from their multilateral cooperation were conducive to increased mutual trade.

Opposition to the League of Nations' sanctions policy

In the second half of the 1930s the political aspects of cooperation between the Oslo states began to increase in importance. This was evident in the reaction to the League of Nations' policy of sanctions against Italy in 1935 (see §16.4). At first the Dutch government responded to the League's call to apply sanctions, but it reversed its position in 1936 when sanctions had proven ineffective (Italy continued with its annexation of Ethiopia regardless) and were damaging to the Dutch economy. Under the leadership of the Netherlands, where the ministry of economics was particularly strongly opposed to sanctions, the Scandinavian states, Spain and Switzerland met in Geneva. Two months later these states announced that they were not willing to implement the League's sanctions any longer.

The Hague trading agreement (1937)

As chairman of the Economic Commission, the Dutch Prime Minister Hendrik Colijn had played an important role in the League's World Economic Conference in 1933. In

1936, as the economy was picking up slightly, he attempted to promote economic cooperation between democratic states. Willingness to participate remained limited to the Oslo states, which concluded a trading agreement in The Hague in 1937. Colijn, whose sympathies lay with free trade and the UK, sought to justify this in the context of the great powers' policy of 'appeasement' towards Germany. By contrast, the Dutch ministry of economics, with the support of the business world, was in favour of a continuation of a German-oriented policy. Colijn therefore felt compelled not to extend the Hague trading agreement in 1938.

The end of cooperation between the Oslo states

There was no longer any question of the Oslo states taking a common position with regard to Germany, on which state they were all economically dependent. During the conflict between Germany and Czechoslovakia in 1938, the Oslo states remained neutral. When in 1939 the possibility arose of cooperation between the Oslo states and the US, the Netherlands was the only opponent. Following the German invasion of Poland, the Netherlands tried to prevent the Assembly of the League being called. However, after the Soviet invasion of Finland the Assembly was called anyway, at the request of Finland. Cooperation among the Oslo states had proved to be worth little and the Netherlands, ever more wary of Germany, was not prepared to offer Finland any assistance.

18.4 The League's World Economic Conference (1933) and the Bruce Committee (1939)

The World Economic Conference (1933)

The Lausanne conference of June 1932, which had led to the cancellation of German reparations, had requested that a further international conference be convened by the League of Nations to discuss possible measures to remedy the continuing international economic crisis. Experts prepared the conference and in 1933 published a plan of action, which included proposals in various fields 'including reflation through "cheap Money," gradual currency stabilization, the abolition of exchange control, and a customs truce, to be followed by negotiations for the reduction of tariffs' (Hill 1946, 65). It was argued that the proposed reduction of tariffs should take place through a periodic percentage decrease and a reduction to a uniform level or commonly agreed ceiling. At the political level, the necessary preparations were made beforehand. But when the World Economic Conference took place in London in June 1933, it became clear that there was insufficient consensus on the monetary and trade objectives. Two months earlier the US had announced its intention to abandon the gold standard and allow the dollar to float. Attempts by the states that were still tied to the gold standard to stabilize their currencies against the dollar had failed. Because of the lack of agreement on monetary policy among the great powers, no agreement on trade was forthcoming either.

Why the World Economic Conference failed

It was obvious from the economic activities of the League that an international economic policy with international instruments was needed, but at the same time it was also clear that the League was not capable of breaking the prevailing deadlock. Edward Carr maintains that its views were based on the wrong set of assumptions. 'Nearly every pronouncement of every international economic conference held since the War has been vitiated by this assumption that there is some "solution" or "plan" which, by a judicious balancing of interests, will be equally favourable to all and prejudicial to none' (Carr 1940, 71). At the same time, according to Robert Cox, the spread of power and the absence of rules at a time of increasing imperialist rivalry meant that it was difficult for states to conform to the rules of a specific order. 'States had more freedom of internal management in a more anarchic system, provided they were able to muster sufficient internal strength in their economies and in their public's sentiments' (Cox 1987, 163). This was why the League's attempts to restore the liberal world order failed. *Laissez-faire* in international relations and in the relationship between capital and labour was 'the paradise of the economically strong. State control, whether in the form of protective legislation or of protective tariffs, is the weapon of self-defence invoked by the economically weak' (Carr 1940, 77). Even the League's World Economic Conference of 1933 did not want to face the fact that the 'lines of economic development' it sought to defend would be disadvantageous for certain states, according to Carr. As such, many of the anticipated benefits for the world were pure utopianism (Carr 1940, 72–73). The failure of the, in any case weak, effort of the League of Nations to achieve economic recovery and monetary stability through international agreements and collective action can partly be attributed to the American dollar policy. This policy was not the result of a weak currency, but rather of domestic economic and political considerations. In fact it seems that the US behaviour was to a large extent experimental: to see what consequences the international reaction would have for domestic prices. The US was not even a member of the League, but this US move was the final nail in the coffin for its attempts to find a solution to the economic crisis through international consultation.

Limitations caused by domestic politics

Two other factors that limited the Conference's success were the divergent views of the negotiators and the effects of domestic politics. The negotiators representing the great powers viewed the negotiations differently from within the same forum. Each power had its own 'conceptual framework' and, because the negotiators did not share the same diagnosis of the problem and had different views on the role of monetary policy, they were unable to arrive at a mutually acceptable solution. Domestic politics in the states concerned also limited the scope for success. The objections of central banks and interest groups could have been overcome if 'side-payments' or resources had been made available to accommodate the demands of such actors. However, in this case no means were provided to compensate for detrimental side effects (Eichengreen and Uzan 1993).

Some successes, despite everything

The League's World Economic Conference was not a total failure, however. For example, a start was made on putting in place international restriction schemes for the supply of primary commodities such as wheat, nitrates, rubber and sugar (Ashworth 1962, 244–45; Yoder 1997, 23). In August 1933 an international wheat agreement was drawn up, followed by an international sugar agreement in May 1937 (see Figure 18.2). The Conference also reached agreement on a number of principles concerning monetary policy. These were included in a research report from the League of Nations' Financial Commission on the functioning of the gold standard and were later incorporated in national law by many states. It included the principle 'that stability should be attained as quickly as practicable and gold re-established as the international measure of exchange values, time and parity being for each country to determine; that it was undesirable to put gold coins or gold certificates into internal circulation; that greater elasticity should be given to central bank legal-cover provisions; that independent central banks with the requisite powers and freedom to carry out an appropriate currency and credit policy should be created in all developed countries; that close and continuous cooperation should be maintained between such banks' (Hill 1946, 66–67). A preparatory commission which investigated the creation of affordable channels of credit also contributed to the recovery of the UK and the states which used the British currency.

New methods of working

The League's attempts to manage international trade processes in the 1920s had consisted of setting up general international agreements, with the aim of improving economic and financial relations between states. At the start of the 1930s, new protectionist attitudes made this way of working more difficult. Instead of general agreements, the League now focused on national economic policies such as tariffs and on issues that required the coordination or gradual adaptation of national policies. These new methods of working involved conventions confined to particular states and the development of models which governments could use during negotiations on bilateral agreements. Examples of the first approach include the 1933 wheat conference in London, which involved wheat-exporting and -importing states, and the League's activities in establishing bilateral currency clearance agreements and foreign exchange controls. During the recovery of the economy in the second half of the 1930s, a League report demonstrated in 1935 how the existing procedures for calculation and control had become simpler and more flexible. An example of the second approach was the issue of double taxation: 'since 1929, a period in which national revenue departments have been more than usually reluctant to make concessions, over a hundred important, and some two hundred minor, conventions dealing with double taxation, very largely based on the models drawn up by the Fiscal Committee of the League, have been concluded'. A model for operating profits followed in 1935: 'the whole range of conventions was overhauled in the light of experience at a series of meetings' (Hill 1946, 74)

Assessing the League's performance in the socio-economic field

The League's economic conferences and the work of the Bank for International Settlements may have lacked support and been unsuccessful in many ways, but their expertise also represented the beginning of a new system for international trade and payments. The ILO, as the League's specialized agency, can be viewed as an example of success in the field of social policy. The economic and social activities which the League had undertaken through its specialized bodies would form the basis of separate international organizations after the Second World War in fields such as health, refugees and intellectual cooperation (Yoder 1997, 13). Negative assessments in the literature on the League of Nations, including economic aspects, do not diminish the fact that this organization, partly because it was unable to achieve much in the area of security, showed increasing leadership in the economic and social fields. With hindsight these activities, which were appreciated least at the time, seem more impressive than what was achieved in the political arena, where expectations had been highest (Claude 1966, 357; Bowett 1982, 60).

The recommendations of the Bruce Committee of 1939

With US support (the US had by now begun to support a strengthening of the League of Nations' economic role), the League set up a committee under the chairmanship of the Australian Stanley Bruce. This committee was charged with studying how cooperation between states could be made more effective, how the instruments at the disposal of the League for handling economic and social issues could be further developed, and how the active participation of states in solving these problems could be achieved. The Bruce Committee met in August 1939, after which it published a report entitled *The Development of International Co-operation in Economic and Social Affairs*. At the heart of its recommendations was the establishment of a Central Committee for Social and Economic Affairs within the League of Nations. This was to take responsibility for the most important economic and social activities of the League, with its own budget and its own annual report. It was to consist of 24 government delegates chosen for their abilities, plus a maximum of eight more members appointed by the delegates themselves. The Bruce Committee hoped that this proposal would bring together all the economic and social work of the League under the direction of one body, which would be both representative and effective. The Committee considered coordination of the diverse economic and social activities of the League important. This also applied to the ILO, which had to become involved. The expectation was that a thorough reform of how the League carried out its economic and social work would lead to new inspiration, especially if the work was to gain public recognition. Finally, a way had to be found for states which were not members of the League, but which were interested in its economic and social work, to become involved. The Bruce Committee saw its proposals as a first step in the direction of reorganizing the whole League of Nations, but it also realized that this would be a long and difficult road.

Long-term effects

The Bruce Committee's vision received sufficient support, and in December 1939 the Assembly passed its proposals. In February 1940 the League of Nations nominated a group of ten states which were to form the basis of the proposed Central Committee, including France, Switzerland and the UK. This group was also made responsible for nominating the remaining states and personnel. Because of the outbreak of the Second World War, the group did not achieve any results. However, the work of the Bruce Committee was not entirely in vain, because in 1945 its recommendations would play a role in the discussions on the establishment of an Economic and Social Council of the United Nations (Hill 1946, 115).

American hegemony and the genesis and evolution of the United Nations system

Part VIII traces the genesis and evolution of the United Nations system as managed by the US. During the Second World War not all activities of the League of Nations came to a standstill, as the ILO and a group of staff members of the League's Secretariat moved to Canada and the US. The outlines of the future UN began to take shape at Allied conferences, eventually showing an improved version of the League, including a socio-economic dimension (Chapter 19). On the basis of its Charter, and to a certain extent also in an independent capacity, the UN proved a dynamic institution producing multiple missions, programmes, funds and world conferences. The UN became a complex bureaucracy, although in fact not that large, but with its own organs, procedures and customs (Chapter 20). Some UN bodies promoted the further development of international law. The UN-related specialized agencies contributed to the objectives of peace and security by looking after economic and social stability. This implied a large-scale focus on technical support (Chapter 21). This part does not restrict itself to the period in which the UN came into existence, but shows the entire line of development of the UN system until today in order to prevent fragmentation of information on the organizational dimension.

Multilateral cooperation during the Second World War

Upon the foundation laid by the League, the economic and social organization of the future is being built

(Hill 1946, 119)

19.1 The ILO flees to Montreal, the League of Nations' staff to Princeton (1940)

The ILO continues its work from Montreal

The activities of international organizations did not come to a halt when the relations between states deteriorated and war broke out, but they did decrease. The ILO decided to leave Switzerland. The American John Winant, who in 1939 had succeeded Harold Butler as director-general, regarded the situation in Switzerland as too isolated and threatening. In June 1940 the ILO was unable to hold its annual International Labour Conference for the first time in its existence, after the German occupation of Belgium and the Netherlands in May. Due to the new circumstances it saw itself obliged to cut the number of its employees drastically. To begin with, the ILO considered taking up residence in Vichy, France, as the French foreign office had put some buildings there at the ILO's disposal, but this plan failed when Marshal Philippe Pétain used the buildings as his headquarters for the part of France he was to govern after his armistice with Germany. The US proved not to be an option for the ILO because the American government did not want it to become a haven for international organizations, as it told Winant. Thanks to Winant's personal relationships the ILO managed to move to a university campus in Montreal. Through the kind offices of the Canadian governmental representative on the ILO's Governing Body, the Canadian government allowed the International Labour Office to take up residence in Montreal for the duration of the war. The city's bilingualism and the availability of economic and law libraries were regarded as advantages. In early August the first group of ILO staff members and their families left Geneva for Montreal. Their journey took more than a month. The university chapel and facilities put at the ILO's disposal were rather a disappointment, but its Canadian residence allowed the ILO to continue its essential services and to stay in contact with most of its member states. Many of them continued to send in their reports on the implementation of ILO conventions. The transfer to Canada, which had declared war on Germany in September 1939, implied that the ILO gave up its original neutral position and sided with the Allies. The ILO also made itself independent from the League of Nations. From its new location it began to see the world from a different perspective, one of the consequences being that it intensified its contacts with the Latin American states.

The special session of the Labour Conference in New York (1941)

After Winant's appointment as US ambassador to London in 1941, Edward Phelan was in charge of the ILO. On 27 October 1941 the ILO convened a special session of the International Labour Conference in New York, to discuss its role in the plans and activities for the postwar reconstruction. The American Secretary of Labour Frances Perkins presided at the conference, which lasted for 12 days. President Roosevelt had permitted her to receive the ILO in the US, appreciating the Organization's openly choosing the Allied side, with Germany and Italy having dissociated themselves from the ILO. The session in New York declared that 'the victory of the free peoples in the war against totalitarian aggression is an indispensable condition of the attainment of the objectives' of the ILO (Ghebali 1989, 18). Thirty-five states were present in New York, 22 of them with complete delegations, and they allowed the International Labour Office to continue its work. The conference was future-oriented and, unlike the situation during the First World War, aware of the fact that the postwar reconstruction had to be planned in advance. It promised the ILO's full cooperation in the implementation of the economic and social provisions of the Atlantic Charter. On 6 November all participants adjourned to Washington DC, where President Roosevelt received them at the White House and assured them that the ILO, with its representation of labour and management, its technical knowledge and experience, would have an essential role to play in building a stable international system of social justice for all people everywhere (Alcock 1971, 169).

Reorganization of the League of Nations' staff

The expansion of the war in 1940 stopped the League of Nations' staff being able to function. Eventually it became impossible for them to convene international meetings in Switzerland or to keep worldwide contacts with governments and experts, as there were more and more obstacles to sending publications from Geneva. On 31 August 1940 secretary-general Joseph Avenol resigned, due to his growing appreciation of the 'new order', and was succeeded by deputy secretary-general Séan Lester. The Communications and Transit Organization continued to function and its secretariat merged with that of the Economic and Financial Organization into the *Economic, Financial and Transit Department*, which also covered the League's other activities in fields such as health, drugs and social and cultural affairs. Some commissions continued their work, as far as possible, in the Western Hemisphere. The *Nutrition Committee* met in Buenos Aires, the *Fiscal Committee* in Mexico City. In 1941 the section of the League's Secretariat dealing with the opium trade, since 1939 known as the *Drug Control Service*, moved to Washington DC.

Activities continued in Princeton

In June 1940 Princeton University, the Institute for Advanced Study and the Rockefeller Institute of Medical Research invited the secretary-general of the League of Nations to continue its economic and social activities in Princeton, New Jersey. The university was willing to provide offices and facilities. After accepting the invitation the director and several staff members of the Economic, Financial and Transit Department moved to Princeton in August, to open the *Princeton Mission* in the rooms made available by the Institute for Advanced Study. Before leaving Geneva 25,000 files from the Geneva card index were microfilmed and shipped to the US. In 1941 another group of staff members arrived in Princeton, making a total of nearly 40. The Princeton Mission enabled the still functioning sections of the League to remain in contact and to monitor economic and social developments during the war. While a small staff remained in Geneva to keep up with European developments, as it still proved possible to collect and receive information from a number of European states, those in Princeton focused on developments elsewhere. During the rest of the war the Economic, Financial and Transit Department succeeded in remaining informed about economic trends in the world, and the Economic Intelligence Service continued its statistical work. At first the *Monthly Bulletin of Statistics* was still published in Geneva, but by the end of 1942 doing so became too complicated. From January 1943 a new monthly edition was published in Princeton. By 1945 this *Bulletin* was still the fullest regular source of essential economic statistics on many states, including those in Europe (Hill 1946, 122–24).

19.2 The Atlantic Charter (1941) and the first signs of the United Nations

The Atlantic Charter (1941)

As in the First World War, forms of economic cooperation between Allied states in the context of warfare were developed during the Second World War. This time it was soon decided that this cooperation should have an enduring character, even before the US became involved in the war. On 14 August 1941 American President Roosevelt and British Prime Minister Winston Churchill, aboard a ship in the Atlantic Ocean, issued a declaration which became known as the *Atlantic Charter*. The Allied states adopted the ideas in this Charter on 1 January 1942. The Atlantic Charter contains eight principles for a better future for the world (see Figure 19.1). Number 5 articulates the desire to bring about in the economic field 'the fullest collaboration between all nations' with the object – and here the ILO's influence can be noticed – of securing for all 'improved labour standards, economic advancement and social security'. After the defeat of national socialism the goal was to establish a peace in which 'all the men in all the lands may live out their lives in freedom from fear and want' (Number 6). The Charter marks a political turning point in Anglo–American relations, showing that the US was important in enforcing peace and also necessary in addressing the economic and social causes of discontent and war (Williams 1998, 83).

Lend–Lease Act (1941) and the growing understanding of the US role

In December 1940 Roosevelt had proposed the *Lend–Lease Act* to the American Congress as an instrument to help the UK finance the war against the Axis powers Germany, Italy and Japan. Japan had signed an agreement with Germany and Italy in September 1940 and

---

Figure 19.1 The Atlantic Charter (1941) and the Declaration by United Nations (1942)

The Atlantic Charter

August 14, 1941

The President of the United States of America and the Prime Minister, Mr. Churchill, representing His Majesty's Government in the United Kingdom, being met together, deem it right to make known certain common principles in the national policies of their respective countries on which they base their hopes for a better future for the world.

First, their countries seek no aggrandizement, territorial or other;

Second, they desire to see no territorial changes that do not accord with the freely expressed wishes of the peoples concerned;

Third, they respect the right of all peoples to choose the form of government under which they will live; and they wish to see sovereign rights and self government restored to those who have been forcibly deprived of them;

Fourth, they will endeavour, with due respect for their existing obligations, to further the enjoyment by all States, great or small, victor or vanquished, of access, on equal terms, to the trade and to the raw materials of the world which are needed for their economic prosperity;

Fifth, they desire to bring about the fullest collaboration between all nations in the economic field with the object of securing, for all, improved labour standards, economic advancement and social security;

Sixth, after the final destruction of the Nazi tyranny, they hope to see established a peace which will afford to all nations the means of dwelling in safety within their own boundaries, and which will afford assurance that all the men in all the lands may live out their lives in freedom from fear and want;

Seventh, such a peace should enable all men to traverse the high seas and oceans without hindrance;

Eighth, they believe that all of the nations of the world, for realistic as well as spiritual reasons must come to the abandonment of the use of force. Since no future peace can be maintained if land, sea or air armaments continue to be

---

employed by nations which threaten, or may threaten, aggression outside of their frontiers, they believe, pending the establishment of a wider and permanent system of general security, that the disarmament of such nations is essential. They will likewise aid and encourage all other practicable measures which will lighten for peace-loving peoples the crushing burden of armaments.

Franklin D. Roosevelt
Winston S. Churchill

Declaration by United Nations

A Joint Declaration by the United States of America, the United Kingdom of Great Britain and Northern Ireland, the Union of Soviet Socialist Republics, China, Australia, Belgium, Canada, Costa Rica, Cuba, Czechoslovakia, Dominican Republic, El Salvador, Greece, Guatemala, Haiti, Honduras, India, Luxembourg, Netherlands, New Zealand, Nicaragua, Norway, Panama, Poland, South Africa, Yugoslavia.

The Governments signatory hereto,

Having subscribed to a common program of purposes and principles embodied in the Joint Declaration of the President of United States of America and the Prime Minister of the United Kingdom of Great Britain and Northern Ireland dated August 14, 1941, known as the Atlantic Charter.

Being convinced that complete victory over their enemies is essential to defend life, liberty, independence and religious freedom, and to preserve human rights and justice in their own lands as well as in other lands, and that they are now engaged in a common struggle against savage and brutal forces seeking to subjugate the world,

DECLARE:

(1) Each Government pledges itself to employ its full resources, military or economic, against those members of the Tripartite Pact and its adherents with which such government is at war.

(2) Each Government pledges itself to cooperate with the Governments signatory hereto and not to make a separate armistice or peace with the enemies.

The foregoing declaration may be adhered to by other nations which are, or which may be, rendering material assistance and contributions in the struggle for victory over Hitlerism.

DONE at Washington
January First, 1942

Adherents to the Declaration by United Nations, together with the date of communication of adherence: Mexico (5 June 1942), Philippines (10 June 1942), Ethiopia (28 July 1942), Iraq (16 January 1943), Brazil (8 February 1943), Bolivia (27 April 1943), Iran (10 September 1943), Colombia (22 December 1943), Liberia (26 February 1944), France (26 December 1944), Ecuador (7 February 1945), Peru (11 February 1945), Chile (12 February 1945), Paraguay (12 February 1945), Venezuela (16 February 1945), Uruguay (23 February 1945), Turkey (24 February 1945), Egypt (27 February 1945), Saudi Arabia (1 March 1945).

on 7 December 1941 it attacked the US naval base in Pearl Harbour without a declaration of war. Until August 1945 the Lend–Lease Act, passed in March 1941, supplied the UK and the other Allied states with a total of 50 billion dollars' worth of war materials and economic support. What the US government in its discussions with the UK during the years 1941–43 began to understand was that the US had to show leadership in the world. Within American government circles, a gradual and reluctant appreciation grew of the necessity of postwar arrangements in favour of both political and economic stability. At the end of 1942 American policy makers became aware that the US could not leave postwar economic developments to the UK and that a return to strictly nationalistic economic policies should be prevented, as these could give rise to renewed militarism. Knowing that the US was taking on an economic position analogous to that of the UK in the nineteenth century, policy makers began to understand the necessity of the US assuming economic leadership. 'The United States now has and proposes to maintain economic leadership in the Western hemisphere' (cited in Williams 1998, 230). The term Western Hemisphere soon began to cover the entire Western industrial world, including its colonies. The US had a critical attitude towards the close economic and monetary relations between the European states and their colonies. In exchange for Lend–Lease and the promise of postwar economic help, it put strong pressure on the UK to renounce its 'Imperial Preference' (see §18.3). It was not until the US had persuaded the UK by the 'combination of Britain's urgent need for help and a resurgence of belief in the benefits of international cooperation after the war', that the economic clauses of the Atlantic Charter became potentially realizable (Williams 1998, 229).

The Declaration by United Nations (1942)

Meanwhile the outlines of a future 'United Nations' were beginning to take shape at multilateral conferences convened by the Allied states. The term United Nations was first used in the Declaration of 1 January 1942 mentioned above. It was said that Roosevelt invented the term, which to him both expressed hope and referred to the nation-state-related idea of sovereignty. The *Declaration by United Nations* (see Figure 19.1), issued in Washington DC, was first signed by the four major powers (the US, the UK, the Soviet Union and China) and then the next day by the other Allied states. This strategy was devised by the Department of State, run by Cordell Hull. Roosevelt appreciated it, as he believed the four major powers to have special responsibility for the war effort and the organization of peace afterwards. This model, with the US as the leader of the group of major powers, also applied to the creation of the UN. With Churchill's approval the Soviet Union and China had been invited as major powers to sign the Declaration drafted by Roosevelt and Churchill. The signing of the Declaration implied the creation of a traditional war alliance, with each participant state pledging to employ its full resources against the Axis powers and not to make separate armistices and peace. The Declaration also recognized the principles of the Atlantic Charter as a common programme of purposes. The states promised 'to defend life, liberty, independence and religious freedom and to preserve human rights and justice in their own lands as well as in other lands'. The major turn in the war came in early 1943, when Nazi Germany lost the Battle of Stalingrad in Russia. Although from that moment on the Allied forces were winning, the war would still last for another two years. In Europe the war ended with the unconditional written surrender of Germany on 7 May 1945. The war in Asia concluded with unconditional surrender by Japan on 2 September, after the US destruction of the cities of Hiroshima and Nagasaki by a new and very forceful weapon, the atomic bomb.

The Conference on Food and Agriculture in Hot Springs (1943)

In 1943 and 1944, the term United Nations was used during the preparations for the postwar situation regarding food supply, rescue operations for refugees and the postwar economy. From 18 May to 3 June 1943 the *United Nations Conference on Food and Agriculture* took place in Hot Springs, Virginia, to agree on postwar food supply. Forty-four states discussed their food situation and the common measures that would be needed to satisfy their nutritional needs. Special attention was paid to issues such as hunger, under-nourishment, mortality and deficiency diseases which would prevent people working and enjoying a full life. They also considered the lack of knowledge and statistical data concerning these problems, as such insights were necessary for large-scale planning. The League's Economic, Financial and Transit Department and the International Labour Office were asked to furnish the background material. To come to grips with the postwar nutritional situation, the conference developed a programme that included the establishment of a food and agriculture organization. As a result of this programme the *Food and Agriculture Organization* (FAO) was created as a specialized UN agency in October 1945. In the meantime the *Interim Commission on Food and Agriculture*, set up by the Hot Springs conference, began to function.

Relief for refugees and displaced persons by the UNRRA (1943)

On 9 November 1943 the same 44 Allied states agreed in Atlantic City, New Jersey, to establish the *United Nations Relief and Rehabilitation Administration* (UNRRA). This common institution was meant to provide relief to the war-displaced refugees and homeless people in the still to be liberated states of Europe and Asia. The UNRRA became one of the largest non-military intergovernmental organizations at the time: 'it acted as a care and rehabilitation centre for millions of displaced persons and refugees' (Williams 1998, 233). It operated from November 1943 until June 1947 in Europe and until March 1949 in China, disbursing nearly 4 billion dollars in direct aid to some seven million refugees. The largest share of this was borne by the US. The UNRRA was based on the assumption that this relief was a common endeavour that would help to restore relations and therefore would be a temporary measure. In reality something else would happen, because decolonization and the outbreak of the Cold War were to generate new refugees and thus contribute to the establishment of a permanent UN refugee organization. Two representatives of the League's Economic, Financial and Transit Department attended the conference in Atlantic City and the subsequent sessions of the UNRRA Council in Montreal (September 1944) and London (August 1945). In turn the UNRRA was represented at the 1945 meeting of the League's Economic and Financial Committees (Hill 1946, 141).

The International Labour Conference in Philadelphia (1944)

Given the ongoing Allied efforts to set up various intergovernmental structures for postwar cooperation, the ILO had to make its presence felt 'for fear of being overtaken on its home ground. It had to demonstrate effectively that, unlike the League of Nations, it had not left a vacuum to be filled' (Ghebali 1989, 20). Therefore the ILO decided not to convene a special session, as it had in 1941, but a regular International Labour Conference. This took place from 20 April to 12 May 1944 in Philadelphia, and was attended by 41 official delegations, 28 of them tripartite. At the conference the ILO prepared itself for the postwar situation by revising its constitution and adjusting its organization, which included independence from the League of Nations, broadening its objectives, redefining the status and functions of its organs and reforming its international labour legislation machinery. On 12 May the ILO adopted the *Declaration of Philadelphia*, which broadened the ILO's objectives in the light of world social developments, and which in 1946 would become part of the new ILO constitution. The purpose of international labour legislation in 1919 was defined as threefold: to promote social justice, to consolidate international peace, and to correct the pattern of international competition. 'The Declaration of Philadelphia fully spells out the first of these objectives, strongly reaffirms the second and alludes indirectly to the third' (Ghebali 1989, 62). The importance of the Declaration of Philadelphia lay in 'the extremely general scope of the mandate it contains: this is concerned exclusively with the world of labour, but is addressed to "all human beings, irrespective of race, creed or sex"' (Ghebali 1989, 61). The ILO focused on the individual with its multi-dimensional participation in the entire social process, addressed all human beings and explicitly mentioned the relevance of promoting the economic and social advancement of the less developed regions of the world. At the close of the conference proceedings the ILO delegates, once again, were received by President Roosevelt at the White House.

19.3 The Bretton Woods conference on international monetary policy (1944)

Keynes and White

The UK and the US had already developed plans on postwar international monetary cooperation in 1942. The British economist Keynes had devised an international institution to help solve balance of payments problems. He believed in an agreement with the US on an international monetary order that would be expansionary and could keep the trading system open, but would also safeguard against depression (Ikenberry 1992, 314). In the US such a synthesis of liberal and interventionist objectives was supported by Harry Dexter White. As an economist he admired Keynes, but as the US delegation leader at Bretton Woods, where Keynes was to represent the UK, he would be his political opponent. White had a more modest international stabilization fund in mind than Keynes, and he launched a proposal for the establishment of a bank to provide the resources for reconstruction. Whereas Keynes wanted an expansionist financial system, the US government feared the high inflation that might result from it. The US also raised objections to Keynes's plan for a fund that would provide large credits without specific arrangements for repayment. It believed that the amounts of money were too great and demanded that states would be able lend no more than their share in the fund. From 1943 onwards the US and the UK engaged in tough negotiations about these plans and their practical elaborations. The US consulted Canada, the Soviet Union, China and the Latin American states about its plans, the UK conferred with the European governments-in-exile in London on its view. Within the American government, Cordell Hull of the Department of State and Henry Morgenthau of the Treasury supported the new strategy of multilateral economic institutionalization. Morgenthau, however, lacked 'Hull's evangelical belief in multilaterism, possibly because he had been present at Versailles'. But the two men shared the belief that 'the economic causes of war were the most intractable and important' (Williams 1998, 231). Hull's department was involved in the issues related to trade policies, while Morgenthau was given charge of the financial side of the postwar settlement. When the delegations of the Allied states arrived at Bretton Woods, the skeleton of the financial institutions had been prepared, according to White's assistant Edward Bernstein. Only the flesh needed to be added. Crucial for the success of the whole conference was the fact that in June the Allied invasion in Normandy, France, had begun. Everyone was delighted with the progress being made in the Continental war theatre.

Successful consensus

Ikenberry regards 'Bretton Woods' as one of the few moments in history when political elites were open to the new ideas of intellectuals and policy experts. A consensus between experts had met with response from political circles, had played an integrating role and had had practical consequences. The liberal-minded American and British economists and policy specialists were given the room to foster an agreement on a desired postwar monetary order, based on their shared technical and normative views. While existing structures, rules and political coalitions were about to collapse, this transgovernmental alliance of 'new thinkers', as an epistemic community, succeeded in renewing the political debate and in getting hold of the political agenda. Its proposals for solving the complex monetary and financial problems were such that traditional departments found themselves on the sidelines and that new and winning political coalitions discovered new common ground for positions which did not exist before. The experts changed the discourse on postwar policies, by shifting the base of debate from trade to monetary issues, and found a middle way between the two leading states. Then they elaborated more coherent political views in order to achieve broader coalitions within postwar Western capitalist democracies. The experts succeeded in this because they kept looking for the middle ground between an unregulated open system (the nineteenth-century free trade system) and bilateral or regional groupings of states which, as in the 1930s, mostly served national interests. American officials were aware that building a new international economic order on a coercive basis would be costly and ultimately counterproductive. Therefore they paid attention to the normative appeal of these new ideas for the elites of other states and avoided looking as if they were imposing policies on European and other states. To give the system legitimacy, they were willing to make adjustments along the way (Ikenberry 1992, 318–21).

The monetary conference at Bretton Woods (1944)

The United Nations Monetary and Financial Conference took place from 1 to 22 July 1944 in Bretton Woods. The American government decided on in this place in New Hampshire because their minister of finance was Jewish and the Mount Washington Hotel there was one of the few large hotels which at that time did not refuse entry to Jews and blacks. The Bretton Woods conference was attended by 700 delegates from 44 states. Its purpose was to provide a new, stable and predictable international monetary regime, resulting in the drafting of the constitutions (Articles of Agreement) of the *International Monetary Fund* (IMF), which was to control the fluctuation between national currencies, and the *International Bank for Reconstruction and Development* (IBRD), which would provide the finances for the reconstruction of war-damaged states. The US expected that a decrease in trade tariffs, combined with this monetary regime, would lessen the economic nationalism of the interwar period. The Soviet Union attended the Bretton Woods conference as an ally. It signed the final documents, in the expectation that after the war the new institutions would furnish it with the funds necessary for reconstruction as well. The documents allowed for the fact that the economic and monetary system of the Soviet Union did not match that of the free market economy. It was agreed that the Soviet Union would have freedom with regard to the value of its rouble (an exception, given its planned economy), but that it would have to provide the institutions with the same economic information and data as the other states.

Conference results: embedded liberalism

The Bretton Woods conference laid the foundation for an international monetary regime aimed at economic stability as a favourable condition for full employment and stable social relations. The US dollar became the core currency in a system that followed White's views more closely than those of Keynes. The US dollar was made a coequal of gold, guaranteed by the US. The currencies of participatory states could be exchanged according to fixed rates. These rates could be adjusted, but only to correct a fundamental disequilibrium in the balance of payments (that is, chronic trade deficits or surpluses) and with the IMF's agreement. If states were unable to comply with the agreed exchange rates, their central banks had to either sell or buy currencies, so as to bring their own currency back to the fixed rates. The IMF would also help its member states to tackle short-term balance of payments problems by temporary lending. The foreign exchange the IMF provided to states was to be deposited with their central banks to supplement their international reserves and thus to give general balance of payments support. In the case of more serious and longer-lasting problems, states were required to discuss the adjustment of exchange rates with the IMF. While the IMF's function was to promote and guard the stability of the international financial system, the purpose of the IBRD was the financing of the postwar reconstruction and the practical support of development in less-developed states. The essential effect of the Bretton Woods conference was a certain extent of 'planning' for the economic future under US economic and political leadership. International cooperation in an institutionalized form came together with ideas about national planning, such as could be found in states like France, the UK and the Soviet Union. John Ruggie called the result the 'compromise of embedded liberalism'. It 'was driven both by the need to keep Britain involved in the post-war project and by an increasingly acknowledged realisation that Europe and other parts of the world would need reconstruction on a scale to dwarf that of 1919' (Williams 1998, 231).

No consensus on trade

The US was less successful with its plans for a postwar international trade regime than with those for the monetary regime. Although the US and the UK had been negotiating a possible postwar international trade regime since 1943, they had not reached the same level of agreement, mainly because of national interests. The UK persisted in its view of a preferential system for its colonies and dominions. The European states on the Continent had to regain control over their trade balances again, and the 'Third World' states needed aid for economic development (see Appendix 2 for the term Third World). For the time being they were not going to receive this aid, as most states agreed at Bretton Woods upon the priority of European reconstruction. On trade, there was no Anglo–American coalition of experts and policy makers succeeding in decisively influencing decision making about a new international regime.

The Convention on International Civil Aviation (1944)

Another policy field in which the US was unsuccessful was civil aviation. At the end of 1944 a conference of 52 states gathered in Chicago. On 7 December 1944 they adopted the *Convention on International Civil Aviation*, containing the constitution of the *International Civil Aviation Organization* (ICAO), which came into effect on 4 April 1947 after the required number of ratifications was received. The Convention focused on providing safety in civil aviation and on the cooperation of states in agreeing principles and regulations on the basis of equality of opportunity. The US had pressed for such a convention by referring to its views on 'global open skies'. Parallel to the 'freedom of the seas', the US defended the 'freedom of the skies'. But since the US dominated aviation and this was expected to increase after the war, making the US the 'master of the skies', the other states refused to entertain this idea by referring to the sovereignty of their airspace. Because of this split the economic regulation of civil aviation would take place through bilateral aviation agreements with only a restricted monitoring role for the ICAO, rather than on a multilateral basis.

19.4 The establishment of the United Nations as managed by the US (1943–45)

The Declaration of Moscow (1943)

The success of the Bretton Woods conference had an impact on the plans for the creation of a new, improved international organization for peace and security. The first commitment to such an effort was expressed in the *Declaration of Moscow* by the ministers of foreign affairs of the US, the UK and the Soviet Union on 30 October 1943, later also signed by China. In this Declaration they recognized the necessity of establishing, at the earliest practicable moment, a general international organization based on the principle of sovereign equality of all peace-loving states, to maintain international peace and security. This idea was also debated at the conference in Tehran, Iran, at the end of November 1943, where the Allied powers discussed their military strategies against Germany and Japan as well as the postwar power relations and spheres of influence.

Security Council plus ECOSOC

Unlike in 1919, this time the US was in favour of a broad and decentralized world organization, which should have both a 'security council', based on the idea of collective security with joint action against potential aggressors, and a 'functional' body to advance the chances of peace and security by taking care of stable economic and social relations. The US felt supported in this by the recommendations of the Bruce Committee, which in 1939 had assessed the League of Nations' economic and social activities (see §18.4). That the US favoured an Economic and Social Council (ECOSOC) was also related to its critical stance on the economic and monetary relations between the European states and their colonies. The European states in turn regarded this as a reason not to be in favour of such a body and to put up a struggle before agreeing. Not charging the envisaged security body with economic and social affairs was because this body would be too 'political' (despite the fact that decisions on economic and social matters are political ones too). A final argument in favour of a decentralized organization was that the existing international structures already had a strongly decentralized character and that the ILO and the public international unions attached importance to their autonomous position (Claude 1966, 357–58; Hill 1974, 9).

The conference at Dumbarton Oaks (1944)

Shortly after Bretton Woods, from 21 August to 7 October 1944, representatives of the US, the UK, the Soviet Union and China met at Dumbarton Oaks, an estate near Washington DC, where they drafted the first version of the constitution for the organization they wanted to establish. The results were published as the *Proposals for the Establishment of a General International Organization*, which specified the organization's objectives and membership. These objectives were maintaining international peace and security, fostering friendly relations among nations and promoting international cooperation in the solution of international economic, social and other humanitarian problems. The proposals were the first draft of the later UN Charter. A distinction was made between a General Assembly, of which all member states should be members, and a Security Council, with 11 members of whom five (the great powers) would have permanent seats. Without using the word, the idea of a veto was introduced here as substantive Security Council decisions would require the asserting votes of the permanent members. The distinction between General Assembly and Security Council was in line with the experiences of the League of Nations with its Assembly and Council. By creating a specific Security Council, the other states also met the objections of the Soviet Union to the economic and social activities of the new organization. Whereas the Soviet Union preferred to leave these activities to separate specialized agencies, the other states wanted the General Assembly to be involved in, and even to supervise, such activities. Not all issues were solved at Dumbarton Oaks. One concerned the precise voting procedure in the Security Council, another the question of whether a state that was party to a dispute under consideration would be able to vote on it. The US and the UK argued that this should not be the case, while the Soviet Union disagreed, being afraid that this might turn out to be against its interests. The US and the UK, however, wanted to receive support from the smaller states and therefore preferred an arrangement that would give these states some protection against the major powers. No agreement was reached at Dumbarton Oaks on the future of the colonial territories. The US saw this as an important issue, whereas the UK did not want to discuss it.

The UN also discussed at the Yalta Conference in early 1945

The issues left unresolved at Dumbarton Oaks were again considered at the Yalta Conference from 4 to 11 February 1945, where Roosevelt, Churchill and Stalin discussed the coordination of their activities with regard to the forthcoming defeat of Germany, the ongoing war with Japan and the resulting postwar relations. With regard to the new international organization, they came up with more precise regulations for the voting procedure in the Security Council and the question of voting by parties engaged in a dispute. They agreed that the veto should not apply to procedural matters and that it could not be invoked by a state that was party to a dispute under consideration. Permanent membership of the Security Council and 'veto power' were granted to the US, the UK, the Soviet Union, China (and later France) as the 'sponsoring powers' of the new organization. With regard to the colonial territories, it was agreed that British colonial territories could not be placed under UN trusteeship arrangements without the consent of the UK. The new trusteeship arrangement identified three kinds of territories: the mandated territories of the League of Nations, territories to be taken from Germany and Japan after the end of the war, and territories that were to be voluntarily placed under UN trusteeship by the colonial powers. The Soviet Union succeeded in having the Ukraine and Belarus given a separate vote within the UN, although they were parts of the Soviet Union, and committed itself to joining the UN in spite of its objections. A date was set for the inaugural meeting of the new organization in San Francisco. It was agreed that the US would issue invitations to all states that had signed the Declaration by United Nations of 1 January 1942 and had declared war on the Axis powers before 1 March 1945.

The UN Conference on International Organization in San Francisco (1945)

The design of the new global peace organization was finalized during the *United Nations Conference on International Organization* (UNCIO), which took place from 25 April to 26 June 1945 in San Francisco. During this conference, the war in Europe came to an end. The conference was attended by 260 delegates from 50 states, who continued the work of drafting the organization's Charter based on the results achieved by the three great powers at Dumbarton Oaks and Yalta. There were four conference commissions and 12 technical committees. The conference organization made clear that a draft was available (the Dumbarton Oaks proposals and the supplementary Yalta decisions), but that every state should express its preferences. As it was agreed that each commission would decide by a two-thirds majority, the organization set aside the traditional diplomatic rule of unanimity also used in the League of Nations. The conference organization furthermore had decided that the Executive Committee of the sponsoring states was to be enlarged by another ten states, in order to give smaller states a more substantive role during the conference. The fact that commissions elected their own chairs and rapporteurs showed that the Conference Secretariat, presided over by the American diplomat Alger Hiss, played a role of its own and left room for manoeuvre for the various sub-organs. The first issue after the opening ceremony was the question of which states could take part. The 21 Latin American states argued that Argentina should be allowed to participate, which due to its friendly relations with the Axis powers during the war had been refused. The Soviet Union pressed for Poland's partaking, but met with opposition from the three Western great powers, which recognized the government-in-exile in London and not the Soviet-supported government in Lublin. Furthermore, the US had not invited Belarus and Ukraine, although, as agreed at Yalta, they were to be admitted to the UN. After five days of heated debates Argentina, Belarus and the Ukraine received an invitation to participate after all, but Poland did not.

Influence by the smaller states

One of the issues in San Francisco influenced by the smaller states was the competence of the General Assembly, as the Assembly was given control over the UN budget. Due to other proposals by the smaller states, the position of the secretary-general, to be elected by the General Assembly, was enhanced. The secretary-general would be allowed to bring any matter that could threaten international peace and security to the attention of the Security Council. And as long as the Security Council did not have the issue on its agenda, the General Assembly would also be able to discuss security issues and threats to peace. Expanding the competence of the General Assembly helped the smaller states to accept the new institutional arrangements.

Colonialism and self-governing territories

Ending colonial administration was another issue of concern to small states, as some of them had been colonies or mandated territories. France and the UK refused to have the word 'independence' in the Charter, and smaller states arguing in favour of decolonization and full independence succeeded in achieving a compromise based on the term 'self-government'. A special *Declaration Regarding Non-Self-Governing Territories* was inserted in the Charter text as Chapter XI. The regulation of trust territories was specified. The League of Nation's mandate system, established at Versailles in 1919, would be continued by the Trusteeship Council, which was to be one of the principal organs of the UN. The main point of the regulation was a system for the administration and supervision of colonial territories of which the populations had not yet achieved self-determination. A few Pacific Islands taken by the US from Japan during the war and regarded as strategic would remain outside the UN trusteeship arrangement. The distinction between strategic and non-strategic trust areas and limiting the authority of the Trusteeship Council over the former implied a stronger role for the Security Council regarding the strategic areas. The new regulations for colonial territories stipulated that states with responsibility for the administration of such territories had to promote to the utmost the well-being of the inhabitants, develop self-government, take due account of the political aspiration of the peoples and assist them in the progressive development of their free political institutions. Despite their resistance, France and the UK agreed to an arrangement for the regular reporting by the responsible states on the economic, social and educational conditions in their territories.

The position of regional organizations

The American states had met on 11 February 1945 to discuss the position of regional organizations within the proposed UN. After that meeting the Latin and Central American states, without Argentina, had discussed the Dumbarton Oaks proposals again, but this time without the US. Their concern was that the use of the veto in the Security Council could limit the region's ability to deal with hemispheric threats, something allowed in 1919 by the League of Nations' explicit reference to the Monroe doctrine (see §15.3). Therefore they favoured a major role for regional organizations in the field of security and greater freedom from UN Security Council intervention. From the perspective of Union of American Republics practice, the US delegation shared this American concern, but it also feared that the Senate and public opinion in the US would not support the creation of a worldwide Security Council if it was not given full authority to address all threats to peace. As a result, the US agreed to a compromise that recognized the existence of regional arrangements or agencies, provided that such arrangements or agencies and their activities were consistent with the purposes and principles of the UN (Article

52 of the Charter). Furthermore, states had the right to collective self-defence until the Security Council had taken measures necessary to maintain international peace and security. This autonomy, however, was limited by the Security Council's right to investigate and take action on any threat to peace. The new compromise also included the right of any state to bring any dispute directly to the Security Council.

The issue of human rights

In San Francisco the Latin American states insisted on a role for the UN in social, economic and human rights cooperation. They received support from other states in the conference committee on economic and social cooperation. As a result of this pressure, and by referring to the recommendations of the Bruce Committee that had evaluated the economic and social activities of the League, the Economic and Social Council (ECOSOC) was created as one of the principal organs of the UN. Neither the Trusteeship Council nor the ECOSOC had been mentioned in the Dumbarton Oaks proposals. Progress with regard to human rights, however, was less propitious than expected. The promises in this respect in the Declaration by United Nations of 1 January 1942 (see Figure 19.1) were not mentioned as explicitly in the UN Charter, much to the disappointment of the states that had signed the 1942 Declaration and had expected a commitment, given the persecution of Jews and other minorities in Europe by the Nazis. But the US had not received sufficient support on this issue from the other three great powers at Dumbarton Oaks. Due to the pressure from Latin American states, the committee on economic and social cooperation recommended in San Francisco that the UN would promote 'universal respect for, and observance of, human rights and fundamental freedoms for all without distinction as to race, sex, language or religion'. In spite of the approval the likely establishment of a commission on human rights attracted in the media, the San Francisco conference did not succeed in agreeing on it. After intensive lobbying the other states managed to persuade the sponsoring powers to agree to include in Article 68 of the part of the Charter dealing with the ECOSOC the establishment of commissions not only in the economic and social fields but also 'for the promotion of human rights'. The actual creation of a commission on human rights would not happen until February 1946, by the UN itself (see §20.5 for the drafting and significance of the later Universal Declaration on Human Rights).

The role of the Commonwealth

The members of the British Commonwealth (see Figure 18.5), which had been involved in the war effort from the beginning, also discussed the Dumbarton Oaks proposals. In April 1945 the foreign secretaries had met in London for consultations on postwar relations and to discuss the proposed UN. Jan Smuts from South Africa, who had also played a role during the establishment of the League of Nations in Versailles, expressed his conviction that something was missing from the Dumbarton Oaks texts. To him it was a 'legalistic document which did not fit the bill' (Marshall 2001, 57). He believed that the Second World War was one of the greatest struggles in all of history, which at bottom had been a religious one. This sentiment, however, was lacking in the texts, and Smuts stressed that what the world expected was a statement of human faith, of the things that had been fought for and that should be stabilized and preserved in the world. He launched the concept of a preamble to the Charter text, which would declare faith in human rights, belief in the practice of tolerance, belief in the enlargement of freedom and the promotion of social progress, and belief in nations living in peace and peaceful intercourse with each other as good neighbours. It was discovered that the UK had actually drafted a preamble for Dumbarton Oaks, but that it had been lost in circulation. Smuts compared the two texts and produced a draft which was a combination of the two. With the support of the Commonwealth states, Smuts set the idea of a preamble in motion as soon as he arrived in San Francisco. He succeeded in getting the support of the commission and committee concerned, and eventually of the conference itself. The finishing touches were put to the text in consultation with Smuts. The US delegation was delighted with the opening phrase of the Charter's preamble, which resembled the opening words of the American constitution: 'We the Peoples of the United Nations' (Marshall 2001, 59).

The UN headquarters

On 26 June 1945 representatives from 50 states signed the Charter of the United Nations, later followed by Poland. After ratification by the five sponsors and a majority of the other signatories, the Charter came into force on 24 October 1945, later to become United Nations Day. Now the UN, as a new collective security organization, had been established. The General Assembly met for the first time on 10 January 1946 in London's Central Hall, where the Economic and Social Council was set up on 13 January. On 17 January the first meeting of the Security Council took place and on 1 February the Norwegian Trygve Lie began work as the UN's first secretary-general, with the Secretariat located in Church House. At the end of 1945 the American Congress invited the UN to establish a permanent base in the US. In early 1946 the UN Secretariat moved to New York, first to Hunter College in the Bronx, then to Lake Success on Long Island. With financial support from John D. Rockefeller Jr and the City of New York, a site in Manhattan's East Side was bought. In 1949 construction work began on four interconnected buildings: the 39-storey Secretariat Building, the Conference Building, the General Assembly Hall and the Library, financed by the Ford Foundation (from 1961 the Dag Hammarskjöld Library). These buildings have been in use since 1952. The Headquarters Agreement between the UN and the US came into force on 21 November 1947. The chosen colours of the UN flag were light blue (background) and white for the emblem, which is a map of the world as seen from the North Pole surrounded by a wreath of olive branches.

Dissolution of the League of Nations (1946)

Unlike with the League of Nations in 1919, the establishment of the UN was not part of the peace treaty. In 1919 it would have meant that if the American Senate had voted against the League of Nations it would have also refused to accept the peace treaty. The main reason why the US Senate did not ratify the League's Covenant was its uncertainty over the precise implications of the use of economic sanctions by the League (Malanczuk 1997, 24). During the negotiations on establishing the UN, Roosevelt, who had died suddenly in April 1945, and his successor Harry Truman had made sure that the Charter's text and the UN decision-making procedures would not cause any obstacles to ratification by the Senate. Therefore in the case of the UN, the US ratified the Charter and supported the organization in many respects. The League of Nations did not play any role during the establishment of the UN, although its Economic and Financial

Commissions met in 1945 to arrange for the transfer of its activities to the new organization. Because of developments concerning the International Court of Justice it took some time before the League of Nations was dissolved, but on 19 April 1946 it officially dissolved itself.

Differences from the League of Nations

The UN as an organization was stronger than the League, although in practice it would meet similar problems to the League, in particular due to lack of agreement between the two leading actors in the Cold War and their self-chosen freedom of manoeuvre regarding the UN. Among its greatest improvements were decision making by qualified majority (instead of unanimity), a better division of labour between the General Assembly and the Security Council (which was not concerned with general matters), greater powers for the secretary-general (which allowed the organization to develop its own policies), functions in the fields of decolonization and the establishment of new states, and a coordinating body for economic and social activities, including the work of the specialized agencies. Some of the older public international unions joined the UN system as specialized agencies.

The institutional settlement of the peace

Ikenberry regards the peace settlement the US, as the hegemonic power, achieved in 1945 as the most fragmented and most far-reaching of any settlement after a major war. In 1945 no peace treaties were concluded with Germany and Japan, and the UN Charter was not attached to the peace settlement. In fact two interrelated settlements for the postwar period were achieved in 1945. The first was between the US and the Soviet Union. This settlement depicted a bipolar world with two great powers and their respective allies which would balance each other out over a long period of time. The second settlement was between Western industrial countries and Japan, and resulted in 'a dense set of new security, economic and political institutions, almost all involving the United States'. Between 1944 and 1951 the US and the other advanced industrial democracies engaged in 'a flurry of institution building'. The resulting institutionalization of the postwar order was 'vastly greater in scope than in the past, dealing with issues of economic stabilization, trade, finance, and monetary relations as well as political and security relations among the postwar allies' (Ikenberry 2001, 163–64).

Concessions by the US

Although the US emerged from the war as by far the strongest power (militarily, politically and economically) and also used this position to safeguard its national interests, it was prepared not to take maximum advantage of this situation but to establish restraints and commitments on the exercise of its power: 'it offered – in most instances quite reluctantly – to restrain itself by operating within an array of postwar economic, political, and security institutions'. For the sake of the legitimacy of the postwar order, the US as the leading power stressed its democratic character. The democratic character of the European states made it easier for the US to make concessions. 'Western leaders repeatedly justified their unprecedented institutional commitments as necessary for the protection of common democratic values' (Ikenberry 2001, 164). The decentralized and pluralist character of the

American political system reassured European leaders that the exercise of power by the US would be less arbitrary and unpredictable than that of authoritarian regimes. The US applied its strongest leverage to the UK to give up its imperial preference and to the other European states to move toward an open postwar system, characterized by values such as free trade, universal institutions, Atlantic community, geopolitical openness and European integration. These values were meant to lock the democracies into an open, multilateral political and economic order, as already mentioned in the Atlantic Charter of 1941 and now jointly managed through new institutional mechanisms. This 1945 settlement was followed by the weak economic position of Europe after the war, the reconstruction of Germany and Japan and the threat of Soviet Union-led communism. Within this settlement and later developments the US was prepared to accept compromise agreements in order to obtain European participation in postwar international organizations. 'European weakness more than its outright resistance limited American postwar liberal multilateral goals, and soon after the war European integration and reconstruction became the critical component of securing a wider open multilateral order' (Ikenberry 2001, 165). In this new global order the UN and its specialized agencies – together, the United Nations system – occupied centre stage.

The United Nations: an improved security organization with economic coordination

We the Peoples of the United Nations

20.1 Charter, member states and budget of the United Nations

Differences in relation to the Covenant of the League of Nations

At the birth of the UN, there was a deliberate decision to use the term 'charter' instead of the 'covenant' which was adopted for the League of Nations. A covenant is an important but voluntary agreement between parties with the intention of undertaking certain actions and refraining from others. A charter, on the other hand, assigns rights, powers and functions. The Covenant of the League of Nations opened with the words 'The High Contracting Parties', while the UN Charter begins 'the Peoples of the United Nations', who assign to themselves the rights, powers and responsibilities named in the Charter. While the Covenant of the League of Nations suggested a voluntary undertaking not to resort to war, Article 4 of the Charter defines refraining from the use of force as a principle. The phrase 'organized peoples' in the preamble to the Covenant of the League of Nations implied the existence of non-organized or less civilized peoples, whereas the UN Charter refers to the sovereign equality of all states.

The preamble

The Charter contains 111 articles and defines the organization's principles and its aims. The UN seeks to uphold international peace and security by taking effective common action and by striving for the peaceful resolution of disputes. The preamble, inserted at the instigation of Smuts, reaffirms faith in fundamental human rights, the dignity and worth of the human person and the equal rights of men and women and of all nations. The UN also seeks to 'promote social progress and better standards of life in larger freedom'. It sets out to 'employ international machinery for the promotion of the economic and social advancement of all peoples' (see Figure 20.1 for the Preamble and the Charter's division into 19 chapters).

Article 55 on economic and social cooperation

Unlike the League of Nations, the UN is a security organization that also has a role in economic and social coordination. Article 55 of the Charter deals with economic and social cooperation. To make possible peaceful and friendly relations between nations possessing equal rights and self-determination, it is necessary to create 'conditions of stability and well-being'. The UN therefore undertakes to promote 'higher standards of living, full employment, and conditions of economic and social progress and development' as well as 'solutions of international economic, social, health, and related problems, international cultural and educational cooperation and universal respect for human rights and fundamental freedoms'. These economic and social goals were defined in general terms in 1945, but in fact they would attain hitherto unknown prominence and consume the majority of resources: about 80 per cent of the UN's total expenditure. The idea that by engaging in economic and social cooperation, states contribute to the resolution of political conflicts and the prevention of war, is translated into the *functionalist thesis*, according to which greater social stability gained through international cooperation reduces the risk of war. This thesis underlies all the economic and social activities undertaken within the UN system (see §21.2).

Amendments to the Charter

Amendments to the Charter were adopted in 1963, 1965 and 1971, related to Articles 23, 27, 61 and 109. The 1965 amendment to Article 23 increased the number of members of the Security Council from 11 to 15. The amendments to Article 61 expanded the membership of the Economic and Social Council from 18 to 27 in 1965 and to 54 in 1971. The other amendments related to voting rules. On 24 October 1970 the General Assembly adopted a *Declaration on Principles of International Law concerning*

Friendly Relations and Cooperation among States in Accordance with the Charter of the United Nations. Resolution 2625(XXV) approved this Declaration. This was not an amendment to the Charter, but it underlined the consensus on the significance of the principles laid down in it.

Figure 20.1 Preamble and chapter division of the United Nations Charter

Preamble

We the Peoples of the United Nations Determined
- to save succeeding generations from the scourge of war, which twice in our lifetime has brought untold sorrow to mankind, and
- to reaffirm faith in fundamental human rights, in the dignity and worth of the human person, in the equal rights of men and women and of nations large and small, and
- to establish conditions under which justice and respect for the obligations arising from treaties and other sources of international law can be maintained, and
- to promote social progress and better standards of life in larger freedom,

And for these Ends
- to practice tolerance and live together in peace with one another as good neighbours, and
- to unite our strength to maintain international peace and security, and
- to ensure by the acceptance of principles and the institution of methods, that armed force shall not be used, save in the common interest, and
- to employ international machinery for the promotion of the economic and social advancement of all peoples,

Have Resolved to Combine our Efforts to Accomplish these Aims
Accordingly, our respective Governments, through representatives assembled in the city of San Francisco, who have exhibited their full powers found to be in good and due form, have agreed to the present Charter of the United Nations and do hereby establish an international organization to be known as the United Nations.

Chapter division of the Charter:

Chapter I: Purposes and principles, Articles 1–2
Chapter II: Membership, Articles 3–6
Chapter III: Organs, Articles 7–8
Chapter IV: The General Assembly, Articles 9–22
Chapter V: The Security Council, Articles 23–32
Chapter VI: Pacific settlement of disputes, Articles 33–38

Chapter VII: Action with respect to threats to the peace, breaches of the peace, and acts of aggression, Articles 39–51
Chapter VIII: Regional arrangements, Articles 52–54
Chapter IX: International economic and social co-operation, Articles 55–60
Chapter X: The Economic and Social Council, Articles 61–72
Chapter XI: Declaration regarding non-self-governing territories, Articles 73–74
Chapter XII: International trusteeship system, Articles 75–85
Chapter XIII: The Trusteeship Council, Articles 86–91
Chapter XIV: The International Court of Justice, Articles 92–96
Chapter XV: The Secretariat, Articles 97–101
Chapter XVI: Miscellaneous provisions, Articles 102–5
Chapter XVII: Transitional security arrangements, Articles 106–7
Chapter XVIII: Amendments, Articles 108–9
Chapter XIX: Ratification and signature, Articles 110–11

Enlargement of membership

The UN is an intergovernmental organization of sovereign and equal states, each of which, regardless of size or power, possesses a single vote. Its membership has almost quadrupled since its establishment by 51 states in 1945, to 192 states in 2006. In the first ten years of its existence the US and the Soviet Union could seldom agree on the admission of new members, and in the Security Council each used its right of veto to frustrate the candidacies proposed by the other. This impasse was broken in 1955 with the agreement of a 'package deal' that enabled 16 states to join simultaneously and that abolished the use of the veto when admitting new members. The biggest problem was China. The communist party, led by Mao Tse-tung, had come to power in 1949 and the nationalists, led by Chiang Kai-shek, had fled to the island of Taiwan. The nationalists' claim to be the legitimate government of the whole of China was recognized through the intervention of the US, and Taiwan occupied China's seat at the UN between 1949 and 1971. The détente in 1971 between the US under President Richard Nixon and China under Chairman Mao culminated in Taiwan being forced to relinquish this seat, which was taken over by the People's Republic of China. As a result Taiwan ended up outside the UN, because China regards it simply as a rebellious province. Apart from Taiwan, the only non-members of the UN in 2008 are Vatican City and the Palestinian Territories. Since the 1980s China has become a member of most international organizations and is party to many international conventions. In 1980 it began to attend the Conference on Disarmament, in 1982 it started taking part in the UN Commission on Human Rights, and in 1984 it provided a judge for the International Court of Justice. China was no longer just one of the leaders of the Third World, but was becoming conscious of its status as a great power. Its actions within international organizations were motivated to a large extent by national security and economic interests, so that regional and global organizations would all help to boost China's position as a great power and to move it closer to becoming an active permanent member of the UN Security Council. 'China is more willing than ever before to use its status as a rising global power to assert greater influence in shaping the international order' (Lanteigne 2005, 30).

Growing membership as a result of decolonization and disintegration

Since the end of the 1950s the UN has admitted former colonies as new member states. In 1959 it had 83 members, in 1969 125, in 1979 149, and by 1989 there were 159 (see Appendix 1 for admissions by continent). After the end of the Cold War the Russian Federation was quietly admitted in 1991 as the successor to the Soviet Union, inheriting its seat at the Security Council. The disintegration of the Soviet Union and Yugoslavia in the early 1990s brought new UN member states, raising the total membership to 188 in 1999. In 1991 the UN welcomed as new members the three Baltic States, North and South Korea, the Marshall Islands and Micronesia. The last two (micro)states thus gained autonomy *vis-à-vis* the US, although the US continued to take care of their defence. 1992 saw the accession of former Soviet republics such as Armenia, Azerbaijan, Georgia, Kazakhstan, Kyrgyzstan, Moldova, Tajikistan, Turkmenistan and Uzbekistan. After a number of former Yugoslav republics declared their independence (Bosnia and Herzegovina, Croatia, Slovenia and Macedonia), the first three joined the UN in 1992 and Macedonia did so in 1993 under the name of the Former Yugoslav Republic of Macedonia. Yugoslavia itself was expelled from the UN in 1992. It joined again in 2000 as the Federal Republic of Yugoslavia and in 2003 changed its name to Serbia and Montenegro, reflecting the *status quo*, until this combination too broke up in 2006. In 2002 Switzerland, which as a neutral state had had qualms about joining for many years, finally became the 190th member of the UN, followed by East Timor. Montenegro became the 192nd member in 2006.

The budget

For the regular contributions, the most important source of its income, the UN adheres to the principle of 'Capacity to Pay'. That means that wealthy industrialized states pay by far the largest share of the regular budget and many developing states pay insignificant amounts. How much a state pays is determined first and foremost by its total national income compared with that of other states. There is a minimum assessment of 0.01 per cent of a state's national income (initially 0.04 per cent, but this was lowered after 1972). In 1980, 71 states were assessed at the rate of 0.01 per cent, nine at 0.02 per cent and ten at 0.03 per cent of their income. There is also a maximum contribution, expressed as a percentage of the UN's total budget. This ceiling, originally 25 per cent, was reduced in 2001 to 22 per cent. In 1980 the US paid 25 per cent of the UN's budget, the Soviet Union 11 per cent, Japan 9.6 per cent, Germany 8 per cent, France 6 per cent, the UK 4.5 per cent and Italy 3.5 per cent. Currently the US pays 22 per cent of the UN's budget, Japan 19.5 per cent and Germany 10 per cent: these three states together thus contribute more than half of the budget. The UN's large and complex budget is drawn up for a period of two years at a time. First this was done by the secretary-general and later it became the responsibility of the Fifth Committee (see Figure 20.2), supported by a number of advisory committees. This budget is used to pay the administrative and other costs of the Secretariat and other UN bodies. Separate budgets exist for peace operations (see below) and for the international tribunals for the former Yugoslavia and for Rwanda, set up in the 1990s. In addition to this UN programmes such as those for refugees, children and development are funded by voluntary contributions. These contributions amount to more than the UN's regular budget.

Payment of contributions and politics

Collecting UN contributions has become a difficult issue because of the political ramifications. For instance, the Soviet Union and France did not accept that the peace operations in the Middle East that followed the 1956 Suez Crisis and the operations in Congo in the early 1960s (see §22.3) should be included in the organization's expenditure. In 1962 the International Court of Justice was asked for an advisory ruling. The Court confirmed that these costs were part of the organization's expenditure and that member states should pay for them. Meanwhile, the tensions that arose from the question of whether member states should be required to pay even if they had expressed their opposition to certain operations were running high. It initially looked as if dissenting states which had not paid their contributions for more than two years would lose their right to vote in the General Assembly, under Article 19 of the Charter. This situation was avoided by having no votes at all in the General Assembly of 1964. Because the Soviet Union, China and France continued to refuse to pay, peace operations have been financed through voluntary contributions since then. The financial crisis the UN suffered in the 1980s and 1990s also stemmed from political sensitivities. A major factor was the US's disapproval of the conduct of the UN and certain of its specialized agencies and of the soaring costs of the many peace operations. Lengthy negotiations were conducted over the reforms urged by the US and over other modes of financing. In the 1990s the US was one of the largest states withholding contributions from the UN. As a result the UN continued to have severe financial problems. These finally came to an end after the attacks of 11 September 2001, when the US Congress voted to pay the overdue contributions. However, the US has continued to use the withholding of contributions as an instrument to enforce its influence.

Structure of the UN

Like many large bureaucracies, the UN has a fairly complex structure that has expanded over the years. Its primary framework, however, is simple. There are six *principal organs*. The central organ is the *General Assembly*, which is assisted by three councils: the *Security Council*, the *Trusteeship Council* and the *Economic and Social Council*. The other two principal organs are the *Secretariat* (in New York, with external offices in Geneva, Vienna and Nairobi) and the *International Court of Justice* (in The Hague). In addition there are specialized agencies, programmes and funds linked to the UN. This chapter discusses the first five principal organs, while chapter 21 looks at the International Court and the specialized agencies (the UN system).

20.2 The General Assembly as the primary organ of the United Nations

The General Assembly as the highest organ

The highest organ of the UN is the *General Assembly*. This meets annually from mid-September until mid-December in New York and may reconvene for special sessions. In the first few weeks there is a 'general debate' in which each member state can make a speech to indicate its priorities. States usually send their head of state or head of government to do this, to stress how important they consider it to be. This caused a timekeeping problem, since it is difficult to tell heads of state or government to cut their speeches short. However, agreement was reached on a shorter speaking time and most speakers keep to it. Each member state has a single vote in the General Assembly. Their delegation can consist of up to five representatives, as well as five deputies and the necessary advisers: its composition is up to the individual state. For regular business decisions are taken by majority vote, while special issues require a two-thirds majority. The latter applies in the case of peace and security, electing members of UN bodies, the admission, suspension or exclusion of member states, trusteeship questions and the budget. The General Assembly appoints the secretary-general following a recommendation from the Security Council. It can discuss all matters referred to in the Charter and make recommendations. There are no binding decisions, nor does the General Assembly have any powers to compel governments to take action of any kind. All that counts is its moral weight.

Special sessions and Uniting for Peace

Special sessions of the General Assembly may be devoted to subjects or themes requiring particular attention, such as drug use or the unequal treatment of women. In certain cases *special emergency sessions* can be convened to discuss situations about which the Security Council has been unable to reach a decision. Here the *Uniting for Peace Resolution*, which the General Assembly adopted in 1950 at the urging of the US, plays a role. The underlying rationale was that the US wanted to circumvent a veto by the Soviet Union in the Security Council, so that the UN could take action in Korea (see §22.3). Resolution 377(V) amounted to a *de facto* amendment to the Charter without having been placed on the agenda as such. It enables the General Assembly to intervene in a situation in which peace has been violated or is threatened, or in which an act of aggression has been committed. It is authorized to take up the matter immediately and to make recommendations for collective measures, including the use of armed force. If the General Assembly is not in session, a special emergency session can be convened within 24 hours in response to a request to this effect from the Security Council (provided nine of the Council's members have voted in favour of it) or at the request of a majority of the UN's members. Among the situations in which the Resolution has been used were the 1956 Suez Crisis and the violence in Congo in 1960. In 1956 the Soviet Union used the Resolution to take action in the Suez Crisis, which had been caused by the UK and France (see §22.2). When the Soviet Union invaded Hungary later that year, the General Assembly proved incapable of stopping it. The same applied to the Soviet invasion of Afghanistan in 1980 (see §34.1).

Resolutions and conventions

The General Assembly differs from national parliaments in being a deliberative rather than a legislative chamber. Decisions are adopted in the form of resolutions, which may be formulated as agreements, declarations, conventions and protocols to conventions, but regardless of their specific format they are still counted as resolutions. Until 1976 the General Assembly numbered all its resolutions consecutively, with the number of the General Assembly in brackets in Roman numerals. Thus Resolution 22(I) was the 22nd resolution to be adopted at the first General Assembly on 13 February 1946. It contains the *General Convention on Privileges and Immunities of the United Nations*. Resolution 2373 (XXII), passed at the 22nd session on 12 June 1968, comprises the *Treaty on the Non-Proliferation of Nuclear Weapons*. The numbers of resolutions adopted at a 'special' or 'special emergency' session are preceded by the letters S and SE, respectively. Since the 31st General Assembly in 1967, the number of the General Assembly has been followed by another number indicating its sequential position within that session. Resolution 34/93, approved at the 34th General Assembly on 12 December 1979 as decision number 93, contains the *Declaration on South Africa*. Although a *resolution* is no more than an agreement with the status of a *recommendation*, it can acquire more weight. For instance, Resolution 217(III) adopted in 1948 acquired great moral authority as the *Universal Declaration of Human Rights*. Drafting international *conventions* is linked to the practice whereby states conclude conventions and present them to their parliaments for ratification. The same procedure was followed with the conventions adopted by the UN, exactly like those agreed at multilateral conferences, public international unions and the League of Nations. Examples include the UN conventions on the political rights of women (1952), human rights (1966) and racial discrimination (1965). All these conventions are resolutions of the General Assembly. Resolutions can be adopted in the General Assembly in different ways: by acclamation, without objection or without a vote, or the vote may be recorded or taken by roll-call.

The committees of the General Assembly

The General Assembly does its work with the help of six specialized *main committees*, whose most important function is to discuss first every subject that appears on the agenda. The First Committee deals with matters of disarmament and international security, the Second with economic and financial affairs and the Third with social, humanitarian and cultural issues (see Figure 20.2). There were originally seven committees, as a Special Political Committee for political security matters was set up because the First Committee concerned itself almost exclusively with disarmament. In 1993 this Special Political Committee merged with the Fourth Committee to form the Special Political and Decolonization Committee, as the process of decolonization was by then almost complete. In addition the General Assembly has two permanent committees, for the budget and for financial contributions, and two procedural committees, the General Committee and the Credentials Committee. Finally there are other and *ad hoc* committees, many of which have acquired permanent status, such as the International Law Commission (see §21.1). At the beginning of each session of the General Assembly it is decided which matters must be discussed in plenary session and which (the majority) are to be referred to the main committees. In other words, most of the debates take place in the committees. In principle all UN member states are represented on each committee, but in practice the committees tend to be smaller. Their debates culminate in draft resolutions on which the General Assembly subsequently takes a decision, generally at the end of its session. Voting within the committees is by a simple majority of 'those present and voting'.

Groups within the UN

Proposals put before the General Assembly in the form of resolutions may be adopted or rejected. As only these two possibilities exist, what matters is what happens before the vote. This depends on formal procedures (debates in the committees discussed above)

Figure 20.2 The six main and other committees of the General Assembly

Main Committees of the General Assembly, in which all member states can be represented:

- *First Committee:* Political and Security, primarily disarmament
- *Special Political Committee*: Political; merged with the Fourth Committee in 1993
- *Second Committee*: Economic and Financial
- *Third Committee*: Social, Humanitarian and Cultural
- *Fourth Committee*: Initially Trusteeship, including non-self-governing territories; merged with the Special Political Committee in 1993 to form the Special Political and Decolonization Committee
- *Fifth Committee*: Administrative and Budgetary
- *Sixth Committee*: Legal

Permanent Committees:

- *Advisory Committee on Administrative and Budgetary Questions* ACABQ (1946; 16 members appointed for three years)
- *Committee on Contributions* (1946; 18 members appointed for three years)
- *International Civil Service Commission* (1972; 15 members appointed for four years)
- *Committee on Information* (1978; 95 members); previously Committee to Review UN Policies and Activities

Procedural Committees:

- *General Committee* (1946; 28 members: the president and 21 vice-presidents of the current General Assembly plus the chairman of each of the six main committees)
- *Credentials Committee* (1946; nine members elected at each session of the General Assembly)

Other and Ad hoc Committees:

Political and security issues:

- *UN Scientific Committee on the Effects of Atomic Radiation* (1955; 21 members)
- *Committee on the Peaceful Uses of Outer Space* COPUOS (1959; 61 members); with a Legal Sub-Committee and a Scientific and Technical Sub-Committee
- *Special Committee on Peace-keeping Operations* (1965; 124 members)
- *Ad Hoc Committee on the Indian Ocean* (1972; 44 members)
- *Committee on the Exercise of the Inalienable Rights of the Palestinian People* (1975; 25 members)
- *Disarmament Commission* (1978; 61 members); replaced the commission set up in 1952

Development:

- Governing Council UN Environment Programme (UNEP) (1972; 58 members)
- Commission on Science and Technology for Development (1992; 33 members)
- Committee on Energy and Natural Resources for Development (1998; 24 members)

Legal issues:

- International Law Commission ILC (1947; 34 members elected for five years); original name was the Commission on the Progressive Development of International Law and its Codification
- Advisory Committee on the UN Programme of Assistance in Teaching, Study, Dissemination and Wider Appreciation of International Law (1965; 25 members)
- UN Commission on International Trade Law UNCITRAL (1966; 36 members)
- Special Committee on the Charter of the UN and on the Strengthening of the Role of the Organization (1975; all member states)

and on the existence of *caucus groups*. The latter are not mentioned in the Charter, but have arisen and gained acceptance over the course of time. They are geographical groups formed within the UN, such as the African, Asian, Latin American, Eastern European and 'Western European and other' groups of states. There are also combinations of comparable states, such as developing states (G77), states maintaining neutrality in the East–West conflict (Non-Aligned Movement countries), Islamic states, and developed states (Nordic states, the G7, the European Union). With the growth in the number of member states, the preparation of decision making in the General Assembly has increasingly become the responsibility of these groups. Most issues are resolved in the corridors, small seating areas or meeting rooms, where national representatives can discuss their concerns or worries, as well as the precise wording of resolutions or reports that are on the agenda. Groups can help to expedite negotiations on texts, particularly when they represent a common identity or adopt a similar position. Such talks outside the formal sessions continue until the very last moment, that is until agreement is reached on the draft resolution that will be submitted to the General Assembly or the relevant Committee. Through the informal preparations and 'trade-offs' in positions and support, those concerned ensure that the wording of the text and the actions arising from it are acceptable to all and that states do not feel compelled to vote against the motion (for the entire policy process see Peterson 1986). Within these groups issues are seldom put to the vote. Instead, the overall aim is to reach consensus.

Voting behaviour within the UN

When states moved to the group system within the UN they tried to secure a reasonable share of the electable positions for their own group, as this would confer legitimacy when debating items on the agenda. As a result many new initiatives tended to emanate from states that were dissatisfied with the existing situation (Morphet 2000, 224–25). In the voting behaviour of states, patterns are discernible that reflect shifts in the global balance of power. Until the mid-1950s the Western states had a clear ascendancy over the communist states in the General Assembly and the Security Council. As time passed, however, they gradually lost ground to a combination of communist and non-aligned Third World states. Until the 1970s it was the Soviet Union that used its veto most frequently in the Security Council. After that the US took over this role, often taking up an isolated position in relation to its support for Israel. Detailed studies have been made of voting behaviour in the UN (Kim and Russett 1996; Voeten 2000).

Bodies established by the General Assembly

The General Assembly's decisions are implemented by the UN Secretariat, special committees set up by the General Assembly to study and report on specific subjects (such as disarmament, decolonization and apartheid) and other auxiliary bodies created by the General Assembly. The dozens of auxiliary bodies that the General Assembly has appointed to implement tasks have had a variety of forms: *ad hoc* committees, a body that administers law (the Administrative Tribunal), research institutes such as the UN Institute for Training and Research, agencies with a certain political responsibility such as the refugee organization UNHCR, and executive bodies with a secretariat, an intergovernmental administrative structure and their own resources such as the children's fund UNICEF. As a rule, over time these bodies become institutions in their own right. This can be seen with the UN Conference on Trade and Development (UNCTAD), the UN Environment Programme (UNEP), the UN Industrial Development Organization (UNIDO) and the World Food Programme (WFP), and has somewhat blurred the distinction between the General Assembly's auxiliary bodies and independent specialized agencies such as the ILO and IMF. The autonomous character of agencies is further enhanced by the fact that they are financed on a voluntary basis. This complicates relations with the General Assembly and does not make it any easier for the Economic and Social Council (see §20.5) to fulfil its coordinating remit (Bowett 1982, 56–58). Figure 20.3 shows, in chronological order and with reference to the place where each is located, the programmes and funds created by the General Assembly (the main group), the 'other UN entities' and research and training institutes.

Figure 20.3 UN programmes and funds created by the General Assembly

Programmes and funds:

- **UNICEF**: *UN Children's Fund* (11 December 1946), New York
- **UNRWA**: *UN Relief and Works Agency for Palestine Refugees in the Near East* (8 December 1949; became operational in May 1950; reports directly to the General Assembly), Beirut (1950–78), Vienna (1978–96), Gaza and Amman
- **UNHCR**: *Office of the UN High Commissioner for Refugees* (became operational on 1 January 1951; from 15 December 1946 to 1950 *International Refugee Organization*, IRO), Geneva
- **WFP**: *World Food Programme* (24 November 1961; became operational on 1 January 1963; set up by the UN General Assembly and the FAO), Rome. In November 1974 the General Assembly set up a *World Food Council* to monitor

the world food situation and to implement the decisions of the 1974 World Food Conference. The WFP has 36 members and was based in Rome until 1992. After this the WFP secretariat was transferred to New York and brought under the auspices of the UN Secretariat.

- **UNCTAD**: *UN Conference on Trade and Development* (30 December 1964), Geneva
    - **ITC**: *International Trade Centre* (joint cooperation agency of UNCTAD and the WTO, previously GATT (1964), Geneva
- **UNDP**: *UN Development Programme* (21 November 1965), New York
    - **UNCDF**: *UN Capital Development Fund* (1966, fully operational in 1974), New York
    - **UNV**: *UN Volunteers* (1970), Bonn
    - **UNIFEM**: *UN Development Fund for Women* (1976; independent in 1985), New York
- **UNEP**: *UN Environment Programme* (15 December 1972), Nairobi
- **UNFPA**: *UN Population Fund* (18 December 1972; until 1987 *UN Fund for Population Activities*), New York
- **UNDCP**: *UN Drug Control Programme* (1991; came under the UN Office for Drugs Control and Crime Prevention of the UN Secretariat from 1997), Vienna
- **UN-Habitat**: *UN Centre for Human Settlements* UNCHS (Habitat) (1978, upgraded to full programme in 2002: *UN Human Settlements Programme* UNHSP), Nairobi

Other UN entities:

- **OHCHR**: *Office of the UN High Commissioner for Human Rights* (in December 1993 the General Assembly created the position of High Commissioner, to be appointed by the secretary-general with the consent of the General Assembly; the Office is part of the UN Secretariat), Geneva
- **UNAIDS**: *Joint UN Programme on HIV/AIDS* (established in 1994 by a resolution adopted by ECOSOC and operational since January 1996; administered by 22 governments, ten 'co-sponsors' [UNHCR, UNICEF, WFP, UNDP, UNFPA, UNODC, ILO, UNESCO, WHO and IBRD] and five NGOs including those representing people living with HIV/AIDS; classified as 'other UN entity' under the General Assembly), Geneva
- **UNOPS**: *UN Office for Project Services* (operational since 1995, administered by the UNDP and UNFPA), New York

Research and training institutes:

- **UNRISD**: *UN Research Institute for Social Development* (1963), Geneva
- **UNITAR**: *UN Institute for Training and Research* (1965), Geneva
- **UNICRI**: *UN Interregional Crime and Justice Institute* (1968), Turin
- **UNU**: *UN University* (1972), Tokyo
- **INSTRAW**: *International Research and Training Institute for the Advancement of Women* (1976), Santo Domingo, Costa Rica
- **UPEACE**: *University for Peace* (1980), Ciudad Colón, Costa Rica
- **UNIDIR**: *UN Institute for Disarmament Research* (1980; reports directly to the General Assembly), Geneva
- **UNSSC**: *UN System Staff College* (2000), Turin

UN world conferences 1968–2002

In the 1970s the UN developed the habit of addressing major global problems at special 'world conferences'. In Stockholm in 1972 the human environment was on the agenda, in 1974 the population issue was discussed in Bucharest and the world food situation in Rome, in 1975 the position of women was debated in Mexico, and in 1977 in Nairobi the subject was desertification. Figure 20.4 lists the UN world conferences and the subjects they covered, with the number of governments represented at each given in brackets. The most recent event of this kind was in 2002. These conferences provide a forum at which proposals can be discussed and consensus reached. Despite the enormous size of such 'mega-conferences', with all the logistical problems involved, they arouse long-term expectations. They help to mobilize national and subnational authorities and private actors into taking action to solve the problem concerned. At the conferences action programmes with international norms and guidelines for national policy are adopted, which are to be implemented at national level in more or less the same way as international conventions. The conferences set in motion a process in which governments take on certain commitments and report back to the UN regarding their progress.

The working of world conferences

Although world population conferences were held as far back as 1954 and 1965, the basic model for a world conference was developed at the conference on human rights held in Tehran in 1968. This applies both to the framework for intergovernmental talks and to the influence of NGOs on conferences of this kind. It is typical for world conferences to be convened by either the General Assembly or the Economic and Social Council, which makes the necessary resources available and invites the member states. The conferences last from two to six weeks and require very intensive preparation in terms of both substance and practical arrangements. They are convened in response to a new problem or problems that are perceived as global (such as the human environment and race relations), that are highly politicized (environmental pollution or women's rights) or that are expected to lead to certain consequences in the longer term (water shortage and overpopulation). They are prepared by Preparatory Committees or *PrepComs*. The governments represented on these Preparatory Committees rely on the expertise of existing specialized bodies, such as the functional commissions of the Economic and Social Council (see Figure 20.7). Success depends on finding a capable, charismatic secretary-general for the conference, obtaining the support of national delegations to achieve international consensus and good preparation at regional meetings. The caucus groups mentioned above play a vital role here.

World conferences and NGOs

Another key ingredient in a successful world conference is the involvement of NGOs from an early stage in the preparations. The public debates at such a conference make it possible for representatives of civil society to influence the intergovernmental discourse. The human rights organization Amnesty International benefited from this in 1968 (Schechter 2005, 27). The UN has its own internal arrangements for the representation of NGOs (see §20.6), which also gives them access to the world conferences. From 1972 onwards it became customary for the UN to organize a special *parallel* or *shadow conference* for NGOs as representatives of civil society. These non-governmental and official inter-governmental conferences communicate not only through general exchanges of ideas, but also in the drafting of the final document. Plenary sessions of the conference are addressed by speakers able to attract media attention, offering governments a platform for publicizing their positions and endorsing the conclusions of the working groups. At conferences labelled as 'world summits' it is normal for heads of state and government to play a part, enhancing the status of the conference. To ensure that responsibility is taken for the implementation of the decisions and policies that have been agreed, detailed action plans and follow-up conferences are used to monitor implementation and progress. Regular follow-up conferences were held every five years until 2003, when the General Assembly decreed that in future a decision would be made on follow-up conferences on a case-by-case basis (Schechter 2005, 7–11). The world conferences have attracted criticism for their massive scale, but they symbolize efforts to ensure that global problems are discussed at global level by representatives of both states and civil society.

Figure 20.4 World conferences organized by the UN 1968–2002

1968   **Tehran**: *International Conference on Human Rights* (84)
1972   **Stockholm**: *UN Conference on the Human Environment* (113)
1974   **Bucharest**: *Third World Population Conference* (136)
1974   **Rome**: *World Food Conference* (133)
1975   **Mexico City**: *World Conference on the International Women's Year* (133)
1976   **Vancouver**: *UN Conference on Human Settlements* (Habitat I) (132)
1977   **Mar del Plata**: *UN Water Conference* (116)
1977   **Nairobi**: *UN Conference on Desertification* UNCOD (95)
1978   **Geneva**: *World Conference against Racism* (125)
1979   **Vienna**: *UN Conference on Science and Technology for Development* (142)
1980   **Copenhagen**: *World Conference on the UN Decade for Women* (145)
1981   **Nairobi**: *UN Conference on New and Renewable Sources of Energy* (125)
1981   **Paris**: *UN Conference on Least Developed Countries* (142)
1982   **Vienna**: *World Assembly on Ageing* (124)
1983   **Geneva**: *Second World Conference to Combat Racism and Racial Discrimination* (128)
1984   **Mexico City**: *International Conference on Population* (146)
1985   **Nairobi**: *World Conference to Review and Appraise the Achievements of the UN Decade for Women: Equality, Development and Peace* (157)
1990   **Paris**: *Second UN Conference on Least Developed Countries* (149)
1990   **New York**: *World Summit for Children* (153)
1992   **Rio de Janeiro**: *UN Conference on Environment and Development* UNCED (170)
1993   **Vienna**: *World Conference on Human Rights* (171)
1994   **Cairo**: *International Conference on Population and Development* ICPD (178)
1995   **Copenhagen**: *World Summit for Social Development* WSSD (186)
1995   **Beijing**: *Fourth World Conference on Women* (189)
1996   **Istanbul**: *UN Conference on Human Settlements* (Habitat II) (171)
2000   **New York**: *Millennium Summit* (189)

2001 **Brussels**: *Third UN Conference on Least Developed Countries* (159)

2001 **New York**: *UN Conference on Illicit Trade in Small Arms and Light Weapons in All Its Aspects* (171)

2001 **Durban**: *World Conference against Racism, Racial Discrimination, Xenophobia and Related Intolerance* (170)

2002 **Monterrey**: *International Conference on Financing for Development* (190)

2002 **Madrid**: *Second World Assembly on Ageing* (188)

2002 **Johannesburg**: *World Summit on Sustainable Development* WSSD (160)

Source: (Schechter 2005, 205–10). In brackets: the number of governments represented.

Monitoring through reports

All these developments mean that the UN General Assembly is not only the highest organ of the member states, it is also a complex structure with 'internal' committees and groups and numerous 'external' bodies linked to it (programmes, funds, entities and world conferences). As the UN's central organ, the General Assembly receives reports from all the other UN organs and conferences. It has a supervisory role with respect to the Trusteeship Council and ECOSOC, which means that it sees and discusses all their reports and decisions. This does not happen with the Security Council, although it does receive its reports.

20.3 The Security Council and its permanent members

The Security Council and the veto privilege

One of the three councils that assist the General Assembly is the *Security Council*. This Council has primary responsibility for maintaining peace and security in the world. It has had 15 members since 1965 (before that 11), ten of which are elected every two years. The Council's presidency rotates among the members in alphabetical order on a monthly basis. Each member possesses a single vote and procedural matters are decided by nine out of the 15 votes. Nine assenting votes are also needed for substantive matters, but here there is the added requirement that a motion must have the unanimous support of the five permanent members (China, France, the Soviet Union/Russian Federation, the UK and the US). This 'great power unanimity' is known as the *veto privilege*. Permanent members can block decision making, although in practice an abstention by one of them is not counted as a veto. If a Security Council member is involved in the issue concerned, it must abstain. Non-members with an involvement in a matter under discussion by the Security Council may attend the Council's meetings, but they are not permitted to vote. The aim is to achieve as broad a consensus as possible in advance of the decision making. But once tensions rise, debates in the Security Council revolve around hard power politics. While other UN organs can only make recommendations to governments, the Security Council has the power to enforce its decisions. It can do so through coercive measures, economic sanctions such as trade embargoes, and joint military action in the framework of peacekeeping operations. Although it is mandatory under the

Charter for member states to implement the Security Council's decisions, there are practical limitations to enforcement, and as a result many of the Security Council's decisions are only recommendations. The Council's responsibilities also include the regulation of armaments and the exercise of trusteeship in territories that are of strategic interest to the UN. The Security Council's annual and special reports are sent to the General Assembly. The Council and the General Assembly jointly appoint the judges of the International Court of Justice and the Security Council recommends a new secretary-general to the General Assembly.

Change of behaviour among the permanent members

During the Cold War, some developing states perfected the art of playing the permanent members of the Security Council off against each other so as to increase the influence of the non-aligned countries. Other states, such as Canada, Finland and Norway, developed skills as helpful mediators. Although the threat of using the veto did not lose any of its force, it was resorted to less often after the end of the Cold War. In the first 45 years of the UN's existence permanent members used the veto 193 times, while from 1990 to the middle of 2003 it was used only 12 times (Malone 2004, 7). After the end of the Cold War the non-permanent Council members began to feel marginalized, because the permanent members were monopolizing the Council's activities more than previously. This was noticeable in the writing of draft resolutions, the preparation of the agenda and the more limited composition of committees and working groups. After the 1995 Dayton agreements on the conflict in the Balkans, the US was at the forefront in determining the Security Council's agenda and its actions, but ten years later the significance of Russia and China had increased as a result of their stronger economies and disputes over US foreign policy.

Security Council resolutions

Security Council resolutions are numbered consecutively, and since 1994 this is followed by the year in brackets. Thus resolution 1004(1995), adopted on 12 July 1995, called for the immediate withdrawal of Bosnian Serbs from Srebrenica, which had been designated a 'safe haven', and the release of the members of the UN Protection Force who had been taken hostage. In its first year (1946) the Security Council issued 15 resolutions and in 2007, 56. In the period 1946–90 the number of resolutions passed was 683, while substantially more were adopted between 1991 and 2007 than in the previous period: 1,111.

Tensions between states

The sections of the Charter that are of greatest relevance to the Security Council are *Chapter VI* on the pacific settlement of disputes and *Chapter VII* on action with respect to threats to the peace, breaches of the peace and acts of aggression. The Council has the power to look into any dispute and any situation that may lead to tension between two or more states. When a complaint about threats to, or breaches of, the peace is brought before the Security Council (which may be done by Council members, a member state, the General Assembly, the secretary-general or under certain conditions by a non-UN member state), the Council will generally try to formulate recommendations for a peaceful resolution of the dispute. In some cases it may even conduct its own investigation or mediate in an attempt to initiate one. It can send special representatives and ask the UN secretary-general to provide his good offices. The Council may also frame principles for the peaceful settlement of disputes. When hostilities have broken out the Council will seek to end them, and to do so it might despatch UN peacekeeping units to help reduce tension and to keep armies and parties apart. To raise peacekeeping forces of this kind, the UN has to appeal to the member states.

Committees and institutions

Figure 20.5 gives an overview of the committees and other institutions created by the Security Council. They include the UN peacekeeping operations and the war tribunals for the former Yugoslavia and for Rwanda. The Council can appoint *ad hoc* committees and working groups to deal with specific issues or subjects, and has frequently done so over the years. Iraq's invasion of Kuwait in 1990 gave rise to the establishment of a committee for compensation and one to monitor the elimination of weapons of mass destruction. This and other conflicts in the 1990s led to the forming of special sanction committees (see §38.1). In 1990 the Security Council set up the Working Group on Sanctions, followed in 2000 by the Working Group on General Issues on Sanctions.

Changes in the 1990s

In the 1990s the Security Council began to give a broader interpretation to the threats to international relations referred to in Chapter VII of the Charter. Such threats were now taken to include matters such as a *coup d'état* against a democratically-elected government (Haiti, 1993), humanitarian disasters causing large numbers of refugees such as in Bosnia in the early 1990s and East Timor in 1999, and acts of terrorism (especially after 2001). As a result the UN was mandated by the Council temporarily to take over a state's (or territory's) administration (in Cambodia in 1992 and in both Kosovo and East Timor in 1999). Before this it had done so only once (in 1962), in New Guinea. A new development, in contrast to the Cold War period, was that the Security Council had to take more account of other IGOs. This included the North Atlantic Treaty Organization and the continental regional organizations for which space had been created in the Charter (Chapter VIII on regional agreements). During the Cold War these regional organizations had been given barely enough scope to play a part in safeguarding security and they had therefore focused their efforts on other matters, such as economic development (in Latin America) or human rights (in Europe). NGO influence was initially accepted only in relation to ECOSOC and was kept out of the Security Council (see §20.6), but their significance in the field of security increased in the 1990s because of their humanitarian activities in war zones. NGOs succeeded in expanding their ties with the Security Council and making their influence felt in areas such as procedures, transparency, ideological outlook and legal and policy issues (see §38.2). This involved NGOs going through a learning process in terms of dealing with the permanent members and working in the context of hard power politics (Paul 2004). Efforts to change the composition of the Security Council in this period were unsuccessful because of continued opposition from the permanent members. The debate on the subject in 2001 did not lead to an increase in the number of seats or an expansion in the geographical spread of members to include more or all continents, nor were any new or different great powers made permanent members. The General Assembly had appointed an Open-Ended Working

Figure 20.5 Security Council committees and institutions

Standing Committees

- *Military Staff Committee*: based on Article 47 of the Charter; consists of the chiefs of staff of the five permanent members or their representatives, but has been largely neglected since 1946
- *Committee of Experts on Rules and Procedures*
- *Committee on Admission of New Members*

Ad hoc **Committees *(examples)***

- Governing Council of the *UN Compensation Commission* (UNCC): appointed on the basis of resolution 692(1991), intended to provide compensation to the victims of Iraqi aggression and paid out of a levy on Iraqi oil revenue as elaborated in resolution 687 of 3 April 1991
- UNMOVIC: *UN Monitoring, Verification and Inspection Commission* (Iraq) (1999): the successor to UNSCOM (UN Special Commission on Iraq) of 1990, intended to monitor Iraq's compliance with the obligation to eliminate its weapons of mass destruction and permanently to verify that Iraq does not regain weapons such as those which the Security Council has banned; led in the period 2001–3 by Hans Blix
- *Sanctions Committees*
- *Counter-Terrorism Committee* (2001)

Tribunals

- *International Criminal Tribunal for the former Yugoslavia* (1993)
- *International Criminal Tribunal for Rwanda* (1994)

Operations and Missions

- *Peacekeeping Operations and Missions* (see Figures 22.1, 37.1 and 37.3)

Group on this in 1993, but this Group had found that the necessary amendments to the Charter would have to be approved by a two-thirds majority of member states as well as needing the consent of the permanent members.

20.4 The Trusteeship Council as a continuation of the League of Nations' mandate system

The Trusteeship Council

The *Trusteeship Council* is another organ set up to assist the General Assembly. While this Council does not have a prescribed number of members, care is taken to strike a balance between member states that administer territories under trusteeship and those that do not. Currently the Trusteeship Council consists of the five permanent members of the

Security Council, with China having been an inactive member until 1989. The Trusteeship Council helped 11 territories in Africa and the Pacific by way of international administration to independence or incorporation into other states. Palau's admission to the UN in December 1994 brought the last of these trusteeships to an end (see Figure 20.6). The Council has had a moderating influence on the general process of decolonization (Taylor and Groom 2000, 142). But that this has not stopped all such conflicts is clear from the situation surrounding a disputed territory such as the Western Sahara. The Trusteeship Council has not been abolished. Secretary-general Boutros Boutros-Ghali recommended its abolition, but in 1997 Kofi Annan submitted a proposal for its revival which envisaged reshaping the Council into a forum in which member states can use their collective trusteeship to protect the integrity of the global commons (oceans, North and South Poles, the atmosphere and outer space). The General Assembly accepted this proposal but did not change the composition of the Trusteeship Council. The Council can be convened as and when required.

Figure 20.6 Territories administered by the UN Trusteeship Council

- The first territory to acquire independence through the Trusteeship Council was British *Togoland*, which united with the British colony of Gold Coast in 1957 to form the state of **Ghana**.
- Italy ceased to rule *Somaliland* in 1960. This combined with the British part of Somaliland to form **Somalia**.
- France withdrew from French *Togoland* in 1960, as a result of which the *Republic of* **Togo** came into existence.
- French *Cameroon* gained its independence as the *Republic of* **Cameroon** in 1960.
- In 1961 the UK withdrew from its part of Cameroon. The northern part of the territory joined Nigeria to form the *Federal Republic of* **Nigeria**, while the southern part joined the Republic of Cameroon.
- The British-ruled territory of *Tanganyika* became independent in 1961, and when the protectorate of Zanzibar also gained its independence in 1963 the two joined to form the *United Republic of* **Tanzania**.
- In 1962 Belgium granted independence to *Ruanda-Urundi*, from which the states of **Rwanda** and **Burundi** were formed.
- New Zealand ended its rule of *Western Samoa* in 1962. This became the state of **Samoa**.
- Australia withdrew from **Nauru**, which it had governed on behalf of the three administrative authorities of Australia, New Zealand and the UK, in 1968, after which the state gained its independence.
- Australia ceased to rule *New Guinea* in 1975. The territory combined with Papua, which had likewise been ruled by Australia, to form the state of **Papua New Guinea**.
- The trust territories of the *Pacific Islands*:
  - The *Commonwealth of the* **Northern Mariana Islands** became a self-governing territory as a Commonwealth of the US in 1978.
  - The *Republic of the* **Marshall Islands** became a self-governing territory in 1979, with a Compact of Free Association with the US entering into force in 1986.

> The *Federated States of Micronesia* became a self-governing territory in 1986, with a Compact of Free Association with the US entering into force in 1986. The *Republic of Palau* gained its independence from the US after a referendum held in 1994.

20.5 The coordinating function of the Economic and Social Council (ECOSOC)

The Economic and Social Council (ECOSOC)

The third council that assists the General Assembly is the *Economic and Social Council* (ECOSOC). Established in October 1945, this Council works 'under the authority of the General Assembly' and is responsible for coordinating all the economic and social activities of the UN and specialized agencies such as the ILO and FAO. ECOSOC's initial membership of 18 was increased to 27 in 1965 and to 54 in 1973. To preserve continuity the General Assembly elects one-third (18) of the members of ECOSOC each year for a period of three years. Each member has a single vote, and decisions are made by a majority of those present and voting. The five regional groups in ECOSOC are Africa (with 14 members), Western Europe and other states (13), Asia (11), Latin America (ten) and Eastern Europe (six). Any member state wishing to attend ECOSOC meetings can do so, but they are unable to vote. ECOSOC has two brief organizational sessions in New York each year, and holds one substantive session which last four to five weeks (in July) and is held alternately in New York and Geneva. The substantive session includes a special meeting with ministers to discuss major economic and social issues. Since 1998 another meeting is held in April with finance ministers chairing relevant committees of the IMF and IBRD. There are three committees during plenary sessions: the First Committee deals with economic issues, the Second Committee with social topics, and the Third Committee is responsible for the programme and coordination. Resolutions adopted by ECOSOC were numbered consecutively until 1977, as seen in the following examples: 1733(LIV), 1915(ORG-75) and 2046(S-III). The first was adopted at the 54th session as number 1733, the second at the organizational session held in 1975 and the third at the third special meeting as number 2046. By December 1977 a total of 2,130 resolutions had been passed. From 1978 onwards resolutions have been indicated by year followed by number: 1990/47.

The powers vested in ECOSOC

The objectives of economic and social cooperation are defined in Article 55 of Chapter IX of the Charter. Since many of these matters are part of the domestic policies of states, Article 56 stipulates that member states pledge to take joint and separate action, in cooperation with the UN, to achieve these objectives. ECOSOC does not have executive power and can only draft recommendations. The powers vested in ECOSOC under Chapter X include the ability to make recommendations to states, the General Assembly or specialized agencies for the purpose of promoting human rights and fundamental freedoms, to conduct studies, to prepare draft conventions for submission to the General

Assembly and to convene international conferences. ECOSOC may also provide technical assistance to UN bodies, specialized agencies and states. The General Assembly can create special programmes and bodies for this purpose, such as the UN Development Programme. Finally, ECOSOC is responsible for coordinating the work of UN bodies and specialized agencies. If no specialized agencies exist, it may undertake activities in its own right.

ECOSOC commissions and committees

Apart from *ad hoc* bodies ECOSOC has three types of commissions and committees (see Figure 20.7): functional commissions with expertise in specific fields (9), regional economic commissions (5) and standing committees (6). *Functional commissions* have frequently evolved into authoritative institutions in their particular policy areas, such as human rights, the position of women or social development. In these fields they prepare international regulations and draft conventions, as well as measures to monitor their implementation. This last is done by developing voluntary norms and minimum standards, often in the form of model legislation, followed by assessments of states' behaviour. The regulations are accompanied by an extensive amount of information. *Regional economic commissions* deal with a continent (or part of one), with the aim of encouraging cooperation between states in that region. There are regional commissions for Europe, Asia and the Pacific, South and Central America, Africa and Western Asia. *Standing committees* focus on the UN itself (relations with IGOs and NGOs) or on substantive issues (for instance human settlements). In 2000 these were also labelled 'forums'. ECOSOC can set up expert groups and elects the members of the executive committees of a number of UN agencies (see 'other related bodies' in Figure 20.7).

The Universal Declaration of Human Rights (1948)

States had enshrined human rights in their constitutions from the nineteenth century onwards and the UN formulated these rights at international level in the *Universal Declaration of Human Rights*, adopted in 1948. This document established human rights in international law, first as a Declaration and later in two fundamental international conventions, the Human Rights Covenants of 1966, and a number of specialized conventions, including those on the elimination of racial discrimination (1965) and discrimination against women (1979) and on the rights of the child (1989) (see Figure 33.1). When the UN was founded in San Francisco in 1945, respect for human rights and fundamental freedoms was defined as the primary objective of the international community. In this respect the UN went further than the League of Nations, which had merely described 'fair and humane conditions of labour' and the 'just treatment of the native inhabitants' in Article 23 of its Covenant as standards to be upheld. The Declaration by United Nations issued in January 1942 in response to German anti-Semitism (see §19.2) had referred explicitly to human rights and justice. The UN Charter built on this foundation by proclaiming universal respect for human rights in Articles 1 and 55. The San Francisco conference also agreed that these rights should be laid down in a special document. To prevent disagreements over this document hindering the establishment of the UN, the conference decided to leave drafting of the text to a committee. In accordance with Article 68 of the UN Charter ECOSOC in 1946 appointed a *Commission on Human Rights* (CHR). This functional commission, chaired by Eleanor Roosevelt, worked on the Declaration which was finally adopted by the General Assembly in Paris on 10 December 1948, by 48 votes in favour and eight abstentions including the Soviet

Figure 20.7 Functional, regional and standing commissions of ECOSOC

*ECOSOC's nine **Functional Commissions:***

- *Commission on Human Rights* (1946, 53 members); has a Sub-Commission on the Promotion and Protection of Human Rights; the Commission on Human Rights was replaced by the Human Rights Council in 2006
- *Commission on the Status of Women* (1946; 45 members); see Figure 20.8
- *Commission for Social Development* (1946, 46 members); set up as the Social Commission; advises ECOSOC on social issues and community-based development
- *Commission on Population and Development* (1946, 47 members); concerns itself with population issues in relation to socio-economic conditions
- *Commission on Narcotic Drugs* (1946, 53 members); action to curb illicit trade; has a Sub-Commission on Illicit Drug Traffic and Related Matters in the Near and Middle East
- *Commission on Crime Prevention and Criminal Justice* (1992, 40 members); drafts international conventions
- *Commission on Science and Technology for Development* (1992, 33 members)
- *Commission on Sustainable Development* (1993, 53 members); ensures that the objectives in Agenda 21 of the 1992 UNCED conference are integrated into the UN's activities
- *Statistical Commission* (24 members); standardizes statistical terminology and procedures

The number of member states represented in each of these special commissions is changeable. The commissions consist of government representatives assisted by various experts.

*ECOSOC's five **Regional Commissions** focus on the following regions:*

- Europe: **ECE**, *Economic Commission for Europe* in Geneva (1947)
- Asia and the Pacific: **ESCAP**, *Economic and Social Commission for Asia and the Pacific* in Bangkok, Thailand (1947)
- Central and Latin America: **ECLAC**, *Economic Commission for Latin America and the Caribbean* in Santiago, Chile (1948 as Economic Commission for Latin America (ECLA); its name changed in 1984)
- Africa: **ECA**, *Economic Commission for Africa* in Addis Ababa, Ethiopia (1958)
- Western Asia: **ESCWA**, *Economic and Social Commission for Western Asia* in Amman, Jordan (1974)

The underlying assumption is that specific problems are best tackled at regional level. Unlike the functional commissions and standing committees, these regional commissions are executive bodies. They deal directly with governments and report back on their activities to ECOSOC.

*ECOSOC's **Standing Committees** are as follows:*

- *Committee on Negotiations with Intergovernmental Agencies* (1946)
- *Committee on Non-Governmental Organizations* (1946)
- *Committee for Programme and Coordination* (1962)
- *Committee for Development Policy* (1965)
- *Commission on Human Settlements* (1977)
- *Committee on Energy and Natural Resources for Development* (1998)

ECOSOC also has temporary **Expert Bodies**, both of government experts and of members acting in their personal capacity as experts, and **Ad hoc Bodies**.

In 2000 two forums were set up as 'other bodies' of ECOSOC:

- The *UN Forum on Forests* UNFF has universal membership for all members of the UN and its specialized agencies
- The *UN Permanent Forum on Indigenous Issues* PFII (16 independent experts chosen by ECOSOC)

Other related bodies:

ECOSOC maintains direct relations with these bodies, as it elects some, or all, of their members.

- *Executive Board* UNICEF: UN Children's Fund (1946; 36 members elected by ECOSOC)
- *International Narcotics Control Board* (1946; 13 members elected by ECOSOC)
- *Executive Committee* UNHCR: UN refugee agency (1951; 53 members elected by ECOSOC)
- *Executive Board* WFP: World Food Programme (1961; 36 members, half of which are elected by ECOSOC and half by FAO)
- *Executive Board* UNDP: UN Development Programme (1965; 36 members elected by ECOSOC)
- *Executive Board* UNFPA: UN Fund for Population Activities (1969; 36 members elected by ECOSOC)
- *Board of Trustees* of the International Research and Training Institute for the Advancement of Women (1974; ten members elected by ECOSOC)

Union, reportedly at Roosevelt's instigation, with two states absent. The Declaration was based on the 'classical' civil and political human rights, derived from the Enlightenment period and as formulated by states, but it also mentioned economic and social rights. The communist states, which had little sympathy with the civil and political rights and had less and less sympathy with them as the Cold War progressed, supported the economic and social rights. Thanks to India the words 'all men' were replaced by 'all human beings' and women were explicitly mentioned in Article 1. Because the drafters were striving for a moral force that would be binding on everyone, not only on governments, they used the word 'universal' rather than 'international'. Among the civil and political rights in the 30 articles are: all human beings are free and equal, they have a right to life, to equal protection of the law and to property and the right to take part in the government of their state. Also enshrined in the Declaration are freedom of opinion and expression and freedom of assembly and association. The economic and social rights include the right to social security and the economic, social and cultural rights that are indispensable to the dignity and free development of one's personality, the right to work, free choice of employment, just and favourable conditions of work and protection against unemployment. The text was based heavily on Western ideas regarding the family and the breadwinner. The family, as 'the natural and fundamental group unit of society', was entitled to protection 'by society and the State'. After the Declaration was adopted the General Assembly asked ECOSOC to give the Commission on Human Rights a mandate to draft a legally-binding convention with measures to monitor compliance, so that the Declaration, convention and monitoring mechanisms would form a trinity. This was eventually achieved, but it took far longer than anticipated (until 1966; see §33.1).

The Commission on the Status of Women

The *Commission on the Status of Women* (CSW) is a functional commission of ECOSOC. At the founding of the UN and following on from developments within the League of Nations in the 1930s (see §18.1), the international women's organizations that had remained active during the Second World War applied pressure to establish a separate commission to deal with the legal status of women. The Brazilian delegation put their proposals forward at the UN founding conference in San Francisco and defended them. The result was a recommendation to set up a new women's commission as a subcommittee of the human rights commission. At the first General Assembly of the UN in London at the beginning of 1946, all female delegates endorsed this proposal in an open letter, which Eleanor Roosevelt, as a member of the US delegation, presented. On 16 February at its first meeting ECOSOC established the *Commission on the Status of Women*, as a subcommittee of the Commission on Human Rights. As the women were opposed to being dependent on the pace of another commission's work, they successfully urged in June 1946 that the women's commission should become a separate ECOSOC commission (see Figure 20.8).

The uninterrupted expansion of activities and their overlap

Chapters IX and X of the Charter gave the UN a central role and universal competence in the sphere of economic and social cooperation. This was not accompanied, however, by the creation of a central authority within the UN, on which neither the US nor the UK had insisted at its founding. Given their experience with the League of Nations, they had expressed a preference for organizations that could stand on their own feet. They considered the possibility that the UN would not actually be established or that it might become paralysed by political conflicts. If this was to happen, organizations active in economic and social fields would still be able to continue their work. To be able to coordinate the activities of the existing or newly-formed specialized agencies, ECOSOC had to start building relations with them, and the first the UN did this with was the ILO. Tough negotiations culminated in the ILO joining the UN system on 30 May 1946, the first specialized agency to do so. The result was 'an improved and codified version of the practices that

Figure 20.8 The Commission on the Status of Women

The UN **Commission on the Status of Women** met annually until 1971, after which it has met every two years. It consisted of 15 members (increased to 32 in 1966) and was entrusted with the task of preparing recommendations and reports for ECOSOC to promote women's rights in political, economic, social and educational fields. The Commission can also make recommendations on urgent matters, the aim being to apply the principle that women and men possess equal rights. Its activities eventually culminated in a large number of UN viewpoints and conventions on the legal status of women. During the 1960s the emphasis in the Commission's work shifted from equality under the law to equal roles and to the role of women in the development process. This led to an organizational change. In 1973 women's affairs were transferred from the Human Rights Department in the Division for Political and General Assembly Affairs of the UN Secretariat to the Secretariat's Centre for Social Development and Humanitarian Affairs. This Centre moved from New York to Vienna in 1979. The Commission's independent status had the disadvantage that women's rights were debated separately from human rights, with the result that it was some time before the human rights debate incorporated the gender dimension.

Like the Commission on Human Rights, the Commission on the Status of Women was given the authority in 1947 to deal with **complaints**, formally known as *communications*, regarding violations of women's rights. These complaints could be submitted by individuals or NGOs and were studied by a three-person subcommittee. However, as this could do little more than take cognizance of the complaints confidentially because the Commission was not authorized to take action, this work was of limited significance and in the 1970s was discontinued. In 1983, under pressure from the second wave of the women's movement, a new procedure was adopted. The Commission was authorized to study complaints submitted on the grounds of discrimination against women and to draw attention to trends or patterns discernible in these complaints. Compared with the Commission on Human Rights, the Commission on the Status of Women had limited powers. For instance it was not able to take action against states that violated women's rights, set up special subsidiary bodies, hold hearings or ask groups of experts to study certain subjects. Nor could it call on NGOs to make statements on the actual situation in states, in the way Amnesty International does in relation to human rights (see Figure 33.3). But because legal frameworks also create procedures for treating cases and because NGOs such as Women's Rights Action Watch have used and monitored these procedures, in practice improvements were achieved.

had marked the relations between the ILO and the League of Nations' (Ghebali 1989, 24). With this cooperation agreement as a model, the UN subsequently negotiated with other IGOs. Some of these organizations insisted on even greater autonomy, such as the Bretton Woods institutions, while others acquired less. The ILO agreement was also the basis for the arrangement in 1957 with the International Atomic Energy Agency (IAEA), which for political reasons was made directly accountable to the General Assembly. The creation of programmes or funds as auxiliary bodies of the General Assembly created a certain tension with regard to the responsibilities of ECOSOC, as there was no clear demarcation between the two organs. The biggest problem was the constant expansion of activities and programmes, together with a certain overlap between agencies and bodies that were active in the same areas. For instance, the ILO overlapped with the FAO in the area of land reform, with UNESCO in education, with the industrial development organization UNIDO in the sphere of small businesses, and with the WHO in relation to health norms. This overlap of work was caused partly by the lack of some, or indeed any, coordination between ministries within national governments. 'Most countries still lacked systematic arrangements even for keeping the activities of international organizations under central review; let alone for developing co-ordinated positions on issues coming before them' (Taylor and Groom 2000, 108). Such overlapping activities hampered ECOSOC's coordinating work.

Fragmentation

Another coordination problem arose with the creation of umbrella organizations other than ECOSOC. For instance, the Expanded Programme of Technical Assistance (EPTA) was established, which divided its funds between the UN and its specialized agencies. When the EPTA and the Special Fund, set up somewhat later, were merged in 1966 to form the UN Development Programme, relations between the General Assembly and ECOSOC were arranged in a system of such bureaucratic intricacy that it was impenetrable to all but insiders. The growth of regional activities also added layers of complexity. In 1973 the UN decided that ECOSOC's economic Regional Commissions were the most important centres of economic and social activities, but this decision was of little value because the regional centres of the specialized agencies were not the same as those of ECOSOC. Institutional overlap and fragmentation would be increased further by political clashes (see below) and the voluntary funding of specialized activities in line with the preferences of governments. 'The general trend was towards voluntary financing and this tended if anything to promote further fragmentation as funds were contributed more whimsically for governments' favoured projects' (Taylor and Groom 2000, 114). The General Assembly's tendency to organize separate world conferences also fostered fragmentation as they soon developed their own dynamic forces, organizational design and funding.

Differences between the ways in which the North and South view ECOSOC

ECOSOC has received little attention in the literature compared with the Security Council and is not held in very high esteem. It is seen either as a body with a wide-ranging remit but limited powers, or as a very active body with little political weight (Bowett 1982, 62). To make matters clearer, it should be noted that the wealthy industrialized states (the North) and the developing states (the South or Third World) view ECOSOC in different ways. For the wealthy states development comes after peace and security, while poorer states see development as the UN's primary task. What irritates them most is that industrialized states determine ECOSOC's activities and dominate its policies.

The undermining of ECOSOC by politicization

In the late 1960s and early 1970s ECOSOC was undermined by a certain amount of politicization, as the result of the growing divisions between Third World and industrialized states (see §34.2). Rising Third World states were eager for more development aid, but saw ECOSOC, the organ that devised development strategies within the UN, as a bastion of the wealthy industrialized states. When Third World states joined forces as the Group of 77 (G77) and stepped up their political pressure, the industrialized states tried to negotiate development aid in the IMF and IBRD instead, where they knew that their large voting numbers would help secure what they viewed as a more pragmatic policy. The developing states responded by moving the debate to the UN Conference on Trade and Development (UNCTAD), where they had taken the original initiative and in which they could operate more easily as a group (see §29.2). The first conference on trade and development in 1964 led to UNCTAD's establishment as a permanent organ of the General Assembly, with the result that debate shifted to the General Assembly. Many decisions prepared in ECOSOC were transferred to the General Assembly at the request of the G77, which helped to undermine ECOSOC still further. In the debates about the reform of the UN system in the mid-1970s, states stressed the need to strengthen ECOSOC, but North–South divisions continued to pose an obstacle. Nor did the effort to clarify the distribution of responsibilities between the General Assembly and ECOSOC produce any results (White 1996, 155). A UN report issued in 1984 observed that this crisis within the UN in the social and economic fields had come to be regarded as the normal state of affairs. While in 1974 the UN was still viewed as the obvious place in which to conduct negotiations on the world's most pressing problems, ten years later, although the General Assembly and ECOSOC were still discussion forums, they barely functioned as forums for negotiation any longer. By that time ECOSOC was also in crisis, partly as a result of practical problems such as dissatisfaction with the documentation sent to those attending, which delegations complained was too much, inadequate and sent out too late (Dembinski et al. 1985, 125).

US policy during the Reagan presidency

From 1981 onwards the US under President Reagan (see chapters 34 and 35) helped to further weaken ECOSOC in two ways. The US contributed less money to the UN, its specialized agencies and its programmes and funds, and made UN bodies monitor the way budgets were spent. They were responsible for finding out what was done and what was not done with the money. The deferral of the US's contributions, a relatively large proportion of the whole, had a major impact on the UN and led to many activities being scaled down or suspended, without ECOSOC having the opportunity to play a coordinating role. Additionally, the US joined with some other industrialized states in moving the coordination of economic policy to institutions outside the UN. While the industrialized states continued to be dominant within ECOSOC, macro-economic coordination was undertaken more and more by the G7, the system of summits involving the seven most developed states (see §27.3). The Bretton Woods institutions and the GATT, which was becoming more heavily oriented towards free trade, increasingly resisted UN coordination.

A coordinating role after all

Despite these developments, ECOSOC retained its coordinating role within the UN in the social and economic fields. The political scientist Amos Yoder found that ECOSOC was an organ that had worked fairly efficiently at its sessions and that had in fact succeeded in coordinating between UN bodies and agencies, in which both governments and IGOs tried to act consistently. The reporting system at ECOSOC meant that different institutions consulted each other before implementing new policies or programmes. As a result the UN system was more effective than was generally believed. An analysis of the decades-long UN policy on the equal treatment of women and men showed that ECOSOC was constantly informed about, and an active participant in, all important decisions and politically complex situations in which multiple bodies and agencies were involved. In addition the governments represented on ECOSOC in many cases also sit on the managing bodies of the specialized agencies, and representatives of these in turn attended ECOSOC meetings as observers or were consulted if controversial matters were being discussed. Compromises reached in ECOSOC were therefore in line with the policies of governments concerned with specialized agencies. That different bodies and agencies were involved in the same problems may seem chaotic, but it also had certain advantages as they were able to secure more financial resources than a single structure could do (Yoder 1997, 141–43).

Not marginalized

Although the UN's social and economic policies were constrained by pressure exerted by the US in the 1980s and 1990s, the end of the Cold War invested ECOSOC with new significance. This was a result of the threat posed by failing states and the need to rebuild states after the end of military conflicts and civil wars. In addition the European Community began to make its presence felt within the UN as a collective actor advocating coordinated economic and social activities. Due to financial cuts and calls for change, improvements in organizational structure were made, including strengthening the programmatic nature of activities and defining ECOSOC's role more precisely, reshuffles within the UN Secretariat and reforms in the management of programmes and funds. All these changes were aimed at enhancing efficiency and effectiveness, without creating a higher layer of administration or expanding the financial role of agencies such as the IBRD. ECOSOC succeeded in strengthening the norms of the multilateral system in such a way that the actors involved fell into line. This was achieved by bringing those responsible for formulating programmes, contributing resources and implementing policy into closer contact within a single forum. 'Contributors, implementers and formulators were locked into a way of working which supported system rules' (Taylor and Groom 2000, 139). Driven by fear of its abolition and the threatened loss of its advantages, ECOSOC succeeded through diplomacy, namely the leadership of the UN secretary-general, in reversing the process of marginalization.

20.6 The consultative status of non-governmental organizations at ECOSOC

Continuation of the League of Nations practice

Within the UN as a political system actors other than governments, such as NGOs, are active. These private organizations have consultative status under the terms of Article 71 of the UN Charter, which states that ECOSOC can arrange consultations with NGOs. This was a codification of the League of Nations practice, but also a restriction as the article stipulates that NGOs can have a say in economic and social affairs but not on security issues. Had it been left solely to the governments at the founding conference in San Francisco this arrangement would not have been adopted at all, but it was eventually agreed due to pressure from NGOs. Governments considered that NGOs, and women's organizations in particular, had exercised too much influence on the League of Nations' Disarmament Conference in 1932 (see §16.2). However, the reluctant American delegation in San Francisco was lobbied by supporters of NGO influence such as the New Deal adherent James Shotwell and American peace organizations. The Soviet Union, which was no great fan of NGOs, also played a role. It wanted special status for the recently formed World Federation of Trade Unions (see §21.4), which operated to some extent under its influence. It preferred it if the ILO was not mentioned in the UN's founding document and therefore it supported consultative status for NGOs. Diplomats performed a 'damage limitation' exercise, as they saw it, by confining the consultative status of NGOs to the economic and social fields (Williams 1990, 260–61). In view of the widespread publicity given to the founding document in the US and the positive response to it from NGOs, several delegations at the San Francisco conference had added NGO representatives. The American delegation included 42 people from spheres of activity ranging from employment, law, agriculture and trade to education, women's affairs and religion, with the aim of familiarizing NGOs with the UN's work in order to gain their support for it and ensure that they would publicize it. These objectives were achieved, partly through the actions of the so-called world federalists.

The World Movement for World Federal Government

Societies aspiring ultimately to establish a world government had been founded in Chicago in 1924 and 1937 and in the UK in 1938. These 'world federalists' wanted to play a role after the war by disseminating their ideas. In 1946 they founded the *World Movement for World Federal Government* (from 1956 the *World Association of World Federalists* and from 1991 the *World Federalist Movement*). They saw the founding of a world government as the key issue in the international system. Only when this was resolved could other national and international problems be settled. In their opinion there were five paths to world government: cooperating in the development and reform of the UN into a world federal government with the power to make, enforce and implement global laws; promoting the fulfilment of the essential conditions for a constitutional assembly; seeking the support of a true majority in national governments; promoting the forming of national federations with a view to hastening the creation of a world federal government; and elaborating a draft constitution for the world. Publications originating from these circles included *The Anatomy of Peace* by Emery Reves (1947) and *World Peace through World Law* by Grenville Clark and Louis Sohn (1960). The world federalists ensured that the UN received support among citizens and elaborated proposals for practical reforms.

Regulating the consultative status of NGOs

A major factor in the way the UN functioned was that many NGOs played a role in setting the agenda and making decisions on subjects debated in the UN. In 1946 ECOSOC established a committee to draft regulations on NGOs sending observers to ECOSOC's public meetings and relevant committees and other suborgans to explain their position. The procedures were formally accepted in 1950. The degree of participation depended on the category to which the NGO belonged. The revised 1968 regulations laid down three categories: I, II and Roster (initially A, B and Register). *Category I* organizations, with the strictest admission criteria, were given the greatest scope to present their philosophy. This category included organizations that, broadly speaking, represented a sizeable section of the population in a large number of states, were closely connected with social and economic life in the areas they represented, were familiar with most of ECOSOC's activities and had made a recognized contribution to the UN's work. They were permitted to attend all meetings of ECOSOC and its subsidiary bodies, could submit written declarations, could speak and were initially even allowed to propose items for the agenda. Category I included four international trade union federations, the international organization of employers, the International Chamber of Commerce and four international women's organizations. *Category II* was reserved for organizations with an international reputation that had special competencies in a small number of ECOSOC's subject areas. They had the same privileges as Category I organizations, except that they were not permitted to propose subjects for the agenda and their written contributions had to be shorter. *Roster* (or scheduled) organizations were those that made occasional useful contributions to the UN's work or that of its specialized agencies. They were only allowed to attend meetings concerning their specific area of expertise, could submit written statements only if asked to do so and had to keep these brief (500 words, as opposed to 2,000 for Category I and 1,500 for Category II). To protect their own interests, the NGOs with consultative status at the UN have since 1948 been united in CONGO, the *Conference of Non-Governmental Organizations in Consultative Status with the United Nations Economic and Social Council.*

Regulation of consultative status as adopted in 1996

The regulations devised in 1996 were an extension of the two previous sets of regulations. NGOs wishing to be eligible for consultative status had to fulfil a number of requirements, such as having been officially registered with the appropriate national authorities as an NGO or non-profit organization for at least two years. They were required to have democratically-agreed by-laws, possess the authority to speak on behalf of their members and have a representative structure. They needed to have democratic and transparent decision-making processes and accountability arrangements. Finally, the organization needed to function on the basis of resources raised through national branches, units or individuals. They could not have been set up by governments or IGOs. Major international NGOs that addressed most of ECOSOC's subject range and spanned a wide geographical area were to be given *General Consultative status* (formerly classified as A or I). NGOs with special competence in one or more areas tended to be smaller and to have been founded later. These were to be given *Special Consultative status*. NGOs that did not fall into either of these categories and made only occasional contributions were included, as before, in the *Roster*. If an internationally-active national NGO wished to achieve consultative status, this could only be done in consultation with the government concerned. NGOs that already had a certain status with another IGO were to be admitted if they could demonstrate that their work was of significance to the UN. Figure 20.9 shows the number of NGOs that had consultative status at the UN between 1948 and 2005. In 1948 there were 40 thus recognized NGOs, while 20 years later, in 1968, there were 180, 4.5 times as many, while the total number increased almost fourfold between 1992 and 2005, from 744 to 2,719.

Regulations for NGOs at specialized agencies and UN conferences

The UN's specialized agencies and programmes such as the FAO, ILO, UNCTAD, UNESCO, UNHCR, UNIDO and WHO have regulations similar to those adopted by

Figure 20.9 Numbers of NGOs with consultative status at ECOSOC 1948–2005

Year	General (First A, Later I)	Special (First B, Later II)	Roster (First Register)	Total
1948	13	26	1	**40**
1967	12	135	43	**190**
1968	17	78	85	**180**
1980	10	205	373	**588**
1992	38	297	409	**744**
1995	65	406	415	**886**
1998	100	742	663	**1,505**
2000	122	1,048	880	**2,050**
2005	136	1,639	944	**2,719**

ECOSOC, with three categories. Others do not differentiate. At the human rights conference held in Paris in 1968 to mark the twentieth anniversary of the Universal Declaration of Human Rights no substantial NGO presence was allowed, to which CONGO responded by holding a separate NGO conference in Paris. After this CONGO lobbied successfully to ensure that NGOs with consultative status would always be invited to UN world conferences in future and could address the floor and submit documents there. The first UN conference held on the initiative of NGOs was the 1972 conference on the human environment, which NGOs having consultative status at ECOSOC were allowed to attend officially. Swedish NGOs arranged that those without consultative status were able to attend the NGO forum paralleling the official conference. These 'shadow conferences', at which NGOs also took responsibility for daily reporting, became a general pattern at UN world conferences (Stephenson 2000, 280). At the UN Conference on Environment and Development (UNCED) in Rio de Janeiro in 1992 a simpler and less bureaucratic procedure than usual was agreed for the admission of NGOs and the General Assembly decided that the same procedure would apply at the ECOSOC Commission on Sustainable Development launched in 1993.

20.7 The UN Secretariat and the secretary-general

The UN Secretariat modelled on the League of Nations

The Secretariat is the fifth principal organ of the UN. It is led by the secretary-general and implements the organization's decisions. Its position is laid down in Chapter XV of the Charter, which contains only five Articles (97–101). The UN Secretariat is in many respects a continuation of the League of Nations' international Secretariat (see §15.4), as seen in the requirement that staff must be loyal to the international organization and that member states must respect its exclusively international nature (Article 100). The UN took over from the League of Nations the salary system set up in 1921 in accordance with the so-called Noblemaire principle and the pension plan devised in 1923. The *High Administrative Tribunal* that the League of Nations had set up in 1927 to settle disputes between members of staff and the organization was transferred to the ILO in 1946. However, in 1949 the General Assembly founded the *UN Administrative Tribunal*, which is open to UN personnel and some specialized agencies, although most specialized agencies work with the ILO tribunal. The IBRD and IMF each have their own tribunal. In view of the UN's many responsibilities, it was decided at the founding conference that instead of different secretariats existing alongside each other the entire staff would come under the authority of the secretary-general (Beigbeder 2000, 200). Unlike his predecessor, the UN secretary-general was given the right of political initiative. He can bring any matter that in his view poses a threat to international peace and security to the attention of the Security Council (Article 99). As in the case of the League of Nations, the secretary-general is responsible for ensuring that all international conventions are deposited, registered and published in the *United Nations Treaty Series*.

The secretary-general as a political figure

The secretary-general is both a political figure and the UN's chief administrative officer. His appointment is political in nature, as the Security Council nominates and the General Assembly endorses the appointment. This means that the candidate must have the support of the permanent members and that these can propose alternative candidates backed up by the threat of veto. The secretary-general must possess diplomatic as well as political qualities. His working environment consists of a wide range of actors, including great powers and world leaders, numerous medium-sized, small and tiny states, regional groups, IGOs with their own secretaries-general, NGOs, religious leaders, media and social movements. During the Cold War one or other of the two sides would frequently either seek the secretary-general's support or ignore him. In the 1950s the Soviet Union would have preferred to see the post held by a triumvirate or *troika*, which would have undermined the position. In the 1970s Kurt Waldheim was criticized because the Third World viewed his appointments policy as too pro-Western. In the 1990s Boutros Boutros-Ghali and Kofi Annan both had to deal with the attempts by the US to prescribe how the Secretariat should do its work. The UN has had a total of eight secretaries-general to date (see Figure 20.10).

The role of the secretary-general

The secretary-general is the most important member of staff at all meetings of the General Assembly, Security Council, ECOSOC and Trusteeship Council. He exercises all the functions assigned to him in the Charter (Article 98) and delivers an annual report to the General Assembly on the organization's work. The right of initiative that he has under Article 99 also shows the limitations of his position, because in the end it is the members of the Security Council who determine the agenda. They sometimes consider it unnecessary to ask for his opinion and they are generally reluctant to use force against those who infringe UN decisions. The Security Council members tend to be more concerned with the short rather than the longer term and the great powers possess secret 'intelligence' that they are loath to share with others. The secretary-general must therefore ensure that he himself has sufficient reliable information on which to base his opinions and actions. For this reason the Secretariat has always had a political affairs department, with specialists who evaluate all incoming information. Among the most important of its information sources are the representatives of the United Nations Development Programme in more than 100 states. The UNDP employs experienced diplomats who are capable of assessing the value of information and are familiar with the local balance of power. 'The salience of these sources depends on the talents of the field personnel and the efficiency of internal coordination within the Secretariat, and thus raises eternal issues of management in a large public agency' (Gordenker 2005, 37). The advantage of the UN's patchwork structure is that it can yield a great deal of specific information. The scope for the secretary-general to play a political role depends both on his individual qualities and competence and on the room for manoeuvre in a given political context. That most of the instructions to the secretary-general issued by the General Assembly, Security Council and ECOSOC are formulated in fairly vague terms is an advantage, because it gives the secretary-general leeway for action. He can offer his good offices, which is one of the most important instruments available to him, and in so doing he can stress qualities such as independence, impartiality and integrity. He may also seek to initiate or maintain negotiations. This presupposes that he is familiar with the political forces at work and will try to seize whatever opportunities arise to play a role. Examples include the peace operations devised by Hammarskjöld in the 1956 Suez Crisis and in Congo in 1960, Pérez de Cuéllar's initiative in the 1980s on regional peace processes in Central America, his mediation in the war between Iraq and Iran and in the Soviet Union's withdrawal from Afghanistan in 1988, and Annan's mission to Iraq in 1998 in connection with the weapons inspections (see Figure 20.10).

Figure 20.10 The secretaries-general of the United Nations

1 **Trygve Lie** of Norway (February 1946-November 1952). Developed a dynamic leadership. Through his activities during the Korean War he provoked opposition from the Soviet Union. His willingness to dismiss American personnel suspected by US Senator Joseph McCarthy of having communist sympathies reinforced this opposition. When the time came for his reappointment to be considered in 1951 the Soviet Union threatened to use its veto, but the US made it clear that it was not willing to consider any other candidate. When his reappointment was discussed in the General Assembly it decided to 'extend' his term in office. The Soviet Union considered this decision to be unlawful and refused to cooperate with him any longer, which led Lie to resign his office prematurely.

2 **Dag Hammarskjöld** of Sweden (April 1953-September 1961). Elected unanimously and re-elected in 1957. It was through his actions that the *UN Emergency Force* was created in the Middle East in 1956 and the *UN Observation Group in Lebanon* in 1958. He travelled a great deal to familiarize himself with the new states and the local balance of power and reacted immediately to the urgent plea for assistance from the Congolese government in 1960, taking action that led the Security Council to create the *UN Force in the Congo*. He died during his fourth trip to Congo when his plane crashed in Africa.

3 **U Thant** of Burma (now known as Myanmar) (November 1961-December 1971). Succeeded Hammarskjöld and was re-elected unanimously in 1962 and 1966. His term of office saw a great expansion in the economic and social activities conducted in the Third World. Thant, who did not speak French, was frequently opposed by France. He tended to adopt a neutral position in conflicts and felt frustrated at being unable to play a mediator's role in the Vietnam War. His role

in the 1962 Cuban Missile Crisis was modest. He established a peacekeeping force in Cyprus (1964) and another one to keep the peace between India and Pakistan (1965). When he gave in to pressure exerted by President Nasser of Egypt to pull the UN's peacekeepers out of Sinai and Gaza in 1967 he was criticized, as it left a vacuum that was followed by a new Arab-Israeli war.

4 **Kurt Waldheim** of Austria (January 1972-December 1981). Put himself forward but several Third World states opposed his re-election in 1976 and in 1981 his re-election was vetoed by China. His actions led to the Palestine Liberation Organization being invited to attend the General Assembly and acquiring observer status at the UN. It was during his term of office that the UN's world conferences were developed. Waldheim also travelled a great deal. There were major international conflicts in this period, such as the dispute between India and Pakistan in 1971, the war in the Middle East in 1973, Vietnam's invasion of Cambodia, the ten-year war between Iraq and Iran and the Iranian revolutionary change from 1979 to 1981. His attempt to mediate to save American hostages in Tehran was unsuccessful.

5 **Javier Pérez de Cuéllar** of Peru (January 1982-December 1991). Became secretary-general after other candidates had been vetoed. Was immediately faced with the Falklands/Malvinas War, but took initiatives that established his reputation as an impartial mediator. Urged that the Security Council be used as a forum for negotiations and peacekeeping and stressed human rights and the need for the return of refugees. After the end of the Cold War he saw opportunities for the UN to have a bigger role. The growth in activities and of the organization itself that he initiated generated a need for more financial resources, which met with opposition from US President Reagan.

6 **Boutros Boutros-Ghali** of Egypt (January 1992-December 1996). Was one of several candidates and was appointed due to the support of the Organization of African Unity. He proposed the idea of 'peace enforcement' and expanded the activities to include the internal problems of states. The number of UN troops was increased from 11,000 to 44,000 in 1992 and 80,000 in 1993. He mobilized support for intervention in Somalia, where however 18 US soldiers were killed and their bodies dragged through the streets, an incident that was given wide TV coverage and completely changed US attitudes to the UN. The massacre in Rwanda followed in 1994, where the UN once again failed to take decisive action. In response to the criticism Boutros-Ghali froze the organization's budget and embarked on a thorough reorganization. The animosity of the US led to it vetoing his re-election.

7 **Kofi Annan** of Ghana (January 1997-December 2006). Made his career within the UN system. He started immediately on a project for the 'renewal' of the UN, for which he obtained the support of the General Assembly and about which he had consultations with American politicians. He succeeded in playing a role in difficult security issues such as managing to persuade Iraq to readmit the weapons inspectors in 1998. He succeeded in getting the African states to agree on a unified position and fostered the formation of the peacekeeping force in Kosovo, approved by the Security Council but led by NATO, as well as the interim UN administration there in 1999. He supported the establishment of

the International Criminal Court, much to the dislike of the US, and played a role in streamlining the UN's peacekeeping activities that did find favour with the US. In 2000 he published a report about the UN in the twenty-first century, with an ambitious plan to tackle evils such as poverty, inequality and life-threatening diseases by 2015. For this too he succeeded in securing political support. In 2001 he was re-elected for a second term. In the years that followed the US-led fight against terrorism set the agenda, with the invasion of Iraq taking place without the approval of the Security Council. Thanks to Annan the UN's 'responsibility to protect' people against genocide, war crimes, ethnic cleansing and crimes against humanity was recognized. In 2005 a Peacebuilding Commission was established with the aim of helping the UN to play a role after conflicts have come to an end. Annan built up his personal authority and in 2001 he was awarded the Nobel Peace Prize.

8 **Ban Ki-moon** of South Korea (from January 2007). Gained experience with the UN through South Korean foreign policy. Enjoys the support of the US.

Leader of a complex administrative machinery

The power of the UN Secretariat rests in its continuity and its capacity to manage information for the UN's diverse organs and bodies, whose decisions must be prepared and implemented. 'Its permanency provides these bodies with an indispensable institutional memory, research capacity, a tool for the collection and dissemination of information, for diplomatic action with member states and other organizations' (Beigbeder 2000, 196). It has legal, political and economic expertise and the necessary language facilities, including the ability to use language to achieve the objectives of the UN. The UN staff is not large in comparison with national bureaucracies. In 1946 the UN in London had a temporary staff of 300, after which the first secretary-general added another 2,900 personnel in the space of a few months. By 1964 the staff had grown to 3,400, by 1974 it was over 11,000 and in 1984 it was almost 15,000 – as it was in 1994, when staff numbers peaked at 14,691. As a result of cuts and reorganizations effected under US pressure this number fell to about 8,900 by 2006. The principle that members of staff should maintain positions independent of the member states has not proved simple in practice. Thus the communist states kept a close eye on those who were eligible for appointments in the UN system. The primary responsibility of their own people was to their states and their communist beliefs. The UN could hardly ignore the lists submitted for its attention. During the period of US Senator Joseph McCarthy in the early 1950s the US government also had no qualms about interfering directly with the way the UN Secretariat was functioning. It ran checks on the political reliability of American candidates, with the full support of secretary-general Lie (Beigbeder 2000, 201). The problem with staff from new developing states was that they frequently had little experience or had been selected for reasons other than their qualities as a candidate. The latter also applied to more industrialized states, which saw the UN as a useful place to 'dump' their less successful politicians. Notwithstanding all this, the UN succeeded in building up its own army of officials, whose attitudes and efforts were focused on the organization. At the same time the UN, as a huge administrative apparatus, found itself having to deal with incompetent management and neglect of the organization itself, which meant that much of the criticism levelled at the organization was justified. This was also true regarding the lack of proper evaluations of results (something that received plenty of attention in the 1970s but that barely improved) and of a careers policy. Although there were restructuring operations in the 1960s, the secretary-general was not called to account for his management of the organization until the 1990s.

American pressure on the UN

From the 1980s onwards the secretary-general was faced with growing criticism from the US and with restrictive measures. The US criticized the excessive 'politicization' of the UN due to pressure from the Third World. In domestic politics opposition to the UN led to a proposal by Senator Nancy Kassebaum to reduce the US contribution to the UN and in 1985 President Reagan signed legislation that would reduce the contribution from 25 to 20 per cent of the UN's total budget. Problems arose over payment of the contribution because much of the UN's policies was not appreciated in American domestic politics. When the US suspended its payments altogether the UN had no option but to make financial cuts and to have the organization reviewed. In response to the US criticism of UN bureaucracy, the Ford Foundation and a committee chaired by bankers Paul Volcker and Shiguro Ogata issued fairly independent reports on the way the UN functioned. Boutros-Ghali took the criticism seriously and his consequent actions included setting up the *Office of Internal Oversight Services* (OIOS) to ensure better supervision of the UN's costs and activities and freezing the soaring budget for peacekeeping operations.

The Department of Peacekeeping Operations (1992)

Additionally a *Department of Peacekeeping Operations* (DPKO) was established in 1992, improving overall control of these activities. Until then peacekeeping operations authorized by the Security Council or General Assembly had been under the supervision of the undersecretary-general for special political affairs of the *Department of Political Affairs* (DPA). The new Department was an integral part of the secretary-general's *Executive Office* and was headed by an undersecretary-general for peacekeeping. The DPKO acquired departments for planning and support and for training and evaluation. Following a proposal from Annan, who had himself been undersecretary-general for peacekeeping, an evaluation department called the *Lessons Learned Unit* was set up in 1995 to meet the objections of the US. Despite his reforms Boutros-Ghali was unable to defuse American politicians' criticism. When the Republicans gained a majority in the Senate in the mid-1990s and Senator Jesse Helms, a fierce critic of the UN, became chairman of the Senate Foreign Affairs Committee, he made it virtually impossible for secretary-general Boutros-Ghali to implement any reforms. Whatever measures the latter took were regarded almost by definition as inadequate. Under US pressure Boutros-Ghali was not re-elected in 1996 and was replaced by Annan. The US saw Annan as someone who would be capable of effecting a sweeping reorganization, as he had made his career within the UN.

Consolidating the UN Secretariat

After the US suspended its contributions the UN experienced serious financial problems. Annan was compelled to effect drastic reforms of the entire apparatus, including the Department of Peacekeeping Operations. Because the DPKO was constantly overspending as a result of the many appeals the UN received from states, it was subjected to close scrutiny. With the authority of UN troops having been challenged on several occasions, Annan wanted to ensure that the UN had sufficient military capacity to carry through any peacekeeping operation it took upon itself. In the wake of three critical reports (on the atrocities committed against Bosnian Muslims in Srebrenica in 1995, the genocide in Rwanda in 1994, and a comprehensive report issued by the undersecretary-general for special assignments Lakhdar Brahimi from Algeria in 2000), there was support for expanding the UN's ability to take action during conflicts and recommendations were made to achieve this. Annan contributed to the developments by acting as a global diplomat, adopting an active role in conflicts and defining the positions in the reorganized UN Secretariat himself. Through his organizational reforms and his role as secretary-general he strengthened the position of the UN Secretariat, the standing of which had been badly undermined in the 1990s. His 1997 report *Renewing the United Nations* led to the centralization of control of peacekeeping operations. The post of *deputy secretary-general* was created, filled in 1998 by Louise Fréchette from Canada. The 2000 Brahimi Report prompted a further professionalization of peacekeeping operations. Brahimi's panel recommended that a UN force should be able to intervene rapidly and that the secretary-general should be given a budget to launch actions where necessary. Annan managed to gain the confidence of the US and to get the essence of the proposed reforms accepted at the 2001 General Assembly. This in turn led the US to adopt a more accommodating attitude and in October 2001, after the events of 11 September, it paid its overdue contributions.

Peacebuilding Commission and the Support Office (2005)

During his second term of office Annan created two new UN bodies. The report *In Larger Freedom* (2005) led to the establishment of the *Peacebuilding Commission*, which is concerned with UN policy after conflicts have been resolved. Its task is to prevent a state descending into chaos (see §37.2). This committee was given a special position with both the General Assembly and the Security Council as an Advisory Subsidiary Body. It is supported by a *Peacebuilding Fund* set up in 2006 and a *Peacebuilding Support Office* within the UN Secretariat. The second body created by Annan is the *Human Rights Council*, established in 2006 to replace the Commission on Human Rights (see §44.3). Annan proved capable of reforming the UN and by exercising leadership to give it a role to play in a period of difficult conflicts. As a result the Secretariat emerged not weakened but stronger than before.

Figure 20.11 Departments and offices of the UN Secretariat

Secretary-general

EOSG: Executive Office of the Secretary-General
OIOS: Office of Internal Oversight Services
OLA: Office of Legal Affairs

Peace and security

DPA: Department of Political Affairs
DDA: Department for Disarmament Affairs
DPKO: Department of Peacekeeping Operations

OCHA: Office for the Coordination of Humanitarian Affairs
PSO: Peacebuilding Support Office

Economic, social and human rights

DESA: Department of Economic and Social Affairs
UNODC: UN Office on Drugs and Crime; originally ODCCP: Office for Drug Control and Crime Prevention
OHCHR: Office of the UN High Commissioner for Human Rights

Management

DGACM: Department of General Assembly and Conference Management
DM: Department of Management
DPI: Department of Public Information

Reporting to the secretary-general

UNSECOORD: Office of the UN Security Coordinator
OIP: UN Office for the Iraq Programme
CAC: Office of the Special Representative of the Secretary-General for Children and Armed Conflict
OHRLLS: Office of the High Representative for the Least Developed Countries, Landlocked Developing Countries and Small Islands Developing Countries

Offices in cities other than New York:

UNOG: UN Office in Geneva
UNON: UN Office in Nairobi
UNOV: UN Office in Vienna

Structure of the UN Secretariat

Apart from the deputy secretary-general three officials in the executive office are particularly important: the undersecretary-general chief of staff; the assistant secretary-general special adviser and the assistant secretary-general external relations. Currently the Secretariat has seven departments and 11 offices. It has three external offices, in Geneva, Vienna and Nairobi (see Figure 20.11).

The workings of the United Nations system

21.1 The International Court of Justice and the development of international law

The end of the Permanent Court of International Justice (1946)

The *International Court of Justice* is the sixth principal organ of the UN and its legal institution. It is the successor to the Permanent Court of International Justice, which operated within the framework of the League of Nations from 1922 onwards (see §15.7). As the Permanent Court did not function after 1939 and could too easily be linked to the inactivity of the League of Nations, the Allies decided to create a new international court. To prepare the way they set up an Inter-Allied Committee in early 1943, which produced a report at the beginning of 1944. In the interest of continuity the statute of the new court was to be based on that of the Permanent Court. At Dumbarton Oaks the Allies decided that the UN would also have a legal dimension and to give it a stronger position they made the new court a principal organ of the new peace organization. A group of legal experts from 44 states drew up a draft statute, which was further elaborated by a committee at the conference in San Francisco which created the UN. The conference then incorporated the *Statute* of the International Court of Justice into the UN Charter and urged the UN member states to approve the binding jurisdiction of the Court. In October 1945 the Permanent Court met to disband itself and pass on all its possessions to its successor. At the beginning of 1946 the initial meeting of the UN in London chose the first judges. The new Court decided to hold its inaugural session in The Hague and after negotiations between the UN and the board of the Carnegie

Foundation (see §7.5) it was accommodated in the Peace Palace. The International Court of Justice met for the first time in April 1946.

The International Court of Justice

The activities of the International Court, which consists of fifteen judges, are regulated in Chapter XIV of the UN Charter (Articles 92–96). The 'members of the Court' are chosen by the General Assembly and the Security Council by absolute majority, on the basis of nominations from national panels of legal experts. They are elected for their qualities rather than their nationality, although all members must be of different nationality. The judges are appointed for nine years and can be re-appointed immediately. The chair rotates every three years. Voting is by a majority of judges present, with a quorum of nine members. In the event of a split vote the chair has the casting vote. All UN member states are party to the Court's Statute because it is an integral part of the UN Charter.

Competences of the International Court

Only states can be parties in cases brought before the Court. The Court's jurisdiction includes all cases submitted by states with a special agreement to do this, all cases relating to a current international treaty or convention in which the Court is referred to (in 2000 this applied to more than 700 bilateral and multilateral agreements) and legal disagreements between states which have accepted the Court's jurisdiction as compulsory in specific disputes. In 2008, 65 states had accepted this compulsory jurisdiction, while all other states cited sovereignty as the reason for not doing so. The Court decides itself if it is competent. There is no possibility of appeal against a ruling of the Court. The ruling is binding only on the parties and in the specific case involved. Parties which appear before the Court are obliged to implement the ruling and if one does not do so the other can appeal to the Security Council, which will make recommendations and take measures to ensure that the ruling is carried out. The General Assembly and the Security Council may ask the Court for non-binding advice on legal questions, while other organs and specialized UN agencies can ask for legal advice on matters relating to their activities if authorized to do so by the General Assembly. The ILO, which sought the advice of the Permanent Court in the interwar period, and the UN also ascribe to the Court a cassation function. In 1955 an administrative conflict between the ILO and UNESCO was passed to the Court with a request for advice (Rosenne 1989, 180). The ILO also determined that disputes about the interpretation of its constitution and conventions can be put before the Court. The Court can set up separate chambers itself. In 1993 for example it established a chamber to deal with environmental matters, comprising seven members.

The Nuremberg and Tokyo war tribunals 1946–48

The most notable international rulings immediately after the Second World War were not made by the International Court but by the Allies, who set up military tribunals in the German city of Nuremberg and in the Japanese capital Tokyo. After the First World War crimes committed during the war had in effect gone unpunished. Turkey's cruel treatment of the Armenians was denied and the victors' call for Germany to deal with its own war criminals had no real effect, as the German Kaiser was able to flee to the Netherlands. After the Second World War, however, the prominent figures in Germany and Japan were put on trial for 'crimes against humanity', the first time that individual leaders had been brought before an international court for such crimes. In Nuremberg the four Allied powers tried the 'major war criminals of the European Axis' in the *International Military Tribunal*, which passed sentence on 30 September and 1 October 1946. The Nuremberg trials took place on the basis of the *Treaty of London* of 8 August 1945, in which the four major powers had established the charter for the trials. There were charges of crimes against peace, war crimes and crimes against humanity, the last intended to punish those responsible for the persecution and extermination of the Jews. Both individual leaders and organizations set up by the national socialists were put on trial in Nuremberg. Sentences included the death penalty, life imprisonment and other terms of imprisonment, and the banning of certain organizations as illegal. The Tokyo trials lasted from May 1946 to November 1948 and were concerned with Japan's activities from the signing of the Kellogg–Briand Pact in 1928 (see §16.2) until its capitulation in 1945. The *International Military Tribunal for the Far East* was conducted based on a charter drawn up by General Douglas MacArthur, which was almost identical to that of Nuremberg. There were eleven judges, one from each of the victorious states, including the two newly-decolonized states India and the Philippines. Seven death sentences and 16 life sentences were passed, with an Indian and a Dutch judge expressing a dissenting opinion.

The Genocide Convention (1948)

Although both war tribunals worked closely with the UN War Crimes Commission, the trials in Nuremberg and Tokyo were primarily military proceedings. In 1946 the UN General Assembly confirmed the international law principles of the Nuremberg Tribunal and declared genocide to be a crime under international law. The term 'genocide' had been coined by Raphael Lemkin, who was born in East Poland and had fled to the US during the war, where he started lobbying for a law that would make it a punishable offence. He went to Nuremberg and to the UN in New York to attempt to have his concept of genocide incorporated into international law. His perseverance was rewarded in December 1948 when the UN adopted the *Convention on the Prevention and Punishment of the Crime of Genocide*, known as the Genocide Convention. The term would however only enter into common usage in the 1990s, in relation to the wars in the former Yugoslavia and in Rwanda and the establishment of war tribunals and the International Criminal Court. In 2004 the UN secretary-general appointed a Special Representative for the Prevention of Genocide. Until that time the International Court of Justice had not used the Genocide Convention, but in 2007 it identified a violation of it (see §38.3).

The strong and weak points of the Court

Among the strong points of the International Court of Justice are that it preserved the tradition of arbitration in international disputes and has contributed to the further systematization, consolidation, codification and development of international law. It has clarified the rules of the law and added important principles, including the legal personality and powers of international organizations on the basis of what is implicitly laid down in their constitution (the *implied powers* from the *Reparations for Injuries* case of 1949). *Jus cogens* or the principle of peremptory norms falls into this category. Whereas states were initially only considered bound by international norms to which they had agreed, it became accepted that some are so important to the international community that they apply to all states, whether they have agreed to them or not. For instance the abolition of racial discrimination also applied to South Africa. This principle was addressed in 1970 in the *Barcelona Traction* case. One of the weaker points of the International Court is that some judges tend to take too much account of political reality, as shown by the fact that in some cases judges have been known to adopt different opinions at the Court and in their own state. Moreover, the number of cases brought before the Court has been consistently low. Between 1946 and 2000 it dealt with around 80 cases and provided advice on just over 20 occasions. A quarter of the cases were dismissed, withdrawn or not pursued because the Court did not feel competent to hear them. As far as peace and security is concerned, the Court has been of limited significance. 'It has, for the most part, not been a central player, and has served mainly by rendering technical opinions and decisions on those matters that governments were prepared to submit to it' (Ramcharan 2000, 178). Another weak point was that in the 1960s and 1970s the Court did not take a firm stand on apartheid against South Africa (see §28.1). It was, however, more resolute in the case against the US for supporting the Contra rebel movement and mining ports in Nicaragua. The Court ruled against the US for these activities in 1986, with the result that the US withdrew its acceptance of the compulsory jurisdiction of the Court (see §34.1). The Court also took a firm stand in 1996 with its ruling on the legality of using or threatening to use nuclear weapons (see §38.2). In the field of human rights the Court has played no role, as East–West relations made this impossible for the two 1966 Human Rights Covenants.

The International Law Commission (1947) and the codification of international law

The commission of experts set up by the League of Nations in 1924 to codify international law took its task seriously, but was unable to make much headway at the codification conference in The Hague in 1930, which addressed issues such as nationality, territorial waters and state responsibility. It only made real progress on drawing up a convention on nationality (see Figure 18.2). The UN later took over the codification process from the League. Article 13.1.a of the UN Charter speaks of 'encouraging the progressive development of international law and its codification'. The General Assembly, which can commission studies and ask for recommendations, set up the *International Law Commission* (ILC) in 1947. The members (first 15 and since 2001 34) are nominated in the same way as for the International Court and are chosen for five years. Although they sit on the Commission as individuals and not as representatives of their government, the General Assembly decided in 1981 that they would be selected according to the UN group system, with nine members from Africa, eight from Asia, eight from Western Europe and other states, six from Latin America and three from Eastern Europe. The ILC usually meets in Geneva and discusses issues submitted by the General Assembly, the Sixth (legal) Committee and other UN bodies. Once the ILC has drawn up draft articles for a convention the General Assembly can convene a multilateral conference, which then incorporates the articles into an international convention and invites member states to sign it. Several of these conferences have taken place in Vienna. In this way some 20 conventions have been drawn up, including four on the law of the seas (1958), the *Vienna Convention on Diplomatic Relations* (1961), the *Vienna Convention on the Law of Treaties* (1969) and the *Vienna Convention on the Law of Treaties Between States and International Organizations or Between International Organizations* (1986). In 1992 the ILC was commissioned to produce a draft for the Statute of the International Criminal Court, which was adopted in Rome in 1998 (see §38.3). One common complaint about the ILC is that it works too slowly. An example is the *Draft Articles on State Responsibility for Internationally Wrongful Acts*, which the Commission did not complete until 1996. The ILC selected the topic in 1949, but it took over 40 years to reach agreement over the Draft Articles, which are the result of both codification and the progressive development of the idea of state responsibility. The UN General Assembly made its own contribution to the codification of international law, by adopting declarations that were later elaborated into international conventions. 'A large number of multilateral treaties have thus grown out of declarations adopted by the General Assembly: the 1967 Outer Space Treaty, the 1968 Treaty on the Nonproliferation of Nuclear Weapons, the 1971 Seabed Arms Control Treaty.' The list also includes the two 1966 Human Rights Covenants. Through this legislative work the General Assembly emphasized the importance of certain concepts or introduced new ones. 'By introducing new concepts, such as the common heritage of mankind, the right of future generations, and sustainable development, and by legitimating certain principles, such as non-aggression and non-discrimination, it built a sort of common system of reference that can influence states' practices and lead to the emergence of new principles in international law' (Smouts 2000, 51).

The development of international law

International public law now focuses on four main areas: preserving peace and security, the economic expansion of states, the environment and commons (the oceans, the North and South Pole and space), and individual rights (human rights). In the case of preserving peace a distinction can be made between the *law of peace*, which includes the regulation of diplomacy, the law of treaties, arbitration, the law of international organizations and state responsibility, and the *law of war*, which regulates the conditions under which war can be declared and the legitimacy of means that are deployed to wage war (respectively *jus ad bellum* and *jus in bello*). The economic expansion of states includes issues such as improving international communications and the regulation of markets, trade and investment.

The UN Conference on the Law of the Sea 1958–82

The freedom of the seas (see §10.2) underwent a number of changes in the 1950s. After the US had proclaimed in 1945 that all natural resources on or below the seabed up to 200 nautical miles from its coasts fell under its jurisdiction, other states followed its example. The unclear situation created by this proclamation, the Cold War rivalry and a dawning awareness of marine pollution and the threat it posed to fish species led in 1958 to the *UN Conference on the Law of the Sea* (UNCLOS) in Geneva. The 86 states present agreed on four conventions on the law of the seas, which incorporated the traditional law of the seas as well as the then current insights. These conventions came into force in 1962 and 1966, but were still somewhat ambiguous about the distinction between land and seabed. The notion of developing a new, all-encompassing regime came after the second UNCLOS conference in 1960 failed due to the inability to reach agreement. UNCLOS III, the largest international conference ever held up to that time, was more successful. It lasted from 1974 to 1982 and was attended by more than 150 states, which in 1982 in Montego Bay, Jamaica, agreed on the *UN Convention on the Law of the Sea* (also UNCLOS). This Convention, which came into effect in 1994, introduced a territorial zone of a maximum of 12 nautical miles (incorporating the principles of sovereignty and innocent passage) and an exclusive economic zone of 200 nautical miles. States had sole rights to exploit natural resources in these economic zones, but otherwise the freedom of the open sea prevailed. UNCLOS III led to the establishment of three international institutions, the *International Seabed Authority* (1994) in Kingston, Jamaica, the *International Tribunal for the Law of the Sea* (1996) with 21 judges who meet in Hamburg in Germany and the *Commission on the Limits of the Continental Shelf* (1997), with 21 members who meet at the UN in New York. This effectively introduced a comprehensive new regime for the law of the seas.

ICSID (1965) and UNCITRAL (1966)

Within the framework of the International Bank for Reconstruction and Development the *International Centre for Settlement of Investment Disputes* (ICSID) was set up in 1965 to institutionalize the settlement of disputes over investments. ICSID provides an arbitration service similar to that of the Permanent Court of Arbitration, but between states and private investors (usually businesses, but sometimes also individuals). If a dispute is declared admissible, the parties can set up a conciliation commission or an arbitral tribunal. The commission mediates, while the tribunal issues a ruling. Arbitration of business disputes can also be conducted on a private basis, for example by the International Court of Arbitration of the International Chamber of Commerce, established in 1923 (see Figure 12.2), and the International Council for Commercial Arbitration, set up in 1961. In December 1966 the UN General Assembly created the *UN Commission on International Trade Law* (UNCITRAL), with the aim of promoting the gradual harmonization and unification of international trade law. UNCITRAL has 36 members and has continued the work previously undertaken by the League of Nations, such as drafting treaties in the areas of international sale of goods, payments, trade arbitration and shipping legislation.

Crime prevention and criminal justice

The UN was also charged with responsibilities in the fields of crime prevention and criminal justice. In 1950 the General Assembly authorized the convening once every five years of a UN conference on crime prevention and how to deal with offenders. The first conference took place in Geneva in 1955 and after that it was held at a different venue each time. The conferences are attended by criminologists, penologists, senior police officials and experts in criminal law, human rights and rehabilitation, supported by various regional research and training centres. At the conferences minimum rules are drawn up for specific problems. In 1992 ECOSOC emphasized the importance of this work by setting up a functional *Commission on Crime Prevention and Criminal Justice*, which has 40 members and meets annually in Vienna. It was the initiator of a global conference on transnational organized crime in 1994. At its conference in The Hague in 2001 the *Convention against Corruption* was prepared, which was agreed in Merida, Mexico, in 2003 and came into force in 2005 (see §41.6). *Transparency International* puts this Commission under pressure, claiming that the Convention is inadequate if there are not also national anti-corruption programmes (Wang and Rosenau 2001).

International courts and tribunals

The number of international courts and tribunals increased over the course of time. Up to 2001, 132 had been set up, 90 of which were in existence or in development. Of the 42 that

Figure 21.1 Numbers of international courts and tribunals up to 2001

Type of international court or tribunal	Existing	Nascent	Proposed	Aborted	Dormant	Extinct
International judicial bodies						
General jurisdiction	1					1
Law of the sea	1					
Environment			1			
International criminal law/humanitarian law	2	1		1		3
Human rights	2	1	1			
Trade, commerce and investments	1		1			
Regional economic and political integration oagreements	9	1	4		9	3
Quasi-judicial, implementation control and other dispute settlement bodies						
Human rights and humanitarian law bodies	19					1
International administrative tribunals	15					3
Inspection panels	3					
Non-compliance/ implementation monitoring bodies (environmental agreements)	3	8				
International claims and compensation bodies – bilateral and multilateral	7					8
Permanent arbitral tribunals/conciliation commissions	12				4	1
Internationalized criminal courts and tribunals	2	2	1			
Total: 132	*77*	*13*	*8*	*1*	*13*	*20*

Source: www.pict-pcti.org, version 2, August 2001; statistics from Cesare Romano's Project on International Courts and Tribunals presented in table form.

are not functional, eight are proposed, one did not materialize, 13 are dormant and 20 have been wound up (see Figure 21.1). The top three categories of the 77 existing courts and tribunals address regional cooperation (26), human rights (19) and administrative law (15). Figure 21.2 shows courts and tribunals at global (13) and regional level (24).

21.2 Specialized international organizations as part of the UN system

Specialized UN agencies
In addition to the six principal organs and many bodies and institutions that have emerged within them, there is a group of more than 20 'specialized UN agencies' and 'organizations related to the UN' (see Figure 21.3, which lists them in the order in

Figure 21.2 Global and regional courts and tribunals

Global

1899	Permanent Court of Arbitration
1922–46	Permanent Court of International Justice
1923	International Court of Arbitration of the International Chamber of Commerce (NGO)
1946	International Court of Justice
1948	GATT Dispute Settlement Body
1961	International Council for Commercial Arbitration (NGO)
1966	ICSID International Centre for Settlement of Investment Disputes
1981	Iran-US Claims Tribunal
1993	International Criminal Tribunal for the former Yugoslavia
1994	International Criminal Tribunal for Rwanda
1995	WTO Dispute Settlement Body
1996	International Tribunal for the Law of the Sea
2002	International Criminal Court

Regional

1907–17	Central American Court of Justice
1951	European Court of Justice
1953	European Court of Human Rights
1960	Arbitration Tribunal of the Central American Common Market (*ad hoc*)
1964	Settlement of Investment Disputes Council of the Arab Economic Union
1967	Eastern Caribbean Supreme Court of the Organization of Eastern Caribbean States
1976	High Council of the Association of South East Asian Nations (*ad hoc*)
1979	Inter-American Court of Human Rights
1981	Commission for the Settlement of Disputes of the Gulf Cooperation Council (*ad hoc*)
1983	Court of Justice of the Economic Community of Central African States
1984	Court of Justice of the Andean Community of Nations
1989	Court of First Instance of the European Court of Justice
1989	Court of Justice of the Arab Maghreb Union
1991	Brasilia Protocol Appendix III MERCOSUR arrangement
1991	Court of Justice of the Central American Integration System
1994	Dispute Settlement Procedure of the North American Free Trade Agreement
1994	Court of Justice of the Economic and Monetary Community of Central Africa
1994	Court of Justice of the West African Economic and Monetary Union
1998	Court of Justice of the Common Market for Eastern and Southern Africa; replaced the *ad hoc* arrangement of its predecessor Preferential Trade Arrangement
1999	Court of Justice of the East African Community

1999 Court of Justice of the Economic Community of West African States; replaced the older Tribunal
2000 Tribunal of the Southern African Development Community
2001 Caribbean Court of Justice of the Caribbean Community and Common Market; replaced the British Privy Council
Planned Court of Justice of the Eurasian Economic Community

which they became related to the UN). Article 57 of the Charter refers to the conditions under which international organizations can be brought into relationship with the UN and can act as specialized UN agencies. These organizations need to be 'established by intergovernmental agreement and having wide international responsibilities, as defined in their basic instruments, in economic, social, cultural, educational, health, and related fields'. The specialized agencies are autonomous organizations, in principle globally-oriented and with their own budget. Some place a heavy emphasis on service provision, such as supplying financial resources and delivering development or humanitarian aid to children or dependent persons. Others are standard-setting organizations, some in what are called 'technical' or 'functional' fields such as postal or air traffic. However technical these activities may be, they always have political implications, as governments decide on the rules of the regime under which they operate. The relationship of a specialized agency with the UN is established through an agreement between the two organizations. Because the specialized agencies retain their autonomy, the required coordination through the Economic and Social Council is far from easy. However, the agencies need each other because of the complementary nature of their activities and in principle they enjoy mutual observer status (see §21.5). In addition ECOSOC has developed ways of bringing the agencies together (see §20.5). As a minimum intergovernmental organizations know what is on each other's agenda and what happens during negotiations. Coordination and observer status do not, however, mean that there are no turf wars or that competition between agencies does not exist. The fact that NGOs can exert influence within both the UN and the specialized agencies can also lead to tensions, because NGOs working with the latter (which do not always have consultative status) often have more specific expertise than the more general NGOs at the UN. The *specialized agencies* refer to themselves as 'agencies' since it is thus laid down in their agreement with the UN. *Organizations 'related to the UN'* have a weaker form of association, as they come under the auspices of the UN but report only to the General Assembly. There are also differences in autonomy between the specialized agencies. The WTO and the Bretton Woods institutions have significantly more autonomy than UNESCO or the FAO, or the programmes and funds (see Figure 20.3) that have reached a status similar to that of the specialized agencies. A small number of specialized agencies originated as public international unions.

The functionalist thesis

The main functions of the specialized agencies within the UN are to gather and exchange information in their own specific areas of concern (the *clearing house* function), promote international standards in international agreements and provide technical

Figure 21.3 Specialized UN agencies and organizations related to the UN

Specialized UN agencies

ILO   **International Labour Organization**, Geneva, established in 1919, a specialized UN agency since 30 May 1946

FAO   **Food and Agriculture Organization** of the United Nations, Rome, the first specialized UN agency to be set up after the Second World War on 16 October 1945 in Quebec

World Bank Group:

IBRD   **International Bank for Reconstruction and Development** (also World Bank), Washington DC, established on 27 December 1945

IFC   **International Finance Corporation**, Washington DC, established on 25 May 1955. After being approved by ECOSOC on 19 December 1956 and the General Assembly on 20 February 1957, the IFC became a specialized UN agency on the latter date

IDA   **International Development Association**, Washington DC, established on 26 January 1960 and in operation since 24 September 1960

ICSID   **International Centre for Settlement of Investment Disputes**, Washington DC, established on 18 March 1965 and in operation since 14 October 1966

MIGA   **Multilateral Investment Guarantee Agency**, Washington DC, established on 11 October 1985 and in operation since 12 April 1988

IMF   **International Monetary Fund**, Washington DC, established on 27 December 1945

UNESCO   **United Nations Educational, Scientific and Cultural Organization**, Paris, established on 4 November 1946 and in operation since that date

ICAO   **International Civil Aviation Organization**, Montreal, established on 7 December 1944 and in full operation since 4 April 1947 as a specialized UN agency

ITU   **International Telecommunication Union**, Geneva, established as a public international union in 1865, becoming a specialized UN agency on 15 November 1947

WHO   **World Health Organization**, Geneva, established on 22 July 1946 and in operation as a specialized agency UN since 7 April 1948

UPU   **Universal Postal Union**, Bern, established as a public international union in 1875, became a specialized UN agency on 1 July 1948

WMO   **World Meteorological Organization**, Geneva, established in 1891 as the International Meteorological Organization, an NGO which acquired an increasingly intergovernmental character. On 11 October 1947 it was transformed into the intergovernmental WMO, which went into operation on 23 March 1950 and became a specialized UN agency on 20 December 1951

IMO   **International Maritime Organization**, London, established as a specialized agency on 17 March 1958 as the Intergovernmental Maritime Consultative Organization (IMCO) and called IMO since 22 May 1982

WIPO **World Intellectual Property Organization**, Geneva, established as public international unions for the protection of intellectual property (Paris Union, 1883) and copyright (Bern Union, 1886). WIPO was established on 14 July 1967, went into operation on 26 April 1970 and has been a specialized UN agency since 17 December 1974

IFAD **International Fund for Agricultural Development**, Rome, established in November 1974 by the UN World Food Conference, went into operation as a specialized UN agency on 30 November 1977

UNIDO **United Nations Industrial Development Organization**, Vienna, established on 17 November 1966, in operation as an autonomous organization within the UN Secretariat since 1 January 1967 and as a specialized UN agency since 1 January 1986

UNWTO **World Tourism Organization**, Madrid, established in 1925 as an NGO and as an IGO on 27 September 1970. In 1969 the UN General Assembly decided to enter into an agreement with the World Tourism Organization and in 1977 a cooperation agreement and a relationship with the UN were concluded. The UNWTO operates as an implementing agency of UNDP and has been a specialized UN agency since October 2003

Organizations related to the UN

IAEA **International Atomic Energy Agency**, Vienna, established on 26 October 1956, in operation since 29 July 1957. On 14 November 1957 the General Assembly approved the relationship with the UN. The IAEA was established under the protection of the UN and reports annually to the General Assembly. If necessary it also reports to the Security Council and ECOSOC

WTO **World Trade Organization**, Geneva, established on 15 April 1994 and in operation since 1 January 1995 as a continuation of the General Agreement on Tariffs and Trade (GATT). In 1994 the two organizations did not reach consensus on integrating the WTO as a specialized UN agency. The UN regards the WTO as an organization related to the UN

CTBTO **Comprehensive Nuclear-Test-Ban Treaty Organization**, Vienna. The
PrepCom UN General Assembly approved the Comprehensive Nuclear-Test-Ban Treaty on 10 September 1996. It was opened for signature on 24 September, when the number of required signatures was obtained, and on 19 November 1996 the Preparatory Commission was established. There are still insufficient ratifications for the Treaty, and therefore the organization, to become operational. The Preparatory Commission reports to the General Assembly

OPCW **Organization for the Prohibition of Chemical Weapons**, The Hague, established on 13 January 1993. It became operational on 29 April 1997 and reports to the General Assembly

assistance in their specialist fields to states in need of it (Williams 1990, 1). The guiding principle is the so-called *functionalist thesis* that the economic and social activities of the UN and its specialized agencies contribute to a more stable world and thereby promote the probability of peace and security (see §20.1). Keynesian ideas are clearly recognizable in the stimulating and, where necessary, correcting role of government in the economic conjuncture. These ideas, expounded by Keynes in his publications and through his role at Bretton Woods, were also popular among the postwar economists involved in the UN, including Keynes's US disciple John Kenneth Galbraith. Keynesianism was expressed in its purest form in the aid provided to developing states, to which nearly all the specialized agencies have made a contribution.

Technology as a normative force

Xiaowei Luo, who studied the emergence of IGOs and NGOs between 1856 and 1993, identifies a shift in attitudes to technology transfer in these organizations, distinguishing three models: the industrial, professional and social development models. The industrial model focuses on international activities aimed at promoting the interests of specific industries, while the professional model does the same for particular professional groups. These first two models were applied in the nineteenth and the first half of the twentieth century, respectively, while the social development model increasingly dominated in the period after 1945. It focused on the social effects of technology, strengthening social welfare and using technology to promote industrial, social and economic development. In the postwar development regime technology was considered a new norm. 'This new norm held that technology should be regarded as a means toward broad social development goals to enhance equity as well as efficiency in the global society.' It dominated in most of the specialized agencies. 'Granted that various state and nonstate actors have played a role in developing the new norms, I emphasize that once these norms came into being, they have gained a life of their own and powerfully shaped the orientations of [the international organizations] above and beyond the direct influence from the actors within the organizations' (Luo 2000, 149). The activities of the specialized agencies are much more similar in terms of their expected impacts than the often almost impossible to unravel multitude of organizations would suggest. They all share the expectation that developing states will develop once they share the same attitudes to technology as the specialized agencies themselves.

21.3 The International Labour Organization and the transition to technical assistance

'Limited monarchy' and a change of activities

The way in which the ILO is governed has been described as a 'limited monarchy'. From the start the organization had a political system structured around a single central figure (see §17.2). The leading role of the director-general was however subject to limitations from both inside and outside the organization. The main political tensions in the postwar period were caused by the confrontation between East and West. At the end of the 1950s strains also emerged between North and South, as developing states resisted apartheid and persistent colonialism. In this context the American David Morse, who became ILO director-general in 1948, pursued a policy that placed less emphasis on international standard setting through conventions and recommendations and focused more on technical assistance. Whereas in 1950 the ILO had devoted around 80 per cent of its expenditure to establishing norms and 20 per cent to technical assistance, by 1958 these percentages had changed to 44 and 56 per cent, respectively, and even further, to 16 and 84 per cent, in 1967 (Cox 1973, 105). Although the director-general remained the principal architect of the organization's policy, he had to take account of external factors such as the political situation in the US. In the 1950s the US Congress put a limit on its contribution to the ILO, partly because it opposed the membership of the Soviet Union, and this restricted the organization's financial options. The director-general also had to consider internal relations. While part of the ILO's staff continued to work according to the traditional ideology and strategy of establishing international standards, a new and increasingly large younger team with an economic background focused on development aid. That these two groups did not compete with each other but only represented different tendencies within a stable organization was due to the coherent view of the ILO, which continued to see itself primarily as a promoter of international regulations, with supporting tasks. The underlying assumption was that the future world order would be grounded in common legal principles that applied equally to all peoples and cultures. The law was seen as 'a kind of immanent force progressively realized through history'. According to Wilfred Jenks, the British director-general who succeeded Morse in 1970, this left no room for any political ideology whatsoever. The notion that it was the ILO's task to administer that branch of international law that regulated working conditions raised the organization above all ideology and made it the protector of human rights in its area of concern (Cox 1973, 121–22). The ILO displayed a remarkable stability and 'developed a political system capable at best of taking advantage of the opportunities presented by the condition of world politics and at worst of assuring its own survival' (Cox 1973, 136).

Prewar technical assistance

Although the 1919 Treaty of Versailles contained few specific provisions to this effect, the ILO took its task, in addition to drafting conventions and recommendations, of actively gathering and disseminating information seriously. To stay well informed and to promote ratification of its conventions ILO personnel made frequent visits to its member states, maintained contact with government bodies, employers' organizations, trade unions and NGOs and attended important conferences. In the 1930s the ILO developed new activities, in order to increase its understanding of the economic crisis, which had affected it in the sense that fewer conventions were agreed and ratified. The organization posted staff members to member states to help them solve their economic and social problems by providing practical assistance, strengthening ministries of labour, labour inspection systems, labour legislation and social security and employment creation projects. The ILO even helped formulate social policy within the context of the New Deal in the US (Ghebali 1989, 13–14). During the Second World War, when it was located in Canada, the ILO gave support for the development of social security systems in Latin America. Immediately after the war it continued these 'operational activities' in various other states. In 1948 the organization contributed to reconstruction in Europe by setting up a manpower programme to help establish labour exchanges, professional training and migration schemes. These manpower projects were later extended to Asia, Latin America and the Middle East.

Postwar technical assistance

Until 1950 the ILO paid for this 'technical assistance', as it was called after the war, out of its own budget. Although it would continue to contribute, with a percentage varying from 4 to 12 per cent of its total budget (not including administrative costs), after 1950 most of the funds for this assistance came from external sources. In 1950 the ILO decided to take part in the UN's *Expanded Programme of Technical Assistance* (EPTA), which aimed to strengthen the economies of 'less developed' states to promote their economic and political independence. In 1960 the ILO also participated in the *Special UN Fund for Economic Development* (SUNFED), which was concerned with large-scale projects. In the 1960s a new form of financing emerged, known as multi-bilateral funding, which entailed a number of donor states entrusting the responsibility for implementing their bilateral development programmes to UN agencies. This was done because the regional activities of the specialized agencies offered more chance of success than if the states provided the aid directly. In addition, aid provided by the ILO benefited organizations of workers and employers, which governments expected would pursue responsible policies. Between 1950 and 1965 the ILO spent a total of 73.7 million dollars on technical assistance, 6.1 million of which came from its own budget, 43 million from EPTA, 21.5 million from SUNFED and 3.1 million from funds entrusted to the ILO by other IGOs. Most assistance was given to Africa, followed by Asia, Latin America and the Middle East, with least going to Europe. Technical assistance included experts, equipment for training and administration and study grants for tailor-made training courses. For the training courses the ILO set up the *International Institute for Labour Studies* in Geneva in 1960 and the *International Centre for Advanced Technical and Vocational Training* in Turin in 1965, to provide education and conduct research into social and labour policy. Morse's intensification of technical assistance was later counterbalanced by Francis Blanchard, director-general from 1974 to 1989, who once again laid emphasis on setting international standards (Ghebali 1989, 161).

Expansion of the Keynesian welfare state

With its combination of establishing international standards and providing technical assistance, the ILO helped expand the strongly Keynesian postwar welfare state. It promoted the active involvement of employers' organizations and trade unions (the 'social partners') and their contacts with governments, as well as the further development of labour ministries and social security systems. After 1945 many states had a high degree of government intervention in social life in common. Governments concerned themselves with the distribution of income, combating social inequalities and promoting employment and social security for those who could not care for themselves. In its increased contact with trade unions and employers' organizations government became a third party in the social sphere by providing the required general legal framework and establishing national institutions and provisions. Government's role also increased in areas such as industrialization, increasing productivity, promoting trade and the provision of credit and gradually it became a large-scale employer in both the public and private sectors itself. There were also differences between states, such as between liberal democracies, communist states (where the trade union movement's role was to promote production and social welfare) and developing states, where industrialization often still had to take place and the social partners had not yet formed distinct groups. Major differences in labour relations also existed within these groups of states, for example between the Anglo-Saxon world, Scandinavia, Germany (with its 'Rhineland' model) and the South European states. As a universal organization providing regulations that covered the entire field of labour (see Figure 17.2), the ILO encouraged the spread of common characteristics for modern relations between government and citizens in both the industrialized and the developing world. A study of the relationship between the ratification of ILO conventions and spending by the population in the period from 1960 to 1980 shows a clear link in industrialized capitalist states. 'Each ratified convention produces an estimated increase in spending of about 0.8 of national income' (Strang and Chang 1993, 250). In states with strong social security systems, such as the Scandinavian states and the Netherlands, spending increased rapidly, while in states such as France, Italy, Ireland and Japan growth was slower. Some less developed states such as Costa Rica, Cyprus and Malta also showed considerable growth, but in others it was more limited. Nevertheless, in these states too there was a clear link between ratified ILO conventions and national spending (Strang and Chang 1993, 249).

21.4 Freedom of association as a normative force in the East–West conflict

Freedom of association

The Soviet Union had a low opinion of the ILO, of which it had not been a member since being expelled from the League of Nations in 1939. It was largely because of the resistance of the Soviet Union during the negotiations that the organization did not become a specialized UN agency until May 1946. During the discussion in the UN on human rights the Soviet Union felt that freedom of association and violations of that right should come under the remit of ECOSOC rather than the ILO. The *World Federation of Trade Unions* (WFTU), established at the end of the war through the merger of the International Federation of Trade Unions and the international communist trade union movement (see §17.4), expected that the old relations would no longer prevail after the war. This unity movement supported the Soviet Union in its opposition to the ILO and became an important factor in the emerging Cold War, as a majority within the WFTU endorsed the foreign policy of the Soviet Union. In 1947 the WFTU was given consultative status at the UN and it proposed setting up a commission within ECOSOC to investigate violations of trade union rights. The WFTU considered the ILO insufficiently representative because the Soviet Union and other states were not members and it also objected to the tripartite structure of the ILO which gave employers' and workers' rights equal status. The US trade union movement, in turn, also appealed to the UN, but in this case to the Commission on Human Rights, and submitted that the ILO should investigate trade union rights violations. On the basis of Article III of the Agreement between the ILO and the UN, ECOSOC ruled that the ILO was the appropriate agency. The ILO then placed freedom of association on the agenda of its International Labour Conference, which resulted in two important conventions establishing fundamental rights: Convention 87 (1948) on the *Freedom of Association and Protection of the Right to Organize* and Convention 98 (1949) on the *Right to Organize and Collective Bargaining* in the private sector (see Figure 21.4). In consultation with the UN, two special bodies were set up to monitor trade union freedoms in practice.

341

Figure 21.4 Important ILO conventions (with fundamental rights in bold)

Number	Year	Subject
1	1919	Limiting the Hours of Work in Industrial Undertakings to Eight in the Day and Forty-Eight in the Week
3	1919	Maternity Protection
47	1935	Forty-Hour Week
52	1936	Holidays with Pay
81	1947	Labour Inspection
87	**1948**	**Freedom of Association and Protection of the Right to Organize**
89	1948	Night Work (Women) (revised)
98	**1949**	**Right to Organize and Collective Bargaining**
100	**1951**	**Equal Remuneration**
102	1952	Social Security (Minimum Standards)
105	**1957**	**Abolition of Forced Labour**
111	**1958**	**Discrimination (Employment and Occupation)**
117	1962	Social Policy (Basic Aims and Standards)
118	1962	Equality of Treatment (Social Security)
121	1967	Employment Injury Benefits
122	1964	Employment Policy
131	1970	Minimum Wage Fixing
135	**1971**	**Workers' Representatives**
138	1973	Minimum Age
140	1974	Paid Educational Leave
151	**1978**	**Labour Relations (Public Service)**
155	1981	Occupational Safety and Health
156	**1981**	**Workers with Family Responsibilities**
161	1985	Occupational Health Services
170	1990	Chemicals
175	1994	Part-Time Work
177	1996	Home Work
182	**1999**	**Worst Forms of Child Labour**

The ILO Committee on Freedom of Association (1951)

In the discussion on violations of trade union rights the WFTU limited itself to the non-communist world, while the US trade union movement drew attention to Eastern Europe as well. The ILO decided to consult the UN on the creation of a monitoring mechanism for freedom of association, as a number of states were not members of either the ILO or the UN. Secretary-general Trygve Lie however felt that the ILO should be responsible for this monitoring and proposed that it should set up a committee which would first investigate the situation and then make a recommendation. Governments were now faced with the choice of cooperating on this issue with the ILO, and thereby in effect permitting it to intervene in their domestic affairs, or allowing violations to be dealt with by ECOSOC, where NGOs such as the WFTU could influence the matter in public. After some hesitation most of them supported the first option. In August 1949, despite last-minute attempts by the Soviet Union to make ECOSOC the responsible agency, a US–UK proposal to set up the committee within the ILO and to give it a broad mandate was approved. This gave the ILO the authority to investigate complaints from a member state about another member state, or from an industrial organization against a member state, even if the accused state had not ratified the ILO Convention on the Freedom of Association. In 1950–51 the ILO established two bodies to perform this monitoring. The first was a *Commission* to investigate the facts and try to find a solution: 'trying to conciliate, but not arbitrate or judge'. The other was a tripartite *Committee* of nine members, which would conduct a preliminary study on behalf of the Board of Governors to determine whether the complaint should be considered by the Board. The Committee also had to consult with governments to establish whether they consented to violations being submitted to the fact-finding Commission, or wished to seek a solution without the case being investigated by the Commission (Alcock 1971, 267). The real problem for the ILO was what would happen if a government refused to cooperate in an investigation. An example presented itself immediately, when the government of Peru denied that the murder of the secretary of the national trade union federation had anything to do with freedom of association. This confirmed the need for the ILO to consult governments through the Committee but, if they refused to cooperate, to pursue its investigations regardless. In practice the two ILO bodies operated in a different way to what had been intended. The *Fact-Finding and Conciliation Commission* did not become operational until 1964, after a complaint against the Japanese government from Japanese trade unions. The *Committee on Freedom of Association* emerged as the more important of the two. What happened was that the Committee did not restrict itself to determining whether a complaint was admissible, but conducted systematic investigations about the complaint among the parties involved. It then submitted detailed conclusions to the ILO's Board of Governors with recommendations on how to approach the government concerned. Often the submission of the Committee's report was enough in itself to make the case admissible and the relevant government would agree to respond to the recommendations within a reasonable period of time. 'The preliminary examination of the worthiness of a complaint became, in reality, a full investigation of the facts and, where warranted, an effort at ILO conciliation and pressure' (Alcock 1971, 268). The Committee's authority was enhanced by the fact that its recommendations were usually unanimous and generally transcended the level of individual cases, achieving a normative effect (Ghebali 1989, 238). The Fact-Finding Commission, which was initially intended to be the more important of the two bodies, was only involved in the event of 'serious' cases, such as in Greece in 1965, Lesotho and Chile in 1973 and the US in 1978. That the Commission was used in so few cases was because states that had not ratified Convention 87 on the Freedom of Association had to approve its involvement. This did not happen and it also explains why complaints against East European states were not addressed, because they appealed to the formal provisions and thus rejected the practice.

Strengthening the ILO position

The debate on trade union rights within the UN had significant consequences, as the ILO, whose authority had been challenged by the Soviet Union, emerged as the winner, with a far-reaching mechanism for monitoring the principle of freedom of association. It also showed that there were two tendencies in the WFTU that were difficult to unite, which led to a split in 1949. The WFTU became the international trade union of the communist states and a number of large unions in France and Italy, while the breakaway West-oriented unions founded the *International Confederation of Free Trade Unions* (ICFTU), with 'free' deliberately included in the name. As a consequence of the split the WFTU's ambition of taking the trade unions' seat within the ILO failed, as this went to the ICFTU, which became the main representation of the international trade union movement within the ILO. A third branch of the movement was the smaller *International Federation of Christian Trade Unions*, which was renamed the World Confederation of Labour in 1968 and merged with the ICFTU in 2006 to form the International Trade Union Confederation. Another consequence of the political developments was that trade union freedom became a factor in the Cold War, with the ICFTU and Western states emphasizing the freedom of trade unions as a feature of democracy and using it as an example in the ideological debate between East and West. This gave the relevant ILO conventions added weight and also strengthened the ILO's universalism.

Tripartism or universality? The declaration of the Pope (1954)

The 'tripartism' of governments, employers and workers, established in 1919, was discussed in 1945 when the ILO was adapting for a new era, but this remained without result. It did, however, come under pressure with the accession of new member states where freedom of association was more symbolic than real. Increased state intervention in economic processes also made the concept of 'employer' less clear. In the early 1950s tripartism again became an issue, in the debate on whether communist states should be permitted to join the ILO. In particular employers had a problem with it, as they could not find comparable partners in the communist world. They therefore opposed the admission of these states to the organization, unless they first fulfilled the requirement of permitting free organizations of employers and of workers which were independent of government. Internally the ILO succeeded in keeping the various groups together by setting up two commissions, which produced practical solutions and saw tripartism as a function: 'its real purpose was not merely the representation of governments, employers and workers as such, but of their *functions*, consisting of control, management and execution' (Ghebali 1989, 129). In 1954, although there were no official ties between the ILO and the Vatican, the Pope intervened in the debate on membership with his declaration in favour of universality, which director-general Morse was delighted to make use of (Cox 1973, 117–19). In the same year the Soviet Union rejoined the ILO, together with Belarus and the Ukraine, followed in 1956 by Romania. Other communist states which were members but had not paid their contributions now did so. Employers found it difficult at first to adjust to this new situation, but during the 1960s an acceptable modus operandi was found.

21.5 The observer status of intergovernmental organizations at the UN

The origins of the observer status

The fact that the UN General Assembly accords IGOs observer status is not based on the UN Charter. Article 35 does refer to the possibility of non-member states bringing an issue before the UN, but does not specifically mention observer status. Under this article a state that is not a member of the UN can bring a dispute in which it is involved to the attention of the Security Council or the General Assembly. Observer status at the UN, however, resulted from the actions of the secretary-general and the General Assembly. The secretary-general has the authority to decide on whether to allow non-member states to observe and, on the basis of Article 35, has done so on occasion at the request of the General Assembly. In that way three categories of permanent observer status were created: non-member states (so far accorded to two states: Switzerland, which held this status from 1948 to 2002, and the Holy See; Taiwan does not have observer status), national liberation movements (accorded to the PLO in 1974 and in 1988 the UN General Assembly decided to use the designation Palestine in place of the designation PLO in the UN system) and IGOs. In 2008, 63 international organizations, 41 of which were regional, held observer status.

Observer status for regional organizations

Regional organizations are mentioned in Chapter VIII of the Charter, which recognizes the right of states to establish regional arrangements in the interests of maintaining peace and security. Article 52.1 offers the possibility of working together with the UN 'provided that such arrangements or agencies and their activities are consistent with the Purposes and Principles of the United Nations'. This in effect makes regional organizations subordinate to the universalism of the UN. The granting of observer status by the General Assembly and the secretary-general to regional organizations began with the culturally-based 'continental' organizations, such as the Organization of American States in 1948, the Arab League in 1950 and the Organization of African Unity in 1965. The fact that in the Charter regionalism relates to security has not proved an obstacle to primarily economic regional organizations being granted observer status. The European Economic Community for instance was accorded observer status at the end of 1974, after the General Assembly had requested the secretary-general on 11 October to permit the EEC to participate in the sessions and work of the Assembly in the capacity of observer, with the aim of strengthening cooperation between the UN and the EEC. The EEC's request for observer status was the outcome of an internal debate in the Community that had lasted for many years and when it was granted the EEC had in effect already been taking part in UN activities for some time. As a consequence of the observer status the EEC Information Bureau at the UN acquired a new and stronger position. As an observer the EEC is actually allowed two representatives, as the delegation list for the General Assembly mentions both the European Commission and the Presidency (represented by the state that holds the rotating Presidency) (Gregory and Stack 1983, 244).

Observer status for specialized UN agencies

The term observer status is also used with regard to the specialized agencies and their formal relationship with the UN. The agreements between the UN and the agencies vary because they are each the result of specific negotiations, yet they all have in common that both organizations permit each other's representatives to attend meetings of their constituent bodies. Most UN agencies 'agree to consider recommendations made by the General Assembly, and to transmit regular reports to the Economic and Social Council; many of them are given a right to request advisory opinions from the International Court of Justice on questions falling within their competence. Provision is also usually made for the mutual exchange of information and documents, and for the enactment of similar Staff Regulations and Staff Rules by each of the organizations concerned' (Malanczuk 1997, 383). Observer status thus promotes the exchange of documentation, mutual consultation and attending sessions of the General Assembly, commissions and working groups (Gregory and Stack 1983, 244). Several IGOs have an office at UN headquarters: in February 2002 18 had a 'mission' there and 11 specialized agencies had a 'liaison office' (Moore and Pubantz 2002, 228).

Coalition formation in the General Assembly

Having observer status does not mean that observers only observe. Member states of IGOs also use the observer status of their regional organization to form coalitions so as to influence the decision-making process of the UN, especially if the states involved belong to a reasonably coherent IGO. The rapidly institutionalized practice of coordinating the foreign policy of European Community member states at the UN is a good illustration of coalition formation in the sense of policy harmonization and block voting (Gregory and Stack 1983, 245). No matter what the issue under discussion, EEC member states very soon began to coordinate their strategies at the UN, in order to promote their own national interests. They quickly realized that this would give them a greater degree of influence within UN bodies than if they acted alone (although without abandoning this altogether). This amounts to using one IGO (the UN) as a means to promote the national interests of member states of another IGO (the EEC). In the case of the EEC no special relationship developed in the 1980s between the UN and the EEC as organizations, although bureaucratic contacts between officials of the two organizations increased (Feld *et al.* 1994, 203–4).

Subordinate to UN policy in the Security Council

In the practice of peacekeeping in the 1990s the Security Council intervened directly in the activities of a number of specialized agencies, including the IAEA, UNDP, UNHCR and UNICEF, as well as in those of the European Community (Feld *et al.* 1994, 203). Article 52.2 of Chapter VIII of the Charter on regional arrangements specifies that UN member states which establish regional arrangements or bodies must 'make every effort to achieve pacific settlement of local disputes through such regional arrangements or by such regional agencies before referring them to the Security Council'. When in the early 1990s representatives of the European Community were unable to achieve a ceasefire in the war in the former Yugoslavia, the conflict was submitted to the Security Council. This led to a US diplomat being appointed as UN mediator and, after a ceasefire was concluded, the Security Council deploying peacekeeping units in parts of the former Yugoslavia. The Security Council, for its part, can promote the peaceful settlement of local disputes by regional agreements or bodies. According to Article 53, the Security Council can use regional agreements and agencies 'for enforcement action under its authority'. In this way regional organizations can play a role in imposing UN sanctions. While in the case of the General Assembly, as described above, the regional organizations take the initiative (thereby essentially 'using' the UN), with the Security Council this relationship appears to be reversed. The regional organization (in this case the European Community) is the secondary actor, for whom the policy devised by the Security Council serves as a guideline. Universalism therefore precedes regionalism. The chances of influencing UN policy increase the more the regional organization is involved in the formulation of that policy. That can happen through permanent or temporary members of, or more direct consultation by, the Security Council, or through observer status at the General Assembly. All this shows that the UN is a political system with its own dynamics, in which specialized agencies and regional organizations also have a role to play.

Collective security in a bipolar world 1945–80

Part IX examines the operation of the UN and of military alliances under conditions of bipolarity. The relations that were to dominate the Cold War first became evident within the UN as a by-product of the postwar refugee problem. Despite US reluctance the UN developed a permanent refugee regime. The UN Charter makes no reference to peacekeeping, but its peacekeeping missions nevertheless gave the organization an autonomous authority. The rivalry between East and West had a paralysing effect on the UN, but it struggled on, with non-aligned countries playing a particular role at that stage (Chapter 22). At the instigation of the US an alliance was formed with Western European states, eventually including Germany. Eastern Europe's Warsaw Pact was significantly weaker than NATO, but was nonetheless a force to be reckoned with. Other alliances were forged in the Western Hemisphere and in Asia and the Arab World, but in neither Asia nor the Arab region was alliance strategy as dominant as in Europe, where a 'hot war' was a distinct possibility (Chapter 23). The Cuban Missile Crisis was a perilous development, with the UN relegated more or less to the sidelines. But that crisis also brought East and West to reason. The Non-Proliferation Treaty, whereby a system was put in place to monitor the spread of nuclear weapons, was concluded and other forms of arms control were also established (Chapter 24).

Refugees, peacekeeping and Cold War at the United Nations

22.1 The UN refugee regime since 1943

The refugee issue: displaced persons

At the end of the Second World War there were tens of millions of people who had been forced to leave their homes as a consequence of the conflict. These *displaced persons* (DPs) needed help to survive and to return to their country of origin. The *United Nations Relief and Rehabilitation Administration* (see §19.2) was set up by the Allies in November 1943 and operated under Allied military command. Its mandate was restricted to assisting civilians from Allied states and displaced persons in states liberated by their troops. The UNRRA, with a staff of almost 28,000 taken on specifically for that purpose, provided these displaced persons with temporary emergency aid in the form of shelter, food and transport. It was never a true refugee organization, if only because it had no authority for this, but in the first five months after the war in Europe ended the UNRRA succeeded in helping to repatriate three-quarters of all displaced persons. First of all DPs needed to be distinguished from prisoners of war and then, using whatever means of transport was available, they were returned home. The UNRRA continued its relief and rehabilitation operations until June 1947 (Loescher 2001, 35–36).

The refugee issue as a political problem

The conferences in Yalta and Potsdam discussed the question of repatriation to the Soviet Union. The refusal of many Eastern Europeans to return to Soviet-controlled territories was something that, initially at least, the Western powers declined to take seriously. Gradually, however, they were forced to do so and repatriation became an issue at the UN General Assembly. 'East' and 'West' took up diametrically opposed positions, even before the Cold War became a reality. The Soviet Union insisted on repatriation, while the West defended the choice of individuals not to live under a regime to which they were antagonistic. The question was whether the UNRRA was obliged to assist those who did not want to be repatriated. Although a compromise was reached at the UN, at the end of 1946 the US, which contributed the lion's share of its funding, refused to make additional funds available to prolong the UNRRA's existence. Instead it lobbied for the establishment of a temporary *International Refugee Organization* (IRO), which would have a five-year mandate to ensure the settlement of refugees and displaced persons who were victims of the war and its aftermath. The issue prompted heated debates at the UN, with the Soviet Union accusing the US of wanting to abolish the UNRRA as a way to stop providing economic aid for Eastern Europe. At the end of 1945 the Soviet Union had already decided not to ratify the Bretton Woods agreements, because it felt that the US was not particularly willing to support the Soviet Union. The abolition of the UNRRA and the creation of the IRO in 1947 therefore became grounds for political dispute. The communist states were indeed left in a difficult position and they accused the West of political opportunism (Loescher 2001, 40). Thanks to the IRO relatively few people were repatriated to Central and Eastern Europe between 1947 and 1951, and of those who refused repatriation most were allowed to settle in Western Europe and a few in the US.

Refugees as a temporary problem

The fundamental assumption underlying both the UNRRA and the IRO was that the refugee problem was both temporary and local. It should be resolved by voluntary repatriation, settlement of refugees in 'the country of first asylum', or alternatively resettlement in a 'third country'. At a UN-sponsored conference on refugees in 1947 it was argued that anyone fearful of returning to their 'country of origin' should be given refugee status and governments were to assess them without an obligation to offer permanent asylum to any individual refugee or groups of refugees. Once asylum had been granted however, refugees could not be forced to return to their home country in cases where persecution was thought likely. These principles found expression in the 1951 UN Refugee Convention (see below), but the real problem for the UN was that the refugee issue proved not to be temporary. The IRO itself recognized that and, in one of its final reports, emphatically warned the UN General Assembly that refugees had become a potentially permanent problem. But the US and the UK feared that a permanent organization would imply limitless responsibility for the resettlement of refugees and that the costs would fall principally on them. Unintentionally the IRO had indeed become a huge financial burden on the US. Funds allocated to the IRO were three times those of all other UN budgets combined (Loescher 2001, 41), so the US was averse to setting up a new organization. While for political reasons the communist states were opposed to an international agency for refugees, Western European states advocated extensive and generous programmes to solve the problem of the large numbers of refugees still living in their states (Gorman 2001, 63).

Creation of the UNHCR (1951)

In the meantime the Arab-Israeli conflict in 1948 triggered a wave of Palestinian refugees. The following year the UN responded to this by setting up a separate aid programme, the *UN Relief and Works Agency for Palestine Refugees in the Near East* (UNRWA), which began its work in May 1950. Because the refugee problem had still not been resolved the UN General Assembly decided at the end of 1950 to appoint a *UN High Commissioner for Refugees* (UNHCR). The post went not to the director-general of the IRO Donald Kingsley, but to the Dutchman Gerrit Jan van Heuven Goedhart, who took office on 1 January 1951. The High Commissioner had few resources at his disposal: three offices in Geneva and 300,000 dollars. Van Heuven Goedhart went on to become an active organizer, devoting all his social skills and other abilities (he was a talented pianist) to raising funds and winning support. By repeatedly insisting that the UNHCR's role encompassed all refugees he regularly clashed with the US, which wanted to give priority to Eastern European refugees. Despite that divergence of views, and the opposition of the Soviet Union within the UN, he was reappointed in 1953.

The Refugee Convention (1951)

That the refugee problem continued to be regarded as temporary was also evident from the *Convention Relating to the Status of Refugees*. The UN General Assembly had adopted the draft text in December 1950 and subsequently convened a conference of states for the purpose of agreeing the final convention. That happened on 28 July 1951 in Geneva. More than 20 states, most of them Western European but including Canada, the US, Israel, Egypt and three Latin American states, adopted the definitive text of the Refugee Convention, in the presence of the ILO, the IRO and 30 NGOs with consultative status at ECOSOC. After the sixth ratification the Convention came into force on 22 April 1954. The text of the Convention was bold. It consolidated previous conventions adopted by the League of Nations (see §16.1) and made use of the experiences of the UNRRA and IRO. The new Convention laid down minimum standards for the treatment of refugees, without prejudice to states granting more favourable treatment, and those standards had to be applied without discrimination on the grounds of race, religion, political opinion or country of origin. The Convention also provided for the issue of a travel document, the successor to the Nansen passport. Certain provisions of the Convention are so fundamental that no reservations could be raised on them, such as the definition of the term 'refugee' in Article 1, which is couched in extremely general terms, and the principle of *non-refoulement*, which prevents a state which is a party to the Convention expelling or returning (*refouler*) refugees against their will, in any manner whatsoever, to a territory where they fear persecution (Article 33). The Convention uses the term 'country' more often than 'nation' or 'state' because country is a wider concept, implying ties with a particular territory without that territory necessarily being (or as yet being) a state. The Convention's principal limitation was that it covered only persons who became refugees as a result of events prior to 1 January 1951. Nor did it apply to refugees for whom responsibility lay with a UN agency other than the UNHCR, such as the UNWRA.

Growth as an autonomous organization

The IRO was proved right in its view that the refugee problem had become permanent. That permanence was illustrated during the 1950s by two major conflicts, in Europe and in North Africa. The Hungarian uprising of 1956 and the Algerian war of independence at the end of the 1950s were followed by huge waves of refugees from Africa and Asia. Under Van Heuven Goedhart, the emergence of an autonomous role for the UNHCR had begun with his argument that refugees need much more than just assistance with housing and travel. They need to eat and to work. During the 1953 crisis in Berlin the UNHCR confirmed that integration projects were necessary to find permanent solutions for refugees and that, if left unresolved, the refugee problem would result in serious political and social costs. The events in Hungary and Algeria strengthened the UNHCR's view and its successful role during these crises, when it raised funds and did much to arrange permanent solutions, ensured it a central and autonomous role in the international refugee regime (Loescher 2001, 81). Ultimately the UNHCR's nonconformist approach led to the UN General Assembly adopting a *Protocol* in December 1966, which widened the scope of the Convention to include refugees other than those existing before 1951. The Protocol became effective on 4 October 1967. Under successive active High Commissioners the UNHCR has developed into a regime which has responded to emergencies in Africa, Asia and in fact everywhere in the world. In the 1990s the refugee problem again took on serious dimensions as a result of conflicts that caused large numbers of refugees, this time usually within states (see §38.2).

The International Organization for Migration (IOM)

The UNHCR was not the only organization concerned with refugees. In 1951 the *Intergovernmental Committee for the Movements of Migrants from Europe* was established on the initiative of Belgium and the US. It was soon renamed the *Intergovernmental Committee for European Migration* (ICEM) and immediately became involved in the continuing global issue of refugees. It worked to resettle refugees from Hungary in 1956 and in Latin America it developed 'migration for development' programmes in the 1960s. It arranged the relocation of Czechoslovakian refugees who had fled to Austria following the reforms and intervention in Prague of 1968, of Asians from Uganda in 1972 and of Chileans to Europe in 1973 following General Augusto Pinochet's coup. Between 1952 and 2000 the organization helped more than 11 million migrants. In 1980 the ICEM was reshaped into the *Intergovernmental Committee for Migration* (ICM) and in 1989 into the *International Organization for Migration* (IOM), but it was not until 1992 that the IOM was given observer status at the UN. By 2000 it had 79 member states, with a further 43 states and 49 IGOs as observers. The relationship between UNHCR and IOM is competitive since they are often involved with the same groups and in conflicts the distinction between 'refugee' and 'migrant' is rarely clear-cut. However, the two organizations did agree to coordinate their activities to some extent, an agreement endorsed in a Memorandum of Understanding in 1997.

Revision of the Red Cross Conventions (1949)

Among the treaties, declarations and conventions to which the Second World War gave rise were the revised and expanded Geneva Red Cross Conventions (see Figure 5.1). The International Committee of the Red Cross started this process as early as February 1945, when Allied troops were about to cross the Rhine and Oder in a final push to defeat Germany. The Red Cross announced its desire to revise the Geneva Conventions in the light of the experience of six years of war in a memorandum, after which two conferences of experts were held as well as a diplomatic conference convened by the Swiss Federal Council. The last took place from 21 April to 12 August 1949 in Geneva and at that conference 59 states agreed to a radical revision of the existing texts. The number of Geneva Conventions was increased from three to four, with the fourth widening the scope of the humanitarian laws of war to include measures for the protection of civilians in wartime. Also new was a provision common to all four Conventions, protecting the victims of non-international armed conflicts. The Red Cross was given a more robust role in the monitoring mechanism, which had hitherto largely been delegated to neutral states. From a political point of view the adoption of the four Conventions was a major success, since it coincided with the increasing splitting of the Allied powers into two blocs. 'In 1948 this confrontation intensified dramatically at the time of the coup in Prague and the blockade of Berlin, the civil wars in Greece and China, the war in Indochina and the nuclear arms race. It paralyzed nearly all aspects of international relations and brought the threat of a third world war long before the wounds left by the second had been able to heal' (Bugnion 2000, 42).

22.2 How the UN developed to become a respected peacekeeper

Namibia: judicial rather than political action

One of the first problems to confront the UN was South Africa's policy to annex Namibia. The UN General Assembly of 1946 rejected South Africa's policy, but that did not deter South Africa from bringing the territory further under its administration by, *inter alia*, imposing apartheid. In response the General Assembly asked the International Court of Justice for an advisory opinion on Namibia's legal status. The Court ruled that the UN had assumed the powers invested in the League of Nations in relation to Namibia and that South Africa, which had occupied Namibia during the First World War and administered it as a League of Nations mandated territory since 1920, did not have the unilateral right to change that territory's status. But it also upheld South Africa's right not to submit the territory to the jurisdiction of the Trusteeship Council. The General Assembly thus did not act in the matter itself, but left it to another organ, the International Court. It was not until the mid-1960s that further developments took place in the matter of Namibia, when the International Court again issued a ruling in favour of South Africa and against African states opposed to apartheid. In 1966 the question of South Africa's role in Namibia returned once again to the political arena of the General Assembly, which now decided to terminate South Africa's authority to administer the territory (Gorman 2001, 54), in a 'legal' procedure unusual for the UN. More typical was what happened at the end of the 1940s in the Arab-Israeli conflict or in the conflict between India and Pakistan: political intervention by the UN, attempts at mediation and then the monitoring of the implementation of any agreements reached.

The earliest peacekeeping missions 1948–49

In November 1947 the UN voted to approve the partition of Palestine into separate Jewish and Palestinian states, in succession to the British mandate which was due to expire in May 1948. When partition resulted in armed conflict the UN sent Count Folke Bernadotte to mediate and, after he was assassinated by a militant Zionist group, Ralph Bunche as his successor. After lengthy negotiations Israel and Egypt agreed an armistice in early 1949, followed by ceasefires between Israel and other neighbouring states. Thus in June 1948 the UN's first peacekeeping mission was launched. The task assigned to the *UN Truce*

Supervision Organization (UNTSO) was to assist the mediator and, later, to monitor the implementation of the ceasefires between Israel and the Arab states. A similar mission was set up following the clashes in 1947 after the former British colony India was given independence, another conflict which entailed a partition, this time of India (Hindu) and Pakistan (Muslim) on the basis of the so-called 'two-nation' theory. It caused huge numbers of refugees. In January 1949 the Security Council established the *UN Military Observer Group in India and Pakistan* (UNMOGIP), which still exists today, to monitor the skirmishes in Kashmir.

Suez Crisis (1956) and the UNEF

UN missions took on even greater significance following the Suez Crisis of 1956, when the UN deployed the *UN Emergency Force* (UNEF) to monitor the withdrawal of British, French and Israeli forces and to create a buffer zone in the Sinai peninsula between the parties involved. In this case the Security Council failed to reach agreement on how to respond because of the threat of veto from both France and the UK. These two states had come to Israel's aid by invading Egypt after Israel had occupied the Sinai peninsula and Gaza to counter Palestinian attacks and to break Egypt's blockade of the Gulf of Aqaba, which had cut off Israeli access to the Red Sea. The closure and nationalization of the Suez Canal by Egypt in July 1956 played a direct role in the conflict. The US, which had not been informed in advance of the intentions of the UK, France and Israel, and the Soviet Union, which threatened to come to Egypt's aid, were opposed to the intervention by the UK and France. The General Assembly then acted pursuant to the Uniting for Peace resolution (see §20.2). In its first ever emergency special session the General Assembly instructed UN secretary-general Dag Hammarskjöld to establish a UN Emergency Force. The General Assembly by a large majority called for the immediate cessation of hostilities, the withdrawal of Israeli troops to behind earlier ceasefire lines, an embargo on military aid and steps to reopen the Suez Canal. The US publicly criticized the UK and France and put pressure on them and Israel to give in to the UN's demands. With Egypt's consent, the UNEF was deployed in Egyptian territory (Israel rejected the stationing of UN forces in its territory) to act as a buffer while non-Egyptian forces withdrew. The UNEF was under the direct authority of the secretary-general, who acted in close consultation with the General Assembly and the Security Council. UNEF was to remain in the region until May 1967, when U Thant agreed to Egypt's request that it should leave. The situation in the area had not been resolved however and after the Yom Kippur War of 1973 UNEF was re-established as UNEF II. In 1958 a *UN Observation Group in Lebanon* (UNOGIL) was created to prevent troops and weapons entering Lebanon.

Peacekeeping in the 1960s

Between 1960 and 1964 the UN deployed the *UN Operation in the Congo* (ONUC). Its mandate was to monitor the withdrawal of Belgian troops from the newly independent Republic of Congo, prevent civil war and ensure the departure of all mercenaries and foreign troops (see §22.3). In the 1960s peacekeeping operations were carried out in New Guinea over a conflict between the Netherlands and Indonesia, in Yemen to certify the implementation of the disengagement agreement between Saudi Arabia and the United Arab Republic, in Cyprus to secure a buffer zone between Greek and Turkish

Cypriots, in the Dominican Republic to monitor a ceasefire between two factions during the transition to a new government, and in India and Pakistan again, this time because of their border disputes. Peacekeeping troops were deployed between 1948 and 1978 (see Figure 22.1 for a summary of these UN operations), but in the decade up to 1988 no new UN peacekeeping operations were launched.

The temporary UN administration for Dutch New Guinea (1962–69)

The Dutch colony of New Guinea was claimed by Indonesia. Because the parties involved were unable to reach a settlement it was in 1962 handed over to a temporary UN administration, the *UN Temporary Executive Authority* (UNTEA). In 1963 administration of the territory was granted to Indonesia, on condition that a referendum would be held before the end of 1969. A *UN Security Force* (UNSF) was formed to maintain a ceasefire during this transitional period and to operate as a UNTEA police force in collaboration with the indigenous population. On 1 May 1969 the UNTEA finally transferred administration of West Irian (or Irian Jaya, as it was called by then) to Indonesia.

Characteristics of the early UN peacekeeping operations

The term *peacekeeping* does not actually appear in the UN Charter. It is said that the UN developed the practice as a 'middle way' (VI½) between Chapter VI (pacific settlement of disputes) and Chapter VII (action with respect to threats to the peace, breaches of the

Figure 22.1 UN peacekeeping operations 1948–78

Abreviation*	Operation name	Period
UNTSO	UN Truce Supervision Organization	May 1948 –
UNMOGIP	UN Military Observer Group in India and Pakistan	January 1949 –
UNEF I	First UN Emergency Force (Suez Crisis)	November 1956 – June 1967
UNOGIL	UN Observation Group in Lebanon	June 1958 – December 1958
ONUC	UN Operation in the Congo	July 1960 – June 1964
UNSF	UN Security Force (in Dutch New Guinea)	October 1962 – April 1963
UNYOM	UN Yemen Observation Mission	July 1963 – September 1964
UNFICYP	UN Peace-keeping Force in Cyprus	March 1964 –
DOMREP	Mission of the Representative of the Secretary-General in the Dominican Republic	May 1965 – October 1966
UNIPOM	UN India-Pakistan Observation Mission	September 1965 – March 1966
UNEF II	Second UN Emergency Force (Yom Kippur War)	October 1973 – July 1979
UNDOF	UN Disengagement Observer Force (Golan Heights)	June 1974 –
UNIFIL	UN Interim Force in Lebanon	March 1978 –

*Italics indicates that control passed to the Department of Peacekeeping Operations set up in 1992. See Figure 37.1 for UN peacekeeping operations in the period 1988–2007 and Figure 37.2 for operations led by the Department of Political Affairs.

peace and acts of aggression). The concept as it emerged at the end of the 1940s and continued until the 1990s was fairly well defined and had a clear set of objectives. It took the form of joint operations intended to help resolve an international conflict, usually between states, and was conditional on the consent of the states involved. It was only after states had agreed on, for instance, a cessation of hostilities that a UN peacekeeping force could play a role. To respect national sovereignty UN peacekeepers were deployed only after the UN had concluded *Status of Forces Agreements* with the states involved, in which those states authorized UN troops to operate in their territory. The peacekeeping force took up positions between the two sides, to ensure that both took the measures necessary to implement agreements reached and to monitor this implementation. It was only lightly armed, enabling it to defend itself, and usually consisted of troops from states regarded as neutral. Peacekeeping operations were generally characterized by principles such as neutrality, consent and impartiality, which although they reflected the geo-political relationships of the time were a source of authority for the UN Secretariat. 'One important source of authority was its delegated mandate from states to promote peace, but one condition of this delegation was that the UN operate with the consent of parties to the conflict.' The moral authority that the UN acquired was rooted in its operational neutrality. 'The Secretariat's power and influence rested on its authority, which in turn depended on being perceived as impartial and operating with consent' (Barnett and Finnemore 2004, 122). The UN and its Secretariat therefore acquired authority through the peacekeeping missions, with the instantly recognizable 'Blue Helmet' peacekeepers.

22.3 The Cold War at the UN: East, West and non-aligned

The paralysing effect of the rivalry between East and West

The Cold War between 'East' and 'West', between the Soviet Union and the US and their respective allies, was not only a power struggle between two groups of states but also an ideological struggle between two competing systems, communism and liberal capitalism. This competition between two power blocs and two systems and the fact that the 'war' was accompanied by hardly any direct ('hot') military confrontation between them made the Cold War a new phenomenon. The rivalry between the two blocs was felt at the UN as a result of the refugee problem in Europe. It would hamper the UN's effectiveness until the fall of the Berlin Wall in 1989, an event which symbolized the end of the Cold War. Other states could not really avoid the effects of the rivalry, although in the 1960s non-aligned countries did try to do so. US dominance at the UN right from the start had a major impact. Within the organization the US exercised more control than communist states, which had less affinity with international organizations. The replacement of the UNRRA by the IRO demonstrated the perseverance of the US, whose policy to prevent the spread of communism (the policy of *containment* espoused in the Truman doctrine of 1947) also had an impact at the UN. The US obstructed admission to the UN of states allied or sympathetic to the Soviet Union, provoking a response from the Soviet Union. Following the political revolution in China in 1949, the US refused to recognize the People's Republic of China and continued to regard the nationalist Chinese government that had fled to Taiwan as China's sole legal representative, including at the UN. In response the Soviet Union decided in 1950 to boycott meetings of the UN and its organs, including the Security Council, which explains why during the Korean War the US was able to successfully promote its own policies within the UN and why the UN itself became embroiled in US policy.

The Korean War (1950)

The Japanese annexation of Korea, which dated from the early twentieth century, was brought to an end with Japan's defeat in the Second World War. The Soviet Union occupied the north and the US took control of the south. Shortly afterwards, at a conference in Moscow, Korea was declared a trust territory under the administration of four major powers, the US, the Soviet Union, the UK and China. In 1947 the UN General Assembly established the *UN Temporary Commission on Korea* (UNTCOK) to organize free elections. These were held in South Korea in 1948, but the Soviet Union denied UNTCOK access to the north and appointed its own unelected government there. In December 1948 the General Assembly responded by passing Resolution 195(III), which declared that the government of South Korea was the sole legitimate representative of Korea. While the occupying forces withdrew from the two Koreas the UN appointed a commission to work towards its reunification by peaceful means, but this was opposed by the Soviet Union. A new situation developed when in June 1950 North Korean troops crossed the 38th parallel, which had been designated the border between North and South. With the Soviet Union boycotting sessions of the UN, the Security Council under US pressure called on all UN member states to provide support to South Korea, so as to force a withdrawal of North Korean troops and restore peace and security. On 7 July the Security Council called on the US to assume leadership of a UN military force. The US appointed General Douglas MacArthur as commander and ensured a multilateral force was quickly deployed. 42 of the UN's 59 member states gave Korea military, economic or humanitarian support (Gorman 2001, 115). Unlike the UN peacekeeping missions discussed earlier, the *United Nations Command in Korea* (UNC) was not under the authority of the UN secretary-general. The UN's rapid response brought the Soviet Union, which had apparently failed to realize the consequences of its boycott, back to the UN. It objected to the UN's decisions and attempted to prevent the Security Council taking further action incompatible with Soviet interests, but found little support among other UN members. That the UN wished to continue pursuing its own policy, even if the Security Council was now deadlocked, became apparent from the adoption by the General Assembly of the Uniting for Peace Resolution on 3 November 1950 (see §20.2). For the Soviet Union, the Korean War reaffirmed its view that UN peacekeeping operations could culminate in US-led military actions targeting former allies. That the Korean conflict was a 'hot' war was confirmed by Soviet support for North Korea and the intervention of forces from the People's Republic of China on the side of North Korea. The military situation on the ground was such that neither side could secure a decisive victory. In 1953 a ceasefire was agreed, with Korea remaining divided. The polarity between East and West was intensified during the Hungarian uprising in 1956, when the UN Security Council was unable to make a decision and, in line with the Uniting for Peace Resolution, it was left to the General Assembly, in emergency session, to demand the withdrawal of Soviet troops. However, with the Suez Crisis coinciding with the Soviet decision to appoint a new government in Budapest, there was little the UN could do other than use the good offices of the UNHCR to help refugees.

The Congo crisis (1960)

Relations between the US and the Soviet Union deteriorated further when in 1960 the Soviet Union shot down a US spy plane over Soviet territory. This time the Soviet leader Nikita Khrushchev went to the UN to berate the West. An incident in which he pounded on the desk with his shoe was widely reported in the media. The US responded to Soviet criticism by accusing the Soviet Union of bugging its embassy in Moscow. Thus the UN became a forum used by the two powers to play out their mutual hostility. When in 1960 Congo gained independence from Belgium a dangerous situation emerged. Civil strife was threatened, with the Soviet Union supporting one side and the US the other. UN secretary-general Dag Hammarskjöld tried to play a role by quickly responding to an appeal for help from the Congolese government, but at the UN he found an opponent in the Soviet Union, which accused him of being pro-Western. East–West antagonism therefore limited the scope for the secretary-general to pursue an independent policy in response to conflicts. Indeed, Khrushchev demanded Hammarskjöld's resignation and presented a proposal to replace the secretary-general by a 'troika': three secretaries, one from the West, one from the East and one from a neutral state. The General Assembly rejected this proposal and Hammarskjöld refused to resign. The assassination of the Congolese Prime Minister Patrice Lumumba in early 1961 led to renewed Soviet opposition to Hammarskjöld, whom it said was to blame. The Soviet Union refused to work with him any longer and again submitted its proposal for a troika, but once more was unsuccessful because the US continued to back Hammarskjöld. In September Hammarskjöld and his staff were killed in a plane crash in Africa. That accident, tragic enough though it was for the organization, also presented the problem of choosing a successor as secretary-general. The US wanted someone appointed quickly, but the Soviet Union created an impasse by again presenting its proposal for a troika. In November a solution was found when U Thant agreed to complete Hammarskjöld's term of office. The Soviet Union eventually abandoned its troika plan, but the scope for the UN to play a role of any significance in the conflicts in Central Africa remained only modest, as Cold War tensions continued. Ultimately these tensions also triggered a heated dispute over the costs of the four-year-long UN peacekeeping operation in Congo. The Soviet Union refused to pay its share, plunging the UN into an unprecedented and severe financial crisis in 1963 and 1964, which had to be referred to the International Court of Justice to be resolved. A consequence of these difficulties was that peacekeeping operations would no longer be regarded as organizational costs of the UN. Instead, from then on each peacekeeping mission would be financed on a voluntary and *ad hoc* basis (see §20.1).

The Non-Aligned Movement (1961)

After Yugoslavia's abstention in the vote on Korea in 1950 a number of states expressed a desire during the course of the 1950s to become more independent of the two superpowers. It was one of the declared aims of the conference of African and Asian states convened in Bandung, Indonesia, in 1955. Later, in September 1961, more than 20 states attended a similar conference in Belgrade. The term *non-aligned* adopted there had been coined by the Indian Prime Minister Jawaharlal Nehru. He had formulated five 'pillars' to guide Sino-Indian relations: mutual respect for each other's territorial integrity and sovereignty; mutual non-aggression; mutual non-interference in domestic affairs; equality and mutual benefit; and peaceful coexistence. These characteristics of what was in essence the Westphalian state system strongly appealed to colonies that had just achieved or still sought independence. They were consistent with their aim of presenting themselves as nation-states with their own flag and they gave them a sense of self-respect which, in terms of the global relations of that period, counted for a great deal and brought with it great expectations. In addition to being 'non-aligned' those 'countries' were therefore committed to the rapid and universal end of colonialism. The founding fathers of the *Movement of Non-Aligned Countries* formed in Belgrade included Nehru, President Sukarno of Indonesia, Egypt's President Nasser and President Tito, who wanted the support of developing states to bring Yugoslavia out of isolation after its rift with the Soviet Union in 1948. Regular conferences were held, such as in 1964 in Cairo and in 1970 in Lusaka, Zambia (see Figure 22.2). Many new states did not have the resources for an extensive global diplomatic presence, so UN headquarters in New York became a forum in which they could meet representatives from other states and lobby for support for their position. Furthermore, through its regional groups (see §20.2) the UN offered them an opportunity to coordinate their policies. The positions developed within the Non-Aligned Movement were also a frame of reference for broader policy within the UN. The issues that dominated the Movement included an end to colonialism and apartheid and the securing of development aid. Economic issues were included on the agenda of the UNCTAD, which met for the first time in 1964 to discuss relations between trade and development (see §29.2). At that meeting developing states established the Group of 77, which grew into an influential caucus group of the Third World within the UN (see Figure 29.4). In terms of political relations at the UN the voice of the non-aligned countries counted in the 1960s, although it remained difficult for them to avoid the East–West polarity, especially when development aid was being provided by one or other of the two blocs. In the 1970s the movement lost much of its influence, weakened for instance by the fact that a country such as Cuba was both a close ally of the Soviet Union and claimed to be non-aligned.

Figure 22.2 The Movement of Non-Aligned Countries (1961)

The **Movement of Non-Aligned Countries** or Non-Aligned Movement (NAM) has only a limited organizational structure. As a rule the heads of state and government leaders meet every three years. The country hosting a summit conference also serves as its chair for three years and is responsible for its organization and for drafting declarations. 18 months after each summit foreign ministers meet to evaluate the implementation of resolutions adopted and they meet again shortly before the next summit to prepare for it. The permanent mission at the UN of the chair serves as the NAM's secretariat. The member states explicitly opted for informal procedures, something also indicated by the term 'movement', because members expected to be able to act most effectively, both individually and collectively, without a formal constitution and a permanent secretariat. A degree of aversion to the image of IGOs led by the former colonial powers also played a role. Decision making is based on consensus. When reforming its procedures in 1996 members agreed that consensus should not necessarily have to mean unanimity. Responsibility for continuity lies with the chair. To coordinate the work of the movement's task forces, committees and working groups, a *Coordinating Bureau* was established. NAM members with a seat on the Security Council form a caucus. In 1994 a *Joint Coordinating Committee* was set up in collaboration with the G77.

Summit conferences were held in 1961 in Belgrade (Yugoslavia), 1964 in Cairo (Egypt), 1970 in Lusaka (Zambia), 1973 in Algiers (Algeria), 1976 in Colombo (Sri Lanka), 1979 in Havana (Cuba), 1983 in New Delhi (India), 1986 in Harare (Zimbabwe), 1989 in Belgrade again, 1992 in Jakarta (Indonesia), 1995 in Cartagena (Colombia), 1998 in Durban (South Africa), 2003 in Kuala Lumpur (Malaysia) and 2006 once more in Havana. In 2006 the NAM had 115 members. Since the end of the Cold War the Movement has struggled to retain its relevance. The states that emerged from the disintegration of Yugoslavia expressed little interest in joining, preferring to set their sights on membership of the European Union. Also, South Africa, when chair, found it difficult to provide leadership. In January 2001 Richard Holbrooke, the US representative to the UN, argued that African states should quit the NAM because it had lost its significance and had become dominated by a handful of radical leaders. African states rejected this advice, pointing to the growth of the Movement and the concomitant solidarity it represented. Holbrooke suggested that Africa would be better off directing its efforts towards the G77, but the non-aligned countries replied that the responsibilities of the G77 (social and economic issues) were different from those of the NAM. They also pointed to their Joint Coordinating Committee. They rejected Holbrooke's view, with the South African spokesman declaring that the NAM will always be remembered for having stood steadfast in support of the struggle against apartheid and that Holbrooke's statement reflected US annoyance at the NAM's continued and uncompromising support for the Palestinians. Even today the movement continues to be a political means to underline the particular identity of non-aligned countries *vis-à-vis* the major powers.

Regional alliances in the 1940s and 1950s

23.1 US policy on Western European cooperation

US policy with respect to a European problem

The institutional settlement of peace promoted by the US following the Second World War was not restricted to just the UN. In the midst of the growing antagonism between West and East, a classic recourse followed from the balance of power between the states: the alliance. In 1952 the North Atlantic Treaty of 1949 became a permanent body, NATO. In 1955 the Soviet Union formed the Warsaw Pact, an organization more centrally led and less intergovernmental than NATO. The role of both alliances was to counter aggression against one or more member states. The bipolar world and the fact that both blocs had nuclear weapons with which they could eliminate each other (as they realized during the Cuban Missile Crisis in 1962) transformed these alliances into direct instruments of power for the two superpowers, which could be used to demonstrate their superiority and deter attacks that might escalate into nuclear war. The permanent nature of the Western alliance added a further dimension. It offered a visible forum in which states could negotiate on joint policy. The alliance had a public figurehead in the person of the secretary general. The establishment of this Western alliance was politically difficult, because of the German problem. The US and Western Europe had different views on how a *de facto* divided Germany should be integrated into Europe. Western European states themselves were far from unanimous on how to address the problem. When the Federal Republic of Germany (West Germany) was formed in September 1949 and the German Democratic Republic (East Germany) was created the following month, the partitioning of Germany took on a more permanent character. The US believed that Western Europe should contribute as much as possible to deterring the Soviet threat. After some time it was a view to which the UK also subscribed. West Germany should also, it was argued, make a substantial contribution, by participating in the defence of Western Europe and in its economic recovery. To kick-start this economic recovery the US advocated a joint approach within the framework of the Marshall Plan and the creation of a Western European internal market, the engine of which would be West Germany. The US realized that this policy could succeed only if Western European states could be given assurances that there would be no renewal of German dominance (Lieshout 1999, 3). This resulted in a complex of security organizations in Western Europe, with ultimately a central role for NATO, and in a range of economic organizations which would subsequently be subsumed under the term 'Western European integration' (see Chapter 26).

Churchill on the Iron Curtain and European cooperation

In his postwar speeches Winston Churchill pointed out in no uncertain terms that the relationship between Western and Eastern Europe was changing. His March 1946 address delivered in Fulton, Missouri, marked a turning point in relations between the Western allies and the Soviet Union, with his image of an 'iron curtain' that had descended across the Continent, dividing Europe in two. In September, in Zurich, he called for a rapprochement between France and Germany and for a kind of United States of Europe, although the UK would continue to orient itself more towards the Commonwealth than towards Europe. Churchill's ideas regarding European cooperation struck a chord among groups of citizens and politicians who, after the war, aspired to a form of European cooperation. In December 1947 they agreed to coordinate their activities by creating the *International Committee for the Union of European Movements*, which changed its name to *European Movement* in 1948 and was to play a role in influencing public opinion and in the foundation of the Council of Europe in May 1949 (see below).

The Treaty of Brussels (1948)

The developments in the field of security led the UK and France to conclude the *Dunkirk Treaty* on 4 March 1947. This was a reciprocal assistance alliance and it was envisaged that it would remain in force for 50 years. The following year Belgium, the Netherlands and Luxembourg also joined. On 17 March 1948 in Brussels these five states signed the *Treaty of Economic, Social and Cultural Collaboration and Collective Self-Defence*, which also had a duration of 50 years. The Treaty provided for the creation of the *Brussels Treaty Organization* for military cooperation and collective self-defence in the event of renewed German aggression. With the development of the Cold War, such cooperation acquired particular significance as a consequence of events in Prague in February 1948 (when, under pressure from Moscow, a pro-Soviet government was installed) and of the Soviet blockade of Berlin in the summer of 1948 and the airlift response by the Western allies. The first stage of the military cooperation envisaged in the Brussels Treaty Organization began in September 1948 when an integrated air defence and a joint command structure were set up.

The North Atlantic Treaty (1949)

As a result of the Berlin blockade, US plans for security in Europe took the form of an Atlantic alliance between North America (Canada and the US) and, initially, the five members of the Brussels Treaty Organization. With the Organization reaching agreement on the principles of a defensive pact for the North Atlantic region in October 1948, treaty negotiations began in Washington DC in December between the US, Canada and the five Organization members. In early 1949 they invited a further five states to join (Denmark, Iceland, Italy, Norway and Portugal). The *North Atlantic Treaty* was signed in Washington on 4 April 1949 and came into force on 24 August. In September the first session of the North Atlantic Council, established by the Treaty, was held in Washington. Following publication of the Treaty by its 12 member states the Soviet Union protested that it contravened the UN Charter, but this argument was quickly rejected. In its preamble the parties to the Treaty reaffirmed their faith in the purposes and principles of the UN Charter and their desire to live in peace with all peoples and all governments. 'They are determined to safeguard the freedom, common heritage and civilization of their peoples, founded on the principles of democracy, individual liberty and the rule of law. They seek to promote stability and well-being in the North Atlantic area. They are resolved to unite their efforts for collective defence and for the preservation of peace and security.' The provisions made special reference to defence against armed attack. Article 5 stated that an armed attack against one or more of them should be considered an attack against them all.

Creation of the Council of Europe (1949)

The European Movement which Churchill had done much to encourage succeeded in attracting more than 600 influential figures from 16 states to a congress on Europe in The Hague in May 1948. This led to ten Western European states signing the Statute of the *Council of Europe* in London on 5 May 1949: Belgium, Denmark, France, Ireland, Italy, Luxembourg, the Netherlands, Norway, Sweden and the UK. They invited Greece, Turkey and Iceland to join as well. The first two joined immediately, while Iceland followed in 1950. West Germany became an associate member in 1950 and a full member in 1951 and Austria joined in 1956. Saarland was an associate member from 1950 to 1957. This territory had been occupied by France in 1945, becoming a protectorate under French control, economically tied to France, in 1947, but in 1957 it was reunited with Germany. The aim of the Council of Europe was to achieve greater unity between its members, so as to safeguard and realize the ideals and principles which are their common heritage and to facilitate their economic and social progress. These principles include true democracy, the rule of law and fundamental human rights and freedoms, and they were precisely and extensively set down in the *Convention for the Protection of Human Rights and Fundamental Freedoms*, adopted by the Council of Europe on 4 November 1950. The Convention introduced into international law the concept that states have legally-binding and moral responsibilities towards their own citizens and all persons subject to their jurisdiction. It established the *European Court of Human Rights* (see §33.5) to implement it. Like the Council of Europe, the European Court of Human Rights is based in Strasbourg, France. A novel feature of the structure of the Council of Europe (see Figure 23.1) is the *Consultative Assembly*, or *Parliamentary Assembly* as it has become known since February 1994, an interparliamentary body. It has no legislative authority, but in terms of composition and procedures it resembles a parliament. Each member state can decide how to select its representatives to the Parliamentary Assembly, with delegations usually reflecting the political composition of their national parliaments. The number of representatives for each state is determined by the size of its population. The Parliamentary Assembly developed into an active body to counterbalance the Committee of Ministers, especially on issues of human rights. In terms of national politics, what was important was that its parliamentarians were directly involved in collective European developments.

Figure 23.1 The Council of Europe (1949)

The three main organs of the **Council of Europe** are the *Committee of Ministers*, which represents governments, the *Parliamentary Assembly*, representing the parliaments of member states, and the *General Secretariat*. The work of ministers is prepared by committees of government experts, that of the Parliamentary Assembly by committees and working groups. The Committee and the Parliamentary Assembly meet in the Joint Committee, on which both are represented.

The Council of Europe is active not just on human rights but also in a wide range of other fields, including social and economic, through its *European Social Charter* (1961). Over the course of half a century the Council has been responsible for more than 170 **European conventions**. Apart from in the field of human rights the organization was for a time overshadowed by the institutions of the European Union and its predecessors. However, the Council's importance revived at the end of the Cold War, when it became a Pan-European organization engaged in dialogue with Central and Eastern European states on the principles underlying the European conventions, principles that would now also apply to these states.

23.2 From North Atlantic Treaty (1949) to NATO (1952)

Towards an international organization

After the foundation of West and East Germany in the autumn of 1949 the US government put a great deal of effort into its policy of securing an integrated defence of the North Atlantic region, including making the necessary financial resources available. The North Atlantic Council, comprising the foreign ministers of the North Atlantic Treaty's 12 contracting parties, in September 1949 established a Defence Committee, consisting of ministers of defence, to integrate plans for the defence of the North Atlantic region. A number of military bodies were founded to advise the Council on military affairs, as were a Defence Financial and Economic Committee, made up of finance ministers, and a Military Production and Supply Board. The latter two were important because of the huge investments that member states were required to make as part of the rearmament drive. In 1950 the Council adopted a four-year defence plan. It soon became apparent that the Council was no longer able to coordinate the meetings of all these military and civilian agencies, so in May 1950 a non-military body was created to coordinate policy. It was composed of delegates representing the foreign ministers, who met in London in continuous session. The political developments on the international scene, and especially the 1950 Korean War, bolstered this process of further institutionalization.

The Korean War and the forward strategy

The Korean War raised the question of how to defend the North Atlantic area in the event of an attack from Eastern Europe. The North Atlantic Council's response in 1950 was to develop the *forward strategy*. To defend the whole region, signatory members would have to be able to resist aggression as far to the east as possible. That would necessitate deploying considerable military forces over a large territory and, given the geographical position of West Germany, the participation of the Federal Republic. For the rest of Europe the prospect of West German participation was controversial. Ultimately a solution was found through the Western European Union, but not until 1954 (see below). In the meantime the North Atlantic Treaty's military organization continued to develop. At the end of 1950 the Council resolved to set up an integrated European military force under a central command. The member states of the Brussels Treaty Organization transferred their military responsibilities to the military organization emerging within the framework of the North Atlantic Treaty. The Council also decided to reorganize the military structure and asked the US President to appoint General Dwight D. Eisenhower *Supreme Allied Commander Europe* (SACEUR). President Truman agreed to the request and Eisenhower was appointed in December 1950. SACEUR was to be supported by an international staff, drawn from all member states participating in the integrated military force. In early April 1951 SACEUR and the *Supreme Headquarters Allied Powers Europe* (SHAPE) were sited in Rocquencourt on the outskirts of Paris. The Supreme Commander is always an American.

Reorganization as NATO (1952)

After May 1951 the civilian agencies of the North Atlantic Treaty were reorganized. The Council delegates now formed the permanent working body of the North Atlantic Council. Their status was enhanced because they no longer represented just the foreign ministers, but all ministers involved in issues that lay within the scope of the Treaty. In May 1951 a small international working staff was established in London. Agreements were reached on the status of the national military forces which were to operate under NATO command, the various regional headquarters and the civilian staff. A Temporary Council Committee chaired by Jean Monnet circulated a summary of the current military capacity of each member state. It was decided to invite Greece and Turkey to join, which they did at the start of 1952. In February 1952 further reorganizations were implemented. The most important was that the North Atlantic Council became a permanent body, with headquarters in Paris. All ministers concerned with NATO were represented on this Council. For the day-to-day work permanent representatives were appointed, supported by national delegations of advisers and experts. To ensure greater cooperation between the Council and the military authorities it was decided to move the civilian personnel from London to Paris. From April 1952 they were given temporary headquarters in a building in Paris which France had originally earmarked for the UN General Assembly.

The secretary general: an international civil servant

Finally NATO got a secretary general. He was not a delegation member but, as was the case with the League of Nations and the UN, an international civil servant, given control over an international staff. On 28 April 1952 NATO became a permanent IGO with both a civilian and a military structure. The UK's Lord Ismay was its first secretary general, from 1952 to 1957. His successors were Paul-Henri Spaak (Belgium, 1957–61), Dirk Stikker (Netherlands, 1961–64), Manlio Brosio (Italy, 1964–71), Joseph Luns (Netherlands, 1971–84), Lord Carrington (UK, 1984–88), Manfred Wörner (Germany, 1988–94), Willy Claes (Belgium, 1994–95), Javier Solana (Spain, 1995–99), Lord Robertson (UK, 1999–2003) and Jaap de Hoop Scheffer (Netherlands, 2004–).

The European Defence Community (1952)

The attempts by the US to ensure greater cooperation among European states came up against the 'German problem'. On the margins of the North Atlantic Council of September 1949 the US had encouraged France to develop a collective policy on Germany. As a result France in May 1950 presented a plan to bring the production of coal and steel in France and Germany under a single common agency, which other states could also join. The so-called *Schuman Plan* was devised by Jean Monnet and his staff. It offered France an opportunity to control the pace of German economic recovery and was compatible with German Chancellor Konrad Adenauer's aim to have Germany accepted within Europe again (Lieshout 1999, 97). The Schuman Plan led to the creation of the European Coal and Steel Community in April 1951 (see §26.3). As part of the same policy and also prompted by US pressure, the French Prime Minister René Pleven in October 1950 presented plans to create a European army, including German contingents, within the framework of the North Atlantic Treaty. After the North Korean invasion of South Korea in the early months of 1950 the US raised its military aid to Western Europe immensely. The US assumed that Western Europe, like the US itself, would greatly increase its defensive capability and its armaments production and also that West Germany would begin to rearm. A joint European or North Atlantic army seemed an appropriate solution to the German problem, because it would make it easier for other Western European countries to accept German troops. At the instigation of Pleven and Churchill the signatory members of the Brussels Treaty decided on 27 May 1952 to set up the *European Defence Community* (EDC), with the aim of creating a Western European army and of inviting West Germany to participate. But during the negotiating stage the original Pleven Plan of 1950 was changed radically. Other states had more confidence in US military supremacy than in that of France, which was relatively weak, so the EDC ultimately became more Atlantic-oriented and less supranational than Pleven had envisaged. Furthermore, the UK declined to join. French politicians at home were even more critical and in August 1954 France's national assembly voted against ratifying the EDC treaty.

Significance of the Western European Union (1954)

The failure of the EDC meant an alternative solution had to be found for the problem of German rearmament. That alternative was to expand and amend the Treaty of Brussels. At a hastily convened conference attended by Western European states, the US and Canada and held in London between late September and early October 1954, it was decided to invite West Germany and Italy to join the Treaty of Brussels. On 23 October, in Paris, five Protocols based on the EDC Treaty were drawn up, the second of which created the *Western European Union* (WEU). After ratification it came into force on 6 May 1955, with seven members (Belgium, France, Italy, Luxembourg, the Netherlands, the UK and West Germany). The WEU was given responsibility for political, economic, cultural and military cooperation and arms control. Of these, only military cooperation took on any significance. The WEU's economic responsibilities were transferred to the European Economic Community when that was created in 1957 and its social and cultural responsibilities were handed over to the Council of Europe in 1960. The obligation on the part of WEU members to provide reciprocal military support went beyond that of the North Atlantic Treaty. Parties to the WEU had to give each other military assistance if any one of them was attacked. Article 5 of the North Atlantic Treaty defines this obligation in more restrictive terms, since it allows each party to take such action as it deems necessary to restore and maintain the security of the North Atlantic area. The principal significance of the WEU in 1954 was that West Germany was invited to join the North Atlantic Treaty, which by then had become NATO. Furthermore, it was permitted to rearm, although subject to certain limitations: it was prohibited, for instance, from manufacturing or obtaining ABC weapons (atomic, biological or chemical) and from building warships and strategic bombers. With the WEU monitoring these restrictions, West Germany could again be accepted as a military force in postwar Western Europe. In a military sense too the significance of the WEU remained limited, because it had been agreed that it would work closely with NATO. Article IV of the modified Treaty of Brussels of October 1954 recognized the undesirability of duplicating NATO's military staff and so no WEU military command structure was created. In practice the WEU was of some importance, because it acted as a forum for informal contacts between the six European Community members and the UK. President Charles de Gaulle of France in 1968 used this role as an argument in an attempt to block the WEU's work, but his departure as political leader in 1969 meant a crisis was averted. With the UK's accession to the EC in 1973 the WEU's bridging role came to an end. It was not until the mid-1980s that the WEU, at France's instigation, was temporarily reactivated as part of a more active European role in NATO. The WEU continues to exist today.

Figure 23.2 The Interparliamentary Assembly of the Western European Union

The **Western European Union** of 1954 has three main institutions: a *Council*, a *Secretariat* and an *Assembly*. The intergovernmental Council takes decisions on the basis of unanimity. These decisions bind member states only politically, not legally. The presidency of the Council rotates among member states (initially annually, later every six months). The Council meets once every six months at the level of foreign ministers and weekly at the level of permanent representatives (the Permanent Council). The Secretariat is based in London.

The **Interparliamentary Assembly** meets twice a year in plenary session in Paris. It consists of those members of the national parliaments who are delegates to the Council of Europe. The Assembly deliberates on the WEU's activities and may submit proposals. It also has committees, which can appoint rapporteurs who draft reports and resolutions for their committees, which can then revise them and submit them to the Assembly. The Assembly's Charter was adopted in October 1955. As earlier with the Council of Europe, the underlying principle is that cooperation between governments at European level implies cooperation between national parliamentarians. It was expected that interparliamentary scrutiny would lead to greater transparency and democratic responsibility than would be the case if scrutiny was limited to just the national level, and that the involvement of parliamentarians would enhance the legitimacy of cooperation within the WEU. In practice the interparliamentary cooperation created a forum in which specialist national parliamentarians could meet each other regularly. This fostered informed debates on security issues, with background reports on specific concerns. The

> Assembly was thus able to play a particular role in the acceptance by national parliaments of issues such as armaments, the harmonization of views on military resources, changes in East–West relations and the gradual emergence of a coherent European security dimension.

Greater political cooperation

Amid the changing international scene in 1955, with West Germany's accession to NATO, and 1956, with the Hungarian uprising and the Suez Crisis, the view gradually emerged within NATO that member states should work together more closely on political issues and that its Council should act as a forum for that purpose. A committee of three wise men was appointed, which proposed that member states should inform the North Atlantic Council of any developments significantly affecting the policy of the Alliance. The foreign ministers could then consult and draw up an assessment based on a summary prepared by the secretary general. In the event of disputes the secretary general could set procedures in motion for their resolution, including offering his good offices. The three wise men also advised NATO that the Council should, from time to time, meet in different capital cities. That would cause greater direct contact with national politics and enhance NATO's status in the member states. The first such meeting of the North Atlantic Council took place in Bonn in May 1957. As a result of these political contacts the role of secretary general took on a greater importance. Within NATO, too, an interparliamentary assembly was set up. The *North Atlantic Assembly* was founded in 1955 as the *Conference of NATO Parliamentarians*, a name that continued to be used until 1966. This Assembly, which is independent of NATO, aims to bring North American and European legislators more closely together. It intends to foster cooperation between Alliance members and to promote within national parliaments a collective sense of Atlantic solidarity. It meets twice a year in plenary session, as do its committees. It is customary for civilian and military authorities engaged in NATO policies and activities to address the Assembly. Within NATO informing politicians and citizens has taken on a higher priority. In pursuit of its foreign policy the US has relied not just on military alliances such as NATO, but has also supplemented these with a common embargo policy as part of COCOM (see Figure 23.3).

23.3 The Warsaw Pact in Eastern Europe (1955)

The Warsaw Pact (1955)

On 14 May 1955 eight communist states (Albania, Bulgaria, Czechoslovakia, East Germany, Hungary, Poland, Romania and the Soviet Union) signed the *Treaty of Friendship, Cooperation and Mutual Assistance* in Warsaw. This organization became known as the *Warsaw Pact* (or *Warsaw Treaty Organization*) and was set up in response to the Paris Protocols which created the WEU and West Germany's accession to NATO on 5 May. As with NATO the Warsaw Pact referred to the objects and principles of the UN and its members pledged to defend each other if one or more members were attacked. The Treaty established a Political Consultative Committee (consisting of foreign and defence ministers, heads of state and the general secretaries of the national communist parties), a Joint Secretariat and

---

Figure 23.3 The COCOM embargo list (1949)

In 1949 the US took the initiative of setting up a committee to coordinate trade policy between East and West. This was the **Coordinating Committee for Multi-lateral Export Controls**, or COCOM. COCOM was not an organization in the formal sense, but a more or less confidential consultative forum which met on a regular basis – with an annual meeting of economics ministers in Paris – to discuss the export of strategic goods to the Soviet Union and other communist states. Until 1983 European states rejected the idea of a permanent committee and so COCOM had no permanent secretariat and seldom acted publicly. Its main weapon was a **common embargo policy**, with a 'blacklist' of goods (Commodity Control List) whose export was prohibited. Decisions were reached by consensus, with states at liberty to pursue a stricter policy if they wished. COCOM had no executive powers. The states themselves maintained the list and monitored its implementation, although the US kept a close eye on developments. NATO's European members took part in COCOM from the start and Japan and Australia joined later. The list of commodities had meanwhile become longer and successfully hampered the export of goods and modern technology to communist states.

With East–West relations changing after 1989, the COCOM list began to lose its significance and former Warsaw Pact states were given access to Western goods and technology. In April 1994 COCOM dissolved itself. However, at an international meeting in Wassenaar in the Netherlands on 12 July 1996 a proposal was approved to set up a successor, composed more broadly than COCOM but still focused on controlling exports to certain states. This successor is known as the ***Wassenaar Arrangement on Export Controls for Conventional Arms and Dual-Use Goods and Technologies***.

---

a Permanent Commission to provide policy recommendations. For military issues a Joint Command of the combined armed forces was established and, following the invasion by the Warsaw Pact of Czechoslovakia in 1968 (see below), a Committee of Ministers of Defence. Although in its set-up the organization resembled NATO, there were differences. The Warsaw Pact was grounded largely in bilateral treaties for mutual assistance between member states, mirroring the accords between the Soviet Union and these states in relation to the status of their armed forces. Compared with NATO, this meant a central position for the Soviet Union at the expense of the organization as a whole. The Soviet Union assumed all the organization's key positions, including supreme command of its military forces, and there was little consultation between member states. Its various committees met infrequently. It was not until 1976 that a Committee of Foreign Ministers was set up to further political cooperation. Compared with the military integration under Soviet leadership, political integration remained significantly weaker.

Intervention in communist states

Although the Warsaw Pact was established as the military counterweight to NATO, the rivalry between the two blocs was fought out largely in ideological terms. There was never actually any direct military confrontation between the two. The creation of

NATO and the Warsaw Pact did, however, lead to the expansion and integration of their respective military forces. In response to the Hungarian uprising of 1956, which was triggered by a show of support for the reform movement taking place in Poland, Soviet troops invaded Hungary. The new government in Budapest responded by pulling Hungary out of the Warsaw Pact on 1 November. Hungary declared its neutrality and asked the Western powers and the UN to recognize it as a neutral state, but Soviet troops crushed the uprising and installed a pro-Soviet government. More than 200,000 Hungarians fled abroad. The Cold War had left Europe split. Hungary was part of the Soviet sphere of influence and was given no opportunity to adopt a neutral position. The Soviet Union ignored a UN resolution calling on it to end its intervention and UN observers were denied access to Hungary, while the new government reversed Hungary's decision to pull out of the Pact. After the 'Prague Spring' of 1968 Warsaw Pact troops, including troops from Hungary, invaded Czechoslovakia to suppress the cautious reforms of the government under Alexander Dubček. The Soviet leader Leonid Brezhnev justified the intervention in terms of the need to save socialism, but Romania's leader Nicolae Ceauşescu spoke out against it as a violation of international principles. He reminded the communist states that the Warsaw Pact had been established to defend its members against external aggression. Romania subsequently refused to take part in any military exercises involving Warsaw Pact forces. Albania, which had barely taken part in the organization since 1961, pulled out of the Treaty in the same year, also because of the ideological split between the Soviet Union and China, to which Albania was more oriented.

23.4 Cooperation on security in the Western Hemisphere and Asia

The Rio Pact (1947) and CONDECA (1963)

Regional mutual assistance agreements were also instituted outside Europe and the North Atlantic region: in the Western Hemisphere, in Southeast Asia and in the Middle East. On 30 August 1947, at an Inter-American conference on peace and security near Rio de Janeiro, 18 states signed the *Inter-American Treaty of Reciprocal Assistance*, known as the *Rio Pact*. This Treaty came into force on 3 December 1948 and was to be integrated into the security system of the Organization of American States (OAS) (see Figure 23.4). By 1990 25 states were party to the Treaty. Under its terms states were obliged to support each other in the event of an attack by an external aggressor. The geographical

Figure 23.4 The Organization of American States (OAS) (1948)

Like the Council of Europe, the **Organization of American States** (OAS) is a culturally (rather than economically) determined regional organization. It was the successor to the *International Union of American Republics* established in 1890, known from 1910 as the *Union of American Republics*, with the *Pan-American Union* as its secretariat (see §11.5). In 1948 the Union was reshaped into the Organization of American States and the Pan-American Union became the OAS General Secretariat. The objectives of the OAS are to strengthen peace and security on the continent, promote and consolidate representative democracy (with 'due respect for the principle of non-intervention'), prevent possible causes of difficulties and ensure the pacific settlement of disputes that may arise between member states. It stipulates common action by states in the event of aggression, the promotion of economic and social development and the limitation of conventional weapons. The OAS, with 35 members, has a General Assembly (a consultative meeting of foreign ministers), various councils (the Permanent Council, the Inter-American Economic and Social Council, the Inter-American Council for Education, Science and Culture – the latter two were replaced in 1996 by the Inter-American Council for Integral Development), the Inter-American Commission on Human Rights, the Inter-American Council of Jurists, a General Secretariat and six specialist agencies dating from before the Second World War: for health, children, women, geography and history, indigenous people and agricultural cooperation (see Figure 18.6). In 1948 the OAS adopted the *American Declaration of the Rights and Duties of Man* shortly before the UN Declaration of Human Rights of the same year. The *American Convention on Human Rights* followed in 1969 and an *Additional Protocol in the Area of Economic, Social and Cultural Rights* in 1988 (see §33.5).

Until 1965 the US succeeded in justifying **OAS intervention** in disputes between states in the Western Hemisphere by pointing to the communist threat, but after that it was less successful in doing so. Initially therefore US interests and those of other member states coincided, or at least such was the perception. The US generally acted as leader and financed and supplied military aid. The OAS 'did well in insignificant as well as in moderately intense disputes, in cases of limited fighting as well as in disputes without fighting. It did even better when war was waged seriously. It coped better with bilateral and local than with regional disputes but even there the record was good' (Haas 1983, 212). A regional example was OAS efforts to limit Cuba's influence in the Caribbean. Cuba was excluded from participation in the OAS in 1962 and the US supplied a wide range of aid to Caribbean states. After 1965 US leadership began to be challenged. Mexico and Venezuela for instance defied the US on issues such as Cuba and US opposition to the Sandinistas in Nicaragua. 'Jamaica, Panama and Andean states are no longer reliable clients' (Haas 1983, 213). The OAS complements the work of the UN. Awareness of that was stronger prior to 1965 than subsequently.

region covered by the Treaty is defined precisely and comprises the entire Western Hemisphere, including Canada, which was not in fact a party to the Treaty. The mechanism has been invoked on several occasions in response to border disputes and military intervention, such as in 1965 in the Dominican Republic, although it was not invoked in the Falklands/Malvinas War. Cuba was excluded from the Rio Pact in 1962. On 14 December 1963 the *Central American Defence Council* (CONDECA) (Consejo de defensa centroamericano) was set up in Guatemala City, with seven member states and the US as an advisory member. Its purpose was to defend members in the event of an attack by a non-member. CONDECA was formed in direct response to the Cuban Missile Crisis of 1962. From the early 1980s it became an instrument of US policy against Nicaragua's Sandinista government. Nicaragua left in 1979 and was subsequently excluded from membership. This political shift meant CONDECA lost its original *raison d'être*.

371

The ANZUS Pact (1951) and SEATO (1954)

In 1951 Australia, New Zealand and the US concluded the *Pacific Defence Pact*, also known as the *ANZUS Pact* from the initial letters of the names of the three states. The Pact, designed to defend the Pacific region in the event of an attack, was prompted by fears of a communist threat and by the desire to protect democratic values. The Pact's significance declined with the creation of the Southeast Asia Treaty Organization (see below) in 1954, but at the end of the 1960s it revived because of problems over the roles of France and Pakistan within SEATO. In 1982 New Zealand decided to limit its role in the ANZUS Pact after its government refused to allow US nuclear-powered or nuclear-armed warships to use its ports, as part of New Zealand's support for a nuclear-free zone in the region. The US responded by suspending its formal obligations to New Zealand under the treaty and downgraded official ties. The conflict has to date not been resolved, with the US continuing to insist on the need for nuclear weapons in the region and New Zealand maintaining its support for a nuclear-free zone. In formal terms the three states are still ANZUS members and there is consultation between the US and Australia. In practical terms, however, the ANZUS Pact is more or less inoperative. Unlike NATO, the *Southeast Asia Treaty Organization* (SEATO) was not an exemplary success. It was founded on 8 September 1954 by Australia, France, New Zealand, Pakistan, the Philippines, Thailand, the UK and the US, whose initiative it was. This collective defence Treaty came into effect in 1955. In a Declaration appended to the Treaty the US limited its involvement to countering 'communist aggression'. The organization's demise can be attributed to the lack of a joint military command and the refusal of states such as Burma, India and Indonesia to join. Cambodia, Laos and South Vietnam, which were prevented from signing the Treaty but included in the area protected under SEATO, rejected that protection. Pakistan left in 1973 after the recognition of Bangladesh by Australia, the UK and New Zealand. France seceded in 1974, having been only a nominal member for several years. In 1977 SEATO was dissolved. On 16 April 1971 a defence pact between five members of the British Commonwealth, known as ANZUK (after Australia, New Zealand and the UK), was concluded. The other two members were Malaysia and Singapore.

The Baghdad Pact (1955)

The *Baghdad Pact* came into being in 1955 as a means to counter communist aggression in the Middle East and to promote economic and social cooperation between members. The members of the Baghdad Pact and the corresponding *Middle East Treaty Organization* (METO) were Iran, Iraq, Pakistan, Turkey and the UK. In 1959 Iraq pulled out because of political changes at home. The organization continued as the *Central Treaty Organization* (CENTO) and its secretariat was transferred to Ankara in Turkey. The US became an associate member and concluded bilateral agreements with Iran, Pakistan and Turkey. CENTO acted more as a security alliance than an organization also aiming to promote cooperation in economic and other fields, although communications and transport infrastructure were developed. Operations under the CENTO flag were also conducted against what were termed 'subversive activities' in member states. CENTO weakened after 1974 when Turkey invaded Cyprus and ceased to exist after the Iranian revolution of 1979. The organization made no effort to persuade Arab states to join. Apparently in the 1950s the importance of a broad multilateral strategy was felt less acutely in Asia and the Arab world than in Europe and the Western Hemisphere.

Peaceful coexistence and nuclear weapons control at the United Nations

24.1 Nuclear weapons control: the IAEA (1957) and the Non-Proliferation Treaty (1968)

The definition of aggression

Debates on the definition of aggression and of disarmament were, from a time point of view, a significant element of UN processes. It took almost a quarter of a century to decide on the definition of aggression. Aggression had already been a discussion item during the Kellogg–Briand Pact of 1928 (see §16.2) and it returned within the context of the Nuremburg Tribunal, when the question was considered of whether planning an aggressive war was a crime against peace (see §21.1). In 1950 the Soviet Union proposed that the UN should formulate a definition of aggression, a proposal that was sent to the International Law Commission for further study. In 1952 the General Assembly set up a special committee on the subject, which was remodelled a number of times. This committee submitted a draft definition in 1973, adopted by the UN in 1974, but it only referred to armed aggression by states, or groups of states, against each other and disregarded other forms of aggression. Despite these limitations, attempts such as this fulfilled 'the general desire of the international community to avoid war' (Gorman 2001, 119). Compared with the debate on aggression, the way the issue of nuclear weapons control was dealt with seems fairly straightforward. The discussions started in 1946 and resulted in a treaty on the non-proliferation of nuclear weapons in 1968. Although the term *disarmament* (the partial or total abolition of weapons, without them being replaced by new ones) is often used in this context, what is really meant is generally *arms control*: the containment of the arms process with a view to reducing the risk of war (and to managing the costs involved).

Nuclear weapons control (1946)

After the US had used nuclear weapons in 1945 to halt the war with Japan, it soon became clear that the Soviet Union also was working on the development of such weapons. The task for the UN seemed to be to monitor the growth and development of the arsenals. Nuclear weapons, together with biological and chemical weapons ('ABC weapons'), were classified as *weapons of mass destruction*. In contrast to 'conventional' weapons, they were deemed to cause mass destruction because a single nuclear bomb was capable of wiping out an entire city. The US and the Soviet Union confronted each other in the *UN Atomic Energy Commission* (UNAEC), which the UN set up in 1946. The US proposed banning the production and possession of nuclear weapons and, with regard to the peaceful use of atomic energy, placing all atomic material, uranium mines and reprocessing plants under international control, with a supranational Atomic Development Authority. The Soviet Union rejected this 'Baruch plan', named after the American UNAEC representative Bernard Baruch. The reason given was that this would in practice amount to an American monopoly. Instead the Soviet Union wanted a moratorium, which the US turned down because the Soviet Union would then be able to continue its development programmes while the US would be unable to do the same. This stalemate meant that the two powers blocked progress by demanding the impossible from each other.

Establishment of the IAEA (1957): peaceful use of atomic energy

With a view to ensuring that progress was nevertheless made, the UN in 1952 arranged the merger of the Atomic Energy Commission and the Commission on Conventional Armaments which had been established in 1947. However, the new *UN Disarmament Commission* (UNDC) made just as little progress during the 1950s. While the US wanted first to tackle conventional weapons and then nuclear weapons, the Soviet Union wanted precisely the opposite. Nonetheless, the US, the Soviet Union, the UK, France and Canada all engaged in secret discussions within the framework of the *Subcommittee on Disarmament*, established in 1954. It was partly as a result of this that the *International Atomic Energy Agency* (IAEA) became operative in July 1957, with the aim of promoting the peaceful use of atomic energy. At the end of 1953 President Dwight D. Eisenhower had laid the basis for a solution to the impasse in his *Atoms for Peace* speech to the General Assembly. Given that the nuclear powers (the US, the Soviet Union, the UK and soon France) were not prepared to transfer part of their nuclear arsenals to an international body, the way forward seemed to be to cooperate on research to find *peaceful* applications for nuclear power. With this goal in mind an institution was set up to oversee the international situation, with the development of atomic energy for peaceful use only permitted subject to *safeguards*. Four years of diplomatic negotiations resulted in an independent IGO under UN patronage. The IAEA was not a specialized UN agency, but one 'related' to the UN (see Figure 21.3). It had its headquarters in Vienna because slightly earlier the former Allies had declared Austria to be a neutral state. The objectives of the IAEA included speeding up and increasing the contribution made by nuclear power to peace, health and welfare throughout the world and preventing it being used for military purposes. The IAEA has set up programmes to verify developments and has encouraged security, the use of atomic energy and the exchange of technology.

Public unease

By the end of the 1950s the US and the Soviet Union had amassed large arsenals of nuclear weapons, which were much more powerful and more destructive than the atomic bombs used in 1945. Moreover the two states had developed many ways of transporting them, such as on strategic bombers, intercontinental missiles and, before long, submarines. Other states were also trying to obtain these weapons, with the UK carrying out its first nuclear test in 1952 and France doing so in 1960. India equally wanted its own nuclear weapons and even a neutral state such as Sweden considered producing them. The UN Disarmament Commission therefore discussed proposals to impose restraints on tests, end the production of fissionable material, limit stocks of weapons and increase the number of inspection possibilities. The growth in the number of UN member states led to a gradual increase in the size of the Disarmament Commission to also include non-aligned countries, which went some way towards easing East–West tensions. At the same time physicists expressed concern over the possibility that, if used, nuclear weapons could lead to the wholesale destruction of life on earth. The worried scientists joined forces in the *Pugwash Movement*, with the aim to raise public awareness, via the media, of the dangers of nuclear weapons (see Figure 24.1).

Figure 24.1 The Russell–Einstein Manifesto (1955) and the Pugwash Movement (1957)

The **Pugwash Movement** relied on support from socially-aware physicists, who themselves had played an active role in the development of nuclear weapons. Nuclear fission had been discovered in Germany in 1939. Thanks to mediation by Albert Einstein the US government had been informed of the military possibilities which this discovery implied and of the danger of Germany being able to produce a nuclear weapon. During the Second World War the US managed to produce precisely such a weapon in a top secret programme carried out in Los Alamos, New Mexico. The US was able to benefit from the knowledge and skill of physicists, some of whom had worked on a nuclear project in the UK. A first and successful test was performed in July 1945. Not all physicists thought that such a bomb would ever actually be used, but they were proven wrong when the US dropped nuclear bombs on two densely-populated cities in Japan. The scientists' concerns about what these weapons could do increased as a result of the postwar research into the H-bomb, or hydrogen bomb, with explosive power of more than a thousand times that of the A-bomb. They again decided to protest, but this time publicly.

The concern was bolstered by a speech broadcast on radio by the British philosopher Bertrand Russell in December 1954 on the danger that mankind was facing. He drew up a manifesto that was signed by Einstein (a few days before his death) and other leading scientists, including a number of Nobel Prize winners. This manifesto was published on 9 July 1955 and became known internationally as the **Russell–Einstein Manifesto**. 'We have to learn to ask ourselves, not what steps can be taken to give military victory to whatever group we prefer, for there no longer are such steps; the question we have to ask ourselves is: what steps can be taken to prevent a military contest of which the issue must be disastrous to all parties?' The manifesto called for an international conference to be organized which would instigate impartial research into the nature and size of the threats and would seek ways of reducing them.

Originally the conference was to take place in India in January 1957, following an invitation from Nehru, but this was made impossible by the Suez Crisis. The American railway tycoon Cyrus Eaton then decided to make his country house in Pugwash, Canada, available, where the first **Pugwash conference** took place in July 1957. Russell had invited 22 scientists, including seven from the US and three from the Soviet Union. The most important subject to be dealt with in detail at the conference was the danger of atomic energy because of radiation, something about which little was known, certainly as far as the public was concerned. A *Continuing Committee* was set up in London to organize subsequent conferences. Although these conferences were confidential, the results were published in press releases and in various journals and the scientists also sent their reports and statements to governments. John F. Kennedy and Nikita Khrushchev responded at the beginning of the 1960s by submitting their own views and arguments to the meetings. Regional and national Pugwash committees were set up in addition to the international Pugwash committees, which organized regional and national conferences that enhanced the movement's image. The Pugwash Movement's authority was based primarily on the expertise of the scientists involved, who were questioning political developments.

The Cuban Missile Crisis (1962)

The nadir, and at the same time the turning point, in the Cold War was the Cuban Missile Crisis in 1962. Through the use of spy planes the US had discovered that the Soviet Union was moving missiles carrying nuclear warheads to Cuba. Fidel Castro had come to power there at the beginning of 1959 and had offered the Soviet Union a missile base on the island. Adlai Stevenson, the US representative to the UN, showed the Security Council aerial photos which clearly revealed what the Soviet Union was doing and he also indicated what military action the US was prepared to take against Cuba and the Soviet Union. In the meantime the US set up a blockade around Cuba. The US government, in which John and Robert Kennedy were determining the strategic framework of the conflict, wanted secretary-general U Thant to become involved and Khrushchev also assented to UN mediation. In the end the UN did not need to become involved, as the key players agreed on compromises and the removal of the missiles through direct consultations. The world had escaped a war in which nuclear weapons would undoubtedly have been used, as was revealed at the end of the Cold War in a reconstruction of the conflict by the surviving decision makers (Blight *et al.* 1993). Both the US and the Soviet governments had understood that such a war should be avoided and in 1963 they set up direct telephone connections (*hot lines*) between Washington and Moscow to facilitate communication in the event of a military threat and to avoid any misunderstandings. Arms control agreements were concluded and steps taken to ensure conflicts were averted. Although the Cuban Missile Crisis reduced the global tensions between East and West, promoting *peaceful coexistence*, their relationship at the UN continued to be poor, as they used the organization as a forum in which to criticize each other.

Consultation in Geneva and the Partial Test Ban Treaty (1963)

The consultations on nuclear weapons control at the UN had reached deadlock, but progress was being made in parallel negotiations. The US, the UK, France and the Soviet Union, as well as other NATO and Warsaw Pact states, had set up the *Ten-Nation Committee on Disarmament* in Geneva in September 1959, which initiated discussions in March 1960. However, these talks failed. The Committee was independent, although the UN had agreed to its formation and there were also personal and institutional ties, as was the case with the *Eighteen-Nation Disarmament Committee* (ENDC) which was established to continue the work in 1961. This new Committee had a broader base and included states from the West, the East and the Third World. Meetings were held in the former League of Nations building and were chaired alternately by the US and the Soviet Union. In November 1961 the UN General Assembly adopted a resolution stating that the use of nuclear weapons was contrary to international law, the UN Charter and humanitarian laws and that their use therefore had to be banned. Some progress was made in 1962, partly as a result of the Cuban Missile Crisis, and the US and the Soviet Union agreed the *Partial Test Ban Treaty* (PTBT) in Moscow on 5 August 1963. This banned all above-ground tests and from then on only underground tests were permitted. The General Assembly saw this Treaty as a step towards a total ban on nuclear tests in the sea, the atmosphere and space. No agreement was reached on how to ensure compliance. Nuclear tests could be measured seismically and monitored by local inspections, but the Soviet Union did not want any inspections to take place in its territory.

Realization of the Non-Proliferation Treaty (1968)

In the meantime discussions within the ENDC in Geneva were beginning to advance. At the UN the idea had been developed that states which had nuclear weapons should promise not to transfer them to other states. In Geneva the great powers agreed that the group of states with nuclear weapons should be kept as small as possible, resulting in the use of the term *non-proliferation*. Following the Partial Test Ban Treaty of 1963 talks continued about the guidelines for nuclear (*haves*) and non-nuclear (*have nots*) states. In 1965 the US and the Soviet Union drew up similar draft treaties intended to prevent the proliferation of nuclear weapons. One question was how this should be dealt with within the military alliances. In the eyes of the Soviet Union the North Atlantic Treaty Organization (see §23.2) was a structure that would allow non-nuclear states to take part in the decision making about the use of nuclear weapons. It also feared that NATO would let the Federal Republic of Germany 'get its finger on the trigger' of the nuclear weapons pointed at the Soviet Union. It was therefore prepared to cooperate on an international inspection system, such as the IAEA, albeit on condition that nuclear states did not need to agree to inspections. Here the problem was that the European Atomic Energy

Community (Euratom), which was established in 1957 (see §26.3), already provided an inspection system. Negotiations between the US, the Soviet Union and the six European states on how a global inspection system would relate to a regional system complicated the discussions in Geneva. Despite all these problems the US and the Soviet Union submitted a joint draft to the ENDC on 24 August 1967, which was adopted. The three nuclear states which were prepared to do so, the US, the UK and the Soviet Union, signed the definitive text of the *Treaty on the Non-Proliferation of Nuclear Weapons,* known as the *Non-Proliferation Treaty* (NPT), on 1 July 1968 in Washington DC, London and Moscow, respectively. The Treaty was not signed by France and China, which by then also had nuclear weapons, but it was signed by 58 non-nuclear weapons states. This happened because the UN General Assembly, which had emphasized the importance of such a treaty in 1966 and 1967, adopted it as Resolution 2373(XXII) on 12 June 1968. The Treaty came into effect on 5 March 1970.

Strengthening the IAEA by controlling non-proliferation

The Non-Proliferation Treaty specified that nuclear weapons states were not allowed to transfer nuclear weapons, nuclear explosives or nuclear weapons technology to non-nuclear states and that the latter were not allowed to acquire nuclear weapons or nuclear explosives. Research and the peaceful use of atomic energy, however, were permitted. *Nuclear Weapons States* (NWS) are states which possessed nuclear weapons on 1 January 1967, which in effect meant the five permanent members of the Security Council. All other states were *Non-Nuclear Weapons States* (NNWS). There was also a group of states that 'were on the threshold' of possessing nuclear weapons, such as Argentina, Brazil, India (which carried out a nuclear test in 1974), Israel and South Africa. The Treaty placed the responsibility for supervising non-proliferation on the IAEA. Through inspections the IAEA can check locally whether the non-nuclear weapons states are

Figure 24.2 The IAEA inspection regime in the twentieth century

During the first 25 years of its existence the number of inspections by the IAEA within the framework of the Non-Proliferation Treaty averaged a thousand per year. The **IAEA inspection regime** operated well as a whole, despite restrictions due to the fact that inspections were only allowed at locations indicated by a particular state. For instance after the Gulf War of 1991 Iraq proved to have been more active than was thought on the basis of the information provided. Other restrictions were the nuclear programmes of the nuclear weapons states (which were not covered by the inspections), the non-notified activities of threshold states (in 1993 South Africa admitted having nuclear facilities for military purposes) and secret activities (which led, for example, to Pakistan acquiring nuclear weapons). The establishment of the IAEA was the product of a calculated US policy which developed from the institutional regulation of peace, in which others were also involved. During the détente between East and West which characterized the initial period of the organization's existence the IAEA was able to develop into a fairly autonomous institution, within which it was quite easy to achieve consensus between the states involved (Scheinman 1973).

During the 1970s more developing states joined the IAEA, because they felt they were underrepresented and that they received relatively little support for the possibilities open to them for the peaceful use of atomic energy. This led to conflicts over the filling of posts and the distribution of the budget, which were discussed against the backdrop of **politicization** (see §34.2). However, even at times of political tension such as during the Gulf War, the IAEA managed to preserve, and even increase, its own authority and autonomy. This was partly due to internal factors, such as leadership and decision making based on consensus, but also to its ability to use situations in which an international regime was failing. The IAEA used the assessment of its weak performance to great effect in order to strengthen the organization's own inspection regime which, despite all the deficiencies, was regarded as indispensable (Colijn 1998, 105). South Africa signed the Non-Proliferation Treaty in 1991 and France and China did so in 1992. In 2008 189 states were party to the Treaty. Four states were not: Cuba, India, Israel and Pakistan. The 1968 Treaty had stipulated that a decision on its extension had to be taken 25 years after it had come into force. In 1995 the parties to it decided to extend it for an indefinite period.

using the 'fissionable material' needed for atomic energy for peaceful purposes. The nuclear weapons states themselves are not obliged to allow checks, but they are bound, on the basis of Article I, to ensure that no transfers take place to non-nuclear weapons states and to strive for a speedy end to the nuclear arms race by negotiating in good faith (Article VI). Article III lays down rules for the safeguards to be used by the IAEA to prevent the non-peaceful use of atomic energy. The 'exporting' states bear considerable responsibility and have to ensure that their trading activities do not result in proliferation. In order to check this IAEA enters into *Safeguard Agreements* with individual states, in which procedures are laid down in accordance with a model agreement. The IAEA also uses a 'trigger list' of nuclear goods that may only be exported under the supervision of the IAEA and which play a key role in the fissionable material cycle so relevant to nuclear weapons. The list was compiled by the so-called Zangger Committee set up in 1971. Opinions differed as to how strict an export policy had to be, as an excessively liberal policy could lead to situations in which a state such as India could effect a nuclear explosion. Despite restrictions and fluctuations, the IAEA regime worked (see Figure 24.2).

Strengthening of the Geneva disarmament committee

The creation of the Non-Proliferation Treaty strengthened not only the IAEA but also the Geneva-based disarmament committee ENDC. In 1969, when the number of participating states was increased to include amongst others Japan, the name was changed from the Eighteen-Nation Disarmament Committee to the *Conference of the Committee on Disarmament* (CCD) and in 1978 it was renamed the *Conference on Disarmament* (CD). This independent committee, which nevertheless has ties with the UN, continues to be active today. It decides on its own procedures but takes account of recommendations from the UN General Assembly. The number of members has risen from 40 to 65.

24.2 Continuing nuclear weapons control and the UN Biological Weapons Convention (1972)

Continuing nuclear weapons control

The goal of nuclear weapons control was not achieved solely by the IAEA (1957), the Partial Test Ban Treaty (1963) and the Non-Proliferation Treaty (1968). Not all nuclear weapons states were party to the 1963 Treaty, while the ban on above-ground nuclear tests encouraged the staging of underground tests. Based on their fear of the consequences of a nuclear war, the US and the Soviet Union continued to regulate their mutual relations in this respect. In 1971 they signed a treaty designed to prevent an accidental war by agreeing to give warning of serious accidents involving missiles or nuclear weapons, followed in 1973 by an agreement to warn each other if there was a risk of a nuclear war breaking out between them. They also agreed to mutual consultations in the event of a nuclear war erupting elsewhere in the world, even if they (or one of them) were not involved. The idea was to be alert to any signs of imminent nuclear war. On 3 July 1974 the two powers signed an agreement which banned underground nuclear tests of a military nature with an explosive capacity of more than 150 kilotons. This *Treaty on the Limitation of Underground Nuclear Weapon Tests* (abbreviated to TTBT, *Threshold Test Ban Treaty*) was followed in April 1976 by the *Treaty on Underground Nuclear Explosions for Peaceful Purposes* (*Peaceful Nuclear Explosions Treaty*, PNET). This imposed the same limit as regards explosive power and a limit of 1,500 kilotons in the event of more than one peaceful explosion taking place at the same time. As both states took a long time to ratify, the impact of these two Treaties was limited, although in 1976 each party had declared that it would observe the Treaties pending ratification. Other discussions between the US and the Soviet Union concerned the way in which these Treaties could be verified and a general treaty banning nuclear activities. In 1982 these discussions were stopped because of a disagreement on how compliance should be monitored. The Soviet Union was prepared to permit some inspections, but the two powers could not reach a definitive agreement. This did only happen at the end of the Cold War and both Treaties were finally ratified in 1990.

Space, the sea bed and the environment

The ENDC, later CCD, in Geneva also continued to be active. The efforts of an ENDC subcommittee on the peaceful use of outer space led on 23 January 1967 to the *Treaty on Principles Governing the Activities of States in the Exploration and Use of Outer Space, Including the Moon and Other Celestial Bodies*. This 'Outer Space Treaty' was signed in Washington DC, Moscow and London and contains the principles which govern state activities in outer space. The parties to the Treaty are banned from launching nuclear weapons or other weapons of mass destruction into an orbit around the earth or into space. Nor may military bases and the like be constructed on the moon or other celestial bodies, which unlike space itself are demilitarized. Weapons systems may be installed in space, as long as they do not include weapons of mass destruction. Research in space is also permitted. All the major states apart from China signed up to this Treaty. The *Treaty on the Prohibition of the Emplacement of Nuclear Weapons and Other Weapons of Mass Destruction on the Sea-Bed and the Ocean Floor and in the Subsoil Thereof* followed on 11 February 1971. The scope of this Treaty is restricted, because these weapons can be transported in submarines and ships and all weapons are permitted in coastal waters (a 12-mile zone). The UN General Assembly adopted the *Convention on the Prohibition of Military or Any Other Hostile Use of Environmental Modification Techniques*, abbreviated to the ENMOD Convention, drawn up in Geneva, on 10 December 1976. The term 'environmental modification techniques' refers to any technique for changing the dynamics, composition or structure of the earth, including its various spheres, and of outer space through the deliberate manipulation of natural processes. States were able to sign up to the Convention in Geneva from May 1977 onwards and it came into effect on 5 October 1978.

Regional agreements

In addition to these general treaties relating to space, the seabed and the environment, regional agreements also imposed restrictions on the use of nuclear weapons. On 1 December 1959 the US, the Soviet Union, France, the UK and a further eight states active in the Antarctic during the International Geophysical Year 1957–58 signed the *Antarctic Treaty*, agreeing to use the South Pole region only for peaceful purposes. The International Geophysical Year was modelled on the International Polar Years of 1882–83 and 1932–33, which allowed scientists from around the world to take part in a series of coordinated observations of various geophysical phenomena. This first postwar arms control Treaty was based on the determination to demilitarize an area, as would be the case with regard to space and celestial bodies in 1967. As well as military activities, nuclear explosions and the storage of nuclear waste are also forbidden at the South Pole. The Treaty also included regulations governing inspections. The next regional treaty was the *Treaty of Tlatelolco* of 14 February 1967, in which Latin America and the Caribbean region were declared nuclear-free zones. This had two Protocols intended to ensure that third-party states with territories in the continent would announce that they respect the provisions of the Treaty and that nuclear weapons states would declare that they will not use any nuclear weapons against signatories to the Treaty. One of the shortcomings of the Treaty of Tlatelolco was that two potential nuclear weapons states, Argentina and Brazil, did not participate due to a disagreement on the interpretation of Article 18 on nuclear explosions for peaceful purposes. However, in 1991 they signed a bilateral agreement banning this. Thanks to the IAEA guarantee agreements, which take account of the attitude of the states that signed up to this Treaty, compliance is verified in practice and a regional control organization was established in Mexico City, known as the *Agency for the Prohibition of Nuclear Weapons in Latin America and the Caribbean* (OPANAL, Organismo para la proscripción de las armas nuclearas en la América Latina y el Caribe). In 1985 the *Treaty of Rarotonga* was signed, making the southern part of the Pacific Ocean a nuclear-free zone. The greatest problem in this case was that France carried out its nuclear tests on the atoll of Mururoa, which forms part of the Tuamotu Archipelago. The Treaty of Rarotonga linked up geographically with the Antarctic Treaty and the Treaty of Tlatelolco. A number of supplementary Protocols were drawn up for states outside the area, but none of the nuclear weapons states felt the need to become party to these (see Figure 24.3 for an overview of the arms control treaties entered into between 1959 and 1985). The 1995 *Treaty of Bangkok* defined a nuclear-free zone in Southeast Asia. This was followed by the *Treaty of Pelindaba* in 1996, which provided the basis for a nuclear-free zone in Africa (see Figure 36.1).

Figure 24.3 Arms control treaties and conventions 1959–85

1959 Antarctic Treaty (40)
1963 Treaty Banning Nuclear Weapon Tests in the Atmosphere, Outer Space, and Under Water (**Partial Test Ban Treaty**, PTBT) (120)
1967 Treaty on Principles Governing the Activities of States in the Exploration and Use of Outer Space, Including the Moon and Other Celestial Bodies (**Outer Space Treaty**) (93)
1967 Treaty for the Prohibition of Nuclear Weapons in Latin America and the Caribbean (**Treaty of Tlatelolco**) (24)
1968 Treaty on the Non-Proliferation of Nuclear Weapons (**Non-Proliferation Treaty**) (156)
1971 Treaty on the Prohibition of the Emplacement of Nuclear Weapons and Other Weapons of Mass Destruction on the Sea-Bed and the Ocean Floor and in the Subsoil Thereof (**Sea-Bed Treaty**) (88)
1972 Convention on the Prohibition of the Development, Production and Stockpiling of Bacteriological (Biological) and Toxin Weapons and on Their Destruction (**Biological Weapons Convention**) (126)
1972 Interim Agreement on Certain Measures with Respect to the Limitation of Strategic Offensive Arms (with Protocol) (**SALT I** with the ABM Treaty as result) (2)
1972 Treaty on the Limitation of Anti-Ballistic Missile Systems (**ABM Treaty**) (2)
1973 Agreement Relating to Basic Principles of Negotiations on the Further Limitation of Strategic Offensive Arms (within the framework of SALT II)
1974 Treaty on the Limitation of Underground Nuclear Weapon Tests (**Threshold Test Ban Treaty**) (2)
1976 Treaty on Underground Nuclear Explosions for Peaceful Purposes (**Peaceful Nuclear Explosions Treaty**) (2)
1976 Convention on the Prohibition of Military or Any Other Hostile Use of Environmental Modification Techniques (**ENMOD Convention**) (59)
1979 Agreement Governing the Activities of States on the Moon and Other Celestial Bodies (**Agreement on Celestial Bodies**) (7)
1979 Treaty on the Limitation of Strategic Offensive Arms (resulting in **SALT II**) (2)
1980 Convention on Prohibitions or Restrictions on the Use of Certain Conventional Weapons Which May Be Deemed to Be Excessively Injurious or to Have Indiscriminate Effects (**Inhumane Weapons Convention, or Convention on Conventional Weapons**, CCW) (35)
1985 South Pacific Nuclear-Free-Zone Treaty (**Treaty of Rarotonga**) (11)

See Figure 36.1 for the treaties and conventions in the period 1987–2002.
The number of parties to a treaty in 1995 is shown in brackets; source for these numbers (Bailey and Daws 1995, 75).

The Biological Weapons Convention (1972)

The idea of restricting the deployment of biological weapons which use pathogenic bacteria, viruses and other microbes is based on the Protocol adopted in Geneva in 1925 that banned the use of poison gases and bacteriological weapons (see §16.2). At the Conference of the Committee on Disarmament in Geneva, the successor to the ENDC, exhaustive discussions were held on the destruction of existing stockpiles. The fear was that such weapons could infect large groups of unprotected people via the air. The US owned substantial supplies and regarded the issue as problematic, given the presumption that the number of states producing biological weapons was increasing. In 1972 the *Convention on the Prohibition of the Development, Production and Stockpiling of Bacteriological (Biological) and Toxin Weapons and on Their Destruction* was agreed. It was referred to as the *Biological Weapons Convention* (BWC) and came into effect in 1975. It stipulated that the weapons in question had to be destroyed within nine months. When the Convention was agreed it applied to four states and at the end of the Cold War this number had risen to ten. According to information which later became available from Russia, it was clear that the Soviet Union had been conducting experiments involving anthrax. This first arms limitation agreement of the Cold War was weak on supervision, given that this task was assigned to the states themselves. Any complaints had to be made through the Security Council. Once it transpired that there was insufficient mutual trust to implement the agreement, negotiations started on a protocol designed to make improvements. These negotiations, which took place between 1991 and 2001, proved to be an attempt to reformulate the entire issue however, rather than an effort to reinforce supervision. 'Rather than clarify the collective understanding and interpretation of the obligations contained in the BWC or agree politically binding measures which states parties were encouraged to undertake to enhance implementation of the Convention, its states parties attempted to develop a new, supplemental, legally-binding agreement which would have radically overhauled the implementation of the BWC' (Littlewood 2005, 9). The failure of the negotiations meant that agreement could not be reached in 2001 on the protocol and the supervisory *Organization for the Prohibition of Biological Weapons* (OPBW). Six review conferences have been held within the framework of the Convention since 1980, with the latest one in 2006.

The Inhumane Weapons Convention (1980)

Nuclear and biological weapons are weapons of mass destruction, but as regards conventional weapons 51 states in 1980 signed the *Convention on Prohibitions or Restrictions on the Use of Certain Conventional Weapons Which May Be Deemed to Be Excessively Injurious or to Have Indiscriminate Effects*. This became known as the Inhumane Weapons Convention or, in diplomat speak, the *Convention on Conventional Weapons* (CCW). The aim of this Convention was to protect military personnel from certain kinds of injuries and to prevent the accidental wounding or killing of civilians by specific types of weapons. When the Convention came into effect in December 1983 these weapons were described in three Protocols: weapons which left very small fragments in a person's body (Protocol I), landmines, 'booby traps' and similar devices (Protocol II) and weapons which used fire (Protocol III). The preamble to the Convention refers to two principles enshrined in international law. The first is that the parties involved in an armed conflict do not have the unrestricted right to choose the way they want to fight, the second that certain weapons and methods of combat are of such a nature that they 'cause superfluous injury or unnecessary suffering'. It was not until 1990 that agreement was reached on how to monitor the implementation of the Convention. Protocol II on landmines was amended in 1996 and in the same year a fourth Protocol on blinding laser beams was added, while in 2003 a fifth Protocol was included covering explosives left behind on the battlefield after conflicts. The work on the *jus in bello*, initiated at the Peace Conference held in The Hague in 1899, had not yet been completed.

24.3 Limitation of arsenals and numbers of military personnel: SALT, MBFR and CSCE

The SALT discussions 1969–79 and the ABM Treaty (1972)

The international conventions discussed have in common that they not only limit the use of certain kinds of weapon, but also ensure that their quantities are known. In the 1950s and 1960s the US and the Soviet Union produced large numbers of weapons of mass destruction. By the beginning of the 1960s they had amassed so many of these weapons that they were capable of destroying each other completely, a situation referred to as MAD: *Mutual Assured Destruction*. Between November 1969 and June 1979 the two powers held discussions on achieving parity and at the same time limiting their strategic arsenals. These discussions are known as the *Strategic Arms Limitation Talks* or SALT. They resulted in a number of agreements. The issues discussed were the types of weapons system (multiple payloads and the interchangeability of means of conveyance on land, by sea and in the air), the differences in arms quality between the two states and the verification of implementation. The basis for the discussions was laid in 1967 by US President Lyndon B. Johnson and Soviet Prime Minister Alexei Kosygin and the first results, referred to as SALT I, were achieved in 1972 by Richard Nixon and Leonid Brezhnev. They signed an interim agreement on the limitation of offensive weapons and the *Treaty on the Limitation of Anti-Ballistic Missile Systems*. This *ABM Treaty* had been the specific goal of Secretary of State Henry Kissinger, who managed to achieve an agreement whereby the US and the Soviet Union were each only allowed to have two strategic defence systems against ballistic missiles. The number of such systems was amended to one each in a *Protocol* dated 1974 which came into force in 1976. The Treaty was agreed for an indefinite period of time but could be cancelled (which the US did in 2001). By the second half of the 1970s the SALT discussions had stalled and an attempt by President Jimmy Carter to revive them resulted in an exchange of new proposals. On 18 June 1979 an agreement was reached on the limitation of strategic weapons to various 'ceilings', intended to replace the interim agreement of 1974. Carter and Brezhnev signed this SALT II Treaty in Vienna and Carter submitted it for ratification to the US Senate. However, following the Soviet invasion of Afghanistan, he suspended the ratification process at the beginning of 1980. Nevertheless the US and the Soviet Union both declared in that same year, and also on later occasions, that they would respect the Treaty's aims.

MBFR discussions between NATO and the Warsaw Pact 1973–89

Within the same framework as SALT, NATO and the Warsaw Pact held discussions in Vienna from October 1973 until February 1989 about *Mutual and Balanced Force Reductions* (MBFR). These discussions were a NATO initiative in the hope that troop cuts would help reduce tension in Central Europe, which was the location of the potentially 'hot' front of the Cold War. In 1978 the two alliances reached agreement about the numbers of military personnel on land and in the air and on the principle of parity that was to be applied. They not only examined reductions but also acknowledged the idea of 'equal ceilings', which meant that each side would have no more than 900,000 military personnel. Because of disagreement on verification and on the correlation of the numbers of military personnel and of weapons, the MBFR discussions in the 1970s and 1980s did not result in a treaty. However, encouraged partly by the success of the CSCE process (see below), the discussions would continue in 1990 to reach an agreement on drastic restrictions on conventional armed forces in Europe (CFE: Conventional Armed Forces in Europe; see §36.1).

The Conference on Security and Cooperation in Europe (CSCE) (1975)

The CSCE process was important for détente in Europe and resulted from the *Conference on Security and Cooperation in Europe* (CSCE). The Soviet Union had talked about the possibility of a European security conference on the formal recognition of the situation after the end of the Second World War, but in the 1950s this could not take place due to the Western European cooperation in the field of security. However, during the course of the 1960s possible discussions on the *status quo* in Europe were made more feasible by the *Ost-Politik* of the German Chancellor Willy Brandt, which led to treaties with Poland, the German Democratic Republic and the Soviet Union. The Warsaw Pact invasion of Czechoslovakia in 1968 also had an effect because of the violence involved. Finland, which itself occupied a difficult position between East and West, offered to organize a conference in Helsinki. Between November 1972 and June 1973 a preparatory process of negotiations took place involving all European states with the exception of Albania, plus the US and Canada. All 35 states were to take part in the Conference as sovereign entities and the Conference itself would not be linked to any military alliances (which would start their own MBFR discussions shortly after the preparatory CSCE negotiations). The Eastern European states vetoed participation by the Council of Europe. It was agreed that decisions would be made by consensus and that the chairpersons of the meetings would change each day in alphabetical order. Three main issues were identified, which became known as the 'three baskets' of Helsinki: security, cooperation in the fields of economics, science, technology and environment, and cooperation in the area of humanitarian and human rights. The actual Conference on Security and Cooperation in Europe started on 3 July 1973 in the Finnish capital and lasted until 21 July 1975 when, only a year later than expected, the text of the *Final Act* was ready. This was duly signed on 1 August.

The Final Act of Helsinki (1975)

In contrast to the treaties discussed so far, the Final Act of Helsinki was not an international treaty but a document that urged the states involved to comply with the principles of the three baskets, as referred to in the document. The *first basket* contained principles relating to security such as sovereignty and the peaceful settlement of disputes, as well as respect for human rights and fundamental freedoms (Principle 7). The greatest value of this lay in confidence-building measures such as the announcement of military exercises and major troop movements, the exchanging of observers and the recognition of the importance of disarmament. The *second basket* covered the promotion of trade, industrial cooperation, improving cooperation in science and technology and protecting the environment. The *third basket* focused on expanding the contacts between European citizens and stimulating the exchange of information, cultural relations and cooperation in the field of education. This third basket would primarily become known, together with Principle 7 on human rights, as the 'human dimension of the CSCE process'. The emphasis was not on the general principles, but on concrete measures to improve existing practices: not on the right to leave a country, but on improving the practicalities of visa provision; not on freedom of information, but on agreements to make information more accessible. The Final Act provided for a number of assessment and follow-up conferences, which took place in Belgrade (1977–78), Madrid (1980–83), Vienna (1986–89) and Helsinki (1992). The publication of the Final Act in the press caused citizens in the Soviet Union and a number of Eastern European states to form so-called Helsinki Groups. However, their demand that human rights should be respected led to arrests and opposition from the authorities, as well as sympathy and expressions of support from Western Europe.

24.4 Measures against aircraft hijackings and terrorism in the 1960s and 1970s

The use of violence for political reasons

The use of violence for political reasons is not a new phenomenon. During the French Revolution Maximilien de Robespierre regarded this as a way of accelerating revolutionary developments, particularly by getting rid of opponents. In 1866, after the American Civil War, the Ku Klux Klan was formed in the south and its members used violence to suppress black Americans and frighten northerners. Some anarchists hoped that killing certain leaders would hasten political and social change. With a view to freeing themselves from the UK, Irish nationalists in the Irish Republican Army waged a guerrilla war against the British, which resulted in Irish independence in 1921. In 1937 the League of Nations had adopted the *Convention for the Prevention and Punishment of Terrorism*, to discourage crimes against internationally-protected people such as heads of state and diplomats, although it never came into effect due to insufficient ratification. After the Second World War there was a return to the use of violence for political reasons. During the decolonization process violence was used against colonial powers, for example during the fight for independence in Indonesia and in Algeria. In the Middle East Palestinians and Israelis used violence against each other because they laid claim to the same territory and each wanted to deter the other. In Northern Ireland the motivation for the use of violence was the antagonism between nationalists, predominantly Roman Catholics and in favour of reunification with Ireland, and Unionists, predominantly Protestants who wanted Northern Ireland to remain part of the UK. The revolutionary expectations of the 1960s were a new development. Following the success of Fidel Castro, who had seized power in Cuba with a small group of comrades, groups such as the Tupamaros in Uruguay and the Montoneros in Argentina focused on taking power by force. In Western Europe radical groups of young people began to use violence in the hope that this would weaken capitalism and thus create a better society. At the end of the 1960s such groups included the Baader–Meinhof Gang in Germany and the Red Brigade in Italy. Nor did extreme right-wing groups shrink from using bombs and murders in the hope of curbing left-wing popularity.

Aircraft hijackings in the 1960s and the ICAO

Another new development was the hijacking of aircraft with the intention of forcing them to land somewhere other than their planned destination. In the US, Cuban exiles coerced aircraft crews into diverting to Cuba in 1961, sometimes in order to return to the country of their birth, on other occasions to demand money. This led to the use of the term *skyjacking*, although the older term *hijacking* remained more common. The latter dates from the 1920s, when lorries or train loads of alcohol were hijacked in the US and driven to an alternative destination. From 1968 onwards a new type of hijacking was practised, when politically motivated Palestinians and sympathetic Arabs began to hijack aircraft. Their aim was to negotiate the release of imprisoned compatriots in exchange for the release of the passengers. If they failed to achieve their goal they were prepared to blow up the aircraft. The International Civil Aviation Organization (ICAO) devised measures to combat hijackings. They adopted the *Convention on Offences and Certain Other Acts Committed on Board Aircraft* in Tokyo in 1963. In 1970 this was followed in The Hague by the *Convention for the Suppression of Unlawful Seizure of Aircraft*. This second Convention made the unlawful possession of an aircraft and the use of violence, or threat thereof, a crime for which states could extradite hijackers they had captured. In 1971 the *Convention for the Suppression of Unlawful Acts against the Safety of Civil Aviation* was adopted in Montreal. This also covered acts of sabotage on the ground (airports, air traffic installations), unlike the Hague Convention that was limited to actions on board an aircraft.

Terrorism and the UN during the 1970s

In 1972 secretary-general Kurt Waldheim asked the UN General Assembly to place the issue of terrorism on its agenda, because it was increasingly becoming an international phenomenon. The background to this step was the murder that year of Israeli athletes during the Olympic Games in Munich. Many states were reticent. The US wanted to discuss a draft treaty for the prevention and punishment of acts of international terrorism at a special international conference, but the Soviet Union advocated proceeding through the International Law Commission. Developing states accused the Northern wealthy states of having turned a blind eye to the cruel treatment amounting to terrorism of suppressed and colonized nations and of only deciding to protest when international terrorism actually affected them directly. They did not want to combat the symptoms but rather highlight the underlying causes. While Israel accused the Arab states of being directly or indirectly responsible for terrorism, Arab states maintained that the Palestinians involved were not terrorists but freedom fighters seeking self-determination. China supported this stance and accused Israel, Portugal and South Africa of being sources of imperialism, colonialism, racism and Zionism. Eventually three resolutions were drawn up by, respectively, the US, various Western states and 16 developing states. Because the Third World states formed a majority, only the last resolution was voted on (Gorman 2001, 220), which led to the setting up of an Ad Hoc Committee on International Terrorism. On 14 December 1973 the UN passed the *Convention on the Prevention and Punishment of Crimes against Internationally Protected Persons, including Diplomatic Agents*. After the debate had calmed down this was followed by the *International Convention against the Taking of Hostages* on 17 December 1979. These Conventions are restricted to specific measures, because it proved impossible to reach agreement on what terrorism is. In March 1980 the IAEA adopted the *Convention on the Physical Protection of Nuclear Material* in an attempt to protect its own domain against terrorism.

Regional treaties against terrorism

More robust treaties were drawn up at regional level. In 1971 the Organization of American States drew up the *Convention to Prevent and Punish Acts of Terrorism Taking the Form of Crimes against Persons and Related Extortion that Are of International Significance*. The Council of Europe followed in 1977 with the *European Convention on the Suppression of Terrorism*. In 1976 the foreign affairs and justice ministers set up the TREVI Group (Terrorism, Radicalism, Extremism, Violence International) within the European Community, to monitor developments permanently. Seven states (Canada, France, Germany, Italy, Japan, the UK and the US) met in Bonn in 1978 and decided to impose sanctions on states which provided any manner of support for hijackings. In 1979 the European Community also decided to enforce measures such as a boycott of states that sympathized with hijackings and the revocation of landing rights for their aircraft, which proved to be an effective way of changing the behaviour of certain states. From the beginning of the 1970s, a lasting consequence of the hijackings was the inspection of passengers and their luggage before planes were boarded, for which special security gates and detecting equipment were developed.

Part X

Economic cooperation in a bipolar world 1945–70

The tenth part deals with the global and regional economic organizations which emerged from the institutional settlement of the peace under the leadership of the US. The IBRD and IMF, as set up at Bretton Woods, had a slow start and the proposed trade organization was amended at the UN in such a way that the US did not ratify the charter. However, an international free trade regime was established based on the charter's Annex on the GATT and this regime gradually became institutionalized (Chapter 25). Against the background of emerging East–West tensions and as compensation for the IBRD and IMF, the US proposed aid under the Marshall Plan. The rejection of this by the communist states resulted in an Eastern European process of integration in the Council for Mutual Economic Assistance, the focus of which was on nationalization and industrialization. In Western Europe, under US guidance, a variety of forms of cooperation emerged, including the Europe of the 'Six' (ECSC, EEC and Euratom) and of the 'Seven' (EFTA). The Organization for European Economic Cooperation, which was linked to the Marshall Plan, led to the setting up of the OECD in 1961, in which the industrialized states coordinate their economic policies (Chapter 26). From the 1960s onwards the Bretton Woods system started to weaken. Strategic consultation between the US, Japan and Western Europe led to a new coordinating mechanism. This was not an IGO but rather a consultative body, most closely resembling an Allied war council, of the major industrialized states (Chapter 27).

The troubled start of the Bretton Woods institutions IBRD and IMF and the GATT regime

25.1 The troubled start of the International Bank for Reconstruction and Development

Dollars instead of gold

A stable monetary climate and the recovery of the European economies were essential to restart international trade after the Second World War. The *International Monetary Fund* (IMF) had been devised at Bretton Woods in 1944 to deal with the former. The US government, which had decided to abandon the gold standard in 1933 (see §18.4), supported the idea of paper money being used as a standard. However, the fact that American bankers were pro-gold meant that Harry Dexter White had to find a compromise at Bretton Woods between 'a full paper standard and a return to the gold standard'. In order to counter the objections of the New York bankers, White worked out a solution based on equating the American dollar to gold. 'As a store of value, gold and the dollar were considered equals' (Moffit 1983, 21). It was agreed that foreigners could exchange dollars at a rate equal to the price of an ounce of gold in 1934 (35 dollars). With a view to avoiding monetary disagreement and in order to ensure stability, the decision was taken at Bretton Woods to impose fixed exchange rates. This meant that states which wanted to change the value of their monetary unit required the agreement of the IMF. So as to end the prewar situation in which states were dependent on private creditors or emergency government loans, both of which were unreliable mechanisms, a new scheme was developed under which states that had to adapt their policy in line with economic problems would automatically be given access to IMF credit facilities. The conditions for getting credit were not worked out in any great detail at Bretton Woods, because of disagreement between Keynes, who represented a state with substantial debts, and White, who represented the state that would have to provide the funds. It was expected that the rules would be devised within the organization itself. The result was that Keynes reported back to the UK that 'use of fund credit would not bring foreign intervention into domestic economic policy making in Britain', while White in the US indicated that the IMF 'would not simply dole out money to debtor countries' (Moffit 1983, 22).

The reason behind being based in Washington and the unequal allocation of votes

Acceptance of the Bretton Woods agreements was not a foregone conclusion within the framework of US domestic politics. Bankers objected to an international institution which the government could use to undermine their international lending options. However, the government initiated a campaign to make clear that it was essential to restore international economic trust and that this was in the interest of American business. If the Bretton Woods agreements were not ratified, the risk of a crisis like the one that occurred during the 1930s would increase. This was an argument against which the bankers had no defence, as their position had been weakened by that crisis, and Congress ratified the Bretton Woods agreements. It was this domestic resistance to the plans that led to both institutions being based in Washington DC, so that the US government could maintain direct supervision. Because the US had to provide most of the resources, it was decided that decision making in the IMF and the *International Bank for Reconstruction and Development* (IBRD) 'would be vested with the Executive Board, in which the U.S. executive director had a veto, rather than in the hands of international civil servants' (Moffit 1983, 25). Based on the principle of 'the greater the contribution, the greater the number of votes', rather than the usual one vote per state rule, the US was allocated so many votes that it had the *de facto* ability to veto. White, who was the first US-appointed director of the IMF (although he only held the post for a short period of time), ensured that IMF staff included prominent economists from the American Treasury. 'Given the vague wording of many key Bretton Woods resolutions, control over the staff was a crucial element in shaping the policies of the new institution' (Moffit 1983, 25).

American bankers

As far as US domestic politics was concerned, the IBRD was less controversial than the IMF. People understood the necessity of lending money to rebuild the infrastructure of Europe that had been devastated by war. Politicians and bankers however were concerned that too much money would be 'given away' to recipient states. With a view to keeping control over this, it was decided that states that wanted to borrow from the IBRD first had to join the IMF. The government also ensured that money-lending Wall Street bankers were appointed to the Bank's management. The result of this was that the IBRD was often seen as an 'American' institution. 'The United States put up most of the seed money, and the Bank's financial survival depended on the success of its bond issues on Wall Street' (Moffit 1983, 25).

Governance structure

The IBRD was established on 27 December 1945 on the basis of the *Articles of Agreement* drawn up at Bretton Woods. Most of the states present there ratified the agreements (something that had to happen before the end of 1945), with the exception of the Soviet Union, which refused to ratify once it realized that the US was not fully prepared to support the Soviet Union as regards reconstruction. The US government refused a loan of 10 billion dollars because it expected that Congress would not agree. The IMF did not want to lend more than one billion dollars. The Soviet Union was concerned that it would become dependent on the US through the IBRD and therefore opted for isolation. The Bank started operations in June 1946. Of the 45 member states in 1947, 32 were European or Latin American. West Germany and Japan joined in 1953, while due to pressure from the Soviet Union a number of Eastern European states (among them Czechoslovakia and Poland) withdrew at the beginning of the 1950s. Many Asian states joined in the 1950s and many African states in the 1960s. The aim of the IBRD was to be a universal organization, but most communist states avoided it during the Cold War. In 1966 there were 103 member states and this rose to 151 in 1989, when the Cold War ended. After that the number increased again to 177 in 1993 and 185 by 2008. Each member state has a representative on the *Board of Governors*, which meets once a year. A more important role is played by the (currently) 24 *Executive Directors*, who are responsible for the organization's day-to-day running. Five are appointed by the states that have the largest number of shares and the largest number of votes, the US, the UK, Germany, France and Japan. The other 19 are elected every two years as representatives of groups of states, with Saudi Arabia and China counting as a group each. The US originally held 25 per cent of the votes. In 2001 the US had 16.5 per cent, Japan 7.9, Germany 4.5 and France and the UK 4.3 per cent each. The votes held by the other groups of states vary from 2 to 4.8 per cent. The IBRD has a relatively large staff: 6,000 people at the beginning of the 1980s and 10,000 in 2008. This is more than the personnel employed at the UN. The chairperson of the Executive Board holds the title of president and, based on an agreement made at Bretton Woods, is always an American (a European is always head of the IMF) (see Figure 25.2).

Relationship with the UN

Although the UN and the IBRD were established on the basis of different arrangements and in different locations, they reached a formal agreement in 1947. This made the IBRD a specialized UN agency, although it remained an independent IGO. With a view to ensuring proper cooperation, it was agreed that relevant information would be exchanged. Representatives of the IBRD are able to attend the meetings of the General Assembly and ECOSOC and participate in the work of the committees. Conversely, representatives of the General Assembly can attend the meetings of the IBRD's Board of Governors. The IBRD initially entered into formal partnership agreements with the specialized UN agencies, but this later took the form of practical cooperation on projects and programmes.

Method of working: infrastructural projects and technical assistance

Rather than being an actual 'World Bank', the name by which it is generally known, the IBRD is a bank with just two tasks, as expressed in its full name: reconstruction and development (in that order). The IBRD lends funds to member states with the aim of initiating international flows of capital for productive purposes. Apart from assistance with reconstruction and development, the focus is on promoting private foreign investments, ensuring balanced growth as far as international trade is concerned and maintaining a balance of payments equilibrium. The IBRD facilitates capital investments, issues loans and encourages international investment. It has capital provided by the member states at its disposal and borrows in the international money markets when necessary. Important sources of income also include repayments and retained and non-taxable profit. As well as making project-based loans, the IBRD provides technical support in the form of project consultation, feasibility studies and assistance with the coordination of programmes. In the first two to three decades of its existence the IBRD mainly provided credit for the supply of electricity (via dams) and transport infrastructure (such as roads and bridges). The expectation was that such large-scale infrastructural projects would boost the economy of the developing states concerned. First an estimate was made of the costs and returns for each project and if these were considered acceptable the IBRD and a number of supporting states would supply funding. By the end of 1965 the IBRD had provided 446 loans to 77 states or trust areas, with a value of 9.3 billion dollars. Of this, 3.2 billion had gone to Asia and the Middle East, 2.4 billion to the Western Hemisphere, 2 billion to Europe, 1.2 billion to Africa and 0.5 billion to the Pacific Ocean area. India was the largest borrower state, receiving almost one billion dollars.

From reconstruction to development (at the end of the 1950s)

The support for the postwar reconstruction and recovery of Western European economies lasted for approximately ten years. This lending by the IBRD was generally called conservative. The loans had to be repaid in hard currency at more or less the market interest rate, because the European states were barely able to contribute to the Bank's capital and the IBRD therefore had to borrow money from conservative Wall Street banks which imposed the condition that repayment was guaranteed. This limited the scope of the activities. The attitude of the IBRD towards the Third World was also cautious. At Bretton Woods the Latin American states had fought hard to ensure that development was given equal priority with reconstruction and on paper it appeared that a number of commitments had been made to them. However, in the first decade after the war the focus of the IBRD was on the reconstruction of Western Europe and not on development. The Bank's governance structure, which was dominated by the 'North' (the industrialized states) for which this priority was the point of departure, exacerbated the neglect of the 'South'. The IBRD was keen to limit funds for the 'less developed' states, in line with its business philosophy of not competing with the private money sector but promoting the inflow of private capital. As a result of political developments this conservative policy began to change from the mid-1950s onwards. This was partly because of pressure from the Southern states, which had manifested themselves as a separate group through the conference of non-aligned countries in Bandung, Indonesia, in 1955. They were starting to cause a stir as the 'Third World' at the UN (see §22.3 and Appendix 2 for the term Third World), partly due to the Soviet Union's policy at the end of the 1950s of establishing links with developing states. Development assistance therefore became a weapon in the East–West conflict. The assumption was that assistance would lead to development, development to political stability and all this, according to the provider of the assistance, to sympathy for one of the two blocs. At the insistence of the major Western states the IBRD started to expand its loans to the Third World and to focus them more specifically on the organization of their economic infrastructure (Spero 1985, 187; Yoder 1997, 167).

Results of the World Bank Group

In 1956 the IBRD established a subsidiary, referred to as the *International Finance Corporation* (IFC), which has the same management as the IBRD. While the Bank itself focuses on government activities, the IFC was assigned the supplementary task of using investments to promote the private production sector and entrepreneurship in developing states with the goal of boosting economic development. The IFC issues loans but can also provide part of companies' share capital, as long as it does not give it a majority interest, without this requiring government guarantees. The IFC's conditions are the same as those of the market. At the end of 1965 112 investments had been made in 34 states with a total value of 150 million dollars. In 1960 the IBRD set up another subsidiary, the *International Development Association* (IDA). The reason for this was the emergence of new developing states with only limited economic capacity. The IDA issues long-term loans to these new states, later referred to as the 'poorest' developing states, at low interest rates. Repayments do not start for ten years and can then be made over a period of between 35 and 40 years. The IDA does not have any capital itself, but is able to do its work thanks to donations from industrialized states and income of the IBRD which is transferred to it. As in the case of the IFC, the IDA is an independent institution affiliated to the IBRD and shares staff and management with the Bank. The IBRD, IFC and IDA form the *World Bank Group* (see Figure 25.1) together with two other organizations, one of which is the International Centre for Settlement of Investment Disputes ICSID (see §21.1). Despite its troubled start, the IBRD had evolved into a substantial multilateral development bank with more than 100 member states by 1966.

25.2 The International Monetary Fund and unilateral US management

An inherent contradiction

Like the IBRD, the International Monetary Fund was established on 27 December 1945 on the basis of the *Articles of Agreement* adopted at Bretton Woods. It became operational in May 1946, when it had 39 member states, with the number of members increasing during the 1960s to reach 103 in 1966. As well as developing states, several communist states joined before the end of the Cold War: Romania in 1972, Hungary in 1982 and Poland in 1986. After the end of the Cold War these were followed by Bulgaria and Czechoslovakia in 1990 and by 12 former constituent republics of the Soviet Union in 1992. China was represented by Taiwan until the People's Republic of China joined in April 1980. The IMF had 151 member states in 1989, 177 in 1993 and 185 in 2008. As with the IBRD the IMF has a *Board of Governors* on which all member states are represented and that meets once a year, usually in September, at a joint meeting with the IBRD. The governors are generally finance ministers or central bank presidents who are able to speak on behalf of their government. Most decisions are taken on the basis of a simple majority, although a majority of 70 or 85 per cent is required on a number of specific issues. These include matters which are fundamental to the policy of the IMF such as an increase in quotas, the sale or use of gold and the creation of drawing rights. This is because of the inherent conflict between developing states which want to expand the resources of the IMF and the industrialized states that have to generate those

Figure 25.1 The World Bank Group

The **World Bank Group** includes:

- the *International Bank for Reconstruction and Development* **IBRD**, established in 1944 (with 185 member states in 2008);
- the *International Finance Corporation* **IFC**, established in 1956 (with 179 member states in 2008);
- the *International Development Association* **IDA**, established in 1960 (with 167 member states in 2008);
- the *International Centre for Settlement of Investment Disputes* **ICSID**, established in 1966 as an institution for the settlement of disputes between foreign investors and governments of the state in which investments are made (with 143 member states in 2008). In 2001 a total of 81 disputes had been submitted, of which judgement had been passed in 46, with 35 still pending;
- the *Multilateral Investment Guarantee Agency* **MIGA**, established in 1988 with the aim to facilitate private investments in developing states by insuring investors against long-term political risks and by providing advice (with 172 member states in 2008).

resources and are often not prepared to do so. The more the IMF membership extended towards the Third World, the more the industrialized states have requested and acquired a continual extension of the decisions covered by the 85 per cent rule.

Governance structure in favour of wealthy states

The daily activities at the IMF are delegated to (currently) 24 executive directors. The *Executive Board* consists of five directors appointed by the member states that make the greatest contribution (quota) to the Fund: the US, the UK, Germany, France and Japan. China, which substantially increased its quota during the course of 1980, and Saudi Arabia are also allowed to appoint a director, while the other 17 directors are elected by groups of states. Weighted votes apply at the IMF: in 2008 the US had 16.77 per cent, Japan 6.02, Germany 5.88, France and the UK 4.86 per cent each, China 3.66 per cent and Saudi Arabia 3.16 per cent. Western country or electoral groups (see below) are those led by Belgium (5.14), the Netherlands (4.76), Italy (4.10), Australia (3.85), Canada (3.64), Sweden (3.44) and Switzerland (2.79). The majority of the votes are therefore held by the 'wealthy states'. Apart from China and Saudi Arabia, the non-Western country groups are those led by Venezuela (4.45), Egypt (3.20), Indonesia (3.11), Kenya (3.01), Russia (2.69), Brazil and Iran (2.42 each), India (2.35), Argentina (1.96) and Rwanda (1.39). The managing director of the IMF is always a European (see Figure 25.2). He is chair of the Executive Board and head of the staff. In 2006 the IMF had approximately 2,800 staff members, in 2008 2,600, fewer than the IBRD, of which two thirds are economists. Since 1974 an *Interim Committee*, made up of the 24 finance ministers of the states represented on the Executive Board, advises the Board of Governors on general monetary matters. The word 'interim' referred to the statutory possibility of converting the Committee into a Board with the authority to make decisions, which proved to be unnecessary. This body meets twice a year (just before the annual meeting and in the spring) and has been known since 1999 as the *International Monetary and Financial Committee* (IMFC). In effect this Committee determines the main themes of IMF policy. There is a joint IMF/IBRD *Development Committee* that advises on development policy and matters relating to developing states.

Figure 25.2 The managing directors of the IMF and the presidents of the IBRD

Managing directors of the IMF		Presidents of the IBRD	
Camille Gutt, Belgium	1946–51	Eugene Meyer, US	1946
Ivar Rooth, Sweden	1951–6	John J. McCloy, US	1947–9
Per Jacobssen, Sweden	1956–63	Eugene R. Black, US	1949–63
Pierre-Paul Schweitzer, France	1963–73	George D. Woods, US	1963–8
H. Johannes Witteveen, Netherlands	1973–8	Robert S. McNamarra, US	1968–81
Jacques de Larosière, France	1978–87	Alden W. Clausen, US	1981–6
Michel Camdessus, France	1987–2000	Barber B. Conable, US	1986–91
Horst Köhler, Germany	2000–04	Lewis T. Preston, US	1991–05
Rodrigo de Rato y Figaredo, Spain	2004–07	James D. Wolfensohn, US	1995–2005
Dominique Strauss-Kahn, France	2007–	Paul Wolfowitz, US	2005–07
		Robert B. Zoellick, US	2007–

Electoral groups

The electoral or country groups which elect the other members of the Executive Board have weighted votes varying from 1.39 to 5.14 per cent, as mentioned above. The electoral group led by Belgium includes Austria, Belarus, the Czech Republic, Hungary, Kazakhstan, Luxembourg, the Slovak Republic, Slovenia and Turkey. Each electoral group was created on the basis of which states were looking for a place and whether these states were eligible for a seat on the Board. The system means there are special consultations between the states prior to and during a meeting, with the aim of achieving joint positions and agreement on negotiating techniques and voting behaviour.

Objectives

The IMF's objectives refer to international monetary cooperation, stable growth as far as international trade is concerned, exchange rate stability, a multilateral payment system and the removal of inequalities in balances of payments. By achieving stable world trade growth the IMF wants to help promote and maintain 'high levels of employment and real income, and the development of the production capacity of all member states'. In order to realise these goals the IMF sells foreign currency to states that have problems with their balance of payments and advises their governments on their financial situation. From the very start the IMF fulfilled three functions. It drew up a code of conduct for exchange rates, it provided financial resources to help member states solve or prevent balance of payments problems and it created a forum in which to discuss international monetary matters.

Results achieved by the mid-1960s

At the end of 1965 the IMF had 2.7 billion dollars in gold and 13.5 billion dollars in currency, deposited by the member states, which either had to contribute 25 per cent of their quota in gold or 10 per cent of what they officially had at their disposal in gold and dollars. In 1962 ten major states promised to lend the IMF six billion in their own currency should this be necessary because of a disruption in the monetary system. Between 1 March 1947, when the exchange rate activities of the IMF started, and 1966 the IMF granted permission to 27 states to adjust their exchange rates. During that period exchange rate transactions were being carried out with 56 member states. Exchange rate alterations were always accompanied by consultations with the state involved, with the IMF providing technical support in the form of expertise and training, carrying out studies and generating reports and publications. In contrast to the IBRD or development banks, the IMF does not give support in financing projects or activities, it provides financial support to help states solve their balance of payment problems and to enhance the possibilities for economic growth. This support is temporary and based on the assumption that states will adjust their policy. The service is provided on the basis of market-related interest and costs. In 1952 the IMF developed the so-called *Stand-By Arrangements*, which entitle a state to receive money if that is necessary. Belgium was the first state to make use of this in order to boost its international reserves. In 1963 the IMF set up a *Compensating Financing Facility*, to provide states which traded in primary goods and were confronted with problems due to late payments or falling prices with temporary balance of payments support. Despite this attention to monetary stability and support measures, the IMF was viewed in a generally negative light during its first two to three decades. Although the Fund was considered necessary for the sound regulation of exchange rates, it was not able to deal with the key problems of the time. 'The United States itself judged the organization unsuitable to deal with the most pressing post-war problem – that of financing the recovery of Western Europe. Later the Fund was acknowledged to be inadequate to deal with all the stresses and strains of the 1960s and had to be extensively supplemented with additional machinery or international financial collaboration' (Strange 1973, 263).

Amendments to the Articles of Agreement (1969 and 1976)

The IMF's Articles of Agreement were revised twice. In 1967 a change became necessary because world trade was growing faster than the available financial resources. In order to counteract the deficit in international payment instruments a fictitious monetary unit was introduced in 1969, also accepted by the central banks of the various states, known as the *Special Drawing Rights* (SDRs). In 1976 the Articles were amended for a second time, because the fixed exchangeability of dollars for gold had come to an end in 1971 and because a different exchange rate mechanism had been introduced (see §27.1).

Limited space for the IMF: unilateral US management

No matter how emphatically the US insisted on implementation of the Bretton Woods system shortly after the war, the Europeans were barely able to do so because of the war damage they had suffered. Trade and production had come to a standstill and people's basic needs had become so acute that the states' balance of payments deficits had increased significantly and their monetary reserves were inadequate. The solution was for the US to take charge of the international monetary system. This 'Pax Americana' turned Bretton Woods into a myth of multiterism. Between 1947 and 1960 there was no *multilateral* Bretton Woods system, there was *unilateral* US management. In addition the US provided the funds and facilitated the convertability of currencies, with the result that the dollar became an international monetary unit (Spero 1985, 40). The US compensated for its own trade surplus and the European and Japanese trade deficits by using foreign assistance in the form of Marshall Aid (see §26.1) and military expenditure. This system worked well until about 1960, when the number of dollars outside the US began to exceed the American gold stocks and international speculators wanted to exchange their dollars for gold, something the US was unable to deal with on its own. Only then did the IMF have the chance, partly because the European reconstruction work had at last been completed, to play a more independent role as an international financial institution. However, even after that the US continued to exert considerable influence.

Division of tasks between the IMF and IBRD

The IMF entered into an agreement with the UN comparable to that of the IBRD. As a result it also became a specialized UN agency which continued to function as an independent organization. Within the UN system the division of tasks between the IMF and IBRD was based on the concept that the IMF was responsible for the international monetary system. In addition, the IMF was able to help member states solve balance of payments problems *in the short term*: it was able to assist any member state that had insufficient currency to fulfil its financial obligations *vis-à-vis* creditors in another state. By contrast the task of the IBRD was to encourage economic growth *in the long term*. It could only lend money to states that needed it as the result of a situation related to reconstruction or inadequate economic development, or to states that were too poor to initiate development.

25.3 1947–48: no International Trade Organization, but GATT instead

World trade and employment

The fact that free trade did not happen of its own accord but had to be promoted by international organizations was one of the lessons learned during the interwar period. However, the two Bretton Woods institutions were restricted in this respect. Although they were able to create conditions for free trade, they were unable to coerce states into actually engaging in free trade practices. During the Second World War the US and the UK had discussed the possibility of a multilateral treaty relating to commercial trade policy, but they had been unable to reach agreement. While the US assumed the goal to be free trade, the UK held the view that full employment had to be achieved first before trade could be liberalized. The US government regarded it as very important to reach international agreement on this matter. During the war Secretary of State Cordell Hull, who had been the driving force behind the American Reciprocal Trade Agreements Act of 1934 (see §18.3), had argued consistently in favour of free trade as a means of promoting peace. Due to his efforts free trade was a feature of the Lend–Lease Act and the Atlantic Charter of 1941. In October 1945 the US demonstrated that it was taking notice of the UK's views by inviting 15 states, including the Soviet Union, to a conference on trade and employment under the auspices of the UN (Curzon and Curzon 1973, 298). In December the US presented proposals for expanding world trade and increasing employment. The Netherlands objected to the composition of the selected group of states, as it thought the representation of the UK with the five Commonwealth states of Australia, Canada, India, New Zealand and South Africa too strong compared with that of the European Continent. Only six Continental states attended: Belgium, Czechoslovakia, France, Luxembourg, the Netherlands and the Soviet Union (which, because it had a different economic system, would later drop out). However, the US rejected the proposal to include Norway because it wanted to limit the number of states. The Netherlands had problems over agricultural products and wanted to be able to negotiate as the Benelux, based on the customs union agreed in 1944 between Belgium, the Netherlands and Luxembourg. The US clarified the details of its views on the conference in a memorandum dated 6 February 1946, after which the UN Economic and Social Council proposed that an international conference on trade and employment should be organized later that year. The ECOSOC set up a *Preparatory Committee* and added the ECOSOC members Chile, Lebanon and Norway to the states invited by the US. In this way Norway was included and in the end the Committee had 23 members.

A free market or restrictions as well?

The UN secretary-general decided that the first session of the Preparatory Committee would take place in London on 15 October. On the agenda was a draft treaty for an International Trade Organization. In July the US presented its plan for a *Charter for an International Trade Organization of the UN*. This ITO draft was based to a considerable degree on the idea of a free market. At a session of the Food and Agriculture Organization in Copenhagen in September, FAO director-general Sir John Boyd Orr put forward very different views. He wanted to set up a world food council to combat famines and also advocated restricting the free market through regulations governing the production and sale of foodstuffs, global commodity agreements, minimum price guarantees for producers, buffer stocks and the sale of surpluses. The US resisted these proposals and argued that the FAO ought to conform to the regulations to be formulated by the ITO. The conference on the new trade organization in London, which lasted until 22 November, resulted in the *London Draft* for an ITO charter. This was developed in more detail at the beginning of 1947 and was discussed at the second session of the Preparatory Committee in Geneva, which lasted from 10 April to 22 August and resulted in what was referred to as the *Geneva Draft* for a charter. This was not as strict as the London Draft and clearly weaker than the US intended. The London Draft was based on 'the unity of the world economy, maintained by fairly stringent international rules'. The Geneva draft tended more towards 'separate national economic systems on the basis of which domestic economies and foreign economic relations were arranged' (Moquette 1993, 330).

The Havana Charter (1948)

The Geneva Draft was on the agenda of the *UN Conference on Trade and Employment* which took place in Havana, Cuba, from 21 November 1947 to 24 March 1948. As well as the 23 members of the Preparatory Committee a further 35 states participated. During the conference a conflict arose between the 'industrialized' and the 'developing' states (partly Latin American states, partly former colonies). While the ambition of the first group was more free trade, the second group emphasized the need to strengthen their economies first. Although the US tried to defend the Geneva Draft against further changes a number of escape clauses were included, such as possibilities to deviate temporarily from the main free trade principles in favour of national economic development. At the close the Havana conference adopted the *Charter for an International Trade Organization*. This *Havana Charter* not only contained a chapter on commercial trade policy aimed at promoting free trade, but also chapters on employment and economic activity, economic development and reconstruction, practices to limit competition on the part of companies and intergovernmental raw materials agreements. The idea was to enable the ITO to become a broad-based specialized UN agency for trade and economic development. However, the Havana Charter did not correspond to US policy.

Signing the GATT (1947)

On the basis of the Reciprocal Trade Agreements Act of 1945 Congress had given the US government three years to enter into trade agreements with other states. As a result it had proposed concluding agreements with states that showed interest, such as the members of the Preparatory Committee for the UN conference. The related negotiations had to take place simultaneously and be reflected in 'one multilateral treaty with more or less similar rules for all participating countries, the rules differing only in the individual tariff schedules applied by each country'. According to the US government, this general agreement on tariffs and trade 'should incorporate the commercial policy provisions of the draft ITO charter' (Curzon and Curzon 1973, 298). As a result of this policy tariff negotiations were started parallel to the negotiations on the ITO Charter. The US added an *Annex* to the London Draft containing a regulation for the tariff negotiations which would apply for as long as the ITO had not yet come into force. The title of Annex 10 reads: 'Multilateral Trade-Agreement Negotiations, Procedures for Giving Effect to Certain Provisions of the Charter of the International Trade Organization by Means of a General Agreement on Tariffs and Trade Among the Members of the Preparatory Committee'. This Annex was based on Chapter IV of the London Draft on commercial trade policy. The US aim of completing the negotiations before the end of 1946 turned out to be unfeasible. The negotiations on mutual trade between the states focused on reducing customs tariffs and counteracting other trade restrictions affecting their mutual trade and the main joint negotiations took place during the second session of the Preparatory Committee in Geneva from April to August 1947. During these GATT negotiations the Netherlands repeated its demands regarding agricultural products. The result was basically that the Netherlands could retain its system for the import and export of these products in the context of the customs union, despite this being contrary to the notion of a free market. Because it was in need of political support for the agreement, the US assented to an exception to the free trade principle of equal treatment, which later was to have important consequences. 'Later the EEC [European Economic Community] would use this provision in the GATT treaty to defend its common agricultural policy which had been engrafted onto these Dutch agriculture political principles by the Dutch former Minister of Agriculture and later EEC Commissioner, S.L. Mansholt' (Moquette 1993, 331). The negotiations on tariffs in Geneva resulted in 23 states signing a multilateral treaty on 30 October 1947 called the *General Agreement on Tariffs and Trade* (GATT). This contained a description of the trade concessions the states had made, plus a number of rules and principles to prevent concessions made being reversed by other protective measures. The Agreement was to come into effect via a Protocol on 1 January 1948.

No ratification of the Havana Charter

Because the GATT was intended to be a temporary solution until the ITO came into effect, it was essential that the Havana Charter was ratified as soon as possible. However, there was a lot of criticism of this Charter in US domestic politics. The opposition believed that it did not go far enough as regards free trade (insufficiently liberal and too many exceptions) and the business community was of the opinion that the government would be given too large a role concerning trade regulation. President Harry Truman decided not to submit the Charter to Congress because it was certain to be rejected. Other states also expressed objections and when the US failed to proceed with ratification they followed suit. As a result the intended International Trade Organization did not materialize. The new situation had far-reaching consequences for the GATT. This Agreement continued to be the only international trade mechanism with rules which the key trading states had accepted, but due to the Protocol it remained provisional. Article XXV included an arrangement whereby the parties would meet to renew those provisions that required joint action and to promote the aims of the Agreement, which had been added to prevent the existing agreement being lost. Now, however, this made it possible to carry on jointly, as happened previously with follow-up conferences to multilateral conferences. As a result the GATT replaced the non-established ITO, despite it not being an organization but rather a multilateral treaty with contracting parties.

Institutionalization of the GATT Agreement

The history of the GATT is one of gradual institutionalization. Its continuation was only secured in 1995 with the setting up of the World Trade Organization. Initially the GATT was seen as an interim situation, as the UN's *Interim Commission for the International Trade Organization* continued to provide it with secretarial support. Eventually however the GATT acquired its own organizational structure, although its Secretariat remained small in comparison with the UN specialized agencies and the director-general was originally referred to as the 'executive secretary'. Nor did it have a permanent address in the beginning: it did not acquire its own building in Geneva until 1977. At first the GATT, which continued to be US-dominated, only held an annual *Session of Contracting Parties*, at which all the parties had a single vote and decisions were, in principle, taken on the basis of a two-thirds majority. In practice, however, they were made by consensus. In 1960 a *Council of Representatives* was set up to improve the handling of daily affairs between the annual meetings. From 1975 onwards a *Consultative Group of Eighteen* attended the annual sessions, which was able to raise new topics informally. Committees were set up for issues such as trade and development, balance of payments restrictions and textiles. Since 1965 the executive secretary has been known as the director-general. The post has been held by Eric Wyndham-White (UK, 1948–68), Olivier Long (Switzerland, 1968–80), Arthur Dunkel (Switzerland, 1980–93) and Peter Sutherland (Ireland, 1993–94). In the early 1980s the staff had increased to 300. In 1964 the GATT set up the *International Trade Centre* (ITC) in Geneva to help developing states with their export trade. The Centre has been run jointly by the GATT and UNCTAD since 1968. The GATT continued to be dominated by the industrialized states. It was said that by the time about two-thirds of the parties to it were developing states, the developed states had control over two-thirds of world trade.

Discussion forum and code of conduct

Apart from being a discussion forum for international trade, the GATT was also a code of conduct. In the areas of trade and economics the GATT wanted to help improve the standard of living and ensure full employment, the gradual and substantial growth in real incomes and effective demand, the comprehensive use of the world's resources and the expansion of production and exchanges of goods. With these goals in mind the GATT oversaw the drawing up of mutually beneficial agreements which, according to the preamble to the GATT Agreement, were designed to achieve a substantial reduction in customs tariffs and other trade barriers and the elimination of discrimination in international trade. In order not to jeopardize the code of conduct structure that had developed in practice, the parties preferred not to amend the Agreement itself. The most important exception was in 1965, when a Fourth Part was added on trade and development. Whenever it was confronted by new developments the GATT tried to ensure a pragmatic application of the Agreement or it drew up separate regulations. Examples are the Multi-Fibre Arrangement (designed to impose restraints on the export of textiles from the Third World to industrial states, which first came into effect in 1976 for a period of five years and which could then be extended; see Figure 39.1) and the specific codes agreed during the GATT trade rounds (see below).

The three most important standards

With its principles, standards, rules and decision-making procedures, the GATT is a regime for the regulation of trade barriers (Finlayson and Zacher 1981; Haus 1991). There are three substantial and two procedural standards, as well as a number of exceptions. The most important standard is *non-discrimination*, also referred to as the *most-favoured-nation treatment*. This means that in its trade relations a state may not discriminate between individual partners and that the favourable trade conditions agreed with one state also have to apply to all others. The second substantial standard is *liberalization*, or the removal of trade barriers through the lowering of customs tariffs and the limitation of non-tariff barriers such as technical demands regarding an import product. This standard became more prominent at the end of the 1950s, only to lose significance again in the 1970s. The third standard is *reciprocity*, which means that in the event of a reduction in customs tariffs states do not need to make unilateral concessions but instead an agreement must lead to mutual benefits.

Escape clauses

Escape clauses applied to a number of articles in the Agreement in the event of economic problems. If their interests were seriously damaged because of a change in the international or their internal situation, states could be exempted from their GATT obligations. Provided two-thirds of the parties agreed a state could even get a *waiver* for matters not covered by the Agreement. Originally the so-called Grandfather Clause also offered acceding states the option of withdrawing from GATT obligations if these were contrary to their own legislation. This flexibility dated from the early days of the Agreement and was intended to ensure that new parties were not discouraged from joining. After the Fourth Part of the Agreement was added in 1965, the *development standard* made it possible for developing states to receive special treatment. For example the General Preferential System (GPS) of the European Economic Community, dating from 1971, was a form of discrimination because it ensured preferential treatment for goods imported from developing states. The GATT agreed to this, despite it being a violation of the most-favoured-nation treatment.

Regional cooperation subordinate to GATT

Preferential trade areas, free trade zones and customs unions are other exceptions to the most-favoured-nation principle. They were based on the compromises agreed during the GATT negotiations of 1947, such as that on customs unions discussed above. Article XXIV regulates the regional joining together of states by formulating the conditions for regional free trade policy. The reason behind this is that regional cooperation should lead to trade creation rather than trade diversion (see §18.3). Moreover, such cooperation may not lead to higher tariffs or other barriers *vis-à-vis* third parties. The commercial trade cooperation also had to be linked to 'substantially all trade'. The GATT developed a notification and approvals system through which the legitimacy of the regional economic cooperation is recognized. Between 1948 and 1994 the GATT received notification of 124 regional trade arrangements. This institutional GATT regulation meant that the same subordination of regionalism to universalism was created in the field of economics as in that of security (as laid down in Article 52 of the UN Charter; see §19.4).

Two procedural standards

The two procedural standards of the GATT are slightly at odds with each other. The *multilaterism standard* assumes that the parties have a legitimate interest in each other's policy and behaviour. Multilaterism expresses the preparedness of governments to take part in conferences which agree rules and to accept multilateral supervision and control of their trade policy. By contrast, the *greatest interests standard* states that some aspects of decision making are reserved for those most concerned with a certain issue. As regards drawing up rules multilaterism only became significant midway through the 1960s, particularly in the context of codes for non-tariff barriers. Multilaterism also applies to the *monitoring* of parties' behaviour. However, the interpretation of rules and the settlement of disputes were subject to the greatest interests standard (Finlayson and Zacher 1981, 298). A process was put in place at the GATT to regulate disputes between states, referred to as the *Dispute Settlement Procedure*. A state which considered itself disadvantaged could file a complaint against another state based on its behaviour having led to the full, or partial, *nullification* or *impairment* of concessions granted earlier in a GATT context. The accused state could respond by cancelling trade concessions granted to it of approximately the same value. This was done on the basis of reciprocity. Initially an attempt would be made to solve a dispute by means of consultation and reconciliation. If that failed a panel of independent experts was set up. Provided the Council of Representatives accepted the panel's verdict unanimously, the aggrieved state was able to impose countermeasures. The process worked in practice, but it was hampered by the Council decision having to be unanimous. The fact that states learned to settle their disputes using this procedure boosted the institutionalization of the GATT regime.

The GATT trade rounds

The multilateral negotiations on a further reduction in barriers to international trade were referred to as *rounds* (see Figure 25.3). The first was the GATT tariff negotiations round of 1947. Up to and including the fifth, the so-called Dillon Round (1960–61), the negotiations revolved around reducing customs tariffs for individual products. The primary providers of a product first tried to reach mutually beneficial agreements, after which the agreements were 'multilateralized' according to the standard of non-discrimination. During the sixth, Kennedy, Round (1964–67) the negotiations no longer focused on individual products, but rather on achieving a reduction in tariffs of several tens per cent across the board. This simplified the negotiations and significantly reduced the average tariffs. In addition to customs tariffs, more and more attention was paid to tackling non-tariff trade barriers, particularly during the seventh, Tokyo, Round (1973–79). This led to a review of the Anti-Dumping Code and codes of conduct for subsidies and compensating levies, input permits, customs valuations and product standards. The final round, the Uruguay Round, would last for eight years (1986–94) and was fundamental because it led to a number of innovative developments. Examples are the inclusion of services in the Agreement because they could be traded in the same way as goods and the increase in the number of states involved in the Agreement, partly as a result of the end of the Cold War. In 1981 there were 84 parties to the GATT Agreement, including a number of communist states. Czechoslovakia had been a signatory since the beginning, Poland acceded in 1967, Romania in 1971 and Hungary in 1973. Some states also implemented the Agreement without being party to it, with 30 states doing so in the 1980s. In 1989 the number of parties to the Agreement was 97 and this increased to 128 by the end of 1994 (five more than the 123 states participating in the Uruguay Round). This meant that the GATT trailed behind the IMF and the IBRD as far as participating states was concerned. The Soviet Union, under Mikhail Gorbachev, asked permission to join the GATT in 1986 and on being unsuccessful repeated the request in 1990, in the hope that opposition to the idea would by then have diminished. Following the collapse of the Soviet Union Russia made the same application in 1993, but the observer status granted in 1991 continued. One of the decisions of the Uruguay Round was the acknowledgement that the GATT was, in fact, an IGO.

Figure 25.3 The eight GATT trade rounds 1947–94

1947 Geneva, 23 states on tariffs

1949 Annecy, France, 13 states on tariffs

1951 Torquay, the UK, 38 states on tariffs

1956 Geneva II, 26 states on tariffs

1960–61 Geneva, 26 states on tariffs (**Dillon Round**)

1964–67 Geneva, 62 states on tariffs and anti-dumping measures (**Kennedy Round**)

1973–79 Geneva, 102 states on tariffs, non-tariff measures, framework agreements (**Tokyo Round**)

1986–94 Geneva, 123 states on tariffs, non-tariff measures, rules, services, intellectual property, disputes settlement, textiles, agriculture, establishment of the WTO (**Uruguay Round**)

26

Marshall Aid, Eastern European integration, Western European integration and the workings of the OECD

26.1 Marshall Aid and the Organization for European Economic Cooperation (1948)

IBRD and IMF fail to come up to the mark

That the Bretton Woods institutions IBRD and IMF were unable to finance the recovery of the European economies was the *economic* background to the aid provided for the reconstruction of Europe, as announced in 1947 by US Secretary of State George Marshall. In effect both institutions hindered the transition to postwar recovery. 'Keynes had been right. The IMF and IBRD were too small to do what they were supposed to do, namely provide the huge sums needed to finance the European recovery.' At the beginning of 1947 the European economic recovery was stagnating and 'the Fund and Bank were proving inadequate to do much about it' (Moffit 1983, 26). The problem was that the US had the largest production capacity and fewer import needs than the rest of the world and also exported large quantities of goods, but a lack of dollars and gold meant that the European states were unable to pay for their imports. If the US was to avoid European bankruptcy it had to tackle this problem on a grand scale, without involving the IBRD and IMF. The solution was the Marshall Plan, that lent and donated more than 12 billion dollars to Western Europe and Japan between 1948 and 1952. During the same period the expenditure of the IBRD and IMF did not even reach three billion dollars.

A matter for the US rather than the UN

The *political* background to Marshall Aid was the failure of the conference organized by the four occupying powers on the future of Germany, which was held in Moscow at the beginning of 1947. During the conference Marshall resisted the Soviet policy, which was based on high reparations by Germany and its industrial dismantlement. He was similarly unimpressed by the French attitude of opposing the economic reconstruction of Germany and also demanding reparations. The solution which Marshall devised involved accommodating France and the Western-occupied zones of Germany in a single coordinated aid programme, which would help start the economic recovery in West Germany and nullify the French resistance to the reconstruction of Germany. During the preparations for the Marshall Plan the experiences of the US with the relief organization UNRRA played a role (see §22.1). The American Department of State was of the opinion that the US had not had sufficient control over the coordination of UNRRA and Assistant Secretary of State William Clayton wanted to avoid a situation in which the UN could dictate policy making on the European recovery. He did not want to end up with a 'new' UNRRA, nor did he have much faith in the UN's Economic Commission for Europe (established in December 1946) due to the likelihood of Soviet opposition. His preference was for Western European economic cooperation sponsored by the US, which could engender a structured approach to Western European recovery. As Clayton said, 'The States must run this show'.

Marshall's speech (1947)

In the US domestic situation of 1945, a Marshall Plan would have been unimaginable, but this all changed in 1947 as a result of the increasing tension with the communist world. While the US government started to develop its ideas on a European aid programme, President Harry Truman announced to Congress at the beginning of 1947 that, because of the instability in the Middle East and the Mediterranean area, a policy was required of US support for 'free peoples' who resisted attempts by armed minorities or outside pressure to suppress them. Secretary of State Marshall concurred with the Truman doctrine when he discussed the situation in Europe in his speech after receiving an honorary degree at Harvard University on 5 June 1947. He predicted a serious decline in European economic, social and political relations if Europe did not receive the necessary financial support, which only the US was able to provide. In his speech, which received widespread attention, he invited Europe to take the initiative and draw up a joint programme of requirements. In the context of US domestic politics it was important in getting the political support needed for such a programme that the initiative came from Europe. However, Marshall also wanted to make the European states jointly responsible for a programme which the US would supervise. The Plan was 'sold' in the US as a means of preventing Europe coming under communist control and as a step in the direction of a new, more united Europe. After Congress had incorporated the necessary guarantees and an agreement had been reached in early April 1948, Truman signed the *Economic Cooperation Act* as the basis for the aid.

The division of Europe (1947)

Bringing together the European states was by no means an easy task. The UK, France, Italy and the Netherlands were the first to respond positively to the Marshall Plan, with the UK and France taking the lead. However, there was no real clarity over what the US considered to be a joint approach. It had to be a joint initiative covering a limited period of time and the outcome had to be acceptable to the American Congress. The programme needed to be more than just the sum of the 'shopping lists' of individual states. The US was of the opinion that Germany, or at least the American-occupied zone, would be part of the recovery programme and that Germany had to contribute to European recovery (Van der Beugel 1966, 64–65). The UK and France decided to invite the Soviet Union for consultations in Paris. The views on this state's participation in the plan diverged, as some believed that Europe should not be allowed to become divided and others feared that Soviet participation would jeopardize the joint position demanded by the US. Inviting the Soviet Union to take part meant that the UK and France accepted that this issue should be resolved and they had kept the Soviet Union informed of all developments. However, Soviet foreign minister Vyacheslav Molotov made it easy for them by not wanting to go any further than bilateral 'shopping lists', as a coordinated approach would mean interfering in the domestic affairs of sovereign states and the existing entirety of bilateral trade agreements. France, which acknowledged the problem of sovereignty, failed to change the Soviet Union's mind (Van der Beugel 1966, 61). On 2 July 1947 the Soviet Union announced that it was rejecting the Marshall Plan. The division of Europe soon followed, with Albania, Hungary, Romania and Yugoslavia immediately siding with the Soviet Union by also rejecting the plan. Czechoslovakia, Finland and Poland were put under pressure and an attempt by the Czechoslovakians Klement Gottwald and Jan Masaryk to change the Soviet Union's stance failed. These three states therefore also supported the dismissive Soviet position, fearing a new German hegemony as a consequence of a European initiative to collaborate with Germany.

The Committee of European Economic Cooperation (1947)

In the meantime the UK and France had reached agreement on how to draw up the common programme, which was to be done at a conference with working groups and a committee. On 4 July they sent invitations to 22 states, with the Soviet Union, Spain and the German occupied zones not invited. Austria, Belgium, Denmark, Greece, Iceland, Ireland, Italy, Luxembourg, the Netherlands, Norway, Portugal, Sweden, Switzerland and Turkey accepted the invitation and the conference of these 16 states opened in Paris on 12 July. The committee of high-level civil servants that was to prepare the recovery programme was given the name of *Committee of European Economic Cooperation* (CEEC). Not much progress was made, partly because the states were more interested in what they could get out of the programme individually rather than jointly and partly because not all the civil servants had received adequate economic training. The greatest political problem was the question of whether Germany should be involved in the programme, which caused serious delay. Weeks of negotiations were required to achieve French agreement with the recovery programme framework and France arranged a separate conference on Germany, with the result that the deadline of 1 September was missed. The US was not represented at the conference, but its embassy maintained informal contacts and Clayton came to Paris in the summer. Towards the end of August the US had clearer views on Western European cooperation than had been the case some months before. The political sensitivity of the German situation meant that Clayton continued to be reticent on that subject. However, as regards economic issues, the US encouraged the formation of a more liberal trade and payment system. It saw the European plans as insufficiently coherent and as more of a sum of shopping lists than a programme. Too much money was being asked for and a permanent organization needed to be created to remove the barriers to European trade and payments. Due to American efforts and despite a certain amount of irritation between Europe and the US, the conference was concluded on 22 September with the presentation of the *European Recovery Programme*. In the meantime discussions continued on the shape of European cooperation. A joint position became more feasible when a number of members of the Committee were invited to the US in connection with the approval the US government needed from Congress. 'The Group acted on behalf of the sixteen countries and was forced to represent the European point of view and to defend European interests' rather than national ones (Van der Beugel 1966, 87).

Creation of the OEEC (1948)

It was not until February 1948 that France agreed, at the conference organized that year, to the participation of the three Western-occupied zones of Germany in the recovery programme. The Six Powers Conference, involving the US, the UK, France, Belgium, the Netherlands and Luxembourg, which was organized by the UK in London, decided to include the three occupied zones in the Marshall Plan. The increase in Soviet Union control over Czechoslovakia in February 1948 strengthened their cooperation. A pro-Soviet government was installed in Prague and Masaryk died in mysterious circumstances. On 17 March the UK, France and the Benelux states signed the *Treaty of Brussels*, which regulated their mutual defence (see §23.1). Once an agreement had been reached that the German occupied zones would be included in the recovery programme, the CEEC was able to convene a new conference on 15 and 16 March to draw up the convention on which the organization that was to be set up would be based. On 16 April the 16 states which were to receive Marshall Aid signed the *Convention for the Establishment of the Organization for European Economic Cooperation* (OEEC). This was preceded by various disputes. While the report of September 1947 still referred to a temporary organization for the duration of the reconstruction-related aid, the focus in March 1948 was on the creation of a permanent organization which would continue to exist even after the assistance had ended. It was not a supranational body as France had proposed (with a high degree of autonomy, a strong executive board and an international secretariat), but it was intergovernmental in accordance with British wishes. The *Council of Ministers* would take decisions unanimously and would be chaired by politicians such as Paul-Henri Spaak, Dirk Stikker and Anthony Eden. The Council was assigned an *Executive Committee* with seven members who would attend to matters between Council meetings. The post of secretary-general of the OEEC was held successively by Robert Marjolin (1948–55) and René Sergent (1955–61).

Strong American guidance

The influence of the US on European developments was strongest in the first two years of the OEEC's existence. 'In these years the United States not only possessed the monopoly of economic strength in the Western world but it used this strength to initiate and promote every step on the road to greater European unity' (Van der Beugel 1966, 137). The Schuman Plan and the European Payments Union (see below) tied in with American intentions because of the European support for these endeavours. Some of the most important tasks of the OEEC in the early years were the programming and distribution of the aid funds to the states involved and the promotion of European payment transactions and trade. The distribution of the aid required a certain level of agreement, and even a special committee of wise men, to solve conflicting positions. The chairman and secretary-general of the OEEC mediated in solving the British monetary crisis and the devaluation of the British pound in 1949, so as to reach agreement on the consequences for other states. Once the distribution of the funds had been arranged more attention was paid to cooperation in the field of payment transactions and trade, again under American pressure.

The European Payments Union (1950–58)

In November 1947 France, Italy and the Benelux states had signed an initial agreement on multilateral monetary cooperation, using claims against one state as payment for debts to other states. The Bank for International Settlements from 1930 (see §18.2) was responsible for clearing these payment obligations, but this was not very successful due to the predominantly bilateral nature of the system. The creation of the OEEC offered new possibilities. In October 1948 the OEEC states signed a treaty on Western European payment transactions and set up a fund in which they could make their currency available to each other. On 19 September 1950 the *European Payments Union* (EPU) was established which, thanks to start-up capital provided by Marshall Aid, was able to settle claims and debts for inter-European goods and services transactions. The BIS was involved in these settlements. The increased multilateral nature of trade meant that this system was able to develop more effectively than when only bilateral settlements were possible. On a number of occasions the European Payments Union provided mutual assistance, which helped states learn how to coordinate their policies. When the national currencies became fully convertible in 1958 the organization was surplus to requirements and it was dissolved at the end of that year.

Liberalization of trade in Europe

At the end of 1949 US criticism of the inadequate functioning of the OEEC resulted in a more rigorous US policy of using Marshall Aid to further economic integration. The US also promoted the appointment of a 'political conciliator' at the OEEC. In February 1950 the Dutch foreign minister Dirk Stikker was chosen for this post, but after he had been elected Council chairman in April the position of 'conciliator' lost its prominence and the US gave up its attempts to acquire more direct influence within the organization. Stikker's aim was to further liberalization within the OEEC and in June 1950 he proposed tackling this by liberalizing various branches of trade in succession, in what was referred to as the 'sector' approach. Stikker advocated full liberalization coupled with compensating measures for certain economic activities, for which a European fund would have to be set up. This idea was amended by French and Italian plans. Although Stikker's plan received a very limited response from the OEEC, the organization began to promote mutual trade under US pressure. In 1950 a *Code of Liberalization of Trade* was agreed, intended to make three-quarters of mutual trade quota-free from February 1951 onwards. It was also meant to end discrimination between the member states. This trade liberalization continued gradually, with 84 per cent of trade being exempt from quantitative restrictions in 1955 and 95 per cent of trade within the OEEC and 90 per cent of trade with the US free of quotas in 1960. The main limitation on the possibilities offered by Stikker's plan was not related to the OEEC, but rather to the launching of the Schuman Plan in May 1950 which would lead to the establishment of the European Coal and Steel Community.

A shift in US policy

The OEEC ran into trouble when the US changed its aid policy as a consequence of the Korean War of 1950. It decided to combine military and economic aid and, once Marshall Aid had finished in 1952, its preferred approach was to provide assistance via the North Atlantic Treaty Organization (see §23.2). The focus was on reinforcing the weapons capability of the alliance, in conjunction with making available and allocating vital related raw materials. With regard to the latter a semi-permanent *International Raw Materials Conference* was set up in Washington DC, in which the US, the UK and France took part. Stikker's role in this was to coordinate its policy with the OEEC states. Similarly to the US, the UK's preferred focus was on the economic development of NATO. However, the OEEC under Stikker managed to achieve a compromise and continued to protect European economic aid matters, including NATO's.

Increasing productivity and professional mobility

That the OEEC member states regularly had to submit statistical information on how their economies were functioning was one of the unexpected strengths of the OEEC. This information improved the insight into each other's economic development and clarified the possibilities for cooperation. At the same time it stimulated mutual competition, because states became more aware of what was happening in the market. This also enhanced productivity. In 1951 European productivity was already 50 per cent higher than it had been in 1939. Increasing productivity was also boosted by the OEEC, because the US invited entrepreneurs and others to visit the country to study the American production system. The US encouraged others to adopt efficient business methods in order to reinforce international competition. These paid-for visits by European entrepreneurs, labour experts and trade union leaders to the US took place under the auspices of the OEEC. A new element for Europe was the provision of relevant public information, with governments intensifying their contacts with the press and launching public information campaigns. The OEEC also tried to stimulate the geographical and professional mobility of workers in Europe. Its *Manpower Committee* used regular reports on national situations to instigate measures to make it easier to find employment and professional training. The expectation that labour shortages in one state could be met by workers from other states proved not to be viable in Europe. Despite all the reconstruction activities, unemployment continued to be a problem. With regard to the free movement of workers, it transpired that not much more could be achieved than the introduction of a few liberal principles governing the provision of work permits. It turned out to be almost impossible to simplify the fairly complex administrative procedures which regulated the admission, employment and residency of foreign workers and their families. While there was a shortage of trained workers in the north of Europe midway through the 1950s, unemployment continued to be a problem in the southern states. Transferring workers from southern to northern Europe was not feasible, because the north needed skilled workers and the unemployed in southern Europe were largely unskilled. Social and housing problems also played a role. Moreover, there was the fear that immigrants would cause lower wages and contribute to future unemployment-related problems. However, with hindsight the liberalization by the OEEC of the rules for worker migration facilitated the 'foreign labour' of the 1960s, during which period there was in fact a need for low-skilled workers.

26.2 Eastern European integration: the Council for Mutual Economic Assistance (1949)

Socialist integration

The communist states, together referred to as the Second World (see Appendix 2 for this term), did not regard the international system primarily as a system of states, but as an economically-determined whole. In their view part of the world had withdrawn from the capitalist world economy. Russia had managed to do this in 1917 and in the early 1920s the area was expanded to include parts of southeastern Europe and central Asia, in what became the Soviet Union. Eastern European states followed this path after 1945, as did Third World states such as Cuba, North Korea and Vietnam. The group also included the People's Republic of China, although the cultural and later ideological divisions between the Soviet Union and China prevented these superpowers from adopting a joint policy. The view in the 1970s was that the communist world had, on the basis of a different type of economy, been able to develop into a global system which could compete with capitalism. This system was characterized by socialist economic integration through the Council for Mutual Economic Assistance which was set up in 1949 (see below) and a socialist international division of labour based on systematic economic development, mutual assistance and cooperation between states. The communist world called itself 'socialist', because the term 'communism' referred to a higher phase of development. Between the socialist and the capitalist 'world systems' (both seen as power constellations of states based on their own world economy) 'system competition' existed (rivalry between two international systems which were each other's opposites), but the two systems also maintained relations. They would face the same problems and resemble each other in their functioning ('convergence'), while also trying to coexist ('peaceful coexistence'). In reality the mutual communist relations were based on political and economic subordination to the Soviet Union and its controlled division of labour. Within the framework of the communist world it would be better to refer to a Core-Periphery relationship. However, a socialist world system did not exist according to Immanuel Wallerstein, because the world economy is, by definition, capitalist. The Soviet Union and other communist states continued to be part of this world economy, despite their own characteristics. As soon as they engaged in trade in raw materials, goods or services, the prices on the world market applied rather than any mutually agreed prices or exchange arrangements (Wallerstein 1979, 35).

Communist view of international organizations

The view of communist states of IGOs was formalist and conservative. An organization's charter expressed the will of the founding states. As a result the organization had a certain autonomy *vis-à-vis* those states, but the resources that the organization was able to apply could not exceed those which the original states had agreed to, unless they reached a new agreement on further action (Archer 1992, 111–13). As with international treaties, IGOs also had to give the communist world the opportunity to apply its own principles. The 1960s were characterized by peaceful coexistence, with the UN as a forum and showcase for the different blocs. The independent activities of Third World states at the UNCTAD conference in 1964 were an embarrassment to the communist world, because the 'Southern' states included communist states in the rich, industrialized 'North'. The communist states' response to the development problem was not different to that of the capitalist industrialized states, as they too offered technical and financial assistance and expected this to generate economic growth as well as sympathy for the donor. However, sometimes they provided social or medical assistance which was tailored more specifically to local needs than that from the Western states. The attitude of communist states regarding IGOs remained limited to participating when it suited them, for example at the UN and certain specialized agencies, or withdrawing, for instance from the IBRD, IMF and GATT. The emerging divisions with the West, the rejection of Marshall Aid by the Soviet Union and the creation of the Western European OEEC contributed to the creation of their own organization, focused on the integration of communist states.

The Council for Mutual Economic Assistance (1949)

As support for reconstruction was not forthcoming from the US because of the attitude of the Soviet Union, discussions on the need for and problems of economic cooperation were held between Bulgaria, Czechoslovakia, Hungary, Poland, Romania and the Soviet Union in Moscow from 5 to 8 January 1949. On 25 January a press communiqué was issued which gave notice of the establishment of the *Council for Mutual Economic Assistance* (CMEA, referred to in the West as 'Comecon'). Its member states participated on the basis of equality, with cooperation built on principles such as respect for national sovereignty, independence and national interests, no interference in domestic matters, equal rights, mutual benefits and fraternal mutual assistance. With regard to the economy the focus was on sharing experiences and on providing each other with technical support and assistance relating to the exchange of raw materials, foodstuffs, machinery and equipment. Four months later a meeting was convened at which the provisional structure of the CMEA was worked out in more detail. Albania joined in 1949 (and remained an active member until 1962), followed by the German Democratic Republic in 1950, Mongolia in 1962, Cuba in 1972 and Vietnam in 1978. Yugoslavia became an associate member in 1964. The CMEA entered into cooperation agreements with Finland (1963), Mexico (1975) and Nicaragua (1983). Afghanistan, Angola, Ethiopia, Nicaragua, Laos, Mozambique and Yemen were assigned observer status in the 1970s and 1980s.

Nationalization and industrialization

At the end of the 1940s and the beginning of the 1950s the CMEA coordinated the nationalizations of industries, transport, communications, banks and foreign trade, as well as the reforms in agriculture to set up cooperatives in the Eastern European states. The main themes of these changes were the abolition of capitalist relations and transformation oriented towards the rapid growth of national economies in accordance with the production method which had been developed in the Soviet Union. As in Western Europe the focus was on recovering from war damage and increasing production. The Eastern

413

European states were barely industrialized, apart from the west of Czechoslovakia and part of Poland, which meant that industrialization was a high priority in Eastern Europe, as was the case later in many developing states. 'The control of international transactions is designed to render trade subservient to the overriding goal of comprehensive, planned, industrial growth' (Macbean and Snowden 1981, 195). Exporters in the Eastern European states, originally oriented towards the West, rejected free international trade and focused on the member states of the CMEA, which promoted the central planning in these states in favour of industrialization 'on a larger scale than could have been achieved alone' (Macbean and Snowden 1981, 209).

Late expansion of the organization

As an organization the CMEA did not at first carry much weight. Its highest body was a *Council* that met periodically and there was also a *Council Bureau*. The Council meetings circulated with the host state supplying the chair. In the first few years the emphasis was on implementing general guidelines for bilateral goods trading and in effect the Soviet government took the key decisions. In 1954 the number of CMEA activities increased, because the mutual trade relations required more coordination. From then on the organization began to be more structured and in 1954 the Council Bureau was replaced by a permanent *Secretariat*. In 1957 the first permanent committees were set up, in 1958 the Council laid down principles for the determination of prices for trade within the CMEA and in 1959 it adopted a *Statute* in which its tasks were specified, which came into effect in April 1960 (Bethkenhagen and Machowski 1976). This Statute included a convention on legal security, privileges and the immunities of the members of the Council and its bodies. It was revised in 1962 and 1974. The Soviet Union benefited from the international division of labour within the CMEA, but also bore the costs of the industrial development of the member states. In 1962 it proposed the formation of a supranational economic schedule similar to that of the European Economic Community. This plan was objected to by Romania, which was averse to any increase in central control. The Council then drew up the basic principles for an international socialist division of labour, with coordination of the national economic plans becoming the main method of cooperation. This decision led to the first amendment of the Statute. With a view to making mutual trade more multilateral, Hungary and Poland advocated the reinforcement of monetary and financial instruments. In 1962 a Committee for Monetary and Financial Questions was established, charged with developing a multiple settlement plan. With this in mind the *International Bank for Economic Cooperation* was set up in Moscow in October 1964. Its task was to issue credits and arrange international payments with the 'transferable rouble' as a common monetary unit. In 1970 the *International Investment Bank* was established in Moscow to provide credit for major investment projects which were of common importance, for example in the energy and raw materials sectors. Ten CMEA member states entered into an agreement with this Bank by 1973, which granted credits to the banks and economic enterprises of the member states. They also created a fund to finance the economic and technical assistance provided by the CMEA and its member states to developing states.

Socialist integration

Within the CMEA the term 'socialist integration' was used for the first time in 1970. The Council adopted a *Comprehensive Programme* in 1971 that referred to concrete objectives and deadlines. In order to realize this integration the Council had at its disposal mechanisms such as the coordination of the member states' medium- and long-term plans, specialization agreements, specific common investment programmes and scientific and technical cooperation. New committees were set up for planning and scientific cooperation and separate institutions were established to oversee coordination in the various sectors of trade. Once Cuba had joined in 1972 and after the cooperation agreement with Finland had been concluded in 1973, a joint policy was formulated with regard to third-party states. This led to the second amendment of the Statute in 1974, as a result of which the CMEA was authorized to conclude treaties with member states, third-party states and IGOs and to maintain relations with them. In the 1960s and at the beginning of the 1970s the CMEA evolved more and more into an IGO. However, the international economic developments of the 1970s, including the oil crisis, would reveal the organization's weaknesses, particularly because of the unequal relationship between the Soviet Union and the other member states (see Figure 26.1).

Figure 26.1 The influence of the world market on the CMEA

In **the 1970s** the **Council for Mutual Economic Assistance** reinforced the coordination of the national plans. At the same time the Soviet Union and the other member states were affected by the consequences of the global economic crisis. Although a variety of factors stimulated the further integration of the CMEA, the costs for the Soviet Union increased. This prompted the question of whether the Soviet Union ought to continue supporting the process of continued integration (Marer 1976), for example through its exports to the CMEA member states. 'As primary goods they would be readily convertible into foreign exchange which in turn could be used to purchase high quality goods in the West.' Moreover, the consequences of the 1973 oil crisis were tangible: 'intra-CMEA price changes in 1975 favoured primary commodities with a doubling of the oil price and a 52 per cent rise in raw material prices. This represented a major terms of trade loss for the European members' (Macbean and Snowden 1981, 209). These external influences, the problems relating to the supply of raw materials by the Soviet Union and the completion of the construction of heavy industries forced the Eastern European states to consider improving their economic efficiency. States such as Hungary and Poland were the first to become aware of this, but they too were confronted by an organization with little flexibility.

The CMEA's influence waned during **the 1980s** due to the poorly functioning planned economies, which played a role in the reform processes taking place at the time in the Soviet Union and other CMEA member states. The CMEA was dissolved in June 1991 during the disintegration of the Soviet Union, without leaving too much of a mark. Both Banks adapted to the circumstances. The International Bank for Economic Cooperation began performing transactions in all currencies and functioning as an international trade bank, while the International Investment Bank also adapted to the capitalist international market economy. Together with some sections of the former CMEA it was superseded in 1991 by the *Organization for International Economic Cooperation*, which was set up as an advisory body to promote cooperation between the Eastern European states on a market basis.

26.3 Western European integration: ECSC (1951), Treaties of Rome (1957) and EFTA (1960)

The Benelux (1948)

That Western European cooperation was difficult to realize was borne out by the economic cooperation between Belgium, the Netherlands and Luxembourg. During the wartime exile of their governments in London they had realized that they shared the aim of reducing the significance of their mutual economic borders after the war. In 1943 they agreed a treaty on reciprocal free currency transactions and in 1944 one on a customs union. Their purpose was to create a stronger position for themselves in the context of international relations dominated by superpowers. The customs union took a long time to materialize and only came into effect as far as import duties were concerned on 1 January 1948. The intended convertibility of the currencies proved to be even more difficult to achieve, even after a joint decision on this in June 1948. The reason it took so long was because of the differences between the Netherlands and Belgium over available production facilities and foreign currency, while the Netherlands was also afraid that Belgium would become more France-oriented. They had a shared interest in the recovery of the German economy, however. At a hearing involving the four occupying powers at the end of January 1947 the Netherlands rejected anything that constituted a drastic obstacle to the rebuilding of Germany's heavy industry, as it did not want to be dependent on Belgium and France for its iron and steel requirements. The Netherlands and Belgium were both of the opinion that the German steel industry had to become internationally competitive again. Attempts by France to initiate economic cooperation with the Netherlands and Belgium in the form of a Conseil Tripartite failed to produce any results. The interests of both states were quite different from France's ideas on how to restrict Germany economically. France wanted to make the cooperation too subordinate to its own solution to the German question, while the Netherlands resisted French pressure during negotiations on how to arrange mutual trade and payment transactions. In discussions on cooperation in the economic and military fields in 1947 and 1948 the Benelux states took the opportunity to express their joint views more vociferously. This happened during the preparations for Marshall Aid, the discussions on the future of the German occupied zones and the establishment of North Atlantic cooperation involving the Benelux states. In 1955 the Benelux would do the same in discussions on a common European market.

Attempts to expand the Benelux

Attempts within the Organization for European Economic Cooperation at the end of the 1940s to expand the Benelux failed. In 1949 France suggested the inclusion of France and Italy to form 'Fritalux', while Belgium proposed 'Finebel'. The Netherlands was worried that such a new customs union would come under excessive French influence and demanded that the German zones and the UK participated as well. However, German participation did not fit in with French policy and the UK had no desire to join. German membership of the Benelux ('Gerbenelux') was a non-starter. Within the OEEC the Benelux did not provide a basis for broader Western European cooperation.

416

The Schuman plan (1950)

In 1950 Stikker's plan to liberalize the European economies by using a sector approach was a response to the Fritalux plan to expand the Benelux, but it received little support within the OEEC. The French foreign minister Robert Schuman thwarted Stikker's idea on 9 May 1950 by presenting his plan for cooperation between the European coal and steel producers and placing their industries under the control of a supranational High Authority with independent powers. This policy was prepared by Jean Monnet, who at the time was responsible for economic planning in France. Schuman's aim was the economic and political integration of the Federal Republic of Germany into Western Europe, in order to prevent Germany becoming a bone of contention between the superpowers and therefore remaining a risk to peace. Monnet himself had excellent contacts with the American decision makers in the US and Germany and had identified possibilities for protecting French interests through cooperation. Monnet's plan helped Schuman, whom the US expected to achieve results (Lieshout 1999, 95). He had secured the cooperation of the German Chancellor Konrad Adenauer for the scheme, who believed it offered an opportunity to change Germany's isolated position. In this way France demonstrated a willingness to reconcile with Germany and it would allow other states to participate in Franco–German cooperation on coal and steel. The idea of a supranational body had been put forward on numerous occasions. The decisive factor this time was that the largest stocks of coal in Europe, needed for reconstruction purposes, were located in the Ruhr region of Germany. Local problems were the strong cartel structure of heavy industry and the lack of an international policy on European use of this energy source. The idea of uniting the French and German coal and steel industries into an international 'pool' was based on the model of the international authority for the Ruhr area that was operational at that time. Both states were to participate on an equal footing in the proposed High Authority and the management of the two industries would become the responsibility of this Authority and not directly of the two states. Due to this external pressure Adenauer managed to open up the heavy industry cartel in the Ruhr region. Supranationality in this case was not a new model for international cooperation, but rather a means of solving international and national impasses. From the French point of view the aim was to have control over West German recovery. The US government had played a regulatory role in the background and responded positively because this was a European initiative. The UK reacted less enthusiastically because of the supranational nature of the initiative and after a while refused to take part in the discussions. The Dutch government was divided, but decided to participate nonetheless, although it registered a reservation with regard to the supranational character of the scheme. The fact that France and Germany were looking for partner states to broaden the basis of support meant that the Benelux states were for some time able to stand up to larger states.

Establishment of the ECSC (1951)

Negotiations in June and July 1950 between the six states involved (France, Germany, Italy and the Benelux states) led to the establishment of an intergovernmental *Council of Ministers* in addition to the proposed supranational *High Authority*. This Council was a concession to the Dutch objections and limited the significance of the supranationalism. A proposed arbitration committee was upgraded to become a *Court of Justice*, which the

Benelux regarded as providing protection against the larger states because it would assess the decisions of the High Authority against the Treaty without power politics coming into play. The negotiations did not finish until April 1951. At the last moment compromises were reached on the composition of the High Authority and the voting procedure in the Council of Ministers. As a result neither France and Germany, nor Italy and the Benelux states, were able to form a majority. Although there were traces of Stikker's sectoral approach, a more limited geographical area was involved. Stikker himself had reservations about this restricted membership. The six states signed the treaty for the *European Coal and Steel Community* (ECSC) in Paris on 18 April 1951. After all six had ratified the ECSC was established on 10 August 1952 for a period of 50 years, with Jean Monnet as the first president of the High Authority (1952–55) (Duchêne 1994).

Significance of the ECSC

In practice the common markets for coal and steel that were created had limited significance. The Italian steel industry was forced to be more competitive, a common scrap policy was devised and Belgium received support during the crisis in 1958 when the Belgian coal industry collapsed (Milward 1995, chapter 3). Despite the influence of the ECSC producer organizations and national governments soon regained control when it came to drawing up regulations for the production of coal and steel. As president, Monnet fell out with the entrepreneurs on a number of occasions. The ECSC's significance lay primarily in the European political cooperation between France and Germany that occurred in the early 1950s with US approval. That the German economy was up and running midway through the 1950s meant that Germany then started to become the powerhouse of the Western European economy. The German *Wirtschaftswunder* as part of the ECSC political constellation enabled Germany to integrate into Western Europe. Hence, this integration was achieved not through the intergovernmental OEEC under Stikker's leadership, but through the limited supranational ECSC that Schuman and Monnet had proposed.

Failure of the European Defence Community (1954)

Once the ECSC had been set up it looked for a time as if the cooperation on coal and steel would be extended to include security. This French aim, presented by Prime Minister Pleven and also inspired by Monnet, received support from outside France. On 27 May 1952 the six ECSC members signed the treaty for a *European Defence Community* (EDC), which was followed in March 1953 by an agreement on a *European Political Community* (EPC). However, the plan failed in August 1954 when France was unable to ratify the European Defence Community because of domestic opposition (see §23.2). The other states, apart from Italy, had already ratified. The Dutch foreign minister Jan-Willem Beijen, who had been a director at the IBRD and the IMF, regarded the ECSC as a more realistic framework for economic cooperation than the OEEC. He saw the European Political Community as a way of achieving greater European unity, despite it being limited to six states. He did not want to use the EPC for military or political cooperation, but rather for customs unification and further economic integration. His 'general' vision was a departure from the branches of trade, or 'sectoral', approach which was dominant at the time. Beijen proposed his notion to the other ECSC members in December 1952 and included it in the discussions on the political community, but he found little support for his views and they ceased to be relevant when France failed to ratify the EDC in 1954.

The 'relance européenne' (1955)

In November 1954 Monnet indicated that he did not want to serve a second term as chairman of the High Authority of the ECSC. Discussions between him and the Belgian foreign minister Spaak resulted in April 1955 in proposals being submitted to the foreign ministers of France, Germany and Italy on additional integration between branches of trade (such as traffic, energy and a new community for atomic energy) and a conference to debate these proposals. Spaak contacted his Benelux colleagues. Beijen wanted to breathe new life into the cooperation and drafted his own memorandum, which was based not on Monnet's integration of branches of trade but rather on a general path for economic integration from customs union to common market. After Monnet and Spaak had discussed the issue, Spaak and Beijen reached agreement on a compromise, which they submitted to France, Germany and Italy on 18 May. This 'Benelux memorandum' advocated greater unity in economic sectors which were related to the ECSC. Branches of trade or sectoral expansion in the three areas referred to would, however, only be possible within the framework of general economic integration in the form of an economic community. For this to happen common institutions had to be created, a common market formed and social policy gradually harmonized. The Benelux memorandum was discussed at the ECSC conference in Messina on 1 and 2 June 1955, during which a successor to Monnet was appointed. The memorandum played a role in the *relance européenne* which took place in Messina thanks to the efforts of the Benelux states. The Benelux ministers decided not to oppose issues contributed by their colleagues from the other states as long as their procedural proposals were accepted. These referred to the setting up of a committee of government representatives, supported by experts and led by a 'political figure', whose assignment was to study the different aspects of European cooperation and develop them into a proposal for an intergovernmental conference. This plan was successful, even though it took considerable effort and time to get France to agree. The committee was led by Spaak and produced the 'Spaak report', which was accepted by the foreign ministers of the ECSC in Venice on 29 May 1956. This made it possible to start discussions on branches of trade integration (atomic energy) and further economic integration (a common market), with separate treaties for the two organizations. On 25 March 1957 this resulted in the signing in Rome of a treaty for the *European Economic Community* (EEC) and another for the *European Atomic Energy Community* (Euratom). Both *Treaties of Rome* came into effect on 1 January 1958.

Creation of Euratom (1957)

When Monnet announced at the end of 1954 that he was stepping down from his role at the ECSC, he was aware of the political situation that had resulted from the failure of the European Defence Community. He was also aware of the importance of atomic energy, which appeared to be overtaking coal as a more modern source of power and which was also important in the French desire to develop nuclear weapons. With a view to influencing public opinion in favour of European cooperation, Monnet set up the *Action Committee for the Unites States of Europe* in 1955. This provided a platform from which politicians, employers and trade union leaders could work publicly towards

European integration. Monnet's proposal to set up a European Atomic Energy Community linked up well with the existing US wish for European cooperation and also tied in with Eisenhower's UN-based Atoms for Peace initiative for the peaceful use of atomic energy (see §24.1). Cooperation would mean the high atomic energy development costs could be shared. However, the efforts by the French government to establish such a community caused distrust among the ECSC members, which also considered creating a common market to be a more important form of cooperation. A variety of factors contributed to what eventually happened. At the beginning of 1956 a change of government took place in France, with the new government more in favour of European cooperation. The new Prime Minister Guy Mollet was a member of Monnet's Action Committee. Germany expressed a wish to combine atomic energy and economic cooperation, based on the notion of no Euratom without a common market and no common market without Euratom. Spaak's idea of creating two communities ultimately made it possible to increase the cooperation of the six ECSC member states. Unlike with the European Defence Community, the Mollet government received backing for the idea from the French parliament in 1956, not least because Euratom did not block France's military nuclear programme, the only restriction being that no testing was allowed before 1961. The creation of Euratom facilitated the use of atomic energy in Europe. A common market was set up for atomic energy products, four research centres were established and nuclear power stations were built in, amongst others, France and Germany. In the event Euratom would not have major significance as a separate community, partly due to the distrust of the other member states about French military intentions, and in the end it became marginalized by the EEC. The ECSC met the same fate, as was shown by the merger of the institutions of the three Communities in 1967 (see §26.5). Further expansion of Euratom was also hampered by the large quantities of oil available in the 1960s and the problem of security at nuclear power stations which was discovered later.

Negotiating structures within the EEC

Although it would not be until 1968 that the European Economic Community agreed on a common external tariff and a common market was set up, the EEC encouraged mutual trade and the creation of transport and communication opportunities during the 1960s. This was partly made possible by the completion of reconstruction work at the end of the 1950s and the development of the welfare state and a consumer society during the 1960s. Rising incomes meant that people from lower and middle classes had more spending power, so contributing to economic development through spending at home and also abroad because of the increase in tourism. The Treaties of Rome stimulated mutual free trade, the abolition of barriers for the free traffic in factors of production used in the production of goods, the creation of a common agricultural policy and framing a common policy in areas such as transport, competition and economic coordination. To facilitate decision making four institutions were set up: a *Commission*, a *Council of Ministers*, a *Parliament* and a *Court of Justice*. The last two continued to build on the work and the experiences of similar ECSC institutes (see §26.5 for details of their development). The *EEC Commission* originally had nine members (with not more than two from any one state) whose expertise was of primary importance. The Commission fulfilled three functions, which were to develop initiatives, to monitor the Treaty and the decisions taken and to ensure the execution of joint decisions. The Commission's initiating function (making recommendations or giving opinions on matters resulting from the Treaty) in particular acquired significance. The task was performed in cooperation with the Council of Ministers, in which ministers represented their national governments and which could accept or reject the Commission's proposals. This combination of Commission and Council led to a new form of negotiating between the member states, due to the fact that the Council could reject a proposal by a two-thirds majority but could also amend it, albeit only unanimously. The Commission and the Council engaged in a negotiating game in which the Commission was able to contribute detailed proposals, but had at an early stage to take account of the political wishes of the member states. This happened as early as when drafting proposals, because the Commission had to consult with the permanent representatives of the member states in Brussels, the *Committee of Permanent Representatives* (Coreper, after its French name). An additional factor was that relations within the Council could be such that voting by qualified majority was not possible. The Commission's initiating function would then continue to play a 'pushing' role, but there would be intergovernmental negotiations in the Council at the same time as negotiations between the Commission and the Council.

The common agricultural policy

One of the first areas in which the Commission was successful was with the EEC's common agricultural policy. At a conference in Stresa, Italy, in July 1958 the member states defined the main features of such a policy, based on common prices, market rules and incentives to increase productivity. Once again France's strategic motives were influential. France had agreed to greater competition in industry in exchange for a common agricultural policy that would support its farmers. The Commission, in which Sicco Mansholt had the agriculture portfolio, managed to develop these main features in such a way that the Council was able to endorse the policy in 1962. Together with a related fund it resulted in guaranteed prices for farmers, significant subsidies (which meant that products would be cheaper in the world market) and the modernization of agriculture, followed by increases in scale. This policy provided a support base for European cooperation. Its negative consequences were overproduction, referred to as 'milk and wine lakes' and 'butter mountains'. The Commission increased its own authority by engaging in implementation-related negotiations with trade partners in Europe and elsewhere, which reinforced the image of European 'unity', but also had a number of unwanted side effects. The European policy complicated the GATT negotiations, because agricultural products were excluded under exception rules established in 1947 (see §25.3). This led to other states, including the US, also introducing agriculture subsidization. That the EEC took little notice of international criticism of its agricultural policy was the result of the internal negotiating process between the Commission and the Council. The feeling that it helped to ensure joint progress meant that the interests of non-member states were ignored in Brussels (Macbean and Snowden 1981, 148).

The European Free Trade Association (1960)

In addition to the Europe of the 'six' (the member states of the ECSC, EEC and Euratom), there was a Europe of the 'seven'. During discussions within the framework of the OEEC the UK had expressed a preference for establishing a free trade area on an intergovernmental basis, rather than a customs union and a common market. While the 'six'

421

pursued their goal of a common market, the UK's idea was supported by Austria, the Scandinavian states and Switzerland. This setting up of a free trade area was also influenced by President Charles de Gaulle coming to power in France in 1958. This general and politician, who succeeded in bringing the faltering French decolonization process in Algeria firmly to a conclusion, was keen on European cooperation with France and Germany at its core, while excluding the UK because of its orientation towards the US. This resulted in a French foreign policy of reconciliation and rapprochement with Germany, which Adenauer reciprocated. De Gaulle was also an advocate of détente with the Soviet Union, because this would give the Continent the opportunity to develop. His policy meant a hostile attitude towards cooperation with the UK and the alienation of the US (see §26.5). The new policy was shown in the first French atomic test in 1960 (although this was contrary to the Euratom agreement not to perform tests before 1961) and later in the curtailment of French participation in NATO. France's anti-British policy was one reason why the seven states, Austria, Denmark, Norway, Portugal, Sweden, Switzerland and the UK, in 1960 signed a convention in Stockholm to establish the *European Free Trade Association* (EFTA). Finland decided to take advantage of its position between East and West and became an associate member of EFTA a year later. Abolishing mutual trade barriers was achieved in 1966. Despite this economic success, the UK in 1961 decided nonetheless to pursue membership of the EEC, which was achieving higher rates of economic growth than the UK. The British Prime Minister Harold Macmillan had realized that there was less to be gained from the British orientation towards the Commonwealth (the UK exported more goods to Europe than to the Commonwealth) and that the same applied to EFTA. Denmark, which was dependent on the British economy, supported Macmillan's choice to apply for EEC membership. However, after starting negotiations the UK's accession to the EEC was vetoed by De Gaulle in January 1963. The UK's second application in 1967 was also vetoed. As a result the EEC retained a Continental character, while the UK became more isolated in Europe. EFTA continued to exist as a free trade agreement, although the UK and Denmark left in 1973 and joined the EEC. Prime Minister Edward Heath was pro-European, but British membership and the entry terms negotiated by his government were controversial.

European cooperation versus Atlanticism

The existence of the Europe of the 'six' and of the 'seven' meant that Western European integration became a controversial element of foreign policy in Europe. First and foremost it affected whether or not states would participate in the three European Communities which were, in fact, dominated by France and Germany. In addition to a choice between free trade (EFTA) and further-reaching economic cooperation (EEC), there was a political dimension tinged with a certain 'European idealism' stimulated by the European Movement and Monnet's Action Committee, which existed until 1975. This struck a sympathetic chord among pro-integration politicians and higher civil servants and was based on the idea that cooperation in the form of Communities, in which certain powers were transferred to joint supranational institutions (the Commission, the Court and Parliament), would bring a democratic and peaceful Europe closer to reality. A federate Europe was a possible final phase, although the term 'federation' would later become controversial. European cooperation as a new element meant that future foreign policy in Europe would have more than one focus. One would be European integration with a view to facilitating mutual European security and economic development, while the other focus would be on the US in order to ensure global security and economic development, more oriented on intergovernmental free trade than on supranational cooperation. In addition to the strain between 'European cooperation' and 'Atlanticism', the Europe of the 'six' was also prone to tensions due to differing French and German political intentions.

26.4 From OEEC to the Organization for Economic Cooperation and Development (1961)

From OEEC to OECD (1961)

When reconstruction had been completed and cooperation within Western Europe and between Western Europe and North America had proven to be fruitful, the 18 OEEC states decided, together with the US and Canada, to transform the organization into the *Organization for Economic Cooperation and Development* (OECD). 'European' was removed from the name and 'development' added. The 20 member states of the OECD decided to increase cooperation because the economic recovery that was taking place and the development of the Western European economy offered new opportunities. The OEEC regarded a strong European economy as a means to maintaining peace. However, as far as the OECD was concerned broader cooperation would make a vital contribution to peaceful and harmonious relations between the peoples of the world. Given the increased interdependence of their economies, the OECD states wanted to focus through consultation and cooperation on a more effective use of their capacities and possibilities for economic and social purposes. In addition, the 'economically more advanced' states needed to cooperate when it came to assisting states that were 'in a process of economic development'. The OECD assigned itself the goal, in advance and in accordance with its Convention of 14 December 1960, to 'achieve the most sustainable economic growth and employment and a rising standard of living in the member states, while maintaining financial stability, and by doing so to contribute to the development of the global economy'. Other goals included healthy economic expansion in member and non-member states and an increase in world trade on a multilateral, non-discriminatory basis, in accordance with international obligations. The OECD Convention came into effect on 30 September 1961, after 17 of its 20 member states had ratified it. On the same day the intercontinental OECD replaced the European OEEC. In addition to the 20 founding states, Japan (1964), Finland (1969) and, after having special status for some time, Australia (1971) and New Zealand (1973) joined the organization. Together they became known as the group of rich industrialized states with a market economy. Yugoslavia acquired special status in 1961.

The OECD as an organization

The highest body of the OECD, and the one that makes the decisions, is the *Council*, consisting of a government representative from each member state. All member states also have a permanent delegation, headed by an ambassador who acts as the Permanent Representative. The Council in the form of the *Permanent Representatives* meets weekly (or more often) under the leadership of the secretary-general of the OECD. Once a year, usually at the end of the May or the beginning of June, the Council meets at ministerial level and is then chaired by a minister from a member state who is elected for a year, together with two vice-chairmen. The Council is assisted by a fourteen-member *Executive Commission* that does the preparatory work. The basic aim of the Council is to achieve consensus. This can result either in decisions which are binding on the member states or in recommendations. No member state can be bound by an OECD decision against its will. Although decisions and recommendations have to be agreed unanimously ('by mutual agreement of all the Members'), states that do not agree can abstain. This does not halt the decision making as there is no right of veto, but it does mean that the decisions and recommendations only apply to those member states that voted in favour. Generally the standards that have not been adopted by all members still function in practice, even in those states that abstained. There is no reason to conclude that the Council has no power because it is not supranational (Bowett 1982, 191). The Council has more than 25 important committees. Foremost is the *Economic Policy Committee*, which is responsible for the current economic trends and prospects of the member states and formulates the appropriate economic and financial policy. The *Economic and Development Review Committee* conducts the, in principle annual, evaluations of the economic situation in the member states and it publishes the authoritative *Economic Surveys* (see below). Other committees deal with industry, trade, agriculture, energy, environment, development assistance, education and social affairs. The Council appoints the secretary-general of the OECD for a period of five years. From 1961 to 1969 this post was held by the Dane Thorkil Kristensen, from 1969 to 1984 by the Dutchman Emile van Lennep, from 1984 to 1996 by the Frenchman Jean-Claude Paye, from 1996 to 2006 by the Canadian Donald Johnston and from 2006 onwards by the Mexican Angel Gurria. Activities are overseen by an international *Secretariat* in Paris, which employs 1,800 staff of whom 600 are economists and statisticians.

OECD institutes and inter-IGO relationships

Because of the decentralization of functions the OECD has several (semi)autonomous institutions with their own administrative bodies, established in the period up to 1974. These are the *Nuclear Energy Agency* (1958), the *Development Centre* (1962), the *Centre for Educational Research and Innovation* (1968), the *Club du Sahel* (1973) and the *International Energy Agency* which was set up in 1974 in response to the oil crisis of the previous year. The OECD Convention has a Protocol which allows the Commission of the European Communities to officially participate in the work of the OECD, albeit without voting rights. The European Free Trade Association can send representatives to OECD meetings. Links were established with the Council of Europe in 1962, when a Liaison Committee with this organization was created. The OECD has official relations with the IBRD, IMF, GATT, ILO, FAO and other specialized UN agencies. Cooperation with the ILO dates back to 1948, when ILO representatives took part in the meetings of the OEEC *Manpower Committee* and also attended other OEEC meetings. When the OECD was set up a decision was made to continue this cooperation through participation in meetings, the exchange of documentation, consultation and advice. The OECD thus became a transatlantic framework for permanent consultation and consensus building on a broad range of economic issues, on which a large number of international economic agreements have been based.

Collecting statistical data

Although the OECD is not able to coerce member states, its *Economic Surveys* constitute a subtle and influential international policy mechanism based on the regular collection and mutual comparison of the states' economic core data. This links up with the intention of Article 3 of the OECD Convention to 'keep each other informed and furnish the

Organization with the information necessary for the accomplishment of its tasks'. Building on OEEC practice the OECD developed quickly into an international statistics bureau that provides data to the member states as a service. That all the data is published widens the effect, since non-member states are also able to benefit. In order to make sensible use of statistical data and policy information from so many states, these have to be mutually comparable. When this is not the case the OECD uses experts to try and reach agreement on definitions, meanings and research procedures. It has acquired a great deal of expertise in areas such as standardization and bringing together statistical and policy information from a great many states relating to a large number of fields.

The confrontation technique

The annual *Economic Surveys* fulfil a signalling function for the economic policy of individual member states and for any policy coordination by the OECD. They assess the short- and long-term economic situation of individual states, which themselves submit most of the data required for these analyses. A panel of experts from other states then evaluates the national situation in the context of international criteria. This involves delegations of high-level national civil servants coming to Paris to explain policy to the Economic and Development Review Committee, with ordinary Committee members and members who have studied the draft *Survey* in detail (the 'examiners') asking questions. This is referred to as the *confrontation technique*, because member states are subjected to a 'cross examination' on their own data. The discussions are frank, as they are subject-based and confidential and the OECD experts who prepare the *Surveys* are well informed. These visits give governments the chance to exercise some, but certainly not unlimited, influence over the end result. This confrontation technique and the regular publication of the surveys enable the OECD to realize a significant degree of unanimity over policy. Although it is based on voluntary cooperation, the OECD as an organization is strengthened in practice due to the quality of the annual assessments (Bowett 1982, 197).

Policy coordination and ideational authority

The regular overviews of the performance of member states also make it possible to attune policy, although there has to be the political will to do so. The need for policy harmonization and coordination can arise if the comparison and analysis of the collected economic core data show that member states are pursuing (excessively) different policies, or have no policy, in certain key areas. In such situations there may be a need to formulate common standards, rules or codes of conduct for specific issues or policy fields, which indicate a general direction and allow the member states to decide for themselves whether to follow this or not. A comparison of the data included in the *Economic Surveys* can reveal which options are available. The OECD's regulating approach in this context is 'soft' rather than 'hard'. 'At best, it creates recommendations and "good practice", and leaves it to the member states to enact these general guidelines in day-to-day policy making.' This 'soft' regulation has turned the OECD into an *ideational authority* with a directing and controlling effect. In contrast to the IMF and IBRD, the OECD has no financial resources to support policy but works on the basis of reasoning. 'Soft regulatory measures have allowed the OECD to deal explicitly with highly controversial issues (e.g. development economics and the paradigmatic shift from Keynesianism to monetarism) while maintaining its ideational authority in the member states. In full accordance with the principle of subsidiarity, the OECD has left it to the member states themselves to work out how their national models, routines, practices and ways of thinking fit into the conceptual framework developed within, and author- ized by, the OECD' (Marcussen 2004, 90). The fact that this OECD mechanism has a coercive effect is because the statistics and analyses regularly show which developments occur and the extent to which states deviate from common standards or rules. Members are free to determine their own behaviour, but they also know that deviating from the norm too far, or for too long, will cause them to be in a disadvantageous position as far as global competition is concerned: in the end the market will punish them mercilessly. As a result, they will tend to take account of these standards or rules of behaviour, even if not forced by the circumstances, despite a preference for not doing so because of their domestic situation. Only a very bold member state would dare to adhere to an economic policy that is at odds with that pursued by everyone else (Bowett 1982, 197).

Political appreciation

The presentation of statistical data by an international organization can also have political implications. For example, when Van Lennep became secretary-general in 1969 he soon became embroiled in conflict with the staff that was preparing the *Economic Outlook* for the OECD Secretariat. This is a detailed economic forecast for all OECD member states, which is published twice a year (in June and December) and which is usually the focus of media attention. Van Lennep was convinced that at that time the Secretariat was inclined to be overly-pessimistic as regards economic growth. In the Netherlands he had discovered that the official planning models often focused too much on reduced growth. However, making pessimistic growth predictions can be dangerous because they provide grounds for advocating the stimulation of demand. With regard to the next issue of the *Economic Outlook* Van Lennep was afraid that, due to the organization's authority, pessimistic OECD forecasts would have a 'self-fulfilling' effect. Despite protests from his economists he therefore gave the text a 'more optimistic tone'. In the long term, however, this kind of manipulation is unsustainable, because experts can see through it and because an incorrect presentation of the state of affairs hinders politicians more than it helps them.

The DAC: Development Assistance Committee

Although technical support was already provided to developing states during the OEEC period, it was in the 1960s, during the first few years of the OECD's existence, that development assistance became a new and important task. A *Development Directorate* – which later became known as the Development Support Directorate – was created within the Secretariat. Two committees were established at Council level, the *Technical Cooperation Committee* and the *Development Assistance Committee* (DAC) which would gain in importance (see below), followed in 1962 by the scientific and independent *Development Centre* for policy-oriented research, rational policy solutions, exchange of experiences and information and informal discussions.

Common policy on the Third World

The goals of the OECD's development policy have been to support developing states in realizing lasting economic growth, to ensure the provision of more and effective assistance by its member states and to contribute in that way to a successful and mutually beneficial integration of developing states into the international economy. Within the framework of the Development Assistance Committee the OECD was involved in matters such as the extent and kinds of development assistance being provided. Another key issue was the role of NGOs, which are capable of tapping into large sums of money for aid to the Third World, in 1985 amounting in DAC states to 1.5 billion dollars from governments and 2.9 billion from private contributions. The DAC also discussed the role of women in development and guidelines were adopted in 1984 designed to combat the negative effects of aid on women. Work was carried out at the OECD to achieve greater cohesion in the policy of the member states towards developing states. The confrontation technique again paid off in the annual assessments of the members' development policy. The results were specific recommendations to the member states and a general mutual agreement on OECD policy, as a result of which the industrialized states during the 1970s increasingly began to approach developing states as a bloc. During the attempt to create a 'dialogue' between North and South at the *Conference for International Economic Cooperation* in 1975–77 OECD states adopted a common stance. The OECD was present as an observer and functioned as a central meeting point where, if possible and desirable, the positions of the member states were unified and harmonized. As far as developing states were concerned the OECD had now become a new opponent, because the industrialized states, which were already powerful, began to coordinate their policy *vis-à-vis* developing states in the OECD and by doing so created an even more closely-knit bloc.

26.5 Ongoing and stagnating Western European integration 1960–80

Economic progress: creation of the customs union (1968)

In the 1960s the European Economic Community began to develop economically. During the GATT Dillon Round of 1960–61 (see Figure 25.3) the EEC presented its planned common external tariff and in May 1961 the GATT accepted this plan to create a customs union. A number of states now wanted to enter into association agreements with the EEC. Greece submitted such a request in 1961 and neutral European states such as Austria, Sweden and Switzerland followed. Spain and Iran wanted to establish closer trade relations and African states were also interested in association agreements. The EEC concluded an association agreement with a number of African states in Yaunde, Cameroon, in 1963 and with Nigeria and the three states of what was later to become the East African Community (see §30.4) later the same year, followed by Turkey. The six EEC member states proceeded to abolish customs tariffs, a process that was completed in 1968, followed by the introduction of a fully common external tariff. The EEC had now become a customs union.

Laborious political decision making

At the beginning of the 1960s the political discussions between the six member states became significantly more laborious. France had declared in 1961 that it could only agree to additional steps towards a common market if agreement on agricultural policy was reached. A plan for a political union presented under the leadership of French politician Christian Fouchet was not approved, as to the displeasure of the small states the larger members claimed special responsibility for foreign policy. As a result the work of the Commission was limited to economics. In the meantime President Charles de Gaulle began to put forward his vision of a 'Europe of states' (*Europe des états*), which contradicted the idea of a 'united Europe'. This became more clearly defined in January 1963, when at a press conference he refused to agree to the UK joining the EEC. A week later he signed a Franco–German cooperation treaty. Negotiations with the UK were stopped (see §26.3). In March France refused to take part in the conference of ministers from the Western European Union because the relationship between the UK and the EEC was an item on the agenda. In May the EEC made some progress, when the ministers reached agreement on a further extension of the agricultural policy. There was also agreement with the GATT on the proposals submitted by the US during the Kennedy Round. In the summer of 1964 France and Germany decided to reopen discussions on a possible political union. Various plans were put forward, with the Belgian foreign minister proposing to try out Fouchet's plan within the Western European Union. However, foreign policy continued to be problematic. Although the UK wanted to join the Community, it was of the opinion that it needed to be able to pursue an independent foreign policy. A conference on political union of the foreign ministers of the six organized for March 1965 was cancelled at the request of France. From an organizational point of view the member states of the three Communities (ECSC, EEC and Euratom) did make progress. In May 1965 they decided to merge the bodies of the three Communities and as a result the High Authority of the ECSC, the EEC Commission and the Euratom Commission were amalgamated into a single European Commission on 1 July 1967, as was also the case with the Councils of Ministers.

The empty French chair (1965) and the Luxembourg 'compromise' (1966)

Walter Hallstein, the first president of the European Commission, advocated a strong Commission. He put forward a daring proposal to give the three Communities control over their own finances, to be sourced from levies at the external borders within the framework of the common agricultural policy, with the European Parliament having budgetary verification powers. This put him in direct conflict with De Gaulle, who was completely opposed to giving either the Commission or the Parliament greater authority. Warnings from Robert Marjolin failed to change Hallstein's mind and De Gaulle responded by withdrawing France from the Council of Ministers and the Committee of Permanent Representatives. This paralysing and unique situation became known as the crisis of the 'empty chair'. De Gaulle also objected to the introduction of majority voting in the Council of Ministers. This was to be implemented from January 1966 in accordance with the Treaty of Rome, but there was no room in De Gaulle's vision for being outvoted. His condition for France returning to the Council was that discussions on majority voting would cease. The other member states did not want to comply and domestic politics forced De Gaulle back to the negotiating table, because although he had won the elections in December 1965 François Mitterrand, who favoured a pro-European approach, had achieved a good result. The six met again midway through January 1966 and the crisis was resolved at the end of the month at a meeting of the foreign ministers in Luxembourg. This Luxembourg 'compromise' was in effect a victory for De Gaulle. A temporary arrangement was put in place to fund the common agricultural policy and the proposal for more power for the Commission and the Parliament was rejected. Although voting by majority was to be allowed in the Council, it was also stipulated that in the event of 'very important issues' discussions would have to continue until an agreement was reached between all the parties. The consequence of this 'compromise' was that the ministers in the Council were aware of each other's national interests, even if it did not concern 'very important' issues, and that future decision making took this into account. With a view to underlining his notion of Europe, De Gaulle decided to distance France even further from the US. In February 1966 he announced at a press conference that France was withdrawing from NATO's military activities, with the result that in September NATO moved its headquarters from Paris to Brussels. At the same time De Gaulle sought a rapprochement with Eastern Europe, paid a month-long visit to the Soviet Union and spent a week in Poland. He continued to disapprove of the UK joining the EEC and again made this known publicly at the end of 1967.

The summit in The Hague (1969)

Although the six could do little about the fact that they disagreed on a number of issues, such as British accession and plans for economic and technological cooperation, there appeared to be fewer differences with regard to international monetary problems. In early 1968 the Luxembourg Prime Minister Pierre Werner proposed that a common view-point should be formulated. 1968 was to become an eventful year, with student unrest in Paris before the summer (during which De Gaulle had the students removed from the Sorbonne) and the invasion of Czechoslovakia by the Soviet Union in September. Within the EEC there was again disagreement, when France first refused to accept a proposal from the German socialist leader Willy Brandt for a trade arrangement with the UK and later declined to join discussions on this. Within the framework of the Western European Union, France rejected a plan for closer cooperation on foreign policy. In February 1969 disagreement on the Middle East led to the announcement by France that it no longer wished to participate in the activities of the WEU. However, De Gaulle's domestic position continued to weaken and after his proposals for political changes were rejected in a referendum he stood down as president at the end of April 1969. His departure gave the European Economic Community the opportunity to move ahead. A summit was prepared based on a suggestion from Brandt, who was by then German Chancellor. This led to agreement on the issues at hand (completion, deepening and expansion of the Communities) and the presence of the Commission at discussions on Community issues. The summit took place in The Hague at the beginning of December 1969, where the leaders agreed to find funding for the common agricultural policy, proceed to a new phase in establishing the common market (with a readiness to accelerate progress towards an economic union on the basis of a step-by-step plan) and increase the number of member states by initiating negotiations.

New European vigour

After the summit in The Hague a new European vigour emerged. The Council reached agreement on agricultural policy funding in December 1969 and in 1970 an arrangement was framed to make resources available to the Community from customs duties and the newly introduced value added tax. In February 1970 the ministers agreed to give the European Parliament some influence over the Community's expenditure. This led to an agreement on greater authority for the Parliament and the allocation of resources to the Community, which was signed in Luxembourg in April. Hallstein's initiative had brought

429

results after all. As regards the accession of new member states, negotiations were started with Denmark, Ireland, Norway and the UK in June 1970. A year later a settlement had been concluded with the UK on the conditions governing entrance into the EEC and in January 1972 the conditions applicable to the four candidate states were signed. France submitted the proposed expansion to the French people in a referendum and it was approved by a majority in April. As a result Denmark, Ireland and the UK joined the Community in 1973, bringing the number of member states to nine (see Figure 43.4), but Norway did not proceed after a referendum in 1972 in which its population rejected the idea. Relations between France and the Western European Union were also restored. The WEU met in January 1970 without France, but in April the six EEC member states reached agreement on the conditions for France's participation in the WEU and it returned in June. In March the six also took the decision to charge senior civil servants with the task of drawing up a report on *European Political Cooperation* (EPC) or European foreign policy. They held their first meeting in November. The Davignon report which resulted, adopted in 1970, enabled the foreign ministers and their senior civil servants to begin exchanging views on a regular basis. The idea was to reach a situation where the states would 'speak with one voice' and in which 'joint action' was possible. Although this was only a beginning, a mechanism came into being through which consultations between the ministries and between ministries and European institutions would gradually intensify.

No EMU, but EMS instead (1979)

A start was also made on further integration. Monetary problems had led to a 12.5 per cent devaluation of the French franc and a revaluation of the German mark by more than 9 per cent. A committee with Werner as chair investigated the possibilities of *economic and monetary union* (EMU) in April 1970. In June the Council of Ministers indicated that such a union could be in place by 1980 and in October Werner submitted a report which detailed the related plans in seven steps, covering both monetary measures and economic policy coordination. The Council of Ministers reached agreement on the first step as early as February 1971 and at their summit in October 1972 the heads of state and government declared that EMU would be in place in 1980. However, economic reality combined with disagreement between France and Germany over the consequences of achieving such a goal meant that the 'Werner Plan' was never implemented and EMU would only start to become a reality at the end of the 1980s. The economic setbacks at the time included Nixon's decision to bring an end to the practice of converting dollars into gold, the ensuing monetary instability and the oil crisis of 1973–74. These problems meant that states became less committed to economic and monetary union. However, the Werner Plan did help to get some control of monetary developments. The collapse of the Bretton Woods system forced the member states, which in monetary matters had adopted an 'each for itself' attitude, to achieve mutual coordination of their exchange rates. In 1972 they proposed a 'snake' with maximum permissible margins. Denmark, Ireland and the UK also participated, although they were not yet members. Political and economic problems, including the British contributions to the EEC and compensation payments linked to agricultural policy, delayed developments further. Nevertheless the *European Monetary System* (EMS) was introduced in March 1979, with regulations for exchange rates and interventions and with the ecu as its monetary unit. EMS proved to be effective and helped to ensure monetary stability in Western Europe. Regular consultations assisted in the member states gaining each other's trust and this led to increased harmonization of their monetary and economic policy structures.

The Social Action Programme (1974)

At their summit in October 1972 the heads of state and government had formulated an action programme for the enlarged European Community that was not only concerned with economic and monetary policies, but with social, regional and industrial, technological and scientific policy as well. With regard to social policies they stipulated that the Council would decide in January 1974 on a 'social action programme' for matters such as living and working conditions, vocational training, workers' participation, European collective employment contracts and the protection of consumer interests. Several articles of the 1957 Treaty of Rome were devoted to social policy, although this was only of minor importance compared with economic policy. In Article 117 the member states acknowledge the need to improve the standard of living and the terms and conditions of employment, Article 119 refers to equal remuneration, while Article 118 sets out areas in which the Commission has to encourage cooperation. In addition, there was a requirement to consult the advisory Economic and Social Committee of the EEC, consisting of representatives from social sectors including employers and trade unions. The statement during the 1972 summit was an invitation to the social partners to become active in this field, which was expected to lead to support for more European cooperation. This came at a time when the trade union movement was becoming more radical and more active than it had been before. After the necessary preparations had been completed in 1973 the Council adopted the *Social Action Programme*, in the shape of a resolution, on 21 January 1974. Its aims were full employment, an improvement in living and employment conditions and greater influence from workers on economic and social decisions taken by businesses.

Positive influence of the feminist movement

Contrary to the Council's expectations this Social Action Programme had been influenced more by the feminist movement than by the trade unions. Actions by women led to a European directive on equal pay for women and men in 1975, a directive on equal treatment in working conditions, access to jobs and professional training in 1976 and a directive ordering the gradual application of equal treatment in social security systems in 1978. Whereas Article 119 of the Treaty of Rome had failed to achieve much progress with regard to equal pay, the three directives enabled the new feminist movement to enhance the position of women regarding paid work and equal treatment. That this featured so prominently on the EC agenda was due to the existence of a small group of inspired women, who put forward well thought-out proposals to the European institutions and mobilized political support. Factors that played a role in the background were the UN's International Women's Year (1975) and the realization among European politicians that in the long term there would not be enough adequately trained people to fill all the vacancies in the employment market. If this market was to function properly access would have to be improved, resulting in more women and other excluded groups performing paid work. The increase in the number of 'women's directives' (two more followed in the 1980s) was a matter of political mobilization by women inside and outside European institutions. Just as at the UN, new generations of women became involved in a male political stronghold, which then started to implement a policy that was favourable to women as a result of their actions. An increasing number of women began to realize how important the European directives were and used them to put pressure on national attitudes and they also exploited the opportunities offered by the European Community itself to exert influence (Reinalda 1997). This included obtaining positions within the bureaucratic organization and setting up an *ad hoc* Committee on Women's Rights at the European Parliament, as was done in 1979. Women also used legal proceedings, at both national level and the level of the European Court of Justice, which refined the Council directives in its judgements and often decided in women's favour.

Limited influence of the trade unions

The contribution of the trade unions to the Social Action Programme was significantly smaller than that of the feminist movement. A few new directives were implemented in areas such as mass redundancy and workers' rights, but these had less effect than the three women-oriented directives of 1975–78. Most rules relating to employees focused on health and safety in the workplace. The greatest expectations were raised by the proposed Vredeling–Davignon directive on informing and consulting workers in enterprises with complex structures, in particular transnational corporations. As regards the supervision of transnational corporations these expectations were the same as those harboured by the UN (see §31.3). However, the proposed directive encountered resistance from employers, who thought that it went too far beyond national regulations. The 1980 proposal was amended in 1983 and was abandoned due to the 'spirit of the 1980s', exemplified by the British Prime Minister Margaret Thatcher's demand for deregulation and liberalization. Nonetheless, the women-oriented directives and the proposed Vredeling–Davignon directive widely stimulated political debate on European integration and had a favourable mobilizing effect on European cooperation.

The European Parliament elected directly (1979)

International parliamentary structures from the 1950s, as with the Council of Europe, the WEU and the ECSC, had a legitimizing function (see §23.1–2): there had to be accountability for what was being done by an organization. The *Common Assembly* of the ECSC consisted of 78 members, who were elected by and from the national parliaments of the six member states. The High Authority had to submit an annual report on its activities to this Common Assembly and if the report was rejected by a two-thirds majority all members of the High Authority were forced to step down. In 1958 this ECSC institution was perpetuated as the *European Parliamentary Assembly*. This *European Parliament*, as it would be called from 1962, met for the first time in Strasbourg in March 1958 and had 142 members. This number increased in line with the number of member states to 198 after the 1973 expansion. On the basis of a clause in the Treaty of Rome the heads of state and government decided at the summit in December 1974 to bring in direct elections, as part of their strategy to engender support for further European integration. Following a final decision in 1976 the first direct elections were held in June 1979 to choose 410 members. The new European Parliament had a supervisory function and was able, just as in the case of the ECSC, to force the Commission to resign, but it had no power over the Council of Ministers. However, in practice it gradually acquired the authority to submit written and verbal questions to both the Commission and the Council. As their questioning became better informed, the members of the European Parliament found they were able to achieve more, both in the form of substantive contributions and by bringing matters to the attention of the general public. Their influence was therefore indirect and based on the extent to which the Parliament managed to exert its authority. This also applied to the consultative function that resulted from the obligation in the Treaties for the Commission and the Council, in certain cases, to consult the Parliament about their proposals. An interaction ensued whereby the Commission and the Parliament were jointly able to achieve some progress. The Parliament's *ad hoc* Committee on Women's Rights was able to make such significant and substantive contributions that the Commission had to take it seriously when preparing long-term policy and new proposals showed clearly that the women in the Parliament had made their presence felt. From 1975 onwards the Parliament also had budgetary powers relating to the Community's non-obligatory expenditure. Although the Council continued to be responsible for expenditure that was obligatory (around 70 per cent within the framework of the common agricultural policy), the Parliament still had to approve the budget in the final instance. Because the role of the European Parliament had never been precisely described and because it operated on the basis of a combination of intergovernmentalism (Council, summits) and supranationalism (Commission), it had sufficient room to take initiatives itself. The Parliament put forward detailed proposals for a more effective structuring of the Community on a number of occasions. It was also insistent that it should have more authority. Due to these initiatives and to making the most of the opportunities that presented themselves, the Parliament was able to develop and strengthen its own position. In September 1968, while De Gaulle was still in power, the European Parliament asked the Commission to submit new proposals to the Council designed to strengthen the Parliament's position, the first in a lengthy series of such requests.

The European Council and the European Court of Justice

The institutional modernization of the European Community included in 1974 transforming the summit meetings of the heads of state and government into the European Council, which was to meet at least twice a year. The Treaty of Rome did not provide a basis for this European Council and it would not be until 1986 that it was put on a formal footing (in the Single European Act). It had effectively been formed at the start of the 1970s, when the G7 was also established. It reinforced the intergovernmental nature of the Community, but also functioned on the basis of a combination of intergovernmentalism and supranationalism. As with the Parliament, the role of the European Court of Justice originated in the ECSC. The Court of the ECSC had been set up for political reasons. In line with the French legal system, which had a body to protect citizens against government wrongdoing, it was an institution that was meant to protect companies and states against decisions by the High Authority and was authorized to reverse these. During its conversion into the *European Court for the European Communities* the legal system was moderated, as the High Authority of the ECSC had been authorized to impose fines while the Commission did not have this power and, as a consequence, neither did the new Court. However, the Court would play a unique role within the Community because of its daring judgements in cases submitted to it by national courts under Article 177, which allowed it to make so-called 'prejudicial judgements'. A number of the European Court's judgements based on this procedure had a far-reaching effect. Its judgement in the *Van Gend en Loos* case of 1963 led to Community law being directly applicable in the member states, without any legal action required first by the state in question. This principle of 'direct effect' meant that the European Treaties created individual citizens' rights which national courts then had to protect. The *Costa/ENEL* case of 1964 led the European Court to establish the principle of precedence of Community law over national law. Judgements such as these went against the wishes of the governments, but they nevertheless accepted the rulings of the European Court. This demonstrates how strongly the European Community is based on a legal order with authorities, Treaties and the power of a Court. Citizens and companies were also able to involve the European Court in national policy debates. In the 1970s the Court played a role in the acceptance of the directives on the equal treatment of women, when it was called upon to interpret prejudicial decisions and gave judgements in a variety of cases. On a number of occasions this led to an article in a Treaty being given a broader or different meaning than the member states had intended when it was drawn up, for example with the definition of equal pay (*Defrenne-1*, *Barber*) and equal treatment (*Marshall*). The Court strengthened the agenda-creating power of the Commission by stipulating that the objectives formulated in a Treaty provision or directive cannot be implemented by using pre-existing regulations (Van der Vleuten 2007, 186–87). The individual role of supranational bodies like the Parliament and Court in this way contributed to the dynamism which had been created earlier in the negotiating process between the Commission and the Council (see §26.3). It made the administrative entirety of Western European integration complicated and progress continued to be dependent on political will.

Failure of the European Council in Luxembourg (1980)

Despite the continuing integration in the 1970s the focus on the common perspective gradually grew weaker, partly for economic and partly for political reasons. A change of government in the UK in 1974 led to difficult renegotiations on the British contribution to the European budget. Although the accession applications from Greece, Portugal and Spain in 1975 and 1977 meant political profit (expansion), they were accompanied by considerable costs because of the substantial differences in development between the existing member states and these Southern European states. Problems continued over the British contribution to the European budget, which was seen as excessive. The fact that the UK had a relatively small agricultural sector meant that it received few subsidies from Brussels, while it had to pay a great deal due to its extensive trade in agricultural products with the Commonwealth. The problems became worse when the British government, in a new attempt to protect its own interests, linked the issue of budgetary contribution to agricultural subsidies. This led to the failure of the European Council in Luxembourg in 1980. Although the impression was given that no mutually-acceptable solution was possible, a month of intensive political negotiations resulted in agreement in sub-areas including agricultural support and the common fisheries policy. The view that the weak economic position of a member state should be taken into account also gained ground. The Commission was charged with the task of preparing procedural reforms to reflect this. During the late 1970s overproduction led to a serious crisis in the metal working industry, which resulted in price decreases, bankruptcies and mass redundancies. Although the Commission was authorized on the basis of the ECSC Treaty to act by setting production quotas, the common decision making in 1980 and subsequent years was slow and laborious, given that unanimity was required among the ministers in the Council. This was, however, almost impossible to achieve because the member states continued to put their own interests first.

The weakening of the Bretton Woods system and the emergence of the G7 (1975)

27.1 The weakening of the Bretton Woods system during the 1960s

Monetary crises during the early 1960s

In the early 1960s the Bretton Woods system began to weaken due to problems with the American dollar and the British pound sterling. It started when in 1960 the total amount of dollars exceeded the US holdings of gold. When speculators demanded gold for their notes the US was not able to solve the problem by itself. An international solution had to be found. The same was true of the sterling crisis of 1961. The IMF facilities were simply insufficient to handle these crises. A number of international institutions developed *ad hoc* management and looked for solutions. The Bank for International Settlements founded in 1930 (BIS, see Figure 18.4) had provided European central bank governors with the opportunity to meet regularly in Basel, Switzerland, and if required to work out solutions. The US was not a BIS member and had not participated in these meetings, as it regarded the IMF and IBRD as the main international financial institutions. At Bretton Woods it had even proposed to the Europeans that the BIS should be wound up, but the European central bankers had ignored this suggestion. The dollar crisis of 1960 caused the chairman and higher-ranked staff members of the US Federal Reserve Board to join the monthly BIS meetings. To help the US the BIS created a 'gold pool', in which bankers agreed to centralize their gold dealings and thus regulate the price of gold (Spero 1985, 45). Although the BIS and its monthly meetings proved helpful to the US, the American government did not consider finding a solution through this institution. President Kennedy proposed that the OECD should establish a working party to discuss the coordination of the balance of payment positions of its member states. This became known as *Working Party Three*, or in jargon WP3, and consisted of the ministers of finance and their deputies. It was agreed that the IMF and the BIS would attend WP3 meetings.

435

Creation and importance of the GAB and the G10 (1961)

In 1961, on the initiative of the US government, some important IMF members agreed an arrangement where they would lend money to the IMF if any of the major states needed to appeal to the IMF for help. The European states and Canada were willing to contribute such additional funds, but on condition that they as a group controlled them. Given the circumstances, the US had to accept. The *General Agreement to Borrow* (GAB), which came into force in 1962, created a further international financial facility, which has been used some eight times since. The GAB was outside the IMF's jurisdiction and was controlled by the newly formed *Group of 10*, or G10: Belgium, Canada, France, Germany, Italy, Japan (from 1964), the Netherlands, Sweden, the UK and the US. In 1964 Switzerland became its 11th member, but this did not change the group's name. The G10 developed into more than a group of states willing to lend. It would meet regularly in Basel at the BIS to discuss monetary cooperation and reform. The continuity and intensification of these consultations were the result of the higher levels of interdependence, in particular the expansion and complexity of international financial transactions and the ongoing monetary crises at the time. Manifestations of this interdependence were the internationalization of US banks and the growth of transnational corporations. In 1963 only 13 US banks had branches abroad, compared with 125 in 1974. Large transnational corporations also dealt with the movement of huge amounts of money from one state to another because of the internationalization of production that was taking place in the 1960s. These corporations did this partly through internal management, but they also appealed to banks and governments if that was profitable for them. Their behaviour made them players in the international financial markets, or at least it made them have an impact there. Another new development was the market in 'Eurocurrencies', among them the so-called Eurodollars – dollars in the form of bank deposits held and traded outside the US, primarily in Europe – and German marks and Swiss francs held abroad (Spero 1985, 48–49).

Multilateral management under US leadership

As with the WP3, the G10 consisted of the ministers of finance and their deputies. The G10 meetings were attended by representatives of the BIS, WP3, IMF and European Commission. This meant that the ministers of finance and the central bank governors of some wealthy states began to coordinate their monetary policies within a number of forums, with certain divisions of the work. Since the US was leading this conglomerate during most of the 1960s, Joan Spero speaks of multilateral management under US leadership, rather than unilateral US management. During the 1960s it was not the IMF that was playing the leading role among the institutions, but rather the fairly independent G10. Between 1965 and 1967 the G10 devised a new international currency facility for the IMF, the *Special Drawing Rights* (SDRs). To use it the IMF had to adapt its Articles of Agreement in 1969 (see §25.2). Once again it was the G10 which had control over this facility, as the Europeans had stipulated veto rights. During the gold crisis of 1968 also it was the G10 that came up with a solution (Spero 1985, 53).

The weakening of Bretton Woods (early 1970s)

All these mechanisms, however, could not control the events that took place from 1968 on. Monetary interdependence grew faster than multilateral management could handle. Another factor that played a role was the rise of the European Economic Community and Japan as economic rivals to the US. That the US got into trouble was also due to the overvaluation of the dollar as a result of the Vietnam War, the military costs of which were partly financed by printing dollars. When other states refused to revalue their currencies against the dollar, as the US demanded, the US began to renounce monetary leadership and monetary cooperation. 'There was benign neglect from 1968 onward, first, in managing the system. The United States let others defend the existing rate system; it permitted a huge foreign dollar buildup; and it was passive in the currency crises of 1969 and 1971' (Spero 1985, 54). American domestic politics took precedence over international stability, but as a result of this policy of neglect the US economy also deteriorated. On 15 August 1971 President Richard Nixon announced that the dollar was no longer convertible into gold, without consulting any of the other states or any of the institutions. His move clearly marked the end of the Bretton Woods system, as this was based on the dollar being coequal to gold. Although its accompanying international institutions continued to exist, new monetary management of the exchange rates was required.

Smithsonian Agreement (1971) and the Committee of Twenty (1972)

The G10 first tried to repair the Bretton Woods system. A meeting in the Smithsonian Institution in Washington DC in December 1971 produced the *Smithsonian Agreement*, but this was mainly crisis management rather than a reform of the system. It made the US lose interest in the G10, as it found this group to be mostly 'nine against one'. The G10 therefore weakened, although it continued its monthly meetings in Basel. The US then tried to reform the monetary system through the *Committee of Twenty* (C20), which was established in 1972 within the IMF by the G10 plus ten of the larger developing states. This make-up had the effect, much to the US's relief, of the European states carrying less weight. However, this effort to achieve a stable exchange rate mechanism also failed. Because of the 1973 oil crisis (see §31.1) there was no unity among the participant states. The Committee of Twenty showed that a new, more flexible system was needed, but the US was not prepared to accept its proposals. In 1974 the newly created *Interim Committee* of the IMF, composed of selected ministers of finance and central bank governors from both developed and developing states, took charge of the process. The 1976 amendment of Article 4 of its Articles of Agreement, known as the 'second amendment' after the first one in 1969 for the Special Drawing Rights, obliged states to collaborate with the IMF and to follow domestic politics which would ensure orderly exchange arrangements and promote a stable system. This amendment became effective in April 1978. In the meantime private banks acted as international monetary managers, for instance by lending to oil-importing states money that came from oil-exporting ones. This enabled the latter to profit once again from their artificially-high oil prices. The IMF and the IBRD were affected by this situation too, which eventually would contribute to an unstable banking world and the huge debt crisis of the 1980s (see §35.2) (Spero 1985, 56–59).

27.2 The Trilateral Commission (1973) and its reflection on American hegemony

The Trilateral Commission (1973)

In March 1973 the unofficial *Trilateral Commission* began to meet on the initiative of the American national security adviser Zbigniew Brzezinski. The Commission consisted of representatives from the economic and political policy elites of the US, Western Europe and Japan, who discussed the question of whether the power in the international system, which after 1945 had remained firmly in the hands of the US, had become dispersed. The Commission worked toward a relatively permanent alliance between the major capitalist states, with the aim of promoting or sustaining a stable world order which was congenial to their dominant interests (Gill 1991, 1). When the Trilateral Commission was established the reputation of the US had been seriously damaged by the Vietnam War and the weak position of the dollar. That competition between the three areas, the US, Western Europe and Japan, began to play a more significant role was related to the growing economic importance of the latter two. Both Western Europe and Japan had successfully accepted the 'American challenge' that was part of the Marshall Plan. By following and partly copying the US economic model they had become strong industrially developed powers. In the early 1970s Western Europe gave its integration process new impetus and used protectionism and larger markets as a means of improving its competitiveness. After its defeat by the US in 1945 Japan had developed into an economic world power with its own characteristics. It had specialized in the technological field (electronics and cars) and had developed a special relationship between government and the business world that promoted the modernization of business and boosted the quality of products. Japan's industrial relations system was built on trade unions and workers who were loyal to their companies and had a strong focus on high quality. The combination of these characteristics was so successful that in industry the 'Japanese model' of industrial relations even became a challenge in the rivalry between the three areas.

No decline of American hegemony

The issue of whether American hegemony was declining in those days was debated from various perspectives, among them the idea of inter-imperialist rivalry. According to that view the US, as leader of the West, encountered serious competition from other major powers, which made continuity of American hegemony anything but self-evident. Others, however, argued that the international position of the US had weakened, but that American dominance in global security and economics was not endangered. The changes taking place in the late 1960s and the 1970s may be regarded as a 'crisis of hegemony', which involved a structural transformation in the nature of the postwar economic and political order and the political consensus between the major capitalist states. But this crisis did not affect American centrality in the global political economy. The relevance of the Trilateral Commission, which was dominated by American national interests and frameworks of thought, therefore was that it brought together the internationalist elements of the civil societies and policy circles of the states from the three areas, with the aim of influencing domestic politics through internationally-oriented views on foreign policy. The political influence of the Trilateral Commission on American politics was strongest on economic rather than security issues. That the two other areas had gained in economic weight in the international system, as was demonstrated by their inclusion in the Trilateral Commission, did not change the fact that American hegemony in the 1970s was far from over. Both the scale of the American economy and its position in the internationalizing world economy at the time were such that the US succeeded in substantially profiting from its structural dominance. Stephen Gill therefore did not accept the argument of declining hegemony, but rather regards the period of change as one in which American centrality is re-emphasized (Gill 1991, 3). The Trilateral Commission was a helpful instrument in analyzing this period of change, as the 1970s were also characterized by oil crises, worldwide inflation, unprecedented high unemployment, new forms of protectionism and the beginning awareness of environmental problems. Halfway through the 1970s a growing need for stronger international economic and political coordination was felt, that could not be satisfied by the remnants of the Bretton Woods system and the Economic and Social Council as the coordinating mechanism of the UN system.

27.3 The emergence of the G7 (1975) and its consequences for the UN system

The Library Group and the summit in Rambouillet (1975)

The Trilateral Commission was not the only forum in which developed states discussed the need for international coordination. A form of regular high-level consultation between wealthy industrial states began with the *Library Group*, consisting of the ministers of finance of France, Germany, the UK and the US. Between 1973 and 1975 they met in the library of the White House to discuss the world's major economic problems. In November 1975 the four states and Japan convened the first international summit at a castle in Rambouillet, France, on the initiative of the French President Valéry Giscard d'Estaing, supported by the German Chancellor Helmut Schmidt. The European Community already had some experience in summitry (see §26.5). The aim of both the Library Group and this summitry was to consult each other about problems on the agenda but also to take the lead. While the IMF still discussed ways to reform the monetary system, the political leaders of the five major industrial states during their three days of discussing solutions for some of the main economic problems agreed upon the reform of the international monetary system through the IMF.

Amendment of IMF Article 4 (1976)

In January 1976 this Rambouillet agreement was discussed at the IMF meeting in Jamaica, where 'the final details were hammered out' on the second amendment to the Articles of Agreement of the IMF (Spero 1985, 60). Amending Article 4 allowed new multilateral public management of the monetary system. For the time being the step taken was a gesture rather than a transparent or effective new practice, as the system of floating exchange rates that was operating left too many problems unresolved. The IMF's main difficulty was that it had virtually no influence over the national monetary policies of the major states and therefore found it difficult to achieve the expected coordination. The Interim Committee of 1974, which would play a leading role within the IMF, had no mandate for policy coordination. The result was that sometimes national and regional monetary mechanisms would be more important than the IMF mechanism. One competitor to the IMF was the *European Monetary System* (EMS), which came into effect within the European Community in 1979, with the aim of stabilizing the exchange rates of the member states and supporting the currencies of weaker states. Despite its shortcomings, the amendment of the IMF's Articles of Agreement in 1976 meant a 'first step toward a new system of international monetary management different from that of Bretton Woods' (Spero 1985, 61), but its real effect would not show until the 1980s.

The G7 economic summits

From 1976 'Rambouillet' was followed by annual international summits (see Figure 27.1 for an overview), usually between May and July. Canada joined this forum at the summit in Puerto Rico in 1976, mainly because the US did not want to be the sole representative of a whole continent, while Europe managed to also have Italy included in this group of, as they saw it, the seven richest states in the world: Canada, France, Germany, Italy, Japan, the UK and the US, or the G7. It was agreed at the London summit of 1977 that the president of the European Commission would be present at the summits, together with the state that holds the Presidency of the European Community unless this is one of the G7 members (the EC, later the EU, has a Presidency that rotates every six months among the member states). Although the original idea of these summits was based on an informal talk between leaders without too much bureaucracy, 'at the fireside' and with an open agenda, the summits developed into jumbo meetings and large-scale media events. The Munich summit of 1992 for instance was attended by 4,000 journalists. The leaders were accompanied by 2,000 officials and security was provided by 9,000 police officers. The summit meetings are thoroughly prepared by the leaders' personal advisers (see below) and are fine-tuned beforehand at meetings such as those of the OECD, IMF and IBRD. The summit meetings always take place after the OECD ministerial meeting in the spring. The US considered this OECD meeting as a preparation for the summit, not entirely to the OECD's liking. Before the leaders meet there are special meetings of ministers or high-ranking civil servants, dealing with specific issues. Russia attended the G7 for the first time in 1997 (with the G7 also called G7/8) and became a full member at the summit in Birmingham in 1998. Here the term G8 was used for the first time, albeit that the institution's essence still is referred to as G7.

Objectives of the G7 system

The G7 system of regular international summits of an elite group of states was meant as collective management for the global political economy, replacing the previous unilateral US leadership. The G7 had to reconcile domestic and foreign pressures resulting from interdependence and to mobilize leadership for issues that were beyond the control of national bureaucracies. Instead of *interdependence*, the catchword of the 1970s, *globalization* became the catchword of the 1980s. After some time issues other than economic ones also appeared on the G7 agenda, but this did not change the objectives of the summits. As a system it provided heads of state and government leaders with opportunities to meet in person. The meetings enabled them to understand each other's views and to draw common conclusions about the basic ideas and main lines of economic and other issues and their solutions. In this way the G7 sidestepped international organizations and national bureaucracies.

The Sherpa system

However, since the issues on the G7 agenda were complex and solutions chosen had a national impact, a good relationship with the national bureaucracies remained crucial. This was solved by the establishment of the so-called *Sherpa system*. In the G7 process every government leader or head of state has someone from the official national bureaucracy available, often from their personal staff or from a central department within the governmental apparatus. This 'Sherpa' prepares the G7 summits for the head of state or government leader by making sure that the G7 agenda issues are in line with the state's domestic and foreign policies and interests. Together the Sherpas prepare the G7 agenda and the draft texts, often motivated by the wish that the G7 leaders will work in an innovative way. It was however soon discovered that old issues remained on the agenda and had to be discussed again. Once the Sherpas have agreed on the agenda they start working towards potential agreements. They ensure these will receive endorsement at lower levels of their own bureaucracies and also from the other summit participants. Whoever wants to become a Sherpa needs the intuition necessary to precisely understand both domestic and international political relations and nuances. The Sherpa system expanded in such a way that 'sous-Sherpas' were introduced. By the end of the 1990s the government leaders believed that the Sherpas had gained too much power and they decided to involve themselves more directly in the summit preparation. Another aspect of the institutionalization of the G7 summits was that the foreign affairs ministers and the ministers of finance, who had been involved in the summits from the beginning, began to show more independence. During the 1980s the ministers of finance started convening their own summit meetings within the G7 context. From 1998 onwards the foreign affairs ministers met before the official summit started, which they no longer attended. Because the number of issues on the agenda kept growing, ministers other than of foreign affairs and finance also became engaged in the G7 summits. In 2000 the Japanese government invited some transnational corporations for consultation during the summit. NGOs also made their presence felt. As they had no access to the summits in the way they had to IGOs through consultative status, they showed their engagement, in particular their dissatisfaction with G7 policies, in street demonstrations (see §41.4).

The G5 sets the tone

Complementing the summits of the seven richest industrial states, the *Group of Five* (G5) began to play a role during the second half of the 1970s. This group consisted of the ministers of finance of the Library Group plus Japan: France, Germany, Japan, the UK and the US. They met at regular intervals to discuss monetary issues. Their action weakened the G10, as the G5 began to set the tone for the G7 summits on monetary topics. During the 1980s the IMF would gain a role of its own with regard to monitoring G7 decisions, which made the IMF part of the G7 machinery (see §35.3) in a similar way to the OECD playing a role in the preparation for the summits.

Consequences for the UN system

The emergence and evolution of the G7 cycle of summits under US leadership meant the existence of another coordinating mechanism in the global multilateral structure. The G7 is not an IGO, such as would have been set up during the institutional peace

Figure 27.1 G7/G8 conferences from 1975

Innovation and establishment	Maturity	Renewal
The first series, 1975–78	**The fourth series, 1989–93**	**The fifth series, 1994–97**
1975 Rambouillet	1989 Paris (Arch)	1994 Naples
1976 Puerto Rico1977 London I	1990 Houston1991 London III	1995 Halifax
1978 Bonn I	1992 Munich	1996 Lyon
The second series, 1979–82	1993 Tokyo III	1997 Denver
1979 Tokyo I		**The sixth series, 1998–**
1980 Venice I		1998 Birmingham
1981 Ottawa		1999 Cologne
1982 Versailles		2000 Okinawa
The third series, 1983–88		2001 Genoa
1983 Williamsburg		2002 Kananaskis
1984 London II		2003 Evian
1985 Bonn II		2004 Sea Island
1986 Tokyo II		2005 Gleneagles
1987 Venice II		2006 St. Petersburg
1988 Toronto		2007 Heiligendamm
		2008 Hokkaido Toyako

With regard to the **G7/8 summits,** Nicholas Bayne refers to a summit cycle and discerns phases such as 'innovation and establishment' (1975–88), 'maturity' (1989–93) and 'renewal' (from 1994) (Bayne 2000, 4). It shows that the G7 as an institution was developing. The G7, however, is not an IGO because it does not meet the criteria of having a written constitution and a permanent secretariat.

settlement of 1945. Instead it has a conference form with an elitist character and, not like the UN, a universal one. Only a few major states were members. There was no international secretariat, merely a joint structure that best resembled an Allied war council (see §18.1), with a small group of high-ranking national officials representing their government and preparing joint agreements. As in 1945 the coordination of international economic and social activities had been given to the Economic and Social Council of the UN, the creation of the G7, with the increasing involvement of the OECD and IMF, meant a weakening of the ECOSOC's capacity. It also made the connections between the UN and the Bretton Woods institutions IMF and IBRD, which already had a fairly autonomous position within the UN system, even looser. Although these institutions remained part of the UN system, their practical ties with the G7 would be reinforced during the 1980s and become stronger than those with the UN. The US, Western Europe and Japan, the three groups that were engaged in the Trilateral Commission, run the show within the G7, the IMF and the G5. The US had remained dominant in this group of three, but it was not so strong as to be able to set the tone unilaterally. However, the Trilateral Commission and the creation of the G7 had helped the US to ward off the crisis of hegemony of the early 1970s in an institutional way, albeit a different institutional way to that of 1945.

Decolonization, the North–South divide and Third World experiences with global and regional international organizations 1960–80

Part XI discusses the economic and political divide between 'North' (the developed and industrialized states) and 'South' (the less developed and industrialized states) during the 1960s and 1970s. Among the related political issues were the white minority governments in Southern Rhodesia and South Africa, which were faced with embargoes imposed by the UN. The Vietnam War was not a UN concern, but given the regional consequences of the war in Indochina it was a UNHCR concern (Chapter 28). In the economic field the developing states were lagging behind the European states, which had completed their postwar reconstruction by the end of the 1950s. The North then devised an economic strategy for the South, in the form of the UN Development Decade, that worked out in favour of the North. The South, also referred to as the Third World, developed alternative strategies, among them import substitution, but it had difficulty in persevering with this in view of opposition from the Northern states and the IGOs they controlled. Besides, the Third World itself was divided (Chapter 29). One of the alternative strategies of the South was the creation of regional economic organizations, which was done with some success during the 1960s (Chapter 30). The debate about strengthening developing states resulted in a UN Declaration on a New International Economic Order (NIEO), but this turned out to be a Pyrrhic victory (Chapter 31).

Decolonization, anti-apartheid and the consequences of the Vietnam War

28.1 Decolonization and anti-apartheid as normative forces in international relations

The Trusteeship Council in operation

For the first 15 years after the Second World War the main decolonization issues in the UN were handled by the Trusteeship Council, which was based on a reinforced version of the mandate system of the League of Nations. The General Assembly set up an *ad hoc* commission to monitor the decolonization process through the required reports, but this was of little significance. Its existence was renewed every three years, but it did not evolve into a permanent body nor did it have the authority to comment on political developments, as that was the privilege of the Trusteeship Council. From the beginning the US had favoured self-determination and independence as the eventual outcome for the mandates, whereas the European colonial states refused to commit themselves to this result although they had agreed to it. This was particularly true for the areas still under their control and less so for the mandates under the supervision of the Trusteeship Council. But the Declaration Regarding Non-Self-Governing Territories in Chapter XI of the UN Charter did call upon the colonial states to be active in promoting the well-being of the people and working towards self-government. However, it took some time before the colonial states were prepared to gradually move in that direction. At first the decision about granting independence was entirely theirs, but by the end of the 1950s their attitude began to change, as they started to regard their colonial territories more and more as a burden. It became more difficult to deny the colonies the liberty and self-determination that they valued so much for themselves. The pursuit of independence by colonial territories also sometimes became violent and forced colonial governments to engage in expensive military operations against liberation movements. This increased their willingness to grant independence, albeit that this often coincided with controversies in domestic politics. During the 1960s 42 states were to gain independence.

Decolonization and Cold War

In 1960 the Soviet Union submitted a draft resolution to the General Assembly calling for the immediate and complete liberation of all colonial peoples from foreign domination. This move was an attempt to make the Second (or communist) World the 'proper' ally of the rising Third World. Western states reacted by stressing that immediate decolonization would destabilize the world and they reminded the Soviet Union of its annexation of the Baltic states. This debate could not prevent an East–West divide on this issue within the UN for years to come. That the developing states preferred greater speed was shown by the draft resolution introduced by Cambodia on behalf of 26 African and Asian states, which gained the support of 43 states. These tried to prevent the issue becoming a Cold War matter. They recognized the operations of the Trusteeship Council, but also believed that the decolonization process was too slow and that political independence needed more economic freedom. Within the General Assembly competition sprang up between the Soviet Union and the Third World states. However, all amendments to the draft resolution of the 43 states proposed by the Soviet Union were rejected. The resolution of the 43 was adopted on 14 December 1960 with 89 votes in favour and nine abstentions (from Western states) as the *Declaration on the Granting of Independence to Colonial Countries and Peoples*. This UN Declaration regarded alien domination, subjection and exploitation as violations of human rights and confirmed the right to self-determination. The victory by the Third World had an impact on the UN. As not much progress was being made a *Special Committee* was set up to monitor the implementation of the Declaration. A year later the Special Committee was enlarged from 17 to 24 members. Known as the *Special Committee of 24*, it would become the most influential UN body on decolonization issues, alongside the Trusteeship Council and the Special Committee against Apartheid (see below). Although the Special Committee of 24 did not have the authority to enforce them, its requests and recommendations were taken seriously (Gorman 2001, 154). By the mid-1970s most colonies had gained independence, with the exception of some microstates with extremely small populations.

The UN embargo imposed on Southern Rhodesia (1966) and the first UN sanctions

One of the biggest conflicts the UN had to deal with in the early 1960s was the Congo crisis (see §22.3) and the major clashes after that all concerned states in Southern Africa: Angola, Mozambique, Namibia, Southern Rhodesia and South Africa. In 1962, as a result of action by the Special Committee of 24, the UN had become involved in the British colony Southern Rhodesia. The white minority government did not want to give up power and in 1965 it made a unilateral declaration of independence. The UK asked the world not to recognize this new state and imposed an embargo on the export of all arms. It asked the UN to act along the same lines. The Security Council followed the UK's lead and called upon all states to impose a weapons embargo and to break off all economic relations with Southern Rhodesia. This had little effect and the Security

Council therefore decided in December 1966 to invoke Chapter VII of the UN Charter and, for the first time in the history of the UN, to impose economic sanctions. In 1968 the number of items subject to economic sanctions was expanded and a committee was set up to monitor the implementation of the resolution. This committee created a list of states that did not abide by the embargo, such as Portugal and South Africa. During the 1970s the Security Council tightened its sanctions against Southern Rhodesia and the General Assembly passed resolutions in favour of action against Rhodesia and of tighter sanctions. In December 1979 the Security Council was able to revoke the embargo and sanctions, because a solution to the conflict had been reached in negotiations that resulted in the colony becoming independent under the name of Zimbabwe. The embargo as an economic and normative force had contributed to the undermining of white minority rule, but in the end other factors had been more decisive in achieving independence, in particular black guerrilla warfare, independence for Angola and Mozambique and pressure from South Africa, which had an interest in settling the ongoing conflict in this neighbouring state. A side effect of the embargo was that it contributed to the economic 'self-reliance' of the isolated regime. A state that has great difficulties in obtaining certain goods and services becomes creative in finding solutions for these needs (Simons 1999, 88).

The UN against apartheid: an arms embargo without sanctions

The UN became involved in the issue of apartheid in South Africa at an early stage. In 1946 India complained to the UN about South African discrimination against Asians. In 1947 it was joined in this by Pakistan, but South Africa felt no need for UN engagement when it offered to mediate in the complaints from India and Pakistan. Later, when criticized by a small UN commission that had studied the racial policies of the state in relation to the UN Charter, South Africa responded that apartheid was a domestic issue and not an international one. It claimed that apartheid was not a matter of the superiority of the 'white' population, but rather of various groups within the population being 'different'. This stance did not stop the UN from calling upon South Africa to end apartheid. During the 1950s the General Assembly passed a number of resolutions on the subject which referred to the Universal Declaration of Human Rights. The situation changed after the Sharpville incident in March 1960, when the mainly white police force shot dead 69 unarmed black protesters. This provoked worldwide outrage and caused the UN to discuss apartheid as an issue that affected international relations. In 1962 the General Assembly for the first time declared apartheid to be a danger to international peace and security. It set up a *Special Committee against Apartheid* and asked its members to break off diplomatic relations, impose export embargoes on South Africa and boycott South African goods. Not all states voted in favour of the resolution or felt inclined to act. In 1963 the Security Council called for a voluntary embargo on the sale of arms to South Africa. This embargo was made mandatory in 1977, but no economic sanctions were imposed. Up to 1988 the Security Council adopted 25 resolutions on apartheid.

The conflict over Namibia

The UN had another and related dispute with South Africa, which involved the mandate of Namibia or South West Africa. The League of Nations had given South Africa a mandate over Namibia, but after the Second World War many new African states expressed dislike of the apartheid that South Africa enforced in Namibia in 1948. In

1963 the African states established a regional organization for the African continent, the Organization of African Unity (OAU) (see Figure 28.1), which actively engaged in the struggle against apartheid and also pressurized the UN. Two African states filed a complaint with the International Court of Justice over South Africa's administration of Namibia, but the Court ruled that the two states did not have the standing to bring suit against South Africa (see §22.2). For the UN, however, this was sufficient reason to revoke South Africa's mandate over Namibia.

Figure 28.1 The Organization of African Unity (OAU) 1963–2001

On 25 May 1963 30 African states established the **Organization of African Unity** (OAU) in Addis Ababa, Ethiopia, with the purpose of promoting the unity and solidarity of African states and of coordinating their policies in various fields. Its creation had not been straightforward because of regional, political and linguistic differences, which to a large extent were related to the colonial subjection and division of Africa. The first initiative to establish an African regional organization came from Ghana and Guinea. In 1958 they drafted a charter and in 1961 they called a conference in Casablanca, Morocco, which decided to set up an African military command and to pursue a common market. In 1960 and 1961 a number of conferences of French-speaking African states took place, which in 1965 resulted in the *Organisation commune africaine et mauricienne* (OCAM). OCAM's main aim was economic cooperation. In the meantime 19 other states had met in Monrovia, Liberia, in May 1961 and had decided to cooperate. In early 1962 they established a permanent secretariat in Lagos, Nigeria. Contacts between the various initiatives and evolving structures resulted in the conference in Addis Ababa in May 1963, which decided to establish an organization to cover the entire African continent. The result was a compromise between the federal form favoured by Ghana and the Casablanca group and the looser association preferred by the Monrovia group. Like the UN the OAU succeeded in its practical significance, as it had many poor member states.

Between 1963 and 1980 the OAU was involved in 43 **territorial and other disputes** between member states. Generally speaking the organization did not prove a very effective agent for conflict management. In internal disputes and in international conflicts that involved allegations of subversion the OAU clearly showed its limitations. However, the organization did succeed in isolating intraregional disputes from becoming entangled in more complex global disputes and thus relieved the UN of the potential burden of numerous local conflicts, albeit that the OAU's involvement depended heavily on policy decisions by the US and the Soviet Union (Meyers 1974). With regard to the UN observer status of African liberation movements the UN decided in 1974 to grant this automatically to all liberation movements recognized by the OAU. Immanuel Wallerstein analysed the emergence of the Organization of African Unity as a regional organization that did not have just the African continent as its territory for action but rather the whole world. Despite the organization's objectives of changes in Africa, it could only change Africa by changing the world (Wallerstein 1969). Wallerstein noticed that development aid in Africa did not match the real situation and that African leaders succeeded in changing sides easily in the East–West conflict. He therefore began to regard the world as an economic system which determined the room for manoeuvre for states (Wallerstein 1974).

The OAU's principal bodies were the *Assembly of Heads of State and Government*, which met at least once a year behind closed doors (and voted by a two-thirds majority), a *Council of Ministers*, consisting of the ministers of foreign affairs meeting at least twice a year, some standing commissions (among them of economic and social affairs) and a *General Secretariat* in Addis Ababa. From 1964 the OAU also had an Arbitration Commission. In 1994 South Africa became the organization's 53rd member state. In 2000 the organization decided to transform itself into the *African Union*, which happened in 2001 (see §42.5).

Crisis in the ILO due to apartheid 1961–63

Within the International Labour Organization the issue of apartheid became a crisis, after some newly independent African states were admitted to ILO membership in 1961 and, on the initiative of Nigeria, submitted a resolution on it. The International Labour Conference adopted this and thus condemned apartheid and invited South Africa to withdraw from ILO membership, as apartheid was not in line with the aims and purposes of the organization. South Africa was not prepared to comply. A year later a new dispute arose when an objection to the South African delegation's credentials was filed. These two events resulted in a crisis in 1963 that brought the ILO to the verge of breaking up. That the organization managed to survive was the result of two important changes to its Constitution and some related measures. The amended Constitution offered the possibility of excluding a member from the organization and apartheid was explicitly mentioned as a form of racial discrimination. Among the measures taken were a Declaration, a Programme of Action, special meetings and annual reports on anti-apartheid activities (Ghebali 1989, 46–47, 83–84). South Africa finally withdrew from membership in 1966.

Normative condemnation of apartheid by the UN

Within the UN the normative aspect of the apartheid issue acquired additional significance. In 1963 the General Assembly, aware of the events within the ILO and the strong feelings against South Africa's racial politics, adopted the *Declaration on the Elimination of All Forms of Racial Discrimination*. This was followed by a stronger instrument on 21 December 1965, when the General Assembly, in the absence of South Africa, adopted the *International Convention on the Elimination of All Forms of Racial Discrimination* (ICERD). This Convention came into effect in 1969 and was accompanied by a Committee that monitors the implementation of the Convention, which allows it to receive reports and to hear complaints (see Figure 28.2). During the 1960s racial discrimination was an issue in a number of places around the world. The black civil rights movement in the US put up a vigorous fight against the forms of segregation existing there. Many black representatives of the newly independent African states who came to visit the UN headquarters in New York were surprised by the segregation they came across in airport facilities and on transport services between New York and Washington. The civil rights movement found an unexpected ally for domestic reform in the Department of State, which was ashamed of these racial relations that did not correspond to the democratic appeal of the US abroad (Banton 2002, 99). The UN persisted in the field of anti-apartheid. On 30 November 1973 it adopted the *International Convention on the Suppression and Punishment of the Crime of Apartheid*, which came into force in 1976. It condemned the policy of apartheid as a crime against humanity and in certain respects as a form of genocide. In 1974 the General Assembly recommended that South Africa should not be allowed to participate in international organizations and bodies, but the Security Council refused a proposal to expel South Africa from the UN. The IMF and IBRD also refused expulsion, as they could only exclude states if they had not fulfilled their financial obligations (Klotz 1995, 49). In 1979 the General Assembly called on the member states to impose an oil embargo on South Africa. During the 1980s the UN continued its pressure on South Africa through calls for Namibia's independence and actions against apartheid. 1982 was the international year of mobilization of sanctions against South Africa. States and corporations increased their pressure on South Africa through stronger economic sanctions. A special session of the UN General Assembly in 1989 adopted the *Declaration on Apartheid and its Destructive Consequences in Southern Africa*. Gradually the tide was turning. Partly as a result of changes in South Africa's domestic politics Namibia became independent in 1990. In 1994, after 31 years, the UN could revoke its arms embargo and other restrictions on South Africa. The government under President F.W. de Klerk, which had received a mandate to end the apartheid system, had released black leader Nelson Mandela from prison in 1990. It began constitutional talks and held democratic general elections, which were monitored by the UN and in 1994 led to Mandela's election as South Africa's president.

Effect of UN policies against apartheid

Although the UN arms embargo, in combination with sanctions by states and corporations, had affected South Africa, the intended effect remained restricted as the UN had failed to impose comprehensive economic sanctions. As in the case of Southern Rhodesia, South Africa had become creative and skilful at circumventing economic sanctions and finding solutions to solve the problems created by the arms embargo (Simons 1999, 81). The main explanation of why the UN in this case did not impose economic sanctions was that although the Third World could successfully apply pressure in organizational settings where majority voting prevailed such as in the General Assembly, it could not do so in the Security Council, where permanent members vetoed comprehensive mandatory sanctions. The same was true for the IMF and IBRD, where major states with most votes refused to take action. Nonetheless, the UN had been the main forum in which to discuss and defend international norms (non-discrimination) and expose and condemn an abuse (apartheid). From the 1960s onward the General Assembly had been the primary forum for criticizing and isolating South Africa further (Klotz 1995, 53).

Figure 28.2 The Committee on the Elimination of Racial Discrimination (CERD)

The 1965 *International Convention on the Elimination of All Forms of Racial Discrimination* entered into force on 4 January 1969, which was even before the two UN Human Rights Covenants of 1966 came into effect. 128 states were parties to the Convention by 1989, in which Article 5 at length sets out the rights that everyone should enjoy. A **Committee on the Elimination of Racial Discrimination** (CERD) was established to monitor its implementation. It consists of 18 independent experts, among them only a few jurists, who meet twice a year in New York. States submit reports on the legislative, judicial and administrative measures which they have adopted. If one state has a complaint about another state that in its opinion is not implementing the Convention's provisions, it can bring the matter to the attention of the Committee, which may appoint an *ad hoc Conciliation Commission*.

The Committee may also receive and consider communications from individuals or groups of individuals within its jurisdiction claiming to be victims of a violation by a state of a right set forth in the Convention. However, this can only happen if the relevant state has recognized this competence of the Committee. The Netherlands did this when ratifying the Convention in 1971, but by 1988 only ten states had acknowledged this competence. Ironically the first case against a state concerned the Netherlands, which had taken the leading role in arguing for the Committee's competence to receive complaints from individuals. The Netherlands was convicted in 1988 of discriminating against a Turkish working woman who had complained to the Committee (Banton 2002, 78).

The anti-apartheid movement

The fight against apartheid was not only a matter of governments and the UN, but also of citizens who spoke out publicly on this political and moral issue. Among them were blacks who had left South Africa, leaders of liberation movements who condemned South African influence in Africa and apartheid as a regime, as well as large groups of non-black citizens elsewhere who protested against apartheid in ways similar to those employed by the nineteenth-century anti-slavery movement. These citizens established working groups or committees on the issue of apartheid, which studied the problem and investigated issues such as justification and refutation of the system, its effects on black citizens, the economic involvement of states and corporations and the ways in which they tried to circumvent the embargo. This resulted in the publication of brochures and journals. These groups also held demonstrations or protests in front of South African embassies and they organized consumer boycotts, such as the one against South African fruit: 'boycott Outspan oranges'. That the UN persevered in its condemnation of apartheid was important for these groups of citizens, as the UN statements legitimized their actions (Klotz 1995, 53). These actions in turn endowed the UN with authority. Similar working groups and committees were established for other African states, among them Angola. During the 1960s a younger generation became informed about problems in the world through the activities of these kinds of committees. This helped them to have opinions about international political issues. The groups also had transnational ties with similar groups in other states, mostly to exchange written information and, to some extent, to coordinate actions.

Impact on US domestic politics

The anti-apartheid movement also had an impact on the black civil rights movement in the US, which had already been influenced by views on non-violent resistance as

451

developed by Mahatma Gandhi (see Figure 28.3). The decolonization process in Africa during the 1960s aroused renewed American interest in this continent. In 1962 the American civil rights activist Martin Luther King Jr and the South African anti-apartheid fighter Albert Luthuli jointly issued a declaration on the necessity of imposing international sanctions on South Africa. Conferences on Africa in the US enhanced the self-consciousness of black Americans, now called African-Americans, and supported the international anti-apartheid struggle. Malcolm X founded the *Organization of Afro-American Unity*, modelled on the Organization of African Unity. The *Black Power* movement was an expression of the increased conviction that 'blacks' were not second-class people. At the end of the 1960s the civil rights movement in the US had gained so much influence that it became a factor in changes in American foreign policy on South Africa. It pressurized both corporations and the government. American corporations were approached with the so-called *Sullivan Principles*, guidelines for corporate strategies to enhance the living and working conditions of black South Africans, devised by the Reverend Leon Sullivan who also was an African-American corporate board member (Klotz 1995, 93). In addition to this appeal to corporate responsibility there was an appeal to the government. As a result the US government began to take a stronger stance on apartheid. The changes in domestic politics, which in 1964 resulted in the Civil Rights Act that outlawed most forms of racial discrimination, explain why the US government, despite its former restraint, eventually during the mid-1980s initiated sanctions against South Africa. 'Prior to the mid-1980s, policy toward Africa was generally insulated from domestic pressures as the United States pursued its strategic and economic interests. Access to minerals and markets seemed ensured under conservative South African governments. But in response to growing vocal public support for racial equality and reform in South Africa, top policy makers in the mid-1980s disrupted this easy correspondence between U.S. interests and white minority rule. Redefining U.S. interests in the region to include support for racial equality, indeed as a prerequisite for – rather than an alternative to – strategic and economic interests, congressional leaders initiated sanctions against South Africa' (Klotz 1995, 110–11).

Figure 28.3 The black civil rights movement in the US

The **black civil rights movement in the US** dates back to the early twentieth century. In 1909 a group of mainly black, but also a few white, Americans founded the *National Association for the Advancement of Colored People* (NAACP). This lobbied government institutions over what it considered injustice against African-Americans and brought legal cases to local and national courts. It established a Legal Defence Fund and in 1919 the NAACP sent representatives to the peace conference in Versailles to defend the cause of African states and of slaves and their descendants of African origin. Until the mid-1950s the NAACP was the most influential organization working for racial justice in the US (Chabot 2001, 233). In this movement the influence of Mahatma Gandhi's action repertoire of **non-violence**, as devised for the nationalist movement in India, could be noticed. It aimed to mobilize large crowds of people, who themselves would avoid any violence, in order to publicly pressurize the authorities. During the 1930s black Americans had become interested in this action repertoire, in particular in African-American colleges, and began experimenting with Gandhian non-violent action themselves. During the Second World War they successfully pressurized President Roosevelt by threatening him with organizing a March on Washington, in view of the oppression at home, while African-American soldiers risked their lives as members of strictly segregated armed forces. Between 1955 and 1965 this Gandhian action repertoire was applied in boycott actions such as the Montgomery bus boycott, student sit-ins, Freedom Rides, voter registration projects and marches on Birmingham, Alabama, and Washington DC (Chabot 2001, 237–41). President Dwight D. Eisenhower was not a strong proponent of racial equality. After having opposed desegregation of the armed forces in 1948 he refused to endorse the Supreme Court's unanimous 1954 decision in the *Brown Case* on school desegregation. He declared racial issues to be matters of the heart, not of legislation. However, the growing influence of the civil rights movement and the sight of National Guard soldiers preventing nine black pupils from entering a high school in Little Rock, Arkansas, in 1957 forced him to mobilize federal troops to enforce integration and protect the pupils. It was followed by a weak Civil Rights Act and a Civil Rights Commission in the same year (Banton 2002, 99).

The violence used by the opponents of the civil rights movement, as in Birmingham, Alabama, in 1960, inflated negative publicity for the US abroad. This issue in US domestic politics became an element in the **Cold War propaganda struggle**, as the Soviet Union regarded these racial conflicts as proof that capitalism and racism went hand in hand. In combination with the fact that successive US governments failed to ratify the UN Human Rights Covenants of 1966 this added to a loss of American prestige. It resulted in the charge that the US saw human rights as for export only, rather than also for its own citizens (Banton 2002, 99). For the time being the US did not ratify the 1965 International Convention on the Elimination of All Forms of Racial Discrimination. President Jimmy Carter forwarded it to the Senate for ratification in 1978, but it was not until October 1994 that the US, under President Bill Clinton, with many reservations ratified the Convention.

28.2 The Vietnam War not a UN but a UNHCR concern

The division of Vietnam

The civil rights movement in the US also became a critic of the Vietnam War of the 1960s and 1970s, but unlike apartheid this war was barely an issue within the UN. In 1949 France had recognized the independence of its colony in Indochina, but it had disregarded the nationalist and partly communist movement which had gained influence during the Japanese occupation. Differences of opinion existed on the virtual division of the territory and on the preferable political system. China and the Soviet Union supported the northern part, which to a large extent already had the form of a state under the leadership of Ho Chi Minh. The US and the UK supported the southern part which as a political system was weakly organized. France also supported the south militarily, but lost the battle of Dien Bien Phu in 1954. The support promised to France within the North Atlantic Council had not been provided. Diplomatic negotiations in Geneva by

France, the UK, China, the Soviet Union, the two parts of Vietnam, Cambodia and Laos divided Vietnam into two zones, with the 17th degree of latitude as their border. In the *Geneva Accords* it was agreed that in both zones elections were to be held in 1955. An *International Control Commission*, consisting of Canada, India and Poland, was set up to oversee the implementation of the Accords. The US had remained aloof and declared that it would refrain from any action that might endanger the implementation. However, it would take any form of aggression seriously. For the US the struggle against communism in the region would become more important than decolonization, as was proven in 1954 by the establishment of the Southeast Asia Treaty Organization (see §23.4) and later its involvement in Vietnamese developments.

The US and the Vietnam War

While China economically supported the north, the US rather than France began to support the south. The state of South Vietnam which was established after the elections had to contend with instability and corruption and refused to fully implement the Geneva Accords. In 1960 the *National Liberation Front* (NLF, or FNL, *Front national de liberation*) was set up in South Vietnam which, like the People's Republic of North Vietnam, aimed at reunification of the two states. In 1961 and 1962 the US began to send military advisers (in fact a number of troops) to South Vietnam, which according to the International Control Commission conflicted with the Geneva Accords. Because of the instability of South Vietnam the US military presence became stronger. In the summer of 1964, according to the US, North Vietnamese torpedo boats attacked US vessels in the Gulf of Tonkin, which was followed by President Lyndon B. Johnson's decision to bomb the base and the stores of these boats. Military actions by the NLF led to further bombings and an escalation of the war. US behaviour was criticized, as negotiations in the framework of the Geneva Accords seemed a more proper solution. However, the US refused to recognize the NLF, which by then had become an important actor. In 1966 the US itself brought the conflict to the attention of the Security Council. Given its East–West character this did not look very promising, since neither North nor South Vietnam were UN member states, as Bulgaria pointed out. The US tried to blame North Vietnam, communist China, which at the time was not a UN member, and the Soviet Union. The Soviet Union, however, argued that it was not the Security Council but rather the Geneva Accords which was the appropriate forum for finding a peaceful solution. It condemned the American aggression (Gorman 2001, 177). Much to the disappointment of the Burmese UN secretary-general U Thant the solution to the Vietnam War was largely found outside the UN.

The US criticized internationally

The foreign policy of President Johnson was sharply criticized because of the Vietnam War, partly by resistance from American baby boomers who did not see a need to fight and die for this cause, partly by intellectual commentary. The American journalist Isy Stone in his independent *I.F. Stone's Weekly* analysed the political relations in the US, among them the civil rights movement, and US foreign policies. By preference he based his analyses on governmental documents, Congressional reports of hearings and other official papers and documents, which he used to demonstrate contradictions in governmental policies and statements. He published the weaknesses or incorrectness of official statements, such as the one on the alleged North Vietnamese aggression in the Gulf of Tonkin. His weekly became widely read both in the US and elsewhere and contributed to the arguments opposing the war effort. In 1966 and 1967 the philosophers Bertrand Russell and Jean-Paul Sartre organized the *Vietnam Tribunal* in Roskilde, Denmark. They compared US behaviour with the norms of the war tribunals at Nuremberg and Tokyo and judged that according to those norms the US was committing war crimes. The anti-war movement, as with the anti-apartheid movement, first took the form of small committees in various parts of the world which analysed the conflict and organized anti-US demonstrations. But unlike with apartheid there were no UN norms they could appeal to. The Vietnam Tribunal referred to older international norms, but these had not been repeated or elaborated by the UN or any other international organization. Despite its efforts to treat the Vietnam War as part of the Cold War, the US began to loose prestige as a result of the criticisms, whereas the tenacious resistance of the Vietnamese during a brutal war with a great power received sympathy. The US did not succeed in settling the conflict in favour of South Vietnam, despite sending more and more troops, returning to and escalating bombings, using chemical defoliants (*Agent Orange*) to destroy the shelters of the NLF from 1965 on and other modern ways of warfare. 'Vietnamizing' the war by training and arming South Vietnamese troops did not change the outcome either. In May 1968 diplomatic negotiations began in Paris between the US, North and South Vietnam and the NLF. The US broke these off in 1971, as it expected that heavy bombing of North Vietnam would bring a military victory. However, negotiations were resumed, as the NLF resistance proved too fierce and the number of protests against the bombings grew. Furthermore the US had begun a different foreign policy approach towards China in the early 1970s. In January 1973 in Paris the American Secretary of State Henry Kissinger and the North Vietnamese special envoy Le Duc Tho concluded the *Paris Peace Accords*, which resulted in an armistice. The US found itself in a situation where it had to withdraw from South Vietnam within two months. The International Control Commission could not accomplish much. Military developments in Vietnam resulted in the reunification of the two states in 1976 as the Socialist Republic of Vietnam. No elections were held and in 1977 Vietnam became a UN member state.

Expansion of UNHCR activities

During the 1960s the specialized UN agencies were not involved in this political and military conflict. This changed in March 1970, when a combined US-South Vietnamese force intervened in Cambodia and caused a stream of 'ethnic' Vietnamese refugees from Cambodia to South Vietnam. Since they were refugees within the UNHCR mandate, South Vietnam asked the UN High Commissioner for Refugees for assistance. This was a reason for the UNHCR to help the refugees, but it also decided to monitor what was happening in the region closely, as 'the fluid situation in the Indochinese peninsula may cause further movements of population which could be of direct concern to UNHCR' (cited in Loescher 2001, 189). In 1972 it opened an office in Bangkok, Thailand, in October 1974 a regional office in Vientiane, Laos, and in November of that year a branch office in Hanoi, North Vietnam. Following the Paris Peace Accords the children's fund UNICEF and other UN specialized agencies and programmes also became operative in the region. The rest of the world regarded the streams of refugees resulting from the Vietnam War and its political aftermath in the Indochinese peninsula (Cambodia, Laos and Thailand) as the responsibility of the US. Although the US requested assistance from the UNHCR and the Intergovernmental Committee for European Migration (see §22.1), it met with little response in its attempts to share the burden and to relocate the refugees in 'third countries'. In Europe only France was prepared to help. 'Most of the UN, including the UN Secretary-General, Kurt Waldheim, and Prince Sadruddin [the Aga Khan, the UN High Commissioner for Refugees], viewed the Indo-China crisis as an American problem and as the almost inevitable aftermath of years of American involvement.' The UNHCR doubted that the Indochinese were bona fide refugees and did not want to become too closely identified 'with the former Vietnamese client regime of the United States so as to offend the victorious Communist regimes in Indo-China' (Loescher 2001, 190).

The political consequences of the American defeat

The US efforts to prevent communist regimes coming to power in Indochina had the opposite effect. In 1975 Vietnam's neighbouring state Laos became a people's republic. During the same year the communist Khmer Rouge obtained power in Cambodia, another neighbouring state. The solution to the resettlement of refugees who were admitted temporarily to another state was problematic, as none of the states in the region was a signatory to the 1951 Refugee Convention and its 1966 Protocol. Hence, they acknowledged no obligation to provide asylum for arriving Indochinese. In July 1975 the UNHCR signed an agreement with Thailand to provide temporary assistance to new arrivals and other states followed suit. As the US had not succeeded in attracting reset-tlement offers from its Western allies, it had little choice but to admit most of the evacuees (130,000 people) to the US, after a temporary stay at US military bases. Another 60,000 people fled to Thailand and some 12,000 to other states throughout the region (Loescher 2001, 191). At first the UNHCR resisted promoting the resettlement in third countries of the so-called 'boat people', who from 1978 on began to flee Viet-nam, as it believed that such programmes would only open a migration channel to the West. However, both the Southeast Asian states and the US put pressure on the UNHCR to respond to this crisis. The UNHCR was involved in the resettlement of over two million people up to the mid-1990s.

The United Nations Development Decade

North versus South during the 1960s

29.1 Multilateral development aid, the UNDP (1965) and regional development banks

Rostow's economic growth theory

Because the economic development of the Latin American states and the newly independent former colonies was lagging behind and this economic vulnerability might create a window of opportunity for communism, American economists began to discuss the question of how to develop these states. What developing states needed was economic growth, according to the US economic elite that took its own economy as the point of departure. At the time of establishing the IBRD Harry Dexter White believed that foreign investments had to be made, as the American economy would profit from this and it would contribute to stable trade. He was convinced that 'the US needed to reconstruct Europe, and create a stable world market in the Third World to secure outlets for American products ... This would necessitate huge investments abroad' (Nustad 2004, 13). Economic growth, conceptualized as income and consumption problems, occupied centre stage in the postwar economic reflections on development. Growth could be enhanced by pushing and supporting the performance of weaker economies, according to Walt Rostow in the early 1960s. He regarded the wealthy industrial states of Western Europe and Northern America as states that had developed on their own. In accordance with liberal economic growth theory other, younger states could develop similarly, if they progressed faster through the five stages of economic growth: traditional society, the preconditions for take-off, the take-off, the drive to maturity and the age of high mass consumption. 'Take off' was the crucial stage for development on its own, to be compared with an airplane gaining speed on the ground and then taking off (Rostow 1960). His view discussed development in terms of *backward areas* and *making up arrears* with some help. In sociology the distinction was referred to as *modernization*. Rostow predicted that the functioning of a free market would eventually result in mass consumption and welfare comparable to that in the wealthier states. He regarded his economic vision as a blueprint for developing states and as an alternative to communism. His book *The Stages of Economic Growth* (1960) was subtitled *A Non-Communist Manifesto*.

The UN Development Decade (1960s)

Rostow became an adviser to the US government of President John F. Kennedy, who in early 1961 took office at a time of strong economic growth and high expectations, in particular from younger people. Kennedy shared Rostow's view on development and would financially support the UN more generously than any of his predecessors. In September 1961 he proposed that the General Assembly should bring more unity to the UN's efforts to develop the many young states in the Third World. Following this, at the end of 1961 the UN declared the 1960s to be the *United Nations Development Decade*. To achieve a more balanced and sound development the UN decided to use the experience of the more industrialized states and to coordinate the economic and social planning procedures of states better. Referring to growing differences in income per capita in the economically-developed and the less developed states, it decided that by the end of the Decade the economies of the developing states should be growing by five per cent a year. Despite its obvious zeal the new economic growth strategy was more restricted than the goals in the 1945 UN Charter, which in addition to economic and social progress also mentioned the promotion of higher standards of living and full employment (Article 55). During the 1960s these other values were pushed into the background as a result of the organizational changes taking place within the UN, where soon only economic growth would matter.

The creation of the UNDP (1965)

Halfway through the Development Decade the UN General Assembly of 1965 decided to merge two of its older agencies for technical support and development assistance, the *Expanded Programme of Technical Assistance* (EPTA) of 1949 and the *Special UN Fund for Economic Development* (SUNFED) of 1958 (see §21.3), into one new programme, the *UN Development Programme* (UNDP). The Special Fund had been set up by the former manager of the Marshall Plan, Paul Hoffman, and had restricted goals, the main one being 'to provide for pre-investment opportunities for poor countries'. Both predecessors would pass on their practical working methods to the new UNDP. This implied that the 'UNDP assimilated the practical goals of the agencies it replaced and thus continued that trend' (St Clair 2004, 178). The *modus operandi* the UNDP inherited from the Expanded Programme was that it only dealt with governments of states and did not have any contacts with lower authorities or representatives of business and civil society. Furthermore, it gave pre-eminence to the poorest of the developing states and gave its funds in the form of grants that had to be paid back. It also distributed parts of its funds not to the states themselves, but to specialized UN agencies such as the ILO, WHO and UNICEF for their sectoral projects. The Expanded Programme worked in every state through a country office. These laid the foundation for the UNDP's network of field offices that later would become the UN Secretariat's main source of information about what is going on in various member states. The other predecessor of the UNDP, SUNFED, used to restrict itself to technical support, mainly in the form of training and equipment.

The UNDP's significance

The UNDP has an *Executive Board*, consisting of 36 members from developed and developing states, that endorses its main programmes and policy decisions. It receives its resources through voluntary contributions from member states and specialized agencies. The UNDP became the largest multilateral programme for technical assistance and within the UN the organizational centrepiece of development activities. Between 1959 and 1985 the amount of contributions rose from 55 million to a total of 8.5 billion dollars. During the 1990s the UNDP spent more than a billion dollars a year. Technical assistance included teaching and training, feasibility studies and the introduction of new technologies. These kinds of assistance preceded the capital investments White and Rostow had in mind. In 1966 the UN also founded, as a participant and executive body of the UNDP, the *UN Industrial Development Organization* (UNIDO), tasked with providing industrial assistance to developing states at their request (see Figure 29.1). By the end of the UN Development Decade the so-called *Jackson Report*, named after the leading figure in development cooperation at the time, Robert Jackson, concluded that the UNDP was too focused on economics. The report stated that the UNDP lacked a think tank to work out ideas and launch them as directives for policies. It emphasized that the UNDP 'could only provide training and well-being to people if the needs of the LDCs [least-developed countries], not some other view of aid, were the starting point of UNDP's programme design'. However, the New York-based UNDP leadership did not truly embrace the critical comments of the Jackson report, although it officially accepted some suggestions. It created opportunities for states to describe their priorities, but as an institution the UNDP did not reflect on the wider problem of development and the ways to solve it. It was 'a morally concerned and even obliged international actor; but it did not include this ethical concern in its conceptual tools' (St Clair 2004, 181).

Figure 29.1 The UN Industrial Development Organization (UNIDO) (1966)

The **UN Industrial Development Organization** (UNIDO) which was founded in 1966 began as an autonomous organization within the UN Secretariat in Vienna, but in 1985 became a specialized agency in the UN system, assisting in industrial projects aimed at promoting and accelerating industrial development in developing states. UNIDO promotes international cooperation for industrialization on global, regional, national and sectoral levels. It functions as a forum for consultation and negotiation. It organizes panels on investment promotion, foreign investment, technology markets and technology transfer. It prepares studies, conducts research and maintains information banks. UNIDO has its own budget and its own governance structure, with a General Conference, an Industrial Development Board, a

Programme and Budget Committee and a Secretariat. In 1993 and 1994 UNIDO provided technical assistance worth 225 million dollars, related to investment projects with a total value of 1.1 billion dollars. UNIDO was not regarded as a successful institution at the time. In the field of biotechnology for instance the developing states were completely outplayed by the wealthy states. In 1995 the US decided to disengage, as it believed UNIDO to be redundant. According to the US, which provided a quarter of the budget, industrial development should be a matter of business and of the states themselves. In 1996 Germany also decided to leave the organization, referring to its own domestic cutbacks. UNIDO, however, managed to survive by playing a role in new issues such as sustainable industrial development, poverty reduction through productive activities, trade capacity building, and energy and environment.

Regional development banks

During the 1960s regional *multilateral development banks* (MDBs) were set up as part of the development strategy advocated by Rostow and the UN. The first of these regional banks was the *Inter-American Development Bank*. It was created in 1959 on the initiative of Brazil, because of dissatisfaction with the slow and complicated procedures of the International Bank for Reconstruction and Development. Brazil was supported by 19 Latin American states and the US. Multilateral development banks are owned and administered by the governments of developed and developing states. They are the main official international channels for transferring capital between these two groups of states, mainly in the form of loans and repayments. The regional banks are more conscious of regional and local needs than the IBRD. During the 1950s and 1960s the IBRD had been the primary source of finance for infrastructural investment in power, transport and water supply, as well as for industrial investment. By the end of the 1960s and during the 1970s the IBRD and the regional banks branched out into financing agriculture and the social sector, favouring education, health, nutrition, population, poverty alleviation and rural and urban development. The multilateral development banks were largely concentrated in Asia, Latin America and Africa and, after the collapse of communism, also in Eastern Europe and other parts of the former Soviet Union (Mistry 1995, 2–3) (see Figure 29.2). Halfway through the 1990s the IBRD and four regional banks for Latin America, Africa, Asia and Eastern Europe accounted for more than 85 per cent of all multilateral bank lending, with the IBRD alone responsible for nearly 60 per cent. The regional multilateral development banks as a group, together with the IBRD, were 'the largest source of development aid for middle- and low-income countries. They lent or invested nearly $40 billion in 2000, four-fifths of it at market-related terms and the rest on concessional terms. The World Bank accounted for half of all MDB aid and 62% of all MDB concessional aid in 1997. In the World Bank and most regional MDBs, the U.S., European Union, and Japan control over half of the vote' (Sanford 2002, i). Other multilateral lending institutions are much smaller. These include the International Fund for Agricultural Development (IFAD), the Islamic Development Bank, the Arab Fund for Economic and Social Development and the Arab-African Development Bank. Economic regional organizations also have created development banks, such as the Andean Development Bank of the Andean Community of Nations and the East African Development Bank of the East African Community.

Figure 29.2 Five regional development banks

1959 *Inter-American Development Bank* (**IDB**). Established by 19 Latin American states and the US. Seat: Washington DC. In 1976 membership was increased to include states outside the region. In 2007, 26 states in the Americas and 21 from outside the region were members.

1963 *African Development Bank* (**AfDB**). Established by 30 independent African states. Seat: Abidjan, Côte d'Ivoire (Ivory Coast). In 2007, 53 African and 24 non-African states were members.

1965 *Asian Development Bank* (**ADB**). Established by 31 members. Seat: Manila, Philippines. In 2007, 48 states belonging to the UN regional commission ESCAP (Economic and Social Commission for Asia and the Pacific) and 19 from outside the region were members.

1969 *Caribbean Development Bank* (**CDB**). Established by independent states and territories in the Caribbean plus Canada, France and the UK. Seat: Wildey, Barbados. In 2007, 18 states in the Caribbean, three Latin American states and five states from outside the region were members.

1990 *European Bank for Reconstruction and Development* (**EBRD**). Established by 41 initial members. Seat: London. In 2007, the EBRD had 61 states and the European Community and the European Investment Bank as members, among them 29 'countries of operation'.

The Paris Club for debt restructuring

Where money is borrowed there are debts and because of liquidity problems and economic setbacks states may not always be able to pay them back. In 1956, a meeting of Argentina and its public creditors took place in Paris to agree on an arrangement to solve its payment difficulties. From this gathering arose an informal forum, referred to as the *Paris Club*, with meetings chaired by a senior official from the French treasury. In 1974, the treasury established a secretariat, but the term 'club' is somewhat misleading, as there are no members and no regulations. The meetings are convened at the request of a debtor state seeking solutions for its payments difficulties by rescheduling its debts. Involved international organizations may also participate. The Paris Club decides by consensus among the creditor states and functions on the basis of informal rules and custom-based procedures. It seeks to apply similar norms in comparable situations and since the debt crisis of the 1980s attempts to agree on an adjustment programme with the IMF, while no creditor can demand more favourable terms or larger payments than agreed within the Paris Club. It has reached more than 400 agreements covering 84 debtor states. The *London Club* is another informal forum, but one of commercial banks that meet to negotiate their claims against a sovereign debtor. Here too the debtor initiates the process, which in this case takes the form of an Advisory Committee that is dissolved when a restructuring agreement has been signed.

The Latin American Parliament (1964)

Sometimes multilateral development banks also support activities other than financing for development. In December 1964 the *Latin American Parliament* (*Parlamento latinoamericano*) was established on the initiative of the Inter-American Development Bank, with the general aim of promoting representative democracy in the southern part of the American continent and of integration on the model of Western Europe. The Parliament consists of delegations from national parliaments (with a maximum of 16 people), which all have the same number of votes (12). In 1972 it was agreed with the European Parliament to convene an interparliamentary conference biennially. The first one took place in Bogota, Colombia, in 1974. Later a similar agreement was made by the Parliament of the Andean Community of Nations (see §30.2).

UNICEF and development aid for children

The availability of large amounts of money for development had a stimulating effect on the activities of the specialized agencies and funds and contributed to the expansion of their organizations. This had already occurred during the 1950s, but happened far more strongly during the UN Development Decade. UNICEF had been established on a temporary basis, with the E in its name standing for Emergency: an international emergency fund for children who were victims of the Second World War. But in 1952 UNICEF became a permanent organization with broader objectives. From then on UNICEF would stand for the *UN Children's Fund*, although keeping the I and E in its acronym. UNICEF would now also devise technical assistance programmes for children, intended to help governments to promote the well-being of children in fields such as health and food. From the 1960s onwards UNICEF has developed into an important player in development aid, with its own activities, focusing on children in particular. As a continuation of these new activities, the UN itself became a standard-setting organization with regard to children when in 1959 the Economic and Social Council issued the *Declaration on the Rights of the Child*. ECOSOC also monitored whether governments incorporated the Declaration's standards in their national laws and regulations. An evaluation of this practice eventually resulted in the adoption of the *UN Convention on the Rights of the Child* in 1989, which spells out the basic rights that children everywhere are entitled to.

The WHO and development aid

In 1948 the *World Health Organization* (WHO) became operative (see Figure 14.2) to help all people attain the highest possible level of health. It tried to prevent and control disease and epidemics, stop them spreading and eradicate them by improving the general level of health. The WHO also provided assistance in setting up health care systems and it developed training programmes and seminars for health workers, pilot projects and other forms of technical assistance, often in cooperation with the FAO. Like UNICEF the WHO expanded as an organization and became a big player in development aid. This did not cause controversy, given its useful work. However, problems arose during the 1960s when the WHO began to set up regional commissions. The way this was done to a large extent depended on the local interests that the organization had built up, which made it difficult to coordinate between regions in the world and it led to a wasteful duplication of efforts. While it was expected that the WHO would produce an integrated global system of health cooperation, it in fact resulted in a loose combination of locally- and nationally-focused activities: 'in fact much of the organization's budget is spent on programs meant to enhance and strengthen the independent capacity of each member state's health sector to provide contained health services within their own territories' (Gorman 2001, 93). The debates about health were also marred by political issues, such as apartheid and the Middle East dispute, but especially in the area of family planning.

Population control: UNFPA

Population trends were an early issue for the UN when in 1947 the Economic and Social Council began to collect population data, which at the time were still scarce. In 1950 the first international census was conducted and in 1954 the World Population Conference in Rome debated standardized statistical measures and census instruments. The issue soon proved controversial, as many in the Western world regarded the increase in the world's population as problematic, given doubts about sufficient availability of food, housing and other necessities of life. Family size was another sensitive topic. Traditionally families in agricultural societies had been larger, while family size tended to decrease in industrialized and urbanized areas. Population control policies and issues such as family planning and means of contraception proved highly controversial because of the underlying moral, religious and ethical questions. In 1962 the debate in the UN General Assembly on whether the UN was to be authorized to provide technical assistance on birth control was heated. The proposed resolution failed as the vote was equally divided. The second World Population Conference in Belgrade in 1965 resulted in a 1966 UN resolution that the number of children in a family should be decided by the free will of each family. But in the 1969 *Declaration on Social Progress and Development* it was also laid down that families should be provided with the knowledge and means that would enable them to decide on the number of their children. In 1966 the UN decided to establish a Trust Fund for Population Activities to assist developing states in studying demographic problems and their effects on social and economic development. The *UN Fund for Population Activities* (UNFPA) became operational in 1969. In 1972 it became a fund of the UN General Assembly and in 1979 it was made a subsidiary body of the General Assembly, with the UNDP Executive Board as its governing body. In 1987 the name was changed to *UN Population Fund*, while retaining the acronym. The UNFPA increasingly became 'the focal point for lobbying by governments and family planning nongovernmental organizations (NGOs) for the wider dissemination of family planning services in the developing world' (Gorman 2001, 135).

29.2 The Third World view: dependency, UNCTAD (1964) and the G77

Frank's dependency approach

The growth strategy devised by Rostow and the UN was based on liberal terms of exchange, with exports of goods by states specializing in what they were best at producing and trading them with other states. In the case of developing states these were mainly raw materials and agricultural products. In reality this strategy proved not to enhance the position of developing states after 1945. This outcome led to a Latin American search into the causes of the continuing dependency (or *dependencia*). Dependency theorists then related the political and socio-economic developments in the Third

World to international structures that were 'asymmetric' and benefited certain groups of states, the 'Core' states or metropolitans, and put other states, the 'Peripheral' or satellite states, at a disadvantage. Disadvantaged states had no autonomous history, as they were subjected to the workings of a larger complex that they as separate parts did not control. This position made them different from the developed and industrialized states, which controlled the complex in all respects, economically, militarily and politically. Generally speaking trade relations between the Core, with its highly developed capitalism, and the Periphery, mainly consisting of former colonies, had been an 'unequal exchange'. The Periphery with its fairly weak economies had to compete with huge, technologically-advanced transnational corporations from the Core states. The 'underdevelopment' which resulted from this and characterized the Periphery was not, as assumed by Rostow, a preceding stage of modernization or economic growth, but rather the draw-back of capitalism. According to Andre Gunder Frank the Periphery served and enriched the Core and this lasting dependency prevented the economic growth that Rostow had predicted (Frank 1969). During the 1960s Frank had been involved in debates about American and multilateral development aid that had resulted in this dependency rather than in an improvement of the Latin American economies. It occurred to him that development assistance had a political dimension and was itself part of the problem. Frank then concluded that development would have a chance only if it could break out of the existing structures that benefited the Core states.

Prebisch's analysis: external dependency

Frank's view linked up with the ideas of the Argentine economist Raul Prebisch, who was the secretary of the UN *Economic Commission for Latin America* (ECLA) from 1950 to 1963. ECLA aimed to promote regional economic development and looked for a common strategy. Prebisch had conducted research which showed that Latin American trade after the Second World War had worked out badly. The terms of trade between industrialized and less-industrialized states had deteriorated, which meant that the Per-ipheral states with their raw materials and agricultural products were having to export more to get the same value of industrial products. The demand for Latin American export products lagged behind the import of industrial goods from Western Europe and Northern America. Technological progress and an increase in productivity in the export sectors had not resulted in stronger Latin American sales, but in price reductions for Western European and American importers. Due to their dependency on imports Latin American states had been forced to continue exporting, even when prices were low. This deterioration in terms of trade motivated Prebisch's pursuit of a way to break out of this 'external dependency' through a common economic strategy.

Benefiting developed states

In developing their Latin American strategy the experiences of the 1940s were taken into account. In the economic discussions during the Second World War the Latin American states had favoured a vision of postwar international economic organizations 'that would allow national regulation of international economic relations while seeing to it that those national regulations conflicted with each other as little as possible' (Murphy 1997, 201). However, towards the end of the war and shortly after the US view on these organiza-tions, aimed at abolishing national restrictions on the international economy rather than merely national regulation, became dominant. Furthermore, the Latin American and other Third World states expected that the principles of states' economic rights and duties would allow them to receive assistance similar to that which had been given to Europe during and after the war. However, this was not the US position, as it prioritized European reconstruction over support for developing states, as became clear at Bretton Woods. The consequences of the international economic regulations based on the American view, such as in the GATT, were soon shown to be to the disadvantage of the developing states. The economic organizations of the UN proved to benefit the wealthier states rather than support the weaker ones. When Prebisch showed in publications what was actually happening in the case of Latin America, the Third World began to discuss this imbalance within the UN. The liberal GATT economist Gottfried Haberler reached similar conclusions to those of Prebisch. In a report published in 1958 he blamed the industrialized states for the declining Third World share of trade. 'Northern trade policies, like those associated with strategic stockpiling, created tariff and non-tariff barriers to increasing the Third World's share of trade.' The free trade system of the GATT as such was not to blame, but rather 'the exceptions to the system, which had been granted mostly to Northern states' (Murphy 1997, 205).

Import substitution and regional free trade

To break out of this external dependency Prebisch preferred an economic policy for developing states which aimed at self-reliant industrialization and an improvement in the terms of trade. *Import substitution industrialization* became one of the strategies that Latin American and Asian states adopted during the 1960s. The strategy promoted the domestic production of goods that so far had been imported. This industrialization policy for the domestic market only needed to be combined with larger export markets in the form of regional free trade zones. This meant that states had to establish economic forms of cooperation in their region, such as free trade areas, custom unions and even common markets. After first promoting economic development within a small group of similar developing states, an attempt could then be made to improve their terms of trade globally from a stronger common position.

Prebisch's connection with the UN

In addition to this economic strategy of import substitution and regional cooperation, Prebisch was also in favour of concerted political action within the UN and its specialized agencies. This action had to focus on securing trade preferences and international commodity agreements favouring developing states and, in line with the Western view on development aid, on more international assistance and investments. Prebisch made out a case for this strategy within the ECLA and the ECOSOC. In 1961 Argentina and 16 other Third World states introduced a resolution on international trade as the primary instrument for economic development. The ECOSOC called upon the UN secretary-general to question all members on the advisability of holding a conference on this topic. The resolution was approved. Not all dependency theorists supported Prebisch's 'reformist' strategy. Some argued that breaking out of the unequal structure could be achieved only by a 'revolutionary' change of society and that participation in intergovernmental organizations would simply render that unequal structure permanent.

UNCTAD as a counterbalance to the IMF and GATT (1964)

Within the UN Prebisch kept arguing that the arrangement of international economic relations through the IMF and GATT was in the interests of the industrialized rather than the less developed world. However, in multilateral negotiation processes these organizations did not show much understanding of the inequalities and 'trade gap' between the two groups of states or of the necessity for developing states to protect their burgeoning industries. His arguments nevertheless persuaded the UN to convene the *UN Conference on Trade and Development* (UNCTAD) in Geneva in 1964. At this conference the developing states indicated that they wanted a permanent organization to study and discuss the problems of trade and development. The General Assembly, which regarded development as a priority goal, agreed and made UNCTAD a permanent body with regular conferences every four years (see Figure 29.3). Many industrialized states expressed their reservations over the final document and had ensured that UNCTAD could not demand that resolutions should be implemented. Between 1964 and 1968 Prebisch served as an enterprising UNCTAD secretary-general, who thanks to his ability to form coalitions succeeded in creating a number of commodity agreements and establishing a general system of preferences. Under Prebisch UNCTAD reached a membership of 135 states, compared with the 87 contracting parties of the GATT. In a way Prebisch made UNCTAD a 'counterbalance' to the IMF and GATT, which were dominated by the industrialized world, for the developing states. This helped UNCTAD to mobilize public opinion in its favour. Many 'Northern' development NGOs felt motivated to align their development aid with the needs of developing states in the South. Whoever analyses the UN system as a configuration of organizations and bodies which helped crystallize the supremacy of the dominant worldviews and the dominant social forces, may find that these global agencies 'also provided political space in which opposing social forces could articulate their own world-views and develop counterhegemonic alliances' (Cox 1980, 374; Murphy 1994, 32).

Figure 29.3 UNCTAD as a UN body from 1964

In December 1964 **UNCTAD** became a permanent body of the UN General Assembly. The UNCTAD conference sessions are numbered:

- **UNCTAD 1**: 1964 Geneva, Switzerland
- **UNCTAD 2**: 1968 New Delhi, India
- **UNCTAD 3**: 1972 Santiago, Chile
- **UNCTAD 4**: 1976 Nairobi, Kenya
- **UNCTAD 5**: 1979 Manila, Philippines
- **UNCTAD 6**: 1983 Belgrade, Yugoslavia
- **UNCTAD 7**: 1987 Geneva, Switzerland
- **UNCTAD 8**: 1992 Cartagena, Colombia
- **UNCTAD 9**: 1996 Midrand, South Africa
- **UNCTAD 10**: 2000 Bangkok, Thailand
- **UNCTAD 11**: 2004 São Paulo, Brazil
- **UNCTAD 12**: 2008 Accra, Ghana

In 1995 the *UN Conference on Trade and Development* had 188 member states (three more than the UN), in 2007 it had 192 (including the Holy See). The UNCTAD Secretariat is located in Geneva. Between the sessions, in which policy guidelines are established, the **Trade and Development Board** as an executive body is responsible for continuity. It meets biennially in two stages and reports to the UN General Assembly through ECOSOC, although it is virtually independent of ECOSOC. At one meeting the Board discusses the international implications of macro-economic policies and, against the background of UNCTAD's annual *Trade and Development Report*, issues concerning interdependence. At the other meeting the Board discusses trade policies and problems of structural adjustment and economic reform. Since 1992 there have been four standing commissions and since 1994 four working groups. They cover issues such as trade in goods and services, poverty, economic cooperation, environment and development, and transnational corporations.

The Group of 77 developing states (G77)

According to informal UN practice UNCTAD member states were geographically classified in line with the then existing regional group structure in the UN (see §20.2). At the Geneva conference of 1964 the states in groups A (Africa and Asia) and C (Latin America and the Caribbean) united by establishing the *Group of 77* or G77 (see Figure 29.4) and by issuing a joint declaration at the end of the first session. Prebisch had succeeded in his efforts to unite these groups of developing states and to let them show a more or less united front in negotiations with the industrialized states. This was remarkable, given the political and cultural differences among them as well as the differences in development. The industrialized states belonged to groups B and D, with a capitalist and a communist character, respectively. The G77 soon developed the habit of preparing for UNCTAD sessions through preliminary meetings where they tried to reach joint positions. This made the G77 into an influential caucus group of the Third World within the UN system, where its numbers counted when it came to voting. This unexpected grouping at the UNCTAD conference in Geneva had several effects. It came as a shock to the states of the North, which gave the conference as a whole a sense of increased political importance. The Third World unity meant that the Western and communist states were nearly always in minority positions, which led to special conciliation provisions and it stimulated the Western states into strengthening their own solidarity by prior coordination in the OECD (see §26.4). This had 'both a rigidifying and a conservative effect, since Western group solidarity was essentially based on an agreement not to embarrass each other on vulnerable points' (Nye 1973, 335).

UNCTAD results in the long term

UNCTAD conferences have had varying success. UNCTAD 2 in 1968 had modest results in the form of some carefully-worded trade preferences with a number of European states and a new sugar agreement, but UNCTAD 3 in 1972, unexpectedly, remained without concrete results. In the longer term UNCTAD has contributed to some favourable arrangements for developing states. In 1970 an agreement was achieved on the adoption of a generalized system of preferences, involving tariff concessions by the

Figure 29.4 The Group of 77 developing states (G77)

The **Group of 77 developing states**, the G77, originally consisted of 75 Third World states from the A and C groups at the UN Conference on Trade and Development in Geneva in 1964. In October 1967 it officially became the Group of 77 at its first ministerial meeting in Algiers, Algeria, where the 77 adopted the *Charter of Algiers*. At this meeting economic issues dominated the agenda as a result of the instability of the Bretton Woods system. Membership of the G77 grew to 131 in 2000 and fell to 130 in 2007, but the group retained its original name because of its historical significance. The Group of 77 remained active in spite of its mixed composition, the absence of a formal organization and the varying effects of capitalism on its member states. The organizational structure of the Group has gradually expanded and has led to the creation of so-called *Chapters* in several locations. In each Chapter a chairman acts as its spokesperson and coordinates the Group's actions. The chairmanship rotates on a regional basis and is held for one year. One Chapter prepares for the meetings of the UN in New York through the permanent representatives, other Chapters are associated with the UN specialized agencies that are most important to developing states, such as UNCTAD, UNEP, UNESCO, FAO and IFAD, and UNIDO. The *Committee of 24* represented the interests of the G77 at the IMF and IBRD. It was established in 1971 to harmonize the position of developing states on monetary and development finance issues and was later known as the *Intergovernmental Group of 24* (G24). The annual meeting of foreign ministers of the G77 is convened at the beginning of the regular session of the UN General Assembly. If required there are sectoral ministerial meetings. From 2000 onwards the G77 has called *South Summits*, as its supreme decision-making body of the heads of state and government. It is convened once every five years. In 2000 the South Summit took place in Havana and in 2005 in Doha, Qatar. The third one will be held in Africa in 2010.

industrialized states. In 1980 UNCTAD adopted guidelines for international action in the area of debt rescheduling and for the control of restrictive business practices. UNCTAD also worked to establish international commodity agreements. Although this helped to clarify the trade problems of developing states with only few products, UNCTAD did not succeed in achieving a strong cooperation of producing states on the marketing of their raw materials, with the objective of stabilizing prices.

International commodity agreements

International commodity agreements are meant to control the imbalance between supply and demand that gives rise to wide price fluctuations. The GATT considered commodity agreements as exceptions to the general rules and principles of free trade, which however could be defended, given the potentially strong fluctuations in commodity prices and the resulting instability of the involved economies. During the adoption of the GATT agreement states had opposed such arrangements, but despite their principled objections five international commodity agreements were set up under the GATT regime up to 1964, among them one for tin (1956) and one for coffee (1962). In 1964 UNCTAD gave the commodity agreements a completely different meaning, compared with the GATT of 1947, as they could contribute to an improvement in the terms of trade for the young developing states and to 'remunerative and equitable prices' for their goods. In 1976 UNCTAD's new principles were reinforced in the *Integrated Programme for Commodities*. This programme consisted of a globally-integrated approach for 18 commodities, including a time schedule for negotiations, arrangements for buffer stocks and a common fund to finance the programme. The expectations of this programme were high, as it aimed for prices that were such that poorer states would earn a larger share of world income. But the disappointment was great as the results remained meagre. The number of commodity agreements after 1964 was no more than three, one of them for rubber (1979). Most agreements expired during the 1980s and it was not until 1980 that the agreement creating the common fund was adopted, to be followed by a long period of it not coming into force. The main explanations for this failure of international commodity agreements were the lack of political will on the side of the industrialized world, the asymmetry in the distribution of bargaining power between industrialized and developing states and the ideological antagonism between the supporters of economic intervention and of free trade (Zang 1985, 111). The US, as an opponent of the UNCTAD policies, slowed down the process and by the end of the 1980s withdrew from the sugar, cocoa and coffee agreements. UNCTAD's role had been to clarify the contrasts between the proponents and opponents of intervention, to bring new meanings to an older form of an international arrangement and to try to make the adopted agreements function for at least the poorest states.

The Common Fund for Commodities (1989)

In 1980 the agreement on the *Common Fund for Commodities* (CFC) was adopted, but it then took another nine years before it became operative. The Common Fund, based in Amsterdam, had a membership of 106 states and seven regional international organizations in 2008. The tragic part of its existence was that by the time it eventually began functioning (1989) it had lost most of its potential for UNCTAD's Integrated Programme for Commodities of 1976, given the in the meantime strong global orientation towards free trade. Nonetheless, it is still in existence.

29.3 Alternative strategies: collective self-reliance and the Asian Tigers

Amin's alternative strategy: collective self-reliance

Based on a radical interpretation of the dependency theory, the Egyptian Samir Amin had little faith in international organizations as a means of promoting the Periphery's development, since Peripheral economies were unable to extract themselves from their unbalanced position *vis-à-vis* Core economies. Their own markets were too small and their industries were not equipped to compete in the Core markets. Social and political relations also played a restraining role, as the 'national' bourgeoisie of a Peripheral state was bound by self-interest to the foreign transnational corporations in its state. This non-autonomous bourgeoisie, referred to by Amin as a bourgeoisie of *compradores*, had in its national and international policies to stay close to the economic interests of the North. To break out of this lasting dependency the Periphery needed to disconnect itself from the world market. Amin advocated a more self-reliant development with mutual assistance between Third World states, a reduction in trade with the industrialized world and thus a loosening of dependence (Archer 1992, 121). Amin's politics of 'collective self-reliance' advocated that Peripheral states should use their natural and human resources for their own needs. National self-reliance had to balance several economic sectors, in particular agriculture and industry. Transactions with Core states that sustained existing inequalities or resulted in unwanted political influence had to be discontinued. Internationally and regionally the Peripheral states had to cooperate economically and politically to solve common problems and to collectively break out of international dependency relations. Amin's plea for radical social change (replacing global capitalism with global socialism) at the time meant choosing China, which was regarded as a successful example of national self-reliance, rather than the Soviet Union, which Amin described as having a disguised form of capitalism.

The Non-Aligned Movement: From East–West to North–South (1973)

In the early 1970s Amin's politics of collective self-reliance was greeted with sympathy within the Non-Aligned Movement (see Figure 22.2), which aimed at decolonization and an independent position between East and West. Despite their non-aligned status many Third World states felt some affinity with China or the Soviet Union, as they regarded these states as allies against discrimination, colonialism and US aggression in Vietnam. At the time the East–West divide was beginning to narrow, while the economic problems of the developing states became a new binding force for the Third World. At the third conference of the Non-Aligned Movement in Lusaka, Zambia, in 1970 54 states came to the conclusion that the UN Development Decade had not brought the results hoped for. The divide between rich and poor states had even become wider and now threatened the independence of the new states, as they did not have the right to economic equality and effective participation in technological development and international progress. To discourage this trend the Lusaka conference devised its own development strategy, based on mobilization of the states' own potential, better use of raw materials, promotion of technology and social reforms with the objective of creating the conditions for the envisaged economic development. In 1973 the Non-Aligned Movement, meeting in Algiers, added the right to nationalize foreign corporations to this strategy. For developing states 1973, also the year of the oil crisis, marked the shift from the East–West to the North–South conflict, as Amin's collective self-reliance strategy gained political momentum within the Non-Aligned Movement. The Movement regarded itself as a 'catalyst' within the G77 because of its stronger views on the North–South divide. Although the basic problem in the North–South divide was an economic one, the Non-Aligned Movement focused on political cooperation. This also influenced the UN and other international organizations through the G77, notwithstanding differences of opinion between the G77 and the Non-Aligned Movement. One of the issues was that various non-aligned countries developed friendly relations with the Soviet Union, which made the Movement lose credibility as far as being 'non-aligned' was concerned.

Import substitution reaching deadlock

The import substitution industrialization policy advocated by Prebisch, which promoted the domestic production of goods that so far had been imported, also had its downside, as the developing states needed to protect their new industries with tariffs and to find finance for the necessary investments. Foreign bankers from the North, however, condemned the tariffs and were not willing to finance these investments, which meant that it became almost impossible to start the new industries up. An increase in exports of raw materials and agricultural products proved insufficient to find the necessary capital. Although theoretically it was possible to be successful with import substitution, the strategy failed in many states at the end of the 1960s as a result of a declining trade balance, lack of financial resources, insufficient technology transfer and inefficient production methods. This failure resulted in economic stagnation, trade obstacles and international isolation rather than economic development.

Export industrialization: the Asian Tigers

The weaknesses of the import substitution strategy inspired some Southeast Asian states to employ a different strategy, based on economic liberalism. With regard to industrialization they followed the Japanese policy of exporting for the world market. In the early 1970s Hong Kong, Singapore, South Korea and Taiwan, later called the four 'Asian Tigers', initiated this with export-oriented industrialization policies. Their inputs were cheap labour and special facilities for foreign corporations, such as a friendly tax environment and the suppression of trade unions.

Transnational corporations during the 1970s

Large internationally-oriented transnational corporations converged on these new Asian opportunities. Modern process technology, as well as communications and transport technology enabled them to split up their production processes. By switching over to transnational production in a number of states they succeeded in lowering their production costs. The textile industry was in the forefront of this by moving its labour-intensive sections from Western Europe and Northern America to developing states that had the required semi- and unskilled labour in abundance. Large parts of the work were done by young women, whose labour was particularly cheap. These new industrial investments resulted in economic growth in these states, but they also harmed traditional social structures. The wealthy states gained doubly from the investment, as they had found cheap labour, far cheaper than in Europe and Northern America, and they managed to profit from the competition for the new investment among the developing states. Other industries followed suit, such as consumer electronics, steel, shipbuilding, cars and trucks. Overall these movements resulted in a hitherto unknown shift of the means of production from the North to some parts of the South. The number of transnational corporations increased and as a result of mergers the corporations became even larger. These large-scale developments furthermore affected the industrialized states themselves, because massive shutdowns and business reorganization took place to enable the corporations to adapt to the new international developments.

The success of the NICs

The arrival of transnational corporations in less developed states meant that investments no longer were merely a matter of raw materials and markets for products, but also of creating attractive conditions for production compared with those in the advanced

471

industrialized states themselves. The latter remained market leaders, but in the longer run the 'tigers' and other *Newly-Industrializing Countries* (NICs) managed to achieve their own comparative advantages. These enabled them to expand their industrial sectors and to develop the required entrepreneurship and training, often at first only in certain regions or cities but later elsewhere too. These domestic developments turned NICs into states with Western-oriented and to foreigners open economies, with generally stable but not very democratic political regimes. With regard to citizen participation and compliance with general and economic human rights the NICs showed a poor record. Hong Kong, as a British Crown colony (returned to China in 1997), was a special case, but Singapore, South Korea and Taiwan became known as examples of developing states that managed to create export-oriented economic growth by themselves. Other states in this category were Malaysia and Thailand in Asia and Brazil and Mexico in Latin America. During the 1980s South Korea and Taiwan succeeded in setting up capital-intensive industries and improving domestic relations.

The other side of the success of the NICs

Among the consequences of the success of the NICs' export-oriented strategy was the reaction from advanced industrialized states in the form of protectionist measures, to counter the drastic effects of the 'cheap imports' on their home markets (reorganization of entire industries followed by massive redundancies, with all ensuing social effects) or to protect their own industrial standards. Trade barriers may have been limited in sectors where international production was most advanced, but they remained high in sectors with little business concentration and advanced production techniques. The US believed that the successful NICs should no longer categorize themselves as developing states, but rather as potential members of the group of wealthy industrialized states. A further drawback was that the NICs damaged the idea of solidarity of the Third World, as had been advocated by Prebisch and the G77 in the early 1970s.

The creation of regional economic organizations in the Third World in the 1960s

30.1 Regional economic cooperation outside Europe

Creation of regional organizations in the South

The policy that the Northern states initiated at Bretton Woods to tackle development after the reconstruction of Europe encouraged the South to reflect on a strategy of its own. This resulted in import substitution and regional economic cooperation as policies to enhance the world market position of Southern states. Southern regional cooperation was not an imitation of European integration (albeit that European experience was taken into account), but a development that had its main roots in the North–South divide and in analyses such as the dependency theory (see §29.2). This strategy resulted in the ongoing creation of economic regional international organizations, which over time had their ups and downs (see §30.2), but which remained a permanent component of the Southern strategy (see Figure 30.1).

Figure 30.1 The number of regional economic cooperative arrangements 1945–2000

REGIONS	1945–49	1950–59	1960–69	1970–79	1980–89	1990–99
Western Europe	2	5	3	2	1	3
Eastern Europe	1				1	11
Elsewhere	1	5	18	20	17	26

In the 1950s the number of regional economic forms of international cooperation set up outside Europe was five, in the 1960s 18 and in the 1970s 20. The number of multilateral monetary institutions, including regional development banks, was three in the 1950s, eight in the 1960s and six in the 1970s (Reinalda 2007). The most important regional economic cooperative arrangements in the 1950s, 1960s and 1970s outside Europe are mentioned in Figure 30.2. Those printed in bold are discussed in this chapter.

30.2 Regional economic organizations in Latin and Central America

Latin American pursuit of mutual free trade: LAFTA (1960)

In February 1960 ten Latin American states adopted the *Treaty of Montevideo*, thereby establishing the *Latin American Free Trade Association* (LAFTA; *Asociación latinoamericana de libre cambio*, ALALC). They sought to promote trade among themselves by removing trade barriers and thereby encourage the rate of economic and social development of their states. The envisaged free trade area, to be reached in 1980, would be the foundation for a Latin American common market. Although Raul Prebisch sympathized with this idea, which originated from the UN Economic Commission for Latin America, he also believed that LAFTA's set-up disregarded the differences in development and size between the member states. He therefore expected that it would be difficult for LAFTA to achieve success and was later proven right. Cooperation between the states did strengthen their industrialization process, but free trade and the other objectives were effectively not realized. The Treaty of Montevideo included too many escape clauses, which allowed renegotiations in situations where tariff cuts had caused major domestic problems. Because the Treaty did not include a provision for establishing

Figure 30.2 Regional economic cooperative arrangements in four regions 1950–80

Africa:

1959: Union douanière des états de l'Afrique occidentale UDAO (7)
1960: Brazzaville Group; from 1965: Organisation commune africaine et mauricienne OCAM (14)
1964: Union monétaire ouest africaine UMOA (8)
1964: Union douanière et économique de l'Afrique centrale UDEAC (6)
1967: **East African Community EAC** (3)
1974: Communauté économique de l'Afrique de l'ouest CEAO (7)
1975: **Economic Community of West African States ECOWAS** (16)
1980: Southern African Development Coordination Conference SADDC (10)

Asia and the Pacific:

1950: Colombo Plan for Cooperative Economic and Social Development in Asia and the Pacific (26)
1967: **Association of Southeast Asian Nations ASEAN** (10)
1971: South Pacific Forum SPF (16)

Latin and Central America

1960: **Latin American Free Trade Association LAFTA** (10)
1960: **Central American Common Market CACM** (5)
1968: Caribbean Free Trade Association CARIFTA (12)
1968: East Caribbean Common Market ECCM (7)
1969: **Andean Group/Pact** (6)
1973: Caribbean Community and Common Market CARICOM (14)
1975: Latin American Economic System SELA (27)
1980: **Latin American Integration Association LAIA** (12)

The Middle East and West Asia:

1957: **Council of Arab Economic Unity CAEU** (10)
1964: **Arab Common Market ACM** (6)
1964: Regional Cooperation for Development RCD (3)

Only the most important arrangements are included; in brackets: the largest membership achieved.

across-the-board cuts in tariffs, as in the EEC and the European Free Trade Association, the members of LAFTA needed to periodically negotiate, which, however, often resulted in discussing previous agreements again and thus in a lack of progress. Another difference compared with the EEC was that with LAFTA the stimulating negotiation process between the ministers (Council) and the common institution (Commission) was absent. In Western European integration the Commission's roots lay in France's foreign policy, which had resulted in a High Authority for the European Coal and Steel Community meant to overcome deadlocks in international and national negotiations. Both in the ECSC and the EEC this *vis-à-vis* the member states fairly autonomous common institution had resulted in creating a dynamic of its own (see §26.3), which in LAFTA was missing.

From LAFTA to LAIA (1980)

In 1980 another *Treaty of Montevideo* replaced the Latin American Free Trade Association with the less ambitious and more flexible *Latin American Integration Association* (LAIA; *Asociación latinoamericana de integración*, ALADI) which, more than LAFTA, relied on restricted preferential and 'partial scope' agreements. It also took into consideration the differences between the member states by establishing three categories: most developed, intermediate and least-developed. Various LAFTA institutions in the fields of credits and payments were retained, adapted and extended. Like LAFTA LAIA had difficulties in carrying out the reduction in tariffs and other trade barriers. Among the partial scope agreements of LAIA was the establishment of the Southern Common Market MERCOSUR in 1991 by four member states, which in fact meant a weakening of LAIA. This was also true for Mexico's accession to the North American Free Trade Agreement a few years later. Despite these weaknesses LAIA continues to exist, with some 100 agreements concluded by the end of the twentieth century. In 1999 Cuba became a member.

The Central American Common Market (1960)

In December 1960 El Salvador, Guatemala, Honduras and Nicaragua adopted a treaty in Managua, Nicaragua, to create the *Central American Common Market* (CACM; *Mercado común centroamericano*, MCCA). It came into force in June 1961, while Costa Rica joined in 1962. It envisaged the liberalization of intra-regional trade and the establishment of a customs union and, within six years, a common market. The last was established in 1969. The reduction and abolition of tariffs contributed to an increase in mutual trade during the 1960s and 1970s. There was also progress on the supply of electricity and on road construction. The success of this Common Market was remarkable, given the long-time laborious and varying cooperation between these states (see §7.4). In 1960 they founded the *Central American Bank for Economic Integration* (CABEI), in 1964 the *Central American Monetary Council*, in which the central bank governors coordinated their policies, and in 1968 the *Central American Fund for Monetary Stabilization* to give financial support to the balance of payments of the states. An older, more far-reaching 1958 agreement on integration of industries did not come into effect. It had been aimed at enhancing specific industries in each state and thus a division of labour between the states, based on the assumption that a larger market with stronger industries would attract larger investments. This specialization, however, came up against much national rivalry, a lack of support from the US which did not want to support this plan and also structural imbalances between the five states trying to implement it.

Growth and stagnation areas

The main problem of the Central American Common Market was the uneven distribution of gains and losses between its member states. While Guatemala and El Salvador profited most, Honduras and Nicaragua were far worse off, with Costa Rica in an intermediate position. These differences became evident in the emergence of growth and stagnation areas, not only in this common market, but also in other forms of regional cooperation in Latin America and elsewhere in the Third World. In addition to the fact that richer states became richer and poorer states poorer, political difficulties arose, which in turn made it even more difficult to reach agreement on further economic cooperation. These results meant that regional economic cooperation could be successful only if distribution mechanisms in the form of regional funds were devised and applied, so as to stimulate the disadvantaged ('stagnation') areas into growth. In the 1980s the Central American Common Market would weaken due to the lack of such correcting mechanisms. This decline began in 1980, when Costa Rica and Nicaragua imposed restrictive trade measures. The situation worsened as a result of internal military tensions and guerrilla warfare during the 1980s. An armed conflict between El Salvador and Honduras in 1969 had at one point stopped the market functioning, but that dispute had been settled. It was not until the end of the 1980s that mutual trade began to grow again, after a new agreement on tariffs was reached in 1986. In 1993 the five states plus Panama decided to bring the Common Market to life again, supported by a cooperation agreement with the European Union. The Central American Common Market illustrates another aspect of regional cooperation: if political cooperation becomes more difficult, or even comes to a standstill, the common institutions continue to function, albeit in a weaker and more vulnerable way. Dissolution obviously does not happen that quickly.

The Andean Group (1969): promising

The most promising regional project in Latin America seemed to be the *Andean Group* (or *Pact*). In May 1969 five states in the Andes (Bolivia, Chile, Colombia, Ecuador and Peru) signed the *Cartagena Agreement*. Venezuela joined the Group in 1974, but Chile withdrew in 1976. Concerned about the slow pace of integration within LAFTA, they wanted to profit from the experiences of LAFTA, CACM and EEC and learn how to improve their bargaining power as a more cohesive group. In addition to a decision-making body of governmental representatives (normally the ministers of trade), the *Commission*, they set up a *Council*, called the *Junta*, which like the Commission in the EEC and EU was to promote the interests of the integration process, had the right of initiative and took care of the permanent Secretariat. Decisions were taken by both the Commission and the Council: the latter prepared the proposals and negotiated them with the Commission. Consultation was part of this process, through a *Consultative Committee* of experts and a *Consultative Economic and Social Committee*. Hence in this case European experience played a role, unlike in the Central American Common Market, although compared with the EEC, the terms Commission and Council were used the other way round. The Andean Group did not only discuss trade, but also adopted agreements in the fields of education, health and industrial relations. The Group established a number of institutions, among them the *Andean Development Bank*, with a completely Latin American governance structure, and, also following the European example, a *Court of Justice* (1979) and a Parliament. The *Andean Parliament* (*Parlamento andino*, also: Parlandino) began to function in 1984 and had five representatives from each member state. It voted by absolute majority, but had only a marginal position in the Group's decision-making process. The main objectives of this regional economic cooperation project were trade liberalization, a common external tariff and, based on the Central American experience, preferential treatment for the least-developed states. The Group adopted a programme for industrial development and one for sectoral industrial development. The latter was regarded as innovative, as it would allocate resources to specific industrial activities and thus promote economic growth in those industries. In 1970 an *Andean Investment Code* was agreed as part of this policy. Although it was not intended to exclude foreign investors, the US and other states interpreted it as such and agitated against it. The Andean Group had drafted it to provide the Group with a more equal position in negotiations with foreign transnational corporations. Within LAFTA the Andean Group clashed several times with more conservative LAFTA members.

Decline during the 1970s

During the first three years of its existence the Andean Group was a promising project, given both internationally and nationally favourable conditions. But during two crises, in 1974–77 and 1981–85, many well-thought-through policy instruments were 'changed, severely curtailed or completely abandoned', among them the investment code, leaving the Group 'but only a pale imitation of the original project' (Gordon Mace in Axline 1994, 45). Among the causes of this decline were the protectionist measures of US President Richard Nixon in 1971, which kept Latin American products out of the US market and made them more expensive on the world market. Other impediments were the 1973 oil crisis, the coup in Chile in the same year which caused Chile's withdrawal from the Andean Group, and the joining of Venezuela. In 1969 domestic political relations had prevented Venezuela from joining. Its admittance in 1973, however, led to a renegotiation of the Cartagena Agreement and resulted in a far weaker version of this constitution of the Andean Group. The second oil crisis of 1979 and the global recession of 1980–82 further undermined the Group. This collective instrument for economic growth (and political tool in the North–South divide) was promising and innovative in the early 1970s, but by the early 1980s it was too weak to adequately adapt to the changes that were taking place in the world economy. Although various policy instruments which permitted the Group to make progress were lost, the Andean Group was not dissolved.

30.3 The emergence of ASEAN (1967)

The Asian way of cooperation

Cooperation between the states in Southeast Asia in the *Association of Southeast Asian Nations* (ASEAN) had its roots in their strained relations in the 1960s. In July 1961 Malaya, the Philippines and Thailand established the *Association of Southeast Asia*, but other states in the region regarded this association as too Western-oriented. Conflicts in the region, such as the formation of Malaysia, the military coup in Indonesia in 1965 and the secession of Singapore from Malaysia, added to the tensions, but also to discussions about more friendly intra-regional relations. Thailand played a role in forging unity among the states, as it worried about the impact of the Vietnam War on the neighbouring states. Its efforts resulted in the issuing of the *ASEAN* or *Bangkok Declaration* in August 1967 in Bangkok, Thailand, by the foreign ministers of Indonesia, Malaysia, the Philippines, Singapore and Thailand. These five states established ASEAN, with the aim of common action to promote regional cooperation in a spirit of equality and partnership and thereby contribute towards peace, progress and prosperity in the region. The Declaration is not a traditional treaty which binds the parties, but rather an impetus for voluntary cooperation, describing in a general way the aims and purposes of the association, with a fairly light organizational structure in which the states ('nations') had to learn how to cooperate and find solutions for Asian issues. Given the intensification of conflicts and the threat of communism in the region, the ASEAN states began to discuss their foreign policies from a regional rather than a nationalist perspective. In accordance with the Bangkok Declaration, and in contrast to many international organizations, the structure of ASEAN remained restricted to an Annual Meeting of foreign ministers, a Standing Committee under the chairmanship of the host state, *ad hoc* and permanent committees on specific subjects and a National Secretariat in each foreign ministry to coordinate ASEAN-related affairs and to liaise with the Standing Committee.

Inspiring mutual confidence

ASEAN member states used the first ten years to explore the possibilities of the Association and to learn to feel at ease with each other. Although the Bangkok Declaration emphasized non-political cooperation, the members in 1971 signed the *Declaration on the Zone of Peace, Freedom and Neutrality* (ZOPFAN), in which they expressed their wish to keep the region free of any form or manner of interference by outside powers. They also stated that the states in the region should make concerted efforts to broaden the areas of cooperation. It was not until February 1976, when the Vietnam War was over and the three states in Indochina had come under communist rule, that ASEAN began to define further ways of cooperation. The first summit of heads of government was held, resulting in the *Treaty of Amity and Cooperation in Southeast Asia*, with principles for their relations, rules for cooperation and a peaceful settlement of disputes, and the *Declaration of ASEAN Concord*, which contained a programme of action as a framework for ASEAN cooperation. Given the greater need for coordination the *ASEAN Secretariat* was set up in Jakarta, Indonesia, which however still was a body without any room for manoeuvre of its own as it was given a non-functional role. The position of secretary-general rotated among the members. Although an increase in transactions among ASEAN members took place, no movement towards regional community formation or in the direction of a security community could be observed at the time (Monte Hill 1978, 575). However, the cautious cooperation created a climate of trust among the governments, which watchfully approached problems that were prepared by civil servants in committees with the purpose of reaching consensus. This meant that it took a long time for discussions to result in agreements. Nonetheless, the member states gradually grew towards common foreign positions. They showed this during the second half of the 1970s, when refugees and 'boat people' from the states in Indochina were looking for help. The common position of the ASEAN members meant that these refugees found only temporary shelter in the ASEAN states and were then resettled elsewhere, in states such as Australia, France and the US. The ASEAN member states also prevented the Cambodian regime installed by Vietnam after its intervention to expel Pol Pot taking over the Cambodian seat at the UN (see §34.1).

ASEAN and economic cooperation

Originally economic cooperation within ASEAN seemed relevant only because of the threat of communism. The UN proposed that ASEAN should coordinate industrial activities as a way towards regional cooperation and development. In 1970 a UN-sponsored foreign team was set up to evaluate the options available. Two years later it identified trade and industry as priority areas and in particular proposed selective trade liberalization, industrial complementarity agreements and a package deal of industrial products. 'The report suggested thirteen chemical and engineering projects that could be initiated on a regional basis with the participation of all member states, enabling them to enjoy the benefits of large-scale operations through regional trade. Each member would then select one from among the list based on its natural advantages' (Thambipillai 1994, 112). As with security, ASEAN took its time in establishing economic cooperation. Whereas Singapore was in favour of free trade, Indonesia was strongly opposed. The main problem for the larger states was that their products were fairly similar. The summit of heads of governments of 1976 agreed that the package deal could be an area for cooperation and gave the economics ministers the responsibility of studying the scheme. The five member states then each selected an industrial project. 'What in fact appeared more important was for each country to "select" an industrial project in line with its national programme than to act in accordance with the rational[e] expressed in the UN report. In fact by 1976 the original report was a mere reference point from which to embark on a "national project" though it was referred to as AIP [ASEAN Industrial Project]' (Thambipillai 1994, 113). In 1977 ASEAN adopted the *Agreement on Preferential Trading Arrangements*, with preferential access to selected items from member states, which can be seen as a minimal form of free trade. In 1980 ASEAN and the European Community signed a Cooperation Agreement to encourage increased trade between the two organizations. ASEAN itself continued its industrial cooperation, but only one project from its 1980 basic agreement on 'industrial projects' was realized, an Indonesian-Malaysian fertilizer project. In 1981 a basic agreement on industrial complementarity was signed and in 1983 one on industrial joint ventures by ASEAN member states. 'The initial eagerness slowly evaporated, but not without a lingering uncertainty that took about fifteen years finally to eclipse the AIP as an ASEAN showpiece.' It showed that ASEAN member states were 'not exceptions to the rule that national interests determine all forms of external interactions' (Thambipillai 1994, 114). But it also showed that slowly and gradually economic cooperation was moving forward.

30.4 Regional organizations in Africa and the Arab world

Regional cooperation in Africa

Regional cooperation in Africa was based on traditional political and social unities older than many newly-independent African states themselves and on local colonial traditions. The Portuguese colonizers had not allowed any cooperation between their colonies, whereas France in its colonies had maintained its centralized policies but with mutual agreements on investments in, and trade between, those colonies. The strongest common economic tie was the link between their currencies and the French franc in the *Franc zône*. Unlike the French, British policies emphasized the separate development of its colonies, but with a considerable degree of coordination through the Commonwealth (see Figure 18.5). In certain regions it also mattered whether a large and relatively strong state existed, such as Nigeria in West Africa (Schulz *et al.* 2001, 63). Regional cooperation was in the 1960s part of the pursuit of independence and the construction of new states, but it remained limited. In 1960 a monetary union of seven francophone states in West Africa was established, followed by a customs union in Central Africa and the so-called Brazzaville Group as an early sign of regional cooperation in East Africa.

The East African Community (1967–77)

The most promising regional project in East Africa was the *East African Community* (EAC) of 1967 between Kenya, Uganda and Tanzania. Not completely in line with British tradition these three states had enjoyed a long history of close regional economic cooperation based in common cultural roots. In 1917 a customs union between Kenya and Uganda had been established, which (then) Tanganyika joined in 1927. Between 1948 and 1961 the *East African High Commission* and between 1961 and 1967 the *East African Common Services Organization* promoted closer economic cooperation, followed in 1967 by the establishment of the EAC. The latter included the *East African Authority*, the *East African Legislative Assembly*, the *Secretariat* to further common interests and the joint *East African Development Bank*. For some time the EAC served as the ideal African model for regional economic cooperation and as a successful customs union. Although its beginning was promising and indeed showed an increase in mutual trade, local self-interest soon began to dominate national policies. The public corporations set up by the EAC had to provide a balance between the three states. Commitments to help the poorer states in order to achieve a more equal level of development, as written into the basic statutes of the Community, resulted in 'losses' for Kenya in the short term, but also in it having pre-ferential access to markets in Tanzania and Uganda. However, its agreement to postpone some of its own development in exchange for economies of scale was combined with 'temptations to secure expatriate investments outside the framework of balanced Community growth, and it has stretched upward its formal allocations of Community investments'. This profiting from its growth capacities harmed mutual trust (Dresang and Sharkansky 1973, 307). Ideological and political factors also began to play a role, as Kenya had a stronger capitalist focus than Tanzania, which began to move in a 'socialist' direction. The rise of dictator Idi Amin in Uganda caused economic discord and the paralysis of the EAC, followed by its dissolution in 1977. But after Amin's removal in 1979 the borders between the formerly united Community members still remained closed.

The inception of ECOWAS (1975)

The *Economic Community of West African States* (ECOWAS) of 1975 developed into an economic cooperation arrangement and later into the regional peacekeeper in West Africa. It covers an area of 6.1 million square kilometres with three landlocked states, 11 (originally 12) coastline states and one island state. Among its many mineral resources is Nigerian oil. Although large tracts of land remained uncultivated, agricultural products such as cocoa beans from Ghana were the principal exports. Despite this natural richness the region had remained poor and economically underdeveloped. The inspiration for the creation of ECOWAS came from the UN Economic Commission for Africa. In the mid-1960s it had divided Africa into regions for the purpose of economic development in each region. In 1966 and 1967 the Economic Commission for Africa called two meetings for West Africa, in Niger and Ghana. The Ghana meeting led to the signing of an Article of Agreement on a proposed economic community and the creation of an Interim Council of Ministers. This Interim Council met in 1967 in Senegal and prepared the ground for a summit of heads of state in Liberia in 1968 which resulted in the establishment of the West African Regional Grouping, but only nine of the 14 states attended the meeting and signed the protocol for a common market. A follow-up con-ference failed. Combined efforts by Nigeria and Togo, however, resulted in renewed progress, with a commission of experts making recommendations for broad areas of coop-eration between the two states. They then called a summit conference of West African leaders to discuss the proposals from a regional perspective. The Nigerian-Togo commis-sion of experts produced a draft treaty for the creation of ECOWAS, which was discussed in depth at a number of ministerial meetings. This led to the signing of the treaty establishing ECOWAS in Lagos, Nigeria, in May 1975 (Emeka Okolo 1985, 125–28).

A weak but firm organization

In November 1976 five Protocols to the Treaty of Lagos were signed in Lomé, Togo, which were meant to promote trade, cooperation and self-reliance in the region. Despite these diplomatic successes ECOWAS was not an immediate economic success. This can be partly attributed to the creation of the francophone *Communauté économique de l'Afri-que de l'ouest* (CEAO) in 1974, which was continued as the West African Economic and Monetary Union in 1994. The reluctance of the francophone states to participate in ECOWAS was based on their fear of economic and political sanctions, as they had remained dependent on France for both money transfers and internal security. Other negative factors preventing ECOWAS from becoming an economic success were the lack of governmental willingness to fully implement agreements and to transfer amounts of money as agreed, a lack of adequate relationships between the ECOWAS Secretariat and governments and a fairly strong nationalism. That ECOWAS nevertheless managed to continue to exist, although it was weak, was the result of its strong organizational set-up. The meticulously worded ECOWAS Treaty guaranteed that economically-important processes such as trade liberalization, free traffic, communication and common plans were set in motion, with the objective of this resulting in a customs union, a common market or even an economic union. The main body of ECOWAS was the *Authority of Heads of State and Government*, with below it the *Council of Ministers* which met twice a year, always with two ministers representing each state. The Council was responsible for the running and monitoring of the Community. This set-up guaranteed the continuation of high-level political support. Although regional policy making was the monopoly of the Authority, it had 'to share this responsibility with the experts and regional bureaucrats of the secretariat, whose proposals, reports, and recommendations on technical issues constitute significant inputs into decision making'. The ECOWAS Treaty had institutionalized a Secretariat of 'more or less supranational officials to strike a balance on technical issues in the politics of national interest and disruptive bargaining that can impede integration'. The Secretariat in practice enjoyed 'significant latitude in fund raising for community programs, execution of projects, and expending budgeted funds; it also awards contracts and supervises work in progress' (Emeka Okolo 1985, 152). Furthermore there were Specialized Technical Commissions and the *Fund for Cooperation, Compensation and Development*, created to offset differences in development. Its compensatory scheme prevented rich member states from becoming richer and poor ones from becoming poorer. 'At the initial stages of integration the more developed member-states may appear to bear a heavier burden than the less developed, but in the long run they are likely to gain more from trade liberalization when the community becomes fully operational.' The leaders of the ECOWAS member states had not lost sight of this fact (Emeka Okolo 1985, 140).

The position of Nigeria

Nigeria gave ECOWAS a strong state whose economic and military power mattered in the region. After its independence in 1960 Nigeria was confronted with strong ethnic tensions. Biafra's secession between 1967 and 1970 and the ensuing civil war resulted in more than two million deaths from fighting and hunger, despite peace initiatives and efforts from international relief organizations. Out of this Biafra crisis arose a new organization, *Médecins Sans Frontières*, which criticized the Nigerian army for its killing of civilians and its blockades which caused the starvation and death of many children. It decided that a new kind of relief organization was needed to prioritize the interests of victims over those of politicians. Due to its income from oil the Nigerian economy soon recovered and the state acquired a leading role in the Organization of African Unity. Within ECOWAS Nigeria as the regional hegemon served as the 'puller' state and as the liaison with the developed states. 'For Nigeria, having declared Africa the centerpiece of its foreign policy, ECOWAS is an excellent vehicle for demonstrating to African states the seriousness of its proclamations and thereby establishing credibility as a Black African leader. In addition, ECOWAS will afford Nigeria the opportunity it has sought to displace France as the power to be reckoned with in francophone West Africa' (Emeka Okolo 1985, 148). However, during the mid-1980s it became doubtful whether the mutual loyalty of ECOWAS states was strong enough. 'The differing political-economic orientations and ideologies of various governments plus the changes in political leadership that have occurred since the treaty was inaugurated raise questions as to whether high-level political support can survive. Furthermore, although the desire to reduce external dependence provided the impetus to move toward integration, there has been no significant change in the low level of trade that characterized West African intraregional interaction in the past' (Emeka Okolo 1985, 151).

Limited cooperation in the Arab world

Little was expected of economic cooperation in the Arab world. The regional organization established in 1945, the *League of Arab States*, did express views on 'Arab unity', but in fact was a combination of a group of states focused on their own independence and sovereignty and with strong mutual suspicions. Other Arab states were afraid that Egypt and Syria would become too powerful, but their coexistence as the United Arab Republic from 1958 collapsed after three years, mainly because Egypt treated Syria as one of its provinces. When Egypt signed a peace treaty with Israel in 1979 it was expelled from the Arab League (for ten years). Within the League 'Arab cold wars' were fought between conservative and somewhat less conservative governments, with their dislike of Israel's existence as the strongest common tie. None of the governments was democratically-elected. Cooperation in the less sensitive areas of education and culture prevailed over economic cooperation (Charles Tripp in Fawcett and Hurrell 2000, 288). In 1958 the Economic Council of the Arab League decided to establish the *Council of Arab Economic Unity*, but it was not until 1964 that this Council actually met. It proclaimed an *Arab Common Market* aimed at eliminating customs duties and other taxes on trade between the member states in annual stages, with the adoption of a full customs union as a further stage. Implementation, however, fell short of expectations. Only a limited group of states participated and there was little willingness to make concessions. Some Arab joint ventures were established in the fields of medical appliances, industrial investments, livestock development and mining and a few specialized federations were set up in industries such as shipping, textiles and tourism. But common efforts to establish cooperative arrangements leading to a common market did not happen in the Arab world.

The Third World struggle for a New International Economic Order (1974)

31.1 The UN Declaration on the New International Economic Order (1974)

1969: social progress and development

Due to political pressure from UNCTAD and the G77, by the end of the 1960s the needs and demands of developing states were heard within the UN, where development aid had turned into a Cold War weapon. The wish to make UN policies more coherent was the reason for the General Assembly of December 1969 adopting the *Declaration on Social Progress and Development*. This was intended to constitute the common basis for national and international policies through its aims of continuously raising the material and spiritual living standards of all members of society, with respect for, and in compliance with, human rights and fundamental freedoms. The real problem however was that the UN Development Decade was not achieving its purpose, as had already become clear halfway through the Decade. Therefore debates had started on new policies and an extension of the Decade.

1970: international development strategy: 1% of GNP and 0.7% in ODA

After lengthy negotiations over the text the UN General Assembly of 24 October 1970 adopted the *International Development Strategy for the Second Development Decade* (1971–80). For most developing states the outcome was disappointing. Preparatory commissions had presented five extensive reports. One of them, drafted under the direction of the economist Jan Tinbergen, contained precise and statistically-underpinned goals and recommendations for improving development. But as the industrialized states raised numerous objections to this text, the preparatory commission had to go through the proposals again. This led to weakened goals, which the developing states regarded as a setback because they already had had to make concessions so often during the previous five years.

Furthermore, the debate in the General Assembly was delayed as a result of disagreement between the US and the Soviet Union on whether both West and East Germany were allowed to participate. This had nothing to do with the actual debate, but it did not improve the atmosphere. Eventually the General Assembly broadly accepted the revised proposals, although very few of the original concrete recommendations were left. Where recommendations based on figures had been mentioned, only the least ambitious ones were adopted. As with the 1969 Declaration on Social Progress and Development, this new strategy provided a common policy. Member states were reminded of their commitment to make arrangements that would help achieve the objectives of the Development Decade. The average annual growth rate of gross national product (GNP) in developing states as a whole should be at least six per cent, with the possibility of accelerating this during the second half of the Decade. Each economically-advanced state should endeavour to provide developing states annually with a financial resources transfer of a minimum net amount of one per cent of its own GNP by 1972. A major part of these financial resource transfers should be in the form of Official Development Assistance (ODA), with a minimum of 0.7 per cent. 'Each economically advanced country will progressively increase its official development assistance to the developing countries and will exert its best efforts to reach a minimum net amount of 0.7 per cent of its gross national product at market prices by the middle of the Decade' (Resolution 2626(XXV) 43).

The 1973 oil crisis and the role of OPEC

Unexpected support for the developing states came from those responsible for the oil crisis of 1973–74. When the price for crude oil had begun to decline by the end of the 1950s Iraq, Iran, Kuwait, Saudi Arabia and Venezuela had established the *Organization of Petroleum Exporting Countries* (OPEC) in 1960. This cartel aimed to unify and coordinate the members' petroleum policies in order to set the price for oil (see Figure 31.1). In 1968 OPEC issued a declaration that it wanted more control over pricing policy and wanted to change existing participation agreements. In the same year Arab oil-exporting states formed an overlapping organization (OAPEC) which soon radicalized politically in line with political changes taking place in Libya, Algeria and Iraq. Against the background of an at that time unstable American dollar, with devaluations in 1971 and 1973, and the Arab-Israeli War of October 1973, OPEC succeeded in raising oil prices and in changing the existing situation, as thereafter price increases were no longer the result of bilateral negotiations but rather of unilateral OPEC decisions. Simultaneously the Arab members of OPEC organized a boycott of those advanced industrialized states that were sympathetic towards the Israeli position. Four OPEC increases in oil prices at the end of 1973 and in January 1974 resulted in an 'oil shock' (raising prices to over 11 dollars a barrel) and a serious economic crisis during the second part of the 1970s because OPEC, which increased its membership, succeeded in keeping oil prices high. The new oil-pricing regime was in fact accepted by both the oil companies and the economically-advanced states. Within the Organization for Economic Cooperation and Development the US initiated the creation of a countervailing consumer group by establishing in 1974 the *International Energy Agency* (IEA) in order to foster cooperation on energy questions among participating states. The IEA did not restrict itself to oil problems and also developed policies for reducing dependency on oil, but within the IEA Japan and Western Europe, which were more dependent on oil imports than the US, favoured a confrontational approach towards OPEC for many years. In 1974 the UN discussed the oil crisis in the context of the North–South divide, with the developing states expecting that the rising oil prices and the political action by the Arab states would increase the pressure of the South on Northern states to make concessions.

Figure 31.1 The OPEC cartel of oil-exporting countries (1960)

In 1984 the **Organization of Petroleum Exporting Countries** (OPEC) had 13 member states: Algeria, Ecuador, Gabon, Indonesia, Iraq, Iran, Kuwait, Libya, Nigeria, Qatar, Saudi Arabia, the United Arab Emirates and Venezuela, with Brunei as a candidate member. Ecuador and Gabon left in 1992 and 1994, respectively. Talks with Angola, Egypt, Oman, Russia and Yemen remained without results. OPEC has a Conference as its supreme authority, a Board of Governors, a Ministerial Monitoring Committee, established in 1988, and a Secretariat. From 1960 to 1965 OPEC's headquarters were in Geneva, but in 1965 they moved to Vienna. OPEC's objective as a cartel is the coordination and unification of petroleum policies, but this goal was 'softened' by the addition that this is done to secure fair and stable prices for petroleum producers, an efficient, economic and regular supply of petroleum to consuming states and a fair return on capital for those investing in the industry. Due to its cartel character OPEC is less transparent in its policy and decision making than most IGOs. During the 1970s OPEC managed to maintain internal unity. It thus controlled the world market and kept oil prices high. During the 1980s OPEC weakened as a result of the discovery of major new oil fields, the IEA policies to reduce dependency on oil and conflicts among OPEC members.

The states that suffered most from OPEC's price increases were the oil-importing Third World states, which were less able to adjust to the new situation than the industrialized states. In 1975 OPEC agreed to support the UN strategy for a New International Economic Order and in 1976 it created the **OPEC Fund for International Development** as a multilateral agency for financial cooperation and assistance. It reinforced financial cooperation between OPEC member states and a number of developing states through the provision of financial support to the latter to assist them in their economic and social development.

Between 1968 and 1979 the **Organization of Arab Petroleum Exporting Countries** (OAPEC) existed. It was established in Kuwait and had as its members Algeria, Bahrain, Iraq, Kuwait, Libya, Qatar, Saudi Arabia, Syria, Tunisia and the United Arab Emirates. It was responsible for Arab oil policies within OPEC.

1974: the New International Economic Order (NIEO)

In May 1974 secretary-general Kurt Waldheim called a Special Session of the UN General Assembly to discuss raw materials and development, after a request from Algeria. The issue of raw materials and development had been on the UNCTAD agenda and was prepared by a conference of the Non-Aligned Movement in Algiers in 1973, where it was determined that the goals of the UN Development Decade had not been reached. The 1974 situation in the Third World seemed, in comparison to 1970, more favourable, given the general price pressure applied by OPEC and the oil embargo imposed on some Northern states. After discussing the question of raw materials and development the

Special Session adopted a *Declaration* and an extensive, more detailed, *Action Programme for the Establishment of a New International Economic Order* (NIEO). The change-oriented Declaration urged the states to work for the establishment of a new international economic order, based on 'equity, sovereign equality, interdependence, common interest and co-operation among all States, irrespective of their economic and social systems which shall correct inequalities and redress existing injustices, make it possible to eliminate the widening gap between the developed and the developing countries and ensure steadily accelerating economic and social development and peace and justice for present and future generations'. The Action Programme reiterated ideas about revising and restructuring North–South relations in line with what had been discussed in UNCTAD. The reforms covered the entire sphere of production, consumption and trade, including reforms in terms of trade, access to the markets of Northern states, reforms in the main economic specialized agencies such as the IMF and IBRD, the problem of burgeoning Third World debt, greater economic assistance, technology transfer and the recognition of rights pertaining to economic sovereignty, including the right of nationalization and the control of transnational corporations. In essence the NIEO represented a detailed view of how to make the position of the Third World less dependent on the industrialized North.

1974: the Charter of Economic Rights and Duties of States

In line with the action programme the session of the December 1974 General Assembly adopted the *Charter of Economic Rights and Duties of States*, which describes the fundamentals of international economic relations and specifies the economic rights and duties of states in 30 articles. The intention of this Charter was to support the NIEO. Each state has the free exercise of its full permanent sovereignty, including possession, use and disposal of all its wealth, natural resources and economic activities, the right to regulate and exercise authority over foreign investment, the right to regulate and supervise the activities of transnational corporations and the right to nationalize, expropriate or transfer ownership of foreign property. In the case of nationalization compensation should be paid and, if a controversy occurs, this should be settled under the domestic law of the nationalizing state, unless it is freely and mutually agreed that other peaceful means should be sought. The Charter recognized the right of states to associate in organizations of primary commodity producers in order to develop their national economies. Furthermore, all states have the right and duty to eliminate colonialism, apartheid, racial discrimination, neo-colonialism and all forms of foreign aggression, occupation and domination as a prerequisite for development.

The NIEO as an expression of power relations and ideological forces

The adoption of the NIEO Declaration was the result of earlier debates on the fact that favourable economic results had failed to materialize for the Third World. The far-reaching character of the adopted texts can be explained by joint political pressure from the Non-Aligned Movement and OPEC, at a time when US international leadership was weak because of international economic and political problems such as the dollar and the Vietnam War. Within the UN General Assembly the joint action and numerical influence of the Third World states mattered. The Declaration and Action Programme were adopted by the Special Session without a vote, but with 39 states voicing reservations and observations. The Charter was passed by 120 votes in favour to six against, among the latter the UK and the US, and ten abstentions. Robert Cox regards the NIEO as the result of negotiations under specific conditions and power relations, but also as a reflection of the fundamental structure of global economic relations. The new term 'NIEO' found a place in the economic discourse next to terms such as liberalism, free trade and development. NIEO became an ideological force that added to expectations and the understanding of what was happening in the world between strong and weak states as well as other actors, such as transnational corporations (Cox 1979).

Lasting dependency

The implementation of the NIEO Action Programme remained far behind the high expectations of the 1970s. Although the adoption of the Declaration and Action Programme within the North–South divide in 1974 was a victory for the developing states, most envisaged structural changes failed to materialize. On the contrary, the Third World was confronted with larger debts, resulting from the rise in energy prices and thus higher prices for other imports, development assistance that fell short of expectations, more protectionism by industrialized states and stronger rather than weaker dependency. Samir Amin described the NIEO as an attempt by the Third World to increase the price of raw materials, obtain more imported technology and thus finance a new stage of development, but also saw this as 'just placing the Third World more in the grip of the neo-colonialist system', as there was no real Third World counterbalance of power (Archer 1992, 121). In as far as developing states were cooperating in economic regional international organizations they had no joint alternative strategy. Instead they supported the NIEO, which might bring them some benefits such as higher prices for their raw materials or some technology, but which did not remove their dependency on stronger states that continued to set the rules.

31.2 The basic needs strategy of the IBRD and ILO as an alternative

The Periphery loses

The industrialized states initiated their counteroffensive as early as 1975. The next round of the Special Session of the UN General Assembly about development and international economic cooperation in September 1975 specified the measures for implementing the NIEO, with the industrialized states neutralizing the issues crucial to them, such as nationalization and the link between raw materials and industrial prices. While developing states pressed for commodity indexation schemes, the industrialized states expressed their reservations and proposed case-by-case negotiations or national preferential trade policies. While a few states affirmed the need to fulfil their 1970 commitment to transfer one per cent of their GNP in financial resources, of which 0.7 per cent of GNP was to be official development assistance, others questioned the usefulness of the targets, expressed concerns about the workability of such transfer arrangements and would not fulfil the commitment.

The North–South Dialogue 1975–77

The industrialized states had begun to coordinate their positions *vis-à-vis* the Third World in the OECD *Development Assistance Committee* (DAC) (see §26.4). The effects of this became noticeable in the *North–South Dialogue*, which started in Paris on the initiative of the French President Valéry Giscard d'Estaing in December 1975 as the *Conference on International Economic Cooperation* (CIEC) and lasted until June 1977. Here the industrialized states and those developing states invited discussed the Third World problems and possible ways of alleviating them further. While the developing states wanted promises about development aid and commodity indexation schemes for raw materials, the industrialized states were mainly interested in agreements about the regular delivery and the pricing of oil. OECD coordination resulted in concerted actions by the industrialized states, whereas the developing states were divided among themselves. While Iran and Saudi Arabia were inclined to have regular consultations between oil-exporting and oil-importing states, the more radical oil-exporters led by Algeria were strongly opposed. While the Africans favoured more development assistance and higher prices for raw materials, the Latin American and Asian states preferred better trade facilities. The North–South Dialogue eventually failed as a result of this discord among the states of the South and the unwillingness of the North to make real concessions. The establishment of a Common Fund for Commodities was endorsed but not implemented. The industrialized states had already opposed the proposed changes in the international division of labour at a UNIDO conference in Lima, Peru, in 1975 and they repeated this in Paris. The only agreement on the price of raw materials that came into being was achieved by the European Economic Community and 46 developing states in 1975 in Lomé, Togo. The *Lomé Convention*, which would be renewed a number of times, covered a wide range of trade and economic cooperation issues and included an export earnings stabilization scheme to provide the African, Caribbean and Pacific parties to the agreement with protection against price and production fluctuations of certain goods.

Anything but effects

In 1977 the UN decided to evaluate the progress of the development issue at another Special Session of the General Assembly on economic problems, which in 1979 concluded that insufficient progress had been made. The UN therefore decided in 1980 to start a round of ongoing negotiations on major issues in the economic field within a specified time schedule. But neither the Special Session in June and July 1980 nor the General Assembly itself succeeded in reaching consensus about the procedures for the envisaged round of negotiations. Not much happened and for want of anything else the UN decided to declare the period 1981–90 the *Third Development Decade*. In 1983 and 1986 it reiterated the necessity of a common approach on development, but this had little significance during the 1980s because the industrialized states were beginning to solve the issue through a stronger market-oriented or neoliberalist approach. As the problems of most developing states had not been solved, the UN could do no better than to issue the *Declaration on International Economic Cooperation, in particular the Revitalization of Economic Growth and Development of the Developing Countries* in 1990 and to declare the 1990s the Fourth Development Decade.

Basic needs receiving attention

With the NIEO approach nearing deadlock in the existing power differences between North and South, some specialized UN agencies developed the new *basic needs strategy*. This policy was based on experiences in a development project in Argentina in the early

1970s, in which the failure of development strategies had been analysed. The conclusion reached was that a poor state in the Third World could achieve development only if the basic needs of all, such as food, shelter, water, health care and education, had been met. As one of the project's staff members also worked for the International Labour Organization, the project's conclusions were discussed by the ILO as well. These insights resulted in country studies by the ILO, IBRD and OECD which showed that economic growth often occurred without meeting basic human needs. This was referred to as 'growth without development'. Ministries in the industrialized states with resources available for development became interested in this new approach, as it proposed a promising reorientation of their development strategy. The economist Johan Galtung, who had an understanding of international economic relations and recognized the weaknesses of the NIEO, called the NIEO a *macro* approach, dealing with relations between regions at global level, and basic needs a *micro* approach, going down to the level of the single individual human being (Galtung 1978).

Optimistic expectations once again

The question of how to define basic needs was open to debate. The minimalist view, which had been used in poor relief in the nineteenth century, referred to the biological subsistence level. The ILO and IBRD in their view did not only take material essentials into account, but also socio-political elements. The ILO for instance included economic equality, participation in decision making and self-reliance. The description of needs cannot be conclusive, as the needs of people increase the more social development and welfare are available. That is also true for socio-political needs such as freedom, self-respect and cultural or sexual identity. The ILO and IBRD focused on combating poverty in the countryside and in urban situations. They aimed at promoting the production of goods and services that would meet the basic needs of the poorest sections of the population, with agricultural and industrial production geared to each other. By not producing for the higher classes or for export the ILO and IBRD expected that the lowest classes, supported by socio-economic measures from above, would begin to be upwardly mobile. Very optimistically it was hoped that improving the population's health, housing and skills would in the long term have a positive effect on overall growth.

MacNamara's absolute poverty

That the International Bank for Reconstruction and Development accepted the basic needs approach followed evaluations which showed that most IBRD projects had far fewer social effects than expected. The IBRD had always assumed that its large infrastructural schemes would be followed by economic growth and that the welfare resulting from this would 'trickle down' to the lower sections of society. The sheer scale of world poverty however became a stick with which critics beat the IBRD during the 1960s. The IBRD presidency of Robert MacNamara (1968–81), the former US Secretary of Defence under Presidents Kennedy and Johnson, saw a rapid expansion in IBRD lending, with a new emphasis on the alleviation of poverty as an objective. His new areas for lending included rural development for very small and middle-sized farmers, urban infrastructure, housing, education and health. Unlike previously the IBRD now expected 'trickle up' effects from its basic human needs approach. The IBRD programme for 1974–78 emphasized the need to assist those in 'absolute poverty': those with an annual income of less than 50 dollars. Most of these 'absolute poor', some 800 million people, lived in the agricultural areas of the Third World, in states such as Bangladesh, India, Indonesia and Pakistan. MacNamara increased lending by the IBRD during the 1970s sixfold, to almost 12 billion dollars by 1980. With similar optimism to that shown when the US government under Kennedy promoted Rostow's take-off policy, MacNamara, who himself was profoundly concerned about world poverty, expected that the problem of absolute poverty could be solved within a generation and before the end of the twentieth century. Developing states, however, saw the basic needs approach as conflicting with the NIEO and believed that it was meant to keep them from getting the structural improvements they were fighting for in UNCTAD and the UN. They also regarded the IBRD policy as an undesired interference in their domestic affairs. The new projects might keep the absolute poor alive, but they were also obstacles to the desired industrial modernization, as the projects were not part of their self-chosen industrial policies aimed at making their economies less dependent on the Northern states. Political scientist Dieter Senghaas spoke about a widely-applied therapy, but unfortunately chosen on the basis of an incorrect diagnosis (Senghaas 1982). He was proven right when during the 1980s drastic cutbacks were begun by Western ministries, based on domestic policies of retrenchment and the insight that these kinds of projects stopped poor states developing their own market-oriented growth strategy. MacNamara in turn believed that the protectionist trade policies of the industrialized states were objectionable and detrimental to global welfare. In the interest of poverty alleviation his IBRD during the 1970s spoke out against the policies of OECD states, 'something which became very muted indeed in the early 1980s. At this time, the term "structural adjustment" was used by the Bank to mean the restructuring of industry in OECD countries after they had dismantled protectionist devices like the Multi-Fibre agreement and the European steel price ring ... As the degree of protectionism in industrial countries continued to increase through the 1980s, the term "structural adjustment" acquired a different application, to the developing countries struggling with rising balance of payments deficits and huge stocks of debt' (Mosley et al. 1991, 22).

31.3 Weak international codes of conduct for transnational corporations

Transnational corporations being criticized

During the early 1970s the rise and effects of transnational corporations, at the time often referred to as multinationals, impressed both South and North. Large and in numerous states active corporations were regarded as relatively new international actors with huge economic and political power. They seemed able to avoid state control or, in the opinion of the developing states, they acted as instruments of industrialized states. Corporations being transnationally active was not new, but rather a trend dating back to the nineteenth century or even earlier. Mercantile houses, colonial firms, banks, shipping agencies, processing firms of raw materials and energy, hotel chains and production firms like Singer (sewing machines) had done this for a long time. New during the 1960s was that large corporations from Northern America and Western Europe succeeded in internationalizing their production and services by relocating their production activities and by establishing subsidiary companies and offices in other states far away. Despite what the term 'multinational' corporations suggests, transnational corporations are national firms with a central board for their subsidiary companies or branches in other states. Usually the parent company remains in the state of origin, unless it opts for another place of business due to fiscal reasons or as the result of a merger. Only a few corporations have dual 'nationality', such as Unilever or (until 2004) Shell–Royal Dutch, both of them British–Dutch. Efforts during the 1970s to establish more 'bi-national' corporations, such as Fokker-VWF and Estel, failed. Corporations have grown as a result of mergers or take-overs, but without this resulting in firms with more than one 'nationality'. The functioning of internationally-active corporations, with annual profits that may be larger than the annual revenue of some states, had long been without criticism. By the end of the 1960s however this changed because of the criticism of transnational corporations from developing states, such as from the G77 within the UN. The economic and social consequences of these giants and their expansion in the developing world were mentioned in particular, because the mere size of their activities and infrastructural demands might reduce the economy of a developing state to a monoculture. Furthermore, these corporations might damage a state's original economic structure and the related social stability and cause the draining away of natural resources, the use of revenues elsewhere and the obstruction of initiatives and efforts to create a more all-embracing infrastructure. Transnational corporations also exerted political influence, as was shown by the involvement of the American concern ITT in the coup against the democratically-elected Chilean President Salvador Allende in 1973, because ITT disagreed with the nationalization of the Chilean copper industry that previously was US-owned.

Motives for and consequences of transnational corporations

While access to raw materials was the original motive for internationalizing corporations, capturing domestic markets and circumventing protectionism became motives for transnational corporations after 1945. US corporations evaded the protectionist measures of the European Economic Community by siting corporations in one of the EEC states or by taking over national businesses. In that way they could sell their products in local markets as European rather than American. Cheap labour and profitable production facilities in certain developing states, such as the Asian Tigers (see §29.3), constituted a new impetus for internationalization. The growth of worldwide competition and technological progress forced corporations to adapt their investments strategies and to further expand internationally. Prime reasons for transnational corporations to invest elsewhere, in both developing and industrialized states, were profit maximization and the suppression of foreign and domestic competition (Gilpin 1975). Steven Hymer regarded transnational corporations as a step forward compared with older ways of organizing international exchange. Transnational corporations eliminated the anarchy of international markets and caused a more extensive and productive international division of labour, releasing great resources of latent energy. But he also recorded that crossing international boundaries pulled at and tore the social and political fabric and eroded the cohesiveness of national states. As these corporations were so powerful, they destroyed the possibility of national seclusion and self-sufficiency and created a universal interdependence. Being private institutions with a biased outlook, they represented only an imperfect solution to the problem of international cooperation. The transnational corporation 'creates hierarchy rather than equality, and it spreads its benefits unequally' (in Radice 1975, 60). Not only developing states felt the consequences, but so also did industrialized states. Although they recognized the necessity for investments by transnational corporations, governments of industrialized states became concerned about the degree of control these corporations had over their economies. The long-term strength of national economies seemed questionable if investment decisions were not taken by national firms but rather by the management of foreign corporations elsewhere. That a foreign company could decide about the survival of a subsidiary raised a spectre. Due to their global strategies and central management transnational corporations succeeded in avoiding national regulations and taxes. Often they were capable of establishing financial arrangements within the firm itself, without using capital markets. Other feared effects were powerful market control with harmful consequences for diversity, the moving of production elsewhere with its consequences for employment and local economic stagnation, the absence of new investment and the prospect of new technologies being applied only on the firm's own conditions, with further consequences for the coherence of national economies. Trade unions saw their negotiation position undermined as a result of the internationalization of production and decision making. This resulted in a decrease in information relevant to local decision making, while the corporations had the opportunity to play off workers from one state against those from another.

Transnational corporations as an issue within the UN

In 1974, through the agency of the G77, the economic and social consequences of transnational corporations had been on the UN agenda as part of the discussion on the NIEO and raw materials and development. This resulted in sections in the text of the programme of action on matters related to transnational corporations, such as the sovereignty of states over natural resources and economic activities, the nationalization issue and the control of transnational corporations. The Charter of Economic Rights and Duties of States of December 1974 also referred to these corporations, with the right of states to regulate and supervise the activities of transnational corporations, that they should not be compelled to grant preferential treatment to foreign investment, and that transnational corporations should not intervene in the internal affairs of a host state. In 1972 the UN Economic and Social Council had asked the advice of a *Group of Eminent Persons on the Impact of Multinational Corporations on Development and on International Relations* to better understand the situation. In 1974 the ECOSOC followed their advice and created the *Information and Research Center on Transnational Corporations* and the *Commission on Transnational Corporations*. The Commission discussed the question of whether a code of conduct for transnational corporations should be established, but its members included both proponents and opponents of a code which incorporated sanctions. During the 1970s various studies were published, but the Commission made little progress and in 1980 only a little more than half a code was settled. Because the US under President Ronald Reagan judged foreign investments as a boost to economic growth positively (see Chapter 35) and the original criticisms from the Third World had faded into the background, no UN code of conduct for transnational corporations was laid down.

The OECD guidelines (1976)

The OECD, however, did adopt a code of conduct, partly as a result of pressure from the trade union movement. Reacting to the criticisms of the unrestrained powers of transnational corporations, the OECD set up the *Committee on International Investments and*

Multinational Corporations (CIME) in 1975. In 1976 the OECD was the first intergovernmental organization to lay down international rules for transnational corporations. This was done in a *Declaration on International Investments and Multinational Corporations* which started with a recognition of the important role these corporations had in international investment, which had assumed increased importance in the world economy. Both the international trade unions and the entrepreneurs had been involved intensively in the preparation of the Declaration through their advisory committees to the OECD, the Trade Union Advisory Committee (TUAC) and the Business and Industry Advisory Committee (BIAC). The balance of the final text was in favour of the entrepreneurs, as the observance of the 'guidelines for multinational enterprises' in an Appendix to the Declaration was meant to be voluntary and not legally enforceable. The trade unions had pressured and hoped for a more encompassing and binding code, but they agreed to the final result with some hesitation. They expected that stern monitoring of the implementation of the code would bring practical results. Monitoring was regulated in a separate decision, which stipulated that CIME should regularly invite the advisory committees of trade unions and entrepreneurs to discuss matters related to the guidelines. If individual corporations were discussed CIME would not draw conclusions about the behaviour of these corporations but restrict itself to the related general principles. With regard to national practices the trade unions concluded that governments were not really active in supervising the guidelines. In practice the role of the so-called National Contact Points remained fairly vague. These are official commissions set up by the governments, mostly within their ministry of economic affairs, to undertake promotional activities, handle inquiries and hold discussions with the parties concerned. Although the OECD guidelines were reasonably successful in the first three years, the parties concerned lost interest in them after that, also because the economic, social and political environment slowly changed in the 1980s (Van Eyk 1995, 243). Sometimes trade unions succeeded in using the guidelines in individual cases, but given the limited pressure that could be applied as a result they shifted from a 'state-oriented' strategy of guidelines to a 'capital-oriented' strategy. These new tactics were based on the creation of 'world councils' for individual transnational corporations, which enabled trade unions to have a say at the level of the international company. The secretary-general of the international trade union secretariat for the chemical industry, Charles Levinson, developed this trade union strategy to 'counterbalance' the power of transnational corporations, using the experience of the early-internationalizing automobile industry in the 1960s. Other international trade union secretariats copied his policy and also created world councils, which enabled trade unions to consult at a higher level than that of national or local industrial relations. Simultaneously trade unions continued their activities within intergovernmental organizations to promote the 'state-oriented' strategy of establishing codes of conduct or of monitoring national implementation and compliance.

Other multilateral codes of conduct

The moderate OECD guidelines cut the ground from under the feet of other IGOs. In 1977 the ILO issued its *Tripartite Declaration of Principles Concerning Multinational Enterprises and Social Policy, Including a List of International Labour Conventions and Recommendations referred to in the Declaration.* This Declaration was a special case as it was not a convention or recommendation. When it became clear beforehand that many governments would not accept the monitoring capacities of its traditional instruments, the Governing Body decided not to submit the issue to the International Labour Conference. But so that its opinion would be heard it issued a Declaration, containing principles regarding the social policy of transnational corporations. It was prepared by a tripartite working group and does not conflict with the OECD guidelines, as it is complementary because it deals with social policies. In 1976 UNCTAD set up a group of experts to study the international regulation of the transfer of technology. This resulted in a conference and was an important issue for the G77 as they wanted to use the transfer of technology to further industrial development. It was extremely difficult for developing states to get access to modern technology, because the industrialized states had arranged the international protection of their industrial property rights extremely well. The World Intellectual Property Organization (WIPO), set up in 1967 as the continuation of the Bern and Paris Unions (see Figure 9.2), looked after these industrial property rights. WIPO came into force in 1970 and in 1974 it became a specialized UN agency. Property rights and the related high costs were obstacles to further development, according to the developing states, as the transnational corporations profited more from these rights than their own industries. As a result of fundamental differences of opinion UNCTAD did not manage to adopt a code of conduct on the transfer of technology. UNCTAD also studied the possibility of a code concerning restrictive business practices, but this equally remained without result. The private International Chamber of Commerce was more successful in this respect, given its *Guidelines for International Investment* (1972), *International Codes of Practice in Marketing* (1973) and *Recommendations to Combat Extortion and Bribery in Business Transactions* (1977). However, as this Chamber represents the interests of the business community, these codes kept to the minimalist view of codes, as shown by the 1972 Guidelines, for which the International Chamber of Commerce emphasized 'strongly' that 'these Guidelines should not be regarded as a rigid code of conduct' (Van Eyk 1995, 21).

The transnational corporation as an accepted international actor

From the 1970s on few international codes of conduct for transnational corporations have been agreed and those that came into existence have not been particularly strong. The paradigmatic change in economic thought during the 1980s (see §35.1) silenced the criticisms of transnational corporations and forced developing states to change their attitude towards international investments. By the end of the 1980s transnational corporations were no longer seen as a threat, but rather as accepted international actors promoting economic growth everywhere. In 1994, with the creation of the World Trade Organization and it replacing GATT on the horizon, the UN decided to transfer its Commission on Transnational Corporations and its related research facilities to UNCTAD, where the Commission continued its existence as the *Commission on International Investment and Transnational Corporations*.

Development aid, environmental protection and human rights as normative powers

NGO pressure on governments through intergovernmental organizations 1960–80

Part XII charts the engagement of non-governmental organizations in issues that during the 1960s had a prominent place on the agenda of intergovernmental organizations and which in society met with sympathy, such as development aid, the role of women and environmental problems (Chapter 32). This also applied to human rights. In this field Amnesty International succeeded in changing the common protocol within the UN of governments not criticizing each other by name (Chapter 33).

NGOs and development aid, the UN International Women's Year (1975) and environmental protection

32.1 NGO contributions to multilateral development aid

Privately organized development aid in the 1960s

Development in the rest of the world caught the imagination of the inhabitants of more developed states early on. In the 1950s this often found expression in church-organized aid for the construction of a school and for money for food in places where there was famine or where a natural disaster had struck. The recent experiences of war in Europe reinforced the sense of willingness to help others. As the prosperity of industrialized states increased during the 1960s, this feeling of wanting to help poor states persisted. The governments of rich states set aside budgets for development aid, which stimulated their industries to export to poor states and at the same time met the UN's call on its member states to help. The assumption in the 1960s, named the *UN Development Decade*, was that any aid which stimulated economic growth was a contribution to development. This was also the doctrine of the first volunteer workers, such as those who followed in the footsteps of the US *Peace Corps* and were posted to Third World states to assist with projects. Between 1960 and 1965 Oxfam raised 7 million pounds in the UK for the Food and Agriculture Organization (FAO) through its *Freedom from Hunger* collection. The Oxfam and FAO campaign aimed to combat food shortages, but also to ensure that people did not remain dependent on food aid and were able to become self-sufficient. In 1965 there was a campaign for providing village water supplies in India. Out of the UNCTAD Conference of 1968 the idea was born of UNCTAD, or Third World, shops selling Third World-produced goods bought in at fair prices. The number of projects in the Third World increased sharply, as did the number of people working there for NGOs. The UN's recommendation that one per cent of GNP should be devoted to support development (see §31.1) was backed by the supporters of NGO aid, who were prepared to contribute financially to NGO activities.

Political inspiration in the early 1970s

In the 1970s young people – who were campaigning on issues such as apartheid and civil rights or on specific states such as Angola, South Africa or Chile – developed their own political analyses. These provided fertile ground for UNCTAD's ideas on the relationship between Core and Periphery and for greater political involvement in the South. Because of the 'unequal struggle' between North and South the concept of 'solidarity' began to look more relevant than 'development aid'. Some saw the North–South relationship in terms of 'poverty as a consequence of capitalism' and their efforts for the Third World as an 'anti-imperialist struggle'. The early 1970s was a politically inspiring time because of events such as the military coup d'état which overthrew the democratically-elected government in Chile in 1973, the end of dictatorships in Portugal, Greece and Spain (1974–75), and the Vietnam War and its conclusion. Political interest in these events, together with a humanitarian vision of aid, meant that public support for development aid in both bilateral (between two states) and multilateral form (via IGOs) remained strong. UNICEF, the FAO and the World Food Programme of 1963 were all UN agencies with popular appeal.

Aid and development

Humanitarian and political disasters affected people's motivation for helping, as well as underlining the necessity of help. The main activities of those NGOs which dealt with emergency situations were food distribution, the provision of shelter and clean water, sanitation and medical help, followed by attempts to enable those affected to return to a normal life. These aid efforts were 'commodity-driven and logistically based, with little programmatic, economic or developmental thought given to how the relief might be more than simply pushing down death rates and saving lives' (Natsios 1995, 407). Many of the NGOs active in the Third World, such as Oxfam, offered practical relief, as did *Médecins Sans Frontières*, which was founded in 1971. Once they were in the field they discovered that relief alone was insufficient: 'they were often drawn to development goals after first providing relief in emergency situations, and came to understand that in developing countries relief was not enough' (Cernea 1988, 10). Steadily the connection between 'aid' and 'development' grew. A distinction began to be made between organizations which carried out relief work only (*Médecins Sans Frontières*) and those which combined this with development. Examples of this latter type were CARE, Catholic Relief Services, Christian Aid, Oxfam, Save the Children and World Vision. Because they were large organizations with a long-term presence in the areas they worked in, they became familiar with local situations. Since the 1985 famine in Ethiopia combining emergency relief and development has become a general trend. Most NGOs 'try to integrate into their relief work developmental components particularly focused in agriculture, microenterprise, primary health care, reforestation and road construction'. The NGOs may provide money, tools, technical support and market surveys for a project chosen by local community leaders as being of long-term benefit for the area (Natsios 1995, 407).

Differences between Northern and Southern NGOs

NGOs were only able to provide relief and stimulate development because they had the resources to do this. Their money came from private sources (collections, appeals, donations) as well as public ones (national governments and, to a lesser extent, IGOs). Some NGOs located their headquarters in a state where they had been active for some time and from there also worked in other states. Others set up development offices in a number of states, which worked independently of each other and sometimes even competed with each other. A third group of NGOs used various agencies to collect funds which were then 'pooled' and, when necessary, distributed through their own local organizations in developing states. A fourth group had a similar structure but distributed the money through independent local organizations. The advantage of this was that the funds went directly to those in need. The disadvantage was the absence of staff to monitor this process. The trend towards using local NGOs (*grassroots organizations*) became more widespread from the 1970s onwards and implied an unequal relationship between 'Northern' NGOs, which had plenty of resources and provided funds and knowledge, and 'Southern' NGOs, which had the support of local, mainly poor groups. Peter Uvin classifies international NGOs within what he calls the 'development aid pyramid', at the summit of which he puts about 20 IGOs, 20 large bilateral donors and those NGOs based in rich states. Although Northern and Southern NGOs share some characteristics and a common concern for development, there are also considerable differences between the two groups. The Northern NGOs 'are conduits of billions of dollars of aid to Southern NGOs. Worldwide, there are about 2000 of them, located in Europe and the US, but maybe 50 of them represent up to 80% of total resources. These resources come from the public (some $5 billion) and from their own governments (around $2.2 billion). They often have programmes in tens of countries, draw on highly capable and well-paid staffs, and have their offices in the same Western capitals as the other summit actors'. The Southern NGOs are far smaller and have little money. 'The differences become clearer still when one looks at the direction of the flows of resources: the hundreds of thousands of Third World NGOs are all competing for pieces of the roughly $50 billion of yearly development aid that is almost exclusively controlled by the 100 or so summit organisations' (Uvin 1995, 497).

Why NGOs work with IGOs

Uvin sees three reasons for NGOs becoming involved with IGOs in their development aid activities. The first is the availability of funding from IGOs. Although NGOs are able to raise considerable funds themselves, they need the IGOs' funding and their contacts if they are to reach the large numbers of people who require aid and ensure the success of their programmes and projects. The second reason is that NGOs often focus on local problems, but these problems need to be tackled at international level to be solved. Cooperation with IGOs offers NGOs the chance to influence this international level.

501

'Some local problems, such as water pollution or depletion of fish stocks, have international causes; only international action can provide solutions' (Uvin 1995, 501). The third reason is that IGOs enable NGOs to achieve better results at governmental level. On the one hand cooperation with IGOs affords NGOs status and greater independence from national governments, on the other IGOs can call on governments to support NGOs with more resources.

Why IGOs work with NGOs

The reasons for IGOs to cultivate relationships with NGOs centre on the funding they bring with them and the ideology coupled with it. The dominant ideology in development aid organizations emphasizes the importance of the private sector. In fact, a liberal ideology predominates among both IGOs and development aid institutions, with notions such as 'state disengagement, privatisation, competition, self-help, and democratisation'. According to this ideology 'the enterprises produce wealth, and NGOs redistribute it' (Uvin 1995, 499). Through their familiarity with local populations NGOs contribute to the effectiveness and sustainability of development programmes. All evaluations have shown that projects organized by IGOs without the participation of NGOs lack effectiveness. This is because IGOs do not focus on engaging local communities. They usually only interact with governments and offer few opportunities for input from societal groups – the very groups that will be affected by the IGOs' policies. NGOs' criticisms of IGOs mean that IGOs feel pressurized into engaging with NGOs and sometimes governments insist on this as well. NGOs help IGOs to gain support for their policies in developing states by making these policies transparent and legitimate. In fact NGOs are obliged to do this under UN rules: an NGO working in partnership with the UN 'shall undertake to support the work of the UN and to promote knowledge of its principles and activities' (Uvin 1995, 500). The UNHCR, for example, admitted that backing for its policies on the ground depended on the support of ordinary people and that NGOs had proved much more capable of influencing their attitudes than the UNHCR itself. This in fact led to a division of labour between the UNHCR and the NGOs. The UNHCR sought to resolve controversies with the governments involved, while the NGOs would discuss the situation with local people. The British *Save the Children Fund* found that this cooperation with IGOs was far from easy, however. This organization became involved with large numbers of refugees in Africa during the 1970s and 1980s. It took the charity some considerable time to discover how to ensure that the right amount of food was in the right place at the right time to avoid large numbers of children dying from starvation. 'It was to discover that the mandates of the UN agencies with responsibility for refugees, the internal structures of those agencies, the relationships between different UN agencies and between UN agencies and other organisations engaging within the system, all had an effect on the ability of the system to work effectively' (Penrose and Seaman 1996, 241). Understanding one organization may have been difficult, but understanding the relationships between all the organizations involved was even more so. Because the UN and the non-UN organizations had not clearly delineated their responsibilities, NGOs could only learn from their practical experience of working with the UNHCR, the World Food Programme or the WHO. 'Gaining knowledge of the system was a gradual process involving a growing understanding of bureaucracies. It was only repeated experience that allowed the organisation to predict what would occur as the original assumptions of how a hierarchy would and should work were often proved to be false' (Penrose and Seaman 1996, 254).

An emphasis on local-level projects: 'everyone for themselves'

The relief and development work undertaken by NGOs at the 'grassroots' level was labour intensive, both in terms of workers from donor states and workers employed locally. Given their expertise in directing this kind of operation in isolated areas, NGOs became skilled at building local infrastructure at the very lowest level – that of families and villages or small districts of towns. The goal was to transform these local groups into functioning units. In practice, however, this meant that NGOs took on those tasks at which they were most skilled, such as 'community-based health care, primary and secondary education, agricultural extension work, water and sanitation projects, small-scale enterprise typically through cooperatives or small loans, road and bridge construction, and environmental programmes, particularly reforestation' (Natsios 1995, 413). This also revealed the weaknesses in NGOs' working practices: the 'everyone for themselves' attitude, which failed to take wider society into account. This method of working meant that the possibility of cooperation with other organizations or government agencies was limited and resulted in a 'reluctance to cede managerial or programme autonomy towards the goal of greater strategic coherence or managerial efficiency'. Underestimating 'national problems of governance, economic reform, planning and policy' increased the risk that problems at national level would jeopardize the success of local-level projects (Natsios 1995, 413–14).

32.2 The international women's movement and the UN International Women's Year (1975)

Women and development

The UN declared 1975 to be the *International Women's Year* for two reasons: the role of women in the development process and its determination to promote equal rights. As early as 1962 a long-term programme for progress on women's rights had been discussed in the context of the UN Development Decade. Developing states insisted that the plan should be put into action, but it was not until 1970 that, as part of the Second Development Decade, the General Assembly adopted a programme of collective international action for the advancement of women. In her book *Women's Role in Economic Development* (1970) the Danish economist Esther Boserup cast doubt on whether the UN was right to argue for the integration of women in the development process, as it did in the 1970 programme, and questioned whether Western development aid in fact had the desired integrating effect. Her research showed that development aid had not previously led to the integration of women, but rather had had a negative effect on their position. Because no attention had been paid to the specific position and problems of women when considering issues of economic development, economists and politicians had failed to notice that Third World development had a different impact on women and men. This was because the Western model of development was based on different assumptions to those which prevailed in the Third World. The Western model broke with the traditional division of labour and put women in developing states at a disadvantage. They lost their previous positions of influence in production and trade, and with it their influence within social and family structures, to a small group of men who took the most important positions of power within the agencies created by development programmes.

Additionally the education and training linked to machinery and technology imported from the West excluded women, because Western donors as a matter of course offered opportunities connected with technology to men only.

The first wave of the women's movement

The other motivating factor behind the International Women's Year was the women's movement, both the 'first wave' – which had won access for women to the League of Nations and was also active within the UN – and the 'second wave'. This second wave consisted of young women who were critical of the existing gender relations and would later find in the UN a forum for the development and expansion of their ideas. The first wave of the women's movement traced its roots back to the end of the nineteenth century and was characterized by its demands for equal rights. To this end it had agitated within the League of Nations, the ILO and the Union of American Republics. This had been interrupted by the Second World War, but through the efforts of women's organizations the UN picked up where the old institutions had left off. In 1946 the ECOSOC established the Commission on the Status of Women (see Figure 20.8). Women's organizations with consultative status at the UN were able to exert influence on this Commission. They were also active within the specialized agencies of the UN. The result of their lobbying of governments and within the UN framework was that the UN and some specialized agencies passed international conventions which laid down equal rights for women in certain areas (see Figure 32.1). After the first resolution concerning the political rights of women was adopted in 1946 the UN drew up a convention on the subject, followed in 1957 by a convention on the nationality of married women, which the League of Nations had previously been unwilling to support. In 1951 the ILO passed its equal remuneration convention (number 100) and a convention concerning discrimination in employment and occupation followed in 1958. UNESCO spoke out against discrimination in education in 1960. Gradually progress was being made towards equal rights for women and men. However, there were contradictions too, such as the

---

Figure 32.1 International statements on women's equality within the UN system

1946 UN Resolution on the Political Rights of Women
1951 ILO Convention 100 on Equal Remuneration
1952 UN Convention on the Political Rights of Women
1957 UN Convention on the Nationality of Married Women
1958 ILO Convention 111 on Discrimination in Employment and Occupation
1960 UNESCO Convention against Discrimination in Education
1962 UN Convention on Consent to Marry, Minimum Age for Marriage and the Registration of Marriages
1966 UN International Covenant on Civil and Political Rights
1966 UN International Covenant on Economic, Social and Cultural Rights
1967 UN Declaration on the Elimination of Discrimination against Women
1979 UN Convention on the Elimination of All Forms of Discrimination against Women

special protection of women workers in a number of ILO conventions since 1919 which had been questioned in 1937 (see §18.1). There was no question yet of more general non-discrimination against women.

Making the International Women's Year (1975) a reality

In 1967 the UN published its *Declaration on the Elimination of Discrimination against Women.* This had moral undertones and called discrimination against women 'fundamentally unjust' and 'an offence against human dignity'. The UN did not see an international convention as suitable, but did create a reporting mechanism for the Declaration. The evaluation of the national reports showed that the principle of non-discrimination was still far from being realized and that a simple declaration of intent was too weak a measure, since it was not binding. The Commission on the Status of Women began work on an international convention, using the International Convention on the Elimination of All Forms of Racial Discrimination of 1965 as a model (see Figure 28.2). Support for this grew during the 1970s, partly due to the developing second wave of the women's movement. Within the Commission changes were also taking place. The battle for equal rights for women and men became less important and the equal role of women in development began to receive greater priority, which led the Commission to broaden its policy. In 1970 the ECOSOC approved a new programme for the Commission. The idea of an International Women's Year was proposed by the Commission on the Status of Women in 1972. It had just marked its 25th anniversary and it seized this as an opportunity to evaluate its work: what had the Commission achieved and what further action should be taken to promote equality between women and men and expand women's contribution to national and international development? The ECOSOC accepted this idea, a decision in which an alliance between women from the Commission and developing states played a role as together they had a majority. In the UN General Assembly of 1974 the Netherlands proposed reducing the year to an 'international women's week', but because of the coalition of women and Third World states the Assembly passed the proposal to declare 1975 the International Women's Year. The year's subtitle – *Equality, Development and Peace* – reflected the broadened interests of the Commission, although the General Assembly had added the 'peace' element. Third World states offered to organize a conference and while Bolivia was not able to do this, Mexico was prepared to take on the task.

The second wave of the women's movement

A new generation of young women from the Americas and Western Europe was taking an interest in social and political affairs. Political change was not the only contributing factor. Developments such as new household appliances, the contraceptive pill and increasing participation in higher education also played a role. Through the social activities and organizations women were becoming more and more involved in, it occurred to them that men consistently occupied the positions of influence. First-hand experience of their second-rate status made women receptive to analyses which showed their unequal status in terms of rights and roles. They read books from an earlier generation of women, such as Simone de Beauvoir's *The Second Sex* and Betty Friedan's *The Feminine Mystique*, and their own publications soon began to appear. Women studied the difficulties that they themselves were experiencing and came to the conclusion that unequal rights were not the only type of discrimination, but that there were also other associated forms. They pejoratively called the set of assumptions which they formulated 'sexism'. The central planks of the second wave of the women's movement were not 'subordination' and 'non-discrimination', but rather 'suppression' and 'liberation'. The analyses by women's groups from the US and Europe began to influence each other and various groups met in autonomous workshops to develop their theories. Such groups felt little affinity for the UN, given their critical view of male-dominated institutions, but the fact that a new women's movement was gaining momentum did help those women who worked within the UN and were pressing for an International Women's Year. Equally, the International Women's Year would support the second wave of the women's movement.

The UN Women's Conference in Mexico City (1975)

The UN revived the tradition of International Women's Day (8 March) which had been initiated by socialist women in 1910. This was celebrated in 1975, albeit a day early, with an international discussion panel at the UN headquarters. The day was officially recognized in 1978. Preparations for the Mexico City conference were organized through the regional Economic Commissions of the UN. The conference took place from 19 June to 1 July and was the first large-scale intergovernmental conference on the position of women, with 133 states, 23 specialized agencies, ten other IGOs, eight recognized liberation movements and 114 NGOs participating. Because of the character of the meeting delegations made sure that they included more women than usual. The secretary-general of the conference was the Finn Helvi Sipilä, who was elected assistant secretary-general of the UN in 1972 and used her high-profile position to support the advancement of women within the organization. The conference adopted a *World Action Plan* for the realization of the aims of the International Women's Year and the *Declaration of Mexico* on the equality of women and their role in development and peace. The World Action Plan contained objectives which should be met within five years, so that states would start to take action at national level immediately. In order to offer continuing support for these national activities and to monitor whether or not progress was being made, the conference advised the UN that the period 1976–85 should be declared the *UN Women's Decade*. At the same time as the UN conference a meeting of NGOs and individual women took place, under the name *Women's Tribune*. The UN-recognized NGOs had organized this 'shadow conference' with the support of the Mexican government and 6,000 women, mostly from South and Central America, took part, plus around 1,500 women from the US. During this meeting considerable differences emerged in the ideas and feelings of the two groups. While the US women resented their situation and expressed this in terms of the balance of power between the sexes, those from the South saw women's issues as part of the conflict between rich and poor. They did not think words such as 'exploitation' and 'suppression' were relevant to the position of women. Despite these differences the success of the shadow conference inspired the women's movement and was also noticed at the UN. The UN accepted the idea of a Women's Decade. For this purpose a special fund was established and the *International Research and Training Institute for the Advancement of Women* (INSTRAW) was set up. The Third World, seeking a New International Economic Order, had managed to set its stamp on the World Action Plan and the Declaration of Mexico. However, although the General Assembly of late 1975 approved both documents, the concepts they contained did not find their way into the economic policy which the Assembly set down at the same time. The expected appointment of more women to UN posts barely materialized at the time either. After the conference in Mexico City several follow-up conferences were held, in 1980 in Copenhagen, 1985 in Nairobi and 1995 in Beijing. They were all accompanied by well-attended shadow conferences, called Women's Forums.

From Declaration (1967) to Convention (1979)

During discussions within the UN at the beginning of 1975 over a convention on discrimination against women the ILO had raised the issue of possible conflict with existing or forthcoming conventions proclaimed by the specialized agencies. The continuation of special protection for women workers, laid down in a number of ILO conventions, played a role in this. Debates had already been going on in the ILO on whether the special protection granted to women by ILO conventions was still permissible, given its discriminatory character. The International Federation of Business and Professional Women had first pointed this out in the 1930s and now repeated its criticisms. Support for this view was increasing and by the mid-1970s advocates of the equal treatment of workers of either sex were in the majority. The ILO made a declaration on this subject in June 1975, accepting that no differentiation could be made between the sexes: all workers were to be treated equally and enjoy equal opportunities. The success of the UN Women's Conference in Mexico City reinforced efforts for a UN convention on discrimination. In 1979, when the formulation of the draft text by the various bodies within the UN appeared to be taking too long, the General Assembly took matters into its own hands and passed the *Convention on the Elimination of All Forms of Discrimination against Women* that same year. The Convention was presented to the UN Women's Conference in Copenhagen (1980) as a contribution to the UN Women's Decade. Because the

---

Figure 32.2 The UN Convention on Discrimination against
Women (1979)

The **Convention on the Elimination of All Forms of Discrimination against Women**, adopted on 18 December 1979, expresses concern in its preamble that in situations of poverty women have inferior access to food, health, education, training, employment opportunities and other basic requirements. The signatories to the Convention believed that the development of states, the welfare of the world and the cause of world peace all require the participation of women on equal terms with men in all areas. In order to realize this goal patterns of behaviour, customs and traditions which are based on the inferiority or superiority of one of the sexes, or on stereotyped roles for men or women, must be changed. The articles refer to various subjects. Article 10 for instance, on education and vocational training, refers in section (a) to equal treatment in career and vocational guidance, in access to education and in the achievement of diplomas in educational establishments of all categories. This equality is to be guaranteed in pre-school education, general education and all types of vocational training. The Convention was signed by 64 states and took effect on 3 September 1981 after 20 states had ratified it. By 2008 the number of ratifications had reached 185.

The **Committee on the Elimination of Discrimination Against Women (CEDAW)**, consisting of 23 experts, was set up to monitor compliance. It has annual meetings and met for the first time in 1982. Participating states are required to submit reports within one year of ratifying and every four years after that, or sooner if required by the Committee. These reports contain details of the legislative, civil, administrative or other steps taken in order to meet the terms of the Convention. In 1984 only 21 of the 50 states which submitted reports had satisfied the require-ments, while in 1987 only 49 out of 92 states which were to report for the first time and 7 out of the 31 which were to report for the second time did so. The Com-mittee may only study reports submitted by the governments themselves. The role of specialized UN agencies is restricted (they are present during negotiations on decisions relating to their field of activity) and there is no role at all for NGOs. Another limitation is that the Committee can discuss the reports, but not make any judgement on whether or not states have met their obligations or make any recommendations on what further steps should be taken. Its recommendations must remain general in nature. A third restriction is that the Committee cannot investigate individual complaints. International women's organizations subse-quently lobbied for an optional protocol to the Convention to enable a complaints procedure for individuals. The World Conference on Human Rights in Vienna in 1993 supported their efforts and the Commission on the Status of Women was finally able to achieve this goal through an open-ended working group. In 1999 the General Assembly passed the *Optional Protocol*, which came into effect at the end of 2000 and by 2008 90 states were participating.

Convention had been rushed through the text had not been through all the usual channels however and therefore it had legal shortcomings. Nonetheless, the character of the Convention was prescriptive and encouraging. It did not contain any binding require-ments, but demanded that states take 'all appropriate measures' to end discrimination (see Figure 32.2). The Convention was effective because women's organizations were able to use it as an international standard through which they could pressurize national governments to amend discriminatory laws and regulations.

Ongoing conceptualization: equal rights

Concepts such as 'equal rights' and '(non-)discrimination against women' evolved over time as a result of incremental decision making. In 1919 the League of Nations had made a start with *equal rights* for its own male and female officials. In the same year the ILO had stated the basic principle of *equal pay for work of equal value* for women and men. In 1923 the Union of American Republics followed with its first declaration on equal civil and political rights and in 1937 this vision was included in an ILO resolution. The UN expressed its faith in equal rights in its 1945 Charter and its 1948 Universal Declaration of Human Rights. The Organization of American States included equal civil and political rights in two conventions in 1948, the Council of Europe did the same in 1950 in the European Convention on Human Rights, as did the UN in its two Human Rights Covenants of 1966.

From equal rights to equal opportunities: the concept of discrimination

The ILO in 1937 was the first IGO to use the term *discrimination*. It was of the opinion that not only equal rights were important, but equal opportunities and treatment were as well. The ILO's new pronouncements on equal opportunities in 1944 set the tone for the direction of policy after the war. In 1958 this found expression in Convention 111, which promoted equal opportunities and treatment and denounced discrimination in employment and occupation. Discrimination was defined, for the first time, as 'any distinction, exclusion or preference made on the basis of race, colour, sex, religion, political opinion, national extraction or social origin, which has the effect of nullifying or impairing equality of opportunity or treatment in employment or occupation' (Article 1).

Progress interrupted

Non-discrimination as a general international standard was codified for the first time in 1944. The ILO's Declaration of Philadelphia spoke of the right to pursue well-being and development 'irrespective of race, creed or sex'. The UN Charter of 1945 echoed this with its exclusion of discrimination 'on the basis of race, sex, language, or religion'. Further development of the concept of discrimination took the 1958 ILO definition as its starting point. Both the 1960 UNESCO Convention against Discrimination in Education and the 1965 UN International Convention on the Elimination of All Forms of Racial Discrimination defined discrimination in the same way. However, after this there was a break in the pattern. While both the UN Human Rights Covenants of 1966 stipulated the grounds on which discrimination was unacceptable, they contained no definition of discrimination itself. Furthermore, the International Covenant on Civil and Political Rights did not refer to 'discrimination', but rather to 'distinction' (see below). Neither did the UN Declaration on the Elimination of Discrimination against Women of 1967 contain a definition of discrimination. This change can be explained by compartmentalization within the UN institutions and by the changing composition of commissions. The Commission on the Status of Women was not involved in the drafting of the Human Rights Covenants or the Convention on Racial Discrimination and as a result the gender dimension of these documents was not developed. Women's organizations did not notice this and they also failed to react adequately to developments elsewhere in the organization in 1967. The 1979 UN Convention on Discrimination against Women however adopted the earlier approach and thus ended the interruption in progress. In terms of its content and definition of discrimination the 1979 Convention had actually more in common with the Convention on Racial Discrimination of 1965 than with the 1967 Declaration, although it formed the legal instrument of the latter.

The concepts of distinction and positive discrimination

During the drafting process of the UN Human Rights Covenants the Indian representative defended the concept of *distinction* in the context of economic and social rights. In this he referred to special measures which were meant to help advance certain socially or educationally disadvantaged groups, which he did not consider to be distinction or discrimination in a negative sense. This view later became known as 'positive discrimination'. However, in 1965 this was the source of some confusion. In Article 2 of the draft text of the International Covenant on Economic, Social and Cultural Rights the concept of 'distinction' was replaced by 'discrimination'. In Article 2 of the International Covenant on Civil and Political Rights, however, the concept of 'distinction' was retained. This was defended by saying that the Charter and the Universal Declaration already included this concept. The term *discrimination* (unlike distinction) thus acquired a specific definition, central to which was the assumption that discrimination required action to be taken (McKean 1983, 146–49).

The second wave of the women's movement as an autonomous actor

During the UN Women's Decade young women from the First and Third Worlds developed their own international structures and strategies. This happened through *international women's networks*, which were less formal than NGOs that resulted from the first wave. They often arranged tribunal-style international conferences on subjects such as violence against women, women and health, reproductive rights and strategies for empowerment. Networks which combined research with the distribution of information and the organization of international conferences proved to be particularly effective. By disseminating information they kept women informed about issues that they considered important. They shared their information (results from research, interpretations, declarations, strategies) with similar groups and encouraged women to be active at international level and participate in the conferences organized by the networks. Meanwhile, these networks were keeping IGOs and governments informed about 'the concerns of many women around the world' and filling 'the void of information available on the situation of women to which many governments have been unwilling to respond' (Stienstra 1994, 142–43). This new feminism was echoed in Latin America and Asia and as a result feminists from these continents also began to take a leading role in their own states and in international forums. Towards the end of the 1970s Latin American women succeeded in persuading European feminists that their campaigns on abortion were too restricted to have a worldwide impact. They helped to broaden these actions into the more comprehensive concept of *reproductive rights*. In addition, they also put the double repression of black and handicapped women on the agenda. A conference on reproductive rights in 1984, also intended as an alternative to the UN International Conference on Population in the same year, confirmed that women's networks should continue to determine their own policy on reproductive rights. In fact the views of the women's NGOs, which had been much more restrained in their criticism of government and UN policies than the feminists, were barely heard at this UN conference.

Involvement of the second wave of the women's movement with the UN

Despite their strategy of autonomy, feminists became increasingly involved with the UN and other IGOs. They drew on the 1979 UN Convention on Discrimination against Women, which proved a useful means of exerting pressure on national governments to introduce changes. The duty of signatory states to report on their progress also meant that feminists became involved in monitoring this. As earlier generations of women left, young feminists took over the running of those women's NGOs which had UN consultative status, such as the Women's International League for Peace and Freedom. Several international networks became professional organizations, which relied on well-informed women's groups in the participating states. In 1986 feminists established the *International Women's Rights Action Watch*, which – just like Amnesty International (see §33.3) – took a critical interest in keeping up to date with national developments and with the work of CEDAW, the monitoring body of the 1979 UN Convention. The UN Women's Conferences held in Copenhagen (1980), Nairobi (1985) and Beijing (1995) encouraged further contacts between feminists and official international politics. The conferences were an opportunity to evaluate and to publicize new ways of thinking. This happened through the Women's Forums and through feminists who were at the same time working for governments and were members of their national delegations. A similar process occurred at the UN world conferences on the environment and development in Rio de Janeiro, human rights in Vienna and population and development in Cairo. By the 1990s women's groups had 'more political vision, know-how and strategies and ... a wider political base than ever before'. They had understood that 'women's voices have little chance of being heard at UN world conferences without deliberate and concerted efforts'. They had also learned that the best moment to influence a global conference was during its preparatory phase. If women's groups wanted to achieve something in the final decision-making phase, it was necessary 'to build consensus and coalitions to bridge ideological and material differences between women' at local, national and international levels before any international action could be taken (Chen 1995, 480–81). They learned how to mount international campaigns, form coalitions, reach consensus between women, prepare policy documents, influence official delegates, mediate between NGO forums and official conferences, as well as to concentrate on the main points and on official documents, maintain contact with all the actors involved and become serious lobbyists. Women from the second wave had gradually become new players on the international level of IGOs and governments, mastering the diplomatic skills necessary for such a multilateral interface. Significant networks developed among women from the South, but there were also networks in which the usual boundaries between North and South became indistinct (Chen 1995, 488–89). The process of *women's empowerment* grew in strength due to three factors: the women's movement as a socio-political force, feminist politicians who had emerged from this movement, and feminist officials or 'femocrats'. Feminists had become experts and advisers and were contributing to national reports submitted by governments to the UN or to other IGOs. They were involved in preparing intergovernmental decisions and during conferences they acted as intermediaries between the official meetings and the NGO meetings. Even when women with a feminist background became delegates, tied to government agendas, they still proved themselves to be delegates 'with a mission' because of their commitment to the feminist cause.

Accommodation by international organizations

Notwithstanding all the influence won by feminists at the UN, other IGOs and multilateral conferences, it is also true that IGOs made a real effort to involve women in their work. To do this they had to find support from women, but they also attempted to tie women into their organizational procedures and policies. While international women's NGOs have influenced agenda setting and have added to the qualities and efficacy of official decisions and the legitimacy of the IGOs, these institutions in turn 'have looked after and interfered with these private organizations through their official procedures in order to make them instrumental to their intergovernmental problem-solving' (Reinalda 2000, 166). Some issues important to feminists received little attention from IGOs, which had other priorities. Violence against women, for example, was not mentioned in any policy document at the Mexico City or Copenhagen conferences and even when

511

concern grew about the issue it was still omitted from the UN's central planning document on women and development (Stienstra 1994, 143). Women's activities within the organizations have not noticeably changed them: 'in spite of their many activities, little change has occurred within international organizations' (Stienstra 1994, 145). The discourse within IGOs has evolved from one which made no mention of gender-specific aspects to one in which women form a specific part of the programme for development. This positive change has had several aspects, including the increased recognition of women at international level, more statements on women's equality and increased support for women's access to education and health care around the world. However, the number of women in positions of authority in IGOs has remained small. Declarations on the subject of women have not been backed by more money, staff or powers. The situation of many women in the world has not improved and in some cases has even worsened due to economic or other crises. The position of women has proved highly dependent on changes in the global political economy, crises and wars. Additionally IGOs have been characterized by a conservatism that is often found in organizations which, as societal institutions, reflect power relationships and which are not required to change those relationships. 'Given this, and the embeddedness of dominant gender relations within international organizations, it is hardly surprising that there has been little change for women within these organizations.' States and IGOs have certainly not been inclined to make the radical changes necessary to meet the demands of women. Instead, small concessions have been made, which has meant 'the inclusion of measures that would not hurt, or would not be costly, and the easiest of these was the inclusion of language that supports broad principles of equality' (Stienstra 1994, 157).

32.3 Consciousness-raising on environmental problems

Conservation: the IUCN (1948) and WWF (1961)

There were three main concerns underlying what was later to become known as environmental policy: conservation of natural habitats, population growth and the human environment. Conservation traced its roots back to a nineteenth-century tradition – a period when nature was being threatened by large-scale mechanized industry, urbanization and new infrastructure projects such as railways, canals and roads. Cultural heritage was in danger, as well as nature itself, and citizens came to their defence by forming private organizations devoted to the conservation of nature. They safeguarded areas of countryside by purchasing them and using them for their own purposes and by lobbying their governments to conserve and restore natural habitats. To be able to exert influence at international level, such as within the UN, the *International Union for the Protection of Nature* was set up in 1948, after 1956 called the *International Union for the Conservation of Nature and Natural Resources – The World Conservation Union* (IUCN). From the 1990s onwards the name *World Conservation Union* was more commonly used, as it summed up the work of the IUCN as a conservation network. This international organization is a hybrid. In 2008 its members included 84 states, 111 government agencies in the field of conservation and 909 NGOs, as well as almost 11,000 experts from 160 states. The *World Wildlife Fund* (WWF), established in 1961, is an INGO. The Fund was set up because of concern over the rapid degradation of fauna and flora in Africa. Julian Huxley, the first director-general of UNESCO who also supported the work of the IUCN, raised awareness of this issue after a visit to Africa. This led to the setting up of the Fund to purchase wildlife areas and mobilize public opinion. A giant panda was chosen as the Fund's symbol. So that the organization would be able to function, 1,001 people were asked to donate 10,000 dollars each. The WWF launched campaigns to protect tigers, tropical rain forests and the oceans. They also recorded the trade in wild animals and plants in the *Trade Records Analysis of Fauna and Flora in Commerce* (TRAFFIC). In 1986 the organization's name was changed to *World Wide Fund for Nature*, although in some parts of the world the old name continued to be used.

Population growth, food shortages and housing

The second concern for environmentalists in the postwar period was the growth in the world's population, which caused some alarm: in 1960 the global population was three billion, in 1974 four billion and in 1987 five billion. Concern about the total numbers and the rate of growth was expressed at UN level during the 1974 World Population Conference in Bucharest. The global food situation had originally been purely a matter of development aid, but now took on another dimension because of the burden food production was placing on the natural environment. So as to stimulate economic and social development through food aid and support at times of special need, the UN and the FAO had set up the *World Food Programme* (WFP) in 1963. This was sponsored by the US, so providing that state with an opportunity to offload some of its food surpluses. At the end of 1974 a World Food Conference was held in Rome, where two new international institutions were created to deal with threatened food shortages resulting from sharp price rises following the oil crisis. These were the *International Fund for Agricultural Development* (IFAD) and the World Food Council. The aim of the IFAD was to combat hunger in low-income states facing chronic food shortages and in the long term to eliminate poverty. This was to be achieved by channelling extra funds into agriculture and rural development. The resources were provided by OECD states (55 per cent), OPEC states, which had gained considerable financial resources during the oil crisis (see §31.1) (43 per cent), and a few developing states. It is debatable whether the OPEC states really had the interests of developing states at heart, but this was certainly the assumption. The *World Food Council* (WFC) was not given an executive role, but was to be a forum in which to develop ideas about food production, distribution and associated problems. The WFC's role was to monitor the work of those IGOs responsible for implementing food programmes, such as the FAO, WFP and IFAD. Relations between these organizations were problematic. Internal tensions, such as those between the US and Saudi Arabia within the IFAD, had a crippling effect. The same was true of the tensions between the WFP and the FAO, which stemmed from the fact that the FAO would not allow the WFP room to develop its own policy. Because the IBRD and the European Community were also elaborating their views on development through food aid, some changes were beginning to be made to the poorly functioning food aid regime. This meant that gradually food aid came to be based more on the requirements of specific states, rather than on simply making food surpluses available to them (Hopkins 1992). These bureaucratic interests and power politics within and between organizations showed that population growth and food policy had become closely linked. Feeding and housing the increasing numbers of people in the Third World was going to place a considerable burden on the natural environment. Housing was discussed in 1976 in Canada at the UN Conference on Human Settlements (Habitat) in Vancouver. On the agenda

513

was the continuing increase in cities of more than a million inhabitants, particularly in developing states. Concern about the global population led to a specifically environmental consciousness and the problem of development was to become intertwined with a growing awareness of the deterioration of the natural and human environment.

The deterioration of the human environment

Some were quicker than others in noticing that the human environment was in peril. Modern technology and the healthy economic performance during the postwar period had raised expectations, but it took people longer to notice the negative consequences. This awareness often came through disasters or environmental abuse, such as the poisoning of people working with mercury, the effects of the pesticide DDT on wildlife in lakes, ditches and other waterways, lung cancer caused by air pollution, the formation of smog in cities, the problem of increasing amounts of refuse as a result of disposable goods and packaging, the increasing quantities of chemicals used by households, disasters involving oil tankers such as the *Torrey Canyon* (1967), the factory accident involving dioxins in Seveso, Italy (1976), the escape of toxic materials from the Union Carbide pesticides factory in Bhopal, India (1984) and the disaster at the Chernobyl nuclear plant in the Soviet Union (1986). Gradually environmental insight was gained into phenomena such as the greenhouse effect (1979), the hole in the ozone layer (1985) and the continued and accelerating disappearance of tropical rainforests in Brazil and Indonesia. Because of the faith in progress resulting from the immediate postwar period, the views of those who saw the dangers earliest were at first barely taken seriously. As early as 1954 Harrison Brown had warned of such dangers in his book *The Challenge of Man's Future* and Rachel Carson had indicated the damage done by DDT and other chemicals in *Silent Spring* (1962). By the end of the 1960s critical scientists and young people began to call into question the assumption that nature could bear any burden human beings might place on it and concerns about the environment grew. They acknowledged that these problems were not confined to single states and demanded an international approach. In 1972 British scientists published their *Blueprint for Survival*.

The Club of Rome and The Limits to Growth *(1972)*

The Limits to Growth, a publication originating from within the Club of Rome, had the greatest impact. This Club was formed in 1968 by scientists who thought that they needed to compensate for the inactivity of governments by investigating the fundamental long-term problems that humanity would face in the future. Young researchers from the Massachusetts Institute of Technology were commissioned to produce *The Limits to Growth*. They used the group-dynamics method and a computer model to predict what would happen if population, food production, pollution and natural resources continued growing (or shrinking) at the rate they were. Donella and Dennis Meadows concluded that the 'limits to growth' would be reached within a century. The report was translated into more than 30 languages and more than 10 million copies were sold. The authors were not against economic development, but pointed out the possible consequences of industrialized states' unthinking pursuit of economic growth. They made the world aware that the planet's natural resources were being used up and that the dominant values and views were ignoring this problem. Serious environmental degradation was to be the result. Discussions about environmental problems influenced views on development. In

1975 the Swedish Dag Hammarskjöld Foundation published a report which argued that development in poorer states should not be based only on their needs, but also be environmentally sensitive. With this understanding came the realization that natural resources in developing states were being exploited in an unbalanced way and that the food relief provided by certain IGOs was not encouraging balanced growth.

The establishment of Greenpeace International (1971)

The wide media coverage of environmental exploits was partly due to the activist NGO *Greenpeace International*. This had started as a group of nature lovers from the US and Canada who were concerned about the nuclear tests being carried out by the US. In 1971 some Canadians decided to employ some of the old tactics used by the American Quakers, who had used boats to sail to the islands of Eniwetok and Bikini, where the US had been carrying out nuclear tests since 1946, hoping their presence would prevent further tests. However, because they were using US boats the US Marines were able to hold them back. The Canadians were aware that the US could not stop Canadian boats and the journalist Robert Hunter attracted wide publicity with reports of their adventurous journey to the island of Amchitka in the north of the Gulf of Alaska, where the US was planning nuclear tests in 1971. This publicity and the terms of the 1963 Partial Test Ban Treaty did not prevent the US from carrying out tests, but because so many protests and demonstrations were held among the general population it decided to call off those at Amchitka. The journey changed Hunter from a reporter to an activist. He and others built the Greenpeace organization up to become an 'ecological police force', which set off for locations where various large-scale, but low-visibility, environmental abuses were taking place to bring them to the world's attention through publicity stunts. This included campaigns against dumping toxic waste at sea and against the hunting of seals and whales. Images of the small Greenpeace dinghies confronting large ships made an impression in the media. Taking his inspiration from Native American legends about warriors attempting to rescue the earth which had become sick because of the greed of man, Hunter called these activists the 'rainbow warriors'. The flagship of the organization would later be given the same name: the *Rainbow Warrior*. In 1985, while on an expedition to Moruroa Atoll to demonstrate against French nuclear tests, this ship was blown up by two explosives on the instructions of the French secret service. Greenpeace grew into an NGO which was able to mobilize public opinion with its high-visibility but carefully chosen publicity stunts. It also became a sizeable business with its own merchandise, millions of members and many sections (Brown and May 1989).

32.4 The UN Conference on the Human Environment and the creation of UNEP (1972)

The UN Conference on the Human Environment in Stockholm (1972)

The increasing environmental consciousness affected the UN too. On the initiative of Sweden the environment was on the agenda by 1968. The report *Man and His Environment* (1969), also known as the *U Thant Report*, pointed out the increasing problems of population growth, the unplanned growth of urban areas, the exhaustion of natural resources, increasing pollution, endangered animal species and threatened food shortages. In 1969 the General Assembly asked UNESCO to hold a number of preparatory conferences for the conference on protecting the human environment, which was to be held in Stockholm in 1972. These were organized by the Economic Commissions of the UN and UNESCO. Prior to the Stockholm conference in June 1972 controversy arose over the attendance of both West and East Germany and when it proved impossible to postpone the conference the Soviet Union and most Eastern European states boycotted it. As a consequence the communist world was not present at the start of international discussions on the environment. The *UN Conference on the Human Environment* (UNCHE) issued a Declaration on the Human Environment in which links were made between environmental problems, underdevelopment and industrial activities. The Declaration was adopted by acclamation, together with an Action Plan containing 109 recommendations. However, objections were raised on some issues. For instance, the US and certain Western states announced that they did not accept the principle that compensation should be paid to developing states when environmental measures restricted their trade. The US, Canada and a number of Western European states also objected to the financial arrangements for the proposed institution for human settlements, which was to become the UN Habitat Centre in 1978. Japan meanwhile did not want to give up its consumption of whale meat and spoke out firmly against the proposed ten-year moratorium on the hunting of whales.

The creation of UNEP (1972)

As a result of the Conference the General Assembly of the UN set up the *United Nations Environment Programme* (UNEP) later in 1972, with a Council, a voluntary fund and an information network called Earthwatch. As a gesture to the Third World the Secretariat of UNEP was located in Nairobi. Although the US understood the importance of environmental policy and was willing to cooperate with and finance an international institution, UNEP had a fairly weak position within the UN. Its founders ruled out making it into a specialized agency, because they saw environmental problems as global problems which, in policy terms, overlapped with the policy areas covered by other specialized agencies. For this reason they opted for a 'programme' instead, which could act as a spur to discussions and actions. The decision not to make it a specialized agency actually was disadvantageous, because existing specialized agencies did not really take the new programme seriously. Compared with these organizations, UNEP was a dwarf and it also found it difficult to gain authority because it lacked expertise and did not have the necessary financial resources. Unlike the specialized agencies with their own budgets, UNEP was financed completely by voluntary contributions. Existing organizations which handled environmental policy as part of a wider remit were able to spend substantially more. UNEP's isolated position in Kenya did not benefit it either. It was not until 1997 that UNEP's mandate was strengthened somewhat.

The UNEP's Mediterranean Action Programme (1975)

One of UNEP's priorities was marine protection. Its director, Maurice Strong, launched a *Regional Seas Programme*, which later developed into a programme for oceans and coastal areas. The Mediterranean Sea was selected as a priority in order to assess whether coastal states could be brought together to set up and implement an action plan on pollution. Representatives from 16 coastal states as well as the European Community attended an intergovernmental meeting in Barcelona in 1975, with only Albania and

Cyprus absent. The states agreed the *Mediterranean Action Programme* (MAP), which consisted of an international framework *Convention for the Protection of the Mediterranean Sea against Pollution* with Protocols on the protection of the marine environment against the dumping of waste from land or at sea, a research and knowledge-sharing programme and a regional development plan. The Convention and Protocols were adopted at the start of 1976, with the Convention coming into force in 1978 (see Figure 32.3) and the Protocols somewhat later. The member states met annually and did indeed combine to tackle pollution. This success was due to a group of environmental experts, who were able to tip the balance in favour of cooperation. The governments themselves had no concrete solutions to the problems discussed, but were presented with such solutions by the experts. Some of the experts were also appointed to national environmental institutions, from where they continued to ensure that momentum was sustained (Haas 1990). The fact that some states did not take on the responsibility themselves but delegated it to a special institute (Nicholson 1998, 87), contributed to the reliability of knowledge about this cross-border problem (Dimitrov 2003). The UNEP's other environmental programmes included the *Global Environmental Monitoring System* (1975), the international register for potentially dangerous chemicals (1976) and a conservation strategy (1980). In 1983 it published its first report into the state of the global environment. Several UN specialized agencies were also active in the environmental field, such as UNESCO with its *Man in the Biosphere* project (1976) and the ILO with its work on dangerous materials in the work place (1977).

32.5 Protection of the natural and human environment through international conventions

Protecting the sea against pollution

The first international treaty on marine safety was passed in 1914 after the tragedy involving the *Titanic* (see §10.2). This *International Convention for the Safety of Life at Sea* (SOLAS) was revised in 1929, 1948 and 1960. The last revision was one of the first tasks of the *Intergovernmental Maritime Consultative Organization* (IMCO), which had begun its function as a specialized UN agency in 1959. The rules were revised to take technical developments in shipping into account and to establish international procedures. In 1974 the SOLAS Convention was amended again. Because oil pollution was something which states had always handled at national level the British government convened a conference in 1954 to establish international procedures, which led to the *International Convention for the Prevention of Pollution of the Sea by Oil*, known as OILPOL (see Figure 32.3). The government thus broke with the UK's long tradition of dominating the world's oceans by acknowledging that it alone could no longer be responsible for procedures at sea. For this reason Britain handed over the ratification process and the associated secretariat to IMCO a year after OILPOL came into effect in 1958: Britannia no longer ruled the waves. The disaster involving the *Torrey Canyon* in 1967 and the resulting pollution caused considerable discussion on the dangers of large tankers. IMCO held a conference which in 1973 led to a new *International Convention on the Prevention of Pollution from Ships* (MARPOL 73), incorporating many elements of the 1954 OILPOL Convention. Because MARPOL was not ratified by enough states and because further environmental disasters involving tankers occurred in the period 1976–77, another conference was held at the beginning of 1978. The results of this were laid down in new Protocols to both the 1974 SOLAS and the 1973 MARPOL Convention. The 1973 MARPOL with its 1978 Protocol was ratified by a sufficient number of states and the new combination came into effect in 1983 (MARPOL 73/78). Several Appendixes to the Convention came into force at later dates (see Figure 32.3). In 1982 IMCO was strengthened and became the *International Maritime Organization* (IMO).

The limitations of the International Whaling Commission of 1946

The *International Whaling Commission* (IWC) was set up in 1946 to prevent whale numbers from falling to a level where whale hunting would no longer be possible, which mutual agreements among fishing companies and the 1931 League of Nations Convention for the Regulation of Whaling had proved unable to achieve. The political situation immediately after the Second World War made it possible for a compromise to be found between hunting and conservation, leading to the *International Convention for the Regulation of Whaling* in 1946 (see Figure 32.3) and the formation of the IWC. However, as the profitability of whaling increased certain species of whales began to face extinction, while some states which were not signatories to the Convention began to hunt whales without taking much notice of its terms. Because of announcements made by the UN Conference on the Human Environment in 1972, the IWC felt compelled to react to the proposed moratorium on whaling and the arguments of the conservationists. The compromise suggested by the IWC was to use scientific research as a basis for categorizing whales and to specify the number of whales which could be caught in each category. In 1974 an *International Observer Scheme* was set up. However, this was difficult to enforce because it relied on bilateral agreements between states and, furthermore, governments were not providing enough funding for research. At this stage, under pressure from NGOs, states which did not have a direct interest in whaling and were more interested in conservation joined the IWC. Leading whaling states such as Japan and Norway reacted by persuading states with an interest in whale products to become members, so that they could conclude bilateral treaties with them. Meanwhile restrictions were being imposed outside the IWC. The European Community banned all trade in whale products, the CITES Convention (see below) listed whales among its endangered species and some states banned whaling within their 200-mile fishing zones. By the early 1980s, as a result of NGO campaigns and pressure from states in the IWC which were concerned with conservation, the IWC felt it had to implement some moratoria. The whaling states however persisted in their search for ways to continue hunting whales. The Reagan government in the US was not prepared to implement the sanctions which it had imposed on Japan and although US NGOs filed lawsuits on this against their government, they lost their case in the Supreme Court. Because the US also failed to hold Japan to agreements made within the IWC Japan was able to continue whaling. Whether certain states were more concerned about whaling or about conservation depended on the power of the NGOs. Within the IWC tensions between the whaling and the conservation camps persisted (Birnie 1991).

The CITES Convention on Endangered Plant and Animal Species (1973)

In 1963 the problem of endangered species of flora and fauna led to an IUCN initiative for an international convention. The underlying assumption was that the trade in plants and animals, or parts of them such as elephant tusks, could threaten their survival. The IUCN, which has both governments and private organizations as members, saw this as a matter for individual states because the trade occurred between states. In March 1973 80 states signed the *Convention on International Trade in Endangered Species of Wild Fauna and Flora* (CITES) in Washington DC. This Convention made a distinction between three kinds of endangered plants and animals: those which faced imminent extinction, those which were endangered and those which states declared to be endangered within their own territory. All three categories are listed by CITES and are part of a licensing scheme for international trade. When CITES was set up it was agreed that its secretariat would be located in the regional UNEP office in Geneva. The Convention was amended in 1979 in Bonn and by 2008 173 states were party to it. In 1980 the UNEP, IUCN and WWF launched their *World Conservation Strategy*, which was designed to promote the coordination of efforts globally. This was in response to the alarming acceleration in the deterioration of flora and fauna. To be able to tackle this effectively they demanded *sustainable development* – the first time this concept was used. In 1982 the UN supported these attempts with the acceptance of the *World Charter for Nature*, which had been prepared by the IUCN.

Desertification, water shortages and the greenhouse effect

Not all the environmental problems identified in the 1970s were taken seriously immediately. The problems of drought and desertification, with their adverse effects on biodiversity and agriculture, were on the agenda of the UN Conference on Desertification in Nairobi in 1977. An international action plan was agreed, but it was not until the 1990s that interest in a large-scale approach to the problems began. The same was true for the 1977 UN Water Conference in Mar del Plata in Argentina. The targets set for 1990 were far from realistic. The results of research into the effects of CO_2 – the *greenhouse effect* – were discussed in detail at the conference of the World Meteorological Organization (WMO) in Geneva in 1979, but this failed to raise concern among governments or the public at large. There was, though, an agreement on acid rain – the *Convention on Long-Range Transboundary Air Pollution* – which was extended through various Protocols in the 1980s and 1990s (see Figure 32.3 and §40.3).

The 'polluter pays' principle (1972)

Concern over the environment reached the Organization for Economic Cooperation and Development at the beginning of the 1970s. The OECD tackled the consequences of environmental measures on international trade, the location of industries and the relationship with economic growth. It supported the harmonization of national decision making with regard to the environment and wanted to eliminate as far as possible discriminatory rules and practices in international trade. In 1972 the OECD passed a resolution on the international economic aspects of environmental policy, which contained the principle that the 'polluter pays'. This seeks to prevent distortions in the price of internationally-traded products by making the polluter pay for the cost of measures imposed by governments to protect the environment. The costs of these measures are therefore included in the cost of goods and services which cause pollution during their production or consumption. Such measures may not include subsidies, since subsidies can cause distortions in international trade. Originally the interpretation of the 'polluter pays' principle was limited because the idea was to discourage subsidies, but in practice it was broadened to include compensatory payments, taxes and levies. At the same time it also came to include all expenses associated with environmental measures. This OECD principle from the early 1970s was so clearly formulated that the GATT and WTO did not state it separately, but they remained alert to distortions in international trade.

Figure 32.3 International conventions on the environment 1946–79

Name of convention (abbreviated name)	Adopted	In force
International Convention for the Regulation of Whaling (**Whaling Convention**)	2.12.1946	10.11.1948
International Convention for the Prevention of Pollution of the Sea by Oil (**OILPOL Convention**)	12.5.1954	26.7.1958
Convention on Fishing and Conservation of Living Resources of the High Seas (**Marine Life Conservation Convention**)	29.4.1958	20.3.1966
Antarctic Treaty	1.12 1959	23.6.1961
International Convention for the Safety of Life at Sea (**SOLAS 1960**)	17.6.1960	26.5.1965
Treaty Banning Nuclear Weapon Tests in the Atmosphere, in Outer Space, and Under Water (**Partial Test Ban Treaty**)	5.8.1963	10.10.1963
Convention on Wetlands of International Importance Especially as Waterfowl Habitat (**Ramsar** or **Wetlands Convention**)	2.2.1971	21.12.1975
Convention on the Prevention of Marine Pollution by Dumping Wastes and Other Matter (**Marine Dumping** or **London Convention**)	29.12.1972	30.8.1975
Convention on International Trade in Endangered Species of Wild Flora and Fauna (**CITES** or **Endangered Species Convention**)	3.3.1973	1.7.1975
International Convention on the Prevention of Pollution from Ships (**MARPOL 73**)	2.11.1973	–
International Convention for the Safety of Life at Sea (**SOLAS 1974**)	1.11.1974	25.5.1980
Convention for the Protection of the Mediterranean Sea against Pollution	16.2.1976	12.2.1978
Convention on the Prohibition of Military or Any Other Hostile Use of Environmental Modification Techniques (**ENMOD or Environmental Modification Convention**)	10.12.1976	5.10.1978
International Convention on the Prevention of Pollution from Ships, 1973, as Modified by the Protocol of 1978 Relating Thereto (**MARPOL 73/78**), with six Appendixes coming into effect: AI and II 2.10.1983, AV 31.12.1988, AIII 1.7.1992, AIV 27.9.2003, AVI 19.5.2005	17.2.1978	2.10.1983 etc.
Convention on Migratory Species of Wild Animals (**Bonn Convention**)	23.6.1979	1.11.1983
Convention on Long-Range Transboundary Air Pollution (**Air Pollution Convention** or **Acid Rain Convention**)	13.11.1979	16.3.1983

See Figure 40.1 for the conventions adopted between 1982 and 2006.

Human rights as a normative power and the Amnesty International model

33.1 The realization of international human rights conventions at the UN

Classical and social fundamental rights

After the acceptance of the Universal Declaration of Human Rights in 1948 the General Assembly of the UN asked ECOSOC to have the Commission on Human Rights draw up a judicially-binding treaty with enforcement measures (see §20.5). The UN chose a covenant rather than a convention as the kind of treaty it wanted. Owing to the differences between classical fundamental rights, which do not require government intervention, and social and economic fundamental rights, the UN decided to draw up two covenants. *Classical fundamental rights* are the political and civil rights that stem from the ideas of the American and French Revolutions and are widely incorporated in national constitutions (see Figure 4.1). They grant freedoms to individuals which the state or government may not interfere with and are therefore also called 'negative' rights, which individuals in principle can enforce via the courts. *Social fundamental rights* are often 'positive' rights, as they require governments to take positive action to protect or favour individuals. They are less often embedded in constitutions and mostly cannot be demanded by individuals.

Transformation of the Declaration into two International Covenants (1966)

Owing to the limited resources of the Commission on Human Rights and the need for states that were not Commission members to have the opportunity to submit proposals, the General Assembly was not able to adopt the two Covenants until 19 December 1966. The first is the *International Covenant on Civil and Political Rights* on classical human rights, the second the *International Covenant on Economic, Social and Cultural Rights*. New in relation to the Universal Declaration was the peoples' right of self-determination, which reflected the progress made in the process of decolonization since 1948. Some rights however, such as asylum, nationality and ownership, had disappeared as a result of political controversy. Ownership was omitted because of an irreconcilable difference of opinion between West and East about individual and collective ownership. It had taken an enormous effort to reach agreement on the enforcement measures in both Covenants. Thanks to the Netherlands the individual right of complaint was upheld in that on civil and political rights, although states had to become party to an Optional Protocol.

International Bill of Human Rights

Although it was initially assumed that one human rights treaty would be sufficient, there ultimately was a whole complex of conventions. In addition to the two 1966 Covenants, the UN included other conventions on specific subjects in the field of human rights, such as the conventions discussed earlier on racial discrimination (1965, see §28.1) and discrimination against women (1979, see Figure 32.2). The conventions on torture (1984), children (1989), migrant workers (1990) and the disabled (2006) also form part of the so-called *International Bill of Human Rights* (which in a stricter interpretation consists only of the Universal Declaration and the two Covenants). In addition to the conventions themselves, the UN human rights regime includes the related optional protocols and monitoring commissions (see Figure 33.1).

Three functions of the Commission on Human Rights

In the context of the UN human rights regime the Commission on Human Rights (see Figure 33.2 for its composition) had three functions: international standard setting, monitoring and promotion. The *standard setting function* proved to be useful when the Universal Declaration, both Human Rights Covenants and the other conventions were drawn up. The *monitoring function* was virtually non-existent for the first 20 years of the Universal Declaration, but was more in evidence from 1967 after the adoption of both Covenants. The monitoring procedure was, however, weak and there were no possibilities to enforce. This combination of normative power and procedural weakness was the result of political decision making, linked to the intentions and willingness of governments at global level. Thanks to the moral weight of the Universal Declaration, of which the two Human Rights Covenants were the judicial result, the two 1966 Covenants formed a relatively strong promotional regime (Donnelly 1986, 613–14). The extent to which states at the time were prepared to monitor compliance properly was evident from the limited resources they made available to the UN for human rights. These comprised 0.7 per cent of the entire UN budget and six staff members at the UN Secretariat in Geneva. Thus the remaining function, the *promotion* of the implementation of international norms at national level, became the most important. Although the procedures were initially rarely put into practice, their very existence had a certain effect, as the Commission on Human Rights publicly discussed the human rights situation every year (Farer 1988).

Figure 33.1 UN human rights conventions 1965–2006

Abbreviation and convention name, monitoring committee, number of signatories, number of parties in 2008, optional protocols	Adopted respectively In force
ICERD: International Convention on the Elimination of All Forms of Racial Discrimination CERD: Committee on the Elimination of Racial Discrimination 85 signatories, 173 ratifications in 2008	21 December **1965** 4 January 1969
ICCPR: International Covenant on Civil and Political Rights HRC: Human Rights Committee 70 signatories, 162 ratifications in 2008 * 16 Dec 1966 ICCPR–OP1: *Optional Protocol to the International Covenant on Civil and Political Rights; in force:* 23 March 1976; 35 signatories, 111 ratifications in 2008 * 15 Dec 1989 ICCPR–OP2: *Second Optional Protocol to the International Covenant on Civil and Political Rights, Aiming at the Abolition of the Death Penalty; in force:* 11 July 1991; 35 signatories, 66 ratifications in 2008	16 December **1966** 23 March 1976
ICESCR: International Covenant on Economic, Social and Cultural Rights CESCR: Committee on Economic, Social and Cultural Rights 67 signatories, 159 ratifications in 2008	16 December **1966** 3 January 1976
CEDAW: Convention on the Elimination of All Forms of Discrimination against Women CEDAW: Committee on the Elimination of Discrimination against Women 98 signatories, 185 ratifications in 2008 * 10 Dec 1999 OP-CEDAW: *Optional Protocol to the Convention on the Elimination of Discrimination against Women;* in force: 22 December 2000; 77 signatories, 90 ratifications in 2008	18 December **1979** 3 September 1981
CAT: Convention against Torture and Other Cruel, Inhuman or Degrading Treatment or Punishment CAT: Committee Against Torture 75 signatories, 145 ratifications in 2008 * 18 Dec 2002 OP-CAT: *Optional Protocol to the Convention against Torture and Other Cruel, Inhuman or Degrading Treatment or Punishment;* in force: 22 June 2006; 61 signatories, 35 ratifications in 2008	10 December **1984** 26 June 1987

Figure 33.1 (continued)

Abbreviation and convention name, monitoring committee, number of signatories, number of parties in 2008, optional protocols	*Adopted respectively In force*
CRC: Convention on the Rights of the Child CRC: Committee on the Rights of the Child 140 signatories, 193 ratifications in 2008 ★ 25 May 2000 OP–CRC–AC: *Optional Protocol to the Convention on the Rights of the Child on the Involvement of Children in Armed Conflict; in force: 12 February 2002; 123 signatories, 122 ratifications in 2008* ★ 25 May 2000 OP–CRC–SC: *Optional Protocol to the Convention on the Rights of the Child on the Sale of Children, Child Prostitution and Child Pornography; in force: 18 January 2002; 115 signatories, 128 ratifications in 2008*	20 November **1989** 2 September 1990
ICRMW: International Convention on the Protection of the Rights of All Migrant Workers and Members of Their Families CMW: Committee on Migrant Workers 28 signatories, 37 ratifications in 2008	18 December **1990** 11 July 2003
CRPD: Convention on the Rights of Persons with Disabilities CRPD: Committee on the Rights of Persons with Disabilities 131 signatories, 34 ratification in 2008 ★ 13 December 2006 OP–CRPD: *Optional Protocol to the Convention on the Rights of Persons with Disabilities; in force 3 May 2008;* 71 signatories, 20 ratifications in 2008	13 December **2006** 3 May 2008

Figure 33.2 Composition of the Commission on Human Rights 1946–2006

The **Commission on Human Rights (CHR)** did not only have the task of drawing up the Universal Declaration of 1948 and the two Covenants of 1966, it was also responsible for civil liberties, the protection of minorities and the prevention of discrimination on the grounds of race, gender, language and religion. The Commission initially had 18 members, which was increased at various times to 43 in 1982, of which 11 were from Africa, nine from Asia, eight from Latin America, ten from Western Europe and other states, and five from Eastern Europe. In 1992 the Commission was enlarged to 53 members. They were chosen for three years and met annually for six weeks in March and April in Geneva. In addition to the members of the Commission, representatives of IGOs and various UN organs (about 15), observers from states that were not members of the Commission (80), and representatives of NGOs (more than 100) – a huge assembly of people – attended the meetings in the 1980s and 1990s. In 2006 the Commission was replaced by the *Human Rights Council* (HRC, see §44.3).

The Commission had a **Sub-Commission on Prevention of Discrimination and Protection of Minorities**, composed of 26 experts chosen by the Commission. In 1999 it was renamed the Subcommission on the Promotion and Protection of Human Rights. Both the Commission and the Sub-Commission had working groups and special rapporteurs on themes and specific states.

33.2 Monitoring the implementation of UN human rights conventions through reports

Complaints about violations

Initially the Commission on Human Rights was not in a position to take action in connection with the many complaints the UN received about violations: between 1947 and 1967 some 65,000. This situation improved in 1967, when the Commission and its Sub-Commission for Minorities were authorized to collect information on gross violations and to investigate situations showing a consistent pattern of violations. The Commission could then submit a report with recommendations to ECOSOC. In 1970 action was taken to deal with complaints made by individuals and private organizations. A *Working Group on Communications* of the Sub-Commission, composed of five of the latter's members, would then further investigate complaints indicating a consistent pattern of gross and conclusive violations. This Working Group met for four weeks every year prior to the meeting of the Sub-Commission. Owing to the complicated procedure (Working Group, Sub-Commission, Commission and possibly a review committee) and the large number of complaints (for instance 54,000 in 1976 alone), dealing with the complaints was a lengthy and not very satisfactory affair. After the Working Group and Sub-Commission had completed their work and if there was reason to do so, the Commission could instigate an investigation following the 1967 procedure and inform the ECOSOC. The Commission could, with the approval of and in cooperation with the state involved, establish an *ad hoc* review committee, which worked confidentially, endeavoured to find a favourable solution, and reported to the Commission. The entire process, known as Procedure 1503 after the ECOSOC resolution of 1967, was substantially amended in 2000 to make it more efficient. The procedure also included a Working Group on Situations. In 1983 a division of labour was agreed with the Commission on the Status of Women, which was also authorized by the 1979 Convention to investigate complaints, but only those on grounds of gender.

Diverse reporting regulations

The UN system has two sources of information for monitoring violations of its conventions: complaints and reports. The International Labour Organization has the strictest regulations of the specialized UN agencies, as it is compulsory for governments to submit reports. As well as governments the social partners report and the various regulations for reports, complaints and powers are harmonized. The ILO also has a special complaints regime through the Committee on Freedom of Association, introduced in 1950 in consultation with the UN to monitor ILO Convention 87 on the Freedom of Association (see §21.4). Rules for reporting were also introduced by the Food and Agriculture Organization, the International Maritime Organization, UNESCO and the World Meteorological Organization. The regulations of the World Health Organization fell into disuse (Ghebali 1989, 221 note 1). At the UN itself a diversity of reporting and complaints procedures with regard to the many conventions evolved as a consequence of political decision making in various settings over many years, with a mixture of compromises. Not all of these regulations have been equally effective. A first group of conventions makes no provision for reporting at all, such as those on the political rights of women (1952), the nationality of married women (1957) and the consent to marry (1962). In 1953 ECOSOC added a biennial reporting system to the Convention on the Political Rights of Women, which was in 1963 even extended to states that had not ratified. This regulation, however, had little success, owing to a lack of cooperation. A second group of conventions had limited obligations to report, such as the 1949 Convention for the Suppression of the Traffic in Persons and of the Exploitation of the Prostitution of Others and the 1956 Supplementary Convention on the Abolition of Slavery. In these cases states must keep the secretary-general informed of the laws, rules and measures taken. He then forwards these reports to ECOSOC as part of the documentation for any discussion ECOSOC may start. Little is usually done with the reports after this. In the mid-1960s prostitution as an issue for special attention even disappeared from the work programme of the ECOSOC commission concerned for a period of ten years.

Problems with the reporting regulations

Most reporting regulations have had various problems in common. Many states either did not participate at all or only did so half-heartedly and many reports often gave little, or hardly any, relevant information. Answers were not consistent or of a general nature. Data were often out of date and difficult to check. More important was whether the monitoring committees concerned had the necessary capacity to analyse the data they had received and whether they could do anything with the information. Institutional restrictions, such as available staff and resources, played a role in this, while higher organs could do what they wanted with data discussed at a lower level. Moreover, it was 'not done' for governments to criticize each other strongly. An additional handicap was that the information and data originated from governments, which were inclined to mask problems and to claim that they were making progress. In the 1967 UN Declaration on the Elimination of Discrimination against Women, ECOSOC introduced a procedure for monitoring progress whereby not only states but also NGOs could provide information. Although ECOSOC had thus introduced an element of independent criticism, for the time being the results remained limited, as most NGOs were not up to this task due to a lack of resources and experience. Furthermore the basis on which they worked was generally too limited, being mostly restricted to the industrialized world, a situation that would not change until the 1970s and 1980s. The involvement of NGOs received a boost when in 1974 the Sub-Commission for Minorities of the Commission on Human Rights opted for an 'open procedure'. The reason for this was that the reports received from governments were not up to standard, both qualitatively and quantitatively. This step meant that the Sub-Commission also took into consideration reports produced by NGOs on concrete situations.

33.3 The UN human rights conference in Tehran (1968) and the Amnesty International model

The International Conference on Human Rights in Tehran (1968)

The breakthrough for NGOs occurred during the *International Conference on Human Rights* in Tehran in 1968, on the twentieth anniversary of the Universal Declaration. Iran (also called Persia) was prepared to pay the costs of a international conference organized by the UN, the first in a long series of UN world conferences (see Figure 20.4). The sister of the Persian shah, Ashraf Pahlevi, who devoted herself to human rights within the UN, was chosen as the conference's chairperson. The UN Secretariat made sure that the executive conference secretariat came from its own ranks and that the director of the Human Rights Department of the Secretariat was put in charge of it. 2,000 delegates from 48 states and 61 IGOs attended the conference. Representatives of NGOs were not invited, but because of the violation of human rights in states such as Vietnam, Congo and South Africa Sean MacBride, co-founder and chairperson of Amnesty International, brought various NGOs together. 'In those years Amnesty International did not want much from the UN and the UN did not want much from it – Amnesty International's advocacy focused on the power of international public opinion in general and specifically on individual prisoner-of-conscience releases. It relied mainly on correspondence between Amnesty International members and the relevant national governments.' MacBride, however, had mobilized a coalition of religious NGOs with a large membership in many states, which acted as a subgroup within the association of NGOs with consultative status at ECOSOC. He had also brought human rights NGOs and experts together in Geneva and Montreal, to develop and elaborate ideas for the UN world conference. 'MacBride also co-chaired a Geneva meeting of seventy-six UN human rights NGOs and of fifty experts sitting as the Montreal Assembly of Human Rights. Both of these gatherings generated recommendations for the Tehran conference, including MacBride's personal priorities, namely heightened protection for victims of armed conflict and the appointment of a UN High Commissioner for Human Rights' (Schechter 2005, 22). The NGOs were also present in Tehran, but as they had neither observer nor any other formal status they exercised their influence by proposing or writing draft resolutions for delegations they were acquainted with.

Authoritative reports of Amnesty International

The meticulous country reports by Amnesty had a unique effect within the UN. Amnesty took the Human Rights Covenants seriously and tested violations against the norms officially recognized in them. It published its own reports on violations in states and held discussions with the governments involved, with the aim of focusing their attention on these violations. This public criticism was a break from the diplomatic practice of governments within the UN. The UN protocol 'dictated that governments not criticize one another by name in the proceedings of the Commission on Human Rights. Consultative NGOs were limited even further by explicit rules and unspoken expectations' (Clark 2001, 13). Unlike Amnesty, the Anti-Slavery Society had pursued its strategy of not mentioning states by name in the UN between 1946 and 1966, expecting that this would win the support of governments and IGOs. Owing to a lack of success, however, the Anti-Slavery Society reversed its decision in the mid-1960s and, with disappointment, ended its self-chosen confidentiality by also seeking public support. The break with the existing UN protocol initiated by Amnesty International was inspired by a renewed confidence in the ideals of human rights and was meant to remind governments of their own words, 'that states themselves should control how and when human rights promises should be fulfilled' (Clark 2001, 13). The basis of the strength of Amnesty's reports was that its allegations were confirmed by various independent sources. Amnesty's method of working developed into an ideal model that other NGOs would follow (see Figure 33.3). Other human rights NGOs included Human Rights Watch, founded in 1979 in the US, and Helsinki Watch. Human Rights Watch also began to collect information on violations of human rights throughout the world and to publicize these. Its field of operations is broader than that of Amnesty, which with a view to effectiveness restricts itself to classical human rights and the protection of individuals. Human Rights Watch also looks at issues such as censorship, racial discrimination and forced labour, in the hope of influencing US foreign policy. Helsinki Watch was formed when committees which had been monitoring the observance of human rights in Eastern Europe, in the framework of the Conference on Security and Cooperation in Europe, joined forces (see §24.3). In addition to Charta 77 from Czechoslovakia and groups from the Soviet Union, committees from Western Europe also belonged to this group. The International Confederation of Free Trade Unions has published its annual *Trade Unions Rights, Survey of Violations* since 1984, to draw attention to violations of the rights of trade unions.

33.4 Reporting with a monitoring commission and a complaints procedure

Reporting regulations with a monitoring commission

A stronger category of monitoring mechanisms based on reporting exists for conventions that combine reporting obligations with a monitoring commission. Such commissions now exist for all human rights conventions (see Figure 33.1). Sometimes these commissions are not established by treaty but by the ECOSOC, for instance the Committee on Economic, Social and Cultural Rights (see below). The strength of these specialized

Figure 33.3 The Amnesty International model

Amnesty International resulted from an initiative by the London lawyer Peter Benenson in 1961. He was enraged that in Portugal two students had received long prison sentences simply because they had proposed a toast to liberty whilst enjoying a drink. Amnesty made an 'Appeal for Amnesty' and started a campaign for 'forgotten prisoners'. Since 1961 it has adopted tens of thousands of prisoners, sent observers to their trials and supported their families. It asked people to write to prisoners to strengthen the involvement of individual citizens and to show the prisoners that something was being done for them. Amnesty has developed into an NGO that works fervently for the observance of human rights worldwide. It publishes country reports and an annual survey of violations of human rights across the world in its yearbook, as well as waging campaigns against specific issues such as the death penalty. Although Amnesty is on the whole not involved in the field of social and economic rights, it has extended its interest to the oppression of specific groups, including the persecution of homosexuals and the violation of the human rights of women.

Amnesty International has consultative status at the UN ECOSOC, giving its findings an audience within this forum. According to Ann Marie Clark, the activities of Amnesty demonstrate **three unique attributes**, which she refers to as loyalty to principle, political impartiality and attention to facts. By **loyalty to principle** she means that Amnesty bases all its activities on the moral principles of human rights as formulated in the international conventions, regardless of the political ideas, religion, gender, race or age of a person. By placing itself above politics it can pursue independent activities and campaigns. Amnesty takes the international norms in the field of human rights extremely seriously and expects states that have signed and ratified such conventions to do the same. **Political impartiality** means that Amnesty is consciously politically independent and campaigns for the rights of individuals regardless of what kind of government or regime they live under. Contacts with governments promote constructive dialogue. To maintain its independent position, Amnesty always strives to be self-sufficient and does not accept subsidies or other support from governments. By **attention to facts** Clark means that Amnesty conscientiously searches for facts in connection with violations of human rights brought to its attention. Each case must be confirmed by three independent sources before Amnesty will give an opinion. It provides an interpretation of the facts that clarifies the meaning of the international norms that are at issue. It does not only search for facts, it also submits them to the governments involved. In this way it can raise incorrect or misleading explanations from governments for discussion and correct them and hence clarify the norms in the international conventions. The result of this method of working is that Amnesty's reports have become authoritative and that Amnesty has helped international law to develop further by its involvement (Clark 2001, 18).

Amnesty International uses its consultative status at the UN to contribute its information on violations to discussions on the reports submitted by governments regarding claims and violations. This is the moment when at international level the *contra* information originating from a private source can correct the data from governments and influence the decision making on further implementation. Other

NGOs have begun to follow this Amnesty International model, but this does not necessarily mean that they always achieve the same level of independence and quality as Amnesty. In her question on whether facts obtained from research are relevant to internationally-active NGOs, Caroline Harper argues that NGOs that want to be successful must make serious use of this. 'Seen by many to be self-appointed advocates, NGOs will have to identify more clearly who they represent, and by what standards they act in their role as advocates for change' (Harper 2001, 256). NGOs must therefore strengthen their own involvement through research, develop the research capacity of their partners, for example in the Third World, and build up good contacts with researchers. They must be aware of the values held by the researchers involved. Harper's investigation of the successful campaign against child labour showed that during the campaign NGOs and trade unions sometimes failed to present their case strongly enough, because they could not provide hard facts based on research. The consequence of this was an unintended disruption to the policy process that they wanted to influence, with even the risk of negative effects for the children involved. When confrontation with governments is sought, it is essential that one's own arguments are supported by serious evidence. 'NGOs must therefore develop their ability to gain, understand, and use research-based evidence to greater effect' (Harper 2001, 257).

commissions lies in the expertise they build up over time, which enables them to see through the pretensions of states. This is more successful when NGOs also have access to these commissions and can submit their own information. In 1986 women set up the International Women's Rights Action Watch as a watchdog to monitor the 1979 UN Convention on Discrimination against Women. The UN Committee on the Rights of the Child can only study government documents relating to the 1989 Convention on the Rights of the Child, but Defence for Children International fulfils the same watchdog function as in the case of women. In 2002 a Protocol to the 1984 Convention against Torture was adopted, against the wishes of the US, which provides for the establishment of a worldwide system for the inspection of prisons by independent organizations in order to prevent the maltreatment and abuse of detainees.

The monitoring of economic, social and cultural human rights

Economic and social human rights are just as fundamental as civil and political rights but, in comparison with the latter, it is only recently that more attention has been paid to them. It was more than ten years before the monitoring procedure of the 1966 International Covenant on Economic, Social and Cultural Rights took shape. This system is weaker and does not have the character of a judicial, or semi-judicial, complaints procedure, as it is based on reports about the legal and other measures taken by states with regard to the rights recognized in the Covenant. Nonetheless, these reports indicate factors and difficulties which have had an adverse influence on the implementation of rights. The UN secretary-general passes on the reports to ECOSOC and, if relevant, to the specialized UN agencies. ECOSOC may make arrangements with these agencies for them to report on the progress that has been made in relation to rights in their field. It can then inform the Commission on Human Rights, send reports with general recommendations to the General Assembly and direct the attention of other UN organs and agencies to problems identified in the report. The intention is that these organs and agencies take international measures aimed at contributing to the efficient and gradual implementation of the Covenant, for example through technical assistance. Initially three groups of articles in the Covenant had to be reported on alternately every two years (Articles 6–9, 10–12 and 13–15, respectively), resulting in a cycle of six years. At the end of 1978 only 24 of the by then 58 participating states had done this. A Sessional Working Group of 15 government representatives from the five regional groups in the UN was then charged with the monitoring. The composition of this group was changed in 1981, as the representatives did not always have sufficient expertise. From then on the Working Group was made up of government experts. An evaluation of the Working Group by ECOSOC in 1985 revealed that their ties with governments were an obstacle to independent discussion, as their debates were 'politicized' and superficial. The analyses continued to be limited to the policy and legal measures that had been taken and gave little idea of the actual implementation. The Working Group was therefore replaced in 1986 by the *Committee on Economic, Social and Cultural Rights*, consisting of 18 independent experts acting in a personal capacity. To gain better insight into the working of the Covenant, the Committee regularly discusses a specific right. In 1989 and 1990 for instance Article 11 and the right to an adequate standard of living were highlighted. The Committee's method of working is energetic and dynamic, aimed at giving actual substance to its mandate. In contrast to this, not all states fulfil their obligations or submit reports. The three-phased report procedure was replaced in 1988 by a single phase, which requires a report on all 15 articles every five years. This prevents fragmentation and lightens the workload of the states. In 1990 the Committee formulated new directives, which are geared more towards the practical situation than towards the regulations. Besides being more specific, more detailed and more extensive, the directives contain more questions.

Complaints by individuals and groups

The complaints regulations of the UN are limited in scope, as states have to sign a special protocol on this and the competence of the related commissions is limited. The International Covenant on Civil and Political Rights has a complaints procedure between states. Individuals can also complain about their own state, provided it has signed the relevant Optional Protocol. Between 1977 and the end of 1990 the Committee received 419 complaints from individuals about violations of the Covenant. In 112 cases the Committee made a judgement, 118 proved to be non-admissible, 65 were withdrawn and the remainder was still being dealt with. In practice member states take notice of the judgement of the Committee. Although the procedure of the Committee is significantly weaker than that of the Convention for the Protection of Human Rights and Fundamental Freedoms of the Council of Europe (see below), this UN process can provide a solution in some cases after a rejection by the Council of Europe. Sometimes the UN procedure is even preferable, as it protects certain rights that the Council of Europe Convention does not. Owing to pressure from NGOs the number of complaints procedures increased. For instance, a complaints measure via an Optional Protocol was introduced in 1999 for the 1979 Convention on the Elimination of Discrimination against Women.

33.5 Regional human rights conventions in Europe, the Americas and Africa

The European Convention on Human Rights (1950)

At the Council of Europe in Strasbourg (see Figure 23.1) classical human rights are laid down in its 1950 Convention on Human Rights and the economic and social rights in the 1961 European Social Charter. The *European Convention for the Protection of Human Rights and Fundamental Freedoms* is the most important of all the 200 conventions drawn up by the Council of Europe. Signed on 4 November 1950, it entered into force on 3 September 1953 and since then 14 additional Protocols have been introduced. These gave additional rights to those protected by the Convention and changed the Convention's machinery (Protocols 2, 3, 5, 8, 9 and 10, which were superseded by Protocol 11, and 14). Protocol 6 (1983), for example, deals with the abolition of the death penalty and Protocol 9 (1990) makes it possible for individual citizens, NGOs or groups of individuals to submit a case to the European Court of Human Rights. The gradual increase in rights and procedures meant a lasting enhancement of the regime. The unexpected driving force behind this expansion proved to be the Parliamentary Assembly of the Council of Europe (Lovecy 2004). The Convention is not a regionally-adapted version of the Universal Declaration of the UN, as it sets out the universal civil and political human rights. Although the Universal Declaration covers more rights, the European Convention, which was inspired by the Declaration, goes further, because the European states were prepared to defer to an international judicial authority. Globally this had not been possible since the Second World War, owing to the rift between West and East. In Western Europe, however, consensus was reached between states with similar political and social experiences that were more or less of the same cultural and judicial inclination and moreover were supported by broad sections of the population (Donnelly 1986, 623).

The European Commission of Human Rights

Two independent organs, composed of the same number of members as there were member states, were responsible for the implementation of and compliance with the European Convention. These were the European Commission of Human Rights, from 1954, and the European Court of Human Rights, from 1959. The Committee of Ministers also played a role in the original procedure. At the *European Commission of Human Rights* both states and individuals could lodge complaints about violations of the Convention by a state. States explicitly had to declare their agreement to this unprecedented individual right to complain, which came into force in 1955. The first thing the Commission did was to investigate whether a complaint could be accepted. It declared less than five per cent of the complaints submitted by individuals to be admissible, hence it was actually functioning as a filter. Once accepted, the Commission investigated the facts and tried to reach an amicable settlement. If that was not possible it gave its judgement in a detailed report, which was sent to the Committee of Ministers and the states involved. The latter had to keep this report confidential.

The European Court of Human Rights

During the following three months the Commission or the state in question could submit the case to the *European Court of Human Rights*. Individuals could not do this until Protocol 9 came into effect in 1994. Once the case had been submitted to the Court, however, individual citizens or their lawyers could also play a role before 1994. The rule was that the decisions of the Court were binding and there was no possibility of appeal. It was up to the Committee of Ministers to ensure that the decision of the Court was implemented, for example by a change in the law. If a case was not submitted to the European Court, the Committee made a decision on whether the Convention had been violated and what the state in question must do about it. Here too the decisions were binding. In the period up to the end of 1989 there were 11 inter-state procedures and the European Commission of Human Rights made 14,241 decisions on individual complaints. Of these 670 were declared admissible, 84 of the completed cases (a number were still in progress) concluded in an amicable settlement and in 355 cases a report was submitted to the Committee of Ministers. One or more violations were confirmed in two-thirds of the 151 completed cases submitted to the Court (Council of Europe 1991, 34–45). The strength of this regime lay in its strict norms and procedures and in the high level of acceptance (Donnelly 1986).

The permanent European Court of Human Rights (1998)

Because of the huge number of complaints and the Eastern European states becoming members of the Council of Europe after the fall of the Berlin Wall in 1989, the Council decided to establish a permanent European Court of Human Rights. In October 1993 the Council of Europe convened its first summit conference in Vienna, thereby confirming its Pan-European dimension. In addition to human rights, its priorities included the protection of national minorities and combating racism and xenophobia. The Council of Europe decided to revise the monitoring mechanism of its Convention on Human Rights and to combine the Commission and the Court. In 1994 the Committee of Ministers presented an 11th Protocol to the Convention, which simplified and strengthened the procedures and entered into force on 1 November 1998. The new *European Court of Human Rights* replaced three other organs: the European Commission of Human Rights, the old Court and the Committee of Ministers. It was responsible for the entire procedure from preparation to judgement, but the European Commission would finish the uncompleted cases it was dealing with. One of the biggest problems for both the old and the new Court has been the heavy workload. The number of cases submitted rose from 5,979 in 1998 to 13,858 in 2001. A steering group was set up to reduce the workload and in 2004 the Council of Europe adopted Protocol 14 to improve the efficiency of the Court's operation. In 1999 the Council appointed a *Commissioner for Human Rights*, who was given the tasks of promoting education and awareness and of supervising the monitoring mechanism. The Council also adopted the *European Convention for the Prevention of Torture* that came into effect in 1989 and a *Framework Convention for the Protection of National Minorities* that entered into force in 1998.

The European Social Charter (1961) as a political compromise

The *European Social Charter* (1961) and the *European Code on Social Security* (1964) are part of the human rights regime of the Council of Europe, but they are significantly weaker than the 1950 Convention. The member states at the time did not agree on the implementation of social rights and hence on their inclusion in the Convention on Human Rights. Their hesitation was linked to the fact that basic social rights were mostly not incorporated in constitutions and that the socio-economic systems and regulations differed considerably from state to state. Agreement within the framework of the 1950 Convention could only be reached on the issues of forced labour, the right of association and non-discrimination. The Secretariat of the Council of Europe, however, instigated a discussion on a 'social charter' after the Convention had come into effect in 1953. The Committee on Social Questions of the Parliamentary Assembly took the initiative with a draft charter, but the Committee on Economic Questions thought his went too far. In a second draft the Committee on Social Questions came out stronger with regard to principles, but had to concede that implementation would not be entrusted to the European Economic and Social Council it had envisaged, but to the existing Social Committee (the permanent government experts of the Council of Ministers). No agreement was reached on this draft, so a third draft was prepared which proposed a European Commissioner for Social Affairs and a European Social Chamber. The obvious aspirations of the Parliamentary Assembly for real 'European social standards' went further than the Committee of Ministers wanted, which took control and asked its Social Committee (the government experts) to work on a social charter. They did not consider this to be a binding treaty, but rather a declaratory instrument confined to general principles. Although the ministers gave some guidance, taking into account the ideas of the Parliamentary Assembly, the result achieved by the government experts was in 'a much less progressive spirit' than the 'far reaching and idealistic view' of the drafts of the Parliamentary Assembly (Council of Europe 1991, 12–13). The draft charter was submitted for advice at the end of 1958 to a tripartite conference in Strasbourg, convened by the ILO at the request of the Council of Europe in order to enable the trade unions and employers to express their opinions. This conference emphasized that all states should accept core obligations. On the initiative of the trade unions amendments were made, extending the draft to include the right to strike and a policy directed at full employment. The Parliamentary Assembly considered the amendments of the tripartite conference to be important, but in its advice it remained close to the original draft of the government experts, as it did not want to cause any further delay and aimed for as many ratifications as possible. The vision of the government experts was therefore dominant in the compromise that was eventually adopted in October 1961.

Restrictions and improvements of the European Social Charter

There were some practical restrictions on the standards mentioned in the European Social Charter. States do not have to ratify all the provisions but only a minimum of five out of seven core rights (the so-called compulsory core) and in addition they may select further provisions on the condition that they are bound by no fewer than ten articles or 45 numbered paragraphs. This arrangement did result in more ratifications, but it also eroded the value of the standards. Article 31 includes another escape clause, as it gives member states the opportunity to apply restrictions which 'are necessary in a democratic society for the protection of the rights and freedoms of others or for the protection of public interest, national security, public health, or morals'. The rights themselves were formulated somewhat flexibly and were diverse in character, varying from rights for both individuals and collectivities to state obligations on organizational measures and specific policies. Whereas the 1950 Convention on Human Rights gave everyone rights, the 1961 Charter only applied to citizens. Some of the articles of the Charter pertained to all citizens, some, however, to workers and employers and some to workers only. That states were unwilling to fulfil the obligations of the European Social Charter adequately was not so much due to the content of the articles, but rather to its weak monitoring procedure. Monitoring was a matter for the government representatives and it was difficult to expect them to cooperate in condemning their own state. Monitoring the observance of the conditions agreed in the Charter was in the form of reporting, in which the members of the Governmental Committee, which consisted of national civil servants, in fact played a double role. As national civil servants they had been involved in writing the biennial reports and as members of the Governmental Committee they monitored their 'own work' and were involved in the interpretation of this international agreement. Consequently, for a long time the Governmental Committee did not submit any conclusions on non-compliance to the Committee of Ministers. This only changed after the nineteenth round of monitoring in 1985–86. At the conference of ministers of the Council of Europe on human rights in Rome in November 1990, secretary general Marcelino Oreja openly spoke out in favour of a better monitoring mechanism for the Charter. If this was to properly complement the Convention on Human Rights a new stimulus was necessary and the ministers therefore established a commission to suggest improvements. On the 30th anniversary of the Charter in 1991 they wanted to give a favourable impression, but they were also under pressure from the European Community, which had accepted the *Charter of Fundamental Social Rights* in December 1989 to highlight the social dimension in the process of creating a single market (see §43.1). In January 1991 human rights NGOs pressed for substantial improvements to the European Social Charter and supported a detailed proposal by the International Commission of Jurists. This led to a revised version of the Charter in 1996, which came into force in 1999 and is gradually replacing the 1961 Charter. It has a stronger monitoring procedure, with the Governmental Committee being assisted by observers representing employers' organizations and trade unions. A 1995 Protocol that became effective in 1998 established a collective complaints procedure for employers' organizations, trade unions and NGOs.

The Council of Europe and other IGOs

The Council of Europe's image profited from its strong human rights regime. This was the inspiration behind that of the Organization of American States (see below) and itself profited from the work in the field of human rights of the Conference on Security and Cooperation in Europe between 1972 and 1989 (see §24.3). For a long time the Council of Europe overshadowed the European Community, which itself did not have regulations on human rights: the preamble of the 1986 Single European Act referred to the European Convention on Human Rights and the European Social Charter of the Council of Europe. But in 1989 the European Community presented its own Charter of Fundamental Social Rights, while the *Charter of Fundamental Rights* which the European Union adopted in Nice in December 2001 is based on the common values of the EU member states and on those expressed in other international conventions, including those of the Council of Europe. It is difficult to compare the effect of this EU Charter and the 1989 Charter of Fundamental Social Rights to the conventions with monitoring mechanisms of the Council of Europe. The EU Charter of Fundamental Rights was announced a second time in December 2007 in the Treaty of Lisbon (see Figure 43.3), this time in a more binding way through the insertion of a clause in the Treaty which conferred on the Charter the same legal value as the EU Treaties have. However, the Treaty of Lisbon has not yet come into force in 2008.

The American Convention of Human Rights (1969)

Like the Council of Europe, the Organization of American States (OAS) is a culturally-determined continental regional organization (see Figure 23.4). Shortly before the UN Universal Declaration of 1948 the OAS adopted the *American Declaration of the Rights and Duties of Man*. This was followed in 1969 by the *American Convention on Human Rights*, which was inspired by the Council of Europe's Convention, and in 1988 by the *Additional Protocol in the Area of Economic, Social and Cultural Rights*. Although inspired by the European Convention, the American Convention is less far reaching. The task of the *Inter-American Commission on Human Rights* is to promote the preservation and protection of human rights and to advise the OAS on this. Regarding the promotion of democracy, the secretary general of the OAS can send civil missions to monitor elections at the express request of governments. This happened, for example, in Nicaragua, Haiti, El Salvador, Surinam and Paraguay. It is also possible to send OAS observers to areas of tension. The organization sometimes expresses an opinion on political developments, as in 1991 in Haiti. In 1985 the OAS adopted the *Inter-American Convention to Prevent and Punish Torture*.

Organizational dynamics of the OAS

The OAS developed its own monitoring mechanisms, with the dynamics of human rights being greater than expected. The *Inter-American Commission on Human Rights* was established in 1959 as an 'autonomous unit' within the OAS. It 'has vigorously exploited this autonomy, especially in the 1970s and 1980s, in the face of strongly resistant states'. The Commission makes decisions and drafts resolutions 'arising from individual communications from more than 20 countries in the region, including the United States. Country Reports documenting particularly serious human rights situations in more than a dozen countries have been issued, usually followed up by renewed and intensified monitoring. The Commission has also adopted special resolutions on major regional problems, such as states of siege' (Donnelly 2003, 142). The Commission can act independently because its members are chosen in a personal capacity and form more of a technical, quasi-judicial unit than a political body. Two other factors that explain the dynamics are the widespread, abstract starting point in the Western Hemisphere that the liberal-democratic state is the legitimate state and the relative disinterest of the US. The US does set limits on what happens, but sometimes it is not interested and sometimes it is. 'Very little happens in the OAS that is strongly opposed by the United States. More positively, the US on occasion has used the OAS to push for such things as the American Declaration, diplomatic pressure against particular rights-violating governments at particular times, and more recently the OAS supervision of elections in places like Central America' (Forsythe 2000, 129). After the 1969 American Convention on Human Rights came into force, the *Inter-American Court of Human Rights* was established in 1979 in San José, Costa Rica.

This 'may take binding enforcement action, although its adjudicatory jurisdiction is optional. The Court may also issue advisory opinions requested by members of the Organization of American States' (Donnelly 2003, 141–42).

The African Charter on Human and Peoples' Rights (1981)

In 1981 the Organization of African Unity (OAU, see Figure 28.1) adopted the *Charter of Banjul*, or to give it its proper name, *The African Charter on Human and Peoples' Rights*. It was drawn up in Banjul, Gambia, and was an African initiative. It added collective rights, such as those of 'peoples', to the existing regulations, with the right to peace and the right to development. Individual obligations have an important position in this Charter. But 'the substantive guarantees are narrower or more subject to state discretion than in other international human rights regimes' (Donnelly 2003, 143). The *African Commission on Human and Peoples' Rights* can deal with interstate and private complaints. The activities of this Commission, however, are 'severely hampered by woefully inadequate administrative resources and a requirement of complete confidentiality until an investigation has been completed'. This resulted in little of substance being achieved, although the existence of the Commission did stimulate the development of local and regional human rights NGOs (Donnelly 2003, 144).

The Arab Charter (2004)

The League of Arab States drew up the *Arab Charter on Human Rights* in 1994, which provided for the establishment of a committee of experts to look at reports from states. This version of the Charter could not be implemented, as there were insufficient ratifications. Negotiations in May 2004 led to a new version, which entered into force on 15 March 2008 after seven ratifications and provoked tension by equating Zionism with racism.

International organizations in the 1980s

The Cold War intensifies and neoliberalism replaces Keynesianism

Part XIII deals with the period in which the US, led by President Reagan, intensified the Cold War and restricted the room for manoeuvre of the UN and its peacekeeping regime (Chapter 34). Reagan introduced an economic policy based on neoliberalism, the Third World suffered a debt crisis and the IMF and IBRD introduced their structural adjustment policy. This strengthened the position of the IMF, ended the IBRD's struggle against poverty and had the effect of the Third World ultimately paying more money to the two organizations than they received (Chapter 35). The Cold War ended with the fall of the Berlin Wall. This was accompanied by multilateral treaties on arms control and reduction and the institutionalization of the Conference on Security and Cooperation in Europe. The Warsaw Pact came to an end, but NATO did not. International financial institutions guided the transformation process of former communist states (Chapter 36).

US President Reagan intensifies the Cold War

34.1 The end of the 1970s, the end of the UN peacekeeping regime?

Centres of conflict

Despite the success of the arms control agreements between East and West in the 1960s and 1970s (see §24.2–3), conflicts arose in the second half of the 1970s that would develop into serious confrontations in the 1980s. The UN and other international organizations were closely involved, but could exert little influence as from 1981 they were faced with a US government led by President Ronald Reagan, who played a personal role in these conflicts, and from 1979 with the invasion of Afghanistan by the Soviet Union. Despite peaceful coexistence and détente in the 1970s, the Cold War continued to influence the hostilities. The most important centres of conflict were in Central America (Nicaragua, El Salvador and Guatemala), Asia (East Timor, Cambodia and Afghanistan), the Middle East (the Israeli–Palestinian conflict and the war between Iraq and Iran) and Southern Africa (Angola).

Central America: victory of the left in Nicaragua (1979)

With regard to Latin America the US continued to fear that others would follow the example of Fidel Castro's success in Cuba, helped by the ideological and material support for left-wing movements provided by the Soviet Union and Cuba. That Che Guevara had 'exported' the Cuban revolution to Latin America in 1965 and become a cult figure after his execution in 1967 contributed to this anxiety. American fears were confirmed when left-wing Sandinistas in Nicaragua succeeded in ousting the corrupt and dynastic regime of the dictator Anastasio Somoza in 1979. Somoza supporters fled to Honduras and Costa Rica, where they formed opposition groups, while the Marxist-oriented regime in Nicaragua led by Daniel Ortega gained the support of the Soviet Union and Cuba. These developments affected the neighbouring state of El Salvador, where a military coup in 1979 was followed by civil war, with the Sandinistas supporting the opposition and the US the military government. The huge numbers of refugees increased further because of the instability in Guatemala, where the military had annulled elections in 1982 and had started a campaign against the indigenous Indian population, who were suspected of communist sympathies. In 1978 Venezuela raised the events in Nicaragua at the Security Council, which warned Nicaragua that border incidents with Costa Rica must not violate the territorial integrity of that state. The UN General Assembly condemned the threat to Costa Rica's security and the oppression of the Nicaraguan population and after the victory of the Sandinistas it set up an aid programme for Nicaragua to strengthen the state after years of corruption, despite US protests.

East Timor annexed by Indonesia

The first conflict to emerge in Asia at this time was linked to political changes in Portugal in 1974, where a democratic regime in favour of decolonization replaced the dictatorship. This change in Portuguese policy led to violence in East Timor between the Fretilin movement, striving for independence, and pro-Indonesian groups. The latter asked for help from Indonesia, which sent troops. Portugal no longer had control over developments and asked Australia, Indonesia and the International Red Cross for help. The parties involved and other states in the area informed the Security Council in detail about the situation in December 1975. While the Security Council and the General Assembly stated that Indonesia should withdraw its troops, Indonesia gained more and more control over East Timor and eventually annexed it in 1976, without other states or the UN either wanting or being able to intervene.

Genocide in Cambodia

In the meantime the situation in and around Cambodia deteriorated. Civil war had broken out after intervention by US troops within the framework of the Vietnam War, with the US unsuccessfully supplying the Cambodian government with military support. The new regime of the Khmer Rouge under the leadership of Pol Pot, which took power in 1975 and changed the name of Cambodia in January 1976 to Kampuchea, resulted in large-scale violence, with almost two million Cambodians killed over a period of four years. After continual border conflicts Vietnam decided to invade its neighbouring state, to stop the incursions across the border and the internal violence. In January 1979 Vietnamese troops took the Cambodian capital Phnom Penh, putting an end to Pol Pot's regime. The political situation deteriorated when China came to the aid of the Khmer Rouge, but Vietnam, which had the support of the Soviet Union, quickly drove out the Chinese troops. Because of the involvement of the great powers the Security Council could do little. At the end of 1979 the General Assembly called for Vietnam to withdraw its troops from Cambodia, while the UNHCR, UNICEF and the International Red Cross were involved in the refugee problems and offered humanitarian assistance. Vietnam, however, received no recognition for ending Pol Pot's rule, because it replaced this China-oriented regime with the Moscow-oriented regime of Hun Sen. Cold War relations and lobbying by ASEAN prevented the new government from taking the Cambodian seat at the UN (see §30.3). In 1982 three groups that had formed an opposition front against Hun Sen were allowed to occupy the Cambodian seat as a government-in-exile.

The Soviet invasion of Afghanistan (1979)

The Security Council became directly involved in the events in Afghanistan, which had seen a number of coups in the 1970s. The regime that came to power in 1978 concluded a treaty of friendship with the Soviet Union, but this did not end the internal unrest. The Soviet Union therefore decided in December 1979 to intervene in the formation of the Afghan government and large numbers of Soviet troops entered Afghanistan during a coup on 27 December. China condemned this Soviet action on 31 December in a letter to the Security Council, which, despite the objections of the Soviet Union, debated the issue at length. No fewer than 32 states were invited to attend the meeting. A resolution proposed by Third World states condemning the Soviet military involvement received wide support, but was vetoed by the Soviet Union. Against its wishes the Security Council decided to request an emergency meeting of the General Assembly, which when held passed a resolution demanding the withdrawal of all foreign troops. However, the UN itself could do little. The Soviet Union became increasingly involved in a guerrilla war in Afghanistan that was virtually impossible to win and the US intervened by actively supporting the militant Islamic opposition.

The Israeli–Palestinian conflict

The Middle East remained a scene of confrontation because of the continuing Israeli–Palestinian tensions. After the Yom Kippur War the Security Council in October 1973 had reformed its *UN Emergency Force* as UNEF II (see Figure 22.1) and to create a buffer zone between the Syrian and Israeli troops the Council established the *UN Disengagement Observer Force* (UNDOF) in June 1974 for the area of the Golan Heights. The *UN Interim Force in Lebanon* (UNIFIL) followed in March 1978, after Israel had invaded Lebanon. UNIFIL was to monitor the withdrawal of Israeli troops and the restoration of peace, security and authority in south Lebanon. Despite this Israel invaded Lebanon for a second time in 1982. The conflict also continued to occupy the UN in a different way. In the 1970s and 1980s the UN granted national liberation movements observer status in an attempt to promote decolonization and state building, on the assumption that major liberation movements would form the core of future governments. In November 1974 the General Assembly acknowledged the *Palestine Liberation Organization* (PLO) as the sole representative of the Palestinian people, which gave the Palestinians a recognizable position. However, the 'Zionism is racism' resolution of November 1975, which equated Israel with the racist regimes in Southern Rhodesia and South Africa, sparked heated debates within the UN. The resolution was passed by a large majority and gave the conflict a new ideological connotation.

The war between Iraq and Iran (1980)

The war that broke out between Iraq and Iran in 1980 arose out of Iranian support for the Kurdish minority in the north of Iraq, which had resulted in border conflicts in the 1970s. In 1975 it did briefly appear that both states would settle their differences within the context of OPEC, of which both were members (see Figure 31.1), and they made concessions and agreements. Tensions, however, increased again after the overthrow of the shah in 1979, when the country became the Islamic Republic of Iran under the leadership of Ayatollah Ruholla Khomeini. In 1980 Iraq bombed Iranian airports and

Iran retaliated. The Security Council discussed the situation, but did little more than call for the cessation of hostilities and although secretary-general Kurt Waldheim appointed the Swedish politician Olaf Palme as special envoy the UN was unable to take control of the situation.

Southern Africa: the civil war in Angola

The political changes in Portugal also led to the independence of Angola in 1975. The various liberation organizations made agreements on a transitional government, but fighting very soon broke out between the MPLA (Popular Movement for the Liberation of Angola), supported by the Soviet Union, and UNITA (National Union for the Total Independence of Angola). International relations played a role, as the MPLA had Cuban military help, while UNITA and other groups were reinforced by troops from South Africa. In 1976 the MPLA government was recognized by the Organization of African Unity and the UN. UNITA's resistance continued, however, and it retained the support of South Africa and also gained that of the US. The situation became complicated when SWAPO (South West Africa People's Organisation) from Namibia sought refuge, with the MPLA's approval, in the south of Angola and carried out guerrilla activities inside Namibia from there. The UN could do little, owing to the opposing positions of the US and the Third World. The US attempted to involve South Africa in finding solutions, but the Third World objected to this state because of apartheid, the Namibia issue and its involvement in Angola. Once again there was a regional conflict in which Cold War relations played a role and for which the UN had no solution.

Weakening of the UN peacekeeping regime

It would be possible to question whether the UN peacekeeping regime still existed at the end of the 1970s. The great powers did not demonstrate effective leadership in the centres of conflict and the UN and regional organizations had barely any leeway to pursue a policy. Moreover, between 1978 and 1988 the UN did not establish any new peacekeeping missions. An investigation of the peacekeeping regime in about 1980 concluded that no fundamental changes had occurred in its principles, rules and decision-making procedures, but that the regime itself had lost coherence. 'Universality of membership became a source of discontent as it was extended de facto to the Palestine Liberation Organization and the South West African People's Organization; the watered-down domestic jurisdiction norm was applied asymmetrically to burden colonial and right-wing governments; its further extension to human rights concerns was aimed mostly at Israel and South Africa. The Security Council continued to be sidestepped on occasion, primarily to restrain Israel, South Africa, and white-ruled Rhodesia. Earlier adaptations were not used when Indonesia conquered Timor, China attacked Vietnam, Vietnam invaded Kampuchea, Iraq moved into Iran, India aided secessionist Bangladesh, and several Middle East countries fuelled the civil wars in Eritrea and Chad' (Haas 1983, 226–27). One of the explanations for this diminishing of coherence was the emergence of the non-aligned countries. It was not only their numerical increase that influenced decision making within the UN, but also the fact that various Latin American and African states, which initially had been on its side, had turned their backs on the US. With the decreasing importance of Cold War relations and the decolonization debate, local rivalries had become more prominent. This was a determining factor when non-aligned countries were involved. It was easy for them as a group to present a united front against a common enemy, but that changed when they themselves were directly involved. All these developments caused divisions between the participants in the UN regime of conflict management. 'The norms have not disappeared, the rules remain in effect, and the procedures continue to be used; but the members cannot agree on the circumstances under which they ought to be applied' (Haas 1983, 227–28). The peacekeeping operations in Israel and Lebanon, as more or less independent agencies, had in effect removed themselves from UN procedures and the presence in a state of troops from other continents, such as the Cubans in Angola, was not a subject for discussion within the UN. 'The regime has not died, but it has decayed' (Haas 1983, 228).

34.2 The US and the politicization of the United Nations 1977–85

Politicization as an argument

The weakening of the peacekeeping regime was directly related to the dissatisfaction of the US with the UN's functioning. During the second half of the 1970s the US considered the UN and its specialized agencies to be a problem, as they were 'politicized', especially by the communist and many Third World states. This resulted in the US leaving or suspending its membership of some UN agencies between 1977 and 1985. Politicization had been an issue in the International Labour Organization in the 1950s during the debate on universalism and the membership of communist states (see §21.4). Despite it choosing universalism, the US continued to view the ILO membership of communist states with suspicion. In the 1970s and 1980s a new discussion about the 'politicization' of IGOs developed, with far-reaching consequences for the US. In 1975 it announced that it was withdrawing from the ILO with effect from 1977 (although it rejoined in 1980). Between 1982 and 1983 the US suspended its membership of the IAEA, followed in 1985 by a long-lasting withdrawal from membership of UNESCO. Although political discussions have a place in meetings of international organizations, the introduction of political topics which are not part of the work of those organizations can be regarded as problematic. At the same time it can be true that governments deliberately qualify subjects to which they object as 'politicized', so as to influence relations within the organization.

The US leaves the ILO (1977)

The US objections to the ILO included the appointment of a Soviet representative as assistant director-general in 1970, the condemnation of the Israeli labour policy in the occupied territories in 1974 and the admission of the PLO as an observer at the ILO in 1975. This accumulation of matters that the US found objectionable led to its decision to withdraw from the ILO. The decision was not implemented with enthusiasm, even though there was strong support for withdrawal especially from the trade union federation AFL-CIO, which had heavily influenced US foreign policy. The expectation was that the ILO, when it found that its most important member state was no longer participating, would react by pursuing a policy that was more agreeable to the US. The ILO did indeed implement some reforms that were to the liking of the US, but this was much later (in 1986) and a number of its objections were ignored completely. Meanwhile the US was immediately confronted with a negative effect of its action, because the reduction in ILO staff as a result of the loss of income from the US meant that in practice the proportion of American high officials at the ILO was reduced. In 1980 the US felt forced to rejoin, as further absence would damage its interests too much. Both the ILO and the US appreciated this return, although the announcement on the reasons for the US rejoining was 'a mixture of both sound and naive judgements, some consistent and some, frankly, selective principles' (Imber 1989, 69). The US had attempted to make the ILO follow its policy through bureaucratic control, but its behaviour seemed to have had a beneficial effect on the ILO rather than a punitive one. The US expected the ILO to stay within the limits of the ideology and power relations it prescribed, which in practice proved not to be the case, even when it actually withdrew from the organization. That the situation had reached this stage was also due to the poor relationship between director-general Jenks and the US. In American eyes, Jenks placed too much emphasis on international standardization rather than technical assistance (see §21.3), which it considered unhelpful (Cox 1977, 406–7).

Threatened withdrawal of Poland from the ILO

In the early 1980s the discussion on the politicization of the ILO resurfaced. Lech Walesa's Solidarity trade union and the communist government had signed the Gdansk Agreement in 1980, which permitted independent trade unions. In December 1981, however, Prime Minister Wojciech Jaruzelski declared a state of emergency, which led to a military council for national salvation and an end to liberalization. The Governing Body of the ILO decided in 1983 to establish a commission to investigate the violation of trade union rights in Poland. However, the communist states submitted a memorandum to the ILO, arguing that its monitoring mechanism had gradually become out of date, as it did not take into account the experiences and legal concepts of communist and developing states. Due to the misuse of the mechanism by certain Western states for their own self-interest the ILO functioned as a supranational tribunal, which involved itself in the internal affairs of states and then put them in the dock, according to the memorandum. Poland drew the obvious conclusion from this and announced it would withdraw from the organization at the end of 1984. Domestic changes, however, resulted in Poland increasing the period of notice and then cancelling its withdrawal in 1987. This debate did not reach the stage of unwelcome politicization. The Committee that monitored observance of the freedom of organization (see §21.4) acted reticently and opted for caution.

The US boycotts the IAEA (1982–83)

The admission of many developing states in the 1970s formed the background to the politicization of the International Atomic Energy Agency. It broke the numerical dominance of the industrialized states and played a role in the decision of the General Conference in 1982 to reject the credentials of the Israeli delegation in a vote. The attempt to exclude Israel from the activities of the IAEA and the use of procedural means (voting on credentials) were not received well by the US. Its withdrawal did not mean that it actually intended to leave the organization, although President Reagan did consider this, but rather that boycotting its activities was seen as a means of pressurizing the organization to avoid certain actions. This proved successful, because in 1983 Israel was neither suspended, nor did the General Conference reject the credentials of the Israeli delegation (Imber 1989, 2).

The US leaves UNESCO (1985–2002)

In 1983 the US, following statutory rules, informed the director-general of UNESCO that it would leave the organization on 31 December 1984. Some of the American objections concerned the administration and financial resources of UNESCO, others its 'politiciza-tion', in the sense that parts of the UNESCO programme were concerned with issues that did not fall within its mandate or were founded on preconceptions about the West. This time the US did indeed leave the organization, which resulted in a long-lasting break with UNESCO. When UNESCO was founded it was given a political connota-tion against the political background of fascism and national socialism. At that time many states were not democracies, which meant that through its strong emphasis on promoting democratic principles in line with the ideas of Enlightenment the task of the organization had political overtones. In the 1950s UNESCO began to encourage scientific research in developing states and established the *International Council of Scientific Unions*. By the end of the 1970s it was clear that these attempts had produced few results and that there was virtually no effective link between the researchers, whose work was based on scientific insights, and the politicians in the capital cities who were responsible for the distribution of resources. Within the decision-making organs of UNESCO, and also other IGOs, the delegations had a preference for projects that were politically attractive, rather than those stemming from research recommendations (Williams 1990, 152). After the accession of many developing states in the 1970s political relations within UNESCO began to over-shadow intellectual matters. This was evident when Arab states, supported by the Soviet Union, introduced anti-Israel resolutions in the General Conference, with the intention of having Israel expelled from the group of European and other states. Furthermore, the director-general of UNESCO was discredited through poor administrative and financial management, including corruption, which could not be discussed due to a majority of states blocking such a debate. There was also disagreement over a 'new information order', which developing states successfully influenced with their ideas about a New Interna-tional Economic Order (see §31.1). These various developments damaged the organization, which had had a good reputation with the public due to its work in education and the restoration of cultural heritage. The departure of the US resulted in a drop in UNESCO's financial resources. The UK and Singapore followed its example, with the UK rejoining in 1996. It was not until 1999 that a new director-general managed to put the budget in order and implement far-reaching reforms, so that the organization was again focusing on objectives on which there was consensus. The US renewed its membership at the end of 2002, with political motives playing a role once more, as the US under President George W. Bush sought to form an international front against Iraq and in that connection wanted to promote human rights, tolerance and education, as Bush explained in the UN General Assembly.

34.3 US President Reagan intensifies the Cold War and puts financial pressure on the UN

From détente to tension

Unlike his predecessors from the 1960s and 1970s, détente and peaceful coexistence were not the main aims of US President Ronald Reagan. When he came to power in 1981 he thought that pressure on the Soviet Union should be increased in various ways. In the military field he did this by increasing the defence expenditure of the US (ultimately by 35 per cent) and by putting forward a plan for a *Strategic Defence Initiative* (SDI, also known as 'star wars') in 1983. The object of this was not *Mutual Assured Destruction* (MAD), it was to prevent Soviet missiles with nuclear weapons being able to reach the US through the building of a 'space shield'. This expensive undertaking would increase the technological lead of the US and challenge the Soviet Union to do the same. It was accompanied by an embargo policy through the COCOM (see Figure 23.3) to prevent the Soviet Union and communist states having access to technology developed in the West. At the same time Reagan supported anticommunist movements in the conflicts that developed at the end of the 1970s (see §34.1). In Afghanistan he provided the opponents of the invading Soviet Union with weapons and in Eastern Europe the independent Polish trade union movement Solidarity received financial support. Reagan supported the opposition forces against the Marxist government in Angola and in Central America he backed the military government in El Salvador, thereby playing a role in the continuing civil war. In Nicaragua he supplied weapons to the Contra rebel movement, which, remarkably, were paid for by the sale of weapons to Iran, a state that had officially been an enemy of the US since its embassy staff had been held hostage there in 1979. When this 'deal' was made public in 1986 it resulted in the *Iran-Contra* scandal. In the same year the International Court of Justice condemned US behaviour in Nicaragua (see §21.1), calling the arming and training of the Contra movement by the US a violation of the non-intervention principle and the laying of mines in the territorial waters of Nicaragua an unlawful misuse of violence. US permanent representative to the UN Jeanne Kirkpatrick showed little respect for the International Court and the US took no notice of the judgement.

The NATO double-track decision (1979)

Reagan's policy of increasing tension in the Cold War also had consequences for the talks between East and West from the late 1970s. The Strategic Arms Limitation Talks between the US and the Soviet Union in 1979 had led to Carter and Brezhnev signing the SALT II agreement in Vienna, with ceilings on and parity of strategic weapons (see §24.3). As a result of the Soviet invasion of Afghanistan at the end of 1979 this agreement was not ratified in 1980, although both powers had declared that they wanted to abide by it. In the meantime a discussion had developed within the North Atlantic Treaty Organization on the modernizing of nuclear weapons by the Soviet Union. It had developed so-called SS-20 missiles that, with a range of 5,000 kilometres, were not covered by the limitations that had been negotiated. The first of these SS-20s were deployed in 1977, which forced NATO to modernize its own medium-range nuclear weapons. In Western Europe in particular this imbalance was seen as a threat to relations between Eastern and Western Europe. NATO decided at the end of 1979 to react in two ways, hence 'double-track decision'. One decision was to modernize NATO's medium-range nuclear weapons by deploying Pershing-II missiles and low-flying cruise missiles that could be directed at specific targets. The US resolved to install 572 modernized nuclear weapons in Western Europe between November 1983 and 1988, replacing the older Pershing-I missiles and therefore not resulting in an increase in the NATO nuclear arsenal. The second decision was at the same time to initiate negotiations with the Soviet Union on weapons with a range of between 1,500 and 5,000 kilometres. It was some time before the Soviet Union was prepared to talk about this, but in November 1981 negations began in Geneva.

Failure of the negotiations in Geneva (1983)

The US had little inclination to make concessions in Geneva. Reagan was prepared to abandon siting Pershing-II and cruise missiles in Western Europe if the Soviet Union dismantled its SS-20, SS-5 and SS-4 missiles. He conveyed this 'zero option' in a personal message to Soviet leader Brezhnev, but without it achieving results in Geneva. At the beginning of 1983 Reagan proposed limiting the number of missiles on both sides. Brezhnev's successor Yuri Andropov was prepared to limit the Soviet missiles to the number held jointly by France and the UK, but the US did not want to include the French and British weapons in the agreement. Tension increased as the date when the US was to deploy the first missiles approached, but concessions remained too small for agreement to be reached. On the day after the German parliament had voted in favour of the siting of Pershing-II missiles in the Federal Republic, 23 November 1983, the Soviet Union broke off the talks in Geneva. On 8 December it left the *Strategic Arms Reduction Talks* (START), the continuation of the SALT discussions of 1982 under a slightly different name, and on 15 December the Soviet Union also refused to set a new date for the *Mutual and Balanced Force Reductions* (MBFR) talks between NATO and the Warsaw Pact on the limitation of forces in Central Europe. For the time being there were no further negotiations between the two great powers and their alliances.

The UN under financial pressure (1985–86)

Midway through the 1980s US dissatisfaction with the UN manifested itself in the American attitude towards the politicization of the organization. 'Washington scorned the UN and cast it aside as a bastion of Third World nationalism and procommunism. The UN's peacekeeping operations were tarred with the same brush' (Weiss *et al.* 1994, 56). Even the contribution to the action stimulated by the US itself as part of UNIFIL was not paid. After Israel's war against Lebanon the US in 1982 had provided troops for a multilateral force under a restricted UN mandate to evacuate the PLO from Beirut. It had sent further troops after the bloodbaths in Sabra and Shatila, but shortly after the US headquarters in Beirut were blown up in October 1983, killing 241 American marines, Reagan withdrew all US troops from Lebanon. Two days later the US invaded Grenada. Through this action Reagan wanted to make clear that communism in the Third World would be repelled immediately. 'Intervening in Grenada, bombing Libya, and supporting insurgencies in Nicaragua, Angola, Afghanistan, and Cambodia attested Washington's preferences' (Weiss *et al.* 1994, 56). The Soviet Union was equally active and hence Central America, the Horn of Africa, Southern Africa and parts of South and East Asia became combat zones in a renewed Cold War. The lack of US cooperation with the UN reached an all-time low in 1985–86, when the US refused to pay its contributions. In the summer of 1985 the Senate passed the Kassebaum amendment, named after Senator Nancy Kassebaum, which would reduce the US contribution from 25 to 20 per cent of the UN budget if the General Assembly refused to apply the principle of weighted voting in votes on budget proposals.

Financial pressure and reforms

As a result of US policy the UN was in crisis, because the US provided the UN with little political and financial leeway and pressed for reorganization. In December 1985 a group of 18 experts was set up to investigate the UN, with a view to introducing reforms and improving efficiency. The group made 71 recommendations in August 1986, which the General Assembly approved in December. This resulted in reforms which were necessary for financial reasons, if nothing else, with more control over expenditure and ceilings on additional expenses. Although not all of the American demands were met, the US showed itself satisfied with the results achieved and began to contribute again. It did not, however, abandon its critical stance and stated that it would again take action if the UN did not try to reach consensus on budgetary matters. Because of its reduced income the UN could not avoid taking economy measures, such as not taking on new staff, reducing the Secretariat and restricting travel expenses and meetings.

Reagonomics, the debt crisis in the South and the structural adjustment programmes of the IMF

'Look guys, I don't like taxes, I don't like inflation, I don't like the Russians. Work something up.'
Ronald Reagan to his economic advisers when he took office

35.1 Reagonomics and the new relationship between the G7, IMF and OECD

From Keynes to Hayek and Friedman

The international monetary policy of the US remained largely unpredictable despite the formation of the G7 in 1975 (see §27.3). However, at the G7 summits in the late 1970s President Jimmy Carter defended a policy of multilateral cooperation between the US, Western Europe and Japan, referred to as trilaterism. He expected that, given their balance of payments surpluses, Western Europe and Japan would pursue an expansionist policy to boost economic growth, the so-called 'locomotive function'. Carter proved to be the first postwar president who was prepared to subordinate domestic economic policy to international monetary considerations. At the end of 1978 he followed a restrictive monetary policy to bring high inflation and interest rates under control. He reserved money to be able to intervene actively in the currency market and liberalized the sale of American gold (Spero 1985, 71). Until the mid-1980s, the G7 summit in Bonn in 1978 was the only meeting where real agreements were made, when it was decided that Germany would increase government spending and the US would take anti-inflation measures. According to monetarist economists, however, this high inflation was fanned by the Keynesian policy pursued up to this point, because this would have overstimulated spending. When Ronald Reagan became president in 1981 the monetarist economic school gained the upper hand over Keynes and Galbraith, while in the UK Prime Minister Margaret Thatcher strongly believed in the ideas of the Austrian economist Friedrich von Hayek, who wanted to restrict the role of the state to maintaining the rule of law and defended a return to classical free-market capitalism. Hayek thus contributed to a paradigmatic shift away from the dominant interventionist Keynesian policies. According to the American economist Milton Friedman the increased government influence on the economy was an obstacle to economic development. Like Hayek he argued that the role of government should be subordinate to that of the market ('less government, more market') and that the growth in money supply should be curbed by restricting credit. The government needed to follow a monetary policy of manipulating the available amounts of money to further the optimal working of the market.

Reagonomics and globalization

President Reagan then introduced an economic policy based on Friedman's ideas, aimed at smaller government that would stimulate the free market economy and reduce taxation. He was an advocate of a supply-side economy, which would foster economic growth. If entrepreneurs could produce goods in more favourable conditions, then sales would increase. Simultaneously Reagan showed himself to be in favour of high public expenditure on defence. His Strategic Defence Initiative (SDI) was intended to stimulate technological development and at the same time challenge the Soviet Union. Reagan preferred to leave the value of the dollar to the market, a policy that would become dominant in the international economy and the international economic organizations controlled by the US. His policy put the terms of employment of workers and the power of the trade unions, or in general terms social security and the welfare state, under pressure. 'Reagonomics' would play a role in all relations: North–South, East–West and also West–West, that is between the industrialized states, and became the core of the *globalization process* that the economy underwent, characterized by a continuing internationalization, the strengthening of free trade, a stronger interdependence and, after the end of the Cold War, the enlargement of the world market due to the collapse of the communist world and the transformation of communist into capitalist states. Reagonomics was also central to the management of the international economy by IGOs such as the IMF, OECD and GATT, and the summits of the G7.

IMF versus OECD

Reagan's new policy resulted in monetary management reappearing on the G7's agenda. Many states and individuals saw the globalization that was taking place as a threat. At the 1982 summit in Versailles the other members of the G7 criticized the one-sided monetary position of the US and in both 1982 and 1983 the G7 insisted on more cooperation between the US and the IMF. The G7 agreed in 1982 that the G5 ministers of finance would become involved in the multilateral surveillance of the balance of payments and exchange rate policies of states, with the managing director of the IMF present in a personal capacity. The secretary-general of the OECD, Emile van Lennep, asked the

Americans to explain why the G5 and the IMF managing director had been chosen to do this and not the more obvious Working Party 3 (WP3) of his organization and the G10 (see §27.3). He was told that the US considered the OECD to be too Keynesian and too much in favour of government regulation. Now that the IMF, due to this surveillance role, had acquired a function in combination with the G7, Van Lennep was intent on a countermove. He found an ally in the French finance minister Jacques Delors, who was annoyed that the US primarily regarded OECD ministerial meetings as preparations for G7 summits. He proposed holding a separate OECD meeting which would be timed not to connect with the summits, but which was to work on a new global policy. Delors considered it necessary to achieve consensus on international policy, as neither Keynesianism nor the laissez-faire thinking of Reagan's supply-side economy offered any prospect of a collective international monetary and economic policy. At the OECD meeting that took place in February 1984 Delors succeeded in establishing a new consensus on the policy to be pursued, with flexibility of the labour, commodity and capital markets, more room for the private sector rather than government aid and the restriction of social taxes as core elements. After the meeting even the US, which had previously spoken scornfully about 'that Delors meeting', had to admit that there was agreement again among the industrialized states on the fundamentals of global policy. The OECD was thus 'back' in the international sphere of influence, albeit it was in a weaker position than before and was still used as a preparatory phase for the G7 summits.

Change of paradigm in the economy

Between the 1978 G7 summit in Bonn and the 1984 Delors meeting a paradigmatic change occurred in the economy. While the Bonn summit was still based on internationally-coordinated Keynesian fine-tuning, at the subsequent summits there was little more than policy convergence. During that period Keynesianism, with its intervention from above, was replaced by a mixture of ideas about monetarism, balanced budgets, a strengthening of the supply side of the economy and an improvement in the labour market through, for example, more compatibility between education and training courses and the market's needs. This was a somewhat eclectic totality of ideas and therefore the consensus Delors achieved in 1984 was important.

35.2 The Brandt Reports and the debt crisis in the South from 1982

A new life for the North–South Dialogue?

The Independent Commission on International Development Issues, led by the former German Chancellor Willy Brandt, endeavoured in the late 1970s to inject new life into the North–South Dialogue (see §31.2). This Commission, set up on the initiative of IBRD president Robert McNamara and the Netherlands, proposed an integrated approach to problems such as dependency, overpopulation, the environment, the arms race and the negative effects of globalization. After two years of discussions and study the Commission issued the report *North–South: A Programme for Survival* in 1980, followed in 1982 by *Common Crisis North–South: Cooperation for World Recovery*. These 'Brandt Reports' exposed the unequal position of the South and included measures to counter poverty, reform the existing international order, modify the monetary system and place the states from the South in a better position in international decision making. The underlying assumption of these reports, which partly repeated arguments from earlier debates and appealed to governments and public opinion in the rich industrialized states, was that cooperation in an increasingly interdependent world could help solve global problems and facilitate the specific needs of the Third World. However, by being an expression of international Keynesian liberalism the Brandt Reports went against the spirit of Reagonomics, which meant that there was little chance of the proposed measures being implemented.

Enlightened self-interest

The Third World itself was also critical of the Brandt Reports. Developing states considered the advocated reforms and generosity as, at very best, 'enlightened self-interest' from the North and described them as correct in an abstract sense, but based on the wrong premise of the North and the South sharing common interests in tackling the poverty issue. In reality there were too many differences to be able to assume this. A few companies might be interested in expanding the market in the South, but the conditions the rich states had imposed on the developing states through development aid in fact restricted incomes and hence also the demand for imports from the North. It was possible that parts of the North would indeed like to see higher incomes in the South, but its protectionist measures, which were an obstacle to the export of agricultural products by the South, also showed that the interests of North and South were not always the same. The Brandt Commission, composed of reformist-inclined but still capitalist politicians, took too little notice of the political dimension of the differences between North and South. These 'abstract and utopian expressions of aristocratic good will' therefore created illusions about the possible effectiveness of a North–South Dialogue (Hadjor 1993, 56–57).

The debt crisis of 1982

The debt crisis in the South provided an even harsher judgement of the Brandt Reports than the Third World gave in words. The term 'debt crisis' refers to the collective debt of the Third World, which was rising to such an extent that in 1982 developing states were unable to repay the industrialized states and the international financial institutions. This debt rose from 100 billion dollars in 1970 to 850 billion in 1982 and 1,300 billion in 1990. The financial problem began with the oil crisis of 1973, when the higher oil prices upset the balance of payments of many states and the oil-exporting states channelled the extra dollars they had obtained through private banks back into the international monetary circuit. The deficits of states could be financed with these 'oil dollars'. As a consequence of the high oil prices and the resulting higher prices of products, however, the non-oil-exporting states in the South could not cover the deficits themselves and had to make use of development cooperation in the form of soft loans from the IBRD and IMF or borrow from private banks. Because of the oil dollars the private banks' terms were more favourable than those of the IMF and IBRD and more than half of the deficits were covered through loans from private banks. In 1982 a new debt crisis occurred as a result of the many loans that had been arranged and the economic recession after the second oil crisis in 1979. This second oil crisis resulted in the North importing less, although the South had more goods available as it needed to increase its exports because of its debts. Since the exchange rate of the dollar and interest rates had gone up, states in the South saw their exports declining, their terms of exchange deteriorating and the interest they owed increasing, which meant that the approaching debt crisis was predictable. Mexico was the first state to announce in 1982 that it could no longer meet its repayment obligations.

Mexico bankrupt (1982)

The US began to pay more attention to global financial stability in solving this debt crisis as a result of Mexico's problems, because US banks had huge interests there. The IMF rushed to Mexico's aid so that it could repay its debts again, but this was at a high domestic price. 'Mexico' then became the quintessential example of crisis solution, as advocated by the IMF in the 1980s. Basically this involved either the states that were interested parties or the Bank for International Settlements coming to the immediate assistance of a state in difficulty. Once the crisis was averted the state made an agreement with the IMF on repayment and possible new private loans. The vital point of this agreement from the IMF's point of view was a vigorous programme of domestic economy measures. It considered the chance for a government to introduce and implement the tough policy measures necessary to be able to make the repayments as more important than the amount of money it provided. This 'reorganization' of the domestic economy was an adjustment of international economic policy in line with the basic ideas of Reagonomics (less government, more market) and brought with it the expectation that the state's economy would then grow and thus enable the state to repay its debts. If the state was unable or unwilling to comply due to domestic political considerations, then the IMF would stop its contribution (Spero 1985, 82).

35.3 The structural adjustment programmes of the IMF and IBRD and their consequences

Overambitious

The interventions of the IMF in the structural difficulties of developing states in the early 1980s were overambitious, given the scale of the problems. By 1985 it was evident that the policy had not resulted in the success hoped for, due to the rising exchange rate of the dollar, the fall in the price of Latin American exports, the flight of capital and the protectionist measures of the industrialized states. Moreover, the IMF adjustment policy had far-reaching consequences in domestic affairs, such as economy measures, unemployment, wage cuts and an increase in social differences. While Mexico, Chile and Uruguay persevered with the IMF policy, political considerations in states returning to democracy, such as Argentina and Brazil, reduced the will to continue with the structural programmes. To end the problems US Secretary of the Treasury James Baker put forward a plan.

Baker's initiative for a new policy

At the end of 1985 Baker introduced the *Adjustment for Growth* initiative to resolve the situation in which the economic environment slowed down growth, or pushed it into decline, in developing states. To achieve this he adopted a 1979 IBRD idea for structural adjustment, the so-called *Sectoral Adjustment Loans* (in jargon: SECALs), which were meant to facilitate the purchase of foreign goods in particular sectors. To ensure that adjustment did in fact take place these IBRD loans were subject to a 'specific monitoring action program'. In his initiative Baker removed the restriction to specific sectors and stipulated that the new programmes had to be set up and monitored by both the IBRD and the IMF. The two institutions accepted Baker's initiative. In 1986 the IMF introduced the *Structural Adjustment Facility* and the IBRD the *Structural Adjustment Loan*, followed in 1987 by the IMF's *Enhanced Structural Adjustment Facility*. However, this initiative did not make any real progress, because the private banks refused to cooperate. The IMF therefore decided to provide extra resources for states that wanted to continue with the IMF adjustment programmes.

Four steps

The *structural adjustment programmes* (SAPs), which resulted from the facilities mentioned above, are set up in four steps. The first step is that a state in a poor economic situation approaches the IMF and the IBRD for substantial financial resources. The second step consists of consultations with both organizations about a structural adjustment of the state's economy. The IMF and IBRD, sometimes separately, sometimes together, then send missions to the state in question to discuss the possible political, economic and monetary responsibilities. If these discussions are successful, the IMF and IBRD draw up a *Policy Framework Paper* (PFP) as the basis for formal negotiations on the adjustment programme. The actual programme is formulated during the third step and comprises a package of measures which define the minimum standards regarding the economy and the monetary policy of the state in question. The IMF and IBRD in fact have a standard package of measures and the details are set down during the talks, leaving governments that are in a weak position as the supplicant party little room for negotiation. The result of this process is a 'structural adjustment programme' that must be approved by the Executive Board of both the IMF and the IBRD. It specifies what resources the state can borrow from the two institutions, as well as the conditions attached. The approval of such a programme is usually a sign for private credit suppliers that it is relatively safe to lend money to the state concerned. The fourth and last step is the implementation of the programme and its monitoring. Specialized UN agencies such as the ILO, UNDP, FAO and UNICEF may be involved in the implementation of the programme, but the IMF and IBRD carry out the annual monitoring.

SAPs more at the centre of the IMF policy

Since the oil crisis in the early 1970s the IMF had not really succeeded in maintaining the stability of exchange rates on a global level, while at regional level the European Monetary System was more successful. While the monetary role of the IMF as a whole thus remained limited, its development role became increasingly important because of the structural adjustment programmes, although this meant that the IMF was actually working in the IBRD's domain. The prominent role of the IMF was due to the fact that it was by far the biggest supplier of credit to the adjustment programmes, as the IBRD had statutory limitations and could not provide more than 20 per cent of its own resources. The IMF's new role did not enhance its image with the developing states: because of the negative effects of the structural adjustment programmes the IMF was mainly seen as a fervent defender of international capitalism. Initially an organization with a monetary role (including the required support mechanisms), the IMF changed into an agency confronted with typical development problems. However, the IMF had neither the correct structure to handle these problems nor the means to act as a development agency. Critics were therefore of the opinion that the IMF should orientate itself on a new monetary role and that it would be better to leave development problems to the World Bank Group and the developing states themselves. In its own interests, however, the IMF was not in favour of this.

The net result: continuing dependency of the South

It was not until 1989 that a new plan was put forward to alleviate the Third World debts, this time by US Secretary of the Treasury Nicholas Brady, who suggested that the IMF should guarantee restructured loans. However, the G7 summit rejected this proposal in the same year with the argument that it did not want to use taxpayers' money to help private banks solve their problems. Due to economic reforms the developing states regained international confidence in the first half of the 1990s, which enabled them to make arrangements with the banks about their debts and to attract new investments. Overall the policy of the IMF and the industrialized states had resulted in a greater and continuing dependency of the developing states, with debts owed to the banks (in Latin America) and to governments and the international financial institutions (in Africa). The saddest aspect of the adjustment policy was that the IMF had to admit by the end of the 1980s that the Northern states as a whole had received more money from the Third World than the IMF had provided for them. 'As a result of the debts the poor are sending resources to the rich' (Hadjor 1993, 92).

Division of labour between the IMF and IBRD under pressure

As a result of the policy pursued by the IMF, the original statutory division of labour between the IMF and IBRD (see §25.2) was less clear from the mid-1980s onwards. The IMF's measures regarding the exchange rate policy formed part of the intervention on the demand side, while the IBRD's measures were part of the supply side. Moreover, IMF policy was aimed at the short term, the IBRD's at the long term. While structural economic adjustment was the task of the IBRD, the IMF, with its monitoring of the implementation of internationally-agreed macro-economic policy and the structural adjustment policy, was increasingly active in the IBRD's domain. The cooperation between the two organizations was therefore not without tensions and made it even more difficult for the IBRD, already wrestling with problems, to function.

The IBRD understands criticism of the SAPs better than the IMF

The IBRD had to look on while the IMF became active in its sphere and, given the strong position of the IMF in the multilateral management of the world economy, even made its mark in it. The IBRD took the censure of the structural adjustment programmes more seriously than the IMF. One criticism was the standardized approach of the SAPs and the inherent assumption that free market principles could be imposed through similar measures on states that had diverse political, economic and social characteristics. A second complaint concerned the assumption that the greatest responsibility for the situations and the solutions that had developed lay with the governments of the states in question, but that in solving the problems private forces worked more efficiently than governments. This ignored the fact that governments also have functions that the private sector is unwilling or unable to fulfil. After some time the IBRD recognized that these government functions are as important for the viability of an economic system in the long term as intervention in the financial market and the infrastructure of a state. A third criticism involved the obsession with exports in the adjustment programmes and the fact that insufficient attention was paid to the limitations of poor states within the international trade system of the GATT, which was dominated by the industrialized states. The fourth problem was the huge social consequences. As a result of the adjustment programmes some social services, which were already less than adequate, were halted. Large parts of the population were plunged into deeper poverty, with access to health care and education, especially for women, deteriorating. The IBRD conceded this point earlier than the IMF and had to acknowledge that its own countermeasures were insufficient to compensate for the negative effects of the SAPs. When drawing up and implementing the programmes the IMF and the IBRD only consulted governments and had no contact with NGOs or other private organizations such as trade unions or employers' organizations. That the population of the states was not consulted in some way made it more difficult to take steps to offset the negative social consequences of the structural adjustment programmes.

Pressure from the international trade unions

The reactions of the international trade unions to the social effects of the policy resulted in a meeting between the IMF, IBRD, ILO and international trade unions in 1985. The trade unions objected in particular to the social consequences of the IMF and IBRD policy for the working population and emphasized the role that trade unions could play with regard to successful economic policy. Given the criticism of their work the leadership of the IMF and IBRD showed interest in closer contacts with the international trade unions, but they maintained the view that consulting with governments should take place at national rather than international level. However, the experience at the annual meetings of the IMF and IBRD showed that most governments did not see any need for the trade unions to have a role in solving economic problems. Despite this the international trade unions continued to monitor the policy of the IMF and IBRD closely and in 1987 there were talks with high-level IBRD officials and the IMF managing director, followed in 1988 by talks with the IBRD president and the IMF managing director. The trade unions urged the two international institutions to pay more attention to the social effects of their structural adjustment policy and to involve workers' representatives. From 1987 onwards the international trade unions were given observer status at the annual meetings of the IBRD and IMF. Because this did not allow them to speak at the meetings they always issued a written statement, so that their views could be expressed by national delegates sympathetic towards them. In cooperation with the IBRD, the UN Development Programme and the African Development Bank the trade unions set up a project for the 'social dimensions of adjustment' (SDA) in 1987 and reached agreement in 1990 on the IBRD including trade unions in the national commissions that monitored the implementation of this SDA project. The IBRD also provided speakers and contributions to trade union seminars. These closer ties with the IBRD, however, were undermined by a long-lasting conflict with the Bank, which employed a company that did not tolerate trade unions to clean its offices in Washington DC. Moreover, there proved to be a deep gulf between what the leadership of the two institutions thought and what the bureaucratic machine was used to doing. Many of the conditions in actual aid programmes were such that governments were deterred from consulting trade unions. IBRD economists considered this, in their economic view, to be in line with the fundamentals of Reagonomics and in practice they excluded trade unions from the implementation of the SDA project.

35.4 From combating poverty to adjustment policy: the IBRD in trouble

Combating poverty and Reagonomics

Despite the economic recession during the 1970s, led by McNamara the IBRD's loan programme increased sixfold to almost 12 billion dollars in 1980 (see §31.2). Initially the Bank assumed that economic growth would follow from its infrastructural projects and that prosperity would then 'trickle down' to the poor at the bottom of society. Because this did not happen, combating poverty became the top priority in the IBRD's policy, with projects that had to benefit the poorest directly through investment in agriculture, rural development, health care, education and family planning. This was done in the expectation that it would increase productivity from the bottom up. But this policy of social improvement had its limitations, not least because many agricultural projects failed due to the incompatibility of the Bank's project aid with government policy in several developing states of keeping agricultural prices artificially low so as to get or maintain the support of the population. The primary explanation for the IBRD's lack of results in combating poverty was the change in the international economic and political climate in the early 1980s, with increases in oil prices and soaring debts dating from the 1970s placing economic restrictions on any IBRD initiative. The political will to pursue a strategy of social support disappeared when Reagan took office and introduced his new economic policy. During the 1980s combating poverty faded into the background with the original IBRD approach in favour of the IMF and IBRD structural adjustment programmes again to the fore. This included measures such as higher agricultural prices, the devaluation of currencies and, due to the debt crisis, privatization and reductions in government expenditure. It remained unclear what 'adjustment' actually meant to the IBRD and especially how it could combat poverty, as it aimed to do, through liberalization, which had such negative social effects.

Banking institution and development agency

As a result of the new direction the *International Development Association* (IDA; see §25.1), which was part of the so-called World Bank Group, developed into an agency providing multilateral development aid within the framework of the IBRD policy for states in which people had to exist on just one dollar a day. The money, on a long-term low interest rate, that was made available for this was meant to provide the basis on which economic, political and social advancement could be founded. The IBRD and IDA thus formed a combination of a banking institution and a development agency. The IDA only provided loans, but towards the end of the century, given the debt crisis of the developing states in the 1980s and 1990s, a discussion developed on whether the IDA should not also be able to cancel debts and give grants. The debts of *Heavily Indebted Poor*

Countries (HIPCs) had in fact already been cancelled, but this idea had consequences for the way the IBRD financed it, as internal calculations indicated that in time this would become virtually impossible (see Figure 35.1).

Figure 35.1 The financial limitations of the IDA in the long term

The **International Development Association** was in the main financed by repayments and would have to draw on reserves if debt remission and grants became more standard. In 2001 the **long-term expectations** were that 'Under current policies, IDA's cash balance will decline from $11.78 billion (2001) to about $1.4 billion (2013) and then will roughly stabilize for several decades. The World Bank and its member countries anticipate that loan repayments will account for 70% of the resources needed to fund IDA's loan program between 2032 and 2041'. By 2002 the IBRD had already cancelled nine billion dollars' worth of debts of Heavily Indebted Poor Countries. 'It has booked most of this debt but – because most of the repayments are not due for many years – it has not yet realized most of the loss.' The IBRD's plan to ensure that the IDA could in future for the greater part finance itself assumed that the donor states 'will reimburse its HIPC debt forgiveness in full. If the forgiven loan reflows are not restored, IDA will deplete its cash balance in 2009 and need to start shrinking its aid program. The cost of funding the lost reflow will be roughly $500 million to $600 million a year for the next 20 years' (Sanford 2002, i).

The need for a change in culture at the IBRD

The IBRD itself also had financial problems. The debt crisis was so serious that in the mid-1980s the Bank was approaching its financial limits. Moreover, the organization and staff were obviously not functioning effectively, as they had paid little attention to new agenda items such as the environment and the role of women in the development process. The IBRD only recognized in the second half of the 1980s, a decade later than the ECOSOC (see §32.2), that a great deal of the development aid was disadvantageous to women. Similarly the IBRD only at a late stage became interested in the social and environmental consequences of large-scale projects such as dams in Thailand and India, after criticism of the Bank's policy by environmental and other NGOs. Previously the IBRD had always brushed aside such censure as unimportant and irrelevant. The result of this financial pressure and the mounting criticism was a far-reaching reorganization of the IBRD in 1987. This did not proceed without difficulties, however, and the Bank struggled to project a new image. The need for a change in culture was talked about, which should result in an improvement in the monitoring of projects. To counter the continuing condemnation – in 1988 the IBRD also received more money from the Third World than it provided in loans – the Bank began to act more positively towards NGOs in the late 1980s and early 1990s. In 1992 some IBRD staff admitted that the criticism of environmental and Third World NGOs was right and acknowledged that one in three IBRD projects had to be considered a failure in this respect. Once more there were pleas from within the Bank to combat poverty and maintain a policy with a 'social face', which meant support for labour-intensive sectors combined with improved training, health care and birth control. Health care expenditure should be directed more at basic medical needs than high-quality medical help. Whether assistance should be linked to the level of military spending by Third World states was also considered. Attracting money for aid to the poorest states remained a problem, as the IDA found out in 1992. After the end of the Cold War it became more difficult to interest donors, because the IBRD began to also help the former Second World. A separate development bank, the European Bank for Reconstruction and Development (see Figure 29.2 and §36.4), had been established for this, but the IBRD set up its own Eastern Europe department. Another complication was that trade liberalization was a *sine qua non* for the IBRD in promoting exports from developing states. The strong drive towards free trade in the context of the GATT, and from 1995 the WTO, however, hindered support for social issues, which within the dominant trade regime were considered to be an impediment to free trade. There was little the IBRD could do.

35.5 Strengthening of the G7 and the surveillance role of the IMF (1985)

The Plaza Accord (1985) and the G7

At a secret meeting of the G5 ministers of finance and central bank governors in September 1985 at the New York Plaza Hotel the US abandoned its opposition to international monetary management. It relinquished its laissez-faire policy and approved interventions in the exchange markets in cooperation with the G5. The position of the G5 finance ministers was strengthened by the inclusion of Canada and Italy, so extending the G7 to this level. This change in US policy was prompted by concern over the influence of the rising exchange rate of the dollar on the current account of the US balance of payments, with ensuing protectionism. Acting together made it possible to hasten a fall in the value of the dollar. The so-called Plaza Accord also included a more active participation by Japan in international monetary management. Following the Plaza Accord, the G7 reached agreement on multilateral surveillance in Tokyo in May 1986. This was delegated to the ministers of finance and the central bank governors of the G7 states. As the coordination of monetary policy was now the responsibility of the ministers of finance, government leaders were able to pay more attention to other matters at the G7 summits. It was agreed that the finance ministers would meet for international monetary consultations during the summits of government leaders and also at least once a year separately. There was agreement as well in Tokyo on cooperation in interventions in exchange markets and on coordination of domestic policy to achieve steady economic growth with minimum inflation.

Crisis management

A few months before the Plaza Accord a report by the G10, strongly influenced by the US, had raised the question of whether the US was really prepared to accept international management. The crux of the US stance was that stable exchange rates should not be achieved by a *system*, but by aspiring to a healthy, credible and stable economic *policy*. The economic vision accompanying this stance focused on free trade, making the

561

financial and labour markets flexible and strengthening the supply structure of the economy. The US compliance with the Plaza Accord was seen as a form of crisis management, whereby the instrument of the exchange rate was used to avert an imminent wave of protectionism in the US. However, when this threat had passed the US continued with collective international monetary management, as was shown by the Louvre Accord on exchange rates in 1987 and by G7 agreements. Shortly afterwards, though, the Louvre Accord could not survive Black Monday, the stock exchange crash in October 1987, when the US did not abide by it but sought its own solution. These developments demonstrate that the stabilization of exchange rates and international economic management continued to be dependent on the position taken by the US, which seemed more willing to cooperate in the small circle of the G7 than in the wider framework of the IMF.

The surveillance function of the IMF

While the G7 had acquired the function of harmonizing the monetary policy of the richest states, the IMF had a task in the field of exchange rates. The further development of the G7 and the apparent willingness of the US to accept international coordination gave the IMF, strengthened by its role in solving the debt crisis of 1982, from 1986 more room to fulfil its surveillance function under the 1976 amendment to Article 4 of its Articles of Agreement (see §25.2), for which the IMF Board drew up guidelines. Although the IMF did not tamper with the right of autonomous states to determine their own exchange rate policy, they did have to cooperate with the IMF. This meant that member states had to keep the IMF informed and explain their national monetary policy and the effects aspired to in relation to international monetary developments, as well as having to take advice on this from the IMF. In principle confidential consultations were held annually between IMF staff members and high national representatives. Within three months of a visit by its staff the IMF administrators produced a report, initially confidential, in the form of 'conclusions'. Between April 1986 and April 1987 the IMF conducted these missions in 124 states, 81 per cent of its members. The extent and frequency of this advice was determined by whether a state was dependent on the IMF or not (see Figure 35.2 for the effects of the mission in the Netherlands in 1990–91).

Figure 35.2 IMF surveillance in the Netherlands 1990–91

An **IMF mission visited the Netherlands at the end of 1990** within the framework of the new surveillance regime and in February 1991 the IMF directors discussed the economic and monetary situation in the Netherlands. They were critical of the continuing financial deficit, the large number of non-active people of working age and the big surplus on the current account of the balance of payments. In the eyes of the IMF the Netherlands would benefit economically from removing the link between wages and benefits, although for diplomatic reasons it was not expressed in this way. The IMF regretted that finance minister Wim Kok had not continued the policy of his predecessor, ex-IMF director Onno Ruding. This confidential comment from the IMF leaked out shortly after the publication of the government's so-called *Tussenbalans* or Mid-Term Review, not long after the OECD in its annual analysis of the Netherlands had also criticized the large number of non-active people and had stated the need for reform of the Dutch social security system. Although this was a coincidence, it did mean that when they became public knowledge, with alarming headlines in the newspapers, these international comments influenced politicians and public opinion. An anonymous IMF expert gave it as his opinion in the press that the Netherlands, as a result of the policy pursued, 'was exporting its problems abroad' but without 'abroad' having a seat in parliament. 'Abroad' was therefore in a disadvantageous position compared with interest groups in the Netherlands. 'Only international organizations such as the OECD and the IMF can warn, on behalf of "abroad", that the Netherlands is trying to transfer its domestic adjustment across its borders', according to this IMF expert (*NRC Handelsblad*, 2 March 1991).

Economists did not consider the IMF surveillance within the framework of the exchange rate policy to have greatly influenced domestic politics. It was only a **soft obligation**, as the Netherlands was not dependent on the IMF for loans, unlike many developing states. Nevertheless this form of influence on policy must not be underestimated. In the context of global policy coordination IMF statements, however mildly phrased, can certainly, just like OECD criticism, strengthen or weaken a policy almost unnoticed. This is particularly the case when a government, such as in the Netherlands, values international economic management and its surveillance. From the point of view of international policy mechanisms, such as the OECD, the G7 summits and the IMF with its surveillance function under Article 4, that is exactly the intention of the arrangement.

36

The fall of the Berlin Wall (1989) and the end of the Cold War

36.1 The fall of the Berlin Wall (1989) and the significance of the CSCE/OSCE

Reagan and Gorbachev

Relations between the US and the Soviet Union changed at the beginning of 1985 with the arrival of a new leader of the Soviet Communist Party, Mikhail Gorbachev, who embarked on economic and political reforms. At the end of 1985 Gorbachev launched a programme for economic reform in the Soviet Union that became known as 'perestroika'. He made major personnel changes in the party and later the army leadership and replaced the long-serving foreign minister Andrei Gromyko with Eduard Shevardnadze. In their foreign policy Gorbachev and Shevardnadze embraced an approach known as 'new thinking'. In March 1985 the Soviet Union resumed negotiations with the US on medium-range missiles (see §24.3), even though the earlier demand that these missiles be withdrawn from Western Europe had not yet been met. In October 1985 Gorbachev visited France, where he stated in a speech to parliament that nuclear weapons within range of each other's territories would have to be abolished. In November Gorbachev met US President Reagan in Geneva, where he dropped the earlier Soviet demand that further negotiations would be conditional on the US abandoning its SDI project. Although no concrete results ensued, the relaxed atmosphere of the talks led to a rapprochement. Even so, there was a renewed chill in relations after this as a result of the US's refusal to relinquish the Strategic Defence Initiative and its announcement in May 1986 that it no longer considered itself to be bound by the terms of SALT II, the

Strategic Arms Limitation Talks which in 1979 had resulted in the unratified Treaty on the Limitation of Strategic Offensive Arms.

The INF Treaty (1987)

As a result the follow-up meeting between Reagan and Gorbachev was postponed. It was eventually held not in the US, as originally planned, but in Reykjavik, Iceland, and proved unexpectedly fruitful, with the leaders reaching agreement on removing the medium-range missile systems and resuming START, the Strategic Arms Reduction Talks, which had been broken off in 1983 (see §34.3). This progress resulted in the US and the Soviet Union signing the *Intermediate-Range Nuclear Forces Treaty* (INF Treaty) in 1987. They undertook to completely dismantle their medium-range nuclear missile systems and implemented this agreement, with the destruction of these missiles complete in 1991.

Progress at the CSCE in Vienna (1986–89)

At the Conference on Security and Cooperation in Europe (CSCE), which in 1975 had led to the Helsinki Final Act (see §24.3), the atmosphere had also deteriorated in the early 1980s. The review conference held in Madrid from 1980 to 1983 seemed unlikely to produce results, partly due to the influence of political events and incidents, such as the proclamation of the state of emergency in Poland (1981) and the shooting down of a South Korean passenger plane over the Soviet island of Sakhalin (1983). The review conference ended with an agreement to hold a follow-up conference in Vienna. This was to last from 1986 to 1989 and would benefit from the new foreign policy of the Soviet Union under Gorbachev. Shevardnadze even suggested having a conference on human rights in Moscow. After a good deal of hesitation this was eventually accepted, as was a Hungarian proposal on the treatment of minorities. To revive the MBFR talks on mutual and balanced force reductions between NATO and the Warsaw Pact, a separate negotiation platform was created under the name of CFE: *Conventional Armed Forces in Europe*. Unlike the early 1980s, the late 1980s saw a rapprochement between East and West, between both the great powers and Eastern and Western Europe.

The stagnating Soviet economy

But the policy of reform within the Soviet Union pursued by Gorbachev and Shevardnadze had unforeseen adverse consequences. 'Perestroika' was meant to strengthen the ailing centrally-planned economy, but it failed because senior officials dug in their heels and resisted the proposed changes. The policy of open debate and democratization, known as 'glasnost', did not produce the anticipated result of generating criticism that would undermine the officials' positions. Instead, the people simply rejected the system altogether: 'once glasnost and democratization let people say what they were thinking, and vote on it, many people said, "We want out. There is no new form of Soviet man. This is an imperial dynasty, and we do not belong in this empire"' (Nye 2003, 131). The Soviet economic system and the loss of legitimacy of communist thinking led to a stagnation in the economy and to Gorbachev losing control over domestic relations and developments.

The fall of the Berlin Wall (1989)

Gorbachev soon realized that maintaining Soviet control in the Eastern European states was becoming unaffordable, as was the war in Afghanistan. He therefore decided to allow the Eastern European states more scope to pursue their own policies. In 1988 he began moving Soviet troops out of Afghanistan and appealed to the UN for help to ensure that the withdrawal went smoothly (see §37.1). In the summer of 1988 the people of Eastern Europe started clamouring to pull down the 'iron curtain'. This happened first in Hungary, where people from the German Democratic Republic had cut through barbed wire fences and were making their way into Austria, with the Hungarian government doing nothing to stop them passing through. This put pressure on the government of East Germany to relax restrictions on its nationals who wanted to leave the country. Because the governments of Eastern Europe were no longer feeling pressure from the Soviet Union, they gradually gave in to the popular protests in the streets. The East–West divide in Europe finally came to an end on 9 November 1989, when people climbed onto the Berlin Wall and started hacking pieces out of it. The frontier crossings were opened without any show of force. This 'fall of the wall' symbolized the end of the Cold War. Gorbachev proposed bringing forward to 1990 the CSCE conference that had been planned for March 1992. The Western European states agreed, on condition that a treaty on conventional armed forces would be tabled. In the meantime fairly peaceful changes were being effected in a number of Central European states. In Czechoslovakia people flooded onto the streets in response to calls from the Citizens' Platform and political changes got under way. In Romania the crowds first jeered at President Nicolae Ceauşescu, who was then taken into custody and, with his wife, executed in rather unseemly haste.

German reunification (1990)

German reunification dominated the year 1990. At the end of 1989 Chancellor Helmut Kohl presented a plan for a German confederation that could culminate in German reunification. When Kohl visited Gorbachev in Moscow in February 1990, it became clear that Gorbachev would respect the Germans' desire for reunification. Despite some reservations on the part of France and the UK, there was support for reunification within NATO, provided NATO's security guarantee was extended to cover the entire German territory. In July Gorbachev indicated his willingness to agree. He had received assurances from the US, which favoured German reunification, that the German armed forces would remain limited in size. This breakthrough reinvigorated the stalled talks on conventional armed forces in Europe. Gorbachev also withdrew the Soviet troops from Eastern Europe. The new president of Czechoslovakia, the former dissident Václav Havel, had requested the troops' withdrawal in January 1990 within the framework of the Warsaw Pact and the two states signed a treaty to this effect when Havel visited Moscow, after which the troops began moving out. Hungary followed in March. Poland waited until the Federal Republic of Germany had signed a treaty formally recognizing their common frontier in November. But Gorbachev was unwilling to withdraw his troops from Poland at that stage, since he saw them as a link to the Soviet troops that were still based in East Germany which would not be withdrawn, under the terms of agreements with the West, until 1992–94. The status of the two Germanies after the Second World War meant that reunification was only possible with the consent of the

Allies. On 12 September 1990 all the negotiations were concluded in Moscow at a 'Four plus Two' meeting. At this the four Allies (the US, the Soviet Union, the UK and France) and the two Germanies signed an agreement that revoked all occupation privileges and restored German sovereignty. The formal reunification of Germany followed on 3 October.

CFE Treaty and the Charter of Paris (1990)

On 19 November 1990 the 16 member states of NATO and the six member states of the Warsaw Pact met in Paris, where they signed the *Treaty* on *Conventional Armed Forces in Europe* (CFE Treaty). This Treaty included agreements on the numbers of tanks, artillery and planes that each of the alliances was permitted to keep. From then on the two alliances would view each other not as adversaries, but as partners. The CFE Treaty fulfilled the condition for holding the CSCE conference, which had been brought forward at Gorbachev's request. The CFE ceremony of the two alliances was followed by the conference of the 34 states of the Conference on Security and Cooperation in Europe. This lasted from 19 to 21 November and concluded with the adoption of the *Charter of Paris for a New Europe*. This Charter emphasized principles such as democracy, human rights and the constitutional state, recognized German reunification and contained agreements designed to further extend the 'human dimension', embark on new disarmament negotiations and promote economic cooperation. CSCE meetings would be held regularly, both at the level of ministers and at that of government leaders and heads of state. The institutional structure of the CSCE would be strengthened. This Charter of Paris brought to an end the political division that had existed in Europe since the beginning of the Cold War.

The Treaty on Open Skies (1992)

The members of NATO and the Warsaw Pact had met earlier in February that year, on the initiative of Canada and Hungary. They explored ways in which they would be able to monitor each other's military movements in the framework of the new détente. Using CSCE facilities in Vienna, they continued their negotiations to examine the scope for unarmed inspection flights over the area covered by their two alliances, Europe and North America. This idea had already been put forward in 1955 by US President Eisenhower, but without Soviet agreement. Now it was debated again. The negotiations resulted in the *Treaty on Open Skies*, which was signed by the 27 member states of the two alliances in March 1992. The Treaty is seen as supplementary to the CFE Treaty and as a far-reaching agreement which regulates precisely which state is permitted to conduct which flights, as well as how and how frequently. Each state is required to allow a set number of flights, with implementation monitored by the *Open Skies Consultative Committee* in Vienna. The Treaty on Open Skies came into effect on 1 January 2002. By 2008, 34 states had signed it. The first aerial inspection over the US by Russia and Belarus took place on 7 June 2004. In July 2008 the 500th flight under this Treaty took place.

Institutionalization of the CSCE

The 1990 CSCE conference in Paris had decided that the CSCE would develop a supervisory mechanism to monitor compliance with the 'human dimension', which included human rights and fundamental freedoms, human contacts and other humanitarian matters. This would be done through exchanges of information, bilateral consultations, announcements to other states and talks at an annual CSCE meeting on this dimension. The conference also welcomed the accession of Eastern European states to the Council of Europe, because of the Council's contribution in areas such as human rights, democratic principles, the formation of a constitutional state and cultural cooperation. The Council of Europe, which the communist states had initially excluded from the CSCE, offered to place its experience at the CSCE's disposal. It hoped that cooperation would prevent an overlap of activities and pointed out that CSCE agreements, unlike those made in the Council of Europe, were not legally binding and that their implementation could not be enforced. The CSCE was institutionalized at the conference in Paris, with the creation of a *Council* (of foreign ministers), a *Committee* (of high-ranking officials), a *Secretariat* in Prague and a *Parliamentary Assembly* (from April 1991). The Parliamentary Assembly met for the first time in July 1992 and consisted of 317 members of parliament from the signatory states. It meets once a year. The CSCE also acquired a *Conflict Prevention Centre* in Vienna and an *Office for Free Elections* in Warsaw. In January 1992 the Council of the CSCE changed the latter to the *Office for Democratic Institutions and Human Rights* (ODIHR) with a wider-ranging remit, which became the CSCE's most important institution for the human dimension. The CSCE's fourth follow-up conference took place in Helsinki from March to July 1992. This 'Helsinki Bis' led to the creation of a *High Commissioner on National Minorities*, a further regulation of the human dimension in the concluding document of the conference and the expansion of the role of NGOs. In 1998 the CSCE would also appoint a *Representative on Freedom of the Media*. The position of High Commissioner was held from 1993 to 2001 by Max van der Stoel, who had previously been politically active supporting dissidents under the Greek dictatorship and in communist Czechoslovakia. As High Commissioner for the CSCE he sought to use behind-the-scenes diplomacy to prevent conflicts breaking out in the disintegrating former communist world. Another prominent task of the CSCE was monitoring the fair conduct of elections.

Transformation of the CSCE into the OSCE (1994)

The CSCE conference of December 1994 in Budapest transformed the CSCE into the *Organization for Security and Cooperation in Europe* (OSCE), reflecting the proposed efforts to promote security and cooperation as well as its ongoing institutionalization: the conference changed 'Conference' in the name to 'Organization' and 'on' to 'for'. It also adopted a *Code of Conduct on Politico-Military Aspects of Security*. This Code was not a treaty incurring legal obligations, but a politically-binding document that had the objective of strengthening the cooperation among OSCE states by formulating standards of behaviour for the political and military aspects of security. The Code of Conduct contained international standards that had been formulated in the past, but it also laid down a connection between the constitutional structure of the states concerned and the supervision of their armed forces, paramilitary units, security services and police forces. The OSCE aimed to make it impossible for individuals or groups to make undemocratic use of the means of force at their disposal, which could jeopardize national security as well as security within the OSCE as a whole. With the break-up of the Soviet Union, Yugoslavia and Czechoslovakia, the number of OSCE member states rose from 35 in 1990 to 55 in 1997. The OSCE's primary organs were now the *Ministerial Council* (foreign ministers meeting once a year), the *Senior Council* (high-ranking officials meeting twice a year and also once as an Economic Forum), the *Summit Conferences* (summits of government leaders and heads of state held in alternate years), the *Chairman-in-Office* and the secretary-general. This last position was created in 1992 and reorganized in 2000.

The OSCE and the Council of Europe

At its Vienna summit in October 1993 the Council of Europe decided to develop closer cooperation with the OSCE in the human dimension. Taking into account the OSCE's different character (mainly political) and the primarily legal character of the Council of Europe's 1950 Convention on Human Rights and Fundamental Freedoms, the Council and the OSCE would complement each other in operational practice. This difference also highlights the weakness of the OSCE, the efforts of which stand or fall by the political will of those concerned. But in the transformation of Eastern Europe the OSCE played a leading role in building mutual confidence between Western and Eastern Europe by facilitating new political processes and preventing or resolving conflicts.

36.2 Abolition of the Warsaw Pact (1991) and the continued existence of NATO

Abolition of the Warsaw Pact (1991)

The Warsaw Pact did not endure long after the fall of the Berlin Wall. After East Germany had ceased to exist in October 1990 the six remaining member states (Bulgaria, Czechoslovakia, Hungary, Poland, Romania and the Soviet Union) signed a document in February 1991 in which they ended their mutual obligations. After they had dismantled their common organs on 1 July 1991 they followed this up by signing an agreement dissolving the Warsaw Pact as a political entity.

End of the Soviet Union and formation of the CIS (1991)

The Soviet Union also ceased to exist. On 8 December 1991 the heads of state of Belarus, the Russian Federation (Russia) and the Ukraine signed the *Minsk Agreement*, providing for the establishment of a commonwealth of independent states. This was followed on 21 December by the *Declaration of Alma-Ata*, signed by 11 states, setting up the *Commonwealth of Independent States* (CIS) and abolishing the Soviet Union. The number of states in the CIS grew to 12 when Georgia joined in 1993 (until 2008). In addition to the four already mentioned, these were Armenia, Azerbaijan, Kazakhstan, Kyrgyzstan, Moldova, Tajikistan, Turkmenistan and Uzbekistan. In March 1992 a committee was appointed to examine the legal and other consequences of this successor to the Soviet Union. In April an *Inter-Parliamentary Assembly* (IPA) was set up, consisting of members of the national parliaments of seven member states. They held their first meeting in September and sought contact with the Parliamentary Assemblies of the Council of Europe and the OSCE. Within the CIS the Inter-Parliamentary Assembly has served to provide a legal basis for the Declaration of Alma-Ata and has played a role in harmonizing national legislation. In January 1993 the *Charter* of the CIS was formally adopted. From this point on the CIS could function as a security alliance and it was furnished with an inter-state

Economic Council. An inter-state court of justice was planned, but this has not yet materialized. Since most of the CIS member states focused on domestic concerns, the CIS in the beginning had little opportunity to develop. Furthermore, disputes about paying off debts to the former Soviet Union hampered progress, with Russia being frequently criticized for failing to honour its agreements. Despite this the organizational structure of the CIS was strengthened towards the end of the twentieth century. The CIS remained on the whole fairly limited and strictly intergovernmental. Its highest organ is the *Council of Heads of State*, which meets twice a year. The *Council of Heads of Government* meets every three months and if needed can also meet together with the heads of state. The *Executive Committee* supervises the Secretariat, the inter-state Economic Council and the working groups.

NATO's adjustment to the new situation

Unlike the Warsaw Pact, NATO was not disbanded after the fall of the Berlin Wall. It adapted to the situation by seeking a new role in the promotion of stability in Europe, a military strategy focusing on regional conflicts and even action beyond the Treaty borders. In 1991 the NATO member states established the organization's permanent importance as a common defence organization. Its task was defined as promoting stability and peace throughout Europe. NATO was no longer oriented towards preparing for a large-scale conflict such as had been anticipated during the Cold War, but towards intervention and the containment of regional conflicts and their consequences. Nuclear weapons were regarded as being of limited importance in defending the Treaty territory. What mattered was creating forces within NATO's integrated military structure that could be deployed rapidly in the event of a regional conflict. These forces would have to consist of different military units and represent different nationalities, but the actual formation of such multinational intervention forces was greatly delayed by problems among the Western European states.

The Partnership for Peace (1994)

NATO's top priority after the end of the Cold War was cooperation with Eastern Europe. To this end it launched the *North Atlantic Cooperation Council* (NACC) in December 1991 to serve as a platform for consultations. This Cooperation Council was attended by the 16 NATO member states, together with the former Warsaw Pact states and the successor states of the Soviet Union. Apart from the members of the CIS these also included the three Baltic states. Although the emphasis was on political and security matters, information was also exchanged on issues such as education, science and the environment. In 1994 NATO established the *Partnership for Peace* (PfP) to strengthen cooperation. This partnership, involving 27 non-NATO member states, consisted of cooperative agreements between NATO and individual states, the aim being to establish armed forces as democratically accepted units of a national society. The agreements focused on securing democratic control of the armed forces, achieving a good understanding of their methods and funding and a public debate on military strategies. States that signed up to these partnerships could look forward to NATO membership in due course. Several states from the former Second World were interested in joining NATO, but Russia refused to accept this. NATO demonstrated its understanding of this position by ensuring that NATO's expansion was accompanied by a deepening of its relations with Russia. This was confirmed in May 1997 in special agreements with Russia and the

Ukraine. The North Atlantic Cooperation Council was replaced in the same month by the *Euro-Atlantic Partnership Council*. NATO's secretary general Javier Solana worked hard to forge good relations between NATO and Russia. However, the US insisted in 1997 that the Czech Republic, Hungary and Poland would be able to join NATO, with full membership in 1999. On NATO's 50th anniversary in 1999 the three states were welcomed as members and other states were offered support to achieve membership. This was followed in 2004 by the accession of Bulgaria, Estonia, Latvia, Lithuania, Romania, Slovakia and Slovenia, bringing NATO membership to 26 states.

Revival of the Western European Union (1984)

The Western European Union (WEU), which had made Germany's NATO membership possible in the 1950s (see §23.2), had never been disbanded, but it had left the security-related tasks to NATO and had itself led a slumbering existence. In 1984, against the background of the negotiations on arms control between the US and the Soviet Union, France had taken the initiative of reactivating the WEU. The underlying idea was to follow the negotiations from the perspective of Western Europe. In 1987 the WEU member states reached agreement on their 'Western European' security interests, the main points of which were to promote a common defence identity among the member states of the European Community and to strengthen the European pillar of NATO. This led to Spain and Portugal joining the WEU and to the expansion of the WEU Secretariat. Furthermore, in 1988 the WEU undertook its first collective military task by clearing mines in the Persian Gulf, followed by the coordination of the activities of its member states during the Gulf War of 1990–91.

The Petersberg Declaration (1992)

In June 1992 the WEU issued the *Petersberg Declaration*, which contained a description of its responsibilities for crisis control. These 'Petersberg tasks' embraced humanitarian and rescue actions, peacekeeping and armed tasks including peace enforcement. The European Community's aim for the reactivated WEU was formulated in the 1991 Maastricht Treaty, which laid the foundations for a Common Foreign and Security Policy (CFSP) for the European Union. The WEU could take on the security role by becoming the EU's 'defence component' and the European 'pillar' within NATO. The 1994 NATO summit confirmed this latter objective, by identifying the WEU as the central element in strengthening the so-called European Security and Defence Identity within NATO. This was complicated as far as WEU membership was concerned, however, as Denmark, Austria, Finland, Ireland and Sweden were not members of the WEU but only observers. In 1996 the last four states, which are not NATO members, announced their willingness to take part in the WEU's Petersberg tasks on an *ad hoc* basis. To forge ties with the Eastern European states Bulgaria, Estonia, Latvia, Lithuania, Romania, Slovakia and Slovenia were made 'associate partners' of the WEU and the Czech Republic, Hungary and Poland (all members of NATO) became 'associate members' during the 1990s.

The WEU active but once again marginalized

The Petersberg tasks meant that the WEU worked alongside NATO in the 1990s. Its activities included having ships and aeroplanes in the Adriatic to monitor compliance with UN sanctions against Serbia and Montenegro in connection with the wars in the former Yugoslavia (see §37.3). The WEU was given a policing task in Mostar, Bosnia, as part of the EU mission to build a new local government structure there and it took charge of training the police in Albania. In May 1992 Germany and France announced their intention of raising a joint defence force, to be based in Strasbourg, that could operate as a European army under the aegis of the WEU. This plan for a 'Eurocorps' provoked concern within NATO. The US and the UK saw it as an attempt to undermine NATO's role in Europe, partly because France was still not part of NATO's military structure. In response to this concern Germany and France finally agreed in November that the Eurocorps could also operate under NATO command. The January 1994 NATO summit accepted the idea of rapid reaction intervention forces, called *Combined Joint Task Forces* in NATO terminology. After several pledges had been received the Eurocorps became formally operational at the end of 1995. France, Italy, Spain and Portugal announced the formation of two more intervention forces that could be placed at the disposal of the WEU, NATO and the UN. The 1997 Treaty of Amsterdam, which was important for the further integration of the EU (see §43.4), defined the WEU as the EU's operational capacity in the realm of defence. However, this provision was discarded again in the 2001 Treaty of Nice, since by then the conclusion had been reached that it was preferable for collective defence to come under the competence of NATO rather than the WEU. In view of NATO's existing policy for rapid reaction intervention forces and the fact that France has now oriented itself more closely towards NATO, partly because of the Eurocorps, there appears to be little scope for the WEU to play a specific role within the EU, which is still struggling to develop a common foreign and security policy. The WEU has once again been marginalized, but without being abolished.

36.3 Arms control, the OPCW (1997) and the comprehensive nuclear test ban

From SALT to START I (1991)

The arms control discussions between the US and the Soviet Union on START (Strategic Arms Reduction Talks) had begun in 1982 as a continuation of the earlier SALT (Strategic Arms Limitation Talks) (see §24.3). A result of SALT had been the *ABM Treaty* which allowed each state to have only two anti-ballistic missile systems (later changed to a single system each). In 1979 the two states concluded the SALT II Treaty, which set the limits of strategic nuclear weapons at a specified maximum number of warheads. The talks in the second half of the 1980s aimed to halve the number of strategic weapons. This ambition was not achieved, but in the *START I Treaty* signed on 31 July 1991 (see Figure 36.1) the US and the Soviet Union reached accord on a 30 per cent reduction in these weapons within seven years, with agreed ceilings. Cruise missiles launched from ships were excluded from the Treaty, although both states did accept a maximum number. The August 1991 coup in the Soviet Union prompted US President George Bush to dismantle a number of short-range missile systems. Gorbachev followed suit, so ensuring progress in arms reduction. Both the US and the Soviet Union then started to withdraw all their short-range nuclear missiles to their own territories. The dissolution of the Soviet Union in December 1991 meant that four of its successor states (Belarus, Kazakhstan, Russia and the Ukraine) had nuclear weapons in their territories. Between

September 1991 and March 1992, although the Treaty had not yet come into force, large numbers of intercontinental missiles, rockets that could be launched from submarines and bomber aircraft were destroyed. The disintegration of the Soviet Union delayed the Treaty becoming effective by more than three years, as the four successor states first had to become parties to the Treaty, in addition to which Belarus, Kazakhstan and the Ukraine, as formerly non-nuclear states, had to accede to the 1968 Non-Proliferation Treaty. By December 1994 all the ratifications had been completed and START I could enter into force for a period of fifteen years. The START Treaty contained detailed provisions on keeping each other informed of the progress made and laid down 12 types of on-site inspection and other kinds of monitoring. The Treaty was successful, as by the end of 2001 the US and Russia had reduced their strategic weapons to the agreed level and all nuclear arms had been removed from the other three states.

START II (1993) and the beginnings of START III (2000)

In the summer of 1992 Presidents George Bush and Boris Yeltsin reached agreement on further reductions in the number of long-range nuclear missiles. On 15 January 1993 these agreements were formulated in the *START II Treaty*, in which the two powers agreed to reduce the number of their long-range nuclear missiles to 3,500 within a period of ten years. The US ratified the new Treaty in 1996, but differences of opinion in the Russian Duma, in which communists and nationalists opposed the agreement, hampered Russia's ratification. The situation did not change until the election of President Vladimir Putin, who wanted to resolve this long drawn-out problem before his first visit to the West. Russia ratified the Treaty in April 2000 and Putin was able to leave for London. New rounds of talks could now begin in the framework of START III, aimed at achieving a further reduction in the number of long-range nuclear missiles to about 2,500 by the end of 2007, on which Presidents Yeltsin and Bill Clinton had reached agreement in 1997.

The Chemical Weapons Convention (1993) and the OPCW (1997)

Following the use of poison gases in the First World War, the so-called Geneva Poison Gas Protocol was concluded in 1925 (see §16.2). However, states reserved the right to possess such weapons in order to be able to strike back in kind if attacked with chemical weapons and rejected the idea of verification measures. The Biological Weapons Convention that had been agreed in 1972 was also undermined by a lack of proper regulations for verification and monitoring compliance (see §24.2). As certain states had again resorted to the use of poison gas and chemical weapons (Egypt had used gas in the war against Yemen and the US had used defoliating agents in Vietnam), Sweden had placed the issue on the agenda of the Eighteen-Nation Disarmament Committee (ENDC) in Geneva in 1968. An attempt by the US and the Soviet Union to engage in bilateral talks on this subject in 1977 stalled in the early 1980s because of the tense relations between the powers at that time. But in 1984 the Conference on Disarmament, the ENDC's successor, put the subject on the agenda again. Progress was achieved in 1987, when the Soviet Union accepted the introduction of a verification regime. In 1990 the US and the Soviet Union also reached agreement on reducing the quantities of their stockpiled combat gases. The Conference on Disarmament agreed the text of a convention in September 1992, followed on 13 January 1993 by the signing of the *Convention on the*

Figure 36.1 Arms control treaties and conventions 1987–2002

1987	Treaty between the United States of America and the Union of Soviet Socialist Republics on the Elimination of Their Intermediate-Range and Shorter-Range Missiles (***Intermediate-Range Nuclear Forces, INF Treaty***) (2)
1990	Treaty on Conventional Armed Forces in Europe (***Conventional Forces in Europe***, CFE) (22)
1990	Charter of Paris for a New Europe (in the framework of CSCE) (34)
1991	Treaty between the United States of America and the Union of Soviet Socialist Republics on the Reduction and Limitation of Strategic Offensive Arms (***Strategic Arms Reduction Treaty, START I***) (2)
1991	United Nations Register of Conventional Arms (95 in 1992)
1992	Treaty on Open Skies (between NATO and the Warsaw Pact) (27)
1993	Convention on the Prohibition of the Development, Production, Stockpiling and Use of Chemical Weapons (***Chemical Weapons Convention***, CWC) (130)
1993	Treaty between the United States of America and the Union of Soviet Socialist Republics on the Reduction and Limitation of Strategic Offensive Arms (***Strategic Arms Reduction Treaty, START II***) (2)
1995	Southeast Asia Nuclear-Weapon-Free-Zone Treaty (*Treaty of Bangkok*) (10)
1996	African Nuclear-Weapon-Free Zone-Treaty (***Treaty of Pelindaba***) (45)
1996	Comprehensive Test Ban Treaty (CTBT) (71)
1997	Convention on the Prohibition of the Use, Stockpiling, Production and Transfer of Anti-Personnel Mines and on Their Destruction (***Landmines Treaty***, or ***Ottawa Convention***) (121)
1997	Helsinki Agreement (between Boris Yeltsin and Bill Clinton on a possible ***START III***) (2)
2002	Treaty on Strategic Offensive Reductions (American name, abbreviated to ***SORT***) or Agreement on the Reduction of Strategic Offensive Potentials (Russian name), known as ***Treaty of Moscow***) (2)

See Figure 24.3 for the treaties and conventions concluded in the period 1959–85.
The numbers given in brackets indicate the number of states that signed the treaty or convention.

Prohibition of the Development, Production, Stockpiling and Use of Chemical Weapons in Paris by 130 states. Since universality was a prerequisite for this Convention's success, efforts were made to get the largest possible number of signatory states. By 2008 the Convention had a total of 184 state parties and another four states had signed but not yet ratified it. The verification system is based on routine inspections, roles for national authorities and 'challenge inspections' if one state suspects another of a violation. The Convention also promotes the peaceful and environmentally-sound use of chemical substances. The Convention entered into effect on 29 April 1997. Compliance is monitored by the *Organization for the Prohibition of Chemical Weapons* (OPCW), based in The Hague. This independent organization collaborates with the UN by reporting to the General Assembly and is regarded as a UN-related organization (see Figure 21.3). The Chemical Weapons Convention was the first multilateral convention that covered the abolition of a category of weapons classified as weapons of mass destruction and that through the OPCW acquired an extensive system of verification. The Convention provoked vehement opposition in the US, led by Senator Jesse Helms. He maintained that the lack of certainty on whether other states would live up their obligations would endanger the security of the US, but the US government under President Clinton at the last minute managed to get the Senate's approval. In 2002 the Brazilian director-general of the OPCW, José Bustani, was dismissed after pressure from the US, because he had tried to persuade Iraq to sign the Convention and accede to the OPCW, so as to acquire more control over Iraq's chemical weapons. The first conference to monitor compliance with the Convention was held in The Hague in 2003, while the second one took place in April 2008.

The Comprehensive Nuclear-Test-Ban Treaty (1996)

In 1963 the US, the UK and the Soviet Union had concluded the *Partial Test Ban Treaty*, which China and France had not signed. In 1974 the US and the Soviet Union had agreed the Threshold Test Ban Treaty, prohibiting tests having an explosive capacity of more than 150 kilotons (see §24.2). As a result of the changing balance of power in the world the Protocols to this Treaty that regulated verification could come into force in December 1990. In 1991 the parties to the Partial Test Ban Treaty held a conference to investigate the possibility of converting it into a treaty that would ban all nuclear tests. With the support of the UN General Assembly talks aiming to complete such a treaty got under way at the Conference on Disarmament in Geneva in 1993 and on 10 September 1996 the General Assembly adopted the *Comprehensive Nuclear-Test-Ban Treaty* (CTBT) that had emerged from this process. The CTBT prohibits all nuclear tests, military as well as non-military. In November 1996 a *Preparatory Commission* was appointed to prepare for the new Treaty coming into force, after which it was to be converted into the *Comprehensive Nuclear-Test-Ban Treaty Organization* (CTBTO) in Vienna. However, the Treaty cannot enter into effect until all the states listed in *Annex 2* have ratified it. These are all states that possess nuclear energy capacity and related research capacity. The Treaty had 179 state parties in 2008, 144 of which had ratified. Of the 44 states listed in Annex 2, 41 had signed and 35 ratified. The states that have not signed are India, Pakistan and North Korea. In the US the Senate rejected ratification in October 1999 by three votes, with those opposing it claiming that the Treaty would not enhance the security of the US. The Senate's opposition was a blow to President Clinton, who had signed the Treaty, and cast doubt on the future of the Comprehensive Nuclear-Test-Ban Treaty.

36.4 International financial institutions and the transformation of communist states

The fall of the Berlin Wall and the role of the IFIs

The fall of the Berlin Wall in 1989 and the later disintegration of the Soviet Union compelled the old and new former communist states to introduce drastic economic reforms. As communist states their economies had performed poorly, but reforms towards capitalism would take a heavy social toll, for all the prospect of improvement they presented. The new rulers would be judged at home by the success of their reforms, but they had little room for manoeuvre as they were not free to pursue policies of their own choosing because of their need for the financial support of the IFIs, the international financial institutions, to achieve the necessary transformation. The most important of these bodies were the European Bank for Reconstruction and Development, the IMF and the IBRD. Many communist states did not belong to the existing international financial institutions, so they now began to apply for membership. The IFIs were willing to lend money and to provide technical assistance, but only on the condition that their policies were followed. Within this 'conditionality' the international financial institutions displayed a preference for *shock therapy*, which meant taking policy measures that would constitute a rapid and complete break with the existing economic and social modes of production and distribution. It included the introduction of market mechanisms as quickly as possible through ceasing to control prices and stabilizing the government budget. Public expenditure had to be cut, combined with large-scale privatization. Liberalization of prices and lowering public expenditure were also necessary to curb the inflation that would arise in the transition to a capitalist economy. However, the new rulers had to cooperate with former company directors who were unwilling to relinquish their power, as well as with citizens who were concerned about their jobs, incomes, benefits and pensions. These groups therefore favoured *gradual change* rather than shock therapy. In this policy variant existing institutions would continue longer, concrete problems would receive more attention and new institutions would be formed more gradually. Poland opted for shock therapy, Hungary for a gradual reform in which the population would receive more protection from the hard consequences of the economic transformation. But whichever variant was chosen, all former communist states went through a process of dramatic social change in the 1990s, because their citizens now bore responsibility for finding their own jobs and securing their own income. While some people benefited from these new conditions, others, who were dependent on benefits and pensions, found themselves facing serious problems as prices continued to rise. The security that the communist states had given their citizens in the areas of social and medical provision had evaporated (Henderson and Robinson 1997, 176–79).

The European Bank for Reconstruction and Development (1990)

At the G7 summit in July 1989 the economic development of Eastern Europe was one of the matters on the agenda. It was agreed that the European Commission would coordinate the West's economic assistance to Hungary and Poland. From the summer of 1989 onwards consultations were held among the OECD member states on economic aid for these two states. The fall of the Berlin wall and the revolutions in Czechoslovakia, Bulgaria and Romania were followed in December by the decision to set up the *European Bank for Reconstruction and Development* (EBRD). This was an initiative by the French President François Mitterrand and it was given a name similar to that of the IBRD. Through a combination of circumstances, decisions on the coordination of aid and the actual setting up of the Bank appeared to be making little progress. Coordination by the European Community was not significant, since the large member states preferred bilateral aid. The recently formed EBRD was hampered by poor policy making and in 1993 it was compelled to make sweeping changes at the top. After a brief period of preparation it had been set up at the end of May 1990, with a complex structure and consequently a ponderous administrative system. It has four groups of shareholders: states in transition ('Countries of Operation', for which the support is intended), EU member states, member states of the European Free Trade Association and 13 'other states'. The European Community, later the EU, and the European Investment Bank (EIB) are also members. The EBRD's Agreement lays down that the EU member states, the EU and the EIB together hold the majority of the share capital. But as a result of pressure exerted by the US in the G7, the US became, at 10 per cent, the largest single shareholder in the EBRD. Non-EU member states objected to the proposed membership of the EIB (preferring membership to be open to other international institutions as well) but were unable to reject this proposal. The initial reservations over the admission of the Soviet Union were dropped when it expressed its willingness to make certain commitments. A political deal had been forged between the UK and France to the effect that the EBRD would be headed by a Frenchman but have its headquarters in London, where it was officially opened in the premises of the International Maritime Organization, the only IGO with its seat in London.

The EBRD in operational practice

The towering costs incurred for the EBRD's premises (including for a lot of expensive marble) and its failure to meet expectations meant that the Bank's French president, Jacques Attali, found himself in difficulties. He was replaced in 1993 by his fellow-countryman Jacques de Larosière, who used his experience in the IMF to put the EBRD's finances in order and to improve the Bank's reputation. After De Larosière's departure in 1998 the Bank was briefly led by the German Horst Köhler, but he was succeeded in 2000 by another Frenchman, Jean Lemierre. The EBRD's main working method has consisted of providing loans. It started by compiling a *Country Strategy Paper* for each individual state. This paper was to be re-evaluated every year before any further decisions were made on aid. In the 1990s the aid focused on the privatization of state enterprises, the conversion from military to peacetime production and the reform of the state banks. The EBRD was much criticized for late payments, which was partly related to restrictions laid down in its Agreement. For instance, only a certain proportion of resources can be allocated to government projects and aid may not impede commercial financial sources. Other problems arose out of a lingering lack of clarity on the legal position of property. The EBRD soon discovered that the transitional problems arising from inflation and rising budgetary deficits were greater than anticipated. National government bodies continued to play a bigger role than intended and relations needed to stabilize before investments could be made. In this area the EBRD collaborated with the IMF and IBRD. The EBRD differs from other international financial institutions, which are obliged to refrain from official political considerations, because explicit political conditions are attached to its work, such as the promotion of multi-party democracy, a sound legal system and respect for human rights. In 1996 the EBRD decided to double its capital. However, Russia's economic crisis in 1998 had serious consequences for the investments in which the Bank was involved and caused many projects to suffer setbacks, leading the EBRD to adopt a new strategy focused on the health of the financial sector. The EBRD helped to offset the financial consequences of the closure of the nuclear power station in Chernobyl in 2000. The states that had arisen from the former Yugoslavia also joined.

The OECD and the transformation

In December 1989 the Organization for Economic Cooperation and Development had also begun to concern itself with the situation in Eastern Europe. A meeting between foreign ministers and high-ranking representatives from Poland and Hungary examined the existing state of affairs and explored the scope for OECD help. This was followed in March 1990 by the establishment of an OECD Directorship, named the *Centre for Cooperation with the European Economies in Transition* (CCEET). The OECD saw this as a body to which governments that were pursuing a path towards a market economy could apply for advice and guidance and where they could take advantage of the expertise of the OECD Directorships. The Centre was mandated to prepare country studies, in the way the OECD did for member states, to convene meetings, to follow developments in the region and to maintain contact about them with other IGOs. The first *Economic Surveys* of the states in transition appeared in 1991 on Hungary and Czechoslovakia and in 1992 on Poland. Although other states expressed interest, agreements were concluded with only these three states, which were the furthest developed in Central Europe in June 1991 and which thereby acquired the status of *Partners in Transition Countries* (PIT).

According to the OECD this PIT status reflected the states' declared intention to develop into market economies and pluralist democracies and they were permitted to attend diverse meetings of OECD committees and working groups. Special programmes were set up for them and their economies were assessed on a regular basis. The OECD viewed the developments in Central and Eastern Europe as problematic, because of political instability, civil wars and disintegration (most notably of Yugoslavia, which previously had special OECD status), as well as these states' poor economic achievements and resulting high unemployment. Many of these problems could not be solved through OECD influence. After the collapse of the Soviet Union the word 'European' was deleted from the Centre's name, to remove its regional restrictions. Global developments led to an expansion in OECD membership. In 1994 Mexico became the first (and as yet only) Latin American state to join the OECD. In 1995 the Czech Republic was granted membership, followed in 1996 by Hungary and Poland. The OECD pursued a restrictive admissions policy, because it feared that the admission of new members would make the organization less homogeneous and less effective. Russia was given observer status in 1994, but it was not granted the requested membership. South Korea became the 29th member state at the end of 1996 and Slovakia the 30th in 2000. In 2007 Chile, Estonia, Israel, Russia and Slovenia were invited to open discussions on membership, while Brazil, China, India, Indonesia and South Africa were offered enhanced engagement, with a view to possible membership.

The IMF in the former Second World

At the G7 summit in July 1990 the G7 appealed to the IMF, IBRD, OECD and EBRD, at the suggestion of the US, to prepare a joint economic analysis of the Soviet Union, in view of the rapidly deteriorating financial situation. The resulting report, *A Study of the Soviet Economy* (1991), identified a great many imbalances and established that the primary cause of the Soviet Union's problems was the non-payment of the debts owed to it. This problem only worsened with the disintegration of the Soviet Union and the formation of the Commonwealth of Independent States. IMF missions to the states in transition led to the conclusion that, in addition to the need to stabilize their economies, they had to create institutions that would enable the market system to work properly. This prompted the IMF to devise programmes for adjustment and structural reform with the aim of achieving monetary stability. The main problems were outstanding debts, a lack of foreign currency reserves and arrears in international payments. The IMF faced the task of providing financial resources to smooth the path for these external adjustments. An additional problem was that the break-up of the Soviet Union, Yugoslavia and Czechoslovakia meant that in many places new currencies were introduced. To curb inflation and to promote monetary stability the IMF launched programmes to support the effects that the shock therapy was designed to achieve. Between 1989 and 1997 it provided credits with a total value of 27 billion dollars. The first 'wave' of credits in 1991 focused on Central Europe, while the second in 1994–95 targeted the Baltic states, Russia and the former Soviet republics. The IMF classified Central European states as the 'most advanced', while those in Eastern and Southeast Europe and Central Asia were categorized as 'less advanced'. The more advanced states were relatively able to keep inflation under control, while the less advanced states were burdened with hyperinflation, dual-currency economies (the use of dollars alongside their own ailing currencies) and a lack of public confidence in the government.

The position of the central banks

The *Basel Committee on Bank Supervision* (BCBS), a body linked to the Bank for International Settlements, was involved in efforts to strengthen the central banks in the new states. This Committee tried to ensure that the *Basel Capital Accord*, adopted in 1988, which contains the most important standards for the supervision of private banks, was also implemented in the states in transition. Slovenia, where the banks had to make a new start after the collapse of Yugoslavia, had greater success in setting up a supervisory structure for its central bank than Hungary, where relations between the banks and industry were an obstacle in introducing the new standards. Another key impediment was that the banks were the only strong sector of the economy in the early 1990s, making them the primary source of income for the Hungarian government. Because the state owed substantial debts to the international financial institutions, Hungarian policy was directed not at strengthening the effective supervision of the central bank, but rather at securing as much revenue as possible from the banking sector (Piroska 2005).

The IBRD in the former Second World

Both the G7 and the US encouraged the IBRD to become active in Eastern Europe. However, the IBRD had no experience with the dramatic economic and political changes that were taking place there and furthermore it first had to build up contacts and raise the necessary funds. It took some time before the states concerned became members of the IBRD, but by 1992 more stable relations began to develop between the IBRD and the former communist states. Offices were opened and missions sent to take stock of the problems. The first reconstruction loans were provided in 1993 as 'fast loans', intended to finance imports to protect important production facilities or infrastructural works. In addition a great deal of technical support was provided to teach the workings of market institutions, frequently in the form of courses, seminars and training sessions. In training public servants the focus was on subjects such as accountability as an element of legitimacy and the provision of services to clients and members of the public. The idea was to change the mentality of 'state institutions' into one of 'public services'. Through their activities, first in Central and Eastern Europe and later also in Central Asia, the IMF and IBRD became increasingly involved in national and regional developments. To some extent they were the standard-bearers of Western aid, but more importantly they were the institutions that through their policies placed their stamp on the developments, provided that national institutional traditions allowed them to do so. With the consolidation of the transitional process, the IBRD was forced to deal more and more with those in power and with the institutions and influences that kept them there.

Technical support by the ILO from 1993 onwards

The support provided to states in transition included technical support by the International Labour Organization. In 1993 the ILO set up a *Central and Eastern European Team* (CEET) in Budapest for all states in transition, including the former Soviet republics. The help it gave involved ILO experts going to the states to support their governments with expertise, for instance in setting up new institutions and training the staff to operate them. The ILO's activities focused on areas such as integrating vulnerable groups into the labour market, local employment agencies, training and retraining employees and developing social security systems in line with the new market economy. The main problem for the ILO was that the existing trade unions had lost many members and were adjusting to the new economic and political balance of power. In this new situation trade unions were not taken for granted and employers' organizations were lacking entirely, which also meant that governments felt little pressure to develop systems for employment relations.

The Energy Charter Treaty (1994)

At the instigation of the Dutch Prime Minister Ruud Lubbers an *Energy Charter* was signed in The Hague in 1991, which was intended as a basic treaty for East–West cooperation in the area of energy. While the 'East' was rich in natural energy resources but lacked the means to tap into them, the 'West' needed energy and had the means to invest in this sector. This led in 1994 to the *Energy Charter Treaty* (ECT), with a Protocol on efficiency and environmental issues. In 1996 the Secretariat of the Energy Charter Treaty was established in Brussels. A total of 51 states and the EU became parties to the Treaty, with other states, including the US, acquiring observer status. The underlying intention was not to create a kind of Marshall Plan, but to find private sources that would be willing to invest capital. In view of the instability in the Central Asian region it was essential to create 'a level playing field of rules to be observed by all participating governments, thus minimizing the risks associated with energy-related investments and trade'. The most important areas of this large-scale energy investment regime were the protection and promotion of foreign investment, free trade, the free transit of energy, the reduction of environmental damage and the creation of a structure to resolve conflicts between states and between investors and states. Despite the instability in the region the investment regime developed gradually and steadily. To bring the Charter into line with WTO rules an amendment to the Treaty was adopted in 1998.

The Stability Pact for Southeastern Europe (1999)

The *Stability Pact for Southeastern Europe* was a political initiative by 33 states and seven international financial institutions for the states that had suffered from NATO's attack on the former Yugoslavia: Albania, Bosnia and Herzegovina, Bulgaria, Croatia, Macedonia and Romania (see §37.7). The Pact was adopted at a meeting of the IMF and IBRD in Washington DC in 1999 and became known as the Stability Pact for the Balkans. After political agreement had been reached money was collected at a much-publicized donors' conference, for the purpose of funding infrastructural projects in these states over the medium term. A great deal of money was pledged, but not all of it actually came in and some of the projects took a long time to materialize, partly depending on which international organization was involved. As a joint initiative the Stability Pact lacked an organizational structure to monitor its implementation. An earlier non-institutionalized form of regional cooperation had been launched at the initiative of Bulgaria in 1996, known as the *South-East European Cooperation Process* (SEECP). The participating states were Albania, Bulgaria, Greece, Macedonia, Romania, Serbia and Montenegro and Turkey, with Bosnia and Herzegovina and Croatia joining at a later stage. The SEECP helped to promote stabilization in the region and to build up new networks, and fostered the acceptance of economic standards in mutual relations. After some time a process of institutionalization of the SEECP began.

Cooperation in Central Europe and the Baltic

The cooperation promoted by former communist states themselves remained confined to a handful of Central European and the Baltic states. Generally speaking the former Eastern European states had been dissatisfied with the cooperation in the Council for Mutual Economic Assistance (see §26.2), which had foundered in 1991, because of the Soviet Union's dominance. However, in 1991 a number of Central European states set up a cooperative framework to promote their economic interests and to assist integration with the West. This *Visegrad Group* was an informal consultative platform, involving Czechoslovakia, Hungary and Poland. It was followed in 1992 by the *Central European Free Trade Agreement* (CEFTA), which several other Central European states also signed. In the longer term this cooperation would benefit these states when they joined the European Union, as it gave them experience in a different kind of cooperation and enabled them to collectively master the rules and customs of European integration. The three Baltic states had created their own *Baltic Council* in 1990, based on a joint structure dating from the 1930s (see §18.3). In 1993 they also established a free trade zone. The *Council of Baltic Sea States* (CBSS), formed in 1992, had a stronger security component than the Baltic Council and included more states. The states around the Baltic Sea feared being exposed to undue regional influence from Russia after the collapse of the Soviet Union, fears they tried to allay by setting up a wide-ranging economic and cultural cooperative framework that included Russia. In addition to promoting mutual relations through regular conferences and specialized bodies, the emphasis within this CBSS framework was on the democratic development of the region.

The 1990s and new challenges for the United Nations as peacekeeper

Part XIV examines the turbulent 1990s and the new challenges that arose for the UN as peacekeeper in this decade. Although the UN was initially able to play a major role in this respect, it was later confronted with virtually impossible tasks arising from new forms of conflict, failing states and political complications. The UN met with failure several times (Somalia, Rwanda, Srebrenica) and was forced to witness a steady decline in the authority of its peacekeepers, despite efforts to adjust its peace operations to changing circumstances (Chapter 37). To a greater extent than in the past, the UN attempted to back up its peace operations with sanctions. NGOs developed their own policies on humanitarian aid, which sometimes conflicted with those of the UN. They supported controls on land mines, light weapons and cluster bombs. A number of UN tribunals and criminal courts were established to try war crimes and crimes against humanity. All these developments were aimed at maintaining collective security. Although the UN's experience of humanitarian interventions was far from positive, the 'responsibility to protect' gave the organization a new strength (Chapter 38).

A new world order and an agenda for peace? Hope and bitter failure for UN peacekeeping missions

37.1 Afghanistan (1988) and the Gulf War (1990–91): the return of the UN as peacekeeper

Gorbachev addresses the General Assembly (1988)

It was unclear in the transitional phase how the new era in international relations after the bipolarity of the Cold War would develop. The UN benefited towards the end of the 1980s from détente between East and West however. In 1987 Gorbachev decided to meet Soviet debts to the UN and to call on the organization for support. He set out his 'new thinking' on the Soviet Union's foreign policy in an address to the UN General Assembly in December 1988. He emphasized that this should lead to a joint approach in international conflicts. In his view the ideological struggle between East and West within the UN was over. He needed UN support for his efforts to strengthen the Soviet economy and to reduce Soviet support for parties in regional conflicts such as Cuba, Ethiopia, Vietnam, Yemen and above all Afghanistan. 'UN peacekeeping provided a face-saving means to withdraw from what Gorbachev described as the "bleeding wound" of Afghanistan' (Weiss *et al.* 1994, 60).

The Soviet withdrawal from Afghanistan (1988)

Gorbachev received the support he had requested for Soviet withdrawal from Afghanistan. In April 1988 Afghanistan and Pakistan signed the *Geneva Accords*, in which the US and the Soviet Union were directly involved. The Accords laid down the withdrawal of Soviet troops, non-interference in the internal affairs of Afghanistan and the voluntary return of refugees. To ensure the smooth implementation of the Accords the UN set up the *UN Good Offices Mission in Afghanistan and Pakistan* in the same year (UNGOMAP; see Figure 37.1 for the UN peace operations since 1988). This Mission monitored the withdrawal of troops between February 1989 and March 1990. However, this solution did not mean that Soviet support for the communist government or US support for the Afghan resistance came to an end (see §34.1). Both superpowers continued their involvement, but the course chosen enabled the Soviet Union to withdraw its troops from Afghanistan. The General Assembly authorized secretary-general Javier Pérez de Cuéllar to play a role in seeking a solution to the internal power struggle. He appointed a personal representative and in May 1991 called for an 'intra-Afghan dialogue' leading to free and fair elections, while the superpowers in the same year agreed to end their support for the various parties. Thanks to the efforts of the UN Afghan resistance groups that had been excluded from the Geneva Accords were involved in the talks, but as a result of the collapse of the Soviet Union local divisions became decisive. Although this meant that the UN was ultimately unable to be very effective, it did play a role. In December 1993 the General Assembly established the *UN Special Mission to Afghanistan* (UNSMA). UN involvement included a special rapporteur for human rights in Afghanistan (appointed by the Commission on Human Rights in 1984) and a special envoy of the secretary-general. As a result of the latter's effort the 'Six plus Two' group, consisting of six neighbouring states plus Russia and the US, was launched in 1997. But none of these efforts prevented the outbreak of civil war or the Islamic fundamentalist Taliban assuming power in 1996. Through its involvement in the Soviet withdrawal, however, the UN did resume its role of peacekeeper.

US support for the UN (1988)

Gorbachev's reconciliation with the UN also influenced the attitude of the US. In 1988 President Ronald Reagan publicly abandoned his previously extremely critical attitude towards the UN and expressed his appreciation for the work of the organization, its secretary-general and UN peacekeepers in the General Assembly. In his opinion the UN now had the opportunity to function as it never had been able to before. The US also decided to meet its debts to the UN, a policy which was continued in 1989 by Reagan's successor, George Bush, who for a short time had been the US representative at the UN. In September 1990 Bush told the US Congress: 'We are now in sight of a United Nations that performs as envisioned by its founders' (cited in Bourantonis and Wiener 1995, 41). The 'return' of both superpowers to the UN meant an increase in the authority of the Security Council as the UN organ in which the great powers could coordinate their policies.

The Gulf War (1990–91)

The UN had had little impact on the war between Iran and Iraq that broke out in 1980 (see §34.1). Although the Security Council had adopted various resolutions, the cautious attitude taken by the great powers meant that it took no action, not even when the Iraqi

Figure 37.1 UN peacekeeping operations 1988–2007

Acronym*	Full name	Period
UNGOMAP	UN Good Offices Mission in Afghanistan and Pakistan	May 1988–March 1990
UNIIMOG	UN Iran–Iraq Military Observer Group	August 1988–February 1991
UNAVEM I	UN Angola Verification Mission I	January 1989–June 1991
UNTAG	UN Transition Assistance Group (Namibia)	April 1989–March 1990
ONUCA	UN Observer Group in Central America	November 1989–January 1992
UNIKOM	UN Iraq–Kuwait Observation Mission	April 1991–October 2003
MINURSO	UN Mission for the Referendum in Western Sahara	April 1991–
UNAVEM II	UN Angola Verification Mission II	June 1991–February 1995
ONUSAL	UN Observer Mission in El Salvador	July 1991–April 1995
UNAMIC	UN Advance Mission in Cambodia	October 1991–March 1992
UNPROFOR	UN Protection Force (former Yugoslavia)	February 1992–December 1995
UNTAC	UN Transitional Authority in Cambodia	March 1992–September 1993
UNOSOM I	UN Operation in Somalia I	April 1992–March 1993
UNOMOZ	UN Operation in Mozambique	December 1992–December 1994
UNOSOM II	UN Operation in Somalia II	March 1993–March 1995
UNOMUR	UN Observer Mission in Uganda-Rwanda	June 1993–September 1994
UNOMIG	UN Observer Mission in Georgia	August 1993–
UNOMIL	UN Observer Mission in Liberia	September 1993–September 1997
UNMIH	UN Mission in Haiti	September 1993–June 1996
UNAMIR	UN Assistance Mission for Rwanda	October 1993–March 1996
UNASOG	UN Aouzou Strip Observer Group	May 1994–June 1994
UNMOT	UN Mission of Observers in Tajikistan	December 1994–May 2000
UNAVEM III	UN Angola Verification Mission III	February 1995–June 1997
UNCRO	UN Confidence Restoration Organization in Croatia	March 1995–January 1996
UNPREDEP	UN Preventive Deployment Force (Macedonia)	March 1995–February 1999
UNMIBH	UN Mission in Bosnia and Herzegovina	December 1995–December 2002
UNTAES	UN Transitional Administration for Eastern Slavonia, Baranja and Western Sirmium	January 1996–January 1998
UNMOP	UN Mission of Observers in Prevlaka (Croatia)	January 1996–December 2002
UNSMIH	UN Support Mission in Haiti	July 1996–July 1997
MINUGUA	UN Verification Mission in Guatemala	January–May 1997
MONUA	UN Observer Mission in Angola	June 1997–February 1999
UNTMIH	UN Transition Mission in Haiti	August–November 1997
MINOPUH	UN Civilian Police Mission in Haiti	December 1997–March 2000
UNPSG	UN Civilian Police Support Group	January 1998–October 1998
MINURCA	UN Mission in the Central African Republic	April 1998–February 2000
UNOMSIL	UN Observer Mission in Sierra Leone	July 1998–October 1999
UNMIK	UN Interim Administration Mission for Kosovo	June 1999–
UNAMSIL	UN Assistance Mission in Sierra Leone	October 1999–December 2005
UNTAET	UN Transitional Administration in East Timor	October 1999–May 2002
MONUC	UN Organization Mission in the Democratic Republic of Congo	November 1999–
UNMEE	UN Mission in Eritrea and Ethiopia	July 2000–
UNAMA	UN Assistance Mission in Afghanistan	March 2002-
UNMISET	UN Mission of Support in East Timor	May 2002–May 2005
UNMIL	UN Mission in Liberia	September 2003–

Figure 37.1 (continued)

Acronym*	Full name	Period
UNOCI	UN Operation in Côte d'Ivoire (Ivory Coast)	April 2004–
MINUSTAH	UN Stabilization Mission in Haiti	June 2004–
ONUB	UN Operation in Burundi	June 2004–December 2006
UNMIS	UN Mission in the Sudan	March 2005–
UNIOSIL	UN Integrated Office in Sierra Leone	January 2006-
UNMIT	UN Integrated Mission in Timor-Leste	August 2006–
BINUB	UN Integrated Office in Burundi	January 2007-
UNAMID	African Union/UN Hybrid Operation in Darfur	July 2007–
MINURCAT	UN Mission in the Central African Republic and Chad	September 2007–

*Acronyms in italics: operations led by the Department of Peacekeeping Operations set up in 1992. See Figure 22.1 for UN peacekeeping operations in the period 1948–78 and Figure 37.2 for operations led by the Department of Political Affairs.

army used mustard and nerve gas. When, after the end of the war with Iran, Iraq occupied Kuwait at the beginning of August 1990 the situation changed. Prompted by the threat to oil supplies, the US initiated a resolution strongly condemning Iraq as the aggressor and invoking Chapter VII of the UN Charter. The Security Council adopted a dozen resolutions aimed at isolating Iraq through condemnation of the invasion, economic sanctions and a naval blockade. At the same time the US was building a military coalition against Iraq of NATO members (although NATO itself was not involved) and most of the Middle Eastern states, including Saudi Arabia, Egypt and Syria. On 29 November 1990 the Security Council adopted Resolution 678, which authorized the member states under Chapter VII of the Charter to 'use all necessary means', for only the second time in the history of the UN, to end the Iraqi occupation of Kuwait. The first time such an authorization was given had been in relation to Korea in 1950. In practical terms this meant that the coalition formed and led by the US could take military action under the auspices of the UN. Diplomatic pressure on Iraq, including that exerted by the UN, had no effect. In January 1991 the aerial bombardment part of the operation the US called *Desert Storm* began. An attempt by Iraq to break up the coalition by carrying out SCUD missile attacks on Israel failed. At the end of February, having been driven out of Kuwait, Iraq admitted defeat and accepted the conditions formulated by the Security Council, which included withdrawal from Kuwait, the release of prisoners and reparations. The precise conditions for peace were set out in Security Council Resolution 687, adopted in April. This led to the creation of a number of institutions, including a compensation fund and the *UN Iraq-Kuwait Observation Mission* (UNIKOM) to monitor the demilitarized zone between the two states. UNIKOM's mandate lasted from April 1991 to October 2003. The *Sanctions Committee* (see §38.1) set up in August 1990 by the Security Council was also responsible for humanitarian aid to the Iraqi people. The Security Council also established the *UN Special Commission on Iraq* (UNSCOM) to ensure Iraq's compliance with UN resolutions. UNSCOM was authorized to carry out unannounced inspections in Iraq to identify and destroy weapons of mass destruction, including chemical weapons. The IAEA was also involved in inspections. UNSCOM was often only able to take action after US and British airpower had compelled Iraq to admit the inspectors. Following reprisals by the Iraqi government against Shiite Muslims in the south and Kurds in the north of Iraq, the US, the UK, France and Turkey set up no-fly zones over both north and south. This coalition carried out air strikes and dropped aid packages over Kurdish enclaves within Iraq. It also believed that the UN should take over the administration of these enclaves. Secretary-general Pérez de Cuéllar was not in favour, but ultimately agreed as long as the consent of the Iraqi government had been obtained, which he received in April 1991. As the coalition transferred responsibility to the UN almost immediately, the organization was underprepared to implement the necessary tasks in a state which was not well-disposed towards it. UNSCOM carried out the work with great difficulty until Iraq withdrew its cooperation in 1998.

37.2 Towards a new world order? Ethnic wars and failing states

The US and the new world order

When asked in January 1991 how global stability was to be maintained after the end of Cold War, President Bush's reply was that the US was the only power that could mobilize the forces for peace in the world. After forming the coalition against Iraq and at the beginning of Operation Desert Storm, it seemed to the Americans that bipolar stability would be replaced by consensus between the great powers. This consensus would be based on American leadership and on a 'new world order' in which the UN occupied a key position. The US seemed destined to take on this leadership role, but Bush also saw this as a problematic issue and as early as 1992 it became clear that the new world order was merely wishful thinking. Under his successor, Bill Clinton, the US distanced itself more and its willingness to take on the role of leader became questionable. 'In stark contrast to the overwhelming commitment of the US to the Gulf War – both politically and in terms of resources – the Clinton administration defined US foreign policy in terms of "assertive multilateralism", which proved not to be very assertive.' The limited leadership role for the US was soon associated with 'lamentations of an apparent disinclination of the US to lead' (Bourantonis and Wiener 1995, 41).

A new kind of war: ethnic conflict

This 'disinclination to lead' was reinforced by the conflicts in Bosnia and Somalia (see below). Where foreign policy was concerned, US self-interest proved stronger than any effort to display leadership in a world soon to be riven by discord. The numerous hot spots included Yugoslavia and the series of wars prompted by its disintegration, the conflicts in and between former Soviet republics and civil wars in Africa and Asia. A common characteristic of many of these clashes was their *ethnic* nature. The warring parties defined themselves in terms of cultural norms based on religion, language and other common features. Of the 111 conflicts that arose between the end of the Cold War and the end of the twentieth century, 95 were purely internal. Eight others were internal but involved foreign intervention, while only the remaining eight were 'classic' wars between states (Nye 2003, 150). Traditional mediation mechanisms were of little use in ethnic clashes. The post-Cold War world was characterized by 'nonstructured or destructured conflict', in which in many cases there were 'multiple parties or interlocutors, and often none had real authority or decisive force' (Shawcross 2000, 13). What is more, the parties in these conflicts, whether guerrillas or governments, had to find the funds for their weapons themselves. This created close ties between political objectives and crime, as arms were needed wherever there was fighting. Local warlords or bandits developed their own strategies, unencumbered by any political morality. 'Mafias armed with cheap weapons multiplied.' Warlords in particular proved unpredictable: 'The malign force has been most visible in the warlords who have dominated the 1990s' (Shawcross 2000, 11).

The UN and the new world order: failing states

The inability of governments to mediate in these new conflicts played a role in the collapse of the new states that had emerged from European colonies in the developing world and in the disintegration of the Soviet Union in the Caucasus and Central Asia. The states in difficulty there were unable to solve their own problems. 'Such "failed states" either never had a strong government or their governments have been undermined by economic conditions, loss of legitimacy, or outside intervention. Thus even though the end of the bipolar conflict of the Cold War led to the withdrawal of foreign troops from Afghanistan, Cambodia, Angola and Somalia, communal war continued' (Nye 2003, 151). In the mid-1990s the International Red Cross calculated that the human cost of such man-made disasters exceeded the resources governments had at their disposal to deal with them. 'There were fifty-six wars being waged around the world; there were at least seventeen million refugees and twenty-six million who had lost their homes, plus another 300 million affected by disasters unrelated to war' (Shawcross 2000, 13–14). The burden of resolving these conflicts fell on the UN. Although the expansion of its tasks was initially accompanied by expectations of a major role for the UN in a new world order, the Security Council was to fail in several respects in assessing and resolving such clashes. This happened 'because of the application of insufficient or inappropriate resources, wishful thinking, and a flight from reality that seemed to overtake the Council in the years 1992–95' (Malone 2004, 11). As a result the prestige the UN and its 'Blue Helmets' had built up (see §22.2), still intact at the beginning of the 1990s, began to decline, as became painfully clear during the conflicts in the Balkans and in Africa.

37.3 The disintegration of Yugoslavia and the Balkan Wars 1991–95: the UN sidelined

Ethnic cleansing

After the death of President Tito in 1980 and against a background of growing détente between East and West at the end of the 1980s, nationalistic movements became ever stronger in multi-ethnic Yugoslavia. In 1987 Serbia's President Slobodan Milošević increased the strains on that multi-ethnic character in an election speech to the Serbian minority in the largely ethnic-Albanian province of Kosovo. In 1991 political differences within the federal government and declarations of independence from Slovenia and Croatia led Milošević, who could count on the support of the Serb-dominated army, to attack Slovenia and carry out 'ethnic cleansing' in parts of Croatia where there was a Serb majority. Slovenia achieved independence in July 1991 and Croatia in December of that year, albeit with the loss of parts of its territory and ongoing fighting to recover them. Although the US and the European states were in favour of preserving the unity of Yugoslavia, Germany broke with this policy by quickly recognizing the independence of

Slovenia and Croatia. It also succeeded in getting the backing of the rest of the EU, which, unlike the US, then recognized the independence of the two states. Because of this Bosnia and Herzegovina announced a referendum on independence and Milošević's suspicions of the EU grew. Bosnia declared independence in March 1992, but became a theatre of war with Serbian militias led by General Ratko Mladic systematically persecuting and driving out the Muslim population. Photos of emaciated people behind barbed wire published in the summer of 1992 revived memories of Nazi concentration camps.

UN involvement

In September 1991 the UN became involved in the conflict when the Security Council imposed an arms embargo on Yugoslavia. The unintended result of this was that it disadvantaged the Croatians and the non-Serb Bosnians, because the Serbs had access to sufficient weapons through the Yugoslavian army and the others did not. In February 1992 the Security Council decided to establish a *UN Protection Force* (UNPROFOR) to monitor the three areas in Croatia with large Serb populations which were protected by the UN. The expectation was that Croatia and Yugoslavia would reach an agreement. UNPROFOR's mandate was gradually expanded to include zones between the three areas, as well as the Bosnian capital Sarajevo and its airport. In August, invoking Chapter VII of the UN Charter, the Security Council charged UNPROFOR with supporting the delivery of humanitarian relief throughout Bosnia. In the meantime secretary-general Boutros Boutros-Ghali had appointed a representative (first Cyrus Vance, later Thorvald Stoltenberg) to coordinate the UN activities with those of the EU, which had appointed Lord Owen as mediator. Boutros-Ghali attempted to achieve a ceasefire, if only so that the UN peacekeepers and humanitarian organizations such as UNHCR, WHO and UNICEF could do their work. Between 18 and 20 May 1992 the General Assembly recommended UN membership for Bosnia and Herzegovina, Croatia, and Slovenia and informed Serbia that it had to apply for membership in its own right rather than continue to occupy Yugoslavia's seat. A conference organized by the EU and the OSCE laid the foundations for Vance and Owen's peace initiative, but their plan to divide Bosnia into 'cantons' ultimately failed to gain support in Bosnia in May 1993.

Failing 'safe havens': the fall of Srebrenica (1995)

Because the situation in Bosnia and Croatia was deteriorating and UNPROFOR's control over it was inadequate, the Security Council decided on 30 May 1992 to impose economic sanctions on the Federal Republic of Yugoslavia. UNPROFOR was reinforced a number of times, a military no-fly zone was established over Bosnia and the UNPROFOR mandate was extended to include Macedonia. But because it had not been charged by the Security Council to do so, UNPROFOR was unable to halt the spread of Serb violence. Even condemnations of ethnic cleansing by the General Assembly brought no change to this situation. The Security Council did, however, at the beginning of 1993 set up an international tribunal to prosecute persons responsible for violations of international humanitarian law, the Yugoslavia Tribunal, in The Hague (see §38.3). In response to a Serb offensive early in 1993 the Security Council decided to designate a number of cities *safe havens*, expecting that the Serbs would not attack them and that UNPROFOR would protect refugees who gathered there. This proved illusory: the Serb militias did attack the safe havens and the UN troops could do little to prevent them. During the fall of Srebrenica in July 1995 thousands of men were separated from their families and killed outside the enclave. Because their presence obviously had very little impact UN peacekeepers lost much of their authority. On several occasions the Serbs held UN soldiers hostage and publicly humiliated them.

NATO involvement

NATO initially failed to reach agreement on military action to end the conflict, but in 1994 started air bombardments of Serb positions. Eventually, in 1995, this together with US support for Croatia changed the balance of power. After a mortar attack on a market in Sarajevo in August 1995 NATO intensified its air strikes. The strikes and Croat military successes in Krajina finally forced Milošević to the negotiating table. The war ended with the *Dayton Peace Accords*. Under the firm leadership of US representative to the UN Richard Holbrooke negotiations between Bosnia, Croatia and Yugoslavia were concluded at an air force base in Dayton, Ohio. The Accords were signed in Paris on 14 December 1995 and brought UN involvement through UNPROFOR to an end. Monitoring implementation of the Dayton Accords was entrusted to the multilateral *Implementation Force* (IFOR), under NATO leadership but including non-NATO participants. Although in December 1995 the *UN Mission in Bosnia and Herzegovina* (UNMIBH) was established to oversee demilitarization and to support the election process, the role of the UN was drastically reduced while that of NATO was reinforced.

37.4 Humanitarian assistance and the failure of the US and UN in Somalia (1993)

Humanitarian intervention in Somalia (1992)

The disintegration of Yugoslavia was not the only fiasco to befall the UN in the early 1990s. The 1992 UN operation in Somalia, a state experiencing drought and civil war, was a new type of intervention, designed to provide humanitarian assistance to the population of a 'failing' state which did not have a functional government. After the Somali government fell in 1991 the UN had done little more than express concern about the civil war that ensued between the various warlords. The UN relief organizations present in Somalia, including UNHCR, left the country on account of the violence and only NGOs such as the International Red Cross, Save the Children and Oxfam remained. It was not until January 1992 that the UN took action. The Security Council decided to impose a full arms embargo and appealed to states and international organizations for assistance in view of the humanitarian situation in Somalia. Thanks to mediation by the Organization of African Unity, the League of Arab States and the Organization of the Islamic Conference a ceasefire agreement was signed in March 1992. In April the UN established the *UN Operation in Somalia* (UNOSOM) to provide humanitarian assistance. At the request of secretary-general Boutros-Ghali Somalia was divided into four operational zones for the provision of food aid by the World Food Programme. If the NGOs had had their way the

UN would have confined its role to logistical support and the protection of food transports, with food distribution left to the NGOs, which the population trusted more than it did the UN. 'The UN aid operation is marred by disputes between the different UN organizations. Their efforts have to date been ineffective. The UN agencies were the first to flee, even before the fighting really began, and they were the last to return', said a Save the Children spokesperson in September 1992. One of the examples of inefficiency he cited was the fact that the development programme UNDP had held on to 68 million dollars in food aid for three months because one of the four signatures needed was missing: that of the health minister who had fled Somalia (*NRC Handelsblad*, 14 September 1992).

US operation Restore Hope (1992)

Although the UN reinforced UNOSOM, Pakistani UN peacekeepers were attacked and killed, vehicles and food supplies were stolen, personnel held hostage and stores looted. Respect for UN troops was completely lacking. The secretary-general asked the Security Council to deploy a military force in Somalia. US President Bush was prepared to supply troops to restore security, expecting to receive support from other states at a later date. In December 1992 the Security Council decided to reinforce UNOSOM and to deploy the *Unified Task Force* (UNITAF) as its military branch under Chapter VII of the UN Charter, allowing the US and other states to restore peace. On 4 December President Bush initiated the deployment and on 9 December the first American soldiers landed in Somalia in an operation which the US code-named *Restore Hope*, but which was formally a UNITAF exercise. Ultimately 35,000 soldiers were deployed in UNITAF, 25,000 from the US and 10,000 from 20 other states. Organized and led by the US, the task force reduced tensions and enabled UN humanitarian assistance to begin, but it could not change the fact that Somalia lacked a functioning government and that the aid reached only half the population.

Failure of the US and UN (1993)

In March 1993 the Security Council authorized the secretary-general to develop a programme designed to reach a settlement in Somalia. A conference was held in Addis Ababa with the intention of achieving national reconciliation. UNOSOM II took over from UNITAF on 4 May, but warlord Mohammed Aideed refused to accept the situation. He attacked UNOSOM II and killed dozens of peacekeepers. Despite a price being put on his head the fighting between his troops and UNOSOM II continued. US soldiers attempting to restore order were ambushed on 3 October. 18 of them were killed and their bodies were dragged through the streets of the capital Mogadishu. This humiliation had so much media impact that President Clinton announced that US troops would withdraw from UNOSOM II on 31 March 1994. Other states made similar announcements and pressure exerted by regional IGOs had little effect. At the end of 1993 the Security Council set up a commission of inquiry to investigate the armed attacks on UNOSOM II. However, the situation in Somalia continued to deteriorate and UN and NGO personnel repeatedly came under fire. Although UNOSOM II's mandate was extended several times, the Security Council decided in November to follow the recommendations of a special investigation mission to Somalia and bring UNOSOM II to an end in March 1995. All remaining efforts were devoted to ensuring that the UN peacekeepers could leave safely. Somalia was then left to its fate. The result was total failure to achieve the UN's aims in carrying out this humanitarian intervention (see §38.4). It undermined the UN's authority, as did the decision by the US to withdraw so rapidly from a joint mission.

37.5 Greater success in Mozambique, Cambodia and Haiti, but failure in Rwanda 1992–94

The UN Operation in Mozambique (1992–94)

The UN operation in Mozambique was much more successful. This state had had to cope with the departure of the Portuguese following independence in 1975, a conflict with its neighbour Southern Rhodesia and a long civil war between the Frelimo government and the Renamo resistance movement. The UN offered assistance as early as 1987, but it was not until 1992 that a ceasefire was achieved. In December 1992 the Security Council set up the *UN Operation in Mozambique* (UNOMOZ) to monitor the ceasefire and the collection and destruction of weapons, separate the opposing parties, coordinate and monitor humanitarian assistance and ensure a smooth electoral process. The UN succeeded in restoring relations in Mozambique and considered the elections to have been free and fair. After two years it was able to wind up UNOMOZ.

The UN Transitional Authority in Cambodia (1992–93)

The UN's attempts to find an international solution to the problems in Cambodia following the Vietnamese invasion in 1979 were initially unsuccessful (see §34.1). Vietnam was forced to withdraw from Cambodia in 1988 when the operation became too costly. Through the efforts of the great powers an international agreement on a comprehensive political settlement in Cambodia was concluded at a peace conference in Paris in October 1991. In February 1992 the UN set up the *UN Transitional Authority in Cambodia* (UNTAC) to implement this agreement. UNTAC was in existence for 15 months. Its tasks included promoting the reconciliation process, domestic governance and foreign relations and it had more than 20,000 military and civilian personnel. In May 1993 elections took place. Although Hun Sen, the prime minister in the government installed by the Vietnamese, lost the elections, he remained in government. Both Hun Sen and the winner of the elections, Prince Norodom Ranariddh, were supported by their own armies, which had effectively refused to cooperate with UNTAC's efforts to disarm them. In 1997 Hun Sen seized power from his co-prime minister. Although the UN then refused to allow him to take up Cambodia's seat at the UN, the seat was re-occupied after controversial elections in 1998. Again the UN's authority was undermined. The situation became the responsibility of the states in the region, which had always pursued their own policy. In 1999 Cambodia became a member of ASEAN.

UN and OAS cooperation in Haiti (1993)

A military coup against the democratically-elected government of Jean-Bertrand Aristide in 1991 put democracy at risk in Haiti. The UN decided to take combined action with the Organization of American States and like the OAS sent a special envoy to explore the scope for a civilian mission. A joint OAS and UN mission, the *International Civilian*

Mission to Haiti (MICIVIH), was established in April 1991. The problems continued, however, and in June 1993 the Security Council imposed an arms embargo in an attempt to increase the pressure on the military rulers. In September this was followed by the establishment of the *UN Mission in Haiti* (UNMIH), which was to lend assistance to the democratic government when it returned. Although talks were making headway the military government was reluctant to yield on certain issues. In October this caused the Security Council to fully restore the embargo, which had been somewhat relaxed. At the beginning of 1994 the situation deteriorated and MICIVIH reported that human rights violations were increasing. The Security Council decided to tighten the embargo further and UNMIH temporarily withdrew. At the initiative of China a debate was held in the Security Council, resulting in the conclusion that this tightening of the embargo was an exceptional measure and did not set a precedent. In July 1994 the Security Council adopted a resolution making it possible to deploy an international force under Chapter VII, to ensure the departure of the military government. The force was in fact deployed in September after the military government had already indicated it would step down and was composed of 10,000 US soldiers and troops from Bangladesh and India. At the end of the month sanctions were lifted and MICIVIH and UNMIH returned. Brazil and Russia both questioned the form this action took and the speed with which it was taken: they regarded the intervention as the US putting its own backyard in order. President Aristide returned in October. UNMIH was terminated in June 1996, but was succeeded by a number of different missions, the last being still active in 2008 (UNSMIH, 1996–97; UNTMIH, 1997, MINOPUH, 1997–2000; MINUSTAH, 2004–; see Figure 37.1).

The UN's failure in Rwanda (1994)

In 1994 800,000 people were massacred in Rwanda in a period of three months, most of them belonging to the minority Tutsi tribe. After the 1993 peace agreement that had brought the civil war to an end, the UN installed the *UN Observer Mission in Uganda-Rwanda* (UNOMUR) at the request of Uganda and Rwanda, with the aim of preventing arms being smuggled into Rwanda. Another mission, the *UN Assistance Mission for Rwanda* (UNAMIR), was set up shortly after this to monitor the ceasefire and take any other measures necessary to ensure that the new government, once elected, could function. However, the Assistance Mission's Canadian commander, Roméo Dallaire, was given fewer than half the envisaged 5,500 peacekeepers. Even more serious was that the UN ignored information sent by Dallaire about plans to murder the Tutsi population and failed to answer his pleas for more troops and powers to take action to prevent the massacre. As soon as it was known in Rwanda that the UN could be ignored, the drama unfolded rapidly. The Security Council subsequently expanded UNAMIR's mandate, but after Belgian peacekeepers were tortured and murdered Belgium withdrew its troops. Under pressure from its non-permanent members and from the non-aligned countries the Security Council condemned the events in Rwanda. It also decided to increase the troop numbers and to impose an arms embargo. However, few states were willing to provide troops and after two months only 500 had been made available. France in the end set up its own operation, providing humanitarian assistance in the south of Rwanda. The situation for the refugees in neighbouring states and in Rwanda itself was so appalling though that even the NGOs could do little to help. UNHCR later admitted that it had not been prepared for what happened in Rwanda. During the slaughter its personnel in Rwanda was faced with a lack of coordination from Geneva. Attempts to organize evacuations and to bring in goods put such pressure on air transport that it came to a halt for several weeks due to lack of fuel. As a result UNHCR itself could do little and delegated the work in the camps as far as possible to the NGOs that were still present (Loescher 2001, 308). Whenever UNHCR set up new camps for the refugees they had to be closed again immediately, since the Hutus waited until refugees emerged from the forests to go to the camps and then slaughtered them (Loescher 2001, 313). The UN and the states involved had failed to cope with the crisis. Not only that, but it also led to destabilization in the region of the Great Lakes and indeed in all of Central Africa.

Reasons for failure

Initially the unwillingness of the great powers to address the crisis was seen as the only reason for the UN's failure in Rwanda. With the tragedy of Somalia still fresh in US minds, President Clinton had no desire to become embroiled in an equally intractable political situation. He decided to ignore the crisis, as he afterwards explained in what became known as 'the Clinton apology' (Gorman 2001, 363). Later attention turned to what had happened within the UN as a bureaucracy, a process that can only be described as a kind of collective 'tunnel vision', in which UN staff interpreted incoming information such as data and urgent appeals for help from Dallaire in a different way to the senders of that information. The UN Secretariat in New York interpreted the events in Rwanda as a civil war rather than genocide, even though in view of what they were hearing from Dallaire 'genocide' appeared the appropriate label for what was happening on the ground. Because of this interpretation the Secretariat's policy was not directed at halting genocide, but at being careful not to become embroiled in a civil war. That the events could be interpreted in this way was linked to the type of peacekeeping operations the UN undertook in the first half of the 1990s. Unlike in the 1950s and 1960s, peacekeepers were becoming increasingly involved in internal conflicts and were having to provide humanitarian assistance and to try to support failing states. This resulted in unprecedented problems both for peacekeepers on the ground (facing violence from the warring factions) and for the organization (withdrawal of troops by states whose soldiers had been killed). As a consequence the Secretariat and the Security Council had become vividly aware of the need to comply with all the rules before taking action. They even engaged in reinterpreting those rules to avoid making the same mistakes again. 'To ensure that peacekeeping would be effective, and to shore up the organization's authority and political support, the Secretariat and the Security Council narrowed the conditions under which peacekeepers were deployed (emphasizing the need for stability on the ground before deployment) and restraining their actions in the field (reemphasizing consent and impartiality).' In view of earlier failures and the criticism that followed, and in the light of the seriousness of the situation in Rwanda, the UN came to the conclusion that it should exercise caution. 'Peacekeepers were no longer to be used in civil wars where there was no peace to keep' (Barnett and Finnemore 2004, 123).

No reference to genocide

The Security Council explicitly avoided the term 'genocide' in connection with the events in Rwanda, because any reference to the 1948 Genocide Convention (see §21.1) would have committed all states which were party to that Convention to take action. As a result the UN did not take any measures to halt the massacre of Tutsis. Despite the fact that the killings attracted widespread attention the UN did not analyse its own failings in order to learn a lesson, although the Security Council did set up the International Criminal Tribunal for Rwanda in 1994 (see §38.3). It was not until five years later that secretary-general Kofi Annan commissioned an independent inquiry into the failure. Published in 1999, the inquiry team's report summed up the repeated failures of the UN throughout the tragedy: the wrong mandate, lack of resources, lack of training for UNAMIR personnel, unclear rules, the desire to remain neutral as events unfolded, failure on the part of states to provide support, the focus of the Security Council on achieving a ceasefire while genocide was being carried out, and the complicating factor of Rwanda being a member of the Security Council during the crisis. The conclusion was that by averting its gaze and refusing for a long time to acknowledge what was really going on, the UN organization in New York had lost all sight of reality in this conflict. Although its conduct could be explained on the grounds of bureaucratic restrictions and the lack of political will on the part of great and small powers alike, the UN's failure to learn lessons contributed to a further loss of authority for the organization. Following the publication of the report Annan, who as undersecretary-general had been responsible for peace operations at the time, offered his apologies.

37.6 An agenda for peace (1992) and new generations of UN peacekeeping

An agenda for peace (1992)

At the request of the Security Council secretary-general Boutros-Ghali, who took office in January 1992, compiled a report into how UN capacity could be increased so it could play a role in the new type of conflicts confronting states and the UN. The request was made in January and Boutros-Ghali presented the report, entitled *An Agenda for Peace*, in June 1992. His view was that the UN had to be strengthened so that it could take timely steps to support at-risk states and enable them to preserve their sovereignty, internal order and security. The UN should have military units that could rapidly be deployed in times of crisis at its disposal, which in less developed states should be accompanied by humanitarian, political and economic support. Important concepts in the report (some of them new) were preventive diplomacy, peacemaking, peacekeeping and post-conflict peacebuilding. The concept of preventive diplomacy aimed to prevent conflict within or between states before it broke out, or prevent the spread of violence. In other words, crises must be foreseen and prevented. Peacemaking was intended to bring the warring parties together through negotiation and mediation. Peacekeeping meant the stationing of UN troops in areas where fighting was in progress or imminent. Post-conflict peacebuilding was important because sustainable peace can only be achieved if economic, social, cultural or humanitarian problems have been tackled. Not only must a crisis be resolved, steps must be taken to prevent it reigniting. The consequence of this report and its implementation was that the UN developed a different kind of peacekeeping to that of the past.

Second generation peace operations

The peace operations undertaken by the UN after the end of Cold War were different to those from the end of the 1940s into the 1970s (see §22.2). The earlier operations

597

were based on the consent of the states involved, UN troops were only lightly armed for defence purposes and the UN acted impartially in separating the warring parties. The 'second generation' peace operations that began after the Cold War shared some of the characteristics of the earlier interventions, but also included UN aid activities designed to achieve sustainable peace in the area of conflict. This meant that civilian personnel was also used, for example to carry out reconstruction work or to monitor elections. In practice those second generation operations went even further, as the use of force was given greater prominence in what came to be called 'peace enforcement'. With terms such as 'peacebuilding' and even 'peace enforcement' Boutros-Ghali drew a distinction between this and the older form of peacekeeping. The involvement of UN troops had clearly broadened and the consent of all parties involved in a conflict was no longer required, even if the conflict was within a sovereign state. Boutros-Ghali's policy in the many conflicts confronting the UN led to a substantial expansion of UN peace operations. While in 1988 around 10,000 peacekeepers were active, this figure rose to 11,500 at the beginning of 1992, 44,000 in mid-1992 and even reached 80,000 at the beginning of 1993. Associated costs rose proportionately, from 364 million dollars in 1988 to 4 billion dollars in 1993.

Third and fourth generation peace operations

'Third generation' peace operations originated in decisions taken by the Security Council under Chapter VII of the UN Charter, which authorized the UN to use force even if the parties opposed UN intervention, for instance to disarm them. The first time this approach was used was in Somalia (UNOSOM) in 1992–93. The abysmal failure of the operation, leading to the death of 18 US soldiers, was harmful to the UN. The same was true of the bloodbath in Rwanda in 1994, which the UN failed to halt. As a result of these experiences the UN began to talk of 'fourth generation' peace operations, based on better trained troops capable of defending themselves and protecting refugees. A panel set up in 2000 by Annan and headed by Lakhdar Brahimi, who at the time served as undersecretary-general for special assignments, evaluated the past experience of UN peace operations and published recommendations in the same year designed to put them on a more professional footing. This would require improved information-gathering and analysis, an integrated approach to operations, a broader interpretation of self-defence to enable UN troops in dangerous situations to act more effectively, and a more discerning assessment of impartiality. Critics of UN peace operations took the view that their quality could improve as a result of Brahimi's reforms, but they expected no miracles: 'Significant improvement will not happen because of the UN's organizational culture, the way its members use it, and the nature of today's conflicts' (Jett 1999, xvii).

Distribution of tasks between DPKO and DPA

Restructuring of the UN Secretariat led from 1997 to a distribution of tasks between two departments. These are the *Department of Political Affairs* (DPA) and the *Department of Peacekeeping Operations* (DPKO) (see §20.7). In May 2007 the DPKO headed 18 existing and new peace missions (see Figure 22.1 and Figure 37.1). The DPKO assists member states and the secretary-general in their efforts to maintain international peace and security. The DPA is responsible for special political missions and 'peacebuilding support offices engaged in conflict prevention, peacemaking and post-conflict peacebuilding in

Figure 37.2 Political and peacebuilding missions of the Department of Political Affairs

Acronym	Full name	Period
UNPOS	UN Political Office for Somalia	April 1995–
UNOGBIS	UN Peacebuilding Support Office in Guinea-Bissau	March 1999–
UNSCO	Office of the UN Special Coordinator for the Middle East	October 1999–
BONUCA	UN Peacebuilding Office in the Central African Republic	February 2000–
UNTOP	UN Tajiskistan Office of Peacebuilding	June 2000–
UNOWA	Office of the Special Representative of the Secretary-General forWest Africa	November 2001–
UNAMI	UN Assistance Mission for Iraq	August 2003–
UNMIN	UN Mission in Nepal	January 2007–
UNSCOL	Office of the UN Special Coordinator of the Secretary-General for Lebanon	February 2007–

West and Central Africa, Central Asia and the Middle East' (see Figure 37.2). Here the emphasis is on 'post-conflict peacebuilding'.

37.7 Violence in Sierra Leone, Kosovo, East Timor and Congo 1998–2000

UN peace operation in Sierra Leone (1998–2000)

One of the UN's largest peace operations took place at the end of the 1990s in Sierra Leone. It revealed the impasse in which UN peacekeeping found itself in Africa. Some years after the 1992 army coup in Sierra Leone demands for a return to civilian rule produced results. In 1995 secretary-general Boutros-Ghali appointed a special envoy to work towards a settlement. The UN, the OAU and the Economic Community of West African States (ECOWAS) worked closely together. Elections were held in 1996, but a year later a new coup took place. In October 1997 the Security Council imposed an oil and arms embargo (see Figure 38.1). It was agreed that with the help of its military wing ECOMOG, ECOWAS would monitor compliance with the sanctions. However, the ECOMOG mission consisted largely of Nigerian soldiers, which weakened its neutral position. When the situation normalized in 1998 the UN established the *UN Observer Mission in Sierra Leone* (UNOMSIL). Armed peacekeepers supervised the disarming of combatants and advised on restructuring the security forces. Unarmed members of UNOMSIL reported human rights violations however. Talks took place between the UN, ECOWAS and the government of Sierra Leone and after the conclusion of a peace agreement in July 1999 the UN set up the *UN Assistance Mission in Sierra Leone* (UNAMSIL). This consisted of 18,000 personnel, but it failed to prevent Sierra Leone becoming embroiled once again in civil war. One of the largest UN peace missions became one of its greatest failures when in May 2000 rebels took 500 UN soldiers hostage. The peacekeepers handed over their weapons to the rebels without firing a shot. Shortly afterwards a force of 1,600 British soldiers arrived and secured the release of the hostages. Because the British troops then rapidly withdrew the UN increased the number of peacekeepers, but it was still unable to achieve much because of the mediocre quality of the troops deployed and ineffectual UN leadership. 'The force commander, Indian general Vijay

Jetley, in a memo that was leaked to the press, accused Nigerian officials of dealing in stolen diamonds with the rebels. The UN's reaction was not to investigate, but to remove Jetley instead. The Indian government, in response, pulled its troops out of the operation' (Jett 1999, xii).

The diamond trade

The UN initially ignored the illegal diamond trade because it needed to work with the African governments. Its troops proved unable to take control of the situation in Sierra Leone and Liberia. Nor could the regional ECOMOG force provide a military solution in either state. A complicating factor was that Liberian President Charles Taylor had become involved in the situation in Sierra Leone and there were reports that he himself was benefiting from the trade in diamonds with the rebels in that state. But the UN ignored the trade once again. 'The key to peace is therefore not more peacekeepers; it is curbing Taylor's greed.' The links between peacekeeping and illegal trade also played a role elsewhere in Africa. 'Angola, Namibia, Zimbabwe, Rwanda, and Uganda, for strategic reasons – or the personal profit of their presidents – all have troops involved. Instead of walking away or punishing those responsible, the UN keeps looking for a chance to plunge 5,000 peacekeepers into a truly hopeless situation' (Jett 1999, xii). This meant that UN peacekeeping, already undermined by the hostage-taking, could not be effective. The UN was equally incapable of controlling the concurrent trade in diamonds in Angola, while the situation in Congo was if possible even more difficult.

War in Kosovo without a UN mandate (1999)

At the same time a NATO military operation conducted without the backing of the Security Council further undermined the already weak position of the UN in the former Yugoslavia. Although the UN was supplying humanitarian aid and specialist assistance for reconstruction in Bosnia and Herzegovina, it was not involved in maintaining security (see §37.3). That task was carried out by the NATO-led *Implementation Force* (IFOR), established in 1995, and its successor from 1996, the *Stabilization Force* (SFOR). Russia and the Ukraine were also part of IFOR and SFOR. The solution to the 1999 Kosovo crisis was not the result of UN efforts, but of those of NATO. In March 1998 increasing tensions between Serbs and ethnic Albanians in Kosovo prompted the Security Council to impose an arms embargo on the Federal Republic of Yugoslavia, pursuant to Chapter VII. In October a new resolution followed to enable the Organization for Security and Cooperation in Europe (OSCE) to monitor the situation in Kosovo, with NATO air support. The main political decisions concerning the former Yugoslavia were not taken in the Security Council but in the international *Contact Group*, made up of France, Germany, Italy, Russia, the UK and the US. The Group's objective was peace negotiations after the withdrawal of Yugoslavian troops, their replacement by NATO units and restoration of Kosovo's autonomous status within Yugoslavia which had ended in 1989. The Kosovan Albanians, whose aim was independence, agreed to this plan under pressure from the Contact Group, but Yugoslavia did not. Following the failure of negotiations NATO began a military intervention in March 1999 under the code name *Allied Force*. The 78-day bombardment of Serbian targets in Kosovo and of towns and cities in Yugoslavia aimed to end the humanitarian catastrophe unfolding for ethnic Albanians. The operation was remarkable because NATO acted for the first time outside the parameters of its Treaty and there was no mandate from the Security Council. According to NATO it would have been impossible to obtain a mandate in view of the position taken by China and Russia, which opposed intervention in Kosovo. Cases brought before the International Court of Justice by Yugoslavia were unsuccessful, although the Court was critical of the procedure followed by NATO. In June President Milošević yielded and withdrew his forces from Kosovo.

UNMIK: the UN interim administration in Kosovo (1999)

A peace agreement followed, which was approved by the UN. Security Council Resolution 1244 authorized the secretary-general to establish the *UN Interim Administration Mission for Kosovo* (UNMIK). The *Kosovo Force* (KFOR), made up of NATO and Russian troops, was responsible for keeping the peace under a UN mandate. Through operation *Allied Harbour* NATO also played a role in coping with the flow of refugees caused by the war. Although the NATO strikes had defused the crisis, states such as Brazil, Cuba, Mexico and Russia expressed their dissatisfaction with the marginalization of the UN by the US and the European states in the Security Council. China pointed out that NATO had stated that it wanted to avoid a humanitarian crisis, but that its bombardments had in fact created one. NATO operations in Kosovo without Security Council backing undermined UN authority and cooled relations between NATO and Russia, which had traditional ties with the Serbs. UNMIK and the specialized UN agencies were given the task of rebuilding civilian government and infrastructure in Kosovo and providing further humanitarian aid. In fact the UN was engaged in nation building. Through the *Joint Interim Administrative Structure* (JIAS) it worked to restore a democratic and civil society. The Serbs had lost control over Kosovo as a result of the NATO operation. Most ethnic Serbs fled to Serbia, with only a few remaining in northern Kosovo.

The EU versus the UN in Cyprus and Kosovo

Appointed in November 2005, UN special envoy Martti Ahtisaari focused on independence under supervision in the talks on Kosovo's future status, although Serbia and Russia opposed this. Kosovo declared independence in February 2008, when an EU mission was to be deployed to further develop Kosovo's police and justice sector. The EU being in favour of an independent Kosovo meant that the UN was no longer able to pursue its policy aimed at meeting both Kosovan and Serbian interests. A similar situation had arisen in the past, when in 2002 a plan drawn up by secretary-general Annan to reunite a divided Cyprus did not get the agreement of either side. When the EU subsequently offered (Greek) Cyprus membership the UN could no longer pursue its stick-and-carrot strategy to put pressure on both sides. In both Cyprus and Kosovo the EU would appear to have acted more out of regional interest than in the interests of UN policy, which is in contravention of Article 52 of the UN Charter.

The UN administration in East Timor (1999)

In East Timor the UN also formed a temporary administration. This former Portuguese colony was occupied by Indonesia in 1975 and annexed by it in 1976 (see §34.1), with the FRETILIN resistance movement continuing to wage a guerrilla war against the occupation. Every year the UN adopted resolutions on East Timor's right to self-determination, but it could do nothing effective to change the situation. It was however instrumental in arranging talks between Indonesia and Portugal in the 1980s, which later included the East Timorese. New opportunities arose when the Indonesian President Suharto was forced to resign in 1998 and the UN reached agreement with Indonesia and Portugal on a referendum. The *UN Mission in East Timor* (UNAMET) was set up to organize and conduct the 'popular consultation'. Indonesia offered the East Timorese 'special autonomy', but almost 80 per cent of the population rejected the proposal in August 1999. When this outcome led to disturbances the Security Council first agreed to the establishment of an international force under Australian leadership and subsequently set up the *UN Transitional Administration in East Timor* (UNTAET). After military intervention in September the Indonesian army withdrew. In October the transitional administration began to function, under one of the broadest mandates a peace mission has ever received. It organized the first parliamentary elections in 2001 and stayed until the independence of East Timor was declared in May 2002. It remained a weak state, however, which required the support of the UN (and Australia) again following rioting in 2006 and renewed outbreaks of violence in 2007.

The UN peace operation in Congo

The *UN Organization Mission in the Democratic Republic of Congo* (MONUC), established in November 1999, became the most expensive and largest UN peacekeeping operation ever. The situation in the Democratic Republic of Congo was a result of the destabilization of Central Africa caused by the massacres in Rwanda in 1994. MONUC was responsible for supporting the implementation of the agreement concluded in the Zambian capital Lusaka in July 1999, in which the OAU had also played a role. This peace agreement consisted of a ceasefire between Angola, Namibia, Rwanda, Uganda and Zimbabwe and a call for inter-Congolese dialogue to arrive at a political settlement and reconciliation. MONUC succeeded in retaining the trust of all the parties, but that did not mean that the rebels and militias ceased fighting or that UN troops could avoid combat, quite apart from the huge problems associated with large-scale chaos, corruption, maladministration and the illegal diamond trade. In 2004 the number of troops was raised from more than 10,000 to just under 17,000. Attempts by the UN to restore order from 2006 onwards focused on holding elections and raising funds at a donor conference for projects aiming to combat poverty and to build education and healthcare infrastructure. A new constitution was adopted in May 2005 and the first democratic election since 1970 was held in July 2006. However, in August 2007 battles between a militia and the Congolese army brought Congo back to civil war. In January 2008 the government and the rebels signed an agreement. The UN presence is expected to continue for some considerable time.

The UN fails to enhance its prestige

Unlike during the first generation of peace operations, in the second and later generations after the end of Cold War the UN did not gain new authority, even though the organization was willing to undertake virtually impossible tasks. The reason for this can be found in the difficulties caused by the new types of conflict confronting the world in this period. But it was also due to the self-willed policies the great powers continued to pursue in these circumstances, sometimes with and sometimes without the backing of the

UN. In addition, the troops provided by UN member states were often a ragbag of soldiers with vastly different levels of training and equipment. Frequently the soldiers were from developing states and participation in UN missions gave them a relatively luxurious lifestyle because they were paid more than at home. As a rule the number of troops actually deployed was lower than states had promised. But the fact that the UN lost prestige was also due to its own failures (or those of its specialized agencies), such as in the administration of the Oil-for-Food Programme in Iraq or in Rwanda in 1994. That weak peace operations were ineffective also worked to the UN's disadvantage, particularly when UN soldiers were taken hostage or disarmed, as happened in the former Yugoslavia and in Sierra Leone. The UN's already shaky authority was further undermined by the moral decline among some of its soldiers, as shown by reports of sexual abuse committed by UN troops, and its difficulty in publicly addressing such misconduct. Like any bureaucracy the UN initially ignored whistleblowing, but was eventually forced to acknowledge the facts (Cain *et al.* 2004). Another problem for which the UN was blamed was that its missions tended to disrupt the local economy. In places where a peace mission was established the price of housing and food rose rapidly and the high salaries paid to UN personnel upset the economic balance. Furthermore, the impact of a mission's presence tended to continue long after it had departed.

38

Efforts to maintain collective security

Sanctions, NGOs and UN tribunals

38.1 UN sanctions policies in the 1990s

UN sanctions policies

Of the total of 170 bilateral and multilateral sanctions imposed between 1914 and 1999 35 per cent, or one third, was effective (Cortright and Lopez 2000, 15). At first the UN rarely applied sanctions, with the exceptions of those against Southern Rhodesia and South Africa in 1966 and 1974, respectively (see §28.1). This policy however changed during the 1990s, when the UN began to use sanctions for a diverse range of purposes: 'to reverse territorial aggression, restore democratically elected leaders, promote human rights, deter and punish terrorism, and promote disarmament' (Cortright and Lopez 2000, 2). Some sanctions proved effective, such as those against Iraq after its occupation of Kuwait in 1990, in the wars in the former Yugoslavia during the early 1990s and against Libya because of its terrorist support. Other sanctions had no success, such as those against Angola, Liberia, Rwanda and Sierra Leone (see Figure 38.1). Most sanctions consist of economic measures which aim at distorting trade, but an economic impact does not necessarily imply political success. Sanctions may also have serious unintended side effects, as became clear during the arms embargo against Yugoslavia which weakened the Croats and Bosnians and not the well-armed Serbs, while the opposite effect was intended. The suffering of the population can be an undesired effect of economic sanctions, as happened in Iraq (see below). Sanctions may also cause new acts of violence. In addition to these difficulties in effectively imposing sanctions, administering and monitoring the implementation processes was another problem for IGOs. The UN bureaucratic machinery at the time proved inadequate for this. 'In an era of financial constraint at the UN, the Security Council and its sanctions committees lacked sufficient resources to evaluate and implement sanctions.' Furthermore, the sanctions committees established to oversee implementation varied in effectiveness according to the degree of 'politicization of the particular episode, its relative priority for the major powers, and the leadership provided by the committee chairs' (Cortright and Lopez 2000, 5). In practice improvements in tracing the implementation of sanction regimes were made when the UN began to employ experts and monitoring panels. The first such panel was established to monitor the weapons embargo against Rwanda in 1995, while others were set up for Angola, Sierra Leone and Afghanistan. The use of these monitoring panels soon became routine. They were complemented by the creation of investigative panels and the involvement of NGOs, which increasingly began to play roles 'in exposing those who violate sanctions, and the humanitarian impact that sanctions may have on a population' (Chesterman and Pouligny 2003, 506). Governments also became creative in better targeting sanctions, such as through the *Interlaken Process*, set in motion by the Swiss government, with its procedures for refining targeted financial sanctions. In 1999 the German government sponsored a similar initiative to improve the implementation of arms embargoes and travel sanctions (Cortright and Lopez 2000, 5).

Punitive or bargaining model?

The economic sanctions the UN Security Council imposed on Iraq after its invasion of Kuwait in 1990 (see §37.1) were among the longest, most comprehensive and most severe in UN history. They were effective in the sense that the pressure applied forced the Iraqi government to make certain moves. However, an investigation into the use of the sanction model showed that during the implementation of the sanctions a 'bargaining model' developed rather than a 'punitive model', with a process of negotiation and concessions for partial compliance, rather than full compliance without reciprocal favours. This can be explained through the understanding that implementation of measures requires efforts from both sides. It is not only a matter of a command from the imposer of sanctions, requiring the punished state to do as it is told. If a certain behaviour is wanted it needs the cooperation of the punished state as well. This means that both sides might enter into talks about how precisely to implement and bring about a negotiated solution which includes carrots and sticks rather than just sticks. It is debatable whether in the case of Iraq the UN did not rely too strongly on the punitive model. If better use had been made of the bargaining model that was developing it might have achieved greater compliance and avoided the deepening of distrust and animosity that took place (Rose 2005). Among the negative results of the sanctions was the serious humanitarian crisis which developed in the isolated state, with many children dying unnecessarily.

The UN Oil-for-Food Programme in Iraq (1991)

Concerned about the suffering of the population as a result of the sanctions, the UN had already devised the *Oil-for-Food Programme* in 1991. This permitted the sale of Iraqi oil of a certain value and the use of the proceeds to buy food and other necessities, among other things, for the Iraqi population. The UN-administered programme was an attempt by the Security Council to address the shortages of food and medicines. However, the implementation of the programme was plagued by the unwillingness of the Iraqi authorities to participate in its execution. It was not until 1996 that they accepted the programme and even then they undermined its fulfilment in various ways. But implementation was

605

Figure 38.1 UN Security Council sanctions 1966–2000

State	Period	Type of sanctions	Effects in the 1990s
Southern Rhodesia	1966–79	Oil and other commodities embargo	See §28.1
South Africa	1974–94	Arms embargo	See §28.1
Iraq/occupied Kuwait	1990–2003	1990–2003: comprehensive embargo from 1990: arms embargo	**Moderate to high**: 'Of eight provisions in SCR 687 six partially or fully met; weapons dismantlement partially achieved; Iraqi military threat reduced'
Yugoslavia	1991–96 1998–2001	1991–96: arms embargo 1992–96: comprehensive embargo 1998–2001: arms embargo	**Moderate to high**: 'Sanctions were major bargaining chip in negotiations leading to Dayton accord'
Cambodia (Khmer Rouge)	1992	Oil embargo and ban on exports of timber, minerals and gems	**Moderate**: 'Paris accord and sanctions contributed to isolation and weakening of Khmer Rouge'
Somalia	1992–	Arms embargo	**Low**: 'UN embargo sparked limited cease-fire; fighting in 1996 ended due to lack of ammunition'
Libya	1992–99	Arms embargo, aviation sanctions, partial assets freeze, ban on oil equipment imports (suspended)	**Moderate to high**: 'Sanctions a factor in negotiations that brought suspected terrorists to the Netherlands for trial in 1999; Libyan support for international terrorism reportedly reduced'
Liberia	1992–2001 2001–07	1992–2001: arms embargo 2001–: arms and diamond embargo; travel ban	**None**: 'UN arms embargo ineffective in constraining NPFL; threat of ECOWAS sanctions following NPFL military rampage in 1996 put peace process back on track and led to elections'
Haiti	1993 1993–4	1993: arms and oil embargo (suspended) 1993–4: comprehensive embargo	**Low**: 'UN sanctions led to Governors Island agreement, but inconsistency and hesitancy reduced impact'
Angola (UNITA)	1993–2002	1993–2002: oil and arms embargo 1997–2002: travel and diplomatic sanctions 1998–2002: financial sanctions and diamond embargo	**None**: 'Sanctions provided little or no bargaining leverage and did not prevent UNITA from waging war and becoming a large well-armed military force'
Rwanda	1994–96	Arms embargo	**None**: 'UN arms embargo too late and too little to prevent genocide; unable to halt widening of conflict to eastern Congo'
Sudan	1996–2001	Diplomatic sanctions, aviation sanctions (threatened but not imposed)	**None**: 'No response to demand for extradition of terrorist suspects; no reported change in support for international terrorism'
Sierra Leone	1997–98 1998–2003	1997–98: oil and arms embargo, travel ban 1998–: arms embargo and travel ban on RUF 2000–03: partial diamond embargo (expired)	**None**: 'Sanctions sparked negotiations but did not prevent rebel movement from accumulating arms and launching military offensives'
Afghanistan (Taliban)	1999–	1999–2002: aviation sanctions 1999–: financial sanctions	**None**
Eritrea and Ethiopia	2000–01	Arms embargo (expired)	**None**

Sources: (Chesterman and Pouligny 2003, 505), column 4: (Cortright and Lopez 2000, 205–7).

also hampered by bureaucratic UN procedures. 'Administrative difficulties at the UN stemmed from the sanctions committee's case-by-case review of applications for humanitarian imports and the frequent holds placed on items that could be considered dual use' (Cortright and Lopez 2000, 49). Efforts to improve the process were slow and met with partial success only. A report on the entire UN programme, published in 2005 by external investigator Paul Volcker, concluded that implementation had not been firmly in the UN's grasp as a result of careless surveillance, a shortage of accountants and a conflict of interest for the programme director. Secretary-general Annan himself was mentioned negatively in the conclusion, as it was discovered that his son was employed by a company working for the programme. The failure of the UN to handle a programme which was far too large and too difficult for its bureaucracy harmed its reputation. As an organization it was not sufficiently equipped for the task, also because it had been unable to prevent Iraqi politicians selling oil and keeping the money themselves.

Sanctions against Libya (1992–99)

UN sanctions against Libya imposed in 1992 and in 1993 (see Figure 38.1) after an assault on American soldiers in a Berlin disco were preceded by unilateral US sanctions in the 1980s, including an air strike on Tripoli in 1986. The bombing of an American aircraft over Lockerbie, Scotland, in December 1988 and of a French plane over Nigeria in September 1989 resulted in arrest warrants for high Libyan officials and in domestic public pressure in the UK and the US for tougher action against Libya, which showed a lack of cooperation with the criminal investigations. The resulting UN sanctions were selective (oil equipment, travel and finance) and appropriately tailored to the offence, the bombing of airliners. They had modest impacts on Libya's economy, but the pressure of both the UN and the US was sufficient to cause serious inconvenience. Libya resented diplomatic isolation and could not solve some of the economic hardships caused. The fact that the sanctions remained in force for more than seven years after 1992 contributed to the emergence of a bargaining dynamic, with both sides making some concessions. Neighbouring states and regional organizations such as the Arab League and the Organization of African Unity in particular applied pressure on the permanent members of the UN Security Council to adopt more flexible diplomacy or face an end to sanctions compliance (Cortright and Lopez 2000, 109). Finally Libya, faced with international isolation, in the Arab world as well, announced it was prepared to turn over the suspected officials and to have them tried by a Scottish tribunal sitting in the Netherlands. During the legal process Libya championed the norms and standards of international law and respect for international organizations, responding to the fact that the proponents of the sanctions had built their case on these norms and procedures. This unexpected tactic, based on liberal internationalism, created a dilemma for the pro-sanctions states: 'continuing to insist on the sanctions regime in the face of rising defections by UN members increased the risk to the credibility of the Council. Faced with a trade-off between defending sanctions and defending the Council itself, the United States and United Kingdom (UK) eventually agreed to a compromise in 1998 that they had earlier rejected' (Hurd 2005, 496).

Regional organizations and sanctions

Regional organizations played a role in sanctions against Haiti, Sierra Leone and Liberia. The sanctions the Organization of American States imposed on Haiti in 1991 after the military takeover there were based on the strongest-ever resolution adopted by the OAS, condemning the coup and demanding the return of the legitimately-elected government. The sanctions aimed at diplomatic and economic isolation and the UN General Assembly supported this. However, the OAS lacked the authority and the institutional capacity to enforce compliance with trade sanctions. Two years later the UN Security Council became involved more actively by imposing sanctions and establishing a sanctions committee, but its efforts were piecemeal and lacked credibility, with non-OAS states not imposing sanctions and OAS members widely circumventing them (Cortright and Lopez 2000, 99). In 1997 the Economic Community of West African States and the UN instituted economic sanctions against Sierra Leone in reaction to a military coup (see §37.7). The enforcement effort however was impeded by a lack of institutional capacity on the part of the UN and inadequate resources on the part of ECOWAS. Therefore they were unable to prevent the rebels expanding their military power and winning significant victories, giving them a more favourable position at the negotiating table. 'In one of the most impoverished regions of the World, with both Sierra Leone and Liberia ravaged by war, the means for enforcing sanctions simply did not exist' (Cortright and Lopez 2000, 174). Liberia's President Charles Taylor had his own disagreement with ECOWAS and succeeded in circumventing the arms embargo by allowing weapons to be transported to Sierra Leone via Liberia. The ECOWAS sanctions and the military actions by its monitoring force ECOMOG for a time constrained Taylor, but they did not stop him. The UN Observer Mission in Liberia attempted to monitor the implementation of demobilization agreements, but it did not have the means to respond to the numerous violations, which meant that the ECOWAS and UN sanctions finally had little impact (Cortright and Lopez 2000, 191–92). By the end of the 1990s this commitment of regional organizations met with public appreciation, particularly in cases of humanitarian intervention. However, the relationship between regional action and the general UN security responsibility as defined in the UN Charter became a matter of dispute. In the UN General Assembly of 1999 US President Clinton defended NATO's military intervention in Kosovo without UN approval (see §37.7), as he regarded it as being based on previous UN resolutions. He believed that regional organizations had the right to undertake military action in their own vicinity against mass murder, as long as this was done under UN auspices. He illustrated this by citing the example of ECOWAS and of the military force in East Timor led by Australia. The conclusion of the debate at the time was that the UN had been and remained responsible for peace and security and that military intervention by regional organizations without UN approval should not become the rule in international relations. Nonetheless, the ultimate UN responsibility as defined in Chapter VIII and Article 52 of the Charter (see §19.4) had been questioned and even undermined.

38.2 The increased role of NGOs in security after the end of the Cold War

Another type of war, another context for NGOs

Changes in the conduct of war and the related peacekeeping operations after the end of the Cold War also had consequences for the functioning of the specialized agencies and NGOs, in particular for relief organizations helping people affected by natural or man-made disasters, such as wars and genocide. The 'original' model for the behaviour of relief organizations was based on conflicts between states, with three processes taking place. First of all states and IGOs undertook action to bring warring parties to the negotiating table to end their conflicts. Then security was provided for refugees and humanitarian organizations, such as the International Red Cross and relief IGOs and NGOs, based on the international procedures and protocols of the Geneva Conventions and the 1951 UN Refugee Convention. This enabled them to meet refugees or prisoners of war so they could assess their needs and take action. If no procedure was relevant because one or more of the states were not signatories, then signing became a matter to be negotiated first. In most cases the belligerent states themselves provided the guarantees of safe access for relief workers. Finally the specialized agencies, such as UNHCR, WFP and UNICEF, and the humanitarian NGOs provided their humanitarian assistance through the delivery of food, water, sanitation, medical aid and refugee relocation (Lindenberg and Bryant 2001, 69). The new ethnic conflicts, mostly taking place within states, provided a completely different context for relief IGOs and NGOs, as there were no procedures available for dealing with states falling apart as a result of intrastate conflicts between parties and warlords. In Somalia in 1993 the humanitarian NGOs had to negotiate with a number of factions, whose territories and coalitions kept changing. Many of these factions did not have any knowledge of international law, nor did they feel the need to cooperate with humanitarian agencies. The increase in the number of child soldiers (see Figure 38.2) added to the weakening of traditional military discipline. Furthermore, as a result of these trends neither states nor IGOs felt encouraged to undertake diplomatic action to bring belligerents in Africa to the negotiating table. This complicated the roles of peacekeeping forces and made it difficult to guarantee security for refugees and aid workers. 'As a result, in the new world of complex emergencies, humanitarian action by the NGO's and ICRC [International Committee of the Red Cross] has been provided without adequate security and without world pressure to bring belligerents to the bargaining table to get them to accept international human rights

Figure 38.2 The phenomenon of child soldiers and the UN Protocol (2000)

In the **UN Convention on the Rights of the Child** of 1989 (see Figure 33.1) the minimum age for recruitment of soldiers was 15 years old. In 2000 an Optional Protocol was adopted which set 18 as the minimum age for recruitment and participation in hostilities. States may accept volunteers from the age of 16, but only under certain safeguards. The adoption of this Protocol was promoted by the **Coalition to Stop the Use of Child Soldiers**. This NGO federation was established by human rights and humanitarian relief NGOs in 1988 and had strong ties to UNICEF and the International Red Cross. It was estimated that when the Protocol entered into force in February 2002 some 300,000 children were used as child soldiers in 35 conflicts, in both guerrilla and civil wars. Many of these children were between 15 and 17 years old, but often they were younger. They are cheap troops and can be easily influenced and told what to do. Their opportunities to go to school and to develop into normal citizens are severely restricted, in addition to the traumatization resulting from their work and duties as soldiers.

protocols, anti-genocide protocols, or normal guarantees to refugees and innocent civilians' (Lindenberg and Bryant 2001, 71). In some situations NGOs became the actors doing the 'dirty' work, as they were taking medicines and food to places where states were no longer willing to send their troops. Such situations made NGOs believe that they were 'being used' by states, as a less expensive substitute for long-term international action to deal with the causes of conflicts and to bring warring parties to the negotiating table.

Limitations of relief organizations

The specialized UN agencies were also insufficiently prepared for these new security relations. The mandate of the refugee organization UNHCR covered refugees living outside their country of origin, but not those remaining within a state as IDPs or *Internally Displaced Persons*. Since the 1970s UNHCR had progressively included IDPs in its work, but mostly on an informal and self-elected basis. Although IDPs had the same needs and difficulties as refugees the international community had long ignored them, as they had not crossed international borders. During the 1990s UNHCR began to increase its work with IDPs, but without changing its mandate. A formal expansion of the mandate would have disturbed relations among those involved in refugee activities within UNHCR and would have burdened it with a for the organization harmful responsibility. Although a number of states and NGOs urged UNHCR to also engage with IDPs, the organization itself remained hesitant about this until 2000. There was no agreement among the states on the question of UNHCR policies towards IDPs, with the ensuing responsibilities to protect and assist them, and many G77 states in particular stressed their sovereignty in this respect. UNHCR therefore preferred to continue without an expanded mandate, rather than with one that was unclear with regard to possible action (Freitas 2004, 127–28). 'Instead, it opted to ensure policy flexibility and retain decision-making capacity on a case-by-case basis, thus satisfying the different actors as the situations occurred' (Freitas 2004, 134). This left much of the work to humanitarian NGOs. But even when UNHCR itself was active and had the authority to protect refugees it sometimes was unable to do so because of a lack of adequate protection. During the 1990s the reluctance of states to provide the UN with troops had increased, given the large risk of casualties in unsafe areas. Relief organizations therefore had to function with less, or even without, military protection. Even for the international forces in East Timor in 1999 it was weeks before Annan had found one state (Australia) willing to contribute some troops. Security for humanitarian workers thus became a problem through both the nature of the conflicts and this lack of official protection, while warring parties were increasingly willing to target aid workers and to capitalize on their deaths for political purposes. 'For example, in 1996 and 1997, seven ICRC medical personnel in Chechnya, three Médecins Sans Frontières staff in Rwanda, and three UN human rights monitors' in Rwanda were assassinated (Lindenberg and Bryant 2001, 79).

Doctors Without Borders

As inconvenient as independent NGOs could be for governments, given their open criticisms and autonomous strategies, governments also if required made themselves less visible, by adopting a policy of official non-interference while letting NGOs act as their informal agents to achieve certain goals. This happened when NGOs expressed opinions that governments for political reasons did not want to air, or did not want to state that explicitly. Sometimes the chance of success was greater if aid was provided through NGOs rather than directly, as this avoided any suggestion of paternalism or political influence. The other side to this coin was that NGOs were able to operate and achieve some measure of success in humanitarian activities, such as providing medical aid, food, child care and educational benefits (Feld *et al.* 1994, 219–20). During the 1980s and 1990s NGOs increasingly became co-implementers of UN development and aid policies. In addition a number of them began to play roles of their own in humanitarian interventions, attaching great value to their independence. In 1974 the initiators of *Médecins Sans Frontières* (MSF) had created a new organization because, as workers for the International Red Cross, they had been able to work in a foreign state only with the consent of its government. This was contrary to their view that all victims in a state should be helped, whether the government or leading power permitted it or not. The work of these brave NGOs was highly appreciated by the public and citizens, while governments were prepared to support them financially.

Undermining NGO impartiality

During the 1990s humanitarian NGO work was undermined by the increasing acceptance of humanitarian activities being carried out by intervention forces. During the operation in Kosovo in 1999 NATO soldiers were also engaged in refugee relief, food drops and other relief work. This involvement in activities that used to be carried out by humanitarian IGOs and NGOs and the fact that military personnel worked in civilian clothes or used non-military vehicles blurred the roles of armed forces and relief workers. It left unclear to refugees who was helping them: the soldiers involved or independent relief workers. The view expressed in the Brahimi report that integrated UN operations of military and non-military units should be used resulted in a similar mixture of identities. This report had been written for the UN by Brahimi in 2000 in an effort to strengthen UN peacekeeping operations (see §37.6). The consequence of this development was that NGOs lost the independent and impartial position they had always claimed and emphasized. Later their independence was to be undermined even further, when they became involved in political campaigns of states and organizations such as the 'war on terror', or were allowed into combat areas only in the military vehicles of the involved states or the UN. In other situations NGOs could not even begin their activities because states, or the UN, were still negotiating on the conditions for access and relief in a conflict area. During the negotiations, or if they failed, NGOs had to remain inactive, which was exactly what they wanted to avoid given their objective of helping all victims under all conditions.

CARE: no reason to withdraw

In the late 1990s relief NGOs began to re-evaluate their roles and responses to crises and discussed the question of under which conditions they would stop relief work if neutral roles during complex emergencies were no longer possible. Given their mandates they were not in favour of withdrawing from operational responses. In 1997 the American private organization CARE decided to stick to 'active humanitarianism'. CARE was established by a number of US NGOs in 1945 to provide relief to the survivors of the Second World War. They sent millions of lifesaving aid packages, first to the states in Europe and later to Asia. During the 1950s and 1960s CARE used American food surpluses to feed the hungry in the developing world and it gradually developed long-term programmes for large-scale problems such as health care and famines. This shift in purpose caused it to change its name from 'Cooperative for American Remittances to Europe' to 'Cooperative for Assistance and Relief Everywhere'. Citizens in conflict areas, according to NGOs such as this, have the right to stay alive and survive during both natural and man-made disasters. Huge organizations like CARE (with a total revenue of more than 423 million dollars in 2000 and 606 million dollars in 2007) deeply believed that an operational response was necessary and that they could work positively and constructively for innocent people who needed help to rebuild their lives once emergencies were over. If such states of emergency arose, organizations such as CARE would attempt to respond. However, in complex emergencies their operations could not start if there was no guaranteed safe access to the people who needed help. This meant that CARE would first negotiate with belligerents over when and where access was possible. If required, CARE would ask for UN protection. Given their inclination to stick to active humanitarianism and to look for ways of remaining neutral, NGOs like Médecins Sans Frontières and CARE seemed more enterprising under the new conditions of the 1990s than the UN and its specialized agencies.

The World Court Project on the use of nuclear weapons (1996)

The original UN restriction to economic and social affairs on the consultative status for NGOs (see §20.6) lost some of its meaning with the increasing NGO influence on security issues in the International Court of Justice and the UN Security Council during the 1990s. With regard to the International Court, NGOs had decided to ask for an advisory opinion from the Court on the legality of nuclear weapons. The resulting *World Court Project* to request such an opinion received the support of New Zealand, which began to look for further state and NGO support. The International Physicians for the Prevention of Nuclear War, an NGO awarded the Nobel Peace Prize in 1985, endorsed the project and succeeded in convincing the World Health Organization to adopt a resolution on the topic in May 1993. Supported by international lawyers and parliamentarians the First Committee of the UN General Assembly in November 1994 also passed a resolution, which was fairly similar to that of the WHO. With the backing of the Non-Aligned Movement the General Assembly then adopted this resolution on the legality of the use of nuclear weapons. 'Within days the case arrived at the World Court, which decided to consider WHO and General Assembly questions separately but simultaneously.' On 8 July 1996 the International Court of Justice delivered its decision. It regarded the threat or use of nuclear weapons contrary to the law of armed conflict, in particular international humanitarian law, but could not conclude whether it would be lawful or unlawful in an extreme case of self-defence, in which the very survival of a state would be at stake. 'NGOs in this case used access through states and through consultative status with ECOSOC, coupled with legal expertise and social movement organizing, to obtain a result from the International Court of Justice that powerful nuclear states had opposed' (Stephenson 2000, 287). The entire case was 'NGO driven. Heavy and well organized lobbying had led to the organizations seeking an opinion from the Court'. Despite pressure for the Court to recognize the written information from NGOs, it decided not to make this part of the case. But it also decided that it would not simply throw these documents out. 'They were placed in the library, and every judge knew from week to week what was coming in, and it was up to each judge to decide if he wished to go beyond the already voluminous official pleadings and to read the other materials' (Higgings 1998, 2). The possibility was even discussed that the Court 'might in the future be able to receive briefs *amicus curiae* from NGOs or from other knowledgeable persons'. Many national superior courts admit these 'intervening arguments' in written form, as they add to the spectrum of data upon which they are able to base their decision (Higgings 1998, 1–2).

The Security Council and NGO consultation (1997)

When Kofi Annan began his first term as UN secretary-general some NGOs, such as the International Red Cross, CARE, Oxfam and Médecins Sans Frontières, were in February 1997 given the opportunity to take their views about the problems of global humanitarian response to the Security Council. The meeting with the Council members lasted twice as long as planned and was followed by a meeting with Annan himself. These talks resulted in additional Security Council briefings by NGOs on special problems. Given their involvement in the consequences of armed conflicts and their provision of humanitarian aid the NGOs proved interesting partners for Security Council members. During 1997 the focus of these briefings was Africa, with some 30 NGOs participating. The outcome of this was a code of conduct which was supported by 144 NGOs, the inclusion of regular NGO representation in the *UN Interagency Standing Committee on Emergency Response* and better access to UN special envoys (Lindenberg and Bryant 2001, 93–94). The approach showed some mutual reliance between NGOs and the UN in this respect. It was an informal way of cooperating for NGOs and Security Council members based on political willingness, which could be terminated at any time. But this cooperation also showed that during the 1990s NGOs were playing a role that was recognized and approved within, and by, the UN. This did not alter the independent commitment of NGOs to go to disaster areas and to assist victims under all circumstances, even if their staff members were threatened, held hostage or killed, or if IGOs were not ready to cooperate with NGO missions. Political relations however decided about their presence and the extent of available facilities. Médecins Sans Frontières was in Iraq during the Gulf War, but was expelled by the Iraqi government later and did not return until the end of 2002. In 2003, during the siege of the capital Baghdad by the US army (see §44.2), part of the organization there remained functional. But when in 2004 even aid workers were being abducted and taken hostage the organization felt obliged to restrict its activities and eventually, as the risks were too great, to leave Iraq. In 2004 Médecins Sans Frontières left Afghanistan as well, as the US-led military forces also undertook relief work and MSF could no longer function independently.

The Ottawa Convention on Landmines (1997)

At a time when states increased and modernized their armaments NGOs devoted themselves to promoting bans on the use of weapons that were particularly harmful to citizens, such as landmines, light arms and cluster bombs. The adoption of a convention on landmines in 1997 by 122 states was initiated by NGOs. The *Convention of Ottawa* aimed at prohibiting the production and use of a type of weapon that had been used for many years, but that had also been criticized from a humanitarian point of view. The Convention was a part of international humanitarian law (measures that make up the laws of armed conflict, or *jus in bello*) rather than of the arms control agreements that had

613

resulted from the Geneva Conference on Disarmament (see §24.1) (Thakur and Maley 1999). The initiative was taken by the *International Campaign to Ban Landmines* (ICBL), a network of NGOs first started in November 1991 by American Vietnam War veterans and the German NGO Medico International. Together with Handicap International, Human Rights Watch, the Mines Advisory Group and Physicians for Human Rights they established ICBL in October 1992. This fairly flexible network, which included some 1,100 NGOs from 60 states in 2006, launched a campaign to ban landmines. ICBL aimed at both politicians and public opinion, by alerting them to the existence of 110 million landmines in 64 states and the disastrous effects of people stepping on landmines which had been placed or which were left when conflicts ended. The campaign showed that the Inhumane Weapons Convention of 1980 (see §24.2) was ineffective with regard to these mines. The first conference on landmines which included states was held in Cambodia in early 1995, with a follow-up conference in Ottawa in 1996. That the Convention of Ottawa was realized was due to the combination of a number of well-motivated states led by Canada (including Austria, New Zealand, Norway and South Africa), the NGOs as part of the ICBL led by the American Jody Williams and the active support of UN secretary-general Boutros-Ghali. Under the leadership of Canada the unanimous group of states succeeded in drafting a convention in a relatively short time and in finding sufficient political support. On 3 December 1997 in Ottawa 122 states signed the *Convention on the Prohibition of the Use, Stockpiling, Production and Transfer of Anti-Personnel Mines and on Their Destruction*. It came into force on 1 March 1999. The ICBL and its coordinator Jody Williams were awarded the Nobel Peace Prize in 1997, which added to the legitimacy of their efforts. Some 40 states, among them the US, did not sign. The US refused to sign because its attempt to change the draft in September 1997 had been rejected. This stance put it in a difficult situation, given the wide support and sympathy for the campaign. When the Inhumane Weapons Convention was revised in 1996 ICBL had been present and had succeeded in emphasizing its Second Protocol on landmines. Even if this did not prohibit landmines, it regulated their use more precisely. This revised Second Protocol entered into force in 1998 and received the support of the major landmine-producing states that did not want to be signatories to the Convention of Ottawa, such as China, India, Israel, Pakistan, Russia and the US. By 2008 156 states had signed the Convention of Ottawa, of which 151 had also ratified.

Action against light weapons

The success of the Convention of Ottawa on landmines gave new impetus to the older discussion on *Small Arms and Light Weapons* (SALW in jargon). The UN had opened its Register for Conventional Arms in 1992 (see Figure 36.1) and at the end of 1997 NGOs began to campaign for a convention on light weapons. Their efforts were supported by regional organizations such as ECOWAS, EU and OAS and were also discussed within the UN in the functional ECOSOC Commission on Crime Prevention and Criminal Justice, because of the illegal trade in light weapons. A Panel of Governmental Experts set up by the secretary-general produced a definition, while NGOs drafted a code of conduct on small arms transfer, which should be considered as a gentlemen's agreement on which states can be held politically accountable. In July 2001 the UN convened a conference of 174 participating states, which discussed the wide availability of light arms and adopted a programme of action to prevent and eradicate the illegal trade in small arms and light weapons. The outcome, a programme but no convention, fell short of the expectations of many NGOs, but it was also the spur for creating the *International Action Network on Small Arms* (IANSA), which has dedicated itself to achieving a binding instrument. Official progress however was limited. In 2005 an agreement was reached on marking and tracing illegal weapons and the UN review conference in 2006 did evaluate the implementation of the programme. However, it failed to agree on an outcome document.

Cluster bombs

A further coalition of NGOs was set up to attain an international convention prohibiting the use of cluster bombs. The *Cluster Munition Coalition* (CMC), formed in November 2003, campaigned in similar ways to the ICBL. When states party to the 1980 Convention on Conventional Weapons failed to agree to begin negotiations on cluster bombs, it prompted Norway to declare in November 2006 that it would spearhead a campaign for an international ban on these weapons. This resulted in the *Oslo Conference on Cluster Munitions* (OCCM) in February 2007, which discussed the humanitarian problems caused by cluster bombs. The states present committed themselves to establishing a legally-binding international instrument to prohibit the use, production, transfer and stockpiling of cluster bombs. Of the 49 participating states Japan, Poland and Romania did not agree with the final declaration, while China, Russia and the US were not represented at Oslo. The diplomatic conference of May 2008 in Dublin adopted the *Convention on Cluster Munitions*, which was open for signature from December. This conference was attended by more than 100 states.

38.3 War crimes, crimes against humanity and UN tribunals

The Yugoslavia Tribunal established (1993)

After the Second World War, war crimes were tried by military tribunals at Nuremberg and Tokyo. In 1948 the UN adopted the Genocide Convention (see §21.1), while the International Red Cross revised and expanded the Geneva Conventions. From 1948 on the UN International Law Commission (ILC) discussed whether, and if so how, an international criminal court should be created. Drafts were produced in 1951 and 1953, but the General Assembly preferred to wait for the requested definition of aggression (see §24.1) and then became inactive. The debate about a criminal court was not resurrected until after the end of the Cold War. In 1989 Trinidad and Tobago asked for the establishment of an international criminal court that would also deal with the illegal drug trade and the ILC presented its draft for such a court to the UN General Assembly in 1993. But because decision making would take some time and meanwhile serious violations of international humanitarian law seemed to be taking place in the wars in the former Yugoslavia, the UN Security Council, acting under Chapter VII of the Charter, decided in May 1993 to establish the *International Tribunal for the Prosecution of Persons Responsible for Serious Violations of International Humanitarian Law Committed in the Territory of the Former Yugoslavia Since 1991*, commonly referred to as the *International Criminal Tribunal for the Former Yugoslavia* (ICTY), or Yugoslavia Tribunal. The Council had reacted to the developments in the former Yugoslavia on the advice of a committee of experts that had closely followed and documented the events. The Yugoslavia Tribunal was established in The Hague and was the first institution for international criminal prosecution since the end of the Second World War. It could not start functioning until a prosecutor had been found, who was to be responsible for investigating crimes, gathering evidence and prosecuting the indicted. The chief prosecutor is appointed by the Security Council on nomination by the secretary-general. South Africa was willing to make its judge Richard Goldstone available, who was prosecutor between 1994 and 1996. He was succeeded by Louise Arbour (1996–99), Carla del Ponte (1999–2008) and Serge Brammertz. This *ad hoc* Tribunal aims to complete all trials and appeals by 2010. It has jurisdiction over four groups of crimes: crimes against humanity (murder, extermination, enslavement, deportation, imprisonment, torture and persecutions on political, racial and religious grounds), grave breaches of the 1949 Geneva Conventions, genocide, and violations of the laws or customs of war. The last include the use of toxic weapons or other weapons calculated to cause unnecessary suffering, wanton destruction of cities, towns or villages, or devastation not justified by military necessity; attack, or bombardment, by whatever means, of undefended towns, villages, dwellings or buildings; seizure of, destruction or wilful damage done to institutions dedicated to religion, charity and education, the arts and sciences, historic monuments and works of art and science; and plunder of public or private property. The Tribunal can try individuals only. It cannot sentence in absentia, but it may collect evidence, publish this and call witnesses, something decided in order to draw attention to suspected persons and to have warrants out to arrest them. For the actual arrests the Tribunal is dependent on states and on NATO. After a reform-oriented president had came to power in the Federal Republic of Yugoslavia in 2000, President Milošević was handed over to the Tribunal. His trial, in which he conducted his own defence, ended without a verdict because he died in 2006 during the proceedings. By that time the Tribunal had filed complaints against 161 people.

The International Court on Genocide in Bosnia (2007)

In February 2007 the International Court of Justice, also located in The Hague, gave its judgement on what had happened in the former Yugoslavia. This had been set in motion by an American law professor, Francis Boyle, and was unrelated to what was happening at the Yugoslavia Tribunal. In the case of Bosnia and Herzegovina versus Serbia and Montenegro the International Court of Justice concluded that the crimes committed in Srebrenica in 1995 were acts of genocide. However, it cleared Serbia of direct involvement in genocide during the Bosnian War, although it also ruled that Serbia did breach the Genocide Convention by failing to prevent the Srebrenica genocide and failing to deliver the persons accused of genocide to the Yugoslavia Tribunal. In August 2008, however, Serbia delivered Radovan Karadzic to the Tribunal in The Hague.

The Rwanda Tribunal (1994)

In November 1994 the UN Security Council established the *International Criminal Tribunal for Rwanda* (ICTR), following the genocide that had taken place in that state in 1994 (see §37.5). This *ad hoc* Tribunal, modelled on the Yugoslavia Tribunal, was sited in Arusha, Tanzania, with its prosecutor located in Kigali, Rwanda. Its aims are to contribute to the process of national reconciliation and the maintenance of peace in the region. It also deals with violations perpetrated in neighbouring states, such as Burundi and Congo. From 1999 to 2003 Carla del Ponte was prosecutor at both the Rwanda and the Yugoslavia Tribunal. In May 2008 the Tribunal had handed down 30 judgements involving 36 accused.

The establishment of the International Criminal Court (1998)

On 17 July 1998 negotiations resulted in the establishment of the envisaged *International Criminal Court* (ICC). The diplomatic conference in Rome which adopted its Statute was convened by the UN and attended by 148 states, 33 IGOs and 236 NGOs, the last belonging to the *Coalition for an International Criminal Court* which had been created by 25 NGOs in 1995. They were not only observers but also participants, with special representation in each of the five regional groups. 120 states voted for the ICC's Statute, seven including the US were against and 21 abstained. Unlike the Yugoslavia and Rwanda Tribunals the ICC was not set up by the Security Council, but was established on the basis of a multilateral treaty with state parties. The ICC is a court of last resort, investigating and prosecuting only when national courts have failed. As long as a case is dealt with by a national court the ICC does not become involved, unless a show trial is taking place. It is not allowed to exercise universal jurisdiction but can operate only under limited circumstances, due in large part to opposition from the US. Despite their objections states such as Iran, Israel and the US signed the Statute on the very last day possible. Because of its ambivalent attitude the US government under President Clinton had instructed its delegation only four weeks before the start of the Rome conference. As a result of this hesitancy the delegation had not enough time to informally and properly discuss its wishes and demands. The US was not strongly in favour of such a Court, as it was afraid of politicization, given the fact that the US as a major power was often in a position to solve international problems militarily, which implied a larger risk of extradition to the Court for Americans than for other nationals. The US also believed that the Court should be allowed to initiate cases only if the state whose nationals were involved agreed. Furthermore, it believed that aggression should not be mentioned in the Statute and that investigations should be started at the request of the Security Council rather than the prosecutor. The International Criminal Court's Rome Statute became a binding treaty when 60 states had ratified. It came into force on 1 July 2002 and the Court can only prosecute crimes committed after that date. By 2006 just over 100 states were members of the ICC. The Court is located in The Hague, where an inaugural ceremony took place in March 2003. In 2004 it concluded a relationship agreement with the UN. The ICC is independent of the UN, although it granted certain powers to the Security Council and it reports on its activities to the UN each year. In April 2003 chief prosecutor Luis Moreno-Ocampo was appointed. He launched the first ICC cases, against Uganda (the Lord's Resistance Army), the Democratic Republic of Congo (situation in Ituri), the Central African Republic and Sudan (because of Darfur). This last case was referred to the ICC by the Security Council in March 2005. In July 2008 Moreno-Ocampo presented evidence showing that the Sudanese President Omar Al Bashir committed genocide, crimes against humanity and war crimes in Darfur. If the ICC's pre-trial chamber confirms these charges, it will mark the ICC's first indictment of a head of state.

The US as an opponent of the ICC

One of the main opponents of the International Criminal Court proved to be the US under President George W. Bush, who set in motion a policy of isolating the ICC over fears that the politicized Court would unfairly target US military personnel abroad with charges of war crimes. In 2002 the US and Israel both 'unsigned' the Rome Statute, which in diplomacy is a fairly ambiguous act, because they no longer wanted to be party to it or have legal obligations arising from their signatures. Furthermore, in August 2002 Congress passed the *American Servicemembers' Protection Act*. It was introduced by Senator Jesse Helms as an amendment to the *Defense Authorization Act*, with the purpose 'to protect United States military personnel and other elected and appointed officials of the United States government against criminal prosecution by an international criminal court to which the United States is not party'. The Act allowed the US government to protect US citizens from extradition to the ICC and also authorized any necessary action 'to free US soldiers improperly handed over to that Court', which is why it was also called *The Hague Invasion Act*. The Act also prohibited the US from providing military aid to states which had ratified the Rome Statute, with a number of exceptions such as NATO members and major non-NATO allies. In addition to the Act the US began to enter into *Bilateral Immunity Agreements* with states, which stipulated that they would not hand over US nationals to the ICC. Out of the first 99 members of the ICC 49 refused to sign such an agreement, as they regarded it to be contrary to the Rome Statute. Many of the states that refused to sign were to all intents and purposes punished and lost US military aid or economic support. According to the US it had entered into these agreements with nearly 100 states by 2005. Within the UN the US in July 2002 demanded that the Security Council should agree to permanently exempt US nationals from the ICC's jurisdiction and threatened to use its veto to block renewal of the mandates of UN peacekeeping operations. The US met with opposition and the UK succeeded in brokering a weaker arrangement to run for a year, which was renewed for another year in 2003, but did not get a majority in 2004 after the abuse of prisoners in Abu Ghraib prison in Iraq by American military personnel. The US then ended its efforts to exempt US nationals from ICC jurisdiction through the Security Council. In practice the US gradually reconciled itself to the ICC's existence, without openly confirming this, but with the Security Council in 2005 referring the situation in Darfur to the ICC.

The Special Court for Sierra Leone (2002)

The establishment of the International Criminal Court did not stop the creation of more *ad hoc* tribunals. This happened for Sierra Leone (2002) and Cambodia (2005) and to investigate the murder of the former Lebanese Prime Minister Rafiq Hariri (2007). The *Special Court for Sierra Leone* had its roots in the civil war that broke out in 1991 and was ended with an agreement in November 1996, but had a sequel until 2002 (see §37.7 and §38.1). On the initiative of the Sierra Leonean President Ahmad Tejan Kabbah, who contacted the UN secretary-general, the Special Court was established jointly by the government of Sierra Leone and the UN in January 2002. It is located in Freetown and aims to try those who bear the greatest responsibility for the war crimes and crimes against humanity committed in Sierra Leone since 30 November 1996. Compared with the Yugoslavia and Rwanda Tribunals, this Special Court is an internationalized version of the Sierra Leonean judicial system. Sierra Leone provides the Special Court with personnel and appoints some of the judges, who use both Sierra Leonean and international law. The non-Sierra Leonean judges are appointed by the UN. The US and the UK bear most of the costs. The trials began in 2004. 11 people were indicted, among them the former Liberian President Charles Taylor. After his expulsion from Liberia and arrest in Nigeria in early 2006 Taylor was transferred to prison in The Hague in order to be tried there by the Special Court which uses the facilities of the International Criminal

Court. This was done for safety reasons and allowed by the UN Security Council, but it meant that Taylor's prosecution was to take place far from where the violations had occurred. Another side effect of the existence of the Special Court was that it obscured the activities of the truth and reconciliation commission that had started work in Sierra Leone simultaneously. By 2008 the trials of five people were concluded.

The UN and the Cambodia Tribunal (2005)

Compared with the independent tribunals for the former Yugoslavia, Rwanda and also Sierra Leone, the *Special Tribunal for Cambodia* is different, as it is a less independent institution restricted to prosecuting the former leaders of the Khmer Rouge for crimes committed between 1975 and 1979. After a request from Cambodia in 1997 the UN wanted to establish another *ad hoc* tribunal, but the Cambodian government refused this. Negotiations resulted in a memorandum of understanding, followed by Cambodian legislation of a nature that forced the UN to withdraw from the talks in early 2002. In 2003 an amended agreement was achieved, which was followed by revised Cambodian legislation and in 2005 resulted in the establishment of Extraordinary Chambers for the prosecution of crimes committed by the Khmer Rouge within the existing Cambodian court structure. The scope for the UN to establish an independent tribunal was limited due to its own involvement in Cambodia (see §34.1 and §37.5), but the UN had insisted that the crimes by the Pol Pot regime should be brought before a criminal court. The two Extraordinary Chambers of this hybrid 'international court' consist of 13 foreign and 16 Cambodian judges, who have to investigate crimes committed up to 30 years earlier. The process followed is mainly based on Cambodian law, but no judgement is possible without the agreement of at least one international judge. Close reading of the proceedings by NGOs, however, showed that the procedures could favour Cambodian judges. NGOs also criticized other factors, such as the Tribunal's location at an army base and in a state without a critical tradition, as well as the sluggish start. However, it was argued that time was pressing given the age of the main leaders and that it was better to have a least a certain number of them brought to justice.

38.4 The issue of humanitarian intervention and the responsibility to protect (R2P)

Non-intervention and a suffering population

Interventions by a state, a group of states and/or an IGO in the domestic affairs of another state are in violation of the fundamental non-intervention principle. Article 2.7 of the UN Charter lays down that there is nothing that authorizes the UN to intervene in matters which are essentially within the jurisdiction of any given state. It can be argued, however, that there are situations in which for humanitarian reasons interventions should take place in order to save, or liberate, a suffering population. Realists may ask whether good intentions are not a cover for other, more egoistic motives of intervening states, whether or not they are supported by IGOs (see Figure 44.1), but in a world in which human rights have turned into pivotal values and where a consciousness exists that the 'world' or the international community has failed too often, humanitarian intervention for ethical reasons received new impetus during the 1990s. In such cases the respect for human rights and fundamental freedoms, as mentioned in Article 1.3 of the Charter, gained supremacy over the non-intervention principle in Article 2.7. During the Cold War Tanzania intervened in Uganda (1978) and Vietnam in Cambodia (1979) in reaction to the huge death tolls resulting from, respectively, the Amin and the Khmer Rouge regimes. These interventions though were not explained by humanitarian principles but rather by the aggression that the neighbouring states had encountered. After the end of the Cold War, however, humanitarian sentiments became more important and resulted in intervention for the sake of helping a population suffering from harsh intrastate conflicts. Examples are the 'safe havens' for Kurds in Northern Iraq (1991), the American intervention in Somalia (1992–93), the French intervention in Rwanda (1994) and the intervention by ten NATO members in Kosovo in the Federal Republic of Yugoslavia (1999).

Problems related to humanitarian intervention

The main problems related to humanitarian intervention are its inconsistency with state sovereignty, the use of violence (which is in fact not allowed) and its weak legal basis. The only body able to provide legitimacy is the UN Security Council, but the UN itself as an organization is far from equipped for such interventions. Legitimacy remains restricted in any case, as Chapter VII of the Charter only mentions action with respect to threats to the peace, breaches of the peace and acts of aggression, and does not give humanitarian grounds. Public opinion plays a bigger role in this respect, because governments feel pressurized by citizens or NGOs to act and discuss this within the UN. This was dubbed the *CNN factor*, after the American news network that began to broadcast television news 24 hours a day worldwide, paying intense attention to conflicts and situations in which people suffer (Newman 1995). But the role of ethical motives and public opinion in domestic politics has its limitations. Public support for foreign actions decreases as soon as the intervening forces are suffering (too many) casualties. This is referred to as the *body bags syndrome* and can stop governments being willing to intervene. The other main problem is the huge, often unquantifiable effort that is needed to improve the situation after a successful intervention and to return it to normality. These reservations do not alter the fact that during the 1990s a shift occurred with regard to the thinking on humanitarian intervention, which gave the idea wider support despite problems with its legal and practical feasibility.

Human security as an international norm

So as to get a better understanding of the range of humanitarian interventions, the UN Development Programme in its annual *Human Development Report* of 1994 introduced the term *human security*. There are various views on what human security means, but they have in common a focus on suffering individuals, the waning of state sovereignty and the arrival of 'saving strangers' through humanitarian interventions and peacekeeping operations. A narrow view of human security centres on the natural rights of people and the rule of law anchored in basic human rights. A wider approach understands human security to be a tool for deepening and strengthening efforts to tackle issues such as war crimes and genocide and finally for preparing the ground for humanitarian intervention. A still broader approach links human security with the state of the global economy, development and globalization (Oberleitner 2005, 188). Canada took the idea of human security seriously, as an element that required priority in states' foreign policies. In 1999 it brought various states that agreed with this together in the *Human Security Network*. In the same year the UN created the *UN Trust Fund for Human Security*, followed in 2003 by a high-level advisory body. As regards content the concept of human security gradually began to take the form of an international norm, in a way similar to 'security' becoming a norm in international law in relation to conflicts between states. The assumption of human security is interventionist. 'As a concept of security based on values, it extends the security obligations of states beyond their borders. Under a human security concept, the use of force would be applied for more "cosmopolitan" goals – to manage human security threats' (Oberleitner 2005, 194).

The Responsibility to Protect

The *International Commission on Intervention and State Sovereignty* (ICISS), set up by Canada in 2000, regarded human security as the wider context for the relationship between state sovereignty and humanitarian intervention. ICISS did not want to emphasize the *right* to intervene, but rather the *responsibility to protect* (in SMS language: R2P). By changing the discourse from the right to intervene to the describing of intervention as a duty if a state is unwilling or unable to fulfil its responsibility to respect the human rights of its population, ICISS strengthened the idea of justifying humanitarian intervention as the responsibility of the other members of the international community to protect these rights. As a result of secretary-general Annan's devotion to this interpretation the idea of responsibility to protect became accepted within the UN and in 2004 was endorsed by a high-level panel. Humanitarian intervention in response to human rights abuses would be permissible under certain conditions, when the threat to human security was sufficiently great to justify the use of force to eliminate this threat. In line with this argument were measures already mentioned by Boutros-Ghali as 'post-conflict peacebuilding', which had the aim of reconstructing human security in weak states, or ensuring that a state would not fall back into chaos. This was expressed by the term *peacebuilding* (see §20.7). UNDP supported post-conflict reconstruction projects in Mozambique and Rwanda, in order to assist these states with eliminating uncertainties in a post-conflict situation and redesigning the institutional environments, 'hence rebuilding trust among the citizens and between them and the state'. The accompanying term used by UNDP was *social capital building* (Fred-Mensah 2004, 437). The emergence and acceptance of the term 'responsibility to protect' provided the UN, at a time when it was losing authority, with a new leading idea that once again supported its work as the world's peacekeeper and now also its peacebuilder.

Globalization in the 1990s

New challenges for the United Nations system as promoter of economic and social stability

Part XV discusses the consequences of globalization in relation to another US-instigated free trade drive. After an intervention by US President Reagan, the GATT began to discuss trade in services and intellectual property rights in addition to trade in goods. The GATT institutionalized further and the resulting WTO became a dominant organization with influential policies, which put a number of specialized UN agencies under pressure. But during the new Doha negotiation round and with regard to medical property rights the WTO also met with resistance from Third World states, which were getting stronger. UNCTAD, which was criticized but managed to survive despite being left in a weaker position, was overshadowed by the WTO (Chapter 39). The new free trade focus did not leave much room for international environmental and social policies. In the environmental field, however, conventions were adopted on the ozone layer, biodiversity, desertification and climate change, including the Kyoto Protocol, although not all major states supported these hard-won arrangements. The welfare state also came under pressure from the new free trade regime, but it succeeded in adapting to the new circumstances. Western Europe did not choose the IGO-supported American approach to tackling unemployment, but preferred the EEC approach. The ILO, also put under strain by the WTO, succeeded in fighting back and resumed its, previously threatened, position (Chapter 40). By the end of the 1990s the IMF and the IBRD were in trouble, mainly due to failures during the financial crises and lesser need for their services. They were criticized by developing states that were growing stronger and by the movement of 'anti'-and 'alter'-globalizationists. Citizens were also criticizing some international business behaviour, which resulted in principles for business in the UN Global Compact (Chapter 41).

Boosting free trade again

From GATT to World Trade Organization (1995)

39.1 Reagan's intervention in the deadlocked GATT: the Uruguay Round 1986–94

Beggar thy neighbour

Because of his dedication to free trade promotion, Reagan becoming US President in 1981 also had an impact on the GATT. At the time the free trade agreement functioned poorly and, although it took years, Reagan succeeded in actuating it again. Despite initial successes in reductions in tariffs and in promoting free trade (see §25.3) the GATT had run into trouble during the 1970s, when states began to make undesirable market agreements, called 'grey zones' or 'voluntary export restraints'. The GATT had not succeeded in concluding an arrangement for agricultural products and trade with the Third World advanced with difficulty. The causes of this paralysis in the early 1980s were partly structural, partly related to the absence of US leadership and the increased interdependence between industrially-developed states. The economies of OECD member states had become more and more similar. Imports from and labour in the Third World played an increasing role in the worldwide competition between the industrialized states, with strong pressure on governments from industrial business sectors in favour of protectionist policies. In the industrialized states new sectors and technologies, such as telecommunication and automation as well as growing services sectors, were becoming more important than traditional production. Due to international competition governments became more involved in the direction of the economic development of their states. They generated national industrial policies with tax advantages, subsidies, cartels and other favourable arrangements for the 'strategic' sectors of their national businesses. However, as they were new forms of protectionism these politico-economic trends constituted obstacles to international trade. The breakdown of the international monetary regime in the 1970s had contributed to the weakening of the GATT, because governments had devised a number of trade measures to protect their balance of payments, such as exchange controls, exchange rate manipulation, special duties and capital controls. Economic recession and inflation had enticed governments into creating disruptive national action and international management breakdown by adopting beggar-thy-neighbour policies. But that was contrary to what the GATT was about (Spero 1985, 103).

The US no longer the director

The increased interdependence between industrially-developed states from the late 1960s onwards demanded a different kind of trade coordination than that provided by the traditional GATT regime with its rounds of tariff negotiations. By then trade policies were no longer functions of general foreign policy (free trade supporting peace and security against the communist world), but were becoming policies in their own right. As domestic support for a multilateral trade regime had been rapidly weakening, the US government had become inactive regarding the GATT after the Kennedy Round of 1964–67 (see Figure 25.3). It met with stronger competition from two protectionist-oriented economic powers, the European Economic Community and Japan, and was losing its dominant leadership position. Instead of being the director of the free trade regime, the US became one of the leading actors. The weakening of US industry, the deterioration of its trade balance and the continuing protectionism of the EEC and Japan, which both had profited from the US-initiated tariff reductions in the Kennedy Round, created a serious problem. Both industry and trade unions in the US pressed for protection, even though the influential trade union federation AFL-CIO was a free trade proponent by tradition. This domestic situation left the US government with virtually no room to conclude international free trade agreements.

New protectionism in the 1970s

In August 1971 the US under President Nixon, with an economy suffering from stagnant productivity, rising inflation and a trade deficit, took the initiative by demanding major unilateral concessions from the EEC and Japan. Both rejected these demands, but made gestures of reconciliation and agreed to some minor concessions to appease protectionist forces in the American Congress. This resulted in a kind of truce, followed by bilateral agreements between the US, Japan and the EEC in 1972. At the suggestion of the US a high-level committee had been established within the OECD in 1971 to discuss proposals for trade and economic reform. For the industrialized states this made the OECD a more important forum in which to discuss international trade than the GATT, although the OECD discussion resulted in an agreement to begin new multilateral trade negotiations within the GATT framework (Spero 1985, 111). The negotiations started in 1973 in Tokyo, with nearly 100 states participating, and focused on non-tariff obstacles to trade. The opening of this Tokyo Round coincided with 'a retreat from liberalism and the beginning of a period of what many have called "the new protectionism"' in the form of, often secret, voluntary export restraint arrangements (Spero 1985, 112). The US no longer was the moving force behind a liberal trading order, but was instead the major force behind the new protectionism. The Tokyo Round lasted until 1979, when it was concluded with progress on regulating non-tariff barriers to trade, albeit that many developing states were not convinced of the value of the agreed codes and chose to remain outside the codes' purview. This left them 'open to discrimination that is legal under GATT's rules'. But the agreed codes were incomplete in another way, as they did not specify which forms of government intervention beyond direct export subsidies were to be considered trade barriers. There was no agreement on how to bring the rapid proliferation of voluntary export restraint arrangements under multilateral management, no agreement on agriculture and the topic of trade in services had not been discussed (Spero 1985, 116).

Reagan's initiative (1982)

In 1982 President Reagan changed the situation. For the first time since 1973 the US initiated a ministerial GATT meeting on international trade, demanding a halt to protectionism, progress in the trade in agricultural products and discussions on trade in services, investments and modern high-grade technology. The meeting in November, however, failed because of indecision, conflict and the sticking to national interests. The economic crisis prevented the EEC adopting any policy of liberalization, while the Third World was not in favour of liberalizing trade in services as long as trade in goods, such as textiles, was not achieving GATT objectives. Their experience with the Multi-Fibre Arrangement, which as an exception to free trade in principle aimed to offer developing states a chance of economic growth, was seldom positive. In practice the industrialized states mainly used the Arrangement as an instrument favouring their protectionism (see Figure 39.1). Within US domestic politics the pressure to reach international consensus increased as a result of the growing trade deficit, the unstable dollar, loss of markets for agricultural products to the EEC and the increasing necessity to conclude international agreements on patents, industrial design and trade secrets. Reagan's initiative resulted in a new ministerial GATT meeting in Punta del Este, Uruguay, in 1986 and in the beginning of a new round of negotiations, the Uruguay Round.

Figure 39.1 The Multi-Fibre Arrangement between North and South 1974–2005

The ***Arrangement Regarding International Trade in Textiles***, better known as the ***Multi-Fibre Arrangement***, was agreed by the GATT in 1974. It was renewed twice by the GATT, until the end of 1994, and the WTO then replaced it with the *Agreement on Textiles and Clothing* for the period 1995–2005. In 1961 a 'Cotton Arrangement' had come into existence within the GATT as a departure from free trade, covering the imports of cotton by industrialized states. The Arrangement was concluded after long negotiations, in which it was agreed that textile and clothing were labour-intensive industries that could help cotton-exporting states to strengthen their economies and so enhance their economic growth, thus allowing a temporary exception to free trade. Market access in the industrialized states was important because of the revenues for developing states. The *Long-Term Arrangement*

Regarding International Trade in Cotton Textiles, the Arrangement's full name, covered the period 1962–73. It allowed cotton-importing states to negotiate bilaterally with exporting states about quotas, covered by the rules of the multilateral Arrangement, with the explicit objective of achieving more free trade in the longer term. The replacement of the Cotton Arrangement by the Multi-Fibre Arrangement in 1974 allowed more fibres to be covered by a similar scheme. This extension was achieved against the background of the failure of the UN Development Decade and the negotiations about a New International Economic Order in the early 1970s (see §31.1). Developing states agreed, since the Multi-Fibre Arrangement allowed the control of protectionism in this business to some extent. Problems that might occur and the promotion of free trade were negotiable and industrialized states had to agree to a certain amount of growth in their textile imports.

The **implementation of the Multi-Fibre Arrangement**, however, showed many shortcomings. The EEC, for instance, imposed strong protection measures on its textile and clothing markets in 1977, when a textile crisis occurred as a result of the moving of production processes to the Third World, followed by the large-scale closure of textile factories in Western Europe. Although the Multi-Fibre Arrangement was meant as an interim phase aimed at more free trade, the policies of the EEC and other industrialized states virtually turned the Arrangement into an instrument for more protectionism. By the end of the 1980s nearly half of the trade in textiles and clothing under this Arrangement was subjected to protection in line with agreed GATT rules. This favourable situation for industrialized states explains why developing states considered the inclusion of textiles and clothing in the negotiations a condition for their participation in the Uruguay Round.

Eventually the **Agreement on Textiles and Clothing** was adopted in 1994 by the new World Trade Organization, as a continuation of the Multi-Fibre Arrangement but with the ultimate removal of all quotas as its aim. Between 1995 and 2005 all trade in textiles and clothing between WTO member states was to be brought under normal free trade rules without quotas. A *Textiles Monitoring Body* was set up to oversee the implementation process. Once again the practice was a disappointment for developing states, because implementation again made the Agreement an instrument of protectionism rather than of free trade. The wording of parts of the text was vague and seemed to allow the extension of quotas, rather than their removal, until the end of the Agreement. The European Commission presented this interpretation several times by declaring that it wanted to continue with the quotas for longer. After making some minor concessions to the protests of the developing states the quota system eventually remained in place until 2005.

When on 1 January 2005 the Agreement on Textiles and Clothing expired, **China** showed that it had prepared itself for the new situation without quotas by shipping large quantities of textile products to the US and Europe. This created tensions as the industrialized states saw their markets 'flooded'. The US and Turkey made an appeal to special measures agreed when China became a WTO member, while the European Commission prevented Chinese textile products from entering the EU market by stopping them at the borders. In June 2005 the EU concluded a three-year agreement with China, with further quotas and another delay in the agreed liberalization.

The Uruguay Round 1986–94

The Uruguay Round was meant to last four years and dealt with both goods and services. The aim with regard to goods, among them textiles and agricultural products, was to bring trade arrangements conflicting with GATT obligations to a *standstill* and to develop a programme to gradually *roll back* these types of arrangements. The extension of the talks to trade in services aimed at devising a coherent set of principles and rules for this increasing trade and, if possible, to elaborate these for specific sectors such as banking and insurance. But after four years the Uruguay Round had still far from finished its deliberations. Although progress was made in 1989, this was insufficient to make the then envisaged final meeting in Brussels in 1990 into a success. Pressure from the G7 summit of 1991 did not change the situation by the end of that year. The delay was caused by the aggressive negotiation position of the US, the defensive stance of the EEC, which could not take a leading role due to the conflicting interests of its member states, and the disengagement of Japan. The poor trade relations between the US and the EEC blocked the entire GATT round. In early 1993 37 states complained about this in a letter to the US, the EEC and Japan. The end of the East–West conflict had created more room for disagreements among Western states, which would have remained undisclosed during the Cold War, to become public. These differences of opinion made the negotiations more political and also a matter of higher-placed politicians, such as heads of government and state rather than just trade ministers. In November 1992 the US and EEC settled most of their differences on agriculture in the so-called Blair House Accord. It was important to the US in 1993 to speed up the process and reach an agreement in the GATT, as it had nearly finished its negotiations with Canada and Mexico about their regional free trade agreement NAFTA. President Clinton also succeeded in concluding a trade agreement with Japan during the G7 summit in Tokyo in July 1993, as well as an agreement between the US, the Commission of the EEC, Japan and Canada (referred to as the Quad) about the liberalization of trade in industrial goods. At last there was progress. In December 1993 most negotiations of the Uruguay Round ended, except from some on market access. In April 1994 the various agreements were signed in Marrakesh, Morocco, by most of the 123 participating governments. They came into force in January 1995 and created the WTO as the successor of the GATT.

Trade in services

To meet the Third World's reservations, it had been agreed that the discussion on trade in services would take place within the GATT round but outside its official scope. Among these services are transborder activities such as transport, insurance, telecommunication, advertising and management, as well as professional, technical and financial services. The OECD was the first to use the term 'trade' in services in 1973, in the context of the internationalization of the services sector. That services crossed borders was not a new development, but the idea that they were traded was (Drake and Nicolaides 1992, 41). Given the expected rapid expansion of trade in services, a high-level OECD group pointed out the need to avoid any tendencies to protectionism and to aim at achieving thorough liberalization. During the 1970s a discussion took place on whether, and to what extent, governments should restrict the transmission of computerized information across borders via telecommunication, also referred to as the 'transborder data flow'. A 1980 OECD guideline advised governments not to introduce new laws or regulations, with the exception of privacy protection. The discussion covered high-grade technology aspects as well as trade-related property rights, given the imitation and counterfeit of expensive brands, industrial design rights, trade secrets and revenues from foreign investments. Whereas Canada, France, Japan, Switzerland and the UK sided with the US in its approach to services negotiations, Third World states led by Brazil and India were almost unanimously opposed. They feared that the industrialized states, with far stronger services divisions, would soon erode their own services sectors. UNCTAD undertook studies on the role of services in the development process and the reports published stressed the problems and fears of the developing states. As a result it was difficult to reach a compromise on trade in services within the GATT. To keep the issue alive and explore areas of agreement and disagreement a group of delegates began a series of informal 'minilateral' meetings before approaching the broader membership (Drake and Nicolaides 1992, 55). After laborious discussions on definitions, enforcement of rules and possible exceptions the contours of a General Agreement on Trade in Services were beginning to show by 1990.

Labour mobility and migration

One of the open questions was whether labour mobility should be included in the definition of services. The industrialized states were against this, as it would imply the liberalization of their immigration laws, while the Third World saw chances for international competition (Drake and Nicolaides 1992, 94). The US was in favour of giving access rights only to skilled labour, but Third World states wanted unskilled labour also included. They referred to the actual presence of Mexican migrant workers and domestic servants in the US, Korean and Pakistani building labourers and Philippine and Sri Lankan housemaids in the Middle East, and Korean workers on drilling platforms. That by the end of the 1980s so many women and men were working abroad was partly caused by the high debts of most Third World states at the time and the strict IMF prescriptions for indebted governments. In order to maximize a state's ability to repay its outstanding loans with interest, the IMF insisted that governments cut their social service budgets. On the list of standard IMF demands were keeping down wages, cutting back public works, reducing the numbers of government employees and limiting health and education budgets. Because of these measures and the high unemployment, working abroad was often the only solution to finding paid work for many of the poor. Women and men working abroad not only earned enough to live on, they also supported their national economies with the money they sent home (Enloe 1989, 184–85).

39.2 The World Trade Organization as the successor of GATT (1995)

The WTO as a result of the Uruguay Round

As a result of the Uruguay Round, which eventually was concluded in 1994, the *World Trade Organization* (WTO) began to function on 1 January 1995. Its objectives were the same as those of the GATT, including the original views on raising standards of living, ensuring full employment and a large and steadily growing amount of real income and effective demand. The GATT phrase 'developing the full use of the resources of the world and expanding the production and exchange of goods' was replaced by 'expanding the production of and trade in goods and services, while allowing for the optimal use of the world's resources in accordance with the objective of sustainable development, seeking both to protect and preserve the environment and to enhance the means for doing so in a manner consistent with their respective needs and concerns at different levels of economic development'. In its free trade endeavour the WTO acknowledges two restrictions: the aim of sustainable development as mentioned and the necessity of positive discrimination in favour of developing states, in particular the least-developed among them. The WTO has a number of functions. It administers WTO trade agreements, is a forum for trade negotiations, handles trade disputes, monitors national trade policies, provides technical assistance and training for developing states and cooperates with other IGOs. The WTO sees its status within the UN system as equal to that of the IMF and IBRD, which means a fairly independent position, while the UN regards the WTO as a 'related' organization (see Figure 21.3).

Differences with the GATT

The Uruguay Round resulted in three agreements which formed the foundation of the WTO: the *General Agreement on Trade in Services* (GATS), the *Agreement on Trade-Related Intellectual Property Rights* (TRIPS; see Figure 39.2) and the updated *General Agreement on Tariffs and Trade* (on trade in goods; also referred to as 'GATT 1994' in contrast to 'GATT 1947'). Unlike the GATT the WTO is a permanent organization, the members of which have to ratify the three WTO agreements. The GATT was an economic agreement that was not sent to parliaments for ratification. The WTO has members (both states and customs territories), while the GATT had 'contracting parties' (although sometimes referred to as 'GATT members' or 'signatories'). The WTO dispute settlement system is faster than the GATT system and gives rulings that cannot be quashed. While the GATT only dealt with trade in goods, the WTO also deals with trade in services and with intellectual property in relation to trade. The WTO has some overlap with the World Intellectual Property Organization. Although the WTO was only concerned with some modern high-tech developments, its new activities restricted WIPO's operation. However, a division of work was arrived at, with WIPO covering violations of intellectual property and the WTO dealing with unfair practices in international trade (see Figure 39.2).

The WTO structure and accession procedure

The WTO structure consists of a *Ministerial Conference*, which is the highest authority and meets at least once every two years, a *General Council*, which conducts much of the day-to-day work in between the Ministerial Conferences, three *Councils* for the three agreements (trade in goods, trade in services and trade-related aspects of intellectual property rights) and three standing committees (on trade and development, balance of payments problems and the WTO budget). The WTO *Secretariat* is located in Geneva, with a staff of 635 in 2006, which is far below the numbers of IMF and IBRD personnel. Any state or customs union with full autonomy in the conduct of its trade policies may become a WTO member ('accede to'), albeit that existing WTO members must agree on the terms of joining. There are four stages in the accession procedure. The first is: 'tell us about yourself', in which a government that is applying has to describe all aspects of its trade and economic policies that have a bearing on WTO agreements; second: 'work out with

Figure 39.2 Intellectual property according to WIPO and WTO (TRIPS)

During the 1880s intellectual property had become a topic covered for industrial property by the Paris Union of 1883 and for copyrights by the Bern Union of 1886. The two established a joint secretariat or Bureau, referred to as BIRPI. In 1967 the **World Intellectual Property Organization (WIPO)** was established, based on the two agreements and the Bureau. WIPO became a specialized UN agency in 1974 (see Figure 9.2). During the Uruguay Round of the GATT (1986–94) the *Agreement on Trade-Related Intellectual Property Rights* **(TRIPS)** was concluded, which laid down the intellectual property rules in the multilateral trading system of the WTO. Its assumption was that ideas and knowledge had become an increasingly important part of both the economy, referred to as the 'knowledge economy', and international trade. This was even true for goods such as clothes, given the greater role of design, inventions and brand names needed to stay in line with trends in the world market. Bringing high-tech products and new medicines to the market required an enormous amount of invention, innovation, research and testing before these products could be sold. Creators therefore wanted to protect their inventions, creations, improvements and designs from those who would use them without payment. This could be partly met by arrangements developed by WIPO, such as copyright, patents for inventions and trademark registration for brand names and product logos. But many modern forms of intellectual property as part of trade processes were not, or only partly, covered by the WIPO arrangements. The TRIPS agreement changed this situation by establishing rules for intellectual property in the context of international trade and by defining the basic principles and procedures. TRIPS includes *basic principles for trade*: national treatment, most-favoured-nation treatment and 'balanced protection', since intellectual property protection should also contribute to technical innovation and the transfer of technology; *common ground rules to protect intellectual property*: trademarks, geographical indications such as *Champagne* and *Scotch*, industrial design, integrated circuits layout designs, undisclosed information and trade secrets which must be protected against breach of confidence and other acts contrary to honest commercial practices (among them test data submitted to governments in order to obtain marketing approval) and curbing anti-competitive licensing contracts; *'tough but fair' enforcement of intellectual property laws*: governments have to ensure that the rights can be enforced under their laws and that penalties for infringement are tough enough to deter further violations, with fair and equitable procedures. When TRIPS entered into force in 1995 developed states were given one year to ensure that their laws conformed with the TRIPS agreement. Developing states and, under certain conditions, states in transformation (from communism to capitalism) were given five years (until 2000). Least-developed states were allowed 11 years (until 2006), which for pharmaceutical patents was extended to 2016. Everything related to TRIPS within the WTO is handled by the **TRIPS Council**, which consists of all WTO members. By the end of 1995 this Council and WIPO decided to work together under a cooperation agreement. This facilitated the implementation of the TRIPS agreement and resulted in two joint technical cooperation agreements, one for developing states (1998) and one for least-developed states (2001). Television broadcasts showing heavy machinery destroying imitation and counterfeit products can be the result of either WIPO action (violated property rights) or WTO action (unfair practices in international trade based on the TRIPS agreement).

There are also some specific arrangements which touch upon WIPO and WTO rules. In 1961 the **International Union for the Protection of New Varieties of Plants** (UPOV) was established by an international convention. It grants the breeders of new varieties intellectual property right on the basis of certain principles. The convention was revised several times. A cooperation agreement with WIPO made the director-general of WIPO the secretary-general of UPOV. With regard to **performing artists** and the technical progress in recording, duplicating and broadcasting sounds and images, including domain names and downloading from the Internet, WIPO has not been very successful. In 2000 the US adopted the *Digital Millennium Copyright Act* and in 2001 the EU followed with the *Directive on the Harmonization of Certain Aspects of Copyright and Related Rights in the Information Society*, which was highly controversial. It was regarded as a victory for copyright-owning companies over copyright users' interests and included a definition of copyright, exceptions and limitations, technological measures and implementation procedures.

us individually what you have to offer'; third: 'let's draft membership terms'; and fourth: 'the decision'. If the working party dealing with the accession during the first stage has made sufficient progress on principles and policies, then during the second stage parallel bilateral talks begin between the prospective new member and individual states on tariff rates, market access and other policies. This was decided because different states have different trading interests. It is a highly complicated matter, as all states need to respect the non-discrimination rules *vis-à-vis* other states. When the negotiations in the second stage and the examination of the applicant's trade regime are complete, the results are recorded in a report, a draft membership treaty, a protocol of accession and 'schedules' or lists of the applicant's commitments. These third-stage documents show to what extent the applicant is willing to bind itself. When the final package is complete (report, treaty, protocol and commitments) the General Council or Ministerial Conference will make the decision about accession by a two-thirds majority. If the vote is in favour the applicant signs the protocol and completes the process by asking its parliament to ratify its agreement with the WTO.

Accession of China and Taiwan, but not yet Russia

The WTO commenced on 1 January 1995, with 85 members of the by then 128 GATT parties having ratified the agreements. Membership rose to 132 by 1997 and 153 by 2008. China joined in December 2001 after long-lasting negotiations. It had first expressed interest in joining the GATT in 1986. It became a major global exporter and was given 'most-favored-nation' status, later 'normal trade relations' status, by the US, which had to be renewed every year. This status and its drive to develop into a market economy helped China to become a WTO member, for which it had to rescind 570 laws and adapt a further 140. Shortly after China, in January 2002, Taiwan also became a

WTO member, not under its own name but as the Separate Customs Territory of Taiwan, Penghu, Kinmen and Matsu, also referred to as Chinese Taipei. Negotiations on Russia's membership were still continuing in 2008. The working party for this application had been set up in 1993, but progress regarding Russia's market economy and the adaptation of its legislation has been insufficient to allow membership. Nonetheless headway has been made in bilateral discussions and in 2006 the US and Russia achieved political agreement over Russia's WTO accession.

Groups of states within the WTO: Quad, Cairns and EU

Within the WTO decision-making process groups of states can also play a role, for instance by building coalitions. The most important group is referred to as the *Quad* and consists of Canada, the Commission of the EU, Japan and the US. Agreement from the Quad may be a condition for progress. Another group of states active within the WTO is the *Cairns Group*, consisting of Argentina, Australia, Brazil, Canada, Chile, Colombia, Fiji, Hungary, Indonesia, Malaysia, New Zealand, Paraguay, the Philippines, Thailand and Uruguay, which have in common that they are exporters of agricultural products. Growing regional cooperation through customs unions or free trade zones is another reason to act as a group within the WTO. The main such group is the European Union, which legally is referred to as the *European Communities in WTO Business*. Both EU member states and the EU itself are WTO members, the EU as a single customs union with a single trade policy and tariff. EU member states coordinate their policies in both Brussels and Geneva and within the WTO the European Commission acts on behalf of the EU. This arrangement evolved within the GATT after the success of the Commission's external EEC trade policy in the 1960s (see §26.3) and was formalized in the 1991 Maastricht Treaty. The WTO negotiating process, which aims at consensus despite the tough negotiations and interests involved, contributed to the relatively autonomous position of the Commission within the WTO. The Commission facilitates this aim, in particular among EU member states. In its negotiations on behalf of the member states the Commission seeks to remain in control and in the construction of package deals and negotiating on controversial issues it retains its room for manoeuvre. While shielding its activities from continuous member state scrutiny, it simultaneously makes sure within the *Committee 133* (named after the relevant Treaty of Rome article) that member states understand its negotiating space and games within the WTO and support the Commission. 'In order to ensure that the member states will understand the rationale for concessions made, the Commission needs to expose their representatives directly to the WTO negotiating process. Due to its central position between the external WTO process and the internal EU process ... , and due to the opportunities the WTO process provides to engage in informal negotiations without member state attendance, the Commission can control the member state representatives' involvement ... to a certain extent so as to strike the right balance between its negotiating autonomy and the need to get member states' backing for its activities' (Kerremans 2004, 55–56). ASEAN member states also coordinate among themselves, albeit that the role of spokesperson on behalf of ASEAN is a rotating one and can be assigned according to topic. Other regional international organizations may also act as a group, such as the Latin American Economic System SELA, NAFTA, MERCOSUR and the ACP, the African, Caribbean and Pacific group of developing states, which are former colonies of EU member states and are treated equally in EU policies.

Tough trade wars

WTO members can have serious disputes with each other, with national interests at stake. The US and EU have had disputes and even 'trade wars' over the use of hormones in cattle, bananas, subsidy schemes for aircraft builders and the American Foreign Sales Corporation Act. This last special US taxation facility was created in 1971 when the US had a trade deficit. American corporations exporting through an offshore address, also called a 'tax haven', received a reduction in US federal income taxes on profits of about 15 per cent. The EEC challenged this as violating the provisions in the GATT and in 1984 the US adopted another, revised, law that matched GATT regulations more closely. The EEC lodged new complaints, but dropped these during the negotiations in the Uruguay Round. In 1997 however, after unsuccessful discussions with the US, the EU launched proceedings against the tax provisions in the WTO, claiming that they were a prohibited export subsidy and in 2000 the WTO Appellate Body (see below) agreed. Although the US Congress replaced the existing law with a new one in 2001, the Extraterritorial Income Exclusion Act, the EU once again appealed and in 2002 the WTO ruled that if the US did not comply with the Appellate Body's decision the EU could impose more than four billion dollars' worth of sanctions on US products. In March 2002 a 'steel war' began between the US and the rest of the world, against the background of US elections in which President George W. Bush was looking for support from the workers in the by then obsolete US steel industry. The US government decided to protect the American steel industry for three years by imposing import restrictions of 30 per cent for most steel products. The EU and several states complained about this protectionism and in 2003 a WTO Appellate Body ruled in favour of the EU, calling the US policy a violation of WTO rules and allowing the EU to impose tariffs on goods to the value of 2.2 billion dollars in retaliation if the US did not abide by the WTO ruling. The EU imposed the sanctions and the US eventually gave in, but in the meantime the US steel industry, which had gone through various bankruptcies, had profited from the policy and had begun to reconsolidate.

The dispute settlement mechanism

The WTO has a more complicated dispute settlement mechanism than the GATT, which was based on two articles (XXII, XXIII) and a document entitled 'Understanding Regarding Notification, Consultation, Dispute Settlement and Surveillance', which was adopted in 1979. Its precise legal status was not clear, but it formed a kind of accepted 'constitutional framework' for GATT processes, including the procedures for dispute settlement (Jackson 1998, 68). By contrast the WTO mechanism is based on 27 articles, totalling 143 paragraphs, plus four appendices. The time schedules of the WTO are stricter than under the GATT and there is a *Dispute Settlement Body* (DSB), which decides on whether a member has violated one or more rules of the WTO agreements or of the multilateral trade agreements. The DSB is virtually the same as the General Council as it consists of a representative of each member, but it has its specific function. When a dispute arises between two or more members they are not allowed to impose unilateral sanctions, but have to find a solution through the WTO disputes procedure. This was agreed in order to make members comply with the WTO rules. During the process the Dispute Settlement Body may be assisted by the good offices of the director-general, the *Disputes Panel* and, possibly, the *Appellate Body*, which is established by the DSB. In the first phase bilateral consultations are organized to find out whether the dispute can be settled. If consultations fail within two months the complainant can ask for the establishment of a Disputes Panel, consisting of three to five independent panellists. The Panel's investigation in general should not exceed six months. If a party to a dispute disagrees with a Panel's recommendation it can appeal to a standing Appellate Body, consisting of seven people who serve a four-year term each. The Appellate Body's findings must be accepted by the parties to the dispute, who are then expected to abide by the WTO ruling. This WTO dispute settlement mechanism, which came into force immediately in 1995, in practice showed a fairly strong 'rule-oriented approach', with rights and obligations for members. The expectation is that the mechanism will face more and more 'jurisprudential' issues, in the same way as has happened in national legal systems. This may result in specific judicial terms used by the WTO. As with other international tribunals, the WTO dispute settlement mechanism may lead to 'results not easily anticipated by the original draftspersons of the treaty clauses or by governments that accepted them' (Jackson 1998, 100).

39.3 The North–South divide within the WTO

Changes in consensus building

Achieving consensus was the main type of decision making within the GATT, based on the assumption that states had to 'do business' and should leave 'political rhetoric' to the UN and its agencies: 'no votes on senseless resolutions, no decision by majority rule'. Experience showed that the consensus rule was not abused. 'Developed countries, particularly the United States and the European Community, drove the GATT agenda and negotiations but did not insist on full participation by all countries. In turn, developing countries did not block progress in trade talks – both because the accords posed few demands on them and because they made huge gains from the commitments of the developed countries extended to them on a most favored nations basis. Moreover, as the weaker partners in the GATT, they benefited significantly from the well-functioning multilateral rules-based system' (Schott and Watal 2000, 284). The number of WTO members grew much larger than the number of GATT parties and 'free riding' on negotiated agreements became harder, as states had to participate in negotiated agreements as part of 'a single undertaking' with obligations. This also affected the way in which consensus was built. The 'green room' procedure of the GATT referred to the green-decorated rooms in the GATT/WTO building, where small groups of states met for as long as necessary to agree on compromises between their positions. This process did not function as well in the WTO, as was discovered in December 1999 during the preparations for another round of negotiations at the 2000 WTO Ministerial Conference in Seattle, Washington. The industrialized states were experienced in using the 'green room' arrangement, while many new members and developing states were unaware of, or inexperienced in, this traditional procedure. Yet they were the states that were asked to loosen their trade barriers and reform their trade practices.

Unforeseen deadlock between North and South in Seattle (2000)

This poor functioning of the old mechanism meant that the WTO, which continued with consensus building on bilateral agreements in a multilateral context, had to make reaching decisions more inclusive. As the developing states had refused to accept a structure similar to those of the IMF and IBRD, it became obvious that they needed 'more of a voice in the WTO's decision-making process' (Schott and Watal 2000, 286). Two measurable criteria that could help improve participation were ranking by value of foreign trade and a better global geographic representation. 'This is both objective and relevant to decision making in the WTO and causes the least disruption to existing green room players, while bringing in others previously excluded' (Schott and Watal 2000, 292). The core political problem at the meeting in Seattle, however, was the difference of opinion between highly-developed industrial states and developing states on how to continue the discussion about free trade and its consequences for the Third World. As working parties were unable to reach agreement, deliberations were ended. The WTO leadership had not foreseen such a deadlock.

Changes in leadership (2002)

The WTO directors-general were Peter Sutherland (Ireland; 1995), Renato Ruggiero (Italy; 1995–99), Mike Moore (Australia; 1999–2002), Supachai Panitchpakdi (Thailand; 2002–5) and Pascal Lamy (France; from 2005). In September 2002 Supachai from Thailand became the new WTO leader. He had been jointly elected to become the director-general in September 1999 with Mike Moore, when a decision on who should fill the post could not be reached. Moore, who had taken the first half of the six-year term, was blamed for the failure of the meeting in Seattle through the internal differences of opinion. In November 2001, however, the WTO succeeded in restoring such unity at the Ministerial Conference in Doha, Qatar, that the deliberations about a new round of negotiations were resumed. The developing states, led by India, kept expressing their unhappiness with the way the WTO promoted the interests of the wealthy states however. Supachai, who believed that since Seattle the developing states had made their presence felt, aimed to improve their position at the negotiating table, given their majority in the by then 144 WTO members. He would regard his three-year term as a success if at the end of it the developing states had achieved the position they were entitled to and if interests between the groups of states had become better balanced. He also proclaimed that the WTO had to cooperate more closely with the UN agencies and bodies, because of their work for development. He agreed that his vision deviated from what was common in the WTO, but he hoped to achieve more coherence between the policies of those organizations and the WTO. His ambition as director-general was to establish a new world trade order, which could not be done without coordinating these international agencies. However, when in 2005 a new director-general had to be elected the Southern candidates were defeated by the experienced EU Commissioner for trade Pascal Lamy, who defended the WTO as the main forum for regulating world trade and achieving economic growth and development. Supachai was appointed UNCTAD's new secretary-general in 2005.

The laborious Doha development agenda (2001)

In November 2001 the WTO Ministerial Conference in Doha began a new round of negotiations, including those on agriculture and services which had started in early 2000 and on the problems developing states faced in implementing the WTO agreements. Despite the start of this new Doha Round progress was poor. The original mandate was revised a number of times at Ministerial Conferences in Cancun, Mexico (2003), Geneva (2004) and Hong Kong (2005). In Cancun the efforts of the developing states were focused on a reduction in farming subsidies in the EU and the US, but the Conference disagreed on agricultural affairs, including cotton, and ended in deadlock on the *Singapore issues*, stressed by the EU. These topics had been on the agenda of the Ministerial Conference in Singapore in 1996 and included investment protection, competition policy, transparency in government procurement and simplifying trade procedures (known as 'trade facilitation'). European business was strongly in favour of a liberal investment code and had pressurized the EU to discuss these issues. The EU, however, made an erroneous assessment of relations within the WTO, although during the preparation for the Cancun Conference it had become clear that the overwhelming majority of developing states did not want to discuss these topics at all. NGOs had also warned against including the Singapore issues. During the 1990s they, and the so-called anti-globalizationists, had strongly rejected the OECD endeavour to draft a Multilateral Agreement on Investments (MAI), given its far too liberal character (see §41.4). Furthermore, the EU underestimated the frustration on the side of developing states over the constant failing to adapt the WTO agreements to the needs of the least-developed states and over the unresolved issue of patented medicines in the context of the TRIPS Agreement (see below). An alliance of 22 developing states, including large states such as Argentina, Brazil, China, India and South Africa, continued to argue in favour of ending farming subsidies and Northern trade barriers, despite the great differences in development between large and small developing states in the G22, as it would be called. Because the EU stuck to the Singapore issues and the G22 proposal on farming subsidies was left out of the draft final statement at Cancun, the WTO found itself unable to make decisions. The behaviour of the wealthy Northern states had promoted the cohesion of the G22 as a new and successful group of developing states *vis-à-vis* the EU and US. In 2004 at the Conference in Geneva three of the four Singapore issues were dropped, as there was no consensus, with only trade facilitation remaining on the agenda. The Ministerial Conference in Hong Kong in 2005 agreed on a new timetable, to finish the negotiations by the end of 2006 instead of the original but missed deadline of January 2005. Some progress was made in the negotiations about agriculture due to a US proposal to reduce farming subsidies by lowering the upper limits, but as the US and the EU did not agree and the EU did not present a reduction proposal of its own, the Northern states were in fact further strengthening the solidarity of the developing states. The US's refusal to refine its general proposal by specifying actual reductions in particular meant that the negotiations were deadlocked. Oxfam calculated that the US, based on its own proposal to reduce upper limits, would still have room for increasing subsidies. Paul Wolfowitz of the IBRD agreed with Oxfam and stated publicly that the US should present realistic and concrete proposals. The General Council meeting in Geneva in July 2006 did not solve the situation and supported Lamy's recommendation to suspend the Doha negotiations. Despite political efforts at the World Economic Forum and the G8 summit in 2007 to move the US, the EU and the G22 towards agreement, the Doha negotiations were not resumed. The creation of the 'G4', consisting of the US, the EU, Brazil and India, in an attempt to bridge major disagreements between them also ended in an impasse, as they could not find a compromise on how to reduce farming subsidies and how to open up agricultural and industrial markets in various types of states. The attempt to settle the differences in July 2008 also failed, with India acting as the main opponent to the industrialized states, in particular the US, over the protection of agricultural products from developing states, which demanded more room for economic growth rather than remaining dependent on imports.

Patented medicines for poorer developing states

The conclusion of the Trade-Related Intellectual Property Rights Agreement in 1994 was strongly influenced by a group of US transnational corporations, which in 1986 had set up the *Intellectual Property Committee* (IPC) as an interest group during the negotiations in the GATT Uruguay Round. Their main concern was the global protection of their intellectual property. They succeeded in getting support from businesses in Europe and the US which initially had not been interested, but they also lobbied the US government in favour of a comprehensive intellectual property code. The IPC itself was surprised by how much it achieved. 'The IPC's activities notwithstanding, there would be no TRIP [S] accord if the US had not changed its domestic attitudes towards strong IP protection. The US state, embedded in the context of the changing structure of global capitalism, redefined its interests and adopted a competitive strategy that made it particularly receptive to the IPC's policy advocacy' (Sell 2000, 103). The corporations' interests showed most clearly in the issue of 'patented medicines for poorer developing states'. The patents made these medicines (too) expensive for these states. There was doubt over whether corporations were willing to develop medicines for states and regions with no well-functioning market at all. Within the WTO wealthy and poor states clashed in the struggle over generic versions of patented medicines. As a result of the African Group's lasting pressure the WTO in August 2003 decided on a waiver that made it easier for poorer states to obtain cheaper generic versions of patented medicines. The waiver set aside a provision in the TRIPS Agreement that hindered exports of pharmaceuticals manufactured under compulsory licence to states that were unable to produce then. The struggle for the developing states now became transforming this temporary arrangement into a permanent one. It was not until December 2005 that this was agreed by the WTO members, also influenced by public opinion and pressure from NGOs. To make the waiver permanent Article 31f of the TRIPS Agreement needed to be adapted, which required ratification by a two-thirds majority before 1 December 2007. Since only 13 states and the EU had ratified by that date it was decided to extend the term by two years to December 2009. Until then the waiver remains in force. If ratification is successful it will be the first amendment of a central WTO agreement.

39.4 WTO impact on the functioning of UNCTAD

Change in its environment

The transformation of GATT into WTO during the 1990s changed the international context in which UNCTAD, as part of the UN system, was functioning. UNCTAD's role also changed. During its early period (see §29.2) UNCTAD promoted the international trade of the developing states and emphasized control of fluctuating commodity prices and achieving Official Development Assistance (ODA) in conformity with the 0.7 per cent guideline of 1970 (see §31.1). But the Common Fund for Commodities barely functioned and the few commodity agreements concluded had a temporary character, with the exception of that for rubber. The debt crises of the 1980s made the 0.7 per cent guideline less relevant. Debt relief and (partial) remission of debts, or rescheduling of official debts through instalment and interest rates, became new themes. Import substitution was replaced by export-oriented growth, as a result of the structural adjustment programmes of the IMF and IBRD as well as the opening up of markets through Northern and GATT/WTO pressure. More and more developing states applied the IMF and IBRD prescriptions, sometimes even without the formal necessity to do so. Privatization lost its taboo character and the end of the Cold War also meant the ending of that part of official aid that was given with political motives. If developing states still wanted to receive official aid they needed to conform with the new principles of free trade and liberalization of the dominant economic discourse. Some of the developing states were no longer developing states in the strict sense of the word. States such as Argentina, Brazil, Malaysia, Singapore and South Korea were Semi-peripheral rather than Peripheral, or at least moving towards the Semi-periphery.

Changes in UNCTAD

The changes in its environment caused UNCTAD to curtail its role as the political advocate of the New International Economic Order and in fact to adapt to the new economic reality based on Friedman's ideas, the IMF and IBRD's adjustment policies and the changes in the trade regime that were being discussed in the Uruguay Round, with trade in services as the one topic on which UNCTAD tried not to give in. UNCTAD gradually turned into a forum for developing states that was also addressed by the developed states. Given the increased competition from the growing number of Newly-Industrializing Countries (NICs), the industrialized states addressed UNCTAD with questions that could be best discussed there. The *Cartagena Commitment*, adopted at UNCTAD 8 in Cartagena, Colombia, in 1992, reflected the new sense of partnership for development, based on a commitment to multilaterism and involving a strengthened development dialogue and cooperation between rich and poor states. It included an institutional reform, which was meant as a contribution to the restructuring of the economic and social sectors of the UN that was taking place. In addition UNCTAD continued its efforts to help the least-developed states, sometimes together with the WTO. In 1997 the WTO convened a Ministerial Conference in Geneva to enhance export facilities for the poorest states. However, in practice changes for these states remained minimal. The wealthiest industrialized states did not react with promises, although richer developing states, such as Malaysia, Morocco and South Korea, showed willingness to give the poorest states more market access for their products. The WTO, UNCTAD, ITC (International Trade Centre), IMF, IBRD and UNDP created a partnership to train and advise developing states on how to adapt to the new globalization.

Overlap between WTO and UNCTAD

The UNCTAD conference in Bangkok, Thailand, in February 2000 (UNCTAD 10) was regarded as an exercise in further trade negotiations within the WTO. Due to the failure of its Ministerial Conference in Seattle the WTO was the main topic of conversation within UNCTAD, more so than ever before. A large overlap between the two organizations existed. Both had the word 'trade' in their name, both were located in Geneva and the national civil servants that represented their states in the two organizations and at their meetings were to a great extent the same people. There were major differences between UNCTAD and the WTO as regards authority and weight of decisions. Decisions of the far stronger WTO were binding, in contrast to the declarations of intent of the weaker UNCTAD. The UNCTAD conference in São Paulo in 2004 (UNCTAD 11) decided to give new impetus to the *Global System of Trade Preferences among Developing Countries* (GSTP), which had been established in 1988 with a view to promoting trade among developing states. The idea was unfolded by the G77 in 1976, then gradually elaborated and finally an agreement was adopted in 1988, with the first round of negotiations concluded in Belgrade. The GSTP slowly institutionalized into a stable forum, proceeding with step-by-step negotiations in successive stages, and had its own dispute settlement arrangement. By 2004 43 states had ratified the GSTP agreement. On the occasion of UNCTAD 11 the Committee of Participants of the GSTP decided to launch a new, third, round of negotiations.

39.5 Diminished importance and criticisms of UNDP: a matter of survival

Survival of the UNDP in the early 1990s

The 1965 UN Development Programme was meant to become the most important UN agency for multilateral development aid (see §29.1). But UNDP's share of development aid given through the UN declined from 65 per cent of the UN total in 1968 to 39 per cent in 1985. The contributions of OECD states to the UNDP as a percentage of their total multilateral expenditure decreased in the same period from 13.5 per cent to 6.8 per cent (Williams 1990, 168). The main explanation for this slide was the fragmentation taking place within the UN system, with more and more specialized agencies, funds, programmes and other institutions being established to which governments contributed. Another factor explaining the decline was that the UNDP relied on the recipient government's decision about its economic and social priorities when deciding on the allocation of the technical assistance funds to individual states. For donor states this became a reason to give less to the UNDP, as they did not like to see the resources they provided lost in a general pool of funds and preferred to have more say in how the money was used (Williams 1990, 169). By the end of the 1980s the UNDP came under fire. The US was critical, as it preferred the aid to be used for 'adjustment' of the economies and not for other purposes, and it even threatened the UNDP with dissolution. Its declining share of aid and the criticisms resulted in careful consideration of its position and effectiveness within the UNDP in the early 1990s. In 1994 the UNDP presented a new objective, with the promotion of *sustainable human development* as its guiding principle. The four priority aims were poverty elimination and sustainable livelihoods; good governance; environmental protection and regeneration; and the advancement and empowerment of women. Each of these four objectives was allocated roughly a quarter of the budget. Furthermore, the UNDP wanted to play a more active and integrating role within the UN system, using its network of national offices. In 1995 it succeeded in receiving backing for this new set-up at the UN World Summit for Social Development in Copenhagen, which supported the reorientation of UNDP programming activities to target poverty as its overriding concern (Schechter 2005, 143).

The Human Development Index

That the UNDP survived was partly the result of its network of offices in many member states, which constituted a to the UN Secretariat invaluable network of information sources. But its survival was also related to the expertise on development and developing states that the UNDP had available and could employ. In 1990 the UNDP decided to no longer use Gross National Product (GNP) to measure the level of a state's development, as this was not very informative about the differences between rich and poor within a state. Instead it developed a different index, the *Human Development Index* (HDI), based on three indicators: life expectancy, educational attainment and GNP per capita at purchasing power parity. The new measure presented sharper pictures than GNP and began to function as an accepted ranking list. In 1994 the UNDP advocated an 'alarm system' to predict poverty and instability in developing states, based on criteria such as available food, employment, distribution of income, human rights, ethnic violence, environmental damage, regional inequality and disproportionately high military expenditure. The UNDP introduced a further index, the *Human Poverty Index* (HPI) in 1997. Whereas the Human Development Index focuses on the advancement of a society, the poverty index reflects the extent of deprivation in a society by trying to quantify the poorest groups, with criteria such as longevity (the proportion of the population not expected to survive to the age of 40), the adult illiteracy rate and the standard of living (related to access to clean water, health services and the proportion of children under the age of five who are underweight). Other new measures were the *Gender-Related Development Index* and the *Gender Empowerment Measure*. Through these indexes the UNDP proved able to produce useful contributions to development issues and policies, which were published in several series of reports.

Figure 39.3 Topics of the Human Development Reports 1990–2007

*The topics of the global **Human Development Reports** of the UNDP are:*

1990	*Concept and Measurement of Human Development*
1991	*Financing Human Development*
1992	*Global Dimensions of Human Development*
1993	*People's Participation*
1994	*New Dimensions of Human Security*
1995	*Gender and Human Development*
1996	*Economic Growth and Human Development*
1997	*Human Development to Eradicate Poverty*
1998	*Consumption for Human Development*
1999	*Globalization with a Human Face*
2000	*Human Rights and Human Development*
2001	*Making New Technologies Work for Human Development*
2002	*Deepening Democracy in a Fragmented World*
2003	*Millennium Development Goals: A Compact Among Nations to End Human Poverty*
2004	*Cultural Liberty in Today's Diverse World*
2005	*International Cooperation at a Crossroads: Aid, Trade and Security in an Unequal World*
2006	*Beyond Scarcity: Power, Poverty and the Global Water Crisis*
2007–08	*Fighting Climate Change: Human Solidarity in a Divided World*

The Human Development Reports

From 1990 onwards the UNDP has published the annual *Human Development Report*. It is an independent report, put together by a select team of experts (academics, practitioners and also UNDP staff) and commissioned by the UNDP. These reports aim at presenting insights into concepts, measures and policy instruments used in the promotion of human development. The first report laid the foundation for the Human Development Index (see Figure 39.3 for the topics of the global reports). In addition to these global reports UNDP has also published *National Human Development Reports* and *Regional Human Development Reports*. National reports were issued on Serbia and Montenegro in 2000 and Haiti and East Timor in 2006. In 2002 and 2003 the *Arab Human Development Reports* received much public attention. They were put together by Arab teams, under the guidance of the Egyptian political scientist Nader Fergamy, and presented information on issues such as democracy, the extent of freedom, gender equality and the use of the Internet. These reports were notably critical and assumed that changes had to come from within the Arab world itself. The third publication about the Arab world in 2004 was delayed, due to US interference because of dissatisfaction with certain passages in the final text. Although the UN denied this, the US had threatened to withhold its payments to the UNDP if these sections were not modified. As a result the third report was not published until 2005. In contrast to the early 1990s when its authority was disputed and extremely weak, the UNDP added to its authority with all these reports.

39.6 The International Telecommunication Union's involvement with the Internet

Transborder data flows

One of the most important innovations in the International Telecommunication Union of 1865 (see Figure 8.1) resulted from its decision in 1959 to also consider space communication. This was not a matter of task expansion, but rather of enabling the ITU to keep up with changing technology. 'Had this decision not been taken, the ITU's activities would have lagged behind technical progress, a situation that would have left a tempting vacuum for organizational entrepreneurs outside the union' (Jacobson 1973, 64). From then on technical progress was related to direct broadcasting via satellite (with routes of satellites that move in an arc which keeps them above the same location on the rotating earth) and the linking of computers to telecommunications systems. This allowed unprecedented transborder data flows. While keeping satellites in their proper path was mainly a technical matter, the use of satellites and computers raised international legal and political issues. Governments of states regarded 'direct broadcasting satellites' and radio and television broadcasts from abroad as an intrusion on their sovereignty. They could bring undesired political or commercial influence and constituted a violation of the national monopoly on television broadcasting. The satellites could also be used for the observation of domestic activities. Large transnational corporations soon profited from the linking of computers and telecommunication. Transborder data flows have 'revolutionized the management of multinational corporations that have been quick to take advantage of the possibilities of modern communication networks for coordinating domestic and foreign operations on functions such as production schedules, financial management, accounting, planning, inventory controls, and marketing' (Soroos 1989, 330). Information-intensive sectors such as international banking, insurance and tourism benefited from these technological innovations. Although the ITU devoted special conferences to space communication and set up regulations for the use of the geosynchronous orbit in 1985 and 1988, other international institutions were also established, such as the UN *Committee on the Peaceful Use of Outer Space* (COPUOS; 1958) and UNISPACE, which resulted from the Second UN Conference on the Exploration and Peaceful Uses of Outer Space in 1982. This conference was held at the insistence of Third World states that were afraid they would be excluded from the benefits of space technologies. The roles of COPUOS and UNISPACE remained secondary to that of the ITU, but the regulation of transborder data flows became a matter for IGOs such as the OECD, Council of Europe, UNCTAD, the GATT/WTO and other organizations. 'International public policy on telecommunications is of special interest to a host of IGOs' (Soroos 1989, 333).

Creation of the Internet

During the 1980s the telecommunications regime was influenced by the policy of deregulation and liberalization initiated by the US under President Reagan. 'This also affected the international telecommunications regime, which began to transform itself from a predominantly intergovernmental arrangement and self-sufficient technical co-ordination, into a more open, less centralized cluster of private and public organizations blending many issues of technical co-ordination with strategic business interests.' During the 1990s the ITU underwent substantial reforms. 'Nevertheless, its tradition as an intergovernmental organization determined by the habits of representatives of sovereign nation-states has left its mark on the telecommunications regime' (Werle and Leib 2000, 103). The simultaneously created Internet, however, remained outside the ITU's activities. This global computer network with a joint technical protocol and a common addressing system enables the sending and receiving of electronic mail, texts and other forms of information. The Internet was first developed by a US defence agency in the 1970s, but from 1983 onwards it evolved from a mainly academic system into a popular means of communication and at the same time an economic network with many unprecedented uses, which facilitated worldwide communications and transborder data flows further.

The ITU interferes with Internet policies

The original responsibility for the functioning of the Internet was guaranteed by the US government. The *Internet Society*, established in 1992 as an NGO, was given part of the governance duties and in 1998 the also private and not-for-profit *Internet Corporation for Assigned Names and Numbers* (ICANN) obtained the responsibility for Internet names and addresses from the US government, which, however, kept control of the central 'A root' server. The Internet Society tried to become an IGO, but 'the struggle for recognition in the international realm and at the national level of the US proved to be a tedious, if not altogether futile, task' (Werle and Leib 2000, 102). Governments were represented in ICANN, although only in an advisory role. But despite this for them unusual set-up the *Governmental Advisory Committee* (GAC) would achieve more influence than expected or intended. The European Commission, which sits on the GAC in the capacity of a 'state', continually expressed its concern that ICANN's policy remit covered issues which historically would have been the preserve of governments. This stance, supported by a number of critical governments, meant that ICANN met with problems when implementing its policies. Furthermore, the Commission succeeded in establishing the domain name '.eu', while ICANN only allowed domain names for states. As a result of these developments ICANN began to identify itself as a 'public-private partnership' rather than a private arrangement. The GAC expanded considerably and opened its doors to the ITU and the WIPO, which received observer status. Because the US government and interest groups had viewed the ITU as representing the traditional values of the telecommunications sector, they had largely sidelined it with regard to the Internet. By the end of the 1990s, however, the ITU was modernizing in line with the liberalization and deregulation tendencies. Reflecting on its position and the political dimensions of the Internet, the ITU convened two *World Summits on the Information Society*, the first in 2003 in Geneva and the second in 2005 in Tunis. The first summit issued a *Declaration of Principles* and a *Plan of Action*, which stated explicitly that 'the international management of the Internet should be multilateral, transparent and democratic with the full involvement of governments, the private sector, civil society and international organisations' (Christou and Simpson 2008, 83). A Working Group on Internet Governance was set up, which put forward a number of alternative models for future Internet governance and criticized the existing situation for its lack of opportunities for developing economies to take part in global Internet governance. In 2006, as a result of the outcome of the second ITU summit, the renewed contract between ICANN and the US Department of Commerce showed 'something of a loosening of control exercised by the US government over ICANN'. Although the US government and ICANN succeeded in resisting more radical changes, they had to reckon with the policies developed by the ITU and its World Summits, both in ICANN's decision making and in implementation (Christou and Simpson 2008, 84).

40

The dominant free trade regime: environment and welfare state under pressure

40.1 Free trade versus environmental and social clauses: GATT and NAFTA

GATT and the Tuna-Dolphin case (1991)

By the end of the 1980s the GATT was confronted with the conflict between free trade policies and environmentally-friendly regulations. Unlike the OECD, which had determined the 'polluter pays' principle in 1972 (see §32.5), and the EEC, which had included this principle in its Single European Act in 1986, the GATT had not been sensitive to views on the environment. It had been set up to promote free trade and to remove any tariffs, restrictions and other trade barriers. Advocates of free trade regarded environmental regulations as veiled protectionism and the GATT therefore opposed trade rules which told other states how to deal with the environment. The US, for instance, could not embargo tuna products from Mexico simply because Mexican regulations on the way tuna was fished did not conform to US rules. The US Marine Mammal Protection Act banned the import of tuna caught with nets that killed dolphins (which generally swim above schools of tuna) in excess of certain US standards, unless the exporting state had regulations comparable to the US Act. In 1991 Mexico, as a fish-exporting state, complained about the US regulations under the GATT dispute settlement procedure, supported by other states which handled the tuna en route from Mexico to the US. The GATT Panel ruled that a state is not allowed to enforce its domestic laws in another state. Director-general Arthur Dunkel argued that the US government should supply Mexico with better fishing nets, which he regarded as a useful form of development aid, as that would result in saving dolphins' lives and in fair competition between Mexican and US vessels. However, the implication of the GATT Panel's report was that in practice the GATT was able to challenge national environmental regulations. GATT Panels also ruled in cases of tropical timber (Indonesia) and lead (Canada). Because the Panel's report of 1991 was not 'adopted', as was required in the GATT procedure (the US and Mexico settled 'out of court'), it did not receive legal status. But the Tuna-Dolphin case attracted a lot of attention and stimulated the debate on whether GATT and the Uruguay Round should pay more attention to the protection of the environment.

A new form of protectionism?

The environmental movement and some governments regarded trade regulations that induced more environmentally-friendly ways of production as advantageous for the protection of nature and environment. However, the GATT rules were an unconditional prerequisite in international trade and these prohibited any regulations and agreements which discriminated on the basis of the ways of production. Free trade and the protection of nature and environment thus seemed to be diametrically opposed to each other. Nonetheless the environmental movement and certain governments were in favour of trade rules as a means to achieve compliance with international agreements on the environment. This happened with the limiting of the use of CFCs by some governments, as agreed in the 1987 Montreal Protocol on the protection of the ozone layer (see §40.2), but the GATT declared such regulations to be a new form of protectionism. In 1992 a GATT working group on trade and environment, which had existed without much activity since 1971, produced a report on the relationship between international trade and environment that was published by the Secretariat. The authors argued that the world economy and the environment would not profit from unilateral trade rules such as import bans. To improve the environment more welfare was required, particularly in poorer states, and to improve welfare more trade was needed. Transborder environmental problems such as the greenhouse effect required not unilateral but multilateral regulations. Damage to tropical forests should be prevented not by import bans, but by rewarding states that had such forests. Rewarding them for their natural approach to the greenhouse effect would prevent deforestation, according to this 1992 GATT report, which acknowledged that a careful examination of existing rules was needed to be certain that they did not hinder multilateral efforts to deal with environmental problems. The environmental movement regarded the expectation of the GATT that more free trade would result in more economic growth and thus allow more environmentally-friendly investment as far too optimistic. It wanted the GATT to recognize the 'polluter pays' principle and to include the costs of environmental regulations in trade prices. An agreement to equally pass on the costs of pollution would have the advantage that non-complying states could be excluded from profitable GATT conditions. The GATT itself, however, had not yet moved even as far as the authors of its report.

The creation of NAFTA (1993)

How threatening the environmental issue could be for international trade was discovered during the creation of NAFTA. From the late 1980s onwards the US, Canada and

Mexico, which had become a signatory to the GATT in 1987, had been working towards the *North American Free Trade Agreement* coming into force by 1994. The US had the wider objective of promoting free trade in the Western Hemisphere, but was also trying to strengthen its position *vis-à-vis* the EEC and Japan. Japan reacted by asking the GATT whether NAFTA was consistent with GATT rules. In the summer of 1992 the three American states drafted an agreement on the conditions for their mutual trade in goods, including some restrictions such as import tariffs and quotas which, however, were to be reduced and removed. In 1993 the preparation of this large-scale operation – with, as US trade unions feared, large-scale social consequences – was in an advanced phase. All that needed to be settled were additional agreements on workers' rights and the environment, two issues that were heatedly debated in US domestic politics.

Trade unions and NAFTA

That workers' rights were to be respected in NAFTA was related to the support from trade unions that the US government needed in order to be successful in having this regional free trade agreement ratified. The first reaction of US trade unions to the NAFTA project had been that it would be detrimental to American workers because of the lower labour standards of Mexican workers. The unions also feared that too many Mexican workers would come to the US and that US companies would move to Mexico. Since a harmonizing effect of the agreement on domestic labour law in the three states could be expected, the trade unions were in fact faced with a common challenge. This also applied to gender relations, as it remained unclear whether more women than men would be able to find jobs in Mexico and whether more Mexican women than men could find work in the informal sector in the US and Canada. The issue was raised because of the export-oriented industrialization programme that had been set up in Mexico in 1965 near the US border. This *maquiladora system* had been introduced to combat rising unemployment among Mexican males after the US unilaterally terminated its policy of allowing Mexican agricultural labourers to work in the southwest of the US during harvest time, but by 1980 almost all the jobs in electronics and clothing in the maquiladora zone were held by female workers (Mitter 1986, 42). Despite uncertainty about future developments the trade unions in the three states managed to pressurize their governments into laying down a number of workers' rights in a NAFTA 'side agreement'.

The environmental movement and NAFTA

Once this side agreement was concluded it was expected that there would be sufficient support for the successful ratification of NAFTA. However, in a case brought by environmental groups a US judge put a spoke in the wheel by forcing the US government to first seriously scrutinize the draft NAFTA agreement regarding its environmental consequences. This might delay ratification, not something President Bill Clinton wanted. The US government therefore was prepared to make concessions, in this case in the form of another side agreement, on the environment. 'As the price of hard-won congressional support for NAFTA as a whole, the Clinton administration advocated the two side agreements as preventing "eco-dumping" or, put another way, as preventing the creation of pollution havens for footloose U.S. corporations with no sense of social responsibility' (MacLaren 2004, 266). The two side agreements were accompanied by two commissions, despite the fact that NAFTA was set up as an agreement without institutions.

These were the *Commission for Labour Cooperation* and the *North American Commission for Environmental Cooperation*. The former was meant to monitor implementation of labour accords and to foster cooperation in that area. The latter aimed to combat pollution, ensure that economic development was not environmentally damaging and monitor compliance with national and NAFTA environmental regulations. In 1995 the North American Fund for Environmental Cooperation was established for this purpose. Both side agreements were concluded at a time when the GATT considered labour and environment extraneous to the formulation of international trade policy.

Social clauses and free trade

These NAFTA developments had repercussions for the GATT. That the almost finished NAFTA agreement went beyond the GATT created some panic in its leadership, as it still had to make a success of the Uruguay Round. The GATT therefore stepped on the brake and argued that it would be on a slippery slope if the principle of trade restrictions being allowed in cases where one state could not accept the environmental policy of another state was also applied to social relations. In 1992 Richard Eglin of the GATT Secretariat asked why a state that enforced a minimum wage should not prohibit imports from another state with low wages. In 1993 director-general Arthur Dunkel also warned against linking social conditions to imports. He took the imports of carpets made by 12-year-old children as an example and argued that he did not want to interfere in the question of whether it would be better for children to work in a small Brazilian family factory or hang around in the Rio de Janeiro slums. But he imagined that a modern industrial entrepreneur producing carpets would be very keen to get excited over child labour, as he secretly would wish to keep Brazilian carpets out of the market. Child labour in Dunkel's view was an ILO matter, to be handled through labour conventions and recommendations, and should not play a role in trade negotiations, because in the end that would lead to new protectionism. Against this GATT revulsion stood the statement by the Belgian foreign minister in July 1993, when Belgium accepted the Presidency of the European Community, that environmental and social policies should increasingly become topics of discussion in international trade policy talks. The European Community, he argued, should include clauses to protect the environment and workers' rights in future trade agreements. As such topics should not be a burden on the current negotiations in the Uruguay Round, he expected that for the time being respect for minimum standards on the environment and labour relations would be limited to the EC and its trading partners in Central and Eastern Europe. The Dutch government showed willingness to support the creation of a GATT working group, to place the issue of international trade and workers' rights on the agenda. This would enable a discussion on including minimum labour standards in the GATT. It stated it was aware that implementation of this might be followed by a misuse of protectionism, under the guise of 'protectionism with a human face', but it did not want to circumvent this dilemma.

No trade regime with social clauses

Despite this debate about 'social clauses', no such type of regulation existed or came into being either in the WTO or the ILO. 'Within the WTO, labour standards have not become a part of its policy, despite the fact that they are sometimes included in the trade policy reviews.' The ILO 'has chosen not to promote the enforcement of core labour standards by means of trade sanctions'. The main reason why social clauses were not developed was that most states agreed that the regimes of trade and labour were incompatible. 'While the principles underlying the trading regime increasingly include trade-related non-tariff issues, most actors do not see labour rights as being related to trade' (Van Roozendaal 2002, 202). Furthermore, it was questioned whether trade sanctions were the best way to address violations of workers' rights. Most developing states opposed almost all labour and environmental regulations, assuming that such rules would be 'exploitable by protectionists, but would also be a major invasion of national sovereignty' (MacLaren 2004, 267).

Attention to social aspects however

Nonetheless, something had changed in the discourse. In India attention was paid to the issue of child labour and in the US labour standards had become part of foreign and development policies. Even the IMF had become aware of issues related to labour standards. The EU had included labour standards in its development programmes and the OECD used these norms as a decisive factor in accepting new member states. When South Korea, which widely suppressed its trade unions, joined the OECD in 1997, it was only allowed to do so after a compromise was reached that allowed the South Korean trade unions more freedom. In the area of environmental policies and international trade the debate continued, as it was no longer possible to deny the environmental consequences of economic policies given the explicit position taken by both NAFTA and the European Community.

40.2 Protection of the ozone layer and the establishment of the IPCC (1988)

CFCs and the hole in the ozone layer

After the rise of the environmental movement in the 1970s (see §32.3), international environmental conventions in the 1980s were restricted to a number of Protocols to the 1979 Acid Rain Convention (see Figure 32.3), the Vienna Convention for the Protection of the Ozone Layer (1985) and a Protocol to the latter (1987) (see Figure 40.1). 'Acid rain' had given reason for concern when acute problems occurred and had resulted in international regulations for air pollution abatement. Anxiety about the ozone layer was first expressed in 1974, when the scientific journal *Nature* published an article on the effects of CFCs (chlorofluorocarbons) used in aerosol cans. These industrial chemicals caused ozone depletion or destruction of ozone molecules in the so-called ozone layer in the stratosphere, which protects life on earth from dangerous radiation from the sun. This resulted in actions to stop the use of aerosols during the late 1970s. Public awareness of the ozone layer problem became greater and the older concern was given a more serious and alarming dimension after the discovery of a 'hole' in the ozone layer in 1984 by British scientists who had studied it from the South Pole over a longer period. The issue of ozone depletion had been discussed earlier in the UN Environment Programme and the World Meteorological Organization. In 1976 the WMO had mapped the condition of the ozone layer for the first time and in 1977 the WMO and UNEP set up a coordinating committee to periodically assess ozone depletion. In 1981 intergovernmental negotiations, based on these assessments, started on an international agreement to phase out ozone-depleting substances, which were concluded in March 1985 with the adoption of the *Vienna Convention for the Protection of the Ozone Layer*. This came into force in 1988. The general Convention was followed by the adoption of the *Montreal Protocol on Substances that Deplete the Ozone Layer* at the headquarters of the International Civil Aviation Organization in Montreal in September 1987, which came into effect in 1989. The Vienna Convention created the conditions for intergovernmental cooperation on research, the systematic observation of the ozone layer, the monitoring of CFC production and the exchange of information, while the Montreal Protocol contained specific commitments and phase-out schedules.

The Ozone Secretariat of the UN (1989)

Once the parties to the Vienna Convention had adopted the Montreal Protocol, UNEP's Ozone Unit evolved into the permanent *Ozone Secretariat* for the Vienna Convention and the Montreal Protocol. Although this is a modest institution, the Ozone Secretariat, based at the UNEP's offices in Nairobi, is responsible for maintaining awareness among the parties, even at times when governmental concern for the environment is lessening. It has to arrange the monitoring of the Convention and Protocol and the implementation of decisions resulting from the meetings of the Conference of the Parties. The Convention and Protocol were designed in such a way that the phase-out schedules can be revised and accelerated on the basis of periodic assessments. The Ozone Secretariat maintains a low profile. Expertise, an institutional memory and specific technical knowledge are its main instruments and it does not play the entrepreneurial role that UNEP experts had during the drafting process of the Convention and Protocol. During the establishment of the ozone regime these experts succeeded in drafting texts and gaining support for them in a relatively short time. 'Thus, the Secretariat's role as an authoritative broker of complex knowledge for all kinds of stakeholders remains important, even if it currently plays an ostensibly less dramatic role in implementation than it did during the regime creation phase' (Bauer 2006, 65). Its work resulted in amendments to the Protocol in 1990 (London), 1992 (Copenhagen), 1997 (Montreal) and 1999 (Beijing), introducing stricter control measures. The US strongly supported the new regime, but hesitated when it realized during the ratification process of the Protocol that it was difficult to get the developing states' cooperation, in particular major ones such as Brazil, China and India. They refused to ratify, as they had not caused the problem and 'should either be allowed to continue using CFCs or receive "clean" technology transfer or financial assistance to use and develop substitutes'. This problem was resolved, to the displeasure of the US, by the creation of a fund: 'a multilateral fund for developing countries was agreed in London in 1990 and China and India finally came on board' (Dobson 2004, 54).

The Brundtland report (1987): Our Common Future

During the 1980s environmental concerns were also discussed in relation to the development issue. In 1983 the UN General Assembly established the *World Commission on Environment and Development*, which published its report *Our Common Future* in 1987, generally called the *Brundtland report* after the Commission's chairwoman Norwegian Prime Minister Gro Harlem Brundtland. This report connected the development problem and environmental issues, with the latter being the result of the immense and prolonged poverty of the South and the non-sustainable patterns of production and consumption in the North. In order to ensure that future generations would be able to meet their needs, the report called for a strategy that combined development with the environment. Economic growth remained necessary, but it needed to be based on policies that sustained and expanded the environmental resource base. The report was debated by the UN General Assembly of 1989, which then decided to convene a world conference on the environment and development in 1992, 20 years after the Stockholm UN Conference on the Human Environment. The new term 'sustainability' was also used in the 1991 report *Caring for the Earth: A Strategy for Sustainable Living* by UNEP, the World Conservation Union IUCN and the World Wide Fund for Nature. Their strategy was a sequel to the World Conservation Strategy of 1980 (see §32.5). Given the UN decision to convene a world conference, this report was devised in a policy-oriented way.

The Intergovernmental Panel on Climate Change IPCC (1988)

In 1979 the WMO had convened the *World Climate Conference*, which indicated concern that 'continued expansion of man's activities on earth may cause significant extended regional and even global changes of climate'. In 1985 a joint conference with UNEP followed, which expressed the fear that as a result of the increasing greenhouse gases a rise in global mean temperature could occur, 'which is greater than in any man's history' (IPCC 2004, 2). These conferences resulted in the establishment of an advisory group on greenhouse gases and in 1988 the WMO and UNEP jointly created the *Intergovernmental Panel on Climate Change* (IPCC). The IPCC does not carry out research, nor does it check climate-related data. Instead it monitors and assesses peer-reviewed and published scientific and technical articles. Based on this the IPCC attempts to understand and gauge the risks of human-induced climate change, its potential impacts and the options for adaptation and mitigation. The IPCC Secretariat is located in Geneva at WMO headquarters. Three working groups were established to prepare assessment reports of available scientific information on climate change, the environmental and socio-economic impacts of climate change and the formulation of response strategies. The IPCC agreed a special procedure for the preparation of its reports, which are written by a team of authors selected on the basis of their expertise for the task. The reports are reviewed twice, first by experts only and the second time by experts and governments. The final reports are accepted at a plenary session, which approves the *Summary for Policymakers* line by line. At the request of the UN General Assembly the IPCC adopted its first *Assessment Report* in 1990. Based on the findings of this report the General Assembly of that year decided to initiate negotiations on an effective framework convention on climate change, which had to be completed before the envisaged world conference on environment and development in 1992.

The IPCC Assessment Reports of 1995 and 2001

In 1995 the IPCC adopted and published its second *Assessment Report* in Madrid. This also covered the socio-economic aspects of climate change. Pressure exerted by the OPEC states resulted in less strong statements concerning human influence on climate change. In the phrase about the balance of evidence with regard to appreciable human influence, the word 'appreciable' in the draft text was replaced in the final text by the weaker 'discernible'. When the IPCC presented its report in Shanghai in 2001 its experts had reached greater unanimity about human influence. The IPCC now referred to new and stronger evidence that most of the warming over the last 50 years was attributable to human activities. The word 'likely' used in the context of it being related to human activities referred to the IPCC being certain of this being so for 66 to 90 per cent. With regard to the warming over the last century it seemed 'very unlikely' to the IPCC that this was attributable to natural climate variation. Opponents of the IPCC reports, who believed that climate change was not exceptional, attacked the credibility of individual experts rather than the IPCC arguments. In 1996 one of the authors of the 1995 report, Ben Santer, was publicly accused of having changed the text after its adoption. It was later shown that Santer had respected the entire protocol and that there had not been any changes to the text. Michael Mann, one of the authors of the 2001 report, was accused of manipulating the graph of temperature trends, called the 'hockey stick', based on reconstructions of the past several millennia from tree ring and other data. Later, independent studies showed the same hockey stick-like curves as those produced by Mann. Both Santer and Mann had left the IPCC, but in fact after false accusations.

40.3 The UNCED Conference in Rio de Janeiro (1992) and its international conventions

The UNCED Conference in Rio (1992)

The *UN Conference on Environment and Development* (UNCED) took place in Rio de Janeiro from 3 to 14 June 1992. It raised high expectations from governments and NGOs alike. During the preparatory committee meetings (PrepComs) an 'Earth Charter' was proposed, containing all necessary principles and an action plan. However, during the preparations a vast divide between industrialized and developing states soon showed. The South felt that it was 'under attack', as the proposals by the North meant international environmental restrictions on their attempts to develop. The Northern concern focused on the destruction of rainforests through human endeavours, the large-scale use of natural fuels and water pollution by chemicals. The G77 states took a joint position, aiming to defend their development strategies against environmental protection by the wealthy states and calling for additional resources from the North for the environmental regulations they were asked to implement. The Conference itself, referred to as the 'Earth Summit', was huge, attracted enormous media attention and was attended by 172 governments, 108 of them at the level of heads of state or government, and by representatives of 2,400 NGOs, out of which 1,500 had accredited status. The parallel *Global Forum* for NGOs attracted 17,000 participants. The original high expectations of this Conference were not met, albeit that the Rio Conference had a huge impact on notions about the environment. The terms 'Rio' and 'Earth Summit' became widely used references. The North–South divide seemed unbridgeable, as was shown by the unwillingness of the wealthy states to provide more resources for environmental regulations in combination with development. The US showed little confidence in the entire Conference project, because it did not want to take on new obligations, and its limiting stance influenced other states. However, the Rio Conference was not without results. The most important documents that resulted from it were the *Rio Declaration on Environment and Development*, *Agenda 21*, two conventions (one on biodiversity and another on climate change) and the *Statement of Principles to Guide the Management, Conservation and Sustainable Development of all Types of Forests*. The Rio Declaration stipulated 26 general principles about the rights and duties of states, among them the 'polluter pays' principle. Agenda 21 was a comprehensive document with over a thousand specific recommendations in four sections: social and economic dimensions, conservation and management of resources for development, strengthening the role of major groups and means of implementation.

The Commission on Sustainable Development (1993)

As a consequence of Agenda 21 the UN General Assembly of December 1992 established the *Commission on Sustainable Development* (CSD) as a functional commission of ECOSOC, with 53 members elected for three years each. It is responsible for reviewing progress in the implementation of Agenda 21 and the Rio Declaration, which was later supplemented by the Johannesburg Plan of Implementation, adopted at the World Summit on Sustainable Development in 2002. Its annual monitoring of these agreements, however, is weak, due to the fact that states are not obliged to send reports on their implementation process. The willingness to do so has remained limited, not least as a result of the North–South conflict about environmental protection and economic development of the South. International environmental policies that interfere with domestic politics are generally countered with sovereignty claims. The CSD responded by monitoring activities in particular topics and in 1997, after five years, it convened an Earth+5 meeting for the assessment of specific issues. Efforts to establish a special fund for the implementation of Agenda 21 had been unsuccessful. The IBRD is the only IGO with a facility to support environmental projects in relation to development.

The environmental U-turn of the IBRD: Polonoroeste

In 1985 the IBRD employed only five environmental specialists, but ten years later their number had increased to 300. This U-turn by the IBRD with regard to environmental policies was described as a move from Old Testament harshness (growth versus environment) to New Testament reconciliation (environmentally-sustainable development) (Wade 2004, 92). While the IBRD before 1987 favoured 'frontier economics', it embraced environmental protection in the early 1990s and arrived at a more comprehensive environmental management approach. This paradigmatic shift was far from a deliberative response to new knowledge and opportunities, but rather the result of a coincidental combination of pressure from Southern and Northern NGOs as well as the US Treasury and learning processes within the IBRD. That the IBRD began to develop environmental policies in 1987 was caused by external pressure, as NGOs had criticized the Bank for its lack of environmental consciousness and the US Treasury had shown concern about the use of US taxpayers' money in the *Polonoroeste Project*. The principal objective of this large-scale poverty project was to build a 1,500-kilometre highway from Brazil's densely populated south-central region into the sparsely populated northwest area (Polonoroeste). Although some people within the IBRD had warned that better ways existed to promote agricultural development in Brazil, the Bank continued with this project by any means, notwithstanding a poor performance on the ground with too many negative side effects. This resulted in critical campaigns by NGOs, in hearings by the US Congress which had to approve US contributions to the IBRD's lending resources and in an alarmed Treasury, which led to the IBRD having to publicly recognize that the project's set-up and implementation were justly criticized. Similar concerns were raised about the

Narmada project in India, which also fell short of environmental expectations. In the meantime, however, the IBRD had completed its U-turn. 'By 1992–93, however, the legitimacy of "environment" inside the Bank began to turn strongly positive. Not only in *World Development Report 1992* but also in all its publications, it began to promote itself, evangelically, as a champion of environmental sustainability' (Wade 2004, 92).

The Convention on Biological Diversity (1992)

The UNCED Conference in Rio passed two international conventions, one on biodiversity (signed by 153 states and the European Community) and another on climate change (signed by 155 states and the EC). The US did not sign the *Convention on Biological Diversity*, as it had difficulties with the embedded view on technology transfer and with its financial set-up. The Convention's main objectives are the conservation of biological diversity, the sustainable use of its components and the fair and equitable sharing of the benefits from the use of genetic resources. In 2000 the *Cartagena Protocol on Biosafety* was adopted by the Conference of the Parties to the 1992 Convention, which seeks to protect biological diversity from the potential risks posed by living modified organisms resulting from modern biotechnology. It has a mechanism for ensuring that states are provided with the information necessary to decide before agreeing to the import of such organisms into their territory. In 2008 the number of ratifications of the Convention was 168 and of the Cartagena Protocol 103 (the number of signatories 191 and 147, respectively).

The UN Framework Convention on Climate Change (1992)

The *UN Framework Convention on Climate Change* raised high expectations. Its main aim was to achieve stabilization of greenhouse gas concentrations in the atmosphere at a level that would prevent dangerous anthropogenic interference with the climate system. It entered into effect in 1994 and in 2008 it had been ratified by 192 states. Its main body is the *Conference of Parties* (COP), which meets annually and is supported by the *Climate Change Secretariat*, at first located in Geneva, but from 1996 in Bonn in the building where the Marshall Plan had been signed. The Convention itself does not limit any gas emissions, nor has it provisions to enforce decisions. Therefore it is not legally binding, but the parties may conclude protocols through which states take on commitments. States that will do so are mentioned in Annex I. They have recognized the aim of returning to their 1990 emission levels. These are in particular Western and Eastern European states (40 states and the European Community). Annex II states are developed states that are prepared to provide financial resources for the costs incurred by developing countries, which are mainly Western states (24 states and the European Community). For the benefit of the first Conference of Parties in 1994 the Intergovernmental Panel on Climate Change published a *Special Report* with topical assessments of climate change. The definitions used by the Framework Convention on Climate Change and the IPCC were not entirely identical, as the Convention made a clearer distinction between climate change caused by human activities and natural climate variation than the IPCC.

The Kyoto Protocol (1997)

The adoption of a protocol to reduce greenhouse gas emissions over the period 2008–12 to on average at least five per cent below 1990 levels required an intensive political

Figure 40.1 International conventions on the environment 1982–2006

Name of convention (plus abbreviated name)	Adopted	Into effect
United Nations Convention on the Law of the Sea (UNCLOS)	10.12.1982	16.11.1994
International Tropical Timber Agreement (Tropical Timber 83)	18.11.1983	1.4.1985
Protocol (1) to the 1979 Convention on Long-Range Transboundary Air Pollution on Long-Term Financing of the Cooperative Programme for Monitoring and Evaluation of the Long-Range Transmission of Air Pollutants in Europe (EMEP) (Air Pollution-EMEP Protocol)	28.9.1984	28.1.1988
Vienna Convention for the Protection of the Ozone Layer (Ozone Layer Protection Convention)	22.3.1985	22.9.1988
Protocol (2) to the 1979 Convention on Long-Range Transboundary Air Pollution on the Reduction of Sulphur Emissions or Their Transboundary Fluxes by at Least 30% (Air-Pollution-Sulphur 85 Protocol)	8.7.1985	2.9.1987
Convention on Early Notification of a Nuclear Accident	26.9.1986	27.10.1986
Convention on Assistance in the Case of a Nuclear Accident or Radiological Emergency	26.9.1986	26.2.1987
Montreal Protocol on Substances that Deplete the Ozone Layer (Montreal Protocol Ozone Layer Protection)	16.9.1987	1.1.1989
Protocol (3) to the 1979 Convention on Long-Range Transboundary Air Pollution Concerning the Control of Emissions of Nitrogen Oxides or Their Transboundary Fluxes (Air Pollution-Nitrogen Oxides Protocol)	31.10.1988	14.2.1991
Basel Convention on the Control of Transboundary Movements of Hazardous Wastes and Their Disposal (Hazardous Wastes Convention)	22.3.1989	5.5.1992
Protocol on Environmental Protection to the Antarctic Treaty (Antarctic Environmental Protocol)	4.10.1991	14.1.1998
Protocol (4) to the 1979 Convention on Long-Range Transboundary Air Pollution Concerning the Control of Emissions of Volatile Organic Compounds or Their Transboundary Fluxes (Air Pollution-Volatile Organic Compounds Protocol)	18.11.1991	29.9.1997
United Nations Framework Convention on Climate Change (FCCC, Climate Change Convention)	9.5.1992	21.3.1994
Convention on Biological Diversity(CBD, Biodiversity Convention)	5.6.1992	29.12.1993
Rio Declaration on Environment and Development	14.6.1992	–
Agenda 21	14.6.1992	–

Figure 40.1 (continued)

Name of convention (plus abbreviated name)	Adopted	Into effect
Statement of Principles to Guide the Management, Conservation and Sustainable Development of all Types of Forests (**Forest Principles**)	14.6.1992	–
International Tropical Timber Agreement 1994 (**Tropical Timber 94**)	26.1.1994	1.1.1997
Protocol (5) to the 1979 Convention on Long–Range Transboundary Air Pollution on Further Reduction of Sulphur Emissions (**Air Pollution–Sulphur 94 Protocol**)	14.6.1994	5.8.1998
United Nations Convention to Combat Desertification in Those Countries Experiencing Serious Drought and/or Desertification, Particularly in Africa (**Desertification Convention**)	14.10.1994	26.12.1996
Kyoto Protocol to the United Nations Framework Convention on Climate Change (**Climate Change–Kyoto Protocol**)	11.12.1997	16.2.2005
Protocol (6) to the 1979 Convention on Long–Range Transboundary Air Pollution on Heavy Metals (**Air Pollution–Heavy Metals Protocol**)	24.6.1998	29.12.2003
Protocol (7) to the 1979 Convention on Long–Range Transboundary Air Pollution on Persistent Organic Pollutants (**Air Pollution–Persistent Organic Pollutants [POP] Protocol**)	24.6.1998	23.10.2003
Rotterdam Convention on Trade in Hazardous Chemicals and Pesticides (**Rotterdam Convention**)	11.9.1998	24.2.2004
Protocol (8) to the 1979 Convention on Long–Range Transboundary Air Pollution to Abate Acidification, Eutrophication and Ground-Level Ozone (**Air Pollution–Abating Acidification Protocol**)	1.12.1999	17.5.2005
Cartagena Protocol on Biosafety to the 1992 Convention on Biological Diversity (**CBD Cartagena Protocol**)	29.1.2000	11.9.2003
Stockholm Convention on Persistent Organic Pollutants (POPs) (**Stockholm Convention**)	22.5.2001	17.5.2004
International Tropical Timber Agreement 2006 (**Tropical Timber 06**)	27.1.2006	1.2.2008 envisaged, but not yet in effect

See Figure 32.3 for the conventions adopted between 1946 and 1979.

struggle. Even it coming into force was controversial, but despite that delegates to the third meeting of the Conference of Parties to the UN Climate Change Convention in the Japanese city Kyoto adopted the *Kyoto Protocol* in 1997, which came into effect in 2005 and set targets for 37 states and the European Union for reducing greenhouse gas emissions. While the Convention encouraged the states to stabilize their emissions, the Protocol committed them to doing so. The Protocol placed a heavier burden on industrialized states, as these were mainly responsible for the high levels of emissions, under the principle of 'common but differentiated responsibilities'. While the Convention stipulated that states should meet their targets through national measures, the Kyoto Protocol offered additional means to achieve this, through market-based mechanisms that stimulate green investment and help to meet targets in a cost-effective way. The *Emission Trading Market* created is often called the 'carbon market' (carbon dioxide or CO_2 being the principal greenhouse gas), with emission reductions as a new tradable commodity. States' targets are expressed in 'assigned amounts' and allowed emissions are divided in 'assigned amount units'. If states have emission units to spare because they have not been used, they may sell them to states that have exceeded their targets. Registry systems to control this market were created. Another way to stimulate states to meet their targets was the *Clean Development Mechanism*, through which some states might implement an emission reduction in developing states and thereby earn credits which are counted towards meeting their targets. Joint Implementation between two states was also a way to earn such credits. In 1998 the fourth Conference of Parties (COP-4) adopted the *Buenos Aires Action Plan*, establishing deadlines for finalizing work on the Kyoto mechanisms and for a number of compliance issues. In 2001 in Marrakesh, Morocco (COP-7), further agreement was achieved on flexibility structures, compliance rules, carbon sinks and financing details for developing states. These rules are known as the *Marrakesh Accords*. However, at the 2000 conference in The Hague (COP-6) a serious difference of opinion between the US and the other states had arisen about a number of US proposals, which would have added certain factors favourable to the US, about the question of what to do if states did not meet their commitments and about the issue of financial support to developing states. In order to prevent deadlock chairman Jan Pronk adjourned the conference, which was resumed in July 2001 in Bonn as COP-6 Bis. In the meantime US President George W. Bush announced that the US was not willing to ratify the Kyoto Protocol as there was insufficient support in US domestic politics, given the large number of objections to the entire regulation. In his opinion it would be better to move forward through voluntary reduction goals. At the Bonn meeting the US was present only in an observer capacity, which helped the other states in settling the remaining issues. The Kyoto Protocol coming into effect then depended on ratification by Russia, which happened in 2004.

The Desertification Convention (1994)

The third UN convention that resulted from the UNCED Conference in Rio de Janeiro was the 1994 *UN Convention to Combat Desertification* (UNCCD). A UN conference had already recognized desertification as an environmental issue in 1977, but it was not until the early 1990s that sufficient support for joint action was achieved. The issue was debated at the 1992 UNCED Conference, which called on the UN General Assembly to establish an intergovernmental negotiating committee to prepare an international convention. Those who had prepared the topic had framed the problem not as 'dryland degradation', which was the actual ecological problem, but rather as 'desertification', which also included social matters. The new term had a political appeal that dryland degradation did not have and it turned the issue from a regional problem into a collective and global one (Bauer 2006, 67–68). This new integrated strategy was successful, leading to the signing of the Convention in 1994 and it coming into force in 1996. The Convention aimed at an inclusive approach, promoting national, subregional and regional action plans. In 1997 the *Global Mechanism* was set up to provide an overview of the various bilateral and multilateral resources, in 1999 the permanent *UNCCD Secretariat* was established in Bonn and in 2001 the *Committee for the Review of the Implementation of the Convention* (CRIC) began to function. In 2003 the *Global Environment Facility* (GEF) was designated a financial mechanism of the Convention. GEF had been established in 1991 to help developing states fund projects and programmes for protecting the global environment in areas such as biodiversity, climate change, international waters, land degradation, the ozone layer and persistent organic pollutants.

Panels on forests: IPF, IFF, UNFF

The forest principles adopted by the UNCED Conference in Rio were a 'non-legally binding authoritative statement' of principles for a global consensus on the management, conservation and sustainable development of all types of forests. This statement character was a compromise, as the Rio Conference had not succeeded in drafting a convention. Within the UN two intergovernmental processes followed Rio: the *Intergovernmental Panel on Forests* (IPF), set up by the Commission on Sustainable Development for the period 1995–97, and the *Intergovernmental Forum on Forests* (IFF), established by ECOSOC for 1997–2000. In 2000 ECOSOC created the *United Nations Forum on Forests* (UNFF) as a permanent body to implement the proposals developed by the IPF and IFF. The envisaged general convention has not yet received sufficient support. The trade in tropical timber was also on the agenda of the *International Tropical Timber Organization* (ITTO), which was set up in 1985 in the context of UNCTAD (see Figure 40.2) and which struggled with the conflicts between the economy (trade) and the environment (conservation of forests) and between North and South.

Figure 40.2 The International Tropical Timber Organization (ITTO) (1985)

For many states the **trade in tropical timber** has been an important source of income, but with increasing worldwide concern over the fate of tropical forests because of rapid deforestation this trade also became problematic. In the 1970s both producers and consumers recognized the threat. After eight years of tough negotiations within the UNCTAD's programme for commodities the *International Tropical Timber Agreement* (ITTA) was achieved by 1983 (see Figure 40.1). In essence this Agreement was a trade-oriented commodity agreement, but it had an environmental component, given its attention to forest conservation and management. As a result of the Agreement the **International Tropical Timber Organization** (ITTO) was set up in 1985 and became effective in November 1986. In 1990 19 producing and 25 consuming states were members, covering most of the forests and the global trade. A small Secretariat was established in Yokohama, Japan. The

ITTO depends on funds contributed on a voluntary basis, with Japan, Switzerland and the US as its major donor states.

In 1994 49 producing and consuming states concluded a new **International Tropical Timber Agreement** (*Tropical Timber 94*). In addition to regulating the trade in tropical timber they agreed that by the year 2000 all exports of tropical timber should be from sustainably-managed sources. Western states such as France insisted that references to the conservation of their forests were kept out of the final text, which was contrary to the global approach agreed at the UNCED Conference in Rio of not discerning between tropical timber and timber from other geographical regions and climatic zones. The new Agreement did not enter into force in 1995 due to an insufficient number of ratifications. Brazil resisted, as it expected the industrialized states to confirm that they would protect their forests as well. Eventually the Agreement came into effect in 1997, superseding the 1983 Agreement. NGOs criticized the EU and major Western states, because the support they gave to developing states lacked precise demands with regard to forest conservation and management. The developing states adopted forest laws, but these barely changed the actual situation. Furthermore, as a result of the structural adjustment policies of the IMF and IBRD developing states had been forced to sell large quantities of timber in order to settle their debts and in most of these cases reforestation had not taken place. NGOs also criticized the industrialized states for backing out of their obligations. In early 2006 negotiators under the auspices of UNCTAD agreed a new agreement, *Tropical Timber 06*, which should enter into effect in 2008, depending on the required number of specified ratifications. This has the double role of promoting the expansion and diversification of international trade in tropical timber on the one hand and encouraging the sustainable management of tropical timber-producing forests on the other.

The World Summit on Sustainable Development in Johannesburg (2002)

The *World Summit on Sustainable Development* (WSSD) which took place in Johannesburg, South Africa, in the summer of 2002 was regarded as an evaluation of the ten years after 'Rio'. It was generally agreed that progress in achieving sustainable development had been extremely disappointing, with some speaking of a 'crisis of implementation'. 'Poverty was deepening and environmental degradation was worsening.' The Global Environment Facility remained 'at best a designer niche in the development business' (Schechter 2005, 187–88). Although this summit, which was attended by 22,000 people, among them 8,000 representatives of NGOs, had raised expectations, there were also signs that it was not considered very important, seeing that many heads of state and government, including the presidents of the US and Russia, were absent. A new Johannesburg Plan of Implementation was agreed, but this included neither a timetable nor specific financial promises (Schechter 2005, 191).

Lack of global governance

Although UNEP is the global institution with most expertise on environmental aspects available to international conferences and conventions, the environmental issue has lacked an authoritative and comprehensive international organization. Instead of a 'super-UNEP' or a global environmental organization (Najam 2003), the existing world environmental regime is based on a patchwork of internationally-active NGOs, bilateral and multilateral conventions and several series of UN conferences and related institutions such as the IPCC or ITTO (Meyer *et al.* 1997). This international regime has made progress in some fields, but still struggles with general governance problems, also because the UN has discussed the environment in connection with development (sustainable development). The factors explaining the success of the *ozone regime* of the late 1980s were scientific consensus, political acceptance of this consensus, support from the US ('the energetic lobbying and diplomacy on behalf of restricting ozone-depleting chemicals by the major international power, the United States of America') and equity in arriving at legitimate solutions, in particular with regard to the distribution of the burden of expenses between North and South (Dobson 2004, 54). By contrast, scientific consensus in the *climate change regime* was debatable. The IPCC 'has struggled for over a decade to convince major political players that global warming is actually occurring, and that this warming is caused by human activities rather than by natural fluctuations' (Dobson 2004, 55). Political acceptance of the regime was weakened when the US positioned itself outside the agreement during the Kyoto Protocol negotiations because it believed that it was hurting its interests and was too profitable for developing states, which in contrast to the ozone regime resulted in a lack of support from the US and of fairness in sharing the burden (Dobson 2004, 57).

The environment back on the agenda (2006)

During 2006 the environment returned to the international agenda, underlined by an awareness of extreme weather conditions in many places around the globe, among them the retreat of glaciers, melting of the permafrost, extreme rainfall, high temperatures hitherto unknown and early springs. Consciousness of the issue's seriousness was demonstrated by the 2006 film *An Inconvenient Truth*, made by former US Vice-President Al Gore, which drew world-wide attention. Gore was awarded the Nobel Peace Prize, jointly with the IPCC, in 2007. In October 2006 the British former IBRD economist Nicholas Stern released a report in which he described climate change as an economic externality that should be taken into account by calculating the impacts of both non-action and action. He argued that non-action in the long term would be very costly. The Conference of Parties to the UN Climate Change Convention in Nairobi in November 2006 (COP-12) concluded that the greenhouse gas emissions by the industrialized world had increased and continued increasing. However, since the two largest 'polluters', China and the US, had not ratified the Kyoto Protocol this covered only 30 per cent of world-wide emissions. But even these figures did not help to achieve agreement on how to proceed. In February 2007 the IPCC published its fourth *Assessment Report*. While in 2001 the IPCC had used the word 'likely' with regard to observed warming over the last 50 years due to increases in anthropogenic greenhouse gas concentrations, it now used the words 'very likely' in respect of human activities.

The climate summit in Bali (2007): a US defeat

In June 2007 the G8 summit in Germany did not accept the proposal of German Chancellor Angela Merkel to reduce greenhouse gas emissions to 50 per cent of 1990 levels midway through the century, as the US and Russia were only prepared to consider this. US President Bush agreed to discuss the climate change issue further within the UN, but repeated his view that individual states needed to show commitment rather than world-wide objectives being formulated. Environmental regulations should not impede economic growth and developing states such as China and India should also take responsibility. China replied that the industrialized states needed to make the first move. In December 2007 at the climate change conference in Bali, in Indonesia, where future commitments for industrialized states under the Kyoto Protocol were discussed, the US demanded leadership, but in fact blocked every compromise. Its continuing criticism of other states made the representative of Papua New Guinea remark that if the US did not want to lead it should leave this to others: 'please, get out of the way'. Somewhat later the US declared: 'we join consensus'. 'Bali' was saved.

40.4 Full employment and the welfare state under pressure by Reagonomics

Full employment as an international standard

During the 1980s full employment as an international norm came under pressure from Reagonomics and globalization. This international standard dates back to the 1919 Treaty of Versailles. In the section on the International Labour Organization's preamble, the 'regulation of the labour supply' and 'prevention of unemployment' were mentioned as contributing to social justice and hence to peace. Some early ILO conventions and recommendations elaborated this starting point. Due to the magnitude of the economic crisis of the 1930s the standard acquired new moral weight: never again such unemployment! In 1935 the ILO recommended government policies for combating unemployment through public works. The ILO's 1944 Declaration of Philadelphia went further, by embracing 'full employment and the raising of standards of living' as objectives. This view can also be found in Article 55 of the UN Charter, which in the context of stability and well-being speaks of 'higher standards of living, full employment, and conditions of economic and social progress and development'. The Universal Declaration of Human Rights of 1948 restricted itself to the right to 'protection against unemployment' (Article 23.1), but Article 6 of the 1966 International Covenant on Economic, Social and Cultural Rights spoke about policies 'to achieve steady economic, social and cultural development and full and productive employment'. This concern over employment also played a role at Bretton Woods and during the establishment of the International Trade Organization in 1946–48. The IMF Articles of Agreement, somewhat thriftily, referred to 'high levels of employment and real income', while the GATT (and later the WTO) spoke of 'ensuring full employment'.

Arguing in favour of an international division of labour (1980)

In the European reconstruction period after the Second World War full employment had had a real chance, as in Western Europe government measures in favour of social well-being and economic growth also counted as contributions to the desired stability in the East–West relationship. This was reflected in the policies of the OECD's predecessor, the Organization for European Economic Cooperation (see §26.1). As a result of the

662

decolonization process and the economic growth in the North full employment became a global issue during the 1960s. In 1969 the ILO published a World Employment Programme as its contribution to the UN's Second Development Decade. Another global employment plan was launched in 1980, in accordance with the ideas about an international division of labour between North and South of development economist Jan Tinbergen, who argued that international coordination was required. This should not focus on economic growth or an increased standard of living in general, but on maximization of employment in both North and South. However, just like the Brandt Reports (see §35.2), this Keynesian plan went against the politico-economic tide of the 1980s. At the G7 summits in London (1977) and Bonn (1978) unemployment had still been on the agenda, but under the influence of Reagonomics employment became a derivative of economic growth during the 1980s. The G7 summits were more successful with regard to inflation and economic growth than employment. Between 1983 and 1988 unemployment in the OECD states, despite the new liberalization policies, only decreased from 8.9 to 7.5 per cent, while within the OECD the EEC had fallen considerably behind, referred to as 'Eurosclerosis'.

The Kreisky Commission (1989): the crisis of the welfare state

That the G7, OECD and IMF framed employment as a matter of the supply economy implied a passionate plea for lower wages and higher productivity, which had to contribute – in that order – to economic growth and employment. Other advocated measures were the privatization of public enterprises to give them more free market opportunities, less government intervention in the market, the reform of the social security systems in order to reduce costs, a more flexible labour market and a relaxation of labour law and of rules in collective agreements. These G7 policies were politically contradicted in Europe by the Kreisky Commission. This Commission of some 100 people, among them representatives of the ILO, OECD, trade unions and business, was chaired by the former Austrian Chancellor Bruno Kreisky. Between 1986 and 1989 it discussed a programme for full employment in the 1990s, which was published in 1989. It functioned independently, although Austria, Luxembourg and the Scandinavian states supported it financially. The Kreisky Commission discussed the unemployment issue of the 1980s in the context of the crisis in the welfare state, which was founded on full employment, government policies securing income during periods of work interruption and full-time male breadwinners. A combination of circumstances had disturbed the balance between the labour market and social security, which was based on these assumptions. This had resulted in an increase in the need for income transfers such as social security, unemployment benefits, early retirement costs and subsidies for employment projects, while revenues had decreased because of the large numbers of unemployed and the growing number of part-time jobs. In addition to this financial side other factors had come into play, such as slow economic growth, demographical changes (the rise in the ageing population and increasing numbers of women in the labour market), and different types of work (part-time and less well-paid).

A joint European approach

The Kreisky Commission did not regard the rigidness of the labour market or the high wages and generous unemployment benefits as the causes of the new forms of mass

663

unemployment and therefore did not expect that a more flexible policy would solve this problem. Rather, this would result in more 'working poor' like in the US, increase global imbalances and not end unemployment. Instead of the low-paid and unskilled labour policy of flexibility the Commission advocated a joint European approach, which should upgrade and fully use the skilled and educated work, stimulate long-term economic developments and 'bend' economic growth in such a way that it would minimize environmental damage, produce high-quality work and create more jobs for those long-term unemployed market forces had neglected for so long. Due to its focus on, for all European citizens, a better quality of life, satisfying employment, environmental improvement and cultural enrichment, this joint approach had a far wider purpose than economic growth. Governments needed to coordinate the various components of such an approach and to handle both inflation and unemployment. In their labour market policies education, training and retraining should re-engage vulnerable groups, while shorter and more flexible working hours would increase employment opportunities. Regional policies as well as environmental protection were regarded as other means to create more jobs, while governments at the European level should implement huge infrastructural investment schemes, in addition to the 'Europe 1992' project of creating a single market within the EEC (see §40.5). The finances for this approach should come from cooperation between the private and government sectors. The European states also had to combine their technology and innovation policies in order to generate new employment facilities and to rival the US and Japan in the long term. They had to make better use of modern communication and information technology, as it was expected that these would generate many jobs in the infrastructural and services areas (Kreisky Commission 1989).

The welfare state under pressure

The welfare state in Europe was under pressure as a result of the new economic paradigm set by Milton Friedman. This also applied to the trade unions, which increasingly were seen as obstacles to the envisaged supply economy. In the UK Margaret Thatcher, Prime Minister from 1979 to 1990, bore down hard on the trade unions, as labour conflicts continued to block her attempts to revitalize industries that had become obsolete. Her plan to close loss-making coal mines provoked a long-lasting strike in 1984, which however was broken in 1985. She closed many mines and succeeded in keeping the unions under control. By first selling small public companies to their employees she began a process of privatizing a large number of public companies. Unlike in the UK, the majority of people on the Continent supported the idea that the welfare state had to be adapted, but that citizens at the same time did need protection against the impact of economic liberalization and globalization. The general view expressed by the Kreisky Commission was also relevant to the joint approach of the European Community (see below). As a result of greater liberalization trade unions on the Continent lost ground as well, but in most Western European states they remained social partners during the 1990s. Although they might oppose liberalization and privatization, they nonetheless contributed to the successful adaptation of the European welfare state. In the 1990s the debate about this process of adaptation took place at the international level of OECD, G7 and IMF and at the level of the European Community.

40.5 European unemployment: the 'American' solution (OECD, G7 and IMF) or the European?

European unemployment a matter for IMF or G7?

During the IMF Spring Meeting in April 1993 in Washington DC IMF experts argued on the basis of the recently published biannual *World Economic Outlook* (see Figure 40.3) that, despite some rays of hope, the world economy was still facing serious problems. The IMF was pessimistic with regard to European unemployment, which seemed structural as a result of the high minimum wages and lack of workers' mobility. The IMF believed that more coordination by the industrialized states was needed to improve the world economy. Managing-director Michel Camdessus preferred it if the IMF Interim Committee were to be given this coordinating task, rather than the G7, as more states would be involved. However, Camdessus did not receive enough support from US President Clinton for such an IMF role and the measures necessary to fulfil that role. Many states in fact did not yet assist in the IMF exercising the monitoring role it had been given for decisions taken by the G7 (see §35.5). Shortly before the IMF meeting the G7 ministers of finance had met separately and had expressed, thanks to US Secretary of the Treasury Lloyd Bentsen, their willingness to engage in international economic coordination, in contrast to the previous Reagan and Bush eras. As was discovered later, at this meeting Bentsen had created a sound foundation for the July meeting of the heads of state and government of the G7 in Tokyo. After the meeting of G7 finance ministers

Figure 40.3 The World Economic Outlook of the IMF

The biannual **World Economic Outlook** is based on the data the IMF is continually collecting in a large number of states. These enable it to discern trends and also to produce forecasts that ministers of finance might take into account. At IMF meetings they then base their common decisions on these trends and analyses. Because the biannual reports regularly draw the attention of the media, IMF data, forecasts and warnings often play a role in domestic politics.

If one places the **newspaper headings** on the *World Economic Outlook* in a row it is possible to get an overview of how the IMF thinks about the world economy and its fluctuations. 'The IMF warns of lower interest.' 'The IMF forecasts growth of the economy by only one per cent' (1991). 'IMF gravely concerned about the world economy' (1992). 'Recovery of the world economy still hesitant' (1993). 'IMF optimism about growth despite exchange fluctuation.' 'World economy in a "growth interval"' (1995). 'IMF sees vast economic growth in many developing states' (1996). 'IMF: influence Asia Crisis restricted' (1998). 'IMF not pessimistic but unresolved' (1999). 'IMF: economic performance disappoints' (2001). 'Sun breaks through in the world economy.' 'IMF: recovery of world growth slows down' (2002). 'IMF predicts recovery world economy not before 2004.' 'Lopsided growth characterizes recovery' (2003). 'IMF positive about recovery of economies' (2005). 'Good results everywhere not without dangers' (2006). 'World economy picks up speed' (2007) and 'IMF alarm' (2008).

Camdessus proved to be a good loser. Although the IMF was not given the envisaged coordinating role, he said he was 'delighted' with the results the ministers of finance had achieved. The IMF was in favour of cooperation and would strengthen its monitoring role.

The OECD as preparation ground for the G7 summit (1993)

The annual OECD meeting of economic and trade ministers in Paris in early June 1993 was attended by a strong US delegation led by Bentsen. There was much debate among the ministers on how to solve European unemployment, which according to their conclusion was related to a fundamental technological and social process that was taking place. The provision of modern high-tech-based services was increasing, while traditional production was likely to move to low-wage states. This implied that economic growth was no longer able to provide jobs for everyone. Combined with economic stagnation and growing pressure on the welfare state this might even result in a 'social explosion'. A drastic change in policy was required to prevent persistent structural unemployment, as well as macro-economic policies aimed at a reduction of budget deficits and social security payments. It was necessary on the one hand to create new products and jobs and arrange that highly-qualified workers were adequately trained and retrained, while on the other labour market and income policies had to be adapted. The OECD ministers referred to the US situation, where low minimum wages and a flexible law governing dismissal made it easy to hire more people when the economy improved. They queried to what extent minimum wages and collective agreements might constitute obstacles to the creation of sufficient numbers of jobs in Europe. The OECD message was clear, even if the organization itself had no unambiguous policies available. Unemployment was to rise further, as was confirmed by the OECD *Economic Outlook* in June, and the labour market still needed to be made more flexible.

The European Council on unemployment (1993)

The European Community was also analysing its unemployment issue and pondering over policies. On the eve of the European Council of 21 and 22 June 1993 in Copenhagen Commissioner Padraig Flynn pointed to the necessity of strong economic growth, but also argued that this alone was insufficient to solve the unemployment problem. In order to help more people find jobs he believed that wage restraint and a decrease in labour costs were necessary. After this first move Commission President Jacques Delors made it clear to the European Council that unemployment was a structural issue and that drastic wage restraint was required to make labour cheaper and labour participation had to be increased to relieve social security. Given the question he raised about the number of porters working in the Community, Delors obviously was interested in expanding cheap services, but he was unwilling to take the 'American way' as discussed within the OECD. That he did not refer to a cutback in social security as an opportunity to lower wage costs did not alter the fact that the European Council also thought in terms of global competition. The British government for instance argued strongly against any obstacles to more competition, such as those in the European Working Time Directive with a maximum 48-hour working week which had been adopted shortly before. At this meeting the European Council began to realize that a more flexible labour market and change in the usual level of wages were unavoidable. However, political relations meant it was not yet possible to say this aloud. News analysts concluded that Delors had not proposed a cutback in social security, but had made it a subject of discussion. The European Council made Delors responsible for drafting a new employment programme and at its meeting in December 1993 in Brussels the Council would discuss what came to be known as 'Delors' White Book' on growth, competitiveness and employment with measures for economic recovery.

The G7 summit in Tokyo (1993)

On the eve of the G7 summit in Tokyo in July 1993 leading American economists emphasized again that greater export opportunities were the best way to enlarge employment. This would promote a rapid conclusion of the GATT negotiations and thus stimulate international trade, and also help to tackle the problem of the too rigid European labour market. President Clinton took the initiative by – prior to the conference – sending an invitation to the other G7 members to come to the US in the autumn for a special summit meeting on unemployment. This made European employment a US-guided issue. The special autumn summit was not to be a meeting of heads of state but of high representatives, as was also the case in Tokyo, because the serious talks on this matter were not taking place at the summit itself, but at a simultaneous meeting of the finance ministers. They concluded that rigid labour market regulations and high wage and social security costs were causing unemployment and considered reform of the labour market regulations, making the law governing dismissal more flexible, and lower costs for social security and health care as necessary. Public services needed to be well-adjusted and the ministers expected that the trade unions would be prepared to accept agreements with more flexible arrangements for working hours and dismissals. These events made a number of things clear. The US was in charge, the G7 had precedence over the IMF, the OECD ministerial meeting once again had been the preparation ground for the G7 summit and policy convergence was taking place, with, if the G7 was to decide, European social relations subordinate to global relations.

The enduring welfare state

Developments in Western Europe would not follow this 'American way' as closely as proposed and would be closer to the recommendations of the Kreisky Commission and the European Community. The situation varied by region, depending on the position of the trade unions within the national labour relations systems. The trade union attitude with regard to social security in Scandinavia was different to that in the 'Rhineland', in southern Europe or in the UK. Despite these differences the common trend in the reform of the welfare state in Western Europe was 'a move away from universal forms of state protection towards means-testing, tighter eligibility requirements, increased private-sector involvement and greater decentralization' (Page 2004, 31). The variations in tax regulation and the often drastic expenditure cuts by European governments were mostly pragmatic responses to the economic difficulties, rather than fundamental decisions about challenging the underpinnings of the welfare state. However, allowances became less generous, as was shown by reductions in unemployment benefit schemes, more individualized state pension arrangements and some increased flexibility in labour law. In addition it was made easier for companies to be active internationally, which would also have its impact on the labour markets, as these became more dynamic: many jobs would disappear due to the relocation of production to other states, initially mostly in the Third

World, but in the 1990s also to Eastern European states in transformation after the end of the Cold War. Many new jobs would be created as a result of the development of new services, such as in communication and information technology. As national industries began to function under global competition conditions the industrialized states became more and more dependent on the dynamics of their labour markets, with a general tendency of disappearing manufacturing industry and expanding services. This implied that low-skilled workers with a weak labour market position were hit hardest by the loss of jobs and had few opportunities to return to work.

The importance of the European single market

The trump card the European Community members had in defending their welfare states proved to be the programme for a European 'single market', launched in 1985 and led with a firm hand by Delors, which had to be completed by the end of 1992. It was a comprehensive set of measures designed to stimulate economic recovery, guarantee the free movement of persons, goods, services and capital and merge the national markets into one single market. It aimed to eliminate the remaining legal, fiscal and technical obstacles to a single market and had a strict time schedule (see §43.1). The preparations for a wider European market stimulated the national economies, for instance through mergers and large-scale investments, and restored trust in economic performance. Eventually the completion of the single market would be closely related to economic recovery during the 1990s. The positive economic results allowed the EC member states to make compromises with the trade unions in their reform of the welfare state and to not take the 'American way' the G7, OECD and IMF had advocated. The European Commission acted as coordinator of the various employment schemes that were set up. In 1995 Commission President Jacques Santer proposed a so-called 'confidence pact' as a force for employment. He brought employers, trade unions and governments together and proposed measures to strengthen the single market, decrease government support, bolster education and schooling and improve the position of small and medium-sized businesses. His comprehensive pact furthermore included large-scale projects at the European level, such as train and road connections, but these were turned down by the UK and Germany. At that time the maintenance of the welfare state was regarded as an exclusively national affair, albeit that the member states' economic power was also the result of the European single market. They had not only profited from the larger European market, but also from the fact that their corporations, enlarged as a result of mergers, were better able to compete in the world market. In the Treaty of Amsterdam (1997) the promotion of 'a high level of employment' was included as one of the objectives of the European Union.

40.6 The ILO in a corner: core labour standards as the way out

The end of the Cold War: international labour standards under pressure

The fall of the Berlin wall in 1989 had consequences for the International Labour Organization. During the Cold War governments, employers and workers had combined to take a firm stand on fundamental human rights such as the freedom of association and the right to collective bargaining. The disappearance of the East–West divide weakened the ILO's human rights regime severely, since the need to remind the communist states to respect those rights no longer existed. Third World states, referring to specific cultures and traditions, furthermore argued that human rights could be of different importance in one continent than in another. As industrializing states they did not have an urgent need for social rights in the field of labour, which they regarded as obstacles to their development opportunities imposed on them by the industrialized states. This putting the situation into perspective meant that the international labour standards threatened to lose their universal character and that the ILO's International Labour Code (see §17.3) was under strain. The declining support for this code could be seen in the fact that ratification of ILO conventions had stagnated. In the early 1990s the drive of Reagonomics for liberalization and privatization had put pressure on the social arrangements the ILO promoted, as was shown in the GATT debate on social clauses in the context of more free trade. The GATT referred the regulating of labour issues to the ILO, but at the same time regarded such regulation as an impediment to free trade (see §40.1). Then the ILO discovered that the UN, without consulting it, had decided to organize a World Summit for Social Development, to take place in 1995 in Copenhagen, with the aim of giving a new direction to social policies. The ILO had long been involved in the three core issues on the agenda of this summit, which were the lessening and elimination of widespread poverty, productive employment and a reduction in unemployment, and social integration. That the UN was going its own way, without involving the ILO, came as a shock to the organization.

The director-general's report on the 75th anniversary (1994)

In 1994 the ILO celebrated its 75th anniversary, but given the many pressures on the organization there was not much of a festive atmosphere. Director-general Michel Hansenne understood that something had to be done: 'the ILO must seize the initiative in a number of difficult fields which have too long lain fallow, or risk losing its relevance, and the values it has always defended' (ILO 1994, 9). He wrote a report entitled *Defending Values, Promoting Change, Social Justice in a Global Economy: An ILO Agenda*, with the aim 'to ensure that the ILO is recognized as an essential agent in the new economic regulatory framework' which was evolving in the new WTO and in other international arrangements (ILO 1994, 17). He succeeded in stimulating discussions within his own organization to find the means to fight back successfully.

The way out: selecting a restricted number of labour standards

The way out of the impasse which the ILO found, thanks to Hansenne's report, resulted from its realization that its full International Labour Code (see Figure 17.2) was too much of a good thing. Given the changed circumstances, it would be better to focus on a few core labour standards. This was not something that had happened in the debate on social clauses, when the ILO took it for granted it should stick to its entire Code, despite the dominant trend of reducing the number of social regulations in favour of more market influence. The International Labour Conference of 1994 therefore decided to select some 'core labour standards' and to ensure that institutions and processes would be assessed according to these standards. The ILO conventions involved were numbers 29 on forced labour, 87 on the freedom of association, 98 on the right to organize and collective bargaining, 100 on the equal remuneration of women and men, 105 on the abolition of forced labour, 111 on discrimination in employment and occupation, 138 on the minimum age and, later, 182 on the worst forms of child labour. The ILO also established a working group to better understand the social dimensions of trade liberalization. The UN World Summit for Social Development then offered a forum where the ILO could make its new policy public, in the same way the UNDP did, which also was struggling to survive and used the World Summit to receive support for its new policies (see §39.5).

The UN Social Summit in Copenhagen (1995)

The convening of the *World Summit for Social Development* in Copenhagen by the UN had not been without debate on its significance. States had warned about raising unrealistic hopes for a topic as difficult as poverty and the related social and economic issues. Within the UN however the idea existed that it was precisely issues such as poverty, employment and social integration that had to be discussed, as a kind of synthesis of all that had gone before. This coherence was confirmed in the discussions at the World Summit and even resulted in innovative ideas. The UNDP and UNICEF, for instance, had developed a plan based on the principle of spending 20 per cent of development aid on basic social services, in return for agreements from the poor states to devote 20 per cent of their budgets to such programmes. However, in the final summit document such ideas were either omitted or mentioned only as suggestions, much to the disappointment of the organizations and NGOs. A G77 proposal for the establishment of an international fund for social development did not receive enough support from the participating states either. Although the final document of the Copenhagen Summit contained ten commitments, the *Copenhagen Alternative Declaration*, drafted by the NGOs, seemed a more realistic document, given its call for more forthright action on issues such as Third World debt, democratization of the IMF and IBRD and regulation of transnational corporations and financial transactions. The main effects of this UN World Summit were a stronger orientation of the UNDP on targeting its activities to tackle poverty (Schechter 2005, 143) and the recognition of the core labour standards of the ILO. The ILO had succeeded in putting its new views on core labour standards on the agenda of the World Summit and in having them recognized in the debates. Section 54 of the action programme that was adopted called on states to ratify these core conventions.

The ILO matters again

Following this support from the UN system the ILO started an intensive and soon successful ratification campaign, which was backed by ministerial statements at the WTO conference in Singapore in 1996 and by EU pressure on those member states that had not yet ratified the core conventions. Although the WTO was not keen to discuss social issues, as these could easily turn into impediments to free trade, reference to a limited set of fundamental labour standards proved an acceptable way of monitoring the social dimension of international trade. Once again (see §19.2) the ILO had succeeded in surviving an external crisis. Led by Hansenne, it had found a way out and then transformed itself into an IGO that mattered again, as was shown by an enthusiastic worldwide campaign against the worst forms of child labour. This campaign supported the adoption of an ILO convention that became part of the set of core standards.

Worldwide ILO campaign against child labour

As had happened for the rights of the child, with an international convention adopted in 1989 (see Figure 33.1), child labour became an important international theme during the 1990s. In 1992 the ILO had started a programme of technical assistance, named the *International Programme on the Elimination of Child Labour* (IPEC). In addition to its 1973 Minimum Age Convention (number 138) the ILO aimed at a convention on the elimination of the worst kinds of child labour. These are all forms of slavery or practices similar to slavery, prostitution, illicit activities in particular in relation to drugs, and work that is likely to harm the health, safety or morals of children. The ILO campaign was supported by the *Global March Against Child Labour*, run by trade unions and NGOs, which organized marches on all continents in order to mobilize public awareness. In 1998 these marches culminated at the International Labour Conference in Geneva, which in 1999 unanimously adopted the proposed ILO convention. The international trade unions launched a campaign to ensure ratification by the member states. The *Worst Forms of Child Labour Convention* (number 182) became the fastest ratified convention in ILO history, with 161 ratifications by 2006 (of which 49 were in Africa, 48 in Europe, 33 in the Western Hemisphere and 31 in Asia, where even China ratified) and 169 by 2008. In 2002 the campaign against the worst forms of child labour was extended by the *Education For All* programme that the ILO set up together with UNESCO, UNICEF, the IBRD and the Global March Against Child Labour. The ILO campaign resulted in a decrease in child labour of some 25 per cent in four years, although in 2004 there were still 218 million children trapped in child labour, including 126 million in hazardous work. Progress was greatest in Latin America and least in sub-Saharan Africa, where child labour remained alarmingly high.

The UN Millennium Development Goals (2000)

Following its 1995 World Summit for Social Development, the UN prepared a huge world summit at the beginning of the new century. This Millennium Summit formulated the UN *Millennium Development Goals* (in jargon MDGs) in areas such as poverty, hunger, disease, illiteracy, environmental degradation and discrimination against women. The goals were concrete and measurable, and had to be met by 2015. The innovative aspect of measurable goals was used, as it would be easier to hold governments to their promises. After the Millennium Summit the UN, its specialized agencies, among them the IMF and IBRD, and the OECD worked on the definition of nearly 50 relevant indicators, so as to regularly assess progress over the period 1990 to 2015. In 2005 UN secretary-general Kofi Annan published an ambitious plan of action for poverty reduction. He had invited the well-known economist Geoffrey Sachs to become his special adviser for the Millennium Development Goals. On the occasion of the UN's 60th anniversary in September 2005 a millennium follow-up conference was convened, where it was revealed that the UN was in serious trouble because of US demands for organizational reforms. It was also clear that the UN poverty reduction policies were barely making progress. The US negotiators tried to keep the Millennium Development Goals out of the final text of this conference, a ploy which however failed as a result of widespread resistance. According to Sachs the weakness of the goals lay in the lack of an approach on how to deal with them. He argued that as long as the goals are not embedded in the work programmes of the specialized and other agencies, in particular those of the IMF and IBRD, they will remain without much significance, apart from rhetorical.

IMF, IBRD and WTO criticized by states and the anti-globalization movement

41.1 The Asian financial crisis (1997–98) and the clash between ASEAN and IMF

New financial crises and crisis prevention

During the huge financial crisis that hit Mexico in 1994 and 1995 the IMF played a poor role as a result of groupthink among those of its personnel involved (see Figure 41.1). They did not see the crisis coming and reacted wrongly, with the result that the Mexican currency lost its value. New financial crises hit East Asia in 1997–98, Russia in 1998 and Turkey and Argentina in 2000 and 2001. Because the IMF's attempts to control these crises were inadequate, it was forced to rethink and reform its operations in three areas: crisis prevention, crisis management and its role in economic development, including its division of labour with the IBRD. Crisis prevention focused on the creation of international standards and codes of good financial practices and the promotion of sound financial institutions in developing states, with responsibility for increased transparency and accountability. It was argued that the greater openness and the better insight these provided would make it easier to follow developments and signal potential dangers. The

IMF decided to keep its documents on individual states no longer confidential. From then on most documents would be published on the Internet.

The Financial Stability Forum (1999)

The *Financial Stability Forum* (FSF) was set up in response to the Asian crisis in 1999, as an attempt to foster international financial stability through regular exchange of information and cooperation on overseeing financial developments, for example in the area of corruption. However, the standards and the information exchange remained weak instruments. 'While the benefits of accounting standards and information transparency may seem apparent, some critics note that the implementation of these standards may be difficult. Acceptance is voluntary, and there is no overt mechanism for enforcement' (Weiss 2002, 3). One of the successful ways in which the Financial Stability Forum tackled tax havens and dubious financial practices was by publishing 'blacklists' containing information on states that were flouting the criteria. This tough measure of blacklisting soon had an impact on tax havens, but in the long term a more institutional approach was required to generate ongoing stability and sustainable arrangements (Sharman 2008).

IMF crisis management

When implementing the crisis management reforms that were obviously necessary, the IMF tried to improve its use of resources during times of crisis. The priorities during a crisis were to prevent it from spreading and to mitigate the damage. The IMF set up two working groups, whose remit was to improve understanding of 'the international capital markets, the forces driving the supply of capital, and the constraints these capital flows place on economic policy makers' (Weiss 2002, 4). From March 2002 onwards the IMF published the quarterly *Global Financial Stability Report*, in an attempt to chart long-term stability and instability. It looked primarily at debt sustainability, arguing that high debts that could not in fact be repaid, such as those of Argentina, were an obstacle to retrenchment. Something had to be done, but in this respect the IMF's practices were still inadequate. Other procedures that the IMF was working on were intended for situations in which states went bankrupt. To address this issue it formulated collective action clauses among other measures, which were to be incorporated into loan contracts.

The Asian crisis 1997–98

The Asian financial crisis erupted in the summer of 1997, when the Thai central bank allowed its national currency to float. It had previously used a large part of its foreign reserves (mostly dollars) to protect the currency, but this intervention had failed. Following its floatation the Thai currency went into free fall, ultimately stabilizing at 60 per cent of its initial value. Thailand's action dragged most East Asian currencies down with it, except those of Japan, Singapore and South Korea. There had already been several conflicts over regional and monetary policy within the Asian Development Bank (ADB) between the Asian and the Western states. In 1994 the US had urged the ADB to increase its capital with the aim of reducing poverty and educating women, but the Asian states wanted to prioritize infrastructural works. The US referred to the IBRD and its human welfare standard, while the Asians regarded the US and IBRD policy as interference in their sovereign and regional politics.

Figure 41.1 Groupthink in the IMF: the Mexican financial crisis of 1994

The 'middle-range' theory of **groupthink** by Irving Janis offers a means of obtaining a deeper understanding of poor decision making within bureaucratic organizations, including IGOs. This socio-psychological approach concerns decision-making situations in small groups during crises. According to Janis, social pressure within a group augments the tendency of group members to adopt each other's ideas and behaviour. In certain circumstances, such as in a crisis, the social pressure can produce such a strong common vision and cohesion within the group that the members make dysfunctional policy choices. This happens because in such circumstances the group members have a greater tendency to agree with each other than to compare alternatives and try to arrive at a realistic decision that is appropriate to the situation (Janis 1982). Ngaire Woods applied this theory to the **Mexican national currency crisis in 1994**, which erupted somewhat abruptly, and the IMF's incorrect response to it. The IMF had a clear and consistent framework for analysing and describing, in accordance with its policy, financial and related developments in its member states. The staff members responsible for evaluating the sudden currency crisis in Mexico were blinded by their belief in that analytical framework. They simply could not imagine that a state which had implemented IMF policy could become embroiled in a crisis: 'believing that because IMF-prescribed structural reforms had been undertaken by the Mexican government, its economy simply could not and would not go into crisis'. Non-IMF analysts who employed more than one particular analysis framework did see signs of trouble. The fact that the IMF staff had hardly any contact with experts outside their own small group exacerbated their tendency to cling to 'just one scenario – that of successful transition'. They were unreceptive to information from external sources and continued on their course even when contrary evidence presented itself. The culture and practices within the department prevented correction of the staff members' behaviour (Woods 2000, 11–12).

Clash between ASEAN and IMF

The response to the financial crisis sparked by Thailand in 1997 was also marked by tense relations. ASEAN sought to establish its own regional currency fund to combat this kind of monetary crisis, but met with strong opposition from the IMF, which saw it as a threat to its own role. However, the IMF was forced to back down in the face of support for such a regional arrangement from other developing states. The matter was also raised at the annual meeting of the Asia Pacific Economic Cooperation (see §42.4). The IMF ultimately had to acknowledge the importance of strengthening regional mutual monitoring between states. Agreements on this were made between the ASEAN and other Asian states at the ADB annual meeting in 1998 and ASEAN, China, Japan and South Korea in 2000 announced their intention to establish an Asian monetary fund to provide financial assistance when their national currencies were under threat (see §42.4 on the Chiang Mai Initiative). In response to the crisis the Asian states completely reorganized and reinforced their central banks (Thies 2004). The crisis ended relatively quickly and fairly soon afterwards Asian states were transformed into international capital providers as a result of domestic investments and their huge trade surpluses.

Forming the G20 (1999)

The G20 was established in Berlin in December 1999 on the recommendation of the G7 finance ministers. This group of 19 states plus the EU was set up to strengthen the 'international financial architecture' after the crises of the 1990s. Headed by the finance ministers and central bank governors of its members, this informal forum is intended to provide a venue for 'open and constructive dialogue' between industrialized states and 'emerging market economies' such as Algeria, Brazil, China, India, Saudi Arabia, Russia and Turkey. There is no secretariat, but there is a rotating presidency that prepares the meetings. The IMF and the IBRD attend the meetings to prevent the G20 from making policy that is incompatible with theirs. In fact, the creation of the G20 was a recognition that large developing states were inadequately represented in the international organizations that determine global policies on economic developments.

Supervision of banks: Basel I (1988) and II (2003)

One of the international financial crisis management reforms was a set of requirements for banks, which was arranged not by the IMF, but by a committee associated with the Bank for International Settlements in Basel (see Figure 18.4). Following the failure of large banks in the 1970s and 1980s, the central bank governors deliberated on the requirements that should be imposed on banks to enable them to fulfil their obligations. In 1984 the *Basel Committee on Bank Supervision* (BCBS) began to formulate international standards for this purpose. The Basel Committee had been established in 1974 by the central bank governors of the G10, comprising the richest IMF members (see §27.1). It has no formal competences or legal powers, but functions under the authority of the central banks and reports to the G10 central bank governors. The BIS supports the Basel Committee's secretariat. Although initially there was no need for international regulations, the US Federal Reserve Board and the Bank of England pressed for an international regime that would not harm their interests in an environment of evolving economic relationships. 'It would strengthen the international payments system without placing the American and British banks at a competitive disadvantage, and it would maintain the primacy of New York and London over Tokyo and Brussels as the centres in which fundamental decisions concerning the payments system were made' (Kapstein 1992, 286). This led to the *Basel Capital Accord* of 1988, known as *Basel I*, which contained the first international principles on the minimum capital reserves that banks should hold to cover outstanding loans. These solvency requirements reduced the banks' risk to a responsible level. The Asian crisis of 1997–98 and the stock market crash of 2000 necessitated a revision of this system, in part due to the increasing complexity of financial markets and the internationalization of banking. This led to agreement on a second capital accord in 2003, *Basel II*, consisting of principles that banks have to adhere to in order to guarantee the stability of their own institution and the financial sector. Basically, the banks can introduce any risk management system of their choice, as long as it meets the requirements of the supervisory authorities under Basel II, which entered into force in 2007.

Improving SAPs and the relationship with the IBRD

In 1999 the third IMF reform, relating to economic development, led to a new facility for issuing loans to developing states. As a result of the Enhanced Structural Adjustment Facility, used in the context of structural adjustment programmes (SAPs, see §35.3), the IMF created the *Poverty Reduction and Growth Facility* (PRGF) to improve effectiveness in the poorest states, in particular in Africa. Poverty reduction became an objective of certain loans. Opinions on the IMF's relationship with the IBRD differed. The options were for both institutions to return to their original core tasks or to enhance their cooperation with each other. The latter solution was encapsulated in the *Financial Sector Assessment Programme* (FSAP), established jointly by the IMF and IBRD in 1999 to assess financial institutions in their member states and, as necessary, create healthy financial institutions. 'These reforms most likely will be implemented by the World Bank and the Multilateral Development Banks through IMF-sponsored adjustment programs' (Weiss 2002, 5). Cooperation on poverty reduction and growth was another obvious course for the two institutions.

41.2 Washington Consensus, Good Governance and IMF mistakes during the Argentine crisis (2000)

Washington Consensus

Despite these reforms, the IMF failed to design programmes that met the needs of borrower states. It was also unsuccessful in retaining the confidence and support of the states from which it needed to obtain money to operate. 'In many cases, the gap between the goals and expectations of the borrower countries and the donor countries is great' (Weiss 2002, 5). The same was true with the so-called *Washington Consensus*. Since 1989 this term has been used in reference to a set of policy reforms based on privatization, liberalization and democratization which the Washington-based financial institutions presented to developing states. It covers a wide range of principles, such as fiscal discipline, tax reform, variable interest rates, a competitive exchange rate, trade liberalization, open capital markets, private property rights, privatization and deregulation. 'Many borrower countries, by contrast, believe that these policies are too narrow and lack sufficient appreciation for their real needs and the limits of their political and economic situations. As developing countries are now the primary recipient of IMF assistance and policy advice, divergence between lenders and creditors has grown, with protests against the IMF in general and specific IMF loan programs' (Weiss 2002, 6).

Good Governance in the 1990s

In the 1990s the term *Good Governance* acquired special significance at the IMF and the IBRD. Both presented Good Governance as a necessary precondition for the neoliberal reforms they were promulgating. Good Governance thus became a new instrument of control over developing states in the hands of international financial institutions (Taylor 2004, 130). Against the backdrop of the financial crises in the 1980s and 1990s, the IMF and IBRD demanded increased discipline in compliance with their policy, although both institutions were themselves supporting many corrupt regimes and knew that states were in practice flouting the standards they now imposed. The rise of Good Governance as an instrument was also related to the political desire to foster liberal democracy, which was prominent in the 1990s. The IMF assumed that there was consensus about what Good Governance was in democratic and transparent systems and that acceptance of this definition of Good Governance would make developing states attractive to investors. IMF managing director Camdessus: 'in a world in which private capital has become more mobile, there is mounting evidence that corruption undermines the confidence of the most serious investors and adversely affects private capital inflows' (Taylor 2004, 124). While the IMF and IBRD assumed that their vision of Good Governance was self-evident, the Asian Development Bank had different ideas. Certain concepts were cited, but they had a different meaning in the region (see Figure 41.2).

IMF mistakes during the Argentine crisis of 2000–2001

The IMF's share of responsibility for the Argentine debt crisis was particularly great because Argentina had been under close IMF supervision virtually throughout the 1990s.

Figure 41.2 The meaning of Good Governance within IBRD, DAC and ADB

The simple fact that the IMF and the IBRD could not interfere in domestic relations in their member states put them in a difficult position with regard to structural adjustment policy and the financial crises. Based on the debt issues and the vision of Good Governance formulated in the 1990s, the **IBRD** presented **Good Governance** as 'administrative governance', while states applied Good Governance as 'political governance' in their bilateral relations (Masujima 2004, 151–52).

Good Governance was also an issue for the OECD's **Development Assistance Committee** (DAC), in which OECD member states coordinate their policy towards developing states. This is a relatively homogeneous group of states involved in development assistance. Despite their recognition of the connection between economics and politics, they were never able to develop the idea of Good Governance fully. This was primarily due to organizational limitations and a difference of opinion between states that advocated restraint and the US, which considered democracy and Good Governance to be natural objectives of development aid (Masujima 2004, 161).

The **Asian Development Bank** (ADB) accepted the Good Governance policy because Western donor states required it. In negotiations concerning resources for certain ADB funds, the ADB was forced to accept wording on Good Governance. But because it was a negotiating process, the final text differed from what Western donors had wanted. Japan played a mediating role. Expressions on the role of the state and the principles of sound development management were reformulated. The final results contained 'terminology borrowed from the Washington Consensus and neoliberal economics to give the Western donors what they wanted'. But this was coupled 'with a redefinition of key concepts, as well as an emphatic restatement of the "apolitical" role of the Bank to protect the integrity of its charter' (Jokinen 2004, 148).

In other crises, such as those in Indonesia, South Korea and Thailand during the Asian crisis and in Brazil in 1998–99, the IMF had become involved only after the crisis had emerged. 'For Argentina, the failures of the Fund are clearly associated with the core of the Fund's most intense involvement with a member: when it is providing financial assistance and when the policies and performance of the member are subject to the intense scrutiny of Fund conditionality' (Mussa 2002, 3). The IMF had become involved in Argentina during the debt crisis of the 1980s. The government at the time had failed to comply with IMF requirements, but the government of President Carlos Menem, which took office in 1988, pursued a course of far-reaching liberalization and privatization of state-owned enterprises in accordance with IMF policy. This checked inflation and stimulated economic growth, but because the peso was pegged to the US dollar it was impossible to adjust the exchange rate in order to mitigate economic shocks. The IMF did nothing to interfere with the connection between the currencies, because it considered this a domestic Argentine matter. It did, however, press for the privatization of pensions and for social security cuts. These reforms led to large budget deficits and in December 2004 to a popular uprising when people were prevented from withdrawing money from their bank accounts. The IMF made at least two mistakes with respect to Argentina: '(1) in failing to press the Argentine authorities much harder to have a more responsible fiscal policy, especially during the high growth years of the early through mid 1990s; and (2) in extending substantial additional financial support to Argentina during the summer of 2001, after it had become abundantly clear that the Argentine government's efforts to avoid default and maintain the exchange rate peg had no reasonable chance of success' (Mussa 2002, 4). The policy that Argentina wanted and conducted was, according to the IMF, a matter for the Argentine government and it supported this policy with explanations and loans. However, it failed to bring pressure to bear on the Argentine government when it adopted policies which it had no intention of implementing, or to discourage the government from pursuing policies that were likely to intensify the crisis. The IMF was therefore to blame for a failure to act: 'either failures of the Fund to press hard enough and soon enough for policies of the Argentine government that would have been likely to improve the outcome; or failures of the Fund to discourage sufficiently forcefully policies that exacerbated the tragedy' (Mussa 2002, 7). The IMF, however, had difficulty acknowledging its own failures.

The changing world economy and the consequences for the IMF

At the beginning of the twenty-first century major changes in the world economy forced the IMF once again to reflect on its own performance. During the financial crises of the 1990s the IMF could act as lender of last resort and impose conditions for loans of tens of billions of dollars. The unprecedented economic growth in Asia and in parts of Latin America, and the high revenues Russia was receiving as a result of rocketing oil prices, had allowed these states to repay all, or most, of their debts. Asia, including China, had been able to accumulate huge reserves in the order of 2,000 billion dollars. For the time being they would not need IMF funds. In this respect the US trade deficits also played a role. Asia not only supplied goods to the US, but it also financed them by buying US shares and government bonds. The IMF is not equipped either financially or administratively to deal with a world economy so out of balance. Financially the IMF, which covers its costs out of interest income, was looking at an increasing lack of funds. It also had an administrative problem in that the larger Asian and Latin American states and

Russia are subordinate in the Western-dominated structures of the IMF and IBDR. Given this situation, it was understandable that Asian states pursued their plans to set up a regional monetary fund. The problem of inadequate and insufficient representation was also a factor in the IMF's relationship with the G8, where states like Brazil, China and India are excluded from decision making. The international financial architecture in which the IMF is a key pillar was under pressure. It was up to the IMF to decide whether or not to play a role in the necessary changes. It could do this by becoming the discussion forum for this issue, but then it would have to be willing to adapt its management structure and reflect on its remit in a changed world economy. Given the entrenched relations and the difficulty that large bureaucracies with long-held traditions have with change, this would seem to be an onerous task. On the other hand IGOs under pressure are capable of adapting and surviving.

41.3 Wolfensohn reorganizes the criticized IBRD (1997)

Wolfensohn reorganizes the IBRD

By the mid-1990s the IBRD's financial position had deteriorated and it was clear that the Bank was functioning badly. In 1997 its new president James Wolfensohn undertook a sweeping reorganization, which his predecessors had tried to do before but without success. Redundancy schemes for 600 of the 6,000 members of staff were very expensive, as were the organizational changes aimed at increasing efficiency in the fight against global poverty. Wolfensohn implemented a large-scale cost reduction plan and rejected the objections from the large states to the high costs of the reorganization. He received 400 million of the 570 million dollars he had requested. His policy led to the cultural change within the organization that had been sought previously (see §35.4). There was greater openness. Through the agency of NGOs and international trade unions dialogues were held between on the one side NGOs and trade unions and on the other the IBRD and IMF. The IBRD was more receptive to criticism than the IMF: anyone visiting the neighbouring institutions in Washington DC could feel the difference. Visitors to the IBRD encountered an inviting bookstore, well-stocked with publications from UN agencies and publishers but also with works by critical groups, including anti-globalizationists. A book by Noreena Herz was chosen by IBRD staff as the favourite of 2002 and was consequently sold at a discount. By contrast, visitors to the IMF across the street found a few expensive IMF reports in a dark corner of the building's entrance.

Criticism of the IBRD from outsiders

The IBRD was facing serious problems, as donor states reduced their contributions so as to make the spending cuts required by their domestic political and economic situation. These states were critical of staff performance and thought IBRD staff salaries were excessive. While less money was coming in, the international community at the same time was calling on the IBRD to help solve new problems, such as those of the economies in transition, the reconstruction of states devastated by ethnic conflict, HIV/AIDS, debt relief and, later, poverty as a root cause of terrorism. Recipient states were critical too, especially of the strict conditions the IBRD imposed under the Washington Consensus. The growth in the number of private investments was a separate problem, as it left the IBRD with less room for manoeuvre and limited its role to issuing loans when a financial crisis arose. The IBRD also faced sharp criticism from NGOs, which expressed their dissatisfaction through the slogan 'Fifty Years is Enough' on the occasion of the IBRD's 50th anniversary in 1994 and through demonstrations during annual meetings (Oxfam 1995). A group of people set up the *Reinventing Bretton Woods Committee*, aimed at finding ways to improve both institutions, which advocated a 'public-private dialogue by drawing market participants into discussions with government officials and leaders of multinational institutions to examine for systemic change in the Bretton Woods institutions'.

Internal criticism and changes

The IBRD also faced criticism from within. A report compiled by Willi Wapenhans, a former vice-president of the Bank, in 1992 showed that the effectiveness of IBRD projects was low and declining. The organizational structure of the Bank aided adverse effects, as the internal promotion system favoured the development of 'as many projects as possible', regardless of whether these were desirable or not. Project evaluations were overly optimistic, because a positive assessment increased the chances of gaining the support of recipient governments. Wolfensohn initiated the *Strategic Compact* reform programme in April 1997, which set out measures aimed at making projects more compatible with the needs of states to invest in neglected areas, and proposed to capture the IBRD's expertise on development processes in a 'knowledge bank'. He also introduced a better management system, which included involving representatives of civil society, often originating from NGOs, in the local IBRD offices and in the drafting and assessment of reports on states.

Personnel problems

Wolfensohn's reform operation was completed in 2000. The IBRD had weathered another critical period in its existence, although it remains to be seen whether it has succeeded in truly changing its in-house culture. Tensions arose internally as a result of the redundancies, financial limitations and uncertainty about the future. 'This created distrust between Wolfensohn, senior management, and staff as well as a general malaise, stress, work overload and "change fatigue" within the organization' (Weaver and Leiteritz 2005, 378). New president Paul Wolfowitz's involvement in a scandal exacerbated those tensions. After taking office in 2005 Wolfowitz introduced a management style that conflicted with the changes that had been made under his predecessor. Furthermore, he had arranged a generous salary increase for his girlfriend when she was transferred, while at the same time criticizing developing states for their failure to fight corruption. Wolfowitz's protracted refusal to resign when the situation came to light in 2007 aggravated internal relations and did damage to the IBRD's reputation, although this did not seem to bother the US. Wolfowitz resigned only when his position became untenable.

Stiglitz's criticism (2002) of the IBRD, IMF and WTO

In 2002 the contrast between the IBRD and the IMF was expressed in the book *Globalization and its Discontents* by Joseph Stiglitz, who had won the Nobel Prize for Economics the year before and previously had worked at the IBRD. He was influenced by the criticism of others on the way the IMF and IBRD operated. In his book he censured the major international economic organizations, attributing 'failures of globalization to the fact that in setting the rules of the game, commercial and financial interests and mind-sets have seemingly prevailed within the international economic institutions' (Stiglitz 2002, 224). The explanation was not difficult to find. 'It is the finance ministers and central bank governors who sit around the table at the IMF making decisions, the trade ministers at the WTO. Even when they stretch to push policies, that are in their countries' broader national interests (or occasionally, stretching further, to push policies that are in a broader global interest), they see the world through particular, inevitably more parochial, perspectives' (Stiglitz 2002, 225). In his view a change of mentality was needed, but he also realized the difficulty of changing people who were so deeply attached to the vested interests of the institutions: 'there has been more of a concern with finding a leader whose views are congruent with the dominant "shareholders" than with finding one that has expertise in the problems of the developing countries, the mainstay of the Fund's business today'. In the WTO the situation was even more complicated than in the IMF. 'As at the IMF, it is the voices of trade ministers that are heard. No wonder, then, that little attention is often paid to concerns about the environment. Yet, while the voting arrangements at the IMF ensure that the rich countries predominate, at the WTO each country has a single vote, and decisions are largely by consensus. But in practice, the United States, Europe, and Japan have dominated in the past' (Stiglitz 2002, 225). He had hope, however, for the WTO, because the developing states began to unite in the context of the Doha Round negotiations and were threatening to withhold agreement on a new round of negotiations. With the accession of China they would have support (see §44.6). What was needed most to guide globalization along the right path was a 'change in governance'. Bringing about the necessary changes would require greater transparency and reforms within the IMF, the global financial system, the IBRD, the WTO and development assistance, and the imbalance in the trade system would need to be rectified. The chief economist at the IMF, Kenneth Rogoff, lashed out at Stiglitz but did not tackle him on the substance of his book. Invited by the IBRD to respond, Rogoff called Stiglitz a good scientist but one who had failed as an IBRD economist. He also accused Stiglitz of attacking aid workers who were busy taking care of the wounded. The newspaper headlines painted a picture of a neighbours' quarrel in Washington, which did neither organization any good.

The World Development Report

At the beginning of the twenty-first century the IBRD played a leading role in elaborating the concept of 'social capital', in the context of knowledge on development and the establishment of the IBRD's knowledge bank (McNeill 2004). The furtherance of the knowledge bank raised questions, because 'creating knowledge and sharing research to promote development serves the interests primarily of the institutions advocating the knowledge agenda and the researchers in their orbit' (Stone 2003, 43). The legitimacy and credibility of the IBRD's expertise appear to be a 'circular process between the knowledge it produces and the audiences that legitimize that knowledge' (Lera St Clair 2006, 77). Whether this process has improved knowledge about current development issues or has merely produced knowledge that helped the IBRD defend its position remains unclear. Nonetheless, it has made the IBRD's *World Development Reports* more interesting (see Figure 41.3). The crucial question, however, is how the IBRD analyses development issues in the new world economy. The problem of poverty continues in many (failing) developing states and neither the IBRD nor the IMF has been able to do much about it or show how improvements can be made. In the meantime China has become actively engaged in its own practical

Figure 41.3 The World Development Report of the IBRD

The IBRD has published its annual **World Development Report** since 1978. Each report is devoted to a particular theme and contains data and trends that the IBRD has knowledge of through implementing its policy. The themes of recent reports have been health care (1993), development infrastructure (1994), workers in an integrating world (1995), the state in a changing world (1997), knowledge for development (1999), attacking poverty (2000), building institutions for markets (2002), sustainable development in a dynamic world (2003), transforming institutions, growth, and quality of life: making services work for poor people (2004), a better investment climate for everyone (2005), equity and development (2006), development and the next generation (2007) and agriculture for development (2008). The reports improved during and after the reorganization because criticism of the IBRD had increased its awareness of development problems.

development policy, especially in Africa, where China is a direct competitor of the IBRD and tackles development problems that the IBRD and IMF have neglected (see §42.5). China's activity is linked to the energy demands of a rapidly industrializing state that, unlike the IBRD, does not impose political or other requirements.

41.4 The Battle of Seattle (1999) and the criticisms by the 'anti'- and 'alter'-globalization movements

Anti-globalizationists versus IGOs

Relations between NGOs and IGOs changed in the 1990s. NGOs tended to target their criticism mostly at national governments and used IGOs to bring pressure to bear on governments by invoking the norms and standards set by these organizations. In as far as NGOs aimed criticism at IGOs they expressed it mainly internally, while IGOs remained an ally against governments and certain forces in society. Another kind of relationship emerged in the 1990s with the rise of the social movements known as *anti-globalizationists*, *globophobes* or, in more positive terms, *alter-globalizationists*. Although these international social movements are broader in nature, many internationally-engaged NGOs are participants. The anti-globalization movement manifested itself in the streets, sometimes as mass demonstrations, during IGO meetings. The IGOs themselves were among the targets, which was especially true for the major international economic organizations such as the IMF, IBRD and WTO. Demonstrators used slogans to express their opposition to the consequences of the 'globalization' championed by these IGOs and also used violence against symbols of international power, such as offices of international banks and corporations. Simultaneously the movement was characterized by idealism and sought small-scale alternatives to the dominant form of globalization.

Dissatisfaction with the EU and NAFTA

The main causes of disaffection among anti-globalizationists emerged at the end of the 1980s. In Europe it was the continuing economic unification of Western Europe and in

North America the free trade agreements between the US and Canada and, later, Mexico (NAFTA) (see §40.1). Environmental groups, farmers' organizations, women's groups, trade unions and urban activists spoke out against the economic, social and environmental consequences for existing industries, small companies and local communities of removing trade barriers and opening up national markets. Anti-globalizationists regarded the expansion of markets via the European single market, US free trade agreements and free trade in the framework of GATT as a threat, because of the opportunities this was generating for large transnational corporations. Opposition to globalization was not a purely 'leftist' position, as there were also objections on the 'right' based on nationalist, conservative sentiments (Rupert 2000). Disaffection with the developments inspired the idea of holding demonstrations against the IMF and IBRD, as these embodied the free trade and liberalization (that is globalization) ambitions of rich states. Demonstrations were staged at the annual meeting of the IMF and IBRD in Madrid in 1994 and became an annual occurrence from 1995 onwards, wherever these organizations met. Rallies were also held at the meetings of the European Council in Amsterdam in 1997 and in Cologne in 1999, as well as at meetings of the WTO, the World Economic Forum in Davos and the G7/G8 summits. By disseminating information on the Internet activists gradually drew more and more people to these 'anti-summit' protests. Related campaigns also evolved, such as that of French sheep farmer José Bové, who attempted to stop the spread of McDonald's in France by any means possible.

The OECD Multilateral Agreement on Investments 1995–98

In the OECD's attempt in the 1990s to frame a *Multilateral Agreement on Investments* (MAI) the international business community failed to gain international acceptance of its proposals for far-reaching liberalization and strong restrictions on and barriers to the powers of national authorities. Anti-globalizationists saw the MAI as a perfect example of the underhanded methods employed by international economic organizations to impose their will. The OECD began to confer on the MAI in 1995, but the agreement negotiations attracted little attention from outside. However, when a Canadian citizens' group learned of the plans in 1997 it concluded that the rich industrialized states were attempting to secretly draft their own international investment code, with the OECD as their obvious forum of choice, since it was an organization whose members were all wealthy states. Such an investment code would enable corporations to make investments all over the world with little regard for national laws and human rights. The OECD's intention was indeed to draft a general agreement on investment opportunities, to which non-members could also sign up. This was an unusual approach for the OECD (see §26.4). Trade unions, social and environmental NGOs and anti-globalizationists were virulently opposed to the MAI. A North American campaign protested against the agreement, posing the question: 'who will we be governed by in the twenty-first century: politically responsible governments or large corporations?'. In February 1998 France's public and fierce criticism of the OECD agreement brought it to an end. The anti-globalizationists saw the defeat of the MAI as their victory.

The business community's weak lobby

In fact, representatives of trade unions and environmental NGOs were in this case more successful than representatives of business in influencing public opinion and the negotiations

within the OECD. 'Opponents have been able to use the context of inter-state negotiations to begin to redress the shifting imbalance of power between citizens and capital
either through shoring up national authority or through transferring it to the global level
via international regulation which reflects more than the interests of multinational capital'
(Smythe 2000, 88). The citizens' groups used the Internet to their advantage in the campaigns against the MAI (Deibert 2000). With regard to influencing multilateral negotiations
the business community had proved inadequate and in response to the developments
transnational corporations began developing 'more sophisticated transnational political
capacities' and improving their ability 'to co-ordinate their activities at the national and
international level' (Levy and Egan 2000, 150). But when the WTO, under pressure
from European businesses, tried to reintroduce the investment code under the so-called
Singapore subjects in Cancun in 2003 (see §39.3), the anti-globalizationists protested
vehemently and immediately renewed their strong opposition. This time it was the
developing states that formed the opposition within the WTO and they succeeded in
having the item removed from the agenda.

The Battle of Seattle (1999)

The anti-globalization demonstrations had their biggest media impact during the WTO
meeting in Seattle, Washington, in December 1999 (which came to be known as the
Battle of Seattle), the meeting of the World Economic Forum in Switzerland in 2000,
the IMF and IBRD meetings in Washington DC in April and in Prague in September
2000, the meeting of the European Council in Gothenburg in June 2001 and the G8
meeting in Genoa in July 2001, where the police shot and killed a demonstrator. The
WTO meeting in Seattle was already ill-fated, since the differences of opinion on free
trade between industrialized and developing states appeared to be unbridgeable (see
§39.3). But neither the WTO nor the city council had anticipated the massive turnout or
the vehemence of the anti-globalization demonstrations. Between 50,000 and 100,000
people came from all over the world, among them human rights activists, labour activists,
representatives of environmental and women's groups and right-wing anti-globalizationists.
They braved the rain and demonstrated en masse against the WTO. Their presence disrupted traffic and prevented the WTO participants from reaching the meeting on time.
Although most of the anti-globalizationists demonstrated peacefully, there were groups
that used violence and threw stones. This provoked a tough police response and a state
of emergency was declared. The violence was shown on television and established the
image of stone-throwing anti-globalizationists.

The World Economic Forum of 2000

The *World Economic Forum* began in 1970 as a meeting place for members of the European business community and politicians and was aimed at showing the Americans that
Europeans too reflected on economic and political issues. Every year directors of major
corporations, politicians and other personalities gathered in Davos to discuss themes
related to the development of the world economy. In the 1990s globalization became a
prominent issue and the World Economic Forum, which presented itself as being
'committed to improving the state of the world', managed to attract considerable media
coverage (Pigman 2002, 302). The Forum was a draw for major personalities. At the
30th meeting in 2000 the speakers included US President Bill Clinton and Microsoft's

chief executive Bill Gates. The discussions examined the social impact of the world economy in greater depth than the WTO meeting in Seattle had done. While Clinton was calling for a dialogue on free trade, demonstrations against the Forum were taking place outside. As in Seattle, the police, who were unaccustomed to these kinds of demonstrations, took a heavy-handed approach. In 2001 the US government under George W. Bush, which had recently taken office, did not attend, but security was tighter than ever. In 2002 the Forum was not even held in Davos, but was in New York, where UN secretary-general Kofi Annan counselled his audience that business and industry bore a share of the responsibility for poverty and other social problems in the world and referred to the UN Global Compact (see §41.6). In 2003 the World Economic Forum returned to Davos.

The World Social Forum (2001)

Demonstrators travelling to Davos in 2001 found the road blocked, so they went to Zurich instead, where disturbances erupted. However, the majority of demonstrators were not even in Switzerland, but were in Porto Alegre, Brazil, where they had come together under the motto 'Another world is possible'. Alter-globalizationists had initiated an annual *World Social Forum* (WSF), for which they received subsidies from a number of governments. This Forum was intended as an alternative to the World Economic Forum, with the objective of a world economy that was more mindful of human rights and social consequences. Although there was a satellite link-up between Porto Alegre and Davos there was little consultation between the two forums, as the differences between the two worlds were too great. In the many workshops of the World Social Forum in Porto Alegre representatives of NGOs, social movements and other organizations met, discussed their opposition to neoliberalism, shared their experiences and visions and worked together to shape a 'new' politics. The World Social Forum met again in Porto Alegre in 2002 and 2003. In 2004 it took place in Mumbai, India, and in 2005 in several cities at the same time: Athens, Bamako (Mali), Caracas (Venezuela) and Karachi (Pakistan). The number of participants grew from 10,000 in 2001 to 150,000 in 2005. They considered the fact that they formed a heterogeneous group culturally, socially and geographically important in joint initiatives. Participation in the World Social Forum strengthened their self-confidence and heightened their awareness of 'their fundamental values as members of the human community and as citizens who build societies, cultures, polities, and economies. The WSF meets the challenge of repoliticizing life to make another world possible in the face of the homogenization of a globalization carried out by, and at the service of, big corporations – a globalization that concentrates wealth, is socially exclusionary, and destroys the environment' (Grzybowski 2006, 7).

Characteristics of anti-/alter-globalizationists

More and more people turned against the trends towards free trade and market expansion, coalescing into a mass movement in little more than a decade. The movement was able to draw many tens of thousands of people to places all over the world on a regular basis to demonstrate against IGOs, governments and corporations. Around the world, in the North as well as the South, this socio-political movement had roots in groups whose activities and interests often overlapped with those of a range of NGOs. Because many NGOs also participated in the demonstrations, a situation emerged in which NGOs were

685

demonstrating against IGOs which they already were trying to influence in different, more traditional ways (lobbying and using their consultative status) and with which they were associated by virtue of their involvement in policy formulation and implementation. Unlike the UN and many of its specialized agencies, though, large economic IGOs such as the IMF, IBRD and WTO did not grant consultative status to NGOs. They considered them outsiders, although their criticisms and that of anti-globalizationists had led these IGOs to recognize a need for contact with NGOs. Various 'dialogues' had been initiated and these continued after the Battle of Seattle. In 2001 the WTO proposed that IGOs, governments and NGOs draft a code of conduct for campaigners that would address such matters as the rejection of violence and transparency with respect to the membership, funding and decision making of NGOs. In exchange the NGOs would be given the opportunity to present their views within the organizations. NGOs that entered into dialogue with the economic IGOs can be considered 'instrumental' groups, that is groups whose objectives and the means to achieve them are separate (see Figure 41.4). These NGOs consider themselves to be *alter*-globalizationists rather than *anti*-globalizationists. A smaller section of the demonstrators focused more on protest as such and limited themselves to expressing their opposition to certain developments. A small core of these protestors was willing to use violence and presented itself as a 'counter-cultural' movement. Hence, the entire body of demonstrators did not form a united front, as one group could not keep another from using violence. They did not have their own 'order troops' like those deployed by 'old' and 'new' social movements, such as the workers' movement and the Black Panthers, which knew that demonstrations also attracted people who would exploit them for their own purposes. This meant that small groups that were intent on doing so could use violence during the anti-globalization demonstrations. However, the police responded with force. The result was escalation, a typical feature of countercultural movements, as during the next conference more police officers were deployed and the proponents of violence had come better prepared. The level of emphasis on this combative element was illustrated by the titles and covers of books such as *The Battle of Seattle: The New Challenge to Capitalist Globalization* (Yuen et al. 2001) and *On Fire: The Battle of Genoa and the Anti-Capitalist Movement* (NN 2001), as well as the name of the group ATTAC: *Association for the Taxation of Financial Transactions in the Interest of the Citizen* (see below). The anti-globalizationists were, at first, an oppositional movement (*against* free trade, as defined by rich states in the 1990s, *against* the major international economic organizations) that had the features of both instrumental and countercultural groups. The 'anti' character conveyed in the media was gradually replaced by an attitude that came across as more positive and focused on alternatives. This was expressed in the term alter-globalizationists. This stance was substantively defended by the movement's own analyses of global capitalism in books such as those authored by Michael Hardt and Antonio Negri, *Empire* (2000), Naomi Klein, *No Logo, No Space, No Choice, No Jobs* (2000) and Noreena Herz, *The Silent Takeover, Global Capitalism and the Death of Democracy* (2001).

The lilliput strategy: fix it or nix it

Anti- and alter-globalizationists considered the development of globalized capitalism as a 'race to the bottom', in which 'workers, communities, and whole countries are forced to compete by lowering wages, working conditions, environmental protections, and social spending'. This downward pressure caused resistance all over the world and activists

Figure 41.4 Instrumental and identity-oriented social movements

The theory of **collective social action** argues that collective action is engendered by social tensions, such as foreign aggression, relative deprivation or structural inequalities in a society, in the presence of resources and political opportunities. Citizens who are frustrated and dissatisfied with their situation in life have three options, according to Albert Hirschman. They can withdraw (the *exit* option), they can adapt to the existing situation (the *loyalty* option) or they can speak out (the *voice* option) (Hirschman 1970). The last alternative includes taking collective action to break down the barriers keeping them from fulfilling their ambitions and to change the system by ending their exclusion from it. *'Old' social movements*, such as the workers' and women's movements of the nineteenth and early twentieth centuries, are examples of the relative deprivation approach, in which movements arise from a situation of social disorganization and structural tensions. By forming organizations these groups, which were originally excluded from society's social and political institutions, were able to play a role and emancipate themselves. The *'new' social movements*, which emerged in the last four decades of the twentieth century, are thought to have replaced the old social movements. The latter were considered to have lost their relevance because they had been absorbed by the established political system, as universal suffrage, collective labour bargaining and the welfare state have served to dispel tensions and generate social balance. In their place came 'new' movements, such as environmental groups, women's groups, black power and also peace movements, representing 'post-material' values and 'alternative' solutions, because they were protests against the excessive growth and inherent rationalities of the modern state and its social and other inequalities. The goal of the new social movements was to transform the system and its established institutions in such a way that the policy-making process and its results would be radically different.

A distinction can be drawn between *instrumental* and *identity-oriented* movements. **Instrumental social movements** maintain a strict division between goals and the means to achieve them. Collective action is judged by how much it contributes to the attainment of a goal that lies outside, and not within, the action. Examples include the solidarity movement encompassing the Third World and environmental and peace movements. Means and goals tend to converge in **identity-oriented social movements**. Campaigning for a goal is at the same time part of the attainment of that goal, which is brought closer to fulfilment through the very act of campaigning. Within identity-oriented movements a further distinction can be made between *subcultural* and *countercultural* movements. *Subcultural* movements create their own, more or less closed, world with its own style, preferences and practices (for instance the hippies' world). Relatively speaking, they tend to stay out of the public eye. By contrast *countercultural* movements have a more or less revolutionary identity and aim to achieve their goals through continuous and public confrontation with their opponents. Examples include the squatters' movement and the violent anti-globalizationists. External goals are important to these groups, but are often so abstract and radical that their attainment is difficult, if not impossible, to measure in terms of success. When authorities take steps in the direction advocated by a movement, these groups often dismiss the action as insignificant or as a strategic manoeuvre. Counter-cultural movements are unimpressed by repressive measures and even sometimes deliberately provoke them (Kriesi *et al.* 1995).

sought to consolidate that resistance in order to unleash a counterforce of 'globalization from below', 'a common interest in resisting the race to the bottom, which is reflected in developing alliances among workers, farmers, environmentalists, consumers, poor people, and people of conscience that cross national borders and the global division of North and South' (Brecher and Costello 1998, xvii). The movement's approach was named the 'lilliput strategy'. These 'lilliputians' turned against the powerful adherents of globaliza-tion who, from above, dominate most governments and transnational corporations and who control most of the world's wealth (Brecher *et al.* 2000, 19). The apparent impos-sibility of challenging that power was countered with the argument that other social movements had also tackled situations that had at first seemed irreversible, such as slavery, apartheid and brutal dictatorships. It is therefore not surprising that the experiences of older and different social movements became relevant again (Panitch and Leys 2002). The movement gradually accumulated power, as other movements had in the past. 'In response to globalization from above, movements are emerging all over the world in social locations that are marginal to the dominant power centres. These are linking up by means of networks that cut across national borders. They are beginning to develop a sense of solidarity, a common belief system, and a common program. They are utilizing these networks to impose new norms on corporations, governments, and international institutions.' The abandonment of the OECD's Multilateral Agreement on Investments and the disruption of WTO decision making in Seattle were considered victories. The strategy employed against IGOs was 'fix it or nix it'. 'Unless you accede to operating within these norms [as defined by the alter-globalizationists], you will face threats (from us and from others) that will block your objectives and undermine your power' (Brecher *et al.* 2000, 26).

The alter-globalizationists' grievances

There are many books expounding on the grievances of the movement against globali-zation and international governance (Bircham and Charlton 2001). In his *No-Nonsense Guide to Globalization* (2001) Wayne Ellwood listed five main objections related to IGOs. First, the major economic IGOs, including the IMF, IBRD, WTO, EU and NAFTA as well as the G7, were to be considered the cornerstones of the discreditable *status quo* in the world. Others wrote about 'The WTO's slow-motion coup d'état over democratic society' (Wallach and Sforza 1999, 13) and the 'silent takeover' (Herz). Second, the policies of these IGOs perpetuated the Third World's debt burden. Third, the policy of liberalization and deregulation that gave large transnational corporations extraordinary latitude had produced the 'corporate century'. As a result, states had no influence over 'corporate power'. The fourth objection was that international financial policy had gen-erated a 'global casino', where international 'flash capital' was given free rein. Casino capitalism and the practice of speculation (short-term investment) undermined long-term investments and the connection between funding and production. Finally, it seemed as though poverty and the environment no longer mattered, as in international policies these issues were subordinated to market thinking (Ellwood 2001, chapters 2–6).

Alternatives put forward by alter-globalizationists

In essence, the main grievance of alter-globalizationists was that governments and the main economic IGOs were abusing their control over global economic forces. The solution was therefore to be found in a course adjustment: 'redesigning the global economy'. IGOs as such were not at issue. The five solutions included the following elements. First, IGOs such as the IMF and IBRD required a complete overhaul because they lacked the support of civil society and exhibited a 'democratic deficit'. The organizations would need to be reformed in a way that allowed citizen participation. Second, a global central bank, a new IGO, was needed to counteract the vulnerability and inefficiency of the global financial markets. Third, the movement advocated a so-called 'Tobin tax' to discourage international financial speculation. This tax was named after economist and Nobel Prize winner James Tobin, who had once postulated that a small tax on foreign exchange transactions would curb speculation. However, as a proponent of globalization he did not advocate such a tax, but the aforementioned ATTAC group had its roots in this notion: an aggressive name but a practical solution. The fourth solution involved setting up a new global organization for the environment under the auspices of the UN. Finally, an alternative investment code would need to be established, based on international principles such as civil rights, state responsibility, obligations for corporations, fair treatment of foreign companies, social obligations and quality standards: 'control capital for the public good' (Ellwood 2001, 108–36). In short, the course that certain IGOs were on would need to be adjusted and a path would need to be set out for policy areas, such the environment and global banking, for which no (strong) IGOs existed.

41.5 Consumer actions against transnational corporations

Social responsibility and the private sector

Corporate social responsibility was frequently a topic of debate in the wake of disasters. For example, a major industrial accident occurred in Seveso, Italy, in 1976 and the world was shocked by two serious industrial catastrophes in 1984, when a gas explosion rocked Mexico City and two weeks later a toxic cloud of gas escaped from the premises of US chemical corporation Union Carbide in Bhopal, India. Union Carbide had relaxed its safety requirements, because it needed to cut costs so as to remain competitive. In other incidents, problems with the tankers *Torrey Canyon* in 1967 and *Exxon Valdez* in 1989 caused environmental pollution. International and national laws were introduced or tightened as a result of disasters like these (see §32.5).

Nestlé and the WHO/UNICEF code for baby food (1981)

In protest against apartheid NGOs as well as governments and IGOs asked corporations explicitly not to invest in South Africa (see §28.1). Although transnational corporations did not look favourably on international codes of conduct and the OECD code of conduct for transnational companies had little effect (see §31.3), NGOs occasionally succeeded in persuading a large corporation to sign up to such a code. In January 1984, after a seven-year boycott, the *International Nestlé Boycott Committee* reached an agreement with Nestlé, which announced that it would comply with the WHO/UNICEF code for baby food (Sikkink 1986). NGOs had been instrumental in the code's development. Action groups arising from the women's movement had objections to the large number of expensive breastmilk substitutes that major food producers brought onto the market, claiming they were better for babies. These groups persuaded the World Health Organization and UNICEF to convene a joint conference on food for babies and young children. Following the conference the pressure groups in 1979 set up the *International Baby Food Action Network* (IBFAN), which called for a code of conduct. This resulted in the introduction of the *International Code of Marketing of Breastmilk Substitutes* in 1981, which was intended to protect parents and children from the promotion of breastmilk substitutes. The IBFAN was rather loosely organized, but managed to effectively oversee compliance with the International Code on several continents. Its co-supervision of compliance resulted in several resolutions which elaborated the International Code.

The WHO Tobacco Control Convention (1999)

The issue of tobacco use and its harmful effects became a permanent item on the WHO agenda from 1975. Campaigns were waged, but encountered resistance from the tobacco industry. In 1995, however, opinions about tobacco use were transformed as people realized the need to reduce the extent of tobacco-related illness and mortality. It was not until 1999 that director-general Gro Brundtland set up a structure for drafting a convention. Five years later, in 2003, the World Health Assembly adopted the *Framework Convention on Tobacco Control*, which imposed restrictions on advertising, sponsorship and the promotion of tobacco products, required warnings to be placed on packaging, contained measures to protect people from exposure to smoke and included procedures to combat the illicit trade in tobacco products. The Framework Convention entered into force in February 2005. In 2008 it had 168 signatories and 157 parties.

Transnational corporations publicly criticized (1990s)

IGOs were not the only targets of criticism because of the disaffection with globalization in the 1990s. Transnational corporations also came under fire. As in the 1970s, they were seen as international actors whose power was so great that they could barely be controlled (see Figure 41.5). They were also the embodiment of the liberalization and privatization ambitions of the 1980s. The Multilateral Agreement on Investments that appeared on the OECD agenda in 1995 was evidence for the anti-globalizationists that these corporations could do what they wanted virtually without restrictions (see §41.4). In the 1990s NGOs were able to influence public opinion and consumer behaviour, so large transnational corporations had to take their arguments into consideration. After protests and boycott campaigns Shell, which had intended to dispose of the Brent Spar oil storage buoy at sea, and Heineken, which had plans to construct a brewery in Myanmar (Burma) where the regime was responsible for severe human rights violations, were forced to reconsider their decisions. Shell initially responded by calling for a code of conduct for internationally-operating action groups and NGOs. However, the corporation, which had decided on deep-sea disposal only after thorough study, understood from the vehement reaction to its plan that transnational corporations needed to demonstrate greater concern for public opinion and circumstances in society than they were used to doing. In the end Shell developed an internal code of conduct and promised to audit its compliance with this code and with environmental requirements on an annual basis. In 1997, in response to criticism that it was too unresponsive, Shell produced a more rigorous version of the code, with provisions for protecting human rights and the environment. Other transnational corporations bowed to pressure and followed Shell's example. Heineken, PepsiCo and Budweiser withdrew from Myanmar. In April 1997 a federal judge in Los Angeles ruled that a company which was building a pipeline in Myanmar could be held responsible for human rights violations perpetrated by the military regime there against its own citizens. Shortly after that the US president banned further investment in Myanmar and campaigns aimed at influencing public opinion forced other corporations to abandon greater investment or withdraw from the country. Following actions by the Clean Clothes Campaign, the C&A clothing company implemented a code of conduct in 1997 requiring suppliers in Third World states to provide decent working conditions and also stopped importing textiles from Myanmar. In the same period US clothing and shoe manufacturers reached agreement on improving working conditions in the factories where their products were made. They received support from President Clinton, who sought to enhance working conditions in textile plants through codes of conduct of this nature. Shoe manufacturer Nike received a huge blow to its reputation when it became public how little workers in states such as Indonesia were being paid for their work.

Corporations' preference for self-regulation

Generally speaking, the private sector prefers self-regulation to public regulation. Self-regulation entails cooperating to form private international regimes in sectors such as pricing, supply, market share and advertising. Private international insurance regimes, for example, set out principles, standards, rules and decision-making procedures for standard terms of contract and political risks (Haufler 1993, 102–3). Globalization and a lack of global governance seem to have encouraged the development of private arrangements in such areas as product standardization, security of transactions and information transfer and social responsibility codes (Haufler 2000). The dyestuffs industry played a largely unobserved but pioneering role in the field of private environmental regulation. 'On a

---

Figure 41.5 The ten largest transnational corporations of the late 1990s

Listed in order of balance sheet total, the **largest transnational corporations in 1997** were: *Shell, Ford, General Electric Company, Exxon, General Motors, Volkswagen, IBM, Toyota, Nestlé* and *Mitsubishi*. The US was home to 30 of the 100 largest transnational corporations, Japan had 18, the UK and France 11 each, Germany nine, Switzerland five, Canada four, Australia, the Netherlands and Sweden three each, Belgium and Italy two each and Venezuela and South Korea one each. Three of these transnational corporations were 'binational', which accounts for the total adding up to 103.

voluntary basis a number of rules, guidelines, and codes have been adopted and implemented to avoid public intervention which, it was feared, could not be based on the same degree of expertise held by the association and the scientific information provided by member firms' (Ronit 2000, 95). As a result of budget restrictions, a lack of expertise on complex technological developments, ideological obligations, the difficulty of negotiating international agreements and sheer negligence, it was common practice for public authorities to legitimize such private arrangements in the 1990s. Despite its private nature, the organization of global governance in this respect often involved negotiations between corporations, governments and NGOs, which gave it a 'shared and multifaceted character' with 'a variety of actors playing an increasingly important role in addition to states' (Higgott *et al.* 2000, 9). Furthermore, there were adjustments in the relations between the market and government. While a policy of 'retreating government' had taken hold in the 1980s and 1990s, the large number of accounting scandals in big corporations at the turn of the twenty-first century clearly showed that the business community was not necessarily regulating itself. A new call for public regulation and control followed.

Rotary, Soroptimists and Round Tables

Interest organizations associated with the international business community such as the International Chamber of Commerce (see §12.2) also have a preference for self-regulation. The Round Tables of business and professional people, international Rotary Clubs and Soroptimist associations are evidence of the importance businesses attach to good conduct in relations between them. These organizations devote themselves to promulgating rules of good conduct for inter-business relations. Entrepreneurs monitor political developments closely, with top industrialists and international political figures coming together annually at Bilderberg Conferences and the World Economic Forum to discuss policy-related issues. The developments in the 1990s, when corporations enjoyed great freedom but were criticized for their conduct with regard to the environment and human rights, had two results. First, corporations began to take the international forums more seriously. When the MAI failed the international business community responded by developing 'more sophisticated transnational political capacities' and coordinating their activities at national and international level more effectively (Levy and Egan 2000, 150). In response to the criticism initiated by NGOs, transnational corporations and their interest organizations changed their strategies on climate change, as discussed at multilateral conferences. They moved from a defensive, reactive approach towards more proactive tactics, with greater support for international initiatives (Kolk 2001). Second, they became more receptive to the appeals from IGOs.

41.6 Principles for business: the UN Global Compact (1999)

Annan's Global Compact (1999)

In the 1990s NGOs such as the baby food network IBFAN, the World Rainforest Movement, the Pesticides Action Network and the international trade union movement put the problematic behaviour of transnational corporations on the agenda of the UN and other IGOs (Willetts 1997, 295). They forced the international business community to account for its conduct in the forums of IGOs and to assess its behaviour against established international standards on environmental protection and conservation, health, labour conditions and child labour. In 1999 at the World Economic Forum in Davos Kofi Annan called upon corporations to adhere to international standards, both in their business practice and by supporting public policy. This appeal ultimately took the shape of the *Global Compact for the New Century*, which sets out principles in the fields of human rights, labour and the environment, based on the Universal Declaration of Human Rights, the ILO Declaration on Fundamental Principles and Rights at Work and the Rio Declaration on Environment and Development (see Figure 41.6). The original nine principles became ten after the adoption of the UN Convention against Corruption in October 2003. This Convention entered into force in December 2005 and had 140 signatories and 122 parties in 2008.

Ties between business and IGOs

The closer ties between the UN and the private sector became apparent when the founder of the CNN television network held out the prospect of contributing a billion dollars to the UN in 1997. In contrast to the previous period, the UN and the international business community began cooperating to promote sustainability in the field of

---

Figure 41.6 Business principles in the UN Global Compact (1999)

Human rights

Principle 1: Businesses should support and respect the protection of internationally proclaimed human rights within their sphere of influence; and
Principle 2: make sure that they are not complicit in human rights abuses.

Labour standards

Principle 3: Businesses should uphold the freedom of association and the effective recognition of the right to collective bargaining;
Principle 4: the elimination of all forms of forced and compulsory labour;
Principle 5: the effective abolition of child labour; and
Principle 6: eliminate discrimination in respect of employment and occupation.

Environment

Principle 7: Businesses should support a precautionary approach of the environmental challenges;
Principle 8: undertake initiatives to promote greater environmental responsibility; and
Principle 9: encourage the development and diffusion of environmentally-friendly technologies.

Anti-corruption

Principle 10: Businesses should work against corruption in all its forms, including extortion and bribery.

---

development assistance. This entailed an increase in resources donated by business, while also showing how political the issue of development assistance is (Ruggie 2001; Thérien and Pouliot 2006). Within the OECD changes with regard to transnational corporations also had an impact, as in 2000 the OECD somewhat improved its relatively weak code of conduct dating from 1976 in terms of substance and procedures (see §31.3). The private sector's involvement in these improvements reflected 'growing comfort on the part of international business, both individually and collectively, to participate in initiatives emanating from governments at the multilateral level that can aid in the management of thorny social issues' (Wilkie 2004, 297).

National corporatism

Just as interest groups representing business are part of a pluralistic society, so they can also be part of a corporatist society, in which the state has incorporated social organizations. The extent to which corporatism was imbedded nationally influenced the international orientation of these interest groups (Levy and Egan 2000, 141–42). Shortly after the Second World War this was seen in interest groups in the agricultural sector in modern Western states, when public authorities and agricultural interest groups formed partnerships aimed at modernizing the agricultural sectors in the states concerned. National arrangements were created because of the strategic importance of the agricultural sector (it contributed to crucial national policy objectives) and high risk (due to the potential impact of unpredictable weather and market conditions). Special schemes were developed, such as income support for farmers and their families, preservation of small-scale businesses and advancement of modern technologies. This situation resulted in interest groups becoming embedded at national level, but left little room for international agricultural NGOs to advocate common interests at regional or global level. National interests weighed more heavily than international interests and the international NGOs could do little more than try to coordinate common positions in international forums.

The liberal market paradigm

The shift towards a liberal market paradigm in the 1980s brought pressure to bear on the original partnerships between public authorities and interest groups in the agricultural sector. However, these interest groups were so deeply embedded in their respective national states that the search for ways of dealing with privatization and globalization led to solutions that resembled, or tended towards, the original partnerships. Although the interest groups had far fewer members because farms and related companies had become larger as a result of mergers and scale efficiencies, they were able to hold their own and exercise sufficient influence in the national political systems. This meant that the international interest groups in this sector remained weak. In the new situation, as in the old, little more than limited coordination of national activities was possible. Any common policy was made on the basis of trade alliances in the form of an EU or Cairns group of agricultural exporting states within the WTO. Within the EU the European federations of agricultural interest groups also remained weak. They had been Europeanized, but had gained little influence. The positions they took in Brussels were the result of consensus on national interests rather than joint policy. The national interest organizations had many more representatives in Brussels than the European federation (Halpin 2005).

Regional international organizations from the 1980s onwards

Part XVI deals with regional organizations beyond and within Europe from the 1980s onwards. Third World states set up new regional economic groupings, or transformed existing ones, to strengthen their position in the world market *vis-à-vis* neoliberalism and the far-reaching forms of free trade promoted by the GATT/WTO. This took place on all continents and helped the states to stimulate reciprocal trade and economic growth (Chapter 42). In Western Europe the European Community evolved into the European Union, whose most important economic achievements were the formation of a single market and the introduction of a common currency. This reinforced the EU's position in the global market. The political evolution of the EU encountered much greater difficulties, but did not prevent enlargement of the EU into Eastern Europe (Chapter 43).

The Third World answer to globalization

Continued and new regionalism

42.1 Continued and new regionalism in the Third World during the 1980s and 1990s

Reaction to an external threat

In the 1980s and 1990s three factors encouraged regional economic cooperation between states outside Europe and North America: the external threat presented by globalization, the end of bipolarity and the pressure exerted by the global free trade regime. The first factor was the external threat to states in the form of the continuing internationalization and globalization of the economy, discernible in the consequences of the coercive economic policies of Reagonomics as pursued by US President Ronald Reagan through the G7, the structural adjustment policy of the IMF and IBRD and the far-reaching free trade policies introduced by the GATT/WTO. To be able to resist this external pressure more effectively, states formed 'alliances' or economic organizations of states in their region. Some of these were new, others were adaptations of existing organizations. In the 1980s 17 regional economic organizations in total were established, or revived, outside Europe and in the

1990s the number was 26 (see Figure 30.1). The general tendency in this period was to move towards a limited form of trade liberalization 'often on the basis of overlapping bilateral agreements rather than multilateral regional obligations'. In Latin America the Andean Group (see §30.2) adjusted to the new global economic relations in this way. Another approach was 'specific cooperation on individual programmes among several countries'. This was the course adopted by MERCOSUR in Latin America and the Southern African Development Community (SADC) in Africa (Axline 1994, 4).

Regional exceptions notified to the GATT/WTO

The strength of these new and transformed alliances was that they were usually based on a proactive policy developed by Third World states themselves. However, they did need the consent of the GATT/WTO in the case of trade agreements. States were allowed to conclude regional free trade agreements as exceptions to the global GATT regime, provided this ultimately contributed to the global free trade system by producing a greater volume of trade. These states could also move further in the direction of customs unions, common markets or even economic unions. GATT contracting parties (later WTO members) have been obliged to notify the GATT/WTO of any regional agreements and seek approval for them. Between 1948 and 1995 GATT received 124 notifications of regional trade agreements applying to goods. In the decade between 1995 and 2005 the WTO was informed of 130 regional agreements on trade in goods and services, slightly more than the number received by GATT throughout its existence.

The end of bipolarity

The second factor that encouraged regional cooperation in the Third World was the disappearance of bipolarity after the end of the Cold War in 1989. This reduced the control exercised over regional relations by the two former superpowers, the US and the Soviet Union, and allowed regional cooperation to flourish. Furthermore, both powers began to engage in regional cooperation on their own account. The US did this in the form of NAFTA (see §40.1) and in its active efforts to create a free trade area covering the entire Western Hemisphere, the Free Trade Area of the Americas (FTAA). Russia too became involved in regional organizations. For historical reasons, cooperation was difficult within the Commonwealth of Independent States. The most successful effort would appear to be an organization that emerged from the CIS in 2000, the Eurasian Economic Community (EURASEC), in which Russia works with Belarus, Kazakhstan, Kyrgyzstan and Tajikistan (see §42.6).

Conflict regulation and support for domestic reforms

The third factor stimulating regional cooperation was the large degree of interdependence in trade matters that had arisen in the 1990s as a result of internationalization and globalization. Working as an active intergovernmental regime, the GATT/WTO promoted international trade through regulations. The great powers were willing to submit trade disputes to the GATT and the WTO for mediation under their dispute settlement system (see §39.2). This increased the confidence of less powerful states, despite the fact that the GATT and the WTO were pursuing a far-reaching form of free trade. Unlike in previous decades, free trade agreements were instrumental in bringing about domestic political changes favourable to international trade. The formation of regional international organizations helped 'prompt and consolidate economic and political reforms in prospective members' (Mansfield and Milner 1999, 601).

Significance of regional trade

Figure 42.1 gives an indication of the significance of regional economic organizations in the period 1975–94. Intra-regional exports (within the regional organization) are shown as a percentage of the total exports of the states in question. In brackets is the organization's share in world trade (total exports of the organization as a percentage of world exports). Together these 12 organizations were responsible for around 70 per cent of world trade in 1994. The EU was by far the biggest in terms of intra-regional trade (58.3 per cent), followed by NAFTA (47.6 per cent), ASEAN (21.8 per cent) and MERCOSUR (18.1 per cent). Where the share of world trade is concerned, the EU and NAFTA dominated once again with 33.9 and 17.5 per cent, respectively. ASEAN achieved 6 per cent, the other blocs remained below this level. These figures reflect the enduring contrast between North and South. While ASEAN's share of world trade rose from 2.6 per cent in 1975 to 6 per cent in 1994, that of ECOWAS fell from 1.4 to 0.5 per cent and the Andean Group's share was halved (from 1.6 to 0.8 per cent). In other words, there are great differences between the regional organizations. This does not alter the fact that they all share an interest in intra-regional trade. Later the resulting expansion of trade *within* the regional organizations would be followed by expansion through agreements *between* them.

Figure 42.1 Intra-regional exports and world trade share 1975–94

Regional organization	1975	1985	1994
Western Hemisphere			
CUSTA 1989: *Canada US Free Trade Agreement*	30.6 (16.8)	38.0 (16.7)	36.7 (16.1)
NAFTA 1994: *North American Free Trade Agreement*	34.8 (18.3)	43.9 (18.1)	47.6 (17.5)
CACM 1960: *Central American Common Market*	23.3 (0.3)	14.7 (0.2)	14.4 (0.2)
LAFTA/LAIA 1960: *Latin American Free Trade Association;* 1980: *Latin American Integration Association*	13.6 (3.5)	8.3 (4.7)	15.7 (4.0)
ANDEAN Group 1969	3.7 (1.6)	3.4 (1.2)	8.9 (0.8)
MERCOSUR 1991: *Southern Common Market*	7.2 (1.6)	5.9 (2.0)	18.1 (1.5)
Asia and Oceania			
ASEAN 1967: *Association of Southeast Asian Nations*	15.9 (2.6)	18.4 (3.9)	21.8 (6.0)
ANZCERTA 1983: *Australia New Zealand Closer Economic Relations Trade Agreement*	6.2 (1.7)	7.0 (1.6)	9.5 (1.4)
Africa			
ECOWAS 1973: *Economic Community of West African States*	4.2 (1.4)	5.3 (1.1)	10.4 (0.5)
PTA 1987: *Preferential Trade Area for Eastern and Southern African States*	9.4 (0.5)	7.0 (0.3)	7.8 (0.3)
Europe			
EC/EU 1957: *European Communities;* 1993: *European Union*	50.0 (35.9)	54.5 (35.6)	58.3 (33.9)
EFTA 1960: *European Free Trade Association*	35.2 (6.3)	31.2 (6.3)	13.8 (5.8)

Source: (Hout 1996, 256, Table 2), but grouped according to continent. The first figure represents intra-regional exports, with share in world trade in brackets.

42.2 The creation of MERCOSUR (1991) and the Andean Community of Nations (1996)

LAIA and SELA

The four leading regional economic organizations in Latin America in this period were the Andean Community with five member states, MERCOSUR with four, and two organizations (LAIA and SELA), comprising 12 and 27 members, respectively, whose aim was generally to promote economic cooperation (see Figure 42.2). Efforts to establish free trade in Latin America were formalized in 1960 in the *Latin American Free Trade Association* (LAFTA), which was transformed in 1980 into the more widely oriented but weaker *Latin American Integration Association* (see §30.2). Membership of LAIA was confined to states on the Latin American mainland (with the exception of Cuba since 1999). The *Latin American Economic System* with its Spanish acronym SELA (*Sistema económico latinoamericano*), set up in 1975, was broader-based in that it included the Central American and Caribbean states. Its aim was to promote regional cooperation and to coordinate policy towards other states and IGOs. As an umbrella organization SELA played a role within UNCTAD and in the regional approach to the debt crisis in the 1980s. In that decade South America witnessed a move towards more obvious trade liberalization, accompanied by the formation of regional organizations. Unlike the EU, where the various organs work together to produce initiatives and implement common policies, these regional organizations give their heads of state a leading role. Latin American cooperation is first and foremost a presidential matter (see below). SELA's importance declined as a result of the establishment of new regional organizations (MERCOSUR in 1991), the revival of the Andean Group in 1996 and the setting up of organizations in the Caribbean area.

Dictatorial regimes in decline

MERCOSUR embodies the efforts of two large and two smaller Latin American states to set up a common market. However, political developments and the dictatorships in

---

Figure 42.2 Regional economic cooperation in Latin America

- 1960 LAFTA; from 1980 **LAIA** *Latin American Integration Association*: Argentina, Bolivia, Brazil, Chile, Colombia, Cuba (since 1999), Ecuador, Mexico, Paraguay, Peru, Uruguay, Venezuela (12)
- 1969 ANDEAN Group; from 1996 **CAN** *Andean Community of Nations*: Bolivia, Colombia, Ecuador, Peru, Venezuela (up to 2006) (5)
- 1975 **SELA** *Latin American Economic System*: Argentina, Bahamas, Barbados, Bolivia, Brazil, Chile, Colombia, Costa Rica, Cuba, Dominican Republic, Ecuador, El Salvador, Grenada, Guatemala, Guyana, Haiti, Honduras, Jamaica, Mexico, Nicaragua, Panama, Paraguay, Peru, Surinam, Trinidad and Tobago, Uruguay, Venezuela (27)
- 1991 **MERCOSUR** *Southern Common Market*: Argentina, Brazil, Paraguay, Uruguay; Venezuela (applied in 2006) (4)

power in the 1970s, as well as disputes over water in the border areas between Argentina and Brazil, did not favour cooperation. In 1979, during the period in which dictatorial regimes began to weaken, Argentina, Brazil and Paraguay concluded an agreement re-establishing their diplomatic ties. The initial reaction to the international debt crisis in 1982 (see §35.2) was strongly protectionist, but the return to democracy put economic cooperation back on the agenda and both LAIA and SELA played a role in this. In 1986 Argentina and Brazil agreed on a Programme for Integration and Economic Cooperation (PICE), based on sectoral agreements covering areas such as capital goods, food and the steel and automotive industries. This assisted both states in planning and consolidating their national industries. Their aim was a mutually-balanced trade in each of the sectors, which was vital to removing the fears of national entrepreneurs that cooperation would lead to losses. Argentina and Brazil were gradually beginning to realize that the Latin American states lay outside the industrialized world's area of interest and that they therefore had no choice but to expand trade between them. This led to the signing of a treaty on integration, cooperation and development in November 1988, with the goal of establishing a common market within ten years. Shortly afterwards 1995 was designated the target year and talks were conducted with Uruguay and Paraguay on the extension of existing trade agreements (Roett 1999, 8–9).

Establishment of MERCOSUR (1991)

In March 1991 the four states concluded the *Treaty of Asunción*, establishing the *Mercadó común del cono sur*, the Southern Common Market (MERCOSUR, in Portuguese MERCOSUL). The primary aim was to achieve the economic integration of the member states through a free flow of goods and services between them, setting a common external tariff, accepting a common trade policy and coordinating macro-economic and sectoral policy. In December 1994 the member states signed the *Ouro Preto Protocol*, which gave MERCOSUR legal personality under public international law, making it capable of concluding treaties with other states, groups of states and IGOs. MERCOSUR's supreme institution is the *Common Market Council*, responsible for directing the integration process and for decision making. The *Common Market Group* implements policies and has a small *Administrative Secretariat* in Montevideo, Uruguay. Other institutions include the *Trade Commission*, the *Common Parliamentary Commission* and the *Economic and Social Consultative Forum*, in which the social partners are represented. The Parliamentary Commission's role is to promote national implementation of common decisions, rather than to participate in the decision-making process. In 1996 it declared that only democratic states could join MERCOSUR.

Economic progress and expansion of trade

From the end of the 1980s the governments of the member states became convinced that, together with mutual trade, liberalization was the only way to economic progress. This meant that the integration process shifted from sectoral agreements to broader liberalization. MERCOSUR's free trade zone came into effect on 1 January 1995. It was agreed that members would move towards full free trade at different speeds. The two large states had a deadline of four years, the two smaller of five years. A customs union was also established in 1995. Mutual trade tripled between 1991 and 1995 and continued to rise after that, until the international situation resulting from the Asian financial crisis put a brake on developments. In 1996 Chile signed a free trade agreement with MERCOSUR, as did Bolivia, which applied for associate membership at the same time. In December 1995 MERCOSUR and the EU signed a framework agreement on cooperation in the trade and economic fields. In addition to reciprocal free trade and policy harmonization MERCOSUR's strategic aim was expansion of trade with the Andean Group, the EU and Mexico, the latter mainly because of trade between Brazil and Mexico.

MERCOSUR as a group vis-à-vis the US

MERCOSUR also presented itself as a group in relation to US plans to establish a Free Trade Area of the Americas by 2005. Its policy was to create the strongest possible position as a group before entering into the negotiations between the American states at the *Summits of the Americas*, where the US wanted to advance the process of establishing the FTAA. MERCOSUR managed to have a separate negotiating group set up to discuss agricultural issues. Two factors strengthened the resolve of the MERCOSUR states, especially Brazil, to 'retain as much autonomy as possible to further strengthen the common market before entering into more ample negotiations for an FTAA' (Roett 1999, 111). These were MERCOSUR's growing strength in the 1990s and the fact that the US was in favour of the FTAA. However, President Clinton failed to obtain fast-track negotiating power from Congress before the second Summit of the Americas in 1998 in Santiago, which impeded the negotiations.

Brazil's position within MERCOSUR

Around the turn of the twenty-first century MERCOSUR was hit by the international economic and monetary crisis and associated domestic problems. The economic policy pursued by Brazil, the largest member state, slowed integration in 1997, as the Brazilian government chose to resolve its own trade deficits first by imposing levies on all kinds of imports. Growth within MERCOSUR was also affected by the serious financial crisis in Argentina in 2001, which led to the fall of the government and the unpegging of the Argentinean peso from the US dollar. It became doubtful whether the creation of a regional trade strategy was receiving sufficient priority and whether economic and political imbalances would not delay and distort this process irreparably. On the other hand Brazil continued to dominate MERCOSUR as an organization. 'Brazil's economic performance and the design of its macro- and microeconomic policies (especially industrial and foreign trade policies) largely define the other partners' perceptions of the costs and benefits of integration. The emergence of tensions among the member states of MERCOSUR, as well as their capacity to absorb and manage them, depends heavily on these factors.' Brazil's negotiating position remains one of the most important explanations of MERCOSUR's profile at the time, 'halfway between a free trade area and a customs union with few mechanisms for institutionalization and limited positive discrimination for the benefit of the smaller economies of the bloc' (Da Motta Velga 1999, 25).

Presidentialism as a characteristic of MERCOSUR

Amongst MERCOSUR's successes are the promotion of intra-regional trade and a better position in the world market. This made Argentina and Brazil into more powerful players in global markets and encouraged foreign companies to invest in the MERCOSUR states again. But relations with the US deteriorated because of President George W. Bush's concentrated efforts to achieve more far-reaching liberalization within the FTAA. The events of 11 September 2001 and US foreign policy as pursued thereafter created even more distance between the US and MERCOSUR. In 2003 the member states decided to strengthen their mutual trade relations and to reinvigorate MERCOSUR, partly through institutional changes. The experiences of the EU were examined as part of this process, but the institutional changes remained very limited. The central role played by the presidents, which was a major feature of the organization at its inception, remained unaffected. Their decisions were not restricted to trade between the member states. In 1990 they drew up a declaration on a common nuclear energy policy. This contributed to the further implementation of the 1967 Treaty of Tlatelolco, banning nuclear weapons (see Figure 24.3), and strengthened mutual peaceful relations (Malamud 2003, 63). Other matters of concern to the presidents at the organization's inception had been a return to democracy, reducing hostile perceptions and pursuing an externally-oriented economic policy. Latin American 'presidentialism' played a role not only in initiating new developments, but also in settling disputes. 'Once the bulk of a given bargain has been done, presidents exert a decisive influence to get their preferred outcome – sometimes even in contradiction with the proposals drafted by the national negotiators' (Malamud 2003, 67). This is also MERCOSUR's weakness, in that any deterioration in relations between the presidents makes it more difficult to reach common agreement. Other institutional actors, such as the Commission and Parliament within the EU, are either absent or lack power.

Revival of the Andean Group (1991)

Regional organizations can offer policy makers a window of opportunity, even in situations where there is strong domestic opposition to liberalizing trade. Policymakers can overcome this opposition by emphasizing regional trade rather than liberalization. Such future-oriented changes in a regional context played a role in the domestic politics of Colombia and Venezuela. In 1991 the governments of these two states decided to revive the Andean Group set up in 1969, which had until then been fairly unsuccessful (see §30.2). 'Policymakers in these countries explain their decision as a politically easy way to dismantle protectionist barriers to an extent that their domestic legislatures would never have allowed had the policy not been pursued in a regional context' (Mansfield and Milner 1999, 605). Here too the influence of the presidents, who had been meeting at summits since 1989, was a major factor. At the 1991 summit they decided to form a free trade area in 1992 (which became 1993) and to set a common external tariff. The latter aim was delayed because of Peru's wish to have exemptions and through the political situation in that state. The common external tariff finally came into effect in February 1995.

Transformation into the Andean Community of Nations (1996)

In 1996 a Protocol reforming the Andean Group was added to the original *Cartagena Agreement* of 1969. The Group was to be renamed the *Comunidad andina de naciones* (CAN), the Andean Community of Nations. In the second half of the 1990s this Andean Community worked towards Peru's gradual inclusion in the free trade area and for the establishment of a free trade zone between the Andean Community and MERCOSUR. The latter required more negotiations and time. Election results in various states in 2005 and 2006, which brought leftist candidates to power, led to tensions between them. More than anything else, the nationalization of Bolivian gas by newly-elected president Evo Morales in 2006 created tense relations with neighbouring states dependent on those gas supplies. In April 2006 the left-wing Venezuelan President Hugo Chávez decided to withdraw from the Andean Community because he considered the policies of other member states – Colombia and Peru had concluded a free trade agreement with the US – to be overly focused on the US and in July Venezuela left the Andean Community and applied to join MERCOSUR.

Towards a Union of South American Nations (2004)

In December 2004, as the result of a Brazilian initiative, 12 Latin American states, including the member states of MERCOSUR and the Andean Community, joined together to set up a South American Community of Nations. The objective was to create a free trade area with a common currency, capable of negotiating with the US and EU, within a period of 15 years. During a summit of the heads of state in September 2005 it was decided that to avoid bureaucracy no new institutions would be created at the beginning, but that they instead would use the institutions of the existing organizations. At a South American energy summit in April 2007 the name of the endeavour was changed to the *Union of South American Nations* (USAN or UNASUR, *Unión de naciones sudamericanas*). Its Constitutive Treaty was signed on 23 May 2008 at the third summit of the heads of state in Brasília. The Union's headquarters will be located in Quito, Ecuador, with a (proposed) South American Parliament in Cochabamba, Bolivia, and the Bank of the South (*Banco del Sur*), which was established in 2007, in Caracas, Venezuela (see §44.6).

42.3 Central American and Caribbean cooperation

CACM and SICA

The two most important regional economic organizations in Central America during this period were the *Central American Common Market* (CACM), which had five member states, and the *Central American Integration System* (SICA), a regional organization with six members, concerned generally with promoting integration (see Figure 42.3). Developments in the 1980s were not favourable for the CACM because of armed conflict within and between certain states (see §34.1). In 1990 the presidents of the five states drew up a declaration supporting peace in El Salvador, Guatemala and Nicaragua. They also wanted to strengthen the Common Market in the interests of peace. In December 1991 the SICA (*Sistema de la integración centroamericana*), a new framework for regional integration, was established within the Organization of Central American States. The SICA had six member states, including Panama, and three observers (Belize, the Dominican Republic and Taiwan). After the US recognition of the People's Republic of China, Taiwan had found support in Latin America to compensate for its loss of UN status. It being an observer expanded the scope of the SICA and increased its impact. The organization was given its own secretariat. The CACM continued as part of the SICA and in 1998 the two secretariats merged. The Central American Parliament established within the CACM in 1989 continued within the SICA, which also has a Court of Justice. In 1998 Panama signed a declaration of intent on free trade with the Andean Community,

Figure 42.3 Central American and Caribbean economic cooperation

CENTRAL AMERICA

- 1960 **CACM Central American Common Market**: Costa Rica, El Salvador, Guatemala, Honduras, Nicaragua (5)
- 1991 **SICA Central American Integration System**: Costa Rica, El Salvador, Guatemala, Honduras, Nicaragua, Panama (6)

THE CARIBBEAN

- 1973 **CARICOM Caribbean Community and Common Market**: Antigua and Barbuda, Bahamas, Barbados, Belize, Dominica, Grenada, Guyana, Haiti (from 1998 conditionally, in 2002 full membership, but suspended from 2004–6), Jamaica, Montserrat, Saint Christopher [later: Kitts] and Nevis, Saint Lucia, Saint Vincent and the Grenadines, Surinam, Trinidad and Tobago; associate members: Anguilla, Bermuda, British Virgin Islands, Cayman Islands, Turks and Caicos Islands (15+5)
- 1981 **OECS Organization of Eastern Caribbean States**: Antigua and Barbuda, Dominica, Grenada, Montserrat, Saint Kitts and Nevis, Saint Lucia, Saint Vincent and the Grenadines; associate members: Anguilla, British Virgin Islands (7+2)
- 1994 **ACS Association of Caribbean States**: Antigua and Barbuda, Bahamas, Barbados, Belize, Colombia, Costa Rica, Cuba, Dominica, Dominican Republic, El Salvador, Grenada, Guatemala, Guyana, Haiti, Honduras, Jamaica, Mexico, Nicaragua, Panama, Saint Kitts and Nevis, Saint Lucia, Saint Vincent and the Grenadines, Surinam, Trinidad and Togo, Venezuela (25)

followed by the so-called Northern Triangle (El Salvador, Guatemala and Honduras) a year later. In 2004 the SICA and the Andean Community signed an agreement to strengthen their mutual economic relations.

From CARIFTA to CARICOM (1973)

During this period the three most important regional economic organizations in the Caribbean were the CARICOM common market with 15 member states, the smaller and partially overlapping OECS with seven member states and the more general ACS with 25 members (see Figure 42.3). In 1968 a free trade agreement for the Caribbean area, *CARIFTA*, was concluded. Former British colonies within CARIFTA that had formed a customs union among themselves were also allied in the *East Caribbean Common Market*. In 1973 the two organizations were replaced by CARICOM, the *Caribbean Community and Common Market*. The main problem facing this successful regional organization is that it is composed of small island states. The international economic crisis at the beginning of the 1980s led to protectionism and a decline in intra-regional trade. This disruption of their reciprocal trade induced the states to return to completely free trade in 1987. A commission set up by the heads of government in 1989 advised them not to form a confederation, but to allow CARICOM to continue as an economic community of sovereign states. It recommended further integration within CARICOM and the formation of a broader *Association of Caribbean States* (ACS). The latter was established in 1994, its objectives being the promotion of economic development, strengthening security and the harmonization of foreign policy. The most important ACS institutions are the Ministerial Council and the Secretariat.

The Caribbean Community and the CSME (2006)

In 2005 CARICOM launched a project aimed at establishing the *CARICOM Single Market and Economy* (CSME). In 2001 the member states revised the *Treaty of Chaguaramas*, subsuming CARICOM into the newly established *Caribbean Community* and giving the CSME a legal basis. A ruling by the Judicial Committee of the Privy Council, the highest court of appeal for several Commonwealth states set up by the British Crown in 1833, delayed the establishment of the CSME. It finally came into effect for six member states on 1 January 2006 and on 3 July for six more. The revision of the Treaty led to reform of the institutions, including the setting up of the *Caribbean Court of Justice*. Installed in 2005, the Court of Justice replaced the Privy Council. The CARICOM Secretariat is located in Georgetown, Guyana. Relations between the more and the less developed states play a major role in the functioning of CARICOM, which is to a considerable degree dependent on the larger states (Payne 1994, 100). The *Organization of Eastern Caribbean States*, which was set up in 1981, emerged from a common colonial past. It promoted the interests of these small islands and established its own institutions, such as the *Eastern Caribbean Supreme Court* (created in 1967 by the West Indies Associated States, a free association of some Caribbean islands with the UK) and a common monetary authority (the *Eastern Caribbean Central Bank*, set up in 1983) and it created the Eastern Caribbean dollar as a common currency. Where necessary, the OECS promotes the interests of its member states within CARICOM.

42.4 The significance of SAARC, ASEAN and APEC for Asian development

Developments in South Asia

The three most important regional economic organizations in South and Southeast Asia during this period were the SAARC and ASEAN, with seven and ten member states, respectively, and APEC, active in the whole of the Pacific Rim, which in 2008 has 21 member states on both sides of the ocean (see Figure 42.4). The characteristic feature of Asian development is the unprecedented economic growth achieved without outside help by certain Asian economies in the 1990s and more specifically at the turn of the twenty-first century. This was based on the same world market oriented strategy pursued by the Asian Tigers earlier in the twentieth century (see §29.3). A difference with the earlier period was the increased influence of the WTO as a coordinating free trade regime. The same applies to the regional superpower China, which due to its size nevertheless plays an individual role and is managing to combine a communist political system with a successful capitalist industrialization process. The regional organizations promoted reciprocal trade and economic growth in South and Southeast Asia, as well as having a security dimension *vis-à-vis* greater powers such as China, India and Pakistan.

Figure 42.4 Regional economic cooperation in South and East Asia

- 1967 **ASEAN** *Association of Southeast Asian Nations*: Brunei, Cambodia, Indonesia, Laos, Malaysia, Myanmar, the Philippines, Singapore, Thailand, Vietnam (10)
- 1985 **SAARC** *South Asian Association for Regional Cooperation*: Bangladesh, Bhutan, India, the Maldives, Nepal, Pakistan, Sri Lanka (7)
- 1989 **APEC** *Asia Pacific Economic Cooperation*: Australia, Brunei, Canada, Chile, China, Hong Kong (China), Indonesia, Japan, Malaysia, Mexico, New Zealand, Papua New Guinea, Peru, the Philippines, Russia, Singapore, South Korea, Thailand, Taiwan, the US, Vietnam (21)

SAARC (1985)

Established in South Asia in 1985, the *South Asian Association for Regional Cooperation* (SAARC) was an initiative of the foreign ministers of its future member states. Although they had for some time been convinced that more common action was necessary to promote economic and social progress, they were aware of the tensions between states in the region. In 1983 they drew up an integrated programme to bring improvements in the fields of agriculture, rural development, health, population issues and communications. The *Dhaka Declaration*, issued at the first SAARC Summit in 1985, spoke of a 'logical answer' to the problems of poverty and underdevelopment. The organization holds an annual *Summit* attended by heads of government and has a *Council of Ministers*, a *Permanent Committee* liaising between the foreign ministries and a *Secretariat* set up in 1987. It is dependent on the willingness of governments to work with each other, a particular difficulty being relations between India and Pakistan. The SAARC institutions are small and sometimes dependent on foreign aid. In the 1990s economic cooperation grew in significance. In 1995 the *SAARC Preferential Trading Arrangement* (SAPTA) came into effect, which represents the least far-reaching form of common trade promotion. SAPTA led to four negotiating rounds involving 5,000 products. In 1996 an Inter-Governmental Expert Group was set up to explore the scope for a free trade area. A Committee of Experts drew up an agreement in 1998 and in 2004 the 12th SAARC Summit adopted the *Agreement on the South Asian Free Trade Area* (SAFTA), which included a programme for trade liberalization up to 2016. The aim is that a planned and gradual process will ultimately lead to the creation of a *South Asian Economic Union* (SAEU).

The rapid economic development of ASEAN

ASEAN was created in 1967 against a background of strained relations in Southeast Asia and developed an approach that gradually promoted a climate of mutual confidence. Economic cooperation slowly but surely evolved (see §30.3). In the early 1990s ASEAN had earned international political recognition for the role it had played in resolving the conflict in Cambodia and the withdrawal of Vietnamese troops from that state. This recognition was closely related to a revival of the organization, which had expanded to ten member states by the end of the decade. Vietnam acceded in 1995, Laos and

Myanmar (formerly Burma) in 1997 and Cambodia in 1999. The member states had decided in 1987 to promote intra-regional trade, since this had not come up to expectation. In 1992 an agreement was concluded aiming to create an *ASEAN Free Trade Area* (AFTA) by 2008. To speed up progress a *Common Effective Preferential Tariff* (CEPT) was established in 1993 to reduce import levies. CEPT soon needed to be amended, because it was not sufficiently effective, while in 1994 the decision was made to bring the introduction of AFTA forward to within seven to ten years. In 1998 the Hanoi Plan of Action was approved, which had the aim of increasing macro-economic and financial cooperation and promoting economic integration. In early 2003 ASEAN adopted a Protocol again adjusting the plans for the CEPT and AFTA. The original six members (ASEAN-6) in this way managed to achieve substantial tariff reductions. The four members that joined later were given more gradual schedules. During the economic boom that marked these years ASEAN benefited in 2004 from the fact that Malaysia was able to introduce reductions earlier than planned and by 2007 there was a well-advanced free trade area within ASEAN, certainly within the ASEAN-6.

ASEAN's institutional structure

The relations between the member states were expanded in the 1990s to include ministries other than those of foreign affairs and trade and senior officials, with regular meetings taking place. In practice a recognizable organizational structure was established, despite ASEAN's efforts to avoid overbearing institutions. In addition to the *Summit Meetings* attended by the heads of government there were regular *Ministerial Meetings* of foreign, economic and other ministers. They met separately or in certain combinations prior to the Summit Meetings. After the Summit Meetings *Post-Ministerial Conferences* (PMCs) were held to consult with other states, the *Dialogue Partners* (Australia, Canada, the EU, Japan, New Zealand, South Korea and the US) and the *Consultative Partners* (China, New Guinea and Russia). The *Standing Committee* met every two months. It consisted of the ambassadors of states accredited to the host state and was chaired by the foreign minister of that state. The *ASEAN Secretariat* in Jakarta expanded proportionately to form a coordinating body with four bureaus (economic cooperation, functional cooperation, ASEAN cooperation and dialogue relations, and AFTA). In 2003 ASEAN decided that it would henceforth consist of three 'pillars': the *ASEAN Economic Community* (AEC), the *ASEAN Socio-Cultural Community* (ASCC), and the *ASEAN Security Community* (ASC). The goal of the first pillar is to expand the free trade area into a broad internal market. The second aims to expand the partnership into a community of caring societies based on a common regional identity and the objective of the third pillar is for the member states to 'live at peace with one another and with the world at large in a just, democratic and harmonious environment'.

Security: the ASEAN Regional Forum (1994)

ASEAN decided in July 1993 to set up an *ASEAN Regional Forum* (ARF) to discuss security issues and the Forum met for the first time a year later. As early as 1971 the ASEAN states had declared that they wanted to establish a zone of peace, freedom and neutrality (see §30.3). In 1992 they decided that more cooperation was needed in the interest of security in the region, partly influenced by the new global relations that had come into being after the end of the Cold War. ASEAN was not the only party that wanted to discuss security in the region. In 1990 Canada set up an informal *North Pacific Cooperative Security Dialogue* in which experts from nine states participated. The Japanese foreign minister proposed in 1991 that official regional security dialogues should be held under the auspices of the ASEAN Post-Ministerial Conferences. ASEAN politicians had initially dismissed this proposal, because they did not feel the need to put security on the agenda. However, a group of think tanks promoted by ASEAN (ASEAN ISIS) convinced the heads of government at their summit in 1992 that it would be quite a good move. Pressure to start such dialogues also came from Australia and the US (Johnston 1999, 292). An advantage of using the Post-Ministerial Conferences was that the Dialogue Partners and the Consultative Partners could be involved without too much difficulty. These developments led to the 1993 decision to launch the ASEAN Regional Forum (see Figure 42.5 for its process of institutionalization). In 2008 there were 26 participants, including Asian non-member states and non-Asian states such as Australia, Canada, Russia and the US, as well as the EU. On the agenda were confidence building, developing preventive diplomacy and elaborating approaches to conflict. After a decade of negotiations and drafting efforts in December 1995 the ASEAN member states adopted the Treaty of Bangkok, or the *Southeast Asia Nuclear-Weapon-Free-Zone Treaty* (see Figure 36.1).

Figure 42.5 Institutionalization of the ASEAN Regional Forum set up in 1994

The **ASEAN Regional Forum (ARF)** had virtually no formal organizational structure. Its members did not even call themselves members. 'The correct term is "participants". "Membership" sounds too permanent. The ARF's first meeting lasted three hours. It now meets once a year for about a day. There is no secretariat. It doesn't call the groups that do intersessional work "working groups". This, too, sounds too permanent. Rather they are called "intersessional support groups" (ISG) and "intersessional meetings" (ISM). This because "meetings" do not sound very institutionalized' (Johnston 1999, 285). The choice of such an informal set-up was dictated by the great variety in levels of economic power and security interests among Forum members. There were few conflicts in the region. The early 1990s were a period of rapid economic development, when all the member states benefited from increased trade and investment liberalization policy. What could be observed was 'prisoner's delight': 'states in the region are individually pursuing economic liberalization strategies with little coordination while apparently unconcerned about defection by others' (Johnston 1999, 288). A security mechanism was apparently unnecessary. Yet in the end, 'given the multiplicity of state interests in the region, there was sufficient uncertainty about the regional security environment to create a demand for some mechanism to increase predictability'. What the ASEAN states in fact wanted was to preserve economic prosperity while being able to predict what they should do if things went wrong, but they regarded all the usual mechanisms for this, such as an arms programme and alliance building, as too costly. They believed a cautious type of organization was a better alternative. Furthermore, they did not know where the threat to security would come from. But anyone who thought this through came to the conclusion that 'even a weak institution, supporting sustained interaction among senior officials, could provide information to clarify and change estimations about intentions'. The state presenting the greatest danger in the region seemed to be China and if they wanted more information about China's intentions in order to reduce uncertainty they needed China to cooperate in the Forum. However, China also should not feel threatened, a consideration that too underlay the decision to keep the 'organiza-tion' of the Forum as weak as possible. This proved acceptable to most of the states. That the Forum was under ASEAN leadership was regarded as sensible, 'because the "ASEAN Way's" stress on consensus decision-making and weak institutionalization ensured the ARF would be minimally threatening to China' (Johnston 1999, 290).

The further development of the ASEAN Regional Forum was dominated by **path dependency** and **mutual constitution**. Consultations began and certain methods of working were found to be useful, leading to follow-up meetings and the exchange of information. By 1997 the Forum had all the necessary structures, such as 'a series of intersessional governmental working groups examining everything from templates for defence white papers, to military observers at military exercises, to the South China Sea, to nuclear weapons free zones, to peacekeeping standby arrangements. There is now a complex division of labour between track I (official) and track II (non-governmental) process that allow controversial issues to be examined in a less controversial way' (Johnston 1999, 290). The whole dialogue led to more organization, because those who were responsible for policy regarding China underwent a socialization process. This led to incremental institutionalization in ways that would have been unacceptable when the Forum was first established. In 1996 the criteria for participation were formalized and in June 2004 an *ARF Unit* was added to the ASEAN Secretariat.

ASEAN Plus Three (1997) and the Chiang Mai Initiative (2000)

In 1997 ASEAN established contacts with China, Japan and South Korea with the aim of expanding its relations to include the whole of East Asia. At an equally informal summit of this expanded ASEAN, *ASEAN Plus Three* (APT), which immediately followed an ASEAN Summit Meeting in November 1999, it was decided to work more closely together, both within the group and within organizations such as the UN and the WTO (the ASEAN member states had become GATT contracting partners in 1980). This led to bilateral trade agreements between ASEAN and China and Japan, opening up the prospect of an *East Asia Free Trade Area* (EAFTA). Against the background of the Asian financial crisis at the end of the 1990s, ASEAN Plus Three in 2000 also reached agreement on regional cooperation during financial crises and on the necessary regional support for each other's currencies rather than being dependent on the IMF. This took the form of the *Chiang Mai Initiative* (CMI), a network of bilateral swap arrangements. During the boom at the beginning of the twenty-first century ASEAN Plus Three took steps to enhance the facility's effectiveness. The financial crisis had heightened the member states' awareness of their economic inter-dependence, influenced by the manner in which the crisis 'was managed by the IMF (International Monetary Fund), resentment against the United States and its (at least perceived) domination of international monetary and financial affairs' (Webber 2003,

127) (see below). At the annual Summits of ASEAN Plus Three issues such as political and security cooperation to combat terrorism and transnational organized crime were also discussed. The ASEAN Secretariat has had an *ASEAN Plus Three Unit* since 2003.

Political problems for ASEAN

At the end of the 1990s ASEAN was also confronted with political problems and a loss of authority. These problems included the Asian financial crisis, the military coup in Cambodia just before its accession to ASEAN and the cross-border environmental problems that were caused by the continuing forest fires in Indonesia. These last were started deliberately every year by farmers trying to expand the land available for agriculture and occurred on such a scale that other states were faced with smog problems. ASEAN proved unable to influence any of these crises (Webber 2003, 135). Other matters for which ASEAN was called to account included the continuing violations of human rights in states such as Cambodia and Myanmar, where opposition leader and Nobel Prize winner Aung San Suu Kyi was either held under house arrest or severely restricted in her movements. As a result of foreign demands ASEAN appealed for her release in 2003 and in 2005 it put pressure on Myanmar not to take up the rotating chairmanship in 2006. Both actions went against ASEAN's principle of non-intervention in the domestic affairs of its member states.

The APEC summits (from 1993)

APEC, the *Asia Pacific Economic Cooperation*, aims to promote economic development based on free trade in the Asia-Pacific region. At the end of 1989 Australia took the initiative by setting up an informal forum for consultation, in order to see whether trade and investment in the region could be promoted through multilateral economic cooperation. This led in November 1993 to the first summit of government leaders of states bordering the Pacific, that is those on the westernmost coasts of the Western Hemisphere and the eastern coasts of Australasia. This summit resulted in annual meetings of foreign and economic ministers, followed by an informal meeting of heads of government to discuss economic development aims in the region. In APEC the US for the first time since 1945 joined an organization that did not include European partners. A small APEC Secretariat was set up in 1993 to assist with the APEC meetings, while 1996 saw the creation of the *APEC Business Advisory Council* (ABAC), in which each member economy has three representatives. Trade liberalization in the region was the main theme in the 1990s. 'The initiation of the annual leaders' meeting in 1993 gave the organization a new sense of dynamism, which was reflected in the following year, at Bogor, in the adoption of a bold long-term programme for trade liberalization between member states' (Webber 2003, 125). The member economies appreciated the fact that the US contributed to the successful conclusion of the GATT Uruguay Round by exerting pressure on the EU.

Troubled relations between the Asian states and the IMF

Relations within APEC were affected at the end of the 1990s by tensions between Asian and Western members. In 1998 the organization failed to reach agreement on the implementation of the trade liberalization programme agreed at Bogor in Indonesia. This was the result of 'irreconcilable conflicts over trade liberalization between the US, backed by the most developed "Anglo-Saxon" member states, on the one hand, and Japan, supported by most of the East Asian states, on the other'. Efforts to resolve the Asian financial crisis in particular created great resentment. Through the mediation of the US, representatives of the IMF, IBRD and the Asian Development Bank attended the APEC summit in 1997 (see §41.1). At that meeting the finance ministers agreed that the IMF would continue to play a leading role in trying to bring the Asian crisis under control, while the IMF in turn agreed that a separate Asian financial facility should be set up. But to the astonishment of the Asian states the IMF later publicly rejected the idea of such a facility, which confirmed their impression that the US wished to push its own trade interests at a time when the Asian states were in deep financial trouble. This undermined relations within APEC: 'the fact that APEC itself did little to alleviate the crisis and that, in as far as it did anything, it backed the IMF's crisis-management prescription, severely damaged the organization's reputation and credibility in East Asia' (Webber 2003, 141). In practice this weakened the initial US leadership of the organization and Japan began to play an increasingly important role, often with the agreement of the Asian states. As a result the dominance of the Asian states grew, even though they could not take over the leadership of APEC. Their position became even stronger as a consequence of the economic growth they experienced at the beginning of the twenty-first century.

The Asia Europe Meetings (from 1996)

The EU established its own forum with the Asian states in the form of the *Asia Europe Meeting* (ASEM), which gathered for the first time in 1996. This was followed by regular biennial meetings, in 1998, 2000, 2002, 2004, 2006 and 2008. The catalyst in this case was the changing political climate at the end of the 1990s, with ASEM described as an informal process of dialogue and cooperation on economic and political issues. The participants are the member states of the EU, the European Commission, 16 Asian states and the ASEAN Secretariat.

42.5 Continued and new regionalism in Africa

Developments in Africa

The developments in Africa in this period were less encouraging than those in Asia. The main problems were an unstable security situation throughout the continent (civil wars and interventions) and the unstable and failing states this gave rise to. These problems were also an obstacle to regional cooperation. Africa has been more dependent than Latin America and Asia on development aid from the industrialized states and the IBRD. The six leading regional economic organizations in Africa are located in three different regions (see Figure 42.6). In West Africa they are UEMOA and ECOWAS with eight and 15 member states, respectively, in Southern and East Africa the SADC and COMESA with 14 and 20 member states and in East Africa the EAC and IGAD with three and seven members.

Review of the ECOWAS Treaty (1993)

A Committee of Eminent Persons was created at the beginning of the 1990s to revise the 1975 Treaty of Lagos, in the hope of ending the stagnation of ECOWAS that had begun

Figure 42.6 Regional economic cooperation in Africa

WEST AFRICA

- 1974 CEAO; from 1994 **UEMOA West African Economic and Monetary Union**: Benin, Burkina Faso, Côte d'Ivoire (Ivory Coast), Guinea-Bissau, Mali, Niger, Senegal, Togo (8)
- 1975 **ECOWAS Economic Community of West African States**: Benin, Burkina Faso, Cape Verde, Côte d'Ivoire (Ivory Coast), Gambia, Ghana, Guinea, Guinea-Bissau, Liberia, Mali, Mauritania (left in 2000), Niger, Nigeria, Senegal, Sierra Leone, Togo (15)

SOUTHERN AND EAST AFRICA

- 1980 SADCC; 1992 **SADC Southern African Development Community**: Angola, Botswana, Democratic Republic of the Congo, Lesotho, Malawi, Mauritius, Mozambique, Namibia, Seychelles, South Africa, Swaziland, Tanzania, Zambia, Zimbabwe (14)
- 1981 PTA; 1994 **COMESA Common Market for Eastern and Southern Africa**: Angola, Burundi, Comoros, Democratic Republic of the Congo, Djibouti, Egypt (1999), Eritrea, Ethiopia, Kenya, Lesotho (left in 1997), Libya (2005), Madagascar, Malawi, Mauritius, Mozambique (left in 1997), Namibia (left in 2004), Rwanda, Seychelles (2001), Sudan, Swaziland, Tanzania (left in 2000), Uganda, Zambia, Zimbabwe (20)

EAST AFRICA

- 1967–77; 1999 **EAC East African Community**: Kenya, Tanzania, Uganda (3)
- 1986 IGADD; 1996 **IGAD Inter-Governmental Authority on Development**: Djibouti, Eritrea (suspended its own membership in 2007), Ethiopia, Kenya, Sudan, Somalia, Uganda (7)

in the mid-1980s (see §30.4). The Committee saw scope for transforming ECOWAS into a stronger trading bloc, for movement towards economic and monetary union and for strengthening the organization's institutions. In July 1993 a summit was held in Cotonou, Benin, where the revised *Treaty of Lagos* was signed. Its economic goals were a common economic market and a single currency. The political objectives included the establishment of an Economic and Social Council and a Court of Justice to replace the existing Tribunal, which lacked authority. The new Court would be able to enforce Community decisions. The revised Treaty also gave the Community responsibility for preventing and where necessary settling regional conflicts. In 1994 a Protocol was signed, setting up the West African Parliament to strengthen ECOWAS's legitimacy. In July 1995 a sufficient number of ratifications had been received for the revised Treaty of Lagos to enter into force. Institutional reform proceeded gradually. The *ECOWAS Parliament* began to function in 2000 and the *Court of Justice* in 2002. The removal of trade barriers was slowly getting under way. By 1997 the number of industrial goods that could be freely traded had risen to 400. In 1996 ECOWAS introduced value-added tax, followed in 1998 by harmonization of policy and rules on customs formalities. Measures were also taken in the fields of transport and communications, although not as swiftly as ECOWAS leaders had hoped. Monetary cooperation progressed primarily in the English-speaking states. The West African Clearing House set up in 1975 was transformed in 1996 into the *West African Monetary Agency* (WAMA), with the goal of simplifying monetary relations between the member states. In 2000 five states (Gambia, Ghana, Guinea, Nigeria and Sierra Leone) established the *West African Monetary Zone* (WAMZ), aiming to form a monetary union by 2005 with the eco as its currency. The intention was that the associated monetary institute, which started work in 2002, would become a West African Central Bank when the monetary union was realized. These plans were however thwarted as a result of the civil conflicts that began in the 1990s in Liberia and Sierra Leone, greater political instability in various member states including Nigeria, and continued disagreement over the choice between orientation towards the French franc (later the euro) and the monetary policy of the WAMA. Francophone member states had in 1994 formed the *West African Economic and Monetary Union* (UEMOA, *Union économique et monétaire ouest-africaine*), a continuation of an older institution, and they had insufficient confidence in the WAMA. These complications meant that the introduction of the single currency, the eco, was postponed until 2009. The main obstacle to further expansion of ECOWAS as a trading bloc was security, characterized by the weakening of various member states because of civil wars and ethnic conflict.

Significance of ECOMOG in West Africa

The civil war in Liberia broke out in 1990 when President Charles Taylor, acting in concert with a group of dissidents, provoked a conflict. ECOWAS established a Standing Mediation Committee to mediate in such conflicts in member states. At the Committee's suggestion it also set up the *ECOWAS Cease-Fire Monitoring Group* (ECOMOG), which was utilized in Liberia and remained there until well into 1997. It finally managed to bring the civil war to a peaceful end and oversaw the elections held in that year, an outcome which reinforced ECOWAS's authority (Van Walraven 1999). In view of these difficulties a separate chapter on regional security policy was incorporated into the revised ECOWAS Treaty of 1993. This required the member states to work in the interests of peace, stability and security. An armed rebellion in Sierra Leone prompted another intervention by ECOMOG in 1998, where its troops contributed to a fragile cease-fire between government and rebels in 1999 (see §37.7). In 1998 ECOMOG was also deployed in Guinea-Bissau and in 1999 ECOWAS decided to make it a permanent institution. In 2001 it was used yet again, on this occasion on the border between Liberia and Guinea-Bissau to prevent infiltration by guerrilla fighters. In 2002 it was deployed in Ivory Coast. However, support for ECOMOG within ECOWAS became a contested issue. The Francophone states in particular expressed criticism because of Nigeria's perceived self-interest in ECOMOG's operations in Liberia. 'From the beginning, neither Nigeria nor the ECOMOG were perceived as neutral in the conflict' (Dennis and Brown 2003, 245). Political instability, with a military regime in power from 1993 to 1998, a return to civilian rule (but with disputed elections), ethnic and other conflicts in the Niger Delta where most of the oil was produced and rampant corruption prevented Nigeria from acting as ECOWAS's leading power. Other member states too were struggling with domestic conflicts and corruption, which hampered ECOWAS in its operations and prevented expansion.

Southern Africa: from SADCC to SADC (1992)

In Southern Africa developments were slightly more favourable. In 1979 nine states in this region had allied themselves in Arusha, Tanzania, in the *Southern African Development Coordination Conference* (SADCC). They wanted to be able to adopt a more independent position *vis-à-vis* the great power in the region, South Africa, through coordination of their economic policy and they also positioned themselves as the frontline states against apartheid. SADCC was seen as a successful regional organization in Africa, even when it became clear that it lacked the institutional capacity to promote economic development. Partly because of South Africa's position as a relatively industrialized state and the authority of Nelson Mandela, who was released from prison in 1991 and in 1994 became president of South Africa, SADC (the successor of SADCC) acquired considerable prestige. After apartheid ended SADCC had in August 1992 been transformed into the *Southern African Development Community* (SADC, with one C and 'Community' instead of 'Conference'). The former frontline states and their former opponent South Africa launched institutional changes and designed the *SADC Programme of Action* (SPA). The core of this was the conclusion of economic sector programmes between specific states aimed at promoting economic development. More than 400 of these were set in motion at the beginning of the twenty-first century, of which 90 per cent were however financed by external sources. SADC managed to extract substantial amounts, proportionally speaking, of support and development aid from the IBRD (Poku 2001, 101–3). The Programme also had a *Trade Protocol*, adopted and in force from 2000, that aimed to make SADC a free trade area by 2008.

From PTA to COMESA (1994)

The *Preferential Trade Area for Eastern and Southern African States* (PTA), established in 1981, also benefited from the calm that returned to the region in the early 1990s as a result of the political changes in South Africa. It was expanded and transformed in 1994 into the *Common Market for Eastern and Southern Africa* (COMESA). With 20 member states, COMESA covers a large part of Southern Africa and the whole of East Africa. Its main priority is trade promotion. Nine member states within COMESA concluded a free trade agreement in 2000 and intended to expand it gradually. In 2004 two more states acceded to the agreement. They have also been working towards a customs union for the whole of COMESA by 2008. COMESA has a *Trade and Development Bank*, a *Clearing House* and a *Court of Justice*, which began to function in 1998. Despite severe conflicts in Eastern and Central Africa, the organization seems to be making gradual but steady progress.

Transformation of the OAU into the African Union (2002)

Developments in South Africa also sped up the reconstruction of the Organization of African Unity (OAU), established in 1963 (see Figure 28.1) and seen as outdated, as the *African Union* (AU) in 2002 with 53 members. All African states with the exception of Morocco joined the Union. Its aims include the promotion of democracy, human rights and a sustainable economy and the creation of a single market. The last objective has meant that the economic dimension of this in origin culturally-based continental organization has grown in importance. At its inception there was rivalry between South

Africa and Libya over organization and leadership, which eventually turned in South Africa's favour. The African Union acquired an extensive organizational structure, with an *Executive Council, Permanent Representatives*, a *Pan-African Parliament* and an *Economic, Social and Cultural Council*.

NEPAD (2001) as a strategy

In 2001 the OAU launched the *New Partnership for Africa's Development* (NEPAD), a 'multi-sector, sustainable development policy framework', designed 'to reduce poverty, increase economic growth, and improve socio-economic development prospects across Africa' (Cook 2002, 1). NEPAD was an initiative of the African states themselves, under the leadership of South Africa. In essence it was the merger, supported by the UN, of two regeneration plans, one launched by South Africa, the other by Senegal. It was adopted as a single programme by the OAU in 2001 and endorsed by the G8. NEPAD has its own Secretariat, although it became an African Union programme. The AU supplemented NEPAD with a *Declaration on Democracy, Political, Economic and Corporate Governance* in 2002, with the aim of strengthening state institutions and social processes. Much was expected from NEPAD and the African Union, despite scepticism caused by the fact that the position of many long-established regimes remained the same. The AU, for instance, expressed virtually no criticism of human rights violations in Zimbabwe or the suppression of the opposition during the 2008 elections and did little to counter the economic collapse of that state as a result of the eviction of white farmers by the government. There has been criticism too of NEPAD's dependence on the IBRD, IMF and G8, because the conditions they set for financial aid are seen as preventing Africa from developing in its own way.

Instability in Central Africa

The AU took on a coordinating role with regard to regional organizations in the four principal regions of Africa. In addition to the three regions referred to above this included Central Africa, where conflicts and intervention after the Rwandan massacres in 1994 had left the regional organizations in disarray. These are the *Economic Community of Central African States* (ECCAS or CEEAC, *Communauté économique des états de l'Afrique centrale*), founded in 1983 and the legacy of French colonial rule, and the *Economic and Monetary Community of Central Africa* (EMCCA or CEMAC, *Communauté économique et monétaire de l'Afrique centrale*), which emerged in 1994 from a predecessor organization. From the beginning of the twenty-first century the African Union became increasingly involved in peace and security issues. Despite its limited resources it demanded a leading role in resolving conflicts such as those in Congo, Burundi and Sudan and was prepared to send peace forces to those states. The first time this happened was in 2003 in Burundi. It made a successful contribution, under South African leadership, to the resolution of crises in Burundi and Congo and to cooperation between its forces and the UN. In 2007 the African Union also deployed troops in Somalia.

East Africa: revival of the EAC

After its collapse in 1977 the *East African Community* (see §30.4) was revived in 1984, after mediation between the three member states was brought to a successful conclusion.

A *Permanent Tripartite Commission for East-African Cooperation* was set up in 1993, on the basis of a recommendation that the possibilities for economic cooperation should be explored. At the end of 1999 this Commission managed to breathe new life into the East African Community and a new Treaty came into force in July 2000, establishing joint institutions in areas such as taxes, defence and transport. The organization is managed through meetings of heads of state and government and of ministers. It has a *Secretariat*, a *Court of Justice* and a parliament, the *East African Legislative Assembly*. The new EAC has succeeded in attracting foreign investment. The three states form one of the few regional organizations which are aware of the possibility of establishing a political federation, to which end they set up a Committee on Fast Tracking East African Federation in 2004.

From IGADD to IGAD (1995)

The driving forces behind the creation in 1986 of the *Inter-Governmental Authority on Drought and Development* (IGADD) were drought, desertification and diminishing food supplies, leading to the famines of the early 1980s. Founded under the auspices of the UN, this regional organization was primarily concerned with technical assistance. Organizational and structural problems made implementation so ineffective that it was decided in 1995 to revitalize the organization by transforming it into the IGAD, with only one D (for development). Following discussions within the OAU, the member states decided to build on the experiences of SADC and COMESA in Southern Africa and of ECOWAS in West Africa. It was even envisaged that IGAD would form the northern sector of the COMESA trade area, with SADC representing the southern sector. IGAD's main policy areas were the development of agriculture and economic cooperation between the member states and with other regional organizations. Another major concern was promoting peace and security in order to safeguard food supplies and sustainable development. In practice this has meant that IGAD had to facilitate peace talks in Sudan and Somalia. The IGAD Secretariat developed a number of projects designed to increase understanding of the complex relations between the warring parties and enable states to work on the prevention, management and resolution of conflicts. With EU support the *Conflict Early Warning and Response Mechanism* (CEWARN) was established in 2002. The great cultural differences, as well as numerous domestic and external conflicts and their links with international terrorism, meant IGAD had a virtually impossible task, even after the comprehensive peace agreement in Sudan was concluded in 2005. From 2005 IGAD has been involved in the African Union's attempt to maintain peace in Somalia. These military complications are the main obstacle to IGAD's economic activities.

The conflicts in Sudan and Darfur

The conflict between Northern and Southern Sudan dates from Sudan's independence in 1956. The government and the People's Liberation Movement fought each other for 20 years in the south of the state, with two million deaths, four million internally displaced people and almost a million refugees as a result. Mediation was arranged through IGAD. The UN followed and supported IGAD's initiative. This led to an agreement in the summer of 2002, followed by further agreements in the first half of 2004. In June 2004 the UN Security Council decided to send a political mission to Sudan to assist the peace process, the *UN Advance Mission in the Sudan* (UNAMIS) and the UN supported the peace talks in Nairobi that led to a peace agreement in January 2005. The follow-up to this was the creation in March 2005 of the *UN Mission in the Sudan* (UNMIS). In the meantime the African Union had arranged mediation in the conflict that had broken out in Darfur, in western Sudan, in 2003. The causes of this conflict were the disaffection of rebel groups, brutal responses by the army and ethnic cleansing. This led to extra tasks for UNAMIS. The African Union sent troops to Darfur, but these were too weak to achieve any control over the situation and the Sudanese government did not want UN peace-keepers on its soil. In April 2005 the AU asked NATO to provide air transport to take its peace force to Darfur, as well as help with training. Attempts to put together a stronger force with the UN met with little success. AU efforts to solve the crisis in Darfur resulted in the Darfur Peace Agreement in May 2006, which however was not signed by all parties. This meant that the fighting continued. It was not until April 2007 that Sudan accepted the deployment of UN peacekeepers. However, both the AU and the UN could do little to prevent the spread of the conflict to states elsewhere in the region, such as Chad and the Central African Republic, partly due to the fact that the two organizations were unable to raise enough forces.

Strategic importance of Africa to the US

For a variety of reasons, the US began in the twenty-first century to attach greater importance to Africa than it had before. Until then the continent had been seen as poss-essing little strategic value, riddled with conflict and the source of less than pleasant experiences for the US. When US President George W. Bush started his 'war against terror' this view changed, partly because various weakened African states provided a breeding ground for terrorist groups. In addition, the presence of oil increased the US's willingness to boost its development aid to Africa. The same applied to the G8, which in 2005 expressed its readiness to cancel the debts of 14 African and four Latin American 'poorest countries' as part of an IMF programme. It was also prepared to increase development aid by 50 billion dollars, half of which was intended for Africa. One of the reasons for the focus on Africa during the G8 summit was the public support mobilized by rock stars such as Bono, through the Live 8 concerts. Confidence in these measures declined when NGOs revealed that many industrialized states had failed to keep their financial promises.

Strategic importance of Africa to China

In the same period a new development emerged, as China sought closer relations with the African states in its pursuit of oil and other raw materials. It was willing to invest in these states and to provide direct assistance in building roads, railways, schools and other facilities damaged or fallen into disrepair in failing states plagued by conflict. In November 2006 China invited all the African states to a three-day Sino-African summit in Beijing, with the goal of expanding mutual trade. China promised to double its bilateral aid within three years and signed 14 agreements with African states on investment in infrastructure, telecommunications and mining. Western states reproached China for failing to discuss human rights violations, the fight against corruption or the issue of Good Governance when investing in Africa or giving aid. The IMF pointed out that Chinese loans entailed new, hidden debts for Africa that the IMF could not monitor. Africans too have difficulties with China's methods. They accuse China of carrying out much of the work using its own people rather than Africans, with the result that local businesses and individuals benefit only to a very limited extent from Chinese activities in their state. China resembles the former colonial powers rather than the modern partner Africans expected.

Economic growth in Africa at last

At the beginning of the twenty-first century Africa started to benefit from global economic growth, partly due to its raw materials but also because of increased investment. In 2000 the *African Venture Capital Association* brought together investors in African trade and industry. In 2006 foreign investment in developing states totalled 379 billion dollars. The bulk went to Asia (China, Hong Kong and Singapore), while Africa received 35.5 billion, with two-thirds of this going to North Africa (Egypt, Morocco and Tunisia) and 4 billion to Sub-Saharan Africa. Oil attracted capital to states such as Cape Verde, Gambia and Madagascar and encouraged investment in South Africa. The IMF recorded economic growth of over 6 per cent in Sub-Saharan Africa in 2006, which remained nevertheless heavily dependent on aid, at the time around 40 billion dollars, in other words ten times the amount of investment.

42.6 Economic cooperation in the Arab world and West Asia

The Gulf Cooperation Council (1981)

The two most important regional economic organizations in the Arab world are the GCC in the Gulf region (six member states) and the North African AMU with five member states (see Figure 42.7). The *Gulf Cooperation Council* was founded in 1981 in response to Iran's threatening stance *vis-à-vis* the Gulf states. Nevertheless, economic cooperation became its main trademark, overshadowing security considerations. The achievements of this economically successful organization include the abolition of customs duties in mutual trade, a common external tariff and fully integrated capital markets (Cooper and Taylor 2003, 107–8). Cooperation reinforced the Gulf states' orientation towards the WTO and encouraged the signing of free trade agreements with other states or organizations. Furthermore, it gave rise to interest in matters such as the environment and building sustainable infrastructures. Since January 2008 the Gulf states have a common market with free movement of capital, goods and persons. Their currencies are pegged to the dollar, with plans to introduce a common currency in 2010.

The Arab Maghreb Union (1989)

In 1989 the North African *Arab Maghreb Union* (AMU) was established in response to the liberalization of the international economy and partly modelled on European developments. Several states have close connections with the European Union through labour migration and trade, but cannot join the EU as they are outside the European Continent. Tensions between Algeria and Morocco, revolving in particular around the issue of Western Sahara, occupied by Morocco, were an obstacle to the development of the AMU. Although institutions were established, they were largely unsuccessful in creating a catalytic role for the AMU.

719

Figure 42.7 Regional cooperation in the Arab world and West Asia

THE ARAB WORLD

- 1981 **GCC** *Gulf Cooperation Council*: Bahrain, Kuwait, Oman, Qatar, Saudi Arabia, United Arab Emirates (6)
- 1989 **AMU** *Arab Maghreb Union*: Algeria, Libya, Morocco, Mauritania, Tunisia (5)

WEST ASIA

- 1985 **ECO** *Economic Cooperation Organization*: Afghanistan, Azerbaijan, Iran, Kazakhstan, Kyrgyzstan, Pakistan, Tajikistan, Turkey, Turkmenistan, Uzbekistan (10)
- 1992 **BSEC** *Black Sea Economic Cooperation*: Albania, Armenia, Azerbaijan, Bulgaria, Georgia, Greece, Moldova, Romania, Russia, Turkey, Ukraine (11)
- 2000 **EURASEC** *Eurasian Economic Community*: Belarus, Kazakhstan, Kyrgyzstan, Russia, Tajikistan (5)
- 2001 **SCO** *Shanghai Cooperation Organization*: China, Kazakhstan, Kyrgyzstan, Russia, Tajikistan, Uzbekistan (6)

West Asia: ECO (1985)

The two most important regional economic organizations in West Asia are ECO with ten member states and the BSEC with 11 members. In what is known as the Eurasian area, the regional organizations are the EURASEC, founded in 2000 with five members, and the six-member SCO, concerned with both security and economic issues (see Figure 42.7). The *Economic Cooperation Organization* (ECO) is the successor to a regional development organization comprising Iran, Pakistan and Turkey set up in 1964, which was expanded to include other states in 1992. Cooperation has focused primarily on areas such as transport, communications and energy. It was not until 2000 that a programme to strengthen intra-regional trade was agreed. Progress has been made in this field, but instability in the region has limited trade and growth.

The Black Sea Economic Cooperation pact (1992)

The *Organization of the Black Sea Economic Cooperation* (BSEC) aims to increase economic cooperation in the Black Sea region. Although founded in 1992, it was not until 1999 that its Charter came into force and the organization could begin its work. Cooperation is primarily technical in nature. A BSEC Business Council and an Environmental Programme for the Black Sea have been established.

Developments within the CIS

The move towards cooperation was a difficult and lengthy process for the states that emerged from the collapse of the Soviet Union. This was partly due to their desire for independence from Moscow, partly to the fact that their economies and infrastructures were and have remained closely linked to those of Russia. Within the Commonwealth of Independent States (see §36.2) groups of states developed several initiatives aimed at greater economic cooperation, which had little impact because of instability within and between states and their lack of experience in this field. In 1994 Kazakhstan, Kyrgyzstan and Uzbekistan formed a 'common economic area', which Tajikistan and Turkmenistan then joined. In 1996 Georgia, Ukraine, Azerbaijan and Moldova formed the *GUAM Group* (the first letters of their names), which after Uzbekistan joined in 1999 became the *GUUAM Group*. Cooperation focused primarily on energy production.

The Eurasian Economic Community (2000)

In 2000 the *Eurasian Economic Community* (EURASEC) emanated from various customs unions (from 1995 onwards, the first was between Russia and Belarus) and a 1996 Treaty, drawn up to deepen economic integration, social cooperation and coordination of foreign policies. The members of EURASEC are Belarus, Kazakhstan, Kyrgyzstan, Russia and Tajikistan. The Treaty came into effect in May 2001 and aims to create a new customs union and a common economic area. Its institutions include an *Interstate Council*, an *Integration Committee* and an *Inter-Parliamentary Assembly*. Preparations for the establishment of a court of justice are under way. Cooperation is exclusively intergovernmental, largely at the level of heads of state and government, like in Latin America. EURASEC's major achievements lie in the facilitation of intra-regional trade and the setting of a common external tariff. Organizational development is proceeding steadily, as is mutual trade. Nevertheless, economic growth has increased as a result of the economic development achieved by Russia and the other states at the turn of the twenty-first century through selling oil, gas and other raw materials.

The Shanghai Cooperation Organization (2001)

Cooperation between China and Russia, Kazakhstan, Kyrgyzstan, Tajikistan and Uzbekistan in the *Shanghai Cooperation Organization* (SCO) founded in 2001 constitutes the most important security project in the region where Europe meets Asia. Cooperation began at a summit in Shanghai in 1995, where five states signed an agreement on 'deepening military trust in border regions'. The initiative came from China, which had been following instability in the region with great concern. Annual summits to discuss the situation followed, attended by heads of state, security service heads, defence ministers and foreign ministers. These regular meetings of the 'Shanghai Five' (expanded to include Uzbekistan in 2001) took on institutional form. In 2001 they established the SCO by adopting the *Declaration on the Establishment of the Shanghai Cooperation Organization*. At the same time they concluded the *Shanghai Convention on Fighting Terrorism, Separatism and Extremism*. In December 2004 the SCO was granted observer status at the UN General Assembly. In addition to cooperation on security matters, the SCO explores the scope for promoting economic cooperation. Economic and trade ministers meet regularly, after having met for the first time in 2002 when they concluded an agreement expressing willingness to cooperate and establishing a mechanism for regular meetings. They also set up a Business Council. The SCO is slowly building up its institutions, learning lessons and showing greater willingness to cooperate. Its creation and expansion strengthened Russia's ties with Central Asia and increased China's control over relations with Russia and the former Soviet republics in the Eurasian region.

43

From European Community to European Union (1993)

Deepening and enlargement

43.1 Continued European integration: the creation of the single market (1993)

Towards institutional renewal

Because national interests predominated, no progress was made towards Western European integration in the early 1980s (see §26.5). The UK, under Margaret Thatcher, made renegotiating Britain's contribution a pivotal issue in its relationship with the European Community, and Thatcher worked with the institutions of the EC to achieve her objectives. In 1981 she began to involve the European Parliament more directly in European Council decision making by informing it of Council decisions immediately after the Council had met, a practice that was later formalized. One solution considered during that period of stagnation was a 'two-speed Europe', an idea expressed in the 1976 *Tindemans Report*, in which the Belgian Prime Minister Leo Tindemans sought not a 'federal' solution, but a reform of the EC's existing institutions by expanding their powers. He suggested the possibility of different 'speeds' for member states, depending on their political ambitions and the practical opportunities for progress. While this idea was rejected politically, it was a feature of the European Monetary System of 1979.

The federalists' solution: subsidiarity

In the midst of this impasse the governments of member states gave precedence to national interests, while so-called federalists within the European Parliament offered a way out of the difficulties. In 1982 former Commissioner and by then Member of the European Parliament Altiero Spinelli and several federalist supporters in the Crocodile Club, after the 'Au Crocodile' restaurant where their meetings were held, persuaded the European Parliament to set up a commission to consider institutional reform of the Communities. This commission was invited to draw up an entirely new treaty for that purpose and its work culminated in the comprehensive *Draft Treaty Establishing the European Union*, which the European Parliament adopted in 1984 by an overwhelming majority. As a fairly pragmatic draft treaty it attracted the support of several government leaders, including President François Mitterrand of France. The solution Spinelli and his fellow federalists advocated was actually an elaboration of the principle of *subsidiarity*, which has its origins in the teachings of the Roman Catholic Church. The principle holds that as far as possible communities should be self-governing. A 'higher-level' organization should assume responsibilities only if they are beneficial to everyone and only if those responsibilities cannot be undertaken by a 'lower-level' organization. In the case of the EC this meant that the EC would act collectively only for those objectives that could be better achieved at the European level and that other action should be left to individual member states. In effect a supranational institution did not need to keep striving for greater power, but it could instead impose a degree of self-restraint on itself. The principle of subsidiarity helped assuage fears of an untrammelled increase in the EC's powers.

Stuttgart 1983: towards a political union

Governments also sought a solution. The *Genscher–Colombo Plan*, named after the German and Italian foreign ministers who co-authored it, initially had little support, but at the European Council in Stuttgart in 1983 it prompted a *Solemn Declaration on European Union*, in which governments expressed a political desire to reform the structures of the three Communities and to increase the powers of the European Parliament. These reforms would be set out in a new Treaty on European Union. Although the European Council did not go as far as the European Parliament wished, its decision to advance the integration process was significant. It seemed as if governments were putting themselves under pressure by adopting far-reaching political ambitions, which included transforming the Communities into a 'political union', allowing the European Council to play an integrating role and strengthening European Political Cooperation (which refers to the EC's foreign policy). To counter the economic recession the Declaration set out a number of economic objectives and strategies, which included agreeing a comprehensive economic strategy to fight unemployment and inflation and a further convergence of national economies. To achieve the latter it contained proposals to strengthen the European Monetary System, complete the 'single market' which European businesses were strongly advocating and develop a joint industrial policy. After years of Euro-pessimism the Stuttgart Solemn Declaration offered renewed hope of agreeing a set of common objectives. The European Council in Fontainebleau reached agreement in 1984 on a reduction in the level of the UK's contribution and in the associated costs of the common agricultural policy. It represented a victory for Thatcher, but also paved the way for

Figure 43.1 European Commission Presidents since 1958

1958–67	**Walter Hallstein**	Germany
1967–70	**Jean Rey**	Belgium
1970–72	**Franco Malfatti**	Italy
1972–73	**Sicco Mansholt**	The Netherlands
1973–77	**François-Xavier Ortoli**	France
1977–81	**Roy Jenkins**	UK
1981–85	**Gaston Thorn**	Luxembourg
1985–95	**Jacques Delors**	France
1995–99	**Jacques Santer**	Luxembourg
1999	**Manuel Marín**	Spain
1999–2004	**Romano Prodi**	Italy
2004–	**José Manuel Barroso**	Portugal

institutional reforms and the accession of Spain and Portugal (Dedman 1996, 126). As was often the case, a solution to an impasse had been found through a combination of political ambition and economic projects.

The White Paper of the European Commission (1985)

Under Jacques Delors, who became President of the European Commission in January 1985 (see Figure 43.1 for the Commission Presidents), the Commission began to design economic projects, with the purpose of releasing the dynamic advantages for European trade and industry of a single large unified market. While Japan and the Asian industrial Tigers had high rates of economic growth and Japanese and US companies seemed to be overtaking their European counterparts, the European Community itself was suffering from 'Eurosclerosis'. To address that growing paralysis European companies had to become globally competitive, with the European Community as their main base, and therefore in early 1985 the Commission presented a plan to the European Parliament that aimed to revitalize Europe's economy. Within a few months European Commissioner Lord Cockfield had drawn up a *White Paper* on completing the single European market by the end of 1992 – hence the plan's name 'Europe 1992'. In June 1985 the European Council approved the White Paper, which set out what needed to be done, and a timetable for doing it, to complete the single (or internal) market as an area without internal frontiers in which goods, persons, services and capital could move freely. Cockfield and Delors also drew on the ruling of the European Court of Justice in the *Cassis de Dijon* case of 1979, which had established the basic principle that if a particular product was safe enough for the French, it should be deemed safe enough for consumers in other member states. This ruling made it possible for national product regulations to be reciprocally recognized, paving the way for an increase in mutual trade without a need to harmonize the very diverse national-level product regulations (Dedman 1996, 126–27). The White Paper and the *Cassis de Dijon* judgement gave impetus to the next stage of Western European integration, during which the European Community was able to weather the crisis in the welfare state caused by Reaganomics and strong free trade and to continue pursuing a European rather than an 'American' solution to unemployment (see §40.4–5).

The tortuous passage of the Single European Act (1986)

Politically, the issue was more emotive. The intergovernmental conference convened for the purpose of shaping institutional reform by amending the Treaties of Rome (see §26.3 and Figure 43.3) lasted from September to December 1985. No consensus could be reached, other than on the need to strengthen the single market. There was considerable disagreement on qualified majority voting in the Council of Ministers, since the UK, Denmark and Greece wished to limit that to single market issues. Eventually, in February 1986, member states assented, but it was not until July 1987 that the *Single European Act* actually came into force. Danish voters approved the Act in a referendum the following February, after Denmark's parliament had rejected it. The Irish government asked for more time to consider the issue and needed to amend Ireland's constitution after the ruling of its Supreme Court that the constitution as it stood did not permit Ireland to ratify the Single European Act. This challenge, set in motion by a citizen, necessitated a referendum and in May 1987 the Irish voted to approve the Act. The Single European Act was the first substantial, though by no means fundamental, change to the Treaties of 1951 and 1957, which created the three Communities (ECSC, EEC and Euratom), since the decision in 1965 to set up a single Council and a single Commission for all three Communities. It gave a legal basis to the informally introduced European Council and European Political Cooperation. The system of qualified majority voting, which had its origins in the Treaty of Rome, was extended particularly on matters relating to the completion of the single market. In response to the objection that the legislative powers of the European Parliament were too limited, a *cooperation procedure* was introduced, which gave it the right to amend legislative proposals in a four-stage process involving the Council of Ministers. Although the Single European Act failed to live up to the expectations of the members of the European Parliament, it once again granted greater *de facto* influence to that body (see §26.5). Finally, the Single European Act gave 'Europe 1992' a clear practical form and included additional provisions to promote its realization.

Completion of the single market (1993)

Delors was a forceful leader on the completion of the internal market. One of his first acts was to ask his officials to calculate what it would cost member states if they were to pull out of the EC. The psychologically-important result showed how high those costs would be and that further cooperation could only be beneficial. He then instituted a process that involved the removal of physical barriers, including customs procedures and border controls limiting the movement of persons and goods, the removal of technical barriers, including those contained in national legislation, to ensure goods, persons, capital and services could move freely, and the removal of fiscal barriers. At the end of 1992 almost all the measures necessary to complete the single market in goods and services by 1 January 1993 had been approved. On the unrestricted movement of persons, an implementation regulation came into force in 1995 among several members that had signed the *Schengen Agreement* of 1985, which led to the abolition of border controls and the introduction of the freedom of movement of persons within Schengen states. Gradually more and more states joined Schengen, including Norway, which is not an EU member. Norway twice rejected joining the EU in referendums (in 1972 and 1994), but it has nonetheless adopted much EU legislation. In 1991 the EU reached agreement with the European Free Trade Association (EFTA) on establishing the *European Economic Area*

(EEA) with a common single market between the EC and EFTA. A dispute then arose with the European Court of Justice over proposals to set up a separate Court for the European Economic Area. This led to a new treaty in which the powers of the existing European Court of Justice were extended to cover the EEA, in part because EFTA states adopted the *acquis communautaire* (the total body of EC law and regulations), except in a few areas. The EEA came into effect in 1994, but without Switzerland, as the Swiss rejected a proposal to join in a referendum at the end of 1992. Switzerland's application for membership of the EU submitted earlier that year was subsequently withdrawn. EFTA's members are now just Iceland, Liechtenstein, Norway and Switzerland.

Towards EMU and political union

Delors also revived efforts to create an economic and monetary union (EMU), which he regarded as a necessary corollary to the single market. During the 1980s the European Monetary System began to function more effectively (see §26.5), with stability being achieved by the end of the 1980s after a period of exchange rate instability from 1979 to 1983 and less volatility from 1983 to 1987. The EMS was supervised by the ministers of economics and finance (the ECOFIN Council) and a Committee of Central Bank Governors, which met each month in Basel at the Bank for International Settlements. A report drawn up in 1989 by a commission chaired by Delors advocated the creation of a European Monetary Institute (EMI) to replace this Committee, a European Central Bank, fixed exchange rates and a single currency. The report proposed that *Economic and Monetary Union* (EMU) be achieved in three stages. It was adopted by the European Council in December 1988. With only the UK opposed, the European Council decided in 1989 to convene an intergovernmental conference on EMU to draft Treaty revisions and to pave the way for the final stages of EMU. It was settled that the first stage of EMU would be implemented on 1 July 1990. The European Council also resolved to convene a second intergovernmental conference, on *European Political Union* (EPU). In the meantime, with the fall of the Berlin Wall in November 1989, changed political relations began to play a role alongside the economic momentum created by 'Europe 1992' and the pursuit of EMU. With Germany reunified, France threw its weight behind a European currency, preferring a greater Germany that was firmly entrenched within an integrated Europe. Germany was prepared to support a single currency, but on condition that it was supervised by a supranational agency. Germany wanted a strong currency, rather like the Deutschmark had ultimately become after the war. With political relations shifting in Eastern Europe as well, EC members looked to strengthen cooperation on security, an issue about which discussions had been going on for many years within the Western European Union (see §36.2). Cooperation increasingly became a matter of concern for individual member states, especially Germany.

43.2 The Maastricht Treaty on European Union (1992)

Black Monday for the Dutch (1991)

The outcome of the intergovernmental conferences on EMU and EPU was the 1992 *Treaty on European Union*, also known as the *Maastricht Treaty* (see Figure 43.3). The negotiations on EMU continued to build upon the extensive work carried out on the single market and EMU by the European Commission under Jacques Delors. There were problems though, because both the UK and Denmark were sceptical about the entire process and because Germany doubted whether German voters would support it. Ultimately a three-stage plan was adopted, which allowed Denmark and the UK to opt out of the transition to a single currency supervised by a European Central Bank. The conference on political union was a more intractable affair, in part because less preparatory work had been carried out. In 1991 a Luxembourg-sponsored draft treaty was agreed which envisaged three 'pillars', originating in the 'temple' model submitted by Denmark, but the UK objected to its federalist aims. The Dutch alternative to the Luxembourg draft met with so much resistance because of its unitary 'tree' structure that its rejection on 30 September became known as 'Black Monday' among the Dutch. That second rejection was a major setback for the conference and led to a reconsideration of the Danish temple model and its pillars, which was eventually approved in December 1991 by the European Council, although the UK ensured all references to federalism were removed from the text.

The Maastricht Treaty (1992)

The Treaty on European Union signed in Maastricht in February 1992 came into force in November 1993. The Treaty was a complicated document, as it comprised a number of provisions, amendments to the original Treaties of the three Communities, measures for a common foreign and security policy as the 'second pillar' alongside the first, which was the economy, and provisions on cooperation in justice and home affairs, which constituted the 'third pillar'. The European Economic Community (EEC) would be known henceforth as the *European Community* (EC). The third pillar was necessitated by the removal of frontiers in the single European market, which led to a greater need for cooperation between ministers of home affairs and of justice in the member states. The Treaty proper was followed by 17 explanatory Protocols, among them the Statute of the European Central Bank and a Protocol on Social Policy, and 34 interpretative Declarations, including one relating to the Western European Union as the defence component of the EU. The Treaty established the *European Union*, founded on the three original Communities and supplemented by the policies and forms of cooperation agreed in Maastricht. One objective of the Treaty was to maintain and then build on the full *acquis communautaire*. The Treaty itself claimed that the Union marked 'a new stage in the process of creating an ever closer union among the peoples of Europe, in which decisions are taken as closely as possible to the citizen'. Because some issues had already been agreed in detail, while others were only provisional, it was decided to convene a new intergovernmental conference in 1996 to revise certain clauses of the Treaty in the light of whether they were effective or not.

Strengthening the European Council

The Maastricht Treaty strengthened the role of the European Council in setting the main outlines of European policy. The Council consists of the heads of state or government of the member states and the President of the Commission. It is assisted by the ministers of foreign affairs and a member of the Commission. According to the Treaty, the European Council 'shall provide the Union with the necessary impetus for its development and shall define the general political guidelines thereof'. That stipulation illustrates how increasingly important within the EU the European Council had become, because it can take decisions on priorities and controversial issues. The Council of

727

Ministers, now renamed the Council of the European Union, and the European Commission are responsible for effecting coherence of policy in the fields of external relations, security, the economy and development. Each in its own way is responsible for ensuring that policy is implemented. The Commission plays a role in this, but so too do the governments of member states. Although the right to initiate legislation remained with the Commission, its position was weakened. The Maastricht Treaty further expanded the powers of the European Parliament, in part by introducing the *codecision procedure*, which was more far-reaching than the previous cooperation procedure.

Ratification of the Maastricht Treaty (1993)

The ratification of the Maastricht Treaty was an exciting process, since several member states submitted it to a referendum. In Denmark the Treaty failed to secure a sufficient majority in parliament and was then rejected in a referendum, with 50.7 per cent of those voting opposing it. The French government also chose to submit it to a referendum, in which it was approved by only 51.05 per cent of voters. The British parliament agreed to ratify the Treaty only after a rebellion by Conservative members of parliament. Within the European Council Denmark won a series of permanent opt-out clauses, which gave it the right to opt out of each of the three stages of EMU. Nor would Denmark be obliged to participate in decision making where defence issues were concerned. After these concessions Danish voters approved the Treaty in a second referendum by a majority of 56.8 per cent. In Germany opponents of ratification referred the Treaty to the Constitutional Court in Karlsruhe, which was asked to rule on whether the Treaty violated Article 24 of the German constitution on allowing the transfer of sovereign powers to intergovernmental organizations. Because the Treaty envisaged a union that went beyond intergovernmentalism, opponents asked the Court to rule on the constitutionality of the proposed transfer of powers. The Constitutional Court, however, adjudged that since the European Union's three pillars are essentially intergovernmental, the European Union was not a (new) genuine state. The EU had more the character of a confederation of states than of a federal state like Germany itself. The European Parliament retained sufficient supervisory powers in relation to EMU, and so there too the Court ruled that the Maastricht Treaty did not violate the democratic guarantees of the German constitution. Its judgement paved the way for the Maastricht Treaty to be ratified by Germany, the last member state to do so, after which the Treaty came into force in November 1993.

43.3 The establishment of the European Central Bank (1998) and the euro

Establishment of the European Central Bank (1998)

As envisaged by the Maastricht Treaty, EMU was a three-stage process. The first stage, from 1990–94, was intended to secure the free movement of capital between member states, closer coordination of economic policy and closer collaboration between central banks. The second stage, from 1994–98, would see the convergence of economic and monetary policy and during the third stage from 1999 onwards a European Central Bank, a fixed exchange rate and a single currency would be introduced. Although the German Chancellor Helmut Kohl had not initially supported a date for implementing stage two, he eventually relented after German reunification in 1990, but on condition that the European Central Bank (ECB), like the Bundesbank, would be completely independent and its sole responsibility was to be to maintain price stability. In 1994 the *European Monetary Institute* (EMI), the precursor of the ECB, was founded in Frankfurt to replace the Committee of Central Bank Governors. The EMI was given responsibility for promoting collaboration between central banks, coordinating monetary policy and supervising the EMS and in 1998 it also took on the job of advising the European Council on which states were eligible to participate in stage three of EMU, for which so-called *convergence criteria* had been set out in the Maastricht Treaty. The criteria were: price stability (inflation not more than 1.5 per cent above that of the three best performing member states), a budget deficit not exceeding 3 per cent of Gross Domestic Product and a government debt not exceeding 60 per cent of GDP, no currency devaluation within the past two years and long-term interest rates no higher than two percentage points above the average for the three best performing member states. Furthermore, at their European Council in Dublin in 1995 member states agreed a *Stability and Growth Pact*. The purpose of this, the outcome of a plan launched by the German finance ministry, was to ensure that member states maintained budgetary discipline beyond the introduction of the single currency. The pact entitled the Council to impose financial penalties on member states failing to demonstrate adequate budgetary discipline. Ironically, Germany's financial position deteriorated during the course of 1997 as a consequence of reunification to such an extent that it in fact failed to meet the criteria. To prevent EMU and the ECB failing, the German government ignored this, although France's position was strengthened as a result. Based on the convergence criteria, in 1998 11 of the 15 member states were invited to participate in stage three. Two others (Denmark and the UK) declined to join, while Greece and Sweden had not met the criteria. The announcement in May 1998 of that favourable result was overshadowed by a conflict over the future president of the ECB. President Jacques Chirac put Germany in a difficult position by nominating, at the last minute, Jean-Claude Trichet as ECB president, after Germany had already expressed its support for the Dutch candidate Wim Duisenberg. The French suggestion forced a protracted debate in the European Council and the comprise eventually reached was vague, with Duisenberg being appointed for eight years, but in the expectation that he would not serve his entire term of office.

The ECB and the introduction of the euro (2002)

The *European Central Bank* came into being on 1 June 1998 and began operating on 1 July, with Wim Duisenberg as president. Trichet eventually succeeded him on 1 November 2003. The Governing Council of this supranational institution consists of the Executive Board of the ECB (president, vice-president and four other members) and the governors of the national central banks of member states that have adopted the euro. The ECB reports to the European Parliament. Alongside the ECB is a *European System of Central Banks* (ESCB), comprising the ECB and the central banks of all EU member states. The ESCB's chief purpose is to maintain price stability by implementing monetary policy, conduct foreign exchange operations, hold and manage the foreign reserves of the member states and promote the smooth operation of payment systems. The ECB quickly built up a solid reputation, which paralleled that of the Federal Reserve Board, the US central banking system, which from 1987 to 2005 was personified by Alan Greenspan. In December 1995 the European Council resolved to proceed with the phased introduction of the *euro* on 1 January 1999. From that date central banks and the banking system carried out transactions in euros and government-issued debt too was euro-denominated. On 1 January 2002 the ECB then introduced the euro in 12 of the 15 member states, with Denmark, Sweden and the UK remaining outside the *eurozone*. In 2007 Slovenia adopted the single currency, the first of the states that joined in 2004 to do so. In 2002 Germany, France and Portugal were reprimanded by the European Commission for their excessive budget deficits and required to address the problem by the following year, under the rules of the Stability and Growth Pact. The Commission recommended giving Germany and France until 2005 to restore order to their budgets, but the Council of Ministers set aside that recommendation and determined to give them more time. In 2006 the Commission decided not to propose imposing financial penalties on the two states, but it did do so in the case of Greece, which had systematically understated its deficits for a number of years. Talks initially convened to discuss strengthening the deficit rules of the Stability and Growth Pact ended with these rules, which their initiator Germany had most notably contravened, being eased.

The Lisbon Strategy and the open method of coordination (2000)

The European Council in Lisbon in 2000 set out an ambitious strategic aim to improve economic productivity within the EU, hoping to make the EU 'the most dynamic and competitive knowledge-based economy in the world capable of sustainable economic growth with more and better jobs and greater social cohesion' by 2010. In a global context that long-term policy implied member states working towards transition to a knowledge-based economy and information society, in which all citizens would participate. The 'European model' of living and working would have to be modernized, with investments in human resources and the promotion of solidarity. Moreover, the need to maintain a healthy approach to economic growth was emphasized. This ambitious strategy became known as the *Lisbon Strategy* and as part of it many projects were set up, including a social agenda and a regional policy to promote innovation. Gradually the approach was broadened to include new aims and areas. To implement these projects the EU relied on the 'open method of coordination', which involved setting timetables for achieving agreed objectives, drawing up indicators and benchmarks, the sharing of best practice and instituting regular monitoring procedures to assess progress, including evaluation and assessment through peer review. This was the 'soft law' mechanism, which contrasted with the 'hard' approach represented by EU directives which had to be 'transposed' into national legislation. The underlying idea was that best practice invites imitation, and an open method of coordination was applied in many policy areas, including higher education. Although under the principle of subsidiarity higher education was a national prerogative, the EU managed to get a foot in the door by other means, such as a Pan-European approach. An initiative taken by several ministers led to the Bologna Process, which is becoming institutionalized (see Figure 43.2).

43.4 Amending the Treaties and enlargement into Central Europe

The Treaty of Amsterdam (1997)

After an intergovernmental conference lasting about a year the follow-up treaty envisaged at Maastricht was approved. The aim of this new treaty was to promote a greater understanding of the EU among citizens. It was also to set out how the EU could be enlarged

Figure 43.2 The Bologna Process (1999) and the reform of higher education

In an attempt to reform higher education, an important step in the development of a knowledge-based economy (but also with a view to cutting costs), a *European Higher Education Area* was set up along the lines of the European Economic Area. The European Higher Education Area was initiated by the education ministers of France, Germany, Italy and the UK in the **Bologna Declaration** in 1999. That document contains six lines of action intended to harmonize higher education in Europe, including the introduction of a more or less identical bachelor/master structure for universities and institutions for professional higher education in all European states. Although the Declaration is not a treaty, it has over the years acquired the status of one. The intergovernmental process took on an impetus and organizational structure all its own, in which the European Commission also procured a role alongside the now 46 states that are 'parties' to the Bologna Declaration. It was significant that instead of going through the EU, where education was a national prerogative, the four education ministers adopted a Pan-European strategy and almost all European states were involved in the 'process', including Russia and Turkey. In terms of form the **Bologna Process** developed into the model of a series of nineteenth-century multilateral conferences which meet regularly (every two years), make decisions incrementally and monitor progress on implementing agreements by means of stocktaking exercises. A secretariat was set up, which is currently provided by whichever state is organizing the next ministerial conference. The secretariat is expected to acquire permanent status at some stage. When it does, the Bologna Process will meet all the criteria of an IGO (Reinalda and Kulesza 2006).

to include Central and Eastern European states. At Maastricht it had been agreed that all European states could apply to join the EU and many did so. The European Council meeting in Amsterdam adopted the *Treaty of Amsterdam* in June 1997, but it was to encounter a myriad of political difficulties. The Treaty of Amsterdam was an extremely complicated document, including little that was new. Moreover, agreement on a number of issues relating to the decision-making process in an enlarged EU was postponed until a next treaty. Although the Treaty of Amsterdam made it possible to begin the process of expanding the EU eastwards, it failed to indicate how this could be best achieved, given the organizational consequences of further enlargement. The powers of the European Parliament were strengthened again, with the codecision procedure broadened to embrace more areas, including transport, the environment, social policy, public health and development aid. Although employment policy remained a national matter, the Treaty of Amsterdam gave the EU a role in coordinating the employment policies of its member states and in supporting the exchange of information and best practices in the field. The promotion of a high level of employment was added to the EU's objectives (see §40.5).

The Treaty of Nice (2001)

In February 2000 the next intergovernmental conference opened in Nice to discuss the issues left unresolved in Amsterdam, including the composition and procedures of the

EU's various institutions. The conference culminated in February 2001 in the *Treaty of Nice*. The EU's five largest member states relinquished their right to appoint a second commissioner, but at the same time the provisions relating to qualified majority voting and to the European Parliament after the enlargement reinforced the position of these states. In Nice the number of policy areas on which decisions would be taken by qualified majority voting was increased. Fundamental rights had first been mentioned in the Treaty of Amsterdam (human rights were actually a matter for the Council of Europe) and a separate *Charter of Fundamental Rights of the European Union*, drafted by a Convention set up by the European Council, was appended to the Treaty of Nice.

The Treaty Establishing a Constitution for Europe (2004) rejected

Because the different treaties contained so many revisions and provisions but were not collectively designed for a larger number of member states, a Declaration was annexed in Nice to the Treaty regarding the future of the EU. This led at the end of 2001 to the establishment of the *European Convention on the Future of Europe*. 217 representatives of governments, national parliaments, the European Commission and the European Parliament were appointed to this body, which was asked to produce a draft 'constitution' for the EU. Candidate member states and various institutions could attend as observers. Chaired by the former French President Valéry Giscard d'Estaing, the Convention drew up a

Figure 43.3 Treaties of the European Union since 1951

Year	Name of treaty	Signed	Effective
1951	Treaty Constituting the European Coal and Steel Community (ECSC), signed in Paris	18 April 1951	23 July 1952 to 23 July 2002
1957	Treaty Establishing the European Economic Community (EEC), signed in Rome	25 March 1957	1 January 1958
1957	Treaty Establishing the European Atomic Energy Community (Euratom), signed in Rome	25 March 1957	1 January 1958
1965	Treaty Instituting a Single Council and a Single Commission of the European Communities (Merger Treaty), signed in Brussels	8 April 1965	1 July 1967
1984	Draft Treaty Establishing the European Union (of the European Parliament)	14 February 1984	–
1986	Single European Act, signed in Luxembourg and The Hague	17 February 1986 28 February 1986	1 July 1987
1992	Treaty on European Union (EU), signed in Maastricht	7 February 1992	1 November 1993
1997	Treaty of Amsterdam Amending the Treaty on European Union, the Treaties Establishing the European Communities and Certain Related Acts	2 October 1997	1 May 1999
2001	Treaty of Nice Amending the Treaty on European Union, the Treaties Establishing the European Communities and Certain Related Acts	26 February 2001	1 February 2003
2004	Treaty Establishing a Constitution for Europe, signed in Rome	29 October 2004	–
2007	Treaty of Lisbon Amending the Treaty on European Union and the Treaty Establishing the European Community	13 December 2007	

'draft EU constitution' over a period of 18 months. It was presented for finalization by member states to an intergovernmental conference which convened from October 2003 to June 2004. The *Treaty Establishing a Constitution for Europe* was then submitted to member states for approval and in some states was the subject of a referendum. Early in the process French and Dutch voters rejected the Treaty in referendums held in May and June 2005, respectively, although more for domestic political reasons than because of the contents of the Treaty itself. Most other member states approved the proposed Treaty. The opposition of France and the Netherlands left the EU with a problem of legitimacy and with serious internal divisions. Moreover, its institutional structure remained inadequate, because the number of member states had meanwhile risen to 25, reaching 27 soon after.

The Treaty of Lisbon (2007)

In 2006 and 2007 a solution was sought by paring down what had been intended as a 'constitution' and transforming it into a 'reform treaty', if only to enhance the efficiency of EU institutions. In October 2007 government leaders reached agreement on a new text, which was largely identical to the previous one except that clauses resembling a constitution had been removed. Government leaders and foreign ministers signed the *Treaty of Lisbon* in December 2007, with the intention and expectation that it would be ratified by all member states before 2009. But the aim of achieving a text that could be understood and accepted by EU citizens had been lost sight of and the accumulation of treaty texts and amendments rendered this Treaty anything but comprehensible. A referendum in Ireland in June 2008 rejected the Treaty of Lisbon.

Enlargement of the EU to 25 members (2004) and to 27 (2007)

European Community enlargement was initially gradual, with the number of member states rising from six to nine in 1973, to ten in 1981, 12 in 1986 and 15 in 1995 (see Figure 43.4). In March 1998 the EU resolved to open negotiations on the accession of six potential new members, Cyprus, the Czech Republic, Estonia, Hungary, Poland and Slovenia, and in February 2000 negotiations began with another six states: Bulgaria, Latvia, Lithuania, Malta, Romania and Slovakia. It was difficult to refuse these states membership, because the Maastricht Treaty contained an invitation to apply. Moreover, the candidate member states and their supporters claimed to share the same values, norms and identities that EU members regarded as paramount (Schimmelfennig 2003). The EU had drawn up its criteria for joining in June 1993. Candidates for membership were required to have stable institutions guaranteeing democracy, the rule of law, human rights and the protection of minorities. They needed to have a functioning market economy able to compete within the EU and they would have to take on the obligations of membership, including adherence to the aims of political, economic and monetary union. Candidate member states could prepare for accession through negotiation and initiatives. They were, for example, required to assimilate the *acquis communautaire* of the single market and to adopt EU norms in other areas. In May 2004 the EU admitted ten new states, bringing the total number of members to 25. Bulgaria and Romania failed to qualify at that time, but were admitted in 2007 despite not being able to comply with all the criteria. Turkey's application to join the EU has been highly controversial. The EU and Turkey have enjoyed trade relations since 1988, when military rule in Turkey came to an end. Turkey had submitted a formal application to join the EU in 1987, when political obstacles to its application were initially related to human rights, but other objections of a more religious and political nature have since also been raised and made accession no less problematic. Furthermore, global political relationships have complicated the situation.

Figure 43.4 Member states of the European Communities and European Union

Accession	Number of member states	Member states
23 July 1951	6	Belgium, France, Germany, Italy, Luxembourg, Netherlands
1 January 1958	6	Ditto
1 January 1973	9	+ Denmark, Ireland, UK
1 January 1981	10	+ Greece
1 January 1986	12	+ Portugal, Spain
1 January 1995	15	+ Austria, Finland, Sweden
1 May 2004	25	+ Cyprus, Czech Republic, Estonia, Hungary, Latvia, Lithuania, Malta, Poland, Slovakia, Slovenia
1 January 2007	27	+ Bulgaria, Romania

Candidate member states: Croatia, Former Yugoslav Republic of Macedonia, Turkey.
Possible candidate member states: Albania, Bosnia and Herzegovina, Montenegro, Serbia (including Kosovo).

The character of the EU

For some supporters of European integration the ultimate objective has always been a federation of states. However, that was a concept which attracted little support among politicians and even drew fierce opposition because of its association with state formation. The EU has been called various things, including a market without a state and a postmodern state, but these are not particularly meaningful terms. With the development of treaties that are becoming more and more far-reaching, a comparison with the Westphalian state suggests an equivalence with constitutionalization, although the term constitution has encountered political objections similar to those evoked by federation. The most appropriate term seems to be *polity*, or 'polity-in-the-making'. As an administrative system covering a number of states and as an international organization, the EU has some special characteristics which include a combination of confederal elements (the cooperation procedure in the European legislative process) and federal ones (the allocation of powers between EU and member states). The EU has central institutions, although none as substantial as those at the national level. It lacks an overall political architecture (Caporaso 1996). Large sections of norm creation are done at the mesolevel of governance, by middle-ranking officials in combination with players from private and semi-public bodies (Weiler 1999). Powers are functionally separate. The EU has a permanent negotiation structure in which states hold one another hostage and the European identity is weak. According to Simon Hix, the EU as a polity has an extremely stable basic institutional ('constitutional') architecture and is so structured that there are few losers: 'a myriad of checks-and-balances ensure that there are few losers from EU policies'. However, it also means that the EU limits the policy autonomy of member states and that there is a strong degree of path dependency: 'the design of the EU constrains domestic policy choices, and it is difficult to change EU policies once they have been adopted' (Hix 2007, 142).

Security and the international economy on the threshold of the twenty-first century

Part XVII addresses developments in security and the economy in the first years of the twenty-first century. The events of 11 September 2001 and the subsequent 'war on terror' changed the global security landscape. The US sidelined the UN and opted for unilateralism. This had consequences for the human rights regime and various security regimes. The stance of the US also weakened the performance of economic IGOs (Chapter 44).

International organizations under pressure

44.1 Emergence of terrorism, 11 September 2001 and the invasion of Afghanistan

Emergence of terrorism in the 1990s

After the attacks on the American and French barracks in Beirut in 1983 and on aircraft over Lockerbie and Niger in 1988 and 1989, further attacks were carried out in the 1990s against mainly American targets, such as the World Trade Center in New York (1993), the US military barracks in Saudi Arabia (1996), the American embassies in Nairobi and Dar es Salaam (1998) and the *USS Cole* (2000). Osama Bin Laden, who was in Afghanistan and had established camps there to train a new kind of international terrorist, was held responsible for the embassy bombings in Africa. The terrorists, motivated by radical Islamic beliefs, carried out attacks using explosives and other deadly weapons and did not care who their victims were, including the hundreds of Africans who died in the bombings in Kenya and Tanzania. The US retaliated for the African bombings by firing rockets at Bin Laden's camp in Afghanistan, but without success, and the Taliban government ignored US extradition requests. In 1994 the UN cited terrorist attacks as a threat to international peace and security. The UN General Assembly, which had established an *ad hoc* committee to study the issue, adopted a resolution in 1997 stating that terrorism was a violation of the right to life, liberty and security. It was no more than a declaration: 97 states voted in favour, 57 abstained. In December 1998 the UN called on the Taliban to stop providing sanctuary for terrorists and condoning training camps within its territory. The Security Council repeated this demand in 1999, requested the extradition of Bin Laden and imposed sanctions on Afghanistan for a year. The relationship

737

between the UN and the Taliban was already on a bad footing due to the suppression of women in Afghanistan and violence against local UN offices, while the UNHCR was assisting the nearly four million Afghan refugees in Pakistan, Iran and elsewhere. This relationship deteriorated further when the Taliban decided to destroy statues in Afghanistan. UNESCO was unable to stop the regime blowing up two towering Buddha statues in Bamiyan province in early 2001.

International conventions against terrorism 1987–99

Emulating its response to the hijackings of the 1970s (see §24.4), the UN General Assembly adopted two conventions related to the terrorist bombings. The first, passed on 15 December 1997, was aimed at preventing terrorist attacks and the second, approved on 9 December 1999, targeted the financing of terrorism. Regional organizations adopted similar conventions. The South Asian Association for Regional Cooperation, whose members include India and Pakistan, had already done this on 4 November 1987. The League of Arab States did so on 22 April 1998, the Commonwealth of Independent States on 4 June 1999, the Organization of the Islamic Conference on 1 July 1999 and the Organization of African Unity on 14 July 1999. All these conventions introduced measures aimed at preventing bombings and at the punishment of perpetrators.

11 September 2001 and the UN response

Although the dangers of the new international terrorism were known, it was a major shock on 11 September 2001 when members of Bin Laden's Al Qaeda network hijacked four passenger aircraft. The hijackers flew two of the planes into the World Trade Center towers in New York, which collapsed shortly afterwards, killing some 3,000 people. A third plane destroyed part of the Pentagon in Washington DC and the fourth crashed after its passengers struggled with the hijackers. The US called the events a declaration of war and appealed to the UN. Up to then this new form of terrorism had been primarily a matter for the General Assembly, but now the Security Council took centre stage. On 12 September it adopted a resolution declaring terrorism a threat to peace and security, with the members voting while standing in an unusual move. On 28 September the Security Council passed Resolution 1373, invoking Chapter VII of the Charter and requiring states to take action to block the financing of terrorist activity by freezing the funds of suspected terrorist groups. Another resolution (1390), containing general guidelines for combating terrorism, followed in 2002. With these resolutions the Security Council involved itself in the internal affairs of states. The sanctions connected to the resolutions would affect individuals if, for example, they appeared on a list of persons suspected of terrorist activity. Resolution 1373 also led to the creation of the Security Council's Counter-Terrorism Committee.

NATO response to 11 September

NATO secretary general George Robertson responded immediately to the Al Qaeda attacks, declaring that they came under Article 5 of the North Atlantic Treaty: an attack on one is an attack on all. Although this principle had always been thought of in terms of the US coming to Europe's aid, this time the situation was reversed. As the US preferred to act independently, NATO's role in what President George W. Bush called the 'war on terror' remained limited to providing AWACS radar aircraft. Later NATO was assigned tasks in Afghanistan, where in August 2003 it assumed command of the International Security Assistance Force established by the UN Security Council, and in Iraq, where it began training security troops in June 2004. NATO, which had recently expanded its membership, acquired a new international role through these activities, which like its previous involvement in the former Yugoslavia fell outside the parameters of its Treaty.

The fall of the Taliban in Afghanistan (2001)

After 11 September the US gave Afghanistan an ultimatum, demanding it hand over Bin Laden and close down the training camps. The Taliban refused to comply, ended all international aid programmes and closed the UN's offices in Afghanistan. The US and the UK, which had been working to establish a coalition against Taliban rule, received support from neighbouring states Pakistan and Uzbekistan. At the beginning of October they initiated air strikes against military targets and training camps in Afghanistan. The Taliban regime was willing to negotiate on the extradition of Bin Laden to a third state in exchange for a cease-fire, but the US rejected this offer. The UN and NGOs were concerned about the flows of refugees that ensued and the consequences of the attacks for innocent civilians, but the coalition forces kept control of humanitarian aid and dropped food packages from aircraft. The US saw 'nation building' as a task for the UN, but only after the Taliban had been ousted. In the final months of the year the US operation *Enduring Freedom*, in which the US had forged ties with the Northern Alliance of Afghanistan, succeeded in routing the Taliban regime. UN secretary-general Annan and UN special representative Lakhdar Brahimi were opposed to the coalition's suggestion of establishing a temporary UN administration. Brahimi developed a plan for the Afghans to play a greater political role, with a multilateral security force to be deployed and the UN to provide support. A conference was convened in Bonn in December under the auspices of the UN, to form a transitional administration to be led by Hamid Karzai. An international force would provide security. For this purpose the Security Council established the *International Security Assistance Force* (ISAF) on 20 December, which would operate in and around Kabul under US military command. The Bonn Conference charged the transitional government with the task of summoning a national council of representatives. This Loya Jirga assembled in June 2002 and elected the new transitional administration, with Karzai as president. In the meantime the UN was providing food aid through the World Food Programme and financial support for reconstruction. The UN Development Programme, the IBRD and the Asian Development Bank convened a planning conference in November and a donor conference in Tokyo in January 2002. Annan travelled to states to secure more money than had been pledged.

The UN Assistance Mission in Afghanistan (2002)

In March 2002 the Security Council created the *UN Assistance Mission in Afghanistan* (UNAMA) to support the process of reconstruction and national reconciliation initiated in Bonn. UNAMA was managed by the Department of Peacekeeping Operations of the UN Secretariat. It was not considered a regular peacekeeping operation, but rather a political 'peacebuilding' mission, with both a political and a development function. Its political mission included guiding the transitional government's efforts to build public institutions and institutionalize human rights. In 2004 UNAMA arranged and oversaw successful elections, which Karzai won. Its development mission included creating an employment policy, with UNAMA engaging more than 1,000 people. In August 2003 NATO assumed command of ISAF, a responsibility that first the UK and then Turkey had had previously. The Security Council in October extended ISAF's mandate to allow operations beyond Kabul. Among the many problems encountered by the organizations involved were fighting among Afghan factions, violence against UN and NGO personnel, poppy cultivation and the related drug trade and the gradual return of the Taliban. More-over, Bin Laden was still at large. NGOs were more or less forced to leave because military operations were severely impeding their ability to function. The ISAF mission consisted of approximately 35,000 personnel, but it faced a difficult situation in Afghanistan. More military force was needed to cope with it, but NATO member states were not willing to provide the troops and material required to reverse and normalize the conditions. The worsening of the security situation reduced the scope for development work, which meant less room for manoeuvre for UNAMA, whose mandate was renewed annually.

44.2 The US war in Iraq (2003)

IAEA inspections in Iraq 1991–98

The US response to 11 September 2001 went beyond Afghanistan and also affected Iraq. Relations with Iraq had been difficult since its invasion of Kuwait and the subsequent Gulf War of 1990 (see §37.1) and the UN was directly involved in the developments there. In 1991 the Security Council had charged the International Atomic Energy Agency with the task of locating and dismantling Iraq's clandestine nuclear weapons programmes and setting up a system of *Ongoing Monitoring and Verification* (OMV). The *Iraq Nuclear Verification Office* (INVO) was created for this purpose and shared responsibility with the *UN Special Commission* (UNSCOM) for finding chemical, biological and other kinds of weapons of mass destruction. They created multinational inspection teams and began to track down and dismantle Iraq's weapons facilities. Between 1994 and the end of 1998 the IAEA had a virtually permanent presence in Iraq, while it set up the monitoring system intended to prevent Iraq undertaking activities prohibited by the Security Council. However, faced with Iraq's increasing hostility towards its inspectors the IAEA felt it had no choice but to withdraw them in December 1998. A UNSCOM team was pre-vented from inspecting a suspicious site and at the beginning of 1999 secretary-general Annan had to recall his personnel, who had been overseeing the UN Oil-for-Food Programme (see §38.1). The Security Council confirmed the IAEA's mandate to carry out inspections and replaced UNSCOM with the *UN Monitoring, Verification and Inspec-tion Commission* (UNMOVIC) at the end of 1999, appointing Hans Blix its chairman in January 2000. Negotiations on new weapons inspections in Iraq did not take place until the spring of 2001. Based on its inspections in Iraq between November 2002 and March 2003, the IAEA informed the Security Council that it had found no proof or evidence that Iraq was capable of resuming a nuclear weapons programme.

The Security Council on Iraq (2003)

In November 2002 the Security Council unanimously adopted Resolution 1441, giving Iraq a final opportunity to comply with its obligations regarding weapons of mass destruction and establishing a stricter inspection regime. Should Iraq fail to meet the requirements this time, the consequences would be severe. Nevertheless, the new UN weapons inspectors found Iraq still unwilling to unconditionally cooperate with inspections. Inspectors were unable to provide conclusive proof that Iraq no longer had weapons of mass destruction, although the IAEA was convinced that it did not have a nuclear weapons capability. On 5 February 2003 US Secretary of State Colin Powell attempted to persuade the Security Council that Iraq did in fact still have weapons of mass destruction and continued to pose a security threat. He presented evidence gathered by the US, but it was unconvincing and was later proved incorrect when the US failed to find weapons of mass destruction in Iraq. Disagreement now arose within the Security Council. China, France and Russia, as well as Germany, which had a temporary seat and chaired the Council at the time, urged that the inspectors should be given more time, while the US and the UK wanted to intervene in Iraq. Since the end of 2002 President Bush's neo-conservative advisers had favoured taking unilateral action and occupying Iraq, as in their view it was necessary to make a 'pre-emptive' move to disable it. Occupation was seen as the path to 'regime change' (see Figure 44.1). Bush won support for this policy from the UK and Spain, although Prime Minister Tony Blair made British support conditional on Security Council approval. In the meantime they were drawing together a large military force around Iraq. Because Resolution 1441 did not clearly state under what conditions military violence could be used against Iraq, opponents of immediate intervention favoured adopting a second resolution to legitimize military action. The US, the UK and Spain had drafted their own 'war resolution', but on 17 March decided against presenting it to the Security Council because France had vowed to veto it. Communication between the great powers had broken down in this crisis (Marfleet and Miller 2005). The British parliament voted the next day in favour of participating in the war. On 20 March the US and the UK launched their military campaign against Iraq, without Security Council approval under the UN Charter. On 9 April US troops took Baghdad and Saddam Hussein's regime collapsed. Chaos ensued, as public buildings, hospitals and shops were looted. The International Red Cross urged the US and the UK, which were doing nothing to stop this, to restore order. Aboard a US warship on 1 May Bush announced that major military operations in Iraq had ended. He named Paul Bremer as his envoy in Iraq with responsibility for guiding the country through the transition to democracy.

Figure 44.1 Armed intervention to produce regime change

Wilsonianism is an illustration of a hegemon's assumption of the right to intervene in other states. This term refers to US President Woodrow Wilson, whose support for the establishment of the League of Nations in 1919 was based on strong notions of sovereignty and self-determination of states. In other words, in 1919 he gave precedence to moral principles and rejected direct power politics in international relations. He was also the architect of the **Wilson doctrine** of 1913, which condoned US intervention in other American states if it felt a government was pursuing the wrong policies. The principle of the justified 'pre-emptive strike' against potentially dangerous states that evolved after 11 September 2001 and the explicit aim of 'regime change' are developments of the Wilson doctrine. Great and regional powers are commonly inclined to use military force to install or prop up friendly governments that rule on the basis of political structures that are acceptable to the dominant powers. Henk Leurdijk counted 82 cases between 1815 and 2000 in which regular army units of a state intervened in a regime conflict in another state. **Armed interventions** are usually carried out by major powers (60 of the 82 interventions) and regional powers (22 cases). 49 of the 60 interventions by major powers were for the purpose of maintaining existing relationships of dependency (*hegemonic interventions*). In 11 cases the aim was to create new dependency relationships (*imperial interventions*). Armed intervention is a component of asymmetric power relations in the international system and the victims are usually small states. There were 28 armed interventions between 1815 and 1914, 11 between 1914 and 1945, none between 1945 and 1956, 23 between 1956 and 1981, six between 1981 and 1989 and 14 between 1990 and 1998. Three of the most recent, in Somalia, Rwanda and Bosnia and Herzegovina, were humanitarian operations (Leurdijk 2006).

The UN in Iraq: the death of De Mello (2003)

Although the US had established an interim government in Iraq that was to its liking, secretary-general Annan insisted that the UN should be given an important role in the reconstruction effort because only the UN could provide sufficient legitimacy. But the US opposed this idea, although the Senate urged such an arrangement. In May the Security Council repealed the sanctions against Iraq and created a Development Fund for Iraq and an International Advisory and Monitoring Board to oversee it. However, little was heard from this body. Annan appointed the High Commissioner for Human Rights, Sergio Vieira de Mello, as his special representative in Iraq for four months. De Mello went to Baghdad at the beginning of June to try to procure a stronger role for the UN, while Annan pressed for a clear timetable on the withdrawal of troops. Attacks on US soldiers were increasing and the UN also met with resistance, because it was seen as an extension of the US due to its history of sanctions and inspections in Iraq. On 19 August a bomb devastated the UN headquarters in Baghdad, killing 24 people including De Mello. The UN subsequently withdrew from Iraq.

Limited involvement of the UN

The US had managed to secure the support of a few dozen allies, forming the *Coalition of the Willing*. Increasing resistance in Iraq to the foreign occupation forced the US to seek more help from the international community, including the UN. In September it pressed for a solution, but without giving the UN or any other state the prospect of ever having much influence. Annan was fiercely opposed to this, because he saw US unilateralism as a threat to security and the future of the UN. In October the Security Council adopted a resolution on the future of Iraq that gained some support from opponents of the war, such as France, Germany and Russia, but it gave the UN only a limited role, if circumstances would permit this. Annan believed the situation was too dangerous to send UN personnel to Iraq at that time and both Secretary of State Powell and the Governing Council the US had established in Iraq criticized the UN for doing too little. France,

Germany and Russia suggested holding an international conference, as was done for Afghanistan, to which Annan attached the condition that Iraq's six neighbouring states should be involved. In January 2004 he appointed Brahimi as his special envoy to Iraq and sent in a team of election experts. Through Brahimi's mediation the US agreed to expedite the transfer of sovereignty and to postpone the promised elections until January 2005. Brahimi wanted the Governing Council to be replaced by a new government composed of prominent Iraqis which would be subject to a UN mandate. The US agreed with the first part, but preferred technocrats rather than prominent individuals. In June the Security Council confirmed a role for the UN in organizing the elections and drafting a new constitution, which led to its limited return to Iraq in August 2004. Although the UN's contribution was successful in both matters, the dilemma remained unresolved. The UN was involved, but the US and the multilateral force under its command had *de facto* power and set policy. Another problem was that the US had difficulty assessing existing relations in Iraq and rather than controlling events allowed itself to be guided by them. Under those conditions Annan was willing to accept only a limited role for the UN. A larger role would be plausible only after the occupation had ended.

Civil war and regional instability

The US was failing to suppress the growing civil disorder in Iraq that was bringing the country to the brink of civil war. It was also unable to curb the daily violence, involving car bombs and other explosive devices, which started almost immediately. Relations between Iraqis and US soldiers were damaged by the latter's rough treatment of civilians and scandals such as the humiliation and mistreatment of inmates at Abu Ghraib prison near Baghdad in early 2004. The Abu Ghraib abuses added to the unease felt over the holding of international terrorists in a special prison at Guantanamo Bay, a US enclave on Cuba. The foreign nationals held there had virtually no access to the justice system and the rules of the Geneva Conventions were not applied. This was, as Annan put it, incompatible with UN human rights policy and would eventually spark criticism within the US as well. Bush and Blair continued to pursue their occupation policy, which fanned the flames of civil war in Iraq and undermined stability in the region, and there was little either the UN or political forces within the US could do to change the situation. Gradually, however, political sentiment in the US began to turn against the government's policy. With refugee numbers increasing, the UNHCR tried to find more resources within and around Iraq and sought to strengthen its ties with the Arab world. The original policy of integrating returning Iraqis was abandoned in favour of preventing instability in neighbouring states receiving refugees. Iraq's neighbours had to accommodate unprecedented numbers of refugees, without being able to offer sufficient employment opportunities or adequate services.

Persistent problems in the Middle East

The Israeli–Palestinian conflict was one of the most persistent and intricate problems that the UN faced at the beginning of the twenty-first century. A US-orchestrated peace process had been launched in the Middle East after the 'intifada' of 1987, which led to the Oslo Peace Accords of 1993 and 1995. Through Norwegian mediation Israel and the PLO began talks that revived hopes of a two-state solution. The UN had been excluded from the conflict since 1973, but President Clinton involved the organization in further peace talks in 1999 and 2000. However, the UN's diplomatic efforts failed when another intifada began in 2001. After the events of 11 September Palestinian resistance came to be viewed within the broader context of terrorism and the US tolerated Israeli policies, with its involvement limited to the provision of general guidelines in the form of the *Road Map* of 2003. This included no role for the UN other than a monitoring one after Israel's war with Lebanon in 2006 (through UNIFIL) and participation in an impotent consultation body, the so-called Quartet, comprised of the US, Russia, the European Union and the UN. The US-organized summit in Annapolis, Maryland, in October 2007 did nothing to change the situation. Various Arab states, Israel and the president of the Palestinian Authority attended the summit, but Hamas, which had won the Palestinian elections and later assumed power in Gaza, was not represented. The UN could do little other than support the consultations and there was no UN contribution to speak of.

44.3 The UN human rights regime after the end of the Cold War

The end of the Cold War

Because human rights constituted an ideological benchmark in East–West relations, the end of the Cold War signified changes in the international human rights regimes. With the political changes that took place in East–West relations at the end of the 1980s, opportunities to strengthen human rights in the Second World seemed to appear. The idea of organizing a global human rights conference emerged at the UN in 1989. The General Assembly wanted ECOSOC to extend the Commission on Human Rights geographically and decided to explore ways to strengthen the functioning of the Commission. However, in early 1990 the proposals for reinforcing the Commission itself met with opposition from the countries of the Non-Aligned Movement, which objected to Western proposals aimed at giving the Commission more autonomy. Instead they wanted to replace the Special Rapporteurs with working groups and to restrict the scope of action of NGOs. This controversy between the states that attempted to strengthen the UN's human rights mechanism and the Third World states which opposed this development and sought to weaken the regime rematerialized in the run-up to, and during, the World Conference on Human Rights in Vienna in June 1993. In 1992 Indonesia launched an offensive by calling for recognition of regional differences in the formulation and exercise of human rights. Indonesia wanted to see less emphasis on individual rights and stressed the need to achieve economic development first. It contrasted what it saw as a traditional Western emphasis on individual rights with the emphasis on community rights and obligations in other cultures. Japan sided with the West, but Indonesia was supported by China, the Non-Aligned Movement (of which Indonesia had recently assumed the chairmanship) and the Asian preparatory meeting in April 1993 for the Vienna World Conference. This preparatory meeting accused the West of using its power to impose its ideas on human rights and democracy on other states, particularly by linking human rights compliance with development aid.

The Good Governance criterion

The growing trend among donors to tie development aid not only to specific economic growth models but also to specific social models caused anger in the Third World. The

IMF, IBRD and OECD called for cuts in arms spending as a component of Good Governance in development (see §41.2). The criteria they set also included fighting corruption and compliance with human rights. In addition to human rights and democratic principles, these organizations wanted 'soft' values based on universal principles to play a role in international cooperation. Ultimately these soft values would need to be pooled in a 'code of conduct for good public policy', with incentives (both carrots and sticks) to encourage compliance. Developing states opposed this because, in their view, such values were connected to Western principles and positions of power. They accused the West of paternalism and neo-colonialist interference in their social choices.

Trade unions as a touchstone for human rights

The international trade union movement suggested that the cultural argument posited by Third World governments was fairly static and conservative. It was used primarily to maintain control over women and children by depriving them of the ability to exercise their rights, as was the idea that an increase in freedom would be justified only after progress had been made in economic development. Autonomous trade unions were seen as a threat by rulers in industrializing states, with the result that they were either banned or crippled by government supervision. In some cases the law granted rights, but governments did not allow them to be exercised, as in the case of the right to strike in Indonesia. The right to strike was enshrined in the constitution but was not tolerated in practice, because it would be damaging to everyone involved. In Newly-Industrializing Countries in southeast Asia the designation of priority industries impeded the recognition of trade unions. In Malaysia, the national trade union of electronics industry workers finally received recognition after using ILO procedures persistently for several years. However, this lasted just five days. After withdrawing the recognition the authorities encouraged weaker company unions, but even these were hampered by a rule requiring a rate of organization exceeding 50 per cent and by the dismissal of active employees.

The UN human rights conference in Vienna (1993)

At the UN human rights conference in Vienna in June 1993 180 states and more than 1,500 NGOs were represented, including Amnesty International, Human Rights Watch, Helsinki Watch, Asia Watch, the International Commission of Jurists, women's organizations and trade unions. The Third World states called for cultural differences, non-interference in internal affairs and the importance of economic development to be given priority over political and civil rights, which they considered 'luxuries'. The West was committed to enforcing the universality and indivisibility of individual and collective rights and of civil and economic rights. Western states also considered strengthening the UN by providing more facilities and resources, establishing a Political Freedom Index and appointing a High Commissioner for Human Rights. However, this idea, already proposed by the US in 1952 and by Amnesty International chairman Sean MacBride in 1968, stood little chance of being implemented. Before and during the UN conference there was an overriding sense that it would fail. NGOs were barred from attending the discussions about the concluding statement. Ultimately the final declaration benefited the Third World, in that it recognized development as a fundamental human right, albeit without specifying the relationship between human rights and development aid. However the declaration did emphasize the universality of human rights (that is, their independence from

745

cultural differences) and the indivisibility of individual and collective rights and of political and economic rights. It explicitly stated that the rights of women and girls were an inalienable, integral and inseparable part of the body of universal human rights and went so far as to establish a special rapporteur on violence against women. The declaration also stressed the importance of NGOs. A compromise was reached on additional resources and the establishment of a High Commissioner for Human Rights by asking the General Assembly to give these matters priority. Although the final declaration limited the damage, it was clear that views on human rights diverged around the world.

The High Commissioner for Human Rights

In December 1993 the UN General Assembly decided to appoint a High Commissioner for Human Rights, who would be responsible for promoting and protecting all human rights, while recognizing religious, historical and cultural differences between the member states. This phraseology won over reluctant developing states. The High Commissioner has a four-year mandate and may be reappointed for one further term. The *Office of the UN High Commissioner for Human Rights* (OHCHR) is in Geneva and operates under the UN Secretariat. Mary Robinson, President of Ireland at the time, was appointed High Commissioner in 1997. She was known to be independent and critical, particularly when human rights were subordinated to trade interests. After the attacks on the US of 11 September 2001 she openly warned of the risk of human rights being sacrificed in the war against terror, which cost her the position of High Commissioner. Although she had wanted to serve a second term, she resigned in the summer of 2002 under US pressure. 'I understand very well that the US was traumatized and considered itself in a state of war. As a result, it was not giving human rights the same emphasis and it was my responsibility to explain that human rights are even more important in such situations' (*NRC Handelsblad*, 31 July 2002). Her successor, the Brazilian Sergio Vieira de Mello, called his sphere of activity a political minefield. According to informed sources he knew where the boundaries lay. 'He will identify human rights violations, but will stop short of frontal assaults on governments – except in the case of atrocities such as genocide' (*NRC Handelsblad*, 23 July 2002). He died in 2003 in the attack on UN headquarters in Baghdad. Louise Arbour of Canada was appointed High Commissioner in 2004.

From Commission to Human Rights Council (2006)

Because of its growing membership and the continuing human rights violations, the Commission on Human Rights had an increasing number of member states that violated human rights. They used their membership to evade criticism or demonstrate that the situation in their view was not all that bad. This meant that the Commission lost its authority and contributed to the weakening of the human rights regime that was the result of the polarized positions of North and South. The US urged reform and after a long struggle and without clear new procedures for going forward the Commission on Human Rights was abolished in June 2006. The first meeting of the *UN Human Rights Council* (HRC) took place on 19 June 2006. It had 47 members (13 from Africa, 13 from Asia, 6 from Eastern Europe, 8 from Latin America and 7 from Western Europe and other states). Members are elected by majority vote for three-year terms, although the US would have preferred a two-thirds majority system to make the selection procedure more discriminating. The US did not stand for election. Members of the Council are judged on their own human rights record and the Council meets three times a year. In principle, the Council took over all the activities of the Commission, including those involving the High Commissioner. Unlike the Commission the Human Rights Council is not an organ of ECOSOC but of the General Assembly.

44.4 Dilution of the nuclear non-proliferation regime

The non-proliferation regime at the beginning of the twenty-first century

Although the nuclear non-proliferation regime (see §24.1) had never been robust, it did function during the Cold War and in the 1990s (see Figure 24.2). Technological advances were making it easier for states to produce nuclear weapons and the required technology became an object of espionage. The Pakistani nuclear physicist Abdul Khan had been able to acquire specific knowledge in the Netherlands and put it to use in Pakistan's nuclear weapons programme. It was later discovered that at the end of the twentieth century he was involved in the sale of this technology to other states which were seeking to acquire nuclear weapons. That other states were developing nuclear weapons programmes in defiance of the Nuclear Non-Proliferation Treaty of 1968 was demonstrated by the nuclear tests carried out by Pakistan and India, a programme in South Africa that had been established in secret and was later dismantled, the exposure of Iraq's clandestine programme in 1991 and the discovery in 2002 and 2003 that North Korea and Iran were conducting uranium enrichment and other nuclear-related activities. The non-proliferation regime proved incapable of preventing the group of nuclear states from growing. In 1997 the IAEA adopted the *Additional Protocol* to expand its options for uncovering unreported nuclear activity, but the problem with this Protocol was that not many states signed and ratified it. By 2006 there were only 54 signatories and 18 ratifications, so that its effectiveness was limited. In 2003 the IAEA announced that a new non-proliferation regime was needed. The new regime would need to incorporate multilateral oversight of nuclear material, energy systems that do not use material that can also be used to produce nuclear weapons and a reduction in the number of storage places for spent nuclear fuel rods and nuclear waste, which would also have to come under multilateral supervision. However, it seemed unlikely that agreement on a solution of this nature could be reached. Another problem with the existing regime was that the five original nuclear powers were doing little to reduce their stockpiles and at the beginning of the twenty-first century they began to invest in the modernization of their arsenals and the related systems. The US was unwilling to ratify the Comprehensive Nuclear-Test-Ban Treaty of 1996 (see §36.3). Unlike the conferences of 1995 and 2000, the 2005 Nuclear Non-Proliferation Treaty review conference failed. The parties could not agree on a final declaration. The US was represented only by an under-secretary and refused to accept criticism of its inadequate nuclear disarmament efforts. Iran objected to being singled out by the US as a treaty violator and it was unclear how to deal with states that threatened to withdraw from the Treaty, such as North Korea.

Tensions surrounding North Korea

In 2002 it became clear that North Korea had been running a clandestine uranium enrichment programme, aided in part by technology provided by Abdul Khan. President

Bush identified Iraq, Iran and North Korea as the 'axis of evil' because their arms activity posed a threat to peace and security. In January 2003 North Korea announced its intention to withdraw from the Nuclear Non-Proliferation Treaty and in February 2005 it declared that it had nuclear weapons. North Korea had already threatened to withdraw from the Treaty in 1993, but had then negotiated a compromise with the US, agreeing to accept some inspections of its nuclear installations in exchange for assistance in generating non-military nuclear energy. It was using the Nuclear Non-Proliferation Treaty mainly as a negotiating lever to obtain nuclear energy assistance and food aid, as because of failed harvests its regime was unable to feed the population. North Korea's nuclear activity and food aid became the subjects of Six-Party Talks involving China, Japan, North and South Korea, Russia and the US. The forum succeeded in getting concessions from North Korea, but the other five members felt that it was using the threat of nuclear attacks to blackmail them. In a new round of negotiations following North Korea's first nuclear test in 2006 the government was promised new food aid and the release of frozen funds in exchange for it abandoning its nuclear programme. North Korea subsequently invited the IAEA for talks about dismantling the programme, which were held in 2008, with some success but without settling the issue. Russia and China also used the Six-Party Talks to seek strategic partnerships and regional multilateralism in Asia (Kerr 2005).

Tensions surrounding Iran

In 2003 the IAEA discovered that Abdul Khan had also provided technology to Iran and that it was carrying out uranium enrichment. The IAEA visited the country in 2003, but found no proof that it was developing nuclear weapons. Iran's lack of cooperation with IAEA inspections and its insistence on the right to develop nuclear energy caused protest from the US, which was convinced that Iran had a nuclear weapons programme. This also triggered multilateral talks, involving three EU member states (France, Germany and the UK) and a kind of mediation role for Russia. However, relations were strained because of the Iranian president's aggressive tone towards the US and Israel, Iran's geographical position as a neighbour of Iraq and the US's dismissive stance. When Iran openly continued its nuclear programme the Security Council adopted a resolution in July 2006, demanding under threat of economic and diplomatic sanctions that it stop its uranium enrichment. These measures were tightened in two subsequent resolutions. Due to Iran's lack of cooperation the role of the IAEA remained limited, while the US under Bush's leadership persisted in its attitude towards Iran.

El Baradei stays on (2005)

As the US's political problems with specific states mounted, it became more critical of the IAEA. In the view of the US government the organization had failed to fully support the American line on Iraq and Iran. For this reason the US in 2005 resisted the reappointment of director-general Mohamed El Baradei for several months. However, in June 2005 the US unexpectedly withdrew its objections, enabling El Baradei – who together with the IAEA was awarded the Nobel Peace Prize shortly afterwards – to stay on for a third term. When the US government concluded a partnership agreement with India in 2006 it became clear that it was continuing to pursue its own policies in the areas of nuclear energy. It showed that it was willing to deliver nuclear technology to India, a state that was not a party to the Nuclear Non-Proliferation Treaty. India did, however, agree to accept international inspections of its civil nuclear plants. The IAEA objected in principle, but it considered these inspections a step forward because this guaranteed a certain degree of oversight, on the basis of which increased oversight might be possible in the future. The agreement met with internal opposition in both the US and India, but in 2008 the American Congress approved it.

44.5 Weakening of the OSCE and cooling US–Russia relations

Changes within the OSCE

The Organization for Security and Cooperation in Europe played an undisputed role in conflict prevention and crisis management in Central and Eastern Europe and the Balkans in the 1990s (see §36.1). This allowed the High Commissioner on National Minorities, Max van der Stoel, who had been appointed in 1993, to tackle impending conflicts with minorities and work on solutions with various parties. The Office for Democratic Institutions and Human Rights also had considerable freedom of movement and sent out teams of observers to monitor election processes. The OSCE's on-site activities included training politicians, police officers and other public servants, as well as promoting independent media, campaigning, political education and judicial reforms. There was a need for all these activities and the OSCE worked with the Council of Europe and the European Union to meet that need. However, relations between the OSCE and Russia gradually deteriorated, due to factors such as the US-instigated expansion of NATO into Eastern Europe (in 1999 and 2004), the enlargement of the EU (in 2004 and 2007) and Russia's stabilization and economic recovery in the early twenty-first century, facilitated by oil and gas revenues. Russia remained outside NATO and the EU, but both organizations were committed to conferring with Russia on a regular basis. NATO consultations with Russia took place within the forum of the North Atlantic Cooperation Council, established in 1991, and the Euro-Atlantic Partnership Council which replaced it in 1997 (see §36.2). The NATO operation in Kosovo in 1999 was problematic for Russia because of its traditional ties with Serbia and relations between Russia and NATO cooled as a result. This changed after the events of 11 September 2001, which Russia also condemned. The establishment of the NATO-Russia Council in May 2002 demonstrated that the relationship had improved.

The OSCE weakened

NATO's operation in Kosovo also had consequences for the OSCE, as it in fact weakened the Organization's position. The OSCE's *Kosovo Prevention Force* had to withdraw from Kosovo shortly before the NATO air strikes in 1999 and did not return afterwards, while the UN mission UNMIK, rather than the OSCE, was given responsibility for overseeing the future course of events (see §37.7). At the beginning of the twenty-first century Russia felt that the OSCE was encroaching on its direct, although declining, sphere of influence in Eastern Europe. OSCE observers played a role in the changes taking place in Georgia in 2003, when the 'Rose Revolution' resulted in President Eduard Shevardnadze being replaced by the Western-oriented Mikheil Saakashvili. In 2004 OSCE observers found fraud during the presidential elections in Ukraine, which necessitated new elections. Fraud was also noticed by the OSCE during the parliamentary elections in Kyrgyzstan in 2005. Russia reacted to this interference by making objections to the OSCE. It stopped paying membership dues and pressed for centralization of the organization. In 2005 a group of eminent persons wrote a report on the future of the OSCE, confirming that the organization had obligations in the 'human dimension' and had the authority to act within states. But the report was also conciliatory towards Russia, calling for more centralization and greater sensitivity over Russian sentiments on developments within its immediate sphere of influence.

Continuing wars in Chechnya

Russia was particularly sensitive about the developments taking place in Chechnya. Excluded from all involvement in the conflict, the OSCE was frustrated by the persistent fighting and human rights violations. Chechnya, an autonomous republic of the Russian Federation, had declared independence in 1991, which led to the 'First Chechen War' with Russian troops in 1994. A ceasefire was achieved two years later, but the 'Second Chechen War' broke out in 1999 after bombings in Moscow and the Chechen invasion of Dagestan. The conflict in Chechnya continued, despite the deployment of huge numbers of Russian troops. After the hostage crises involving the audience of the Russian musical *Nord-Ost* in Moscow in 2002 and a school in Beslan in North Ossetia in 2004 Russia labelled the conflict 'Chechen terrorism'. Russia made clear that this was a problem it would resolve on its own (and by its own, primarily military, means). There was no role for the OSCE.

Abrogation of the ABM Treaty (2001)

While the OSCE's significance as a regime for easing tensions between European states was declining, the relationship between the US and Russia in regard to strategic arms was also changing. After the end of the Cold War the détente in US–Russian relations had been enshrined in various arms control agreements between the two powers (see §36.3). But when the Republican government took office in the US in January 2001, President Bush introduced a new defence policy. In his opinion the US needed fewer nuclear and more defensive weapons, now that the Cold War was over. He therefore sought to unilaterally reduce the strategic nuclear arms arsenal and intended to introduce a national anti-missile shield. Bush did not want his plans for the shield defence system to be dependent on Russia's cooperation. In November 2001 he announced that the US would cut its nuclear arsenal to approximately 2,200 warheads. Because his new policy conflicted with the ABM Treaty concluded with the Soviet Union in 1972, he informed Vladimir Putin during the Russian president's visit to the US in December that the US intended to withdraw from the Treaty, which permitted only one strategic defence system.

Signing of SORT (2002)

Putin responded by saying that he would reduce Russia's nuclear arsenal as well, but he wanted to maintain a formal process with the US. In January 2002 Russia and the US thus began negotiations on a new consultative forum, which led to the *Strategic Offensive Reductions Treaty* (SORT), which was signed on 24 May 2002. This extremely succinct agreement stated that both parties would reduce their arsenal of long-range nuclear weapons to between 1,700 and 2,200 by the end of 2012, which would meet the commitments for 2007 of the START III arms reduction talks. Unlike START III, however, SORT contained no agreements about destroying long-range weapons or limiting the numbers of tactical nuclear weapons. The dual name of the treaty is symbolic of the parties' inability to reach agreement on various issues. They could not even agree on the title (see Figure 36.1). The US decision to withdraw from the ABM Treaty prompted Russia to withdraw from START II in June 2002, as the new American defence policy had rendered it meaningless. The US Senate ratified SORT in March 2003 and the Russian Duma did so in May.

A new arms race

Amid escalating tensions, particularly in the Middle East and Iraq, and problems with states such as North Korea and Iran, a new arms race began to take shape. The US priority was the further development of its missile defence shield. Poland and the Czech Republic expressed their willingness to host a European component of the shield, much to Russia's displeasure, given the closeness of the two states to its borders and its sphere of influence in Eastern Europe. In 2007 Russia tested a new ballistic missile that could transport multiple nuclear warheads over long distances. In addition Putin warned the US in October that Russia would withdraw from the 1987 INF Treaty in which Reagan and Gorbachev had agreed to destroy their intermediate range missiles. If Russia carried out this threat there would be consequences for the balance of military power in Europe.

Suspension of the CFE Treaty (2007)

The Treaty on Conventional Armed Forces in Europe (CFE) concluded by NATO and the Warsaw Pact in 1990 (see §36.1) also played a role in the deteriorating situation. The CFE Treaty had come into force in 1992 and because of the dissolution of the Warsaw Pact and the enlargement of NATO the parties to the CFE Treaty concluded an *Adaptation Agreement* in 1999. Despite their consensus on these changes the NATO member states refused to ratify this agreement unless Russia withdrew its troops from Georgia and Moldova. With tensions rising because of the siting of the US missile defence shield in the Czech Republic and Poland, Putin signed a law, with the consent of the Duma, in November 2007 suspending Russia's participation in the CFE Treaty. The relations between Russia and the West, including NATO, cooled further after the short war between Georgia and Russia over the separatist region South Ossetia in early August 2008.

Deadlock at the Geneva disarmament conference

At the beginning of the twenty-first century no progress was made in the Geneva Conference on Disarmament (see §24.1). Pakistan blocked a US proposal on the negotiation of a treaty that would ban the production of fissionable material for use in nuclear weapons. However, a proposal by Russia and China for a treaty that would ban all weapons from space was discussed. Underlying this proposal was the idea that satellites intended for civil purposes could also be used militarily. However, the US government did not wish to limit its military options in space and rejected the Russian-Chinese proposal, which caused deadlock.

44.6 Lack of global economic coordination at the beginning of the twenty-first century

The US economy as the locomotive

In 2000 the world economy grew dramatically, pulled along by the US economy. In the EU unemployment fell. Japan experienced slow economic growth, but the other Asian states recovered from the financial crisis of the late 1990s (see §41.1). However, the world economy seemed to be far from stable. The price of oil rose as a result of declining US oil reserves and increasing consumption in Asia. In addition the dollar exchange rate continued to rise, as the influx of foreign capital, with which the US offset its trade deficit, continued. Inflation increased in the US and the euro exchange rate fell. All these factors, combined with high consumer debt, made the US economy unstable. To slow it down the US Federal Reserve Board raised the interest rate in phases. The IMF and OECD criticized this policy because of the inflation risk, but the European Central Bank and other central banks did the same.

The US Congress on the IMF and IBRD

Within the IMF there was a difference of opinion in 2000 over who would succeed managing director Camdessus. The US found a candidate proposed by Europe lacking in substance, but accepted Horst Köhler of the EBRD. The US Congress debated the tasks of the IMF and IBRD in the new century and the committee considering these matters could see no more than a limited role for each organization. It concluded that the IMF should function strictly as a *lender of last resort*, in other words it would not impose policy on states and it would be involved in monetary relations only in emergencies. Similarly, the IBRD's activities should be limited to assisting the poorest countries. These recommendations were not welcomed within the organizations. Köhler had a broader view of the IMF's purpose, based on the need – as perceived by the IMF – to safeguard financial order in the world. IBDR president Wolfensohn stressed the importance of several issues on the IBRD agenda, including advancing the economic infrastructure, health care and the environment.

Central banks more important than the IMF, IBRD and WTO

The world economy deteriorated as a result of setbacks in the information technology sector in 2001 and the events of 11 September in the US. To stimulate the economy the Federal Reserve Board cut its key interest rate several times. The ECB, which initially withstood political pressure from European governments and the IMF and OECD, eventually felt compelled to do so as well. The sluggish economic performance of the US and Europe also affected growth in Asia, particularly in states such as Malaysia, Singapore and Taiwan which were heavily dependent on electronics exports. However, states like China (which joined the WTO in 2001), India and Indonesia were able to maintain economic growth. In the Western Hemisphere Mexico, strongly oriented towards the US as a member of NAFTA, and Argentina, which had linked its currency to the dollar and was no longer able to pay its debts (see §41.2), felt the impact of the economic downturn. There was little global coordination by economic IGOs, because the American and European central banks set the most important macro-economic policy. Furthermore, there was no consensus on international trade policy. After the WTO had failed to achieve agreement in Seattle in 1999, agreement needed to be secured in Doha, Qatar (see §39.3), with the round of talks scheduled for conclusion in 2005. However, France refused to discuss Europe's agricultural policy, which was based on subsidies and protectionism, within the WTO. The IMF and IBRD failed to achieve consensus on funding for the UN Millennium Development Goals aimed at reducing poverty and improving health and education (see §40.6). They agreed to work towards a solution at a special UN conference in Monterrey, Mexico, at the beginning of 2002.

Asian and Latin American states go their own way

The US, and consequently the world, economy hit another rough patch in 2002. In the US consumer spending was encouraged by rising house prices and home equity and by interest-free loans from car manufacturers, but consumer confidence was undermined by massive redundancies and bankruptcies. This was compounded by corporate accounting scandals, such as the questionable speculation and fraudulent financial reporting practices that led to the downfall of energy company Enron and accounting firm Arthur Andersen. The economy was further weakened as a result of poor market performance and uncertainty surrounding pensions and social security. The European economy was also stagnating, but the Asian economies were showing strong growth, boosted by ASEAN's efforts to promote free trade with other Asian states, including China. These economies also began to focus on the consumption patterns of their own populations. The IMF continued to control developments in Latin America, because Argentina and Brazil were forced to borrow from the Fund. The US and the IMF both had misgivings about Brazil's newly-elected president, trade union leader Luiz Lula da Silva. Despite these restrictions Latin American governments acquired more control over domestic economic growth, which was stimulated in part by regional cooperation.

Lack of coordination among IGOs

Little came of the debt relief policy trumpeted by wealthy states, aimed at cancelling the debts of the world's poorest development states. Many debtor states were unable to comply with the Good Governance criteria (see §41.2) and consequently were not fully eligible, if at all, for debt remission. UNCTAD pointed out that it would be better to use IBRD income support to strengthen the economic production of the very poorest nations. The IBRD in turn argued that poor states were unlikely to achieve economic growth as long as wealthy kept their borders closed to agricultural products and textiles. The WTO's Doha Round failed to make progress and nothing was accomplished at the UN World Summit on Sustainable Development in Johannesburg, South Africa, or the special poverty conference in Monterrey, Mexico, in 2002. No concrete agreements were made. The global economic organizations failed to coordinate their efforts and neither the US nor the G8 provided leadership.

The G22 at the WTO conference in Cancun (2003)

Trade relations continued to deteriorate. In view of the upcoming elections, the US government had introduced an import duty on steel in violation of WTO rules (see §39.2) and to win votes it also increased farming subsidies. The WTO conference in

Cancun, Mexico, in September 2003 failed, even though EU member states were gradually beginning to accept the idea of concessions on agricultural subsidies and, shortly before the conference, the EU and the US had drafted a joint proposal to limit such support. The EU-US proposal was not enough. The G22, under the leadership of large developing states such as Brazil, China, India and South Africa, were able to formulate joint demands (see §39.3), calling for better access to the markets of wealthy states. They also opposed the requirement to open up their own markets to services, because doing so would give wealthy states yet another economic advantage. The Doha Round of negotiations foundered as a result.

Yes to CAFTA, no to FTAA (2005)

At a joint conference in November 2003 the American states agreed to form a *Free Trade Area of the Americas* (FTAA) in 2005. However, this US free trade effort, for which a series of conferences were held starting in 1994, failed as a result of domestic opposition and the new configuration of relations in Latin America. In December 2003 the US concluded a free trade agreement with four Central American states (Costa Rica, El Salvador, Guatemala and Nicaragua), joined later by the Dominican Republic. The *Central American Free Trade Agreement* (CAFTA) faced strong political opposition in the US, mainly because of the fear of job losses. In July 2005 the House of Representatives adopted CAFTA by a vote of 217 in favour and 215 against. This wafer-thin majority gave little hope of success for further trade agreements. The FTAA attempt ended for different reasons at the FTAA summit in Mar del Plata, Argentina, in November 2005. Venezuelan president Hugo Chávez, Bolivian presidential candidate Evo Morales and others protested against a full free trade zone in advance of the summit. Brazil's Lula da Silva and Argentina's Néstor Kirchner had little interest in an FTAA unless the US was willing to end agricultural subsidies. Because no agreement could be reached on that issue, the summit and the US's efforts to form a free trade area in the Americas failed. In Latin America the leftist presidents were adding anti-US weight to the scale and thus to the significance of the MERCOSUR and the Andean Community (see §42.2). In 2007, on the initiative of President Chávez, seven Latin American states set up the *Banco del Sur*, a regional development bank, as a counterweight and alternative to the IBRD.

Weakening of the IMF and the G7

In Asia the significance of ASEAN's free trade promotion continued to grow, as India and Japan also became involved. As with Latin America, Asia went its own way both monetarily and economically. The WTO failed to break the deadlock over agricultural subsidies and get negotiations back on track in 2004. The G22 stood its ground and the EU and the US did not move far enough. Equally, little progress was made on the issue of debt relief for the poorest states. The IMF, IBRD and G8 agreed that debt relief was desirable, but could not reach consensus on how to frame it. A British proposal to use part of the IMF's gold reserves for this purpose did not get a majority. The IMF's position gradually weakened. Due to economic growth states such as Argentina and Brazil were able to accelerate their debt repayment and Asian states were accumulating their own financial reserves under the Chiang Mai Initiative (see §42.4), with the result that the IMF faced a falling demand for credit. The IMF covers its costs out of interest revenues, but since this was bringing in less money it would need to economize, while to retain its significance it would have to implement reforms. However, as the board structure was still based on the dominance of highly-developed states, there was little inclination to reconstruct in favour of states such as Brazil, China and India. As a result the IMF lost influence. According to economist Stephen Roach, the world economy was out of balance. While the US was expending on credit, Asia was providing the goods and the related financing by buying up American shares and government bonds. The IMF, IBRD and G7 were incapable of offering solutions. 'We have the wrong architecture for solving the problems of globalization. The IMF and the World Bank are products of the post-Second World War world order. I do not see how these two organizations can cope with the demands of today's international economy in a globalizing world. The G7 should become the G5 and incorporate China and India. We need a permanent organization with directors who are authorized by their national governments to analyse the problems and, if necessary, present difficult solutions. We don't have an organization like this now' (*NRC Handelsblad*, 19 March 2005). Roach predicted that only a serious crisis would precipitate change in this respect, but equated that to shutting the stable door after the horse has bolted.

Private equity and hedge funds

The pattern of international investment also demonstrated that economic globalization had made states more dependent on each other. In 2006 there was an increase in foreign investment around the world which surpassed even the previous top year 2000. Private equity and hedge funds were special forms of investment. Since the 1990s private investors had been buying into successful companies everywhere and during shareholders' meetings they urged these companies to pursue activities that produced short-term high returns. If necessary they prompted companies to split up and sell off the parts, which was advantageous because it allowed rigid relationships to be severed and facilitated the modernization of activities. The disadvantages were that companies stopped making long-term investments, lost their coherence and reserve capital and deprioritized considerations such as employee interests and the environment. This caused unrest in companies and among trade unions and public authorities. In a related development sovereign wealth funds were able to acquire control of companies in Europe and the US, where the influence of public authorities on the private sector had diminished at the end of the twentieth century. The 'golden share', which provided governments with effective control over companies that were important to the national economy or strategically significant, had been abolished. However, private equity funds and foreign government securities had the financial resources to acquire large blocks of shares when capital was urgently needed. This gave them a degree of influence over national economies that was neither intended nor in the national interest. Cash-rich investors from Asia and states with raw materials such as Russia and the Arab oil states obtained control in economic sectors where rich states had hitherto shaped policy. The debate on this development is taking place primarily at national level and has not reached the IGOs yet. Foreign government securities have gained similar opportunities following the outbreak of the 2007–8 credit crisis.

The credit crisis of 2007–8

The international credit crisis of 2007–8 stemmed from modernizations in the financial world and was generated by problems in the US mortgage market. Due to rising interest rates in the summer of 2007 many homeowners were unable to pay their mortgages and house prices fell as a result. The fact that lending institutions had sold a large volume of high-risk so-called sub-prime mortgages to people with few possessions or low incomes played a large role. This sub-prime crisis ignited problems in the credit market, when it emerged that investors worldwide were caught up in the housing crisis through complex financial constructions and reinsurance. Credit rating agencies were forced to substantially devalue securities and bank assets, which meant that banks found themselves in trouble and confidence was undermined. Once again the central banks tried to resolve the crisis. They made short-term loans of hundreds of billions of dollars to banks in order to stabilize the financial system. They also tried to save banks that had, for example, supported hedge funds and had invested their money in the sub-prime market. The US and European governments that had given up many of their oversight functions found themselves barely capable of assessing the impact of the many new financial products on the market. Given the ensuing loss of confidence in the financial system during the summer of 2008 they became heavily involved in the takeover and even nationalization of banks and insurance companies, as well as in the setting up of national rescue plans in order to keep the financial system functioning. It can be expected that public authorities and central banks will be working, both nationally and internationally, to develop stronger oversight mechanisms for private banks and investors, as also happened after previous financial crises and the accounting scandals of 2002. However, in this credit crisis IGOs such as the IMF, IBRD, BIS, Financial Stability Forum and even the European Union more closely resembled forums in which finance ministers met than actors involved in the management of the international economy in trouble. This is also true with worldwide economic problems such as the plummeting dollar (which the G8 and the IMF do little about), the rising prices of oil and raw materials, prompted primarily by the needs of Asian and Latin American economies, and rising food prices, of which the FAO had warned.

44.7 What happens to international organizations under pressure?

IGOs and institutional endurance: dynamism

This book has provided a comprehensive answer to the question of how intergovernmental organizations come into being. They are either created (as in the case of the Central Commission for the Navigation of the Rhine in 1815 and the IMF in 1944) or they evolve from a process of institutionalization subsequent to multilateral conferences and follow-up conferences (as in the case of public international unions). How IGOs continue their existence is a different question altogether. Their continued existence may be related to factors other than those involved in their inception. IGOs are not easily terminated, although it has happened a few times in the past. This corresponds with the sociological understanding that it is easier to create organizations than to dismantle them. There are at least two factors that account for the continuing existence of IGOs: dynamism and expertise. Once they have been established, IGOs frequently prove themselves to be dynamic rather than passive actors. Even when their founders have imposed strict limitations on them, organizations often develop in directions that the founders never wanted or predicted. However, nation-states may influence the endurance of IGOs by giving them new tasks or responsibilities. In order to do so, they can even amend the constitution of the organization, as occurred in the case of the IMF. But the continuing of an organization may also be facilitated by its staff: 'international bureaucracies created to serve international organizations may add new ambitions to those of the states: from the pursuit of specific technical goals the aim might be extended to the desire to make international relations more peaceful or to redistribute the wealth between rich and poor countries. Thus, once established, organizations take on a life of their own and develop their own inner dynamics' (Cox and Jacobson 1973, 7). In such cases there are limitations, but these IGOs manage to successfully argue that the new tasks fall within the scope of their objectives and, consequently, they have implicit powers, as needed, to fulfil those tasks. In other words, IGOs play a role in their own continued existence, interpret their constitutions broadly to that end and succeed in persuading the state parties to agree and to provide the necessary resources.

IGOs and institutional endurance: expertise

The second factor that contributes to the continuing existence of IGOs is expertise. An IGO garners expertise by regularly examining the effects of its regulatory activities or provided services. Because states are required to draft periodic reports on the implementation of joint policies and IGOs have an institutional memory that is inherent in modern bureaucracy, the organizations accumulate knowledge by observing trends in time and acquiring multi-country comparative perspectives. IGOs can use this expertise to fortify their authority. Their openness to input from multiple sources allows them also to absorb information and ideas of non-government origin, such as from experts, NGOs and transnational advocacy networks. IGOs combine this kind of expertise with their own when trying to find appropriate solutions to current problems. These solutions are often extensions of previously conceived paths upon which they build, as can be seen in revisions of international conventions (incremental decision making and path dependency). Because IGOs have to take into account what states want and because states do not always seek the most appropriate solutions but rather solutions that uphold the balance of power, according to the logic of consequentialism, the pathways of IGO activity sometimes meander. However, an appealing characteristic of IGOs (and the NGOs that support them) is that they demonstrate a degree of tenacity in their search for appropriate solutions, whether this takes time or not. Even the most powerful state, the US, has difficulty exercising control over organizations such as the IMF and IBRD. Irrespective of whether their actions are effective, IGOs tenaciously pursue the tasks they are given, debate issues expertly and demand resources for their activities. It is not insignificant that states are willing to make huge financial resources available to facilitate problem solving through international organizations.

Why do IGOs never die?

Political scientist Susan Strange pondered the question of why IGOs never, or rarely, die. Even the 'exogenous shock' of the First World War precipitated the end of no more than one-fifth of the existing IGOs (see Figure 8.2) and IGOs also survived the Second World War or were revived in an improved version. This book discusses several IGOs that have exhibited serious shortcomings or have been short-listed for dissolution. Yet the actual number of 'deaths' and terminations remains small. Strange believes that this is related to the fact that international bureaucracies are closely intertwined with the national bureaucracies from which many international officials emanate. She holds that bureaucracies 'that have a symbiotic relationship with well-entrenched national bureaucracies staff them' (Strange 1998, 217). Many national officials are well acquainted with IGOs and even receive training and experience at IGOs. Strange lists the IMF, ILO and Western European Union as examples of IGOs that at a certain point in time have functioned inadequately but were not abolished. In all these cases, 'the staffs of international organizations were allowed to carry on their jobs and to enjoy a comparatively enjoyable lifestyle'. The additional explanation she gives is a more legalistic one, related to the agreements binding member states of these IGOs to observe certain responsibilities towards the staff members of the international secretariats (Strange 1998, 218).

IGOs under pressure

There is another additional explanation of why IGOs rarely die, which is that situations in which IGOs function poorly can be evaluated so as to help these organizations improve their performance. If an IGO is subjected to pressure and criticism, it is to be expected that its personnel will do their best to ensure the organization survives. This can be done by evaluating the situation, making use of the organization's expertise and authority and marshalling resources to demonstrate that the organization still has value. When the IAEA came under criticism in the 1990s for its inadequate oversight performance the organization was able to consolidate resources and improve its performance. When the UNDP was at risk of dissolution, it warded off its demise by developing new indices and insightful publications. The ILO was also able to fight back and regain its position. In other words, a period of underperformance can offer a window of opportunity for an organization to adapt and survive. In some cases reform is an ongoing and repeated process. The UN is a good example. In response to criticism from the US in the 1990s Kofi Annan successfully implemented a firm reorganization, which certainly did not weaken the UN Secretariat. Eventually this reorganization made the UN Secretariat under Annan even stronger. International organizations may find themselves under pressure at the beginning of the twenty-first century, but their institutional endurance is not necessarily under threat. They may have to adapt, but they will do their utmost to continue their work.

Appendix 1

Nation-states in the international system since 1815 (by continent, in chronologic order) and League of Nations and United Nations membership

Existence since 1815	Nation-state	Member League of Nations*	Member United Nations*
Europe			
1815–70	Baden		
1815–61	Two Sicilies		
1815–70	Bavaria		
1815–1940; 1945	Denmark	1919★	1945★
1815	United Kingdom	1919★	1945★
1815–1942; 1944	France	1919★	1945★
1815–67	Hesse Grand Ducal /-Darmstadt		
1815–66	Hesse Electoral /-Kassel		
1815–1940; 1945	Netherlands	1919	1945★
1815–1918	Austria-Hungary		
1815–60/70	Papal States		
1815	Portugal	1919★	1955
1815–70	Prussia		
1815–1922	Russia		
1815–67	Saxony		
1815	San Marino		1992
1815–59	Sardinia		
1815	Spain	1919★–39	1955
1815–60	Tuscany		
1815–70	Württemberg		
1815	Sweden	1919★	1946
1815	Switzerland	1919★	2002
1828–1941; 1945	Greece	1919★	1945★
1830–1940; 1945	Belgium	1919★	1945★
1838–66	Hannover		
1842–60	Modena		
1843–67	Mecklenburg-Schwerin		

(continued)

Existence since 1815	Nation-state	Member League of Nations*	Member United Nations*
1851–60	Parma		
1860	Italy	1919*–37	1955
1861	Monaco		1993
1866	Liechtenstein		1990
1871–1945	Germany	1926–33	
1878	Romania	1919*–40	1955
1878–1918	Serbia		
1905–40; 1945	Norway	1919*	1945*
1908	Bulgaria	1920	1955
1914–39; 1944	Albania	1920–39	1955
1918–40; 1991	Estonia	1921	1991
1918–40; 1991	Latvia	1921	1991
1918–40; 1991	Lithuania	1921	1991
1918–39; 1945–1992	Czechoslovakia	1919*	1945*–92
1919	Finland	1920	1955
1919	Hungary	1922–39	1955
1919–41; 1944–2000	Yugoslavia	1919*	1945*–2000
1919–38; 1955	Austria	1920–38	1955
1919–39; 1945	Poland	1919*	1945*
1920–40; 1944	Luxembourg	1920	1945*
1922	Ireland	1923	1955
1922–91	Soviet Union	1934–39	1945*–91
1929	Vatican City/Holy See		Observer
1944	Iceland		1946
1954–90	German Democratic Republic/East Germany		1973–90
1955–90; 1990	Federal Republic of Germany/West Germany		1973–90; 1990
1960	Cyprus		1960
1964	Malta		1964
1991	Ukraine		1945*
1991	Belarus		1945*
1991	Russian Federation		1991
1992	Bosnia and Herzegovina		1992
1992	Croatia		1992
1992	Moldova		1992
1992	Uzbekistan		1992
1992	Slovenia		1992
1992	Former Yugoslav Republic of Macedonia		1993
1993	Andorra		1993
1993	Slovakia		1993
1993	Czech Republic		1993

(continued)

Existence since 1815	Nation-state	Member League of Nations★	Member United Nations★
2000–03; 2003–06	Federal Republic of Yugoslavia/2003: Serbia and Montenegro/2006: Serbia		2000
2006	Montenegro		2006
2008	Republic of Kosovo (self-declared and only recognized by a number of states)		
Western Hemisphere (Americas)			
1815	United States of America		1945★
1826	Brazil	1919★–26	1945★
1831	Colombia	1919★	1945★
1831	Mexico	1931	1945★
1838	Peru	1919★–39	1945★
1839	Chile	1919★–38	1945★
1841	Argentina	1919★	1945★
1841	Venezuela	1919★–38	1945★
1848	Bolivia	1919★	1945★
1849	Guatemala	1919★–36	1945★
1854	Ecuador	1934	1945★
1859	Haiti	1919★–42	1945★
1875	El Salvador	1919★–37	1945★
1882	Uruguay	1919★	1945★
1887	Dominican Republic	1924	1945★
1896	Paraguay	1919★–35	1945★
1899	Honduras	1919★–36	1945★
1900	Nicaragua	1919★–36	1945★
1902	Cuba	1919★	1945★
1920	Canada	1919★	1945★
1920	Costa Rica	1920–25	1945★
1920	Panama	1919★	1945★
1962	Jamaica		1962
1962	Trinidad and Tobago		1962
1966	Barbados		1966
1966	Guyana		1966
1973	Bahamas		1973
1974	Grenada		1974
1975	Surinam		1975
1978	Dominica		1978
1979	Saint Lucia		1979
1979	Saint Vincent and the Grenadines		1980
1981	Antigua and Barbuda		1981
1981	Belize		1981
1983	Saint Kitts and Nevis		1983
Asia and Pacific			
1860	China	1919★	1945★–50; 1971
1860–1945; 1952	Japan	1919★–33	1956
1887	Siam/1948: Thailand	1919★	1946
1888–1905	Korea		
1912–51	Tibet		
1920	Afghanistan	1920–34	1946
1920	Australia	1919★	1945★

(continued)

Existence since 1815	Nation-state	Member League of Nations*	Member United Nations*
1920	Nepal		1955
1920	New Zealand	1919*	1945*
1921	Mongolia		1961
1946	Philippines		1945*
1947	India	1919*	1945*
1947	Pakistan		1947
1948	Burma/1989: Myanmar		1948
1948	Ceylon/1972: Sri Lanka		1955
1948	People's Republic of Korea/North Korea		1991
1948	Republic of Korea/South Korea		1991
1949	Bhutan		1971
1949	Indonesia		1950
1949	Taiwan		1950–71
1953	Cambodia		1955
1954	Laos		1955
1954–76; 1976	Democratic Republic of Vietnam/North Vietnam/ 1976: Socialist Republic of Vietnam		1977
1954–75	Republic of Vietnam/South Vietnam		
1957	Malaysia		1957
1962	Samoa		1976
1965	Maldives		1965
1965	Singapore		1965
1970	Fiji		1970
1970	Tonga		1999
1971	Bangladesh		1974
1975	Papua New Guinea		1975
1978	Solomon Islands		1978
1978	Tuvalu		2000
1979	Kiribati		1999
1980	Vanuatu		1981
1984	Brunei Darussalam		1984
1986	Micronesia		1991
1990	Marshall Islands		1991
1991	Armenia		1992
1992	Azerbaijan		1992
1992	Georgia		1992
1992	Kazakhstan		1992
1992	Kyrgyzstan		1992
1992	Tajikistan		1992
1992	Turkmenistan		1992
1994	Palau		1994
1997	Nauru		1999
1999	East Timor		2002

Middle East

Existence since 1815	Nation-state	Member League of Nations*	Member United Nations*
1815	Turkey	1932	1945*
1847–1911; 1956	Morocco		1956
1855	Persia/1935: Iran	1919*	1945*
1926	Yemen, Arab Republic of/1990: Yemen (= merger Arab Republic of Yemen and Democratic People's Republic of Yemen)		1947; 1990

(continued)

Existence since 1815	Nation-state	Member League of Nations★	Member United Nations★
1927	Saudi Arabia		1945★
1932	Iraq	1932	1945★
1937–58; 1961	Egypt/1958: United Arab Republic (= Egypt and Syria)/1961: Egypt, Arab Republic of	1937	1945★
1946	Jordan		1955
1946	Lebanon		1945★
1946–58; 1961	Syria		1945★–58; 1961
1948	Israel		1949
1952	Libya		1955
1956	Sudan		1956
1956	Tunisia		1956
1961	Kuwait		1963
1962	Algeria		1962
1967–90	Democratic People's Republic of Yemen		1967–90
1970	Oman		1971
1971	Bahrain		1971
1971	Qatar		1971
1971	United Arab Emirates		1971
1974	Palestine Liberation Organization (not a state, but in 1988 the UN General Assembly decided to use the designation 'Palestine' in place of the designation PLO in the UN system)		Observer
Africa			
1898–1936; 1941	Ethiopia	1923	1945★
1920	Liberia	1919★	1945★
1920	South Africa	1919★	1945★
1957	Ghana		1957
1958	Guinea		1958
1960	Central African Republic		1960
1960	Congo (Brazzaville)		1960
1960	Dahomey/1975: Benin		1960
1960	Democratic Republic of the Congo (also Zaire, Congo Kinshasa)		1960
1960	Gabon		1960
1960	Côte d'Ivoire/Ivory Coast		1960
1960	Cameroon		1960
1960	Malagasy Republic/Madagascar		1960
1960	Mali		1960
1960	Mauretania		1961
1960	Niger		1960
1960	Nigeria		1960
1960	Upper Volta/1984: Burkina Faso		1960
1960	Senegal		1960
1960	Somalia		1960
1960	Togo		1960
1960	Chad		1960
1961	Sierra Leone		1961
1961–64	Tanganyika		1961–64
1962	Burundi		1962
1962	Uganda		1962

(continued)

Existence since 1815	Nation-state	Member League of Nations*	Member United Nations*
1962	Rwanda		1962
1963	Kenya		1963
1963–64	Zanzibar		1963–64
1964	Tanzania, United Republic of (= union Tanganyika and Zanzibar)		1964
1964	Malawi		1964
1964	Zambia		1964
1965	Gambia		1965
1966	Botswana		1966
1966	Lesotho		1966
1968	Equatorial Guinea		1968
1968	Mauritius		1968
1968	Swaziland		1968
1974	Guinea–Bissau		1974
1975	Angola		1976
1975	Comoros		1975
1975	Cape Verde		1975
1975	Mozambique		1975
1975	São Tomé and Príncipe		1975
1976	Seychelles		1976
1977	Djibouti		1977
1980	Zimbabwe		1980
1990	Namibia		1990
1993	Eritrea		1993

Source: (Singer and Wallace 1970, 524–5); (Moore and Pubantz 2002, 409–11); (Van Ginneken 2006, 217–8); small corrections and additions: *Encyclopedia Britannica*.

* Co-founder of the League of Nations/United Nations.

Appendix 2

Groups of states (First, Second and Third World, G3-G77)

FIRST WORLD: Umbrella term to identify the advanced, industrialized (capitalist) economies, also referring to democracies and to 'wealthy' states with a high standard of living. To be distinguished from the 'second' or communist world and from the 'third' or developing world. **North:** Economic and political counterpart to South: the rich and industrialized states (both capitalist and communist), most of which are located in the Northern Hemisphere. **Industrialized states:** Counterpart to the states with economies dominated by commodities and agriculture, or less-industrialized states. **Advanced economies:** IMF term for some 30 states, representing the top group of the industrialized states, referring to a high gross domestic product and a high per capita income. **High-income economies** is the term used by the IBRD. **Developed states:** OECD term for some 35 states, representing the top group of the industrialized states.

SECOND WORLD: Umbrella term to identify the communist states, within the sphere of both the Soviet Union and China, although China was also seen as part of the Third World. **Communist states:** States with authoritarian (often one-party) political systems and centrally-planned economies, many of them under the leadership of the Soviet Union and many belonging to the North rather than the South. **Socialist states:** States with public ownership of the means of production. Socialist states have abolished capitalism and are moving towards communism. The 1936 Constitution of the Soviet Union used the term for the first time. Since the 1970s the term **real socialism** was used. **Centrally-planned economies:** Communist economies, often based on the model of the Soviet Union, also called command economies, with the government managing the economic system and the economy. **States in transition:** The former communist states after the end of the Cold War, developing towards market-oriented economies and democracies. **FSU:** Former Soviet Union: group of 15 successor states to the Soviet Union. **FSU/ CEE:** Former Soviet Union and Central and Eastern Europe: group of 27 successor states to the Soviet Union and the former communist states in Central and Eastern Europe. **Near abroad:** Russian term for the other successor states of the Soviet Union.

THIRD WORLD: Umbrella term to identify the 'less developed' states, often former colonies, which had in common that they had been excluded from power positions in the world. Originally the term was meant to avoid the negative connotation of 'backward', 'uncivilized' or 'underdeveloped' states and it referred to the potentially revolutionary perspective of the Third Estate in the French Revolution. During the Cold War this perspective was to a certain extent expressed in the 'third' position of the non-aligned countries between 'West' and 'East' (see §22.3), but the term was also disputed, as it gave the Third World the lowest ranking after the Second and First Worlds. After the end of the Cold War it was replaced by **developing world**. **South:** Economic and political counterpart to North: the states with weaker economies and state institutions, most of which are located in the Southern Hemisphere, although 'South' can also be found in North, even within developed states. **Developing states:** IMF term for some 120 to 140 states with an undeveloped or developing industrial base and a low per capita income. According to the IBRD in 2007 there were 24 developing states in Europe and Central Asia, 23 in East Asia and the Pacific, 8 in South Asia, 29 in Latin and Central America, 13 in the Middle East and North Africa and 47 in Sub-Saharan Africa, totalling 144 developing states. **Low–income and middle–income economies:** From the 1970s the IBRD has considered gross national income the best single indicator for economic capacity and progress. Developing economies are both low- and middle-income economies. In 2007 low was: 935 dollars or less; lower-middle: 936 to 3,705 dollars; upper-middle: 3,706 to 11,455 dollars; and high: 11,456 dollars or more. There are 49 low-income economies, 54 lower-middle-income economies, 41 upper-middle-incomes and 65 high-income economies (including 29 OECD economies), totalling 209 economies (both states and in some cases parts of states). **LDCs:** Least-developed countries, also referred to as **Fourth World**. UN term for some 25 states in 1968 (41 in 1991 and 49 in 2008) with low incomes, a human resource weakness and economic vulnerability. **LLDCs:** Landlocked developing countries, constrained as a result of isolation from world markets. **HIPC:** Highly indebted poor countries, an IMF and IBRD term from 1996 for some 33 poor states that cannot manage their debt burden and can receive support. **Advanced developing states:** Term used for developing states with strong industrial development. **Emerging and developing economies:** IMF term for developing states that have attracted large amounts of foreign direct investment in all sectors of their economy. **Emerging markets:** IBRD term for some 12 large developing states with rapid industrialization. **NICs/NIEs:** Newly-industrializing countries / economies: developing states with rapid industrial development that are more advanced than most developing states, but not yet developed states. **Four Tigers:** four Asian developing states with strong economic growth and rapid industrialization from the 1960s, now belonging to the advanced economies (see §29.3).

G-Groups (G3-G77)

G3   policy coordination between Colombia, Mexico and Venezuela in October 1990

G5   France, Germany, Japan, the UK and the US; informal summitry, established in 1975 when Japan joined the Library Group of finance ministers of the other four states (see §27.3). The G7 superseded the G5 at the level of finance ministers in 1986–87

G7   G5 plus Canada and Italy from 1975 (see §27.3)

G8   G7 plus Russian Federation from 1998 (see §27.3)

G8   Australia, Canada, European Community, Japan, Spain, Sweden, Switzerland and the US; policy coordination between industrialized states during the Conference on International Economic Cooperation (December 1975-June 1977) (see §26.4), established in October 1975 (see also G19)

G10 Belgium, Canada, France, Germany, Italy, Japan, Netherlands, Sweden, Switzerland (from April 1964), the UK and the US; observers: BIS, European Commission, IMF and OECD; participants in the General Agreement to Borrow, established in October 1962 (see §27.1)

G15 Algeria, Argentina, Brazil, Egypt, India, Indonesia, Jamaica, Malaysia, Mexico, Nigeria, Peru, Senegal, Venezuela, Yugoslavia, Zimbabwe; later 17 members: also Chile, Kenya and Sri Lanka, but not Yugoslavia; established in September 1989 by the Non-Aligned Movement (see Figure 22.2), focusing on cooperation in investment, trade and technology

G19 Algeria, Argentina, Brazil, Cameroon, Democratic Republic of the Congo, Egypt, India, Indonesia, Iran, Iraq, Jamaica, Mexico, Nigeria, Pakistan, Peru, Saudi Arabia, Venezuela, Yugoslavia and Zambia; policy coordination between developing states during the Conference on International Economic Cooperation (December 1975-June 1977) (see §26.4), established in October 1975 (see also G8)

G20 Argentina, Australia, Brazil, Canada, China, France, Germany, India, Indonesia, Italy, Japan, Korea, Mexico, Russia, Saudi Arabia, South Africa, Turkey, the UK and the US; established on 15–16 December 1999 (superseding the G33), comprising the finance ministers and central bank governors of the G7, 12 other 'key states' and Russia, plus the European Union Presidency (if not a G7 member), the European Central Bank, the IMF managing director, the International Monetary and Financial Committee chairman, the IBRD president and the Development Committee chairman (see §41.1)

G22 Argentina, Australia, Brazil, China, Hong Kong SAR (Special Administrative Region), India, Indonesia, Korea, Malaysia, Mexico, Poland, Russia, Singapore, South Africa and Thailand; established in November 1997 at the APEC meeting in Vancouver on a temporary basis, comprising the finance ministers and central bank governors from the G7 plus 15 other states; superseded by the G33 in early 1999 and by the G20 later that year

G22 Argentina, Bolivia, Brazil, Chile, China, Columbia, Costa Rica, Cuba, Ecuador, Egypt, Guatemala, India, Indonesia, Mexico, Nigeria, Pakistan, Paraguay, Peru, Philippines, South Africa, Thailand and Venezuela; alliance of 22 developing states within the WTO Doha Round, established on 4 September 2003 (see §44.6)

G24 Algeria, Argentina, Brazil, Colombia, Côte d'Ivoire, Democratic Republic of the Congo, Egypt, Ethiopia, Gabon, Ghana, Guatemala, India, Iran, Lebanon, Mexico, Nigeria, Pakistan, Peru, Philippines, Sri Lanka, Syria, Trinidad and Tobago, Venezuela and Yugoslavia (replaced by South Africa); established in January 1972 to coordinate the positions of developing states within the IMF

G33 Argentina, Australia, Belgium, Brazil, Canada, Chile, China, Côte d'Ivoire, Egypt, France, Germany, Hong Kong SAR, India, Indonesia, Italy, Japan, Korea, Malaysia, Mexico, Morocco, Netherlands, Poland, Russia, Saudi Arabia, Singapore, South Africa, Spain, Sweden, Switzerland, Thailand, Turkey, the UK and the US; established in early 1999, superseding the G22 from 1977 and superseded by the G20 later that year

G77 established on 15 June 1964 by 77 developing states in the context of UNCTAD (see §29.2 and Figure 29.4); with 130 member states in 2008 but retaining its original name

767

Literature

Alcock, A. (1971) *History of the International Labour Organisation*, London: Macmillan.

Alder, K. (2002) *The Measure of All Things. The Seven-Year Odyssey and Hidden Error That Transformed the World*, New York: Free Press.

Archer, C. (1992) *International Organizations*, London: Routledge.

Armstrong, D., Lloyd, L. *et al.* (1996) *From Versailles to Maastricht. International Organisation in the Twentieth Century*, Houndmills: Macmillan.

Ashworth, W. (1962) *A Short History of the International Economy Since 1850*, London: Longman.

Axline, W.A. (ed.) (1994) *The Political Economy of Regional Cooperation. Comparative Case Studies*, London: Pinter Publishers.

Baer, G.W. (1973) 'Sanctions and Security: The League of Nations and the Italian–Ethiopian War, 1935–36', *International Organization*, 27(1): 165–79.

Bailey, S.D. and Daws, S. (1995) *The United Nations. A Concise Political Guide*, 3rd edn, Houndmills: Macmillan.

Bakker, A.F.P. (1996) *International Financial Institutions*, London and New York: Addison Wesley Longman.

Baldwin, D.A. (ed.) (1993) *Neorealism and Neoliberalism. The Contemporary Debate*, New York: Columbia University Press.

Banton, M. (2002) *The International Politics of Race*, Cambridge: Polity.

Barnett, M. and Finnemore, M. (1999) 'The Politics, Power, and Pathologies of International Organizations', *International Organization*, 53(4): 699–732.

——(2004) *Rules for the World. International Organizations in Global Politics*, Ithaca, NY: Cornell University Press.

Bauer, S. (2006) 'Does Bureaucracy Really Matter? The Authority of Intergovernmental Treaty Secretariats in Global Environmental Politics', *Global Environmental Politics*, 6(1): 23–49.

——(2006) 'The United Nations and the Fight against Desertification: What Role for the UNCCD Secretariat?' in P.M. Johnson, K. Mayrand *et al.* (eds) *Governing Global Desertification. Linking Environmental Degradation, Poverty and Participation*, Aldershot: Ashgate.

Bayne, N. (2000) *Hanging in There. The G7 and G8 Summit in Maturity and Renewal*, Aldershot: Ashgate.

Beigbeder, Y. (2000) 'The United Nations Secretariat: Reform in Progress', in P. Taylor and A.J.R. Groom (eds) *The United Nations at Millennium. The Principal Organs*, London and New York: Continuum, 196–223.

Bethkenhagen, J. and Machowski, H. (1976) *Integration im Rat fuer gegenseitigen Wirtschaftshilfe. Entwicklung, Organisation, Erfolge und Grenzen*, Berlin: Berlin-Verlag.

Bircham, E. and Charlton, J. (eds) (2001) *Anticapitalism. A Guide to the Movement*, London: Bookmarks Publications.

Birnie, P. (1991) 'Environmental Diplomacy', in R. Barnston (ed.) *International Politics Since 1945. Key Issues in the Making of the Modern World*, Aldershot: Edward Elgar, 242–72.

Blight, J.G., Allyn, B.J. *et al.* (1993) *Cuba on the Brink. Castro, the Missile Crisis, and the Soviet Collapse*, New York: Pantheon Books.

Boas, M. and McNeill, D. (eds) (2004) *Global Institutions and Development*. London: Routledge.

Bourantonis, D. and Wiener, J. (eds) (1995) *The United Nations in the New World Order. The World Organization at Fifty*, Houndmills: Macmillan.

Bowett, D.W. (1982) *The Law of International Institutions*, London: Stevens & Sons.

Brecher, J. and Costello, T. (1998) *Global Village or Global Pillage. Economic Reconstruction from the Bottom Up*, 2nd edn, Cambridge, MA: South End Press.

Brecher, J., Costello, T. *et al.* (2000) *Globalization from Below. The Power of Solidarity*, Cambridge, MA: South End Press.

Brown, M.H. and May, J. (1989) *The Greenpeace Story*, London and New York: Dorling Kindersley.

Bugnion, F. (2000) 'The Geneva Conventions of 12 August 1949: From the 1949 Diplomatic Conference to the New Millennium', *International Affairs*, 76(1): 41–50.

Buzan, B. and Little, R. (2000) *International Systems in World History. Remaking the Study of International Relations*, Oxford: Oxford University Press.

Cain, K., Postlewait, H. *et al.* (2004) *Emergency Sex and other Desperate Measures. A True Story from Hell on Earth*, New York: Miramax Books.

Caporaso, J.A. (1996) 'The European Union and Forms of State: Westphalian, Regulatory or Post-Modern?' *Journal of Common Market Studies*, 34(1): 29–52.

Carr, E.H. (1940) *The Twenty Years' Crisis 1919–1939. An Introduction to the Study of International Relations*, London: Macmillan.

Carter, A. (1992) *Peace Movements. International Protest and World Politics Since 1945*, London: Longman.

Cernea, M.M. (1988) *Nongovernmental Organizations and Local Development*, Washington, DC: World Bank.

Chabot, S. (2001) 'Building Transnational Advocacy Networks before 1965: Diffusion from the Indian Nationalist Movement to the American Civil Rights Movement', in B. Arts, M. Noortmann *et al.* (eds) *Non-State Actors in International Relations*, Aldershot: Ashgate, 229–45.

Charnovitz, S. (1997) 'Two Centuries of Participation: NGOs and International Governance', *Michigan Journal of International Law*, 18(2): 183–286.

Chen, M.E. (1995) 'Engendering World Conferences: The International Women's Movement and the United Nations', *Third World Quarterly*, 16(3): 477–93.

Chesterman, S. and Pouligny, B. (2003) 'Are Sanctions Meant to Work? The Politics of Creating and Implementing Sanctions Through the United Nations', *Global Governance*, 9(4): 503–18.

Christou, G. and Simpson, S. (2008) 'International Policy Implementation Through Gate Keeping. The Internet Corporation for Assigned Names and Numbers', in J. Joachim, B. Reinalda *et al.* (eds) *International Organizations and Implementation. Enforcers, Managers, Authorities?*, London and New York: Routledge, 75–87.

Cipolla, C.M. (ed.) (1976) *The Fontana Economic History of Europe. Contemporary Economies, Part Two*, Glasgow: Collins/Fontana Books.

Clark, A.M. (2001) *Diplomacy of Conscience. Amnesty International and Changing Human Rights Norms*, Princeton, NJ: Princeton University Press.

Claude Jr, I.L. (1966) *Swords into Plowshares. The Problems and Progress of International Organization*, 3rd edn, London: University of London Press.

Clavin, P. (2000) *The Great Depression in Europe, 1929–1939*, Houndmills: Macmillan.

Cohen, R. and Kennedy, P. (2000) *Global Sociology*, Houndmills: Palgrave Macmillan.

Colijn, K. (1998) 'Non-Proliferation: Reinforcing the IAEA Nuclear Safeguards Regime in the 1990s', in B. Reinalda and B. Verbeek (eds) *Autonomous Policy Making by International Organizations*, London: Routledge, 93–107.

Cook, N. (2002) *New Partnership for Africa's Development (NEPAD). CRS Report for Congress RS21353*, Washington, DC: Congressional Research Service.

Cooper Jr, J.M. (2001) *Breaking the Heart of the World. Woodrow Wilson and the Fight for the League of Nations*, Cambridge: Cambridge University Press.

Cooper, S.E. (1985) 'Goegg, Marie Pouchoulin', in H. Josephson *Biographical Dictionary of Modern Peace Leaders*, Westport, CT: Greenwood Press, 338–39.

Cooper, S. and Taylor, B. (2003) 'Power and Regionalism: Explaining Regional Cooperation in the Persian Gulf', in F. Laursen (ed.) *Comparative Regional Integration. Theoretical Perspectives*, Aldershot: Ashgate, 105–24.

Cortright, D. and Lopez, G.A. (2000) *The Sanctions Decade. Assessing UN Strategies in the 1990s*, Boulder, CO: Lynne Rienner.

Council of Europe (1991) *The Council of Europe and Human Rights*, Strasbourg: Council of Europe.

——(1991) *The European Social Charter. Origin, Operation and Results*, Strasbourg: Council of Europe Press.

Cox, R.W. (1973) 'ILO: Limited Monarchy', in R.W. Cox and H.K. Jacobson (eds) *The Anatomy of Influence. Decision Making in International Organization*, New Haven, CT: Yale University Press, 102–38.

——(1977) 'Labor and Hegemony', *International Organization*, 31(3): 385–424.

——(1979) 'Ideologies and the New International Economic Order. Reflections on Some Recent Literature', *International Organization*, 33(2): 257–302.

——(1980) 'The Crisis of World Order and the Problem of International Organization in the 1980s', *International Journal*, 35(2): 370–95.

——(1987) *Production, Power, and World Order. Social Forces in the Making of History*, New York: Columbia University Press.

Cox, R.W. and Jacobson, H.K. (eds) (1973) *The Anatomy of Influence. Decision Making in International Organization*, New Haven, CT: Yale University Press.

Curzon, G. and Curzon, V. (1973) 'GATT: Traders' Club', in R.W. Cox and H.K. Jacobson (eds) *The Anatomy of Influence. Decision Making in International Organization*, New Haven, CT: Yale University Press, 298–333.

Cutts, M. (ed.) (2000) *The State of the World's Refugees 2000. Fifty Years of Humanitarian Action*. Oxford: Oxford University Press.

Da Motta Velga, P. (1999) 'Brazil in Mercosur: Reciprocal Influence', in R. Roett (ed.) *Mercosur. Regional Integration, World Markets*, Boulder, CO: Lynne Rienner, 25–33.

De Király, F. (1929) 'International Cartels and their Effects on the Progress of International Law', *Transactions of the Grotius Society*, 15: 17–33.

Dedman, M.J. (1996) *The Origins and Development of the European Union 1945–95. A History of European Integration*, London: Routledge.

Deibert, R.J. (2000) 'International Plug 'n Play? Citizen Activism, the Internet, and Global Public Policy', *International Studies Perspectives*, 1(3): 255–72.

Dembinski, L., O'Regan, R. et al. (eds) (1985) *International Geneva 1985*, Lausanne: Payot.

Dennis, P.M. and Brown, M.L. (2003) 'The ECOWAS: From Regional Economic Organization to Regional Peacekeeper', in F. Laursen (ed.) *Comparative Regional Integration: Theoretical Perspectives*, Aldershot: Ashgate, 229–49.

Dimitrov, R.S. (2003) 'Knowledge, Power, and Interests in Environmental Regime Formation', *International Studies Quarterly*, 47(1): 123–50.

Dobson, A. (2004) 'Globalization and the Environment', in V. George and R.M. Page (eds) *Global Social Problems*, Cambridge: Polity Press, 45–61.

Donnelly, J. (1986) 'International Human Rights: A Regime Analysis', *International Organization*, 40(3): 599–642.

——(2003) *Universal Human Rights in Theory and Practice*, 2nd edn, Ithaca, NY: Cornell University Press.

Drake, W.J. and Nicolaides, K. (1992) 'Ideas, Interests, and Institutionalization: "Trade in Services" and the Uruguay Round', *International Organization*, 46(1): 37–100.

Dresang, D.L. and Sharkansky, I. (1973) 'Public Corporations in Single-Country and Regional Settings: Kenya and the East African Community', *International Organization*, 27(3): 303–27.

Dubin, M.D. (1983) 'Transgovernmental Processes in the League of Nations', *International Organization*, 37(3): 469–93.

Duchêne, F. (1994) *Jean Monnet. The First Statesman of Interdependence*, New York: W.W. Norton & Co.

Eichengreen, B. and Uzan, M. (1993) 'The 1933 World Economic Conference as an Instance of Failed International Cooperation', in P.B. Evans, H.K. Jacobson *et al.* (eds) *Double-Edged Diplomacy. International Bargaining and Domestic Politics*, Berkeley, CA: University of California Press, 171–206.

Ellwood, W. (2001) *The No-Nonsense Guide to Globalization*, Oxford: New Internationalist Publications & Verso.

Emeka Okolo, J. (1985) 'Integrative and Cooperative Regionalism: The Economic Community of West African States', *International Organization*, 39(1): 121–53.

Enloe, C. (1989) *Bananas, Beaches & Bases. Making Feminist Sense of International Politics*, London: Pandora.

Evans, R.J. (1977) *The Feminists. Women's Emancipation Movements in Europe, America and Australasia 1840–1920*, London: Croom Helm.

Eyffinger, A. (1996) *The International Court of Justice 1946–1996*, The Hague: Kluwer Law International.

Farer, T.J. (1988) 'The UN and Human Rights: More than a Whimper, Less than a Roar', in A. Roberts and B. Kingsbury (eds) *United Nations, Divided World. The UN's Roles in International Relations*, Oxford: Clarendon Press, 95–138.

Fawcett, L. and Hurrell, A. (eds) (2000) *Regionalism in World Politics. Regional Organization and International Order*. Oxford: Oxford University Press.

Feld, W.J., Jordan, R.S. *et al.* (1994) *International Organizations. A Comparative Approach*, 3rd edn, Westport, CT: Praeger.

Fennema, M. (1982) *International Networks of Banks and Industry*, Den Haag: Martinus Nijhoff.

Finger, M., Tamiotti, L. *et al.* (eds) (2006) *The Multi-Governance of Water. Four Case Studies*. Albany, NY: State University of New York Press.

Finlayson, J.A. and Zacher, M.W. (1981) 'The GATT and the Regulation of Trade Barriers: Regime Dynamics and Functions', *International Organization*, 35(4): 273–314.

Finnemore, M. (1996) *National Interests in International Society*, Ithaca, NY: Cornell University Press.

Finnemore, M. and Sikkink, K. (1998) 'International Norm Dynamics and Political Change', *International Organization*, 52(4): 887–917.

Forsythe, D.P. (1976) 'The Red Cross as Transnational Movement: Conserving and Changing the Nation-State System', *International Organization*, 30(4): 607–30.

——(2000) *Human Rights in International Relations*, Cambridge: Cambridge University Press.

Frank, A.G. (1969) *Latin America. Underdevelopment and Revolution*, New York: Monthly Review Press.

Fred-Mensah, B.K. (2004) 'Social Capital Building as Capacity for Postconflict Development: The UNDP in Mozambique and Rwanda', *Global Governance*, 10(4): 437–57.

Freitas, R. (2004) 'UNHCR's Decision Making on Internally Displaced Persons: The Impact of External and Internal Factors on Policy Strategy', in B. Reinalda and B. Verbeek (eds) *Decision Making Within International Organizations*, London: Routledge, 123–36.

Galtung, J. (1978) *Toward Self-Reliance and Global Interdependence: Reflections on a New International Order and North–South Cooperation*, Ottawa: Canadian International Development Agency and Environment Canada.

Gathorne-Hardy, G.M. (1952) *A Short History of International Affairs 1920–1939*, 4th edn, London: Oxford University Press.

Ghebali, V.-Y. (1989) *The International Labour Organisation. A Case Study on the Evolution of U.N. Specialised Agencies*, Dordrecht: Martinus Nijhoff.

Gill, S. (1991) *American Hegemony and the Trilateral Commission*, Cambridge: Cambridge University Press.

Gilpin, R. (1975) *U.S. Power and the Multinational Corporation*, New York: Basic Books.

Gordenker, L. (2005) *The UN Secretary-General and Secretariat*, London and New York: Routledge.

Gorman, R.F. (2001) *Great Debates at the United Nations. An Encyclopedia of Fifty Key Issues 1945–2000*, Westport, CT: Greenwood Press.

Gregory, F. and Stack, F. (1983) 'The European Community and International Institutions', in J. Lodge (ed.) *Institutions and Policies of the European Community*, London: Frances Pinter, 240–51.

Grzybowski, C. (2006) 'The World Social Forum: Reinventing Global Politics', *Global Governance*, 12(1): 7–13.

Guyot, E. (1968) *Histoire de la détermination de l'heure*, La Chaux-de-Fonds: Chambre Suisse de L'horhogerie.

771

Haas, E.B. (1968) *Beyond the Nation-State. Functionalism and International Organization*, 2nd edn, Stanford, CA: Stanford University Press.

——(1983) 'Regime Decay: Conflict Management and International Organizations, 1945–81', *International Organization*, 37(2): 189–256.

——(1990) *When Knowledge is Power*, Berkeley, CA: University of California Press.

Haas, P.M. (1990) *Saving the Mediterranean. The Politics of International Environmental Cooperation*, New York: Columbia University Press.

Hadjor, K.B. (1993) *Dictionary of Third World Terms*, London: Penguin Books.

Halpin, D. (ed.) (2005) *Surviving Global Change? Agricultural Interest Groups in Comparative Perspective*, Aldershot: Ashgate.

Harper, C. (2001) 'Do the Facts Matter? NGOs, Research, and International Advocacy', in M. Edwards and J. Gaventa (eds) *Global Citizen Action*, London: Earthscan, 247–58.

Haufler, V. (1993) 'Crossing the Boundary between Public and Private: International Regimes and Non-State Actors', in V. Rittberger and P. Mayer (eds) *Regime Theory and International Relations*, Oxford: Clarendon Press, 94–111.

——(2000) 'Private Sector International Regimes', in R.A. Higgott, G.R.D. Underhill *et al.* (eds) *Non-State Actors and Authority in the Global System*, London: Routledge, 121–37.

Haus, L. (1991) 'The East European Countries and GATT: The Role of Realism, Mercantilism, and Regime Theory in Explaining East-West Trade', *International Organization*, 45(2): 163–82.

Held, D., McGrew, A. *et al.* (eds) (1999) *Global Transformations. Politics, Economics and Culture*, Cambridge: Polity Press.

Henderson, K. and Robinson, N. (1997) *Post-Communist Politics. An Introduction*, London: Prentice Hall.

Higgings, R. (1998) 'Remedies and the International Court of Justice: An Introduction', in M.D. Evans (ed.) *Remedies in International Law: The Institutional Dilemma*, Oxford: Hart, 1–10.

Higgott, R.A., Underhill, G.R.D. *et al.* (2000) 'Introduction. Globalisation and Non-State Actors', in R.A. Higgott, G.R.D. Underhill *et al.* (eds) *Non-State Actors and Authority in the Global System*, London: Routledge, 1–12.

Hill, M. (1946) *The Economic and Financial Organization of the League of Nations. A Survey of Twenty-Five Years' Experience*, Washington, DC: Carnegie Endowment for International Peace.

——(1974) *Towards Greater Order, Coherence and Co-ordination in the United Nations System*, New York: UN Institute for Training and Research.

Hillier, T. (1994) *Public International Law*, London: Cavendish.

Hirschman, A.O. (1970) *Exit, Voice, and Loyalty. Responses to Decline in Firms, Organizations, and States*, Cambridge, MA: Harvard University Press.

Hirst, P. and Thompson, G. (1996) *Globalization in Question. The International Economy and the Possibilities of Governance*, Cambridge: Polity Press.

Hix, S. (2007) 'The European Union as a Polity (I)', in K.E. Joergensen, M.A. Pollack *et al.* (eds) *Handbook of European Union Politics*, London: Sage, 141–58.

Hogan, M.J. and Paterson, T.G. (eds) (1991) *Explaining the History of American Foreign Relations*. Cambridge: Cambridge University Press.

Hopkins, R.F. (1992) 'Reform in the International Food Aid Regime: The Role of Consensual Knowledge', *International Organization*, 46(1): 225–64.

Horne, J. (2004) 'The European Moment between the Two World Wars (1924–33)', in M. De Keizer and S. Tates (eds) *Moderniteit. Modernisme en massacultuur in Nederland 1914–1940*, Zutphen: Walburg Pers, 223–40.

Hout, W. (1996) 'Het "nieuwe regionalisme": mythe of werkelijkheid?' *Internationale Spectator*, 50(5): 254–60.

Huberman, M. and Lewchuk, W. (2003) 'European Economic Integration and the Labour Compact, 1850–1913', *European Review of Economic History*, 7(3): 3–41.

Hurd, I. (2005) 'The Strategic Use of Liberal Internationalism: Libya and the UN Sanctions, 1992–2003', *International Organization*, 59(3): 495–526.

ICC (1981) *Speaking up for Free Enterprise All Over the World*, Paris: International Chamber of Commerce.

772

ICW (1966) *Women in a Changing World. The Dynamic Story of the International Council of Women Since 1888*, London: Routledge & Kegan Paul.

Ikenberry, G.J. (1992) 'A World Economy Restored: Expert Consensus and the Anglo-American Postwar Settlement', *International Organization*, 46(1): 289–321.

——(2001) *After Victory. Institutions, Strategic Restraint, and the Rebuilding of Order After Major Wars*, Princeton, NJ: Princeton University Press.

ILO (1969) *ILO 1919–1969. Vijftig jaar Internationale Arbeidsorganisatie*, Alphen aan den Rijn: Samson.

——(1992) *International Labour Conventions and Recommendations 1919–1991*, Geneva: International Labour Office.

——(1994) *Defending Values, Promoting Change. Social Justice in a Global Economy: An ILO Agenda*, Geneva: International Labour Office.

Imber, M.F. (1989) *The USA, ILO, UNESCO and IAEA. Politicization and Withdrawal in the Specialized Agencies*, Houndmills: Macmillan.

IPCC (2004) *16 Years of Scientific Assessment in Support of the Climate Convention*, Geneva: IPCC.

Jackson, R. (1998) *The World Trade Organization. Constitution and Jurisprudence*, London: Royal Institute of International Affairs.

——(2000) *The Global Covenant. Human Conduct in a World of States*, Oxford: Oxford University Press.

Jacobson, H.K. (1973) 'ITU: A Potpourri of Bureaucrats and Industrialists', in R.W. Cox and H.K. Jacobson (eds) *The Anatomy of Influence. Decision Making in International Organization*, New Haven, CT: Yale University Press, 59–101.

——(1973) 'WHO: Medicine, Regionalism, and Managed Politics', in R.W. Cox and H.K. Jacobson (eds) *The Anatomy of Influence. Decision Making in International Organization*, New Haven, CT: Yale University Press, 175–215.

——(1979) *Networks of Interdependence. International Organizations and the Global Political System*, New York: Alfred A. Knopf.

Janis, I.L. (1982) *Groupthink: Psychological Studies of Policy Decisions and Fiascoes*, 2nd edn, Boston: Houghton Mifflin.

Jett, D.C. (1999) *Why Peace Keeping Fails*, New York: Palgrave Macmillan.

Joachim, J., Reinalda, B. *et al.* (eds) (2008) *International Organizations and Implementation. Enforcers, Managers, Authorities?* London and New York: Routledge.

Johnston, A.I. (1999) 'The Myth of the ASEAN Way? Explaining the Evolution of the ASEAN Regional Forum', in H. Haftendorn, R.O. Keohane *et al.* (eds) *Imperfect Unions. Security Institutions over Time and Space*, Oxford: Oxford University Press, 287–324.

Johnston, G.A. (1924) *International Social Progress. The Work of the International Labour Organisation of the League of Nations*, London: George Allen & Unwin.

——(1970) *The International Labour Organisation. Its Work for Social and Economic Progress*, London: Europa Publications.

Jokinen, J. (2004) 'Balancing between East and West. The Asian Development Bank's Policy on Good Governance', in M. Boas and D. McNeill (eds) *Global Institutions and Development. Framing the World?*, London: Routledge, 137–50.

Kahler, M. (1997) 'Inventing International Relations: International Relations Theory After 1945', in M.W. Doyle and G.J. Ikenberry (eds) *New Thinking in International Relations Theory*, Boulder, CO: Westview Press, 20–53.

Kapstein, E.B. (1992) 'Between Power and Purpose: Central Bankers and the Politics of Regulatory Convergence', *International Organization*, 46(1): 265–87.

Keck, M.E. and Sikkink, K. (1998) *Activists Beyond Borders. Advocacy Networks in International Politics*, Ithaca, NY: Cornell University Press.

Kegley Jr, C.W. (ed.) (1995) *Controversies in International Relations Theory. Realism and the Neoliberal Challenge*. New York: St Martin's Press.

Kegley Jr, C.W. and Wittkopf, E.R. (1996) *American Foreign Policy*, 5th edn, New York: St Martin's Press.

Kenwood, A.G. and Lougheed, A.L. (1971) *The Growth of the International Economy 1820–1960. An Introductory Text*, London: George Allen & Unwin.

Keohane, R.O. (1984) *After Hegemony. Cooperation and Discord in the World Political Economy*, Princeton, NJ: Princeton University Press.

——(2001) 'Governance in a Partially Globalized World', *American Political Science Review*, 95(1): 1–13.

Keohane, R.O. and Nye, J.S. (eds) (1972) *Transnational Relations and World Politics*, Cambridge, MA: Harvard University Press.

Kerr, D. (2005) 'The Sino-Russian Partnership and U.S. Policy Toward North Korea: From Hegemony to Concert in Northeast Asia', *International Studies Quarterly*, 49(3): 411–87.

Kerremans, B. (2004) 'The European Commission and the EU Member States as Actors in the WTO Negotiating Process. Decision Making between Scylla and Charibdis?' in B. Reinalda and B. Verbeek (eds) *Decision Making Within International Organizations*, London: Routledge, 45–58.

Keynes, J.M. (1920) *The Economic Consequences of the Peace*, New York: Harcourt, Brace and Howe.

Kim, S.Y. and Russett, B.M. (1996) 'The New Politics of Voting Alignments in the United Nations General Assembly', *International Organization*, 50(4): 629–52.

Klotz, A. (1995) *Norms in International Relations. The Struggle against Apartheid*, Ithaca, NY: Cornell University Press.

Kolk, A. (2001) 'Multinational Corporations and International Climate Policy', in B. Arts, M. Noortmann *et al.* (eds) *Non-State Actors in International Relations*, Aldershot: Ashgate, 211–25.

Kreisky Commission (1989) *A Programme for Full Employment in the 1990s. Report of the Kreisky Commission on Employment Issues in Europe*, Oxford: Pergamon Press.

Kriesi, H., Koopmans, R. *et al.* (1995) *New Social Movements in Western Europe. A Comparative Analysis*, Minneapolis, MN: University of Minnesota Press.

Lanteigne, M. (2005) *China and International Institutions. Alternate Paths to Global Power*, London: Routledge.

Lee, K. (1996) *Global Telecommunications Regulation. A Political Economy Perspective*, London: Pinter.

Lera St Clair, A. (2006) 'The World Bank as a Transnational Expertised Institution', *Global Governance*, 12(1): 77–95.

Leurdijk, J.H. (2006) *Armed Intervention in International Politics. A Historical and Comparative Analysis*, Nijmegen: Wolf Legal Publishers.

Levin, P.L. (2001) *Edith and Woodrow. The Wilson White House*, New York: Scribner.

Levy, D.L. and Egan, D. (2000) 'Corporate Political Action in the Global Polity', in R.A. Higgott, G.R.D. Underhill *et al.* (eds) *Non-State Actors and Authority in the Global System*, London: Routledge, 138–53.

Lieshout, R.H. (1999) *The Struggle for the Organization of Europe. The Foundations of the European Union*, Cheltenham: Edward Elgar.

Lindenberg, M. and Bryant, C. (2001) *Going Global. Transforming Relief and Development NGOs*, Bloomfield, CT: Kumarian Press.

Littlewood, J. (2005) *The Biological Weapons Convention. A Failed Revolution*, Aldershot: Ashgate.

Lobell, S.E. (1999) 'Second Image Reversed Politics: Britain's Choice of Free Trade or Imperial Preferences, 1903–6, 1917–23, 1930–32', *International Studies Quarterly*, 43(4): 671–94.

Loescher, G. (2001) *The UNHCR and World Politics*, Oxford: Oxford University Press.

Logue, J. (1980) *Toward a Theory of Trade Union Internationalism*, Gothenburg: University of Gothenburg, Department of History.

Lorwin, L.L. (1929) *Labor and Internationalism*, New York: Macmillan.

Lovecy, J. (2004) 'Framing Decisions in the Council of Europe: An Institutionalist Analysis', in B. Reinalda and B. Verbeek (eds) *Decision Making Within International Organizations*, London: Routledge, 59–73.

Luo, X. (2000) 'The Rise of the Social Development Model: Institutional Construction of International Technology Organizations, 1856–1993', *International Studies Quarterly*, 44(1): 147–75.

Lyons, F.S.L. (1963) *Internationalism in Europe 1815–1914*, Leiden: A.W. Sijthoff.

Macbean, A.I. and Snowden, P.N. (1981) *International Institutions in Trade and Finance*, London: George Allen & Unwin.

MacLaren, R. (2004) 'Integrating Environment and Labour into the World Trade Organization', in J.J. Kirton and M.J. Trebilcock (eds) *Hard Choices, Soft Law. Voluntary Standards in Global Trade, Environment and Social Governance*, Aldershot: Ashgate, 266–69.

Malamud, A. (2003) 'Presidentialism and Mercosur: A Hidden Case for a Successful Experience', in F. Laursen (ed.) *Comparative Regional Integration. Theoretical Perspectives*, Aldershot: Ashgate, 53–73.

Malanczuk, P. (1997) *Akehurst's Modern Introduction to International Law*, 7th revised edn, London: Routledge.

Malone, D.M. (ed.) (2004) *The UN Security Council. From the Cold War to the 21st Century*, Boulder, CO and London: Lynne Rienner.

Mansbach, R.W. (1994) *The Global Puzzle. Issues and Actors in World Politics*, Boston, MA: Houghton Mifflin Company.

Mansfield, E.D. and Milner, H.V. (eds) (1997) *The Political Economy of Regionalism*, New York: Columbia University Press.

——(1999) 'The New Wave of Regionalism', *International Organization*, 53(3): 589–627.

March, J.G. and Olsen, J.P. (1989) *Rediscovering Institutions. The Organizational Basis of Politics*, New York and London: The Free Press and Collier Macmillan.

Marcussen, M. (2004) 'The Organization for Economic Cooperation and Development as Ideational Artist and Arbitrator: Reality or Dream?' in B. Reinalda and B. Verbeek (eds) *Decision Making Within International Organizations*, London: Routledge, 90–105.

Marer, P. (1976) 'Prospects for Integration in the Council for Mutual Economic Assistance (CMEA)', *International Organization*, 30(4): 631–48.

Marfleet, G.B. and Miller, C. (2005) 'Failure after 1441: Bush and Chirac in the UN Security Council', *Foreign Policy Analysis*, 1(3): 333–60.

Marshall, P. (2001) 'Smuts and the Preamble to the UN Charter', *The Round Table* (358): 55–65.

Masujima, K. (2004) '"Good Governance" and the Development Assistance Committee', in M. Boas and D. McNeill (eds) *Global Institutions and Development*, London: Routledge, 151–63.

Mattli, W. (1999) *The Logic of Regional Integration. Europe and Beyond*, Cambridge: Cambridge University Press.

McKean, W. (1983) *Equality and Discrimination under International Law*, Oxford: Oxford University Press.

McNeill, D. (2004) 'Social Capital and the World Bank', in M. Boas and D. McNeill (eds) *Global Institutions and Development. Framing the World?* London: Routledge, 108–23.

Meyer, J.W., Frank, D.J. *et al.* (1997) 'The Structuring of a World Environmental Regime, 1870–1990', *International Organization*, 51(4): 623–51.

Meyers, D.B. (1974) 'Intraregional Conflict Management by the Organization of African Unity', *International Organization*, 28(3): 345–73.

Milward, A.S. (1995) *The European Rescue of the Nation-State*, London: Routledge.

Mistry, P.S. (1995) *Multilateral Development Banks. An Assessment of their Financial Structures, Policies and Practices*, The Hague: Fondad.

Mitter, S. (1986) *Common Fate, Common Bond. Women in the Global Economy*, London: Pluto Press.

Moffit, M. (1983) *The World's Money. International Banking from Bretton Woods to the Brink of Insolvency*, New York: Simon and Schuster.

Monte Hill, H. (1978) 'Community Formation within ASEAN', *International Organization*, 32(2): 569–75.

Moore Jr, J.A. and Pubantz, J. (2002) *Encyclopedia of the United Nations*, New York: Facts on File.

Moquette, F.G. (1993) *Van BEP tot BEB. De aanpassing van de bestuurlijke structuren aan de ontwikkelingen van de buitenlandse economische betrekkingen in Nederland sinds 1795*, Leiden: Universiteit Leiden.

Morgenthau, H.J. (1993) *Politics among Nations. The Struggle for Power and Peace*. Brief Edition. Revised by Kenneth W. Thompson, New York: McGraw-Hill.

Morphet, S. (2000) 'States Groups at the United Nations and Growth of Member States at the United Nations', in P. Taylor and A.J.R. Groom (eds) *The United Nations at the Millennium. The Principal Organs*, London and New York: Continuum, 224–70.

Mosley, P., Harrigan, J. *et al.* (1991) *Aid and Power. The World Bank and Policy-Lending. Volume 1. Analysis and Policy Proposals*, London: Routledge.

Murphy, C.N. (1994) *International Organization and Industrial Change. Global Governance since 1850*, Cambridge: Polity Press.

——(1997) 'What the Third World Wants: An Interpretation of the Development and Meaning of the New International Economic Order Ideology', in P.F. Diehl (ed.) *The Politics of Global Governance. International Organizations in an Interdependent World*, Boulder, CO: Lynne Rienner, 201–15.

——(2000) 'Global Governance: Poorly Done and Poorly Understood', *International Affairs*, 76(4): 789–803.

Mussa, M. (2002) *Argentina and the Fund: From Triumph to Tragedy*, Washington, DC: Institute for International Economics.

Myers, D.P. (1935) *Handbook of the League of Nations*, Boston, MA: World Peace Foundation.

Najam, A. (2003) 'The Case against a New International Environmental Organization', *Global Governance*, 9(3): 367–84.

Natsios, A.S. (1995) 'NGOs and the UN System in Complex Humanitarian Emergencies: Conflict or Cooperation?' *Third World Quarterly*, 16(3): 405–19.

Newman, E. (1995) 'Realpolitik and the CNN Factor of Humanitarian Intervention', in D. Bourantonis and J. Wiener (eds) *The United Nations in the New World Order. The World Organization at Fifty*, New York: St Martin's Press, 190–211.

Nicholson, M. (1998) 'A Rational Choice Analysis of International Organizations. How UNEP Helped to Bring About the Mediterranean Action Plan', in B. Reinalda and B. Verbeek (eds) *Autonomous Policy Making by International Organizations*, London: Routledge, 79–90.

NN (2001) *On Fire. The Battle of Genoa and the Anti-Capitalist Movement*, Edinburgh: One-Off Press.

Nustad, K.G. (2004) 'The Development Discourse in the Multilateral System', in M. Boas and D. McNeill (eds) *Global Institutions and Development. Framing the world?* London: Routledge, 13–23.

Nye, J.S. (1973) 'UNCTAD: Poor Nations' Pressure Group', in R.W. Cox and H.K. Jacobson (eds) *The Anatomy of Influence. Decision Making in International Organization*, New Haven, CT: Yale University Press, 334–70.

——(2003) *Understanding International Conflicts. An Introduction to Theory and History*, 4th edn, New York: Pearson Addison Wesley.

Oberleitner, G. (2005) 'Human Security: A Challenge to International Law?' *Global Governance*, 11(2): 185–203.

Oxfam (1995) *A Case for Reform. Fifty Years of the IMF and World Bank*, Oxford: Oxfam Publications.

Page, R.M. (2004) 'Globalization and Social Welfare', in V. George and R.M. Page (eds) *Global Social Problems*, Cambridge: Polity Press, 29–44.

Palmer, R.R. and Colton, J. (1971) *A History of the Modern World*, 4th edn, New York: Alfred A. Knopf.

Pan American Health Organization (1992) *Pro Salute Novi Mundi. A History of the Pan American Health Organization*, Washington, DC: PAHO.

Panitch, L. and Leys, C. (eds) (2002) *A World of Contradictions*. London: Merlin Press, Fernwood Publishing, Monthly Review Press.

Paul, J.A. (2004) 'Working with Nongovernmental Organizations', in D.M. Malone (ed.) *The UN Security Council. From the Cold War to the 21st Century*, Boulder, CO and London: Lynne Rienner Publishers.

Payne, A. (1994) 'The Politics of Regional Cooperation in the Caribbean: The Case of Caricom', in W.A. Axline (ed.) *The Political Economy of Regional Cooperation. Comparative Case Studies*, Madison: Fairleigh Dickinson University Press, 72–104.

Penrose, A. and Seaman, J. (1996) 'The Save the Children Fund and Nutrition for Refugees', in P. Willetts (ed.) *'The Conscience of the World'. The Influence of Non-Governmental Organisations in the UN System*, London: Hurst & Company, 241–69.

Peterson, M.J. (1986) *The General Assembly in World Politics*, Boston, MA: Unwin Hyman.

Pierson, R.R. (ed.) (1987) *Women and Peace. Theoretical, Historical and Practical Perspectives*, London: Croom Helm.

Pigman, G.A. (2002) 'A Multifunctional Case Study for Teaching International Political Economy: The World Economic Forum as Shar-pei or Wolf in Sheep's Clothing?' *International Studies Perspectives*, 3(3): 291–309.

Pinder, J. (1976) 'Europe in the World Economy 1920–70', in C.M. Cipolla (ed.) *The Fontana Economic History of Europe*, Glasgow: Collins/Fontana Books, 6: 323–75.

Piroska, D. (2005) *Small Post-Socialist States and Global Finance. A Comparative Study of the Internationalization of State Roles in Banking in Hungary and Slovenia*, Budapest: Central European University.

Plano, J.C. and Olton, R. (1982) *The International Relations Directory*, 3rd edn, Santa Barbara: ABC-CLIO.

Poku, N. (2001) *Regionalization and Security in Southern Africa*, Houndmills: Palgrave Macmillan.

Price, J. (1945) *The International Labour Movement*, London: Oxford University Press.

Radice, H. (ed.) (1975) *International Firms and Modern Imperialism*, Harmondsworth: Penguin.

Ramcharan, B.G. (2000) 'The International Court of Justice', in P. Taylor and A.J.R. Groom (eds) *The United Nations at the Millennium. The Principal Organs*, London and New York: Continuum.

Reinalda, B. (1997) '"Dea ex Machina" or the Interplay between National and International Policy Making ? A Critical Analysis of Women in the European Union', in F. Gardiner (ed.) *Sex Equality Policy in Western Europe*, London: Routledge, 197–215.

——(ed.) (1997) *The International Transportworkers Federation 1914–1945. The Edo Fimmen Era*, Amsterdam: International Institute for Social History.

——(1998) 'Organization Theory and the Autonomy of the International Labour Organization', in B. Reinalda and B. Verbeek (eds) *Autonomous Policy Making by International Organizations*, London: Routledge, 42–61.

——(2000) 'The International Women's Movement as a Private Actor between Change and Accommodation', in K. Ronit and V. Schneider (eds) *Private Organizations in Global Politics*, London: Routledge, 165–86.

——(2007) 'The Question of Input, Control and Output Legitimacy in Economic RIOs', in A. Ribeiro Hoffmann and A. van der Vleuten (eds) *Closing or Widening the Gap? Legitimacy and Democracy in Regional Integration Organizations*, Aldershot: Ashgate, 49–81.

Reinalda, B. and Kulesza, E. (2006) *The Bologna Process – Harmonizing Europe's Higher Education. Including the Essential Original Texts*, Foreword by Hans-Dieter Klingemann, 2nd revised edn, Opladen and Farmington Hills, MI: Barbara Budrich.

Reinalda, B. and Verbeek, B. (eds) (1998) *Autonomous Policy Making by International Organizations*, London: Routledge.

——(eds) (2004) *Decision Making Within International Organizations, With a Foreword by Robert W. Cox*, London and New York: Routledge.

Reinsch, P.S. (1911) *Public International Unions. Their Work and Organization*, Boston: Ginn and Company.

Richardson, D. (1995) *The League of Nations and Disarmament 1920–1930*, Second Pan-European Conference of International Relations, Paris.

Richardson, L. (1999) 'The Concert of Europe and Security Management in the Nineteenth Century', in H. Haftendorn, R.O. Keohane *et al.* (eds) *Imperfect Unions. Security Institutions over Time and Space*, Oxford: Oxford University Press, 48–79.

Riegelman Lubin, C. and Winslow, A. (1990) *Social Justice for Women. The International Labor Organization and Women*, Durham, NC, and London: Duke University Press.

Ripley, W.Z. (1915) *Trusts, Pools and Corporations*, Boston, MA: Ginn and Co.

Roett, R. (ed.) (1999) *MERCOSUR. Regional Integration, World Markets*, Boulder, CO: Lynne Rienner.

Ronit, K. (2000) 'The Good, the Bad, the Ugly? Practices of Global Self-Regulation among Dyestuffs Producers', in K. Ronit and V. Schneider (eds) *Private Organizations in Global Politics*, London: Routledge, 83–101.

Ronit, K. and Schneider, V. (eds) (2000) *Private Organisations in Global Politics*, London: Routledge.

Rose, E.A. (2005) 'From a Punitive to a Bargaining Model of Sanctions: Lessons from Iraq', *International Studies Quarterly*, 49(3): 459–79.

Rosenne, S. (1989) *The World Court. What It Is and How it Works*, 4th revised edn, Dordrecht: Martinus Nijhoff.

Rostow, W.W. (1960) *The Stages of Economic Growth. A Non-Communist Manifesto*. Cambridge: Cambridge University Press.

Rowbotham, S. (1972) *Women, Resistance and Revolution*, Harmondsworth: Penguin.

Ruggie, J.G. (2001) 'global_network.net: The Global Compact as Learning Network', *Global Governance*, 7(4): 371–78.

Rupert, M. (2000) *Ideologies of Globalization. Contending Visions of a New World Order*, London: Routledge.

Rupp, L.J. (1997) *Worlds of Women. The Making of an International Women's Movement*, Princeton, NJ: Princeton University Press.

Sanford, J.E. (2002) *Multilateral Development Banks: Issues for the 107th Congress*, CRS Issue Brief 96008, Washington, DC: Congressional Research Service.

——(2002) *World Bank: Funding IDA's Assistance Program*, CRS Report for Congress RL31418, Washington, DC: Congressional Research Service.

Schechter, M.G. (2005) *United Nations Global Conferences*, London and New York: Routledge.

Scheinman, L. (1973) 'IAEA: Atomic Condominium', in R.W. Cox and H.K. Jacobson (eds) *The Anatomy of Influence. Decision Making in International Organization*, New Haven, CT: Yale University Press, 216–62.

Schemeil, Y. (2004) 'Expertise and Political Competence: Consensus Making Within the World Trade Organization and the World Meteorological Organization', in B. Reinalda and B. Verbeek (eds) *Decision Making Within International Organizations*, London: Routledge, 77–89.

Schimmelfennig, F. (2003) *The EU, NATO and the Integration of Europe. Rules and Rhetoric*, Cambridge: Cambridge University Press.

Schnietz, K.E. (2003) 'The Reaction of Private Interests to the 1934 Reciprocal Trade Agreement Act', *International Organization*, 57(1): 213–33.

Schott, J.J. and Watal, J. (2000) 'Decision Making in the WTO', in J.J. Schott (ed.) *The WTO After Seattle*, Washington, DC: Institute for International Economics, 283–92.

Schroeder, P.W. (1996) *The Transformation of European Politics 1763–1848*, Oxford: Oxford University Press.

Schulz, M., Soderbaum, F. *et al.* (eds) (2001) *Regionalization in a Globalizing World. A Comparative Perspective on Forms, Actors and Processes*, London: ZED Books.

Seary, B. (1996) 'The Early History from the Congress of Vienna to the San Francisco Conference', in P. Willetts (ed.) *'The Conscience of the World'. The Influence of Non-Governmental Organisations in the UN System*, London: Hurst & Company, 15–30.

Sell, S.K. (2000) 'Structures, Agents and Institutions. Private Corporate Power and the Globalisation of Intellectual Property Rights', in R.A. Higgott, G.R.D. Underhill *et al.* (eds) *Non-State Actors and Authority in the Global System*, London: Routledge, 91–106.

Senghaas, D. (ed.) (1982) *Kapitalistische Weltökonomie. Kontroversen über ihren Ursprung und ihre Entwicklungsdynamik*, Frankfurt am Main: Suhrkamp.

Shannon, T.R. (1996) *An Introduction to the World-System Perspective*, 2nd edn, Boulder, CO: Westview Press.

Sharman, J.C. (2008) 'International Organizations and the Implementation of New Financial Regulations by Blacklisting', in J. Joachim, B. Reinalda *et al.* (eds) *International Organizations and Implementation. Enforcers, Managers, Authorities?*, London and New York: Routledge, 48–61.

Shawcross, W. (2000) *Deliver Us from Evil. Warlords & Peacekeepers in a World of Endless Conflict*, London: Bloomsbury.

Sikkink, K. (1986) 'Codes of Conduct for Transnational Corporations: The Case of the WHO/UNICEF Code', *International Organization*, 40(4): 815–40.

Sil, R. (2002) *Managing 'Modernity'. Work, Community, and Authority in Late-Industrializing Japan and Russia*, Ann Arbor: University of Michigan Press.

Simons, G. (1999) *Imposing Economic Sanctions. Legal Remedy or Genocidal Tool?* London: Pluto Press.

Singer, J.D. and Wallace, M. (1970) 'Intergovernmental Organization and the Preservation of Peace, 1816–1964: Some Bivariate Relationships', *International Organization*, 24(3): 520–47.

Smouts, M.-C. (2000) 'The General Assembly: Grandeur and Decadence', in P. Taylor and A.J.R. Groom (eds) *The United Nations at the Millennium. The Principal Organs*, New York and London: Continuum, 21–60.

Smuts, J.C. (1952) *Jan Christian Smuts by his Son*, London: Cassell and Company.

Smythe, E. (2000) 'State Authority and Investment Security: Non-State Actors and the Negotiation of the Multilateral Agreement on Investment at the OECD', in R.A. Higgott, G.R.D. Underhill *et al.* (eds) *Non-State Actors and Authority in the Global System*, London: Routledge, 74–90.

Soroos, M.S. (1989) *Beyond Sovereignty. The Challenge of Global Policy*, Columbia, SC: University of South Carolina Press.

Spero, J.E. (1985) *The Politics of International Economic Relations*, 3rd edn, London: George Allen & Unwin.

St Clair, A.L. (2004) 'The Role of Ideas in the United Nations Development Programme', in M. Boas and D. McNeill (eds) *Global Institutions and Development. Framing the World?*, London: Routledge, 178–92.

Stephenson, C.M. (2000) 'NGOs and the Principal Organs of the United Nations', in P. Taylor and A.J.R. Groom (eds) *The United Nations at the Millennium. The Principal Organs*, London and New York: Continuum, 271–94.

Stienstra, D. (1994) *Women's Movements and International Organizations*, New York: St Martin's Press.

Stiglitz, J.E. (2002) *Globalization and its Discontents*, New York: W.W. Norton & Company.

Stone, D. (2003) 'The "Knowledge Bank" and the Global Development Network', *Global Governance*, 9(1): 43–61.

Strang, D. and Chang, P.M.Y. (1993) 'The International Labour Organization and the Welfare State: Institutional Effects on Natural Welfare Spending, 1960–80', *International Organization*, 47(2): 235–62.

Strange, S. (1973) 'IMF: Monetary Managers', in R.W. Cox and H.K. Jacobson (eds) *The Anatomy of Influence. Decision Making in International Organization*, New Haven, CT: Yale University Press, 263–97.

——(1998) 'Why do International Organizations Never Die?' in B. Reinalda and B. Verbeek (eds) *Autonomous Policy Making by International Organizations*, London: Routledge, 213–20.

Taylor, I. (2004) 'Hegemony, Neoliberal "Good Governance" and the International Monetary Fund', in M. Boas and D. McNeill (eds) *Global Institutions and Development. Framing the World?* London: Routledge, 124–36.

Taylor, P. and Groom, A.J.R. (eds) (2000) *The United Nations at the Millennium. The Principal Organs*, London and New York: Continuum.

Thakur, R. and Maley, W. (1999) 'The Ottawa Convention on Landmines: A Landmark Humanitarian Treaty in Arms Control?' *Global Governance*, 5(3): 273–302.

Thambipillai, P. (1994) 'Continuity and Change in ASEAN: The Politics of Regional Cooperation in South East Asia', in W.A. Axline (ed.) *The Political Economy of Regional Cooperation. Comparative Case Studies*, Madison, WI: Fairleigh Dickinson University Press, 105–35.

Thelen, K. (2003) 'How Institutions Evolve. Insights from Comparative Historical Analysis', in J. Mahoney and D. Rueschemeyer (eds) *Comparative Historical Analysis in the Social Sciences*, Cambridge: Cambridge University Press, 208–40.

Thérien, J-P. and Pouliot, V. (2006) 'The Global Compact: Shifting the Politics of International Development', *Global Governance*, 12(1): 55–75.

Thies, C.G. (2004) 'Individuals, Institutions, and Inflation: Conceptual Complexity, Central Bank Independence, and the Asian Crisis', *International Studies Quarterly*, 48(3): 579–602.

Thorp, W.L. (1924) *The Integration of Industrial Operation*, Washington, DC: Government Printing Office.

Tilly, R. and Welfens, P.J.J. (eds) (2000) *Economic Globalization, International Organizations and Crisis Management. Contemporary and Historical Perspectives on Growth, Impact and Evolution of Major Organizations in an Interdependent World*, Berlin: Springer.

Tuttle, L. (1986) *Encyclopedia of Feminism*, Harlow: Longman.

Uvin, P. (1995) 'Scaling Up the Grass Roots and Scaling Down the Summit: The Relations between Third World Nongovernmental Organizations and the United Nations', *Third World Quarterly*, 16(3): 495–512.

Valticos, N. (1985) 'International Labour Standards and the World Community', in L. Dembinski, R. O'Regan *et al.* (eds) *International Geneva 1985*, Lausanne: Payot, 93–99.

Van der Beugel, E.H. (1966) *European Integration as a Concern of American Foreign Policy. From Marshall Aid to Atlantic Partnership*, Amsterdam: Elsevier.

Van der Linden, M. (ed.) (2000) *The International Confederation of Free Trade Unions*, Bern: Peter Lang.

Van der Linden, W.H. (1987) *The International Peace Movement 1815–1874*, Amsterdam: Tilleul Publications.

Van der Vleuten, A. (2007) *The Price of Gender Equality. Member States and Governance in the European Union*, Aldershot: Ashgate.

Van Eyk, S.C. (1995) *The OECD Declaration and Decisions Concerning Multinational Enterprises: An Attempt to Tame the Shrew*, Nijmegen: Ars Aequi Libri.

Van Eysinga, W.J.M. and Walther, H. (1969) *Geschichte der Zentralkommission fuer die Rheinschiffart 1816 bis 1969*, Strassburg: CCR.

Van Ginneken, A.H.M. (2006) *Historical Dictionary of the League of Nations*, Lanham, MA: The Scarecrow Press.

Van Goethem, G. (2005) *The Amsterdam International. The World of the International Federation of Trade Unions (IFTU), 1913–1945*, Aldershot: Ashgate.

——(2006) 'An International Experiment of Women Workers: The International Federation of Working Women, 1919–24', *Revue belge de philologie et d'histoire*, 84(6): 1025–47.

Van Kersbergen, K., Lieshout, R.H. et al. (eds) (1999) *Expansion and Fragmentation. Internationalization, Political Change and the Transformation of the Nation State*, Amsterdam: Amsterdam University Press.

Van Roozendaal, G. (2002) *Trade Unions and Global Governance. The Debate on a Social Clause*, London: Routledge.

Van Walraven, K. (1999) *The Pretence of Peace-Keeping. ECOMOG, West Africa and Liberia (1990–1998)*, Den Haag: Clingendael.

Verdier, D. (1998) 'Domestic Responses to Capital Market Internationalization Under the Gold Standard, 1870–1914', *International Organization*, 52(1): 1–34.

Voeten, E. (2000) 'Clashes in the Assembly', *International Organization*, 54(2): 185–215.

Wade, R. (2004) 'The World Bank and the Environment', in M. Boas and D. McNeill (eds) *Global Institutions and Development. Framing the World?* London: Routledge, 72–94.

Wallace, M. and Singer, J.D. (1970) 'Intergovernmental Organization in the Global System, 1815–1964: A Quantitative Description', *International Organization*, 24(2): 239–87.

Wallach, L. and Sforza, M. (1999) *The WTO. Five Years of Reasons to Resist Corporate Globalization*, New York: Seven Stories Press.

Wallerstein, I. (1969) *Africa. The Politics of Unity*, New York: Vintage.

——(1974) *The Modern World-System. Capitalist Agriculture and the Origins of the European World-Economy in the Sixteenth Century*, New York: Academic Press.

——(1979) *The Capitalist World-Economy*, Cambridge: Cambridge University Press.

Walters, F.P. (1960) *A History of the League of Nations*, 2nd edn, London: Oxford University Press.

Waltz, K.N. (1979) *Theory of International Politics*, New York: McGraw-Hill.

Wang, H. and Rosenau, J.N. (2001) 'Transparency International and Corruption as an Issue of Global Governance', *Global Governance*, 7(1): 25–49.

Weaver, C. and Leiteritz, R.J. (2005) '"Our Poverty Is a World Full of Dreams": Reforming the World Bank', *Global Governance*, 11(3): 369–88.

Webber, D. (2003) 'Two Funerals and a Wedding? The Ups and Downs of Regionalism in East Asia and Asia Pacific after the Asian Crisis', in F. Laursen (ed.) *Comparative Regional Integration. Theoretical Perspectives*, Aldershot: Ashgate, 125–57.

Weiler, J.H.H. (1999) *The Constitution of Europe. 'Do the New Clothes Have an Emperor?' and Other Essays on European Integration*, Cambridge: Cambridge University Press.

Weiss, M.A. (2002) *CRS Report for Congress. The International Monetary Fund: Current Reforms*, Washington, DC: Congressional Research Service.

Weiss, T.G., Forsythe, D.P. et al. (1994) *The United Nations and Changing World Politics*, Boulder, CO: Westview Press.

Wendt, A. (1992) 'Constructing International Politics', *International Security*, 20(1): 71–81.

Werle, R. and Leib, V. (2000) 'The Internet Society and its Struggle for Recognition and Influence', in K. Ronit and V. Schneider (eds) *Private Organizations in International Politics*, London: Routledge, 102–23.

White, N.D. (1996) *The Law of International Organisations*, Manchester: Manchester University Press.

Wibaut, F.M. (1935) *A World Production Order*, London: George Allen & Unwin.

Wilkie, C. (2004) 'Enhancing Global Governance: Corporate Social Responsibility and the International Trade and Investment Framework', in J.J. Kirton and M.J. Trebilcock (eds) *Hard Choices, Soft Law. Voluntary Standards in Global Trade, Environment and Social Governance*, Aldershot: Ashgate, 288–322.

Willetts, P. (ed.) (1996) *'The Conscience of the World'. The Influence of Non-Governmental Organisations in the UN System*, London: Hurst & Company.

——(1997) 'Transnational Actors and International Organizations in Global Politics', in J. Baylis and S. Smith (eds) *The Globalization of World Politics*, Oxford: Oxford University Press, 287–310.

Williams, A. (1998) *Failed Imagination? New World Orders of the Twentieth Century*, Manchester: Manchester University Press.

Williams, D. (1990) *The Specialized Agencies and the United Nations. The System in Crisis*, London: Hurst & Company.

Windmuller, J.P. (1980) *The International Trade Union Movement*, Deventer: Kluwer.

Woods, N. (2000) 'Groupthink and Decision-Making within International Financial Institutions', *ECPR News*, 11(3): 11–12.

Woolf, L.S. (1916) *International Government*, New York: Brentano's.

Yoder, A. (1997) *The Evolution of the United Nations System*, 3rd edn, Washington, DC: Taylor & Francis.

Yuen, E., Burton Rose, D. *et al.* (eds) (2001) *The Battle of Seattle: The New Challenge to Capitalist Globalization*. New York: Soft Skull Press.

Zang, L. (1985) 'International Commodity Agreements: What Future?' in L. Dembinski, R. O'Regan *et al.* (eds) *International Geneva 1985*, Geneva: Payot, 107–13.

Index